POLITICS IN AMERICA

Seventh Edition

Thomas R. Dye

Emeritus McKenzie
Professor of Government
Florida State University

PEARSON

Prentice
Hall

Upper Saddle River, New Jersey 07458

Library of Congress Cataloging-in-Publication Data
Dye, Thomas R.
   Politics in America / Thomas R. Dye. — 7th ed.
     p. cm.
   Includes bibliographical references and index.
   ISBN 0-13-613220-0 (alk. paper)
1. United States—Politics and government.   I. Title.
JK276.D926 2006b
320.473—dc22   2006038781

Editorial Director: Charlyce Jones Owen
Executive Editor: Dickson Musslewhite
Associate Editor: Rob DeGeorge
Editorial Assistant: Jennifer Murphy
Senior Marketing Manager: Kate Mitchell
Marketing Manager: Emily Cleary
Marketing Assistant: Jennifer Lang
Senior Managing Editor: Lisa Iarkowski
Production Liaison: Fran Russello
Permissions Coordinator: Lisa Black
Manufacturing Buyer: Mary Ann Gloriande
Design Manager: Amy Rosen
Interior Design: Jonathan Boylan
Cover Design: Jonathan Boylan/Laura Gardner
Cover Illustration/Photo: Tomi/Photolink/Photodisc Green/Getty Images, Inc.
Director, Image Resource Center: Melinda Reo
Manager, Rights and Permissions: Zina Arabia
Manager, Visual Research: Beth Brenzel
Manager, Cover Visual Research & Permissions: Karen Sanatar
Image Permission Coordinator: Debbie Hewitson
Photo Researcher: Kathy Ringrose
Composition/Full-Service Project Management: Margaret Pinette/
Stratford Publishing Services, Inc.
Printer/Binder: Courier Companies, Inc.
Cover Printer: Phoenix Color Corp.

Credits and acknowledgments borrowed from other sources and reproduced, with permission, in this textbook appear on appropriate page within text (or on page PC-1).

Pearson Education LTD. London
Pearson Education Singapore, Pte. Ltd
Pearson Education, Canada, Ltd
Pearson Education–Japan

Pearson Education Australia PTY, Limited
Pearson Education North Asia Ltd
Pearson Educación de Mexico, S.A. de C.V.
Pearson Education Malaysia, Pte. Ltd

PEARSON
Prentice
Hall

10 9 8 7 6 5 4 3 2 1

ISBN 0-13-613220-0
ISBN 978-0-13-613220-2

To my students over the years,
who taught me more than I taught them.

BRIEF CONTENTS

CONTENTS

Part One   POLITICS

*The study of politics is the study of influence and the influential. . . .
The influential are those who get the most of what there is to get. Those
who get the most are elite; the rest are mass.*
                                                    Harold Lasswell

Part Two   CONSTITUTION

*The ascendancy of any elite depends upon the success of the practices
it adopts. . . . The Constitution, written and unwritten, embodies the
practices which are deemed most fundamental to the governmental
and social order.*
                                                    Harold Lasswell

Part Three PARTICIPANTS

People strive for power—to get the most of what there is to get.
Harold Lasswell

Part Four INSTITUTIONS

Authority is the expected and legitimate possession of power.
Harold Lasswell

Part Five   OUTCOMES

*That political science concentrates upon the influential does not imply
the neglect of the total distribution of values throughout the community.
. . . The emphasis upon the probability that the few (elite) will get the
most does not imply that the many (mass) do not profit from some
political changes.*
                                                    Harold Lasswell

APPENDIX

PREFACE

Politics is an activity by which people try to get more of whatever there is to get. It is not about the pursuit of liberty as much as it is about the struggle over the allocation of values in society. Simply put, it is about "who gets what, when, and how."

By using Lasswell's classic definition of politics as the unifying framework, *Politics in America, Seventh Edition,* strives to present a clear, concise, and stimulating introduction to the American political system. Politics consists of all of the activities—reasonable discussion, impassioned oratory, campaigning, balloting, fund raising, advertising, lobbying, demonstrating, rioting, street fighting, and waging war—by which conflict is carried on. Managing conflict is the principal function of the political system and power is the ultimate goal.

By examining the struggle for power—the participants, the stakes, the processes, and the institutional arenas—*Politics in America, Seventh Edition,* introduces students to the political struggles that drive democracy.

Why Politics in America?

Instructors teaching the Introductory American Government course find engaging their students to be the most difficult task facing them. *Politics in America, Seventh Edition,* is written to be lively and absorbing, reflecting the teaching philosophy that *stimulating students' interest in politics and public affairs is the most important goal of an introductory course.* Interesting examples and controversial debates spark students' interest and keep them connected to the material. The struggle for power in society is not a dull topic, and textbooks should not make it so.

Politics in America, Seventh Edition, strives for a balanced presentation, but "balanced" does not mean boring. It does not mean the avoidance of controversy. Liberal and conservative arguments are set forth clearly and forcefully. Race and gender are given particular attention, not because it is currently fashionable to do so, but because American politics has long been driven by these factors.

Organization

Part I, "Politics," begins with Lasswell's classic definition of politics and proceeds to describe the nature and functions of government and the meaning of democracy. It poses the question, How democratic is the American political system? It describes the American political culture: its contradictions between law and liberty, political equality and economic inequality, equality of opportunity and inequality of

results, and the role of ideology—liberalism and conservatism, thus laying the groundwork for understanding the struggle over who gets what.

Part II, "Constitution," describes the politics of constitution making—deciding how to decide. It describes how the struggle over the U.S. Constitution reflected the distribution of power in the new nation. It focuses on the classic arguments of the Founders for limiting and dividing governmental power and the structural arrangements designed to accomplish this end.

Part III, "Participants," begins by examining individual participation in politics—the way people acquire and hold political opinions and act on them through voting and protest activity. It examines the influences of family, school, gender, race, and the role of media in shaping political opinion. It describes how organization concentrates power—to win public office in the case of party organizations, and to influence policy in the case of interest groups. It assesses the role of personal ambition in politics and the role of money.

Part IV, "Institutions," describes the various governmental arenas in which the struggle for power takes place—the Congress, the presidency, the bureaucracy, the courts. More important, it evaluates the power that comes with control of each of these institutions.

Part V, "Outcomes," deals with public policies—the result of the struggle over the allocation of values. It is especially concerned with the two fundamental values of American society—liberty and equality. Each is examined in separate chapters, as are economic policies, welfare policies, and national security policies.

New to the Seventh Edition

The struggle for political power in America has been particularly intense since the controversy over the election of George W. Bush in 2000. In that election Bush's opponent, Al Gore, won more popular votes than Bush, but following a bitter controversy over Electoral College votes from Florida—a controversy that was finally resolved by the Supreme Court—Bush occupied the White House. The bitterness of that election helped to polarize Americans—Democrats versus Republicans, liberals versus conservatives, religious versus secular, supporters versus opponents of the Iraq war, feminists versus nonfeminists, civil libertarians versus supporters of restrictive measures in the war on terror, supporters versus opponents of immigration, and a host of other conflicts. Americans seemed to become more polarized than at any other time since the Vietnam War. And all of these conflicts resounded in the halls of Congress, the White House, the Supreme Court, and the federal bureaucracy.

The seventh edition of *Politics in America* tries to capture these conflicts and how they affect our political system. Few of these conflicts were resolved with Bush's reelection in 2004. Indeed, it seemed as if the nation became even more polarized, especially as the war in Iraq continued unabated. A textbook focusing on conflict and the struggle for power seems more relevant today than in previous decades.

Among the topics given special attention in the seventh edition are the war in Iraq and its impact on domestic politics; the war on terror and its potential threats to civil liberty; religious and secular conflicts; immigration and its impact on politics and the economy; social issues, including abortion, marijuana for medical use, same-sex marriages, the conservative fight against the mainstream media, and the battle between liberal and conservative 527s; the continuing struggle over affirmative action, particularly in universities; the controversy over the extent of "executive power"; the reorganization of the intelligence community after 9/11; the heated controversies over the selection of Supreme Court justices; and the Democratic and Republican efforts to capture the growing Hispanic vote.

Politics in America is designed to invite controversy and spirited discussion in the classroom. It does not hesitate to raise all of the "politically incorrect" issues—affirmative action and "diversity" in education; when is it right to disobey the law; what is the appropriate justification for the use of military force; what, if any, restrictions should be placed on abortion; should the states or the federal government attempt to ban gay marriages; what constitutional rights, if any, should be given to enemy combatants captured on foreign battlefields or inside the United States; and even whether the Pledge of Allegiance should include the words "under God." Discussions of these conflicts and how and where they are carried on leads students to better understand our political system and how it works.

The congressional election of 2006 is described and analyzed in terms of popular perceptions of the role of Congress in resolving some of these conflicts. President Bush's policies and popularity are assessed as components of voters' decisions in the congressional election.

Educators and citizens have become distressed in recent years over the lack of knowledge of the U.S. Constitution by college graduates. To address this issue, the seventh edition of *Politics in America* not only includes an *annotated* Constitution, but also a new feature—*A Constitutional Note*—at the end of each chapter that discusses constitutional issues raised by the topic in that chapter.

Supplementary Books and Readings for American Government

Each of the following books features specialized topical coverage allowing you to tailor your American Government course to suit the needs of your region or your particular teaching style. Featuring contemporary issues or timely readings, any of the following books are available for a discount when bundled with *Politics in America*. Please visit our Online Catalog at www.prenhall.com/dye for additional details.

Government's Greatest Achievements:
From Civil Rights to Homeland Security, 20th ed.
Paul C. Light, Brookings Institute
ISBN: 0-13-110192-7 © 2004

Issues in American Political Life:
Money, Violence, and Biology, 4th ed.
Robert Thobaben, Wright State University
Donna Schlagheck, Wright State University
Charles Funderburk, Wright State University
ISBN: 0-13-0336726 © 2002

Choices: An American Government Reader—
Custom Publishing
Gregory Scott, University of Central Oklahoma
Katherine Tate, University of California–Irvine
Ronald Weber, University of Wisconsin–Milwaukee
ISBN: 0-13-0219916 © 2002

Civil Rights and Liberties:
Provocative Questions and Evolving Answers, 2nd ed.
Harold Sullivan, The City University of New York
ISBN: 0-13-1174355 © 2001

21 Debated: Issues in American Politics, 2nd ed.
Gregory Scott, University of Central Oklahoma
Loren Gatch, University of Central Oklahoma
ISBN: 0-13-1841785 © 2005

Government and Politics in the Lone Star State:
Theory and Practice, 4th ed.
L. Tucker Gibson, Trinity University
Clay Robison, The Houston Chronicle
ISBN: 0-13-0340502 © 2002

Rethinking California:
Politics and Policy in the Golden State
Matthew Cahn, California State University–Northridge
H. Eric Schockman, University of Southern California
David Shafie, Ohio University
ISBN: 0-13-0282677 © 2001

Strategies for Active Citizenship
Kateri M. Drexler
Gwen Garcelon
ISBN: 0-13-1172956 © 2005

*Political Science: Evaluating Online Resources
    with Research Navigator, 2005*
Melissa Payton
ISBN: 0-13-192288-2

*The Political Science Student Writer's
    Manual, 4th ed.*
Gregory M. Scott, University of
    Central Oklahoma
Stephen M. Garrison, University of
    Central Oklahoma
ISBN: 0-13-0404470 © 2002

*Smoking and Politics: Policy Making and
    the Federal Bureaucracy, 5th ed.*
A. Lee Fritschler, Dickinson College
James M. Hoefler, Dickinson College
ISBN: 0-13-4358015 © 1996

Real Politics in America series is another resource for contemporary instructional material. To bridge the gap between research and relevancy, we have launched a new series of supplemental books with the help of series editor Paul Herrnson of the University of Maryland. More descriptive than quantitative, more case study than data study, these books cut across all topics to bring students relevant details in current political science research. From exploring the growing phenomenon of direct democracy to who runs for the state legislature, these books show students that real political science is meaningful and exciting. Available for a discount when bundled with *Politics in America*. Please see your Prentice Hall representative or access www.prenhall.com for a complete listing of titles in the series.

Acknowledgments

Politics in America, Seventh Edition, reflects the influence of many splendid teachers, students, and colleagues who have helped me over the years. I am grateful for the early guidance of Frank Sorauf, my undergraduate student adviser at Pennsylvania State University, and James G. Coke, my Ph.D. dissertation director at the University of Pennsylvania. Georgia Parthemos at the University of Georgia and Malcolm Parsons at Florida State University gave me my first teaching posts. But my students over the years contributed most to my education—notably Susan MacManus, Kent Portney, Ed Benton, James Ammons, Aubrey Jewitt, and especially John Robey. Several of my colleagues gave advice on various parts of this book. Glen Parker (on Congress), Suzanne Parker (on public opinion), James Gwartney (on economics), Robert Lichter (on the mass media), Charles Barrioux (on bureaucracy), and especially Harmon Zeigler, whose knowledge of politics is unbounded.

I would like to thank James Corey of High Point University for preparing the annotated Constitution and Chris Cardone for editorial management in the early stages of this Seventh edition.

Finally, I would like to thank the many reviewers who evaluated the text and contributed invaluable advice:

Charles W. Chapman, University of Texas at
    Brownsville
John Pratt, Cedar Valley College
James Corey, High Point University
Christopher C. Lovett, Emporia State University
Kevin R. den Dulk, Grand Valley State
    University
Wayne Pryor, Brazosport College
James W. Lamare, Florida Atlantic University
Roger Marietta, Darton College
Paul Davis, Truckee Meadows Community
    College
Earl T. Sheridan, University of North Carolina

Thomas R. Dye

ABOUT THE AUTHOR

THOMAS R. DYE, Emeritus McKenzie Professor of Government at Florida State University, regularly taught large introductory classes in American politics and was University Teacher of the Year in 1987. He received his B.A. and M.A. degrees from Pennsylvania State University and his Ph.D. degree from the University of Pennsylvania. He is the author of numerous books and articles on American government and public policy, including *The Irony of Democracy; Politics in States and Communities; Understanding Public Policy; Who's Running America; American Politics in the Media Age; Power in Society; Politics, Economics, and the Public;* and *American Federalism: Competition Among Governments.* His books have been translated into many languages, including Russian and Chinese, and published abroad. He has served as president of the Southern Political Science Association, president of the Policy Studies Organization, and secretary of the American Political Science Association. He has taught at the University of Pennsylvania, the University of Wisconsin, and the University of Georgia, and served as a visiting scholar at Bar-Ilan University, Israel, the Brookings Institution in Washington, D.C., and elsewhere. He is a member of Phi Beta Kappa, Omicron Delta Kappa, and Phi Kappa Phi and is listed in most major biographical directories. Additional information is available at www.thomasrdye.com.

STUDENT TOOL KIT

1 POLITICS
Who Gets What, When, and How

A Provocative Theme and Lively Narrative

This balanced and exceedingly readable text uses Harold Laswell's classic definition of politics—"who gets what, when and how"—as a framework for presenting a clear, concise, and stimulating introduction to the American political system. The absorbing narrative examines this struggle for power—the participants, the stakes, the processes, and the institutions—in a way that provokes thinking and discussion.

Contemporary and Relevant

The study of politics is the story of not just the past, but the present, of conflict and debate. It is also constantly changing. *Politics in America* captures the essence of politics today. Its many features help students see how our system works, and understand the timely and important issues that are currently challenging our political system. The text consistently helps students understand how what is happening in politics today affects their own lives.

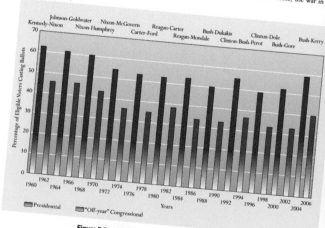

154 CHAPTER 5 • OPINION AND PARTICIPATION: THINKING AND ACTING IN POLITICS

effects on actual turnout at the polls were very limited.[18] Apparently, easy tration does not automatically increase voter turnout.

Why Vote?

Deciding whether to cast a vote in an election is just as important as dec which candidate to vote for. *About half of the voting-age population in the United States cally fails to vote, even in presidential elections.* Voter **turnout**—the number of actual v in relation to the number of people eligible to register and vote—is even lowe off-year congressional and state elections, when presidential elections are not h Turnout in local elections (for example, city, county, school board) is even lo when these elections are held separately from national elections. Voter turnou presidential elections steadily declined for several decades (see Figure 5.5). T three-way presidential race in 1992 temporarily reversed the downward trend. I in 2004 voter turnout surged to levels not seen since the 1960s. Various explai tions have been offered: the expected closeness of the election, the experien of 2000 when only a few votes in Florida decided the outcome, the war in Ira

turnout Number of voters who actually cast ballots in an election, as a percentage of people eligible to register and vote.

Figure 5.5 Voter Turnout in Presidential and Congressional Elections
Voter turnout is always higher in years with a presidential election. However, voter turnout has generally declined since 1960, even in presidential election years. The exception came in 1992, when intense interest in the contest between George H.W. Bush and Bill Clinton—spiced by the entry of independent Ross Perot—led to a higher-than-normal turnout. In 1996 fewer than half of voting-age Americans bothered to cast ballots. However, in 2004 voter turnout rose to levels not seen since the 1960s.

ENGAGING SPECIAL FEATURES

What Do You Think?

This feature helps students to think critically about today's issues and political debates. Controversial questions and national opinion survey data on topics in the national news are included to stimulate classroom discussion.

A Conflicting View

This feature challenges students to rethink conventional notions about American politics. They are designed to be controversial and to start students thinking about the push and pull that is politics.

Compared to What?

Global context is essential to the study of American politics today. This feature provides comparisons of the United States with other nations. Discussions include "Freedom and Democracy around the World," as well as topics such as the size of government, tax burdens, voter turnout, television culture, and health care.

People in Politics

This feature is designed to personalize politics, to illustrate that the participants in the struggle for power are real people. Students are introduced to some of the key participants who have helped shape American politics, their backgrounds, and careers.

Up Close

This feature illustrates the struggles over who gets what and covers a wide variety of current political conflicts.

PEOPLE IN POLITICS

Larry King Live

Who turned presidential politics into talk-show entertainment? A strong argument can be made that Larry King was personally responsible for changing the nature of presidential campaigning. It was Larry King who nudged frequent talk-show guest Ross Perot into the presidential arena. And it was Larry King who demonstrated to the candidates that the talk-show format was a good way to reach out to the American people.

Larry King's supremacy in talk-show politics came late in life, after a half-century of hustling and hard knocks, no college education, bouts of gambling followed by bankruptcy, and multiple marriages. King has written five books about himself, describing his rise from Brooklyn neighborhoods; his friendships with Jackie Gleason, Frank Sinatra, and other celebrities; and his hardscrabble life. As he tells it, he hung around a New York radio station for five years before taking a bus to Miami to try his luck first as a disk jockey and later as a sports announcer. After a decade in Miami, he had his own TV interview show, a talk show on radio, and a newspaper column, and he was color commentator for the Miami Dolphins. He lived the fast life, running up huge debts and dealing in shady financial transactions. He was arrested in 1971 on grand larceny charges; they were dropped only because the statute of limitations had expired. He lost his TV and radio shows and his newspaper column. He ended up in Shreveport, Louisiana, doing play-by-play for the World Football League. In 1978 he bankrupt but back in Miami doing radio. In 1978 he moved to Washington to launch his Mutual Network radio talk show. As radio talk shows gained popular-

ity, so did King. When CNN started twenty-four-hour broadcasting in 1982, the network turned to King to do an evening interview show, *Larry King Live*. At first, the show merely filled the space between the evening and the late news. A decade later, the show was making news itself.

King's success is directly attributable to his accommodating style. He actually listens to his guests; he lets them speak for themselves; he unashamedly plugs their books, records, and movies. He does *not* attack his guests; he does not assume the adversarial, abrasive style preferred by reporters like Mike Wallace, or interviewers like Bill O'Reilly. An old-fashioned liberal himself, King appears comfortable interviewing politicians of every stripe. He lets guests talk about themselves. He tosses "softball" questions: "If I were to interview the president about an alleged sexual affair, I wouldn't ask if he'd had one, I'd ask him, 'How does it feel to read these things about yourself?'"

With his emphasis on feelings, emotions, and motives rather than on facts, it is little wonder that King's style attracts politicians . . . or that *Larry King Live* is the highest rated show on CNN.

Source: Excerpted from "A King Who Can Listen," *Time,* 10/5/92.

COMPARED TO WHAT?

America's TV Culture in Perspective

America is a TV culture. Americans rely more on television for news and entertainment than people in other advanced industrial nations do. Perhaps more important, Americans have greater confidence in the media than other peoples do. Consider, for example, the question "Would you say you have a great deal of confidence, only some confidence, hardly any confidence, or no confidence at all in the media—press, radio, and television?" When this question was asked of a national sample of Americans, 69 percent responded that they had a great deal or at least some confidence in the media. But majorities in four other countries—France, Great Britain, Germany, and Spain—said they had little or no confidence in the media (see "confidence in the media" figure).

How much do the media influence key decisions in society? A majority of people in both the United States and these same European nations believe the media exert a large influence on public opinion. Americans appear to be closer to unanimity on this point (88 percent) than are Europeans. When people are asked how much influence the media exerts on particular governing institutions—the executive, the legislature, and the judiciary—Americans are much more likely to perceive strong media influence than are Europeans (see "media influence" figure).

Source: Adapted from Laurence Parisot, "Attitudes about the Media: A Five Country Study," *Public Opinion* 43 (January/February 1988): 18, 60.

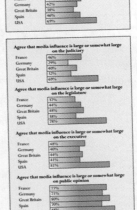

Have confidence in the media

France	48%
Germany	42%
Great Britain	38%
Spain	46%
USA	69%

Agree that media influence is large or somewhat large on the judiciary

France	46%
Germany	29%
Great Britain	40%
Spain	37%
USA	69%

Agree that media influence is large or somewhat large on the legislature

France	37%
Germany	44%
Great Britain	48%
Spain	38%
USA	78%

Agree that media influence is large or somewhat large on the executive

France	48%
Germany	46%
Great Britain	44%
Spain	41%
USA	81%

Agree that media influence is large or somewhat large on public opinion

France	77%
Germany	71%
Great Britain	80%
Spain	70%
USA	88%

---

equal-time rule Federal Communications Commission (FCC) requirement that broadcasters who sell time to any political candidate must make equal time available to opposing candidates at the same price.

libel Writings that are false and malicious and are intended to damage an individual.

amount of airtime at the same price. Stations are not required to give free time to candidates, but if stations choose to give free time to one candidate, they must do so for the candidate's opponents. But this **equal-time rule** does *not* apply to newscasts, news specials, or even long documentaries, nor does it apply to talk shows like *Larry King Live* (see *People in Politics:* "Larry King Live"). Nor does it apply to presidential press conferences or presidential addresses to the nation, although the networks now generally offer free time for a "Democratic response" to a Republican president, and vice versa. A biased news presentation does not require the network or station to grant equal time to opponents of its views. And it is important to note that newspapers, unlike radio and television, have never been required to provide equal time to opposing views (see *Compared to What?* "America's TV Culture in Perspective").

court that the communication caused actual damage and was either false or defamatory. A damaging falsehood or words or phrases that are defamatory (such as "Joe Jones is a rotten son of a bitch") are libelous and are not protected by the First Amendment from lawsuits seeking compensation.

Public Officials Over the years, the media have sought to narrow the protection afforded public officials against libel and slander. In 1964 the U.S. Supreme Court ruled in the case of *New York Times v. Sullivan* that public officials did not have a right to recover damages for false statements unless they are made with "malicious intent."[23] The **Sullivan rule** requires public officials not only to show that the media published or broadcast false and damaging statements but also to prove they did so knowing that their statements were false and damaging or that they did so with

Think Again

Should the media report on all aspects of the private lives of public officials?

The Constitution of the United States

THE PREAMBLE

We the People of the United States, in Order to form a more perfect Union, establish Justice, insure domestic Tranquility, provide for the common defense, promote the general Welfare, and secure the Blessings of Liberty to ourselves and our Posterity, do ordain and establish this Constitution for the United States of America.

"We, the people." Three simple words, yet of profound importance and contentious origin. Every government in the world at the time of the Constitutional Convention was some type of monarchy wherein sovereign power flowed from the top. The Founders of our new country rejected monarchy as a form of government and proposed instead a republic, which would draw its sovereignty from the people.

The Articles of Confederation that governed the U.S. from 1776 until 1789 started with: "We the under signed Delegates of the States." Early drafts of the new constitution started with: "We, the states . . ." But again, the Founders were not interested in another union of states but rather the creation of a new national government. Therefore, "We, the states" was changed to "We, the people."

The remainder of the preamble describes the generic functions of government

of Representatives) organization of the legislative branch.

House of Representatives: Composition, Qualifications; Apportionment, Impeachment Power

Section 2 Clause 1. The House of Representatives shall be composed of Members chosen every second Year by the People of the several States, and the Electors in each State shall have the Qualifications requisite for Electors of the most numerous Branch of the State Legislature.

This section sets the term of office for House members (2 years) and indicates that those voting for Congress will have the same qualifications as those voting for the state legislatures. Originally, states limited voters to white property owners. Some states even had religious disqualifications, such as Catholic or Jewish. Most property and religious qualifications for voting were removed by the 1840s, but race and gender restrictions remained, until the 15th and 19th amendments were passed.

Clause 2. No Person shall be a Representative who shall not have attained to the Age of twenty five Years, and been seven Years a Citizen of the United States, and who shall not, when elected, be an inhabitant of that State in which he shall be chosen.

Annotated Constitution

Politics in America features the most integrated approach to the Constitution for the American Government class. An annotated constitution is included as part of the Constitution chapter. It provides extended commentary on key sections and clauses to give students a deeper insight into the intentions behind this important document.

NEW! A Constitutional Note

A groundbreaking feature at the end of each chapter that expands and integrates coverage of the Constitution into the core concepts of the American Government course.

A CONSTITUTIONAL NOTE

Campaign Finance and Free Speech

Both the Congress and the Supreme Court have confronted the issue of whether or not limiting campaign spending has the effect of limiting free speech. In 1976 in *Buckley v. Valeo*, the Supreme Court struck down Congress's limit on what an individual candidate or independent organization could spend to promote its own views it a campaign. "The First Amendment denies government the power to determine that spending to promote one's political views is... excessive. In the free society ordained by our Constitution, it is not the government but the people who must retain control over the quantity and range of debate in a political campaign."[a] This decision means that wealthy individuals can spend unlimited amounts on their own campaigns, and independent organizations can spend unlimited amounts as long as their spending is independent of a candidate's campaign. However, the Supreme

Court approved limits on *contributions* by individuals and organizations—distinguishing between contributions and expenditures. It approved the Federal Election Commission limits on individual and organizational contributions to political campaigns. Congress sought to remedy the many holes in the original Federal Election Campaign Act of 1974 in the Bipartisan Campaign Reform Act of 2002. It placed limits on "soft money" contributions to political parties, most of which found its way into candidate campaigns. However, Congress did not challenge the Court's *Buckley* decision by trying to prevent individuals or nonprofit organizations from spending money to broadcast their views. Limiting spending for political broadcasting would "place substantial and direct restrictions on the ability of candidates, citizens, and associations to engage in protected political speech."[b] The result was the emergence of independent organizations, known as "527s," in the 2004 election. These organizations spent heavily and played a major role in the presidential campaigns of both parties.

[a]*Buckley v. Valeo*, 424 U.S. 1 (1976).

[b]*McConnell v. Federal Election Commission*, 590 U.S. 93 (2003).

influential as in previous presidential races. The economy was cited as "most important" by about one-fifth of the voters in 2004 and Kerry won the vast majority of these voters.

Issue Voting Casting one's vote exclusively on the basis of the policy positions of the candidates is rare. Most voters are unaware of the specific positions taken by candidates on the issues. Indeed, voters often believe that their pre-

ACROSS THE USA

Reapportionment, 2000

Since 1910, the number of seats in the House of Representatives has remained constant at 435. Each ten-year census requires a reapportionment of seats among states based on their populations. States with rapid population growth such as Arizona, Texas, Georgia, and Florida gain seats (each of these states gained two seats following the 2000 census). States with slow population growth lose seats (New York and Pennsylvania both lost two seats). The newly apportioned House convened in January 2003.

Across the USA

This collection of maps summarizes important statistical and demographic information relevant to American politics.

courts have ruled that only official U.S. Bureau of the Census figures may be used: estimated changes since the last census may *not* be used. In recent years, the courts have insisted on nearly exact mathematical equality in populations in congressional districts in a state.

STUDY AIDS FOR SUCCESS IN THE CLASSROOM

Chapter Outline

- The Power of the Media
- Sources of Media Power
- The Business of the Media
- The Politics of the News
- Polarization of the Media
- Mediated Elections
- Freedom versus Fairness
- Libel and Slander
- Politics and the Internet
- Media Effects: Shaping Political Life

Think About Politics

1 Are media professionals—news reporters, editors, anchors—the true voice of the people in public affairs?
Yes ☐ No ☐

2 Do the media mirror what is really news, rather than deciding themselves what's important and then making it news?
Yes ☐ No ☐

3 Is television your most important source of news?
Yes ☐ No ☐

4 Should the media report on all aspects of the private lives of public officials?
Yes ☐ No ☐

5 Do the media report equally fairly on Democratic and Republican candidates for office?
Yes ☐ No ☐

6 Should the media be legally required to be fair and accurate in reporting political news?
Yes ☐ No ☐

7 Are you more alienated than attracted by the media's coverage of politics?
Yes ☐ No ☐

8 Is your choice of candidates in elections affected by their advertising?
Yes ☐ No ☐

Ask yourself how much of your knowledge about politics in America comes from television and newspapers and the radio. What you know about politics and how you participate are, in fact, largely determined by the power of the media to decide what they want you to know.

★ ★ ★

The Power of the Media

Politics—the struggle over who gets what, when, and how—is largely carried out in the **mass media**. The arenas of political conflict are the various media of mass communication—television, newspapers, magazines, radio, books, recordings, motion pictures, and the Internet. What we know about politics comes to us largely through these media. Unless we ourselves are admitted to the White House Oval Office or the committee rooms of Congress or dinner parties at foreign embassies, or unless we ourselves attend political rallies and demonstrations or travel to distant battlefields, we must rely on the mass media to tell us about politics. Furthermore, few of us ever have the opportunity to personally evaluate the character of presidential candidates or cabinet members or members of Congress, or to learn their views on public issues by talking with them face to face. Instead, we must learn about people as well as events from the mass media.

Great power derives from the control of information. *Who knows what* helps to determine *who gets what*. The media not only provide an arena for politics; they are also themselves players in that arena. The media not only report on the struggles for power in society; they are also themselves participants in those struggles. The media have long been referred to as America's "fourth branch" of government—and for good reason.[1]

The Power of Television Television is the most powerful medium of communication. It is the first true *mass* communication medium. Virtually every home in the United States has a television set, and the average home has the set turned on for about seven hours a day. Television is regularly chosen over other news media by Americans as the most common news source.

Americans turn to local TV news broadcasts as their most regular source of news. Daily newspapers are read by less than half of the adult public (see Figure 6.1). The national network evening news shows (NBC Nightly News, ABC World News Tonight, CBS Evening News) have lost viewership in recent years. But viewership of CNN, Fox News Cable, CNBC, and MSNBC is rising. Television weekly news magazines, notably CBS's *60 Minutes* and ABC's *20/20* have also become major sources of news for many Americans.

169

Chapter Outline

Each chapter begins with an outline that gives students an overview of the topics that are covered.

Thinking About Politics

A brief poll alerts students to crucial issues covered in the chapter. By taking the poll, students can understand their own beliefs on these issues before undertaking their study of the chapter content.

First Gov
Official Web portal to all federal departments and agencies, information on government benefits, agency links, and so forth.
www.firstgov.gov

bureaucracy Departments, agencies, bureaus, and offices that perform the functions of government.

chain of command Hierarchical structure of authority in which command flows downward; typical of a bureaucracy.

division of labor Division of work among many specialized workers in a bureaucracy.

impersonality Treatment of all persons within a bureaucracy on the basis of "merit" and of all "clients" served by the bureaucracy equally according to rules.

Think Again

Do bureaucrats in Washington have too much power?

implementation Development by the federal bureaucracy of procedures and activities to carry out policies legislated by Congress; it includes regulation as well as adjudication.

1. *Needed Expertise and Technological Advances* Congress and the president do not have the time, energy, or expertise to handle the details of policy making. A related explanation is that the increasing complexity and sophistication of technology require technical experts ("technocrats") to actually carry out the intent of Congress and the president. Neither the president nor the 535 members of Congress can look after the myriad details involved in environmental protection, occupational safety, air traffic control, or thousands of other responsibilities of government. So the president and Congress create bureaucracies, appropriate money for them, and authorize them to draw up detailed rules, regulations, and "guidelines" that actually govern the nation. Bureaucratic agencies receive only vague and general directions from the president and Congress. Actual governance is in the hands of the Environmental Protection Agency, the Occupational Safety and Health Administration, the Federal Aviation Administration, and hundreds of similar agencies (see Figure 12.1).

2. *Symbolic Politics* But there are also political explanations for the growth of bureaucratic power. Congress and the president often deliberately pass vague and ambiguous laws. These laws allow elected officials to show symbolically their concerns for environmental protection, occupational safety, and so on, yet avoid the controversies surrounding actual application of those lofty principles. Bureaucracies must then give practical meaning to these symbolic measures by developing specific rules and regulations. If the rules and regulations prove unpopular, Congress and the president can blame the bureaucrats and pretend that these unpopular decisions are a product of an "ungovernable" Washington bureaucracy (see *What Do You Think? "How Would You Rate These Federal Agencies?"*)

3. *Bureaucratic Explanation* There is also a bureaucratic explanation of the growth in the size and influence of government agencies. Bureaucracy has become its own source of power. Bureaucrats have a personal stake in expanding the size of their own agencies and budgets and adding to their own regulatory authority. They can mobilize their "client" groups (interest groups that directly benefit from the agency's programs, such as environmental groups on behalf of the Environmental Protection Agency, farm groups for the Department of Agriculture, the National Education Association for the Department of Education) in support of larger budgets and expanded authority.

4. *Popular Demands* Finally, it has been argued that "big government" is really an expression of democratic sentiments. People want to use the power of government to improve their lives—to regulate and develop the economy, to guarantee civil rights, to develop their communities, and so on. Conservative opponents of the government are really expressing their disdain for popular demands.[3]

Bureaucratic Power: Implementation Bureaucracies are not *constitutionally* empowered to decide policy questions. But they do so, nevertheless, as they perform their tasks of implementation, regulation, and adjudication.

Implementation is the development of procedures and activities to carry out policies legislated by Congress. It may involve creating new agencies or bureaus or assigning new responsibilities to old agencies. It often requires bureaucracies to translate laws into operational rules and regulations and usually to allocate resources—money, personnel, offices, supplies—to the new function. All of these tasks involve decisions by bureaucrats, decisions that drive how the law

---

Marginal Learning Aids

Each chapter contains a **running glossary** in the margin to help students master important concepts. **Website urls** provides sources from which students can obtain additional information. **Think Again** marginal questions are taken from the chapter opening poll to help students revisit their thinking on issues as they move through the content.

End-of-Chapter Resources

Summary Notes and a list of **Key Terms** help students review and test their understanding of the chapter's main topics.

MEDIA RESOURCES
AID LEARNING AND ASSESSMENT

Make it Real 2.0

This comprehensive website contains dynamic simulations, activities on civic participation, interactive timelines and maps, quizzes, primary source documents, Census data, exercises in visual literacy, and self-study quizzes. Students will use information such as real election results, real demographics, maps and voting score cards. Self-study quizzes are available for the student to take to make sure they understand the concepts used in completing the simulations and other activities.
www.prenhall.com/makeitreal2

New! MyPoliSciLab

An easy-to-use online resource that enables students to diagnose their progress by completing an online self-assessment test. Based on the results of this test, each student is provided with a customized study plan, including a variety of tools to help them fully master the material. MyPoliSciLab offers the major resources, including Make It Real online resources and ABC News video clip, in one convenient location. **www.mypoliscilab.com**

Research Navigator

From finding the right articles and journals, to citing sources, drafting and writing effective papers, and completing research assignments, Research Navigator offers extensive help on the research process.

Your instructor resources...

Politics in America is accompanied by an extensive supplements package that delivers classroom support in a variety of media.

A comprehensive Instructor's Resource Manual offers recent news and pop culture examples, discussion topics, activities, and assignments, and a list of related Internet activities for students all correlated to related content in each chapter.

The Faculty Resource CD-ROM contains PowerPoint presentations including a Lecture presentation that covers each chapter in detail, a Special Topic presentation for each chapter and a Graphics presentation that includes all of the chapter's graphs, charts, and illustrations. It also includes the Test Item File and Instructor's Manual.

Custom solutions

It's your course. Why not teach from your book? The Pearson Custom Publishing program allows you to tailor the content and organization of *Politics in America* to the specific needs of your course, including the addition of your own course notes and original content. Pearson custom editions are available in groundbreaking full color. Contact your local Prentice Hall representative today to begin building your ideal text. Visit www.pearsoncustom.com for additional information.

Part One
POLITICS

On the Edge

ABCNEWS

Originally Aired: **April 15, 2004**
Program: **Nightline**
Running Time: **16:16**

When we say "poor" or "poverty-stricken Americans," what image comes to mind? The homeless man sleeping on the grate? The unemployed person standing in line at the unemployment or welfare office? What about someone who has a full-time job making $9 an hour? That sounds like a decent wage, right? Well, that actually comes out to just above $18,000 a year, and for a family with one adult and three children, that means poverty. We've decided to launch a new, occasional series that looks at the working poor: the millions of Americans who live on the edge of poverty.

The genesis of tonight's show was a great new book by former *New York Times* reporter and Pulitzer Prize winner David Shipler. *The Working Poor* takes a comprehensive look at the lives of people set to plunge into the abyss of financial ruin if just one payment isn't met, if their car breaks down, or if they call in sick at work. Such seemingly minor events can have catastrophic effects on this segment of the population and Mr. Shipler has documented many of their lives, weaving economic analysis into the story of what these people face trying to survive from day to day. Ted Koppel sat down with Mr. Shipler for an extensive interview on his findings.

Critical Thinking Questions

1. How does author David Shipler define "working poor"?

2. How does the video's title, "On the Edge," apply to the working poor?

3. The underlying problem of the working poor seems to be their vulnerability in every area of life. Explain how the working poor are vulnerable in ways not experienced by other economic groups.

4. Author David Shipler disagrees with the concept of a "culture of poverty." Instead, he speaks of an "ecological system of interactions." What does he mean?

5. What is the difference between an entitlement and a means-tested entitlement?

1 POLITICS
Who Gets What, When, and How

Think About Politics

1 Can you trust the government to do what is right most of the time?
Yes ☐ No ☐

2 Should any group other than the government have the right to use force?
Yes ☐ No ☐

3 Is it ever right to disobey the law?
Yes ☐ No ☐

4 Should important decisions in a democracy be submitted to voters rather than decided by Congress?
Yes ☐ No ☐

5 Is the government run by a few big interests looking out for themselves?
Yes ☐ No ☐

6 In a democracy should "majority rule" be able to limit the rights of members of an unpopular or dangerous minority?
Yes ☐ No ☐

7 Is government trying to do too many things that should be left to individuals?
Yes ☐ No ☐

8 Does the threat of terrorism on American soil justify increased government surveillance of its citizens?
Yes ☐ No ☐

Who has power and how they use it are the basis of all these questions. Issues of power underlie everything we call politics and the study of political science.

Politics and Political Science

Politics is deciding "who gets what, when, and how."[1] It is an activity by which people try to get more of whatever there is to get—money, prestige, jobs, respect, sex, even power itself. Politics occurs in many different settings. We talk about office politics, student politics, union politics, church politics, and so forth. But political science usually limits its attention to *politics in government.*

Political science is the study of politics, or the study of who gets what, when, and how. The *who* are the participants in politics—voters, special-interest groups, political parties, television and the press, corporations and labor unions, lawyers and lobbyists, foundations and think tanks, and both elected and appointed government officials, including members of Congress, the president and vice president, judges, prosecutors, and bureaucrats. The *what* of politics are public policies—the decisions that governments make concerning social welfare, health care, education, national defense, law enforcement, the environment, taxation, and thousands of other issues that come before governments. The *when* and *how* are the political process—campaigns and elections, political reporting in the news media, television debates, fund raising, lobbying, decision making in the White House and executive agencies, and decision making in the courts.

Political science is generally concerned with three questions. *Who governs? For what ends? By what means?* Throughout this book, we are concerned with who participates in politics, how government decisions are made, who benefits most from those decisions, and who bears their greatest costs (see Figure 1.1).

Politics would be simple if everyone agreed on who should govern, who should get what, who should pay for it, and how and when it should be done. But conflict arises from disagreements over these questions, and sometimes the question of confidence in the government itself underlies the conflict (see *What Do You Think?* "Can You Trust the Government?").

Politics and Government

What distinguishes governmental politics from politics in other institutions in society? After all, parents, teachers, unions, banks, corporations,

politics Deciding who gets what, when, and how.

political science The study of politics: who governs, for what ends, and by what means.

Figure 1.1   Who Gets What, When, and How

Political science is the study of politics. The distinguished political scientist Harold Lasswell entitled his most popular book *Politics: Who Gets What, When and How*. The first topic of politics is "Who?" (that is, who are the participants in politics, both within and outside of government?), "When and how are political decisions made?" (that is, how do the institutions and processes of politics function?), and "What outcomes are produced?" (that is, what public policies are adopted?). Shown here are some of the topics of concern to political science.

Who Governs: Participants

Governmental
President and White House staff
Executive Office of the President, including Office of Management and Budget
Cabinet officers and executive agency heads
Bureaucrats

Congress members
Congressional staff

Supreme Court justices
Federal appellate and district judges

Nongovernmental
Voters
Campaign contributors
Interest-group leaders and members
Party leaders and party identifiers in the electorate
Corporate and union leaders
Media leaders, including press and television anchors and reporters
Lawyers and lobbyists
Think tanks and foundation personnel

When and How: Institutions and Processes

Institutions
Constitution
  Separation of powers
  Checks and balances
  Federalism
  Judicial review
  Amendment procedures
  Electoral system

Presidency
Congress
  Senate
  House of Representatives

Courts
  Supreme Court
  Appellate courts
  District courts

Parties
  National committees
  Conventions
  State and local organizations

Press and television

Processes
Socialization and learning
Opinion formation
Party identification
Voting
Contributing
Joining organizations
Talking politics

Running for office
Campaigning
Polling
Fund raising
Parading and demonstrating
Nonviolent direct action
Violence

Agenda setting
Lobbying
Logrolling
Deciding
Budgeting
Implementing and evaluating
Adjudicating

What Outcomes: Public Policies

Civil liberties
Civil rights
Equality
Criminal justice
Welfare
Social Security
Health
Education
Energy

Environmental protection
Economic development
Economic stability
Taxation
Government spending and deficits
National defense
Foreign affairs
Homeland Security

— Think Again —
Should any group other than the government have the right to use force?

government Organization extending to the whole society that can legitimately use force to carry out its decisions.

and many other organizations make decisions about who gets what in society. The answer is that only **government** decisions can *extend to the whole society*, and only government can *legitimately use force*. Other institutions encompass only a part of society: for example, students and faculty in a college, members of a church or union, employees or customers of a corporation. And individuals have a legal right to voluntarily withdraw from *non*governmental organizations. But governments make decisions affecting everyone, and no one can voluntarily

Conflict exists in all political activities as participants struggle over who gets what, when, and how. From the streets to the Congress to the White House, participants in the political process compete to further their goals and ambitions.

withdraw from government's authority (without leaving the country, and thus becoming subject to some other government's authority). Some individuals and organizations—muggers, gangs, crime families—occasionally use physical force to get what they want. But only governments can use force legitimately—that is, people generally believe it is acceptable for the government to use force if necessary to uphold its laws, but they do not extend this right to other institutions or individuals.

Most people would say that they obey the law in order to avoid fines and stay out of prison. But if large numbers of people all decided to disobey the law at the same time, the government would not have enough police or jails to hold them all.

The government can rely on force only against relatively small numbers of offenders. Most of us, most of the time, obey laws out of habit—the habit of compliance. We have been taught to believe that law and order are necessary and that government is right to punish those who disobey its laws.

Government thus enjoys **legitimacy**, or rightfulness, in its use of force.[2] A democratic government has a special claim to legitimacy because it is based on the consent of its people, who participate in the selection of its leaders and the making of its laws. Those who disagree with a law have the option of working for its change by speaking out, petitioning, demonstrating, forming interest groups or parties, voting against unpopular leaders, or running for office themselves.

American Political Science Association Association of college and university teachers advises students how to study political science.
www.apsanet.org

—Think Again—
Is violence ever justified as a means of bringing about political change?

legitimacy Widespread acceptance of something as necessary, rightful, and legally binding.

WHAT DO YOU THINK?

Can You Trust the Government?

Americans are suspicious of big government. Many do not trust the government in Washington to "do what is right." Trust in government has varied over the years, as measured by polls asking, "How much of the time do you think you can trust the government in Washington to do what is right? Just about always? Most of the time? Some of the time? None of the time?" Low levels of trust and confidence in government may represent profound disaffection with the political system, or more superficial dissatisfaction with current leaders or policies.[a] During the early years of the Johnson Administration (and even earlier, during the Kennedy and Eisenhower presidencies), public confidence in government was high. But in the late '60s and early '70s defeat and humiliation in Vietnam appeared to diminish public confidence. On the heels of the Vietnam experience came the Watergate scandal and President Richard Nixon's forced resignation in 1974—the first resignation of a president in U.S. history—causing public confidence in government to fall further.

Throughout the long years of decline in public confidence in government, television has broadcast many negative images of government and public policy. Television producers seldom consider good news as "news" but instead focus on violence, scandal, corruption, and incompetence (see Chapter 6, "Mass Media: Setting the Political Agenda").

But public confidence in government can be at least partially restored, as it was in part during the Reagan presidency. Perhaps President Reagan's personal popularity was part of the reason that popular confidence in government rose.[b]

Economic recessions erode public confidence in government. People expect the president and Congress to lead them out of "hard times." George H. W. Bush's Gulf War success in 1991 raised public confidence only temporarily; the perceived failure of his administration to act decisively to restore the nation's economic health helped to send public confidence in government back down. Sustained growth in the economy during the 1990s under President Clinton improved public trust in government.

The terrorist attacks of September 11, 2001, rallied Americans behind their government as no other event since the Japanese attack on Pearl Harbor in 1941. American flags sprouted from homes, businesses, and automobiles. Trust in government "to do the right thing" leaped to levels not seen since the 1960s. This dramatic rise in trust after "9/11" leveled off in 2002, but still remained higher than at any time in recent years.

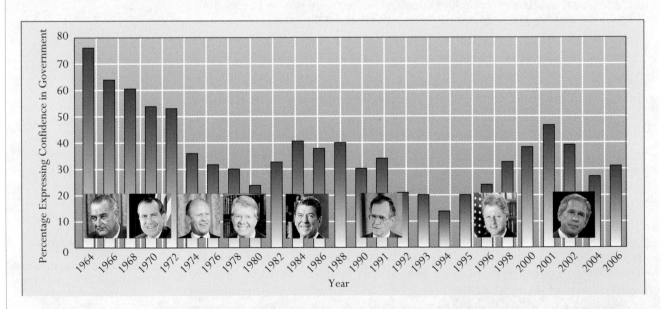

Public Confidence, That the Federal Government Can Be Trusted to "Do What Is Right Most of the Time"

[a]Timothy E. Cook and Paul Gronke, "The Skeptical American," *Journal of Politics* Vol. 67 (Aug., 2005) 784–803

[b]Arthur H. Miller, "Confidence in Government during the 1980s," *American Politics Quarterly* 19 (April 1991): 147–73.

Source: 1992–2006 data from Gallup Opinion Polls (http://www.gallup.com/poll/topics/trust_ gov.asd), Copyright © 1992–2004, The Gallup Organization.

Since people living in a democracy can effect change by "working within the system," they have a greater moral obligation to obey the law than people living under regimes in which they have no voice. However, there may be some occasions when "civil disobedience" even in a democracy may be morally justified (see *A Conflicting View:* "Sometimes It's Right to Disobey the Law").

The Purposes of Government

All governments tax, penalize, punish, restrict, and regulate their people. Governments in the United States—the federal government in Washington, the 50 state governments, and the more than 87,000 local governments—take nearly 40 cents out of every dollar Americans earn. Each year, the Congress enacts about 500 laws; federal bureaucracies publish about 19,000 rules and regulations, the state legislatures enact about 25,000 laws; and cities, counties, school districts, and other local governments enact countless local ordinances. Each of these laws restricts our freedom in some way.

Why do people put up with governments? An answer to this question can be found in the words of the Preamble to the Constitution of the United States:

> We the people of the United States, in Order to form a more perfect Union, establish Justice, insure domestic Tranquility, provide for the common defense, promote the general Welfare, and secure the Blessings of Liberty to ourselves and our Posterity, do ordain and establish this Constitution for the United States of America.

To Establish Justice and Insure Domestic Tranquility   Government manages conflict and maintains order. We might think of government as a **social contract** among people who agree to allow themselves to be regulated and taxed in exchange for protection of their lives and property. No society can allow individuals or groups to settle their conflicts by street fighting, murder, kidnapping, rioting, bombing, or terrorism. Whenever government fails to control such violence, we describe it as "a breakdown in law and order." Without the protection of government, human lives and property are endangered, and only those skilled with fists and weapons have much of a chance of survival. The seventeenth-century English political philosopher Thomas Hobbes described life without government as "a war where every man is enemy to every man," where people live in "continual fear and danger of violent death."[3]

To Provide for the Common Defense   Many anthropologists link the origins of government to warfare—to the need of early communities to protect themselves from raids by outsiders and to organize raids against others. Since the Revolutionary War, the U.S. government has been responsible for the country's defense. During the long Cold War, when America confronted a nuclear-armed, expansionist-minded, communist-governed Soviet Union, the United States spent nearly half of the federal budget on national defense. With the end of the Cold War, defense spending fell to about 15 percent of the federal budget, but defense spending has begun to creep upward again as the nation confronts the new war on terrorism. National defense will always remain a primary responsibility of United States government.

To Promote the General Welfare   Government promotes the general welfare in a number of ways. It provides **public goods**—goods and services that private markets cannot readily furnish either because they are too expensive for individuals to buy for themselves (for example, a national park, a highway, or a

Think Again

Is it ever right to disobey the law?

The King Center   Atlanta-based center commemorates the life and teachings of Martin Luther King, Jr.
www.theKingCenter.com

Internet Encyclopedia of Philosophy   At this site, you can find a concise description of social contract theory along with a discussion of John Locke's writing.
www.utm.edu/research/iep/

social contract   Idea that government originates as an implied contract among individuals who agree to obey laws in exchange for protection of their rights.

DefenseLink   Official site of the U.S. Department of Defense, with current news as well as links to Army, Navy, Air Force, Marine, and other defense agencies.
www.defenselink.gov

public goods   Goods and services that cannot readily be provided by markets, either because they are too expensive for a single individual to buy or because if one person bought them, everyone else would use them without paying.

A CONFLICTING VIEW

Sometimes It's Right to Disobey the Law

Civil disobedience is the nonviolent violation of laws that people believe to be unjust. Civil disobedience denies the *legitimacy,* or rightfulness, of a law and implies that a higher moral authority takes precedence over unjust laws. It is frequently a political tactic of minorities. (Majorities can more easily change laws through conventional political activity.)

Why resort to civil disobedience in a democracy? Why not work within the democratic system to change unjust laws? In 1963 a group of Alabama clergy posed these questions to Martin Luther King, Jr., and asked him to call off mass demonstrations in Birmingham, Alabama. King, who had been arrested in the demonstrations, replied in his now famous "Letter from Birmingham City Jail":

Dr. Martin Luther King, Jr., shown here marching in Mississippi with his wife, Coretta Scott King, and others, used civil disobedience to advance the rights of African Americans during the 1950s and 1960s. (Copyright © Flip Schulke)

> One may well ask, "How can you advocate breaking some laws and obeying others?" The answer is found in the fact that there are unjust laws. I would be the first to advocate obeying just laws. One has not only a legal but a moral responsibility to obey just laws. Conversely, one has a moral responsibility to disobey unjust laws.

King argued that *nonviolent direct action* was a vital aspect of democratic politics. The political purpose of civil disobedience is to call attention or "to bear witness" to the existence of injustices. Only laws regarded as unjust are broken, and they are broken openly, without hatred or violence. Punishment is actively sought rather than avoided, since punishment will further emphasize the injustice of the laws.

The objective of nonviolent civil disobedience is to stir the conscience of an apathetic majority and to win support for measures that will eliminate the injustices. By accepting punishment for the violation of an unjust law, persons practicing civil disobedience demonstrate their sincerity. They hope to shame the majority and to make it ask itself how far it is willing to go to protect the status quo. Thus, according to King's

teachings, civil disobedience is clearly differentiated from hatred and violence:

> One who breaks an unjust law must do it openly, lovingly (not hatefully as the white mothers did in New Orleans when they were seen on television screaming "nigger, nigger, nigger") and with a willingness to accept the penalty. I submit that an individual who breaks a law that conscience tells him is unjust, and willingly accepts the penalty by staying in jail to arouse the conscience of the community over its injustice, is in reality expressing the very highest respect for law.

In 1964 Martin Luther King, Jr., received the Nobel Peace Prize in recognition of his extraordinary contributions to the development of nonviolent methods of social change.

Source: Martin Luther King, Jr., "Letter from Birmingham City Jail," April 16, 1963.

---

free market Free competition for voluntary exchange among individuals, firms, and corporations.

sewage disposal plant) or because if one person bought them, everyone else would "free-ride," or use them without paying (for example, clean air, police protection, or national defense).

Nevertheless, Americans acquire most of their goods and services on the **free market**, through voluntary exchange among individuals, firms, and corporations. The **gross domestic product (GDP)**—the dollar sum of all the goods and services produced in the United States in a year—amounts to more than $12 trillion.

Government spending in the United States—federal, state, and local governments combined—amounts to about $4 trillion, or an amount equivalent to 30 percent of the gross domestic product.

Governments also regulate society. Free markets cannot function effectively if individuals and firms engage in fraud, deception, or unfair competition, or if contracts cannot be enforced. Moreover, many economic activities impose costs on persons who are not direct participants in these activities. Economists refer to such costs as **externalities**. A factory that produces air pollution or wastewater imposes external costs on community residents who would otherwise enjoy cleaner air or water. A junkyard that creates an eyesore makes life less pleasant for neighbors and passersby. Many government regulations are designed to reduce these external costs.

To promote general welfare, governments also use **income transfers** from taxpayers to people who are regarded as deserving. Government agencies and programs provide support and care for individuals who cannot supply these things for themselves through the private job market, for example, ill, elderly, and disabled people, and dependent children who cannot usually be expected to find productive employment. The largest income transfer programs are Social Security and Medicare, which are paid to the elderly regardless of their personal wealth. Other large transfer payments go to farmers, veterans, and the unemployed, as well as to a wide variety of businesses. As we shall see, the struggle of individuals and groups to obtain direct government payments is a major motivator of political activity (see What Do You Think? "What Government Programs Do You Support?").

To Secure the Blessings of Liberty   All governments must maintain order, protect national security, provide public goods, regulate society, and care for those unable to fend for themselves. But *democratic* governments have a special added responsibility—to protect individual liberty by ensuring that all people are treated equally before the law. No one is above the law. The president must obey the Constitution and laws of the United States, and so must members of Congress, governors, judges, and the police. A democratic government must protect people's freedom to speak and write what they please, to practice their religion, to petition, to form groups and parties, to enjoy personal privacy, and to exercise their rights if accused of a crime.

The Meaning of Democracy

Throughout the centuries, thinkers in many different cultures contributed to the development of democratic government. Early Greek philosophers contributed the word **democracy**, which means "rule by the many." But there is no single definition of *democracy*, nor is there a tightly organized system of democratic thought. It is better, perhaps, to speak of democratic traditions than of a single democratic ideology.

Unfortunately, the looseness of the term *democracy* allows it to be perverted by *anti*democratic governments. Hardly a nation in the world exists that does not *claim* to be "democratic." Governments that outlaw political opposition, suppress dissent, discourage religion, and deny fundamental freedoms of speech and press still claim to be "democracies," "democratic republics," or "people's republics" (for example, the Democratic People's Republic of Korea is the official name of Communist North Korea). These governments defend their use of the term *democracy* by claiming that their policies reflect the true interests of their people. But they are unwilling to allow political freedoms or to hold free elections in

gross domestic product (GDP) Measure of economic performance in terms of the nation's total production of goods and services for a single year, valued in terms of market prices.

externalities Costs imposed on people who are not direct participants in an activity.

income transfers Government transfers of income from taxpayers to persons regarded as deserving.

www Council for Excellence in Government
A Washington-based think tank, relatively unbiased, that regularly publishes polls and studies on key issues facing the nation. *www.excelgov.org*

democracy Governing system in which the people govern themselves, from the Greek term meaning "rule by the many."

www U.S. Information Agency
Official government site defining democracy, individual rights, and the culture of democracy. *www.usinfo.state.gov/products/pubs/whatsdem*

WHAT DO YOU THINK?

What Government Programs Do You Support?

Although many Americans lack confidence in their government in general, they support many specific programs of the government. In somewhat of a paradox, Americans often express distrust in the federal government, yet at the same time approve of many of the programs and activities of that government.

The Council on Excellence in Government, which conducted this poll, believes that the most highly regarded programs are those that serve (or potentially serve) all Americans, rather than target groups.

Support for Government Programs

Support a Great Deal	Percent
Social Security	69
The Armed Forces	64
Medicare	64
Enforcing workplace safety	63
Enforcing laws against discrimination	61
Programs for public schools	61
Enforcing food and drug safety	60
College student loans	56
Enforcing minimum wage laws	56
Enforcing environmental protection laws	55
Federal law enforcement, such as the FBI	45
Enforcing family and medical leave laws	40
NASA and the space program	34
Affirmative action programs	29
Welfare programs	24

Source: Council Excellence in Government nationwide survey, February, 1997. www.excelgov.org. Reprinted by permission of Council on Excellence in Government.

democratic ideals
Individual dignity, equality before the law, widespread participation in public decisions, and public decisions by majority rule, with one person having one vote.

order to find out whether their people really agree with their policies. In effect, they use the term as a political slogan rather than a true description of their government.

The actual existence of **democratic ideals** varies considerably from country to country, regardless of their names (see *Compared to What?* "Freedom and Democracy around the World"). A meaningful definition of democracy must include the following ideals: 1) recognition of the dignity of every individual; 2) equal protection under the law for every individual; 3) opportunity for everyone to participate in public decisions; and 4) decision making by majority rule, with one person having one vote.

Individual Dignity   The underlying value of democracy is the dignity of the individual. Human beings are entitled to life and liberty, personal property, and equal protection under the law. These liberties are *not* granted by governments; they belong to every person born into the world. The English political philosopher John Locke (1632–1704) argued that a higher "natural law" guaranteed liberty to every person and that this natural law was morally superior to all human laws and governments. Each individual possesses "certain inalienable Rights, among these are Life, Liberty, and Property."[4] When Thomas Jefferson wrote his eloquent defense of the American Revolution in the Declaration of Independence for the Continental Congress in Philadelphia in 1776, he borrowed heavily from Locke (perhaps even to the point of plagiarism):

> We hold these truths to be self-evident, that all Men are created equal, that they are endowed by their Creator with certain unalienable Rights, that among these are Life, Liberty and the Pursuit of Happiness.

Individual dignity requires personal freedom. People who are directed by governments in every aspect of their lives, people who are "collectivized" and made into workers for the state, people who are enslaved—all are denied the personal

COMPARED TO WHAT?

Freedom and Democracy Around the World

Worldwide progress toward freedom over the past half-century has been impressive. In 1950 there were 22 democracies accounting for 31 percent of the world population that were said to be "free." Another 21 nations with restricted democratic practices were labeled "partly free"; they accounted for an additional 11.9 percent of the world population. By 2005, democracy had spread to 88 "free" countries that constituted 44 percent of the world population; an additional 21 percent lived in nations labeled "partly free." "Not-free" authoritarian and totalitarian regimes governed more than one-third of the world's population.[a]

Worldwide progress toward freedom and democracy has been evident since 1989 notably as a result of the collapse of communism in Eastern Europe and the demise of the Soviet Union.

One way to assess the degree of democracy in a governmental system is to consider its record in ensuring political freedoms—enabling citizens to participate meaningfully in government—and individual liberties. A checklist for political freedoms might include whether the chief executive and national legislature are elected; whether elections are generally fair, with open campaigning and honest tabulation of votes; and whether multiple candidates and parties participate. A checklist for individual liberties might include whether the press and broadcasting are free and independent of the government; whether people are free to assemble, protest, and form opposition parties; whether religious institutions, labor unions, business organizations, and other groups are free and independent of the government; and whether individuals are free to own property, travel, and move their residence.

The Freedom House is a New York-based think tank that regularly surveys political conditions around the world (see map). Russia's score was downgraded by Freedom House in 2004 and its classification remains only "partly free." Freedom House denounced President Vladimir Putin's government takeover of that nation's media.

[a]Freedom House, *Democracy's Century* (New York: Freedom House, 2001).

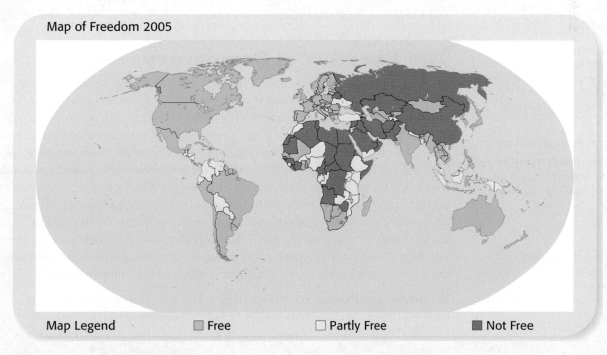

Map of Freedom 2005

Map Legend   ☐ Free   ☐ Partly Free   ■ Not Free

Source: Reprinted by permission of Freedom House.

www **Freedom House**
A think tank
monitoring the ongoing
evolution of global human
rights and liberty; provides an
annual world survey covering
freedom's progress
throughout the state system.
www.freedomhouse.org/

—— Think Again ——

**Should important
decisions in a democracy
be submitted to voters
rather than decided by
Congress?**

www **National
Endowment for
Democracy**
Private advocacy group for
worldwide democracy and
human rights. *www.ned.org*

—— Think Again ——

**In a democracy should
"majority rule" be able to
limit the rights of members
of an unpopular or
dangerous minority?**

—— Think Again ——

**Is government trying to do
too many things that
should be left to
individuals?**

paradox of democracy
Potential for conflict between
individual freedom and
majority rule.

dignity to which all human beings are entitled. Democratic governments try to minimize the role of government in the lives of citizens.

Equality   True democracy requires equal protection of the law for every individual. Democratic governments cannot discriminate between blacks and whites, or men and women, or rich and poor, or any groups of people in applying the law. Not only must a democratic government refrain from discrimination itself, but it must also work to prevent discrimination in society generally. Today our notion of equality extends to equality of opportunity—the obligation of government to ensure that all Americans have an equal opportunity to develop their full potential.

Participation in Decision Making   Democracy means individual participation in the decisions that affect individuals' lives. People should be free to choose for themselves how they want to live. Individual participation in government is necessary for individual dignity. People in a democracy should not have decisions made *for* them but *by* them. Even if they make mistakes, it is better that they be permitted to do so than to take away their rights to make their own decisions. The true democrat would reject even a wise and benevolent dictatorship because it would threaten the individual's character, self-reliance, and dignity. The argument for democracy is not that the people will always choose wise policies for themselves, but that people who cannot choose for themselves are not really free.

Majority Rule: One Person, One Vote   Collective decision making in democracies must be by majority rule, with each person having one vote. That is, each person's vote must be equal to every other person's, regardless of status, money, or fame. Whenever any individual is denied political equality because of race, sex, or wealth, then the government is not truly democratic. Majorities are not always right. But majority *rule* means that all persons have an equal say in decisions affecting them. If people are truly equal, their votes must count equally, and a majority vote must decide the issue, even if the majority decides foolishly.

The Paradox of Democracy

But what if a *majority* of the people decide to attack the rights of some unpopular individuals or minorities? What if hate, prejudice, or racism infects a majority of people and they vote for leaders who promise to "get rid of the Jews" or "put blacks in their place" or "bash a few gays"? What if a majority of people vote to take away the property of wealthy people and distribute it among themselves.[5] Do we abide by the principle of majority rule and allow the majority to do what it wants? Or do we defend the principle of individual liberty and limit the majority's power? If we enshrine the principle of majority rule, we are placing all our confidence in the wisdom and righteousness of the majority of the people. Yet we know that democracy means more than majority rule, that it also means freedom and dignity for the individual. How do we resolve this **paradox of democracy**—the potential for conflict between majority rule and individual freedom?

Limiting the Power of Majorities   The Founders of the American nation were not sure that freedom would be safe in the hands of the majority. In *The Federalist Papers* in 1787, James Madison warned against a direct democracy: "Pure democracy . . . can admit of no cure for the mischiefs of faction. . . . There is nothing to check the inducements to sacrifice the weaker party, or an obnoxious individual."[6] So the Founders wrote a Constitution and adopted a Bill of Rights that limited the power of government over the individual, that placed some personal liberties beyond the reach of majorities. They established the principle

The paradox of democracy balances the principles of majority rule against the principle of individual liberty. When the German people voted Adolf Hitler and the Nazi Party into power, did majority rule give the Nazis free rein to restrict the individual liberties of the people? Or did those who abhorred the trespasses of their government have the right to fight aganinst its power?

of **limited government**—a government that is itself restrained by law. Under a limited government, even if a majority of voters wanted to, they could not prohibit communists or atheists or racists from speaking or writing. Nor could they ban certain religions, set aside the rights of criminal defendants to a fair trial, or prohibit people from moving or quitting their jobs. These rights belong to individuals, not to majorities or governments.

limited government
Principle that government power over the individual is limited, that there are some personal liberties that even a majority cannot regulate, and that government itself is restrained by law.

Totalitarianism: Unlimited Government Power

No government can be truly democratic if it directs every aspect of its citizens' lives. Individuals must be free to shape their own lives, free from the dictates of governments or even majorities of their fellow citizens. Indeed, we call a government with *un*limited power over its citizens totalitarian. Under **totalitarianism**, the individual possesses no personal liberty. Totalitarian governments decide what people can say or write;

totalitarianism Rule by an elite that exercises unlimited power over individuals in all aspects of life.

Political sociologists have observed that the military in totalitarian societies has a distinct body language. Soldiers in Nazi Germany and, as seen here, communist North Korea used a "goose step" when on parade—a march in which the knee is unbent and the foot, encased in a heavy boot, is stamped on the ground, providing a powerful image of authority and force. In democratic societies, the goose step is not employed; indeed, it is regarded as somewhat ridiculous.

what unions, churches, or parties they can join, if any; where people must live; what work they must do; what goods they can find in stores and what they will be allowed to buy and sell; whether citizens will be allowed to travel outside of their country; and so on. Under a totalitarian government, the total life of the individual is subject to government control.

Totalitarian governments undertake to control all agencies of the government, including the military and the police, and virtually all other institutions of society including newspapers, television, schools, churches, businesses, banks, labor unions, and any other organization that might challenge their control. In contrast, democratic societies allow many other institutions to operate independently of the government (see *Up Close:* "Confidence in American Institutions").

Authoritarianism   In many countries throughout the world, a single individual or ruling group monopolizes all *political* power, but allows people to otherwise lead their lives as they wish. **Authoritarianism** is largely concerned with dominating government. People can conduct business and trade, join churches, live where they wish, and otherwise conduct their *private* lives without government interference. They have no role to play in politics, no control over their government, no competitive political parties, no elections, and are otherwise barred from political life. Authoritarianism appears somewhat less oppressive, at least in the everyday lives of the people, than totalitarianism.

Constitutional Government   Constitutions, written or unwritten, are the principal means by which governmental powers are limited. Constitutions set forth the liberties of individuals and restrain governments from interfering with these liberties. Consider, for example, the opening words of the First Amendment to the U.S. Constitution: "Congress shall make no law respecting an establishment of religion, or prohibiting the free exercise thereof." This amendment places religious belief beyond the reach of the government. The government itself is restrained by law. It cannot, even by majority vote, interfere with the personal liberty to worship as one chooses. In addition, armed with the power of judicial review, the courts can declare unconstitutional laws passed by majority vote of Congress or state legislatures (see "Judicial Power" in Chapter 13).

Throughout this book we examine how well limited constitutional government succeeds in preserving individual liberty in the United States. We examine free speech and press, the mass media, religious freedom, the freedom to protest and demonstrate, and the freedom to support political candidates and interest groups of all kinds. We examine how well the U.S. Constitution protects individuals from discrimination and inequality. And we examine how far government should go in protecting society without destroying individual liberty (see *Up Close:* "Terrorism's Threat to Democracy" on page 18).

Direct Versus Representative Democracy

In the Gettysburg Address, Abraham Lincoln spoke about "a government of the people, by the people, for the people," and his ringing phrase remains an American ideal. But can we take this phrase literally? More than 300 million Americans are spread over 4 million square miles. If we brought everyone together, standing shoulder to shoulder, they would occupy 70 square miles. One round of five-minute speeches by everyone would take over 3,000 years. "People could be born, grow old, and die while they waited for the assembly to make one decision."[7]

Direct democracy (also called pure or participatory democracy), where everyone actively participates in every decision, is rare. The closest approximation to direct democracy in American government may be the traditional New England

---

authoritarianism Monopoly of political power by an individual or small group that otherwise allows people to go about their private lives as they wish.

New Rules Project An organization advocating local government solutions and "direct democracy," including the New England town meeting. *www.newrules.org*

direct democracy Governing system in which every person participates actively in every public decision, rather than delegating decision making to representatives.

UP CLOSE

Confidence in American Institutions

American's confidence in their government varies over time, but overall it is much lower than a generation ago. Which institutions in society today enjoy the confidence of the American people? In somewhat of a paradox for a democratic society, the *military* enjoys the greatest confidence of Americans. The *police* also enjoyed a great deal of confidence, although "the criminal justice system" (defined by most respondents as the courts) does not. Among branches of the national government, the president and the Supreme Court rate fairly high in confidence. But Congress is rated very low.

Q. I am going to read you a list of institutions in American society. Please tell me how much confidence you, yourself, have in each one: a great deal, quite a lot, some, or very little."

	Percent Saying a Great Deal or Quite a Lot
The military	74
The police	63
Organized religion	53
Banks	49
The presidency	44
The medical system	42
The U.S. Supreme Court	41
Public schools	37
Television news	28
Newspapers	28
The criminal justice system	26
Organized labor	24
Congress	22
Big business	22
Health maintenance organizations (HMOs)	17

Source: Copyright © 2005 The Gallup Organization.

Americans' patriotism and love of the flag as a symbol of their freedom doesn't always translate into confidence in government institutions.

town meeting, where all of the citizens come together face-to-face to decide about town affairs. But today most New England towns vest authority in a board of officials elected by the townspeople to make policy decisions between town meetings, and professional administrators are appointed to supervise the day-to-day town services. The town meeting is vanishing because citizens cannot spend so much of their time and energy in community decision making.

Representative democracy recognizes that it is impossible to expect millions of people to come together and decide every issue. Instead, representatives of the people are elected by the people to decide issues on behalf of the people. Elections must be open to competition so that the people can choose representatives who reflect their own views. And elections must take place in an environment of free speech and press, so that both candidates and voters can freely express their views. Finally, elections must be held periodically so that representatives can be thrown out of office if they no longer reflect the views of the majority of the people.

No government can claim to be a representative democracy, then, unless

1. Representatives are selected by vote of all the people.

2. Elections are open to competition.

representative democracy
Governing system in which public decision making is delegated to representatives of the people chosen by popular vote in free, open, and periodic elections.

Direct democracy still lives in many New England towns, where citizens come together periodically to pass laws, elect officials, and make decisions about such matters as taxation and land use.

3. Candidates and voters can freely express themselves.

4. Representatives are selected periodically.

So when we hear of "elections" in which only one party is permitted to run candidates, candidates are not free to express their views, or leaders are elected "for life," then we know that these governments are not really democracies, regardless of what they may call themselves.

Throughout this book, as we examine how well representative democracy works in the United States, we consider such issues as participation in elections—why some people vote and others do not—whether parties and candidates offer the voters real alternatives, whether modern political campaigning informs voters or only confuses them, and whether elected representatives are responsive to the wishes of voters. These are the kinds of issues that concern political science.

Who Really Governs?

────Think Again────

Is the government run by a few big interests looking out for themselves?

Democracy is an inspiring ideal. But is democratic government really possible? Is it possible for millions of people to govern themselves, with every voice having equal influence? Or will a small number of people inevitably acquire more power than others? To what extent is democracy attainable in *any* society, and how democratic is the American political system? That is, who really governs?

The Elitist Perspective   "Government is always government by the few, whether in the name of the few, the one, or the many."[8] This quotation from political scientists Harold Lasswell and Daniel Lerner expresses the basic idea of **elitism**. All societies, including democracies, divide themselves into the few who have power and the many who do not. In every society, there is a division of labor. Only a few people are directly involved in governing a nation; most people are content to let others undertake the tasks of government. The *elite* are the few who have power; the *masses* are the many who do not.[9] This theory holds that an elite is inevitable in any social organization. We cannot form a club, a church, a business, or a government without selecting some people to provide leadership. And leaders will always have a perspective on the organization different from that of its members.[10]

In any large, complex society, then, whether or not it is a democracy, decisions are made by tiny minorities. Out of more than 300 million Americans, only

elitism Political system in which power is concentrated in the hands of a relatively small group of individuals or institutions.

a few thousand individuals at most participate directly in decisions about war and peace, wages and prices, employment and production, law and justice, taxes and benefits, health and welfare.

Elitism does *not* mean that leaders always exploit or oppress members. On the contrary, elites may be very concerned for the welfare of the masses. Elite status may be open to ambitious, talented, or educated individuals from the masses or may be closed to all except the wealthy. Elites may be very responsive to public opinion, or they may ignore the usually apathetic and ill-informed masses. But whether elites are self-seeking or public-spirited, open or closed, responsive or unresponsive, it is they and not the masses who actually make the decisions.

Most people do not regularly concern themselves with decision making in Washington. They are more concerned with their jobs, family, sports, and recreation than they are with politics. They are not well informed about tax laws, foreign policy, or even who represents them in Congress. Since the "masses" are largely apathetic and ill informed about policy questions, their views are likely to be influenced more by what they see and hear on television than by their own experience. Most communication flows downward from elites to masses. Elitism argues that the masses have at best only an indirect influence on the decisions of elites.

Opinion polls indicate that many Americans agree with the elitist contention that government is run by "a few big interests" (see Figure 1.2).

The Pluralist Perspective   No one seriously argues that all Americans participate in *all* of the decisions that shape their lives; that majority preferences *always* prevail; that the values of life, liberty, and property are *never* sacrificed; or that every American enjoys equality of opportunity. Nevertheless, most American political scientists argue that the American system of government, which they describe as "pluralist," is the best possible approximation of the democratic ideal in a large, complex society. Pluralism is designed to make the theory of democracy "more realistic."[11]

Pluralism is the belief that democracy can be achieved in a large, complex society by competition, bargaining, and compromise among organized groups and that individuals can participate in decision making through membership in these groups and by choosing among parties and candidates in elections.

Pluralists recognize that the individual acting alone is no match for giant government bureaucracies, big corporations and banks, the television networks,

pluralism Theory that democracy can be achieved through competition among multiple organized groups and that individuals can participate in politics through group memberships and elections.

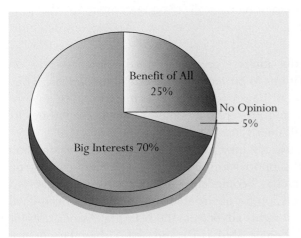

Figure 1.2 Public Opinion about Who Runs the Country

Would you say the government is pretty much run by a few big interests looking out for themselves or that it is run for the benefit of all the people?

Source: The Gallup Poll, July 6–9, 2000. Copyright © 1996–2004 by The Gallup Organization.

UP CLOSE

Terrorism's Threat to Democracy

The horrifying images of "9/11" will not be easily forgotten—America's tallest skyscrapers exploding in flames and crumbling to earth—images projected over and over again on the nation's television screens. Commercial airliners, loaded with fuel and passengers, flown at high speeds directly into the symbols of America's financial and military power—the World Trade Center in New York and the Pentagon in Washington. Within minutes, thousands of lives are lost on American soil—more than at any time since the Civil War. After September 11 America found itself in a new war, a war against worldwide networks of terrorists.

The horrifying images of "9/11" will not be easily forgotten—America's tallest skyscrapers exploding and crumbling to earth—images projected over and over again on the nation's television screens.

The Goal of Terrorism   Terrorism is violence directed against innocent civilians to advance political goals. As barbaric as terrorism appears to civilized peoples, it is not without a rationale. Terrorists are not "crazies." Their first goal is to announce in the most dramatic fashion their own grievances, their commitment to violence, and their disregard for human life, often including their own. In its initial phase the success of a terrorist act is directly related to the publicity it receives. Terrorist groups jubilantly claim responsibility for their acts. The more horrendous, the more media coverage, the more damage, the more dead—all add to the success of the terrorists in attracting attention to themselves.

A prolonged campaign of terrorism is designed to inspire pervasive fear among people, to convince them that their government cannot protect them, and to undermine their confidence in their political system. If the government fails to suppress terrorism, people become ever more fearful, more willing to accept restrictions on liberties, and more open to

the appeals of demagogues who promise to restore order to protect people at any cost. Or a weakened government may resort to "negotiations" with the leaders of terrorist groups, implicitly granting them legitimacy and providing them the opportunity to advance their goals.

America's Response   But America's response to the terrorist attacks of September 11, 2001, was precisely the *opposite* of the intention of the terrorists. National pride, confidence in national leadership, and faith in human nature, all soared among the American people in the aftermath of the attack. Patriotism flourished. Flags flew from businesses, homes, and automobiles. The attack united the country in a way that no other event since the 1941 Japanese attack on Pearl Harbor had done. Trust in government rose to highs not seen since the 1960s. Initial popular support for military action was overwhelming.

Democracy Net
Democracy site of the League of Women Voters linking ZIP codes to your federal, state, and local representatives. *www.dnet.org*

labor unions, or other powerful interest groups. Instead, pluralists rely on *competition* among these organizations to protect the interests of individuals. They hope that countervailing centers of power—big business, big labor, big government—will check one another and prevent any single group from abusing its power and oppressing individual Americans.

Individuals in a pluralist democracy may not participate directly in decision making, but they can join and support *interest groups* whose leaders bargain on their behalf in the political arena. People are more effective in organized groups—for example, the Sierra Club for environmentalists, the American Civil Liberties Union (ACLU) for civil rights advocates, the National Association for the Advancement of Colored People (NAACP) and the Urban League for

However, this "rally 'round the flag" effect could not be sustained. Mass support for the nation's elite over a long war on terrorism—with continuing terrorist attacks, daily casualties among American soldiers, and few reported victories in a largely hidden conflict—declined over time. Political partisanship again replaced national unity, and Washington began "the blame game." Support for the war on terrorism gradually eroded (see Chapter 18).

Security vs. Liberty   Threats to national security have historically resulted in challenges to individual liberty. Abraham Lincoln suspended the *writ of habeas corpus* (the requirement that authorities bring defendants before a judge and show cause for their detention) during the Civil War. (Only after the war did the U.S. Supreme Court hold that he had no authority to suspend the writ.[a])

In February 1942, shortly after the Japanese attack on Pearl Harbor, President Franklin D. Roosevelt authorized the removal and internment of Japanese Americans living on the West Coast. The U.S. Supreme Court upheld this flagrant violation of the Constitution;[b] not until 1988 did the U.S. Congress vote reparations and make public apologies to the surviving victims.

New Restrictions on Liberty   The "9/11" terrorist attack on America inspired Congress and the president to enact and enforce greater restrictions on individual liberty than the nation had experienced since World War II. Congress passed the Patriot Act with near-unanimous support of Democrats and Republicans. Among other things, the Act allows searches without notice to the suspect; grants "roving" wiretap warrants that allow government eavesdropping on any telephones used by suspects; allows the interception of e-mail; allows investiga-

tors to obtain information from credit card companies, banks, libraries, and other businesses; authorizes the seizure of properties used to commit or facilitate terrorism; and allows the detention of noncitizens charged with terrorism. President George W. Bush created a new Department of Homeland Security, reorganizing more than forty federal agencies that have a role in combating terrorism.

President Bush also announced that "enemy combatants" captured on the battlefields of Afghanistan and Iraq would be tried by military tribunals. Prisoners of war have never been entitled to constitutional protection. "Detainees" from the war on terrorism are not officially prisoners of war; most are being held at the U.S. base in Guantanamo Bay, Cuba. As military detainees, they were not given lawyers or access to courts, although a Supreme Court decision in 2004 ordered the U.S. to provide them with lawyers and hearings (see Chapter 14).[c]

Terrorism and Democracy   Terrorism has brought mixed blessings to American democracy. It has succeeded in uniting Americans, inspiring patriotism, and increasing their trust in government. But it has also inspired a greater willingness to accept new restrictions on individual liberty. In the past, restrictions on individual liberty have been relaxed when the perceived crisis has subsided. How long will the "war on terrorism" last? Will Americans be asked to sacrifice additional liberties in this war? How far are Americans willing to go in sacrificing individual liberty to achieve national security?

See Robert A. Pape, "The Strategic Logic of Suicide Terrorism," *American Political Science Review* 97 (August 2003): 343–361.

[a]Ex parte Milligan (1866).
[b]*Korematsu v. U.S.*, 323 U.S. 214 (1944).
[c]*Rasul v. Bush*, June 28, 2004

African Americans, the American Legion and Veterans of Foreign Wars for veterans, and the National Rifle Association (NRA) for opponents of gun control.

According to the pluralist view, the Democratic and Republican parties are really coalitions of groups: the national Democratic Party is a coalition of union members, big-city residents, blacks, Catholics, Jews, and, until recently, southerners; the national Republican Party is a coalition of business and professional people, suburbanites, farmers, and white Protestants. When voters choose candidates and parties, they are helping to determine which interest groups will enjoy a better reception in government.

Pluralists contend that there are multiple leadership groups in society (hence the term *pluralism*). They contend that power is widely dispersed among these

www The Terrorism Research Center
News and information on terrorist attacks around the world and list of terrorist organizations.
www.terrorism.com

A CONFLICTING VIEW

Complaints About the American Political System

Overall, Americans are very patriotic. Indeed, most polls conducted in United States and other democratic nations show Americans to be the most patriotic citizens in the free world.

Nonetheless, many Americans express serious reservations about their political system. They believe strongly in the ideals of democracy but they are realistic in their appraisal of its weaknesses as well. A majority of Americans describe as "a major problem": elected officials caring more about re-election than what's best for the country; good people being discouraged from running for office because of the high costs of campaigns; citizens who don't stay informed about politics; a decline in moral and ethical standards in government; and the role that money plays in elections and influencing decisions.

Q. As I read each item, tell me how much of a problem you think it is for the political system today: a major problem, somewhat of a problem, or not much of a problem.

Women have achieved political prominence in their party and in the U.S. Senate. Hillary Clinton (D-NY), Elizabeth Dole (R-NC), and Kay Bailey Hutchinson (R-TX) are among women leaders in the Senate.

	Major Problem	Somewhat of a Problem	Not much of a Problem
Elected officials caring more about getting reelected than doing what is best for the country	76%	19%	4%
The two major political parties not being responsive enough to people's concerns	58%	32%	7%
Good people being discouraged from running for office by the high costs of campaigns	71%	22%	6%
Political contributions having too much influence on elections and government policy	66%	25%	7%
Citizens not making enough effort to vote or stay informed about politics and government	68%	26%	5%
A decline in moral and ethical values in politics	59%	30%	9%
Elected officials spending too much of their time raising money for election campaigns	61%	30%	6%
Elected officials seeking or receiving political contributions while making decisions about issues of concern to those giving money	65%	27%	6%

Source: From *Beyond Red and Blue,* Pew Research Center for the People and the Press, May 20, 2005. Copyright © 2005 by the Pew Research Center. Reprinted by permission.

groups; that no one group, not even the wealthy upper class, dominates decision making; and that groups that are influential in one area of decision making are not necessarily the same groups that are influential in other areas of decision making. Different groups of leaders make decisions in different issue areas.

Pluralism recognizes that public policy does not always coincide with majority preferences. Instead, public policy is the "equilibrium" reached in the conflict

A CONSTITUTIONAL NOTE

Representative Government, Not Direct Democracy

Nowhere in the Constitution do we find a provision for national referenda voting on any topic, however important for the nation. Indeed, nowhere do we find the word "democracy" in the Constitution. Rather, the founders believed in "republican" government, that is, decision making by representatives of the people, *not* by the people themselves. James Madison wrote, "the public voice, pronounced by representatives of the people, will be more consonant to the public good than if pronounced by the people themselves."

It was not until over a century later that "populism"—a strong political movement mainly in the Midwestern and Western states that appealed especially to farmers—succeeded in getting the initiative and referendum adopted, allowing *state* voters to vote directly on some issues. (The initiative allows citizens to place issues on the ballot by obtaining a certain number of signatures on a petition. The referendum is a popular vote that decides whether the issue becomes part of the state constitution or state law.) Today about half of the states have the initiative and referendum. (The legislatures of all fifty states can place an issue on the ballot if they choose to do so, usually a change in the state constitution.) But Americans cannot vote directly on *national* issues.

among group interests. It is the balance of competing interest groups, and therefore, say the pluralists, it is a reasonable approximation of society's preferences.

Democracy in America

Is democracy alive and well in America today? Elitism raises serious questions about the possibility of achieving true democracy in any large, complex society. Pluralism is more comforting; it offers a way of reaffirming democratic values and providing some practical solutions to the problem of individual participation in a modern society.

There is no doubt about the strength of democratic *ideals* in American society. These ideals—individual dignity, equality, popular participation in government, and majority rule—are the standards by which we judge the performance of the American political system. But we are still faced with the task of describing the *reality* of American politics.

This book explores who gets what, when, and how in the American political system; who participates in politics; what policies are decided upon; and when and how these decisions are made. In so doing, it raises many controversial questions about the realities of democracy, elitism, and pluralism in American life. But this book does not supply the answers; as a responsible citizen, you have to provide your own answers. At the completion of your studies, you will have to decide for yourself whether the American political system is truly democratic. Your studies will help inform your judgment, but, in the end, you yourself must make that judgment. That is the burden of freedom.

Summary Notes

- Politics is deciding who gets what, when, and how. It occurs in many different settings, but political science focuses on politics in government.

- Political science focuses on three central questions:
  Who governs?
  For what ends?
  By what means?

- Government is distinguished from other social organizations in that it
  Extends to the whole society
  Can legitimately use force

- The purposes of government are to
  Maintain order in society
  Provide for national defense
  Provide "public goods"
  Regulate society
  Transfer income
  Protect individual liberty

- The ideals of democracy include
  Recognition of individual dignity and personal freedom
  Equality before the law
  Widespread participation in decision making
  Majority rule, with one person equaling one vote

- The principles of democracy pose a paradox: How can we resolve conflicts between our belief in majority rule and our belief in individual freedom?

- Limited government places individual liberty beyond the reach of majorities. Constitutions are the principal means of limiting government power.

- Direct democracy, in which everyone participates in every public decision, is very rare. Representative democracy means that public decisions are made by representatives elected by the people, in elections held periodically and open to competition, in which candidates and voters freely express themselves.

- Threats to national security have historically reduced the scope of individual liberty in our nation. The terrorist attack on America of September 11, 2001, inspired greater unity, patriotism, and trust in government among the people. But it also brought greater restrictions on individual liberty.

- Who really governs? The elitist perspective on American democracy focuses on the small number of leaders who actually decide national issues, compared to the mass of citizens who are apathetic and ill informed about politics. A pluralist perspective focuses on competition among organized groups in society, with individuals participating through group membership and voting for parties and candidates in elections.

- How democratic is American government today? Democratic ideals are widely shared in our society. But you must make your own informed judgment about the realities of American politics.

Key Terms

politics 3	public goods 7	democracy 9	authoritarianism 14
political science 3	free market 8	democratic ideals 10	direct democracy 14
government 4	gross domestic product (GDP) 8	paradox of democracy 12	representative democracy 15
legitimacy 5	externalities 9	limited government 13	elitism 16
social contract 7	income transfers 9	totalitarianism 13	pluralism 17

Suggested Readings

Cronin, Thomas J. *Direct Democracy*. Cambridge, Mass.: Harvard University Press, 1989. A thoughtful discussion of direct versus representative democracy, as well as a review of initiative, referendum, and recall devices.

Dahl, Robert A. *Democracy and Its Critics*. New Haven, Conn.: Yale University Press, 1989. A defense of modern democracy from the pluralist perspective.

Dye, Thomas R., and Harmon Zeigler. *The Irony of Democracy*. 13th ed. New York: Wadsworth, 2005. An interpretation of American politics from the elitist perspective.

Fukuyama, Francis. *Trust*. New York: Free Press, 1995. Argues that the breakdown of trust in America—not only in the government but at a person-to-person level—is burdening the nation with formal rules and regulations, lengthy contracts, bureaucracy, lawyers, and lawsuits.

Katznelson, Ira, Mark Kesselman, and Alan Draper. *The Politics of Power: A Critical Introduction to American Government*, 5th ed. Belmont, Calif.: Wadsworth, 2006. An argument that the United States "is characterized by massive disparities in wealth, income, and political resources."

Lasswell, Harold. Politics: *Who Gets What, When, and How*. New York: McGraw-Hill, 1936. Classic description of the nature of politics and the study of political science by America's foremost political scientist of the twentieth century.

Mills, C. Wright. *The Power Elite*. New York: Oxford University Press, 1956. Classic Marxist critique of elitism in American society, setting forth the argument that "corporate chieftains," "military warlords," and a "political directorate" come together to form the nation's power elite.

Neiman, Max. *Defending Government: Why Big Government Works*. Upper Saddle River, N.J.: Prentice Hall, 2000. A spirited defense of how big government can improve the lives of people.

Putnam, Robert D. *Bowling Alone: The Collapse and Revival of the American Community*. New York: Simon & Schuster, 2001. An argument that Americans are increasingly disconnected from one another, harming the health of democracy.

Roskin, Michael G. *Political Science: An Introduction*, 9th ed. Upper Saddle River, N.J.: Prentice Hall, 2006. A text introduction to the basic theories and concepts of political science.

2 POLITICAL CULTURE
Ideas in Conflict

Political Culture

Ideas have power. We are all influenced by ideas—beliefs, values, symbols—more than we realize. Political institutions are shaped by ideas, and political leaders are influenced by them.

The term **political culture** refers to widely shared ideas about who should govern, for what ends, and by what means. **Values** are shared ideas about what is good and desirable. Values provide standards for judging what is right or wrong. **Beliefs** are shared ideas about what is true. Values and beliefs are often related. For example, if we believe that human beings are endowed by God with rights to life, liberty, and property, then we will value the protection of these rights. Thus beliefs can justify values.

Cultural descriptions are generalizations about the values and beliefs of many people in society, but these generalizations do not apply to everyone. Important variations in values and beliefs may exist within a society; these variations are frequently referred to as **subcultures** and may arise from such diverse bases as religion, racial or ethnic identity, or political group membership.

Contradictions between Values and Conditions Agreement over values in a political culture is no guarantee that there will not be contradictions between these values and actual conditions. People both in and out of politics frequently act contrary to their professed values. No doubt the most grievous contradiction between professed national beliefs and actual conditions in America is found in the long history of slavery, segregation, and racial discrimination. The contradiction between the words of the Declaration of Independence that "all men are created equal" and the practices of slavery and segregation became the "American dilemma."[1] But this contradiction does not mean that professed values are worthless; the very existence of the gap between values and behavior becomes *a motivation for change.* The history of the civil rights movement might be viewed as an effort to "bear witness" to the contradiction between the belief in equality and the existence of segregation and discrimination.[2] Whatever the obstacles to racial equality in America, these obstacles would be even greater if the nation's political culture did *not* include a professed belief in equality.

Inconsistent Applications And political culture does not mean that shared principles are always applied in every circumstance. For example,

political culture Widely shared views about who should govern, for what ends, and by what means.

values Shared ideas about what is good and desirable.

beliefs Shared ideas about what is true.

subcultures Variations on the prevailing values and beliefs in a society.

people may truly believe in the principle of "free speech for all, no matter what their views might be," and yet when asked whether racists should be allowed to speak on a college campus, many people will say no. Thus general agreement with abstract principles of freedom of speech, freedom of the press, and academic freedom does not always ensure their application to specific individuals or groups.[3] Americans are frequently willing to restrict the freedoms of particularly obnoxious groups. A generation ago it was alleged communists and atheists whose freedoms were questioned. Over time these groups have become less threatening, but today people are still willing to restrict the liberties of racists, pro-abortion or anti-abortion groups, "skinheads" and neo-Nazis, and people who resemble terrorists.

Conflict   The idea of political culture does not mean an absence of conflict over values and beliefs. Indeed, much of politics involves conflict over very fundamental values. The American nation has experienced a bloody civil war, political assassinations, rioting and burning of cities, the forced resignation of a president, and other direct challenges to its political foundations. Indeed, much of this book deals with serious political conflict. Yet Americans do share many common ways of thinking about politics.

Individual Liberty

No political value has been more widely held in the United States than individual liberty. The very beginnings of our history as a nation were shaped by **classical liberalism**, which asserts the worth and dignity of the individual. This political philosophy emphasizes the rational ability of human beings to determine their own destinies, and it rejects ideas, practices, and institutions that submerge individuals into a larger whole and thus deprive them of their dignity. The only restriction on the individual is not to interfere with the liberties of others.

Political Liberty   Classical liberalism grew out of the eighteenth-century Enlightenment, the Age of Reason in which great philosophers such as Voltaire, John Locke, Jean Jacques Rousseau, Adam Smith, and Thomas Jefferson affirmed their faith in reason, virtue, and common sense. Classical liberalism originated as an attack on the hereditary prerogatives and distinctions of a feudal society, the monarchy, the privileged aristocracy, and the state-established church.

   Classical liberalism motivated America's Founders to declare their independence from England, to write the U.S. Constitution, and to establish the Republic. It rationalized their actions and provided ideological legitimacy for the new nation. The founders adopted the language of John Locke, who argued that a natural law, or moral principle, guaranteed every person "certain inalienable Rights," among them "Life, Liberty, and Property," and that human beings form a social contract with one another to establish a government to help protect their rights. Implicit in the social contract and the liberal notion of freedom is the belief that governmental activity and restrictions on the individual should be kept to a minimum.

Economic Freedom   Classical liberalism as a political idea is closely related to capitalism as an *economic* idea. **Capitalism** asserts the individual's right to own private property and to buy, sell, rent, and trade that property in a free market. The economic version of freedom is the freedom to make contracts, to bargain for one's services, to move from job to job, to join labor unions, to start one's own business. In classical liberal *politics*, individuals are free to speak out, to form political parties, and to vote as they please—to pursue their political interests as they think best. In classical liberal *economics*, individuals are free to find work, to

classical liberalism Political philosophy asserting the worth and dignity of the individual and emphasizing the rational ability of human beings to determine their own destinies.

www **Philosophy Pages**
History of Western philosophy and discussion of major democratic philosophers, including John Locke, Jean Jacques Rousseau, and Thomas Hobbes, among others.
www.philosophypages.com

capitalism Economic system asserting the individual's right to own private property and to buy, sell, rent, and trade that property in a free market.

Illegal immigration became an issue in the 2006 congressional elections. Many Hispanic Americans have protested against bills targeting illegal immigrants.

Opposition to illegal immigration is strong, especially among Anglos in the Southwest. Just prior to the 2006 congressional elections, Congress voted to strengthen border security

start businesses, and to spend their money as they please—to pursue their economic interests as they think best. The role of government is restricted to protecting private property, enforcing contracts, and performing only those functions and services that cannot be performed by the private market.

The value of liberty in these political and economic spheres has been paramount throughout our history. Only equality competes with liberty as the most honored value in the American political culture.

 **Heritage Foundation**
This think tank site includes a ranking of over 150 nations on an "Index of Economic Freedom." The U.S. ranks sixth; Hong Kong ranks first.
www.heritage.org

Dilemmas of Equality

Since the bold assertion of the Declaration of Independence that "all men are created equal," Americans have generally believed that no person has greater worth than any other person. The principle of equal worth and dignity was a radical idea in 1776, when much of the world was dominated by hereditary monarchies, titled nobilities, and rigid caste and class systems.

As early as 1835 the French historian and visitor to America, Alexis de Tocqueville, wrote his classic analysis of American political culture, *Democracy in America*. He identified equality as a fundamental aspect of American society—the absence of a privileged nobility or notions of class that characterize European societies. Yet he also warned of the "tyranny of the majority"—the potential for the majority to trample the rights of minorities and individuals—and he believed that an independent judiciary formed a powerful barrier "against the tyranny of political assemblies."[4]

Belief in equality drove the expansion of voting rights in the early 1800s and ultimately destroyed the institution of slavery. Abraham Lincoln understood that equality was not so much a description of reality as an ideal to be aspired to: "a standard maxim for a free society which should be familiar to all, and revered by all; constantly looked to, constantly labored for, and even though never perfectly

In the early 1800s, a visiting French historian, Alexis de Tocqueville, identified *equality* as a central American value that distinguished the new nation from European countries.

attained, constantly approximated and thereby augmenting the happiness and value of life to all people of all colors everywhere."[5] The millions who immigrated to the United States viewed this country as a land not only of opportunity but of *equal* opportunity, where everyone, regardless of birth, could rise in wealth and status based on hard work, natural talents, and perhaps good luck.

Today, most Americans agree that no one is intrinsically "better" than anyone else. This belief in equality, then, is fundamental to Americans, but a closer examination shows that throughout our history it has been tested, as beliefs and values so often are, by political realities.

political equality Belief that the law should apply equally to all and that every person's vote counts equally.

Political Equality   The nation's Founders shared the belief that the law should apply equally to all—that birth, status, or wealth do not justify differential application of the laws. But *legal equality* did not necessarily mean **political equality**, at least not in 1787, when the U.S. Constitution was written. The Constitution left the issue of voter qualifications to the states to decide for themselves. At that time, all states imposed either property or taxpayer qualifications for voting. Neither women nor slaves could vote anywhere. The expansion of voting rights to universal suffrage required many bitter battles over the course of two centuries. The long history of the struggle over voting rights illustrates the contradictions between values and practices (see the section "Securing the Right to Vote" in Chapter 6). Yet in the absence of the *value* of equality, voting rights might have remained restricted.

Center for Equal Opportunity
Think tank advocating equality of opportunity over equality of results.
www.ceousa.org

equality of opportunity
Elimination of artificial barriers to success in life and the opportunity for everyone to strive for success.

Equality of Opportunity   The American ideal of equality extends to **equality of opportunity**—the elimination of artificial barriers to success in life. The term *equality of opportunity* refers to the ability to make of oneself what one can, to develop one's talents and abilities, and to be rewarded for one's work, initiative, and achievement. Equality of opportunity means that everyone comes to the same starting line in life, with the same chance of success, and that whatever differences develop over time do so as a result of abilities, talents, initiative, hard work, and perhaps good luck.

Americans do not generally resent the fact that physicians, engineers, airline pilots, and others who have spent time and energy acquiring particular skills make more money than those whose jobs require fewer skills and less training. Neither do most Americans resent the fact that people who risk their own time and money to build a business, bring new or better products to market, and create jobs for others make more money than their employees. Nor do many Americans begrudge multimillion-dollar incomes to sports figures, rock stars, and movie stars whose talents entertain the public. And few Americans object when someone wins a million-dollar lottery, as long as everyone who entered the lottery had an equal chance at winning. Americans are generally willing to have government act to ensure equality of opportunity—to ensure that everyone has an equal chance at getting an education, landing a job, and buying a home, and that no barriers of race, sex, religion, or ethnicity bar individual advancement.

Equality of Results   Equality of results refers to the equal sharing of income and material rewards. Equality of results means that everyone starts *and finishes* the race together, regardless of ability, talent, initiative, or work. Those who argue on behalf of this notion of equality say that if individuals are truly equal, then everyone should enjoy generally equal conditions in life. According to this belief, we should appreciate an individual's contributions to society without creating inequalities of wealth and income. Government should act to *transfer* wealth and income from the rich to the poor to increase the total happiness of all members of society.

But equality of results, or absolute equality, is *not* a widely shared value in the United States. This notion of equality was referred to as "leveling" by Thomas Jefferson and generally has been denounced by the nation's political leadership—and by most Americans—then and now:

> To take from one, because it is thought his own industry and that of his fathers has acquired too much, in order to spare to others who have not exercised equal industry and skill, is to violate arbitrarily . . . the guarantee to everyone the free exercise of his industry and the fruits acquired by it.[6]

The taking of private property from those who acquired it legitimately, for no other reason than to equalize wealth or income, is widely viewed as morally wrong. Moreover, many people believe that society generally would suffer if incomes were equalized. Absolute equality, in this view, would remove incentives for people to work, save, or produce. Everyone would slack off, production would decline, goods would be in short supply, and everyone would end up poorer than ever. So some inequality may be essential for the well-being of society.

Thus Americans believe strongly in equality of opportunity but not necessarily equality of results (see *What Do You Think?* "Beliefs about Fairness"). Americans seek fairness rather than equality of wealth and income.

Fairness   Americans value "fairness" even though they do not always agree on what is fair. Most Americans support a "floor" on income and material well-being—a level that no one, regardless of his or her condition, should be permitted to fall below—even though they differ over how high that floor should be. Indeed, the belief in a floor is consistent with the belief in equality of opportunity; extreme poverty would deny people, especially children, the opportunity to compete in life.[7] But very few Americans want to place a "ceiling" on income or wealth. This unwillingness to limit top income extends to nearly all groups in the United States, the poor as well as the rich. Generally, Americans want people who cannot provide for themselves to be well cared for, especially children, the elderly, the ill, and the disabled. They are often willing to "soak the rich" when searching for new

equality of results Equal sharing of income and material goods regardless of one's efforts in life.

Monticello Biography, letters, and a "Day in the Life" of Thomas Jefferson. *www.monticello.org*

Thomas Jefferson, the primary author of the Declaration of Independence, was a powerful advocate of equality of opportunity, but opposed government

WHAT DO YOU THINK?

Beliefs about Fairness

Americans believe that there is "plenty of opportunity" to get ahead and that the economic system of the United States is "basically fair." They do NOT believe that everyone's income should be made more equal.

Q. Some people say there's not much opportunity in America today—that the average person doesn't have much chance to really get ahead. Others say there's plenty of opportunity and anyone who works hard can go as far as they want. How do you feel about this?

Plenty of opportunity	81%
Not much opportunity	17
Don't know	2

Q. Do you believe that incomes should be more equal because everybody's contribution to society is equally important?

Yes	37%
No	61
No opinion	2

Q. People should be allowed to accumulate as much wealth as they can even if some make millions while others live in poverty.

Strongly agree or agree	56%
Neither agree nor disagree	11
Strongly disagree or disagree	30

Sources: James R. Kluegel and Eliot R. Smith, *Beliefs about Inequality* (New York: Aldine de Gruyter, 1986); Everett Ladd and Karlyn H. Bowman, *Attitudes toward Economic Inequality* (Washington, DC: AEI Press, 1998).

tax sources, believing that the rich can easily afford to bear the burdens of government. But, unlike citizens in other Western democracies, Americans generally do *not* believe that government should equalize incomes.

Inequality of Income and Wealth

Conflict in society is generated more often by inequalities among people than by hardship or deprivation. Material well-being and standards of living are usually expressed in aggregate measures for a whole society—for example, gross domestic product per capita, income per capita, average life expectancy, infant mortality rate. These measures of societal well-being are vitally important to a nation and its people, but *political* conflict is more likely to occur over the *distribution* of well-being *within* a society. Unequal distributions can generate conflict even in a very affluent society with high levels of income and a high standard of living (see *Compared to What?* "Income and Inequality").

Inequality of Income   Let us examine inequality of income in the United States systematically. Figure 2.1 divides all American households into two groups—the lowest one-fifth in income and the highest one-fifth—and shows the shares (percentage) of total household income received by each of these groups over the years. (If perfect income equality existed, each fifth of American households would receive 20 percent of all personal income.) The poorest one-fifth received only 4.5 percent of all household income in 1929; today, this group does a little worse, at 3.5 percent of household income. The highest one-fifth received 54.0 percent of all household income in 1929; today, its percentage stands at 50.1.

However, while income differences in the United States have declined over the long run, inequality has actually *increased* in recent years. The income of the poorest households declined from 5.4 to 3.5 percent of total income between 1970 and 2004; the income of the highest quintile rose from 40.9 to 50.1 percent of total income. This reversal of historical trends has generated both political rhetoric and serious scholarly inquiry about both its causes and consequences.[8]

— Think Again —

Are income differences in America widening?

Global Policy Forum
Information on many global issues. Click to "social and economic policy" and then to "inequality of wealth and income" for cross-national data.
www.globalpolicy.org

COMPARED TO WHAT?

Income and Inequality

Capitalism has proven successful in creating wealth. The free market system has provided Americans with more purchasing power than any other people. ("Purchasing power parity" is a statistic used by international economists to adjust for the cost of living differences in measuring how much it costs to purchase a standard "basket" of goods and services.)

However, relatively high incomes of average Americans exist side by side with relatively high inequality among Americans. The United States ranks well below many European countries in measures of income inequality. (The "Gini index" is a statistic used by economists to measure income equality/inequality.) But poverty and inequality exist side by side in most of the world's less-developed countries (not ranked below).

Rank by purchasing power

1. **United States**	14. Sweden
2. Switzerland	15. United Kingdom
3. Norway	16. Italy
4. Belgium	17. Taiwan
5. Denmark	18. Israel
6. Canada	19. Spain
7. Japan	20. South Korea
8. Netherlands	21. Portugal
9. Ireland	22. Greece
10. Australia	23. Czech Republic
11. Germany	24. Poland
12. Finland	25. Mexico
13. France	

Rank by equality (Gini index)

1. Denmark	14. Netherlands
2. Czech Republic	15. Taiwan
3. Japan	16. France
4. Sweden	17. Greece
5. Finland	18. Switzerland
6. Norway	19. Portugal
7. Italy	20. Israel
8. Belgium	21. Ireland
9. Germany	22. United Kingdom
10. Canada	23. **United States**
11. South Korea	24. Costa Rica
12. Poland	25. Mexico
13. Spain	

Sources: Rank by purchasing power, *The Economist Pocket World in Figures*, 2003; rank by Gini index, Central Intelligence Agency, *The World Factbook*, 2003. Both sources rank many more nations.

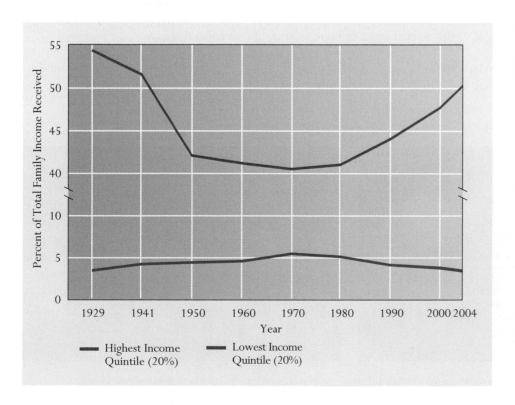

Figure 2.1 Shares of Total Household Income Received by Highest and Lowest Income Groups

Explaining Recent Increases in Income Inequality   Recent increases in income inequality in the United States are a product of several social and economic trends: (1) the decline of the manufacturing sector of the economy (and the loss of many relatively high-paying blue-collar jobs) and the ascendancy of the communications, information, and service sectors of the economy (with a combination of high-paying and low-paying jobs); (2) the rise in the number of two-wage families, making single-wage, female-headed households relatively less affluent; (3) demographic trends, which include larger proportions of aged and larger proportions of female-headed families; and (4) global competition, which restrains wages in unskilled and semiskilled jobs while rewarding people in high-technology, high-productivity occupations.

Social Mobility

social mobility Extent to which people move upward or downward in income and status over a lifetime or generations.

Political conflict over inequality might be greater in the United States if it were not for the prospect of **social mobility**. All societies are stratified, or layered, but societies differ greatly in the extent to which people move upward or downward in income and status over a lifetime or over generations. When there is social mobility, people have a good opportunity to get ahead if they study or work long and hard, save and invest wisely, or display initiative and enterprise in business affairs (however, see *A Conflicting View:* "Success Is Determined by the Bell Curve"). Fairly steep inequalities may be tolerated politically if people have a reasonable expectation of moving up over time, or at least of seeing their children do so.

How Much Mobility?   The United States describes itself as the land of opportunity. The really important political question may be how much real opportunity exists for individual Americans to improve their conditions in life relative to others. The impression given by Figure 2.1 is one of a static distribution system, with families permanently placed in upper or lower fifths of income earners. But there is considerable evidence of both upward and downward movement by people among income groupings.[9] Almost half of the families in the poorest one-fifth will move upward within a decade, and about half of families in the richest one-fifth will fall out of this top category.

Mobility, Class Conflict, and Class Consciousness   Social mobility and the expectation of mobility, over a lifetime or over generations, may be the

Income and wealth differences have increased in America in recent years.

A CONFLICTING VIEW

Success Is Determined by the Bell Curve

Most Americans believe in social mobility—the idea that anyone who studies or works hard, saves and invests wisely, and makes good use of his or her talents, initiative, and enterprise can get ahead. But a controversial book, *The Bell Curve* by Richard J. Herrnstein and Charles Murray, sets forth the argument that general intelligence largely determines success in life. General intelligence, the authors contend, is distributed among the population in a bell-shaped curve, with most people clustered around the median, smaller numbers with higher intelligence (a "cognitive elite") at one end, and an unfortunate few trailing behind at the other end (see graph). Over time, say Herrnstein and Murray, intelligence is becoming ever more necessary for the performance of key jobs in the "information society." The result will be the continuing enhancement of the power and wealth of the cognitive elite and the further erosion of the lifestyle of the less intelligent.

Even more controversial than the authors' claim that general intelligence determines success is their contention that general intelligence is mostly (60 percent) genetic. Because intelligence is mostly inherited, programs to assist the underprivileged are useless or even counterproductive.

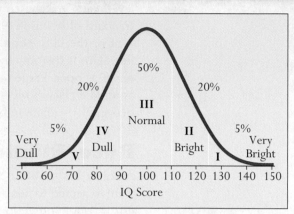

Population Distribution of IQ Scores

Source: Adapted with the permission of The Free Press, a division of Simon & Schuster Adult Publishing Group, from *The Bell Curve: Intelligence and Class Structure in American Life* by Richard J. Herrnstein and Charles Murray. Copyright © 1994 by Richard J. Herrnstein and Charles Murray. All rights reserved.

The cognitive elite, the authors predict, will continue to distance themselves from the masses in knowledge, skills, technical competence, income, and power while social problems will be concentrated among the "dullest." Indeed, they amass statistics showing that educational deficiencies, emotional problems, welfare reliance, early childbirth, and even criminal behavior are disproportionately concentrated in low-intelligence groups (see table).

	Cognitive Class	High School Dropout	Women on Welfare Assistance	Mean Age at First Childbearing	Convictions (young white males)
I	Very Bright	0%	0%	27.2 years	3%
II	Bright	0	2	25.6	7
III	Normal	6	8	23.4	15
IV	Dull	35	17	21.0	21
V	Very Dull	55	31	19.8	14

Source: Adapted with the permission of The Free Press, a Division of Simon & Schuster Adult Publishing Group, from THE BELL CURVE: Intelligence and Class Structure for American Life by Richard J. Hernstein and Charles Murray. Copyright © 1994 by Richard J. Hernstein and Charles Murray. All rights reserved.

key to understanding why **class conflict**—conflict over wealth and power among social classes—is not as widespread or as intense in America as it is in many other nations. The *belief* in social mobility reduces the potential for class conflict because it diminishes **class consciousness**, the awareness of one's class position and the feeling of political solidarity with others in the same class in opposition to other classes. If class lines were impermeable and no one had any reasonable expectation of moving up or seeing his or her children move up, then class consciousness would rise and political conflict among classes would intensify.

class conflict Conflict between upper and lower social classes over wealth and power.

class consciousness Awareness of one's class position and a feeling of political solidarity with others within the same class in opposition to other classes.

Most Americans describe themselves as "middle class" rather than "rich" or "poor" or "lower class" or "upper class." There are no widely accepted income definitions of "middle class." The federal government officially defines a "poverty level" each year based on the annual cash income required to maintain a decent standard of living ($19,223 in 2004 for a family of four). Roughly 12 to 13 percent of the U.S. population lives with annual cash incomes below this poverty line. This is the only income group in which a majority of people describe themselves as poor. Large majorities in every other income group identify themselves as middle class. So it is no surprise that presidents, politicians, and political parties regularly claim to be defenders of America's "middle class"!

Race, Ethnicity, and Immigration

America has always been an ethnically and racially pluralist society. All groups were expected to adopt the American political culture—including individual liberty, economic freedom, political equality, and equality of opportunity—and to learn American history and the English language. The nation's motto "E Pluribus Unum" (from many, one) is inscribed on its coins. Yet each of America's racial and ethnic groups brings its own traditions and values to the American political culture.

African Americans   Historically African Americans constituted the nation's largest minority. Blacks composed about 20 percent of the population at the time the U.S. Constitution was written in 1787 (although as we shall see in Chapter 3 an enslaved African American was to be counted as only 3/5ths of a person in the original Constitution). Heavy European immigration in the late nineteenth century diluted the black population to roughly 12 percent of the nation's total. As late as 1900, most African Americans (90 percent) were still concentrated in the Southern states. But World Wars I and II provided job opportunities in large cities of the Northeast and Midwest. Blacks could not cast ballots in most Southern counties, but they could "vote with their feet." The migration of African Americans from the rural South to the urban North was one of the largest internal migrations in our history. Today only about half of the nation's African Americans live in the South—still more than in any other region but less of a concentration than earlier in American history. Today the nation's 36 million African Americans comprise 12.3 percent of the total population of the United States (see Figure 2.2). "African-American Politics in Historical Perspective" is discussed in Chapter 15, as well as the long struggle against slavery, segregation, and discrimination. This struggle has given African Americans a somewhat different perspective on American politics (see "Race and Opinion" in Chapter 5).

Hispanic Americans   Hispanics are now the nation's largest minority. The term *Hispanic* generally refers to persons of Spanish-speaking ancestry and culture; it includes Mexican Americans, Cuban Americans, and Puerto Ricans. Today there are an estimated 37 million Hispanics in the United States, or 12.5 percent of the total population. The largest subgroup is Mexican Americans, some of whom are descendants of citizens living in Mexican territory that was annexed to the United States in 1848, but most of whom have come to the United States in accelerating numbers in recent years. The largest Mexican American populations are found in Texas, Arizona, New Mexico, and California. The second-largest subgroup is Puerto Ricans, many of whom move back and forth from the island to the mainland, especially New York City. The third-largest subgroup is Cubans, most of whom have fled from Castro's Cuba. They

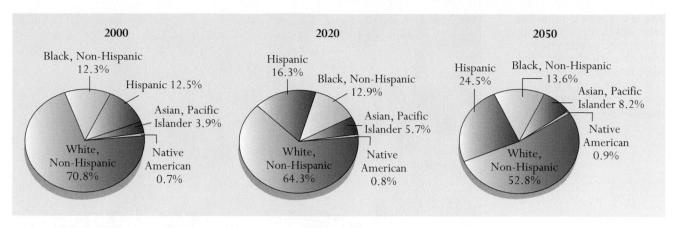

Figure 2.2   Racial and Ethnic Composition of the United States 2000, 2020, 2050

Source: U.S. Bureau of the Census (Middle Series).

live mainly in the Miami metropolitan area. The politics of each of these Hispanic groups differs somewhat (see "Hispanic Politics" in Chapter 15).

A Nation of Immigrants   The United States is a nation of immigrants, from the first "boat people" (Pilgrims) to the latest Haitian refugees and Cuban *balseros* ("rafters"). Historically, most of the people who came to settle in this country did so because they believed their lives would be better here, and American political culture today has been greatly affected by the beliefs and values they brought with them. Americans are proud of their immigrant heritage and the freedom and opportunity the nation has extended to generations of "huddled masses yearning to breathe free"—words emblazoned on the Statue of Liberty in New York's harbor. Today about 8 percent of the U.S. population is foreign-born.

Immigration policy is a responsibility of the national government. It was not until 1882 that Congress passed the first legislation restricting entry into the United States of persons alleged to be "undesirable" and virtually all Asians. After

Immigration places responsibility on public schools to provide for the needs of children from different cultures. Here, Latino pupils assemble in Santa Ana, California.

The U.S. Coast Guard may intercept boats at sea and return their occupants to their country of origin. But once immigrants reach the U.S. shore, they are entitled to a hearing in any deportation proceedings.

World War I, Congress passed the comprehensive Immigration Act of 1921, which established maximum numbers of new immigrants each year and set a quota for immigrants for each foreign country at 3 percent of the number of that nation's foreign-born who were living in the United States in 1910, later reduced to 2 percent of the number living here in 1890. These restrictions reflected antiimmigration feelings that were generally directed at the large wave of Southern and Eastern European Catholic and Jewish immigrants (from Poland, Russia, Hungary, Italy, and Greece) entering the United States prior to World War I (see Figure 2.3). It was not until the Immigration and Naturalization Act of 1965 that national origin

Figure 2.3 Legal Immigration to the United States by Decades

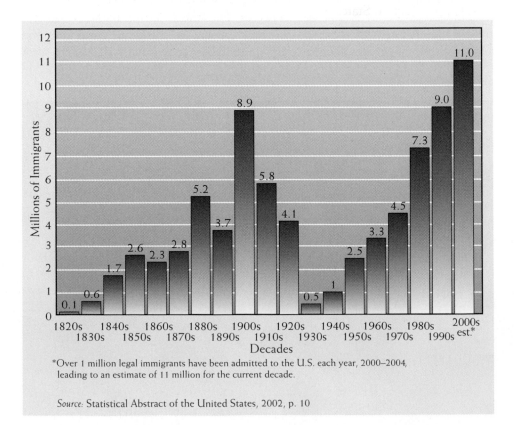

*Over 1 million legal immigrants have been admitted to the U.S. each year, 2000–2004, leading to an estimate of 11 million for the current decade.

Source: Statistical Abstract of the United States, 2002, p. 10

quotas were abolished, replaced by preference categories for close relatives of U.S. citizens, professionals, and skilled workers.

Immigration "reform" was the announced goal of Congress in the Immigration Reform and Control Act of 1986, also known as the Simpson-Mazzoli Act. It sought to control immigration by placing principal responsibility on employers; it set fines for knowingly hiring an illegal alien. However, it allowed employers to accept many different forms of easily forged documentation and at the same time subjected them to penalties for discriminating against legal foreign-born residents. To win political support, the act granted amnesty to illegal aliens who had lived in the United States since 1982. But the act failed to reduce the flow of either legal or illegal immigrants.

Today, more than a million people per year are admitted *legally* to the United States as "lawful permanent residents" (persons who have needed job skills or who have relatives who are U.S. citizens) or as "political refugees" (persons with "a well-founded fear of persecution" in their country of origin). In addition, each year more than 33 million people are awarded temporary visas to enter the United States for study, business, or pleasure (See *What Do You Think?* "Does Immigration Help or Hurt America?").

Illegal Immigration   The United States is a free and prosperous society with more than 5,000 miles of borders (2,000 with Mexico) and hundreds of international air- and seaports. In theory, a sovereign nation should be able to maintain secure borders, but in practice the United States has been unwilling and unable to do so. Estimates of illegal immigration vary widely, from the official U.S. Bureau of Immigration and Citizenship Services (formerly the Immigration and Naturalization Service, INS) estimate of 400,000 per year (about 45 percent of the legal immigration) to unofficial estimates ranging up to 3 million per year. The government estimates that about 4 million illegal immigrants currently reside in the United States; unofficial estimates range up to 12 million or more. Many illegal immigrants slip across U.S. borders or enter ports with false documentation; many more overstay tourist, worker, or student visas.[10] The total number of immigrants, legal and illegal, living in the United States is shown above.

As a free society, the United States is not prepared to undertake massive roundups and summary deportations of millions of illegal residents. The Fifth and Fourteenth Amendments to the U.S. Constitution require that every *person* (not just citizen) be afforded "due process of law." The government may turn back persons at the border or even hold them in detention camps. The Coast Guard may intercept boats at sea and return persons to their country of origin.[11] Aliens have no constitutional right to come to the United States. However, once in the United States, whether legally or illegally, every person is entitled to due process of law and equal protection of the laws. People are thus entitled to a fair hearing prior to any government attempt to deport them. Aliens are entitled to apply for asylum and present evidence at a hearing of their "well-founded fear of prosecution" if returned to their country. Experience has shown that the only way to reduce the flow of illegal immigration is to control it at the border, an expensive and difficult, but not impossible, task. Localized experiments in border enforcement have indicated that, with significant increases in personnel and technology, illegal immigration can be reduced by half or more.

Citizenship   Persons born in the United States are U.S. citizens. People who have been lawfully admitted into the United States and granted permanent

www Center for Immigration Studies
Advocacy organization for strengthening enforcement of immigration law. *www.cis.org*

Source: Steve Kelley.

www Bureau of Citizenship and Immigration Services
Official site with information on immigration laws, citizenship requirements, etc. (previously INS).
www.immigration.gov

WHAT DO YOU THINK?

Does Immigration Help or Hurt America?

Americans are divided over whether *legal* immigration is a "good thing" or a "bad thing." And they are divided over whether immigrants help the economy by taking low-paying hard labor jobs that most Americans shun, or whether they hurt the economy by driving down wages and burdening schools and social services.

Q. On the whole, do you think immigration is a good thing or a bad thing for this country today?

Good thing	52%
Bad thing	42
Mixed or no opinion	6

Q. Do you think immigrants mostly help the economy by providing low-cost labor, or mostly hurt the economy by driving wages down for many Americans?

Mostly hurt	48%
Mostly help	42
Neither	3
Both	1
Don't know	5

It is important to note, however, that most Americans oppose *illegal* immigration. They want illegal immigrants sent back to their home country "immediately" without court hearings, and they favor "stricter penalties" on illegal immigrants.

Q. When people are caught trying to enter the United States illegally, which do you think should be government policy?

Immediately send them back to their home country	61%
Allow them to appeal their case using legal representation and a court hearing	35
Neither, don't know	4

Q. Do you favor or oppose stricter penalties on illegal immigrants?

Favor	77%
Oppose	18
Don't know	5

Q. Do you favor or oppose using the U.S. military to stop illegal immigration at the borders?

Favor	67%
Oppose	24
Unsure	9

Source: Various national polls reported in Public Agenda, www.publicagenda.com

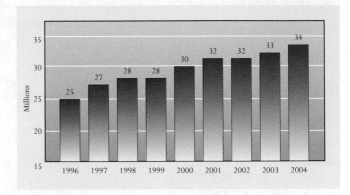

Number of Immigrants Living in the United States

Source: Derived from figures published by the Center for Immigration Studies, 2004.

Border Patrol officers apprehend illegal aliens in the U.S. border city of Nogales, Arizona.

residence, and who have resided in the United States for at least five years and in their home state for the last six months, are eligible for naturalization as U.S. citizens. Federal district courts as well as offices of the CIS may grant applications for citizenship. By law, the applicant must be over age eighteen, be able to read, write, and speak English, possess good moral character, and understand and

WHAT DO YOU THINK?

Could You Pass the Citizenship Test?

To ensure that new citizens "understand" the history, principles, and form of government of the United States, the CIS administers a citizenship test. Could you pass it today?

Answer correctly at least 18 of 30 questions to pass:

1. How many stars are there on our flag?
2. What do the stars on the flag mean?
3. What color are the stripes?
4. What do the stripes on the flag mean?
5. What is the date of Independence Day?
6. Independence from whom?
7. What do we call a change to the Constitution?
8. How many branches are there in our government?
9. How many full terms can a president serve?
10. Who nominates judges of the Supreme Court?
11. How many Supreme Court justices are there?
12. Who was the main writer of the Declaration of Independence?
13. What holiday was celebrated for the first time by American colonists?
14. Who wrote the Star-Spangled Banner?
15. What is the minimum voting age in the U.S.?
16. Who was president during the Civil War?
17. Which president is called the "Father of our Country"?
18. What is the 50th state of the Union?
19. What is the name of the ship that brought the Pilgrims to America?
20. Who has the power to declare war?
21. What were the 13 original states of the U.S. called?
22. In what year was the Constitution written?

A large congregation at Calvary Chapel in Fort Lauderdale, Florida, hears a sermon in 2004 regarding faith and morals in politics and government.

23. What is the introduction to the Constitution called?
24. Which president was the first Commander-in-Chief of the U.S. Army and Navy?
25. In what month do we vote for the president?
26. How many times may a senator be reelected?
27. Who signs bills into law?
28. Who elects the president of the U.S.?
29. How many states are there in the U.S.?
30. Who becomes president if both the president and V.P. die?

Answers to citizenship test: 1. 50; 2. One for each state in the Union; 3. Red and white; 4. They represent the 13 original states; 5. July 4; 6. England; 7. Amendments; 8. 3; 9. 2; 10. The president; 11. 9; 12. Thomas Jefferson; 13. Thanksgiving; 14. Francis Scott Key; 15. 18; 16. Abraham Lincoln; 17. George Washington; 18. Hawaii; 19. *The Mayflower*; 20. The Congress; 21. Colonies; 22. 1787; 23. The Preamble; 24. George Washington; 25. November; 26. There is no limit at the present time; 27. The president; 28. The Electoral College; 29. 50; 30. Speaker of the House of Representatives.

Source: Bureau of Citizenship and Immigration Services.

demonstrate an attachment to the history, principles, and form of government of the United States (see *What Do You Think? "*Could You Pass the Citizenship Test?").

Citizens of the United States are entitled to **passports**, issued by the U.S. State Department upon presentation of photos plus evidence of citizenship—a birth certificate or naturalization papers. A passport enables U.S. citizens to reenter the country after travel abroad. When traveling abroad, your U.S. passport may be your most valuable possession. Fewer than one-quarter of the U.S.

passport Evidence of U.S. citizenship, allowing people to travel abroad and reenter the United States.

visa A document or stamp on a passport allowing a person to visit a foreign country.

population currently hold passports. **Visas** are documents or stamps on a passport, issued by a foreign country, that allow citizens of one nation to visit another. The U.S. allows citizens of some countries, mostly Western European, to visit the United States without visas.

Religion and Secularism in Politics

The United States is one of the most religious societies in the world. Over 90 percent of Americans report in polls that they believe in God. Over 80 percent say that prayer is part of their daily lives, and 60 percent say that they attend church at least once a month. Over 80 percent claim some religious affiliation. Evangelical Protestants are the largest single group and the fastest-growing (see Figure 2.4).

At the same time, however, most Americans are concerned about religious leaders exercising influence in political life. Most respondents say it is "not appropriate for religious leaders to talk about their political beliefs as part of their religious activities" (61 percent), "religious leaders should not try to influence how people vote in elections" (64 percent), and "religious groups should not advance their beliefs by being involved in politics and working to affect policy" (54 percent).[12]

American's religious commitments and their belief in the separation of religion from politics sometimes clash.

Challenging Religion in Public Life   There is a growing divide in America between religious faith and **secular** politics on a number of key public issues. The most religious among us, as determined by frequency of church attendance and

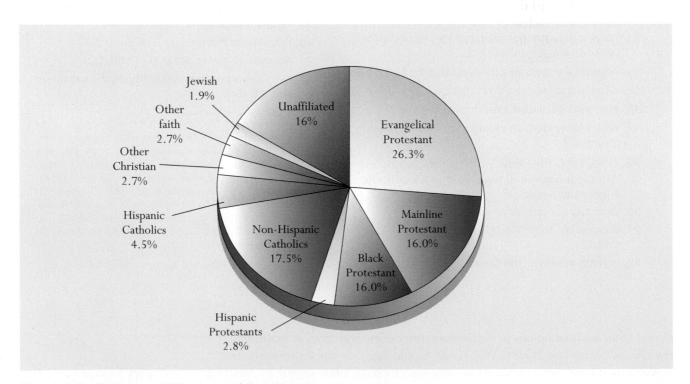

People for the American Way
An influential interest group on the Left which, among other issues, strongly opposes religious symbols in public.
www.pfaw.org

secular In politics, a reference to opposition to religious practices and symbols in public life.

Figure 2.4   Religious Affiliations of Americans

Source: From Pew Forum on Religion & Public Life Survey of 4,000 U.S. adults in March–May 2004. Copyright © 2004 by The Pew Research Center. Reprinted by Permission.

belief in the literal interpretation of the Bible, generally support limitations on abortion, including parental notification when minors seek abortions, and would prohibit partial-birth abortions. They also support abstinence in sex education; oppose same-sex marriage, support the phrase "under God" in the Pledge of Allegiance; support the display of religious symbols in public places; support the public funding of "faith-based" social service organizations; and generally believe that religion should play an important role in addressing "all or most of today's problems."

In contrast, challenges to religion in public life are increasingly being raised in American politics, especially in the courts. Organizations such as the American Civil Liberties Union (see *Up Close*: "The American Civil Liberties Union" in Chapter 14) and Americans United for the Separation of Church and State are challenging many traditional religious practices and symbols in public life. Most of these challenges are based upon the First Amendment's "no establishment of religion" clause (See Freedom of Religion in Chapter 14). Among these challenges: removing "under God" from the Pledge of Allegiance and eliminating the national motto "In God We Trust" from our coins; removing religious symbols— Christmas displays, the Ten Commandments, etc.—from public places; supporting the teaching of evolution and opposing the teaching of "creationism" in the schools; opposing the use of public school vouchers to pay for students attending religious schools; supporting gay rights, including same-sex marriages; and threatening to remove tax exemptions from churches whose religious leaders endorse candidates or involve themselves in politics.

Religious/Political Alignments   Interestingly, the religious-versus-secular division on these issues does *not* depend upon *which* religion (for example, Protestants, Catholic, Jewish) that Americans identify themselves. Rather, this division appears to be more closely aligned with the intensity of people's religious commitments; in polls, for example, their self-identification as "born-again" or "evangelical"; their frequency of church attendance; and their agreement with statements such as "prayer is an important part of my daily life."

An overwhelming majority of Americans (80 percent) say they have "old-fashioned values about family and marriage." And in the 2004 presidential election "moral values" was cited as the single most important issue (see Chapter 8).

Increasingly, this division between religious and secular viewpoints is coming to correspond with the division between liberals and conservatives in American politics. Religious traditionalists are more likely to describe themselves as conservatives or moderates, while secularists are more likely to describe themselves as liberal in politics.[13]

Ideologies: Liberalism and Conservatism

An **ideology** is a consistent and integrated system of ideas, values, and beliefs. A political ideology tells us who *should* get what, when, and how; that is, it tells us who *ought* to govern and what goals they *ought* to pursue. When we use ideological terms such as *liberalism* and *conservatism*, we imply reasonably integrated sets of values and beliefs. And when we pin ideological labels on people, we imply that those people are fairly consistent in the application of these values and beliefs in public affairs. In reality, neither political leaders nor citizens always display integrated or consistent opinions; many hold conservative views on some issues and liberal views on others.[14] Many Americans avoid ideological labeling, either by

Americans United for Separation of Church and State
An interest group formed to keep religion out of public places, especially schools. *www.au.org*

Family Religious Council
An interest group championing religion, family, and marriage, and government support of these values. *www.frc.org*

ideology Consistent and integrated system of ideas, values, and beliefs.

Figure 2.5 Americans: Liberal, Moderate, Conservative

Source: General Social Surveys, National Opinion Research Center, University of Chicago; Updated from *The American Enterprise*, January/February 2000, and Gallup, 2005.

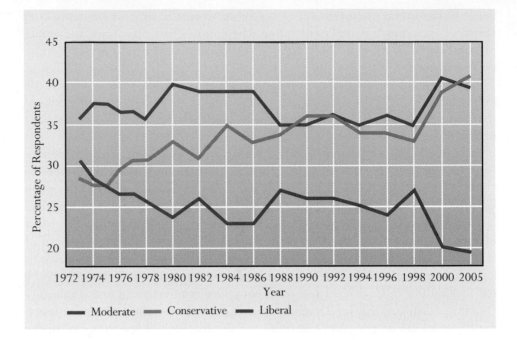

━━ Moderate   ━━ Conservative   ━━ Liberal

— Think Again —

Do you consider yourself politically conservative, moderate, or liberal?

www American Conservative Union
Conservative news and views and rankings of Congress members on conservative index. *www.conservative.org*

conservatism Belief in the value of free markets, limited government, and individual self-reliance in economic affairs, combined with a belief in the value of tradition, law, and morality in social affairs.

www Bill O'Reilly
Popular Web site for conservative views as well as promotion of O'Reilly programs, books, editorials, etc. *www.billoreilly.com*

describing themselves as "moderate" or "middle-of-the-road" or by simply declining to place themselves on an ideological scale. But as Figure 2.5 shows, among those who choose an ideological label to describe their politics, conservatives consistently outnumber liberals. (See also *Across the USA:* "Liberalism and Conservatism" on the facing page)

Despite inconsistencies in opinion and avoidance of labeling, ideology plays an important role in American politics. Political *elites*—elected and appointed officeholders; journalists, editors, and commentators; party officials and interest-group leaders; and others active in politics—are generally more consistent in their political views than nonelites and are more likely to use ideological terms in describing politics.[15]

Modern Conservatism: Individualism plus Traditional Values Modern **conservatism** combines a belief in free markets, limited government, and individual self-reliance in economic affairs with a belief in the value of tradition, law, and morality in social affairs. Conservatives wish to retain our historical commitments to individual freedom from governmental controls; reliance on individual initiative and effort for self-development; a free-enterprise economy with a minimum of governmental intervention; and rewards for initiative, skill, risk, and hard work. These views are consistent with the early classical liberalism of Locke, Jefferson, and the nation's Founders, discussed at the beginning of this chapter. The result is a confusion of ideological labels: modern conservatives claim to be the true inheritors of the (classical) liberal tradition.

Conservatism is less optimistic about human nature. Traditionally, conservatives have recognized that human nature includes elements of irrationality, ignorance, hatred, and violence. Thus they have been more likely to place their faith in *law* and *traditional values* than in popular fads, trends, or emotions. To conservatives, the absence of law does not mean freedom but, rather, exposure to the tyranny of terrorism and violence. They believe that without the guidance of traditional values, people would soon come to grief through the unruliness

ACROSS THE USA

Liberalism and Conservatism

States might be classified in terms of their voters' self-identification in opinion surveys as liberal, moderate, or conservative. The most conservative state is Utah (45 percent conservative, 37 percent moderate, 13 percent liberal), followed by Indiana (42 percent conservative, 39 percent moderate, 13 percent liberal). The most liberal states are Massachusetts (26 percent conservative, 42 percent moderate, 26 percent liberal), New York (29 percent conservative, 39 percent moderate, 26 percent liberal), and New Jersey (28 percent conservative, 40 percent moderate, 26 percent liberal).

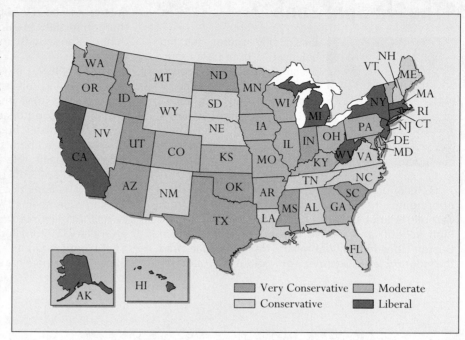

Source: Gerald C. Wright, Robert S. Erikson, and John P. McIver, "Public Opinion and Policy Liberalism in the American States," *American Journal of Political Science* 31 (November 1987): 980–1001. Reprinted by permission of the University of Wisconsin Press.

of their passions, destroying both themselves and others. Conservatives argue that strong institutions—family, church, and community—are needed to control individuals' selfish and immoral impulses and to foster civilized ways of life.

It is important to note that conservatism in America incorporates different views of the role of government in economic versus social affairs. Conservatives generally prefer *limited noninterventionist government in economic affairs*—a government that relies on free markets to provide and distribute goods and services; minimizes its regulatory activity; limits social welfare programs to the "truly needy"; keeps taxes low; and rejects schemes to equalize income or wealth. On the other hand, conservatives would *strengthen government's power to regulate social conduct.* They support restrictions on abortion; endorse school prayer; favor a war on drugs and pornography; oppose the legitimizing of homosexuality; support the death penalty; and advocate tougher criminal penalties.

Modern Liberalism: Governmental Power to "Do Good"   Modern **liberalism** combines a belief in a strong government to provide economic security and protection for civil rights with a belief in freedom from government intervention in social conduct. Modern liberalism retains the classical liberalism commitment to individual dignity, but it emphasizes the importance of social and

Young Americans for Freedom
The "YAF" archives site contains background on the conservative organization and conservative views on key issues of the day.
www.yaf.com

liberalism Belief in the value of strong government to provide economic security and protection for civil rights, combined with a belief in personal freedom from government intervention in social conduct.

PEOPLE IN POLITICS

Bill O'Reilly, "The No Spin Zone"?

Bill O'Reilly assures "fair and balanced" broadcast journalism to Fox News viewers. He describes his popular TV show as a "no spin zone" and refers to himself as an "independent." Yet O'Reilly has emerged as the nation's most popular voice of conservatism on television.

O'Reilly boasts of an Irish Catholic working-class upbringing in Long Island. He graduated from Catholic Marist College, briefly taught in a Miami high school, and earned a master's degree from Boston University in journalism. He bounced around the country as a reporter for various TV stations,

and by 1986 he had become a top correspondent for ABC News. He eventually replaced David Frost as anchor of the TV tabloid *Inside Edition*, but left that job in 1995 to earn a master's degree from the John F. Kennedy School of Government at Harvard University.

The Fox News network recruited O'Reilly to create a new evening talk show, *The O'Reilly Factor*. The show quickly grew into the most watched program on cable news, outdistancing even *Larry King Live*.

O'Reilly mixes humor with bombast. He ferociously attacks liberals bold enough to come on his show as guests. He constantly interrupts guests, both liberal and conservative, to broadcast his own views. He is convinced that liberal "secularists" are waging war against religion and traditional moral values. His favorite targets include Hollywood liberals, Hillary Clinton, Jesse Jackson, and the American Civil Liberties Union. The occasional twinkle in his Irish eyes tempers his often venomous commentary.

Americans for Democratic Action
The ADA is the nation's oldest liberal political action organization. *www.adaction.org*

U.S. Senator Barbara Boxer
The official Web site of U.S. Senator Barbara Boxer of California contains biographical material, information about Boxer's committee assignments, and her stands on various political issues. *www.senate.gov/~boxer/*

economic security for the whole population. In contrast to classical liberalism, which looked at governmental power as a potential threat to personal freedom, modern liberalism looks on the power of government as a positive force for eliminating social and economic conditions that adversely affect people's lives and impede their self-development. The modern liberal approves of the use of governmental power to correct the perceived ills of society (see *People in Politics: "Barbara Boxer, Defending Liberalism in Congress"*). The prevailing impulse is to "do good," to perform public services, and to assist the least fortunate in society, particularly the poor and minorities. Modern liberalism is impatient with what it sees as the slow progress of individual initiative and private enterprise toward solving socioeconomic problems, so it seeks to use the power of the national government to find solutions to society's troubles.

Modern liberalism contends that individual dignity and equality of opportunity depend in some measure on *reduction of absolute inequality* in society. Modern liberals believe that true equality of opportunity cannot be achieved where significant numbers of people are suffering from hopelessness, hunger, treatable illness, or poverty. Thus modern liberalism supports government efforts to reduce inequalities in society.

Liberals also have different views of the role of government in economic versus social affairs. Liberals generally prefer an *active, powerful government in economic affairs*—a government that provides a broad range of public services; regulates business; protects civil rights; protects consumers and the environment; provides generous unemployment, welfare, and Social Security benefits; and reduces economic inequality. But many of these same liberals would *limit the government's power to regulate social conduct*. They oppose restrictions on abortion; oppose school prayer; favor "decriminalizing" marijuana use and "victimless" offenses like public intoxication and vagrancy; support gay rights and tolerance toward alternative

PEOPLE IN POLITICS

Barbara Boxer, Defending Liberalism in Congress

Perhaps no one has been more successful in defending liberal causes in Congress than California's outspoken U.S. senator, Barbara Boxer. Her political résumé boasts awards and honors from such organizations as Planned Parenthood (family planning, reproductive health, and abortion rights), the Sierra Club (environmental causes), Mobilization against AIDS, Anti-Defamation League (civil rights), and Public Citizen (consumer affairs).

A graduate of Brooklyn College with a B.A. in economics, Boxer worked briefly as a stockbroker before moving to San Francisco, where she became a journalist and later a campaign aide to a local congressional representative. Her political career is based in Marin County, a trendy, upper-class, liberal community north of San Francisco, where she first won elected office as a member of the County Board of Supervisors. She was elected to the U.S. House of Representatives from her Marin County district in 1982 and quickly won a reputation as one of the most liberal members of the House. Appointed to the House Armed Services Committee, she became a leading critic of defense spending and virtually every weapon requested by the military.

When her state's liberal Democratic senator, Alan Cranston, announced he would not seek reelection to the Senate in the wake of his censure in the Keating Five affair, Boxer sought the open seat. Her opponent, conservative Republican radio and TV commentator Bruce Herschensohn, hammered at Boxer's 143 overdrafts at the House bank, her frequent absenteeism, and her extensive use of congressional perks. But with the help of Clinton's 1992 landslide (47 to 32 percent) victory over George Bush in California, Boxer eked out a 48 to 46 percent victory over Herschensohn. Her victory, together with that of Dianne Feinstein, gave California a historical first—two women U.S. senators.

Boxer quickly emerged as a powerful force in the U.S. Senate on behalf of abortion rights. She led the Senate fight for a federal law protecting abortion clinics from obstruction by demonstrators. On the Environmental and Public Works Committee she helped block efforts to relax federal environmental regulations. She led the movement to oust Republican senator Bob Packwood from the Senate on charges of sexually harassing staff members. She helped lead the fight for the Family Medical Leave Act, passed in the early days of the Clinton administration, as well as the Freedom of Access to [Abortion] Clinics Act. She was reelected by a wide margin in 1998, 2004, and 2006.

lifestyles; oppose government restrictions on speech, press, and protest; oppose the death penalty; and strive to protect the rights of criminal defendants. Liberalism is the prevailing ideology among college professors (see Figure 2.6).

The Ideological Battlefield   If Americans aligned themselves along a single liberal-conservative dimension, politics in the United States would be easier to describe, but far less interesting. We have already defined liberals as supporting a strong government in economic affairs and civil rights, but opposing government intervention in social affairs. And we have described conservatives as supporting a limited government in economic affairs and civil rights, but favoring government regulation of social conduct. Thus neither liberals or conservatives are really consistent in their view of the role of government in society, each differentiating between economic and social affairs.

Yet some people consistently support strong government to regulate business and provide economic security, and also to closely regulate social conduct. While few people use the term *populist* to describe themselves, these people may actually make up a fairly large proportion of the electorate. Liberal politicians can appeal for their votes by stressing government intervention to provide economic security, while conservative politicians can appeal to them by stressing the maintenance of traditional social values.

Figure 2.6 Ideology Among Professors

Source: American Enterprise, vol. 2, July/August 1991, http://www. TAEmag.com. Published by the American Enterprise Institute for Public Policy Research, Washington, DC.

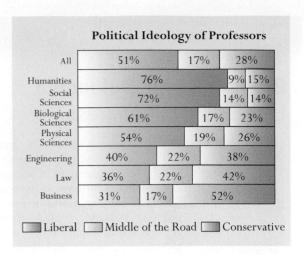

Political Ideology of Professors

	Liberal	Middle of the Road	Conservative
All	51%	17%	28%
Humanities	76%	9%	15%
Social Sciences	72%	14%	14%
Biological Sciences	61%	17%	23%
Physical Sciences	54%	19%	26%
Engineering	40%	22%	38%
Law	36%	22%	42%
Business	31%	17%	52%

☐ Liberal ☐ Middle of the Road ☐ Conservative

libertarian Opposing government intervention in both economic and social affairs, and favoring minimal government in all sectors of society.

And some people, often referred to as **libertarians**, oppose government intervention in *both* economic affairs and in the private lives of citizens. They are against most environmental regulations, consumer protecton laws, antidrug laws, defense spending, foreign aid, and government restrictions on abortion. In other words, they favor minimal government intervention in all sectors of society.

The result may be a two-dimensional ideological battlefield—identifying more or less government intervention and separating economic from social affairs—resulting in four separate groups—liberals, conservatives, populists, and libertarians (see Figure 2.7). (See also *Up Close:* "The Libertarian Party: A Dissenting Voice," in Chapter 7).

left A reference to the liberal, progressive, and/or socialist side of the political spectrum.

Youth and Ideology Young people are more likely to hold liberal views than their elders. Especially on social issues, young people, 18–24, are more likely to describe themselves as liberals (see Table 2.1). Older adults are more likely to describe themselves as conservatives on social as well as economic issues.

right A reference to the conservative, traditional, anticommunist side of the political spectrum.

Dissent in the United States

Dissent from the principal elements of American political culture—individualism, free enterprise, democracy, and equality of opportunity—has arisen over the years from both the *left* and the *right*. The **left** generally refers to socialists and communists, but it is sometimes used to brand liberals. The **right** generally refers to fascists and extreme nationalists, although it is sometimes used to stamp conservatives. Despite their professed hostility toward each other, **radicals** on the left and right share many characteristics. Both are **extremist**. They reject democratic politics, compromise, and coalition building as immoral, and they assert the supremacy of the "people" over laws, institutions, and individual rights. Extremists view politics with hostility, although they may make cynical use of democratic politics as a short-term tactical means to their goals.

radicalism Advocacy of immediate and drastic changes in society, including the complete restructuring of institutions, values, and beliefs. Radicals may exist on either the extreme left or extreme right.

extremism Rejection of democratic politics and the assertion of the supremacy of the "people" over laws, institutions, and individual rights.

Conspiracy theories are popular among extremists. For example, the left sees a conspiracy among high government, corporate, and military chieftains to profit from war; the right sees a conspiracy among communists, intellectuals, the United Nations, and Wall Street bankers to subordinate the United States to a

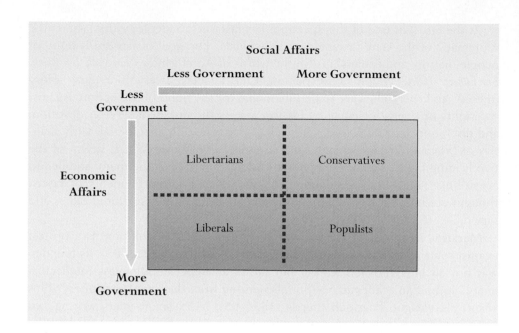

Figure 2.7 Mapping the Ideological Battlefield

We can classify people's views on whether they prefer more or less government intervention, first, in economic affairs (the vertical axis), and, second, in social affairs (the horizontal axis). The result is a fourfold classification scheme distinguishing types (economic and social) of liberals and conservatives.

world government. The historian Richard Hofstadter has referred to this tendency as "the paranoid style of politics."[16] Both the left and right are intolerant of the opinions of others and are willing to disrupt and intimidate those with whom they disagree. Whether shouting down speakers or disrupting meetings or burning crosses and parading in hoods, the impulse to violence is often present in those who subscribe to radical politics.

Antidemocratic Ideologies   Dissent in the United States has historical roots in antidemocratic movements that originated primarily outside its borders. These movements have spanned the political spectrum from the far right to the far left.

Table 2.1   Ideology and Age

Thinking about social issues, would you say your views on social issues are conservative, moderate, or liberal?

Age	Conservative	Moderate	Liberal
18–24	27%	36%	36%
25–38	33	34	31
39 plus	40	38	19

Thinking about economic issues, would you say your views on economic issues are conservative, moderate, or liberal?

Age			
18–24	33%	40%	26%
25–38	39	39	20
39 plus	47	38	12

Source: Gallup Poll reported May 20, 2003. Copyright © 2003 by The Gallup Organization.

fascism Political ideology in which the state and/or race is assumed to be supreme over individuals.

At the far-right end of this spectrum lies **fascism**, an ideology that asserts the supremacy of the state or race over individuals. The goal of fascism is unity of people, nation, and leadership—in the words of Adolf Hitler: *"Ein Volk, Ein Reich, Ein Führer"* (One People, One Nation, One Leader). Every individual, every interest, and every class are to be submerged for the good of the nation. Against the rights of liberty or equality, fascism asserts the duties of service, devotion, and discipline. Its goal is to develop a superior type of human being, with qualities of bravery, courage, genius, and strength. The World War II defeat of the two leading fascist regimes in history—Adolf Hitler's Nazi Germany and Benito Mussolini's fascist Italy—did not extinguish fascist ideas. Elements of fascist thought are found today in extremist movements in both the United States and Europe.

Marxism The theories of Karl Marx, among them that capitalists oppress workers and that worldwide revolution and the emergence of a classless society are inevitable.

Marxism arose out of the turmoil of the Industrial Revolution as a protest against social evils and economic inequalities. Karl Marx (1818–83), its founder, was not an impoverished worker but rather an upper-middle-class intellectual unable to find an academic position. Benefiting from the financial support of his wealthy colleague Friedrich Engels (1820–95), Marx spent years writing *Das Kapital* (1867), a lengthy work describing the evils of capitalism, especially the oppression of factory workers (the proletariat) and the inevitability of revolution. The two men collaborated on a popular pamphlet entitled *The Communist Manifesto* (1848), which called for a workers' revolution: "Workers of the world, unite. You have nothing to lose but your chains."

Leninism The theories of Vladimir Lenin, among them that advanced capitalist countries turned toward war and colonialism to make their own workers relatively prosperous.

It fell to Vladimir Lenin (1870–1924) to implement Marx and Engels's revolutionary ideology in the Russian Revolution in 1917. According to **Leninism**, the key to a successful revolution is the organization of small, disciplined, hard-core groups of professional revolutionaries into a centralized totalitarian party. To explain why Marx's predictions about the ever-worsening conditions of the masses under capitalism proved untrue (workers' standards of living in Western democracies rose rapidly in the twentieth century), Lenin devised the theory of imperialism: advanced capitalist countries turned to war and colonialism, exploiting the Third World, in order to make their own workers relatively prosperous.

Liberals' concern about efforts to curtail social welfare programs reflects their support of strong government, whereas conservatives' demands for tax cuts reflect their preference for government that encourages self-reliance and individual initiative.

WHAT DO YOU THINK?

Are You a Liberal or a Conservative?

Not everyone consistently takes a liberal or a conservative position on every issue. But if you find that you agree with more positions under one of the following "liberal" or "conservative" lists, you are probably ready to label yourself ideologically.

	You are *Liberal* If You Agree That	You Are *Conservative* If You Agree That
Economic policy	Government should regulate business to protect the public interest.	Free-market competition is better at protecting the public than government regulation.
	The rich should pay higher taxes to support public services for all.	Taxes should be kept as low as possible.
	Government spending for social welfare is a good investment in people.	Government welfare programs destroy incentives to work.
Crime	Government should place primary emphasis on alleviating the social conditions (such as poverty and joblessness) that cause crime.	Government should place primary emphasis on providing more police and prisons and stop courts from coddling criminals.
Social policy	Government should protect the right of women to choose abortion and fund abortions for poor women.	Government should restrict abortion and not use taxpayer money for abortions.
	Government should pursue affirmative action programs on behalf of minorities and women in employment, education, and so on.	Government should not grant preferences to anyone based on race or sex.
	Government should keep religious prayers and ceremonies out of schools and public places.	Government should allow prayers and religious observances in schools and public places.
National security policy	Government should support "human rights" throughout the world.	Government should pursue the "national interest" of the United States.
	Military spending should be reduced now that the Cold War is over.	Military spending must reflect a variety of new dangers in this post–Cold War period.

Communism is the outgrowth of Marxist-Leninist ideas about the necessity of class warfare, the inevitability of a worldwide proletarian revolution, and the concentration of all power in the "vanguard of the proletariat"—the Communist Party. Communism justifies violence as a means to attain power by arguing that the bourgeoisie (the capitalistic middle class) will never voluntarily give up its control over "the means of production" (the economy). Democracy is only "window dressing" to disguise capitalist exploitation. The Communist Party justifies authoritarian single-party rule as the "dictatorship of the proletariat." In theory, after a period of rule by the Communist Party, all property will be owned by the government, and a "classless" society of true communism will emerge.

communism System of government in which a single totalitarian party controls all means of production and distribution of goods and services.

Socialism Socialism shares with communism a condemnation of capitalist profit making as exploitative of the working classes. Communists and socialists agree on the "evils" of industrial capitalism: the concentration of wealth, the insensitivity of the profit motive to human needs, the insecurities and suffering brought on by the business cycle, the conflict of class interests, and the tendency of capitalist nations to involve themselves in imperialist wars. However, socialists are committed to the democratic process as a means of replacing capitalism with collective ownership of economic enterprise. Socialists generally reject the notion of violent revolution as a way to replace capitalism and instead advocate

Socialist Party USA News and views from America's Socialist party. *http://sp-usa.org*

socialism System of government involving collective or government ownership of economic enterprise, with the goal being equality of results, not merely equality of opportunity.

Political extremists of the left and right often have more in common than they would like to admit. Although decidedly different in their political philosophies, both members of right-wing American neo-Nazi groups and members of left-wing communist groups reject democratic politics and assert the supremacy of the "people" over laws, institutions, and individual rights. Gregory Johnson (left) was the catalyst for the flag burning controversy that is still raging in Congress today. Buford O'Neal Furrow, Jr. (right), was arrested for opening fire on children in a Jewish day care center in California. Several children died in this attack.

peaceful, constitutional roads to bring about change. Moreover, many socialists are prepared to govern in a free society under democratic principles, including freedom of speech and press and the right to organize political parties and oppose government policy. Socialism is egalitarian, seeking to reduce or eliminate inequalities in the distribution of wealth. It attempts to achieve equality of results, rather than mere equality of opportunity.

The End of History?   Much of the history of the twentieth century was the struggle between democratic capitalism and totalitarian communism. Thus the collapse of communism in Eastern Europe and the Soviet Union, symbolized by the tearing down of the Berlin Wall in 1989 as well as the worldwide movement toward free markets and democracy at the end of the twentieth century, has been labeled the **end of history**.[17] Democratic revolutions were largely inspired by the realization that free-market capitalism provided much higher standards of living than communism. The economies of Eastern Europe were falling further and further behind the economies of the capitalist nations of the West. Similar comparative observations of the successful economies of the Asian capitalist "Four Tigers"—South Korea, Taiwan, Singapore, and Hong Kong—even inspired China's communist leadership to undertake market reforms. Communism destroyed the individual's incentive to work, produce, innovate, save, and invest in the future. Under communism, production for government goals (principally a strong military) came first; production for individual needs came last. The result

end of history The collapse of communism and the worldwide movement toward free markets and political democracy.

A CONSTITUTIONAL NOTE

Natural Born Versus Naturalized Citizenship

The Fourteenth Amendment to the Constitution requires the states, and by implication the national government, to treat natural born and naturalized citizens the same: "all persons born or naturalized in United States, and subject to the jurisdiction thereof, are citizens of the United States . . . . No State shall make or enforce any law which shall abridge the privileges or immunities of citizens of the United States . . ." But there is one key difference between natural born and naturalized citizens written into the original Constitution of 1787: "No Person except a natural born Citizen, or a Citizen of the United States, at the time of the Adoption of this Constitution, shall be eligible to the Office of President . . ."

Requiring that the President be born in the United States is the only constitutional difference between born and naturalized citizens. Perhaps this difference made more sense in 1787 when many aspiring politicians had only recently moved into the country. But is it relevant today? Does it deny some very qualified people the opportunity to run for the nation's highest office?

was long lines at stores, shoddy products, and frequent bribery of bureaucrats to obtain necessary consumer items. More important, the concentration of both economic and political power in the hands of a central bureaucracy proved to be incompatible with democracy. Communism relies on central direction, force, and repression. Communist systems curtail individual freedom and prohibit the development of separate parties and interest groups outside of government.

Capitalism does not *ensure* democracy; some capitalist nations are authoritarian. But economic freedom inspires demands for political freedom. Thus market reforms, initiated by communist leaders to increase productivity, led to democracy movements, and those movements eventually dismantled the communist system in Eastern Europe and the old Soviet Union.

Academic Radicalism   Marxism survives on campuses today largely as an academic critique of the functioning of capitalism.[18] It provides some disaffected academics with ideas and language to attack everything that disturbs them about the United States—from poverty, racism, and environmental hazards to junk food, athletic scholarships, and obnoxious television advertising—conveniently blaming the "profit motive" for many of the ills of American society.

Contemporary radicals argue that the institutions of capitalism have conditioned people to be materialistic, competitive, and even violent. The individual has been transformed into a one-dimensional person in whom genuine humanistic values are repressed.[19] Profitability, rather than humanistic values, remains the primary criterion for decision making in the capitalist economy, and thus profitability is the reason for poverty and misery despite material abundance. Without capitalist institutions, life would be giving, cooperative, and compassionate. Only a *radical restructuring* of social and economic institutions will succeed in liberating people from these institutions to lead humanistic, cooperative lives.

To American radicals, the problem of social change is truly monumental, because capitalist values and institutions are deeply rooted in this country. Since most people are not aware that they are oppressed and victimized, the first step toward social change is consciousness raising—that is, making people aware of their misery.

The agenda of academic radicalism has been labeled **politically correct** (PC) thinking. Politically correct thinking views American society as racist, sexist, and homophobic. Overt bigotry is not the real issue, but rather Western institutions,

 **National Association of Scholars**
Association of college and university professors opposed to PC restrictions on campus. *www.nas.org*

politically correct (PC)
Repression of attitudes, speech, and writings that are deemed racist, sexist, homophobic (anti-homosexual), or otherwise "insensitive."

language, and culture, which systematically oppress and victimize women, people of color, gays, and others.

Academic radicalism "includes the assumption that Western values are inherently oppressive, that the chief purpose of education is political transformation, and that all standards are arbitrary.[20] In PC thinking, "everything is political." Therefore curriculum, courses, and lectures—even language and demeanor—are judged according to whether they are politically correct or not. Universities have always been centers for the critical examination of institutions, values, and culture, but PC thinking does not really tolerate open discussion or debate. Opposition is denounced as "insensitive," racist, sexist, or worse, and intimidation is not infrequent (see *Up Close:* "Political Correctness versus Free Speech on Campus" in Chapter 14).

Summary Notes

- Ideas are sources of power. They provide people with guides for determining right and wrong and with rationales for political action. Political institutions are shaped by the values and beliefs of the political culture, and political leaders are restrained in their exercise of power by these ideas.

- The American political culture is a set of widely shared values and beliefs about who should govern, for what ends, and by what means.

- Americans share many common ways of thinking about politics. Nevertheless, there are often contradictions between professed values and actual conditions, problems in applying abstract beliefs to concrete situations, and even occasional conflict over fundamental values.

- Individual liberty is a fundamental value in American life. The classical liberal tradition that inspired the nation's Founders included both political liberties and economic freedoms.

- Equality is another fundamental American value. The nation's Founders believed in equality before the law; yet political equality, in the form of universal voting rights, required nearly two centuries to bring about.

- Equality of opportunity is a widely shared value; most Americans are opposed to artificial barriers of race, sex, religion, or ethnicity barring individual advancement. But equality of results is not a widely shared value; most Americans support a "floor" on income and well-being for their fellow citizens but oppose placing a "ceiling" on income or wealth.

- Income inequality has increased in recent years primarily as a result of economic and demographic changes. Most Americans believe that opportunities for individual advancement are still available, and this belief diminishes the potential for class conflict.

- A great majority of Americans claim religious affiliation. But there is a growing divide between religious and secular viewpoints on the role of religion in public life. Secularists have challenged many traditional religious practices and symbols, such as the words "under God" in the Pledge of Allegiance.

- Liberal and conservative ideologies in American politics present somewhat different sets of values and beliefs, even though they share a common commitment to individual dignity and private property. Generally, liberals favor an active, powerful government to provide economic security and protection for civil rights but oppose government restrictions on social conduct. Generally, conservatives favor minimal government intervention in economic affairs and civil rights but support many government restrictions on social conduct.

- Many Americans who identify themselves as liberals or conservatives are not always consistent in applying their professed views. Populists are liberal on economic issues but conservative in their views on social issues. Libertarians are conservative on economic issues but liberal in their social views.

- The collapse of communism in Eastern Europe and the former Soviet Union and the worldwide movement toward free markets and democracy have undermined support for socialism throughout the world. Yet Marxism survives in academic circles as a critique of the functioning of capitalism.

Key Terms

political culture 26	equality of results 29	conservatism 42	Marxism 48
values 26	social mobility 32	liberalism 43	Leninism 48
beliefs 26	class conflict 33	libertarian 46	communism 49
subcultures 26	class consciousness 33	left 46	socialism 49
classical liberalism 26	passport 39	right 46	end of history 50
capitalism 26	visa 39	radicalism 46	politically correct (PC) 51
political equality 28	secular 39	extremism 46	
equality of opportunity 28	ideology 41	fascism 48	

Suggested Readings

Baradat, Leon P., *Political Ideologies: Their Origin and Impact.* 9th ed. Upper Saddle River, NJ: Prentice Hall, 2006. Text coverage of evolution of political ideologies over the past three centuries.

de Tocqueville, Alexis. *Democracy in America* (1835). Chicago: University of Chicago Press. 2000. Classic early assessment of American political culture by a French traveler.

Dolbeare, Kenneth M., and Michael S. Cummings, *American Political Thought,* 5th ed. Washington, DC: CQ Press, 2004. A compilation of key writings and speeches from Franklin, Madison, Adams, and Paine, to Bill Clinton, Ronald Reagan, Pat Buchanan, and the Green Party.

Ebenstein, Alan, William Ebenstein, and Edwin Fogelman. *Today's Isms: Communism, Fascism, Capitalism, Socialism.* 11th ed. Upper Saddle River, N.J.: Prentice Hall, 2000. A concise description and history of the major isms.

Herrnstein, Richard J., and Charles Murray. *The Bell Curve: Intelligence and Class Structure in American Life.* New York: Free Press, 1994. A controversial argument that success in life is mainly a result of inherited intelligence and that a very bright "cognitive elite" will continue to distance themselves from the duller masses.

Huntington, Samuel P. *American Politics: The Promise of Disharmony.* Cambridge, Mass.: Harvard University Press,

1981. An examination of the gaps between the promise of the American ideals of liberty and equality and the performance of the American political system.

Ingersoll, David E., Richard K. Matthews, and Andrew Davidson. *The Philosophical Roots of Modern Ideology: Liberalism, Communism, Fascism, Islamism.* 3rd ed. Upper Saddle River, N.J.: Prentice Hall, 2001. Overview of political ideologies, including extensive quotes from original sources, from Locke, Jefferson, Madison, Marx, and Lenin to Gorbachev, Hitler, and Khomeini.

Jacobs, Lawrence R., and Theda Skocpol, eds. *Inequality and American Democracy.* New York: Russell Sage Foundation, 2005. A series of essays on the political consequences of growing income inequality in America.

Ryscavage, Paul. *Income Inequality in America.* Armonk, N.Y.: M.E. Sharpe, 1999. A careful analysis of current trends toward income inequality in the United States.

Wolff, Edward N. *Top Heavy.* 2nd ed. New York: News Press, 2002. A fact-filled report on the increasing inequality of wealth in America, together with a proposal to tax wealth as well as income.

Make It Real

POLITICAL CULTURE
Students take a look at the belief systems that make political movements possible.

Part Two

CONSTITUTION

Moment of Crisis—System Failure

ABCNEWS

Originally Aired: **September 15, 2005**
Program: **Primetime**
Running Time: **29:12**

Katrina ranks as the country's most expensive natural disaster and one of the deadliest in U.S. history. It has killed more than 700 people, uprooted tens of thousands of families, destroyed countless homes, and forced the evacuation of a major American city. Two and a half weeks after the hurricane roared ashore, just east of New Orleans, the country is trying to make sense of the resulting failures of local, state, and federal government. On this program, ABC News will piece together what we know and where the breakdowns occurred.

Born as a garden-variety tropical depression, Katrina grew into a tropical storm and officially earned hurricane status on August 24, 2005. It initially made landfall north of Miami, causing serious flooding and eleven deaths. But only when it marched across the Florida peninsula and hit the warm waters of the Gulf of Mexico did Katrina rapidly intensify and unleash its full fury. And as it evolved into a monster storm, the National Hurricane Center issued pointed warnings to the target communities along the Gulf Coast. The director made phone calls to key officials, including the mayor of New Orleans, saying Katrina could be "the big one" officials had long feared. Simultaneously, weather service bulletins were issued with unusually apocalyptic language. One predicted a storm of "unprecedented strength," "the area will be uninhabitable for weeks," and went on to predict human suffering "incredible by modern standards."

Given the dire warnings, should the deaths and suffering throughout the Gulf region have been as great? Were the recommendations issued by the 9/11 Commission put into practice?

Ted Koppel hosts a Primetime special edition, "Moment of Crisis: System Failure," a moment-by-moment chronology of what went so terribly wrong in the horrific days following Katrina's strike on the Gulf Coast. This was America's first major test of emergency response since 9/11, a test that has received failing grades.

Critical Thinking Questions

1. In "Moment of Crisis—System Failure," state and local officials blame federal officials for the grossly inadequate response to this natural disaster and federal officials blame state and local officials. What are the responsibilities of the federal government, particularly agencies such as the Federal Emergency Management Agency (FEMA) and the Department of Homeland Security, in regard to both natural and man-made disasters? What are the responsibilities of state and local governments?

2. How much of a role did poverty play in the tragic aftermath of Hurricane Katrina? Do you get the impression from viewing the program that race had any impact on the way the federal government responded to the crisis?

3 THE CONSTITUTION
Limiting Governmental Power

Think About Politics

1 Was the original constitution of 1787 a truly democratic document?
Yes ☐ No ☐

2 Should citizens be able to vote directly on national policies such as prayer in public schools or doctor-assisted suicides?
Yes ☐ No ☐

3 Should a large state like California, with 32 million people, elect more U.S. senators than a small state like Wyoming, with only half a million people?
Yes ☐ No ☐

4 Should federal laws always supersede state laws?
Yes ☐ No ☐

5 In which do you have the most trust and confidence?
President ☐ Congress ☐ Supreme Court ☐

6 Should the Constitution be amended to require Congress to pass only balanced budgets?
Yes ☐ No ☐

7 Should the Constitution be amended to guarantee that equal rights shall not be denied based on sex?
Yes ☐ No ☐

In a democracy "of the people, by the people, and for the people," who really has the power to govern? Are strong national government and personal liberty compatible? Can majorities limit individual rights? America's Founders struggled with such questions, and in resolving them established the oldest existing constitutional government.

Constitutional Government

Constitutions govern government. **Constitutionalism**—a government of laws, not of people—means that those who exercise governmental power are restricted in their use of it by a higher law. If individual freedoms are to be placed beyond the reach of government and beyond the reach of majorities, then a constitution must truly limit the exercise of authority by government. It does so by setting forth individual liberties that the government—even with majority support—cannot violate.

A **constitution** legally establishes government authority. It sets up governmental bodies (such as the House of Representatives, the Senate, the presidency, and the Supreme Court in the United States). It grants them powers. It determines how their members are to be chosen. And it prescribes the rules by which they make decisions.

Constitutional decision making is deciding how to decide; that is, it is deciding on the rules for policy making. It is not policy making itself. Policies will be decided later, according to the rules set forth in the constitution.

A constitution cannot be changed by the ordinary acts of governmental bodies; change can come only through a process of general popular consent.[1] The U.S. Constitution, then, is superior to ordinary laws of Congress, orders of the president, decisions of the courts, acts of the state legislatures, and regulations of the bureaucracies. Indeed, the Constitution is "the supreme law of the land."

The Constitutional Tradition

Americans are strongly committed to the idea of a written constitution to establish government and limit its powers. In fact, the Constitutional Convention of 1787 had many important antecedents.

The Magna Carta, 1215 English lords, traditionally required to finance the king's wars, forced King John to sign the Magna Carta, a document guaranteeing their feudal rights and setting the precedent of a limited government and monarchy.

constitutionalism A government of laws, not people, operating on the principle that governmental power must be limited and government officials should be restrained in their exercise of power over individuals.

constitution The legal structure of a political system, establishing governmental bodies, granting their powers, determining how their members are selected, and prescribing the rules by which they make their decisions. Considered basic or fundamental, a constitution cannot be changed by ordinary acts of governmental bodies.

National Constitution Center

Located in Philadelphia's Independence Mall, this museum is devoted to explaining the U.S. Constitution.
www.constitutioncenter.org

The Mayflower Compact, 1620 Puritan colonists, while still aboard the Mayflower, signed a compact establishing a "civil body politic . . . to enact just and equal laws . . . for the general good of the colony, unto which we promise all due submission and obedience." After the Puritans landed at Plymouth, in what is today Massachusetts, they formed a colony based on the Mayflower Compact, thus setting a precedent of a government established by contract with the governed.

The Colonial Charters, 1624–1732 The charters that authorized settlement of the colonies in America were granted by royal action. For some of the colonies, the British king granted official proprietary rights to an individual, as in Maryland (granted to Lord Baltimore), Pennsylvania (to William Penn), and Delaware (also to Penn). For other colonies, the king granted royal commissions to companies to establish governments, as in Virginia, Massachusetts, New Hampshire, New York, New Jersey, Georgia, and North and South Carolina. Royal charters were granted directly to the colonists themselves only in Connecticut and Rhode Island. These colonists drew up their charters and presented them to the king, setting a precedent in America for written contracts defining governmental power.

The "Charter Oak Affair" of 1685–88 began when King James II became displeased with his Connecticut subjects and issued an order for the repeal of the Connecticut Charter. In 1687 Sir Edmund Andros went to Hartford, dissolved the colonial government, and demanded that the charter be returned. But Captain John Wadsworth hid it in an oak tree. After the so-called Glorious Revolution in England in 1688, the charter was taken out and used again as the fundamental law of the colony. Subsequent British monarchs silently acquiesced in this restoration of rights, and the affair strengthened the notion of loyalty to the constitution rather than to the king.

The Declaration of Independence, 1776 The First Continental Congress, a convention of delegates from twelve of the thirteen original colonies, came together in 1774 to protest British interference in American affairs. But the Revolutionary War did not begin until April 19, 1775. The evening before, British regular troops marched out from Boston to seize arms stored by citizens in Lexington and Concord, Massachusetts. At dawn the next morning, the Minutemen—armed citizens organized for the protection of their towns—engaged the British regulars in brief battles, then harassed them all the way back to Boston. In June of that year, the Second Continental Congress appointed George Washington Commander-in-Chief of American forces and sent him to Boston to take command of the American militia surrounding the city. Still, popular support for the Revolution remained limited, and even many members of the Continental Congress hoped only to force changes—not to split off from Britain.

As this hope died, however, members of the Continental Congress came to view a formal Declaration of Independence as necessary to give legitimacy to their cause and establish the basis for a new nation. Accordingly, on July 2, 1776, the Continental Congress "Resolved, that these United Colonies are, and, of right, ought to be free and independent States." Thomas Jefferson had been commissioned to write a justification for the action, which he presented to the congress on July 4, 1776. In writing the Declaration of Independence, Jefferson lifted several phrases directly from the English political philosopher John Locke asserting the rights of individuals, the contract theory of government, and the

PEOPLE IN POLITICS

John Locke, Guiding the Founders

The English political philosopher John Locke had a profound influence on America's founders. Indeed, the Declaration of Independence may be thought of as a restatement of Locke's basic ideas. Writing in 1690, Locke rejected the notion of the divine right of kings to rule and asserted the rights of human beings who are "by nature free, equal, and independent" to establish their own government by "social contract" to gain security from an unstable "state of nature." In other words, people consent to be governed to protect themselves and their property. But if the government they create becomes arbitrary, enslaves its people, or takes away their property, then the people have the "right of revolution" against such a government. Locke had been read by most of the Founders, who accepted his ideas of a "social contract" as the origin of government, and even a "right of revolution" as a last resort to a despotic government.

right of revolution. The declaration was signed first by the president of the Continental Congress, John Hancock.

The Revolutionary War effectively ended when British General Charles Cornwallis surrendered at Yorktown, Virginia, in October 1781. But even as the war was being waged, the new nation was creating the framework of its government.

The Articles of Confederation, 1781–1789   Although Richard Henry Lee, a Virginia delegate to the Continental Congress, first proposed that the newly independent states form a confederation on July 6, 1776, the Continental Congress did not approve the Articles of Confederation until November 15, 1777, and the last state to sign them, Maryland, did not do so until March 1, 1781. Under the Articles, Congress was a single house in which each state had two to seven members but only one vote. Congress itself created and appointed executives, judges, and military officers. It also had the power to make war and peace, conduct foreign affairs, and borrow and print money. But Congress could *not* collect taxes or enforce laws directly; it had to rely on the states to provide money and enforce its laws. The United States under the Articles was really a confederation of nations. Within this "firm league of friendship" (Article III of the Articles of Confederation), the national government was thought of as an alliance of independent states, not as a government "of the people."

www U.S. History
The Independence Hall Association Web site with "Documents of Freedom" including Mayflower Compact, Declaration of Independence, Articles of Confederation, etc.
www.ushistory.org

Troubles Confronting a New Nation

Two centuries ago the United States was struggling to achieve nationhood. The new U.S. government achieved enormous successes under the Articles of Confederation: It won independence from Great Britain, the world's most powerful colonial nation at the time; it defeated vastly superior forces in a prolonged war for independence; it established a viable peace and won powerful allies (notably, France) in the international community; it created an effective army and navy, established a postal system, and laid the foundations for national unity. But despite these successes in war and diplomacy, the political arrangements under the Articles were unsatisfactory to many influential groups—notably, bankers and investors who held U.S. government bonds, plantation owners, real estate developers, and merchants and shippers.

www **Constitution Society**

Web site includes comprehensive list of founding documents, essays, and commentaries on the Constitution.

www.constitution.org

Financial Difficulties   Under the Articles of Confederation, Congress had no power to tax the people directly. Instead, Congress had to ask the states for money to pay its expenses, particularly the expenses of fighting the long and costly War of Independence with Great Britain. There was no way to force the states to make their payments to the national government. In fact, about 90 percent of the funds requisitioned by Congress from the states was never paid, so Congress had to borrow money from wealthy patriot investors to fight the war. Without the power to tax, however, Congress could not pay off these debts. Indeed, the value of U.S. governmental bonds fell to about 10 cents for every dollar's worth because few people believed the bonds would ever be paid off. Congress even stopped making interest payments on these bonds.

Commercial Obstacles   Under the Articles of Confederation, states were free to tax the goods of other states. Without the power to regulate interstate commerce, the national government was unable to protect merchants from heavy tariffs imposed on shipments from state to state. Southern planters could not ship their agricultural products to northern cities without paying state-imposed tariffs, and northern merchants could not ship manufactured products from state to state without interference. Merchants, manufacturers, shippers, and planters all wanted to develop national markets and prevent the states from imposing tariffs or restrictions on interstate trade.

Currency Problems   Under the Articles, the states themselves had the power to issue their own currency, regulate its value, and require that it be accepted in payment of debts. States had their own "legal tender" laws, which required creditors to accept state money if "tendered" in payment of debt. As a result, many forms of money were circulating: Virginia dollars, Rhode Island dollars, Pennsylvania dollars, and so on. Some states (Rhode Island, for example) printed a great deal of money, creating inflation in their currency and alienating banks and investors whose loans were being paid off in this cheap currency. If creditors refused payment in a particular state's currency, the debt could be abolished in that state. So finances throughout the states were very unstable, and banks and creditors were threatened by cheap paper money.

Civil Disorder   In several states, debtors openly revolted against tax collectors and sheriffs attempting to repossess farms on behalf of creditors who held unpaid mortgages. The most serious rebellion broke out in the summer of 1786 in western Massachusetts, where a band of 2,000 insurgent farmers captured the courthouses in several counties and briefly held the city of Springfield. Led by Daniel Shays, a veteran of the Revolutionary War battle at Bunker Hill, the insurgent army posed a direct threat to investors, bankers, creditors, and tax collectors by burning deeds, mortgages, and tax records to wipe out proof of the farmers' debts. Shays's Rebellion, as it was called, was finally put down by a small mercenary army, paid for by well-to-do citizens of Boston.

Reports of Shays's Rebellion filled the newspapers of the large Eastern cities. George Washington, Alexander Hamilton, James Madison, and many other prominent Americans wrote their friends about it. The event galvanized property owners to support the creation of a strong central government capable of dealing with "radicalism." Only a strong central government, they wrote one another, could "insure domestic tranquility," guarantee "a republican form of government," and protect property "against domestic violence." It is no accident that all of these phrases appear in the Constitution of 1787.

In an attempt to prevent the foreclosure of farms by creditors, Revolutionary War veteran Daniel Shays led an armed mass of citizens in a march on a western Massachusetts courthouse. This uprising, which came to be known as Shays's Rebellion, exposed the Confederation's military weakness and increased support for a strong central government.

The Road to the Constitutional Convention   In the spring of 1785, some wealthy merchants from Virginia and Maryland met at Alexandria, Virginia, to try to resolve a conflict between the two states over commerce and navigation on the Potomac River and Chesapeake Bay. George Washington, the new nation's most prominent citizen, took a personal interest in the meeting. As a wealthy plantation owner and a land speculator who owned more than 30,000 acres of land upstream on the Potomac, Washington was keenly interested in commercial problems under the Articles of Confederation. He lent his great prestige to the Alexandria meeting by inviting the participants to his house at Mount Vernon. Out of this conference came the idea for a general economic conference for all of the states, to be held in Annapolis, Maryland, in September 1786.

The Annapolis Convention turned out to be a key stepping-stone to the Constitutional Convention of 1787. Instead of concentrating on commerce and navigation between the states, the delegates at Annapolis, including Alexander Hamilton and James Madison, called for a general constitutional convention to suggest remedies to what they saw as defects in the Articles of Confederation.

On February 21, 1787, the Congress called for a convention to meet in Philadelphia for the "sole and express purpose" of *revising* the Articles of Confederation and reporting to the Congress and the state legislatures "such alterations and provisions therein as shall, when agreed to in Congress and confirmed by the states, render the federal Constitution adequate to the exigencies of government and the preservation of the union." Notice that Congress did not authorize the convention to write a new constitution or to call constitutional conventions in the states to ratify a new constitution. State legislatures sent delegates to Philadelphia expecting that their task would be limited to revising the Articles and that revisions would be sent back to Congress and state legislatures for their approval. But that is not what happened.

George Washington Papers
The life of George Washington with images, maps, documents, and papers.
http://gwpapers.virginia.edu

The Nation's Founders   The fifty-five delegates to the Constitutional Convention, which met in Philadelphia in the summer of 1787, quickly discarded the congressional mandate to merely "revise" the Articles of Confederation. The Virginia delegation, led by James Madison, arrived before a quorum of seven states had assembled and used the time to draw up an entirely new constitutional document. After the first formal session opened on May 25 and George Washington was elected president of the convention, the Virginia Plan became the basis of discussion. Thus, at the very beginning of the convention, the decision was made to scrap the Articles of Confederation altogether, write a new constitution, and form a new national government.[2]

Our Documents
National Archives Web site with access to 100 "milestone documents" in American history.
www.ourdocuments.gov

The Founders were very confident of their powers and abilities. They had been selected by their state legislatures (only Rhode Island, dominated by small farmers, refused to send a delegation). When Thomas Jefferson, then serving in the critical post of ambassador to France (the nation's military ally in the Revolutionary War), first saw the list of delegates, he exclaimed, "It is really an assembly of demigods." Indeed, among the nation's notables, only Jefferson and John Adams (then serving as ambassador to England) were absent. The eventual success of the convention, and the ratification of the new Constitution, resulted in part from the enormous prestige, experience, and achievements of the delegates themselves.

Above all, the delegates at Philadelphia were cosmopolitan. They approached political, economic, and military issues from a "continental" point of view. Unlike most Americans in 1787, their loyalties extended beyond their states. They were truly nationalists.[3]

|Think Again|

Was the original
Constitution of 1787 a truly
democratic document?

Consensus in Philadelphia

The Founders shared many ideas about government. We often focus our attention on *conflict* in the Convention of 1787 and the compromises reached by the participants, but the really important story of the Constitution is the *consensus* that was shared by these men of influence.

Liberty and Property   The Founders had read John Locke and absorbed his idea that the purpose of government is to protect individual liberty and property. They believed in a natural law, superior to any human-made laws, that endowed each person with certain inalienable rights—the rights to life, liberty, and property. They believed that all people were equally entitled to these rights. Most of them, including slave owners George Washington and Thomas Jefferson, understood that the belief in personal liberty conflicted with the practice of slavery and found the inconsistency troubling.

Social Contract   The Founders believed that government originated in an implied contract among people. People agreed to establish government, obey laws, and pay taxes in exchange for protection of their natural rights. This social contract gave government its legitimacy—a legitimacy that rested on the consent of the governed, not with gods or kings or force. If a government violated individual liberty, it broke the social contract and thus lost its legitimacy.

republicanism Government by representatives of the people rather than directly by the people themselves.

Representative Government   Although most of the world's governments in 1787 were hereditary monarchies, the Founders believed the people should have a voice in choosing their own representatives in government. They opposed hereditary aristocracy and titled nobility. Instead, they sought to forge a republic. **Republicanism** meant government by representatives of the people. The Founders expected the masses to consent to be governed by their leaders—men of principle and property with ability, education, and a stake in the preservation of liberty. The Founders believed the people should have only a limited role in directly selecting their representatives: they should vote for members of the House of Representatives, but senators, the president, and members of the Supreme Court should be selected by others more qualified to judge their ability.

Limited Government   The Founders believed unlimited power was corrupting and a concentration of power was dangerous. They believed in a written constitution that limited the scope of governmental power. They also believed in dividing power within government by creating separate bodies able to check and balance one another's powers.

nationalism Belief that shared cultural, historical, linguistic, and social characteristics of a people justify the creation of a government encompassing all of them and that the resulting nation-state should be independent and legally equal to all other nation-states.

Nationalism   Most important, the Founders shared a belief in **nationalism**—a strong and independent national (federal) government with power to govern directly, rather than through state governments. They sought to establish a government that would be recognized around the world as representing "We the people of the United States." Not everyone in America shared this enthusiasm for a strong federal government; indeed, opposition forces, calling themselves Anti-Federalists, almost succeeded in defeating the new Constitution. But the leaders meeting in Philadelphia in the summer of 1787 were convinced of the need for a strong central government that would share power with the states.

Conflict in Philadelphia

Consensus on basic principles of government was essential to the success of the Philadelphia convention. But conflict over the implementation of these principles not only tied up the convention for an entire summer but also later

PEOPLE IN POLITICS

George Washington, Founder of a Nation

From the time he took command of the American Revolutionary forces in 1775 until he gave his Farewell Address to the nation in 1796 and returned to his Mount Vernon plantation, George Washington (1732–99) was, indeed, "First in war, first in peace, first in the hearts of his countrymen." His military success, combined with his diplomacy and practical political acumen, gave him overwhelming moral authority, which he used to inspire the Constitutional Convention, to secure the ratification of the Constitution, and then to guide the new nation through its first years.

Washington was raised on a Virginia plantation and inherited substantial landholdings, including his Mount Vernon plantation on the Potomac River. He began his career as a surveyor. His work took him deep into the wilderness of America's frontier. This experience later served him well when, at age twenty-one, he was appointed an officer in the Virginia militia. In 1754 he led a small force toward the French Fort Duquesne, but after a brief battle at makeshift "Fort Necessity" he was obliged to retreat. In 1755 British Major General Edward Braddock asked the young militia officer to accompany his heavy regiments on a campaign to dislodge the French from Fort Duquesne. Braddock disregarded Washington's warnings about concealed ways of fighting in the New World; Braddock's parading redcoat forces were ambushed by the French and Indians near Pittsburgh, and the general was killed. Washington rallied what remained of the British forces and led them in a successful retreat back to Virginia.

Washington was viewed by Virginians as a hero, and at age twenty-two he was appointed by the Virginia Assembly "Colonel of the Virginia Regiment and Commander in Chief of all Virginia Forces." But regular British officers ridiculed the militia forces and asserted their authority over Washington. British General John Forbes occupied Fort Duquesne, renamed it Fort Pitt, and gave Washington's men the task of garrisoning it.

In 1759, having completed his service in the French and Indian Wars, Washington left his military post and returned to plantation life. He married a wealthy widow, Martha Custis, expanded his plantation holdings, and prospered in western land speculation.

The Virginia legislature elected Washington to attend the First Continental Congress in September 1774. Washington was the most celebrated veteran of the French and Indian Wars who was still young enough (forty-two) to lead military forces in a new struggle. John Adams of Massachusetts was anxious to unite the continent in the coming contest, and he persuaded the Second Continental Congress to give the Virginian command of the American revolutionary forces surrounding the British army in Boston in 1775.

Throughout the Revolutionary War Washington persevered by employing many of the tactics later defined as the principles of guerrilla warfare. By retreating deep into Pennsylvania's Valley Forge, Washington avoided defeat and saved his army. His bold Christmas night attack against Hessian troops at Trenton, New Jersey, encouraged French intervention on America's behalf. Slowly Washington was able to wear down the British resolve to fight. In the end, he succeeded in trapping a British army at Yorktown, Virginia. Assisted by a French naval blockade, he accepted the surrender of Lord Cornwallis and 8,000 of his men on October 19, 1781.

Perhaps Washington's greatest contribution to democratic government occurred in 1783 in Newburgh, New York, near West Point, where the veterans of his Continental Army were encamped. Despite their hardships and ultimate victory in the Revolutionary War, these soldiers remained unpaid by Congress. Indeed, Congress ignored a series of letters, known as the Newburgh Addresses, that threatened military force if Congress continued to deny benefits to the veterans. Washington was invited to Newburgh by officers who hoped he would agree to lead a military coup against the Congress. But when Washington mounted the platform he denounced the use of force and the "infamous propositions" contained in their earlier addresses to Congress. There is little doubt that he could have chosen to march on the Congress with his veteran army and install himself as military dictator. World history is filled with revolutionary army leaders who did so. But Washington chose to preserve representative government.

One of the few noncontroversial decisions of the Constitutional Convention in 1787 was the selection of George Washington to preside over the meetings. He took little part in the debates; however, his enormous prestige helped to hold the convention together and later to win support for the new Constitution.

threatened to prevent the states from ratifying, or voting to approve, the document the convention produced.

Representation   Representation was the most controversial issue in Philadelphia. Following the election of George Washington as president of the convention, Governor Edmund Randolph of Virginia rose to present a draft of a new constitution. This Virginia Plan called for a legislature with two houses: a lower house chosen by the people of the states, with representation according to population and an upper house to be chosen by the lower house (see Table 3.1). Congress was to have the broad power to "legislate in all cases to which the separate States are incompetent, or in which the harmony of the United States may be interrupted." Congress was to have the power to nullify state laws that it believed violated the Constitution, thus ensuring the national government's supremacy over the states. The Virginia Plan also proposed a *parliamentary* form of government, in which the legislature (Congress) chose the principal executive officers of the government as well as federal judges. Finally, the Virginia Plan included a curious "council of revision," with the power to veto acts of Congress.

Delegates from New Jersey and Delaware objected strongly to the great power given to the national government in the Virginia Plan, the larger representation it proposed for the more populous states, and the plan's failure to recognize the role of the states in the composition of the new government. After several weeks of debate, William Paterson of New Jersey submitted a counterproposal.[4] The New Jersey Plan called for a single-chamber Congress in which each state, regardless of its population, had one vote, just as under the Articles of Confederation. But unlike the Articles, the New Jersey Plan proposed separate executive and judicial branches of government and the expansion of the powers of Congress to include levying taxes and regulating commerce. Moreover, the New Jersey Plan included a National Supremacy Clause, declaring that the Constitution and federal laws would supersede state constitutions and laws.

Table 3.1   Constitutional Compromise

The Virginia Plan	The New Jersey Plan	The Connecticut Compromise The Constitution of 1787
Two-house legislature, with the lower house directly elected based on state population and the upper house elected by the lower.	One-house legislature, with equal state representation, regardless of population.	Two-house legislature, with the House directly elected based on state population and the Senate selected by the state legislatures; two senators per state, regardless of population.
Legislature with broad power, including veto power over laws passed by the state legislatures.	Legislature with the same power as under the Articles of Confederation, plus the power to levy some taxes and to regulate commerce.	Legislature with broad power, including the power to tax and to regulate commerce.
President and cabinet elected by the legislature.	Separate multiperson executive, elected by the legislature, removable by petition from a majority of the state governors.	President chosen by an Electoral College.
National judiciary elected by the legislature.	National judiciary appointed by the executive.	National judiciary appointed by the president and confirmed by the Senate.
"Council of Revision" with the power to veto laws of the legislature.	National Supremacy Clause similar to that found in Article VI of the 1787 Constitution.	National Supremacy Clause: the Constitution is "the supreme Law of the Land."

Debate over representation in Congress raged into July 1787. At one point, the convention actually voted for the Virginia Plan, 7 votes to 3, but without New York, New Jersey, and Delaware, the new nation would not have been viable. Eventually, Roger Sherman of Connecticut came forward with a compromise. This Connecticut Compromise—sometimes called the Great Compromise— established two houses of Congress: in the upper house, the Senate, each state would have two members regardless of its size; in the lower body, the House of Representatives, each state would be represented according to population. Members of the House would be directly elected by the people; members of the Senate would be selected by their state legislatures. Legislation would have to pass both houses to be enacted. This compromise was approved by the convention on July 16.

Slavery   Another conflict absorbing the attention of the delegates was slavery. In 1787 slavery was legal everywhere except in Massachusetts. Nevertheless, the delegates were too embarrassed to use the word *slave* or *slavery* in their debates or in the Constitution itself. Instead, they referred to "other persons" and "persons held to service or labour."

Delegates from the Southern states, where slaves were a large proportion of the population, believed slaves should be counted in representation afforded the states, but not counted if taxes were to be levied on a population basis. Delegates from the Northern states, with small slave populations, believed that "the people" counted for representation purposes should include only free persons. The Connecticut Plan included the now-infamous Three-Fifths Compromise: Three-fifths of the slaves of each state would be counted for purposes both of representation in the House of Representatives and for apportionment for direct taxes.

Slave owners also sought protection for their human "property" in the Constitution itself. They were particularly concerned about slaves running away to other states and claiming their freedom. So they succeeded in writing into the Constitution (Article IV, Section 2) a specific guarantee: "No person held to Service or Labour in one State . . . escaping into another, shall . . . be discharged from such Service or Labour, but shall be delivered up on Claim of the Party to whom such Service or Labour may be due."

Yet another compromise dealt with the slave trade. The capture, transportation, and "breaking in" of African slaves was considered a nasty business, even by Southern planters. Many wealthy Maryland and Virginia plantations were already well supplied with slaves and thus could afford the luxury of conscience to call for an end to slave importation. But other planters from the less-developed Southern states, particularly South Carolina and Georgia, wanted additional slave labor. The final compromise prohibited the slave trade—but not before the year 1808, thereby giving the planters twenty years to import all the slaves they needed before the slave trade ended.

Voter Qualifications   Another important conflict centered on qualifications for voting and holding office in the new government. Most of the delegates believed that voters as well as officeholders should be men of property. (Only Benjamin Franklin went so far as to propose universal *male* suffrage.) But delegates argued over the specific wording of property qualifications, their views on the subject reflecting the source of their own wealth. Merchants, bankers, and manufacturers objected to making the ownership of a certain amount of land a qualification for officeholding. James Madison, a plantation owner himself, was forced to admit that "landed possessions were no certain evidence of real wealth. Many enjoyed them who were more in debt than they were worth."

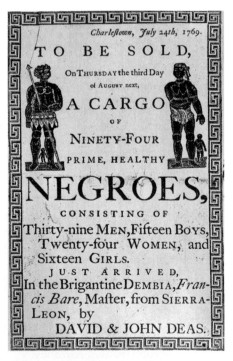

The Great Compromise
James Madison University Web site on Madison with information on constitutional compromises, including the slavery compromise.
www.jmu.edu/madison

Slavery was protected in the Constitution as written in 1787. The buying and selling of slaves was common at the time in the Southern states. The slave trade from Africa to America was given protection for twenty years, until 1808.

After much debate, the convention approved a constitution without any expressed property qualifications for voting or holding office, except those that the states might impose themselves: "The Electors in each State shall have the Qualifications requisite for Electors of the most numerous Branch of the State Legislature." At the time, every state had property qualifications for voting, and women were not permitted to vote or hold office. (The New Jersey Constitution of 1776 enfranchised women as well as men who owned property, but in 1787 a new state law limited the vote to "free white male citizens.")

Resolving the Economic Issues

The Founders were just as concerned with "who gets what, when, and how" as today's politicians are. Important economic interests were at stake in the Constitution. Historian Charles A. Beard pointed out that the delegates to the Constitutional Convention were men of wealth: planters, slaveholders, merchants, manufacturers, shippers, bankers and investors, and land speculators. Moreover, most of the delegates owned Revolutionary War bonds that were now worthless and would remain so unless the national government could obtain the tax revenues to pay them off[5] (see *A Conflicting View:* "An Economic Interpretation of the Constitution"). But it is certainly not true that the Founders acted only out of personal interest. Wealthy delegates were found on both sides of constitutional debates, arguing principles as well as economic interests.[6]

Levying Taxes   A central purpose of the Constitution was to enable the national government to levy its own **taxes**, so that it could end its dependence on state contributions and achieve financial credibility. The very first power given to Congress in Article 1, Section 8, is the power to tax: "The Congress shall have Power to lay and collect Taxes, Duties, Imposts and Excises, to pay the Debts and provide for the common Defence and general Welfare."

The financial credit of the United States and the interests of Revolutionary War bondholders were guaranteed by Article VI in the Constitution, which specifically declared that the new government would be obligated to pay the debts of the old government. Indeed, the nation's first secretary of the treasury, Alexander Hamilton, made repayment of the national debt the first priority of the Washington Administration.

The original Constitution placed most of the tax burden on consumers in the form of **tariffs** on goods imported into the United States. For more than a century, these tariffs provided the national government with its principal source of revenue. Tariffs were generally favored by American manufacturers, who wished to raise the price paid for foreign goods to make their home-produced goods more competitive. No taxes were permitted on *exports,* a protection for southern

taxes Compulsory payments to the government.

Constitutional Law Cornell University Law School overview of the Constitution. *www.law.cornell.edu/topics/ constitutional*

tariff Tax imposed on imported products (also called a customs duty).

Under the Articles of Confederation, each state issued its own currency. Differences in currency regulation from state to state led to financial uncertainty and inflation. By creating a national currency and putting the national government in charge of the money supply, the Founders hoped to restore stability and control inflation.

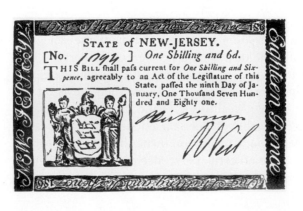

A CONFLICTING VIEW

An Economic Interpretation of the Constitution

Charles Beard, historian and political scientist, provided the most controversial historical interpretation of the origin of American national government in his landmark book, *An Economic Interpretation of the Constitution of the United States* (1913). Not all historians agree with Beard's economic interpretation, but all concede that it is a milestone in understanding the U.S. Constitution. Beard closely studied unpublished financial records of the U.S. Treasury Department and the personal letters and financial accounts of the fifty-five delegates to the Philadelphia convention. He concluded that they represented the following five economic interest groups, each of which benefited from specific provisions of the Constitution:

- *Public security interests* (persons holding U.S. bonds from the Revolutionary War; thirty-seven of the fifty-five delegates). The taxing power was of great benefit to the holders of public securities, particularly when it was combined with the provision in Article VI that "all Debts contracted and Engagements entered into, before the Adoption of this Constitution, shall be as valid against the United States under this Constitution, as under the Confederation." That is, the national government would be obliged to pay off all those investors who held U.S. bonds, and the taxing power would give the national government the ability to do so on its own.
- *Merchants and manufacturers* (persons engaged in shipping and trade; eleven of the fifty-five delegates). The Interstate Commerce Clause, which eliminated state control over commerce, and the provision in Article I, Section 9, which prohibited the states from taxing exports, created a free-trade area, or "common market," among the thirteen states.
- *Bankers and investors* (twenty-four of fifty-five delegates). Congress was given the power to make bankruptcy laws, to coin money and regulate its value, to fix standards of weights and measures, to punish counterfeiting, to establish post offices and post roads, to pass copyright and patent laws to protect authors and inventors, and

to punish piracies and felonies committed on the high seas. Each of these powers is a specific asset to bankers and investors as well as merchants, authors, inventors, and shippers.

- *Western land speculators* (persons who purchased large tracts of land west of the Appalachian Mountains: fourteen of the fifty-five delegates). If western settlers were to be protected from the Indians, and if the British were to be persuaded to give up their forts in Ohio and open the way to American westward expansion, the national government could not rely on state militias but must have an army of its own. Western land speculators welcomed the creation of a national army that would be employed primarily as an Indian-fighting force over the next century.
- *Slave owners* (fifteen of the fifty-five delegates). Protection against domestic insurrection also appealed to the southern slaveholders' deep-seated fear of a slave revolt. The Constitution permitted Congress to outlaw the *import of slaves* after the year 1808. But most Southern planters were more interested in protecting their existing property and slaves than they were in extending the slave trade, and the Constitution provided an explicit advantage to slaveholders in Article IV, Section 2 (later revoked by the Thirteenth Amendment, which abolished slavery), by specifically requiring the forced return of slaves who might escape to free states.

Beard argued that the members of the Philadelphia convention who drafted the Constitution were, with a few exceptions, immediately, directly, and personally interested in, and derived economic advantages from, the establishment of the new system. But many historians disagree with Beard's emphasis on the economic motives of the Founders. The Constitution, they point out, was adopted in a society that was fundamentally democratic, and it was adopted by people who were primarily middle-class property owners, especially farmers, rather than owners of businesses. The Constitution was not just an economic document, although economic factors were certainly important. Since most of the people were middle class and owned private property, practically all Americans were interested in the protection of property.

planters, who exported most of their tobacco and, later, cotton. Direct taxes on individuals were prohibited (Article 1, Section 2) except in proportion to *population*. This provision prevented the national government from levying direct taxes in proportion to income until the Sixteenth Amendment (income tax) was ratified in 1913.

The power to tax and spend was given to Congress, not to the president or executive agencies. Instead, the Constitution was very specific: "No Money shall be drawn from the Treasury, but in Consequence of Appropriations made by Law." This is the constitutional basis of Congress's "power of the purse."

Regulating Commerce   The new Constitution gave Congress the power to "regulate Commerce with foreign Nations, and among the several States" (Article 1, Section 8), and it prohibited the states from imposing tariffs on goods shipped across state lines (Article 1, Section 10). This power created what we call today a **common market**; it protected merchants against state-imposed tariffs and stimulated trade among the states. States were also prohibited from "impairing the Obligation of Contracts"—that is, passing any laws that would allow debtors to avoid their obligations to banks and other lenders.

common market Unified trade area in which all goods and services can be sold or exchanged free from customs or tariffs.

Protecting Money   The Constitution also ensured that the new national government would control the money supply. Congress was given the power to coin money and regulate its value. More important, the states were prohibited from issuing their own paper money, thus protecting bankers and creditors from the repayment of debts in cheap state currencies. (No one wanted to be paid for goods or labor in Rhode Island's inflated dollars.) If only the national government could issue money, the Founders hoped, inflation could be minimized.

Protecting National Security

At the start of the Revolutionary War, the Continental Congress had given George Washington command of a small regular army—"Continentals"—paid for by Congress and also had authorized him to take command of state militia units. During the entire war, most of Washington's troops had been state militia. (The "militia" in those days was composed of every free adult male; each was expected to bring his own gun.) Washington himself had frequently decried the militia units as undisciplined, untrained, and unwilling to follow his orders. He wanted the new United States to have a *regular* army and navy, paid for by the Congress with its new taxing power, to back up the state militia units.

War and the Military Forces   Congress was authorized to "declare War," to raise and support a regular army and navy, and to make rules regulating these forces. It was also authorized to call up the militia, as it had done in the Revolution, in order to "execute the Laws of the Union, suppress Insurrections and repel Invasions." When the militia are called into national service, they come under the rule of Congress and the command of the president.

The United States relied primarily on militia—citizen-soldiers organized in state units—until World War I. The regular U.S. Army, stationed in coastal and frontier forts, directed most of its actions against Native Americans. The major actions in America's nineteenth-century wars—the War of 1812 against the British, the Mexican War of 1846–48, the Civil War in 1861–65, and the Spanish-American War in 1898—were fought largely by citizen-soldiers from these state units.

Commander-in-Chief   Following the precedent set in the Revolutionary War, the new president, whom everyone expected to be George Washington, was made "Commander-in-Chief of the Army and Navy of the United States, and of the Militia of the several States, when called into the actual Service of the

The president's role as Commander-in-Chief was designed at the Constitutional Convention with George Washington in mind, as a reflection of his exploits in the Revolutionary War. Here three wartime presidents—Franklin Delano Roosevelt, Lyndon Baines Johnson, and George W. Bush—are shown reviewing troops.

United States." Clearly, there is some overlap in responsibility for national defense: Congress has the power to declare war, but the president is Commander-in-Chief. During the next two centuries, the president would order U.S. forces into 200 or more military actions, but Congress would pass an official Declaration of War only five times. Conflict between the president and Congress over war-making powers continues to this day (see the section "Commander-in-Chief" in Chapter 11).

Foreign Affairs   The national government also assumed full power over foreign affairs and prohibited the states from entering into any "Treaty, Alliance, or Confederation." The Constitution gave the president, not Congress, the power to "make Treaties" and "appoint Ambassadors." However, the Constitution stipulated that the president could do these things only "by and with the Advice and Consent of the Senate," indicating an unwillingness to allow the president to act autonomously in these matters. The Senate's power to "advise and consent" to treaties and appointments, together with the congressional power over appropriations, gives the Congress important influence in foreign affairs. Nevertheless, the president remains the dominant figure in this arena.

The Structure of the Government

The Constitution that emerged from the Philadelphia convention on September 17, 1787, founded a new government with a unique structure. That structure was designed to implement the Founders' beliefs in nationalism, limited government, republicanism, the social contract, and the protection of liberty and property. The Founders were realists; they did not have any romantic notions about the wisdom and virtue of "the people." James Madison wrote, "A dependence on the people is, no doubt, the primary control on the government, but experience has taught mankind the necessity of auxiliary precautions." The key structural arrangements in the Constitution—national supremacy, federalism, republicanism, separation of powers, checks and balances, and judicial review—all reflect the Founders' desire to create a strong national government while at the same time ensuring that it would not become a threat to liberty or property.

National Supremacy   The heart of the Constitution is the National Supremacy Clause of Article VI:

> This Constitution, and the Laws of the United States which shall be made in Pursuance thereof, and all Treaties made, or which shall be made, under the Authority of the United States, shall be the supreme Law of the Land, and the Judges in every State shall be bound thereby, any Thing in the Constitution or Laws of any State to the Contrary notwithstanding.

This sentence ensures that the Constitution itself is the supreme law of the land and that laws passed by Congress supersede state laws. This National Supremacy Clause establishes the authority of the Constitution and the U.S. government. (See *Up Close*: "The Supremacy Clause at Work: Marijuana for Medical Use?").

Federalism   The Constitution *divides power* between the nation and the states (see Chapter 4). It recognizes that both the national government and the state governments have independent legal authority over their own citizens: both can pass their own laws, levy their own taxes, and maintain their own courts. The states have an important role in the selection of national officeholders—in the apportionment of congressional seats and in the allocation of electoral votes for president. Most important, perhaps, both the Congress and three-quarters of the states must consent to changes in the Constitution itself.

Republicanism   To the Founders, a *republican* government meant the delegation of powers by the people to a small number of gifted individuals "whose wisdom may best discern the true interest of their country, and whose patriotism and love of justice, will be least likely to sacrifice it to temporary or partial considerations."[7] The Founders believed that enlightened leaders of principle and property with ability, education, and a stake in the preservation of liberty could govern the people better than the people could govern themselves. So they gave the voters only a limited voice in the selection of government leaders.

The Constitution of 1787 created *four* decision-making bodies, each with separate numbers of members, terms of office, and selection processes (see

---|Think Again|---

Should a large state like California, with 32 million people, elect more U.S. senators than a small state like Wyoming, with only half a million people?

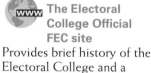

The Electoral College Official FEC site
Provides brief history of the Electoral College and a description of how it works.
www.fec.gov/pages/ecmenu

UP CLOSE

The Supremacy Clause at Work: Marijuana for Medical Use?

Currently, marijuana prohibition applies to everyone across the nation, including the sick and dying. But many doctors, patients, and organizations contend that marijuana, medically known as cannabis, is valuable in the treatment of glaucoma, HIV-AIDS, nausea, and pain relief, especially in cancer patients. Since 1996 voters in nine states—Alaska, Arizona, California, Colorado, Maine, Maryland, Nevada, Oregon, and Washington—have adopted initiatives exempting patitents who use marijuana under a physician's supervision from state marijuana prohibitions. Wherever the issue has appeared on state referenda, it has passed by large margins. National polls regularly report that 75 percent of the American public support making marijuana legally available to seriously ill patients.

Congress, however, has never exempted the medical use of marijuana from its Controlled Substance Act, which makes it a federal crime "to manufacture, distribute, or dispense, or possess . . . a controlled substance." Various petitions to the federal Drug Enforcement Agency to declassify marijuana as a controlled substance and allow physicians to legally prescribe its use have been rejected.

Clearly, federal law is in direct conflict with the laws of many states in this issue. But the Supremacy Clause of the Constitution clearly requires that federal law prevail over state law in cases of conflict.

The issue reached the U.S. Supreme Court in 2001. The Court recognized that whether or not the activities of individuals or organizations regarding marijuana were legal under California law, they nonetheless violated federal law, notably the Controlled Substance Act. The Court further held that "medical necessity" does not allow anyone to violate the Controlled Substance Act; Congress made no exemption in this act for medical necessity. The Supreme Court recognized that the states have concurrent powers with the federal government in regulating drugs and medications. However, "Under the Supremacy Clause, any state law, however clearly within a state's acknowledged power, which interferes with or is contrary to federal laws must yield."[a]

Politically, the federal Drug Enforcement Agency realizes that prosecuting seriously ill patients or their doctors for using marijuana medically is very unpopular. Many individuals, especially in those states that have tried to legalize the medical use of marijuana, have continued to use the drug, knowing that they are violating federal law.

---

[a] *United States v. Oakland Cannabis Buyers Cooperatives* 523 U.S. 483 (2001).

The Supremacy Clause of the Constitution dictates that the laws of Congress prevail over those of the states. Some states have attempted to legalize the use of marijuana for medical purposes. But the laws of Congress have not (yet?) made an exception for such use.

Table 3.2). Note that in the *original* Constitution only one of these four bodies—the House of Representatives—was to be directly elected by the people. The other three were removed from direct popular control: state legislatures selected U.S. senators; "electors" (chosen at the discretion of the state legislatures) selected the president; the president appointed Supreme Court and other federal judges.

Democracy?   The Founders believed that government rests ultimately on "the consent of the governed." But their notion of republicanism envisioned decision

Table 3.2   Decision-Making Bodies in the Constitution of 1787

House of Representatives	Senate	President	Supreme Court
Members alloted to each state "according to their respective numbers," but each state guaranteed at least one member.	"Two senators from each state" (regardless of the size of the state).	Single executive.	No size specified in the Constitution, but by tradition nine.
Two-year term. No limits on number of terms that can be served.	Six-year term. No limits on number of terms that can be served.	Four-year term (later limited to two terms by the Twenty-second Amendment in 1951).	Life term.
Directly elected by "the People of the several States."	Selected by the state legislatures (later changed to direct election by the Seventeenth Amendment in 1913).	Selected by "Electors," appointed in each state "In such Manner as the Legislature thereof may direct" and equal to the total number of U.S. senators and House members to which the state is entitled in Congress.	Appointed by the president, "by and with the Advice and Consent of the Senate."

referenda Proposed laws or constitutional amendments submitted to the voters for their direct approval or rejection, found in state constitutions, but not in the U.S. Constitution.

making by *representatives* of the people, not the people themselves (see *A Conflicting View*: "Let the People Vote on National Issues"). The U.S. Constitution does not provide for *direct* voting by the people on national questions; that is, unlike many state constitutions today, it does *not* provide for national **referenda**. Moreover, as noted earlier, only the House of Representatives (sometimes referred to even today as "the people's house") was to be elected directly by voters in the states.

These republican arrangements may appear "undemocratic" from our perspective today, but in 1787 the U.S. Constitution was more democratic than any other governing system in the world. Although other nations were governed by monarchs, emperors, chieftains, and hereditary aristocracies, the Founders recognized that government depended on the *consent of the governed*. Later democratic impulses in America greatly altered the original Constitution (see "Constitutional Change" later in this chapter) and reshaped it into a much more democratic document.

Separation of Powers and Checks and Balances

separation of powers Constitutional division of powers among the three branches of the national government—legislative, executive, and judicial.

checks and balances Constitutional provisions giving each branch of the national government certain checks over the actions of other branches.

The Founders believed that unlimited power was corrupting and that the concentration of power was dangerous. James Madison wrote, "Ambition must be made to counteract ambition." The **separation of powers** within the national government—the creation of separate legislative, executive, and judicial branches in Articles I, II, and III of the Constitution—was designed to place internal controls on governmental power. Power is not only apportioned among three branches of government, but, perhaps more important, each branch is given important **checks and balances** over the actions of the others (see Figure 3.1 on page 73). According to Madison, "The constant aim is to divide and arrange the several offices in such a manner as that each may be a check on the other." No bill can become a law without the approval of both the House and the Senate. The president shares

A CONFLICTING VIEW

Let the People Vote on National Issues

"Direct democracy" means that the people themselves can initiate and decide policy questions by popular vote. The Founders were profoundly skeptical of this form of democracy. They had read about direct democracy in the ancient Greek city-state of Athens, and they believed the "follies" of direct democracy far outweighed any virtues it might possess. It was not until more than 100 years after the U.S. Constitution was written that widespread support developed in the American states for direct voter participation in policy making. Direct democracy developed in states and communities, and it is to be found today *only* in state and local government.

Why not extend our notion of democracy to include nationwide referenda voting on key public issues? Perhaps Congress should be authorized to place particularly controversial issues on a national ballot. Perhaps a petition signed by at least 1 million voters should also result in a question being placed on a national ballot.

Proponents of direct voting on national issues argue that national referenda would

- Enhance government responsiveness and accountability to the people.
- Stimulate national debate over policy questions.
- Increase voter interest and turnout on election day.
- Increase trust in government and diminish feelings of alienation from Washington.
- Give voters a direct role in policy making.

Opponents of direct democracy, from our nation's Founders to the present, argue that national referenda voting would

- Encourage majorities to sacrifice the rights of individuals and minorities.
- Lead to the adoption of unwise and unsound policies because voters are not sufficiently informed to cast intelligent ballots on many complex issues.
- Prevent consideration of alternative policies or modifications or amendments to the proposition set forth on the ballot. (In contrast, legislators devote a great deal of attention to writing, rewriting, and amending bills, as well as seeking out compromises among interests.)
- Enable special interests to mount expensive referendum campaigns; the outcomes of referenda would be heavily influenced by paid television advertising.

How would voters' decisions in national referenda differ from current government policies? National polls suggest that voters would approve of many policy initiatives that Congress has rejected, including a constitutional requirement to balance the budget (83% favor); making English the official language (82% favor); a constitutional amendment to limit the terms of Congress members (74% favor); and a constitutional amendment to allow prayer in public schools (73% favor).[a]

---

[a]*Gallup Poll Monthly*, May 1996.

---

legislative power through the power to sign or to veto laws of Congress, although Congress may override a presidential veto with a two-thirds vote in each house. The president may also suggest legislation, "give to the Congress Information of the State of the Union, and recommend to their Consideration such Measures as he shall judge necessary and expedient." The president may also convene special sessions of Congress.

However, the president's power of appointment is shared by the Senate, which confirms cabinet and ambassadorial appointments. The president must also secure the advice and consent of the Senate for any treaty. The president must execute the laws, but it is Congress that provides the money to do so. The president and the rest of the executive branch may not spend money that has not been appropriated by Congress. Congress must also authorize the creation of executive departments and agencies. Finally, Congress may impeach and remove the president from office for "Treason, Bribery, or other High Crimes and Misdemeanors."

⊣Think Again⊢

In which do you have the most trust and confidence? President, Congress, Supreme Court

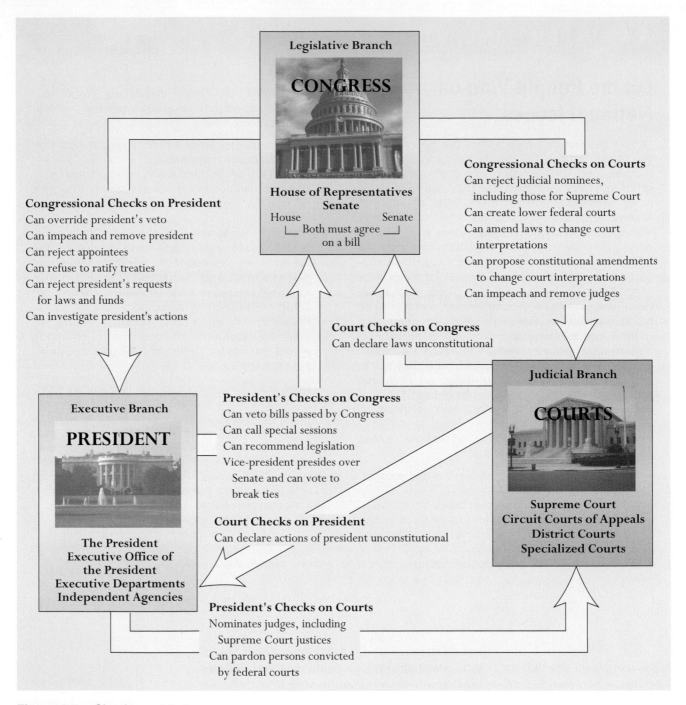

Figure 3.1   Checks and Balances

judicial review Power of the U.S. Supreme Court and federal judiciary to declare laws of Congress and the states and actions of the president unconstitutional and therefore legally invalid.

Members of the Supreme Court are appointed by the president and confirmed by the Senate. Traditionally, this court has nine members, but Congress may determine the number of justices. More important, Congress must create lower federal district courts as well as courts of appeal. Congress must also determine the number of these judgeships and determine the jurisdiction of federal courts. But the most important check of all is the Supreme Court's power of judicial review.

Judicial review, which is not specifically mentioned in the Constitution itself, is the power of the judiciary to overturn laws of Congress and the states and

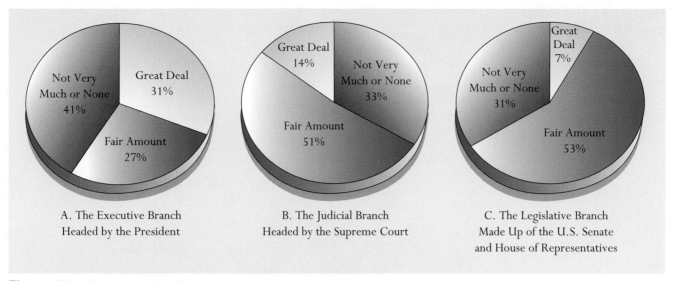

A. The Executive Branch
Headed by the President

B. The Judicial Branch
Headed by the Supreme Court

C. The Legislative Branch
Made Up of the U.S. Senate
and House of Representatives

Figure 3.2   Trust and Confidence in the Three Branches of Government

As you know, the federal government is made up of three branches: an Executive branch, headed by the president, a Judicial branch, headed by the U.S. Supreme Court, and a Legislative branch, made up of the U.S. Senate and House of Representatives. How much trust and confidence do you have at this time: a great deal, a fair amount, not very much, or none at all?

Source: Gallup Poll, July, 2004. Copyright © 2004 by The Gallup Organization.

actions of the president that the courts believe violate the Constitution (see "Judicial Power" in Chapter 13). Judicial review, in short, ensures compliance with the Constitution.

Many Federalists, including Alexander Hamilton, believed the Constitution of 1787 clearly implied that the Supreme Court could invalidate any laws of Congress or presidential actions it believed to be unconstitutional. Hamilton wrote in 1787, "[Limited government] . . . can be preserved in no other way than through the medium of courts of justice, whose duty it is to declare all acts contrary to the manifest tenor of the Constitution void."[8] But it was not until *Marbury v. Madison* in 1803 that Chief Justice John Marshall asserted in a Supreme Court ruling that the Supreme Court possessed the power of judicial review over laws of Congress. (See *People in Politics:* "John Marshall and Early Supreme Court Politics" in Chapter 13.) Today the American people express more trust and confidence in the Supreme Court than in either the president or the Congress (see Figure 3.2).

Conflict over Ratification

Today the U.S. Constitution is a revered document, but in the winter of 1787–88, the Founders had real doubts about whether they could get it accepted as "the supreme Law of the Land." Indeed, the Constitution was ratified by only the narrowest of margins in the key states of Massachusetts, Virginia, and New York.

The Founders adopted a **ratification** procedure that was designed to enhance chances for acceptance of the Constitution. The ratification procedure written into the new Constitution was a complete departure from what was then supposed to be the law of the land, the Articles of Confederation, in two major ways. First, the Articles of Confederation required that amendments be approved

ratification Power of a legislature to approve or reject decisions made by other bodies. State legislators or state conventions must have the power to ratify constitutional amendments submitted by Congress. The U.S. Senate has the power to ratify treaties made by the president.

Figure 3.3 The Fight over Ratification.

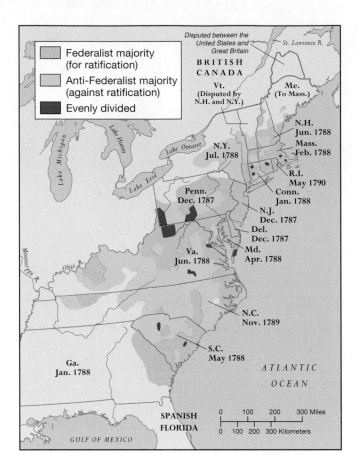

by *all* of the states. But since Rhode Island was firmly in the hands of small farmers, the Founders knew that unanimous approval was unlikely. So they simply wrote into their new Constitution that approval required only nine of the states. Second, the Founders called for special ratifying conventions in the states rather than risk submitting the Constitution to the state legislatures. Because the Constitution placed many prohibitions on the powers of states, the Founders believed that special constitutional ratifying conventions would be more likely to approve the document than would state legislatures.

The Founders enjoyed some important tactical advantages over the opposition. First, the Constitutional Convention was held in secret; potential opponents did not know what was coming out of it. Second, the Founders called for ratifying conventions to be held as quickly as possible so that the opposition could not get itself organized. Many state conventions met during the winter months, so it was difficult for some rural opponents of the Constitution to get to their county seats in order to vote (see Figure 3.3 above).

The Founders also waged a very professional (for 1787–88) media campaign in support of the Constitution. James Madison, Alexander Hamilton, and John Jay issued a series of eighty-five press releases, signed simply "Publius," on behalf of the Constitution. Major newspapers ran these essays, which were later collected and published as *The Federalist Papers*. The essays provide an excellent description and explanation of the Constitution by three of its writers and even today serve as a principal reference for political scientists and judges faced with constitutional ambiguities (see *People in Politics:* "James Madison and the Control

PEOPLE IN POLITICS

James Madison and the Control of "Faction"

The most important contributions to American democracy by James Madison (1751–1836) were his work in helping to write the Constitution and his insightful and scholarly defense of it during the ratification struggle. Indeed, Madison is more highly regarded by political scientists and historians as a *political theorist* than as the fourth president of the United States.

Madison's family owned a large plantation in Virginia. He graduated from the College of New Jersey (now Princeton University) at eighteen and assumed a number of elected and appointed positions in Virginia's colonial government. In 1776 Madison drafted a new Virginia Constitution. While serving in Virginia's Revolutionary assembly, he met Thomas Jefferson; the two became lifetime political allies and friends. In 1787 Madison represented Virginia at the Constitutional Convention and took a leading role in its debates over the form of a new federal government.

Madison's political insights are revealed in *The Federalist Papers*, a series of eighty-five essays published in major newspapers in 1787–88, all signed simply "Publius." Alexander Hamilton and John Jay contributed some of them, but Madison wrote the two most important essays: Number 10, which explains the nature of political conflict (faction) and how it can be "controlled", and Number 51, which explains the system of separation of powers and checks and balances (both reprinted in the Appendix of this textbook). According to Madison, "controlling faction" was the principal task of government.

What creates faction? Madison believed that conflict is part of human nature. In all societies, we find "a zeal for different opinions concerning religion, concerning government, and many other points," as well as "an attachment to different leaders ambitiously contending for preeminence and power." Even when there are no serious differences among people, these "frivolous and fanciful distinctions" will inspire "unfriendly passions" and "violent conflicts."

Clearly, Madison believed conflict could arise over just about any matter. Yet "the most common and durable source of factions, has been the various and unequal distribution of property." That is, economic conflicts between rich and poor and between people with different kinds of wealth and sources of income are the most serious conflicts confronting society.

Madison argued that factions could best be controlled in a republican government extending over a large society with a "variety of parties and interests." He defended republicanism (representative democracy) over "pure democracy," which he believed "incompatible with personal security, or the rights of property." And he argued that protection against "factious combinations" can be achieved by including a great variety of competing interests in the political system so that no one interest will be able to "outnumber and oppress the rest." Modern pluralist political theory (see Chapter 1) claims Madison as a forerunner.

of 'Faction'"). Two of the most important *Federalist Papers* are reprinted in the Appendix to this textbook.

Nevertheless, opponents of the Constitution—the Anti-Federalists—almost succeeded in defeating the document in New York and Virginia. They charged that the new Constitution would create an "aristocratic tyranny" and pose a threat to the "spirit of republicanism." They argued that the new Senate would be an aristocratic upper house and the new president a ruling monarch. They complained that neither the Senate nor the president was directly elected by the people. They also argued that the new national government would trample state governments and deny the people of the states the opportunity to handle their own political and economic affairs. Virginia patriot Patrick Henry urged the defeat of the Constitution "to preserve the poor Commonwealth of Virginia." Finally, their most effective argument was that the new Constitution lacked a bill of rights to protect individual liberty from government abuse (see *A Conflicting View:* "Objections to the Constitution by an Anti-Federalist" on page 82).

A Bill of Rights

Bill of Rights Written guarantees of basic individual liberties; the first ten amendments to the U.S. Constitution.

It may be hard to imagine today, but the original Constitution had no **Bill of Rights**. This was a particularly glaring deficiency because many of the new state constitutions proudly displayed these written guarantees of individual liberty.

The Founders certainly believed in limited government and individual liberty, and they did write a few liberties into the body of the Constitution, including protection against ex post facto laws, a limited definition of treason, a guarantee of the writ of habeas corpus, and a guarantee of trial by jury (see Chapter 14).

enumerated powers Powers specifically mentioned in the Constitution as belonging to the national government.

The Federalists argued that there was really no need for a bill of rights because (1) the national government was one of **enumerated powers** only, meaning it could not exercise any power not expressly enumerated, or granted, in the Constitution; (2) the power to limit free speech or press, establish a religion, or otherwise restrain individual liberty was not among the enumerated powers; (3) therefore it was not necessary to specifically deny these powers to the new government. But the Anti-Federalists were unwilling to rest fundamental freedoms on a thin thread of logical inference from the notion of enumerated powers. They wanted specific written guarantees that the new national government would not interfere with the rights of individuals or the powers of the states. So Federalists at the New York, Massachusetts, and Virginia ratifying conventions promised to support the addition of a bill of rights to the Constitution in the very first Congress.

A young member of the new House of Representatives, James Madison, rose in 1789 and presented a bill of rights that he had drawn up after reviewing more than 200 recommendations sent from the states. Interestingly, the new Congress was so busy debating new tax laws that Madison had a difficult time attracting attention to his bill. Eventually, in September 1789, Congress approved a Bill of Rights as ten **amendments**, or formal changes, to the Constitution and sent them to the states. (Congress actually passed twelve amendments. One was never ratified; another, dealing with pay raises for Congress, was not ratified by the necessary three-quarters of the states until 1992.) The states promptly ratified the first ten amendments to the Constitution (see Table 3.3), and these changes took effect in 1791.

amendment Formal change in a bill, law, or constitution.

The Bill of Rights was originally designed to limit the powers of the new *national* government. The Bill of Rights begins with the command "Congress shall make no law. . . ." It was not until after the Civil War that the Constitution was amended to also prohibit states from violating individual liberties. The Fourteenth Amendment, ratified in 1868, includes the command "No State shall. . . ." It prohibits the states from depriving any person of "life, liberty or property, without due process of law," or abridging "the privileges or immunities of citizens of the United States," or denying any person "equal protection of the laws." Today virtually all of the liberties guaranteed in the Constitution protect individuals not only from the national government but also from state governments.

www **James Madison**
The legacy of Madison organized by topic.
www.jmu.edu/madison

Constitutional Change

⊣Think Again⊢

Should the Constitution be amended to guarantee that equal rights shall not be denied based on sex?

The purpose of a constitution is to govern government—to place limits on governmental power. Thus government itself must not be able to alter or amend a constitution easily. Yet the U.S. Constitution has changed over time, sometimes by formal amendment and other times by judicial interpretation, presidential and congressional action, and general custom and practice.

Table 3.3　The Bill of Rights

Guaranteeing Freedom of Expression
First Amendment prohibits the government from abridging freedoms of speech, press, assembly, and petition.

Guaranteeing Religious Freedom
First Amendment prohibits the government from establishing a religion or interfering with the free exercise of religion.

Affirming the Right to Bear Arms and Protecting Citizens from Quartering Troops
Second Amendment guarantees the right to bear arms.

Third Amendment prohibits troops from occupying citizens' homes in peacetime.

Protecting the Rights of Accused Persons
Fourth Amendment protects against unreasonable searches and seizures.

Fifth Amendment requires an indictment by a grand jury for serious crimes; prohibits the government from trying a person twice for the same crime; prohibits the government from taking life, liberty, or property without due process of law; and prohibits the government from taking private property for public use without fair compensation to the owner.

Sixth Amendment guarantees a speedy and public jury trial, the right to confront witnesses in court, and the right to legal counsel for defense.

Seventh Amendment guarantees the right to a jury trial in civil cases.

Eighth Amendment prohibits the government from setting excessive bail or fines or inflicting cruel and unusual punishment.

Protecting the Rights of People and States
Ninth Amendment protects all other unspecified rights of the people.

Tenth Amendment reserves to the states or to the people those powers neither granted to the federal government nor prohibited to the states in the Constitution.

Amendments　A constitutional amendment must first be proposed, and then it must be ratified. The Constitution allows two methods of *proposing* a constitutional amendment: (1) by passage in the House and the Senate with a two-thirds vote, or (2) by passage in a national convention called by Congress in response to petitions by two-thirds of the state legislatures. Congress then chooses the method of *ratification*, which can be either (1) by vote in the legislatures of three-fourths of the states, or (2) by vote in conventions called for that purpose in three-fourths of the states (see Figure 3.4).

Of the four possible combinations of proposal and ratification, the method involving proposal by a two-thirds vote of Congress and ratification by three-quarters of the legislatures has been used for all the amendments except one. Only for the Twenty-first Amendment's repeal of Prohibition did Congress call for state ratifying conventions (principally because Congress feared that southern Bible Belt state legislatures would vote against repeal). The method of proposal by national convention has never been used.

In addition to the Bill of Rights, most of the constitutional amendments ratified over the nation's 200 years have expanded our notion of democracy. Today

The Anti-Federalist Papers
Essays by Anti-Federalists opposed to the ratification of the Constitution.
www.thisnation.com/library/antifederalist

Figure 3.4
Constitutional
Amendment Process

The Constitution set up
two alternative routes for
proposing amendments
and two for ratifying them.
One of the four possible
combinations has actually
been used for all except
one (the Twenty-first)
amendment. However, in
our time there have been
persistent calls for a constitutional convention to
propose new amendments
permitting school prayer,
making abortion illegal,
and requiring a balanced
national budget.

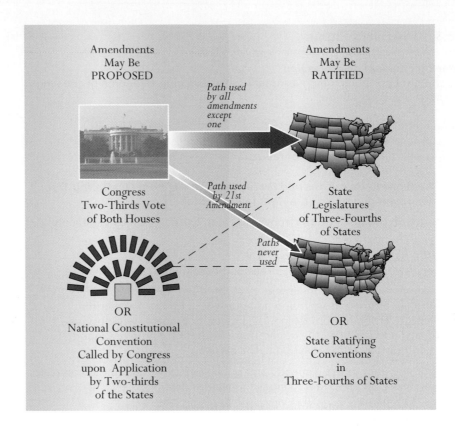

**Equal Rights Amendment
(ERA)** Proposed amendment
to the Constitution guar-
anteeing that equal rights
under the law shall not be
denied or abridged on
account of sex. Passed by
Congress in 1972, the
amendment failed to win
ratification by three of the
necessary three-fourths of
the states.

the Constitution includes 27 amendments, which means that only 17 (out of more than 10,000) proposed amendments have been ratified since the passage of the Bill of Rights. It is possible to classify the amendments that have been ratified into the broad categories of constitutional processes, Prohibition, income tax, individual liberty, and voting rights (see Table 3.4).

Amending the U.S. Constitution requires not only a two-thirds vote in both houses of Congress, reflecting *national* support, but also ratification by three-fourths of the states, reflecting widespread support within the states. The fate of the **Equal Rights Amendment**, popularly known as the ERA, illustrates the need for nationwide consensus in order to amend the Constitution. The Equal Rights Amendment is a simple statement to which the vast majority of Americans agree, according to public opinion polls: "Equality of rights under the law shall not be denied or abridged by the United States or any state on account of sex." Congress passed the ERA in 1972 with far more than the necessary two-thirds vote; both Republicans and Democrats supported the ERA, and it was endorsed by Presidents Nixon, Ford, and Carter as well as most other national political leaders and organizations. By 1978, thirty-five state legislatures had ratified the amendment—three states short of the necessary thirty-eight (three-quarters). (Five states subsequently voted to rescind, or cancel, their earlier ratification. However, because there is no language in the Constitution regarding rescission, there is some disagreement about the constitutionality of this action.) Promising that the "ERA won't go away," proponents of the amendment have continued to press their case. But to date Congress has not acted to resubmit the ERA to the states.

Judicial Interpretations   Some of the greatest changes in the Constitution have come about not by formal amendment but by interpretations of the document by federal courts, notably the U.S. Supreme Court.

Table 3.4   Amendments to the Constitution Since the Bill of Rights

Perfecting Constitutional Processes

Eleventh Amendment (1798) forbids federal lawsuits against a state by citizens of another state or nation

Twelfth Amendment (1804) provides separate ballots for president and vice president in the Electoral College to prevent confusion.

Twentieth Amendment (1933) determines the dates for the beginning of the terms of Congress (January 3) and the president (January 20).

Twenty-second Amendment (1951) limits the president to two terms.

Twenty-fifth Amendment (1967) provides for presidential disability.

Twenty-seventh Amendment (1992) prevents Congress from raising its own pay in a single session.

The Experiment with Prohibition

Eighteenth Amendment (1919) prohibits the manufacture, sale, or transportation of intoxicating liquors.

Twenty-first Amendment (1933) repeals the Eighteenth Amendment.

The Income Tax

Sixteenth Amendment (1913) allows Congress to tax incomes.

Expanding Liberty

Thirteenth Amendment (1865) abolishes slavery.

Fourteenth Amendment (1868) protects life, liberty, and property and the privileges and immunities of citizenship and provides equal protection of the law.

Expanding Voting Rights

Fifteenth Amendment (1870) guarantees that the right to vote shall not be denied because of race.

Seventeenth Amendment (1913) provides for the election of senators by the people of each state.

Nineteenth Amendment (1920) guarantees that the right to vote shall not be denied because of sex.

Twenty-third Amendment (1961) gives the District of Columbia electoral votes for presidential elections.

Twenty-fourth Amendment (1964) guarantees that the right to vote shall not be denied because of failure to pay a poll tax or other tax.

Twenty-sixth Amendment (1971) guarantees that the right to vote shall not be denied to persons eighteen years of age or older.

Indeed, through **judicial review**, the U.S. Supreme Court has come to play the central role in giving meaning to the Constitution. Judicial review is the power of federal courts, and ultimately the Supreme Court, to declare laws of Congress and actions of the president unconstitutional and therefore invalid. This power was first asserted by Chief Justice John Marshall in the case of *Marbury v. Madison* in 1803 (see *People in Politics:* "John Marshall and Early Supreme Court Politics" in Chapter 13). It is now an important part of the system of checks and balances (see Figure 3.1). This power is itself an interpretation of the Constitution, because it is not specifically mentioned in the document.

Supreme Court interpretations of the Constitution have given specific meaning to many of our most important constitutional phrases. Among the most important examples of constitutional change through judicial interpretation are

judicial review The power of federal courts to declare laws of Congress and actions of the president unconstitutional.

A CONFLICTING VIEW

Objections to the Constitution by an Anti-Federalist

Virginia's George Mason was a delegate to the Constitutional Convention of 1787, but he refused to sign the final document and became a leading opponent of the new Constitution. Mason was a wealthy plantation owner and a heavy speculator in western (Ohio) lands. He was a friend of George Washington, but he considered most other political figures of his day to be "babblers" and he generally avoided public office. However, in 1776 he authored Virginia's Declaration of Rights, which was widely copied in other state constitutions and later became the basis for the Bill of Rights. Although an ardent supporter of states' rights, he attended the Constitutional Convention of 1787 and, according to James Madison's notes on the proceedings, was an influential force in shaping the new national government. His refusal to sign the Constitution and his subsequent leadership of the opposition to its ratification made him the recognized early leader of the Anti-Federalists.

Mason's first objection to the Constitution was that it included no Bill of Rights. But he also objected to the powers given to the Senate, which was not directly elected by the people in the original document; to the federal courts; and to the president. He was wary of the Necessary and Proper Clause, which granted Congress the power to "make all laws which shall be necessary and proper" for carrying out the enumerated powers—those specifically mentioned in the Constitution. Mason correctly predicted that this clause would be used to preempt the powers of the states.

In his "objections to the Constitution" Mason wrote,

There is no declaration of rights; and the laws of the general government being paramount to the laws and constitutions of the several States, the declaration of rights in the separate States are no security.

Senators are not the representatives of the people, or amenable to them.

The judiciary of the United States is so constructed and extended as to absorb and destroy the judiciaries of the several States; thereby rendering law as tedious, intricate and expensive. . .

Under their own construction of the general clause at the end of the enumerated powers, the Congress may . . . extend their power as far as they shall think proper; so that the State Legislatures have no security for the powers now presumed to remain to them; or the people for their rights.

Note that virtually all of Mason's objections to the original Constitution had to be remedied at a later date. The Bill of Rights was added as the first ten amendments. Eventually (1913) the Seventeenth Amendment, for the direct election of U.S. senators, was passed. And Mason correctly predicted that the federal judiciary would eventually render the law "tedious, intricate, and expensive" and that the Necessary and Proper Clause, which he refers to as "the general clause at the end of the enumerated powers," would be used to expand congressional powers at the expense of the states.

the meanings given to the Fourteenth Amendment, particularly its provisions that "No State shall . . . deprive any person of life, liberty, or property, without due process of law; nor deny to any person within its jurisdiction the equal protection of the laws":

- Deciding that "equal protection of the laws" requires an end to segregation of the races (*Brown v. Board of Education of Topeka*, 1954, and subsequent decisions).

- Deciding that "liberty" includes a woman's right to choose an abortion, and that the term *person* does not include the unborn fetus (*Roe v. Wade*, 1973, and subsequent decisions).

- Deciding that "equal protection of the laws" requires that every person's vote should be weighed equally in apportionment and districting plans for the House of Representatives, state legislatures, city councils, and so on (*Baker v. Carr*, 1964, and subsequent decisions).

Presidential and Congressional Action   Congress and the president have also undertaken to interpret the Constitution. Nearly every president, for example, has argued that the phrase "executive Power" in Article II includes more than the specific powers mentioned afterward. Thomas Jefferson purchased the Louisiana Territory from France in 1803 even though there is no constitutional authorization for the president, or even the national government, to acquire new territory. Presidents from George Washington to Richard Nixon have argued that Congress cannot force the executive branch to turn over documents it does not wish to disclose (see Chapter 11).

Congress by law has tried to restrict the president's power as Commander-in-Chief of the Armed Forces by requiring the president to notify Congress when U.S. troops are sent to "situations where imminent involvement in hostilities is clearly indicated" and limiting their stay to sixty days unless Congress authorizes an extension. This War Powers Resolution (1973), passed by Congress over President Richard Nixon's veto in the immediate aftermath of the Vietnam War, has been ignored by every president to date (see Chapter 11). Yet it indicates that Congress has its own ideas about interpreting the Constitution.

Custom and Practice   Finally, the Constitution changes over time as a result of generally accepted customs and practice. It is interesting to note, for example, that the Constitution never mentions political parties. (Many of the Founders disapproved of parties because they caused "faction" among the people.) But soon after Thomas Jefferson resigned as President Washington's first secretary of state (in part because he resented the influence of Secretary of the Treasury Alexander Hamilton), the Virginian attracted the support of Anti-Federalists, who believed the national government was too strong. When Washington retired from office, most Federalists supported John Adams as his successor. But many Anti-Federalists ran for posts as presidential electors, promising to be "Jefferson's men." Adams won the presidential election of 1796, but the Anti-Federalists organized themselves into a political party, the Democratic-Republicans, to oppose Adams in the

A CONSTITUTIONAL NOTE

How Democratic Was the Constitution of 1787?

The Constitution established *four* decision-making bodies—the House and the Senate in the legislative branch (Article I); the president in the executive branch (Article II); and the Supreme Court and "such inferior Courts as the Congress may from time to time ordain and establish" in the judicial branch (Article III). But in 1787 only one of these bodies was to be elected by the people—the House of Representatives. The other three bodies were removed from direct popular control: State legislatures selected U.S. Senators; "electors," chosen in a fashion decided by state legislatures, chose the president;

and the president appointed the Supreme Court and other federal judges "with the Advice and Consent of the [then unelected] Senate." Of course, over time state legislatures provided for the direct election of presidential electors and the Seventeenth Amendment provided for the direct election of U.S. Senators.

The Constitution of 1787 also recognized slavery—"persons held to Service or Labor" (Article IV, Section 2)—and even protected it, by requiring states that capture runaway slaves to "deliver up," that is, to return them to their owners. And in terms of representation, the Constitution of 1787 distinguishes between "free persons" and three-fifths of "all other Persons" (Article I, Section 2), that is, slaves.

election of 1800. The party secured pledges from candidates for presidential elector to cast their electoral vote for Jefferson if they won their post, and then the party helped win support for its slate of electors. In this way the Electoral College was transformed from a deliberative body where leading citizens from each state came together to decide for themselves who should be president into a ceremonial body where pledged electors simply cast their presidential vote for the candidate who had carried their state in the presidential election. (For a full discussion of the current operation of the Electoral College, see *Up Close:* "Understanding the Electoral College" in Chapter 8.)

Summary Notes

- The true meaning of constitutionalism is the limitation of governmental power. Constitutions govern governments; they are designed to restrict those who exercise governmental power. Constitutions not only establish governmental bodies and prescribe the rules by which they make their decisions, but, more important, they also limit the powers of government.

- The American tradition of written constitutions extends back through the Articles of Confederation, the colonial charters, and the Mayflower Compact to the thirteenth-century English Magna Carta. The Second Continental Congress in 1776 adopted a written Declaration of Independence to justify the colonies' separation from Great Britain. All of these documents strengthened the idea of a written contract defining governmental power.

- The movement for a Constitutional Convention in 1787 was inspired by the new government's inability to levy taxes under the Articles of Confederation, its inability to fund the Revolutionary War debt, obstacles to interstate commerce, monetary problems, and civil disorders, including Shays's Rebellion.

- The nation's Founders—fifty-five delegates to the Constitutional Convention in Philadelphia in 1787—shared a broad consensus on liberty and property, the social contract, republicanism, limited government, and the need for a national government.

- The Founders compromised their differences over representation by creating two co-equal houses in the Congress: the House of Representatives, with members apportioned to the states on the basis of population and directly elected by the people for two-year terms, and the Senate, with two members allotted to each state regardless of its population and originally selected by state legislatures for six-year terms.

- The infamous slavery provisions in the Constitution—counting each slave as three-fifths of a person for purposes of taxation and representation, guaranteeing the return of escaped slaves, and postponing the end of the slave trade for twenty years—were also compromises. Voter qualifications in national elections were left to the states to determine.

- The structure of the national government reflects the Founders' beliefs in national supremacy, federalism, republicanism, separation of powers, checks and balances, and judicial review.

- The original Constitution gave the people very little influence on their government: only members of the House of Representatives were directly elected; senators were elected by state legislatures; the president was elected indirectly by "electors" chosen in each state; and members of the Supreme Court and federal judiciary were appointed for life by the president and confirmed by the Senate. Over time, the national government became more democratic through the expansion of voting rights, the direct election of senators, the emergence of political parties, and the practice of voting for presidential electors pledged to cast their vote for the candidates of one party.

- The separation of powers and checks and balances written into the Constitution were designed, in Madison's words, "to divide and arrange the several offices in such a manner as that each may be a check on the other." Judicial review was not specifically described in the original Constitution, but the Supreme Court soon asserted its power to overturn laws of Congress and the states, as well as presidential actions, that the Court determined to be in conflict with the Constitution.

- Opposition to the new Constitution was strong. Anti-Federalists argued that it created a national government that was aristocratic, undemocratic, and a threat to the rights of the states and the people. Their concerns resulted in the Bill of Rights: ten amendments added to the original Constitution, all designed to limit the power of the national government and protect the rights of individuals and states.

- Over time, constitutional changes have come about as a result of formal amendments, judicial interpretations, presidential and congressional actions, and changes in custom and practice. The most common method of constitutional amendment has been proposal by two-thirds vote of both houses of Congress followed by ratification by three-fourths of the state legislatures.

Key Terms

constitutionalism   58
constitution   58
republicanism   62
nationalism   62
taxes   66

tariff   66
common market   68
referenda   72
separation of powers   72

checks and balances   72
judicial review   74
ratification   75
Bill of Rights   78

enumerated powers   78
amendment   78
Equal Rights Amendment (ERA)   80
judicial review   81

Suggested Readings

Beard, Charles. *An Economic Interpretation of the Constitution*. New York: Macmillan, 1913. A classic work setting forth the argument that economic self-interest inspired the Founders in writing the Constitution.

Finkelman, Paul. *Slavery and the Founders*. 2nd ed. Armonk, NY: M.E. Sharpe, 2000. A critical account of the Founders' attitudes toward slavery and the resulting three-fifth's compromise.

Frohren, Bruce, ed. *The American Republic: Primary Sources*. Indianapolis: Liberty Fund Inc., 2002. Excellent collection of earliest American documents, from the Mayflower Compact to the Declaration of Independence.

Madison, James, Alexander Hamilton, and John Jay. *The Federalist Papers*. New York: Modern Library, 1937. These eighty-five collected essays, written in 1787–88 in support of ratification of the Constitution, remain the most important commentary on that document. Numbers 10 and 51 (reprinted in the Appendix) ought to be required reading for all students of American government.

Mason, Alpheus Thomas, and Donald Grier Stephenson Jr. *American Constitutional Law*. 14th ed. Upper Saddle River, NJ: Prentice Hall, 2004. The now classic introduction to the Constitution and the Supreme Court through essays and case excerpts.

McDonald, Forrest B. *Novus Ordo Seculorum*. Lawrence: University Press of Kansas, 1986. A description of the intellectual origins of the Constitution and the "new secular order" that it represented.

Peltason, J. W., and Sue Davis. *Understanding the Constitution*. 16th ed. New York: Harcourt Brace, 2004. Of the many books that explain the Constitution, this is one of the best. It contains explanations of the Declaration of Independence, the Articles of Confederation, and the Constitution. The book is written clearly and well suited for undergraduates.

Rossiter, Clinton L. *1787, The Grand Convention*. New York: Macmillan, 1960. A very readable account of the people and events surrounding the Constitutional Convention in 1787, with many insights into the conflicts and compromises that took place there.

Storing, Herbert J. *What the Anti-Federalists Were For*. Chicago: University of Chicago Press, 1981. An examination of the arguments of the Anti-Federalists in opposition to the ratification of the Constitution.

Make It Real

CONSTITUTIONAL DEMOCRACY
This module includes a look at the *Federalist Papers* and the *Articles of Confederation*.

★ ★ *On Reading the Constitution* ★ ★

More than 218 years after its ratification, our Constitution remains the operating charter of our republic. It is neither self-explanatory nor a comprehensive description of our constitutional rules. Still, it remains the starting point. Many Americans who swear by the Constitution have never read it seriously, although copies can be found in most American government and American history textbooks.

Justice Hugo Black, who served on the Supreme Court for 34 years, kept a copy of the Constitution with him at all times. He read it often. Reading the Constitution would be a good way for you to begin (and then reread again to end) your study of the government of the United States. We have therefore included a copy of it at this point in the book. Please read it carefully.

The Constitution of the United States

We the People of the United States, in Order to form a more perfect Union, establish Justice, insure domestic Tranquility, provide for the common defense, promote the general Welfare, and secure the Blessings of Liberty to ourselves and our Posterity, do ordain and establish this Constitution for the United States of America.

"We, the people." Three simple words, yet of profound importance and contentious origin. Every government in the world at the time of the Constitutional Convention was some type of monarchy wherein sovereign power flowed from the top. The Founders of our new country rejected monarchy as a form of government and proposed instead a republic, which would draw its sovereignty from the people.

The Articles of Confederation that governed the U.S. from 1776 until 1789 started with: "We the under signed Delegates of the States." Early drafts of the new constitution started with: "We, the states . . ." But again, the Founders were not interested in another union of states but rather the creation of a new national government. Therefore, "We, the states" was changed to "We, the people."

The remainder of the preamble describes the generic functions of government.

ARTICLE I—THE LEGISLATIVE ARTICLE

Legislative Power

The very first article in the Constitution established the legislative branch of the new national government. Why did the framers start with the legislative power instead of the executive branch? Under the Articles of Confederation, the legislature was the only functional instrument of government. Therefore, the framers truly believed it was the most important component of the new government.

Section 1 All legislative Powers herein granted shall be vested in a Congress of the United States, which shall consist of a Senate and House of Representatives.

Section 1 established a bicameral (two-chamber) legislature of an upper (Senate) and lower (House of Representatives) organization of the legislative branch.

House of Representatives: Composition; Qualifications; Apportionment; Impeachment Power

Section 2 Clause 1. The House of Representatives shall be composed of Members chosen every second Year by the People of the several States, and the Electors in each State shall have the Qualifications requisite for Electors of the most numerous Branch of the State Legislature.

This section sets the term of office for House members (2 years) and indicates that those voting for Congress will have the same qualifications as those voting for the state legislatures. Originally, states limited voters to white property owners. Some states even had religious disqualifications, such as Catholic or Jewish. Most property and religious qualifications for voting were removed by the 1840s, but race and gender restrictions remained, until the 15th and 19th amendments were passed.

Clause 2. No Person shall be a Representative who shall not have attained to the Age of twenty five Years, and been seven Years a Citizen of the United States, and who shall not, when elected, be an inhabitant of that State in which he shall be chosen.

This section sets forth the basic qualifications of a representative: at least 25 years of age, a U.S. citizen for at least 7 years, and a resident of a state. Note that the Constitution does not require a person to be a resident of the district he or she represents. At the time the Constitution was written, life expectancy was about 43 years of age. So a person 25 years old was middle aged. Considering today's life expectancy of about 78 years, the equivalent age of 25 would be about 45. The average age of a current representative is 53.

Clause 2 does not specify how many terms a Representative can serve in Congress. Calls for Congress members to be term limited have never been enacted. Some states passed legislation to limit the terms of their U.S. Representatives. Because of the specificity of the qualifications for office, the USSC ruled in *U.S. Term Limits, Inc. v. Thomton,* 514 U.S. 779 (1995) that term limits for U.S. legislators could not be imposed by any state but would require a constitutional amendment.

Clause 3. Representatives and direct Taxes[1] shall be apportioned among the several States which may be included within this Union, according to their respective Numbers, which shall be determined by adding to the whole Number of free Persons, including those bound to Service for a Term of Years, and excluding Indians not taxed, three fifths of all other Persons.[2] The actual Enumeration shall be made within three Years after the first Meeting of the Congress of the United States, and within every subsequent Term of ten Years in such Manner as they shall by Law direct. The Number of Representatives shall not exceed one for every thirty Thousand, but each State shall have at Least one Representative, and until such enumeration shall be made, the State of New Hampshire shall be entitled to chuse three, Massachusetts eight, Rhode Island and Providence Plantations one, Connecticut five, New York six, New Jersey four, Pennsylvania eight, Delaware one, Maryland six, Virginia ten, North Carolina five, South Carolina five, and Georgia three.

This clause contains the Three-Fifths Compromise wherein American Indians and Blacks were only counted as 3/5 of a person for congressional representation purposes. This clause also addresses the question of congressional reapportionment every 10 years, which requires a census. Since the 1911 Reapportionment Act, the size of the House of Representatives has been set at 435. This is the designated size that is reapportioned every 10 years. Based on changes of population, some states gain and some states lose representatives. This clause also provides that every state, regardless of population, will have at least one (1) representative. Currently, seven states have only one representative.

Clause 4. When vacancies happen in the Representation from any State, the Executive Authority thereof shall issue Writs of Election to fill such Vacancies.

This clause provides a procedure for replacing a U.S. representative in the case of death, resignation, or expulsion from the House. Generally, if less than half a term is left, the governor will appoint a successor. If more than half a term is remaining, most states require a special election to fill the vacancy.

Clause 5. The House of Representatives shall chuse their Speaker and other Officers, and shall have the sole Power of Impeachment.

Only one officer of the House is specified—the Speaker. All other officers are decided by the House. This clause also gives the House authority for impeachments (accusations) against officials of the executive and judicial branches.

Senate Composition: Qualifications, Impeachment Trials

Section 3 Clause 1. The Senate of the United States shall be composed of two Senators from each State, chosen by the Legislature thereof,[3] for six Years and each Senator shall have one Vote.

This clause treats each state equally—all have two senators each. Originally, senators were chosen by

state legislators, but since passage and ratification of the 17th Amendment, they are now elected by popular vote. This clause also establishes the term of a senator—6 years—three times that of a House member.

Clause 2. Immediately after they shall be assembled in Consequence of the first Election, they shall be divided as equally as may be into three Classes. The Seats of the Senators of the first Class shall be vacated at the Expiration of the second Year, of the second Class at the Expiration of the fourth Year, and of the third Class at the Expiration of the sixth Year, so that one third may be chosen every second Year and if Vacancies happen by Resignation, or otherwise, during the Recess of the Legislature of any State, the Executive thereof may make temporary Appointments until the next Meeting of the Legislature which shall then fill such Vacancies.[4]

To prevent a wholesale election of senators every six years, this clause provides that one-third of the Senate will be elected every two years. Senate vacancies are filled similar to the House—either appointment by the governor or a special election.

Clause 3. No person shall be a Senator who shall not have attained to the Age of thirty Years, and been nine Years a Citizen of the United States, and who shall not, when elected, be an Inhabitant of that State for which he shall be chosen.

This clause sets forth the qualifications for U.S. senator: at least 30 years old, a U.S. citizen for at least nine years, and a citizen of a state. The equivalent age of 30 today would be 54 years old. The average age of a U.S. senator at present is 58.3 years.

Clause 4. The Vice President of the United States shall be President of the Senate but shall have no Vote, unless they be equally divided.

The only constitutional duty of the vice president is specified in this clause—president of the Senate. This official only has a vote if there is a tie vote in the Senate; then the vice president's vote breaks the tie.

Clause 5. The Senate shall chuse their other Officers, and also a President pro tempore, in the Absence of the Vice President, or when he shall exercise the Office of President of the United States.

One official office in the U.S. Senate is specified— temporary president, who fills in during the vice president's absence (which is normally the case). All other Senate officers are designated and selected by the Senate.

Clause 6. The Senate shall have the sole Power to try all Impeachments. When sitting for that Purpose, they shall be on Oath or Affirmation. When the President of the United States is tried, the Chief Justice shall preside. And no Person shall be convicted without the Concurrence of two thirds of the Members present.

Judgment in Cases of impeachment shall not extend further than to removal from Office, and disqualification to hold and enjoy any Office of honor, Trust or Profit under the United States, but the Party convicted shall nevertheless be liable and subject to Indictment, Trial, Judgment and Punishment according to Law.

---

[1]Modified by the 16th Amendment
[2]Replaced by Section 2, 14th Amendment
[3]Repealed by the 17th Amendment

---

[4]Modified by the 17th Amendment

THE CONSTITUTION OF THE UNITED STATES **89**

The Senate acts as a trial court for impeached federal officials. If the accused is the president, the Chief Justice of the U.S. Supreme Court presides. Otherwise, the vice president normally presides. Conviction of the charges requires a 2/3 majority vote of those senators present at the time of the vote. Conviction results in the federal official's removal from office and disqualification to hold any other federal appointed office. Removal from office does not bar further prosecution under applicable criminal or civil laws, nor does it apparently bar one from elected office. A current representative, Alcee L. Hastings, was impeached and removed as a federal district judge. He subsequently ran for Congress and now represents Florida's 23rd Congressional District.

Congressional Elections: Times, Places, Manner

Section 4 The Times, Places and Manner of holding Elections for Senators and Representatives, shall be prescribed in each State by the Legislature thereof, but the Congress may at any time by Law make or alter such Regulations, except as to the Places of chusting Senators.

The Congress shall assemble at least once in every Year, and such Meeting shall be on the first Monday in December, unless they shall by Law appoint a different Day.[5]

The states determine the place and manner of electing representatives and senators, but Congress has the right to make or change these laws or regulations, except for the election sites. Congress is required to meet annually, and now, by law, annual meetings begin in January.

Powers and Duties of the Houses

Section 5 Clause 1. Each House shall be the Judge of the Elections, Returns and Qualifications of its own Members, and a Majority of each shall constitute a Quorum to do Business, but a smaller Number may adjourn from day to day, and may be authorized to compel the Attendance of absent Members, in such Manner, and under the Penalties as each House may provide.

This clause enables each legislative branch to essentially make its own rules. Normally, to take a vote, a quorum is necessary. But if no votes are scheduled, fewer than a quorum can convene a session.

Clause 2. Each House may determine the Rules of its Proceedings, punish its Members for disorderly Behaviour, and with the Concurrence of two thirds, expel a Member.

Essentially, each branch promulgates its own rules and punishes its own members. The ultimate punishment is expulsion of the member, which requires a 2/3 vote. Expulsion does not prevent the member from running again.

Clause 3. Each House shall keep a Journal of its Proceedings, and from time to time publish the same, excepting such Parts as may in their Judgment require Secrecy, and the Yeas and Nays of the Members of either House on any question shall, at the Desire of one fifth of those Present, be entered on the Journal.

An official record called the Congressional Record, House Journal, etc., is kept for all sessions. It is a daily account of House and Senate floor debates,

[5]Changed by the 20th Amendment

votes, and members' remarks. However, a record is not printed if a proceeding is closed to the public for security reasons. Many votes are by voice vote, and if at least 1/5 of the members request, a recorded vote of Yeas and Nays will be conducted and recorded. This procedure permits analysis of congressional roll-call votes.

Clause 4. Neither House, during the Session of Congress shall, without the Consent of the other, adjourn for more than three days, nor to any other Place than that in which the two Houses shall be sitting.

This clause prevents one branch from adjourning for a long period or to some other location without the consent of the other branch.

Rights of Members

Section 6 Clause 1. The Senators and Representatives shall receive a Compensation for their Services, to be ascertained by Law, and paid out of the Treasury of the United States. They shall in all Cases, except Treason, Felony and Breach of the Peace, be privileged from Arrest during their Attendance at the Session of their respective Houses, and in going to and returning from the same, and for any Speech or Debate in either House, they shall not be questioned in any other Place.

This section ensures that senators and congressional representatives will be paid a salary from the U.S. Treasury. This salary is determined by no other than the legislature. According to the Library of Congress legislative Web site THOMAS "The current salary for members of Congress is $165,200. A small number of leadership positions, like Speaker of the House, receive a somewhat higher salary." In addition, members of Congress receive many other benefits: free health care, fully funded retirement system, free gyms, 26 free round trips to their home state or district, etc. This section also provides immunity from arrest or prosecution for congressional actions on the floor or in travel to and from the Congress. For example, few members of Congress have ever been charged with drunk driving.

Clause 2. No Senator or Representative, shall, during the Time for which he was elected, be appointed to any civil Office under the Authority of the United States, which shall have been created, or the Emoluments whereof shall have been increased during such time; and no Person holding any Office under the United States, shall be a Member of either House during his Continuance in Office.

This section prevents the U.S. from adopting a parliamentary democracy, since congressional members cannot hold executive offices and members of the executive branch cannot be members of Congress.

Legislative Powers: Bills and Resolutions

Section 7 Clause 1. All Bills for raising Revenue shall originate in the House of Representatives; but the Senate may propose or concur with Amendments as on other Bills.

This clause specifies one of the few powers specific to the U.S. House—revenue bills.

Clause 2. Every Bill which shall have passed the House of Representatives and the Senate, shall, before it becomes a Law, be presented to the President of the United States; If he approve he shall sign it, but if not he shall return it, with his Objections to that House in which it shall have originated, who shall enter the Objections at large on their Journal, and proceed to reconsider it. If after such Reconsideration two thirds of that House shall agree to pass the Bill, it shall be sent, together with the Objections, to the other House, by which it shall likewise be reconsidered, and if approved by two thirds of that House, it shall become a Law. But in all such Cases the Votes of both Houses shall be determined by yeas and Nays, and the Names of the Persons voting for and against the Bill shall be entered on the Journal of each House respectively. If any Bill shall not be returned by the President within ten Days (Sundays excepted) after it shall have been presented to him, the Same shall be a Law, in like Manner as if he had signed it, unless the Congress by their Adjournment prevent its Return, in which Case it shall not be a Law.

The heart of the checks and balances system is contained in this clause. Both the House and Senate must pass a bill and present it to the president. If the president fails to act on the bill within 10 days (not including Sundays), the bill will automatically become law. If the president signs the bill, it becomes law. If the president vetoes the bill and sends it back to Congress, this body may override the veto by a 2/3 vote in each house. This vote must be a recorded vote.

Clause 3. Every Order, Resolution, or Vote to which the Concurrence of the Senate and House of Representatives may be necessary (except on a question of Adjournment) shall be presented to the President of the United States; and before the Same shall take Effect, shall be approved by him, or being disapproved by him, shall be repassed by two thirds of the Senate and House of Representatives, according to the Rules and Limitations prescribed in the Case of a Bill.

This clause covers every other type of legislative action other than a bill. Essentially, the same procedures apply in most cases. There are a few exceptions. For example, a joint resolution proposing a new congressional amendment is not subject to presidential veto.

Powers of Congress

Section 8 Clause 1. The Congress shall have Power to lay and collect Taxes, Duties, Imposts and Excises, to pay the Debts and provide for the common Defence and general Welfare of the United States, but all Duties, Imposts and Excises shall be uniform throughout the United States.

To borrow Money on the credit of the United States;

To regulate Commerce with foreign Nations, and among the several States, and with the Indian Tribes;

To establish an uniform Rule of Naturalization, and uniform Laws on the subject of Bankruptcies throughout the United States;

To coin Money, regulate the Value thereof, and of foreign Coin, and fix the Standard of Weights and Measures;

To provide for the Punishment of counterfeiting the Securities and current Coin of the United States;

To establish Post Offices and post Roads;

To promote the Progress of Science and useful Arts, by securing for limited Times to Authors and Inventors the exclusive Right to their respective Writings and Discoveries;

To constitute Tribunals inferior to the supreme Court;

To define and punish Piracies and Felonies committed on the high Seas, and Offences against the Law of Nations;

To declare War, grant Letters of Marque and Reprisal, and make Rules concerning Captures on Land and Water;

To raise and support Armies, but no Appropriation of Money to that Use shall be for a longer Term than two Years;

To provide and maintain a Navy;

To make Rules for the Government and Regulation of the land and naval Forces;

To provide for calling for the Militia to execute the Laws of the Union, suppress Insurrections and repel Invasions;

To provide for organizing, arming, and disciplining, the Militia, and for governing such Part of them as may be employed in the Service of the United States, reserving to the States respectively, the Appointment of the Officers, and the Authority of training the Militia according to the discipline prescribed by Congress;

This *extensive* clause establishes what are known as the "expressed" or "specified" powers of Congress. In theory, this serves as a limit or brake on congressional power.

Clause 2. To exercise exclusive Legislation in all Cases whatsoever, over such District (not exceeding ten Miles square) as may, by Cession of particular States, and the Acceptance of Congress, become the Seat of the Government of the United States, and to exercise like Authority over all Places purchased by the Consent of the Legislature of the State in which the Same shall be, for the Erection of Forts, Magazines, Arsenals, dock Yards, and other needful Buildings—And

This clause establishes the seat of the federal government, which was first started in New York but eventually was moved to Washington, D.C., when both Maryland and Virginia ceded land to the new national government, which then established the District of Columbia.

Clause 3. To make all Laws which shall be necessary and proper for carrying into Execution the foregoing Powers, and all other Powers vested by this Constitution in the Government of the United States, or in any Department or Officer thereof.

This clause, known as the "Elastic Clause," provides the basis for the doctrine of "implied" congressional powers, which was first introduced in the U.S. Supreme Court case of *McCulloch v. Maryland,* 1819. This doctrine tremendously expanded the power of Congress to pass legislation and make regulations.

Powers Denied to Congress

Section 9 Clause 1. The Migration or Importation of such Persons as any of the States now existing shall think proper to admit, shall not be prohibited by the Congress prior to the Year one thousand eight hundred and eight, but a Tax or duty may be imposed on such Importation, not exceeding ten dollars for each Person.

This clause was part of the Three-Fifths Compromise. Essentially, the new Congress was prohibited from stopping the importation of slaves until 1808, but it could impose a head tax, not to exceed ten dollars for each slave.

Clause 2. The Privilege of the Writ of Habeas Corpus shall not be suspended, unless when in Cases of Rebellion or Invasion the public Safety may require it.

Congress cannot suspend the writ of habeas corpus except in cases of rebellion or invasion. The writ of habeas corpus permits a judge to inquire about the legality of detention or deprivation of liberty of any citizen.

Clause 3. No Bill of Attainder or ex post facto Law shall be passed.

This provision prohibits Congress from passing either a bill of attainder (forfeiture of property in capital cases) or ex post facto laws (retroactive crimes after passage of legislation). Similar restrictions were enshrined in many state constitutions.

Clause 4. No Capitation, or other direct Tax shall be laid, unless in Proportion to the Census or Enumeration herein before directed to be taken.[6]

This clause prevented Congress from passing an Income tax. Only with passage of the 16th Amendment in 1913 did Congress gain this power.

Clause 5. No Tax or Duty shall be laid on Articles exported from any State.

This section establishes free trade within the U.S. The federal government cannot tax state exports.

Clause 6. No Preference shall be given by any Regulation of Commerce or Revenue to the Ports of one State over those of another; nor shall Vessels bound to, or from one State, be obliged to enter, clear, or pay Duties in another.

This clause also applies to free trade within the U.S. The national government cannot show any preference to any state or maritime movements among the states.

Clause 7. No Money shall be drawn from the Treasury, but in Consequence of Appropriations made by Law, and a regular Statement and Account of the Receipts and Expenditures of all public Money shall be published from time to time.

This provision of the Constitution prevents any expenditure unless it has been specifically provided for in an appropriations bill. At the beginning of most fiscal years, Congress has not completed its work on the budget. Technically, the government cannot spend any money according to this provision and would have to shut down. So Congress normally passes a Continuing Resolution providing temporary authority to continue to spend money until the final budget is approved and signed into law.

Clause 8. No Title of Nobility shall be granted by the United States. And no Person holding any Office of Profit or Trust under them, shall, without the Consent of Congress, accept of any present, Emolument, Office, or Title, of any kind whatever, from any King, Prince, or foreign State.

Feudalism would not be established in the new country. We would have no nobles. No federal official can even accept a title of nobility (even honorary) without permission of Congress.

[6]Modified by the 16th Amendment.

Powers Denied to the States

This section sets out the prohibitions on state actions.

Section 10 Clause 1. No State shall enter into any Treaty, Alliance, or Confederation, grant Letters of Marque and Reprisal, coin Money, emit Bills of Credit, make any Thing but gold and silver Coin a Tender in Payment of Debts, pass any Bill of Attainder, ex post facto Law, or Law impairing the Obligation of Contracts of grant any Title of Nobility.

This particular clause is a laundry list of denied powers. Note that these restrictions cannot even be waived by Congress. States are not to engage in foreign relations, nor acts of war. A letter of Marque and Reprisal was used during these times to provide legal cover for privateers. The federal government's currency monopoly is established. The sanctity of contracts is specified. And similar state prohibitions are specified for bills of attainder, ex post facto, etc.

Clause 2. No State shall, without the Consent of the Congress, lay any Imposts or Duties on Imports or Exports, except what may be absolutely necessary for executing its inspection Laws: and the net Produce of all Duties and Imposts, laid by any State on Imports or Exports, shall be for the Use of the Treasury of the United States, and all such Laws shall be subject to the Revision and Controul of the Congress.

This section establishes the monopoly control of the national government in matters of both national and international trade. The only concession to states is health and safety inspections.

Clause 3. No State shall, without the Consent of Congress, lay any Duty of Tonnage, keep Troops, or Ships of War in time of Peace, enter into any Agreement or Compact with another State, or with a foreign Power, or engage in War, unless actually invaded, or in such imminent Danger as will not admit of delay.

This final section of the Legislative article establishes the war monopoly power of the national government. The only exception to state action is actual invasion or threat of imminent danger.

ARTICLE II—THE EXECUTIVE ARTICLE

This article establishes an entirely new concept in government—an elected executive power.

Nature and Scope of Presidential Power

Section 1 Clause 1. The executive Power shall be vested in a President of the United States of America. He shall hold his Office during the Term of four Years and, together with the Vice President, chosen for the same Term, be elected, as follows.

This clause establishes the executive power in the office of the president of the United States of America. It also establishes a second office—vice president. A four-year term was established, but no limit on the number of terms. A limit was later established by the 22nd Amendment.

Clause 2. Each State shall appoint, in such Manner as the Legislature thereof may direct, a Number of Electors, equal to the whole Number of Senators and Representatives to which the State may be entitled in the Congress: but no Senator or Representative, or Person holding an Office of Trust or Profit under the United States, shall be appointed an Elector.

This paragraph essentially establishes the Electoral College to choose the president and vice president.

Clause 3. The Electors shall meet in their respective States, and vote by Ballot for two Persons, of whom one at least shall not be an Inhabitant of the same State with themselves. And they shall make a List of all the Persons voted for, and of the Number of Votes for each; which List they shall sign and certify, and transmit sealed to the Seat of the Government of the United States, directed to the President of the Senate. The President of the Senate shall, in the Presence of the Senate and House of Representatives, open all the Certificates, and the Votes shall then be counted. The Person having the greatest Number of Votes shall be the President, if such Number be a Majority of the whole Number of Electors appointed; and if there be more than one who have such Majority and have an equal Number of Votes, then the House of Representatives shall immediately chuse by Ballot one of them for President; and if no Person have a Majority, then from the five highest on the List the said House shall in like Manner chuse the President. But in chusing the President, the Votes shall be taken by States, the Representation from each State having one Vote; a quorum for this Purpose shall consist of a Member or Members from two thirds of the States, and a Majority of all the States shall be necessary to a Choice. In every Case, after the Choice of the President, the Person having the greatest Number of Votes of the Electors shall be the Vice President. But if there should remain two or more who have equal Votes, the Senate shall chuse from them by Ballot the Vice President.[7]

This paragraph has been superseded by the 12th Amendment. The original language did not require a separate vote for president and vice president. This resulted in a tied vote in the Electoral College in 1800 when both Thomas Jefferson and Aaron Burr received 73 electoral votes. The 12th Amendment requires a separate vote for each. Only one of the two can be from the state of the elector. This means that it is highly unlikely that the presidential and vice presidential candidates would be from the same state. This question arose in the 2000 election when Dick Cheney, who lived and worked in Texas, had to reestablish his residence in Wyoming.

The original language provided for a House election in the case of no majority vote or a tie vote among the top five candidates. The amendment lowered the number of candidates to the top three. The Senate is to select the vice president if a candidate does not have an electoral majority or in the case of a tie vote. The Senate considers only the top two candidates. The amendment also clarifies that the qualifications of the vice president are the same as those for president.

Clause 4. The Congress may determine the Time of chusing the Electors, and the Day on which they shall give their Votes; which Day shall be the same throughout the United States.

Congress is given the power to establish a uniform day and time for the state selection of electors.

Clause 5. No Person except a natural born Citizen, or a Citizen of the United States, at the time of the Adoption of this Constitution, shall be eligible to the Office of President, neither shall any Person be eligible to that Office who shall not have attained to the Age of thirty five Years, and been fourteen Years a Resident within the United States.

The qualifications for the offices of president and vice president are specified here—at least 35 years old, 14 years' resident in the U.S., and a natural-born citizen or citizen of the U.S. The 14th Amendment clarified who is a citizen of the U.S.: a person born or naturalized in the U.S. and subject to its jurisdiction. But the term "natural-born citizen" is unclear and has never been further defined by the judicial branch. Does it mean born in the U.S. or born of U.S. citizens in the U.S. or somewhere else in the world? Unfortunately, there is no definitive answer.

Clause 6. In Case of the Removal of the President from Office, or of his Death, Resignation, or Inability to discharge the Powers and Duties of the said Office, the Same shall devolve on the Vice President, and the Congress may by Law provide for the Case of Removal, Death, Resignation, or Inability, both of the President and Vice President, declaring what Officer shall then act as president, and such Officer shall act accordingly, until the Disability be removed, or a President shall be elected.[8]

This clause has been modified by the 25th Amendment. Upon the death, resignation, or impeachment and conviction of the president, the vice president becomes president. The new president nominates a new vice president, who assumes the office, if approved by a majority vote in both congressional branches. The president is also now able to notify the Congress of his inability to perform his office.

Clause 7. The President shall, at stated Times, receive for his Services, a Compensation which shall neither be increased nor diminished during the Period of which he shall have been elected, and he shall not receive within that Period any other Emolument from the United States, or any of them.

This section covers the compensation of the president, which cannot be increased or decreased during his office. The current salary is $400,000/year.

Clause 8. Before he enter on the Execution of his Office, he shall take the following Oath or Affirmation—"I do solemnly swear (or affirm) that I will faithfully execute the Office of President of the United States, and will to the best of my Ability, preserve, protect and defend the Constitution of the United States."

This final clause in Section 1 is the oath of office administered to the new president.

Powers and Duties of the President

Section 2   Clause 1. The President shall be the Commander in Chief of the Army and Navy of the United States, and of the

---

[7]Changed by the 12th and 20th Amendments

[8]Modified by the 25th Amendment

Militia of the several States; when called into the actual Service of the United States, he may require the Opinion, in writing, of the principal Officer in each of the executive Departments, upon any Subject relating to the Duties of their respective Offices, and he shall have the Power to grant Reprieves and Pardons for Offences against the United States, except in Cases of Impeachment.

This clause establishes the president as Commander-in-Chief of the U.S. armed forces. George Washington actually led U.S. armed forces during the Whiskey Rebellion. The second provision provides the basis for cabinet meetings that are used to acquire the opinions of executive department heads. The last provision provides an absolute pardon or reprieve power from the president. The provision was controversial, but legal, when President Gerald Ford pardoned Richard Nixon following the Watergate scandal.

Clause 2. He shall have Power, by and with the Advice and Consent of the Senate to make Treaties, provided two thirds of the Senators present concur, and he shall nominate, and by and with the Advice and Consent of the Senate, shall appoint Ambassadors, other public Ministers and Consuls, Judges of the supreme Court, and all other Officers of the United States, whose Appointments are not herein otherwise provided for, and which shall be established by Law but the Congress may by Law vest the Appointment of such inferior Officers, as they think proper in the President alone, in the Courts of Law, or in the Heads of Departments.

This clause covers two important presidential powers, treaty making and appointments. The president (via the State Department) can negotiate treaties with other nations, but these do not become official until ratified by a 2/3 vote of the U.S. Senate. The president is empowered to appoint judges, ambassadors, and other U.S. officials (cabinet officers, military officers, agency heads, etc.) subject to Senate approval. The Congress can and does delegate this approval to the president in the case of inferior officers. For example, junior military officer promotions are not submitted to the Senate, but senior officer promotions are.

Clause 3. The President shall have Power to fill up all Vacancies that may happen during the Recess of the Senate, by granting Commissions which shall expire at the End of their next Session.

This provision allows recess appointments of the officials listed in Clause 2 above. These commissions automatically expire unless approved by the Senate by the end of the next session. Presidents have used this provision to fill jobs when the nomination process is stalled. Some of these appointments have been very controversial. The regular nomination was stalled because the Senate did not want to confirm the nominee.

Section 3 He shall from time to time give to the Congress Information of the State of the Union, and recommend to their Consideration such Measures as he shall judge necessary and expedient, he may, on extraordinary Occasions convene both Houses, or either of them and in Case of Disagreement between them, with Respect to the Time of Adjournment, he may adjourn them to such Time as he shall think proper, he shall receive

Ambassadors and other public Ministers, he shall take Care that the Laws be faithfully executed, and shall Commission all the Officers of the United States.

This section provides for the annual State of the Union address to a joint session of Congress and the American people. The president is also authorized to call special meetings of either the House or Senate. If there is disagreement between the House and Senate regarding adjournment, the president is empowered to adjourn them. This would be extremely rare. The president formally receives other nations' ambassadors. The next to last provision to faithfully execute laws provides the basis for the whole administrative apparatus of the presidency. All officers of the U.S. receive a formal commission from the president (most of these are signed with a signature machine).

Section 4 The President, Vice President and all civil Officers of the United States, shall be removed from Office on Impeachment for, and Conviction of, Treason, Bribery, or other high Crimes and Misdemeanors.

This section provides the constitutional authority for the impeachment and trial of the president, vice president, and all civil officers of the U.S. for treason, bribery, or other high crimes and misdemeanors (the exact meaning of this phrase is unclear and is often more political than judicial).

ARTICLE III—THE JUDICIAL ARTICLE

Judicial Power, Courts, Judges

Section 1 The judicial Power of the United States, shall be vested in one supreme Court, and in such inferior Courts as the Congress may from time to time ordain and establish. The Judges, both of the supreme and inferior Courts, shall hold their Offices during good Behaviour, and shall, at stated Times, receive for their Services, a Compensation, which shall not be diminished during their Continuance in Office.

This section establishes the judicial branch in very general terms. It specifically provides only for the Supreme Court. Congress is given the responsibility to flesh out the court system. It initially did so in the Judiciary Act of 1789, when it established 13 district courts (one for each state), and 3 appellate courts. All federal judges hold their offices for life and can only be removed for breaches of good behavior—a very nebulous term. Federal judges have been removed for drunkenness, accepting bribes, and other misdemeanors. To date, no justice of the U.S. Supreme Court has ever been removed.

The salary of federal judges is set by congressional act, but can never be reduced. Although the American Bar Association and the Federal Bar Association consider federal judges' salaries inadequate, most Americans would probably disagree. Federal district judges earn $165,200/year, appellate judges $174,600, and Supreme Court justices $203,000. The Chief Justice is paid $212,100. These are lifetime salaries, even upon retirement.

Jurisdiction

Section 2 The judicial Power shall extend to all Cases, in Law and Equity, arising under this Constitution, the Laws of the United States, and Treaties made, or which shall be made, under their Authority;—to all Cases affecting Ambassadors, other public Ministers and Consuls;—to all Cases of admiralty and maritime Jurisdiction;—to Controversies to which the United States shall be a Party;—to Controversies between two or more States; between a State and Citizens of another State;[9]—between Citizens of different States;—between Citizens of the same State claiming Lands under Grants of different States, and between a State, or the Citizens thereof, and foreign States, Citizens, or Subjects.

In all Cases affecting Ambassadors, other public Ministers and Consuls, and those in which a State shall be Party, the supreme Court shall have original Jurisdiction. In all the other Cases before mentioned, the supreme Court shall have appellate Jurisdiction, both as to Law and Fact, with such Exceptions, and under such Regulations as Congress shall make.

The Trial of all Crimes, except in Cases of Impeachment, shall be by Jury; and such Trial shall be held in the State where the said Crimes shall have been committed, but when not committed within any State, the Trial shall be at such Place or Places as the Congress may by Law have directed.

This section establishes the original and appellate jurisdiction of the U.S. Supreme Court. With the Congress of Vienna's 1815 establishment of "diplomatic immunity," the U.S. Supreme Court no longer hears cases involving ambassadors. Since 1925, the Supreme Court no longer hears every case on appeal but can select which cases it will accept, which is now only about 150 cases per year. This section also establishes the right of trial by jury for federal crimes.

Treason

Section 3 Treason against the United States, shall consist only in levying War against them, or in adhering to their Enemies, giving them Aid and Comfort. No Person shall be convicted of Treason unless on the Testimony of two Witnesses to the same overt Act, or on Confession in open Court.

The Congress shall have Power to declare the Punishment of Treason, but no Attainder of Treason shall work Corruption of Blood, or Forfeiture except during the Life of the Person attainted.

Treason is the only crime defined in the U.S. Constitution. Congress established the penalty of death for treason convictions. Note that two witnesses are required to convict anyone of treason. Even in cases of treasonable conduct, seizure of estates is prohibited.

ARTICLE IV—INTERSTATE RELATIONS

Full Faith and Credit Clause

Section 1 Full Faith and Credit shall be given in each State to the public Acts, Records, and judicial Proceedings of every other State. And the Congress may by general Laws prescribe the Manner in which such Acts, Records and Proceedings shall be proved, and the Effect thereof.

This section provides that the official acts and records of one state will be recognized and given credence by other states, e.g., marriages and divorces.

Privileges and Immunities, Interstate Extradition

Section 2 Clause 1. The Citizens of each State shall be entitled to all Privileges and Immunities of Citizens in the several States.

This clause requires states to treat citizens of other states equally. For example, when driving in another state, one's driver's license is recognized. One area not so clear is that of charging higher tuitions at state educational institutions for out-of-state students.

Clause 2. A person charged in any State with Treason, Felony or other Crime, who shall flee from Justice, and be found in another State, shall on Demand of the executive Authority of the State from which he fled, be delivered up, to be removed to the State having Jurisdiction of the Crime.

Extradition is the name of this clause. A criminal fleeing to another state, if captured, can be returned to the state where the crime was committed. But this is not an absolute. A state's governor can refuse, for good reason, to extradite someone to another state.

Clause 3. No person held to Service or Labour in one State, under the Laws thereof, escaping into another, shall, in Consequence of any Law or Regulation therein, be discharged from such Service or Labour, but shall be delivered up on Claim of the Party to whom such Service or Labour may be due.[10]

This clause was included to cover runaway slaves. It has been made inoperable by the 13th Amendment, which abolished slavery.

Admission of States

Section 3 New States may be admitted by the Congress into this Union but no new State shall be formed or erected within the Jurisdiction of any other State, nor any State to be formed by the Junction of two or more States, or Parts of States, without the Consent of the Legislatures of the States concerned as well as of the Congress.

The Congress shall have Power to dispose of and make all needful Rules and Regulations respecting the Territory or other Property belonging to the United States, and nothing in this Constitution shall be so construed as to Prejudice any Claims of the United States, or of any particular State.

This section concerns the admission of new states to the Union. In theory, no state can be created from part of another state without permission of the state legislature. But West Virginia was formed from Virginia during the Civil War without the permission of Virginia, which was part of the Confederacy. With fifty states now part of the Union, this section has not been used for many decades. The only future use may be in the case of Puerto Rico or perhaps Washington, D.C.

Republican Form of Government

Section 4 The United States shall guarantee to every State in this Union a Republican Form of Government, and shall protect each of them against Invasion, and on Application of the Legislature, or of the Executive (when the Legislature cannot be convened) against domestic Violence.

---

[9]Modified by the 11th Amendment

[10]Repealed by the 13th Amendment

This section commits the federal government to guarantee a republican form of government to each state and protect the state against foreign invasion or domestic insurrection.

ARTICLE V—THE AMENDING POWER

The Congress, whenever two thirds of both Houses shall deem it necessary, shall propose Amendments to this Constitution, or, on the Application of the Legislatures of two thirds of the several States, shall call a Convention for proposing Amendments, which, in either Case, shall be valid to all Intents and Purposes, as Part of this Constitution, when ratified by the Legislatures of three fourths of the several States, or by Conventions in three fourths thereof, as the one or the other Mode of Ratification may be proposed by the Congress; Provided that no Amendment which may be made prior to the Year One thousand eight hundred and eight shall in any Manner affect the first and fourth Clauses in the Ninth Section of the first Article; and that no State, without its Consent, shall be deprived of its equal Suffrage in the Senate.

Amendment to the U.S. Constitution can be originated by a 2/3 vote in both the U.S. House and Senate or by 2/3 of the state legislatures asking for a convention to propose amendments. Proposed amendments, by either route, must be approved by 3/4 of state legislatures or by 3/4 of conventions convened in the states for purposes of ratification. Only one amendment has been ratified by the convention method—Amendment 21 to repeal the 18th Amendment establishing Prohibition.

Thousands of amendments have been proposed; few have been passed by 2/3 vote in each branch of Congress. The Equal Rights Amendment was one such case, but it was not ratified by 3/4 of state legislatures. There have only been 27 successful amendments to the U.S. Constitution.

ARTICLE VI—THE SUPREMACY CLAUSE

Clause 1. All Debts contracted and Engagements entered into, before the Adoption of this Constitution, shall be as valid against the United States under the Constitution, as under the Confederation.

This clause made the new national government responsible for all debts incurred during the Revolutionary War. This was very important to banking and commercial Interests.

Clause 2. This Constitution, and the Laws of the United States which shall be made in Pursuance thereof, and all Treaties made, or which shall be made, under the Authority of the United States, shall be the supreme Law of the Land; and the Judges in every State shall be bound thereby any Thing in the Constitution or Laws of any State to the Contrary notwithstanding.

This is the National Supremacy Clause, which provides the basis for the supremacy of the national government.

Clause 3. The Senators and Representatives before mentioned, and the Members of the several State Legislatures, and all executive and judicial Officers, both of the United States and of the several States, shall be bound by Oath or Affirmation, to support this Constitution, but no religious Test shall ever be required as a Qualification to any Office or public Trust under the United States.

This clause requires essentially all federal and state officials to swear or affirm their allegiance to and support of the U.S. Constitution. Note that a religious test was prohibited for federal office. However, some states used religious tests for voting and office qualification until the 1830s.

ARTICLE VII—RATIFICATION

The Ratification of the Conventions of nine States, shall be sufficient for the Establishment of this Constitution between the States so ratifying the Same.

   Done in Convention by the Unanimous Consent of the States present the Seventeenth Day of September in the Year of our Lord one thousand seven hundred and Eighty seven and of the Independence of the United States of America the Twelfth. *In Witness whereof We have hereunto subscribed our Names.*

Realizing the unanimous ratification of the 13 states of the new Constitution might never have occurred, the framers wisely specified that only 9 states would be needed for ratification. Even this proved to be a test of wills between Federalists and Anti-Federalists, leading to publication of the great political work *The Federalist Papers*.

AMENDMENTS
THE BILL OF RIGHTS

[The first ten amendments were ratified on December 15, 1791, and form what is known as the "Bill of Rights."]

The Bill of Rights applied initially only to the federal government and not to state or local governments. Beginning in 1925 in the case of *Gitlow v. New York,* the U.S. Supreme Court began to selectively incorporate the Bill of Rights, making its provisions applicable to state and local governments. There are only three exceptions, which will be discussed at the appropriate amendment.

AMENDMENT 1—
RELIGION, SPEECH, ASSEMBLY, AND POLITICS

Congress shall make no law respecting an establishment of religion, or prohibiting the free exercise thereof; or abridging the freedom of speech, or of the press; or the right of the people peaceably to assemble, and to petition the Government for a redress of grievances.

This is the godfather of all amendments in that it protects five fundamental freedoms: religion, speech, press, assembly, and petition. Note that the press is the only business that is specifically protected by the U.S. Constitution. Freedom of religion and speech are two of the most contentious issues and generate a multitude of Supreme Court cases.

AMENDMENT 2—MILITIA AND THE RIGHT TO BEAR ARMS

A well-regulated Militia, being necessary to the security of a free State, the right of the people to keep and bear Arms, shall not be infringed.

There is also controversy as to the meaning of this amendment. Some believe that it specifically refers to citizen militias, which were common at the time of the Constitution but now have been replaced by National Guard units. Therefore, is the amendment still applicable? Do private citizens need weapons for the security of a free state?

AMENDMENT 3—QUARTERING OF SOLDIERS

No Soldier shall, in time of peace be quartered in any house, without the consent of the Owner, nor in time of war, but in manner to be prescribed by law.

It was the practice of the British government to insist that colonists provide room and board to British troops. This amendment was designed to prohibit this practice. Today, military and naval bases provide the necessary quarters.

AMENDMENT 4—SEARCHES AND SEIZURES

The right of the people to be secure in their persons, houses, papers, and effects, against unreasonable searches and seizures, shall not be violated, and no Warrants shall issue, but upon probable cause, supported by Oath or affirmation, and particularly describing the place to be searched, and the persons or things to be seized.

This is an extremely important amendment to prevent the abuse of state police powers. Essentially, unreasonable searches or seizures of homes, persons, or property cannot be undertaken without probable cause or a warrant that specifically describes the place to be searched, the person involved, and suspicious things to be seized.

AMENDMENT 5—GRAND JURIES, SELF-INCRIMINATION, DOUBLE JEOPARDY, DUE PROCESS, AND EMINENT DOMAIN

No person shall be held to answer for a capital, or otherwise infamous crime, unless on a presentment or indictment of a Grand jury, except in cases arising in the land or naval forces, or in the Militia, when in actual service in time of War or public danger; nor shall any person be subject for the same offence to be twice put in jeopardy of life or limb, nor shall be compelled in any criminal case to be a witness against himself, nor be deprived of life, liberty, or property, without due process of law, nor shall private property be taken for public use, without just compensation.

Only a grand jury can indict a person for a federal crime. This provision does not apply to state/local governments. This amendment also covers double jeopardy, or being tried twice for the same crime in the same jurisdiction. Note that since the federal government and state governments are different jurisdictions, one could be tried in each jurisdiction for essentially the same crime. For example, it is a federal crime to kill a congressperson. It is also a state crime to murder anyone. Further, this amendment also covers the prohibition of self-incrimination. Pleading the 5th Amendment is common among defendants. The deprivation of life, liberty, or property by any level of government is prohibited unless due process of law is applied. Finally, private property may not be taken under the doctrine of "eminent domain" unless the government provides just compensation and the taking is for public purposes.

AMENDMENT 6—CRIMINAL COURT PROCEDURES

In all criminal prosecutions, the accused shall enjoy the right to a speedy and public trial, by an impartial jury of the State and district wherein the crime shall have been committed, which district shall have been previously ascertained by law, and to be informed of the nature and cause of the accusation, to be confronted with the witnesses against him, to have compulsory process for obtaining witnesses in his favor, and to have the Assistance of Counsel for his defence.

This amendment requires public trials by jury for criminal prosecutions. Anyone accused of a crime is guaranteed the right to be informed of the charges; confront witnesses; to subpoena witnesses for his or her defense; and to have a lawyer for his or her defense. The government must provide a lawyer for a defendant unable to afford one.

AMENDMENT 7—TRIAL BY JURY IN COMMON LAW CASES

In Suits at common law, where the value in controversy shall exceed twenty dollars, the right of trial by jury shall be preserved, and no fact tried by a jury shall be otherwise re-examined in any Court of the United States, than according to the rules of the common law.

This amendment is practically without meaning in modern times. Statutory law has largely superseded common law. Federal civil law suits with a guaranteed jury are now restricted to cases that exceed $50,000. The Bill of Rights, which includes the right to trial by jury, applied orginally only to the national government. Beginning in 1925, the USSC began a selective process of incorporating provisions of the Bill of Rights, applicable to state/local governments as well. There are just a few provisions that have not been thus incorporated. Trial by jury is one. Some state/local governments have trials by judges, not by juries.

AMENDMENT 8— BAIL, CRUEL AND UNUSUAL PUNISHMENT

Excessive bail shall not be required, nor excessive fines imposed, nor cruel and unusual punishments inflicted.

Capital punishment is covered by this amendment, which also prohibits excessive bail. But this is relative. Million-dollar bails are not uncommon in some cases. One federal judge offered voluntary castration for sex offenders in lieu of jail time. Higher courts held this to be a cruel or unusual punishment. But it is the death penalty that generates the most heated controversy. Court cases challenging the constitutionality of capital punishment cite this amendment's language prohibiting cruel and unusual punishment. For a period of 4 years, the USSC banned capital punishment. When states modified their statutes to provide a two-part judicial process of guilt determination and punishment, the USSC allowed the reinstitution of capital punishment by the states.

AMENDMENT 9—RIGHTS RETAINED BY THE PEOPLE

The enumeration in the Constitution of certain rights, shall not be construed to deny or disparage others retained by the people.

This amendment implies that there may be other rights of the people not specified by the previous amendments. Indeed, the Warren Court established the right to privacy even though it is not specifically mentioned in any previous amendment.

AMENDMENT 10—RESERVED POWERS OF THE STATES

The powers not delegated to the United States by the Constitution, nor prohibited by it to the States, are reserved to the States respectively, or to the people.

The 10th Amendment was seen as the reservoir of reserved powers for state governments. If the national government had been limited only to expressed powers in Article 1, Section 8, of the Constitution, this would have been the case. But the doctrine of implied national government powers, which was established by the U.S. Supreme Court in *McCulloch v. Maryland* in 1819, made the intent of this amendment almost meaningless. What reserved powers that were retained by the states were virtually removed by the U.S. Supreme Court's decision in the *Garcia v. San Antonio Metropolitan Transit Authority* case in 1985, which basically told state/local governments not to look to the courts to protect their residual rights but rather to their political representatives. In subsequent cases, the USSC has retreated somewhat from this position when the court found the federal government encroaching in state jurisdictional areas.

AMENDMENT 11—SUITS AGAINST THE STATES

[Ratified February 7, 1795]

The Judicial power of the United States shall not be construed to extend to any suit in law or equity, commenced or prosecuted against one of the United States by Citizens of another State, or by Citizens or Subjects of any Foreign State.

Article 3 of the U.S. Constitution originally allowed federal jurisdiction in cases of one state citizen against another state citizen or state. This amendment removes federal jurisdiction in this area. In essence, states may not be sued in federal court by citizens of another state or country.

AMENDMENT 12—ELECTION OF THE PRESIDENT

[Ratified June 15, 1804]

The Electors shall meet in their respective states, and vote by ballot for President and Vice-President, one of whom, at least, shall not be an inhabitant of the same state with themselves; they shall name in their ballots the person voted for as President, and in distinct ballots the person voted for as Vice-President, and they shall make distinct lists of all persons voted for as President, and of all persons voted for as Vice-President, and of the number of votes for each, which lists they shall sign and certify, and transmit sealed to the seat of the government of the United States, directed to the President of the Senate;—The President of the Senate shall, in presence of the Senate and House of Representatives, open all the certificates and the votes shall then be counted;—The person having the greatest number of votes for President, shall be the President, if such number be a majority of the whole number of Electors appointed; and if no person have such majority, then from the persons having the highest numbers not exceeding three on the list of those voted for as President, the House of Representatives shall choose immediately, by ballot, the President. But in choosing the President, the votes shall be taken by states, the representation from each state having one vote; a quorum for this purpose shall consist of a member or members from two-thirds of the states, and a majority of all states shall be necessary to a choice. And if the House of Representatives shall not choose a President whenever the right of choice shall devolve upon them, before the fourth day of March next following, then the Vice-President shall act as President, as in the case of the death or other constitutional disability of the President.[11] The person having the greatest number of votes as Vice-President, shall be the Vice-President, if such a number be a majority of the whole numbers of Electors appointed, and if no person have a majority, then from the two highest numbers on the list, the Senate shall choose the Vice-President, a quorum for the purpose shall consist of two-thirds of the whole number of Senators, and a majority of the whole number shall be necessary to a choice. But no person constitutionally ineligible to the office of President shall be eligible to that of Vice-President of the United States.

This was a necessary amendment to correct a flaw in the Constitution covering operations of the Electoral College. In the election of 1800, both Thomas Jefferson and Aaron Burr, of the same Democratic-Republican Party, received the same number of electoral votes, 73, for president. Article II of the original Constitution specified that each elector would cast two ballots. It did not specify for whom. This amendment clarifies that the electoral vote must be specific for president and vice president. The original Constitution provided that if no candidate received a majority of electoral votes, the House would decide from the candidates with the top five vote totals. This amendment reduces the candidate field to the top three vote totals. If the House delays in this selection past the fourth day of March, the elected vice president will act as president until the House selects the president. The original Constitution provided that the candidate with the second highest number of electoral votes would become vice president.

This amendment, which requires a separate vote tally for vice president, provides for selection by the U.S. Senate if no vice presidential candidate receives an electoral vote majority.

AMENDMENT 13—PROHIBITION OF SLAVERY

[Ratified December 6, 1865]

Section 1   Neither slavery nor involuntary servitude, except as a punishment for crime whereof the party shall have been duly convicted, shall exist within the United States, or any place subject to their jurisdiction.

Section 2   Congress shall have power to enforce this article by appropriate legislation.

---

[11]Changed by the 20th Amendment

This is the first of the three Civil War amendments. Slavery is prohibited under all circumstances. Involuntary servitude is also prohibited unless it is a punishment for a convicted crime.

AMENDMENT 14—CITIZENSHIP, DUE PROCESS, AND EQUAL PROTECTION OF THE LAWS

[Ratified July 9, 1868]

Section 1   All persons born or naturalized in the United States, and subject to the jurisdiction thereof, are citizens of the United States and of the State wherein they reside. No State shall make or enforce any law which shall abridge the privileges or immunities of citizens of the United States; nor shall any State deprive any person of life, liberty, or property, without due process of law; nor deny to any person within its jurisdiction the equal protection of the laws.

This section defines the meaning of U.S. citizenship and protection of these citizenship rights. It also establishes the Equal Protection Clause that each state must guarantee to its citizens. It extended the provisions of the 5th Amendment of due process and protection of life, liberty, and property and made these applicable to the states.

Section 2   Representatives shall be apportioned among the several States according to their respective numbers, counting the whole number of persons in each State, excluding Indians not taxed. But when the right to vote at any election for the choice of electors for President and Vice President of the United States, Representatives in Congress, the Executive and Judicial officers of a State, or the members of the Legislature thereof, is denied to any of the male inhabitants of such State, being twenty-one[12] years of age, and citizens of the United States, or in any way abridged, except for participation in rebellion, or other crime, the basis of representation therein shall be reduced in the proportion which the number of such male citizens shall bear to the whole number of male citizens twenty-one years of age in such State.

This section changes the Three-Fifths Clause of the original Constitution. Now all male citizens, 21 or older, will be used to calculate representation in the House of Representatives. If a state denies the right to vote to any male 21 or older, the number of denied citizens will be deducted from the overall state total to determine representation.

Section 3   No person shall be a Senator or Representative in Congress, or elector of President and Vice President, or hold any office, civil or military under the United States, or under any State, who, having previously taken an oath, as a member of Congress, or as an officer of the United States, or as a member of any State legislature, or as an executive or judicial officer of any State, to support the Constitution of the United States, shall have engaged in insurrection or rebellion against the same, or given aid or comfort to the enemies thereof. But Congress may by a vote of two-thirds of each House, remove such disability.

This section disqualifies from federal office or elector for president or vice president anyone who rebelled or participated in an insurrection against the Constitution. This was specifically directed against citizens of Southern states. Congress by a 2/3 vote could override this provision.

---

[12]Changed by the 26th Amendment

Section 4   The validity of the public debt of the United States, authorized by law, including debts incurred for payment of pensions and bounties for services in suppressing insurrection or rebellion, shall not be questioned. But neither the United States nor any State shall assume or pay any debt or obligation incurred in aid of insurrection or rebellion against the United States or any claim for the loss or emancipation of any slave, but all such debts, obligations and claims shall be held illegal and void.

Section 5   The Congress shall have power to enforce, by appropriate legislation, the provisions of this article.

These sections guarantee payment of Civil War debts incurred by the U.S. government but declare void any debts incurred by the Confederacy.

AMENDMENT 15—THE RIGHT TO VOTE

[Ratified February 3, 1870]

Section 1   The right of citizens of the United States to vote shall not be denied or abridged by the United States or by any State on account of race, color, or previous condition of servitude.

Section 2   The Congress shall have power to enforce this article by appropriate legislation.

This final Civil War amendment guarantees that voting rights cannot be denied by any states on account of race, color, or previous servitude. Unfortunately, it did not mention gender. Accordingly, all male citizens 21 or over were guaranteed the right to vote by this amendment.

AMENDMENT 16—INCOME TAXES

[Ratified February 3, 1913]

The Congress shall have power to lay and collect taxes on incomes, from whatever source derived, without apportionment among the several States, and without regard to any census or enumeration.

Article 1, Section 9, of the original Constitution prohibited Congress from enacting a direct tax (head tax) unless in proportion to a census. Congress in 1894 passed an income tax law, levying a 2 percent tax on incomes over $4,000. In 1895, the U.S. Supreme Court in a split decision (5–4) found that the income tax was a direct tax not apportioned among the states and was thus unconstitutional. Thus, Congress proposed an amendment allowing it to enact an income tax. Once this amendment was ratified, the flow of tax money to Washington increased tremendously.

AMENDMENT 17—DIRECT ELECTION OF SENATORS

[Ratified April 8, 1913]

The Senate of the United States shall be composed of two Senators from each State, elected by the people thereof, for six years and each Senator shall have one vote. The electors in each State shall have the qualifications requisite for electors of the most numerous branch of the State legislatures.

When vacancies happen in the representation of any State in the Senate, the executive authority of such State shall issue writs of election to fill such vacancies: Provided, That the legislature of any State may empower the executive thereof to make temporary appointment until the people fill the vacancies by election as the legislature may direct.

This amendment shall not be so construed as to affect the election or term of any Senator chosen before it becomes valid as part of the Constitution.

Prior to this amendment, U.S. senators were selected by state legislatures. Now U.S. senators would be selected by popular vote in each state. Further, the governor of each state may fill vacancies, subject to state laws.

AMENDMENT 18—PROHIBITION

[Ratified January 16, 1919, Repealed December 5, 1933 by Amendment 21]

Section 1   After one year from the ratification of this article the manufacture, sale, or transportation of intoxicating liquors within, the importation thereof into, or the exportation thereof from the United States and all territory subject to the jurisdiction thereof for beverage purposes is hereby prohibited.

Section 2   The Congress and the several States shall have concurrent power to enforce this article by appropriate legislation.

Section 3   This article shall be inoperative unless it shall have been ratified as an amendment to the Constitution by the legislatures of the several States, as provided in the Constitution, within seven years from the date of the submission hereof to the States by the Congress.[13]

This amendment was largely the work of the Women's Christian Temperance Union and essentially banned the manufacture, sale, or transportation of alcoholic beverages. Unintended consequences of this attempt to legislate morality were the brewing of "bathtub gin" and moonshine liquor, and the involvement of the mob in importing liquor from Canada. This ill-fated social experiment was corrected by the 21st Amendment. This is also the first amendment for which Congress fixed a period for ratification—7 years.

AMENDMENT 19—WOMEN'S SUFFRAGE

[Ratified August 18, 1920]

The right of the citizens of the United States to vote shall not be denied or abridged by the United States or by any State on account of sex.

Congress shall have power to enforce this article by appropriate legislation .

At long last, women achieved voting parity with men.

AMENDMENT 20—THE LAME DUCK AMENDMENT

[Ratified January 23, 1933]

Section 1   The terms of the President and Vice President shall end at noon on the 20th day of January, and the terms of the Senators and Representatives at noon on the 3d day of January, of the years in which such terms would have ended if this article had not been ratified, and the terms of their successors shall then begin.

Section 2   The Congress shall assemble at least once in every year, and such meeting shall begin at noon on the 3d day of January, unless they shall by law appoint a different day.

Section 3   If, at the time fixed for the beginning of the term of the President, the President elect shall have died, the Vice President elect shall become President. If a President shall not have been chosen before the time fixed for the beginning of his term, or if the President elect shall have failed to qualify, then the Vice President elect shall act as President until a President shall have qualified, and the Congress may by law provide for the case wherein neither a President elect nor a Vice President elect shall have qualified, declaring who shall then act as President, or the manner in which one who is to act shall be selected, and such person shall act accordingly until a President or Vice President shall have qualified.

Section 4   The Congress may by law provide for the case of the death of any of the persons from whom the House of Representatives may choose a President whenever the right of choice shall have devolved upon them, and for the case of the death of any of the persons from whom the Senate may choose a Vice President whenever the right of choice shall have devolved upon them.

Section 5   Sections 1 and 2 shall take effect on the 15th day of October following the ratification of this article.

Section 6   This article shall be inoperative unless it shall have been ratified as an amendment to the Constitution by the legislatures of three-fourths of the several States within seven years from the date of its submission.

Called the Lame Duck amendment, this amendment fixes the dates for the end of presidential and legislative terms. A new president is elected in November, but the current president remains in office until January 20 of the following year. Thus, the term "lame duck." Legislative terms begin earlier, on January 3.

AMENDMENT 21—REPEAL OF PROHIBITION

[Ratified December 5, 1933]

Section 1   The eighteenth article of amendment to the Constitution of the United States is hereby repealed.

Section 2   The transportation or importation into any State, Territory, or possession of the United States for delivery or use therein of intoxicating liquors, in violation of the laws thereof, is hereby prohibited.

Section 3   This article shall be inoperative unless it shall have been ratified as an amendment to the Constitution by conventions in the several States, as provided in the Constitution, within seven years from the date of the submission hereof to the States by the Congress.

This unusual amendment nullified the 18th Amendment. It ended federal Prohibition; now only state laws regulate liquors.

AMENDMENT 22—NUMBER OF PRESIDENTIAL TERMS

[Ratified February 27, 1951]

Section 1   No person shall be elected to the office of the President more than twice, and no person who has held the office of President, or acted as President, for more than two years of a term to which some other person was elected President shall be elected to the office of the President more than once. But this article shall not apply to any person holding the office of President when this article was proposed by the Congress, and shall

---

[13]Repealed by the 21st Amendment

not prevent any person who may be holding the office of President, or acting as President, during the term within which this article becomes operative from holding the office of President or acting as President during the remainder of such term.

Section 2   This article shall be inoperative unless it shall have been ratified as an amendment to the Constitution by the legislatures of three-fourths of the several states within seven years from the date of its submission to the states by the Congress.

This amendment could be called the Franklin D. Roosevelt amendment. It was FDR who broke the previous unwritten custom of no more than two-term presidents. Democrat Roosevelt won an unprecedented four terms as president. When the Republicans took control of the Congress in 1948, they pushed through the 22nd Amendment, limiting the U.S. president to a lifetime of two full four-year terms of office.

AMENDMENT 23—PRESIDENTIAL ELECTORS FOR THE DISTRICT OF COLUMBIA

[Ratified March 29, 1961]

Section 1   The District constituting the seat of government of the United States shall appoint in such manner as the Congress may direct:

A number of electors of President and Vice President equal to the whole number of Senators and Representatives in Congress to which the District would be entitled if it were a state, but in no event more than the least populous state, they shall be in addition to those appointed by the states, but they shall be considered for the purposes of the election of President and Vice President, to be electors appointed by a state, and they shall meet in the District and perform such duties as provided by the twelfth article of amendment.

Section 2   The Congress shall have power to enforce this article by appropriate legislation.

This amendment gave electoral votes to the citizens of Washington, D.C., which is not a state and thus not included in the original scheme of state electoral votes. Currently, Washington, D.C., has 3 electoral votes, bringing the total of presidential electoral votes to 538. Puerto Ricans are citizens of the U.S. but have no electoral votes.

AMENDMENT 24—THE ANTI-POLL TAX AMENDMENT

[Ratified January 23, 1964]

Section 1   The right of citizens of the United States to vote in any primary or other election for President or Vice President, for electors for President or Vice President or for Senator or Representative in Congress, shall not be denied or abridged by the United States or any state by reason of failure to pay any poll tax or other tax.

Section 2   The Congress shall have power to enforce this article by appropriate legislation.

The poll tax was a procedure used mostly in southern states to discourage poor white and black voters from registering to vote. Essentially, one would have to pay a tax to register to vote. The tax was usually not much. But for a poor white or black voter, this might not be disposable income. As part of the assault against disfran-

chisement of voters, the poll tax was abolished. Literacy tests, another device to disqualify voters, were abolished by the Voting Rights Act of 1965.

AMENDMENT 25—PRESIDENTIAL DISABILITY, VICE PRESIDENTIAL VACANCIES

[Ratified February 10, 1967]

Section 1   In case of the removal of the President from office or his death or resignation, the Vice President shall become President.

Section 2   Whenever there is a vacancy in the office of the Vice President, the President shall nominate a Vice President who shall take the office upon confirmation by a majority vote of both Houses of Congress.

Section 3   Whenever the President transmits to the President pro tempore of the Senate and the Speaker of the House of Representatives his written declaration that he is unable to discharge the powers and duties of his office, and until he transmits to them a written declaration to the contrary, such powers and duties shall be discharged by the Vice President as Acting President.

Section 4   Whenever the Vice President and a majority of either the principal officers of the executive departments or of such other body as Congress may by law provide, transmit to the President pro tempore of the Senate and the Speaker of the House of Representatives their written declaration that the President is unable to discharge the powers and duties of his office, the Vice President shall immediately assume the powers and duties of the office as Acting President.

Thereafter, when the President transmits to the President pro tempore of the Senate and the Speaker of the House of Representatives his written declaration that no inability exists, he shall resume the powers and duties of his office unless the Vice President and a majority of either the principal officers of the executive departments, or of such other body as Congress may by law provide, transmit within four days to the President pro tempore of the Senate and the Speaker of the House of Representatives their written declaration that the President is unable to discharge the powers and duties of his office. Thereupon Congress shall decide the issue, assembling within forty-eight hours for that purpose if not in session. If the Congress, within twenty-one days after receipt of the latter written declaration, or, if Congress is not in session, within twenty-one days after Congress is required to assemble, determines by two-thirds vote of both Houses that the President is unable to discharge the powers and duties of his office, the Vice President shall continue to discharge the same as Acting President; otherwise the President shall resume the powers and duties of his office.

During the administration of President Woodrow Wilson, his final year in office, in 1919, was marked by serious illness. It is rumored that his wife acted as president. There was no constitutional provision to cover an incapacitating illness of a president. So this amendment provides a procedure for this eventuality. The president can inform congressional leaders of his incapacitation and the vice president takes over. When he recovers, the president can so inform congressional leaders and he resumes office.

But the amendment also recognizes that the president may not be able or wish to indicate this debilitation; so the vice president and a majority of cabinet members can inform congressional leaders and the vice president takes over. When the president informs congressional leadership that

he is back in form, he resumes the presidency unless the vice president and a majority of the cabinet disagree. Then Congress must decide. The likelihood that this procedure will ever be used is very small.

The most immediate importance of this amendment concerns the office of vice president. The original Constitution did not address the issue of a vacancy in this office. So the 25th Amendment established the procedure, just in time! This amendment was ratified in 1967. In 1973, the sitting vice president, Spiro Agnew, resigned his office. Under the provisions of this amendment, President Nixon nominated Gerald Ford as vice president. A former member of the House, the Congress quickly approved him. But a year later, President Nixon also resigned. Now Vice President Ford became President Ford, and he in turn appointed Nelson Rockefeller as the new vice president. For the first time in our history, we had both a president and vice president, neither of whom was elected by the Electoral College.

Amendment 26—Eighteen-Year-Old Vote

[Ratified July 1, 1971]

Section 1 The right of citizens of the United States, who are 18 years of age or older, to vote, shall not be denied or abridged by the United States or by any state on account of age.

Section 2 The Congress shall have power to enforce this article by appropriate legislation.

During the Vietnam War, 18-year-olds were being drafted and sent out to possibly die in the service of their country. Yet they did not even have the right to vote. This incongruity led to the 26th Amendment, which lowered the legal voting age from 21 to 18.

Amendment 27—Congressional Salaries

[Ratified May 7, 1992]

No law varying the compensation for the services of the Senators and Representatives shall take effect until an election of Representatives shall be intervened.

This is a "sleeper" amendment that was part of 12 amendments originally submitted by the first Congress to the states for ratification. The states only ratified 10 of the 12, which collectively became known as the Bill of Rights. But since Congress did not set a time limit for ratification, the other two amendments remained on the table. Much to the shock of the body politic, in 1992, 3/4 of the states ratified original amendment 12 of 12. This reflected the disgust of seeing Congress continuing to increase its salary and benefits. The amendment delays any increase of compensation for at least one election cycle.*

---

*Annotations by James Corey, High Point University.

4 FEDERALISM
Dividing Governmental Power

Chapter Outline

- Indestructible Union, Indestructible States
- Why Federalism? The Argument for a "Compound Republic"
- The Original Design of Federalism
- The Evolution of American Federalism
- Federalism Revived?
- Money and Power Flow to Washington
- Coercive Federalism: Preemptions and Mandates
- Summary Notes

Think About Politics

1 Which level of government deals best with the problems it faces?
Federal ☐ State ☐ Local ☐

2 In which level of government do you have the most confidence?
Federal ☐ State ☐ Local ☐

3 Should the national government be able to prosecute a high school student for bringing a gun to school?
Yes ☐ No ☐

4 Should welfare benefits be the same in all states?
Yes ☐ No ☐

5 Should each state determine its own minimum age for drinking alcohol?
Yes ☐ No ☐

6 Should each state determine its own maximum highway speed limit?
Yes ☐ No ☐

7 When the federal government requires states to provide safe drinking water, clean air, or access for the handicapped, should it provide funds to carry out these mandates?
Yes ☐ No ☐

What should be the relationship between the national government and the states? Questions like these lie at the heart of the issue of who gets what, when, and how. They affect employment, transportation, health, education, the very air we breathe. And when there has been disagreement, the nation has been plunged into conflict at best and the bloodiest war in its history at worst.

Indestructible Union, Indestructible States

In December 1860 South Carolina seceded from the Union and in April 1861 authorized its state militia to expel U.S. troops from Fort Sumter in Charleston harbor. Although there is no provision in the Constitution for states leaving the Union, eleven southern states—South Carolina, Mississippi, Florida, Alabama, Georgia, Louisiana, Texas, Virginia, Arkansas, Tennessee, and North Carolina, in that order—argued that the Union was a voluntary association and they were entitled to withdraw.[1] President Abraham Lincoln declared these states to be in armed rebellion and sent federal troops to crush the "rebels." The result was the nation's bloodiest war: more than 250,000 battle deaths and another 250,000 deaths from disease and privation, out of a total population of less than 30 million.

Following the Civil War, Chief Justice Salmon P. Chase confirmed what had been decided on the battlefield. "The Constitution in all its provisions looks to an indestructible union, composed of indestructible states."[2]

Federalism divides power between two separate authorities—the nation and the states—each of which enforces its own laws directly on its citizens. Both the nation and the states pass laws, impose taxes, spend money, and maintain their own courts. Neither the nation nor the states can dissolve the Union or amend the Constitution without the consent of the other. The Constitution itself is the only legal source of authority for both the states and the nation, the states do not get their power from the national government, and the national government does not get its power from the states. Both national and state governments derive their power directly from the people.

American federalism differs from a **unitary system** of government, in which formal authority rests with the national government, and whatever powers are exercised by states, provinces, or subdivisions are given to those governments by the national government. Most of the world's governments—including France and Britain—are unitary. Federalism also differs from a **confederation** of states, in which the national government relies on the states for its authority, not the people (see Figure 4.1). Under

Figure 4.1 The Federal, Confederation, and Unitary Systems of Government

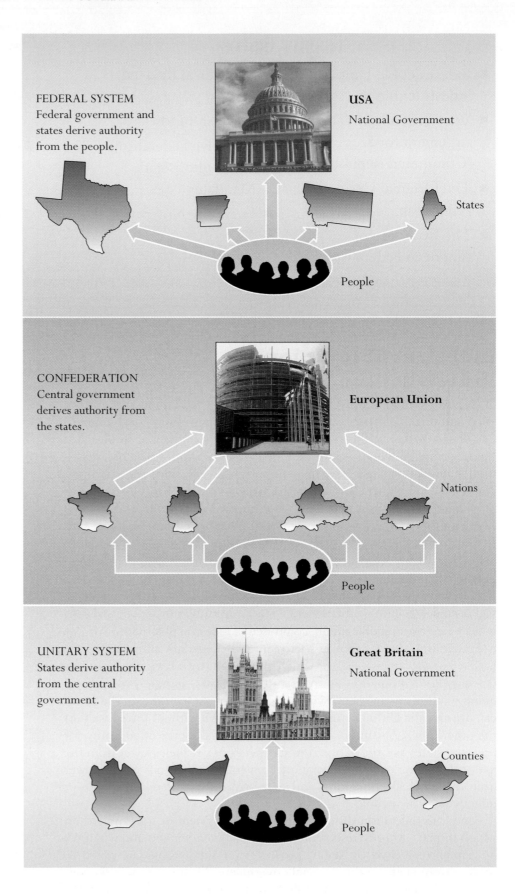

FEDERAL SYSTEM
Federal government and states derive authority from the people.

USA
National Government

States

People

CONFEDERATION
Central government derives authority from the states.

European Union

Nations

People

UNITARY SYSTEM
States derive authority from the central government.

Great Britain
National Government

Counties

People

Table 4.1   How Many American Governments?

U.S. government	1
States	50
Counties	3,034
Municipalities	19,429
Townships	16,504
Special districts	35,052
School districts	13,506
All governments	*87,525*

Source: *Statistical Abstract of the United States*, 2006, p. 272.

the Articles of Confederation of 1781, the United States was a confederation. The national government could not even levy taxes; it had to ask the states for revenue. Like the United States, a number of other countries were confederations before establishing federal systems, and today new types of confederations with limited functions are being formed (see *Compared to What?* "The European Union").

People in the United States often think of the *federal government* when the word *government* comes up. In fact, today there are more than 87,000 American governments. These state and local governments are important in American life, for they provide such essential day-to-day services as schools, water, and police and fire departments (see Table 4.1). However, the U.S. Constitution, the supreme law of the land, recognizes the existence of only the national government and the states. Local governments have no guarantees of power—or even existence—under the U.S. Constitution. Whatever powers they have are given to them by their state governments. States can create or abolish local governments, grant or withhold their powers, or change their boundaries without their consent. Some local governments have powers guaranteed in *state* constitutions, and some are even given **home rule**—the power to pass laws affecting local affairs, so long as those laws do not conflict with state or federal laws. About 60,000 of these 87,000 governments have the power to levy taxes to support activities authorized by state law.

In short, the American federal system is large and complex, with three levels of government—national, state, and local—sharing power. Indeed, the numbers and complexity of governments in the United States make **intergovernmental relations**—all of the interactions among these governments and their officials—a major concern of political scientists and policy makers.

Why Federalism? The Argument for a "Compound Republic"

The nation's Founders believed that "republican principles" would help make government responsible to the people, but they also argued that "auxiliary precautions" were necessary to protect the liberties of minorities and individuals. They believed that majority rule in a democratic government made it particularly important to devise ways to protect minorities and individuals from "unjust" and "interested" *majorities*. They believed that federalism would better protect liberty, disperse power, and manage "faction" (conflict).

federalism A constitutional arrangement whereby power is divided between national and subnational governments, each of which enforces its own laws directly on its citizens and neither of which can alter the arrangement without the consent of the other.

unitary system Constitutional arrangement whereby authority rests with the national government; subnational governments have only those powers given to them by the national government.

confederation Constitutional arrangement whereby the national government is created by and relies on subnational governments for its authority.

home rule Power of local government to pass laws affecting local affairs, so long as those laws do not conflict with state or federal laws.

— Think Again —
Which level of government deals best with the problems it faces?

COMPARED TO WHAT?

The European Union

The European Union (EU) incorporates features of both federalism and confederation. The EU now includes twenty-five member nations and embraces more than 455 million people. It grew slowly from a European Economic Community established in 1957 (designed to reduce and eventually abolish all tariffs among member nations), through a European Community established in 1965 (designed to create a single market free of all barriers to the movement of goods, services, capital, and labor), to its much more unified European Union established in 1991.

European Parliament

Deputies of the European Parliament are directly elected every five years by the EU's 455 million citizens. The major political parties operating in each of the member nations nominate candidates. The Parliament oversees the EU budget and passes on proposals to the Council of Ministers and the Commission. The Parliament also passes on new applicants to the EU.

Distribution of Seats in the European Parliament

Austria	18	Latvia	9
Belgium	24	Lithuania	13
Cyprus	6	Luxembourg	6
Czech Republic	24	Malta	5
Denmark	14	Netherlands	27
Estonia	6	Poland	54
Finland	14	Portugal	24
France	78	Slovakia	14
Germany	99	Slovenia	7
Greece	24	Spain	54
Hungary	24	Sweden	19
Ireland	13	United Kingdom	78
Italy	78		

Council of the EU

The Council is the EU's principal decision-making body. It is composed of the foreign ministers of the member nations. Each country takes the presidency for six months; the Council votes by majority, although each country's vote is weighted differently.

The Commission

The Commission of the EU supervises the implementation of EU treaties, implements EU policies, and manages EU funds. It is composed of 20 commissioners appointed by member governments. The five largest countries—France, Germany, Italy, Spain, and the United Kingdom—appoint two commissioners each; the remaining countries appoint one commissioner each.

The Court of Justice

A Court of Justice hears complaints about member governments' treaty violations and interprets EU treaties and legislation. Its fifteen justices are appointed by the member governments and serve six-year terms.

The "Euro"

Perhaps the most far-reaching accomplishment of the EU was the introduction of the "euro"—a single European currency for use in all member states. The euro was first introduced January 1, 1999, and officially replaced old national currencies—such as francs, marks, pesetas, and lira—on January 1, 2002. However, the United Kingdom, Sweden, and Denmark have refused to substitute the euro for their own currency.

The Future of the Union

The future of the EU remains under discussion. A lengthy EU Constitution was to be submitted to the

---

intergovernmental relations Network of political, financial, and administrative relationships between units of the federal government and those of state and local governments.

European Union Online Official EU site Describes the structure of the organization, its membership, current issues, and so forth.
www.europa.eu.int

Protecting Liberty Constitutional guarantees of individual liberty do not enforce themselves. The Founders argued that to guarantee liberty, government should be structured to encourage "opposite and rival" centers of power *within* and *among* governments. So they settled on both *federalism*—dividing powers between the national and state governments—and *separation of powers*—the dispersal of power among branches within the national government.

In the compound republic of America, the power surrendered by the people is first divided between two distinct governments, and then the portion allotted to each is subdivided among distinct and separate departments. Hence a double security arises to the rights of the people. The different governments will control each other, at the same time that each will be controlled by itself.[3]

voters in each nation. Ten nations approved it, but in 2005 voters in France and the Netherlands rejected it. Inasmuch as all twenty-five nations must approve it in order for it to go into effect, its future is in serious doubt.

At present the EU is more of an economic alliance than a sovereign political state. Voters in member nations may not be as yet willing to enact a common Bill of Rights or depend upon a central government (in Brussels) for the protection of their individual liberties. How much power will be allocated to the central EU government relative to the powers of member nations? Note that these and similar questions were the same as many of those discussed in the American Constitutional Convention of 1787 (see Chapter 3).

This map, produced by the EU, uses the languages of the nations portrayed. Test yourself by translating these names into English, for example Osterreich = Austria.

Source: Reprinted from http://www.europa.eu.int/abc/maps/index_en.htm. Copyright © European Communities, 1995–2006.

Thus the Founders deliberately tried to create competition within and among governmental units as a means of protecting liberty. Rather than rely on the "better motives" of leaders, the Founders sought to construct a system in which governments and government officials would be constrained by competition with other governments and other government officials: "Ambition must be made to counteract ambition."[4]

Dispersing Power   Federalism distributes power widely among different sets of leaders, national as well as state and local officeholders. The Founders believed that multiple leadership groups offered more protection against tyranny than a single set of all-powerful leaders. State and local government offices also provide a political base for the opposition party when it has lost a national election. In this way, state and local governments contribute to party competition in the

Council of State Governments
Official Organization of U.S. states, providing information on their governmental structures, officials, and current issues. *www.csg.org*

UP CLOSE

Federalism Is the Enemy of Uniformity

Should taxes and services be uniform throughout the United States? Or should federalism allow variations among the states in tax burdens as well as provided?

Federalism allows citizens in each state to decide levels of public services (schools, transportation, police and fire protection, and so forth, and other state and local functions), as well as how much they pay in state and local taxes. If some voters want more public services and are willing to pay higher taxes for them, and other voters want fewer public services and enjoy lower taxes, then federalism allows for a better match between citizen preferences and public policy. Of course, the result is a lack of uniformity across the states.

Consider, for example, differences in per capita state and local taxes paid by residents of different states.

Ten high-tax states

New York	$4,640
Connecticut	4,373
New Jersey	4,038
Massachusetts	3,721
Minnesota	3,673
Maryland	3,646
Wyoming	3,644
Maine	3,567
California	3,440
Wisconsin	3,421

Ten low-tax states

Oregon	$2,558
Oklahoma	2,516
Idaho	2,451
South Dakota	2,423
Arkansas	2,387
South Carolina	2,376
Montana	2,346
Mississippi	2,275
Tennessee	2,241
Alabama	2,170

States Without Income Taxes

Alaska	New Hampshire[a]	Texas
Florida	South Dakota	Washington
Nevada	Tennessee[a]	Wyoming

States Taxing Individual Income (rate ranges in parentheses)

Alabama (2.0–5.0)	Kentucky (2.0–6.0)	North Carolina (6.0–8.25)
Arizona (2.8–5.0)	Louisiana (2.0–6.0)	North Dakota (2.1–15.6)
Arkansas (1.0–7.0)	Maine (2.0–8.5)	Ohio (0.7–7.5)
California (1.0–9.3)	Maryland (2.0–4.8)	Oklahoma (0.5–6.75)
Colorado (4.6)	Massachusetts (5)	Oregon (5.0–9.0)
Connecticut (3.0–5)	Michigan (4)	Pennsylvania (2.8)
Delaware (2.2–6.0)	Minnesota (5.3–7.8)	Rhode Island (26% federal)[b]
Georgia (1.0–6.0)	Mississippi (3.0–5.0)	South Carolina (2.5–7.0)
Hawaii (1.4–8.25)	Missouri (1.5–6.0)	Utah (2.3–7.0)
Idaho (1.6–7.8)	Montana (2.0–11.0)	Vermont (3.6–9.5)
Illinois (3.0)	Nebraska (2.5–6.8)	Virginia (2.0–5.75)
Indiana (3.4)	New Jersey (1.4–6.4)	West Virginia (3.0–6.5)
Iowa (0.4–9.0)	New Mexico (1.7–6.8)	Wisconsin (4.6–6.8)
Kansas (3.5–6.5)	New York (4.0–7.7)	

[a]State income tax is limited to dividends and interest only.

[b]State income taxes determined as a percentage of federal income tax liability.

Source: Data from Council of State Governments, Book of the States, 2004–05 (Lexington, KY: Council of State Governments, 2005).

United States by helping to tide over the losing party after electoral defeat at the national level so that it can remain strong enough to challenge incumbents at the next election. And finally, state and local governments often provide a training ground for national political leaders. National leaders can be drawn from a pool of leaders experienced in state and local government.

Increasing Participation   Federalism allows more people to participate in the political system. With more than 87,000 governments in the United States—state, county, municipality, township, special district, and school district—nearly a million people hold some kind of public office.

Improving Efficiency   Federalism also makes government more manageable and efficient. Imagine the bureaucracy, red tape, and confusion if every governmental activity—police, schools, roads, fire fighting, garbage collection, sewage disposal, and so forth—in every local community in the nation were controlled by a centralized administration in Washington. Government can become arbitrary when a bureaucracy far from the scene directs local officials. Thus decentralization often softens the rigidity of law.

Ensuring Policy Responsiveness   Federalism encourages policy responsiveness. The existence of multiple governments offering different packages of benefits and costs allows a better match between citizen preferences and public policy. Americans are very mobile. People and businesses can "vote with their feet" by relocating to those states and communities that most closely conform to their own policy preferences. This mobility not only facilitates a better match between citizen preferences and public policy but also encourages competition between states and communities to offer improved services at lower costs.[5]

Encouraging Policy Innovation   The Founders hoped that federalism would encourage policy experimentation and innovation. Today federalism may seem like a "conservative" idea, but it was once the instrument of liberal reformers. Federal programs as diverse as the income tax, unemployment compensation, Social Security, wage and hour legislation, bank deposit insurance, and food stamps were all state programs before becoming national undertakings. Today much of the current "liberal" policy agenda—mandatory health insurance for workers, child-care programs, notification of plant closings, government support of industrial research and development—has been embraced by various states. The phrase **laboratories of democracies** is generally attributed to the great progressive jurist Supreme Court Justice Louis D. Brandeis, who used it in defense of state experimentation with new solutions to social and economic problems.[6]

laboratories of democracy
A reference to the ability of states to experiment and innovate in public policy.

Some Important Reservations   Despite the strengths of federalism, it has its problems. First of all, federalism can obstruct action on national issues. Although decentralization may reduce conflict at the national level, it may do so at the price of "sweeping under the rug" very serious national injustices (see *A Conflicting View:* "The Dark Side of Federalism" on page 112). Federalism also permits local leaders and citizens to frustrate national policy, to sacrifice national interest to local interests. Decentralized government provides an opportunity for local NIMBYs (people who subscribe to the motto *"Not In My Back Yard"*) to obstruct airports, highways, waste disposal plants, public housing, drug rehabilitation centers, and many other projects that would be in the national interest.

—Think Again—
In which level of government do you have the most confidence?

UP CLOSE

Katrina: Federalism Fails in a Crisis

Hurricane Katrina was the nation's largest natural disaster. Perhaps it was inevitable that government—federal, state, and local—would be unable to respond to such a crisis. But the lack of competence among city, state, and federal officials, the bureaucratic inertia and stupidity, the disorganized relief that led directly to the deaths of many, all combined to make Katrina "the worst man-made relief disaster ever."[a]

Katrina was a powerful Category Four hurricane when it hit east of New Orleans, practically leveling the city of Biloxi, Mississippi. The first day New Orleans seemed to be spared, but the next day the levees began to crumble—levees that had protected the below-sea-level "Big Easy" for over a century. Soon water submerged 80 percent of the city and 100,000 people were stranded with little or no food and water and no electricity. For three days emergency efforts floundered badly. Survivors gathered on rooftops and highway flyovers. The country watched on television as babies, old people, the sick, and diabetic died on live television. Reporters got themselves to the scenes of tragedies, but government agents failed to do so. Soon armed looters appeared on the streets. Hospitals functioned in the dark and in the heat; doctors and nurses cried out for rescue of their patients.

The first rescuers, including private citizens with small boats, dropped people off on highway overpasses, with 100-degree heat and no water or food. Other makeshift rescue efforts took over 25,000 sur-

Federal, state, and local government agencies performed poorly in response to Hurricane Katrina's devastation of New Orleans and the Mississippi Gulf Coast. Only the U.S. Coast Guard, shown here rescuing survivors, was given high marks for its work during the disaster.

The Original Design of Federalism

The U.S. Constitution *originally* defined American federalism in terms of (1) the powers expressly delegated to the national government plus the powers implied by those that are specifically granted, (2) the concurrent powers exercised by both states and the national government, (3) the powers reserved to the states, (4) the powers denied by the Constitution to both the national government and the states, and (5) the constitutional provisions giving the states a role in the composition of the national government (see Figure 4.2).

Delegated Powers   The U.S. Constitution lists seventeen specific grants of power to Congress, in Article I, Section 8. These are usually referred to as the **delegated, or enumerated, powers**. They include authority over war and foreign affairs, authority over the economy ("interstate commerce"), control over the money supply, and the power to tax and spend "to pay the debts and provide for the common defence and general welfare." After these specific grants of power comes the power "to make all laws which shall be necessary and proper for carry-

delegated, or enumerated, powers Powers specifically mentioned in the Constitution as belonging to the national government.

vivors to the leaking Superdome, where there were no light, no air, and no working toilets. Stories of individual bravery as well as bureaucratic bungling were carried on national television.

No one was in charge. Local, state, and federal leaders failed to lead, bureaucrats battled over turf, and government was paralyzed. The mayor urged residents to evacuate, but tens of thousands, especially the poor, had no cars or other means of transportation. The mayor hesitated to order a mandatory evacuation; when he finally did, hundreds of city buses were underwater. Some city police abandoned their posts to help their own families. Some nursing homes were overlooked in evacuation efforts and some elderly died unnecessarily.

Meanwhile, the mayor, FEMA officials, the governor, and even the president were giving press conferences boasting of all the aid that was on its way. But the governor refused to request federal troops or to place the Louisiana National Guard under federal authority. President Bush could have done so on his own, but he hesitated, waiting for the governor's request. The governor, a Democrat, feared that Republican federal officials would claim political credit for rescuing the city. She instructed National Guardsmen to keep people out of the city; in many instances they interpreted that order to keep out rescue workers from other states. Only the U.S. Coast Guard and military helicopters seemed to perform well—indeed heroically, in many cases rescuing survivors from rooftops.

But FEMA's performance was even worse. FEMA's authority is only to "coordinate" relief efforts in a crisis. FEMA had recently been transformed from an independent agency to a bureau in the Department of Homeland Security. Many newer appointees, including its director, had little or no disaster experi-

ence. For three days FEMA sat and waited to be called by the governor. When asked by a TV reporter what he intended to do about the horrid conditions in the Superdome, conditions that had been shown on TV for days, the FEMA director responded that he did not know that anyone was in the Superdome. Hundreds of FEMA house trailers sat outside the city unused, as did truckloads of food and water. As flames consumed buildings in New Orleans, FEMA held back 600 firefighters in order to lecture them on equal opportunity, sexual harassment, and customer service.[b] At the airport, frustrated medics waited in empty helicopters to evacuate patients while FEMA delayed over paperwork. When outside doctors and nurses tried to help, FEMA rejected their assistance because they "weren't certified members of a National Disaster Medical Team." "FEMA kept stonewalling us with paperwork. Meanwhile, every 30 or 40 minutes someone was dying."[c] About 150 trucks full of ice purchased for hurricane victims sat uselessly in a parking lot in Maine.[d] The FEMA emergency number was out of service.

The president was on vacation in Crawford, Texas. Initially he and his advisers failed to understand the seriousness of the situation. When the full extent of the tragedy became known in Crawford, the president flew over New Orleans and later, in a series of speeches, pledged billions to rebuild the city. He finally relieved the FEMA director of his job. But the president's approval ratings fell to their lowest point since he first entered office.

---

[a]*U.S. News and World Report,* September 19, 2005, p. 30.
[b]*Time,* September 19, 2005, p. 18.
[c]*New York Times,* September 18, 2005.
[d]*Ft. Lauderdale Sun-Sentinel,* October 7, 2005, p. 1.

---

ing into execution the foregoing powers, and all other powers vested by this Constitution in the government of the United States or in any department or officer thereof." This statement is generally known as the **Necessary and Proper Clause**, and it is the principal source of the national government's **implied powers**— powers not specifically listed in the Constitution but inferred from those that are.

National Supremacy   The delegated and implied powers, when coupled with the assertion of "national supremacy" (in Article VI), ensure a powerful national government. The **National Supremacy Clause** is very specific in asserting the supremacy of federal laws over state and local laws.

This Constitution, and the laws of the United States which shall be made in pursuance thereof, and all treaties made, or which shall be made, under the authority of the United States, shall be the supreme law of the land, and the Judges in every state shall be bound thereby, any thing in the constitution or laws of any state to the contrary notwithstanding.

Concurrent and Reserved Powers   Despite broad grants of power to the national government, the states retain considerable governing power. **Concurrent powers** are those recognized in the Constitution as belonging to *both* the national

Necessary and Proper Clause Clause in Article I, Section 8, of the U.S. Constitution granting Congress the power to enact all laws that are "necessary and proper" for carrying out those responsibilities specifically delegated to it. Also referred to as the Implied Powers Clause.

implied powers Powers not mentioned specifically in the Constitution as belonging to Congress but inferred as necessary and proper for carrying out the enumerated powers.

A CONFLICTING VIEW

The Dark Side of Federalism

Segregationists once regularly used the argument of "states' rights" to deny equal protection of the law to African Americans. Indeed, *states' rights* became a code word for opposition to federal civil rights laws. In 1963 Governor George Wallace invoked the states' rights argument when he stood in a doorway at the University of Alabama to prevent the execution of a federal court order that the university admit two African American students and thus integrate. Federal marshals were on hand to enforce the order, and Wallace only temporarily delayed them. Shortly after his dramatic stand in front of the television cameras, he retreated to his office. Later in his career, Wallace sought African American votes, declaring, "I was wrong. Those days are over."

Federalism in America remains tainted by its historical association with slavery, segregation, and discrimination. In the Virginia and Kentucky Resolutions of 1798, Thomas Jefferson and James Madison asserted the doctrine of "nullification," claiming that states could nullify unconstitutional laws of Congress. Although the original intent of this doctrine was to counter congressional attacks on a free press under the Alien and Sedition Acts of 1798, it was later revived to defend slavery. John C. Calhoun of South Carolina argued forcefully in the years before the Civil War that slavery was an issue for the states to decide and the Constitution gave Congress no power to interfere with slavery in the southern states or in the new western territories.

In the years immediately following the Civil War, the issues of slavery, racial inequality, and African American voting rights were *nationalized.* Nationalizing these issues meant removing them from the jurisdiction of the states and placing them in the hands of the national government. The Thirteenth, Fourteenth, and Fifteenth Amendments to the Constitution were enforced by federal troops in the southern states during the post–Civil War Reconstruction era. But after the Compromise of 1876 led to the withdrawal of federal troops from the southern states, legal and social segregation of African Americans became a "way of life" in the region. Segregation was *denationalized,*

which reduced national conflict over race but exacted a high price from the nation's African American population. Segregationists asserted the states' rights argument so often in defense of racial discrimination that it became a code phrase for racism. Not until the 1950s and 1960s were questions of segregation and equality again made into national issues. The civil rights movement asserted the supremacy of national law and in 1954 won a landmark decision in the case of *Brown v. Board of Education of Topeka,* when the U.S. Supreme Court ruled that segregation enforced by state (or local) officials violated the Fourteenth Amendment's guarantee that no state could deny any person the equal protection of the law. Later the *national* Civil Rights Act of 1964 outlawed discrimination in private employment and businesses serving the public.

Only now that national constitutional and legal guarantees of equal protection of the law are in place is it possible to reassess the true worth of federalism. Having established that federalism will not mean racial inequality, Americans are now free to explore the values of decentralized government.

In an attempt to block the admission of two African American students to the University of Alabama in 1963, Governor George Wallace barred the door with his body in the face of U.S. federal marshals. The tactic did not succeed, and the two students were admitted.

National Supremacy Clause
Clause in Article VI of the U.S. Constitution declaring the constitution and laws of the national government "the supreme law of the land" superior to the constitutions and laws of the states.

and state governments, including the power to tax and spend, make and enforce laws, and establish courts of justice. The Tenth Amendment reassured the states that "the powers not delegated to the United States . . . are reserved to the States respectively, or to the people." Through these **reserved powers**, the states generally retain control over property and contract law, criminal law, marriage and divorce, and the provision of education, highways, and social welfare activities. The states control the organization and powers of their own local governments. Finally, the states, like the federal government, retain the power to tax and spend for the general welfare.

POWERS GRANTED BY THE CONSTITUTION

NATIONAL GOVERNMENT Delegated Powers	NATIONAL AND STATE GOVERNMENTS Concurrent Powers	STATE GOVERNMENTS Reserved to the States

Military Affairs and Defense
- Provide for the common defense (I-8).
- Declare war (I-8).
- Raise and support armies (I-8).
- Provide and maintain a navy (I-8).
- Define and punish piracies (I-8).
- Define and punish offenses against the law of nations (I-8).
- Provide for calling forth the militia to execute laws, suppress insurrections, and repel invasions (I-8).
- Provide for organizing, arming, and disciplining the militia (I-8).
- Declare the punishment of treason (III-3).

Economic Affairs
- Regulate commerce with foreign nations, among the several states, and with Indian tribes (I-8).
- Establish uniform laws on bankruptcy (I-8).
- Coin money and regulate its value (I-8).
- Fix standards of weights and measures (I-8).
- Provide for patents and copyrights (I-8).
- Establish post offices and post roads (I-8).

Governmental Organization
- Constitute tribunals inferior to the Supreme Court (I-8, III-1).
- Exercise exclusive legislative power over the seat of government and over certain military installations (I-8).
- Admit new states (IV-3).
- Dispose of and regulate territory or property of the United States (IV-3).

"Implied" Powers
- Make laws necessary and proper for carrying the expressed powers into execution (I-8).

Concurrent Powers:
- Levy taxes (I-8).
- Borrow money (I-8).
- Contract and pay debts (I-8).
- Charter banks and corporations (I-8).
- Make and enforce laws (I-8).
- Establish courts (I-8).
- Provide for the general welfare (I-8).

Reserved to the States:
- Regulate intrastate commerce.
- Conduct elections.
- Provide for public health, safety, and morals.
- Establish local government.
- Maintain the militia (National Guard).
- Ratify amendments to the federal Constitution (V).
- Determine voter qualifications (I-2).

"Reserved" Powers
- Powers not delegated to national government nor denied to the States by the Constitution (X).

POWERS DENIED BY THE CONSTITUTION

NATIONAL GOVERNMENT	NATIONAL AND STATE GOVERNMENTS	STATE GOVERNMENTS

National Government:
- Give preference to the ports of any state (I-9).
- Impose a tax or duty on articles exported from any state (I-9).
- Directly tax except by apportionment among the states on a population basis (I-9), now superseded as to income tax (Amendment XVI).
- Draw money from the Treasury except by appropriation (I-9).

National and State Governments:
- Grant titles of nobility (I-9).
- Limit the suspension of habeas corpus (I-9).
- Issue bills of attainder (I-10).
- Make ex post facto laws (I-10).
- Establish a religion or prohibit the free exercise of religion (Amendment I).
- Abridge freedom of speech, press, assembly, or right of petition (Amendment I).
- Deny the right to bear arms (Amendment II).
- Quarter soldiers in private homes (Amendment III).
- Conduct unreasonable searches or seizures. (Amendment IV).
- Deny guarantees of fair trials (Amendment V, Amendment VI, and Amendment VII).
- Impose excessive bail or unusual punishments (Amendment VII).
- Take life, liberty, or property without due process (Amendment V).
- Permit slavery (Amendment XIII).
- Deny life, liberty, or property without due process of law (Amendment XIV).
- Deny voting because of race, color, previous servitude (Amendment XV), sex (Amendment XIX), or age if 18 or over (Amendment XXVI).
- Deny voting because of nonpayment of any tax (Amendment XXIV).

State Governments:

Economic Affairs
- Use legal tender other than gold or silver coin (I-10).
- Issue separate state coinage (I-10).
- Impair the obligation of contracts (I-10).
- Emit bills of credit (I-10).
- Levy import or export duties, except reasonable inspection fees, without the consent of Congress (I-10).
- Abridge the privileges and immunities of national citizenship (Amendment XIV)
- Make any law that violates federal law (Amendment VI).
- Pay for rebellion against the United States or for emancipated slaves (Amendment XIV).

Foreign Affairs
- Enter into treaties, alliances, or confederations (I-10).
- Make compact with a foreign state, except by congressional consent (I-10).

Military Affairs
- Issue letters of marque and reprisal (I-10).
- Maintain standing military forces in peace without congressional consent (I-10).
- Engage in war, without congressional consent, except in imminent danger or when invaded (I-10).

Figure 4.2   Original Constitutional Distribution of Powers
Under the Constitution of 1787, certain powers were delegated to the national government, other powers were shared by the national and state governments, and still other powers were reserved for state governments alone. Similarly, certain powers were denied by the Constitution to the national government, other powers were denied to both the national and state governments, and still other powers were denied only to state governments. Later amendments especially protected individual liberties.

concurrent powers Powers exercised by both the national government and state governments in the American federal system.

reserved powers Powers not granted to the national government or specifically denied to the states in the Constitution that are recognized by the Tenth Amendment as belonging to the state governments. This guarantee, known as the Reserved Powers Clause, embodies the principle of American federalism.

"Look, the American people don't want to be bossed around by federal bureaucrats. They want to be bossed around by state bureaucrats."

Source: © 2002 Robert Mankoff from cartoonbank.com. All Rights Reserved.

Powers Denied to the States   The Constitution denies the states some powers in order to safeguard national unity. States are specifically denied the power to coin money, enter into treaties with foreign nations, interfere with the "obligation of contracts," levy taxes on imports or exports, or engage in war.

Powers Denied to the Nation and the States   The Constitution denies some powers to both national and state government—namely, the powers to abridge individual rights. The Bill of Rights originally applied only to the national government, but the Fourteenth Amendment, passed by Congress in 1866 and ratified by 1868, provided that the states must also adhere to fundamental guarantees of individual liberty.

State Role in National Government   The states are basic units in the organizational scheme of the national government. The House of Representatives apportions members to the states by population, and state legislatures draw up the districts that elect representatives. Every state has at least one member in the House of Representatives, regardless of its population. Each state elects two U.S. senators, regardless of its population. The president is chosen by the electoral votes of the states, with each state having as many electoral votes as it has senators and representatives combined. Finally, three-fourths of the states must ratify amendments to the U.S. Constitution.

State Obligations to Each Other   To promote national unity, the Constitution requires the states to recognize actions and decisions taken by other states. Article IV requires the states to give "Full Faith and Credit . . . to the public Acts, Records, and judiciary Proceedings of every other State." This provision ensures that contracts, property ownership, insurance, civil judgments, marriages and divorces, among other things, made in one state are recognized in all states (see *What Do You Think?*: "Federalism and Same-Sex Marriages").

Recently, controversy has arisen over recognition of gay and lesbian marriages or "civil unions." A strict reading of Article IV would suggest that if any state legalized same-sex marriages, all states would be obliged to recognize them. (In 1999 the Vermont Supreme Court prohibited discrimination against gay marriages.) Anticipating this issue, the Congress passed a Defense of Marriage Act in 1996 stating that "No State . . . shall be required to give effect to any public act, record, or judicial proceeding of any other State respecting a relationship between persons of the same sex that is treated as a marriage. . ." The Congress relied on language in the next sentence of Article IV: "the Congress may by general law prescribe the Manner in which such Acts, Records and Proceedings shall be proved, *and the Effect thereof*" (italics added). It is not altogether clear whether this constitutional language in the second sentence allows Congress to nullify the "Full Faith and Credit" clause in the first sentence. If Vermont or any other state persists in recognizing gay marriages, the issue may end up in the Supreme Court (see also "Privacy and the Constitution" in Chapter 14).

The Evolution of American Federalism

American federalism has evolved over 200 years from a state-centered division of power to a national-centered system of government. Although the original constitutional wordings have remained in place, *power has flowed toward the national government since the earliest days of the Republic.* American federalism has been forged in the fires of political conflicts between states and nation, conflicts that have usually been resolved in favor of the national government. (See *Up Close:* "Historical Markers in the Development of American Federalism."). Generalizing about the

WHAT DO YOU THINK?

Federalism and Same-Sex Marriage

Traditionally, states outlawed sodomy (anal penetration, whether practiced by homo- or heterosexuals). The U.S. Supreme Court upheld these laws in 1986: "There is no constitutional right to sodomy."[a] But in 2003 the Supreme Court reversed itself and held that homosexuals' "right to liberty under the Due Process Clause gives them the full right to engage in private conduct without government interference."[b] This decision was a important victory for the gay rights movement in America and generated additional cases involving the legal status of homosexual relations.

Among the issues confronting homosexuals is that of same-sex marriage. The Supreme Court's decision that homosexual activity among consenting adults was a constitutionally protected liberty inspired several state courts to consider whether the denial of marriage to homosexual couples was discriminatory. Anticipating that some state courts might rule that same-sex marriages were constitutionally protected in their states, Congress passed a Defense of Marriage Act in 1996. This act was designed to circumvent the Full Faith and Credit clause of Article IV of the Constitution requiring every state to recognize the public acts and judiciary proceedings of every other state. The act stated that "No state. . . . shall be required to give effect to any public act, record, or judicial proceeding of any other state respecting a relationship between persons of the same-sex that is treated as a marriage. . . ." The Congress relied on the language of the next sentence of Article IV: "The Congress may by general law prescribe the Manner in which such Acts, Records and Proceedings shall be proved, and the Effect thereof." Congress was trying to prevent the recognition of same-sex marriages by all states if one or more states decided to legalize such marriages.

Public opinion is strongly opposed to same-sex *marriage*, but many Americans have no objection to the alternative of *civil unions* for same-sex couples.[c]

Q. *Do you think marriages between homosexuals should or should not be recognized by the law as valid, with the same rights as traditional marriages?"*

Should be valid	Should not be	Unsure
28%	68%	4%

[a]*Bowers v. Hardwick*, 478 U.S. 186 (1986).

[b]*Lawrence v. Texas*, June 26, 2003.

[c]*ABC News Poll*, April 24, 2005; CNN/*USA Today* Poll, March 20, 2005.

Q. *"Do you think same-sex couples should be allowed to legally marry, should be allowed legally to form civil unions but not to marry, should not be allowed to obtain legal recognition of their relationships?"*

Marriage	Civil unions	No legal recognition	Unsure
27%	29%	40%	4%

Vermont decided in 2000 to sanction "civil unions" between same-sex couples. While avoiding the term "marriage," the Vermont law allows ceremonies to be performed by a judge or clergy member and the couple to be entitled to all the benefits, protections, and responsibilities that are granted to married couples. And in 2003 the Massachusetts Supreme Court ruled that same-sex couples had a right to marriage under the Massachusetts state constitution.[d]

In 2005, forty states had laws against same-sex marriages, many adapted by a statewide voter referendum. It is not altogether clear whether the Congress has a power under the language of Article IV to nullify in effect the Full Faith and Credit clause. It is quite possible that the U.S. Supreme Court will hold that it does not, and that states are obliged to recognize same-sex marriages performed lawfully in any state.

Finally, *if* the federal courts, with the approval of the U.S. Supreme Court, were to decide that denying licenses for same-sex marriages violated the Equal Protection Clause of the Fourteenth Amendment to the Constitution, that such denial was discriminatory, *then all* states would be obliged to grant such licenses and recognize such marriages.

[d]*Goodridge v. Department of Health*, 798 N.E. 2d 941 (2003).

Does the Constitution's "full faith and credit clause" oblige all states to recognize same-sex marriages performed in any state? Congress's "Protection of Marriage Act" says no, but the U.S. Supreme Court has yet to speak on the issue. Here television celebrity Rosie O'Donnell leaves the courthouse following her marriage ceremony.

Battles over same-sex marriages are currently being fought in state capitals across the country. The Constitution requires every state to give "Full Faith and Credit" to the official acts of other states. But Congress' Defense of Marriage Act relieves states from recognizing same-sex marriages consummated in other states. The Supreme Court may end up deciding the issue.

evolution of American federalism is no easy task. But let us try to describe broadly some major periods in the evolution of federalism and then look at five specific historical developments that had far-reaching impact on that evolution.

State-Centered Federalism, 1787–1868   From the adoption of the Constitution of 1787 to the end of the Civil War, the states were the most important units in the American federal system. It is true that during this period the legal foundation for the expansion of national power was being laid, but people looked to the states for resolving most policy questions and providing most public services. Even the issue of slavery was decided by state governments. The supremacy of the national government was frequently questioned, first by the Anti-Federalists (including Thomas Jefferson) and later by John C. Calhoun and other defenders of slavery.

dual federalism Early concept of federalism in which national and state powers were clearly distinguished and functionally separate.

Dual Federalism, 1868–1913   The supremacy of the national government was decided on the battlefields of the Civil War. Yet for nearly a half-century after that conflict, the national government narrowly interpreted its delegated powers, and the states continued to decide most domestic policy issues. The resulting pattern has been described as **dual federalism**. Under this pattern, the states and the nation divided most governmental functions. The national government concentrated its attention on the "delegated" powers—national defense, foreign affairs, tariffs, interstate commerce, the coinage of money, standard weights and measures, post office and post roads, and the admission of new states. State governments decided the important domestic policy issues—education, welfare, health, and criminal justice. The separation of policy responsibilities was once compared to a layer cake, with local governments at the base, state governments in the middle, and the national government at the top.[7]

Cooperative Federalism, 1913–64   The distinction between national and state responsibilities gradually eroded in the first half of the twentieth century. American federalism was transformed by the Industrial Revolution and the development of a national economy, by the federal income tax in 1913, which shifted financial resources to the national government, and by the challenges of two world wars and the Great Depression. In response to the Great Depression of the

UP CLOSE

Historical Markers in the Development of American Federalism

Among the most important events in the development of American federalism: (1) the Supreme Court's decision in *McCulloch v. Maryland* in 1819 giving a broad interpretation of the Necessary and Proper Clause; (2) the victory of the national government in the Civil War 1861–65; (3) the establishment of a national system of civil rights based on the Fourteenth Amendment culminating in the Supreme Court's desegregation decision in *Brown v. Board of Education;* (4) the expansion of the national government's power under the Interstate Commerce Clause during the Great Depression of the 1930s; and (5) the growth of federal revenues after the passage of the Sixteenth (income tax) Amendment in 1913.

McCulloch v. Maryland and the Necessary and Proper Clause

Political conflict over the scope of national power is as old as the nation itself. In 1790 Secretary of the Treasury Alexander Hamilton proposed the establishment of a national bank. Congress acted on Hamilton's suggestion in 1791, establishing a national bank to serve as a depository for federal money and to aid the federal government in borrowing funds. Jeffersonians believed the national bank was a dangerous centralization of government. They objected that the power to establish the bank was nowhere to be found in the enumerated powers of Congress.

Hamilton replied that Congress could derive the power to establish a bank from grants of authority in the Constitution relating to money, in combination with the clause authorizing Congress "to make all laws which shall be necessary and proper for carrying into execution the foregoing powers."

The question finally reached the Supreme Court in 1819, when the State of Maryland levied a tax on the national bank and the bank refused to pay it. In the case of *McCulloch v. Maryland,* Chief Justice Marshall accepted the broader Hamiltonian version of the Necessary and Proper Clause: "Let the end be legitimate, let it be within the scope of the Constitution, and all means which are appropriate, which are plainly adopted to that end, which are not prohibited but consistent with the letter and the spirit of the Constitution, are constitutional."[a]

The *McCulloch* case firmly established the principle that the Necessary and Proper Clause gives Congress the right to choose its means in carrying out the enumerated powers of the national government. Because of this broad interpretation of the Necessary and Proper Clause, today Congress can devise programs, create agencies, and establish national laws on the basis of long chains of reasoning from the most meager phrases of the constitutional text.

Secession and Civil War

The Civil War was the greatest crisis of the American federal system. Did a state have the right to oppose national law to the point of secession, that is, withdrawing from the federal Union? The question of secession was decided on Civil War battlefields between 1861 and 1865. Yet the states' rights doctrine and political disputes over the character of American federalism did not disappear with General Robert E. Lee's surrender at Appomattox. In addition to establishing that states cannot secede from the federal union, the Civil War led to three constitutional amendments clearly aimed at limiting state power in the interests of individual freedom. The Thirteenth Amendment eliminated slavery in the states; the Fifteenth Amendment prevented states from denying the vote on the basis of race, color, or previous enslavement; and the Fourteenth Amendment declared,

> No State shall make or enforce any law which shall abridge the privileges or immunities of citizens of the United States; nor shall any state deprive any person of life, liberty, or property, without due process of law; nor deny to any person within its jurisdiction the equal protection of the laws.

National Guarantees of Civil Rights

In the twentieth century, the Supreme Court began to build a national system of civil rights based on the Fourteenth Amendment. First, the Court held that the Fourteenth Amendment prevented states from interfering with free speech, free press, or religious practices. But it was not until 1954, in the desegregation decision in *Brown v. Board of Education of Topeka,* that the Court began to call for the full assertion of national authority on behalf of civil rights.[b] When it decided that the Fourteenth Amendment prohibited the states from segregating the races in public schools, the Court was asserting national authority over longstanding practices in many of the states.

But in the years following *Brown,* some state officials tried to prevent the enforcement of a national law. Governor Orval Faubus called out the Arkansas National Guard to prevent a federal court from desegregating Little Rock Central High School in 1957. President Dwight D. Eisenhower responded by

---

[a]*McCulloch v. Maryland,* 4 Wheaten 316 (1819).

[b]*Brown v. Board of Education of Topeka, Kansas,* 347 U.S. 483 (1954).

ordering the Arkansas National Guard removed and sent units of the U.S. Army to enforce national authority. This presidential action reinforced the principle of national supremacy in the American political system.

The Expansion of Interstate Commerce

The growth of national power under the Interstate Commerce Clause of the Constitution is another important development in the evolution of American federalism. For many years, the U.S. Supreme Court narrowly defined *interstate commerce* to mean only the movement of goods and services across state lines. Until the late 1930s, it insisted that agriculture, mining, manufacturing, and labor relations were outside the reach of the delegated powers of the national government. However, when confronted with the Great Depression of the 1930s and Franklin Roosevelt's threat to add enough members to the Supreme Court to win

favorable rulings, the Court yielded. It redefined *interstate commerce* to include any activity that "substantially affects" the national economy.[c] Indeed, the Court frequently approved of congressional restrictions on economic activities that had only very indirect effects on interstate commerce.[d]

The Income Tax and Federal Grants

In the famous Northwest Ordinance of 1787, which provided for the governing of the territories west of the Appalachian Mountains, Congress made grants of land for the establishment of public schools. Then in the Morrill Land Grant Act of 1862, Congress provided grants of land to the states to promote higher education, especially agricultural and mechanical studies. Federal support for "A and M" or "land grant" universities continues today.

With the money provided to Washington by the passage of the Sixteenth (income tax) Amendment in 1913, Congress embarked on cash grants to the states. Among the earliest cash grant programs were the Federal Highway Act of 1916 and the Smith-Hughes Act of 1917 (vocational education). With federal money came federal direction. For example, states that wanted federal money for highways after 1916 had to accept uniform standards of construction and even a uniform road-numbering system (U.S. 1, U.S. 30, and so on). Shortly after these programs began, the U.S. Supreme Court considered the claim that these federal grants were unconstitutional intrusions into areas "reserved" for the states. But the Court upheld grants as a legitimate exercise of Congress's power to tax and spend for the general welfare.[e]

[c]*National Labor Relations Board v. Jones & Laughlin Steel Corporation*, 301 U.S. 1 (1937).
[d]*Wickard v. Filburn*, 317 U.S. 128 (1938).
[e]*Massachusetts v. Mellon, Framingham v. Mellon*, 262 U.S. 447 (1923).

1930s, state governors welcomed massive federal public works projects under President Franklin D. Roosevelt's New Deal program. In addition, the federal government intervened directly in economic affairs, labor relations, business practices, and agriculture. Through its grants of money, the national government cooperated with the states in public assistance, employment services, child welfare, public housing, urban renewal, highway building, and vocational education.

This new pattern of federal-state relations was labeled **cooperative federalism**. Both the nation and the states exercised responsibilities for welfare, health, highways, education, and criminal justice. This merging of policy responsibilities was compared to a marble cake: "As the colors are mixed in a marble cake, so functions are mixed in the American federal system."[8] Yet even in this period of shared national-state responsibility, the national government emphasized cooperation in achieving common national and state goals. Congress generally acknowledged that it had no direct constitutional authority to regulate

cooperative federalism
Model of federalism in which national, state, and local governments work together exercising common policy responsibilities.

public health, safety, or welfare. Instead, it relied primarily on its powers to tax and spend for the general welfare, providing financial assistance to state and local governments to achieve shared goals. Congress did not usually legislate directly on local matters.

Centralized Federalism, 1964–80

Over the years, it became increasingly difficult to maintain the fiction that the national government was merely assisting the states to perform their domestic responsibilities. By the time President Lyndon B. Johnson launched the Great Society program in 1964, the federal government clearly had its own *national* goals. Virtually all problems confronting American society—from solid-waste disposal and water and air pollution to consumer safety, home insulation, noise abatement, and even "highway beautification"—were declared to be national problems. Congress legislated directly on any matter it chose, without regard to its *enumerated powers* and without pretending to render only financial assistance. The Supreme Court no longer concerned itself with the reserved powers of the states, and the Tenth Amendment lost most of its meaning. The pattern of national-state relations became **centralized federalism**. As for the cake analogies, one commentator observed, "The frosting had moved to the top, something like a pineapple upside-down cake."[9]

New Federalism, 1980–85

New federalism was a phrase frequently applied to efforts to reverse the flow of power to Washington and to return responsibilities to states and communities. (The phrase originated in the administration of Richard M. Nixon, 1969–74, who used it to describe general revenue sharing—making federal grants to state and local governments with few strings attached.) New Federalism was popular early in the administration of President Ronald Reagan, who tried to reduce federal involvement in domestic programs and encourage states and cities to undertake greater policy responsibilities themselves. The result was that state and local governments were forced to rely more on their own sources of revenue and less on federal money. Still, centralizing tendencies in the American federal system continued. While the general public usually gave better marks to state and local governments than to the federal government, paradoxically that same public also favored greater federal involvement in policy areas traditionally thought to be state or local responsibilities (see Figure 4.3).

The Close Up Foundation
A nonprofit, nonpartisan citizenship education organization with excellent historical materials about federalism's evolution and information about federalism issues. A related link on the Close Up site contains the complete text of the pro-states' rights 1798 Kentucky and Virginia Resolutions (authored by Jefferson and Madison). *www.closeup.org*

centralized federalism
Model of federalism in which the national government assumes primary responsibility for determining national goals in all major policy areas and directs state and local government activity through conditions attached to money grants.

new federalism Attempts to return power and responsibility to the states and reduce the role of the national government in domestic affairs.

During the Great Depression of the 1930s, the massive public works projects sponsored by the federal government under President Franklin Roosevelt's New Deal reflected the emergence of cooperative federalism. Programs of the Works Progress Administration, like the one shown here, were responsible for the construction of buildings, bridges, highways, and airports throughout the country.

Figure 4.3 Public Views about Which Level of Government Should Run Various Programs

Source: Gallup/CNN/*USA Today* Poll, reported in *The Polling Report*, February 10, 1997. Copyright © 1996–2004 by The Gallup Organization.

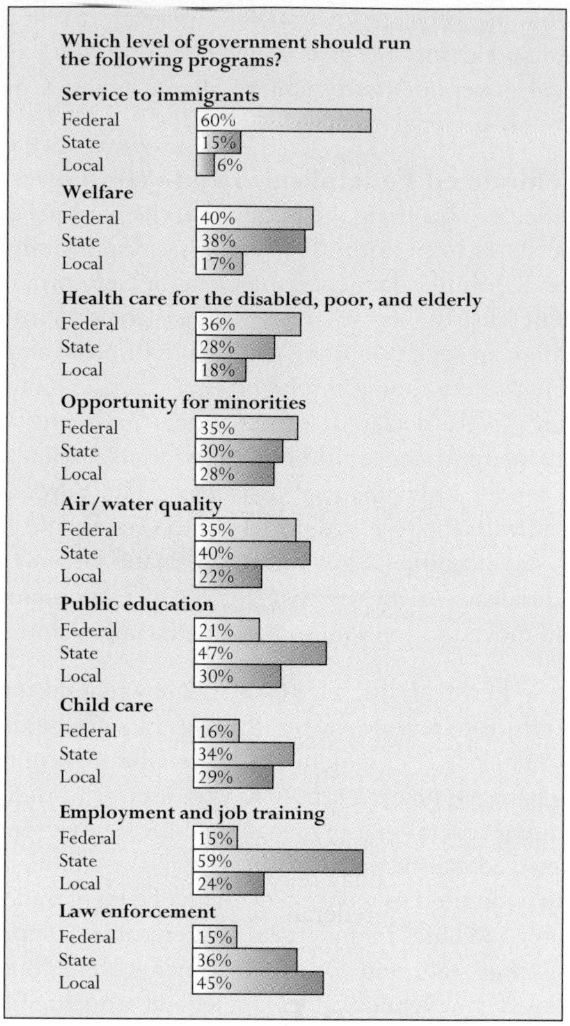

Which level of government should run the following programs?

Service to immigrants
Federal 60%
State 15%
Local 6%

Welfare
Federal 40%
State 38%
Local 17%

Health care for the disabled, poor, and elderly
Federal 36%
State 28%
Local 18%

Opportunity for minorities
Federal 35%
State 30%
Local 28%

Air/water quality
Federal 35%
State 40%
Local 22%

Public education
Federal 21%
State 47%
Local 30%

Child care
Federal 16%
State 34%
Local 29%

Employment and job training
Federal 15%
State 59%
Local 24%

Law enforcement
Federal 15%
State 36%
Local 45%

Representational Federalism, 1985–95   Despite centralizing tendencies, it was still widely assumed prior to 1985 that the Congress could not directly legislate how state and local governments should go about performing their traditional functions. However, in its 1985 *Garcia v. San Antonio Metropolitan Transit Authority* decision, the U.S. Supreme Court appeared to remove all barriers to direct congressional legislation in matters traditionally reserved to the states. The case arose after Congress directly ordered state and local governments to pay minimum wages to their employees. The Court dismissed arguments that the nature of American federalism and the Reserved Powers Clause of the Tenth Amendment prevented Congress from directly legislating in state affairs. It said that the only protection for state powers was to be found in the states' role in electing U.S. senators, members of the U.S. House of Representatives, and the president. The Court's ruling asserts a concept known as **representational federalism**: Federalism is defined by the role of the states in electing members of Congress and the president, not by any constitutional division of powers. The United States is said to retain a federal system because its national officials are selected from subunits of government—the president through the allocation of Electoral College votes to the states and the Congress through the allocation of two Senate seats per state and the apportionment of representatives based on state population. Whatever protection exists for state power and independence

representational federalism
Assertion that no constitutional division of powers exists between the nation and the states but the states retain their constitutional role merely by selecting the president and members of Congress.

Medicare was begun in 1965 as part of President Lyndon B. Johnson's Great Society agenda. A Republican Congress added prescription drug coverage (Part D) beginning in 2004, but protestors like these shown here criticize gaps in coverage.

must be found in the national political process, in the influence of state and district voters on their senators and representatives. In a strongly worded dissenting opinion in *Garcia*, Justice Lewis Powell argued that if federalism is to be retained, the Constitution—not Congress—should divide powers. "The states' role in our system of government is a matter of constitutional law, not legislative grace. . . . [This decision] today rejects almost 200 years of the understanding of the constitutional status of federalism."[10]

Federalism Revived?

In recent years federalism has experienced a modest revival. The U.S. Supreme Court today appears to be somewhat more respectful of the powers of states and somewhat less willing to see these powers trampled upon by the national government.[11]

In 1995 the U.S. Supreme Court issued its first opinion in more than sixty years that recognized a limit on Congress's power over interstate commerce and reaffirmed the Founders' notion of a national government with only the powers enumerated in the Constitution.[12] The Court found that the federal Gun-Free School Zones Act was unconstitutional because it exceeded Congress's powers under the Interstate Commerce Clause. When a student, Alfonso Lopez, was apprehended at his Texas high school carrying a .38 caliber handgun, federal agents charged him with violating the *federal* Gun-Free School Zones Act of 1990.

The U.S. government argued that the act was a constitutional exercise of its interstate commerce power, because "violent crime reduces the willingness of individuals to travel to areas within the country that are perceived to be unsafe." But after reviewing virtually all of the key commerce clause cases in its history, the Court determined that an activity must *substantially affect* interstate commerce in order to be regulated by Congress. Chief Justice William H. Rehnquist, writing for the majority in a 5 to 4 decision in *U.S. v. Lopez*, even cited James Madison with approval: "The powers delegated by the proposed Constitution to the federal government are few and defined. Those which are to remain in the state governments are numerous and indefinite" (*Federalist*, No. 45).

—— **Think Again** ——

Should the national government be able to prosecute a high school student for bringing a gun to school?

 **National Conference of State Legislatures**
This conference site provides information on 50 state legislatures and the issues they confront. *www.ncsl.org*

In another victory for federalism, the U.S. Supreme Court ruled in 1996 in *Seminole Tribe v. Florida* that the Eleventh Amendment shields states from lawsuits by private parties that seek to force states to comply with federal laws enacted under the commerce power.[13] And in 1999 in *Alden v. Maine*, the Supreme Court held that states were also shielded in their own courts from lawsuits in which private parties seek to enforce federal mandates. In an opinion that surveyed the history of American federalism, Justice Kennedy wrote: "Congress has vast power but not all power. . . . When Congress legislates in matters affecting the states it may not treat these sovereign entities as mere prefectures or corporations."[14]

In defense of federalism, the Supreme Court invalidated a provision of a very popular law of Congress—the Brady Handgun Violence Protection Act. The Court decided in 1997 that the law's command to local law enforcement officers to conduct background checks on gun purchasers violated "the very principle of separate state sovereignty." The Court affirmed that the federal government "may neither issue directives requiring the states to address particular problems, nor command the states' officers, or those of their political subdivisions, to administer or enforce the federal regulatory program" (*Printz v. U.S.*, 521 U.S. 890 (1997).[15] And the Court held that in the Violence against Women Act, Congress also invaded the reserved police power of the states[16] (see *What Do You Think?* "Should Violence Against Women Be a Federal Crime?").

The Supreme Court's apparent revival of federalism has been greeted with cautious optimism. However, all of the recent Supreme Court rulings reaffirming federalism have come in narrow 5 to 4 decisions. The closeness of these votes, together with these decisions' contrast to more than a half-century of case law in support of national power, provide no guarantee that in the future the Supreme Court will continue to move in the direction of strengthening federalism.

Former presidential press secretary James Brady was permanently disabled in the assassination attempt on President Reagan in 1981. Brady and his wife led the effort to pass the Brady Act, which, among other things, ordered state and local officials to conduct background checks on gun purchasers. The Supreme Court held that portion of the act to be an unconstitutional violation of the principle of federalism.

WHAT DO YOU THINK?

Should Violence Against Women Be a Federal Crime?

When a student at VPI (Virginia Polytechnic Institute) was raped, she argued that the attack violated the federal Violence against Women Act of 1994, a popular bill that passed overwhelmingly in Congress and was signed by President Bill Clinton. The act allowed victims of "gender-motivated violence," including rape, to sue their attackers for monetary damages in *federal* court. The U.S. government defended its constitutional authority to involve itself in crimes against women by citing the Interstate Commerce Clause, arguing that crimes against women interfered with interstate commerce, the power over which is given to the national government in Article I of the Constitution.

But in 2000 the U.S. Supreme Court said, "If accepted, this reasoning would allow Congress to regulate any crime whose nationwide, aggregated impact has substantial effects on employment, production, transit, or consumption. Moreover, such reasoning will not limit Congress to regulating violence, but may be applied equally as well to family law and other areas of state regulation since the aggregate effect of marriage, divorce, and childrearing on the national economy is undoubtedly significant." The Court reasoned that "the Constitution requires a distinction between what is truly national and what is truly local, and there is no better example of the police power, which the Founders undeniably left reposed in the States and denied the central government." In Justice Scalia's opinion, allowing Congress to claim that violence against women interfered with interstate commerce would open the door to federalizing all crime because all crime affects interstate commerce.

Source: U.S. v. Morrison, May 15, 2000.

Money and Power Flow to Washington

Over the years, power in the federal system has flowed to Washington because tax money has flowed to Washington. With its financial resources, the federal government has been able to offer assistance to state and local governments and thereby involve itself in just about every governmental function performed by these governments. Today the federal government is no longer one of *enumerated* or *delegated* powers. No activities are really *reserved* to the states. Through its power to tax and spend for the *general welfare*, the national government is now deeply involved in welfare, education, transportation, police protection, housing, hospitals, urban development, and other activities that were once the exclusive domain of state and local government (see *Up Close:* "How Congress Set a National Drinking Age").

> ── Think Again ──
> When the federal government requires states to provide safe drinking water, clean air, or access for the handicapped, should it provide funds to carry out these mandates?

Grants-in-aid   Today grant-in-aid programs are the single most important source of federal influence over state and local activity. A **grant-in-aid** is defined as "payment of funds by one level of government (national or state) to be expended by another level (state or local) for a specified purpose, usually on a matching-funds basis (the federal government puts up only as much as the state or locality) and in accordance with prescribed standards of requirements."[17] No state or local government is *required* to accept grants-in-aid. Participation in grant-in-aid programs is voluntary. So in theory, if conditions attached to the grant money are too oppressive, state and local governments can simply decline to participate and pass up these funds.

grants-in-aid Payments of funds from the national government to state or local governments or from a state government to local governments for specific purposes.

About one-quarter of all state and local government revenues currently come from federal grants. Federal grants are available in nearly every major category of state and local government activity. Over 500 separate grant programs are administered by various federal agencies. So numerous and diverse are these

UP CLOSE

How Congress Set a National Drinking Age

Traditionally the *reserved* powers of the states included protection of the health, safety, and well-being of their citizens. The *enumerated* powers of Congress in the Constitution did not include regulating the sale and consumption of alcoholic beverages. Every state determined its own minimum age for drinking.

But the minimum drinking age became a national issue as a result of emotional appeals by groups such as Mothers Against Drunk Driving (MADD). Tragic stories told at televised committee hearings by grieving relatives of dead teenagers swept away federalism arguments. A few Congress members tried to argue that a national drinking age infringed on the powers of the state in a matter traditionally under state control. However, the new law, enacted in 1984, did not directly mandate a national drinking age. Instead, it ordered the withholding of 10 percent of all federal highway funds from any state that failed to raise its minimum drinking age to twenty-one. States retained the rights to ignore the national minimum and give up a portion of their highway funds. (Congress used this same approach in 1974 in establishing a national 55-mile-per-hour speed limit.) Opponents of this device labeled it federal blackmail and a federal intrusion into state responsibilities. For some state officials, then, the issue was not teen drinking but rather the preemption of state authority.

From a purely constitutional perspective, Congress simply exercised its power to spend money for the general welfare; it did not *directly* legislate in an area *reserved* to the states. Technically, states remain free to set their own minimum drinking age. Despite heated arguments in many state legislatures, all of the states adopted the twenty-one-year-old minimum national drinking age by 1990.

Appeals by groups such as Mothers Against Drunk Driving (MADD) helped overcome concerns that legislation effectively setting a national drinking age would infringe on state authority.

grants that state and local officials often lack information about their availability, purpose, and requirements. "Grantsmanship"—knowing where and how to obtain federal grants—is highly valued in state and local governments. Federal grants can be obtained to preserve historic buildings, develop minority-owned businesses, aid foreign refugees, drain abandoned mines, control riots, subsidize school milk programs, and so on. However, welfare (including cash benefits and food stamps) and health (including Medicaid for the poor) account for two-thirds of federal aid money (see Figure 4.4).

Thus many of the special projects and ongoing programs carried out today by state and local governments are funded by grants from the federal government. These funds have generally been dispersed as either categorical grants or block grants.

- *Categorical Grant:* A grant for a specific, narrow project. The project must be approved by a federal administrative agency. About 90 percent of federal aid money is distributed in the form of categorical grants. Categorical grants can be distributed on a project basis or a formula basis. Grants made on a project

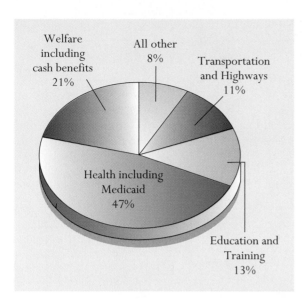

Figure 4.4 Purposes of Federal Grants to State and Local Governments

Over one-fifth of all state and local government revenues are derived from federal grants. Federal grants-in-aid to state and local governments are especially vital in the areas of health and welfare.

Source: Budget of United States Government, 2007.

basis are distributed by federal administrative agencies to state or local governments that compete for project funds in their applications. Federal agencies have a great deal of discretion in selecting specific projects for support, and they can exercise direct control over the projects. Most categorical grants are distributed to state or local governments according to a fixed formula set by Congress. Medicaid and Food Stamps (see Chapter 17) are the largest categorical grant programs.

■ *Block Grant:*   A grant for a general governmental function, such as health, social services, law enforcement, education, or community development. State and local governments have fairly wide discretion in deciding how to spend federal block grant money within a functional area. For example, cities receiving "community development" block grants can decide for themselves about specific neighborhood development projects, housing projects, community facilities, and so on. All block grants are distributed on a formula basis set by Congress. Federal administrative agencies may require reports and adherence to rules and guidelines, but they do not choose which specific projects to fund.

State–Local Dependency on Federal Grants   Prior to 1980 and the presidential administration of Ronald Reagan, state and local governments throughout the United States were becoming increasingly dependent upon federal grant money. From 1960 to 1980 federal grants as a percent of state–local spending rose from 14.8 percent to 27.4 percent. President Reagan made significant cutbacks in the flow of federal funds to state and local governments, and by 1990 federal grants constituted only 18.9 percent of state–local spending (see Figure 4.5). Reagan achieved most of this reduction by transforming categorical grants into block grants and then reducing the size of the block grants below the sum of the categorical grants. But following Reagan's efforts, federal grants again began to creep up under Presidents Bill Clinton and George W. Bush, and today federal grants again account for about one-quarter of all state and local government spending.

"Devolution"   Controversy over federalism—what level of government should do what and who should pay for it—is as old as the nation itself (see *A Conflicting View:* "Liberals, Conservatives, and Federalism"). Beginning in 1995,

Figure 4.5 State and Local Government Dependency on Federal Grants

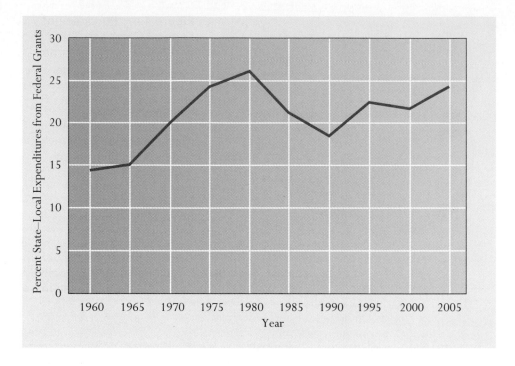

devolution Passing down of responsibilities from the national government to the states.

with a new Republican majority in both houses of Congress and Republicans holding a majority of state governorships, debates over federalism were renewed. The new phrase was **devolution**—the passing down of responsibilities from the national government to the states.

Welfare reform turned out to be the key to devolution. Bill Clinton once promised "to end welfare as we know it," but it was a Republican Congress in 1996 that did so. After President Clinton had twice vetoed welfare reform bills, he and Congress finally agreed to merge welfare reform with devolution. A new Temporary Assistance to Needy Families program (see Chapter 17) replaced direct federal cash aid welfare "entitlements." The new program:

- Establishes block grants with lump-sum allocations to the states for cash welfare payments.

- Grants the states broad flexibility in determining eligibility and benefit levels for persons receiving such aid.

- Limits the use of federally aided cash grants for most recipients to two continuing years and five years over their lifetime.

- Allows states to deny additional cash payments for children born to women already receiving welfare assistance and allowing states to deny cash payments to parents under eighteen who do not live with an adult and attend school.

Since Franklin D. Roosevelt's New Deal, with its federal guarantee of cash Aid to Families with Dependent Children (AFDC), low-income mothers and children had enjoyed a federal "entitlement" to welfare payments. But welfare reform, with its devolution of responsibility to the states, ended this sixty-year-old federal entitlement. Note, however, that Congress continues to place "strings" on the use of federal welfare funds, including a two-year limit on continuing payments to beneficiaries and a five-year lifetime limit.

A CONFLICTING VIEW

Liberals, Conservatives, and Federalism

From the earliest days of the Republic, American leaders and scholars have argued over federalism. Political interests that constitute a majority at the national level and control the national government generally praise the virtue of national supremacy. Political interests that do not control the national government but exercise controlling influence in one or more states generally see great merit in preserving the powers of the states.

In recent years, political conflict over federalism—over the division between national versus state and local responsibilities and finances—has tended to follow traditional "liberal" and "conservative" political cleavages. Generally, liberals seek to enhance the power of the *national* government because they believe people's lives can be changed—and bettered—by the exercise of national governmental power. The government in Washington has more power and resources than do state and local governments, which many liberals regard as too slow, cumbersome, weak, and unresponsive. Thus liberalism and centralization are closely related in American politics.

In contrast, conservatives generally seek to return power to *state and local* governments. Conservatives are skeptical about the "good" that government can do and believe that adding to the power of the national government is not an effective way of resolving society's problems. On the contrary, they argue that "government is the problem, not the solution." Excessive government regulation, burdensome taxation, and inflationary government spending combine to restrict individual freedom, penalize work and savings, and destroy incentives for economic growth. Government should be kept small, controllable, and close to the people.

There is no way to settle the argument over federalism once and for all. Debates about federalism are part of the fabric of American politics.

Political Obstacles to Devolution and Federalism Politicians in Washington are fond of the rhetoric of federalism. They know that Americans generally prefer governments closer to home. Yet at the same time they confront strong political pressures to "DO SOMETHING!" about virtually every problem that confronts individuals, families, or communities, whether or not doing so may overstep the enumerated powers of the national government. Politicians gain very little by telling their constituents that a particular problem—violence in the schools, domestic abuse, physician-assisted suicide, and so on—is not a federal responsibility and should be dealt with at the state or local level of government. So both federal and state politicians compete to address well-publicized problems.[18]

Moreover, neither presidents nor members of Congress are inclined to restrain their own power. Both liberals and conservatives in Washington are motivated to tie their own strings to federal grant-in-aid money, issue their own federal mandates, and otherwise "correct" what they perceive to be errors or inadequacies of state policies.

Urban Institute Washington think tank offers viewpoints on federalism and issues confronting state/local government. *www.urban.org*

Coercive Federalism: Preemptions and Mandates

Traditionally, Congress avoided issuing direct orders to state and local governments. Instead, it sought to influence them by offering grants of money with federal rules, regulations, or "guidelines" attached. In theory at least, states and communities were free to forgo the money and ignore the strings attached to it. But increasingly Congress has undertaken direct regulation of areas traditionally reserved to the states and restricted state authority to regulate these areas. And it has issued direct orders to state and local governments to perform various services and comply with federal law in the performance of these services.

Federal Preemptions   The supremacy of federal laws over those of the states, spelled out in the National Supremacy Clause of the Constitution, permits Congress to decide whether or not there is **preemption** of state laws in a particular field by federal law. In **total preemption**, the federal government assumes all regulatory powers in a particular field—for example, copyrights, bankruptcy, railroads, and airlines. No state regulations in a totally preempted field are permitted. **Partial preemption** stipulates that a state law on the same subject is valid as long as it does not conflict with the federal law in the same area. For example, the Occupational Safety and Health Act of 1970 specifically permits state regulation of any occupational safety or health issue on which the federal Occupational Safety and Health Administration (OSHA) has *not* developed a standard; but once OSHA enacts a standard, all state standards are nullified. A specific form of partial preemption called **standard partial preemption** permits states to regulate activities in a field already regulated by the federal government, as long as state regulatory standards are at least as stringent as those of the federal government. Usually states must submit their regulations to the responsible federal agency for approval; the federal agency may revoke a state's regulating power if that state fails to enforce the approved standards. For example, the federal Environmental Protection Agency (EPA) permits state environmental regulations that meet or exceed EPA standards.

Federal Mandates   Federal **mandates** are direct orders to state and local governments to perform a particular activity or service or to comply with federal laws in the performance of their functions. Federal mandates occur in a wide variety of areas, from civil rights to minimum-wage regulations. Their range is reflected in some recent examples of federal mandates to state and local governments:

- *Age Discrimination Act, 1986:*   Outlaws mandatory retirement ages for public as well as private employees, including police, firefighters, and state college and university faculty.

- *Asbestos Hazard Emergency Act, 1986:*   Orders school districts to inspect for asbestos hazards and remove asbestos from school buildings when necessary.

- *Safe Drinking Water Act, 1986:*   Establishes national requirements for municipal water supplies; regulates municipal waste treatment plants.

- *Clean Air Act, 1990:*   Bans municipal incinerators and requires auto emission inspections in certain urban areas.

- *Americans with Disabilities Act, 1990:*   Requires all state and local government buildings to promote handicapped access.

- *National Voter Registration Act, 1993:*   Requires states to register voters at driver's license, welfare, and unemployment compensation offices.

- *No Child Left Behind Act, 2001:*   Requires states and their school districts to test public school pupils.

State and local governments frequently complain that the costs imposed on them by complying with such federal mandates are seldom reimbursed by Washington.

---

preemption Total or partial federal assumption of power in a particular field, restricting the authority of the states.

total preemption Federal government's assumption of all regulatory powers in a particular field.

partial preemption Federal government's assumption of some regulatory powers in a particular field, with the stipulation that a state law on the same subject as a federal law is valid if it does not conflict with the federal law in the same area.

standard partial preemption Form of partial preemption in which the states are permitted to regulate activities already regulated by the federal government if the state regulatory standards are at least as stringent as the federal government's.

mandate Perception of popular support for a program or policy based on the margin of electoral victory won by a candidate who proposed it during a campaign; direct federal orders to state and local governments requiring them to perform a service or to obey federal laws in the performance of their functions.

A CONSTITUTIONAL NOTE

How Is National and State Power Divided?

The Constitution gives to Congress—that is, to the national government—seventeen specific grants of power, the so-called "enumerated powers." These are followed by an eighteenth "necessary and proper" power—"to make all laws which shall be necessary and proper for carrying into Execution the foregoing powers, and all other Powers vested by this Constitution in the Government of the United States . . ." (Article I, Section 8). It is this last "implied powers" or "elastic" clause that has been used extensively by the national government to greatly expand its power.

But what of the states? The Founders believed that the Constitution left all other governmental powers to the states. The Tenth Amendment solidified that idea: "The powers not delegated to the United States by the Constitution, nor prohibited by it to the States, are reserved to the States respectively, or to the people." The "reserved powers" of the states are limited only by a few paragraphs in the text of the Constitution, notably Article I, Section 10, which, among other things, prohibits the states from entering into treaties with other nations, or coining money, or passing laws impairing the obligation of contracts, or granting any title of nobility, or placing taxes or duties on imports or exports, or engaging in war with a foreign power "unless actually invaded."

In brief, the original Constitution envisioned the states as having the principal responsibility for the health, safety, education, welfare, law enforcement, and protection of their people. This constitutional "division of power" remains in the Constitution, despite great shifts in power to the national government. Subsequent amendments prohibited slavery in the states (Amendment 13); prohibited states from abridging the privileges or immunities of citizens of the United States, or depriving any person of life, liberty, or property without due process of law, or denying any person within this jurisdiction equal protection of the laws (Amendment 14); or prohibiting citizens the right to vote because of race, color, or previous condition of servitude (Amendment 15); or denying the right to vote for failure to pay any poll tax or other tax (Amendment 24); or denying anyone eighteen years of age or older the right to vote on account of age (Amendment 26).

So anyone reading the Constitution, without knowledge of the history of constitutional change in United States, would not really understand the nature of our government.

"Unfunded" Mandates   Federal mandates often impose heavy costs on states and communities. When no federal monies are provided to cover these costs, the mandates are said to be **unfunded mandates**. Governors, mayors, and other state and local officials have often urged Congress to stop imposing unfunded mandates on states and communities. Private industries have long voiced the same complaint. Regulations and mandates allow Congress to address problems while pushing the costs of doing so onto others.

unfunded mandates
Mandates that impose costs on state and local governments (and private industry) without reimbursement from the federal government.

Homeland Security   The Constitution gives the federal government the responsibility for national defense. The terrorist attacks on the World Trade Center in New York and the Pentagon in Washington, on September 11, 2001, began what President George W. Bush described as a long and difficult "war on terrorism." Washington reorganized itself, creating a new Department of Homeland Security (see Chapter 12), and allocated billions of dollars for homeland defenses. But the "first responders" to any terrorist attack are state and local police, fire, medical, and other emergency agencies. States, counties, and cities now face unprecedented and permanent responsibilities in homeland security, even including dealing with the results of nuclear, biological, and chemical attacks. Governors, mayors, city and county officials, and especially police, fire, and emergency officers, have urged the Congress to provide more federal funding and resources to state and local agencies for homeland security. Congress has responded with billions of dollars in additional aid, but states and communities claim that assistance for their "first responders" is inadequate.

Summary Notes

■ The struggle for power between the national government and the states over two centuries has shaped American federalism today.

■ Federalism is the division of power between two separate authorities, the nation and the state, each of which enforces its own laws directly on its citizens and neither of which can change the division of power without the consent of the other.

■ American federalism was designed by the Founders as an additional protection for individual liberty by providing for the division and dispersal of power among multiple units of government.

■ Federalism has also been defended as a means of increasing opportunities to hold public office, improving governmental efficiency, ensuring policy responsiveness, encouraging policy innovation, and managing conflict.

■ However, federalism can also obstruct and frustrate national action. Narrow state interests can sometimes prevail over national interests or the interests of minorities within states. Segregation was long protected by theories of states' rights. Federalism also results in uneven levels of public services through the nation.

■ Power has flowed to the national government over time, as the original state-centered division of power has evolved into a national-centered system of government. Among the most important historical influences on this shift in power toward Washington have been the Supreme Court's broad interpretation of national power, the national government's victory over the secessionist states in the Civil War, the establishment of a national system of civil rights based on the Fourteenth Amendment, the growth of a national economy governed by Congress under its interstate commerce power, and the national government's

accumulation of power through its greater financial resources.

■ Federal grants to state and local governments have greatly expanded the national government's powers in areas previously regarded as *reserved* to the states.

■ Federal grants are available for most state and local government activities, but health and welfare account for about two-thirds of these grants. Grant money flows unevenly to the states, causing complaints from states that send more tax dollars then they get back.

■ Although Congress has generally refrained from directly legislating in areas traditionally *reserved* to the states, federal power in local affairs has grown as a result of federal rules, regulations, and guidelines established as conditions for the receipt of federal funds.

■ The Supreme Court in its *Garcia* decision in 1985 removed all constitutional barriers to direct congressional legislation in matters traditionally reserved to the states. Establishing the principle of representational federalism, the Court said that states could defend their own interests through their representation in the national government.

■ Representational federalism focuses on the role of the states in electing national officials—the president through the allocation of Electoral College votes to the states, the Senate through the allocation of two seats for each state, and the House through the apportionment of representatives based on the state's population.

■ Recent efforts at the "devolution" of federal responsibilities for welfare resulted in an end to federal individual "entitlements" to cash welfare payments and their replacement with block grants for cash aid to the states. But Congress continues to place "strings" on the use of federal welfare grants to the states.

Key Terms

federalism 105	delegated, or enumerated,	reserved powers 114	devolution 126
unitary system 105	powers 110	dual federalism 116	preemption 128
confederation 105	Necessary and Proper	cooperative federalism 118	total preemption 128
home rule 105	Clause 111	centralized federalism 119	partial preemption 128
intergovernmental	implied powers 111	new federalism 119	standard partial
relations 106	National Supremacy	representational	preemption 128
laboratories of	Clause 112	federalism 120	mandate 128
democracy 109	concurrent powers 114	grants-in-aid 123	unfunded mandates 129

Suggested Readings

Beer, Samuel H. *To Make a Nation: The Rediscovery of American Federalism*. Cambridge, Mass.: Harvard University Press, 1993. A historical account of the development of both federalism and nationalism in American political philosophy.

Dye, Thomas R. *American Federalism: Competition among Governments*. Lexington, Mass.: Lexington Books, 1990. A theory of "competitive federalism" arguing that rivalries among governments improve public services while lowering taxes, restrain the growth of government, promote innovation and experimentation in public policies, inspire greater responsiveness to the preferences of citizen-taxpayers, and encourage economic growth.

Ehrenhalt, Alan, ed. *Governing: Issues and Applications from the Front Lines of Government*, 2nd ed. Washington D.C.: CQ Press, 2005. A collection of essays and case studies on state and local government management, with federal relations given prominence.

Elazar, Daniel J. *The American Partnership*. Chicago: University of Chicago Press, 1962. Classic study of the historical evolution of federalism, stressing the nation-state sharing of policy concerns and financing, from the early days of the Republic, and the politics behind the gradual growth of national power.

Nagel, Robert F. *The Implosion of Federalism*. New York: Oxford University Press, 2001. America's political institutions are collapsing into the center, reducing the opportunity for competition and participation.

Ostrum, Vincent. *The Meaning of American Federalism*. San Francisco: ICS Press, 1991. A theoretical examination of federalism, setting forth the conditions for a self-governing society and arguing that multiple, overlapping units of government, with various checks on one another's power, provide a viable democratic system of conflict resolution.

O'Toole, Laurence J., ed. *American Intergovernmental Relations*. 3rd ed. Washington, D.C.: CQ Press, 1999. A collection of readings, both classic and contemporary, describing the theory, history, and current problems of intergovernmental relations in America.

Peterson, Paul E. *The Price of Federalism*. Washington, D.C.: Brookings Institution, 1995. Historical, theoretical, and empirical perspectives merged into a new, timely model of federalism that would allocate social welfare functions to the national government and education and economic development to states and communities.

Van Horn, Carl E. *The State of the States*. 4th ed. Washington, D.C.: CQ Press, 2005. An assessment of the challenges facing state governments as a result of the devolution revolution.

Make It Real

FEDERALISM?

This unit delves into *McCulloch v. Maryland* and Katrina.

Part Three

PARTICIPANTS

God and Country

ABCNEWS

Originally Aired: **November 26, 2002**
Program: **Nightline**
Running Time: **12:41**

Over the last couple of years, what has come to be called the Christian Right has become more and more active in supporting the Sharon government in its war with the Palestinians. And their political clout with the Bush administration is considerable. They are opposed to giving the Palestinians any land, taking a much harder line than many Americans. The reason? Prophecy. Many believe that what is playing out now in the Middle East is all part of the process leading toward the Second Coming. The existence of the state of Israel is crucial to that process and many believe that Israel must cover all of the land, including the occupied territories, in order for this process to move forward. So they send money, take trips to Israel, meet regularly with Israeli officials, including Sharon, and at the same time, seem to be breaking what was a strong alliance between American Jews and the Democratic Party. That would certainly change the political landscape in this country as well. Israel needs friends now, facing serious criticism from much of the world over its tactics in the current conflict.

And so both sides are sort of glossing over a theological issue. According to the prophecies that many Christians believe, as part of the Second Coming, Jews will have the opportunity to either convert to Christianity or perish. In other words, they will disappear as a people, or religion, one way or the other. You might think this would be a point of contention between the two religions but it doesn't appear to be. Ted Koppel interviews Pat Robertson, founder and chairman of the Christian Broadcasting Network. He is a former presidential candidate and arguably one of the most recognized leaders of the evangelical Christian community.

Critical Thinking Questions

1. In "God and Country," conservative Christians explain their strong support for Israel, especially their support of Jewish occupation of the West Bank. Briefly discuss the reasons they give for this support.

2. Not all Jews welcome the support of conservative American Christians. What implications of that support concern them?

3. As a general rule, interest groups rarely have a decisive role in the formulation of foreign policy. How might conservative Christian support for Israel be an exception to that rule?

5 OPINION AND PARTICIPATION
Thinking and Acting in Politics

Think About Politics

1 Should political leaders pay attention to public opinion polls when making decisions for the country?
Yes ☐ No ☐

2 Do you believe that your representative in Congress cares about your personal opinion on important issues?
Yes ☐ No ☐

3 Can you name the two U.S. senators from your state?
Yes ☐ No ☐

4 Is our government really legitimate when only about half the people vote in presidential elections?
Yes ☐ No ☐

5 Do you identify yourself with the same political party as your family?
Yes ☐ No ☐

5 Is it appropriate for religious leaders to try to influence how people vote?
Yes ☐ No ☐

7 Have you ever personally called or written to your representative in Congress?
Yes ☐ No ☐

8 Do you think you will ever run for public office yourself?
Yes ☐ No ☐

By thinking about politics and acting on your political opinions—voting, talking to friends, writing letters, joining organizations, attending meetings and rallies, contributing money, marching in demonstrations, or running for office yourself—you are participating in politics.

Politics and Public Opinion

For most Americans, politics is not as interesting as football or basketball, or the sex lives of celebrities, or prime-time television entertainment. Although politicians, pollsters, and commentators frequently assume that Americans have formed opinions on major public issues, in fact, most have not given them very much thought. Nevertheless, **public opinion** commands the attention of politicians, the news media, and political scientists.

Public opinion is given a lot of attention in democracies because democratic government rests on the consent of the governed. The question of whether public opinion *should* direct government policy has confounded political philosophers for centuries. Edmund Burke, writing in 1790, argued that democratic representatives should serve the *interests* of the people, but not necessarily conform to their *will*, in deciding questions of public policy. In contrast, other political philosophers have evaluated the success of democratic institutions by whether or not they produce policies that conform to popular opinion.

Major shifts in public opinion in the United States generally translate into policy change. Both the president and Congress appear to respond over time to *general* public preferences for "more" or "less" government regulation, "more" or "less" government spending, "getting tough on crime," "reforming welfare," and so on.[1] But public opinion is often weak, unstable, ill informed, or nonexistent on *specific* policy issues. Consequently, elected officials have greater flexibility in dealing with these issues—and, at the same time, there is an increase in the influence of lobbyists, interest groups, reporters, commentators, and others who have direct access to policy makers. Moreover, the absence of well-formed public opinion on an issue provides interest groups and the media with the opportunity to influence policy indirectly by shaping popular opinion.

Politicians read the opinion polls. And even though many elected representatives claim that they exercise independent judgment about what is

UP CLOSE

Can We Believe the Polls?

Survey research is a flourishing political enterprise. The national news media—notably CBS, NBC, ABC, and CNN television networks, the *New York Times* and the *Washington Post*, and *Time* and *Newsweek* magazines—regularly sponsor independent national surveys, especially during election campaigns. Major survey organizations—the American Institute of Public Opinion (Gallup), Louis Harris and Associates, National Opinion Research Center (NORC), the Roper Organization, National Election Studies (University of Michigan)—have been in business for a long time and have files of survey results going back many years. Political candidates also contract with private marketing and opinion research firms to conduct surveys in conjunction with their campaigns.

Public opinion surveys depend on the selection of a *random sample* of persons chosen in a way which ensures that every person in the *universe* of people about whom information is desired has an equal chance of being selected for interviewing. National samples, representative of all adults or all voters, usually include only about 1,000 persons. First, geographical areas (for example, counties or telephone area codes) that are representative of all such areas in the nation are chosen. Then residential telephone numbers are randomly selected within these areas. Once the numbers have been selected at random, the poll taker does not make substitutions but calls back several times if necessary to make contact so as not to bias the sample toward people who stay at home.

Even when random-selection procedures are closely followed, the sample may not be truly representative of the universe. But survey researchers can estimate the *sampling error* through the mathematics of probability. The sampling error is usually expressed as a percentage range—for example, plus or minus 3 percent—above and below the sample response within which there is a 95 percent likelihood that the universe response would be found if the entire universe were questioned. For example, if 65 percent of the survey respondents favor the death penalty and the sampling error is calculated at plus or minus 3 percent, then we can say there is a 95 percent probability that a survey of the whole population (the universe) would produce a response of between 62 and 68 percent in favor of the death penalty.

"Loaded" or "leading" questions are often used by unprofessional pollsters simply to produce results favorable to their side of an argument. An even worse abuse in telephone polling is the "push poll"—questions asked by political campaign workers posing as independent pollsters, deliberately worded to create an opinion—for example, "If you knew that Congressman Smith would soon be indicted for child molestation, would you vote for him?"

Professional pollsters strive for questions that are clear and precise, easily understood by the respondents, and as neutral and unbiased as possible. Nevertheless, because all questions have a potential bias, it is often better to examine *changes over time* in response to identically worded questions. Perhaps the best-known continuing question in public opinion polling is the presidential approval rating: "Do you approve or disapprove of the way _____ is handling his job as president?" Changes over time in public response to this question alert scholars, commentators, and presidents themselves to their public standing (see Chapter 11).

A survey can only measure opinions *at the time* it is taken. A few days later public opinion may change, especially if major events that receive heavy television coverage intervene. Some political pollsters conduct continuous "tracking" surveys until election night in order to catch last-minute opinion changes.

---

public opinion Aggregate of preferences and opinions of individuals on significant issues.

survey research Gathering of information about public opinion by questioning a representative sample of the population.

best for the nation in their decision making, we can be reasonably sure their "independent judgment" is influenced at least in part by what they think their constituents want. The cynical stereotype of the politician who reads the opinion polls before taking stands on the issues is often embarrassingly accurate.

All this attention to public opinion has created a thriving industry in public opinion polling and **survey research**. Polls have become a fixture of American political life (see *Up Close:* "Can We Believe the Polls?"). But how much do Americans really think about politics? How informed, stable, and consistent is public opinion?

Knowledge Levels Most Americans do *not* follow politics closely enough to develop well-informed opinions on many public issues (see Figure 5.1). Low

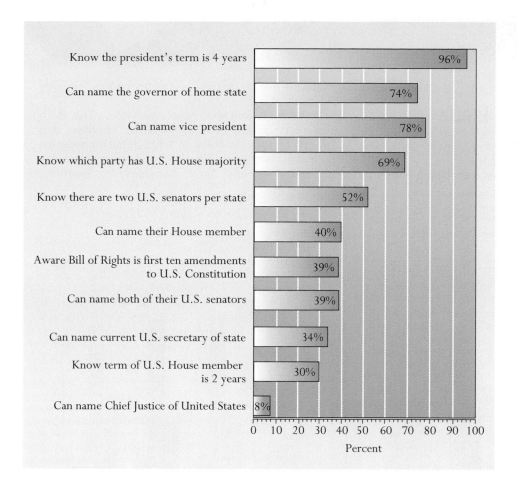

Figure 5.1 What Do Americans Know about Politics?

Politics is not the major interest of most Americans, and as a result knowledge about the political system is limited. Less than one-third of the general public knows the names of their representatives in Congress or their U.S. senators, and knowledge of specific foreign and domestic matters is even more limited.

Source: Data from Robert S. Erikson and Kent L. Tedin, *American Public Opinion*, 6th ed. (New York: Macmillan, 2002). p. 55 citing various polls.

levels of knowledge about government and public affairs make it difficult for people to form opinions on specific issues or policy proposals. Many opinion surveys ask questions about topics that people had not considered before being interviewed. Few respondents are willing to admit that they know nothing about the topic or have "no opinion." Respondents believe they should provide some sort of answer, even if their opinion was nonexistent before the question was asked. The result is that the polls themselves "create" opinions.[2]

Gallup
Oldest public opinion organization, with latest polls and large archive.
www.gallup.com

The "Halo Effect" Many respondents give "good citizen" or socially respectable answers, whether they are truthful or not, even to an anonymous interviewer. This **halo effect** leads to an *underestimation* of the true extent of prejudice, hatred, and bigotry. Another common example of the halo effect is the fact that people do not like to admit that they do not vote. Surveys regularly report higher percentages of people *saying* they voted in an election than the actual number of ballots cast. Moreover, postelection surveys almost always produce higher percentages of people who say they voted for the winner than the actual vote tally for the winner. Apparently poll respondents do not like to admit that they backed the loser.

— Think Again —

Should political leaders pay attention to public opinion polls when making decisions for the country?

halo effect Tendency of survey respondents to provide socially acceptable answers to questions.

Inconsistencies Because so many people hold no real opinion on political issues, the wording of a question frequently determines their response. People respond positively to positive phrases (for example, "helping poor people," "improving education," "cleaning up the environment") and negatively to

UP CLOSE

Abortion: The "Hot-Button" Issue

Although public opinion may be weak or nonexistent on many policy questions, there are a few "hot-button" issues in politics—issues on which virtually everyone has an opinion and many people feel very intensely about.

Abortion is one such highly sensitive issue. Both *pro-choice* proponents of legalized abortion and *pro-life* opponents claim to have public opinion on their side. *Interpretation* of the poll results becomes a political activity itself. Consider, for example,

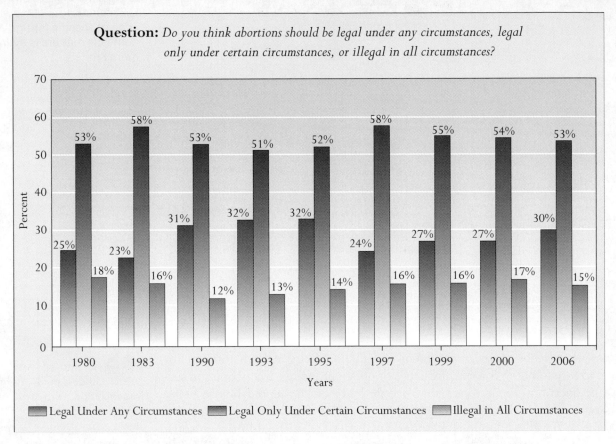

Question: *Do you think abortions should be legal under any circumstances, legal only under certain circumstances, or illegal in all circumstances?*

Legend: ▇ Legal Under Any Circumstances ▇ Legal Only Under Certain Circumstances ▇ Illegal in All Circumstances

Source: Copyright © 1980–2005 by The Gallup Organization.

negative phrases (for example, "raising taxes," "expanding governmental power," "restricting choice").

The wording of questions, combined with weak or nonexistent opinion, often produces inconsistent responses. For example, when asked whether they agreed or disagreed with the statement that "people should have the right to purchase a sexually explicit book, magazine, or movie, if that's what they want to do," an overwhelming 80 percent endorsed the statement. However, when the same respondents were also asked whether they agreed with the opposite statement that "community authorities should be able to prohibit the selling of magazines or movies they consider to be pornographic," 65 percent approved of this view as well.[3]

The Polling Report
Recent public opinion polls on policy issues, political actors, government institutions, etc.
www.pollingreport.com

responses to the general question posed in the graph pictured here.

Pro-choice forces interpret these results as overwhelming support for legalized abortion; pro-life commentators interpret these results as majority support for restricting abortion. Indeed, public opinion appears to support *specific restrictions* on abortion but oppose constitutional ban on abortions.

In short, most Americans appear to want to keep some abortions legal, but they believe that government should place certain restrictions on the practice.

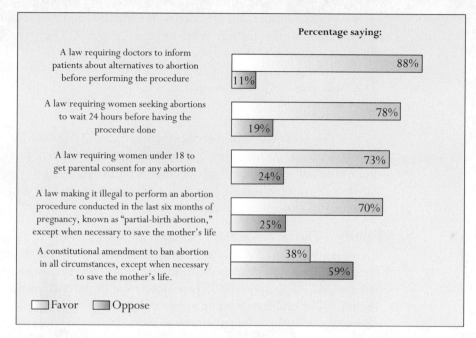

Percentage saying:

A law requiring doctors to inform patients about alternatives to abortion before performing the procedure — 88% / 11%

A law requiring women seeking abortions to wait 24 hours before having the procedure done — 78% / 19%

A law requiring women under 18 to get parental consent for any abortion — 73% / 24%

A law making it illegal to perform an abortion procedure conducted in the last six months of pregnancy, known as "partial-birth abortion," except when necessary to save the mother's life — 70% / 25%

A constitutional amendment to ban abortion in all circumstances, except when necessary to save the mother's life. — 38% / 59%

☐ Favor   ■ Oppose

Source: Gallup, CNN, *USA Today*, as reported on Public Opinion Online, *www.publicagenda.org*, October, 2003. Copyright © 2003 by The Gallup Organization.

Instability   Many people answer survey questions impulsively without very serious consideration. This lack of thought often results in an apparent instability of opinions—people giving contradictory responses to the same question when asked it at different times. Indeed, when identical questions are asked just a few months apart, 20 percent or more of respondents may switch sides! Instability is somewhat less on issues that are intensely debated (for example, abortion); it is somewhat greater on issues that receive less media attention (for example, oil drilling in Alaska).

Salience   People are likely to think about issues that receive a great deal of attention in the mass media—television, newspapers, magazines. **Salient issues** are those that people think about most—issues on which they hold stronger and more stable opinions. These are issues that people feel relate directly to their own lives, such as abortion (see *Up Close:* "Abortion: The 'Hot-Button Issue'"). Salient issues are, therefore, more important in politics.

Salient issues change over time. In general, during recessions the most salient issue is "Jobs, Jobs, Jobs!"—that is, unemployment and the economy. During inflationary periods, the issue is "the high cost of living." During wartime, the war itself becomes the public's principal concern. A gasoline shortage can turn public concern toward energy issues. These salient issues drive the political debate of the times.[4]

Public Agenda Online
Recent opinion polls on a variety of policy issues.
www.publicagenda.org

salient issues Issues about which most people have an opinion.

Socialization: The Origins of Political Opinions

socialization The learning of a culture and its values.

Where do people acquire their political opinions? Political **socialization** is the learning of political values, beliefs, and opinions. It begins early in life when a child acquires images and attitudes toward public authority. Preschool children see "police officer" and "president" as powerful yet benevolent "helpers." These figures—police officer and president—are usually the first recognized sources of authority above the parents who must be obeyed. They are usually positive images of authority at these early ages:

> Q: What does the policeman do?
> A: He catches bad people.[5]

Even the American flag is recognized by most U.S. preschoolers, who pick it out when asked, "Which flag is your favorite?" These early positive perceptions about political figures and symbols may later provide *diffuse support* for the political system—a reservoir of goodwill toward governmental authority that lends legitimacy to the political order.

Family   The family is the first agent of socialization. Children in the early school grades (3 to 5) begin to identify themselves as Republicans or Democrats. These childhood party identifications are almost always the same as those of the parents. Indeed, parent-child correspondence in party identification may last a lifetime.[6] The children who abandon the party of their parents tend to become independents rather than identify with the opposition party. However, party identification appears to be more easily passed on from parent to child than specific opinions on policy questions. Perhaps the reason is that parental party identifications are known to children, but few families conduct specific discussions of policy questions.

School   Political revolutionaries once believed that the school was the key to molding political values and beliefs. After the communist revolutions in Russia in 1917 and China in 1949, the schools became the focus of political indoctrination of the population. Today political battles rage in America over textbooks, teaching methods, prayer in schools, and other manifestations of politics in the classroom. But no strong evidence indicates a causal relationship between what is taught in the schools and the political attitudes of students.

Certainly the schools provide the factual basis for understanding government—how the president is chosen, the three branches of government, how a law is passed. But even this elemental knowledge is likely to fade if not reinforced by additional education or exposure to the news media or discussion with family or peers.

The schools *try* to inculcate "good citizenship" values, including support for democratic rules, tolerance toward others, the importance of voting, and the legitimacy (rightfulness) of government authority. Patriotic symbols and rituals abound in the classroom—the flag, the Pledge of Allegiance—and students are taught to respect the institutions of government. Generally the younger the student, the more positive the attitudes expressed toward political authority.[7] Yet despite the efforts of the schools to inspire support for the political system, distrust and cynicism creep in during the high school years. Although American youth retain a generally positive view of the political system, they share with adults increasing skepticism toward specific institutions and practices. During

Table 5.1   Education and Tolerance

	Percentage Responding "Yes" (by highest degree completed)				
	No High School	**High School**	**Junior College**	**College Degree**	**Total**
If such a person wanted to make a speech in your community, should he be allowed to speak?					
Atheist (antireligion)	47%	72%	83%	88%	69%
Racist	47	61	69	77	61
Homosexual	51	76	85	90	73
Should such a person be allowed to teach in a college or university?					
Atheist (antireligion)	29%	49%	65%	72%	49%
Racist	35	42	52	58	45
Homosexual	40	66	80	83	64

Source: General Social Survey, Cumulative Index, 2000 (Chicago: National Opinion Research Center). Cross tabulations by Nikita Desai, Department of Political Science, Purdue University.

high school, students acquire some ability to think along liberal-conservative dimensions. The college experience appears to produce a "liberalizing" effect: College seniors tend to be more liberal than entering freshmen. But over the years following graduation, liberal views tend to moderate.

Although no direct evidence indicates that the schools can inculcate democratic values, people with more education tend to be more tolerant than those with less education and to be generally more supportive of the political system (see Table 5.1). This pattern suggests that the effects of schooling are gradual and subtle (see also *What Do You Think?* "College Students' Opinions").

Church   Religious beliefs and values may also shape political opinion. *Which* religion an individual identifies with (for example, Protestant, Catholic, Jewish) affects public opinion. So does *how important* religion is in the individual's life. It is difficult to explain exactly how religion affects political values, but we can observe differences in the opinions expressed by Protestants, Catholics, and Jews; by people who say their religious beliefs are strong versus those who say they are not; and between fundamentalists (those who believe in a literal interpretation of the Bible) and nonfundamentalists. Religion shapes political attitudes on a variety of issues, including abortion, drugs, the death penalty, homosexuality, and prayer in public schools[8] (see Table 5.2 on page 142). Religion also plays a measurable role in political ideology. Fundamentalists are more likely to describe themselves as conservatives than as moderates, and very few accept the liberal label.[9]

At the same time, however, most Americans are concerned about religious leaders exercising influence in political life. Most respondents say it is "not appropriate for religious leaders to talk about their political beliefs as part of their religious activities" (61 percent), "religious leaders should not try to influence how people vote in elections" (64 percent), and "religious groups should *not* advance their beliefs by being involved in politics and working to affect policy" (54 percent).[10]

Age and Opinion   Age group differences in politics and public opinion are sometimes referred to as the **generation gap**. On most of the issues shown in Table 5.3, older people appear to be more conservative than younger people.

Think Again
Is it appropriate for religious leaders to try to influence how people vote?

Christian Coalition
Organization advocating greater Christian involvement in politics and government. *www.cc.org*

Americans United for Separation of Church and State
Advocacy organization opposed to religious influence in government. *www.au.org*

generation gap Differences in politics and public opinion among age groups.

WHAT DO YOU THINK?

College Students' Opinions

College students' opinions today appear to be somewhat more conservative then they were a generation ago, in the 1970s. While most students identify themselves politically as "middle-of-the-road," there are somewhat more "conservative" self-identifiers and fewer "liberal" self identifiers than 35 years ago. On policy issues, students today are more likely to support the death penalty, believe the courts are too lenient with criminals, and oppose legalization of marijuana. (However, students are somewhat more liberal on these issues today than in the 1980s and 1990s.) Students in the 1970s confronted an unpopular war in Vietnam, faced a military draft, and were more likely to experiment with drugs and alternative lifestyles. Today's students confront greater economic competition and increased educational requirements for employment. They are more concerned with their financial future than students were a generation ago.

However, college students remain somewhat more liberal than the general population. Moreover, college seniors and graduate students are more liberal than first-year students; students at prestigious Ivy League universities are more liberal than students at state universities and community colleges; and students in humanities and social sciences are more liberal than students in engineering, physical sciences, and business. Over the years following graduation, many of these liberal predispositions tend to moderate.

Political Opinions of College Students

	1972	1995	2000	2005
Political ideology				
Far left	2%	3%	3%	3%
Liberal	33	21	25	26
Middle-of-the road	48	50	51	46
Conservative	16	20	20	22
Far right	1	2	1	2
Policy issues				
Abolish the death penalty	33	21	32	33
Courts are too concerned with rights of criminals	50	73	64	58
Marijuana should be legal	47	34	40	37

Source: Data taken from various issues of *The Chronicle of Higher Education*, reporting annual polls by the American Council on Education.

Table 5.2 Religion and Public Opinion

Opinion	Affiliation			Faith		Belief That the Bible Is		
	Protestant	Catholic	Jew	Strong	Not Very Strong	Literal Word of God	Inspired by God	Book of Fables
Abortion for any reason should be legal	36%	35%	79%	26%	47%	23%	44%	67%
Legalize marijuana	19	23	43	14	28	13	23	45
Support death penalty	60	65	69	68	79	69	78	71
Remove book that favored homosexuality from library	42	31	15	46	31	54	24	17
Support prayer in public school	67	60	17	70	57	78	55	33

Source: General Social Survey, Cumulative Index, 2000 (Chicago: National Opinion Research Center). Cross-tabulations by Nikita Desai, Department of Political Science, Purdue University.

Source: PEANUTS reprinted by permission of United Feature Syndicate, Inc.

Older people are less likely than younger people to favor the legalization of marijuana, to allow abortion for any reason, or to allow homosexuals to teach in college; older people are more likely to identify themselves as "conservative." Younger Americans in general appear to be less interested and involved in politics than older Americans; they are less likely to keep up with political news and, perhaps most importantly, are less likely to vote (see Table 5.3 and the discussion later in this chapter).

Media Influence   Television is the major source of political information for Americans. More than two-thirds report that they receive "all or most" of their news from television, making newspapers, magazines, books, the Internet, and radio secondary to television as a source of political information (see Chapter 6). Moreover, Americans rate television the "most believable" channel of communication.

But the effect of television on opinion is not really in persuading people to take one side of an issue or another. Instead, the principal effect is in *setting the agenda* for thinking and talking about politics. Television does not tell people *what* to think, but it does tell them what to think *about* (see Chapter 6, "Mass Media: Setting the Political Agenda"). Television coverage determines matters of general public concern. Without coverage, the general public would not know about, think about, or discuss most events, personalities, and issues. Media attention creates issues, and the amount of attention given an issue determines its importance. (We return to the discussion of media power in Chapter 6.)

Table 5.3   Age and Public Opinion

	Under 30	55 and Over
Marijuana should be made legal	35%	17%
Allow homosexuals to teach in college	88	61
Allow abortion for any reason	44	32
Describe oneself as:		
Liberal	35	19
Moderate	33	43
Conservative	33	49
Read news about presidential campaign	42	71
Pay attention to national news	33	57
Vote in presidential election	24	65

Source: Questions from various *National Election Studies* and *General Social Surveys*, 1996–2000.

Religion helps to shape politics and public opinion. Here Catholics protest a tax-supported New York museum's showing of an exhibit that included a feces-smeared painting of the Virgin Mary.

Ideology and Opinion

Ideology helps to shape opinion. Many people, especially politically interested and active people, approach policy questions with a fairly consistent and integrated set of principles—that is, an *ideology* (see Chapter 2). Liberal and conservative ideas about the proper role of government in the economy, about the regulation of social conduct, about equality and the distribution of income, and about civil rights influence people's views on specific policy questions.

To what extent do self-described liberals and conservatives differ over specific issues? Can we predict people's stances on particular issues by knowing whether they call themselves liberal or conservative? Generally speaking, self-described liberals and conservatives do differ in their responses to specific policy questions,

Table 5.4   Ideology and Opinion

	Percentage Agreeing			
	Liberals	**Moderates**	**Conservatives**	**Total**
Equality				
"Government should reduce income differences"	33%	24%	20%	25%
"Government should not concern itself with income differences"	27	23	50	32
Courts' treatment of criminals				
"Too harsh"	5	2	0	2
"Not harsh enough"	83	91	92	89
"About right"	12	8	8	9
Social issues				
Favor legalizing marijuana	52	32	20	35
Favor school prayer	43	61	69	58
Oppose busing for racial balance in public schools	70	79	88	77

Source: General Social Survey, Cumulative Index, 2000 (Chicago: National Opinion Research Center). Cross-tabulations by Nikita Desai, Department of Political Science, Purdue University.

although some take policy positions inconsistent with their proclaimed ideology (see Table 5.4). People who describe themselves as liberal generally favor governmental efforts to reduce income inequalities and to improve the positions of African Americans, other minorities, and women. Overall, it appears that ideology and opinion are fairly well linked—that the liberal-conservative dimension is related to opinions on specific policy questions.[11]

Gender and Opinion

A **gender gap** in public opinion—a difference of opinion between men and women—occurs on only a few issues. Interestingly, a gender gap does *not* appear on women's issues: abortion, the role of women in business and politics, whether one would vote for a qualified woman for president, or whether men are better suited for political office. On these issues, men and women do not differ significantly (see Figure 5.2).

However, gender gap differences are apparent on a variety of contemporary issues (see Figure 5.2). Many polls report that women are

- More likely to favor an activist role for government

- More often opposed to U.S. military intervention

- More supportive of restrictions on firearms

- More supportive of spending on social programs

- More supportive of affirmative action

And there is some evidence that these gender gap differences are recognized by many voters and affect their choices at the polls.

Politically, the most important gender gap is in party identification. Women are more likely to identify themselves as Democrats, and men more likely to identify themselves as Republicans. This difference emerged in the 1980s, when men were more likely than women to support Republican president Ronald Reagan.[12] (Group differences in party identification are discussed at length in Chapter 7.)

Race and Opinion

Opinion over the extent of discrimination in the United States and over the causes of and remedies for racial inequality differs sharply across racial lines. Most whites believe there is very little discrimination toward African Americans in jobs, housing, or education and that differences between whites and blacks in society occur as a result of a lack of motivation among black people. Most African Americans strongly disagree with these views and believe that discrimination continues in employment, housing, and education and that differences between whites and blacks in standards of living are "mainly due to discrimination" (see Figure 5.3).

African Americans generally support a more positive role for government in reducing inequality in society. Approximately two out of every three believe that government should do more to reduce income differences between rich and poor. Blacks favor busing to achieve racial balance in public schools, a view not shared by many whites. Given these preferences for a strong role for government, it is not surprising that more blacks than whites identify themselves as liberals. However, about one-quarter of black people identify themselves as conservative. And indeed, on certain social issues—crime, drugs, school prayers—majorities of black people take conservative positions.

gender gap Aggregate differences in political opinions between men and women.

Center for Women in Politics
Extensive information on women officeholders, as well as gender gap data on voting and attitudes on public policy.
www.rci.rutgers.edu/~cawp

National Urban League
Organization devoted to advancing the economic well-being of African Americans, often reflecting opinions of the growing black middle class. Publishes annual *State of Black America*.
www.nul.org

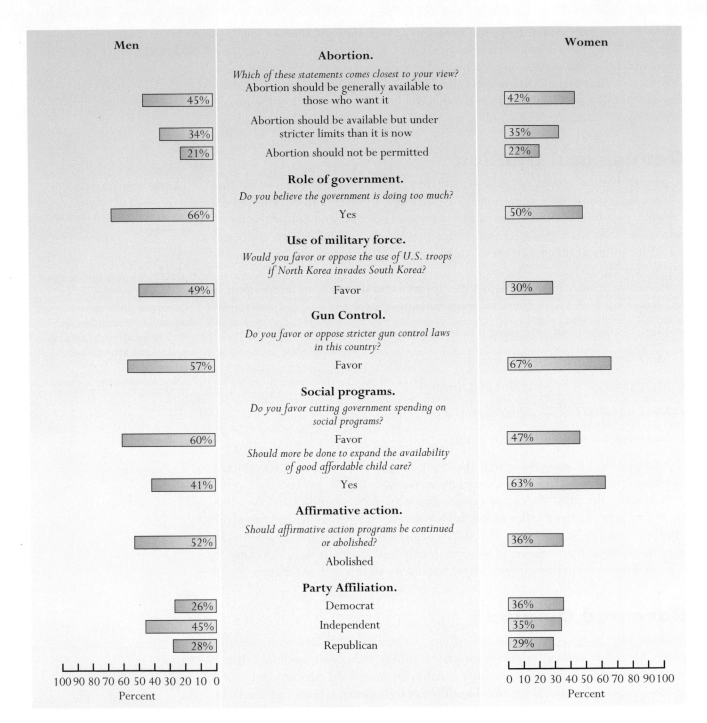

Figure 5.2 The Gender Gap

Source: Reprinted by permission of Center for American Women and Politics, Eagleton Institute of Politics, Rutgers, The State University of New Jersey.

African American perceptions of the criminal justice system are especially negative. Police encounters with black civilians have inspired many of the most destructive riots and demonstrations. Most whites believe the criminal justice system is fundamentally fair; most blacks do not. Whites attribute police brutality to individual malfeasance by officers; blacks see it as racism when the victim is black. Blacks see the disproportionate percentages of blacks in prison as discrimination; whites see it as a product of greater criminality among African Americans.[13]

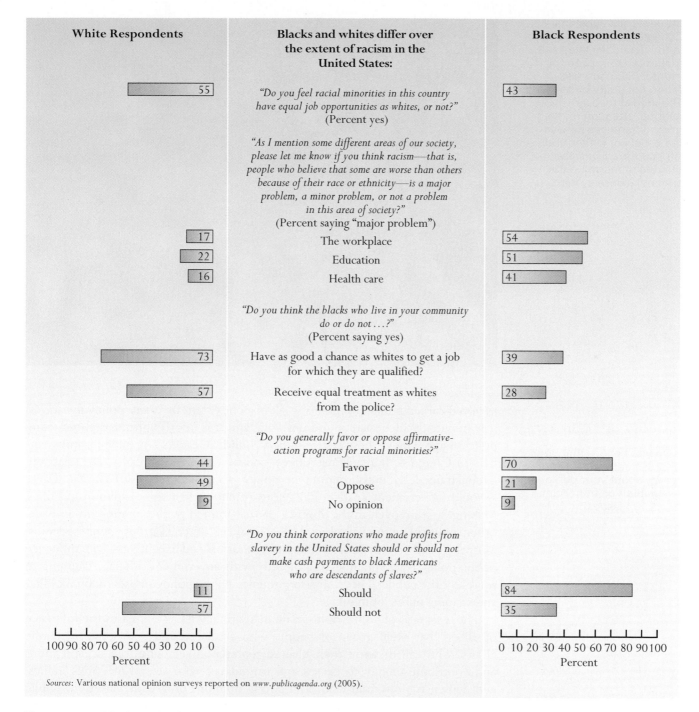

Figure 5.3   Black and White Opinions

African Americans are more likely than whites to support governmental actions and programs to improve the position of black people and other minorities. Levels of support for affirmative action depend on the wording of the question, but regardless of wording, blacks are more likely to support racial and minority preferences than whites.

Policy and Opinion

Does public opinion determine government policy? It is widely assumed that in a democracy, government policy will be heavily influenced by public opinion. Yet,

Students at Augustana College react to the verdict in the nationally televised trial of O.J. Simpson for murder. Simpson was found not guilty by the jury. The verdict focused national attention on the great differences between the beliefs of whites and African Americans about the role of racism in the criminal justice system.

as noted earlier, public opinion is weak or nonexistent on many policy questions; it is frequently inconsistent and unstable; and it is poorly informed about many policy issues. Under these circumstances, political leaders—presidents and members of Congress, bureaucrats, judges, and other public officials—are relatively unconstrained by mass opinion in policy decisions (see *What Do You Think?* "Should Government Leaders Pay More Attention to Public Opinion in Policy Making?"). Moreover, in the absence of well-formed public opinion on an issue, other political actors—lobbyists and lawyers, interest-group spokespersons, journalists and commentators, television reporters and executives—can influence public policy by communicating directly with government officials, claiming to represent the public. They can also influence public policy indirectly by molding and shaping public opinion.

The weakness of public opinion on many policy issues increases the influence of elites, that small group of people who are interested and active in public affairs, who call or write their elected representatives; who join organizations and contribute money to causes and candidates; who attend meetings, rallies, and demonstrations; and who hold strong opinions on a wide variety of public issues. According to political scientist V. O. Key Jr., the linkage between ordinary citizens and democratic government depends heavily on "that thin stratum of persons referred to variously as the political elite, the political activists, the leadership echelons, or the influentials."[14] Thus political *participation* appears to be the essential link between opinion and policy.

Individual Participation in Politics

Democracies provide a variety of ways for individuals to participate in politics. People may run for, and win, public office; take part in marches, demonstrations, and protests; make financial contributions to political candidates or causes; attend political meetings, speeches, and rallies; write letters to public officials or to newspapers; wear a political button or place a bumper sticker on their car; belong to organizations that support or oppose particular candidates or take

WHAT DO YOU THINK?

How Would You Decide These Current Policy Issues?

Salient issues change over time, as political leadership and mass media change the focus of their

attention. In other words, on many issues the degree of public attention is a function of political elites. In early 2005, the Pew Research Center for the People and the Press conducted a national poll on issues that were being talked about in the media. Some partial results follow.

Social Security private accounts	
Favor	46%
Oppose	44%
Increase in minimum wage from $5.15 per hour to $6.45 per hour	
Favor	86%
Oppose	12%
Government guaranteeing health insurance for all citizens	
Favor	65%
Oppose	30%
Limiting the amount patients can be awarded in medical malpractice lawsuits	
Favor	63%
Oppose	30%
Allowing immigrants to enter the United States legally and work here for a limited amount of time	
Favor	50%
Oppose	44%
Raising taxes in order to reduce deficits	
Favor	31%
Oppose	66%
Allowing gays and lesbians to marry legally	
Favor	32%
Oppose	61%
Displaying the Ten Commandments in government buildings	
Proper	74%
Improper	22%
With the next Supreme Court appointment, Bush should make the court . . .	
More liberal	24%
More conservative	28%
About the same as it is now	41%

Source: Pew Research Center, March 2005.

stands on public issues; attempt to influence friends while discussing candidates or issues; and vote in elections. Individuals may also participate in politics passively, by simply following political issues and campaigns in the media, acquiring knowledge, forming opinions about public affairs, and expressing their views to others. These forms of political participation can be ranked according to their order of frequency (see Figure 5.4). Only a little more than half of the voting-age population vote in presidential elections, and far fewer vote in congressional and state and local elections.

Securing the Right to Vote

Popular participation in government is part of the very definition of democracy. The long history of struggle to secure the right to vote—**suffrage**—reflects the democratizing of the American political system.

suffrage Legal right to vote.

WHAT DO YOU THINK?

Should Government Leaders Pay More Attention to Public Opinion in Policy Making?

Over 200 years ago, the British parliamentarian Edmund Burke told his constituents: "Your representative owes you, not his industry only, but his judgment, and he betrays you instead of serving you, if he sacrifices it to your opinion." Since then "Burkian representation" has come to mean using one's own judgment in governmental decision making and paying little or no attention to public opinion polls. Indeed, many politicians boast of their own courage and independence and their willingness to ignore opinion polls on major issues.

But the American people believe that the country would be much better off if politicians paid *more* attention to public opinion.

Q. If the leaders of the nation followed the views of the public more closely, do you think that the nation would be better off or worse off than it is today?

Better	81%
Worse	10%

Indeed, most Americans believe that members of Congress should "read up on the polls" in order to "get a sense of the public's views."

Q. Please tell me which statement you agree with most. (A) When members of Congress are thinking about how to vote on an issue, they should read up on the polls, because this can help them get a sense of the public's views on the issue. (B) When members of Congress are thinking about how to vote on an issue, they should not read the polls, because this will distract them from thinking about what is right.

Should read polls	67%
Should not read polls	26%

But fewer than one-third of the members of Congress believe that the American people know enough to form wise opinions on public issues. When Congress members themselves were questioned—"*Do you think the American public knows enough about the issues you face to form wise opinions about what should be done about these issues, or not?*"—the results (Yes—31 percent, No—47 percent, Maybe—17 percent) indicated that Congress members do not have a very high regard for the "wisdom of the people," no matter what they say in their political speeches.

Source: Center on Policy Alternatives, as reported in *The Polling Report,* February 15, 1999.

The Elimination of Property Qualifications, 1800–40   The Constitution of 1787 left it to the states to determine voter qualifications. The Founders generally believed that only men of property had a sufficient "stake in society" to exercise their vote in a "responsible" fashion. However, the Founders could not agree on the wording of property qualifications for insertion into the Constitution, so they left the issue to the states, feeling safe in the knowledge that at the time every state had property qualifications for voting. Yet over time, Jeffersonian and Jacksonian principles of democracy, including confidence in the judgment of ordinary citizens, spread rapidly in the new Republic. The states themselves eliminated most property qualifications by 1840. Thus before the Civil War (1861–65), the vote had been extended to virtually all *white males* over twenty-one years of age.

The Fifteenth Amendment, 1870   The first important limitation on state powers over voting came with the ratification of the Fifteenth Amendment: "The right of citizens of the United States to vote shall not be denied or abridged by the United States or by any state on account of race, color, or previous condition of servitude." The object of this amendment, passed by the Reconstruction Congress after the Civil War and ratified in 1870, was to extend the vote to former

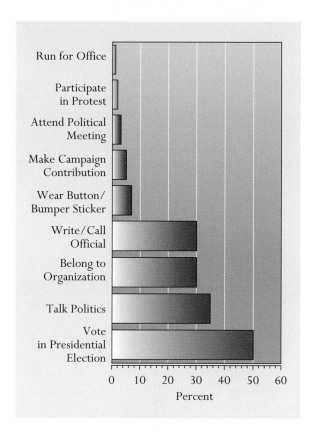

Figure 5.4 Political Participation

Only a small percentage of the American people are actively engaged in the political process, yet they receive most of the media attention. Less than 1 percent of the population runs for office at any level of government, and only about half of all voting-age Americans bother to go to the polls even in a presidential election.

Source: National Election Studies Cumulative File. See also M. Margaret Conway, *Political Participation in the United States,* 3rd ed. (Washington, D.C.: CQ Press, 2000).

black slaves and prohibit voter discrimination on the basis of race. The Fifteenth Amendment also gave Congress the power to enforce black voting rights "by appropriate legislation." The states retain their right to determine voter qualifications, *as long as they do not practice racial discrimination,* and Congress has the power to pass legislation ensuring black voting rights.

Continued Denial of Voting Rights, 1870–1964   For almost 100 years after the adoption of the Fifteenth Amendment, white politicians in the southern states were able to defeat its purposes. Social and economic pressures and threats of violence were used to intimidate many thousands of would-be black voters.

There were also many "legal" methods of disenfranchisement, including a technique known as the **white primary.** So strong was the Democratic Party throughout the South that the Democratic nomination for public office was tantamount to election. Thus *primary elections* to choose the Democratic nominee were the only elections in which real choices were made. If black people were prevented from voting in Democratic primaries, they could be effectively disenfranchised. Therefore, southern state legislatures resorted to the simple device of declaring the Democratic Party in southern states a private club and ruling that only white people could participate in its elections—that is, in primary elections. Blacks were free to vote in "official" general elections, but all whites tacitly agreed to support the Democratic, or "white man's," Party in general elections, regardless of their differences in the primary. Not until 1944, in *Smith v. Allwright,* did the Supreme Court declare the white primary unconstitutional and bring primary elections under the purview of the Fifteenth Amendment.[15]

Despite the Fifteenth Amendment, many local registrars in the South succeeded in barring black registration by an endless variety of obstacles, delays,

white primary Democratic Party primary elections in many southern counties in the early part of the twentieth century that excluded black people from voting.

and frustrations. Application forms for registration were lengthy and complicated; even a minor error, such as underlining rather than circling in the "Mr.—Mrs.—Miss" set of choices, as instructed, would lead to rejection. **Literacy tests** were the most common form of disenfranchisement. Many a black college graduate failed to interpret "properly" the complex legal documents that were part of the test. White applicants for voter registration were seldom asked to go through these lengthy procedures.

The Civil Rights Act, the Twenty-fourth Amendment, and the Voting Rights Act, 1964–65

The Civil Rights Act of 1964 made it unlawful for registrars to apply unequal standards in registration procedures or to reject applications because of immaterial errors. It required that literacy tests be in writing and made a sixth-grade education a presumption of literacy. In 1970 Congress outlawed literacy tests altogether.

The Twenty-fourth Amendment to the Constitution, ratified in 1964, made **poll taxes**—taxes required of all voters—unconstitutional as a requirement for voting in national elections. In 1966 the Supreme Court declared poll taxes unconstitutional in state and local elections as well.[16]

In early 1965 civil rights organizations led by Martin Luther King Jr., effectively demonstrated against local registrars in Selma, Alabama, who were still keeping large numbers of black people off the voting rolls. Registrars there closed their offices for all but a few hours every month, placed limits on the number of applications processed, went out to lunch when black applicants appeared, delayed months before processing black applications, and used a variety of other methods to keep blacks disenfranchised. In response to the Selma march, Congress enacted the strong Voting Rights Act in 1965. The U.S. attorney general, upon evidence of voter discrimination, was empowered to replace local registrars with federal registrars, abolish **literacy tests**, and register voters under simplified federal procedures. Southern counties that had previously discriminated in voting registration hurried to sign up black voters just to avoid the imposition of federal registrars. The Voting Rights Act of 1965 proved to be very effective, and Congress has voted to extend it over the years.

poll taxes Taxes imposed as a prerequisite to voting; prohibited by the Twenty-fourth Amendment.

literacy test Examination of a person's ability to read and write as a prerequisite to voter registration, outlawed by Voting Rights Act (1965) as discriminatory.

Passage of the Voting Rights Act of 1965 opened the voting booth to millions of black voters formerly kept from the polls by a variety of discriminatory regulations in the South. Here African Americans in rural Alabama in 1966 line up at a local store to cast their votes in a primary that focused on an issue central to their existence—segregation.

The turn of the century saw the acceleration of the women's suffrage movement. Although Woodrow Wilson expressed support for granting the vote to women even before he took office in 1912, it took the activities of women "manning the homefront" during World War I to persuade the male electorate to pass the Nineteenth Amendment and give women access to the ballot box throughout the nation.

The Nineteenth Amendment, 1920   Following the Civil War, many of the women who had been active in the abolitionist movement to end slavery turned their attention to the condition of women in the United States. As abolitionists, they had learned to organize, conduct petition campaigns, and parade and demonstrate. Now they sought to improve the legal and political rights of women. In 1869 the Wyoming territory adopted women's suffrage; later, several other western states followed suit. But it was not until the Nineteenth Amendment was added to the U.S. Constitution in 1920 that women's right to vote in all elections was constitutionally guaranteed.

The Twenty-sixth Amendment, 1971   The movement for eighteen-year-old voting received its original impetus during World War II. It was argued successfully in Georgia in 1944 that because eighteen-year-olds were being called upon to fight and die for their country, they deserved to have a voice in the conduct of government. However, this argument failed to convince adult voters in other states; qualifications for military service were not regarded as the same as qualifications for rational decision making in elections. In state after state, voters rejected state constitutional amendments designed to extend the vote to eighteen-year-olds.

Congress intervened on behalf of eighteen-year-old voting with the passage of the Twenty-sixth Amendment to the Constitution.[17] The states quickly ratified this amendment in 1971 during a period of national turbulence over the Vietnam War. Many supporters of the amendment believed that protests on the campuses and streets would be reduced if youthful protesters were given the vote.

The National Voter Registration Act, 1993   The National Voter Registration Act of 1993, popularly known as the "Motor Voter Act," mandates that the states offer people the opportunity to register to vote when they apply for driver's licenses or apply for welfare services. States must also offer registration by mail, and they must accept a simplified registration form prepared by the Federal Election Commission. Finally, it bars states from removing the names of people from registration lists for failure to vote. Did the "**Motor Voter Act**" work? Careful research indicates that it succeeded in increasing voter registration, but its

"Motor Voter Act" Federal mandate that states offer voter registration at driver's licensing and welfare offices.

effects on actual turnout at the polls were very limited.[18] Apparently, easy registration does not automatically increase voter turnout.

Why Vote?

Deciding whether to cast a vote in an election is just as important as deciding which candidate to vote for. *About half of the voting-age population in the United States typically fails to vote, even in presidential elections.* Voter **turnout**—the number of actual voters in relation to the number of people eligible to register and vote—is even lower in off-year congressional and state elections, when presidential elections are not held. Turnout in local elections (for example, city, county, school board) is even lower when these elections are held separately from national elections. Voter turnout in presidential elections steadily declined for several decades (see Figure 5.5). The three-way presidential race in 1992 temporarily reversed the downward trend. But in 2004 voter turnout surged to levels not seen since the 1960s. Various explanations have been offered: the expected closeness of the election, the experience of 2000 when only a few votes in Florida decided the outcome, the war in Iraq,

turnout Number of voters who actually cast ballots in an election, as a percentage of people eligible to register and vote.

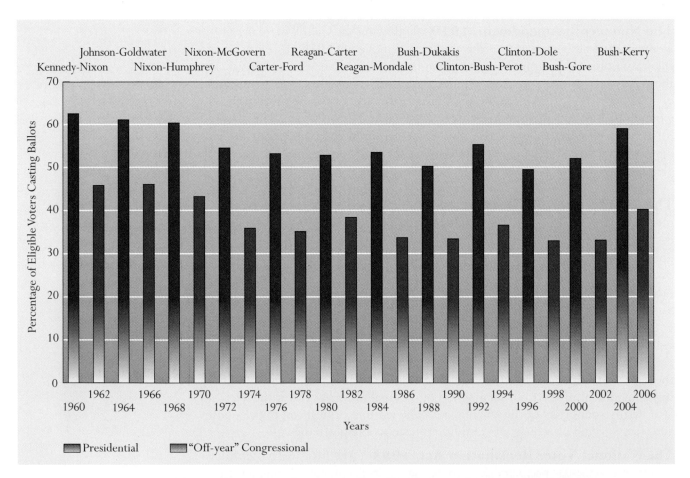

Figure 5.5   Voter Turnout in Presidential and Congressional Elections
Voter turnout is always higher in years with a presidential election. However, voter turnout has generally declined since 1960, even in presidential election years. The exception came in 1992, when intense interest in the contest between George H.W. Bush and Bill Clinton—spiced by the entry of independent Ross Perot—led to a higher-than-normal turnout. In 1996 fewer than half of voting-age Americans bothered to cast ballots. However, in 2004 voter turnout rose to levels not seen since the 1960s.

and an increasing concern with "moral values" that seemed to motivate devout churchgoers to go to the polls.

Why vote? Usually, this question is asked in the negative: Why do so many people fail to register and vote? But greater insight into the question of voter participation can be obtained if we try to understand what motivates the people who do go to the polls.

The Rational Voter From a purely "rational" perspective, an individual should vote only if the costs of voting (time spent in registering, informing oneself about the candidates, and going to the polls) are *less* than the expected value of having the preferred candidate win (the personal benefits gained from having one's candidate win), multiplied by the probability that one's own vote will be the deciding vote. Why vote when registering, following the political news, and getting to the polls take away time from work, family, or leisure activity? Why vote when the winner will not really change one's life for the better, or even do things much differently from what the loser would have done? Most important, why vote when the chance that one individual vote will determine who wins is very small? Thought of in this fashion, the wonder is that millions of Americans continue to vote.

The "rational" model can explain voter turnout only by adding "the intrinsic rewards of voting" to the equation. These rewards include the ethic of voting, patriotism, a sense of duty, and allegiance to democracy. People exercise their right to vote out of respect for that right rather than for any personal tangible benefit they expect to receive. They can look at the voting returns on television later in the evening, knowing they were part of an important national event. These psychological rewards do not depend on whether a single vote determines the outcome. Millions of people vote out of a sense of duty and commitment to democracy.

State of the Vote
Official Web site of the National Association of Secretaries of State (state voting officials) urging young people to register and vote.
www.stateofthevote.org

The Burden of Registration Voter **registration** remains an obstacle to voting, despite the easing of requirements for registration by many states. Not only must citizens care enough to go to the polls on election day; they must also expend time and energy, weeks before the election, to register. This may involve a trip to the county courthouse and a procedure more complicated than voting itself. Approximately 85 percent of *registered voters* turn out for a presidential election, but this figure represents only about 50 percent of the *voting-age population*. This discrepancy suggests that registration is a significant barrier to participation. (see *A Conflicting View*: "Easy Voting Encourages Fraud").

registration Requirement that prospective voters establish their identity and place of residence prior to an election in order to be eligible to vote.

Burdensome Ballots Deciding upon voting times, places, equipment, and ballots is the responsibility of state governments, most of which pass on this responsibility to their county governments. County elected or appointed "supervisors of elections" function throughout the nation preparing ballots and handling the streams of voters on election day. Nationwide, over 1 million "poll workers," usually volunteers from the local Democratic and Republican party organizations, assist in the voting process and later the counting of votes.

The contested 2000 presidential election spotlighted many of the flaws of ballots and vote counting throughout the nation. That election revealed the variety of voting methods used among the states and even within the same state.[19] Some states and counties use traditional paper or mark-sense ballots, others older lever machines and punch-card ballots, while still others are progressing toward electronic voting equipment. Paper and punch-card ballots regularly produce

A CONFLICTING VIEW

Easy Voting Encourages Fraud

Since the civil rights battles of the 1960s, the nation has been primarily concerned with expanding voter participation—to bring more people, especially minorities, into the political process. These efforts have led to an easing of the burdens of registration—registration by mail, mass registration drives, registration on the same day as voting, and so forth—as well as an easing of the burdens of voting itself—absentee voting, voting by mail, voting over an extended period, and so forth. Voting via the Internet is also being advocated in many jurisdictions. Yet there is no strong evidence to suggest that these innovations lead to higher voter turnouts. With the exception of the 2004 presidential election, voting turnouts have generally declined over time.

There are nearly 200,000 voting precincts in United States. Usually representatives of both the Democratic and Republican parties are present at each precinct to ensure the honesty of the vote. Voters who have previously registered show their voter cards or present other identification and then sign their names on the voter registration lists. This ensures that the voters are who they say they are, and that they do not vote more than once.

But registration by mail and absentee voting are rising over time. Voter registration cards are widely distributed, to be filled out by persons eligible to vote, and then collected and sent to the county election office. As the election nears, registered voters may request an absentee ballot, to be filled out and mailed to the county election office.

Increasingly, party operatives as well as independent "get-out-the-vote" organizations are going to nursing homes, assisted-living facilities, and other institutions housing the elderly, as well as large condominium projects, filling out registration forms for the residents as well as absentee ballot requests, and then "helping out" in marking the ballots, collecting them, and mailing them en masse to voting offices. It has been charged that some groups collecting registration forms and absentee ballots conveniently discard those that do not match the group's preferences.[a]

Few states have the resources, and many politicians lack the will, to investigate and prosecute voter fraud. Finding the right balance between promoting greater participation and maintaining the integrity of the electoral system is creating political conflict in many states and cities today.

[a]See Larry J. Sabato and Glenn R. Simpson, *Dirty Little Secrets: The Persistence of Corruption in American Politics* (New York: Random House, 1996).

Voter registration is designed to prevent fraud, but it also tends to discourage people from exercising their right to vote. Spanish language registration forms, where they are used, may ease the burden of registration for some.

"overvotes" (where voters mark or punch votes for more than one candidate for the same office) or "undervotes" (where voters fail to make a selection for a particular office), or otherwise spoil their ballot. These ballots are "uncounted"; nationwide, they usually amount to about 2 percent of all ballots cast. Many state laws are fuzzy regarding when and how to conduct "recounts"—requiring election officials to undertake a second or third counting of the ballots. Reformers generally recommend touch screen voting machines, carefully designed ballot layouts, better training of poll workers, uniform rules for recounts, and better voter education programs, including sample ballots distributed well before election day. Congress passed a Help America Vote Act in 2002 to provide federal grants to states to help replace punch cards and lever voting machines.

Center for Voting and Democracy
Reform organization devoted to expanding voter participation; Web site includes data on voter turnout nationally and by state. *www.fairvote.org*

The Politics of Voter Turnout

Politics drives the debate over easing voter registration requirements. Democrats generally favor minimal requirements—for example, same-day registration, registration by mail, and registration at welfare and motor vehicle licensing offices. They know that nonvoters are heavily drawn from groups that typically support the Democratic Party, including the less-educated, lower-income, and minority groups. Republicans are often less enthusiastic about easing voting requirements, but it is politically embarrassing to appear to oppose increased participation. It is not surprising that the Motor Voter Act of 1993 was a product of a Democratic Congress and a Democratic president, Bill Clinton.[20]

The Stimulus of Competition   The more lively the competition between parties or between candidates, the greater the interest of citizens and the larger the voter turnout. When parties and candidates compete vigorously, they make news and are given large play by the mass media. Consequently, a setting of competitive politics generates more political stimuli than does a setting with weak competition. People are also more likely to perceive that their votes count in a close contest, and thus they are more likely to cast them. Moreover, when parties or candidates are fighting in a close contest, their supporters tend to spend more time and energy campaigning and getting out the vote.

Political Alienation   People who feel politics is irrelevant to their lives—or who feel they cannot personally affect public affairs—are less likely to vote than people who feel they themselves can affect political outcomes and that these outcomes affect their lives. Given the level of **political alienation** (two-thirds of respondents agree with the statement, "Most public officials are not really interested in the problems of people like me"),[21] it is surprising that so many people vote. Alienation is high among voters, and it is even higher among nonvoters.

political alienation Belief that politics is irrelevant to one's life and that one cannot personally affect public affairs.

Intensity   Finally, as we might expect, people who feel strongly about politics and who hold strong opinions about political issues are more likely to vote than people who do not. For example, people who describe themselves as *extreme* liberals or *extreme* conservatives are more likely to vote than people who describe themselves as moderates.

Age and Turnout   Young people do not vote in the same proportions as older people (see Figure 5.6). After the electorate was expanded by the Twenty-sixth Amendment to include persons eighteen years of age and over, voter turnout actually dropped, from 60.9 percent in the 1968 presidential election to 55.2 percent in the 1972 presidential election, the largest turnout decline in successive presidential elections.

Figure 5.6 Voter Turnout by Social Groups

Although there is virtually no gender gap in who goes to the polls, voter turnout increases with education, age, and income. Major efforts to "get out the vote" in the African American community have raised voter turnout to nearly that of whites, but turnout among Hispanics continues to lag.

Source: U.S. Bureau of the Census, *Statistical Abstract of the United States,* 2006. Data for 2004 presidential election.

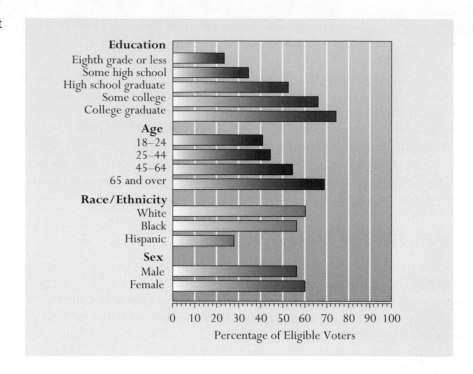

Party Organization   Strong party organizations can help increase turnout. But strong party organizations, or machines, that canvassed neighborhoods, took citizens to the courthouse to register them, contacted them personally during campaigns, and saw to it that they got to the polls on election day have largely disappeared (see Chapter 7).

Regardless of the explanations offered, it is interesting to note that most European democracies report higher voter turnout rates than the United States (see *Compared to What?* "Voter Turnout in Western Democracies").

Voters and Nonvoters

Who votes and who doesn't? The perceived benefits and costs of voting apparently do not fall evenly across all social groups. Nonvoting would generate less concern if voters were a representative cross section of nonvoters. But voters differ from nonvoters in politically important ways.

Voters are better educated than nonvoters. Education appears to be the most important determinant of voter turnout (see Figure 5.5). It may be that schooling promotes an interest in politics, instills the ethic of citizen participation, or gives people a better awareness of public affairs and an understanding of the role of elections in a democracy. Education is associated with a sense of confidence and political *efficacy*, the feeling that one can indeed have a personal impact on public affairs.

Age is another factor affecting voter participation. Perhaps because young people have more distractions, more demands on their time in school, work, or new family responsibilities, nonvoting is greatest among eighteen- to twenty-four-year-olds. In contrast, older Americans are politically influential in part because candidates know they turn out at the polls.

High-income people are more likely to vote than are low-income people. Most of this difference stems from the fact that high-income people are more likely to be well educated and older. But poor people may also feel alienated

COMPARED TO WHAT?

Voter Turnout in Western Democracies

Other Western democracies regularly report higher voter turnout rates than the United States (see figure). Yet in an apparent paradox, Americans seem to be more supportive of their political institutions, less alienated from their political system, and even more patriotic than citizens of Western European nations. Why, then, are voter turnouts in the United States so much lower than in these other democracies?

The answer to this question lies primarily in the legal and institutional differences between the United States and the other democracies. First of all, in Austria, Australia, Belgium, and Italy, voting is *mandatory*. Penalties and the level of enforcement vary within and across these countries. Moreover, registration laws in the United States make voting more difficult than in other countries. In Western Europe, all citizens are required to register with the government and obtain identification cards. These cards are then used for admission to the polls. In contrast, voter registration is entirely voluntary in the United States, and voters must reregister if they change residences. Nearly 50 percent of the U.S. population changes residence at least once in a five-year period, thus necessitating reregistration.

Parties in the United States are more loosely organized, less disciplined, and less able to mobilize voters than are European parties. Moreover, many elections in the United States, notably elections for Congress, are not very competitive. The United States organizes congressional elections by district with winner-take-all rules, whereas many European parliaments are selected by proportional representation, with seats allocated to parties based on national vote totals. Proportional representation means every vote counts toward seats in the legislative body. Thus greater competition and proportional representation may encourage higher voter turnout in European democracies.

But cultural differences may also contribute to differences in turnout. The American political culture, with its tradition of individualism and self-reliance and its reluctance to empower government (see Chapter 2), encourages Americans to resolve their problems through their own efforts rather than looking to government for solutions. Government is not as central to Americans as it is to Europeans, and therefore getting to the polls on election day is not seen as so important.

Average Turnout, 1991–2000

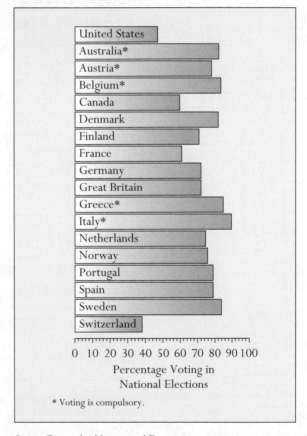

Source: Center for Voting and Democracy, 2002, *www.fairvote.org.* Reprinted by permission.

from the political system—they may lack a sense of political efficacy; they may feel they have little control over their own lives, let alone over public affairs. Or poor people may simply be so absorbed in the problems of life that they have little time or energy to spend on registering and voting.[22]

Income and education differences between participants and nonparticipants are even greater when other forms of political participation are considered. Higher-income, better-educated people are much more likely to be among those who make campaign contributions, who write or call their elected representatives, and who join and work in active political organizations.[23]

Historically, race was a major determinant of nonvoting. Black voter turnout, especially in the South, was markedly lower than white voter turnout. African Americans continue today to have a slightly lower overall voter turnout than whites, but most of the remaining difference is attributable to differences between blacks and whites in educational and income levels. Blacks and whites at the same educational and income levels register and vote with the same frequency. Indeed, in cities where African Americans are well organized politically, black voter turnout may exceed white voter turnout.[24]

The greatest disparity in voter turnout is between Hispanics and others. Low voter participation by Hispanics may be a product of language differences, lack of cultural assimilation, or noncitizenship status.

Nonvoting: What Difference Does It Make?

Think Again

Is our government really legitimate when only about half the people vote in presidential elections?

How concerned should we be about low levels of participation in American politics? Certainly the democratic ideal envisions an active, participating citizenry. Democratic government, asserts the Declaration of Independence, derives its "just powers from the consent of the governed." The legitimacy of democratic government can be more easily questioned when half of the people fail to vote. That is, it is easier to question whether the government truly represents "the people" when only half of the people vote even in a presidential election. Voting is an expression of good citizenship, and it reinforces attachment to the nation and to democratic government. Nonvoting suggests alienation from the political system.

However, the *right* to vote is more important to democratic government than voter turnout. The nineteenth-century English political philosopher John Stuart Mill wrote, "Men, as well as women, do not need political rights in order that they may govern, but in order that they may not be misgoverned."[25] As long as all adult Americans possess the right to vote, politicians must consider their interests. "Rulers and ruling classes are under a necessity of considering the interests of those who have the suffrage."[26] Democratic governments cannot really ignore the interests of anyone who can vote. People who have the right to vote, but who have voluntarily chosen not to exercise it in the past, can always change their minds, go to the polls, and "throw the rascals out."

Voluntary nonvoting is not the same as being denied the suffrage. Politicians can indeed ignore the interests of people denied the vote by restrictive laws or practices or by intimidation or force. But when people choose not to exercise their right to vote, they may be saying that they do not believe their interests are really affected by government. The late Senator Sam Ervin is widely quoted on the topic of nonvoters:

> I'm not going to shed any crocodile tears if people don't care enough to vote. I don't believe in making it easy for apathetic, lazy people. I'd be extremely happy if nobody in the United States voted except for the people who thought about the issues and made up their own minds and wanted to vote.[27]

Protest as Political Participation

Protests, marches, and demonstrations are important forms of political participation. Indeed, the First Amendment guarantees the right "peaceably to assemble, and to petition the government for a redress of grievances." A march to the steps

A CONSTITUTIONAL NOTE

Who Can Vote?

The Founders generally believed that only property-owning free white males, twenty-one or older, should be entitled to vote. But they failed to include these qualifications in the original Constitution of 1787. Instead, they left to the states to decide who should vote: "... the Electors in each State shall have the Qualifications requisite for Electors of the most numerous Branch of the State Legislature" (Article I, Section 2). Why leave it up to the states to decide the voter qualifications for national elections? In committee and in floor discussions the delegates could not agree on what kind of property should qualify a person to vote. Plantation owners argued for qualifications to be expressed in land acreage; bankers wanted them expressed in the size of one's bank account; shippers and businessmen, in the value of their inventories or ships; and so on. In

frustration, the delegates dropped the issue into the laps of the states secure in the knowledge that in 1787 all of the states had some form of property qualifications and no state permitted women, slaves, or persons under twenty-one to vote. But this opening in the Constitution began a long journey toward full voting rights in the United States. Jacksonian democracy swept the nation in the 1840s and property qualifications were dropped by the states themselves. Not until after the Civil War was the Constitution amended to prevent the states from denying the right to vote on account of race (Fifteenth Amendment, 1870). The long fight for women's suffrage finally resulted in a constitutional guarantee of women's right to vote (Nineteenth Amendment, 1920); poll taxes were constitutionally banned (Twenty-fourth Amendment, 1964); and eighteen-year-olds secured the constitutional right to vote (Twenty-sixth Amendment, 1971).

of Congress, a mass assembly of people on the Washington Mall with speakers, sign waving, and songs, and the presentation of petitions to government officials are all forms of participation protected by the First Amendment.

Protests   Protests are generally designed to call attention to an issue and to motivate others to apply pressure on public officials. In fact, protests are usually directed at the news media rather than at public officials themselves. If protesters could persuade public officials directly in the fashion of lobbyists and interest groups, they would not need to protest. Protests are intended to generate attention and support among previously uncommitted people—enough so the ultimate targets of the protest, public officials, will be pressured to act to redress grievances.

Coverage by the news media, especially television, is vital to the success of protest activity. The media not only carry the protesters' message to the mass public but also inform public officials about what is taking place. Protests provide the media with "good visuals"—pictorial dramatizations of political issues. The media welcome opportunities to present political issues in a confrontational fashion because confrontation helps capture larger audiences. Thus protesters and the media use each other to advance their separate goals.

Protests are most commonly employed by groups that have little influence in electoral politics. They were a key device of the civil rights movement at a time when many African Americans were barred from voting. In the absence of protest, the majority white population—and the public officials they elected—were at best unconcerned with the plight of black people in a segregated society. Protests, including a dramatic march on Washington in 1963 at which Martin Luther King Jr. delivered his inspirational "I Have a Dream" speech, called attention to the injustices of segregation and placed civil rights on the agenda of decision makers.

Protests can be effectively employed by groups that are relatively small in number but whose members feel very intensely about the issue. Often the protest

protests Public marches or demonstrations designed to call attention to an issue and motivate others to apply pressure on public officials.

www Protest Net
Radical organization provides calendar of protests against military actions, world trade, animal experiments, and so forth.
www.protest.net

UP CLOSE

How to Run for Office

Many rewards come with elected office—the opportunity to help shape public policy, public attention and name recognition, and many business, professional, and social contacts. But there are many drawbacks as well—the absence of privacy; a microscopic review of one's past; constant calls, meetings, interviews, and handshaking; and, perhaps most onerous of all, the continual need to solicit campaign funds.

Before You Run—Getting Involved

Get involved in various organizations in your community:

- Neighborhood associations.
- Chambers of commerce, business associations.
- Churches and synagogues (become an usher, if possible, for visibility).
- Political groups (Democratic or Republican clubs, League of Women Voters, and so on).
- Parent-Teacher Associations (PTAs).
- Service clubs (Rotary, Kiwanis, Civitan, Toastmasters).
- Recreation organizations (Little League, flag football, soccer leagues, running and walking clubs, for example, as participant, coach, or umpire).

Deciding to Run—Know What You're Doing

In deciding to run, and choosing the office for which you wish to run, you should become thoroughly familiar with the issues, duties, and responsibilities.

- Attend council or commission meetings, state legislative sessions, and/or committee hearings.
- Become familiar with current issues and officeholders, and obtain a copy of and read the budget.
- Learn the demographics of your district (racial, ethnic, and age composition; occupational mix; average income; neighborhood differences). If you do not fit the prevailing racial, ethnic, or age composition, think about moving to another district.
- Memorize a brief (preferably less than seven seconds) answer to the question, "Why are you running?"

Getting in the Race

Contact your county elections department to obtain the following:

- Qualifying forms and information.
- Campaign financing forms and regulations.

- District and street maps for your district.
- Recent election results in your district.
- Election-law book or pamphlet.
- Voter registration lists (usually sold as lists, or labels, or tapes).
- Contact your party's county chairperson for advice; convince the party's leaders that you can win. Ask for a list of their regular campaign contributors.

Raising Money

The easiest way to finance a campaign is to be rich enough to provide your own funds. Failing that, you must:

- Establish a campaign fund, according to the laws of your state.
- Find a treasurer/campaign-finance chairperson who knows many wealthy, politically involved people.
- Invite wealthy, politically involved people to small coffees, cocktail parties, dinners; give a brief campaign speech and then have your finance chairperson solicit contributions.
- Follow up fund-raising events and meetings with personal phone calls.
- Be prepared to continue fund-raising activities throughout your campaign; file accurate financial disclosure statements as required by state law.

Getting Organized

Professional campaign managers and management firms almost always outperform volunteers. If you cannot afford professional management, you must rely on yourself or trusted friends to perform the following:

- Draw up a budget based on reasonable expectations of campaign funding.
- Interview and select a professional campaign-management firm, or appoint a trusted campaign manager.
- Ask trusted friends from various clubs, activities, neighborhoods, churches, and so on, to meet and serve as a campaign committee. If your district is racially or ethnically diverse, make sure all groups are represented on your committee.
- Decide on a campaign theme; research issues important to your community; develop brief, well-articulated positions on these issues.
- Open a campaign headquarters with desks and telephones. Buy a cell phone; use call forwarding; stay in contact. Use your garage if you can't afford an office.

- Arrange to meet with newspaper editors, editorial boards, TV station executives, and political reporters. Be prepared for tough questions.
- Hire a media consultant or advertising agency, or appoint a volunteer media director who knows television, radio, and newspaper advertising.
- Arrange a press conference to announce your candidacy. Notify all media well in advance. Arrange for overflow crowd of supporters to cheer and applaud.
- Produce eyecatching, inspirational 15- or 30-second television and radio ads that present a favorable image of you and stress your campaign theme.
- Prepare and print attractive campaign brochures, signs, and bumper stickers.
- Hire a local survey-research firm to conduct telephone surveys of voters in your district, asking what they think are the most important issues, how they stand on them, whether they recognize your name and your theme, and how they plan to vote. Be prepared to change your theme and your position on issues if surveys show strong opposition to your views.

On the Campaign Trail

Campaigns themselves may be primarily media centered or primarily *door-to-door* ("retail") or some combination of both.

- Buy media time as early as possible from television and radio stations; insist on prime-time slots before, during, and after popular shows.
- Buy newspaper ads; insist on their placement in popular, well-read sections of the paper.
- Attend every community gathering possible, just to be seen, even if you do not give a speech. Keep all speeches short. Focus on one or two issues that your polls show are important to voters.
- Recruit paid or unpaid volunteers to hand out literature door-to-door. Record names and addresses of voters who say they support you.
- Canvass door-to-door with a brief (seven-second) self-introduction and statement of your reasons for running. Use registration lists to identify members of your own party, and try to address them by name. Also canvass offices, factories, coffee shops, shopping malls—anywhere you find a crowd.
- Organize a phone bank, either professional or volunteer. Prepare *brief* introduction and phone statements. Record names of people who say they support you.

- Know your opponent: Research his or her past affiliations, indiscretions if any, previous voting record, and public positions on issues.
- Be prepared to "define" your opponent in negative terms. Negative advertising works. But be fair: Base your comments on your opponent's public record. Emphasize his or her positions that clearly deviate from your district voters' known preferences.

Primary versus General Elections

Remember that you will usually have to campaign in two elections—your party's primary and the general election.

- Before the primary, identify potential opposition in your own party, try to dissuade them from running.
- Allocate your budget first to win the primary election. If you lose the primary, you won't need any funds for the general election.
- In general elections, you must broaden your appeal without distancing your own party supporters. Deemphasize your party affiliation unless your district regularly elects members of your party; in a close district or a district that regularly votes for the opposition party, stress your independence and your commitment to the *district's* interests.

On Election Day

Turning out your voters is the key to success. Election day is the busiest day of the campaign for you and your staff.

- Use your phone bank to place as many calls as possible to party members in your district (especially those who have indicated in previous calls and visits that they support you). Remind them to vote; make sure your phone workers can tell each voter where to go to cast his or her vote.
- Solicit volunteers to drive people to the polls.
- Assign workers to as many polling places as possible. Most state laws require that they stay a specified distance from the voting booths. But they should be in evidence with your signs and literature to buttonhole voters before they go into the booths.
- Show up at city or county election office on election night with prepared victory statement thanking supporters and pledging your service to the district. (Also draft a courteous concession statement pledging your support to the winner, in case you lose.)
- Attend victory party with your supporters; meet many "new" friends.

is a means by which these groups can obtain bargaining power with decision makers. Protests may threaten to tarnish the reputations of government officials or private corporations, or may threaten to disrupt their daily activities or reduce their business through boycotts or pressure on customers. If the protest is successful, protest leaders can then offer to end the protest in exchange for concessions from their targets.

civil disobedience Form of public protest involving the breaking of laws believed to be unjust.

Civil Disobedience   Civil disobedience is a form of protest that involves breaking what are perceived as "unjust" laws. The purpose is to call attention to the existence of injustice. In the words of Martin Luther King Jr., civil disobedience "seeks so to dramatize the issue that it can no longer be ignored"[28] (see *A Conflicting View:* "Sometimes It's Right to Disobey the Law" in Chapter 1). Those truly engaging in civil disobedience do not attempt to evade punishment for breaking the law but instead willingly accept the penalty. By doing so, they demonstrate not only their sincerity and commitment but also the injustice of the law. Cruelty or violence directed at the protesters by police or others contributes further to the drama of injustice. Like other protest activity, the success of civil disobedience depends on the willingness of the mass media to carry the message to both the general public and the political leadership.

Violence   Violence can also be a form of political participation. Indeed, political violence—for example, assassinations, rioting, burning, looting—has been uncomfortably frequent in American politics over the years. It is important to distinguish violence from protest. Peaceful protest is constitutionally protected. Often, organized protest activity harnesses frustrations and hostilities, directs them into constitutionally acceptable activities, and thus avoids violence. Likewise, civil disobedience should be distinguished from violence. Civil disobedience breaks only "unjust" laws, without violence, and willingly accepts punishment without trying to escape.

Cruelty or violence directed at peaceful protesters further dramatizes their cause. In Jackson, Mississippi, in 1963, segregationists poured mustard, ketchup, and sugar over lunch counter sit-in protesters. But far more serious violence, including murder, was perpetrated against civil rights protesters in the 1960s.

Effectiveness   How effective are protests? Protests can be effective in achieving some goals under some conditions. But protests are useless or even counterproductive in pursuit of other goals under other conditions. Here are some generalizations about the effectiveness of protests:

- Protests are more likely to be effective when directed at specific problems or laws rather than at general conditions that cannot readily be remedied by governmental action.

- Protests are more likely to be effective when targeted toward public officials who are capable of granting the desired concession or resolving the specific problem. Protests with no specific targets and protests directed at officials who have no power to change things are generally unproductive.

- Protests are more likely to succeed when the goal is limited to gaining access or representation in decision making or to placing an issue on the agenda of decision makers.

- Protests are not always effective in actually getting laws changed and are even less effective in ensuring that the impact of the changes will really improve the conditions that led to the protest.

Public officials can defuse protest activity in a variety of ways. They may greet protesters with smiles and reassurances that they agree with their goals. They may dispense symbolic satisfaction without any tangible results. They may grant token concessions with great publicity, perhaps remedying a specific case of injustice while doing little to affect general conditions. Or public officials may claim to be constrained either legally or financially from doing anything—the "I-would-like-to-help-you-but-I-can't" strategy. Or public officials can directly confront the protesters by charging that they are unrepresentative of the groups they are trying to help.

Perhaps the most challenging and sometimes most effective kind of "protest" is to run for public office (see *Up Close:* "How to Run for Office" on pages 162–163). Whether at the local level, such as the school board, or at the state or national level, the participation of one individual as a candidate—even when not elected—can make a difference in public affairs.

Summary Notes

- Public opinion commands the attention of elected public officials in a democracy, yet many Americans are poorly informed and unconcerned about politics; their opinions on public issues are often changeable and inconsistent. Only a few highly salient issues generate strong and stable opinions.

- Political socialization—the learning of political values, beliefs, and opinions—starts at an early age. It is influenced by family, school, church, age group, and the media.

- Ideology also shapes opinion, especially among politically interested and active people who employ fairly consistent liberal or conservative ideas in forming their opinions on specific issues.

- Race and gender also influence public opinion. Blacks and whites differ over the extent of discrimination in the United States, as well as over its causes and remedies. Men and women tend to differ over issues involving the use of force. In recent years, women have tended to give greater support to the Democratic Party than men have.

- Individuals can exercise power in a democratic political system in a variety of ways. They can run for public office, take part in demonstrations and protests, make financial contributions to candidates, attend political events, write letters to newspapers or public officials, belong to political organizations, vote in elections, or simply hold and express opinions on public issues.

■ Securing the right to vote for all Americans required nearly 200 years of political struggle. Key victories included the elimination of property qualifications by 1840, the Fifteenth Amendment in 1870 (eliminating restrictions based on race), the Nineteenth Amendment in 1920 (eliminating restrictions based on gender), the Civil Rights Act of 1964 and Voting Rights Act of 1965 (eliminating racial obstacles), the Twenty-fourth Amendment in 1964 (eliminating poll taxes), and the Twenty-sixth Amendment in 1971 (extending the right to vote to eighteen-year-olds).

■ About half of the voting-age population fails to vote even in presidential elections. Voter turnout has steadily declined in recent decades. Voter registration is a major obstacle to voting. Turnout is affected by competition as well as by feelings of political alienation and distrust of government. Young people have the poorest record of voter turnout of any age group.

■ Voluntary nonvoting is not as serious a threat to democracy as denial of the right to vote. Nevertheless, the class bias in voting may tilt the political system toward the interests of higher-income, better-educated, older whites at the expense of lower-income, less-educated, younger minorities.

■ Protest is an important form of participation in politics. Protests are more commonly employed by groups with little direct influence over public officials. The object is to generate attention and support from previously uncommitted people in order to bring new pressure on public officials to redress grievances. Media coverage is vital to the success of protests.

Key Terms

public opinion 136	generation gap 141	literacy tests 152	protests 161
survey research 136	gender gap 145	"Motor Voter Act" 153	civil disobedience 164
halo effect 137	suffrage 149	turnout 154	
salient issues 139	white primary 151	registration 155	
socialization 140	poll taxes 152	political alienation 157	

Suggested Readings

Asher, Herbert. *Polling and the Public: What Every Citizen Should Know.* 6th ed. Washington, D.C.: CQ Press, 2005. Explains methods of polling and how results can be influenced by wording, sampling, and interviewing techniques; also covers how polls are used by the media and in campaigns.

Conway, M. Margaret, Gertrude A. Stevernagel, and David Ahern. *Women and Political Participation.* 2nd ed. Washington, D.C.: CQ Press, 2004. An examination of cultural change and women's participation in politics, including treatment of the gender gap in political attitudes and the impact of women's membership in the political elite.

Drexler, Kateri M., and Gwen Garcelon. *Strategies for Active Citizenship.* Upper Saddle River, N.J.: Prentice Hall, 2005. A handbook for becoming active in politics.

Erikson, Robert S., and Kent L. Tedin. *American Public Opinion,* 6th ed. Longman, 2002. A comprehensive review of the forces influencing public opinion and an assessment of the influence of public opinion in American politics.

Greenstein, Fred I. *Children and Politics.* New Haven, Conn.: Yale University Press, 1985. Early research on what children know about politics and how they learned it.

Page, Benjamin I., and Robert Y. Shapiro. *The Rational Public.* Chicago: University of Chicago Press, 1992. An examination of fifty years of public opinion polls convinces these authors that American government is generally responsive to the views of the majority.

Stimson, James A. *Public Opinion in America: Moods, Cycles, and Swings.* 2nd ed. Boulder, Colo.: Westview Press, 1998. A systematic analysis of swings and cycles in "policy moods" that roughly correspond to liberal and conservative views concerning the effectiveness of government in dealing with perceived problems.

Wald, Kenneth D. *Religion and Politics in the United States.* 4th ed. Rowman & Littlefield, 2003. An explanation of the impact of religion on American political culture, the policy process, and voting behavior.

Walton, Hanes, and Robert C. Smith. *African American Politics and the African American Quest for Universal Freedom.* New York: Pearson Longman, 2002. A comprehensive American government textbook emphasizing the diversity of African American opinions and behavior.

Zaller, John R. *The Nature and Origins of Mass Opinion.* New York: Cambridge University Press, 1992. An effort to develop and test a conceptual model of how people form political preferences, how political views and arguments diffuse through the population, and how people evaluate this information and convert their reactions into public opinion.

★ Make It Real

PUBLIC OPINION, PARTICIPATION AND VOTING

Students look at the 2000 presidential election and how the outcome was affected by using congressional districts to allocate presidential electors.

6 MASS MEDIA
Setting the Political Agenda

Chapter Outline

- The Power of the Media
- Sources of Media Power
- The Business of the Media
- The Politics of the News
- Polarization of the Media
- Mediated Elections
- Freedom versus Fairness
- Libel and Slander
- Politics and the Internet
- Media Effects: Shaping Political Life

The Power of the Media

Politics—the struggle over who gets what, when, and how—is largely carried out in the **mass media**. The arenas of political conflict are the various media of mass communication—television, newspapers, magazines, radio, books, recordings, motion pictures, and the Internet. What we know about politics comes to us largely through these media. Unless we ourselves are admitted to the White House Oval Office or the committee rooms of Congress or dinner parties at foreign embassies, or unless we ourselves attend political rallies and demonstrations or travel to distant battlefields, we must rely on the mass media to tell us about politics. Furthermore, few of us ever have the opportunity to personally evaluate the character of presidential candidates or cabinet members or members of Congress, or to learn their views on public issues by talking with them face to face. Instead, we must learn about people as well as events from the mass media.

Great power derives from the control of information. *Who knows what* helps to determine *who gets what.* The media not only provide an arena for politics; they are also themselves players in that arena. The media not only report on the struggles for power in society; they are also themselves participants in those struggles. The media have long been referred to as America's "fourth branch" of government—and for good reason.[1]

The Power of Television Television is the most powerful medium of communication. It is the first true *mass* communication medium. Virtually every home in the United States has a television set, and the average home has the set turned on for about seven hours a day. Television is regularly chosen over other news media by Americans as the most common news source.

Americans turn to *local* TV news broadcasts as their most regular source of news. Daily newspapers are read by less than half of the adult public (see Figure 6.1). The national network evening news shows (*NBC Nightly News, ABC World News Tonight, CBS Evening News*) have lost viewership in recent years. But viewership of CNN, Fox News Cable, CNBC, and MSNBC is rising. Television weekly news magazines, notably CBS's *60 Minutes* and ABC's *20/20* have also become major sources of news for many Americans.

Figure 6.1 Where Americans Get Their News

Note: More than one answer accepted in survey, so the sum adds up to well over 100%.

Source: Adapted from the Pew Research Center for the People and the Press, "Public News Habits," June 2, 2005. *http://www.people-press.org.*

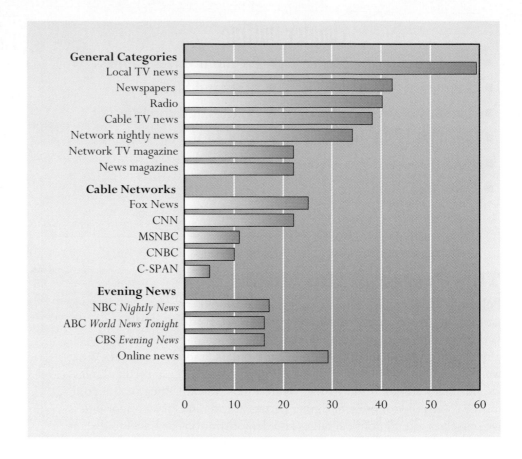

mass media All means of communication with the general public, including television, newspapers, magazines, radio, books, recordings, motion pictures, and the Internet.

A growing number of Americans, especially young people, are turning to online news sources (see *Up Close:* "The Generation Gap in News").

During a national crisis—for example, the terrorist attack of 9/11—Americans become even more dependent on television for their news. When asked "Where would you go first," for information during a crisis, 66 percent of Americans said they would turn on their TV sets. CNN was mentioned most often.[2]

Believability Television is also rated by Americans as the most *believable* medium of communication. Compared to television news, print sources are generally seen as less believable, with one exception, the *Wall Street Journal.* CNN is rated highest among all news sources (see Figure 6.2). Not many people rate the tabloids as very believable.

Newspapers and Magazines Less than one-half of the adult population reads one or another of the nation's 1,500 daily newspapers. But the nation's prestige newspapers—the *New York Times, Washington Post,* and *Wall Street Journal*—are regularly read by government officials, corporate chiefs, interest-group leaders, and other media people. Stories appearing in these newspapers are generally picked up by daily papers around the country, and these stories almost always appear on national network television.

The leading weekly newsmagazines—*Time, Newsweek,* and *U.S. News & World Report*—reach a smaller but more politically attentive audience than do newspapers. Magazines of political commentary—for example, the *Nation* (liberal), *New Republic* (liberal), *National Review* (conservative), *American Spectator* (conservative), *Weekly Standard* (conservative), *Public Interest* (neo-conservative), and *Washington Monthly* (neo-liberal)—reach very small but politically active audiences.

UP CLOSE

The Generation Gap in News

Young people are far less likely to spend time watching the news than older people. Indeed, people 65 and older are nearly twice as likely as those under 30 to watch television news. And older people are more than twice as likely to read a newspaper.

However, young people are more likely than older people to hear radio news, perhaps because radio news periodically interrupts music programming. And young people are the principal consumers of online news. Yet overall, young people are exposed to far less news than seniors.

The News Generation Gap

	18–29	30–49	50–64	65+
Watch TV news	40%	52%	62%	73%
Local TV	28	41	49	52
Network evening news	17	25	38	46
Cable TV news	16	23	30	35
Morning TV news	11	16	21	27
Read newspaper	26	37	52	59
Listen to radio news	34	49	42	29
News magazines	12	13	15	13
Online news	31	30	24	7
No news (yesterday)	33	19	15	12

Source: Pew Research Center for the People and the Press. *http://www.people-press.org.* Reprinted by permission of Pew Research Center for the People and the Press.

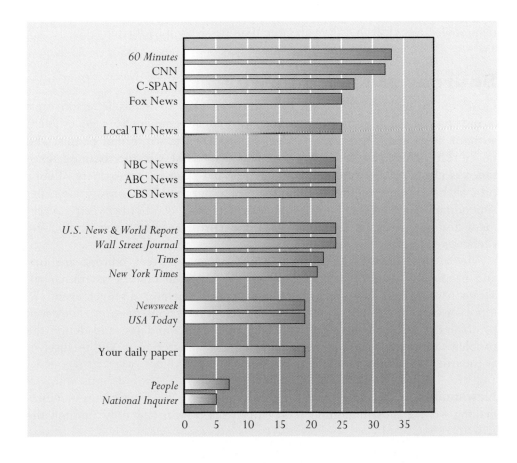

Figure 6.2   Believability of the Media

Source: Data from Pew Research Center for the People and the Press, *http://people-press.org* June 2, 2005.

Network Television
All major networks now maintain news sites on the Web.
www.cbsnews.com
www.abcnews.com
www.cnn.com
www.msnbc.com
www.foxnews.com

Television's Emotional Communication   The power of television derives not only from its large audiences, but also from its ability to communicate emotions as well as information. Television's power is found in its visuals—angry faces in a rioting mob, police beating an African American motorist, wounded soldiers being unloaded from a helicopter—scenes that convey an emotional message. Gripping pictures can inflame public opinion, inspire a clamor for action, and even pressure the government into hasty action. (This "CNN effect"—pictures of starving children and brutal fighting—has been cited as a cause of the disastrous American intervention in Somalia in 1992.)

Moreover, television focuses on the faces of individuals as well as on their words, portraying honesty or deception, humility or arrogance, compassion or indifference, humor or meanness, and a host of other personal characteristics. Skillful politicians understand that *what* one says may not be as importants as *how* one says it. Image triumphs over substance on television.[3]

Influence on Decision Makers   The media's impact on political decision makers is vastly more significant than their impact on ordinary viewers. Media stories often relate more directly to the immediate concerns of politicians and government officials. They are more attentive to these stories; they are often asked to respond or comment upon news stories. They correctly perceive that media coverage of particular events and issues sets the agenda for public discussion. Even media stories that have relatively little widespread public interest can create a buzz "inside the Beltway," that is, within Washington circles.

Pew Research Center for People and the Press
Information, including opinion polls, on the media.
http://www.people-press.org

The Myth of the Mirror   Media people themselves often deny that they exercise great power. They sometimes claim that they only "mirror" reality. They like to think of themselves as unbiased reporters who simply narrate happenings and transmit videotaped portrayals of people and events as they really are. But whether or not the editors, reporters, producers, or anchors acknowledge their own power, it is clear that they do more than passively mirror reality.

Sources of Media Power

Government and the media are natural adversaries. (Thomas Jefferson once wrote that he would prefer newspapers without government to a government without newspapers. But after serving as president, he wrote that people who never read newspapers are better informed than those who do, because ignorance is closer to the truth than the falsehoods spread by newspapers.) Public officials have long been frustrated by the media. But the U.S. Constitution's First Amendment guarantee of a free press anticipates this conflict between government and the media. It prohibits government from resolving this conflict by silencing its critics.

> **Think Again**
> Do the media mirror what is really news, rather than deciding themselves what's important and then making it news?

Media professionals—television and newspaper reporters, editors, anchors, and producers—are not neutral observers of American politics but rather are active participants. They not only report events but· also discover events to report, assign them political meaning, and predict their consequences. They seek to challenge government officials, debate political candidates, and define the problems of society. They see their profession as a "sacred trust" and themselves as the true voice of the people in public affairs.

newsmaking Deciding what events, topics, presentations, and issues will be given coverage in the news.

Newsmaking   Deciding what is "news" and who is "newsworthy"—**newsmaking**—is the most important source of media power. It is only through the

Politicians have a "love-hate" relationship with the media. Democratic presidential candidate John Kerry complains here to reporters that thousands of voters were wrongly prevented from voting in the 2004 presidential election.

media that the general public comes to know about events, personalities, and issues. Media attention makes topics public, creates issues, and elevates personalities from obscurity to celebrity. Each day, editors, producers, and reporters must select from millions of events, topics, and people those that will be videotaped, written about, and talked about. The media can never be a "picture of the world" because the whole world cannot be squeezed into the picture. The media must decide what is and is not "news."

Politicians have a love-hate relationship with the media. They need media attention to promote themselves, their message, and their programs. They crave the exposure, the name recognition, and the celebrity status that the media can confer. At the same time, they fear attack by the media. They know the media are active players in the political game, not just passive spectators. The media seek sensational stories of sin, sexuality, corruption, and scandal in government to attract viewers and readers, and thus the media pose a constant danger to politicians. Politicians understand the power of the media to make or break their careers.

Agenda Setting   Agenda setting is the power to decide what will be decided. It is the power to define society's "problems," to create political issues, and to set forth alternative solutions. Deciding which issues will be addressed by government may be even more important than deciding how the issues will be resolved. The distinguished political scientist E. E. Schattschneider once wrote, "He who determines what politics is about runs the country."[4]

The real power of the media lies in their ability to set the political agenda for the nation. This power grows out of their ability to decide what is news. Media coverage determines what both citizens and public officials regard as "crises" or "problems" or "issues" to be resolved. Conditions ignored by the media seldom get on the agenda of political leaders. Media attention forces public officials to speak on the topic, take positions, and respond to questions. Media inattention allows problems to be ignored by government. "TV is the Great Legitimator. TV confers reality. Nothing happens in America, practically everyone seems to agree, until it happens on television."[5]

 Newspaper Web Sites
Virtually all major daily newspapers have Web sites that summarize each day's stories. For national news the most frequently consulted sites are *USA Today, Wall Street Journal, New York Times, Washington Post.*
www.usatoday.com
www.nytimes.com
www.washingtonpost.com
www.wallstreetjournal.com

agenda setting Deciding what will be decided, defining the problems and issues to be addressed by decision makers.

Groups hoping for free media coverage of their cause can improve their chances by framing their protests in dramatic form. Here, members of an animal-rights group attract the press by getting arrested during a protest against the fur industry, in which they painted themselves with red paint and wore leghold traps.

Political issues do not just "happen." The media are crucial to their development. Organized interest groups, professional public relations firms, government bureaucracies, political candidates, and elected officials all try to solicit the assistance of the media in shaping the political agenda. Creating an issue, publicizing it, dramatizing it, turning it into a "crisis," getting people to talk about it, and ultimately forcing government to do something about it are the tactics of agenda setting. The participation of the mass media is vital to their success.[6]

Interpreting   The media not only decide what will be news; they also interpret the news for us. Editors, reporters, and anchors provide each story with an *angle*, an interpretation that places the story in a context and speculates about its meaning and consequences. The interpretation tells us what to think about the news.

News is presented in "stories." Reporters do not report facts; they tell stories. The story structure gives meaning to various pieces of information. Some common angles or themes of news stories are these:

- *Good guys versus bad guys:* for example, corrupt officials, foreign dictators, corporate polluters, and other assorted villains versus honest citizens, exploited workers, endangered children, or other innocents.

- *Little guys versus big guys:* for example, big corporations, the military, or insensitive bureaucracies versus consumers, taxpayers, poor people, or the elderly.

- *Appearance versus reality:* for example, the public statements of government officials or corporate executives versus whatever contradicting facts hardworking investigative reporters can find.

News is also "pictures." A story without visuals is not likely to be selected as television news in the first place. The use of visuals reinforces the angle. A close-up shot can reveal hostility, insincerity, or anxiety on the face of villains or can show fear, concern, sincerity, or compassion on the face of innocents. To emphasize elements of a story, an editor can stop the action, use slow motion, zoom the lens, add graphics, cut back and forth between antagonists, cut away for audience reaction, and so on. Videotaped interviews can be spliced to make the interviewees appear knowledgeable, informed, and sincere or, alternatively, ignorant, insensitive, and mean-spirited. The media jealously guard the right to edit interviews themselves, rejecting virtually all attempts by interviewees to review and edit their own interviews.

Socializing   The media have power to socialize audiences to the political culture. News, entertainment, and advertising all contribute to **socialization**—to the learning of political values. Socialization through television and motion pictures begins in early childhood and continues throughout life. Most of the political information people learn comes to them through television—specific facts as well as general values. Election coverage, for example, shows "how democracy works," encourages political participation, and legitimizes the winner's control of government. Advertising shows Americans desirable middle-class standards of living even while it encourages people to buy automobiles, detergent, and beer, and entertainment programming socializes them to "acceptable" ways of life. Political values such as racial tolerance, sexual equality, and support for law enforcement are reinforced in movies, situation comedies, and police shows.

socialization The learning of a culture and its values.

Persuading   The media, in both paid advertising and news and entertainment programming, engage in direct efforts to change our attitudes, opinions, and behavior. Newspaper editorials have traditionally been employed for direct persuasion. A great deal of the political commentary on television news and interview programs is aimed at persuading people to adopt the views of the commentators. Even many entertainment programs and movies are intended to promote specific political viewpoints. But most direct persuasion efforts come to us through paid advertising.

Center for Media and Public Affairs
Studies of news and entertainment media, including election coverage. *www.cmpa.com*

Political campaigning is now largely a media battle, with paid political advertisements as the weapons. Candidates rely on professional campaign-management firms, with their pollsters, public relations specialists, advertising-production people, and media consultants, to carry on the fight (see Chapter 8).

Governments and political leaders must rely on persuasion through the mass media to carry out their programs. Presidents can take their message directly to people in televised speeches, news conferences, and the yearly State of the Union message. Presidents by custom are accorded television time whenever they request it. In this way, they can go over the heads of Congress and even the media executives and reporters themselves to communicate directly with the people.

In short, persuasion is central to politics, and the media are the key to persuasion.

The Business of the Media

The business of the media is to gather mass audiences to sell to advertisers. Economic interest drives all media to try to attract and hold the largest numbers of readers and viewers in order to sell time and space to advertisers. Over one-quarter of all prime-time television (8–11 P.M.) is devoted to commercial advertising. Americans get more than one minute of commercials for every three minutes of news and entertainment. Television networks and commercial stations charge advertisers on the basis of audience estimates made by rating services. One rating service, A. C. Nielsen, places electronic boxes in a national sample of television homes and calculates the proportion of these homes that watch a program (the rating), as well as the proportion of homes with their television sets turned on that watch a particular program (the share). Newspapers' and magazines' advertising revenue is based primarily on circulation figures (see Table 6.1).

National Association of Broadcasters
News and views of the media industry from their trade association. *www.nab.org*

Table 6.1   The Largest Circulation U.S. Newspapers and Magazines

Daily Newspapers			Magazines		
Rank	Newspaper	Circulation	Rank	Magazine	Circulation
1. *USA Today* (Arlington, Va.)		2,199,052	1. *AARP The Magazine*		22,668,583
2. *Wall Street Journal* (New York, N.Y.)		1,888,621	2. *Reader's Digest*		10,155,054
3. *The New York Times* (New York, N.Y.)		1,121,623	3. *TV Guide*		9,015,866
4. *The Los Angeles Times* (Los Angeles)		907,997	4. *Better Homes and Gardens*		7,627,256
5. *The Washington Post* (Washington, D.C.)		740,947	5. *National Geographic*		6,471,803
6. *Daily News* (New York, N.Y.)		708,713	6. *Good Housekeeping*		4,631,527
7. *New York Post* (New York, N.Y.)		652,149	7. *Family Circle*		4,252,730
8. *Chicago Tribune* (Chicago)		663,996	8. *Woman's Day*		4,130,507
9. *Houston Chronicle* (Houston)		477,493	9. *Ladies' Home Journal*		4,114,353
10. *Dallas Morning News* (Dallas)		527,744	10. *TIME*		4,034,272

Source: Editor and Publisher International Yearbook 2005. Copyright © 2005–6 VNU Business Media, Inc. Used with permission.

Soft Fluff versus Hard Programming   Lightweight entertainment—"soft fluff"—prevails over serious programming in virtually all media, but particularly on television. Critics of the "boob tube" abound in intellectual circles, but the mass public clearly prefers fluffy entertainment programming. Political scientist Doris Graber writes:

> Although "lightweight" programming draws the wrath of many people, particularly intellectual elites, one can argue that their disdain constitutes intellectual snobbery. Who is to say that the mass public's tastes are inferior to those of elites? . . . Proof is plentiful that the mass public does indeed prefer light entertainment to more serious programs.[7]

And it is the mass public that advertisers want to reach. Channels devoted to highbrow culture, including public television stations, languish with low ratings.

News as TV Entertainment   Increasingly news is being presented as television entertainment. In recent years there has been a dramatic increase in the number of entertainment-oriented, quasi-news programming, sometimes referred to as the "soft news media."[8] Soft news comes mainly in two formats: talk shows, both daytime and nighttime; and tabloid news programs (see Table 6.2). Even

Table 6.2   TV Soft News Programming

Network news magazines	Network TV soft news
Dateline NBC	*Extra*
20/20	*Entertainment Tonight*
Primetime Live	*Inside Edition*
48 Hours	*A Current Affair*
60 Minutes	*Access Hollywood*
Late-night TV talk shows	**Cable TV soft news**
Jay Leno	E! Network
David Letterman	Black Entertainment Television
Conan O'Brien	Comedy Central's *Daily Show*
Politically Incorrect	MTV News
Daytime TV talk shows	
Oprah Winfrey	
Regis and Kelly	

The media are biased in favor of bad news over good. Wars, disasters, scandals, crimes are all well reported. Good news about improved health, a cleaner environment, or rising standards of living is generally overlooked.

late-night entertainment programs—Jay Leno, David Letterman, Conan O'Brien, *Politically Incorrect*—include comedy monologues that occasionally refer to political events or issues.

Soft news is a major source of information for people who are not interested in politics or public affairs. It is true, of course, that most soft news programming favors celebrity gossip, murder trials, sex scandals, disasters, and other human interest stories. But on some high-profile news issues these programs provide an otherwise inattentive public with what little information it absorbs.

60 Minutes attracts more viewers than any other soft news program. *Dateline* and *20/20* are not far behind. (Arguably these programs are oriented toward a somewhat more sophisticated audience than talk shows or tabloid news programs.) These programs, as well as *Entertainment Tonight* and Oprah Winfrey, attract more viewers than any of the nightly network newscasts.

Politicians themselves have come to understand the importance of soft news programming in reaching segments of the public that seldom watch news programs, speeches or debates, or campaign advertising. Presidential candidates welcome invitations to appear with Oprah, or Leno, or Letterman, and try to reformulate their messages in a light, comedic style that fits the program.

The Media Conglomerates   Mega-mergers in recent years have created corporate empires that spread across multiple media—television, film, newspapers, music, and the Internet. Conglomerate media corporations combine television broadcasting and cable programming, movie production and distribution, magazine and book publication, music recording, Internet access, and even sports and recreation. The six multinational corporations listed in Table 6.3 currently dominate world media and cultural interests.

The Politics of the News

The politics of the news media are shaped by (1) their *economic interest*, (2) their *professional environment*, and (3) their *ideological leanings*.

Sensationalism   The economic interest of the media—the need to capture and hold audience attention—creates a bias toward "hype" in the selection of news, its presentation, and its interpretation. To attract viewers and readers, the media bias the news toward violence, conflict, scandal, corruption, sex, scares of various sorts, and the personal lives of politicians and celebrities. News is selected primarily for its emotional impact on audiences; its social, economic, or political significance is secondary to the need to capture attention.

News must "touch" audiences personally, arouse emotions, and hold the interest of people with short attention spans. Scare stories—street crime, drug use, AIDS, nuclear power plant accidents, global warming, and a host of health alarms—make "good" news, for they cause viewers to fear for their personal

Table 6.3   The Media Empires

Time Warner Inc. (formerly known as AOL Time Warner)

Television: HBO, TNT, TBS, CNN, CNNSI, CNNFN, Cinemax, Time Warner Cable
Motion Pictures: Warner Brothers, New Line Cinema, Castle Rock, Looney Tunes
Magazines: Time, People, Sports Illustrated, Fortune, plus twenty-eight other specialty magazines
Books: Warner Books; Little, Brown Publishing; Book-of-the-Month Club
Music: Warner Brothers Records, Atlantic Records, Elektra
Sports and Entertainment: Atlanta Braves, Atlanta Hawks, World Championship Wrestling
Internet: AOL, Netscape, CompuServe

Walt Disney

Television: ABC-TV, plus ten stations; ESPN, ESPN-2, Disney Channel, A&E, E!, Lifetime
Motion Pictures: Walt Disney Pictures, Miramax, Touchstone
Music: Walt Disney Records, Mammoth, Buena Vista Records
Sports and Recreation: Disney theme parks in Florida, California, France, Japan; Disney Cruise Line; Anaheim Mighty Ducks
Consumer Products: Disney stores, Disney toys.

Viacom

Television: CBS, plus forty TV stations: MTV, TNN, Nickelodeon, Showtime, VH1, Nick-At-Nite, Spike TV, BET, Comedy Central
Motion Pictures: Paramount Pictures, Spelling, Viacom
Books: Simon & Schuster, Scribner, Free Press
Radio: Infinity Broadcasting
Music: Famous Music Publishing
Sports and Recreation: SportsLine, plus five Paramount parks

NewsCorp (Fox)

Television: Fox Network plus thirty-five TV stations; Fox News, Fox Entertainment, Fox Sports, Fox Family Channel, National Geographic Channel, DirecTV
Motion Pictures: 20th Century Fox, Searchlight
Books: HarperCollins
Newspaper: New York Post
Magazines: TV Guide
Music: Mushroom Records
Sports and Recreation: Los Angeles Lakers, Los Angeles Kings

Sony

Television: Game Show Network, *Jeopardy, Wheel of Fortune*
Motion Pictures: Columbia Pictures, Sony Pictures, Tri Star
Music: Columbia Records, Epic Records, Sony, Nashville
Sports and Recreation: Sony Theaters

NBC-Universal

Television: NBC Network plus thirteen TV stations; CNBC, MSNBC, Telemundo, Bravo, USA, SciFi
Motion Pictures: Universal Pictures
Sports and Recreation: Universal Studios theme parks in California and Florida
Music: Motown, Geffen, MCA

Source: Thomas R. Dye, *Who's Running America? The Bush Restoration,* 6th ed. (Upper Saddle River, N.J.: Prentice Hall, 2002). Updated by the author.

safety. The sex lives of politicians, once by custom off-limits to the press, are now public "affairs." Scandal and corruption among politicians, as well as selfishness and greed among business executives, are regular media themes.[9]

Negativism   The media are biased toward bad news. Bad news attracts larger audiences than good news. Television news displays a pervasive bias toward the negative in American life—in government, business, the military, politics, education, and everywhere else. Bad-news stories on television vastly outnumber good-news stories.

Good news gets little attention. For example, television news watchers are not likely to know that illegal drug use is declining in the United States, that both the air and water are measurably cleaner today than in past decades, that the nuclear power industry has the best safety record of any major industry in the United States, and that the aged in America are wealthier and enjoy higher incomes than the nonaged. The violent crime rate is down 50 percent since 1990. Teenage pregnancies and abortion rates are both down significantly. Television has generally failed to report these stories or, even worse, has implied that the opposite is true. Good news—stories about improved health statistics, longer life spans, better safety records, higher educational levels, for example—seldom provides the dramatic element needed to capture audience attention. The result is an overwhelming bad-news bias, especially on television.[10]

Muckraking   The professional environment of reporters and editors predisposes them toward an activist style of journalism once dubbed **muckraking**. Reporters today view themselves as "watchdogs" of the public trust. They see themselves in noble terms—enemies of corruption, crusaders for justice, defenders of the disadvantaged. "The watchdog function, once considered remedial and subsidiary. . .[is now] paramount: the primary duty of the journalists is to focus attention on problems and deficits, failures and threats."[11] Their professional models are the crusading "investigative reporters" who expose wrongdoing in government, business, the military, and every other institution in society—except the media.

muckraking Journalistic exposés of corruption, wrongdoing, or mismanagement in government, business, and other institutions of society.

The "Feeding Frenzy"   Occasionally, muckraking episodes grow into "**feeding frenzies**"—intense coverage of a scandal or event that blocks out most other news. Political scientist Larry Sabato describes the feeding frenzy: "In such situations a development is almost inevitably magnified and overscrutinized, the crush of cameras, microphones, and people, combined with the pressure of instant deadlines and live broadcasts, hype events and make it difficult to keep them in perspective. When a frenzy begins to gather, the intensity grows exponentially. . . . Television news time is virtually turned over to the subject of the frenzy."[12] Increasingly stiff competition among the media for attention and the need for round-the-clock cable news to fill long hours contribute to feeding frenzies.

"feeding frenzy" Intense media coverage of a scandal or event that blocks out most other news.

Liberalism in the Newsroom   The activist role that the media have taken upon themselves means that the personal values of reporters, editors, producers, and anchors are a very important element of American politics. The political values of the media are decidedly liberal and reformist. Political scientist Doris A. Graber writes about the politics of the media: "Economic and social liberalism prevails, especially in the most prominent media organizations. So does a preference for an internationalist foreign policy, caution about military intervention, and some suspicion about the ethics of established large institutions, particularly big business and big government."[13] Most Americans agree that media news coverage is biased and the bias is in a liberal direction (see *What Do You Think?* "Are the Media Biased?").

Liberalism in Hollywood   With a few exceptions, Hollywood producers, directors, writers, studio executives, and actors are decidedly liberal in their political views, especially when compared with the general public. Of the Hollywood elite, more than 60 percent describe themselves as liberal and only 14 percent as conservative,[14] whereas in the general public, self-described conservatives outnumber liberals by a significant margin. Hollywood leaders are five times more likely to be Democrats than Republicans, and Hollywood is a major source of Democratic Party campaign funds. On both economic and social issues, the Hollywood elite is significantly more liberal than the nation's general public or college-educated public.[15] (However, see *A Conflicting View*, "Fox News: 'Fair and Balanced'?").

WHAT DO YOU THINK?

Are the Media Biased?

Are the media biased, and if so in what direction—liberal or conservative? Arguments over media bias have grown in intensity as the media have come to play a central role in American politics.

Nearly three out of four Americans (74 percent) see "a fair amount" or "a great deal" of media bias in news coverage (see the following table). And of those who see a bias, over twice as many see a liberal bias rather than a conservative bias. Indeed, even liberals see a liberal bias in the news; it is not a perception limited to conservatives, although they are more likely to see it. The liberal bias is much more likely to be seen by college graduates than by people who did not finish high school. It is also more likely to be seen by political activists than by those who engage in little or no political activity. However, African Americans are likely to see a conservative bias in the news, in contrast to the liberal bias perceived more often by whites.

At the same time, Americans have high expectations of the role of the media in society: they expect the media to protect them from "abuse of power" by government, to hold public officials accountable, and to point out and help solve the problems of society.

Perceptions of Media Bias

	How Much Bias? "A Great Deal" or "Fair Amount" (%)	Direction of Bias	
		Liberal (%)	Conservative (%)
All	74	43	19
Race			
White	75	46	15
Black	64	24	40
Education			
Less than high school	56	29	33
High school graduate	75	42	19
College graduate	81	57	19
Ideology			
Liberal	70	41	22
Moderate	70	30	16
Conservative	81	57	19
Political Activism			
High	82	54	14
Low	76	42	22
None	65	34	22

Source: "Perceptions of Media Bias" from *Media Monitor*, May/June 1997, Center for Media and Public Affairs, Washington, DC. Reprinted by permission.

Accuracy in Media A self-described watchdog organization critical of liberal bias in the media. *www.aim.org*

Conservatism on Talk Radio   Talk radio is the one medium where conservatism prevails. The single most listened-to talk radio show is the *Rush Limbaugh Show*, whose host regularly bashes "limousine liberals," "femi-Nazis," "environmental wackos," and "croissant people."[16] Talk radio might be portrayed as "call-in democracy." Callers respond almost immediately to reported news events. Call-in shows are the first to sense the public mood. Callers are not necessarily representative of the general public. Rather they are usually the most intense and outraged of citizens. But their complaints are early warning signs for wary politicians.

Televised Incivility and Political Trust   Does watching political shows on television, in which hosts, guests, pundits, and others hurl insults at each other, interrupt and shout over each other, and use especially contentious and uncivil

A CONFLICTING VIEW

Fox News: "Fair and Balanced"?

For many years conservatives complained about the liberal tilt of television news. But despite their ample financial resources, conservative investors failed to create their own network or purchase an existing one. It was an Australian billionaire, Rupert Murdoch, who eventually came to the rescue of American conservatives.

Murdoch's global media empire, News Corp, includes Fox Network, Fox News Cable, 20th Century Fox, the *New York Post, The Times* and *The Sun* of London, HarperCollins Publishing, thirty-five local TV stations, and the Los Angeles Dodgers. He began his career by injecting glitz and vulgarity into previously dull Australian newspapers he inherited. The formula worked worldwide: The *New York Post* became a noisy tabloid after Murdoch took over (most memorable headline: "HEADLESS BODY FOUND IN TOPLESS BAR"), and Fox TV entertainment airs even more vulgar shows than the mainstream networks.

Murdoch himself is not particularly conservative in his politics, but he recognized an unfilled market for conservative views on American television. In 1996 he founded Fox News and hired Roger Ailes (former TV ad producer for Richard Nixon, Ronald Reagan, and George H. W. Bush) to head up the new network. Ailes quickly signed Bill O'Reilly (see *People in Politics* in Chapter 2) for an hourlong nightly conservative talk show. Brit Hume, one of the few prominent TV reporters considered to be a conservative, was made managing editor.

Fox proclaims "fair and balanced" news—"We report, you decide." The implication is that mainstream media has a liberal bias and that Fox is rectifying it with its own fair and balanced reporting. According to Fox, if its reporting appears conservative, it is only because the country has become so accustomed to left-leaning media that a truly balanced network just seems conservative.

Regular news reporting on Fox is not much different than other networks, except that Fox may cover some stories ignored by the mainstream media, e.g. political correctness running amok on college campuses, ridiculous environmental regulations, hypocrisy among Hollywood liberals, etc. But it is the talk and commentary shows that outrage liberals and warm the hearts of conservatives. Liberals bold enough to appear on Fox are badgered mercilessly, while conservative guests are tossed softball questions.

The bottom line, financially as well as politically, is that Fox News is now the most watched cable news network, even surpassing CNN. Whatever its flaws, Fox News had added diversity of views to American television.

---

language, reduce levels of trust in politicians and government? Programs such as *The O'Reilly Factor, Meet the Press, Crossfire, Capital Gang,* and *Hardball* regularly resort to confrontational talk, replete with hyperbole and venomous invective. One experiment, with some viewers watching friendly, polite, and simple political discussions, and other viewers watching rude, emotional, quarrelsome political confrontations, concluded that incivility has a detrimental effect on trust in government and attitudes toward political leaders.[17] Yet it is not likely that televised politics will ever become more civil. Politics for most people cannot compete with entertainment shows for TV audiences, so increasingly political shows are creating dramatic tension and uncivil conflict to gain viewers.

News versus Entertainment   Cable television and the Internet have produced dramatic increases in available political information. Yet overall political knowledge and turnout have not changed noticeably. The key to understanding this apparent paradox is the vast expansion in choices now available to viewers.[18] People can now choose from numerous cable channels and Web sites. Increasingly there is a division between people who prefer entertainment programming and those who prefer news shows. There is some evidence that people who prefer news shows acquire greater political knowledge and go to the polls more often than those who mainly watch entertainment shows. Greater media choice, then, appears to widen the "knowledge gap." Because people who like news and take advantage of additional information in the media gain political knowledge, while people who prefer entertainment programming learn less about politics, the mean levels of political knowledge in the population have essentially remained constant.

Polarization of the Media

Increasingly, media audiences are becoming politically polarized, with Republicans and conservatives, and Democrats and liberals, choosing to listen to and view separate media outlets. Listeners and viewers are choosing sides in their sources of news (see Table 6.4).

News audiences in the aggregate are somewhat more conservative than the general public. The Pew Research Center reports that of those who regularly watch, read, or listen to the news, conservatives comprise 36 percent, moderates 38 percent, and liberals 18 percent. The favorites of conservatives are the *Rush Limbaugh Show* on radio and the *O'Reilly Factor* on Fox television, followed by religious radio, Fox News, business magazines, and call-in radio shows. Moderates and liberals turn to *Larry King Live*, the nightly ABC, CBS, and NBC news, National Public Radio, and literary magazines.

Mediated Elections

Political campaigning is largely a media activity, and the media, especially television, shape the nation's electoral politics.

The Media and Candidate-Voter Linkage   The media are the principal link between candidates and the voters. At one time, political party organizations performed this function, with city, ward, and precinct workers knocking on

Table 6.4   Ideology and News Sources

Of those who regularly watch, read or listen to . . .	Conservative	Moderate	Liberal	Don't Know
Rush Limbaugh Show	77%	16%	7%	0%
O'Reilly Factor	72	23	4	1
Religious radio	53	26	12	9
Fox News	52	30	13	5
Business magazines	49	35	14	2
Call-in radio shows	45	33	18	4
Local news	38	41	15	6
Morning news	38	39	17	6
Newspaper	37	41	17	5
Network News Magazines	37	40	17	6
Political magazines	37	29	29	5
CNN	36	39	20	5
Larry King Live	35	41	16	8
CNBC	35	40	18	7
Letterman/Leno	34	41	21	4
MSNBC	33	41	22	4
Nightly Network news	33	41	18	8
NPR	31	33	30	6
Literary magazines	19	38	36	7

Source: Pew Research Center for the People and the Press, June 8, 2004, *http://wwwpeople-press.org*. Reprinted by permission of Pew Research Center for the People and the Press.

Conservative talk-show host Rush Limbaugh has become a symbol of the talk-radio phenomenon.

doors, distributing campaign literature, organizing rallies and candidate appearances, and getting out the vote on election day. But television has largely replaced party organizations and personal contact as the means by which candidates communicate with voters. Candidates come directly into the living room via television—on the nightly news, in broadcast debates and interviews, and in paid advertising (see Table 6.5).

Media campaigning requires candidates to possess great skill in communications. Candidates must be able to project a favorable media *image*. The image is a composite of the candidate's words, mannerisms, appearance, personality, warmth, friendliness, humor, and ease in front of a camera. Policy positions have less to do with image than the candidate's ability to project personal qualities—leadership, compassion, strength, and character.

The Media and Candidate Selection   The media strongly influence the early selection of candidates. Media coverage creates **name recognition**, an essential quality for any candidate. Early media "mentions" of senators, governors, and other political figures as possible presidential contenders help to sort out the field even before the election year begins. Conversely, media inattention can condemn aspiring politicians to obscurity.

name recognition Public awareness of a candidate—whether they even know his or her name.

Serious presidential campaigns now begin at least six months to a year before the New Hampshire primary (or almost two years before the November presidential election). This early time period, "the invisible primary," is increasingly critical for campaigns.[19] Candidates must position themselves relative to competitors in their own party—build their name recognition, raise poll numbers, and build a campaign war chest. Inasmuch as campaign contributions are just beginning to come in, candidates have relatively little money to spend on paid advertising. They are forced to focus their efforts on attracting media attention by staging media events and issuing press releases. But from the media's perspective, campaign news is neither timely nor immediately relevant. Candidates must try to win media coverage by catering to the conflict and horse race stories preferred by the media. Press releases and speeches focused on issues are most likely to be ignored.

The media sort out the serious candidates early in a race. They even assign front-runner status, which may be either a blessing or a curse, depending on subsequent media coverage. In presidential primaries, the media play the *expectations*

Table 6.5 Sources of Political Campaign News in Presidential Election Years

Over time, network news (ABC, CBS, NBC) has been declining as a major source of campaign news, while cable news (CNN, MSNBC, Fox) has been gaining. The Internet has also gained ground as a source of campaign news.

News Sources	1992	1996	2000	2004
Television	82%	72%	70%	76%
Cable	29	21	36	40
Network	55	36	22	29
Local	29	23	21	12
Newspapers	57	60	39	46
Radio	12	19	15	22
Internet	—	3	11	21
Magazines	9	11	4	6

Note: Respondents were asked, "How did you get most of your news about the presidential election campaign? From television, from newspapers, from radio, from magazines or from the Internet?" Television users were then asked, "Did you get most of your news about the presidential campaign from network TV news, from local TV news, or from cable news networks such as CNN or MSNBC?" Respondents could name two sources.

Source: Pew Research Center for the People and the Press, data from a telephone survey of 1,113 voters, November 10–12, 2000, *http://www.people-press.org/post100que.htm.*

Drudge Report Controversial site that links to stories not always carried by mainstream media. Links to all major media outlets.
www.drudgereport.com

game, setting vote margins that the front-runner must meet in order to maintain *momentum*. If the front-runner does not win by a large enough margin, the media may declare the runner-up the "real" winner. This sorting out of candidates by the media influences not only voters, but—more important—financial contributors. The media-designated favorite is more likely to receive campaign contributions; financial backers do not like to waste money on losers. And as contributions roll in, the favorite can buy more television advertising, adding momentum to the campaign.

In presidential elections, the media sorting process places great emphasis on the early primary states, particularly New Hampshire, whose primary in early February is customarily the first contest in a presidential election year. Less than 1 percent of convention delegates are chosen by this small state, but media coverage is intense, and the winner quickly becomes the media-designated front-runner.[20]

The Media as Kingmakers In the early months of a campaign, media coverage of candidates and their standing in public opinion polls tend to move together. Candidates who receive heavy media coverage usually do well in the polls. Good poll ratings create more media coverage. Good poll ratings and increased media coverage inspire campaign contributions, which then allow candidates to buy television advertising to further increase their poll numbers. Media-sponsored public opinion polls play an important role in kingmaking. The CBS/*New York Times* poll, the NBC/Associated Press poll, the ABC/*Washington Post* poll, and the CNN/*USA Today* poll are widely reported; they become the benchmarks for voters, telling them who the winners and losers are.

The name of the game for candidates early in the race is *exposure*. Even appearances on entertainment shows, once considered "unpresidential," are now highly valued by political candidates. They vie to appear on *Larry King Live* and on late-night talk shows hosted by Jay Leno, David Letterman, and Conan O'Brien.

Democratic supporters of Colorado Attorney General Ken Salazar watch early results in the presidential election at a hotel ballroom in Denver, Colorado, on Tuesday night, Nov. 2, 2004. Salazar was in a close race against beer magnate Pete Coors for the open U.S. Senate seat.

Media Effects on the Campaign   Political candidates are aware of the importance of the media to their success. Their campaign managers must be "media-savvy" and they must hire media consultants early in the campaign. Candidates are advised to arrange daily newsworthy events to keep their name and image in the news. Television producers, reporters, and editors do not like to receive position papers on substantive issues or to present "talking heads"—shots only of the faces of speakers. Rather they prefer attention-getting, action-oriented, emotion-laden videotape. Candidates and their managers know this and so they attract media attention and resort to *media events*—staged activities designed to polish the image of the candidate. Candidates arrange to appear at police conventions, at schools, at hazardous waste sites, on aircraft carriers, at flag factories, and so on in order to project an image on television of their concern for crime, education, the environment, national defense, patriotism, and the like. (See also "Campaign Strategies" in Chapter 8.)

The Media and the Horse Race   The media give election campaigns **horse-race coverage**: reporting on who is ahead or behind, what the candidates' strategies are, how much money they are spending, and, above all, what their current standing in the polls is. Such stories account for more than half of all television news coverage of an election. Additional stories are centered on *campaign* issues—controversies that arise on the campaign trail itself, including verbal blunders by the candidate—and *character* issues, such as the sex life of the candidate. In contrast, *policy* issues typically account for only about one-third of the television news stories in a presidential election campaign.[21]

horse-race coverage Media coverage of electoral campaigns that concentrates on who is ahead and who is behind, and neglects the issues at stake.

The Bad News Bias   The media's bad-news bias is evident in election campaigns as well as in general news reporting. Negative stories about all presidential candidates usually outnumber positive stories. The media generally see their function in political campaigns as reporting on the weaknesses, blunders, and vulnerabilities of the candidates. It might be argued that exposing the flaws of the candidates is an important function in a democracy. But the media's negative reporting about candidates and generally skeptical attitude toward their campaign speeches, promises, and advertisements may contribute to political alienation and cynicism among voters.

The media focus intense scrutiny on the personal lives of candidates—their marriages, sex lives, drug or alcohol use, personal finances, past friendships, military service, club memberships, and other potential sources of embarrassment.

UP CLOSE

TV Network News Coverage of the Presidential Campaign, 2004

How did the major TV networks cover the 2004 presidential campaign between Republican George W. Bush and Democrat John Kerry? More time and more stories were devoted to the 2004 campaign than any other campaign since the Clinton–Bush contest in 1996. And in a reversal of past trends, almost as much time was devoted to policy issues as to the horse race.

More people (21 percent) reported that they relied "most" on Fox News, followed by CNN (15 percent), NBC (13 percent), ABC (11 percent), and CBS (9 percent).

But as in previous elections, stories broadcast by the traditional networks—ABC, CBS, and NBC—favored the Democratic candidate by a large margin. Only Fox News reported more favorably on Bush (53 percent of stories with positive evaluations) than Kerry (21 percent of stories with positive evaluations).

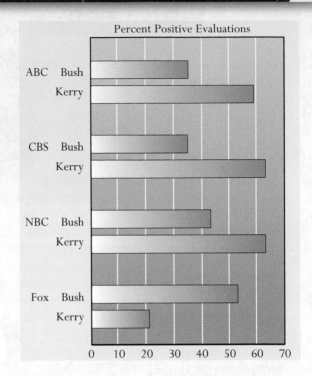

Percent Positive Evaluations

Source: Data derived from various issues of *Media Monitor,* the publication of the Center for Media and Public Affairs.

Virtually any past error in judgment or behavior by a candidate is given heavy coverage. But the media defend their attention to personal scandal on the ground that they are reporting on the "character issue." They argue that voters must have information on candidates' character as well as on their policy positions.

The Shrinking Sound Bite   Reporters and newsroom anchors dominate television broadcasting. They report roughly three-quarters of all campaign news themselves. The candidates are allocated less than 15 percent of the time devoted to campaign news stories. (Other sources—pundits, commentators, voters, and so forth—account for the remaining airtime.) The candidates themselves have very little direct contact with audiences in network news. The average **sound bite**—time allowed the candidates to speak on their own behalf—has shrunk to less than eight seconds!

sound bites Concise and catchy phrases that attract media coverage.

The Media and Political Bias   The media are very sensitive to charges of bias toward candidates or parties. Media people are overwhelmingly liberal and Democratic but generally try to deflect charges of political bias during an election campaign by giving almost equal coverage to both Democratic and Republican candidates. Moreover, the media report negatively on both Republicans and Democrats, although some scholars count more negative stories about Republican candidates.

The media are generally more critical of front-runners than of underdogs during a campaign. A horse race loses audience interest if one horse gets too far ahead, so the media tend to favor the underdog. During the presidential primary season, media attacks on an early favorite may result in gains for the underdog, who then becomes the new object of attack.

Freedom versus Fairness

Complaints about the fairness of media are as old as the printing press. Most early newspapers in the United States were allied with political parties; they were not expected to be fair in their coverage. It was only in the early 1900s that many large newspapers broke their ties with parties and proclaimed themselves independent. And it was not until the 1920s and 1930s that the norms of journalistic professionalism and accuracy gained widespread acceptance.

The Constitution protects the *freedom* of the press; it was not intended to guarantee *fairness.* The First Amendment's guarantee of freedom of the press was originally designed to protect the press from government attempts to silence criticism. Over the years, the U.S. Supreme Court has greatly expanded the meaning of the free-press guarantee.

No Prior Restraint   The Supreme Court has interpreted freedom of the press to mean that government may place no **prior restraint** on speech or publication (that is, before it is said or published). Originally, this doctrine was designed to prevent the government from closing down or seizing newspapers. Today, the doctrine prevents the government from censoring any news items. In the famous case of the Pentagon Papers, the *New York Times* and *Washington Post* undertook to publish secret information stolen from the files of the State Department and Defense Department regarding U.S. policy in Vietnam while the war was still going on. No one disputed the fact that stealing the secret material was illegal. What was at issue was the ability of the government to prevent the publication of stolen documents in order to protect national security. The Supreme Court rejected the national security argument and reaffirmed that the government may place no prior restraint on publication.[22] If the government wishes to keep military secrets, it must not let them fall into the hands of the American press.

prior restraint Government actions to restrict publication of a magazine, newspaper, or books on grounds of libel, obscenity, or other legal violations prior to actual publication of the work.

Press versus Electronic Media   In the early days of radio, broadcast channels were limited, and anyone with a radio transmitter could broadcast on any frequency. As a result, interference was a common frustration of early broadcasters. The industry petitioned the federal government to regulate and license the assignment and use of broadcast frequencies.

The Federal Communications Commission (FCC) was established in 1934 to allocate broadcast frequencies and to license stations for "the public interest, convenience and necessity." The act clearly instructed the FCC: "Nothing in this Act shall be understood or construed to give the Commission the power of censorship." However, the FCC views a broadcast license and exclusive right to use a particular frequency as a *public trust.* Thus broadcasters, unlike newspapers and magazines, are licensed by a government agency and supposed to operate in the *public interest.*

Federal Communication Commission
The FCC's official Web site with announcements and consumer information.
www.fcc.gov

Decency   Recently the FCC decided to crack down on "indecency" on radio and television, presumably doing so in the "public interest." CBS was fined for the Super Bowl halftime "wardrobe malfunction" by singer Janet Jackson. "Shock-jock" Howard Stern incurred millions of dollars in fines for himself and his stations before giving up regular programming and moving to unregulated satellite radio. Government suppression of "indecency" is constitutionally permitted over broadcast waves on the theory that these channels are limited, they belong to the public, and government licenses broadcasters. Otherwise, mere "indecency" that does not constitute "obscenity" is constitutionally protected by the First Amendment (see Chapter 14).

The Equal-Time Requirement   The FCC requires radio and television stations that provide airtime to a political candidate to offer competing candidates the same

— Think Again —

Should the media be legally required to be fair and accurate in reporting political news?

PEOPLE IN POLITICS

Larry King Live

Who turned presidential politics into talk-show entertainment? A strong argument can be made that Larry King was personally responsible for changing the nature of presidential campaigning. It was Larry King who nudged frequent talk-show guest Ross Perot into the presidential arena. And it was Larry King who demonstrated to the candidates that the talk-show format was a good way to reach out to the American people.

Larry King's supremacy in talk-show politics came late in life, after a half-century of hustling and hard knocks, no college education, bouts of gambling followed by bankruptcy, and multiple marriages. King has written five books about himself, describing his rise from Brooklyn neighborhoods; his friendships with Jackie Gleason, Frank Sinatra, and other celebrities; and his hardscrabble life. As he tells it, he hung around a New York radio station for five years before taking a bus to Miami to try his luck first as a disk jockey and later as a sports announcer. After a decade in Miami, he had his own TV interview show, a talk show on radio, and a newspaper column, and he was color commentator for the Miami Dolphins. He lived the fast life, running up huge debts and dealing in shady financial transactions. He was arrested in 1971 on grand larceny charges; they were dropped only because the statute of limitations had expired. He lost his TV and radio shows and his newspaper column. He ended up in Shreveport, Louisiana, doing play-by-play for the World Football League. In 1975 he was bankrupt but back in Miami doing radio. In 1978 he moved to Washington to launch his Mutual Network radio talk show. As radio talk shows gained popular-

ity, so did King. When CNN started twenty-four-hour broadcasting in 1982, the network turned to King to do an evening interview show, *Larry King Live*. At first, the show merely filled the space between the evening and the late news. A decade later, the show was making news itself.

King's success is directly attributable to his accommodating style. He actually listens to his guests; he lets them speak for themselves; he unashamedly plugs their books, records, and movies. He does *not* attack his guests; he does not assume the adversarial, abrasive style preferred by reporters like Mike Wallace, or interviewers like Bill O'Reilly. An old-fashioned liberal himself, King appears comfortable interviewing politicians of every stripe. He lets guests talk about themselves. He tosses "softball" questions: "If I were to interview the president about an alleged sexual affair, I wouldn't ask if he'd had one, I'd ask him, 'How does it feel to read these things about yourself?'"

With his emphasis on feelings, emotions, and motives rather than on facts, it is little wonder that King's style attracts politicians . . . or that *Larry King Live* is the highest rated show on CNN.

Source: Excerpted from "A King Who Can Listen," *Time,* 10/5/92.

---

equal-time rule Federal Communications Commission (FCC) requirement that broadcasters who sell time to any political candidate must make equal time available to opposing candidates at the same price.

libel Writings that are false and malicious and are intended to damage an individual.

slander Oral statements that are false and malicious and are intended to damage an individual.

amount of airtime at the same price. Stations are not required to give free time to candidates, but if stations choose to give free time to one candidate, they must do so for the candidate's opponents. But this **equal-time rule** does *not* apply to newscasts, news specials, or even long documentaries, nor does it apply to talk shows like *Larry King Live* (see *People in Politics:* "Larry King Live"). Nor does it apply to presidential press conferences or presidential addresses to the nation, although the networks now generally offer free time for a "Democratic response" to a Republican president, and vice versa. A biased news presentation does not require the network or station to grant equal time to opponents of its views. And it is important to note that newspapers, unlike radio and television, have never been required to provide equal time to opposing views (see *Compared to What?* "America's TV Culture in Perspective").

Libel and Slander

Communications that wrongly damage an individual are known in law as **libel** (when written) and **slander** (when spoken). The injured party must prove in

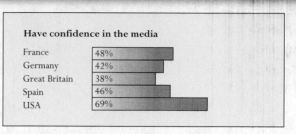

COMPARED TO WHAT?

America's TV Culture in Perspective

America is a TV culture. Americans rely more on television for news and entertainment than people in other advanced industrial nations do. Perhaps more important, Americans have greater confidence in the media than other peoples do. Consider, for example, the question "Would you say you have a great deal of confidence, only some confidence, hardly any confidence, or no confidence at all in the media—press, radio, and television?" When this question was asked of a national sample of Americans, 69 percent responded that they had a great deal or at least some confidence in the media. But majorities in four other countries—France, Great Britain, Germany, and Spain—said they had little or no confidence in the media (see "confidence in the media" figure).

How much do the media influence key decisions in society? A majority of people in both the United States and these same European nations believe the media exert a large influence on public opinion. Americans appear to be closer to unanimity on this point (88 percent) than are Europeans. When people are asked how much influence the media exerts on particular governing institutions—the executive, the legislature, and the judiciary—Americans are much more likely to perceive strong media influence than are Europeans (see "media influence" figure).

Source: Adapted from Laurence Parisot, "Attitudes about the Media: A Five Country Study," *Public Opinion* 43 (January/February 1988): 18, 60.

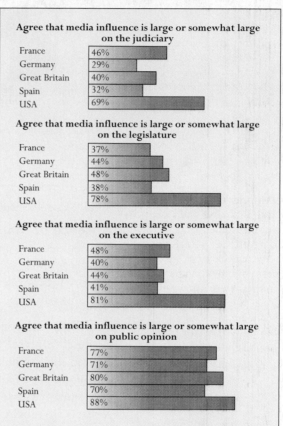

Have confidence in the media

France	48%
Germany	42%
Great Britain	38%
Spain	46%
USA	69%

Agree that media influence is large or somewhat large on the judiciary

France	46%
Germany	29%
Great Britain	40%
Spain	32%
USA	69%

Agree that media influence is large or somewhat large on the legislature

France	37%
Germany	44%
Great Britain	48%
Spain	38%
USA	78%

Agree that media influence is large or somewhat large on the executive

France	48%
Germany	40%
Great Britain	44%
Spain	41%
USA	81%

Agree that media influence is large or somewhat large on public opinion

France	77%
Germany	71%
Great Britain	80%
Spain	70%
USA	88%

---

court that the communication caused actual damage and was either false or defamatory. A damaging falsehood or words or phrases that are defamatory (such as "Joe Jones is a rotten son of a bitch") are libelous and are not protected by the First Amendment from lawsuits seeking compensation.

Public Officials   Over the years, the media have sought to narrow the protection afforded public officials against libel and slander. In 1964 the U.S. Supreme Court ruled in the case of *New York Times v. Sullivan* that public officials did not have a right to recover damages for false statements unless they are made with "malicious intent."[23] The **Sullivan rule** requires public officials not only to show that the media published or broadcast false and damaging statements but also to prove they did so knowing that their statements were false and damaging or that they did so with "reckless disregard" for the truth or falsehood of their statements. The effect of the Sullivan rule is to free the media to say virtually anything about public officials.

Think Again

Should the media report on all aspects of the private lives of public officials?

" INTERESTING.....IT'S LIKE A PORTABLE 500K FILE and YOU DON'T HAVE TO WAIT FOR IT
TO DOWNLOAD.... AND YOU SAY IT'S CALLED A NEWSPAPER ?"

(©1997 Jim Borgman, Cincinnati Enquirer. Reprinted with permission of King Features Syndicate.)

Sullivan rule Court
guideline that false and
malicious statements
regarding public officials are
protected by the First
Amendment unless it can be
proven they were known to
be false at the time they were
made or were made with
"reckless disregard" for their
truth or falsehood.

Indeed, the media have sought to expand the definition of "public officials" to "public figures"—that is, to include anyone they choose as the subject of a story.

"Absence of Malice"   The First Amendment protects the right of the media to be biased, unfair, negative, sensational, and even offensive. Indeed, even *damaging falsehoods* may be printed or broadcast as long as the media can show that the story was not deliberately fabricated by them with malicious intent, that is, if the media can show an "absence of malice."

Shielding Sources   The media argue that the First Amendment allows them to refuse to reveal the names of their sources, even when this information is required in criminal investigations and trials. Thus far, the U.S. Supreme Court has not given blanket protection to reporters to withhold information from court proceedings. However, a number of states have passed *shield laws* protecting reporters from being forced to reveal their sources.

Politics and the Internet

The development of any new medium of communications invariably affects political life. Just as, first, radio and, later, television reshaped politics in America, today the Internet is having its own unique impact on public affairs. The Internet provides a channel for *interactive mass participation* in politics. It is unruly and chaotic by design. It offers the promise of abundant and diverse information and the opportunity for increased political participation. It empowers everyone who can design a Web site to spread their views, whether their views are profound and public-spirited or hateful and obscene.

Chaotic by Design   During the Cold War, the RAND Corporation, a technological research think tank, proposed the Internet as a communications network that might survive a nuclear attack. It was deliberately designed to operate without any central authority or organization. Should any part of the system be destroyed, messages would still find their way to their destinations. The later development of the World Wide Web language allowed any connected computer in the world to communicate with any other connected computer. And introduc-

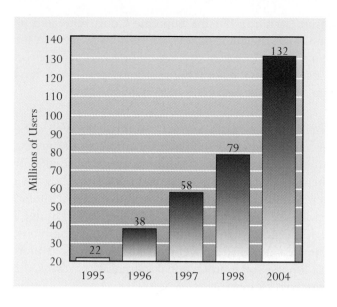

Figure 6.3 Growth of Internet Users

Source: Statistical Abstract of the United States, 2004–05, p. 731.

tion of the World Wide Web in 1992 also meant that users no longer needed computer expertise to communicate. By 1995 Americans were buying more computers than television sets and sending more e-mail than "snail mail." Since then, Internet usage has continued to mushroom (see Figure 6.3).

Political Web Sites Abound   The Internet is awash in political Web sites. The simple query "politics" on a standard search program can return well over a million matches. Almost all federal agencies, including the White House, Congress, the federal judiciary, and executive departments and agencies, maintain Web sites. Individual elected officeholders, including all members of Congress, maintain sites that include personal biographies, committee assignments, legislative accomplishments, issue statements, and press releases. The home pages of the Democratic and Republican parties offer political news, issue positions, opportunities to become active in party affairs, and invitations to send them money. No serious candidate for major public office lacks a Web site; these campaign sites usually include flattering biographies, press releases, and, of course, invitations to contribute financially to the candidates' campaigns. All major interest groups maintain Web sites—business, trade, and professional groups; labor unions; ideological and issue groups; women's, religious, environmental, and civil rights groups. Indeed, this virtual tidal wave of politics on the Internet may turn out to offer too much information in too fragmented a fashion, thereby simply adding to apathy and indifference.[24]

Internet Uncensored   The Internet allows unrestricted freedom of expression, from scientific discourses on particle physics and information on the latest developments in medical science, to invitations to join in paramilitary "militia" and offers to exchange pornographic photos and messages. Commercial sex sites outnumber any other category on the Web.

Congress unsuccessfully attempted to outlaw "indecent" and "patently offensive" material on the Internet with its Communications Decency Act of 1996. But the U.S. Supreme Court gave the Internet First Amendment protection in 1997 in *Reno v. American Civil Liberties Union.*[25] The Court recognized the Internet as an important form of popular expression protected by the Constitution. Congress had sought to make it a federal crime to send or display "indecent" material to persons under 18 years of age (material describing or displaying sexual activities

 Annenberg Public Policy Center
The Annenberg Center of the University of Pennsylvania conducts research on political use of the media, including the Internet.
www.appcpenn.org

or organs in "patently offensive" fashion). But the Supreme Court reiterated its view that government may not limit the adult population to "only what is fit for children." The Court decision places the burden of filtering Internet messages on parents. Filtering software can be installed on home computers, but a First Amendment issue arises when it is installed on computers in public libraries.

The Bloggers   The Internet has spawned a myriad of individual Web sites, commonly known as "blogs," that frequently criticize the professional media. The more reputable blog sites fact-check stories in the mainstream media, or publish stories ignored by them, as well as toss in their own opinions. They have been labeled the media's "back-seat" drivers. (One of the earliest and most quoted bloggers is the "Drudge Report," posted by maverick journalist Matt Drudge.) While many bloggers offer little more than their own often-heated opinions, bloggers have forced the mainstream media to cover stories they may not other-wise have covered, as well as forcing some professional journalists to check the accuracy of their stories before publication.

Media Effects: Shaping Political Life

─ Think Again ─
Is your choice of candidates in elections affected by their advertising?

What effects do the media have on public opinion and political behavior? Let us consider media effects on (1) information and agenda setting, (2) values and opinions, and (3) behavior. These categories of effects are ranked by the degree of influence the media are likely to have over us. The strongest effects of the media are on our information levels and societal concerns. The media also influence values and opinions, but the strength of media effects in these areas is diluted by many other influences. Finally, it is most difficult to establish the independent effect of the media on behavior.

Information and Agenda-Setting Effects   The media strongly influence what we know about our world and how we think and talk about it. Years ago, foreign-policy expert Bernard Cohen, in the first book to assess the effects of the media on foreign policy, put it this way: "The mass media may not be successful in telling people what to think, but the media are stunningly successful in telling their audience what to think about"[26] (see *Up Close:* "The Media Age").

information overload
Situation in which individuals are subjected to so many communications that they cannot make sense of them.

However, **information overload** diminishes the influence of the media in determining what we think about. So many communications are directed at us that we cannot possibly process them all. A person's ability to recall a media report depends on repeated exposure to it and reinforcement through personal experience. For example, an individual who has a brother in a trouble spot in the Middle East is more likely to be aware of reports from that area of the world. But too many voices with too many messages cause most viewers to block out a great deal of information.

Information overload may be especially heavy in political news. Television tells most viewers more about politics than they really want to know. Political scientist Austin Ranney writes, "The fact is that for most Americans politics is still far from being the most interesting and important thing in life. To them, politics is usually confusing, boring, repetitious, and above all irrelevant to the things that really matter in their lives."[27]

American Journalism Review
Features articles on current topics in print and television reporting, together with links to newspapers, television networks and stations, radio stations, media companies, and so forth. *www.ajr.org*

Effects on Values and Opinions   The media often tell us how we *should* feel about news events or issues, especially those about which we have no prior feelings or experiences. The media can reinforce values and attitudes we already hold. However, the media seldom *change* our preexisting values or opinions. Media influ-

UP CLOSE

The Media Age

The print media—newspapers, magazines, and books—have played a major role in American politics since colonial times. But today the electronic media—radio, television, and cable television—dominate in political communication.

Radio was widely introduced into American homes in the 1920s and 1930s, allowing President Franklin D. Roosevelt to become the first "media president," directly communicating with the American people through radio "fireside chats." After World War II, the popularity of television spread quickly; between 1950 and 1960, the percentage of homes with TV sets grew from 9 to 87.

Some notable political media innovations over the years:

- **1952:** The first paid commercial TV ad in a presidential campaign appeared, on behalf of Dwight D. Eisenhower. The black-and-white ad began with a voice-over—"Eisenhower answers the nation!"—followed by citizens asking favorable questions and Eisenhower responding, and ending with a musical jingle: "I like Ike." Although crude by current standards, it nevertheless set a precedent in media campaigning.

- **1952:** The "Checkers speech" by Eisenhower's running mate, Richard M. Nixon, represented the first direct television appeal to the people over the heads of party leaders. Nixon was about to be dumped from the Republican ticket for hiding secret slush-fund money received from campaign contributors. He went on national television with an emotional appeal, claiming that the only personal item he ever took from a campaign contributor was his daughters' little dog, Checkers. Thousands of viewers called and wired in sympathy. Ike kept Nixon on the ticket.

- **1960:** The first televised debate between presidential candidates featured a youthful, handsome John F. Kennedy against a shifty-eyed Richard M. Nixon with a pronounced "five o'clock shadow." Nixon doggedly scored debater points, but JFK presented a cool and confident image and spoke directly to the viewers. The debate swung the popular tide toward Kennedy, who won in a very tight contest. Nixon attributed his defeat to his failure to shave before the broadcast.

- **1964:** The first "negative" TV ad was the "Daisy Girl" commercial sponsored by the Lyndon Johnson campaign against Republican conservative Barry Goldwater. It implied that Goldwater would start a nuclear war. It showed a little girl picking petals off a daisy while an ominous voice counted down "10-9-8-7 . . ." to a nuclear explosion, followed by a statement that

Lyndon Johnson could be trusted to keep the peace.

- **1976:** President Gerald Ford was the first incumbent president to agree to a televised debate. (No televised presidential debates were held in the Nixon-Humphrey race in 1968 or in the Nixon-McGovern race in 1972. Apparently Nixon had learned his lesson.) Ford stumbled badly, and Jimmy Carter went on to victory.

- **1982:** CNN (Cable News Network), introduced by the maverick media mogul Ted Turner, began twenty-four-hour broadcasting.

- **1991:** The Persian Gulf War was the first war to be fought live on television. (Although film and videotape reports of the Vietnam War had been important molders of public opinion in America, the technology of that era did not allow live reporting.) In the Gulf War, the Iraqi government permitted CNN to continue live broadcasts from Baghdad, including spectacular coverage of the first night's air raids on the city.

- **1992:** In the presidential election, television talk shows became a major focus of the campaign. Wealthy independent candidate Ross Perot actually conducted an all-media campaign, rejecting in-person appearances in favor of such media techniques as half-hour "infomercials."

- **1994–95:** The arrest and trial of celebrity O.J. Simpson on murder charges so dominated the national news that more television time was devoted to the O.J. story than to the actions of the president and Congress.

- **1996:** The presidential election was given less television time and newspaper space than previous elections. Clinton's large lead throughout the campaign, public boredom with Whitewater and other scandals, and Dole's lackluster performance frustrated reporters in search of drama. Network TV news gave Clinton twice as much positive coverage as Dole.

- **1997–98:** Sex scandals involving Bill Clinton dominated the news and talk shows, but public opinion polls gave the president the highest approval ratings of his two terms in office.

- **2000:** On election night, the networks prematurely called the presidential election, first for Gore and then for Bush, causing confusion among the public and embarrassment for the networks. A "Florida feeding frenzy" ensued over the next month as television blanketed every phase of that state's recount, from local election officials staring at punch-card ballots to state and U.S. Supreme Court arguments.

- **2001:** Dramatic television coverage of commercial aircraft crashing into the World Trade Center and videotape of the collapse of the twin giant

The first televised presidential election debates were in 1960 between Senator John F. Kennedy and Vice President Richard Nixon. Nixon came armed with statistics, but his dour demeanor, "five o'clock shadow," and stiff presentation fared poorly in contrast to Kennedy's open, relaxed, confident air.

buildings shocked Americans and inspired the "War on Terrorism."

■ **2003:** Reporters were "embedded" with American troops in the Iraqi War, providing ground-level narratives and video of combat.

■ **2004:** Photos from Ahu Ghraib prison in Iraq showing abuse of detainees were broadcast worldwide, inspiring intense opposition in the Muslim world.

selective perception
Mentally screening out information or opinions with which one disagrees.

ence over values and opinions is reduced by **selective perception**, mentally screening out information or opinions we disagree with. People tend to see and hear only what they want to see and hear. For example, television news concentration on scandal, abuse, and corruption in government has not always produced the liberal, reformist values among viewers that media people expected. On the contrary, the focus of network executives on governmental scandals—Watergate, the Iran-Contra scandal, the sexual antics of politicians, congressional check kiting, and so on—has produced feelings of general political distrust and cynicism toward government and the political system. These feelings have been labeled **television malaise**, a combination of social distrust, political cynicism, feelings of powerlessness, and disaffection from parties and politics that seems to stem from television's emphasis on the negative aspects of American life.

television malaise
Generalized feelings of distrust, cynicism, and powerlessness stemming from television's emphasis on the negative aspects of American life.

The media do not *intend* to create television malaise; they are performing their self-declared watchdog role. They expect their stories to encourage liberal reform of our political institutions. But the result is often alienation rather than reform.

Direct Effects on Public Opinion Can the media change public opinion, and if so, how? For many years, political scientists claimed that the media had only minimal effects on public opinions and behavior. This early view was based largely on the fact that newspaper editorial endorsements seldom affected people's votes. But serious research on the effects of television tells a different story.

In an extensive study of eighty policy issues over fifteen years, political scientists examined public opinion polls on various policy issues at a first point in time, then media content over a following interval of time, and finally public opinion on these same issues at the end of the interval. The purpose was to learn if media content—messages scored by their relevance to the issue, their salience in the

─── Think Again ───
Are media professionals—news reporters, editors, anchors—the true voice of the people in public affairs?

Late-night television is now a popular campaign forum. Young people rely heavily on the Jay Leno, David Letterman, and Conan O'Brien shows for their political news.

broadcast, their pro/con direction, the credibility of the news source, and quality of the reporting—changed public opinion. Most people's opinions remained constant over time (opinion at the first point in time is the best predictor of opinion at the second point in time). However, when opinion did change, it changed in the direction supported by the media. "News variables alone account for nearly half the variance in opinion change." Other findings include the following:

- Anchors, reporters, and commentators have the greatest impact on opinion change. Television newscasters have high credibility and trust with the general public. Their opinions are crucial in shaping mass opinion.

- Independent experts interviewed by the media have a substantial impact on opinion, but not as great as newscasters themselves.

- A popular president can also shift public opinion somewhat. Unpopular presidents do not have much success as opinion movers, however.

- Interest groups on the whole have a slightly negative effect on public opinion. "In many instances they seem actually to have antagonized the public and created a genuine adverse effect"; such cases include Vietnam War protesters, nuclear freeze advocates, and other demonstrators and protesters, even peaceful ones.[28]

Effects on Behavior   Many studies have focused on the effects of the media on behavior: studies of the effects of TV violence, studies of the effects of television on children, and studies of the effects of obscenity and pornography.[29] Although it is difficult to generalize from these studies, television appears more likely to reinforce behavioral tendencies than to change them. For example, televised violence may trigger violent behavior in children who are already predisposed to such behavior, but televised violence has little behavioral effect on average children.[30] Nevertheless, we know that television advertising sells products. And we know that political candidates spend millions to persuade audiences to go out and vote for them on election day. Both manufacturers and politicians create name recognition, employ product differentiation, try to associate with audiences, and use repetition to communicate their messages. These tactics are designed to affect our behavior both in the marketplace and in the election booth.

A CONSTITUTIONAL NOTE

Can the Federal Communications Commission Ban Profanity from Radio and Television?

When the Bill of Rights was passed by the nation's first Congress, the First Amendment's reference to freedom of the press could hardly have envisioned radio, television, or the Internet. When radio broadcasting began in the 1920s, there was a scarcity of broadcast frequencies. Stations fought over frequencies and even jammed each other's programming. The industry welcomed the Federal Communications Act of 1934 which created the Federal Communications Commission (FCC) to license stations for the exclusive use of radio frequencies. The law stated that the use of a frequency was a "public trust" and that the FCC should ensure that it was used in "the public interest." Although technology has vastly multiplied radio and television channels, the FCC has continued to fine broadcasters for indecency or profanity. The Supreme Court has continued to uphold the powers of the FCC. "Shock-jock" radio personality Howard Stern has been fined almost $2 million. Janet Jackson's "wardrobe malfunction" during the 2004 Super Bowl half-time performance also cost her network a large fine. In short, the FCC has retained its power over radio and television despite the fact that its original rationale, the scarcity of broadcast frequencies, has disappeared. We can contrast the control that the Supreme Court allows the government to exercise over radio and television with the freedom the same Court grants to users of the Internet. The Supreme Court held that the Communications Decency Act of 1996, making it a federal crime to send or display "indecent" material to persons under eighteen years of age over the Internet, was unconstitutional. The Supreme Court held that the government may not limit the adult population to "only what is fit for children."[a] Commercial sex sites deluge the Internet.

[a]*Reno v. American Civil Liberties Union*, 521 U.S. 471 (1997).

Political ads are more successful in motivating a candidate's supporters to go to the polls than they are in changing opponents into supporters. It is unlikely that voters who dislike a candidate will be persuaded by political advertising to change their votes. But many potential voters are undecided, and the support of many others is dubbed "soft." Going to the polls on Election Day requires effort—people have errands to do, it may be raining, they may be tired. Television advertising is more effective with the marginal voters.

Summary Notes

- The mass media in America not only report on the struggle for power, they are also participants themselves in that struggle.

- It is only through the media that the general public comes to know about political events, personalities, and issues. Newsmaking—deciding what is or is not "news"—is a major source of media power. Media coverage not only influences popular discussion but also forces public officials to respond.

- Media power also derives from the media's ability to set the agenda for public decision making—to determine what citizens and public officials will regard as "crises," "problems," or "issues" to be resolved by government.

- The media also exercise power in their interpretation of the news. News is presented in story form; pictures, words, sources, and story selection all contribute to interpretation.

- The media play a major role in socializing people to the political culture. Socialization occurs in news, entertainment, and advertising.

- The politics of the media are shaped by their economic interest in attracting readers and viewers. This interest largely accounts for the sensational and negative aspects of news reporting.

- The professional environment of newspeople encourages an activist, watchdog role in politics. The politics of most newspeople are liberal and Democratic.

■ Political campaigning is largely a media activity. The media have replaced the parties as the principal linkage between candidates and voters. But the media tend to report the campaign as a horse race, at the expense of issue coverage, and to focus more on candidates' character than on their voting records or issue positions.

■ The First Amendment guarantee of freedom of the press protects the media from government efforts to silence or censor them and allows the media to be "unfair" when they choose to be. The Federal Communications Commission exercises some modest controls over the electronic media, since the right to exclusive use of broadcast frequencies is a *public trust.*

■ Public officials are afforded very little protection by libel and slander laws. The Supreme Court's Sullivan rule allows even damaging falsehoods to be written and broadcast as long as newspeople themselves do not deliberately fabricate lies with "malicious intent" or "reckless disregard."

■ Media effects on political life can be observed in (1) information and agenda setting, (2) values and opinions, and (3) behavior—in that order of influence. The media strongly influence what we know about politics and what we talk about. The media are less effective in changing existing opinions, values, and beliefs than they are in creating new ones. Nevertheless, the media can change many people's opinions, based on the credibility of news anchors and reporters. Direct media effects on behavior are limited. Political ads are more important in motivating supporters to go to the polls, and in swinging undecided or "soft" voters, than in changing the minds of committed voters.

Key Terms

Suggested Readings

Alterman, Eric. *What Liberal Media?* New York: Simon & Schuster, 2003. A contrarian argument that the media does *not* have a liberal bias but rather bends over backward to include conservative views.

Ansolabehere, Stephen, Roy Behr, and Shanto Iyengar. *The Media Game: American Politics in the Television Age.* New York: Longman, 1993. A comprehensive text assessing the changes in the political system brought about by the rise of television since the 1950s.

Fallows, James. *Breaking the News: How the Media Undermine American Democracy.* New York: Pantheon, 1996. An argument that today's arrogant, cynical, and scandal-minded news reporting is turning readers and viewers away and undermining support for democracy.

Goldberg, Bernard. *Bias: A CBS Insider Exposes How the Media Distort the News.* New York: Perennial, 2003. The title says it all.

Graber, Doris A. *Mass Media and American Politics.* 7th ed. Washington, D.C.: CQ Press, 2005. A wide-ranging description of media effects on campaigns, parties, and elections, as well as on social values and public policies.

Lichter, Robert S., Stanley Rothman, and Linda S. Lichter. *The Media Elite.* Bethesda, Md.: Adler and Adler, 1986. A thorough study of the social and political values of top leaders in the mass media, based on extensive interviews of key people in the most influential media outlets.

Patterson, Thomas E. *Out of Order.* New York: Random House, 1994. The antipolitical bias of the media poisons national election campaigns; policy questions are ignored in favor of the personal characteristics of candidates, their campaign strategies, and their standing in the horse race.

Prindle, David F. *Risky Business.* Boulder, Colo.: Westview Press, 1993. An examination of the politics of Hollywood, its liberalism, activism, self-indulgence, and celebrity egotism.

Sabato, Larry J. *Feeding Frenzy: How Attack Journalism Has Transformed American Politics.* New York: Free Press, 1992. A strong argument that the media prefer "to employ titillation rather than scrutiny" and as a result produce "trivialization rather than enlightenment."

West, Darrell M. *Air Wars: Television Advertising in Election Campaigns.* 4th ed. Washington, D.C.: CQ Press, 2005. The evolution of campaign advertising from 1952 to 2004 and how voters are influenced by television ads.

7 POLITICAL PARTIES
Organizing Politics

Think About Politics

1 Generally speaking, how would you identify yourself: as a Republican, Democrat, independent, or something else?
Republican ☐ Democrat ☐
Independent ☐ Other ☐

2 Which major political party better represents the interests of people like yourself?
Republican ☐ Democrat ☐

3 Does the Republican Party favor the rich more than the middle class or poor?
Yes ☐ No ☐

4 Does the Democratic Party favor the poor more than the middle class or rich?
Yes ☐ No ☐

5 Which major party does a better job of protecting the Social Security system?
Republican ☐ Democrat ☐

6 Which major party does a better job of handling foreign affairs?
Republican ☐ Democrat ☐

7 Should elected officials be bound by their party's platform?
Yes ☐ No ☐

8 Do we need a third party to challenge the Republican and Democratic parties?
Yes ☐ No ☐

How much power do political parties really have to determine who gets what in America? We hear the terms Republican and Democratic linked to people and to policies, but do these parties have real power beyond that of organizing for elections?

The Power of Organization

In the struggle for power, organization grants advantage. Italian political scientist Gaetano Mosca once put it succinctly: "A hundred men acting uniformly in concert, with a common understanding, will triumph over a thousand men who are not in accord and can therefore be dealt with one by one."[1] Thus politics centers on organization—on organizing people to win office and to influence public policy.

Political organizations—parties and interest groups—function as intermediaries between individuals and government. They organize individuals to give them power in selecting government officials—who governs—and in determining public policy—for what ends. Generally, **political parties** are more concerned with winning public office in elections than with influencing policy, whereas *interest groups* are more directly concerned with public policy and involve themselves with elections only to advance their policy interests (see Figure 7.1). In other words, parties and interest groups have an informal division of functions, with parties focusing on personnel and interest groups focusing on policy. Yet both organize individuals for more effective political action.

American Parties: A Historical Perspective

Parties are *not* mentioned in the Constitution. Indeed, the nation's Founders regarded both parties and interest groups as "factions," citizens united by "some common impulse of passion, or of interest, adverse to the rights of other citizens, or to the permanent and aggregate interests of the community." The Founders viewed factions as "mischievous" and "dangerous."[2] Yet the emergence of parties was inevitable as people sought to organize themselves to exercise power over who governs (see Figure 7.2).

The Emergence of Parties: Federalists and Democratic-Republicans In his Farewell Address, George Washington warned the nation about political parties: "Let me . . . warn you in the most solemn manner against the baneful effects of the spirit of party generally."[3] As president,

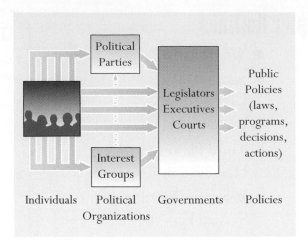

Figure 7.1 Political Organizations as Intermediaries
All political organizations function as intermediaries between individuals and government. Parties are concerned primarily with winning elected office; interest groups are concerned with influencing policy.

political organizations
Parties and interest groups that function as intermediaries between individuals and government.

political parties
Organizations that seek to achieve power by winning public office.

Federalists Those who supported the U.S. Constitution during the ratification process and who later formed a political party in support of John Adams's presidential candidacy.

Anti-Federalists Those who opposed the ratification of the U.S. Constitution and the creation of a strong national government.

majority Election by more than 50 percent of all votes cast in the contest.

Washington stood above the factions that were coalescing around his secretary of the treasury, Alexander Hamilton, and around his former secretary of state, Thomas Jefferson. Jefferson had resigned from Washington's cabinet in 1793 to protest the fiscal policies of Hamilton, notably his creation of a national bank and repayment of the states' Revolutionary War debts with federal funds. Washington had endorsed Hamilton's policies, but so great was the first president's prestige that Jefferson and his followers directed their fire not against Washington but against Hamilton, John Adams, and their supporters, who called themselves **Federalists** after their leaders' outspoken defense of the Constitution during the ratification process. By the 1790s, Jefferson and Madison, as well as many **Anti-Federalists** who had initially opposed the ratification of the Constitution, began calling themselves *Republicans* or *Democratic-Republicans,* terms that had become popular after the French Revolution in 1789.

Adams narrowly defeated Jefferson in the presidential election of 1796. This election was an important milestone in the development of the parties and the presidential election system. For the first time, two candidates campaigned as members of opposing parties, and candidates for presidential elector in each state pledged themselves as "Adams's men" or "Jefferson's men." By committing themselves in advance of the actual presidential vote, these pledged electors enabled voters in each state to determine the outcome of the presidential election.

Jefferson's Democratic-Republicans   Party activity intensified in anticipation of the election of 1800. Jefferson's Democratic-Republican Party first saw the importance of organizing voters, circulating literature, and rallying the masses to their causes. Many Federalists viewed this early party activity with disdain. Indeed, the Federalists even tried to outlaw public criticism of the federal government by means of the Alien and Sedition Acts of 1798, which among other things made it a crime to publish false or malicious writings against the (Federalist) Congress or president or to "stir up hatred" against them. These acts directly challenged the newly adopted First Amendment guarantees of freedom of speech and the press. But in the election of 1800, the Federalists went down to defeat. Democratic-Republican electors won a **majority** (more than half the votes cast) in the Electoral College. (See *A Constitutional Note:* "Political Parties and the Constitution.")

The election of 1800 was a landmark in American democracy—the first time that control of government passed peacefully from one party to another on the basis of an election outcome. As commonplace as that may seem to Americans today, the peaceful transfer of power from one group to another remains a rarity in many political systems around the world.

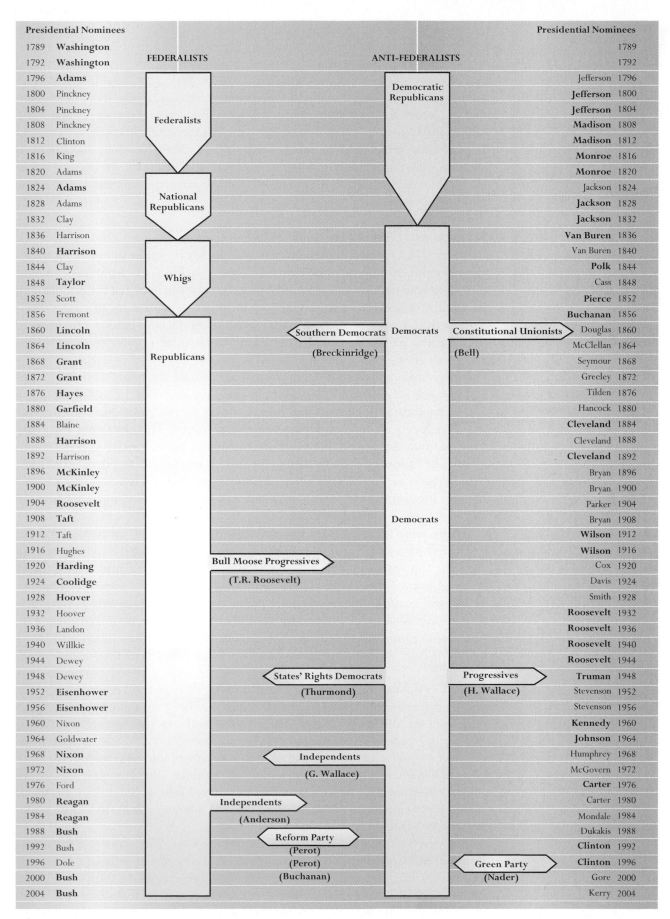

Figure 7.2 Change and Continuity in the American Party System

Jefferson was adept at partisan politics, and his Democratic-Republican Party was a great success.

plurality Election by at least one vote more than any other candidate in the race.

Democratic Party One of the main parties in American politics; it traces its origins to Thomas Jefferson's Democratic-Republican Party, acquiring its current name under Andrew Jackson in 1828.

Republican Party One of the two main parties in American politics, it traces its origins to the antislavery and nationalist forces that united in the 1850s and nominated Abraham Lincoln for president in 1860.

Jefferson's Democratic-Republican Party—later to be called the Democrats—was so successful that the Federalist Party never regained the presidency or control of Congress. The Federalists tended to represent merchants, manufacturers, and shippers, who were concentrated in New York and New England. The Democratic-Republicans tended to represent agrarian interests, from large plantation owners to small farmers. In the mostly agrarian America of the early 1800s, the Democratic-Republican Party prevailed.[4] Jefferson easily won reelection in 1804, and his allies, James Madison and James Monroe, overwhelmed their Federalist opponents in subsequent presidential elections. By 1820, the Federalist Party had ceased to exist. Indeed, for a few years, it seemed as if the new nation had ended party politics.

Jacksonian Democrats and Whigs Partisan politics soon reappeared, however. The Democratic-Republicans had already begun to fight among themselves by the 1824 presidential election. Andrew Jackson won a **plurality** (at least one more vote than anyone else in the race) but not a majority of the popular and Electoral College vote, but he then lost to John Quincy Adams in a close decision by the factionalized House of Representatives. Jackson led his supporters to found a new party, the **Democratic Party**, to organize popular support for his 1828 presidential bid, which succeeded in ousting Adams.

Jacksonian ideas both *democratized* and *nationalized* the party system. Under Jackson, the Democratic Party began to mobilize voters on behalf of the party and its candidates. It pressed the states to lower property qualifications for voting in order to recruit new Democratic Party voters. The electorate expanded from 365,000 voters in 1824 to well over a million in 1828 and over 2 million in 1840. The Democratic Party also pressed the states to choose presidential electors by popular vote rather than by state legislatures. Thus Jackson and his Democratic successor, Martin Van Buren, ran truly national campaigns directed at the voters in every state.

At the same time, Jackson's opponents formed the Whig Party, named after the British party of that name. Like the British Whigs, who opposed the power of the king, the American Whigs charged "King Andrew" with usurping the powers of Congress and the people. The Whigs quickly adopted the Democrats' tactics of national campaigning and popular organizing. By 1840, the Whigs were able to gain the White House, running William Henry Harrison—nicknamed "Old Tippecanoe" from his victory at Tippecanoe over Native Americans in 1811—and John Tyler and featuring the slogan "Tippecanoe and Tyler too."

Post–Civil War Republican Dominance Whigs and Democrats continued to share national power until the slavery conflict that ignited the Civil War destroyed the old party system. The Republican Party had formed in 1854 to oppose the spread of slavery to the western territories. By the election of 1860, the slavery issue so divided the nation that four parties offered presidential candidates: Lincoln, the Republican; Stephen A. Douglas, the northern Democrat; John C. Breckinridge, the southern Democrat; and John Bell, the Constitutional Union Party candidate. No party came close to winning a majority of the popular vote, but Lincoln won in the Electoral College.

The new party system that emerged from the Civil War featured a victorious **Republican Party** that generally represented the northern industrial economy and a struggling Democratic Party that generally represented a southern agricultural economy. The Republican Party won every presidential election from 1860 to 1912 except for two victories by Democratic reformer and New York governor Grover Cleveland (see *Up Close:* "The Donkey and the Elephant").

UP CLOSE

The Donkey and the Elephant

The popular nineteenth-century cartoonist Thomas Nast is generally credited with giving the Democratic and Republican parties their current symbols: the donkey and the elephant. In *Harper's Weekly* cartoons in the 1870s, Nast critically portrayed the Democratic Party as a stubborn mule "without pride of ancestry nor hope of posterity." During this period of Republican Party dominance, Nast portrayed the Republican Party as an elephant, the biggest beast in the political jungle. Now both party symbols are used with pride.

In the 1870 cartoon on the left, published following the death of Lincoln's Secretary of War E. M. Stanton, Nast shows a donkey (labeled "Copperheads," a disparaging term for the mostly Democratic northerners who were sympathetic to the South during the Civil War) kicking the dead Stanton, who is portrayed as a lion. The 1874 cartoon on the right features the elephant as the Republican Vote and the donkey masquerading as a lion.

Yet the Democratic Party offered a serious challenge in the election of 1896 and realigned the party affiliations of the nation's voters. The Democratic Party nominated William Jennings Bryan, a talented orator and a religious fundamentalist. Bryan sought to rally the nation's white "have-nots" to the Democratic Party banner, particularly the debt-ridden farmers of the South and West. His plan was to stimulate inflation (and thus enable debtors to pay their debts with "cheaper," less valuable dollars) through using plentiful, western-mined "free silver," rather than gold, as the monetary standard. He defeated Cleveland's faction and the "Gold Democrats" in the 1896 Democratic Party convention with his famous Cross of Gold speech: "You shall not crucify mankind upon a cross of gold."

But the Republican Party rallied its forces in perhaps the most bitter presidential battle in history. It sought to convince the nation that high tariffs, protection for manufacturers, and a solid monetary standard would lead to prosperity for industrial workers as well as the new tycoons. The campaign, directed by Marcus Alonzo Hanna, attorney for John D. Rockefeller's Standard Oil Company, spent an unprecedented $16 million (an amount in inflation-adjusted dollars that has never been equaled) to elect Republican William McKinley, advertised as the candidate who would bring a "full dinner pail" to all. The battle also produced one of the largest voter turnouts in history. McKinley won in a landslide. Bryan ran twice again but lost by even larger margins. The Republican Party solidified

Negative advertising has a long history in American politics. In the election of 1896, Republican presidential candidate William McKinley portrayed his Democratic opponent William Jennings Bryan as an unpatriotic destroyer of America's interests, represented by the flag.

the loyalty of industrial workers, small-business owners, bankers, and large manufacturers, as well as black voters, who respected "the party of Lincoln" and despised the segregationist practices of the southern Democratic Party.

Republican Split, Democratic Win   So great was the Republican Party's dominance in national elections that only a split among Republicans enabled the Democrat Woodrow Wilson to capture the presidency in 1912. Republican Theodore Roosevelt (who became president following McKinley's assassination and had won reelection in 1904) sought to recapture the presidency from his former protégé, Republican William Howard Taft. In the **GOP** ("Grand Old Party," as the Republicans began labeling themselves) convention, party regulars rejected the unpredictable Roosevelt in favor of Taft, even though Roosevelt had won the few primary elections that had recently been initiated. An irate Teddy Roosevelt launched a third, progressive party, the "Bull Moose," which actually outpolled the Republican Party in the 1912 election—the only time a third party has surpassed one of the two major parties in U.S. history. But the result was a victory for the Democratic candidate, former Princeton political science professor Woodrow Wilson. Following Wilson's two terms, Republicans again reasserted their political dominance with victories by Warren G. Harding, Calvin Coolidge, and Herbert Hoover.

The New Deal Democratic Party   The promise of prosperity that empowered the Republican Party to hold its membership together faded in the light of the Great Depression. The U.S. stock market crashed in 1929, and by the early 1930s, one-quarter of the labor force was unemployed. Having lost confidence in the nation's business and political leadership, in 1932 American voters turned out incumbent Republican President Herbert Hoover in favor of Democrat Franklin D. Roosevelt, who promised the country a **New Deal**.

More than just bringing the Democrats to the White House, the Great Depression marked another party realignment. This time, traditionally Republican voting groups changed their affiliation and enabled the Democratic Party to dominate national politics for a generation. This realignment actually began in 1928, when Democratic presidential candidate Al Smith, a Catholic, won many northern, urban, ethnic voters away from the Republican Party. By 1932, a majority New Deal Democratic coalition had been formed in American politics. It consisted of the following groups:

- Working classes and union members, especially in large cities.

- White ethnic groups who had previously aligned themselves with Republican machines.

- Catholics and Jews.

- African Americans, who ended their historic affiliation with the party of Lincoln to pursue new economic and social goals.

- Poor people, who associated the New Deal with expanded welfare and Social Security programs.

- Southern whites, who had provided the most loyal block of Democratic voters since the Civil War.

To be sure, this majority coalition had many internal factions: southern "Dixiecrats" walked out of the Democratic Party convention in 1948 to protest a party platform that called for an end to racial discrimination in employment. But

---

GOP "Grand Old Party"—popular label for the Republican Party.

— Think Again —

Does the Democratic Party favor the poor more than the middle class or rich?

New Deal Policies of President Franklin D. Roosevelt during the Depression of the 1930s that helped form a Democratic Party coalition of urban working-class, ethnic, Catholic, Jewish, poor, and Southern voters.

 **Franklin D. Roosevelt (FDR) Heritage Center** Biography on F.D.R. and information on the New Deal. *www.fdrheritage.org*

Franklin Roosevelt campaigning among coal miners in West Virginia during the presidential election campaign of 1932. Roosevelt's optimism and "can-do" attitude in the face of the Great Depression helped cement the New Deal Democratic coalition that won him the presidency.

the promise of a New Deal—with its vast array of government supports for workers, elderly and disabled people, widows and children, and farmers—held this coalition together reasonably well. President Harry Truman's **Fair Deal** proved that the coalition could survive its founder, Franklin D. Roosevelt. Republican Dwight D. Eisenhower made inroads into this coalition by virtue of his personal popularity and the Republican Party's acceptance of most New Deal programs. But John F. Kennedy's "New Frontier" demonstrated the continuing appeal of the Democratic Party tradition. Lyndon Johnson's **Great Society** went further than the programs of any of his predecessors in government intervention in the economic and social life of the nation. Indeed, it might be argued that the Great Society laid the foundation for a political reaction that eventually destroyed the old Democratic coalition and led to yet another new party alignment (see Figure 7.3).

A New Republican Majority   The American political system underwent massive convulsions in the late 1960s as a result of both the civil rights revolution at home and an unpopular war in Vietnam. Strains were felt in all of the nation's political institutions, from the courts to the Congress to the presidency. And when Lyndon Johnson announced his decision not to run for reelection in 1968, the Democratic Party erupted in a battle that ultimately destroyed its majority support among presidential voters.

At the 1968 Democratic Party convention in Chicago, Vice President Hubert Humphrey controlled a majority of the delegates inside the convention hall, but antiwar protesters dominated media coverage outside the hall. When Chicago police attacked unruly demonstrators with batons, the media broadcast to the world an image of the nation's turmoil. In the presidential campaign that followed, both candidates—Democrat Hubert Humphrey and Republican Richard Nixon—presented nearly identical positions supporting the U.S. military commitment in Vietnam while endorsing a negotiated, "honorable" settlement of the war. But the image of the Democratic Party became associated with the street protesters. Inside the convention hall, pressure from women and minorities led party leaders to adopt changes in the party's delegate-selection process for future conventions to

Fair Deal Policies of President Harry Truman extending Roosevelt's New Deal and maintaining the Democratic Party's voter coalition.

Great Society Policies of President Lyndon Johnson that promised to solve the nation's social and economic problems through government intervention.

www Democratic Party Web site of the **Democratic National Committee (DNC)** With news, press releases, policy positions, and so forth. *www.democrat.org*

—Think Again—

Does the Republican Party favor the rich more than the middle class or poor?

Figure 7.3   The Parties in Presidential Voting

Despite the dominance of the Democratic Party in terms of numbers of registered voters, Republicans have won more presidential elections since 1952, indicating that, at the presidential level, voters are not always loyal to their party.

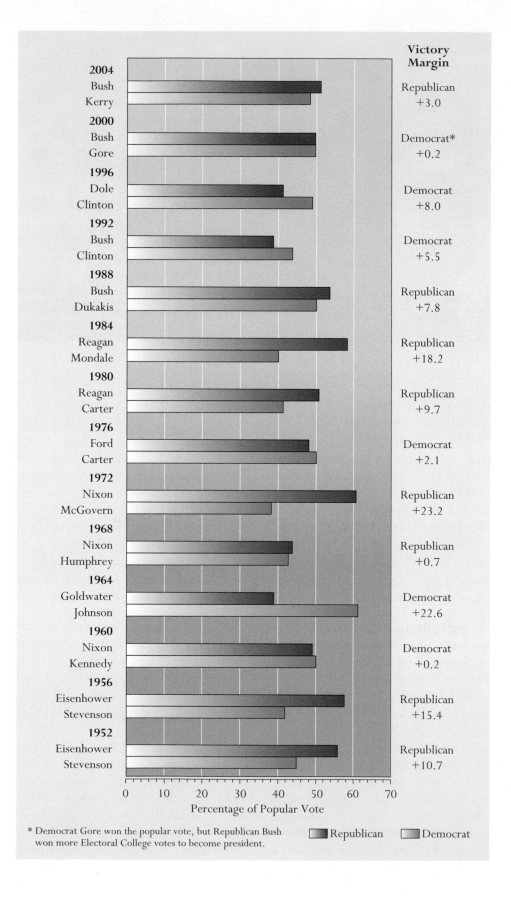

* Democrat Gore won the popular vote, but Republican Bush won more Electoral College votes to become president.

assure better representation of these groups—at the expense of Democratic office-holders (see "Making Party Rules" later in this chapter for more details).

In 1972 the Democratic Party convention strongly reflected the views of anti-war protesters, civil rights advocates, feminist organizations, and liberal activists generally. The visibility of these activists, who appeared to be well to the left of both Democratic Party voters and the electorate in general, allowed the Republican Party to portray the Democratic presidential nominee, George McGovern, as an unpatriotic liberal, willing to "crawl to Hanoi" and to sacrifice the nation's honor for peace. It also allowed the Republicans to characterize the new Democratic Party as soft on crime, tolerant of disorder, and committed to racial and sexual quotas in American life. Richard Nixon, never very popular personally, was able to win in a landslide in 1972. The Watergate scandal and Nixon's forced resignation only temporarily stemmed the tide of "the new Republican majority." Democrat Jimmy Carter's narrow victory over Republican Gerald R. Ford in 1976 owed much to the latter's pardon of Nixon.

The Reagan Coalition   Under the leadership of Ronald Reagan, the Republican Party was able to assemble a majority coalition that dominated presidential elections in the 1980s, giving Reagan landslide victories in 1980 and 1984 and George H.W. Bush a convincing win in 1988. The **Reagan Coalition** consisted of the following groups:

■ Economic conservatives concerned about high taxes and excessive government regulation, including business and professional voters who had traditionally supported the Republican Party.

■ Social conservatives concerned about crime, drugs, and racial conflict, including many white ethnic voters and union members who had traditionally voted Democratic.

■ Religious fundamentalists concerned about such issues as abortion and prayer in schools.

■ Southern whites concerned about racial issues, including affirmative action programs.

■ Internationalists and anticommunists who wanted the United States to maintain a strong military force and to confront Soviet-backed Marxist regimes around the world.

Reagan held this coalition together in large part through his personal popularity and his infectious optimism about the United States and its future. Although sometimes at odds with one another, economic conservatives, religious fundamentalists, and internationalists could unite behind the "Great Communicator." Reagan's presidential victory in 1980 helped to elect a Republican majority to the U.S. Senate and encouraged Democratic conservatives in the Democrat-controlled House of Representatives to frequently vote with Republicans. As a result, Reagan got most of what he asked of Congress in his first term: cuts in personal income taxes, increased spending for national defense, and slower growth of federal regulatory activity. With the assistance of the Federal Reserve Board, inflation was brought under control. But Reagan largely failed to cut government spending as he had promised, and the result was a series of huge federal deficits. Reagan appointed conservatives to the Supreme Court and the federal judiciary (see Chapter 13), but no major decisions were reversed (including the *Roe v. Wade* decision, protecting abortion); social conservatives had to be content with the president's symbolic support.

Republican Party
Web site of the **Republican National Committee (RNC)**
With GOP news, press releases, policy positions, and so forth. ***www.rnc.org***

Reagan Coalition
Combination of economic and social conservatives, religious fundamentalists, and defense-minded anticommunists who rallied behind Republican President Ronald Reagan.

President Ronald Reagan created a Republican majority coalition in the 1980s by uniting Republican factions—economic conservatives, social conservatives, religious fundamentalists, and anti-Communists—and adding many Southern white Democrats.

Democratic Leadership Council Organization of party leaders who sought to create a "new" Democratic Party to appeal to middle-class, moderate voters.

During these years, the national Democratic Party was saddled with an unpopular image as the party of special-interest groups. As more middle-class and working-class voters deserted to the GOP, the key remaining loyal Democratic constituencies were African Americans and other minorities, government employees, union leaders, liberal intellectuals in the media and universities, feminist organizations, and environmentalists. Democratic presidential candidates Walter Mondale in 1984 and Michael Dukakis in 1988 were obliged to take liberal positions to win the support of these groups in the primary elections. Later, both candidates sought to move toward the center of the ideological battleground in the general election. But Republican Party strategists were able to "define" Mondale and Dukakis through negative campaign advertising (see Chapter 8) as liberal defenders of special-interest groups. The general conservative tilt of public opinion in the 1980s added to the effectiveness of the GOP strategy of branding Democratic presidential candidates with the "*L* word" (*liberal*).

Clinton and the "New" Democrats Yet even while Democratic candidates fared poorly in presidential elections, Democrats continued to maintain control of the House of Representatives, to win back control of the U.S. Senate in 1986, and to hold more state governorships and state legislative seats than the Republicans. Thus the Democratic Party retained a strong leadership base on which to rebuild itself.

During the 1980s, Democratic leaders among governors and senators came together in the **Democratic Leadership Council** to create a "new" Democratic Party closer to the center of the political spectrum. The chair of the Democratic Leadership Council was the young, energetic, and successful governor of Arkansas, Bill Clinton. The concern of the council was that the Democratic Party's traditional support for social justice and social welfare programs was overshadowing its commitment to economic prosperity. Many council members argued that a healthy economy was a prerequisite to progress in social welfare. Not all Democrats agreed with the council agenda. African American leaders (including the Reverend Jesse Jackson), as well as liberal and environmental groups, feared that the priorities of

Left to right: President George W. Bush, former President Bill Clinton, former President Jimmy Carter, and former President George H.W. Bush, at the opening of the Clinton Presidential Center (library) in Little Rock, Arkansas. Shared experiences in the White House can bring Republican and Democratic presidents together.

the council would result in the sacrifice of traditional Democratic Party commitments to minorities, poor people, and the environment.

In the 1992 presidential election, Bill Clinton was in a strong position to take advantage of the faltering economy under George H.W. Bush, to stress the "new" Democratic Party's commitment to the middle class, and to avoid being labeled as a liberal defender of special interests. At the same time, he managed to rally the party's core activist groups—liberals, intellectuals, African Americans, feminists, and environmentalists. Many liberals in the party deliberately soft-pedaled their views during the 1992 election in order not to offend voters, hoping to win with Clinton and then fight for liberal programs later. Clinton won with 43 percent of the vote, to Bush's 38 percent. Independent Ross Perot captured a surprising 19 percent of the popular vote, including many voters who were alienated from both the Democratic and Republican parties. Once in office, Clinton appeared to revert to liberal policy directions rather than to pursue the more moderate line he had espoused as a "new" Democrat. As Clinton's ratings sagged, the opportunity arose for a Republican resurgence.

Republican Resurgence   A political earthquake shook Washington in the 1994 congressional elections, when the Republicans for the first time in forty years captured the House of Representatives, regained control of the Senate, and captured a majority of the nation's governorships. For the first time in history Republicans won more seats in the South than the Democrats. This southern swing to the Republicans in congressional elections seemed to confirm the realignment of Southern voters that had begun earlier in presidential elections. Just two years after a Democratic president had been elected, the GOP won its biggest nationwide victory since the Great Depression.

Clinton Holds On   Following the Republican victory, the Democratic Party appeared to be in temporary disarray. The new Republican House Speaker, Newt Gingrich, tried to seize national policy leadership; Clinton was widely viewed as a failed president. But the Republicans quickly squandered their political opportunity. They had made many promises in a well-publicized "Contract with America"—a balanced federal budget, congressional term limits, tax cuts, welfare reform, and more—but they delivered little. Majority Leader Bob Dole failed by one vote to pass the Balanced Budget Amendment in the Senate. President Clinton took an unexpectedly hard line toward GOP spending cuts and vetoed several budget bills. When the federal government officially "closed down" for lack of appropriated funds, the public appeared to blame Republicans. Polls showed a dramatic recovery in the president's approval ratings. Clinton skillfully portrayed GOP leaders, especially Newt Gingrich, as "extremists" and himself as a responsible moderate prepared to trim the budget, reduce the deficit, and reform welfare, "while still protecting Medicare, Medicaid, education, and the environment." By early 1996, Clinton had set the stage for his reelection campaign.

> **MoveOn**
> Website of the liberal wing of the Democratic Party. *www.moveon.org*

Bill Clinton is the first Democratic president to be reelected since Franklin D. Roosevelt. Clinton rode to victory on a robust economy. Voters put aside doubts about Clinton's character, and they ignored Republican Bob Dole's call for tax reductions. Clinton won with 49 percent of the popular vote to Dole's 41 percent and Perot's 8 percent. But Clinton's victory failed to rejuvenate the Democratic Party's fortunes across the country. The GOP retained its majorities in both houses of Congress.

2000—A Nation Divided   The nation was more evenly divided in 2000 between the Democratic and Republican parties than perhaps at any other time in history. Democrat Al Gore won a narrow victory in the popular vote for president.

But after a month-long battle for Florida's electoral vote, Republican George W. Bush, former Texas governor and son of the former President Bush, emerged as the winner of the Electoral College vote, 271 to 267 (see Chapter 8). Not only was the presidential vote almost tied, but also both houses of Congress were split almost evenly between Democrats and Republicans. The Republican Party lost seats in the House of Representatives in 1998 and again in 2000. Yet the GOP still retained a razor-thin margin of control of that body. In the Senate, the 2000 election created a historic 50–50 tie between Democrats and Republicans. The vote of the Senate's presiding officer, Republican Vice President Dick Cheney, would have given the GOP the narrowest of control of that body. But in 2001, Vermont's Republican Senator Jim Jeffords decided to switch his support to the Democratic Party, swinging control of the Senate to the Democrats (see Chapter 10).

The Republican Party defied tradition in 2002 by gaining seats in the Senate and expanding its majority in the House. Historically, the party in control of the White House *lost* seats in midterm elections. But in an era in which presidents are not supposed to have coattails, especially in midterm congressional elections, President George W. Bush campaigned energetically across the country for GOP candidates, focusing attention on the war on terrorism. Democratic complaints about the weak economy were muted. Bush's intense efforts appeared to motivate Republican voters; a higher-than-usual midterm voter turnout resulted in Republican victories in hotly contested Senate and House races across the country.

Republicans Take Control   In 2004, the GOP further consolidated its control over the White House, Senate, and House of Representatives. Throughout the 2004 election campaign, polls showed the nation evenly split, with Republican President Bush and Democratic Senator Kerry running neck and neck. There was considerable fear of another contested presidential election and concern that the popular vote winner might again lose in the Electoral College. But Republicans showed unexpected strength, with Bush winning both the popular vote and the Electoral College vote. Turnout was high—about 59 percent of persons eligible to vote. (Republican turnout may have been helped by referenda banning same-sex marriage that appeared on the ballot in eleven states; polls consistently show regular churchgoers tending to vote Republican.) Republicans added to their controlling margins in both the House and the Senate. Even the Democratic Senate leader, Tom Daschle of South Dakota, lost his bid for reelection. President Bush claimed a mandate for Republican efforts to simplify the tax code and to allow younger workers to invest part of their Social Security taxes in the stock market, and continued to aggressively pursue the war on terrorism throughout the world.

Democrats Recover—2006   The war in Iraq undermined the Republican Party's hold on congressional voters in 2006. For the first time in twelve years, the GOP lost control of the House of Representatives. They also gave up control of the Senate; Democrats won just enough seats to give them a 51 to 49 margin in that body. Polls suggested that voters had lost confidence in President Bush; his approval ratings remained below 40 percent throughout the election year. Midterm elections are seldom a referendum on national policy, but just enough voters in close House and Senate races decided in favor of "change," bringing back Democratic majorities in both houses of Congress.

Political Parties and Democratic Government

"Political parties created democracy, and modern democracy is unthinkable save in terms of the parties."[5] Traditionally, political scientists have praised parties as indispensable to democratic government. They have argued that parties are essential for organizing popular majorities to exercise control over government. The development of political parties in all the democracies of the world testifies to the underlying importance of parties to democratic government. But political parties in the United States have lost their preeminent position as instruments of democracy. Other structures and organizations in society—interest groups, the mass media, independent campaign organizations, primary elections, social welfare agencies—now perform many of the functions traditionally regarded as prerogatives of political parties. Nevertheless, the Democratic and Republican parties remain important organizing structures for politics in the United States.

"Responsible" Parties in Theory   In theory, political parties function in a democracy to organize majorities around broad principles of government in order to win public office and enact these principles into law. A "responsible" party should:

- Adopt a platform setting forth its principles and policy positions.

- Recruit candidates for public office who agree with the party's platform.

- Inform and educate the public about the platform.

- Organize and direct campaigns based on platform principles.

- Organize the legislature to ensure party control in policy making.

- Hold its elected officials responsible for enacting the party's platform.

If responsible, disciplined, policy-oriented parties competed for majority support, *if* they offered clear policy alternatives to the voters, and *if* the voters cast their ballots on the basis of these policy options, *then* the winning party would have a "policy mandate" from the people to guide the course of government. In that way, the democratic ideal of government by majority rule would be implemented.

But Winning Wins over Principle   However, the **responsible party model** never accurately described the American party system. The major American parties have been loose coalitions of individuals and groups seeking to attract sufficient votes to gain control of government. *Winning has generally been more important than any principles or policies.* America's major parties must appeal to tens of millions of voters in every section of the nation and from all walks of life. If a major party is to acquire a majority capable of controlling the U.S. government, it cannot limit its appeal by relying on a single unifying principle. Instead, it must form coalitions of voters from as many sectors of the population as it can. Major American parties therefore usually do not emphasize particular principles or ideologies so much as try to find a common ground of agreement among many different people. This emphasis does not mean no policy differences exist between the American parties. On the contrary, each party tends to appeal to a distinctive coalition of interests, and therefore each party expresses somewhat distinctive policy views (see *What Do You Think?* "Which Party Does a Better Job?").

In their efforts to win, major American political parties strive to attract the support of the large numbers of people near the center of public opinion. Generally more votes are at the center of the ideological spectrum—the middle-of-the-road—than on the extreme liberal or conservative ends. Thus *no real incentive exists for vote-maximizing parties to take strong policy positions in opposition to each other* (see Figure 7.4).

Party and Ideology   Despite incentives for the parties to move to the center of the political spectrum, the Republican and Democratic parties are perceived

---

Think Again

Should elected officials be bound by their party's platform?

---

responsible party model
System in which competitive parties adopt a platform of principles, recruiting candidates and directing campaigns based on the platform, and holding their elected officials responsible for enacting it.

WHAT DO YOU THINK?

Which Party Does a Better Job?

What do Americans think of the Democratic and Republican parties? Generally speaking, the Democratic Party has been able to maintain an image of "the party of the common people," and the Republican Party has long been saddled with an image of "favoring the rich."

But when it comes to popular perceptions of each party's ability to deal with problems confronting the nation, the Democratic and Republican parties appear evenly matched. The Republican Party is trusted to "do a better job" in handling foreign affairs and maintaining a strong national defense. It also enjoys a reputation of being better at "holding down taxes."

The Democratic Party enjoys its greatest advantage on "compassion issues" such as helping poor, elderly, and homeless people. And the Democrats have long enjoyed the support of the high-voter-turnout over-sixty-five age group because it is trusted to do a better job "protecting the Social Security system."

Source: Various polls reported in *The Polling Report,* November 22, 1999, September 10, 2001, January 28, 2002, August 11, 2003.

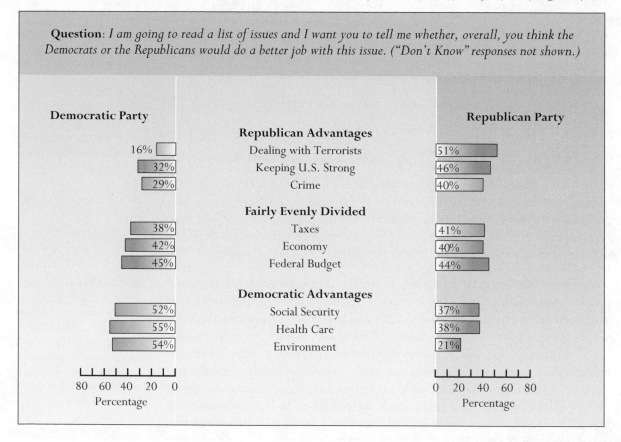

Question: *I am going to read a list of issues and I want you to tell me whether, overall, you think the Democrats or the Republicans would do a better job with this issue. ("Don't Know" responses not shown.)*

Democratic Party		Republican Party
	Republican Advantages	
16%	Dealing with Terrorists	51%
32%	Keeping U.S. Strong	46%
29%	Crime	40%
	Fairly Evenly Divided	
38%	Taxes	41%
42%	Economy	40%
45%	Federal Budget	44%
	Democratic Advantages	
52%	Social Security	37%
55%	Health Care	38%
54%	Environment	21%
80 60 40 20 0 Percentage		0 20 40 60 80 Percentage

by the public as ideologically separate. The electorate tends to perceive the Republican Party as conservative and the Democratic Party as liberal.

Indeed, polls suggest that Republican voters described themselves as conservatives far more often than as liberals. And Democratic voters are more likely to identify themselves as liberals than as conservatives, although many like to think of themselves as moderates (see Table 7.1).

This relationship between ideological self-identification and party self-identification is relatively stable over time. It suggests that the parties are not altogether empty jars. Later we will observe that Democratic and Republican party activists (notably, delegates to the party conventions) are even more ideologically separate than Democratic and Republican Party voters.

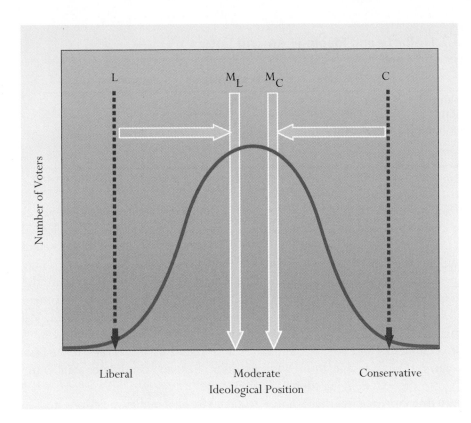

Figure 7.4 Winning versus Principle

Why don't we have a party system based on principles, with a liberal party and a conservative party, each offering the voters a real ideological choice? Let's assume that voters generally choose the party closest to their own ideological position. If the liberal party (L) took a strong ideological position to the left of most voters, the conservative party (C) would move toward the center, winning more moderate votes, even while retaining its conservative supporters, who would still prefer it to the more liberal opposition party. Likewise, if the conservative party took a strong ideological position to the right of most voters, the liberal party would move to the center and win. So both parties must abandon strong ideological positions and move to the center, becoming moderate in the fight for support of moderate voters.

Democratic and Republican party activists have become more ideologically separate in recent years. And voters have become increasingly aware of this **party polarization**. Indeed many voters are now prepared to say that the Democratic Party is more liberal and the Republican Party is more conservative on a variety of high-profile issues, including government services and spending, government provision of health insurance, and government help to African-Americans.[6]

party polarization The tendency of the Democratic Party to take more liberal positions and the Republican Party to take more conservative positions on key issues.

The Republican Party tends to include defenders of the free enterprise system and opponents of government regulation, together with strongly religious people who hold traditional views on moral issues. The Republican Party also appeals to people strongly supportive of the military and an assertive foreign policy. The Democratic Party includes liberals with strong views on social issues such as homosexuality, abortion, and environmental protection, as well as opposition to the use of military force. Yet another part of the Democratic coalition includes the people supportive of the role of government in providing a social safety net— efforts to provide jobs, help to the needy, and economic opportunity for all.

The Erosion of Traditional Party Functions   Parties play only a limited role in campaign organization and finance. *Campaigns are generally directed by professional campaign management firms or by the candidates' personal organizations, not by parties.* Party organizations have largely been displaced in campaign activity by advertising firms, media consultants, pollsters, and others hired by the candidates themselves (see Chapter 8).

Most political candidates today are self-recruited. American political parties also play only a limited role in recruiting candidates for elected office. People initiate their own candidacies, first contacting friends and financial supporters. Often in state and local races, candidates contact party officials only as a courtesy, if at all.

Table 7.1   Party and Ideology Among Voters

	All Voters	Democratic Voters	Republican Voters
Liberals	21%	85%	13%
Moderates	45	54	45
Conservatives	34	15	84

Source: As reported at *www.CNN.com*, November 17, 2004.

nominee Political party's entry in a general election race.

nomination Political party's selection of its candidate for a public office.

primary elections Elections to choose party nominees for public office; may be open or closed.

The major American political parties cannot really control who their **nominee**—*the party's entry in a general election race*—*will be.* Rather, party **nominations** for most elected offices are won in *primary elections*. In a **primary election**, registered voters select who will be their party's nominee in the general election. Party leaders may endorse a candidate in a primary election and may even work to try to ensure the victory of their favorite, but the voters in that party's primary select the nominee.

Candidates usually communicate directly with voters through the mass media. Television has replaced the party organization as the principal medium of communication between candidates and voters. Candidates no longer rely much on party workers to carry their message from door to door. Instead, candidates can come directly into the voters' living rooms via television.

Even if the American parties wanted to take stronger policy positions and to enact them into law, they would not have the means to do so. *American political parties have no way to bind their elected officials to the party platform or even to their campaign promises.* Parties have no strong disciplinary sanctions to use against members of Congress who vote against the party's policy position. The parties cannot deny them renomination. At most, the party's leadership in Congress can threaten the status, privileges, and pet bills of disloyal members (see Chapter 10). Party cohesion, where it exists, is more a product of like-mindedness than of party discipline.

machine Tightly disciplined party organization, headed by a boss, that relies on material rewards—including patronage jobs—to control politics.

patronage Appointment to public office based on party loyalty.

divided party government One party controls the presidency while the other party controls one or both houses of Congress.

American political parties no longer perform social welfare functions—trading off social services, patronage jobs, or petty favors in exchange for votes. Traditional party organizations, or **machines**, especially in large cities, once helped immigrants get settled in, found **patronage** jobs in government for party workers, and occasionally provided aid to impoverished but loyal party voters. But government bureaucracies have replaced the political parties as providers of social services. Government employment agencies, welfare agencies, civil service systems, and other bureaucracies now provide the social services once undertaken by political machines in search of votes.

Divided Party Government   Finally, to further confound the responsible party model, Americans seem to prefer **divided party government**—where one party controls the executive branch while the other party controls one or both houses of the legislative branch. Over the last forty years, American presidents have been more likely to face a Congress in which the opposition party controls one or both houses than to enjoy their own party's full control of Congress.[7] (Divided party government in the states—where one party controls the governorship and the opposition party controls one or both houses of the state legislature—is also increasing over time).[8] Divided party control of government makes it difficult for either party to fully enact its platform.

It is noteworthy that American public opinion seems to prefer divided party government over unified party control: *"Do you think it is better when one party controls both the presidency and the Congress, better when control is split between the Democrats and*

Table 7.2   Party Finances (million $)

	2000	2002	2004	2006
Totals				
Democratic Party	$520	$463	$618	$493
Republican Party	715	691	744	598
National Committees				
Dem. National Com.	260	162	299	119
Rep. National Com.	379	284	330	209
House Party Committees				
Dem. Cong. Camp. Com.	105	103	76	108
Nat'l Rep. Cong. Com.	145	211	156	152
Senate Party Committees				
Dem. Senatorial Camp. Com.	104	143	76	104
Nat'l Rep. Senatorial Camp. Com.	96	125	69	78

Source: Center for Responsive Politics, *www.opensecrets.org*

Republicans, or doesn't it matter?": Better one party—23.8%; Better control split—52.4%; Doesn't matter—23.8%.[9]

Party Finances

Parties as well as candidates raise hundreds of millions of dollars in every election year. (Later, in Chapter 8, we will examine campaign financing by candidates themselves.) At the national level, contributions to the parties go to the Democratic and Republican National Committees, and to the Democratic and Republican House and Senatorial Committees (see Table 7.2).

The Partisan Tilt of Campaign Contributions   The Republican Party has generally been able to raise and spend more money in each election cycle than the Democratic Party. But the dollar differences have narrowed over the years. Perhaps more interesting are the differences in sources of support for each party. Broken down by sector (as in Table 7.3), the Democratic Party relies more heavily on lawyers and law firms, on the TV, movie and music industry (Hollywood), teachers and public sector employee unions, and industrial and building trade unions. Business interests divide their contributions, but they tilt toward the Republican Party, notably the health care industry, insurance, manufacturing, oil and gas, automotive, and general and special contractors.

Center for Responsive Politics
Source of information on campaign finances—contributors, recipients, PACs, lobbyists, and so forth.
www.opensecrets.org

Parties as Organizers of Elections

Despite the erosion of many of their functions, America's political parties survive as the principal institutions for organizing elections. Party nominations organize electoral choice by narrowing the field of aspiring office seekers to the Democratic and Republican candidates in most cases. Very few independents or third-party candidates are elected to high political office in the United States. **Nonpartisan elections**—elections in which there are no party nominations and all candidates run without an official party label—are common only in local elections, for city council, country commission, school board, judgeships, and so on. Only Nebraska has nonpartisan elections for its unicameral (one-house) state

nonpartisan elections
Elections in which candidates do not officially indicate their party affiliation; often used for city, country, school board, and judicial elections.

Table 7.3 Contributors to the Republican and Democratic Parties by Sector

Democratic Party	Republican Party
1. Lawyers/law firms	1. Real estate
2. Securities/investment	2. Health professionals
3. Real estate	3. Securities/investment
4. TV/movies/music	4. Lawyers/law firms
5. Business services	5. Insurance
6. Health professionals	6. Manufacturing/distributing
7. Education	7. Oil and gas
8. Lobbyists	8. Business services
9. Computers/Internet	9. General contractors
10. Insurance	10. Automotive
11. Public sector unions	11. Computers/Internet
12. Commercial banks	12. Commercial banks
13. Industrial unions	13. Special trade contractors
14. Building trade unions	14. Retail sales
15. Liberal/ideological	15. Food and beverage

Source: Center for Responsive Politics. Candidate committees, miscellaneous, and "retired" excluded from this table. Data from 2004 presidential election.

legislature. Party conventions are still held in many states in every presidential year, but these conventions seldom have the power to determine the parties' nominees for public office.

Party Conventions Historically, party nominations were made by caucus or convention. The **caucus** was the earliest nominating process; party leaders (party chairs, elected officials, and "bosses") would simply meet several months before the election and decide on the party's nominee themselves. The early presidents—Thomas Jefferson, James Madison, James Monroe, and John Quincy Adams—were nominated by caucuses of Congress members. Complaints about the exclusion of the people from this process led to nominations by convention—large meetings of delegates sent by local party organizations—starting in 1832. Andrew Jackson was the first president to be nominated by convention. The convention was considered more democratic than the caucus.

For nearly a century, party conventions were held at all levels of government—local, state, and national. City or county conventions included delegates from local **wards** and **precincts**, who nominated candidates for city or county office, for the state legislature, or even for the House of Representatives when a congressional district fell within the city or county. State conventions included delegates from counties, and they nominated governors, U.S. senators, and other statewide officers. State parties chose delegates to the Republican and Democratic national conventions every four years to nominate a president.

Party Primaries Today, primary elections have largely replaced conventions as the means of selecting the Democratic and Republican nominees for public office.[10] Primary elections, introduced as part of the progressive reform movement of the early twentieth century, allow the party's *voters* to choose the party's nominee directly. The primary election was designed to bypass the power of party organizations and party leaders and to further democratize the nomination process. It generally succeeded in doing so, but it also had the effect of seriously

caucus Nominating process in which party leaders select the party's nominee.

ward Division of a city for electoral or administrative purposes or as a unit for organizing political parties.

precinct Subdivision of a city, county, or ward for election purposes.

(a)

(b)

(c)

(d)

Political parties as organizers of elections. (a) The Executive Committee of the Republican National Convention in Chicago in 1880. Conventions emerged as the main way for parties to select candidates in the nineteenth century. (b) Senator Ted Kennedy (D-MA) and Senate Minority Leader Harry Reid (D-NV) lead the Democratic opposition to the policies of Republican President George W. Bush, at a news conference in 2006. (c) Parties also seek to attract voters through registration drives. (d) George W. Bush campaigning on his way to the Republican National Convention in Philadelphia. Parties provide the organizational structure for political campaigns.

weakening political parties, since candidates seeking a party nomination need only appeal to party *voters*—not *leaders*—for support in the primary election.[11]

Types of Primaries   There are some differences among the American states in how they conduct their primary elections. **Closed primaries** allow only voters who have previously registered as Democrats or Republicans (or in some states voters who choose to register as Democrats or Republicans on primary election day) can cast a ballot in their chosen party's primary. Closed primaries tend to discourage people from officially registering as independents, even if they think of themselves as independent, because persons registered as independents cannot cast a ballot in either party's primary.

Open primaries allow voters to choose on election day which party primary they wish to participate in. Anyone, regardless of prior party affiliation, may choose to vote in either party's primary election. Voters simply request the ballot of one party or the other.[12] Open primaries provide opportunities for voters to cross over party lines and vote in the primary of the party they usually do not support. Opponents of open primaries have argued that these types of primary elections allow for **raiding**—

closed primaries Primary elections in which voters must declare (or have previously declared) their party affiliation and can cast a ballot only in their own party's primary election.

open primaries Primary elections in which a voter may cast a ballot in either party's primary election.

raiding Organized efforts by one party to get its members to cross over in a primary and defeat an attractive candidate in the opposition party's primary.

organized efforts by one party to get its members to cross over to the opposition party's primary and defeat an attractive candidate and thereby improve the raiding party's chances of winning the general election. But there is little evidence to show that large numbers of voters connive in such a fashion.

Louisiana is unique in its nonpartisan primary elections. All candidates, regardless of their party affiliation, run in the same primary election. If a candidate gets over 50 percent of the vote, he or she wins the office, without appearing on the general election ballot. If no one receives over 50 percent of the primary election votes, then the top two vote-getters, regardless of party, face each other in the general election.[13]

runoff primary Additional primary held between the top two vote-getters in a primary where no candidate has received a majority of the vote.

Some states hold a **runoff primary** when no candidate receives a majority or a designated percentage of the vote in the party's first primary election. A runoff primary is limited to the two highest vote-getters in the first primary. Runoff elections are more common in the southern United States. In most states, only a plurality of votes is needed to win a primary election.

General Elections   Several months after the primaries and conventions, the **general election** (usually held in November, on the first Tuesday after the first Monday for presidential and most state elections) determines who will occupy elective office. Winners of the Democratic and Republican primary elections must face each other—and any independent or third-party candidates—in the general election. Voters in the general election may choose any candidate, regardless of how they voted earlier in their party's primary or whether they voted in the primary at all.

general election Election to choose among candidates nominated by parties and/or independent candidates who gained access to the ballot by petition.

Independent and minor-party candidates can get on the general election ballot, although the process is usually very difficult. Most states require independent candidates to file a petition with the signatures of several thousand registered voters. The number of signatures varies from state to state and office to office, but it may range up to 5 or 10 percent of *all* registered voters, a very large number that, in a big state especially, presents a difficult obstacle. The same petition requirements usually apply to minor parties, although some states automatically carry a minor party's nominee on the general election ballot if that party's candidate or candidates received a certain percentage (for example, 10 percent) of the vote in the previous general election.

Where's the Party?

The Democratic and Republican parties are found in different political arenas (see Figure 7.5). There is, first of all, the **party-in-the-electorate**—the voters who identify themselves as Democrats or Republicans and who tend to vote for the candidates of their party. The party-in-the-electorate appears to be in decline today. Party loyalties among voters are weakening. More people identify themselves as independents, and more **ticket splitters** divide their votes between candidates of different parties for different offices in the same general election, and more voters cast their ballots without regard to the party affiliation of the candidates than ever before.

party-in-the-electorate Voters who identify themselves with a party.

ticket splitter Person who votes for candidates of different parties for different offices in a general election.

The second locus of party activity is the **party-in-the-government**—officials who received their party's nomination and won the general election. The party-in-the-government includes members of Congress, state legislators and local government officials, and elected members of the executive branch, including the president and governors.

party-in-the-government Public officials who were nominated by their party and who identify themselves in office with their party.

Party identification and loyalty among elected officeholders (the party-in-the-government) are generally stronger than party identification and loyalty among

UP CLOSE

Democratic Presidential Primaries 2004

The Democrats lost their two most popular presidential candidates even before the "pre-primary" when former Vice President Al Gore and New York Senator Hillary Clinton both announced that they would not seek their party's nomination. Both had led in Democratic opinion polls before their announcements. Their decisions to forgo the race brought a small army of Democratic candidates into the race.

The "pre-primary" season began in earnest in August, 2003. Connecticut Senator Joe Lieberman initially led in name recognition but soon fell to fourth or fifth place as a battle progressed. Massachusetts Senator John Kerry and Missouri Congressman Dick Gephardt were getting double-digit numbers in the polls. Former NATO Commander General Wesley Clark also appeared to be a serious contender; he was rumored to be the choice of Bill and Hillary Clinton.

The Dean Bubble

By early November the media began to focus on a little-known Vermont governor, Howard Dean. Dean separated himself from the other candidates with his heated opposition to the war in Iraq and his vitriolic attacks on President Bush. The media was entranced with his lurid anti-Bush rhetoric and his passionate "Hate Bush" followers. Dean was also successful in exploiting the Internet to tap into his most zealous followers to amass $50 million in campaign funds, the largest war chest of any Democratic candidate. But could money and passion win votes in the early primaries?

Iowa and New Hampshire

Grassroots Democrats in the Iowa caucuses and New Hampshire primary appeared unfazed by Dean's intensity or the media attention given him. Many admired his "raw meat" attacks on Bush, but more seemed committed to finding an "electable" Democrat. John Kerry's relatively low-key yet well-organized work in Iowa and New Hampshire paid off. He surprised the pundits, commentators, and pollsters with come-from-behind victories in both states. Dean was stunned. He reacted with a high-volume shouting speech which appeared to confirm the voters' notion that he was too emotional and perhaps too unstable for the presidency.

Front-loaded Victories

Kerry's Iowa and New Hampshire victories gave him much-needed momentum for a series of Democratic primaries that had been moved up into February. By March 2nd, Kerry had effectively won the Democratic nomination. (He lost only to Clark in Oklahoma and Edwards in South Carolina.) His Democratic poll numbers skyrocketed. One by one his competitors dropped out. North Carolina Senator John Edwards ended up a distant second in the primary voting. Although Kerry's liberal voting record matched that of his mentor, Ted Kennedy, he appeared moderate in contrast to Dean. And perhaps the youthful-looking Edwards did not appear to have the necessary experience to win what Democrats expected to be a hard fought election. Kerry's Vietnam War heroism set him apart from the other candidates and reassured voters that he would be a capable Commander-in-Chief. (He had voted for the war in Iraq but later criticized its execution.)

A Long Campaign

The front loading of the primary season in 2004 produced a Democratic challenger to President Bush a full eight months before the general election in November. Kerry's victories reported in the media catapulted the Massachusetts senator to near-even standing with Bush. Indeed, the Bush camp decided to begin running television campaign advertisements in early March. The stage was set for a long and brutal general election campaign.

---

the party-in-the-electorate. Nevertheless, party loyalties among elected officials have also weakened over time. (We examine the role of parties in Congress in Chapter 9 and the president's party role in Chapter 10.)

Finally, there is the **party organization**—national and state party officials and workers, committee members, convention delegates, and others active in the party. The Democratic and Republican party organizations formally resemble the American federal system, with national committees, officers and staffs, and national conventions, 50 state committees, and more than 3,000 county committees with city, ward, and precinct levels under their supervision. State committees are not very responsive to the direction of the national committee; and in most states, city and county party organizations operate quite independently of the state committees. In other words, no real hierarchy of authority exists in American parties.

party organization National and state party officials and workers, committee members, convention delegates, and others active in the party.

UP CLOSE

Off and Running, 2008

Campaigning for the next election begins the day after the polls close from the last election. In presidential politics, candidates have about three years of "precampaigning" before officially announcing their candidacies. During this time, they must seek "media mentions" as possible presidential contenders, get their names in presidential polls, begin recruiting a campaign staff, give speeches to organizations influential in their party, meet with party officials across the country, travel to Iowa and New Hampshire, and, most of all, make contacts with wealthy potential campaign contributors. Knowing that they must first win their party's nomination, most of these activities take place *within* party circles.

Early frontrunners in the polls do not always win their party's nomination. Three or four years is a long time in politics. Relative unknowns have won their party's nomination in the final year, for example, Jimmy Carter in 1976, and Bill Clinton in 1992. But prominence in the polls helps to raise campaign funds and often deters potential competitors.

Senator Hillary Clinton (D-NY)

Former Senator John Edwards (D-NC)

Senator John McCain (R-AZ)

Former New York City Mayor Rudy Giuliani

2008

Democratic Candidates		Republican Candidates	
Respondents: Registered Democrats		**Respondents: Registered Republicans**	
Hillary Clinton	36%	Rudy Giuliani	28%
Al Gore	16%	John McCain	24%
John Edwards	12%	Newt Gingrich	8%
John Kerry	11%	Mitt Romney	6%
Wesley Clark	4%	Bill Frist	6%
Joe Biden	4%	George Allen	5%
Other/None	21%	Other/None	23%

Source: Gallup Poll, June 2006.

Voter turnout among 18- to 21-year-olds is lower than any other age group. Here, University of New Hampshire students register to vote in the 2000 election.

National Party Structure   The Democratic and Republican national party conventions possess *formal* authority over the parties. They meet every four years not only to nominate candidates for president and vice president but also to adopt a party platform, choose party officers, and adopt rules for the party's operation. Because the convention is a large body that meets for only three or four days, however, its real function is to ratify decisions made by national party leaders, as well as to formally nominate presidential and vice presidential candidates.

Election World
Links to party Web sites in many nations of the world, with latest election results.
www.electionsworld.org

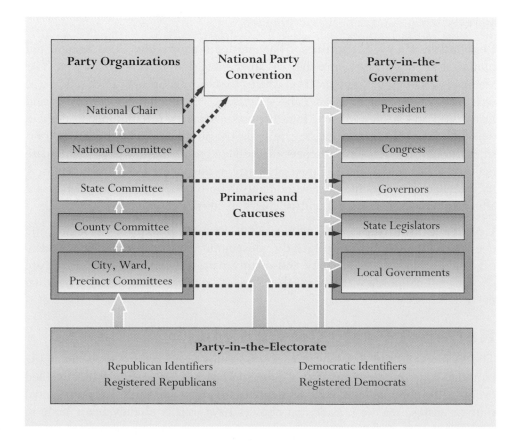

Figure 7.5   Where's the Party?

Even among Americans who strongly identify with a major party, there are differences among those who are strictly members of the party-in-the-electorate (voters), those who are members of the party-in-the-government (elected officials), and those who are members of the party organization (national and state party committee members).

Democratic Party Chairman Howard Dean is widely recognized for his often heated speeches attacking Republican policies.

The Democratic and Republican national committees, made up of delegates from each state and territory, are supposed to govern party affairs *between* conventions. But the *real* work of the national party organizations is undertaken by the national party chairs and staff. The national chair is officially chosen by the national committee but is actually chosen by the party's presidential candidate. If the party wins the presidency, the national chair usually serves as a liaison with the president for party affairs. If the party loses, the chair may be replaced before the next national convention. The national chair is supposed to be neutral in the party's primary battles, but when an incumbent president is seeking reelection, the national chair and staff lean very heavily in the president's favor.

State Party Organizations   State party organizations consist of a state committee, a state chair who heads the committee, and a staff working at the state capital. Democratic and Republican state committees vary from state to state in composition, organization, and function. The state party chair is generally selected by the state committee, but this selection is often dictated by the party's candidate for governor. Membership on the state committee may range from about a dozen up to several hundred. The members may be chosen through party primaries or by state party conventions. Generally, representation on state committees is allocated by counties, but occasionally other units of government are recognized in state party organizations.

Most state party organizations maintain full-time staffs, including an executive director and public relations, fund-raising, and research people. These organizations help to raise campaign funds for their candidates, conduct registration drives, provide advice and services to their nominees, and even recruit candidates to run in election districts and for offices where the party would otherwise have no names on the ballot. Services to candidates may include advertising and media consulting, advice on election-law compliance, polling, research (including research on opponents), registration and voter identification, mailing lists, and even seminars on campaign techniques.

Legislative Party Structures   The parties organize the U.S. Senate and House of Representatives, and they organize most state legislatures as well. The majority party in the House meets in caucus to select the Speaker of the House as well as the House majority leader and whip (see "Organizing Congress: Party and Leadership" in Chapter 10). The minority party elects its own minority leader and whip. The majority party in the Senate elects the president pro tempore, who presides during the (frequent) absences of the vice president, as well as the Senate majority leader and whip. The minority party in the Senate elects its own minority leader and whip. Committee assignments in both the House and the Senate are allocated on a party basis; committee chairs are always majority-party members.

County Committees   The nation's 3,000 Republican and 3,000 Democratic county chairs probably constitute the most important building blocks in party organization in the nation. City and county party officers and committees are chosen in local primary elections; they cannot be removed by state or national party authorities.

National Party Conventions

convention Nominating process in which delegates from local party organizations select the party's nominees.

The Democratic and Republican parties are showcased every four years at the national party **convention**. The official purpose of these four-day fun-filled events is the nomination of the presidential candidates and their vice presidential running mates. Yet the presidential choices have usually already been made in the parties' **presidential primaries** and caucuses earlier in the year. By midsummer convention time, delegates pledged to cast their convention vote for one or another of the presidential candidates have already been selected. Not since 1952, when the Democrats took three convention ballots to select Adlai Stevenson as their presidential candidate, has convention voting gone beyond the first ballot.[14] The possibility exists that in some future presidential race no candidate will win a majority of delegates in the primaries and caucuses, and the result will be a *brokered* convention in which delegates will exercise independent power to select the party nominee. But this event is unlikely.

The Democratic and Republican national conventions are really televised party rallies, designed to showcase the presidential nominee, confirm the nominee's choice for a running mate, and inspire television viewers to support the party and its candidates in the forthcoming general election. Indeed, the national party conventions are largely media events, carefully staged to present an attractive image of the party and its nominees. Party luminaries jockey for key time slots at the podium, and the party prepares slick videotaped commercials touting its nominee for prime-time presentation.

Convention Delegates   Over time, the spread of presidential primary elections has taken the suspense out of the national party conventions. As late as 1968, fewer than half of the delegates were selected in primary elections. But today, the selection of more than 80 percent of pledged delegates by the party's primary voters has greatly diminished the role of party officials in presidential selection.

Both parties award **delegates** to each state in rough proportion to the number of party voters in the state. Democratic Party rules currently require that all popularly elected delegates from each state be awarded to the presidential candidates according to their proportion of that state's primary or caucus vote, after the candidates reach a 15 percent vote threshold. Republican Party rules allow states either to apportion their delegates according to the primary or caucus vote or to adopt a winner-take-all system of awarding all state delegates to the state's primary election victor.

Convention delegates are generally party activists, ideologically motivated and strongly committed to their presidential candidates. Democratic delegates are much more *liberal* than Democratic voters, and Republican delegates are more *conservative* than Republican voters (see Figure 7.6). There is a slight tendency for Democratic and Republican delegates to differ in social backgrounds; usually

presidential primaries
Primary elections in the states in which voters in each party can choose a presidential candidate for their party's nomination. Outcomes help determine the distribution of pledged delegates to each party's national nominating convention.

delegates Accredited voting members of a party's national presidential nominating convention.

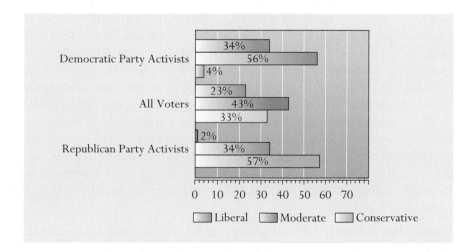

Figure 7.6 Ideologies of Voters versus Party Activists

Democratic and Republican party activists (convention delegates in 2000) are far more likely to hold divergent liberal and conservative views than voters generally.

Source: As reported in the *New York Times,* August 14, 2000.

President George W. Bush formally accepts the Republican Party's presidential nomination at the party's national convention.

superdelegates Delegates to the Democratic Party national convention selected because of their position in the government or the party and not pledged to any candidate.

platform Statement of principles adopted by a political party at its national convention (specific portions of the platform are known as planks); a platform is not binding on the party's candidates.

more African Americans, women, public employees, and union members are found among Democratic delegates than among Republican delegates.

Making Party Rules   National party conventions make rules for the party, including rules governing the selection of delegates at the next party convention. Democrats are especially likely to focus on delegate selection rules. In 1972 the Democratic Party responded to charges that African Americans, women, and other minorities were underrepresented among the delegates by appointing a special commission chaired by Senator George McGovern to "reform" the party. The McGovern Commission took "affirmative steps" to ensure that the next convention would include "goals" for the representation of African Americans, women, and other minorities among the delegates in proportion to their presence in the Democratic electorate. The effect of these reforms was to reduce the influence of Democratic officeholders (members of Congress, governors, state legislators, and mayors) at the convention and to increase the influence of ideologically motivated activists. Later rule changes eliminated the *unit vote,* in which all delegates from a state were required to vote with the majority of the state's delegation and which required that all delegates who were pledged to a candidate vote for that candidate unless *released* by the candidate.

Then, in the 1980s, the Democratic Leadership Council pressed the party to reserve some convention delegate seats for **superdelegates**—elected officials and party leaders not bound to one candidate—with the expectation that these delegates would be more moderate than the liberal party activists. The notion was that the superdelegates would inject more balanced, less ideological political judgments into convention deliberations, thus improving the party's chances of victory in the general elections. As a result, many Democratic senators, governors, and members of Congress now attend the convention as superdelegates. If presidential candidates ever fail to win a majority of delegates in the primaries, these superdelegates may some day control a nomination.

Party Platforms   National conventions also write party **platforms**, setting out the party's goals and policy positions. Because a party's platform is not binding on its nominees, platform *planks* are largely symbolic, although they often provide heated arguments and provide distinct differences between the parties to present to voters (see *Up Close:* "Democratic and Republican Platforms: Can You Tell the Difference?").

Selecting a Running Mate   Perhaps the only suspense remaining in national party conventions centers on the presidential nominee's choice of a vice presidential running mate. Even a presidential candidate who has decided on a running mate well in advance of the convention may choose to wait until the convention to announce the choice, otherwise there would be little real "news value" to the convention, and the television networks would give less coverage to it. By encouraging speculation about who the running mate will be, the candidate and the convention manager can sustain media interest. (For a discussion of various strategies in selecting a running mate, see "The Vice Presidential Waiting Game" in Chapter 11.)

The convention *always* accepts the presidential candidate's recommendation for a running mate. No formal rules require the convention to do so, but it would be politically unacceptable for the convention to override the first important decision of the party's presidential nominee. Convention delegates set aside any personal reservations they may have and unanimously endorse the presidential nominee's choice.

Campaign Kickoff   The final evening of the national conventions is really the kickoff for the general election campaign. The presidential nominee's accept-

UP CLOSE

Democratic and Republican Platforms: Can You Tell the Difference?

Iraq

A "We cannot allow a failed state in Iraq that inevitably would become a haven for terrorists and a destabilizing force in the Middle East."

B "... today there are more than 50 million newly freed people in the nation of Afghanistan and Iraq—America is safer."

Taxes

A "We will roll back the tax cuts for those making more than $200,000."

B "Tax reform is necessary to achieve tax simplicity, efficiency, fairness, and predictability. . . . In particular we must: Make the tax relief of 2001 and 2003 permanent."

Foreign Policy

A "They rush to force before exhausting diplomacy. They bully rather than persuade. They act alone when they could assemble a team."

B "We are defending the peace by taking the fight to the enemy. We are confronting terrorists overseas so that we do not have to confront them here at home."

Health-care

A "We will offer individuals and businesses tax credits to make quality, reliable health coverage more affordable."

B "Enact Health Savings Accounts that allow individuals to save and pay for their healthcare tax-free."

Social Security

A "We are absolutely committed to preserving Social Security."

B "Social Security needs to be strengthened and enhanced for our children and grandchildren . . . Each of today's workers should be free to direct a portion of their payroll taxes to personal investments for their retirement."

Other

A "Their energy policy is simple: government by big oil, of big oil, and for big oil."

B "We will curb the burden of frivolous lawsuits . . . One of their nominees made his fortune as a trial lawyer . . . They offer no hope for reform of this badly broken system."

A "We will raise the minimum wage to $7.00."

B "We strongly support the policy that prevents taxpayers' dollars from being used to encourage the future destruction of human embryos."

A "We will create new jobs and protect existing ones by ending tax breaks for companies that ship jobs overseas."

B "We support legislation requiring a supermajority vote in both houses of Congress to raise taxes."

Source: Excerpts from Democratic [A] and Republican [B] party platforms, 2004.

ance speech tries to set the tone for the fall campaign. Party celebrities, including defeated presidential candidates, join hands at the podium as a symbol of party unity. Presidential and vice presidential candidates, spouses, and families assemble under balloons and streamers, amid the happy noise and hoopla, to signal the start of the general election campaign. TV coverage helps provide the parties with small postconvention "bumps" in the polls.

Party Voters

Traditionally, the Democratic Party has been able to claim to be the majority party in the United States (see Figure 7.7). In opinion polls, those who "identify" with the Democratic Party generally outnumber those who "identify" with the Republican Party. (**Party identification** is determined by response to the question, "Generally speaking, how would you identify yourself: as a Republican, Democrat, independent, or something else?") But the Democratic Party advantage

party identification Self-described identification with a political party, usually in response to the question, "Generally speaking, how would you identify yourself: as a Republican, Democrat, independent, or something else?"

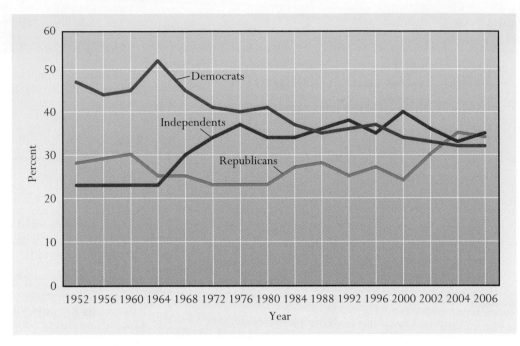

Figure 7.7 Party Identification in the Electorate

For many years, the Democratic Party enjoyed a substantial lead in party identification among voters. This Democratic lead eroded in the late 1960s as more people began to identify themselves as independents. Independent identification suggests that many voters have become disillusioned with both parties.

Source: Data from *National Election Studies,* University of Michigan; 2000–2006, data from Gallup Polls.

among the voters eroded over time, partly as a result of a gradual increase in the number of people who call themselves independents.

dealignment Declining attractiveness of the parties to the voters, a reluctance to identify strongly with a party, and a decrease in reliance on party affiliation in voter choice.

Dealignment Dealignment describes the decline in attractiveness of the political parties to the voters, the growing reluctance of people to identify themselves with either party, and a decrease in reliance on a candidate's party affiliation in voter choice. Dealignment is evident not only in the growing numbers of self-described independents, but also in the declining numbers of those who identify themselves as "strong" Democrats or Republicans. In short, the electorate is less partisan than it once was.

Party Loyalty in Voting Despite the decline in partisan identification in the electorate, it is important to note that *party identification is a strong influence in voter choice in elections.* Most voters cast their ballot for the candidate of their party. This is true in presidential elections (see Figure 7.8) and even more true in congressional and state elections. Those who identify themselves as Democrats are somewhat more likely to vote for a Republican presidential candidate than those who identify themselves as Republicans are to vote for a Democratic presidential candidate. Republican Ronald Reagan was able to win more than one-quarter of self-identified Democrats in 1980 and 1984, earning these crossover voters the label "Reagan Democrats."[15]

realignment Long-term shift in social-group support for various political parties that creates new coalitions in each party.

Realignment? Although Democratic Party loyalty has eroded over the last thirty years, it is not clear whether or not this erosion is a classic party realignment.[16] Most scholars agree that party realignments occurred in the presidential elections of 1824 (Jackson, Democrats), 1860 (Lincoln, Republicans),

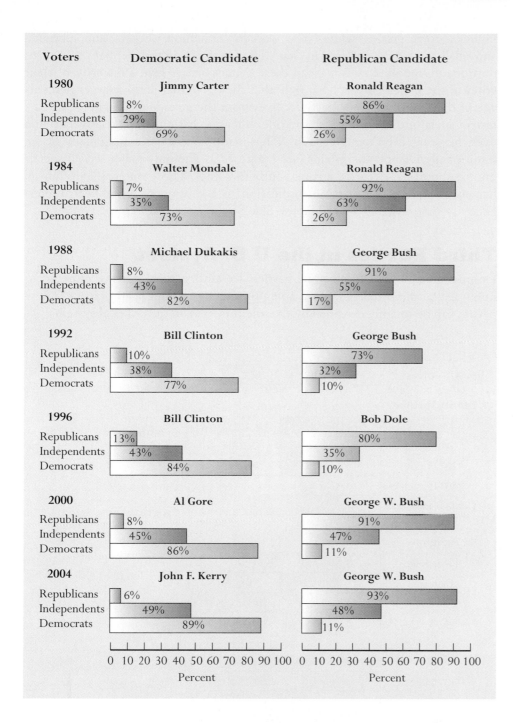

Figure 7.8 Republican, Democratic, and Independent Voters in Presidential Elections

As the percentages here indicate, in recent years registered Democrats have been more likely to "cross over" and vote for a Republican candidate for president than registered Republicans have been to vote for the Democratic presidential candidate.

Source: New York Times.

1896 (Bryan, Democrats), and 1932 (Roosevelt, Democrats). This historical sequence gave rise to a theory that realigning elections occur every thirty-six years. According to this theory, the election of 1968 should have been a realigning one. It is true that Richard Nixon's 1968 victory marked the beginning of a twenty-four-year Republican era in presidential election victories that was broken only by Jimmy Carter in 1976. But there was relatively little shifting of the party loyalties of major social groups, and the Democratic Party remained the dominant party in the electorate and in Congress.

The Democratic Party still receives *disproportionate* support from Catholics, Jews, African Americans, less educated and lower income groups, blue-collar workers, union members, and big-city residents. The Republican Party still receives *disproportionate* support from Protestants, whites, more educated and higher income groups, white-collar workers, nonunion workers, and suburban and small-town dwellers (see *Up Close:* "The Donkey and the Elephant"). Disproportionate support does not mean these groups *always* give a majority of their votes to the indicated party, but only that they give that party a larger percentage of their votes than the party receives from the general electorate. This pattern of social-group voting and party identification has remained relatively stable over the years, even though the GOP has made some gains among many of the traditionally Democratic groups (see Figure 7.9). The only major *shift* in social-group support has occurred among Southern whites. This group has shifted from heavily Democratic in party identification to a substantial Republican preference[17] (see *Across the USA:* "Red States, Blue States").

Third Parties in the U.S. System

Despite the cultural and electoral barriers to victory, **third parties**, more accurately called minor parties, are a common feature of American politics. These parties can be roughly classified by the role they play in the political system.

— Think Again —

Do we need a third party to challenge the Republican and Democratic parties?

---

third party Political party that challenges the two major parties in an election.

Figure 7.9 Social-Group Support for the Democratic and Republican Parties

The Democratic Party draws disproportionate support from low-income, less-educated, Catholic, Jewish, and African American voters. The Republican Party relies more heavily on support from high-income, college-educated, white Protestant voters.

Source: Data from *National Election Studies,* University of Michigan.

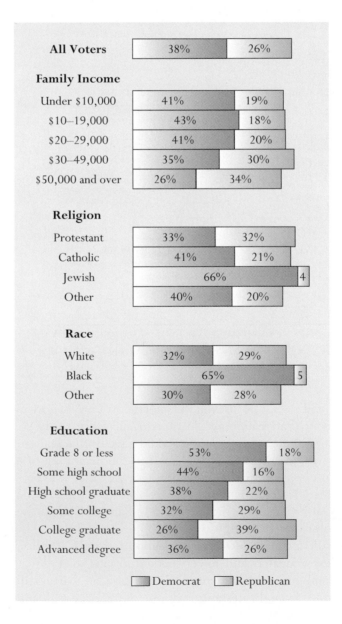

	Democrat	Republican
All Voters	38%	26%
Family Income		
Under $10,000	41%	19%
$10–19,000	43%	18%
$20–29,000	41%	20%
$30–49,000	35%	30%
$50,000 and over	26%	34%
Religion		
Protestant	33%	32%
Catholic	41%	21%
Jewish	66%	4
Other	40%	20%
Race		
White	32%	29%
Black	65%	5
Other	30%	28%
Education		
Grade 8 or less	53%	18%
Some high school	44%	16%
High school graduate	38%	22%
Some college	32%	29%
College graduate	26%	39%
Advanced degree	36%	26%

ACROSS THE USA

Red States, Blue States

The Democratic and Republican Parties compete in every state. But sectionalism was and is evident in the strength of the Republican Party in the Mountain, Plains, and Southern states. The Democratic Party is becoming bicoastal—strong in the Northeast and the Pacific Coasts. Of the four largest states, California and New York lean Democratic, while Texas and Florida lean Republican. At least this has been the pattern in the last few presidential elections; congressional and gubernatorial elections are not quite so sectionalized.

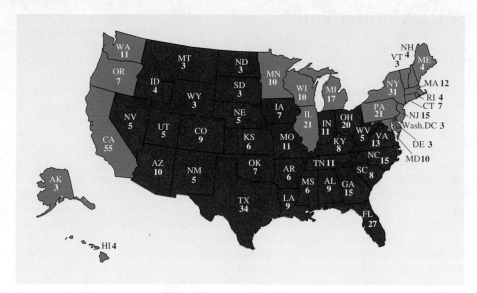

Ideological Parties

Ideological parties exist to promote an ideology rather than to win elections. They use the electoral process to express their views and to rally activists to their cause, and they measure success not by victory at the polls but by their ability to bring their names and their views to the attention of the American public. The socialist parties, which have run candidates in virtually every presidential election in this century, are prime examples of ideological parties in the United States (see also *Up Close:* "The Libertarian Party: A Dissenting Voice").

ideological party Third party that exists to promote an ideology rather than to win elections.

Protest Parties

Protest parties arise around popular issues or concerns that the major parties have failed to address. An important historical example of a protest party is the Populist Party of the late 1800s. It arose as a protest by Midwestern farmers against eastern railroads, "trusts" and monopolies, and the gold standard. The Populists threatened to capture the wave of popular support for railroad regulation, cheap money, and antimonopoly legislation, and thus they endangered the established Democratic and Republican parties. But when the Democratic Party nominated William Jennings Bryan in 1896, the Populist Party officially endorsed Bryan and temporarily disappeared as a significant independent political organization. Populist ideas were set forth again in a new Progressive Party, which nominated Robert M. La Follette for president in 1924; the Democratic and Republican parties both nominated conservative candidates that year, helping La Follette to win almost 17 percent of the popular vote.

Not all major protest movements have been accompanied by the formation of third parties. Indeed, protest leaders have often argued that a third-party effort distracts the movement from a more effective strategy of capturing control of one or both of the major parties. The labor-union-organizing movement of the 1930s and the civil rights and antiwar movements of the 1960s did not spark a

Libertarian Party This Web site reflects the Libertarian Party's strong ideological commitments to individual liberty, free markets, and nonintervention in world affairs. *www.lp.org*

protest party Third party that arises in response to issues of popular concern which have not been addressed by the major parties.

UP CLOSE

The Libertarian Party: A Dissenting Voice

Would you like to see the federal income tax repealed; the Internal Revenue Service abolished; foreign aid ended; all U.S. troops brought home from overseas; and individual choice "in all matters," from abortion to gun control to drug use? Would you like to eliminate government farm subsidies; end federal support for public broadcasting, science, and the arts; and "privatize" education and "charitize" welfare? These are the campaign promises of the Libertarian Party, whose presidential candidates' names appeared on the ballot in most states since 1992.

The Libertarian Party is unique in its uncompromising commitment to the classical liberal, eighteenth-century ideals of John Locke and Adam Smith. Libertarians oppose all interference by government in the private lives of citizens. They support unregulated free markets and the protection of private property rights. Thus they oppose environmental regulations, consumer protection laws, and laws that infringe on private property or "take" property for government use without just compensation to owners. They also oppose government efforts to regulate private morals—including laws outlawing drug use, prostitution, gambling, and pornography—believing these activities should be the exclusive choice of consenting individuals. Libertarians are strict noninterventionists in international affairs; they are opposed to the North Atlantic Treaty Organization (NATO) alliance, to foreign aid, to military involvements outside of U.S. territory, and to virtually all spending for national defense.

Although the Libertarian Party candidate for president regularly receives less than 1 percent of the popular vote, Libertarian ideas have entered the nation's policy debates and influenced both major parties. Republican candidates have frequently adopted Libertarian arguments on behalf of deregulation of market activities; Democratic candidates frequently use Libertarian arguments about individual "choice" in the areas of abortion, school prayer, and homosexual activity. And both the Democratic and the Republican parties have vocal "isolationist" wings that borrow Libertarian, noninterventionist arguments against foreign aid, international alliances, and military expenditures. Thus the Libertarian Party, like other ideological parties, functions to promote ideas rather than win elections.

---

separate third party but instead worked largely *within* the dominant Democratic Party to advance their goals.

single-issue party Third party formed around one particular cause.

Single-Issue Parties   Single-issue parties have frequently formed around a particular cause. Single-issue parties are much like protest parties, although somewhat narrower in their policy focus. The Greenback Party of the late 1800s shared with the Populists a desire for cheap inflated currency in order to ease the burden of debt and mortgage payments by farmers. But the Greenback Party focused on a single remedy: an end to the gold standard and the issuance of cheap currency—"greenbacks."

Perhaps the most persistent of minor parties over the years has been the Prohibition Party. It achieved temporary success with the passage of the Eighteenth Amendment to the U.S. Constitution in 1919, which prohibited the manufacture, sale, or transportation of "intoxicating liquors," only to see its "noble experiment" fail and be repealed by the Twenty-first Amendment.

Today the Green Party provides an example of a single-issue party, with its primary emphasis on environmental protection. However, the Green Party itself contends that it is "part of the worldwide movement that promotes ecological wisdom, social justice, grassroots democracy and non-violence."

splinter party Third party formed by a dissatisfied faction of a major party.

Splinter Parties   Finally, many third parties in American politics are really **splinter parties**, parties formed by a dissatisfied faction of a major party. Splinter parties may form around a particular individual, as did the Progressive (Bull Moose) Party of Theodore Roosevelt in 1912. As a popular former president,

Teddy Roosevelt won more than 27 percent of the popular vote, outpolling Republican candidate William Howard Taft but allowing Democrat Woodrow Wilson to win the presidency.

Splinter parties also may emerge from an intense intraparty policy dispute. For example, in 1948 the States' Rights (Dixiecrat) Party formed in protest to the civil rights (fair employment practices) plank in the Democratic Party platform of that year and nominated Strom Thurmond for president. In 1968 George Wallace's American Independent Party won nearly 14 percent of the popular vote. Wallace attacked school desegregation and busing to achieve racial balance in schools, as well as crime in the streets, welfare "cheats," and meddling federal judges and bureaucrats. He abandoned his third-party organization in 1972 to run in the Democratic presidential primary elections. Following some Democratic primary victories, he was shot and disabled for life.

An Anti-Party Party   Many Americans feel disgusted with "politics as usual." They view both the Democratic and Republican parties as ineffective, unprincipled, and even corrupt. They represent a dealignment from the current party system; that is, they have no party loyalty and they usually describe themselves as "Independents." In 1992 Texas billionaire Ross Perot was able to mobilize many of these independents into a third-party challenge to the two-party system. He spent nearly $100 million of his own money to build a nationwide organization, the Reform Party (originally called United We Stand) and to place his name on the ballot of all fifty states. Early in the campaign his poll numbers mushroomed to 35 percent, higher than any other independent candidate's support in the history of modem polling. His political support came mostly from the center of the political spectrum—people who identified themselves as independents. Perot participated in the first three-way presidential television debates and won 19 percent of the popular vote in the general election, the highest percentage won by a third-party candidate since Teddy Roosevelt in 1912. But he failed to win a single electoral vote. Perot ran again in 1996, but when his early poll numbers languished, he was excluded from the presidential debates. On Election Day he won fewer than half of the votes (9 percent) that he had garnered four years earlier, and again failed to win any state's electoral votes. In 2000 the Reform Party imploded in a raucous convention, with rival factions almost coming to blows over control of the microphone. The party officially nominated conservative firebrand Pat Buchanan, but

Ralph Nader, the nation's most visible interest-group entrepreneur, continues his fight against auto companies, speaking here to Toledo residents unhappy with tax breaks given to Daimler-Chrysler to keep its plant in the city. In the 2000 presidential election, Nader was the Green Party's nominee. But he lost the Green nomination in 2004 and ran as an independent.

www Reform Party
The Reform Party site provides information about founder Ross Perot and the principles of and news about the party.
www.reformparty.org

Buchanan's right-wing rhetoric attracted less than 1 percent of the voters. By 2004 many states had dropped the Reform Party from their ballots.

Third-Party Prospects   In recent years, polls have reported that a majority of Americans favor the idea of a third party. But support for the *general* idea of a third party has never been matched by voter support for *specific* third-party or independent presidential candidates (see Table 7.4). Moreover, it is very difficult for a third party or independent candidate to win electoral votes. Only Theodore Roosevelt, Robert M. La Follette, and George C. Wallace managed to win any electoral votes in the past century. The Reform Party, founded by billionaire Ross Perot in 1992, was the latest serious yet unsuccessful attempt to create a nationwide third party.

Why the Two-Party System Persists

The two-party system is deeply ingrained in American politics. Although third parties have often made appearances in presidential elections, no third-party candidate has ever won the Oval Office. (Lincoln's new Republican Party in 1860 might be counted as an exception, but it quickly became a major party.) Very few third-party candidates have won seats in Congress. Many other democracies have multiple-party systems, so the question arises as to why the United States has had a two-party system throughout its history.[18]

Cultural Consensus   One explanation of the nation's continuing two-party system focuses on the broad consensus supporting the American political culture (see Chapter 2). The values of democracy, capitalism, free enterprise, individual liberty, religious freedom, and equality of opportunity are so widely shared that no party challenging these values has ever won much of a following. There is little support in the American political culture for avowedly fascist, communist, authoritarian, or other antidemocratic parties. Moreover, the American political culture includes a strong belief in the separation of church and state. Political parties with religious affiliations, common in European democracies, are absent from American politics. Socialist parties have frequently appeared on the scene under various

---

Table 7.4   Twentieth-Century Third-Party Presidential Votes

Third-Party Presidential Candidates	Popular Vote (percentage)	Electoral Votes (number)
Theodore Roosevelt (1912), Progressive (Bull Moose) Party	27.4%	88
Robert M. La Follette (1924), Progressive Party	16.6	13
George C. Wallace (1968), American Independent Party	13.5	46
John Anderson (1980), Independent	6.6	0
Ross Perot (1992), Independent	18.9	0
Ross Perot (1996), Reform Party	8.5	0
Ralph Nader (2000), Green Party	2.7	0
Ralph Nader (2004) Independent	0.4	0

A CONSTITUTIONAL NOTE

Political Parties and the Constitution

Political parties had not yet formed in 1787 when the Founders met in Philadelphia to draft the Constitution. Indeed, George Washington and other Founders believed that the new nation might be destroyed by the "baneful effects of the spirit of party." Nowhere in the Constitution do we find any reference to "parties." Indeed, the original Constitution called for presidential electors to cast two votes for president, with the candidate receiving the highest number becoming president and the candidate with the second-highest becoming vice president. But by 1800 parties had formed: the Federalists rallied around John Adams, the second president; and the Democratic-Republicans (often called Republi-

cans, but not to be confused with today's Republican Party) supported Thomas Jefferson. Candidates for the Electoral College ran under these labels (or sometimes as just Adams's men or Jefferson's men). In the 1800 presidential election the Democratic-Republican party won a majority of electors. But all of them had cast their votes for both Jefferson and his intended vice president Aaron Burr. Thus, Jefferson and Burr ended up with the same number of electoral votes, 73, for president. For a while, Burr considered challenging Jefferson for president, but in the end conceded the office. The incident illustrated the failure of the Founders to envision parties as central to the electoral process. Congress and the states were obliged to add the Twelfth Amendment to the Constitution by 1804 in order to separate "in distinct ballots" the persons voted for as president and vice president.

labels—the Socialist Party, the Socialist Labor Party, and the Socialist Workers Party. But the largest popular vote ever garnered by a socialist candidate in a presidential election was the 6 percent won by Eugene V. Debs in 1912. In contrast, socialist parties have frequently won control of European governments.

On broad policy issues, most Americans cluster near the center. This general consensus tends to discourage multiple parties. There does not appear to be sufficient room for them to stake out a position on the ideological spectrum that would detach voters from the two major parties.

This cultural explanation blends with the influence of historical precedents. The American two-party system has gained acceptance through custom. The nation's first party system developed from two coalitions, Federalists and Anti-Federalists, and this dual pattern has been reinforced over two centuries.

Winner-Takes-All Electoral System   Yet another explanation of the American two-party system focuses on the electoral system itself. Winners in presidential and congressional elections, as well as in state gubernatorial and legislative elections, are usually determined by a plurality, winner-takes-all vote. Even in elections that require a majority of more than 50 percent to win—which may involve a runoff election—only one party's candidate wins in the end. Because of the winner-takes-all nature of U.S. elections, parties and candidates have an overriding incentive to broaden their appeal to a plurality or majority of voters. Losers come away empty-handed. There is not much incentive in such a system for a party to form to represent the views of 5 or 10 percent of the electorate.

Americans are so accustomed to winner-takes-all elections that they seldom consider alternatives. In some countries, legislative bodies are elected by **proportional representation**, whereby all voters cast a single ballot for the party of their choice and legislative seats are then apportioned to the parties in proportion to their total vote in the electorate. Minority parties are assured of legislative seats, perhaps with as little as 10 or 15 percent of the vote. If no party wins 50 percent of the votes and seats, the parties try to form a coalition of parties to

proportional representation
Electoral system that allocates seats in a legislature based on the proportion of votes each party receives in a national election.

establish control of the government. In these nations, party coalition building to form a governing majority occurs *after* the election rather than *before* the election, as it does in winner-takes-all election systems.

Legal Access to the Ballot Another factor in the American two-party system may be electoral system barriers to third parties. The Democratic and Republican nominees are automatically included on all general election ballots, but third-party and independent candidates face difficult obstacles in getting their names listed. In presidential elections, a third-party candidate must meet the varied requirements of fifty separate states to appear on their ballots along with the Democratic and Republican nominees. These requirements often include filing petitions signed by up to 5 or 10 percent of registered voters. In addition, states require third parties to win 5 or 10 percent of the vote in the last election in order to retain their position on the ballot in subsequent elections. In 1980 independent John Anderson gained access to the ballot in all fifty states, as did independent Ross Perot in 1992. But just doing so required a considerable expenditure of effort and money that the major parties were able to avoid.

Summary Notes

- Organization grants advantage in the struggle for power. Political parties organize individuals and groups to exercise power in democracies by winning elected office.

- Political parties are not mentioned in the U.S. Constitution, yet they have played a central role in American political history. Major party realignments have occurred at critical points in American history, as major social groups shifted their political loyalties.

- In theory, political parties are "responsible" organizations that adopt a principled platform, recruit candidates who support the platform, educate the public about it, direct an issue-oriented campaign, and then organize the legislature and ensure that their candidates enact the party's platform.

- But in the American two-party system, winning office by appealing to the large numbers of people at the center of the political spectrum becomes more important than promoting strong policy positions. American parties cannot bind elected officials to campaign promises anyway.

- American parties have lost many of their traditional functions over time. Party nominations are won by individual candidates in primary elections rather than through selection by party leaders. Most political candidates are self-selected; they organize their own campaigns. Television has replaced the party as the principal means of educating the public. And government bureaucracies, not party machines, provide social services.

- Party nominations are won in primary elections as earlier caucus and convention methods of nomination have largely disappeared. Party primary elections in the various states may be open or closed and may or may not require runoff primaries. The nominees selected in each party's primary election then battle each other in the general election.

- The parties battle in three major arenas. The *party-in-the-electorate* refers to party identification among voters. The *party-in-the-government* refers to party identification and organization among elected officials. The *party organization* refers to party offices at the local, state, and national levels.

- The Democratic and Republican parties are structured to include national party conventions, national committees with chairs and staff, congressional party organizations, state committees, and county and local committees.

- Since presidential nominations are now generally decided in primary elections—with pledged delegates selected before the opening of the national conventions and with party platforms largely symbolic and wholly unenforceable on the candidates—the conventions have become largely media events designed to kick off the general election campaign.

- *Dealignment* refers to a decline in the attractiveness of the parties to the voters, a growing reluctance of people to identify strongly with either party, and greater voter willingness to cross party lines. Despite dealignment, party identification remains a strong influence in voter choice.

- Opinion polls indicate that most Americans support the general idea of a third party, but throughout the twentieth century no third-party presidential candidate won very many votes.

- In the United States, many aspects of the political system—including cultural consensus, the winner-take-all electoral system, and legal restrictions to ballot access—place major obstacles in the way of success for third parties and independent candidates. Although never successful at gaining federal office in significant numbers, ideological, protest, single-issue, and splinter third parties have often been effective at getting popular issues on the federal agenda.

Key Terms

political organizations   200
political parties   200
Federalists   200
Anti-Federalists   200
majority   200
plurality   202
Democratic Party   202
Republican Party   202
GOP   204
New Deal   204
Fair Deal   205
Great Society   205
Reagan Coalition   207

Democratic Leadership
   Council   208
responsible party model   211
party polarization   213
nominee   214
nomination   214
primary election   214
machine   214
patronage   214
divided party
   government   215
nonpartisan elections   216
caucus   216

ward   217
precinct   216
closed primaries   217
open primaries   217
raiding   217
runoff primary   218
general election   218
party-in-the-electorate   218
ticket splitter   218
party-in-the-government   218
party organization   219
convention   222
presidential primaries   223

delegates   223
superdelegates   224
platform   224
party identification   225
dealignment   226
realignment   226
third party   228
ideological party   229
protest party   229
single-issue party   230
splinter party   230
proportional
   representation   233

Suggested Readings

Beck, Paul, and Marjorie Hershey. *Party Politics in America*. 11th ed. New York: Longman, 2005. An authoritative text on the American party system—party organizations, the parties-in-government, and the parties-in-the-electorate.

Downs, Anthony. *An Economic Theory of Democracy*. New York: Harper & Row, 1957. The classic work describing rational choice winning strategies for political parties and explaining why there is no incentive for vote-maximizing parties in a two-party system to adopt widely separate policy positions.

Kccfe, William J., and Marc J. Hetherington. *Parties, Politics, and Public Policy in America*. 9th ed. Washington, D.C.: CQ Press, 2003. A comprehensive survey of American political parties, from the nominating process to campaign finance and the changing affiliations of voters.

Lowi, Theodore E., and Joseph Romange. *Debating the Two Party System*. Boulder, Colo.: Rowman & Littlefield, 1997. Lowi argues that the two-party system is no longer adequate to represent the people of a diverse nation; Romange counters that two parties help unify the country and instruct Americans about the value of compromise.

Wattenberg, Martin P. *The Decline of American Political Parties, 1952–1992*. Cambridge, Mass.: Harvard University Press, 1994. An authoritative discussion of increasing negative attitudes toward the parties and the growing dealignment in the electorate.

White, John Kenneth, and Daniel M. Shen. *New Party Politics*. 2nd ed. Belmont, Calif.: Wadsworth, 2004. Historical approach to evolution of the American party system.

Make It Real

POLITICAL PARTIES

In this module, students have the opportunity to write their own party platforms.

8 CAMPAIGNS AND ELECTIONS
Deciding Who Governs

Chapter Outline

- Elections in a Democracy
- Power and Ambition
- The Advantages of Incumbency
- Campaign Strategies
- How Much Does It Cost to Get Elected?
- Raising Campaign Cash
- What Do Contributors "Buy"?
- Regulating Campaign Finance
- The Presidential Campaign: The Primary Race
- The Presidential Campaign: The General Election Battle
- The Voter Decides

Think About Politics

1 Should elected officials be bound by their campaign promises?
Yes ☐ No ☐

2 Do you think that personal ambition, rather than civic duty, motivates most politicians?
Yes ☐ No ☐

3 Do career politicians serve their constituents better than those who go into politics for just a short time?
Yes ☐ No ☐

4 Should people vote on the basis of a candidate's personal character rather than his or her policy positions?
Yes ☐ No ☐

5 Would you vote for a candidate who used negative ads to discredit an opponent?
Yes ☐ No ☐

6 Do political campaign contributions have too much influence on elections and government policy?
Yes ☐ No ☐

7 Are high campaign costs discouraging good people from becoming candidates?
Yes ☐ No ☐

8 Should presidents be elected by direct popular vote?
Yes ☐ No ☐

What real power do you have in a democracy? By casting ballots, citizens in a democracy have the power to determine who will represent them, who will make up the government under which they live. You, then, are an integral part of the democratic process every time you vote in an election.

★   ★   ★

Elections in a Democracy

Democratic government is government by "the consent of the governed." Elections give practical meaning to this notion of "consent." Elections allow people to choose among competing candidates and parties and to decide who will occupy public office. Elections give people the opportunity to pass judgment on current officeholders, either by reelecting them (granting continued consent) or by throwing them out of office (withdrawing consent).

In a representative democracy, elections function primarily to choose personnel to occupy public office—to decide "who governs." But elections also have an indirect influence on public policy, allowing voters to influence policy directions by choosing between candidates or parties with different policy priorities. Thus elections indirectly influence "who gets what"—that is, the outcomes of the political process.

Elections as Mandates?   However, it is difficult to argue that elections serve as "policy mandates"—that is, that elections allow voters to direct the course of public policy. Frequently, election winners claim a **mandate**—overwhelming support from the people—for their policies and programs. But for elections to serve as policy mandates, four conditions have to be met:

1. Competing candidates have to offer clear policy alternatives.
2. The voters have to cast their ballots on the basis of these policy alternatives alone.
3. The election results have to clearly indicate the voters' policy preferences.
4. Elected officials have to be bound by their campaign promises.[1]

As we shall see, *none* of these conditions is fully met in American elections. Often candidates do not differ much on policy questions, or they deliberately obscure their policy positions to avoid offending groups of

mandate Perception of popular support for a program or policy based on the margin of electoral victory won by a candidate who proposed it during a campaign.

voters. Voters themselves frequently pay little attention to policy issues in elections but rather vote along traditional party lines or group affiliations, or on the basis of the candidate's character, personality, or media image.

Moreover, even in elections in which issues seem to dominate the campaign, the outcome may not clearly reflect policy preferences. Candidates take stands on a variety of issues. It is never certain on which issues the voters agreed with the winner and on which issues they disagreed yet voted for the candidate anyway.

Finally, candidates often fail to abide by their campaign promises once they are elected. Some simply ignore their promises, assuming voters have forgotten about the campaign. Others point to changes in circumstances or conditions as a justification for abandoning a campaign pledge.

retrospective voting Voting for or against a candidate or party on the basis of past performance in office.

Retrospective Voting   Voters can influence future policy directions through **retrospective voting**—votes cast on the basis of the performance of incumbents, by either reelecting them or throwing them out of office.[2] Voters may not know what politicians will do in the future, but they can evaluate how well politicians performed in the past. When incumbent officeholders are defeated, it is reasonable to assume that voters did not like their performance and that newly elected officials should change policy course if they do not want to meet a similar fate in the next election. But it is not always clear what the defeated incumbents did in office that led to their ouster by the voters. Nor, indeed, can incumbents who won reelection assume that all of their policies are approved of by a majority of voters. Nevertheless, retrospective voting provides an overall judgment of how voters evaluate performance in office.

— **Think Again** —

Should elected officials be bound by their campaign promises?

Protection of Rights   Elections also provide protection against official abuse. The long struggle for African American voting rights in the United States was premised on the belief that once black people acquired the right to vote, government would become more responsive to their concerns. In signing the Voting Rights Act of 1965, President Lyndon Johnson expressed this view: "The vote is the most powerful instrument ever devised by man for breaking down injustice and destroying the terrible walls which imprison men because they are different from other men."[3] The subsequent history of racial politics in America (see Chapter 15) suggests that the vote is more effective in eliminating discriminatory laws than it is in resolving social or economic inequities. Nevertheless, *without* the vote, we can be certain that government would have very little incentive to respond to popular needs.

Power and Ambition

— **Think Again** —

Do you think that personal ambition, rather than civic duty, motivates most politicians?

Personal ambition is a driving force in politics. Politics attracts people for whom *power*—the drive to shape the world according to one's own beliefs and values—and *celebrity*—the public attention, deference, name recognition, and social status that accompany public office—are more rewarding than money, leisure, or privacy. "Political office today flows to those who want it enough to spend the time and energy mastering its pursuit. It flows in the direction of ambition—and talent."[4]

Communication Skills   Another important personal qualification is the ability to communicate with others. Politicians must know how to talk, and talk, and talk—to large audiences, in press conferences and interviews, on television, to reporters, to small groups of financial contributors, on the phone, at airports and commencements, to their staffs, on the floor of Congress or the state legislature. It matters less what politicians say than how they look and sound saying it. They must communicate sincerity, compassion, confidence, and good humor, as well as ideas.

Professionalism   Politics is increasingly characterized by **professionalism**. "Citizen officeholders"—people with business or professional careers who get into politics part time or for short periods of time—are being driven out of political life by career politicians—people who enter politics early in life as a full-time occupation and expect to make it their career. Politics increasingly demands all of a politician's time and energy. At all levels of government, from city council to state legislatures to the U.S. Congress, political work is becoming full-time and year-round.

professionalism In politics, a reference to the increasing number of officeholders for whom politics is a full-time occupation.

Careerism   Professional political careers begin at a relatively early age. **Careerism** in politics begins when ambitious young people seek out internships and staff positions with members of Congress, with congressional committees, in state legislators' or governors' offices, in mayors' offices, or in council chambers. Others volunteer to work in political campaigns. Many find political mentors from whom they learn how to organize campaigns, contact financial contributors, and deal with the media. Soon they are ready to run for local office or the state legislature. Rather than challenge a strong incumbent, they may wait for an open seat to be created by retirement, by reapportionment, or by its holder seeking another office. Over time, running for and holding elective office become their career.

careerism In politics, a reference to people who started young working in politics, running for and holding public office, and made politics their career.

Lawyers in Politics   The prevalence of lawyers in politics is an American tradition. Among the fifty-five delegates to the Constitutional Convention in 1787, some twenty-five were lawyers. The political dominance of lawyers continues today, with lawyers filling about half of U.S. Senate seats and nearly half of the seats in the U.S. House of Representatives.

It is sometimes argued that lawyers dominate in politics because of the parallel skills required in law and politics. Lawyers represent clients, so they can apply their professional experience to represent constituents in Congress. Lawyers are trained to deal with statutory law, so they are assumed to be reasonably familiar

Former President Clinton prepares for an interview with reporters from the television news show *60 Minutes.* Successful politicians are skilled communicators; most truly enjoy the hard work and constant interaction with other people their careers entail.

with the United States Code (the codified laws of the U.S. government) when they arrive in Congress to make or amend these statutes.

But it is more likely that people attracted to politics decide to go to law school fully aware of the tradition of lawyers in American politics. Moreover, political officeholding at the state and local level as well as in the national government can help a struggling lawyer's private practice through free public advertising and opportunities to make contacts with potential clients. Finally, there are many special opportunities for lawyers to acquire public office in "lawyers only" posts as judges and prosecuting attorneys in federal, state, and local governments. Law school graduates who accept modest salaries as U.S. attorneys in the Justice Department or in state or county prosecuting offices can gain valuable experience for later use in either private law practice or politics.

Most of the lawyers in the Congress, however, have become professional politicians over time. They have left their legal practices behind.

The Advantages of Incumbency

incumbent Candidate currently in office seeking reelection.

In theory, elections offer voters the opportunity to "throw the rascals out." But in practice, voters seldom do so. **Incumbents**, people already holding public office, have a strong advantage when they seek reelection. The reelection rates of incumbents for *all* elective offices—city council, mayor, state legislature, governor, and especially Congress—are very high. Since 1950, more than 90 percent of all members of the House of Representatives who have sought reelection have been successful. The success rate of U.S. Senate incumbents is not as great, but it is still impressive; since 1950, more than 70 percent of senators seeking reelection have been successful.[5]

Why do incumbents win so often? This is a particularly vexing question, inasmuch as so many people are distrustful of government and hold politicians in low esteem. Congress itself is the focal point of public disapproval and even ridicule. Yet people seem to distinguish between Congress as an institution—which they distrust—and their own members of Congress—whom they reelect. The result is something of a contradiction: popular members of Congress serving in an unpopular Congress (see *What Do You Think?* "Why Do Voters Reelect Members of an Unpopular Congress?" in Chapter 10). Three major advantages tend to enhance incumbents' chances of winning: name recognition, campaign contributions, and the resources of office.

name recognition Public awareness of a political candidate—whether they know his or her name.

Name Recognition One reason for incumbents' success is that they begin the campaign with greater **name recognition** than their challengers, simply because they are the incumbent and their name has become familiar to their constituents over the previous years. Much of the daily work of all elected officials, especially members of Congress, is really public relations. Name recognition is a strategic advantage at the ballot box, especially if voters have little knowledge of policy positions or voting records. Voters tend to cast ballots for recognizable names over unknowns. Cynics have concluded that there is no such thing as bad publicity, only publicity. Even in cases of well-publicized scandals, incumbent members of Congress have won reelection; presumably voters preferred "the devil they knew" to the one they did not.

The somewhat lower rate of reelection of Senate versus House members may be a result of the fact that Senate challengers are more likely to have held high-visibility offices—for example, governor or member of Congress—before running for the Senate. Thus Senate challengers often enjoy some name recognition even before the campaign begins. Greater media attention to a statewide Senate race also helps to move the challenger closer to the incumbent in public recognition. In contrast, House challengers are likely to have held less visible local or state legislative offices or to be political novices, and House races attract considerably less media attention than Senate races do.

Campaign Contributions   Incumbents have a strong advantage in raising campaign funds, simply because individuals and groups seeking access to those already in office are inspired to make contributions (see Table 8.1). **Challengers** have no immediate favors to offer; they must convince a potential contributor that they will win office and also that they are devoted to the interests of their financial backers.[6]

Contributing individuals and interest groups show a strong preference for incumbents over challengers. They do not wish to offend incumbent officeholders by contributing to their challengers; doing so risks both immediate retribution and future "freezing out" in the likely event of the challengers' defeat. Thus only when an incumbent has been especially hostile to an organization's interest, or in rare cases where an incumbent seems especially vulnerable, will an interest group support a challenger. Yet challengers need even larger campaign war chests than incumbents to be successful. Challengers must overcome the greater name recognition of incumbents, their many office resources, and their records of constituency service. Thus even if incumbents and challengers had equal campaign treasuries, incumbents would enjoy the advantage.

Resources of Office   Successful politicians use their offices to keep their names and faces before the public in various ways—public appearances, interviews, speeches, and press releases. Congressional incumbents make full use of the **franking privilege** (free use of the U.S. mails) to send self-promotional newsletters to tens of thousands of households in their district at taxpayers' expense. They travel on weekends to their district virtually year-round, using tax-funded travel allowances, to make local appearances, speeches, and contacts.

Members of Congress have large staffs working every day over many years with the principal objective of ensuring the reelection of their members. Indeed, Congress is structured as an "incumbent-protection society" organized and staffed to help guarantee the reelection of its members (see "Home Style" in Chapter 10). Service to constituents occupies the energies of congressional office staffs both in Washington and in local district offices established for this purpose. Casework wins voters one at a time: tracing lost Social Security checks,

Senator Joe Lieberman (D-CT) lost in his Democratic Party primary for reelection to the U.S. Senate–a rare occurrence for an incumbent. Lieberman was the Democratic vice-presidential candidate on the ticket with Al Gore in 2000. Liberal activists led the way to his defeat, attacking his support of the invasion of Iraq. Lieberman subsequently was reelected as an independent candidate in the general election.

challengers In politics, a reference to people running against incumbent officeholders.

franking privilege Free use of the U.S. mails granted to members of Congress to promote communication with constituents.

Table 8.1   Incumbent Advantage in Fund Raising

	2002	2004
Senate		
Average Incumbent Raised	$5,803,639	$7,212,068
Average Challenger Raised	1,013,314	869,688
House		
Average Incumbent Raised	898,382	982,941
Average Challenger Raised	197,608	171,551

Source: Center for Responsive Politics; figures for 2002 and 2004 congressional elections.

Campaigns and Elections

The Web site for *Campaigns and Elections*, a magazine directed toward candidates, campaign managers, political TV advertisers, political consultants, and lobbyists.

www.campaignline.com

campaign strategy Plan for a political campaign, usually including a theme, an attempt to define the opponent or the issues, and an effort to coordinate images and messages in news broadcasts and paid advertising.

negative campaigning Speeches, commercials, or advertising attacking a political opponent during a campaign.

ferreting out which federal loans voters qualify for and helping them with their applications, and performing countless other personal favors. These individual "retail-level" favors are supplemented by larger-scale projects that experienced members of Congress can bring to their district or state (roads, dams, post offices, buildings, schools, grants, contracts), as well as undesirable projects (landfills, waste disposal sites, halfway houses) that they can keep out of their district. The longer incumbents have occupied the office, the more favors they have performed and the larger their networks of grateful voters.

Campaign Strategies

Campaigning is largely a media activity, especially in presidential and congressional campaigns. Media campaigns are highly professionalized, relying on public relations and advertising specialists, professional fund raisers, media consultants, and pollsters. Campaign management involves techniques that strongly resemble those employed in marketing commercial products. Professional media campaign management includes developing a **campaign strategy**: compiling computerized mailing lists and invitations for fund-raising events; selecting a campaign theme and coming up with a desirable candidate image; monitoring the progress of the campaign with continual polling of the voters; producing television tapes for commercials, newspaper advertisements, signs, bumper stickers, and radio spots; selecting clothing and hairstyles for the candidate; writing speeches and scheduling appearances; and even planning the victory party.

Selecting a Theme   Finding the right theme or "message" for a campaign is essential; this effort is not greatly different from that of launching an advertising campaign for a new detergent. A successful theme or "message" is one that characterizes the candidate or the electoral choice confronting the voters. A campaign theme need not be controversial; indeed, it need not even focus on a specific issue. It might be as simple as "a leader you can trust"—an attempt to "package" the candidate as competent and trustworthy.

Most media campaigns focus on candidates' personal qualities rather than on their stands on policy issues. Professional campaigns are based on the assumption that a candidate's "image" is the most important factor affecting voter choice. This image is largely devoid of issues, except in very general terms: for example, "tough on crime," "stands up to the special interests," "fights for the taxpayer," or "cares about you."

Negative Campaigning: "Defining" the Opponent   A media campaign also seeks to "define" the opponent in negative terms. The original negative TV ad is generally identified as the 1964 "Daisy Girl" commercial, aired by the Lyndon B. Johnson presidential campaign (see *Up Close*: "Dirty Politics"). Negative ads can serve a purpose in exposing the record of an opponent. But **negative campaigning** risks an opponent's counterattack charges of "mudslinging," "dirty tricks," and "sleaze."

Research into the opponent's public and personal background ("oppo research") provides the data for negative campaigning. Previous speeches and writings can be mined for embarrassing or mean-spirited statements. The voting record of the opponent can be scrutinized for unpopular policy positions. Any evils that occurred during an opponent's term of office can be attributed to him or her, either directly ("She knew and conspired in it") or indirectly ("He should have known and done something about it"). Personal scandals or embarrassments can be developed as evidence of "character." If campaign managers fear that highly personal attacks on an opponent will backfire, they may choose to leak

UP CLOSE

Dirty Politics

Political campaigning frequently turns ugly with negative advertising that is vicious and personal. It is widely believed that television's focus on personal character and private lives—rather than on policy positions and governmental experience—encourages negative campaigning. But vicious personal attacks in political campaigns began long before television. They are nearly as old as the nation itself.

"If Jefferson is elected," proclaimed Yale's president in 1800, "the Bible will be burned and we will see our wives and daughters the victims of legal prostitution." In 1864 *Harper's Weekly* decried the "mudslinging" of the day, lamenting that President Abraham Lincoln was regularly referred to by his opponent as a "filthy storyteller, despot, liar, thief, braggart, buffoon, monster, Ignoramus Abe, robber, swindler, tyrant, fiend, butcher, and pirate."

Television's first memorable attack advertisement was the "Daisy Girl" commercial broadcast by Lyndon Johnson's presidential campaign in 1964 against his Republican opponent, Barry Goldwater. Although never mentioning Goldwater by name, the purpose of the ad was to "define" him as a warmonger who would plunge the world into a nuclear holocaust. The ad opens with a small, innocent girl standing in an open field plucking petals from a daisy and counting, "1, 2, 3 . . ." When she reaches 9, an ominous adult male voice begins a countdown: "10, 9, 8 . . ." as the camera closes in on the child's face. At "zero," a mushroom cloud appears, reflected in her eyes, and envelops the screen. Lyndon Johnson's voice is heard: "These are the stakes."

The infamous Willie Horton ad, broadcast by an independent organization supporting Republican George H. W. Bush in 1988, portrayed Democrat Michael Dukakis as weak on crime prevention. It featured a close-up mug shot of a very threatening convicted murderer, Willie Horton, with a voice proclaiming, "Dukakis not only opposes the death penalty, he allowed first-degree murderers to have weekend passes from prison. One was Willie Horton, who murdered a boy in a robbery, stabbing him nineteen times. Despite a life sentence, Horton received ten weekend passes from prison." A final photo shows Dukakis, with a voice-over announcing, "Weekend prison passes, Dukakis weak on crime."

"Attack ads" have multiplied in recent elections at all levels of government. John Kerry had volunteered for Vietnam following his graduation from Yale. In four months as commander of a small "swift boat" he won a Silver Star, a Bronze Star, and three Purple Hearts. But an independent group, Swift Boat Veterans for the Truth, challenged the legitimacy of Kerry's medals in a series of TV ads. Later, the Swift Boat group redirected their attacks toward Kerry's post-Vietnam behavior as a leader in the Vietnam Veterans against the War. These ads showed a young Kerry at a congressional hearing accusing his fellow veterans of terrible atrocities, "murdering civilians, cutting off heads, and burning villages." These ads corresponded to a slight drop in Kerry's poll numbers.

But Bush's service in the Texas National Guard during the Vietnam War was also a target of attack. Bush joined the Guard with the possible help of family friends, but he won his wings as a fighter pilot and was honorably discharged after five years. The Texas Guard was never called to active duty and Bush never saw combat. But a CBS News report by Dan Rather, based on forged documents, asserted that Bush failed to meet all of his Guard responsibilities. Later CBS News recanted the charge. The affair may have helped Bush somewhat, by convincing viewers that Dan Rather and others at CBS were biased against him.

What are the effects of negative advertising? First of all, it works more often than not. Controlled experiments indicate that targets of attack ads are rated less positively by people who have watched these ads. But another effect of negative advertising is to make voters more cynical about politics and government in general. There is conflicting evidence about whether or not negative campaigning by opposing candidates reduces voter turnout.

What, if anything, can be done? Government regulation of political speech directly contravenes the First Amendment. American democracy has survived negative campaigning for a long time.

VOTE FOR PRESIDENT JOHNSON ON NOVEMBER 3.

Frames from Lyndon Johnson's 1964 "Daisy Girl" commercial.

Source: Kathleen Hall Jamieson, *Dirty Politics: Deception, Distraction, and Democracy* (New York: Oxford University Press, 1992); also Stephen Ansolabehere et al., "Does Attack Advertising Demobilize the Electorate?" *American Political Science Review* 88 (December 1994): 829–38; Kim Fridkin Kahn and Patrick J. Kenney, "Do Negative Campaigns Mobilize or Suppress Turnout?" *American Political Science Review* 93 (December, 1999): 877–89.

the information to reporters and try to avoid attribution of the story to themselves or their candidate.

Negative advertising is often blamed on television's dominant role in political campaigns. "The high cost of television means now that you have to go for the jugular."[7] A political consultant summarized the current rules of political engagement as follows:

1. Advertise early if you have the money.
2. Go negative early, often, and right through Election Day, if necessary.
3. Appeal to the heart and gut, rather than to the head.
4. Define your opponent to the voters before he or she can define him/herself or you.
5. If attacked, hit back even harder.
6. It's easier to give voters a negative impression of your opponent than it is to improve their image of you.[8]

Using Focus Groups and Polling   Focus group techniques can help in selecting campaign themes and identifying negative characteristics in opponents. A **focus group** is a small group of people brought together to view videotapes, listen to specific campaign appeals, and respond to particular topics and issues. Media professionals then develop a campaign strategy around "hot-button" issues—issues that generate strong responses by focus groups—and avoid themes or issues that fail to elicit much interest.

The results of focus group work can then be tested in wider polling. Polling is a central feature of professional campaigning. Serious candidates for national and statewide offices almost always employ their own private polling firms, distinct from the national survey organizations that supply the media with survey data. Initial polling is generally designed to determine candidates' name recognition—the extent to which the voters recognize the candidates—and whatever positive and negative images are already associated with their names.

Campaign polling is highly professionalized, with telephone banks, trained interviewers, and computer-assisted-telephone-interviewing (CATI) software that records and tabulates responses instantly and sends the results to campaign managers. In well-financed campaigns, polling is continual throughout the campaign, so that managers can assess progress on a daily basis. Polls chart the candidate's progress and, perhaps more important, help assess the effectiveness of specific campaign themes. If the candidate appears to be gaining support, the campaign stays on course. But if the candidate appears to be falling in the polls, the campaign manager comes under intense pressure to change themes and strategies. As election day nears, the pressure increases on the trailing candidate to "go negative"—to launch even more scathing attacks on the opponent.

Incumbent versus Challenger Strategies   Campaign strategies vary by the offices being sought, the nature of the times, and the imagination and inventiveness of the candidates' managers. But incumbency is perhaps the most important factor affecting the choice of a strategy. The challenger must attack the record of the incumbent, deplore current conditions in the city, state, or nation; and stress the need for change. Challengers are usually freer to take the offensive; incumbents must defend their record in office and either boast of accomplishments during their term or blame the opposition for blocking them. Challengers frequently opt for the "outsider" strategy, capitalizing on distrust and cynicism toward government.

---

focus group In a political context, a small number of people brought together in a comfortable setting to discuss and respond to themes and issues, allowing campaign managers to develop and analyze strategies.

—Think Again—
Would you vote for a candidate who used negative ads to discredit an opponent?

News Management News management is the key to the media campaign. News coverage of the candidates is more credible in the eyes of viewers than paid advertisements. The campaign is planned to get the maximum favorable "free" exposure on the evening news. Each day a candidate must do something interesting and "newsworthy," that is, likely to be reported as news. Pictures are as important as words. Candidates must provide good **photo ops** for the media—opportunities where they can be photographed in settings or backgrounds that emphasize their themes. For example, if the theme is patriotism, then the candidate appears with war veterans, at a military base, or at a flag factory. If the theme is education, the candidate appears at a school; if crime control, then with police officers; if environmentalism, then in a wilderness area; if the economy, then at a closed factory or unemployment line or soup kitchen for the homeless.

Themes must be stated in concise and catchy **sound bites** that will register in the viewers' minds. Candidates now understand that the news media will select only a few seconds of an entire day of speech making for broadcast. The average length of a network news sound bite has shrunk from forty-five to seven seconds over the last thirty years. Thus extended or serious discussion of issues during a campaign is sacrificed to the need for one-liners on the nightly news. Indeed, if a campaign theme cannot fit on a bumper sticker, it is too complex.

photo ops Staged opportunities for the media to photograph the candidate in a favorable setting.

sound bites Concise and catchy phrases that attract media coverage.

Paid Advertising Television "spot" ads must be prepared prior to and during the campaign. They involve employing expensive television advertising and production firms well in advance of the campaign and keeping them busy revising and producing new ads throughout the campaign to respond to changing issues or opponents' attacks. Commercial advertising is the most expensive aspect of the campaign. Heavy costs are incurred in the production of the ads and in the purchase of broadcast time. The Federal Communications Commission (FCC) does not permit television networks or stations to charge more than standard commercial rates for political ads, but these rates are already high. Networks and stations are required to offer the same rates and times to all candidates, but if one candidate's campaign treasury is weak or exhausted, an opponent can saturate broadcast airtime.

Paid spot ads on television are usually only fifteen or thirty seconds long, owing to the expense of television time. The result is that these ads pay relatively little attention to issues but rather try to appeal to the viewers' emotions. There is some evidence that simply showing enthusiasm for the candidate motivates participation and activates existing supporters to get out and vote, whereas appealing to fear is somewhat more effective in changing behavior, including swinging the votes of undecideds. However, advertising campaigns, whether they are directed at inspiring enthusiasm for the candidate or fear of a candidate's opponent, must be kept going over time. Bursts of emotion are likely to fade if the ad campaign does not keep the drumbeat going.[9] An accumulation of short spot ads, all aimed at the same theme, can have a meaningful impact on the course of an election.

Television ads are much maligned by scholars and commentators. And it is easy to identify particular ads that are silly, offensive, uninformative, and even misleading. Nevertheless, there is increasing evidence that paid political advertising does create a somewhat more attentive, more informed, and more-likely-to-vote citizenry. Moreover, paid ads appear to affect people with less political information and less interest in politics more than the better informed and more active citizens. Thus, campaign ads are often petty, sometimes offensive, and seldom uplifting. But they do serve an important political function.[10]

mobilize In politics, to activate supporters to work for candidates and turn out on Election Day.

Free Airtime   All candidates seek free airtime on news and talk shows, but the need to gain free exposure is much greater for underfunded candidates. They must go to extremes in devising media events, and they must encourage and participate in free televised debates. The debate format is particularly well suited for candidates who cannot match their opponents in paid commercial advertising. Thus well-funded and poorly funded candidates may jockey over the number and times of public debates.

The Effects of Campaigning   Campaigns serve primarily to activate a candidate's supporters—to ensure that they go to the polls on Election Day. They serve secondarily to try to persuade undecideds to become supporters. Campaigns are designed to **mobilize** core supporters more than to persuade undecideds or opponents to vote for candidates.[11] Undecideds must be both persuaded *and* mobilized to vote—a more difficult task than simply activating core supporters. Observers may wonder why candidates appear before partisan crowds, visit with supporters, and advertise in areas that appear to support them anyway. "Core party voters are more likely to receive and respond to campaign information, implying that successful campaigns are those that mobilize their supporters enough to translate their natural predispositions into actual votes."

How Much Does It Cost to Get Elected?

—Think Again—

Are high campaign costs discouraging good people from becoming candidates?

Getting elected to public office has never been more expensive (see *Up Close:* "A Brief History of Money in Politics"). The professionalization of campaigning and the heavy costs of television advertising drive up the costs of running for office. Campaign costs are rising with each election cycle (see Figure 8.1). In the presidential election year 2004, campaign spending by *all* presidential and congressional candidates, the Democratic and Republican parties, and independent political organizations is estimated to have topped *$4 billion.*

Congressional Costs   The typical winning campaign for a seat in the House of Representatives costs nearly $900,000. House members seeking to retain their seats must raise this amount *every two years.* The typical winning campaign for a U.S. Senate seat costs $5 to $7 million. But Senate campaign costs vary a great deal from state to state; Senate seats in the larger states may cost $20 million to $40 million or more.

The upward spiral in congressional campaign spending continued through 2004 with over $1 *billion* spent by all House and Senate candidates (see Table 8.2). New York's high-profile Senate race in 2002 between Democrat Hillary Clinton and Republican Rick Lazio attracted a combined $85 million in contributions from across the nation. A new individual spending record was set by multimillionaire Democrat Jon Corzine in his successful bid for a U.S. Senate seat from New Jersey in 2002; Corzine spent about $60 million of his *own* money.

Spending for House seats also varies a great deal from one race to another. (The spending record for a House seat is held by former Speaker Republican Newt Gingrich of Georgia, who spent more than $7.5 million seeking reelection in 1998.) In nearly two-thirds of all House districts, one candidate (almost always the incumbent) outspends his or her opponent by a factor of ten to one or more. Only about 16 percent of House campaigns are financially competitive; that is, neither candidate spends more than twice as much as his or her opponent. In the remaining 84 percent of House campaigns, one candidate spends more than twice as much as his or her opponent.[12]

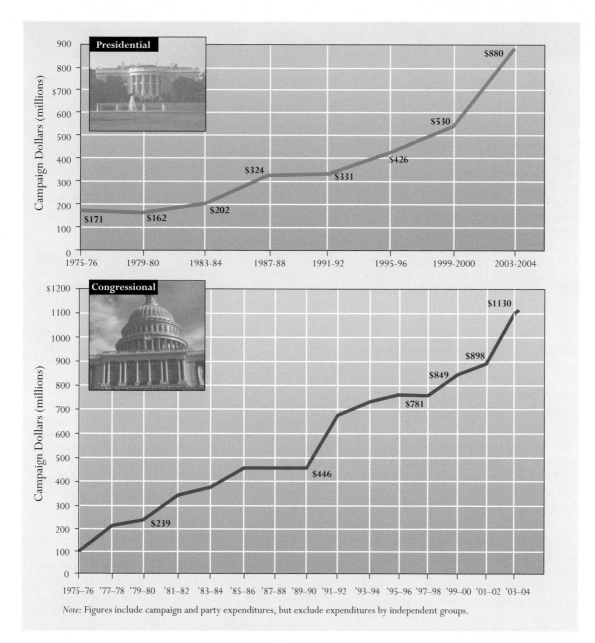

Figure 8.1   The Growing Costs of Campaigns

Source: Reprinted by permission of Center for Responsive Politics.

Raising Campaign Cash

Fund raising to meet the high costs of campaigning is the most important hurdle for any candidate for public office. Campaign funds come from a wide range of sources—small donors, big donors, interest group PACs of every stripe, labor unions, even taxpayers. In some cases, candidates pay their own way (or most of it). More typically, however, candidates for high public office—particularly incumbents—have become adept at running their campaigns using other people's money, not their own.

Public Money   Presidential campaigns can be partly funded with taxpayer money through an income tax checkoff system. Each year taxpayers are urged to check the box on their tax forms that authorizes $3 of their tax payment to go to the Federal Elections Commission for distribution to presidential candidates' campaigns as well

UP CLOSE

A Brief History of Money in Politics

In 1757, in his race for a seat in the Virginia House of Burgesses, George Washington was reprimanded for purchasing and distributing more than a quart of whiskey per voter in his district. But for the first fifty years or so of American independence, campaign costs were relatively low. The population was small, and only white males who owned property—about one of every five adults—were allowed to vote. But as the population grew, and property requirements were abolished, campaign costs rose. By 1840 the practice of buying votes was well established in the nation's cities.

Rising campaign costs in the early nineteenth century required candidates to begin soliciting funds from businesses, industries, and wealthy individuals. These contributors, in turn, increasingly sought favors from a government that was becoming more and more involved in economic matters. During the Civil War, Abraham Lincoln wrote:

As a result of the war, corporations have become enthroned, and an era of corruption in high places will follow. The money power of the country will endeavor to prolong its rule by preying on the prejudices of the people until all wealth is concentrated in a few hands.

During the industrial revolution following the Civil War, historian Richard Hofstadter describes what may have been the high-water mark of corruption in American politics: "Capitalists seeking land grants, tariffs, bounties, favorable currency policies, freedom from regulatory legislation and economic reform, supplied campaign funds, fees, and bribes, and plied politicians with investment opportunities." Banks, railroads, and oil and mining companies became the major sources of campaign cash in national politics; in local politics, campaigns were funded by utilities, saloons, gambling halls, houses of prostitution, and racetracks. According to historian George Thayer, "Standard Oil did everything to the Pennsylvania Legislature except refine it." The presidential election of 1896 set a record for campaign spending that would not be surpassed in equivalent dollars until the 1970s. U.S. Senator Marcus Alonzo Hanna, general counsel for John D. Rockefeller's Standard Oil Company, raised between $6 and $7 million for the winner, Republican William McKinley, while his Democratic opponent William Jennings Bryan spent only about a half million dollars.

Political campaign costs rose again following the Seventeenth Amendment (1913), which instituted the direct election of U.S. senators; the Nineteenth Amendment, which won women the right to vote; and the expanding use of primary elections to choose party candidates. Fortunately for politicians who began to need more campaign money to reach more voters, the New Deal vastly increased government involvement in the economy and thereby raised the incentives for business interests to fork over more money to ensure that their interests would be protected in policy-making. Labor unions became a major source of campaign funds in 1936 when the newly formed Congress of Industrial Organizations (CIO) contributed a half million dollars to Franklin D. Roosevelt's presidential campaign.

During the 1950s and 1960s, each of the major parties enjoyed the support of wealthy "superdonors"—the Mellons and Rockefellers on the Republican side and the Kennedys and Harrimans on the Democratic side. But a turning point in campaign finance history occurred after the Watergate revelations of secret donations to the 1972 Nixon reelection campaign, especially the $2 million individual contribution by insurance magnate Clement Stone. The result was the passage of the Federal Election Campaign Act, creating the Federal Elections Commission (FEC) and placing limits on direct campaign contributions to candidates by individuals and organizations.

But the reforms envisioned by the act were quickly undermined by an explosion in the number of political action committees, vast increases in unlimited "soft money" contributions to the parties, and the U.S. Supreme Court decision in *Buckley v. Valeo* declaring that individuals (and by implication independent organizations) may spend as much as they wish to express their own views and advance their own candidacies. The result was a skyrocketing of political campaign spending and an even greater dependence on big money sources of campaign funds than before the passage of the act.

The Bipartisan Campaign Finance Reform Act of 2002 was designed to close "loopholes" in the earlier reform act. It banned unlimited soft money contributions to the parties, and limited individual contributions to candidates to $2,000 per election. But contributions to independent organizations ("527s") remained unregulated. These groups were prohibited from coordinating their ads with candidates or parties, but they played a major role in the 2004 election (see *Up Close:* "527s: Eroding Campaign Finance Reform").

Source: Excerpted from *A Brief History of Money in Politics*, Center for Responsive Politics, Washington, D.C., 1999.

Table 8.2   The Cost of Getting Elected to Congress

Senate

Average Democratic Incumbent	$8,582,559
Average Democratic Challenger	$772,381
Average Republican Incumbent	$5,750,211
Average Republican Challenger	$1,126,857
Most Expensive Campaign	Tom Daschle (D-S.D.) $17.4 million (lost)

House of Representatives

Average Democratic Incumbent	$918,481
Average Democratic Challenger	$174,694
Average Republican Incumbent	$1,041,327
Average Republican Challenger	$192,960
Most Expensive Campaign	Martin Frost (D-Tex.), $3.9 million (lost)

Source: Center for Responsive Politics. Figures for 2004.

as to political party conventions. However, taxpayers are becoming less and less willing to allow their tax monies to go into political campaigning (even though the $3 checkoff does not add to the taxpayers' total taxes). Only about 11 percent of taxpayers currently check the box. The Presidential Election Campaign Fund has been in jeopardy of not having enough money to make its promised payments to the candidates and parties.

Presidential candidates may opt out of taxpayer-financed funding if they choose to do so. This allows them to spend as much money as they wish, but they receive no public money. Nonetheless, all presidential candidates, and all candidates for Congress, must abide by federal campaign finance laws (see below).

Small Donations   Millions of Americans participate in campaign financing, either by giving directly to candidates or the parties or by giving to political action committees, which then distribute their funds to candidates. For members of Congress, small donors typically make up less than 20 percent of their campaign funds. The proportion is higher for presidential candidates. For donations under $200, contributors' names and addresses are recorded only by the candidates and parties, not passed along to the Federal Election Commission as part of the public record.

Large Individual Donors   "Fat cats" are the preferred donors. These are the donors whose names are on the candidates' Rolodexes. They are the ones in attendance when the president, the Speaker of the House, or other top political dignitaries travel around the country doing fund-raisers. They are also the ones who are wined, dined, prodded, and cajoled in a seemingly ceaseless effort by the parties and the candidates to raise funds for the next election.

In its 2002 campaign finance reform legislation, Congress raised the maximum individual contribution to federal candidates to $2,000 (up from $1,000 in the 2000 election). Fat cats are expected to give the maximum, and indeed even more. They can do so by giving their maximum $2,000 once in the primary election and a second time in the general election. And their spouses can do the same. And, of course, they can also give to the parties and to independent political organizations committed to helping their preferred candidates.

www Center for Responsive Politics
The site of an organization devoted to the study of campaign finance laws, the role of money in elections, PACs, "soft money," and special-interest groups.
www.opensecrets.org

UP CLOSE

How to Spend $7 Million on a Political Campaign

How do you spend $7 million dollars on a Senate campaign? It may sound like a lot of money, but it can disappear quickly in a heated Senate campaign. Indeed, $7 million is the *average* expenditure of winning senators. (U.S. Senator Jon Corzine [D-N.J.] spent $60 million of his own personal wealth to win his New Jersey seat.)

Television advertising is the biggest cost. It may consume 40 to 65 percent of the campaign budget, depending on how many "media markets" (separate cities with groups of TV stations) are in the state and how expensive television time is in each market. Staff salaries may consume a good portion of the budget. Experienced professionals and/or professional campaign management firms do not come cheap; volunteers are helpful, but no match for professionals in knowing how to run a campaign. Polling firms are needed throughout the campaign to keep track of progress or decline and to continue to evaluate the effectiveness of campaign themes, policy positions, negative hits on the opponent, and so on. Travel is another large item, whether the candidate and staff fly by private jet or rent a bus. Lawyers and accountants must supervise spending, submit FEC reports, and see that everyone adheres to campaign laws. A typical Senate campaign budget follows.

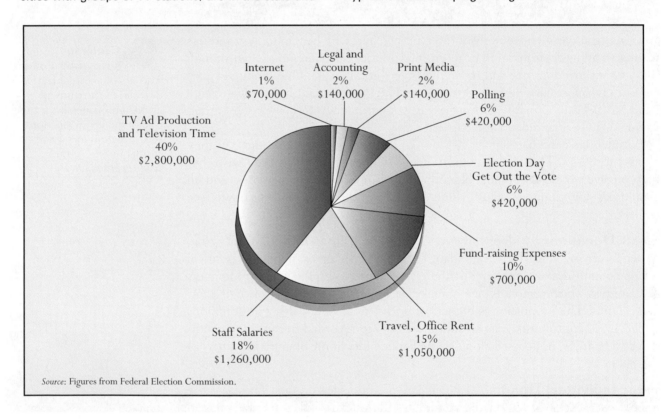

Internet
1%
$70,000

Legal and
Accounting
2%
$140,000

Print Media
2%
$140,000

Polling
6%
$420,000

TV Ad Production
and Television Time
40%
$2,800,000

Election Day
Get Out the Vote
6%
$420,000

Fund-raising Expenses
10%
$700,000

Staff Salaries
18%
$1,260,000

Travel, Office Rent
15%
$1,050,000

Source: Figures from Federal Election Commission.

Candidate Self-Financing   Candidates for federal office also pump millions into their own campaigns. There are no federal restrictions on the amount of money individuals can spend on their own campaign.[13] Senate and House candidates frequently put $50,000 to $100,000 or more of their own money into their campaigns, through outright gifts or personal loans. (Candidates who loan themselves the money to run are able to pay themselves back later from outside contributions.)

issue ads Ads that advocate policy positions rather than explicitly supporting or opposing particular candidates.

Issue Ads   Issue ads advocate policy positions rather than explicitly advising voters to cast their ballots for or against particular candidates. But most of these ads leave little doubt about which candidate is being supported or targeted. The

New Jersey Governor Jon Corzine at his inauguration in 2006. The multimillionaire Corzine still holds the record for a self-financed U.S. senate campaign. There are no limits on the amounts of their personal money that candidates can spend on their own campaigns.

Bipartisan Campaign Reform Act of 2002 bans issue ads 60 days before a general election and 30 days before a primary election. However, there are no dollar limits on the size of contributions to sponsoring groups (often referred to as 527s from the section of the Internal Revenue code under which they operate).

What Do Contributors "Buy"?

What does money buy in politics? A cynic might say that money can buy anything—for example, special appropriations for public works directly benefiting the contributor, special tax breaks, special federal regulations. Public opinion views big-money contributions as a major problem in the American political system. Scandals involving the direct (quid pro quo) purchase of special favors, privileges, exemptions, and treatments have been common enough in the past, and they are likely to continue in the future. But campaign contributions are rarely made in the form of a direct trade-off for a favorable vote. Such an arrangement risks exposure as bribery and may be prosecuted under the law. Campaign contributions are more likely to be made without any *explicit* quid pro quo but rather with a general understanding that the contributor has confidence in the candidate's good judgment on issues directly affecting the contributor. The contributor expects the candidate to be smart enough to figure out how to vote in order to keep the contributions coming in the future.

The Big-Money Contributors   Big-money contributors—businesses, unions, professional associations—pump millions into presidential and congressional elections. Figure 8.2 lists the top fifty contributors to candidates and parties since 1989. Note that union contributions are heavily weighted toward Democrats, as are the contributions of the Association of Trial Lawyers. Businesses and business associations tend to split their contributions between the parties, but Republicans usually get the largest share.

Buying Access to Policy Makers   Large contributors expect to be able to call or visit and present their views directly to "their" officeholders. At the presidential level, major contributors who cannot get a meeting with the president expect to

> ── Think Again ──
>
> Do political campaign contributions have too much influence on elections and government policy?

Rank	Contributor	Total Contributions	% Dem.	% Rep.	Rank	Contributor	Total Contributions	% Dem.	% Rep.
1.	American Federation of State/County/Municipal Employees	$34,944,356	98%	1%	25.	National Rifle Assn	$14,345,042	13%	86%
					26.	AFL-CIO	$14,143,542	88%	11%
2.	National Assn of Realtors	$24,159,780	50%	49%	27.	American Bankers Assn	$13,753,323	39%	60%
3.	National Education Assn	$23,382,034	86%	13%	28.	Time Warner	$13,408,561	70%	28%
4.	Assn of Trial Lawyers of America	$23,310,366	89%	10%	29.	SBC Communications	$13,032,502	34%	65%
					30.	Verizon Communications	$12,617,393	38%	61%
5.	Communications Workers of America	$21,968,716	98%	1%	31.	BellSouth Corp	$12,427,578	43%	56%
					32.	Microsoft Corp	$12,327,062	58%	41%
6.	Service Employees International Union	$21,865,215	88%	11%	33.	National Beer Wholesalers Assn	$12,207,798	30%	69%
7.	Intl Brotherhood of Electrical Workers	$21,522,812	96%	3%	34.	EMILY's List	$11,777,389	100%	0%
					35.	Sheet Metal Workers Union	$11,687,901	97%	2%
8.	Carpenters & Joiners Union	$20,995,637	68%	31%	36.	Ernst & Young	$11,672,581	31%	67%
					37.	Lockheed Martin	$11,486,880	39%	60%
9.	Teamsters Union	$20,838,115	85%	13%	38.	JP Morgan Chase & Co	$11,455,069	49%	50%
10.	American Medical Assn	$20,632,636	28%	71%	39.	RJR Nabisco/ RJ Reynolds Tobacco	$10,959,872	11%	88%
11.	Altria Group (Philip Morris)	$20,567,067	41%	57%	40.	American Dental Assn	$10,898,735	43%	56%
12.	FedEx Corp	$20,500,993	33%	66%	41.	Morgan Stanley	$10,850,938	34%	65%
13.	Laborers Union	$20,497,632	86%	13%	42.	Blue Cross/Blue Shield	$10,757,914	42%	57%
14.	United Auto Workers	$19,832,550	98%	0%	43.	American Hospital Assn	$10,748,440	44%	55%
15.	AT&T	$19,484,567	47%	52%	44.	National Assn of Insurance & Financial Advisors	$10,629,255	37%	62%
16.	American Federation of Teachers	$19,291,514	99%	0%					
17.	Goldman Sachs	$18,607,643	50%	49%	45.	General Electric	$10,596,818	46%	53%
18.	Machinists & Aerospace Workers Union	$18,429,464	98%	0%	46.	American Institute of CPAs	$10,381,169	37%	62%
19.	United Food & Commercial Workers Union	$18,318,526	98%	1%	47.	Union Pacific Corp	$10,131,658	22%	77%
					48.	Credit Union National Assn	$10,110,853	43%	56%
20.	Citigroup Inc	$17,080,206	48%	50%	49.	Deloitte Touche Tohmatsu	$10,108,211	28%	71%
21.	United Parcel Service	$16,859,844	29%	70%					
22.	National Auto Dealers Assn	$16,474,442	29%	70%	50.	United Steelworkers of America	$10,089,196	97%	2%
23.	National Assn of Home Builders	$14,930,228	38%	61%					
24.	National Assn of Letter Carriers	$14,608,734	71%	27%					

Figure 8.2   All Time Big-Money Contributors

Source: Reprinted by permission of Center for Responsive Politics.

political action committees (PACs) Organizations that solicit and receive campaign contributions from corporations, unions, trade associations, and ideological and issue-oriented groups, and their members, then distribute these funds to political candidates.

meet at least with high-level White House staff or cabinet officials. At the congressional level, major contributors usually expect to meet or speak directly with their representative or senator. Members of Congress boast of responding to letters, calls, or visits by any constituent, but contributors can expect a more immediate and direct response than noncontributors can. Lobbyists for contributing organizations routinely expect and receive a hearing from members of Congress.

Political Action Committees   Political action committees (PACs) are the most reliable source of money for reelection campaigns in Congress. Corporations and unions are not allowed to contribute directly to campaigns from corporate or union funds, but they may form PACs to seek contributions from managers and stockholders and their families, or union workers and their families. PACs are organized not only by corporations and unions but also by trade and professional associations, environmental groups, and liberal and conservative ideological groups. The wealthiest PACs are based in Washington, D.C. (see "PAC Power" in Chapter 9). PACs are very cautious; their job is to get a maximum return on their contributions, winning influence and goodwill with as many lawmakers as possible in Washington. There's no return on their investment if their recipients lose at the polls; therefore most PACs—particularly business PACs—give most of their dollars to incumbents seeking reelection.

Individual Contributors Most individual contributors are ideologically motivated. They make their contributions based on their perception of the ideological position of the candidate (or perhaps their perception of the candidate's opponent). They may make contributions to congressional candidates across the country who share their policy views. Liberal and conservative networks of contributors can be contacted through specialized mailing lists—for example, liberals through television producer Norman Lear's People for the American Way. Feminists have been effective in soliciting individual contributions across the country and funneling them very early in a campaign to women candidates through EMILY's List. Ideological contributors may only get the satisfaction of knowing that they are financially backing their cause in the political process. Some contributors simply enjoy the opportunity to be near and to be seen with high-ranking politicians. Politicians pose for photos with contributors, who later frame the photos and hang them in their office to impress their friends, associates, and customers. Contributors are disproportionately high-income, older people with strong partisan views (see Figure 8.3).

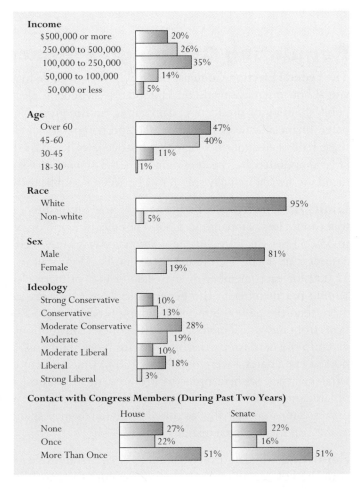

Figure 8.3

Characteristics of Individual Political Contributors

Contributors to political campaigns generally are older and have higher incomes than most Americans. Whites and males contribute more than blacks and females, and conservatives contribute more than liberals.

Source: John Green, Paul Herrnson, Lynda Powell, Clyde Wilcox, "Individual Congressional Campaign Contributors," press release, June 9, 1998, Center for Responsive Politics.

Buying Government Assistance   Many large contributors do business with government agencies. They expect any representative or senator they have supported to intervene on their behalf with these agencies, sometimes acting to cut red tape, ensure fairness, and expedite their cases, and other times pressuring the agencies for a favorable decision. Officials in the White House or the cabinet may also be expected to intervene on behalf of major contributors. There is little question raised when the intervention merely expedites consideration of a contributor's case, but pressure to bend rules or regulations to get favorable decisions raises ethical problems for officeholders (see "Congressional Ethics" in Chapter 10). Corporations that do business with government agencies, and those that are heavily regulated by government agencies, may make contributions simply to "flex their muscles"—to signal bureaucrats that if they wished to do so, they could fight any agency's specific decisions.[14]

Fund-Raising Chores   Fund raising occupies more of a candidate's time than any other campaign activity. Candidates must personally contact as many individual contributors as possible. They work late into the evening on the telephone with potential contributors. Fund-raising dinners, cocktail parties, barbecues, fish frys, and so on, are scheduled nearly every day of a campaign. The candidate is expected to appear personally to "press the flesh" of big contributors. Movie and rock stars and other assorted celebrities may also be asked to appear at fund-raising affairs to generate attendance. Dinners may run to $2,000 a plate in presidential affairs, although often less in Senate or House campaigns. Tickets may be "bundled" to well-heeled individual contributors or sold in blocks to organizations. Fund-raising techniques are limited only by the imagination of the campaign manager.

Regulating Campaign Finance

Federal Election Commission (FEC) Agency charged with enforcing federal election laws and disbursing public presidential campaign funds.

The **Federal Election Commission (FEC)** is responsible for enforcing limits on individual and organizational contributions to all federal elections, administering the public funding of presidential campaigns, and requiring full disclosure of all campaign financial activity in presidential and congressional elections. Enforcement of these federal election and campaign finance laws lies in the hands of the six-member FEC. Appointed by the president to serve staggered six-year terms, commission members are traditionally split 3 to 3 between Republicans and Democrats.

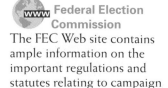

Federal Election Commission
The FEC Web site contains ample information on the important regulations and statutes relating to campaign finance. *http://www.fec.gov*

Limits on Contributions   The FEC now limits direct individual contributions to a candidate's campaign to $2,000 per election and organizational contributions to $5,000 per election. But there are many ways in which individuals and organizations can legally surmount these limits. Contributors may give a candidate $2,000 for each member of their family in a primary election and then another $2,000 per member in the general election. Organizations may generate much more than the $5,000 limit by bundling (combining) $2,000 additional contributions from individual members. (Soft-money contributions—unregulated amounts given to the national parties officially for "party building" but actually used in support of candidates—were banned in 2002.) Independent organizations can spend whatever they wish in order to promote their political views, so long as these organizations do so "without cooperation or consultation with the candidate of his or her campaign." Finally, as noted, individuals may spend as much of their own money on their own campaigns as they wish.

Reporting   By law, every candidate for federal office must file periodic reports with the FEC detailing both the income and the expenditures of his or her cam-

Candidates often seek the help of celebrities in raising campaign money. Here Senator Ted Kennedy (D-MA) appears at a 2006 concert with singer Bono and cellist Yo Yo Ma.

paign. Individual contributors who give an aggregate of $200 or more must be identified by name, address, occupation, and employer. All PAC and party contributions, no matter how large or small, must also be itemized. In addition, PACs themselves must file reports with the FEC at least four times a year, detailing both the contributions received by the PAC and the names of candidates and other groups that received the PAC's donations.

Federal Funding of Presidential Elections   Federal funding, financed by the $3 checkoff box on individual income tax returns, is available to presidential candidates in primary and general elections, as well as to major-party nominating conventions. Candidates seeking the nomination in presidential primary elections can qualify for federal funds by raising $5,000 from private contributions no greater than $250 each in each of twenty states. In the general election, Democratic and Republican nominees are funded equally at levels determined by the FEC. In order to receive federal funding, presidential candidates must agree to FEC limits on their campaign spending in both primary and general elections.

Federal funding pays about one-third of the primary campaign costs of presidential candidates and all the *official* presidential campaign organization costs in the general election. The parties also receive federal funds for their nominating conventions.

Campaign Finance Reform   Unregulated soft-money contributions to the parties grew rapidly during the 1990s. These contributions represented a giant black hole in the original Federal Election Campaign Act of 1974. Contributions made directly to a candidate's campaign—hard money contributions—were limited (originally to $1,000). But individuals, organizations, corporations, and unions could contribute as much as they wanted to the Democratic and Republican national parties. These contributions were supposed to be for party building, voter registration, getting out the vote, and so on, but in fact went into candidate campaigning.

In the 2000 Republican presidential primaries, U.S. Senator John McCain made campaign finance reform his principal issue. He surprised the Republican Party leaders by defeating George W. Bush in the New Hampshire primary that year. Bush and both Democratic and Republican leaders decided to jump on the campaign finance reform bandwagon, although with little real enthusiasm. In

UP CLOSE

Midterm Congressional Elections, 2006: What Do They Mean?

Tip O'Neill, the former Democratic Speaker of the House and wily Boston Irish politician, once said, "All politics is local." Usually midterm congressional elections are decided by personalities, issues, and events with 435 separate House districts and one-third of the states electing U.S. Senators. But in 2006 the war in Iraq was the top concern of voters everywhere. Nearly two of every three Americans cited Iraq as "the top priority for the president and Congress to deal with."[a]

Traditionally the party of a two-term president loses congressional seats in the sixth year of his tenure. The party out of power usually calls for "change," even if it does not make the direction of the change very clear. But the 2006 congressional elections appeared to be in large measure a referendum on George Bush's presidency. Throughout the election year Bush's approval ratings stayed below 40 percent. As U.S. troop casualties in Iraq grew, a large majority of voters turned against the war and especially against Bush's conduct of the war and the decisions of Secretary of Defense Donald Rumsfeld. An early indication of voter dissatisfaction was the defeat of incumbent U.S. Senator Joseph Lieberman in his own Democratic primary in Connecticut. (The defeat of an incumbent senator in his own party's primary is practically unheard-of in American politics.) Lieberman had voted for the war, and although he defeated his primary opponent in the general election, the antiwar handwriting was on the wall.

Throughout the campaign Bush defended the war in Iraq as a necessary part of the broader war on terrorism. He portrayed Democrats as wanting to "cut and run" and argued that a U.S. defeat in Iraq would encourage terrorists around the world. Democratic congressional campaigns attacked Bush's initial decision to go into Iraq, as well as his subsequent conduct of the war. Yet few Democrats proposed any real strategy for U.S. withdrawal from Iraq. Even New York Democratic senatorial candidate Hillary Clinton opposed an immediate and complete withdrawal of U.S. troops.

Senator Hillary Clinton (D-NY) campaigning for reelection in Buffalo, New York, with her husband, former president Bill Clinton, in 2006. He is a popular campaign speaker for Democratic candidates throughout the country.

Democrats captured control of both the House of Representatives and the Senate in the 2006 midterm elections. (The GOP had held the House for the previous 12 years, since 1994.) The new House opened its 2007 session with 232 Democrats and 203 Republicans, and the Democrats held a razor-thin majority—51 to 49 in the U.S. Senate. On the morning after the election, the president announced that he had accepted the resignation of Secretary of Defense Donald Rumsfeld. The immediate replacement of Rumsfeld (with former CIA Director Robert Gates) suggested that Bush understood the unpopularity of the war in Iraq and was prepared to change direction (although exactly what the new direction would be remained unclear).

Only a handful of seats changed from Republican to Democratic. But it was enough to change party control of the House and Senate, to shake up the balance of power in Washington, to cause the president to rethink national security policy, and to bring back divided party government to the nation.

[a] Gallup poll, November 3, 2006. *www.gallup.com*

Table 8.3   Campaign Finance Rules, 2006

General

All federal election contributions and expenditures must be reported to the Federal Election Commission, which may investigate and prosecute violators.

All contributions over $200 must be reported, with name, address, and occupation of contributor.

No foreign contributions can be made.

There are no restrictions on how much individuals may spend on their own campaigns *(Buckley v. Valeo)*.

No large contributions (soft money) may be made to the national parties; party contributions by individuals and committees are limited.

Presidential Primaries

Federal matching funds are available for money raised by candidates from individual donors giving $250 dollars or less. To be eligible, the primary candidate must raise $5,000 in each of twenty states in contributions of $250 or less.

Presidential Elections

The federal government pays all campaign costs of major party candidates and contributes to the costs of party conventions. The federal government will also pay part of the costs of minor party candidates who win between 5 and 25 percent of the vote.

Limits on Contributions

Donor	Candidate	PAC	National Party	State/Local	Special
Individual	$2,100[a]	$5,000	$25,000	$10,000	Biennial total: $101,400[a]
National party	5,000	5,000	—	—	—
State/local party	5,000	5,000	—	—	—
PAC (multi-candidate)	5,000	5,000	1,500	5,000	—
PAC (single-candidate)	2,100[a]	5,000	26,700[a]	10,000	—

Millionaire Amendment

If a candidate spends more of his own money beyond specified thresholds (e.g., $350,000 for House candidates), contribution limits for his or her opponent are tripled.

Independent Group Expenditures

Independent individuals or groups airing TV or radio ads must not coordinate with candidates or parties in order to avoid contribution limits.

Election Communications

Independent individuals or groups may not broadcast TV or radio ads referring to a candidate 60 days prior to a general election or 30 days prior to the primary election.

[a]Contribution limit for 2006. Limits rise with inflation.

Note: This table summarizes the Bipartisan Campaign Finance Reform Act of 2002.

Source: FEC, 2006.

2002 a somewhat reluctant Congress finally passed the Bipartisan Campaign Finance Reform Act (see Table 8.3).

Among other things, this act eliminates soft money contributions to the parties; increases the individual contribution limit to candidates' campaigns from $1,000 to $2,000; prohibits independent groups from coordinating their campaign spending with candidates or parties; does not allow independent groups to mention the name of a candidate in their issue ads; and bans independent groups from broadcasting their views in the final days of a campaign.

But contributions to nonprofit independent groups remain unregulated. Big money contributors who can no longer provide large amounts of cash to candidates or to parties *can* establish nonprofit independent groups (known as "527s,"

UP CLOSE

527s: Eroding Campaign Finance Reform

The Bipartisan Campaign Finance Reform Act was supposed to eliminate big money contributions from national elections. After years of struggle, reformers thought they had eliminated loopholes that allow individuals, corporations, and labor unions to pump millions of dollars into presidential and congressional campaigns.

But campaign cash is like the Pillsbury doughboy: Push it in one place and it pops out in another. The act banned big soft money contributions to the parties. But Congress did not block individuals or non-profit independent groups from spending as much as they want to broadcast their own views. So early in the 2004 election campaign, big money contributors and politically savvy consultants, especially in the Democratic Party, began to build a network of nonprofit organizations—organizations into which they could funnel millions of dollars and expect to see them broadcast issue ads in favor of their candidates during the campaign. (These organizations became popularly known as "527s," in reference to the section in the U.S. Tax Code authorizing them.)

George Soros, one of the world's richest men, has given away billions to promote democracy in former Soviet bloc nations, including his birthplace, Hungary. In addition, Soros funds a wide variety of liberal causes through his Open Society Institute. In 2003, he declared financial war on George Bush. He gave millions to a series of often newly created liberal organizations. Among the recipients of his political generosity:

MoveOn, an organization originally formed by Silicon Valley entrepreneurs to defend President Bill Clinton against impeachment.

Americans Coming Together (ACT), an organization formed by officers of the AFL-CIO, the Sierra Club, and the Service Employees International Union "to mobilize voters to defeat George W. Bush and elect progressive candidates across all America."

America Votes, created by former Texas Gov. Ann Richards and her daughter to coordinate get-out-the-vote of anti-George Bush groups.

Partnership for America's Families, another group formed by the Service Employees International Union to get "progressive" voters to the polls in big cities.

Voices for Working Families, created by the AFL-CIO to "mobilize the votes primarily of minorities and women."

The Media Fund, organized by President Clinton's Deputy White House Chief of Staff to raise big money to buy TV and radio ads.

Moving America Forward, created to increase Hispanic Democratic voting in the southwestern states.

Grassroots Democrats, organized by the Communications Workers of America union and the Association of Trial Lawyers to raise contributions under the new campaign finance law.

Billionaires for Bush, a tongue-in-cheek organization opposed to Bush's reelection.

The only anti-Kerry group to match the Soros-funded organizations was the controversial Swift Boat Veterans for Truth. It ran bitter TV ads challenging Kerry's Vietnam War record.

referring to their Internal Revenue Service code) to accept big contributions to enable them to produce and broadcast campaign advertisements (see *Up Close* "527s: Eroding Campaign Finance Reform").

The act was challenged as a violation of First Amendment free speech rights but upheld by the U.S. Supreme Court.[15]

The Supreme Court has held that state or federal laws that place too *low* a *limit* on how much individuals can contribute to a candidate or party violates the First Amendment's guarantee of free speech. When Vermont placed a $200 limit on campaign contributions for offices in that state, the Court held that limits could not be so low as to prevent challengers from mounting effective campaigns. Vermont's limits were "disproportionately severe."[16]

The Presidential Campaign:
The Primary Race

The phrase *presidential fever* refers to the burning political ambition required to seek the presidency. The grueling presidential campaign is a test of strength, character, endurance, and determination. It is physically exhausting and mentally and emotionally draining. Every aspect of the candidates' lives—and the lives of their families—is subject to microscopic inspection by the news media. Most of this coverage is critical, and much of it is unfair. Yet candidates are expected to handle it all with grace and humor, from the earliest testing of the waters through a full-fledged campaign.

Media Mentions   Politicians with presidential ambitions may begin by promoting presidential *mentions* by media columnists and commentators. The media help to identify "presidential timber" years in advance of a presidential race simply by drawing up lists of potential candidates, commenting on their qualifications, and speculating about their intentions. Mentions are likely to come to prominent governors or senators who start making speeches outside their states, who grab the media spotlight on a national issue, or who simply let it be known to the media "off the record" that they are considering a presidential race. Visiting New Hampshire and Iowa and giving speeches there is viewed as "testing the waters" and a signal of presidential ambitions.

Presidential Credentials   Political experience as vice president, governor, U.S. senator, or member of Congress not only inspires presidential ambition but also provides vital experience in political campaigning. However, virtually all presidential candidates testify that the presidential arena is far more challenging than politics at any other level. The experience of running for and holding high public office appears to be a political requirement for the presidency. Some presidential aspirants have tried to make a virtue of their lack of previous political office holding, no doubt hoping to attract support from the many Americans who disdain "politics as usual." But for over a century no major party nominee for president has not previously held office as vice president, governor, U.S. senator, or member of Congress except World War II hero General Dwight D. Eisenhower.

The Decision to Run   The decision to run for president involves complex personal and political calculations. Ambition to occupy the world's most powerful office must be weighed against the staggering costs—emotional as well as financial—of a presidential campaign.

Serious planning, organizing, and fund-raising must begin at least two years before the general election. A staff must be assembled—campaign managers and strategists, fund-raisers, media experts, pollsters, issues advisers and speech-writers, lawyers and accountants—and supporters must be identified in key states throughout the nation. Paid and volunteer workers must be assembled (see Figure 8.4). Leaders among important interest groups must be contacted. A general campaign strategy must be developed, an organization put in place, and several millions of dollars in campaign contributions pledged in advance of the race. Often the decision to run hinges on whether initial pledges of campaign contributions appear adequate. The serious candidate must be able to anticipate contributions of $25 million or more for primary elections. Most of this work must be accomplished in the preprimary season—the months after Labor Day of the year preceding the election, and before the first primary election.

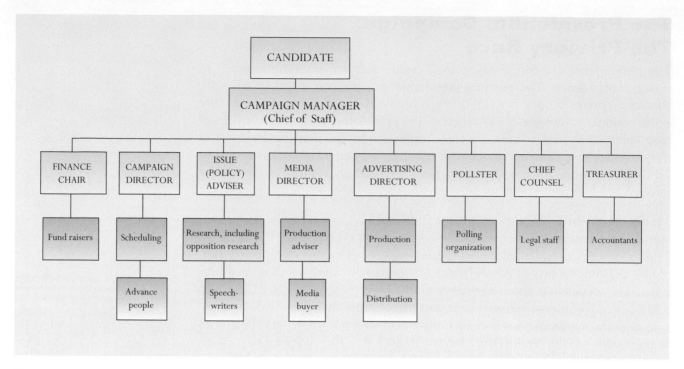

Figure 8.4   Typical Campaign Organization
Campaign organizations vary, but most assign someone to perform these tasks: funding, scheduling appearances, speech writing, media production and buying, polling, advertising, legal compliance, and check writing, even if, in local campaigns, all these tasks must be performed by the candidate or his or her family members.

A Strategy for the Primaries   The road to the White House consists of two separate races: the primary elections and caucuses leading to the Democratic and Republican party nominations, and the general election. Each of these races requires a separate strategy. The primary race requires an appeal to party activists and the more ideologically motivated primary voters in key states. The general election requires an appeal to the less partisan, less attentive, more ideologically moderate general election voters. Thus the campaign strategy developed to win the nomination must give way after the national conventions to a strategy to win the November general election.

Primary Campaigns   Primary campaigns come in different varieties. An incumbent president with no serious competition from within his own party can safely glide through his party's primaries, saving campaign money for the general election. In contrast, the party out of the White House typically goes through a rough-and-tumble primary (and preprimary) season, with multiple presidential aspirants. And when no incumbent president is running for reelection, both parties experience heavy party infighting among multiple presidential hopefuls.

Candidates strive during the preprimary season to win media attention, to climb the poll ratings, and raise campaign funds. Early front runners must beware of stumbles and gaffes; they must be prepared for close scrutiny by the media; and they must expect to be the targets of their competitors. Not infrequently, early front runners lose their momentum even before the first primary elections.[17]

Primary voters are heavily weighted toward party activists, who are more ideologically motivated than the more moderate voters in general elections. Democratic primary voters are more liberal, and Republican primary voters are more

Democratic presidential hopefuls line up for a debate prior to the New Hampshire primary, won by Massachusetts Senator John Kerry (third from right). Others are Missouri's Dick Gephardt, New York's Al Sharpton, Ohio's Dennis Kucinich, Connecticut's Joe Lieberman, North Carolina's John Edwards, Illinois' Carol Moseley-Braun, and Vermont's Howard Dean.

conservative, than the voters in the November general election. Democratic primary voters include large numbers of the party's core constituents—union members, public employees, minorities, environmentalists, and feminists.

Presidential candidates must try to appeal not only to the ideological predispositions of their party's primary voters but also convince them of their "electability"—the likelihood that they can win the party's nomination and more importantly go on to win the presidential election. Often primary voters are torn between voting for their favorite candidate based on his or her ideological and issue positions, or voting for the most electable candidate.

The New Hampshire Primary   The primary season begins in the winter snows of New Hampshire, traditionally the first state to hold a presidential primary election. New Hampshire is far more important *strategically* to a presidential campaign than it is in delegate strength. As a small state, New Hampshire supplies fewer than one percent of the delegates at the Democratic and Republican conventions. But the New Hampshire primary looms very large in media coverage and hence in overall campaign strategy. Although the popular Democratic Iowa party caucuses are held even earlier, New Hampshire is the nation's first primary, and the media begin speculating about its outcome and reporting early state-poll results months in advance.

The New Hampshire primary inspires **retail politics**—direct candidate contact with the voters. Presidential aspirants begin visiting New Hampshire in the year preceding the primary elections, speaking at town hall meetings, visiting with small groups, standing outside of supermarkets, walking through restaurants, greeting workers at factories and offices, and so on. These personal contacts bypass the media's filtering and interpreting of the candidate's personality and message. Retail politics is largely confined to New Hampshire, a small state and a year of pre-primary time to reach voters personally. And there is some evidence that voters who actually meet candidates come away with a more favorable view of them.[18]

The "expectations" game is played with a vengeance in the early primaries. Media polls and commentators set the candidates' expected vote percentages, and the candidates and their spokespersons try to deflate these expectations. On

retail politics Direct candidate contact with individual voters.

spin doctor Practitioner of the art of spin control, or manipulation of media reporting to favor one's own candidate.

election night, the candidates' **spin doctors** sally forth among the crowds of television and newspaper reporters to give a favorable interpretation of the outcome. The candidates themselves appear at campaign headquarters (and, they hope, on national television) to give the same favorable spin to the election results. But the media itself—particularly the television network anchors and reporters and commentators—interpret the results for the American people, determining the early favorites in the presidential horse race.

New Hampshire provides the initial *momentum* for the presidential candidates. "Momentum" is more than just a media catchword. The Democratic and Republican winners in New Hampshire have demonstrated their voter appeal, their "electability." Favorable New Hampshire results inspire more financial contributions and thus the resources needed to carry the fight into the next group of primary elections. Unfavorable New Hampshire results tend to dry up contributions; weaker candidates may be forced into an early withdrawal.

front-end strategy Presidential political campaign strategy in which a candidate focuses on winning early primaries to build momentum.

The Front-End Strategy A **front-end strategy** places heavy emphasis on the results from New Hampshire and other early primary states. This strategy involves spending all or most of the candidate's available resources—time, energy, and money—on the early primary states, in the hopes that early victories will provide the momentum, in media attention and financial contributions, to continue the race.

Big-State Strategy Presidential aspirants who begin the race with widespread support among party activists, heavy financial backing, and strong endorsements from the major interest groups can focus their attention on the big-state primaries. A **big-state strategy** generally requires more money, more workers, and better organization than a front-end strategy. But the big states—California, New York, Texas, Florida, Pennsylvania, Ohio, and Michigan—have the most delegates. The results of these primaries may determine the Democratic and Republican nominees, assuming that most or all of them are won by the same candidates. It is rare that more than two candidates in each party survive as credible candidates after the big states have made their selections. By this stage of the race, many uncommitted delegates begin to commit themselves and their convention votes to the leader.

big-state strategy Presidential political campaign strategy in which a candidate focuses on winning primaries in large states because of their high delegate counts.

Front Loading Presidential nominees are now selected by early March. State legislators in a number of states expressed their frustration over the media attention given to tiny New Hampshire by moving up the dates of their presidential primary elections. (The New Hampshire Legislature responded by officially setting its primary date one week earlier than any other state's primary.) Today many big states, including California, Connecticut, Georgia, Massachusetts, Minnesota, New York, Ohio, Florida, and Texas hold their primary in March.

This **front loading** of presidential primaries appears to favor the candidate who peaks in the polls in the first six weeks of the primary season.[19]

front loading The scheduling of presidential primary elections early in the year.

Convention Showplace Once a presidential candidate has enough votes to assure nomination, this uncrowned winner must prepare for the party's convention. Organizing and orchestrating convention forces, dominating the platform and rules writing, enjoying the nominating speeches and the traditional roll call of the state delegations, mugging for the television camera when the nominating vote goes over the top, submitting the vice presidential nominee's name for convention approval, and preparing and delivering a rousing acceptance speech to begin the fall campaign are just a few of the many tasks awaiting the winner—and the winner's campaign team.

Presidential candidates usually submit their choice for vice president in the run-up to the party's national convention. George W. Bush's 2000 running mate, Dick Cheney, was viewed by some as having been chosen to lend an air of maturity to the Republican ticket. Cheney was Secretary of Defense in Bush's father's administration.

The Presidential Campaign: The General Election Battle

Buoyed by the conventions—and often by postconvention bounces in the polls—the new nominees must now face the general electorate.

General Election Strategies   Strategies in the general election are as varied as the imaginations of campaign advisers, media consultants, pollsters, and the candidates themselves. As noted earlier, campaign strategies are affected by the nature of the times and the state of the economy; by the incumbent or challenger status of the candidate; by the issues, conditions, scandals, or events currently being spotlighted by the media; and by the dynamics of the campaign itself as the candidates attack and defend themselves (see *Up Close*, "Bush v. Kerry, 2004").

Presidential election campaigns must focus on the **Electoral College**. The president is not elected by the national popular vote total but rather by a majority of the *electoral* votes of the states. Electoral votes are won by plurality, winner-take-all popular voting in most of the states. (Exceptions are Nebraska and Maine.) Thus a narrow plurality win in a state delivers *all* of that state's electoral votes. Big-state victories, even by very narrow margins, can deliver big electoral prizes. The biggest prizes are California with 55 electoral votes, New York with 31, and Texas with 34. With a total of 538 electoral votes at stake, *the winner must garner victories in states that total a minimum of 270 electoral votes.* (See *What Do You Think?* "Should We Scrap the Electoral College?" on page 266.)

Electoral College The 538 presidential electors apportioned among the states according to their congressional representation (plus three for the District of Columbia) whose votes officially elect the president and vice president of the United States.

Targeting the Swing States   In focusing on the most populous states, with their large electoral votes, candidates must decide which of these states are "winnable," then direct their time, energy, and money to these **swing states**. Candidates cannot afford to spend too much effort in states that already seem to be solidly in their column, although they must avoid the perception that they are ignoring these strong bases of support. Neither can candidates waste much effort on states that already appear to be solidly in their opponent's column. So the swing states receive most of the candidates' time, attention, and television advertising money.

swing states States that are not considered to be firmly in the Democratic or Republican column.

UP CLOSE

Bush v. Kerry, 2004

John F. Kerry wrapped up the Democratic nomination in the early spring, and his poll numbers quickly matched those of President Bush. Despite one of the most liberal voting records in Congress, Kerry appeared to be a "moderate" in contrast to his boisterous primary opponent, Vermont Governor Howard Dean (See *Up Close*: "Democratic Presidential Primaries 2004" in Chapter 7). At the Democratic National Convention Kerry took the stage with a snappy military salute, "I'm John Kerry and I'm reporting for duty!" The early intent was to use his war hero's status to demonstrate his ability to be Commander-in-Chief in time of war. It was a risky strategic decision because President Bush was perceived in all of the polls as a "strong leader" in the war on terrorism. But events thirty-five years ago seemed irrelevant in 2004. Kerry got very little "bounce" from the Democratic Convention.

George Bush had little choice but to make the war on terrorism his major theme. Bush's advisors believed it was to their candidate's advantage to make terrorism the "chief concern" of Americans, rather than the economy. They believed that in wartime most voters wanted a "strong leader," "decisive," and a "man of his word"—qualities in which the polls indicated Bush was strongest. Kerry was to be cast as a "waffler"—first voting to authorize military force against Iraq and then later voting against a bill to finance operations there. Kerry supported continuing U.S. military efforts in Iraq, but he attacked Bush's decision to invade Iraq without the support of other United Nations members. He referred to Iraq as "the wrong war, the wrong place, the wrong time," and accused Bush of a "colossal error of judgment" in shifting anti-terrorist efforts to catch Osama bin Laden in Afghanistan to the attack on Iraq.

Bush maintained a slim lead in the polls throughout the spring and summer, a lead that he was to lose briefly after the first presidential debate in October. Kerry's carefully crafted image in the debate seemed to reassure many Americans that he too would make a strong Commander-in-Chief. He claimed that Bush had "misled" the American people about the existence of weapons of mass destruction in Iraq, that he failed to "exhaust the remedies of the United Nations," and that he, Kerry, would not commit American troops to battle without satisfying "the global test." Bush jumped on the phrase "the global test" to claim that Kerry would place America's security in the hands of the United Nations: "I'll never turn over America's national security needs to leaders of other countries." Kerry was judged by the polls as the winner of the debates. But Bush had found a theme—that Kerry was indecisive, that he flip-flopped, and that he would hesitate to act when confronted with threats to national security. Within a week, Bush regained his slim lead in the polls.

As Election Day neared, the rhetoric became more bitter. Bush had "lied" about the reasons for the war in Iraq, rather than simply being misinformed by the intelligence community about the existence of weapons of mass destruction in Saddam's hands. It was charged that Bush secretly intended to bring back the draft and that he would cut social security benefits for the elderly. Kerry was "unfit for command": early in his career he had accused his fellow veterans of committing atrocities in Vietnam. The terrorists were hoping for a Kerry victory. The nation would not be "safe" if Kerry won.

Bush succeeded in making Iraq part of the war on terrorism: "We will fight the terrorists abroad, rather than fight them at home." Kerry could never fully take advantage of the controversial war: he had voted for it in the first place. He said he would call upon our allies in the United Nations to help in Iraq, but it seemed unlikely to many Americans that UN members who opposed the war would want to assist the U.S.

Contrary to expectations, Americans went to the polls in record numbers. And while Iraq and terrorism ranked high among their concerns, they cited "moral values" as the most important issue in the election. Bush's folksy image and his moral values seemed to match their own. He was "honest and trustworthy," he "took a clear stand," he was "decisive" and "better at handling the war on terrorism." He not only won a majority of the popular vote (51 to 48%), but also helped to increase the Republican majorities in the House and Senate.

The Presidential Debates   The nationally televised presidential debates are the central feature of the general election campaign. These debates attract more viewers than any other campaign event. Moreover, they enable a candidate to reach undecided voters and the opponent's supporters, as well as the candidate's own partisans. Even people who usually pay little attention to politics may be drawn in by the drama of the confrontation (see *Up Close*: "The Presidential Debates" on page 270).

The debates allow viewers an opportunity to see and hear candidates together and to compare their responses to questions as they stand side by side. The debates give audiences a better view of the candidates than they can get from thirty-second commercial ads or seven-second news sound bites. Viewers can at least judge how the candidates react under pressure.

However, the debates emphasize candidate image over substantive policy issues. Candidates must appear presidential. They must appear confident, compassionate, concerned, and good humored. They must not appear uncertain or unsure of themselves, or aloof or out of touch with viewers, or easily upset by hostile questions. They must avoid verbal slips or gaffes or even unpolished or awkward gestures. They must remember that the debates are not really debates so much as joint press conferences in which the candidates respond to questions with rehearsed mini-speeches and practiced sound bites.

U.S. Senator John McCain (R-AZ) speake during a taping of *Meet the Press* at the NBC studios, August 20, 2006 in Washingdon D.C.

Hitting the Talk Shows   Candidates know that more people watch entertainment talk shows then news shows. Oprah Winfrey, Regis Philbin, Larry King, David Letterman, Jay Leno, and Conan O'Brien all have larger audiences than *Meet the Press, Hardball, Hannity and Colmes, The O'Reilly Factor,* and others. Moreover, entertainment hosts rarely ask policy questions but rather toss "softball" queries about family, feelings, and personal qualities. Responding to these questions "humanizes" the candidate. And these entertainment shows reach audiences that have relatively little political knowledge or awareness. This provides an opportunity for a candidate to actually win over undecideds and persuadable opposition voters with a likable personality, good humor, and a good rapport with the host.[20] Beginning in 2000, presidential candidates expended considerable effort to get themselves on as many entertainment talk shows as possible.

The Electoral College Vote   In recent presidential elections, the Democratic candidates (Clinton in 1992 and 1996 and Gore in 2000) have won the Northeastern states, including New York; the upper Midwestern states, including Michigan and Illinois; and, perhaps most importantly, the West Coast, including California (see *Across the USA:* "How the States Voted" on page 269). Republican presidential candidates (Bush in 1992, Dole in 1996, and Bush in 2000 and 2004) have shown greater strength in the Great Plains and Rocky Mountain states and in the southeastern states (forming a Republican "L" on the Electoral College map). If these patterns continue in presidential elections, Democrats can depend on two of the four largest Electoral College vote states, California (55) and New York (31), while Republicans can feel comfortable in the other two, Texas (34) and Florida (27). The Electoral College battleground may be states such as Ohio, Pennsylvania, and Missouri—"swing states" that have cast their votes alternatively for Democratic and Republican candidates in recent presidential elections.

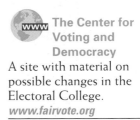

The Center for Voting and Democracy
A site with material on possible changes in the Electoral College.
www.fairvote.org

The Voter Decides

Understanding the reasons behind the voters' choice at the ballot box is a central concern of candidates, campaign strategists, commentators, and political scientists. Perhaps no other area of politics has been investigated as thoroughly as voting behavior. Survey data on voter choice have been collected for presidential elections for the past half century.[21] We know that voters cast ballots for and against candidates for a variety of reasons—party affiliation, group interests, characteristics and images of the candidates themselves, the economy, and policy issues. But forecasting election outcomes remains a risky business.

WHAT DO YOU THINK?

Should We Scrap the Electoral College?

Americans were given a dramatic reminder in 2000 that the president of the United States is *not* elected by nationwide *popular* vote, but rather by a majority of the *electoral votes* of the states.

How the Electoral College Works

The Constitution grants each state a number of electors equal to the number of its congressional representatives and senators combined (see map). Because representatives are apportioned to the states on the basis of population, the electoral vote of the states is subject to change after each ten-year census. No state has fewer than three electoral votes, because the Constitution guarantees every state two U.S. senators and at least one representative. The Twenty-third Amendment granted three electoral votes to the District of Columbia even though it has no voting members of Congress. So winning the presidency requires winning in states with at least 270 of the 538 total electoral votes.

Voters in presidential elections are actually choosing a slate of presidential electors pledged to vote for their party's presidential and vice presidential candidates. The names of electors seldom appear on the ballot, only the names of the candidates and their parties. The slate that wins a *plurality* of the popular vote in a state (more than any other slate, not necessarily a majority) casts *all* of the state's vote in the Electoral College. (This "winner-take-all" system in the states is not mandated by the Constitution; a state legislature could allocate a state's electoral votes in proportion to the split in the popular vote, as happens in Nebraska and Maine. The winner-take-all system in the states helps ensure that the Electoral College produces a majority for one candidate.)

The Electoral College never meets at a single location; rather, electors meet at their respective state capitals to cast their ballots around December 15, following the general election on the first Tuesday after the first Monday of November. The results are sent to the presiding officer of the Senate, the vice president, who in January presides over their count in the presence of both houses of Congress and formally announces the results. These proce-dures are usually considered a formality, but the U.S. Constitution does not *require* that electors cast their vote for the winning presidential candidate in their state, and occasionally "faithless electors" disrupt the process, although none has ever changed the outcome.

If no candidate wins a majority of electoral votes, the House of Representatives chooses the president from among the three candidates with the largest number of electoral votes, with each state casting *one* vote. The Constitution does not specify how House delegations should determine their vote, but by House rules, the state's vote goes to the candidate receiving a majority vote in the delegation.

The Historical Record

Only two presidential elections have ever been decided formally by the House of Representatives. In 1800 Thomas Jefferson and Aaron Burr tied in the Electoral College because the Twelfth Amendment had not yet been adopted to separate presidential from vice presidential voting; all the Democratic-Republican electors voted for both Jefferson and Burr, creating a tie. In 1824 Andrew Jackson won the popular vote and more electoral votes than anyone else but failed to get a majority. The House chose John Quincy Adams over Jackson, causing a popular uproar and ensuring Jackson's election in 1828.

In addition, in 1876, the Congress was called on to decide which electoral results from the Southern states to validate; a Republican Congress chose to validate enough Republican electoral votes to allow Republican Rutherford B. Hayes to win, even though Democrat Samuel Tilden had won more popular votes. Hayes promised the Democratic Southern states that in return for their acknowledgment of his presidential claim, he would end the military occupation of the South.

In 1888, the Electoral College vote failed to reflect the popular vote. Benjamin Harrison received 233 electoral votes to incumbent president Grover Cleveland's 168, even though Cleveland won about 90,000 more popular votes than Harrison. Harrison served a single lackluster term; Cleveland was elected for a second time in 1892, the only president to serve two nonconsecutive terms.

2000—Gore Wins but Loses

Al Gore won the nationwide popular vote, receiving about 500,000 more votes (out of the more than 100

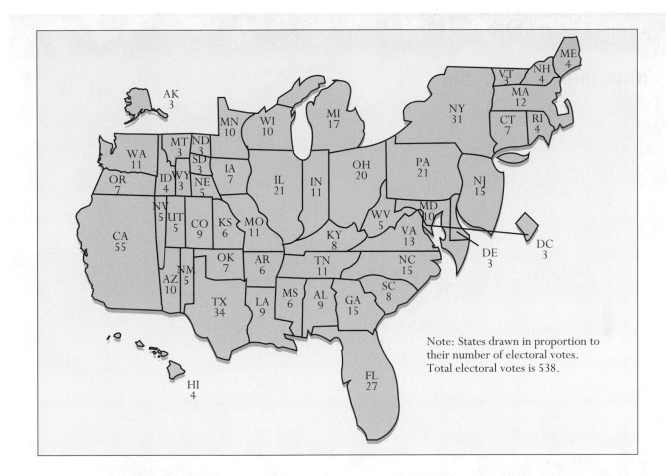

Note: States drawn in proportion to their number of electoral votes. Total electoral votes is 538.

million ballots cast) than George W. Bush. But the vote in several states was extremely close. On election night, Gore was reported to have won 262 electoral votes to Bush's 246—that is, neither candidate had the necessary 270. The key turned out to be Florida's 25 electoral votes. (New Mexico's 5 votes eventually went to Gore.) The Florida secretary of state declared Bush the winner by a few hundred votes out of 6 million cast in that state. The Gore campaign demanded *hand* recounts, especially in heavily Democratic counties in south Florida (including Palm Beach County, where the ballot was said to be confusing to voters). The Bush campaign responded that hand counts are subjective, unreliable, and open to partisan bias. For over a month neither Bush nor Gore would concede the election. Suits were initiated by both candidates in both federal and Florida states courts. Finally the U.S. Supreme Court rejected Gore's appeal; Florida's votes went to Bush and he was declared the winner.

What Would Replace the Electoral College?

Constitutional proposals to reform the Electoral College have circulated for nearly two hundred years, but none has won widespread support. These reform proposals have included (1) election of the president by direct national popular vote; (2) allocation of each state's electoral vote in proportion to the popular vote each candidate received in the state; (3) allocation of electoral votes to winners of each congressional district and two to the statewide winners.

But most reform proposals create as many problems as they resolve. If the president is to be elected by direct nationwide popular vote, should a plurality vote be sufficient to win? Or should a national runoff be held in the event that no one receives a majority in the first election? Would proportional allocation of electoral votes encourage third-party candidates to enter the race in order to deny the leading candidate a majority?

ACROSS THE USA

How the States Voted

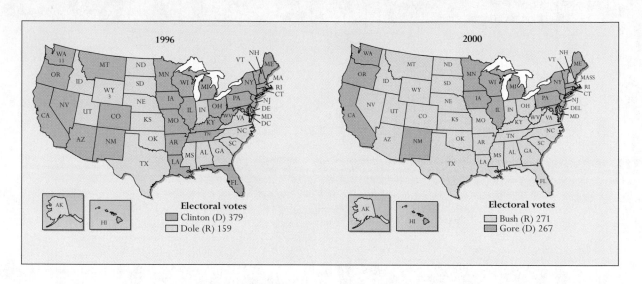

1996

Electoral votes
- Clinton (D) 379
- Dole (R) 159

2000

Electoral votes
- Bush (R) 271
- Gore (D) 267

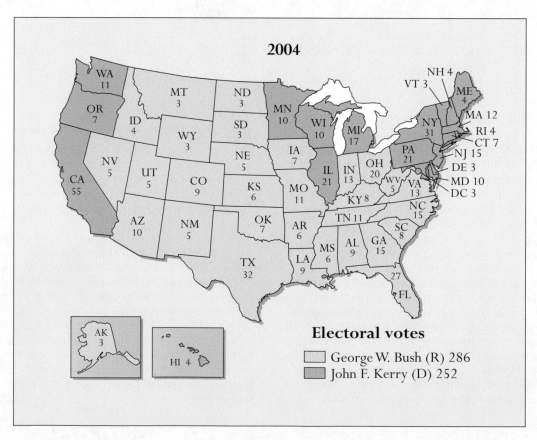

2004

Electoral votes
- George W. Bush (R) 286
- John F. Kerry (D) 252

Party Affiliation   Although many people claim to vote for "the person, not the party," party identification remains a powerful influence in voter choice. Party ties among voters have weakened over time, with increasing proportions of voters labeling themselves as independents or only weak Democrats or Republicans, and more voters opting to split their tickets or cross party lines than did so a generation ago (see Chapter 7). Nevertheless, party identification remains one of the most important influences on voter choice. Party affiliation is more important in congressional than in presidential elections, but even in presidential elections the tendency to see the candidate of one's own party as "the best person" is very strong.

Consider the three presidential elections (see Figure 8.5). Self-identified Republicans voted overwhelmingly for Bush in 1992, for Dole in 1996, and for George W. Bush in 2000 and 2004. Self-identified Democrats voted overwhelmingly for Clinton in 1992 and 1996, for Gore in 2000, and for Kerry in 2004.

Because Republican identifiers are outnumbered in the electorate by Democratic identifiers, Republican presidential candidates, and many Republican congressional candidates as well, *must* appeal to independent and Democratic crossover voters.

Group Voting   We already know that various social and economic groups give disproportionate support to the Democratic and Republican parties (see Chapter 7). So it comes as no surprise that recent Democratic presidential candidates have received disproportionate support from African Americans, Catholics, Jews, the less-educated, and union workers; Republican presidential candidates have fared better among whites, Protestants, and better-educated voters (see Figure 8.6). That is, these groups have given a larger percentage of their vote to the Democratic or Republican candidates than the candidate received from the total electorate.

Race and Gender Gaps   Among the more interesting group voting patterns is the serious *gender gap* affecting recent Republican candidates. Although Reagan won the women's vote in both 1980 and 1984, his vote percentages among men were considerably higher than among women. George H. W. Bush lost the women's vote in both 1988 and 1992. In 1996 the gender gap widened, with 54 percent of women voting for Clinton as opposed to only 38 percent for Dole, and continued in 2000 with women giving Gore 54 percent of the vote as opposed to Bush's 43 percent. Again in 2004 women gave Democrat John F. Kerry 54 percent of their vote. African Americans have long constituted the most loyal group of Democratic voters, regularly giving the Democratic presidential nominee up to 90 percent or more of their vote. The overall Hispanic vote is Democratic, although a significant portion of Hispanics, notably Cuban Americans in Florida, vote Republican.

Candidate Image   In an age of direct communication between candidates and voters via television, the image of candidates and their ability to relate to audiences have emerged as important determinants of voter choice. Candidate image is most important in presidential contests, inasmuch as presidential candidates are personally more visible to the voter than candidates for lesser offices.[22]

It is difficult to identify exactly what personal qualities appeal most to voters. Warmth, compassion, strength, confidence, honesty, sincerity, good humor, appearance, and "character" all seem important. "Character" has become a central feature of media coverage of candidates (see Chapter 6). Reports of extramarital

---

— Think Again —

Should people vote on the basis of a candidate's personal character rather than his or her policy positions?

UP CLOSE

The Presidential Debates

Presidential debates attract more viewers than any other campaign activity. Most campaign activities—speeches, rallies, motorcades—reach only supporters. Such activities may inspire supporters to go to the polls, contribute money, and even work to get others to vote their way. But televised debates reach undecided voters as well as supporters, and they allow candidates to be seen by supporters of their opponent. Even if issues are not really discussed in depth, people see how presidential candidates react as human beings under pressure.

Kennedy-Nixon

Televised presidential debates began in 1960 when John F. Kennedy and Richard M. Nixon confronted each other on a bare stage before an America watching on black-and-white TV sets. Nixon was the vice president in the popular presidential administration of Dwight Eisenhower; he was also an accomplished college debate-team member. He prepared for the debates as if they were college debates, memorizing facts and arguments. But he failed to realize that image triumphs over substance on television. By contrast, Kennedy was handsome, cool, confident; whatever doubts the American people may have had regarding his youth and inexperience were dispelled by his polished manner. Radio listeners tended to think that Nixon won, and debate coaches scored him the winner. But television viewers preferred the glamorous young Kennedy. The polls shifted in Kennedy's direction after the debate, and he won in a very close general election.

Carter-Ford

President Lyndon Johnson avoided debating in 1964, and Nixon, having learned his lesson, declined to debate in 1968 and 1972. Thus televised presidential debates did not resume until 1976, when incumbent president Gerald Ford, perceiving he was behind in the polls, agreed to debate challenger Jimmy Carter. Ford made a series of verbal slips. Carter was widely perceived as having won the debate, and he went on to victory in the general election.

Reagan-Carter and Reagan-Mondale

It was Ronald Reagan who demonstrated the true power of television. Reagan had lived his life in front of a camera. It was the principal tool of both of his trades—actor and politician. In 1980 incumbent president Jimmy Carter talked rapidly and seriously about programs, figures, and budgets. But Reagan was master of the stage; he was relaxed, confident, joking. He appeared to treat the president of the United States as an overly aggressive, impulsive younger man, regrettably given to exaggeration. When it was all over, it was clear to most viewers that Carter had been bested by a true professional in media skills.

However, in the first of two televised debates with Walter Mondale in 1984, Reagan's skills of a lifetime seemed to desert him. He stumbled over statistics and groped for words. Reagan's poor performance raised the only issue that might conceivably defeat him—his age. The president had looked and sounded *old*. But in the second debate, Reagan laid the perfect trap for his questioners. When asked about his age and capacity to lead the nation, he responded with a serious dead-pan expression to a hushed audience and waiting America: "I want you to know that I will not make age an issue in this campaign. I am not going to exploit for political purposes [pause] my opponent's youth and inexperience." The studio audience broke into uncontrolled laughter. Even Mondale had to laugh. With a classic one-liner, Reagan buried the age issue and won not only the debate but also the election.

Bush-Dukakis

In 1988 Michael Dukakis ensured his defeat with a cold, detached performance in the presidential debates, beginning with the very first question. When CNN anchor Bernard Shaw asked, "Governor, if Kitty Dukakis were raped and murdered, would you favor an irrevocable death penalty for the killer?" The question demanded an emotional reply. Instead, Dukakis responded with an impersonal recitation of his stock position on law enforcement. Bush seized the opportunity to establish a more personal relationship with the viewers: Voters responded to Bush, electing him.

Clinton-Bush-Perot

The three-way presidential debates of 1992 drew the largest television audiences in the history of presidential debates. In the first debate, Ross Perot's Texas twang and down-home folksy style stole the show. Chided by his opponents for having no governmental experience, he shot back, "Well, they have a point. I don't have any experience in running up a $4 trillion dollar debt." But it was Bill Clinton's smooth performance in the second debate, with its talk-show format, that seemed to wrap up the election. Ahead in the polls, Clinton appeared at ease walking about the stage and responding to audience questions with sympathy and sincerity. By contrast, George Bush appeared stiff and formal, and somewhat ill-at-ease with the "unpresidential" format.

Clinton-Dole

A desperate Bob Dole, running 20 points behind, faced a newly "presidential" Bill Clinton in their two 1996 debates. (Perot's poor standing in the polls led to his exclusion.) Dole tried to counter his image as a grumpy old man in the first encounter; his humor actually won more laughs from the audience than Clinton's. Dole injected more barbs in the second debate, complaining of "ethical problems in the White House." But Clinton remained cool and comfortable, ignoring the challenger and focusing on the nation's economic health. Viewers, most of whom were already in Clinton's court, judged him the winner of both debates.

Bush-Gore

Separate formats were agreed upon for three debates—the traditional podium, a conference, table, and a town hall setting. Gore was assertive, almost to the point of rudeness, but both candidates focused on policy differences rather than on personal attacks. Viewers gave Gore the edge in these debates but they found Bush more likable. Bush appeared to benefit more in the post-debate polls.

Bush-Kerry

Kerry prepared well for the three debates. He appeared tall, earnest, confident, well-informed, and "presidential." He spoke forcefully, avoiding the qualifying clauses and lengthy sentences that had plagued his speeches in the past. Bush appeared uncomfortable, scowling at Kerry's answers, often repeating himself, and failing to "connect" with his audiences. Polls showed Kerry winning each debate.

2004	Kerry(Democrat)	Bush (Republican)
Party		
Democrat	90%	9%
Republican	7%	92%
Independent	45%	48%
Ideology		
Liberal	84%	12%
Moderate	45%	53%
Conservative	18%	80%
Economy		
Excellent	10%	88%
Good	14%	82%
Not Good	80%	16%

2000	Gore (Democrat)	Bush (Republican)
Party		
Democrat	86%	11%
Republican	8%	91%
Independent	45%	47%
Ideology		
Liberal	80%	13%
Moderate	52%	44%
Conservative	17%	81%
Economy		
Excellent	53%	46%
Good	37%	53%
Not Good	47%	49%

1996	Clinton (Democrat)	Dole (Republican)
Party		
Democrat	84%	10%
Republican	13%	80%
Independent	43%	35%
Ideology		
Liberal	78%	11%
Moderate	57%	33%
Conservative	20%	71%
Economy		
Better	66%	26%
Same	46%	45%
Worse	27%	57%

Figure 8.5 Party, Ideology, and Nature of the Times in Presidential Voting

Those who identify themselves as members of a major political party are highly likely to vote for the presidential candidates of their party. Likewise, those who identify themselves as liberals are more likely than average to vote for Democrats, and those who identify themselves as conservatives are more likely to vote for Republicans in presidential elections. In addition, voters who see the economic picture as better are more likely to vote for the incumbent, those who are concerned about the nation's economy are more likely to vote against the incumbent.

Source: Election exit polls, Voter News Service, National Election Pool.

affairs, experimentation with drugs, draft dodging, cheating in college, shady financial dealings, conflicts of interest, or lying or misrepresenting facts receive heavy media coverage because they attract large audiences. But it is difficult to estimate how many voters are swayed by so-called character issues.

Attractive personal qualities can win support from opposition-party identifiers and people who disagree on the issues. John F. Kennedy's handsome and youthful appearance, charm, self-confidence, and disarming good humor defeated the

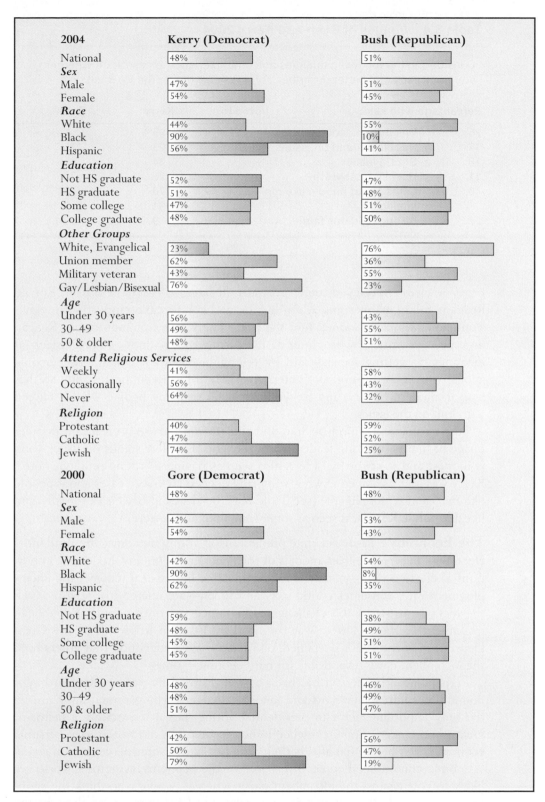

2004	Kerry (Democrat)	Bush (Republican)
National	48%	51%
Sex		
Male	47%	51%
Female	54%	45%
Race		
White	44%	55%
Black	90%	10%
Hispanic	56%	41%
Education		
Not HS graduate	52%	47%
HS graduate	51%	48%
Some college	47%	51%
College graduate	48%	50%
Other Groups		
White, Evangelical	23%	76%
Union member	62%	36%
Military veteran	43%	55%
Gay/Lesbian/Bisexual	76%	23%
Age		
Under 30 years	56%	43%
30–49	49%	55%
50 & older	48%	51%
Attend Religious Services		
Weekly	41%	58%
Occasionally	56%	43%
Never	64%	32%
Religion		
Protestant	40%	59%
Catholic	47%	52%
Jewish	74%	25%

2000	Gore (Democrat)	Bush (Republican)
National	48%	48%
Sex		
Male	42%	53%
Female	54%	43%
Race		
White	42%	54%
Black	90%	8%
Hispanic	62%	35%
Education		
Not HS graduate	59%	38%
HS graduate	48%	49%
Some college	45%	51%
College graduate	45%	51%
Age		
Under 30 years	48%	46%
30–49	48%	49%
50 & older	51%	47%
Religion		
Protestant	42%	56%
Catholic	50%	47%
Jewish	79%	19%

Figure 8.6   Group Voting in Presidential Elections

Democratic presidential candidates regularly do better among African American, Hispanic, lower income, less educated voters. The gender gap—men tending to vote Republican and women Democratic—first emerged in the Reagan years. Increasingly, white religious voters are casting their ballots for Republican candidates.

Source: Election exit polls, Voter News Service, National Election Pool.

Table 8.4   Images of Bush and Kerry 2004

Considering the following qualities and characteristics, please state whether you think each one better describes John F. Kerry or George W. Bush.

Percentage who said:		Voted for:	Kerry	Bush
25%	Will bring needed change		95%	4%
17	Has clear stand on issues		23	75
16	Strong leader		14	85
11	Honest, trustworthy		28	70
10	Cares about people like me		76	23
8	Intelligent		91	7
7	Strong religious faith		9	90

heavy-jowled, shifty-eyed, defensive, and ill-humored Richard Nixon. Ronald Reagan's folksy mannerisms, warm humor, and comfortable rapport with television audiences justly earned him the title "The Great Communicator." Reagan disarmed his critics by laughing at his own personal flubs—falling asleep at meetings, forgetting names—and by telling his own age jokes. His personal appeal won more Democratic voters than any other Republican candidate has won in modern history, and he won the votes of many people who disagreed with him on the issues.

Bush's resolute position on Iraq and the war on terrorism created a popular image of him as "a strong leader," someone who "has clear stands on issues," and is "honest and trustworthy." He is also seen as having a "strong religious faith." Kerry was seen as someone who "will bring needed change," "cares about people like me," and is "intelligent" (see Table 8.4). Bush was also seen as friendly and likeable, while Kerry was seen as somewhat aloof and austere.

The Economy   Fairly accurate predictions of voting outcomes in presidential elections can be made from models of the American economy. Economic conditions at election time—recent growth or decline in personal income, the unemployment rate, consumer confidence, and so on—are related to the vote given the incumbent versus the challenger. Ever since the once-popular Republican incumbent Herbert Hoover was trounced by Franklin Roosevelt as the Great Depression of the 1930s deepened, politicians have understood that voters hold the incumbent party responsible for hard economic times.

Perhaps no other lesson has been as well learned by politicians: Hard economic times hurt incumbents and favor challengers. The economy may not be the only important factor in presidential voting, but it is certainly a factor of great importance.[23] Some evidence indicates that it is not voters' *own* personal economic well-being that affects their vote but rather voter perception of *general* economic conditions. People who perceive the economy as getting worse are likely to vote against the incumbent party, whereas people who think the economy is getting better support the incumbent.[24] Thus voters who thought the economy was getting *worse* in 1992 supported challenger Bill Clinton over incumbent president George H.W. Bush. But the reverse was true in 1996; more people thought the economy was better, and the people who thought so voted heavily for incumbent Bill Clinton. In 2000, Gore won the votes of those who thought the economy was "excellent," but economic voting did not seem to be as

A CONSTITUTIONAL NOTE

Campaign Finance and Free Speech

Both the Congress and the Supreme Court have confronted the issue of whether or not limiting campaign spending has the effect of limiting free speech. In 1976 in *Buckley v. Valeo*, the Supreme Court struck down Congress's limit on what an individual candidate or independent organization could spend to promote its own views it a campaign. "The First Amendment denies government the power to determine that spending to promote one's political views is... excessive. In the free society ordained by our Constitution, it is not the government but the people who must retain control over the quantity and range of debate in a political campaign."[a] This decision means that wealthy individuals can spend unlimited amounts on their own campaigns, and independent organizations can spend unlimited amounts as long as their spending is independent of a candidate's campaign. However, the Supreme Court approved limits on *contributions* by individuals and organizations—distinguishing between contributions and expenditures. It approved the Federal Election Commission limits on individual and organizational contributions to political campaigns. Congress sought to remedy the many holes in the original Federal Election Campaign Act of 1974 in its Bipartisan Campaign Reform Act of 2002. It placed limits on "soft money" contributions to political parties, most of which found its way into candidate campaigns. However, Congress did not challenge the Court's *Buckley* decision by trying to prevent individuals or nonprofit organizations from spending money to broadcast their views. Limiting spending for political broadcasting would "place substantial and direct restrictions on the ability of candidates, citizens, and associations to engage in protected political speech."[b] The result was the emergence of independent organizations, known as "527s," in the 2004 election. These organizations spent heavily and played a major role in the presidential campaigns of both parties.

[a]*Buckley v. Valeo*, 424 U.S. 1 (1976).

[b]*McConnell v. Federal Election Commission*, 590 U.S. 93 (2003).

influential as in previous presidential races. The economy was cited as "most important" by about one-fifth of the voters in 2004 and Kerry won the vast majority of these voters.

Issue Voting   Casting one's vote exclusively on the basis of the policy positions of the candidates is rare. Most voters are unaware of the specific positions taken by candidates on the issues. Indeed, voters often believe that their preferred candidate agrees with them on the issues, even when this is not the case. In other words, voters project their own policy views onto their favorite candidate more often than they decide to vote for a candidate because of his or her position on the issues.

However, when asked specifically about issues, voters are willing to name those they care most about (see Table 8.5). Voters do not always make their choices based on a candidate's stated policy positions, but voters *do* strongly favor candidates whose policy views they assume match their own. Only when a key issue takes center stage do voters really become aware of what the candidates actually propose to do. In the 1992, 1996, and 2000 elections, the economy was the issue that voters cared about most. In all three elections, Clinton and Gore won the votes of the people most concerned about the economy (see Table 8.5).

To the surprise of many commentators, "moral values" was cited as the most important issue by voters leaving the polls in 2004.[25] Bush won over three-quarters of these voters. Faith and family appeared to underlie concern with moral values. Bush had never disguised his religious faith. Bans on same-sex marriage were on referenda ballots in eleven states and may have helped inspire a heavy turnout for Bush.

Table 8.5   Issues the Voters Cared about in 2004

Presidential Vote of Those Who Listed Issue as "Most Important"

Rank	Percentage who said:		Who they voted for:	
			Kerry	Bush
1	21%	Moral values	19%	78%
2	20	Economy/jobs	82	16
3	18	Terrorism	15	85
4	15	Iraq	76	23
5	8	Health care	79	20
6	5	Taxes	47	53
7	4	Education	75	24

Bush had tried to portray the war in Iraq as part of a broader war on terrorism. But while Bush won the votes of people concerned with terrorism, Kerry won the votes of those concerned with the war in Iraq. Voters opposed to the war in Iraq went heavily for Kerry, while supporters of the war voted heavily for Bush.

Summary Notes

■ In a democracy, elections decide "who governs." But they also indirectly affect public policy, influencing "who gets what."

■ Although winning candidates often claim a mandate for their policy proposals, in reality few campaigns present clear policy alternatives to the voters, few voters cast their ballots on the basis of policy considerations, and the policy preferences of the electorate can seldom be determined from election outcomes.

■ Nevertheless, voters can influence future policy directions through retrospective judgments about the performance of incumbents, returning them to office or turning them out. Most retrospective voting appears to center on the economy.

■ Personal ambition for power and celebrity drives the decision to seek public office. Political entrepreneurship, professionalism, and careerism have come to dominate political recruitment; lawyers have traditionally dominated American politics.

■ Incumbents begin campaigns with many advantages: name recognition, financial support, goodwill from services they perform for constituents, large-scale public projects they bring to their districts, and the other resources of office.

■ Campaigning for office is largely a media activity, dominated by professional advertising specialists, fund-raisers, media consultants, and pollsters.

■ The professionalization of campaigning and the heavy costs of a media campaign drive up the costs of running for office. These huge costs make candidates heavily dependent on financial support from individuals and organizations. Fund-raising occupies more of a candidate's time than any other campaign activity.

■ Campaign contributions are made by politically active individuals and organizations, including political action committees. Many contributions are made in order to gain access to policy makers and assistance with government business. Some contributors are ideologically motivated; others merely seek to rub shoulders with powerful people.

■ Presidential primary election strategies emphasize appeals to party activists and core supporters, including the more ideologically motivated primary voters.

■ In the general election campaign, presidential candidates usually seek to broaden their appeal to moderate, centrist voters while holding on to their core supporters. Campaigns must focus on states where the candidate has the best chance of gaining the 270 electoral votes needed to win.

■ Voter choice is influenced by party identification, group membership, perceived image of the candidates, economic conditions, and, to a lesser extent, ideology and issue preferences.

Key Terms

Suggested Readings

Abramson, Paul R., John H. Aldrich, and David W. Rohde. *Change and Continuity in the 2004 Elections.* Washington, D.C.: CQ Press, 2005. An in-depth analysis of the 2004 presidential and congressional elections assessing the impact of party loyalties, presidential performance, group memberships, and policy preferences on voter choice.

DiClerico, Robert, ed. *Political Parties, Campaigns and Elections.* Upper Saddle River, N.J.: Prentice Hall, 2000. Essays by leading scholars on the nominating process, campaign finance, media campaigning, turnout, voter choice, and the party system.

Fiorina, Morris P. *Retrospective Voting in American National Elections.* Princeton, N.J.: Princeton University Press, 1988. Argues that retrospective judgments guide voter choice in presidential elections.

Flanigan, William H., and Nancy H. Zingale. *Political Behavior of the American Electorate.* 11th ed. Washington, D.C.: CQ Press, 2002. A brief but comprehensive summary of the extensive research literature on the effects of party identification, opinion, ideology, the media, and candidate image on voter choice and election outcomes.

Iyengar, Shanto, and Stephen Ansolabehere. *Going Negative: How Political Advertisements Shrink and Polarize the Electorate.* New York: Free Press, 1996. The real problem with negative political ads is not that they sway voters to support one candidate over another, but that they reinforce the belief that all are dishonest and cynical.

Matalin, Mary, and James Carville. *All's Fair: Love, War and Running for President.* New York: Random House and Simon & Schuster, 1994. Inside the presidential campaign of George Bush and Bill Clinton in 1992 by their respective campaign directors, who were romantically involved and were married after the campaign.

Rosenstone, Steven. *Forecasting Presidential Elections.* New Haven, Conn.: Yale University Press, 1985. A discussion of the models employed to forecast presidential election outcomes based on unemployment, inflation, and personal income statistics.

Sabato, Larry J., and Glenn R. Simpson. *Dirty Little Secrets: The Persistence of Corruption in American Politics.* New York: Random House Times Books, 1996. A political scientist and a journalist combine to produce a lurid report on unethical and corrupt practices in campaigns and elections.

9 INTEREST GROUPS
Getting Their Share and More

Interest-Group Power

Organization is a means to power—to determining who gets what in society. Interest groups are organizations that seek to influence government policy. The First Amendment to the Constitution recognizes "the right of the people peaceably to assemble and to petition the government for a redress of grievances." Americans thus enjoy a fundamental right to organize themselves to influence government.

Electoral versus Interest-Group Systems The *electoral system* is organized to represent geographically defined constituencies—states and congressional districts in Congress. The *interest-group system* is organized to represent economic, professional, ideological, religious, racial, gender, and issue constituencies. In other words, the interest-group system supplements the electoral system by providing people with another avenue of participation. Individuals may participate in politics by supporting candidates and parties in elections, and also by joining **interest groups**, organizations that pressure government to advance their interests.[1]

Interest group activity provides more *direct* representation of policy preferences than electoral politics. At best, individual voters can influence government policy only indirectly through elections (see Chapter 8). Elected politicians try to represent many different—and even occasionally conflicting—interests. But interest groups provide concentrated and direct representation of policy views in government.

Checking Majoritarianism The interest-group system gives voice to special interests, whereas parties and the electoral system cater to the majority interest. Indeed, interest groups are often defended as a check on **majoritarianism**, the tendency of democratic governments to allow the faint preferences of a majority to prevail over the intense feelings of minorities. However, the interest-group system is frequently attacked because it obstructs the majority from implementing its preferences in public policy.

Concentrating Benefits While Dispersing Costs Interest groups seek special benefits, subsidies, privileges, and protections from the government. The costs of these *concentrated* benefits are usually *dispersed* to all

Think About Politics

1 Do special-interest groups in America obstruct the majority of citizens' wishes on public policy?
Yes ☐ No ☐

2 Should people join an interest group such as the American Association of Retired Persons for its discounts, magazines, and travel guides even if they disagree with its policy goals?
Yes ☐ No ☐

3 Should state and local governments use taxpayers' money to lobby Congress to get federal funds?
Yes ☐ No ☐

4 Should former government officials be allowed to lobby their former colleagues?
Yes ☐ No ☐

5 Should interest groups be prohibited from making large campaign contributions in their effort to influence public policy?
Yes ☐ No ☐

6 If a lobbyist makes a campaign contribution to a Congress member, hoping to gain support for a bill, is this a form of bribery?
Yes ☐ No ☐

7 Is organized interest-group activity a cause of government gridlock?
Yes ☐ No ☐

What role do interest groups play in politics? Their organization, their money, and their influence in Washington raise the possibility that interest groups, rather than individuals, may in fact hold the real power in politics. They may be the "who" that determines the "what" that the rest of us get.

★   ★   ★

interest group Organization seeking to directly influence government policy.

majoritarianism Tendency of democratic governments to allow the faint preferences of the majority to prevail over the intense feelings of minorities.

organizational sclerosis Society encrusted with so many special benefits to interest groups that everyone's standard of living is lowered.

Think Again

Do special-interest groups in America obstruct the majority of citizens' wishes on public policy?

NAACP
Oldest civil rights organization, working on behalf of African Americans.
www.naacp.org

National Organization for Women
An organization of "feminist activists" concerned with abortion rights, lesbian rights, sexual harassment, affirmative action, and electing feminists.
www.now.org

---

taxpayers, none of whom individually bears enough added cost to merit spending time, energy, or money to organize a group to oppose the benefit. Thus the interest-group system concentrates benefits to the few and disperses costs to the many. The system favors small, well-organized, homogeneous interests that seek the expansion of government activity at the expense of larger but less well-organized citizen-taxpayers. Over long periods of time, the cumulative activities of many special-interest groups, each seeking concentrated benefits to themselves and dispersed costs to others, result in what has been termed **organizational sclerosis**, a society so encrusted with subsidies, benefits, regulations, protections, and special treatments for organized groups that work, productivity, and investment are discouraged and everyone's standard of living is lowered.

Origins of Interest Groups

James Madison viewed interest groups—which he called "factions"—as a necessary evil in politics. He defined a faction as "a number of citizens, whether amounting to a majority or a minority of the whole, who are united and actuated by some common impulse of passion, or of interest, adverse to the rights of other citizens, or to the permanent and aggregate interests of the community." He believed that interest groups not only conflict with each other but, more important, also conflict with the common good. Nevertheless, Madison believed that the origin of interest groups was to be found in human nature—"a zeal for different opinions concerning religion, concerning government, and many other points"—and therefore impossible to eliminate from politics.[2]

Protecting Economic Interests   Madison believed that "the most common and durable source of factions, has been the various and unequal distribution of property." With genuine insight, he identified *economic interests* as the most prevalent in politics: "a landed interest, a manufacturing interest, a mercantile interest, a moneyed interest, with many lesser interests." From Madison's era to the present, businesspeople and professionals, bankers and insurers, farmers and factory workers, merchants and shippers have organized themselves to press their demands on government (see *Up Close:* "Superlobby: The Business Roundtable").

Advancing Social Movements   Major social movements in American history have spawned many interest groups. Abolitionist groups were formed before the Civil War to fight slavery. The National Association for the Advancement of Colored People (NAACP) emerged in 1909 to fight segregation laws and to rally public support against lynching and other violence against African Americans. Farm organizations emerged from the populist movement of the late nineteenth century to press demands for railroad rate regulation and easier credit terms. The small trade unions that workers formed in the nineteenth century to improve their pay and working conditions gave way to large national unions in the 1930s as workers sought protection for the rights to organize, bargain collectively, and strike. The success of the women's suffrage movement led to the formation of the League of Women Voters in the early twentieth century, and a generation later the feminist movement inspired the National Organization for Women (NOW).

Seeking Government Benefits   As government expands its activities, it creates more interest groups. Wars create veterans' organizations. The first large veterans' group—the Grand Army of the Republic—formed after the Civil War and successfully lobbied for bonus payments to veterans over the years. Today the American Legion, the Veterans of Foreign Wars, and the Vietnam Veterans of

UP CLOSE

Superlobby:
The Business Roundtable

The Business Roundtable was established in 1972 "in the belief that business executives should take an increased role in the continuing debates about public policy."[a] The organization is composed of the chief executives of the 200 largest corporations in America and is financed through corporate membership fees.

The Roundtable organizes itself into task forces, each headed by the CEO of a major corporation. Among the recent lobbying goals of these task forces: reducing product liability in the courts, opposing limits on executive pay, limiting environmental protection regulations, seeking corporate tax reductions, and supporting President Bush's proposal to allow workers to invest part of their Social Security taxes in the stock market.

[a]Quotations about the reasons for the establishment of the Business Roundtable from "The History of the Business Roundtable," 1998.

The power of the Business Roundtable stems in part from its "firm rule" that a corporate chief executive officer (CEO) cannot send a substitute to its meetings. Moreover, corporate CEOs lobby the Congress in person rather than sending paid lobbyists. Members of Congress are impressed when the chair of IBM appears at a congressional hearing on business regulation or when the chair of GTE speaks to a congressional committee about taxation, or when the chair of Prudential talks to Congress about Social Security, or when the head of B. F. Goodrich testifies before the Senate Judiciary Committee about antitrust policy. One congressional staff member explained, "If a corporation sends its Washington representative to our office, he's probably going to be shunted over to a legislative assistant. But the chairman of the board is going to get in to see the senator." Another aide echoed those sentiments: "Very few members of Congress would not meet with the president of a Business Roundtable corporation."[b]

[b]*Time*, April 13, 1981, pp. 76–77.

America engage in lobbying the Congress and monitor the activities of the Department of Veterans Affairs. As the welfare state grew, so did organizations seeking to obtain benefits for their members, including the nation's largest interest group, the American Association of Retired Persons (AARP). Over time, organizations seeking to protect and expand welfare benefits for the poor also emerged (see *People in Politics:* "Marian Wright Edelman, Lobbying for the Poor"). Federal grant-in-aid programs to state and local governments inspired the development of governmental interest groups—the Council of State Governments, the National League of Cities, the National Governors Association, the U.S. Conference of Mayors, and so on—so that it is not uncommon today to see governments lobby other governments. Expanded government support for education led to political activity by the National Education Association, the American Federation of Teachers, the American Association of Land Grant Colleges and Universities, and other educational groups.

Responding to Government Regulation   As more businesses and professions came under government regulation in the twentieth century, more organizations formed to protect their interests, including such large and powerful groups as the American Medical Association (doctors), the American Bar Association (lawyers), and the National Association of Broadcasters (broadcasters). Indeed, the issue of regulation—whether of public utilities, interstate transportation, mine safety, medicines, or children's pajamas—always causes the formation of interest groups. Some form to demand regulation; others form to protect their members from regulatory burdens.

Business Roundtable
Organization representing largest U.S. corporations.
www.broundtable.org

Children's Defense Fund
Advocacy organization for welfare programs.
www.childrendefense.org

From (a) the Whiskey Rebellion of 1794 to (b) violent early union protests such as the Haymarket Riot of 1886 to (c) Carrie Nation's battle to ban liquor and (d) the women's suffrage movement of the late nineteenth and early twentieth centuries to (e) the civil rights marches of the 1960s and (f) the gay rights marches of the 1990s, protest has had a long and strong history for interest groups in the United States. Some protests have been violent and others peaceful, but by addressing key issues of the time, all have prompted public debate, and many have resulted in changes in public policy.

PEOPLE IN POLITICS

Marian Wright Edelman, Lobbying for the Poor

As founder and president of the Children's Defense Fund, Marian Wright Edelman has become legendary in Washington as a persuasive and persistent lobbyist on behalf of civil rights and social welfare legislation. A close friend of the Kennedy family, Edelman regularly testifies at Senate committee hearings, providing rapid-fire statistics on the effects of poverty on African American children. Each year the Children's Defense Fund, with a staff of more than a hundred in its Washington headquarters, produces numerous reports on infant mortality, homelessness, prenatal care, child nutrition, drug use, child abuse, teenage pregnancy, and single-parent households.

Marian Wright grew up in segregated rural South Carolina, the academically gifted daughter of a Baptist minister with a strong commitment to social justice. At an early age, she worked at the Wright House for the Aged, which her father had established. She entered all-black Spelman College in Atlanta and studied abroad at the Sorbonne in Paris and the University of Geneva, intending to take up a career in the foreign service. But Wright changed her career plans when she became involved in the early civil rights struggles in Atlanta. After graduating from Spelman, she entered Yale Law School to prepare herself in civil rights law. Upon her graduation in 1963, she immediately went to work for the National Association for the Advancement of Colored People Legal Defense Fund and traveled to Mississippi, where for four years she undertook the dangerous work of defending civil rights workers. In 1967 she met Peter Edelman, a Harvard Law School graduate and legislative aide to Senator Robert Kennedy; together they persuaded Kennedy to personally tour the most poverty-stricken areas of the Mississippi Delta, where the senator directly confronted hungry children living in miserable conditions.

The following year Wright and Edelman were married and settled in Washington, where she established the Washington Research Project, a public-interest research and lobbying organization on behalf of President Lyndon Johnson's War on Poverty. She maintained her Washington base even while directing the Harvard University Center for Law and Education during the several years that her husband served as vice president of the University of Massachusetts. In 1973 she organized the Children's Defense Fund (CDF) in Washington, "a strong national voice for children and family." The Children's Defense Fund describes its mission: "to leave no child behind." It was the principal lobbying group behind the Head Start program as well as federal child care and the Family Leave Act of 1993.

Marian Wright Edelman has been especially effective as an advocate of social welfare programs with her lively style, sense of urgency, and wealth of information about children in poverty. In 2000 Edelman received the Presidential Medal of Freedom, the nation's highest civilian award.

The Organized Interests in Washington

There are more than 1 million nonprofit organizations in the United States, several thousand of which are officially registered in Washington as lobbyists.[3] Trade and professional associations and corporations are the most common lobbies in Washington, but unions, public-interest groups, farm groups, environmental groups, ideological groups, religious and civil rights organizations, women's groups, veterans and defense-related groups, groups organized around a single issue (for example, Mothers Against Drunk Driving), and even organizations representing state and local governments also recognize that they need to be "where the action is." Among this huge assortment of organizations, many of which are very influential in their highly specialized field, there are a number of well-known organized interests. Even a partial list of organized interest groups (see Table 9.1) demonstrates the breadth and complexities of interest-group life in American politics.

Table 9.1   Major Organized Interest Groups, by Type

Business
Business Roundtable
National Association of
  Manufacturers
National Federation of Independent
  Businesses
National Small Business Association
U.S. Chamber of Commerce

Trade
American Bankers Association
American Gas Association
American Iron and Steel Institute
American Petroleum Institute
American Truckers Association
Automobile Dealers Association
Home Builders Association
Motion Picture Association of
  America
National Association of Broadcasters
National Association of Real Estate
  Boards

Professional
American Bar Association
American Medical Association
Association of Trial Lawyers
National Education Association

Union
AFL-CIO
American Federation of State,
  County, and Municipal Employees
American Federation of Teachers
International Brotherhood of
  Teamsters
International Ladies' Garment
  Workers Union
National Association of Letter
  Carriers
United Auto Workers
United Postal Workers
United Steel Workers

Agricultural
American Farm Bureau Federation
National Cattlemen's Association
National Farmers Union
National Grange
National Milk Producers Federation
Tobacco Institute

Women
League of Women Voters
National Organization for Women

Public Interest
Common Cause
Consumer Federation of America
Public Citizen
Public Interest Research Groups

Ideological
American Conservative Union
Americans for Constitutional Action
  (conservative)
Americans for Democratic Action
  (liberal)
People for the American Way (liberal)
MoveOn (liberal)

Single Issue
Mothers Against Drunk Driving
NARAL Pro-Choice America
National Rifle Association
National Right to Life Committee
Planned Parenthood Federation of
  America
National Taxpayers Union

Environmental
Environmental Defense Fund
Greenpeace
National Wildlife Federation
National Resources Defense Council
Nature Conservancy
Sierra Club
Wilderness Society

Religious
American Israel Public Affairs
  Committee
Anti-Defamation League of B'nai
  B'rith
Christian Coalition
National Council of Churches
U.S. Catholic Conference

Civil Rights
American Civil Liberties Union
American Indian Movement
Mexican-American Legal Defense and
  Education Fund
National Association for the
  Advancement of Colored People
National Urban League
Rainbow Coalition
Southern Christian Leadership
  Conference

Age Related
American Association of Retired
  Persons
Children's Defense Fund

Veterans
American Legion
Veterans of Foreign Wars
Vietnam Veterans of America

Defense
Air Force Association
American Security Council
Army Association
Navy Association

Government
National Association of Counties
National Conference of State
  Legislators
National Governors Association
National League of Cities
U.S. Conference of Mayors

**www U.S. Chamber of
Commerce**
Representing business,
"3 million companies of all
sizes." *www.uschamber.com*

Business and Trade Organizations   Traditionally, economic organizations have dominated interest-group politics in Washington. There is ample evidence that economic interests continue to play a major role in national policy making, despite the rapid growth over the last several decades of consumer and environmental organizations. Certainly in terms of the sheer number of organizations with offices and representatives in Washington, business and professional groups and occupational and trade associations predominate. More than half of the organizations with offices in Washington are business or trade associations, and all together these organizations account for about 75 percent of all of the reported lobbying expenditures.[4]

Business interests are represented, first of all, by large inclusive organizations, such as the U.S. Chamber of Commerce, representing thousands of local chambers of commerce across the nation; the National Association of Manufacturers; the Business Roundtable, representing the nation's largest corporations; and the National Federation of Independent Businesses, representing small business. Specific business interests are also represented by thousands of **trade associations**. These associations can closely monitor the interests of their specialized memberships. Among the most powerful of these associations are the American Bankers Association, the American Gas Association, the American Iron and Steel Institute, the National Association of Real Estate Boards, the American Petroleum Institute, and the National Association of Broadcasters. In addition, many individual corporations and firms achieve representation in Washington by opening their own lobbying offices or by hiring experienced professional lobbying and law firms.

trade associations Interest groups composed of businesses in specific industries.

Professional Associations   Professional associations rival business and trade organizations in lobbying influence. The American Bar Association (ABA), the American Medical Association (AMA), and the National Education Association (NEA) are three of the most influential groups in Washington. For example, the ABA, which includes virtually all of the nation's practicing attorneys, and its more specialized offspring, the American Association of Trial Lawyers, have successfully resisted efforts to reform the nation's tort laws (see *A Conflicting View:* "America Is Drowning in a Sea of Lawsuits," Chapter 13).

 American Medical Association
Professional organization of doctors that both lobbies and publishes medical research in the prestigious *Journal of the American Medical Association* (JAMA) *www.ama-assn.org*

Organized Labor   Labor organizations have declined in membership over the last several decades. The percentage of the total workforce belonging to unions has declined from about 37 percent in the 1950s to about 13 percent today. Workers in the private sector have largely deserted unions (see Figure 9.1). The major industrial unions—for example, the United Steelworkers of America, United Automobile Workers, United Mine Workers—have shrunk in membership. Only the unions of government employees—for example, the American Federation of State, Country, and Municipal Employees, the National Education Association—and some transportation and service workers unions—for example, Teamsters Union, Service Employees International, International Brotherhood of Electrical Workers—have gained members in recent years.

Nevertheless, labor unions remain a major political influence in Congress and the Democratic Party. The AFL-CIO is a federation of sixty-eight separate unions with more than 13 million members. The AFL-CIO has long maintained a large and capable lobbying staff in Washington, and it provides both financial contributions and campaign services (registration, get-out-the-vote, information, endorsements) for members of Congress it favors. Many of the larger individual unions also maintain offices in Washington and offer campaign contributions and services.

AFL-CIO
Homepage of labor confederation; includes information on wages, unemployment, strikes, as well as news and press releases on union affairs. *www.alfcio.org*

Today union influence is greatest among government employees, including teachers. About 38 percent of all public sector employees are unionized. The American Federation of State, County, and Municipal Employees (AFSCME), the National Education Association (NEA), the American Federation of Teachers (AFT), and the Teamsters Union (which recruits public employees in sanitation and transportation) are among the few unions growing in membership.

Labor union political campaign contributions (see "PAC Power" below) remain a major source of union influence in Washington. The AFSCME, NEA, Teamsters, United Auto Workers, United Steel Workers, Electrical Workers, Machinists, and Letter Carriers, as well as the AFL-CIO itself, are regularly

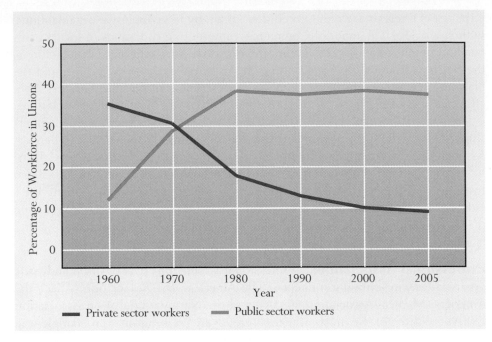

Figure 9.1   Unions and the American Workforce
Source: Statistical Abstract of the United States, 2005.

ranked among the top contributors in congressional elections. Almost all union campaign contributions go to Democratic candidates.

American Farm Bureau

The American Farm Bureau site reveals that the largest farm organization in America represents more than 5 million families in the fifty states and Puerto Rico.
www.fb.com

Farm Organizations   Even though the farm population of the United States has declined from about 25 percent of the total population in the 1930s to less than 3 percent today, farmers—especially large agricultural producers—remain a very potent political force in Washington. Agricultural interests are organized both into large inclusive groups, such as the American Farm Bureau Federation and the National Grange, and into very effective specialized groups, such as the National Milk Producers and the National Cattlemen's Association. Small and low-income farmers are represented by the National Farmers Union.

Women's Organizations   Women's organizations date back to the antislavery societies in pre-Civil War America. The first generation of feminists—Lucretia Mott, Elizabeth Cady Stanton, Lucy Stone, and Susan B. Anthony—learned to organize, hold public meetings, and conduct petition campaigns as abolitionists. After the Civil War, women were successful in changing many state laws that abridged the rights of married women and otherwise treated them as "chattel" (property) of their husbands. Women were also prominent in the Anti-Saloon League, which succeeded in outlawing prostitution and gambling in every state except Nevada and provided a major source of support for the Eighteenth Amendment (Prohibition). In the early twentieth century, the feminist movement concentrated on obtaining the vote (suffrage) for women. Today the League of Women Voters—a broad-based organization that provides information to voters—backs registration and get-out-the-vote drives and generally supports measures seeking to ensure honesty and integrity in government.

Interest in feminist politics revived in the wake of the civil rights movement of the 1960s. New organizations sprang up to compete with the conventional

"A very special interest to see you, Senator."

activities of the League of Women Voters by taking a more activist stance toward women's issues. The largest of these organizations is the National Organization for Women (NOW), founded in 1966.

Religious Groups   Churches and religious groups have a long history of involvement in American politics—from the pre-Civil War antislavery crusades, to the prohibition effort in the early twentieth century, to the civil rights movement of the 1960s. The leadership for the historic Civil Rights Act of 1964 came from the Reverend Martin Luther King Jr. and his Southern Christian Leadership Conference. Today religious groups span the political spectrum, from liberal organizations such as the National Council of Churches and Anti-Defamation League of B'nai B'rith, to conservative and fundamentalist organizations, such as the Christian Coalition, often referred to as the "religious right" (see *Up Close: "The Christian Coalition: Organizing the Faithful"*).

Public-Interest Groups   Public-interest groups claim to represent broad classes of people—consumers, voters, reformers, or the public as a whole. Groups with lofty-sounding names, such as Common Cause, Public Citizen, and the Consumer Federation of America, perceive themselves as balancing the narrow, "selfish" interests of business organizations, trade associations, unions, and other "special" interests. Public-interest groups generally lobby for greater government regulation of consumer products, public safety, campaign finance, and so on. Their reform agenda, as well as their call for a larger regulatory role for government, makes them frequent allies of liberal ideological groups, civil rights organizations, and environmental groups.[5]

Many public-interest groups were initially formed in the 1970s by "entrepreneurs" who saw an untapped "market" for the representation of these interests. Among the most influential public-interest groups are Common Cause, a self-styled "citizens' lobby," and the sprawling network of organizations created by consumer advocate Ralph Nader (see *People in Politics: "Ralph Nader, People's Lobbyist"*). Common Cause tends to focus on election-law reform, public financing of elections, and limitations on political contributions. The Nader organization began as a consumer protection group focusing on auto safety but soon spread to encompass a wide variety of causes.

Single-Issue Groups   Like public-interest groups, **single-issue groups** appeal to principle and belief. But as their name implies, single-issue groups concentrate their attention on a single cause. They attract the support of individuals with a strong commitment to that cause. Single-issue groups have little incentive to compromise their position. They exist for a single cause; no other issues really matter to them. They are by nature passionate and often shrill. Their attraction to members is the intensity of their beliefs.

Among the most vocal single-issue groups in recent years have been the organizations on both sides of the abortion issue. NARAL Pro-Choice America describes itself as "pro-choice" and opposes any restrictions on a woman's right to obtain an abortion. The National Right-to-Life Committee describes itself as "pro-life" and opposes abortion for any reason other than to preserve the life of the mother. Other prominent single-issue groups include the National Rifle Association (opposed to gun control) and Mothers Against Drunk Driving (MADD).

Ideological Groups   **Ideological organizations** pursue liberal or conservative agendas, often with great passion and considerable financial resources derived from true-believing contributors. The ideological groups rely heavily on

---

www **Christian Coalition**
Organization "defending our godly heritage" by giving "people of faith a voice in government".
www.cc.org

public-interest groups
Interest groups that claim to represent broad classes of people or the public as a whole.

www **Public Citizen**
Organization founded by Ralph Nader; devotes its site to "protecting health, safety and democracy" as well as lobbying for "strong citizen and consumer protection laws."
www.publiccitizen.com

single-issue groups
Organizations formed to support or oppose government action on a specific issue.

ideological organizations
Interest groups that pursue ideologically based (liberal or conservative) agendas.

UP CLOSE

The Christian Coalition: Organizing the Faithful

Christian fundamentalists, whose religious beliefs are based on a literal reading of the Bible, have become a significant political force in the United States through effective organization. Perhaps the most influential Christian fundamentalist organization today is the Christian Coalition, with nearly 2 million active members throughout the country.

Fundamentalist Christians are opposed to abortion, pornography, and homosexuality; they favor the recognition of religion in public life, including prayer in schools; and they despair at the decline of traditional family values in American culture, including motion pictures and television broadcasting. Historically, fundamentalist Protestant churches avoided politics as profane and concentrated evangelical efforts on saving individual souls. Their few ventures into worldly politics—notably the prohibition movement in the early twentieth century—ended in defeat. Their strength tended to be in the southern, rural, and poorer regions of the country. They were widely ridiculed in the national media.

In the 1960s, television evangelism emerged as a religious force in the United States. The Reverend Pat Robertson founded the Christian Broadcasting Network (CBN) and later purchased the Family Channel. But efforts by social conservatives to build a "moral majority" for political action largely failed, as did Robertson's presidential candidacy in 1988. Televangelists, including Jerry Falwell and Tammy Faye Bakker, suffered popular disdain following some well-publicized scandals.

Although officially nonpartisan, the Coalition became an important force in Republican politics; religious fundamentalists may constitute as much as one-third of the party's voter support. The Christian Coalition does not officially endorse candidates, but its voter guides at right clearly indicate which candidates reflect the coalition's position on major issues. The political influence of the Christian Coalition in Republican politics, and the "religious right" generally, ensures that most GOP candidates for public office publicly express support for a "profamily" agenda. This agenda includes a constitutional amendment allowing prayer in public schools; vouchers for parents to send their children to private, religious schools; banning late-term abortions as well as banning the use of taxpayer funds to pay for abortions; restrictions on pornography on cable television and the Internet; and opposition to human embryo research and human cloning.

Religious groups can play a key role in elections by informing their members about candidates and getting out the vote. The Christian Coalition is one of the most active religious groups.

2004 Christian Coalition VOTER  GUIDE

PRESIDENTIAL Election

George W. Bush (R)	ISSUES	John F. Kerry (D)
Supports	Passage of a Federal Marriage Protection Amendment	Opposes
Supports	Permanent Extension of the $1,000 Per Child Tax Credit	Opposes
Supports	Educational Choice for Parents (Vouchers)	Opposes
Opposes	Unrestricted Abortion on Demand	No Response
Supports	Federal Funding for Faith-Based Charitable Organizations	No Response
Supports	Permanent Elimination of the Marriage Penalty Tax	Opposes
Supports	Permanent Elimination of the Death Tax	Opposes
Supports	Banning Partial Birth Abortions	Opposes
Opposes	Public Financing of Abortions	Supports
Opposes	Federal Firearms Registration & Licensing of Gun Owners	No Response
Opposes	Adoption of Children by Homosexuals	No Response
Supports	Prescription Drug Benefits for Medicare Recipients	Supports
Opposes	Placing US Troops Under UN Control	No Response
Opposes	Affirmative Action Programs that Provide Preferential Treatment	Supports
Supports	Allowing Younger Workers to Invest a Portion of their Social Security Tax in a Private Account	Opposes

www.georgewbush.com   www.johnkerry.com

Each candidate was sent a 2004 Federal Issue Survey by certified mail and/or facsimile machine. When possible, positions of candidates on issues were verified or determined using voting records and/or public statements.

Authorized by the Christian Coalition of America; PO Box 37030 - Washington, DC 20013

The Christian Coalition of America is a pro-family, citizen action organization. This voter guide is provided for educational purposes only and is not to be construed as an endorsement of any candidate or party.

Please visit our website at www.cc.org, and the Texas website at www.texascc.org

Vote on November 2   F

Photo courtesy: Christian Coalition of America

PEOPLE IN POLITICS

Ralph Nader, People's Lobbyist

Much of the credit for the growth of public-interest groups in recent decades goes to Ralph Nader, the self-appointed "people's lobbyist" who first achieved national celebrity as an advocate of consumer protection laws. From seat belts and nonsmoking sections to nuclear power regulation, insurance rates, food and drug legislation, and worker safety, Nader's influence has been widely felt in American society.

The child of Lebanese immigrants who operated a small bakery in Winsted, Connecticut, Nader graduated from the Woodrow Wilson School of Public and International Affairs at Princeton University magna cum laude, then went on to Harvard Law School.

Later while employed at the Department of Labor, Nader wrote and published his book *Unsafe at Any Speed* (1965), which charged that General Motors Corporation preferred styling to safety. Nader was thrust further into the national spotlight when he sued General Motors for invading his privacy by hiring private detectives to investigate him. With his $16 million in settlement money (plus substantial royalties and speaking income), Nader began to construct an organizational colossus.

In 1971 Nader started Public Citizen, Inc., to enlist members of the general public in a broad array of causes. Among these causes: *Congress Watch*, which directly lobbies Congress on health, safety, and environmental issues, as well as campaign finance reform; *The Health Research Group,* which lobbies the Food and Drug Administration for greater regulation, including tobacco restrictions; *The Litigation Group,* which generates class-action suits against corporations and governments; *The Critical Mass Energy Project,* which opposes nuclear energy and the oil and gas industry; *Global Trade Watch,* which opposes free trade as a threat to the environment; and *Buyers Up,* a home-heating-oil cooperative that also monitors quality of gasoline sold to consumers.

Capitalizing on his campus popularity, Nader formed hundreds of Public Interest Research Groups (PIRGs) and overcame the "free-rider" problem by pressuring university administrators on many campuses to add PIRG dues to student activities fees.

Nader has resigned from direct participation in most of the organizations he founded, leaving them to be managed by a new generation of consumer advocates. Nader ran for president in 1996 as a Green Party (environmental protection) candidate. But he campaigned very little and refused to solicit contributions. In public appearances he often seemed argumentative and self-righteous. He ended up with less than 1 percent of the popular vote nationwide.

Nader's decision to actively campaign for the presidency in 2000 angered many of his liberal Democratic friends. They believed that most of his nearly 3 million votes nationwide (about 3 percent of the popular vote) would otherwise have gone to Democrat Al Gore. Nader ran again in 2004, but not all of the states granted him ballot position. He won less than one percent of the vote.

---

computerized mailings to solicit funds from persons identified as holding liberal or conservative views. The oldest of the established ideological groups is the liberal Americans for Democratic Action (ADA), well known for its annual liberalism ratings of members of the Congress according to their support for or rejection of programs of concern. The American Conservative Union (ACU) also rates members of Congress each year. Overall, Democrats do better on the liberal list and Republicans on the conservative list, although both parties include some Congress members who occasionally vote on the opposite side of the fence from the majority of their fellow party members (see Table 9.2). Other interest groups, such as the AFL-CIO, the National Taxpayers Union, and NARAL Pro-Choice America also rate members of Congress, but these groups have a narrower focus than the ADA and ACU. Yet another prominent ideological group, People for the American Way, was formed by television producer Norman Lear

 **National Rifle Association**

The National Rifle Association site is devoted to opposing gun control legislation as well as employing the Second Amendment in its antigun control argument.
www.nra.org

Table 9.2   Ideological Interest-Group Ratings for U.S. Senators*

ADA Americans for Democratic Action (liberal)		ACU American Conservative Union (conservative)	
"Senate Heroes" **(100% voting with ADA)**		**"Senate Standouts"** **(100% voting with ACU)**	
Corzine	(D-NJ)	Bunning	(R-KY)
Dodd	(D-CT)	Burns	(R-MT)
Feingold	(D-WI)	Cornyn	(R-TX)
Feinstein	(D-CA)	Inhofe	(R-OK)
Harkin	(D-IA)	Kyl	(R-AZ)
Inouye	(D-HI)	Nickles	(R-OK)
Kennedy	(D-MA)	Sununu	(R-NH)
Kohl	(D-WI)	Thomas	(R-WY)
Lautenberg	(D-NJ)		
Leahy	(D-VT)	**"Worst of the Worst"**	
Levin	(D-MI)	Biden	(D-DE)
Mikulski	(D-MD)	Clinton	(D-NY)
Reed	(D-RI)	Edwards	(D-NC)
Sarbanes	(D-MD)	Kennedy	(D-MA)
Schumer	(D-NY)	Kerry	(D-MA)
Stabenow	(D-MI)	Lautenberg	(D-NJ)
Wyden	(D-NY)	Levin	(D-MI)
		Lieberman	(D-CT)
Senate Moderates		Reed	(D-RI)
(40–60% rating with ADA)		Sarbanes	(D-MD)
Chaffee	(R-RI)		
Collins	(R-ME)		
Edwards	(D-NC)		
Smith	(R-OR)		
Specter	(R-PA)		

*Voting in 2004.

Sources: Americans for Democratic Action, *www.adaction.org*; American Conservative Union, *www.conservative.org*

to coordinate the efforts of liberals in the entertainment industry as well as the general public, but it issues no ratings.

Government Lobbies   The federal government's grant-in-aid programs to state and local governments (see Chapter 4) have spawned a host of lobbying efforts by these governments in Washington, D.C. Thus state- and local-government taxpayers foot the bill to lobby Washington to transfer federal taxpayers' revenues to states and communities. The National Governors Association occupies a beautiful marble building, the Hall of the States, in Washington, along with representatives of the separate states and many major cities. The National League of Cities and the National Association of Counties also maintain large Washington offices, as does the U.S. Conference of Mayors. The National Conference of State Legislators sends its lobbyists to Washington from its Denver headquarters. These groups pursue a wide policy agenda and often confront internal disputes. But they are united in their support for increased federal transfers of tax revenues to states and cities.

Leaders and Followers

Organizations require leadership. And over time leaders develop a perspective somewhat different from that of their organizations' membership. A key question in interest-group politics is how well organization leaders represent the views of their members.

Interest-Group Entrepreneurs   People who create organizations and build membership in those organizations—**interest-group entrepreneurs**—have played a major role in strengthening the interest-group system in recent decades. These entrepreneurs help overcome a major obstacle to the formation of strong interest groups—the *free-rider* problem.

Free-riders are people who benefit from the efforts of others but do not contribute to the costs of those efforts. Not everyone feels an obligation to support organizations that represent their interests or views. Some people feel that their own small contribution will not make a difference in the success or failure of the organization's goals and, moreover, that they will benefit from any successes even if they are not members. Indeed, most organizations enroll only a tiny fraction of the people they claim to represent. The task of the interest-group entrepreneur is to convince people to join the organization, either by appealing to their sense of obligation or by attracting them through tangible benefits.

Marketing Membership   Interest-group entrepreneurs make different appeals for membership depending on the nature of the organization. Some appeal to passion or purpose, as, for example, those who seek to create ideological (liberal or conservative) organizations, public-interest organizations committed to environmental or consumer protection or governmental reform, and single-issue organizations devoted to the support or opposition of a single policy issue (gun control, abortion, and so on). Entrepreneurs of these organizations appeal to people's sense of duty and commitment to the cause rather than to material rewards of membership. By using sophisticated computerized mailing lists, they can solicit support from sympathetic people.[6]

Business, trade, and professional organizations usually offer their members many tangible benefits in addition to lobbying on behalf of their economic interests. These benefits may include magazines, journals, and newsletters that provide access to business, trade, and professional information as well as national conventions and meetings that serve as social settings for the development of contacts, friendships, and business and professional relationships. Some organizations also offer discount travel and insurance, credit cards, and the like, that go only to dues-paying members.

It is generally easier to organize smaller, specialized economic interests than larger, general, noneconomic interests. People more easily recognize that their own membership is important to the success of a small organization, and economic interests are more readily calculated in dollar terms.

Large organizations with broad goals—such as advancing the interests of all veterans or all retired people or all automobile drivers—must rely even more heavily on tangible benefits to solicit members. Indeed, some organizations have succeeded in recruiting millions of members (for example, the AARP with 36 million members, the American Automobile Association with 28 million members), most of whom have very little knowledge about the policy positions or lobbying activities of the organization. These members joined to receive specific benefits—magazines, insurance, travel tips, discounts. Leaders of these organizations may

interest-group entrepreneurs Leaders who create organizations and market memberships.

free-riders People who do not belong to an organization or pay dues, yet nevertheless benefit from its activities.

claim to speak for millions of members, but it is unlikely that these millions all share the policy views expressed by the leaders.

Organizational Democracy and Leader/Member Agreement   Most organized interest groups are run by a small group of leaders and activists. Few interest groups are governed democratically; members may drop out if they do not like the direction their organization is taking but rarely do they have the opportunity to directly challenge or replace the organization's leadership. Relatively few members attend national meetings, vote in organizational elections, or try to exercise influence within their organization. Thus the leadership may not always reflect the views of the membership, especially in large organizations that rely heavily on tangible benefits to recruit members. Leaders of these organizations enjoy considerable freedom in adopting policy positions and negotiating, bargaining, and compromising in the political arena.

The exception to this rule is the single-issue group. Because the strength of these groups is in the intensity of their members' beliefs, the leaders of such groups are closely tied to their members' views. They cannot bargain or compromise these views or adopt policy positions at variance with those of their members.

Class Bias in Membership   Americans are joiners. A majority of the population belong to at least one organization, most often a church. Yet membership in organized interest groups is clearly linked to socioeconomic status. Membership is greatest among professional and managerial, college-educated, and high-income persons.[7]

The Washington Lobbyists

lobbyist Person working to influence government policies and actions.

Washington is a labyrinth of interest representatives—lawyers and law firms; independent consultants; public and governmental relations firms; business, professional, and trade associations; and advocates of special causes. It is estimated that more than 15,000 people in Washington fit the definition of **lobbyist**, a person working to influence government policies and actions. This figure suggests at least twenty-eight lobbyists for every member of Congress. Roughly $1.5 *billion* are spent on direct lobbying activities *each year*;[8] this figure does *not* include political campaign contributions. The top spenders for direct lobbying are listed in Table 9.3.

Who Are the Lobbyists?   Lobbyists in Washington share a common goal—to influence the making and enforcing of laws—and common tactics to achieve this goal. Many lobbyists are the employees of interest-group organizations who devote all of their efforts to their sponsors.

Other lobbyists are located in independent law, consulting, or public relations firms that take on clients for fees. Independent lobbyists, especially law firms, are often secretive about whom they represent, especially when they represent foreign governments. Lobbyists frequently prefer to label their activities as "government relations," "public affairs," "regulatory liaison," "legislative counseling," or merely "representation."

In reality, many independent lawyers and lobbyists in Washington are "fixers" who offer to influence government policies for a price. Many are former government officials—former Congress members, cabinet secretaries, White House aides, and the like—who "know their way around." Their personal connections help to "open doors" to allow their paying clients to "just get a chance to talk" with top officials.

Table 9.3	Top Lobbying Spenders	

Rank	Organization	Annual Spending
1	Chamber of Commerce of the U.S.	$26,160,160
2	Business Roundtable	21,480,000
3	American Medical Assn.	16,640,000
4	General Electric	16,020,000
5	Edison Electric Institute	12,000,000
6	American Hospital Assn.	11,950,000
7	Philip Morris	11,220,000
8	Lockheed Martin	11,170,000
9	Verizon Communications	10,480,000
10	Schering-Plough Corp.	9,180,000
11	Seniors Coalition	9,022,096
12	National Assn. of Realtors	8,920,000
13	General Motors	8,805,620
14	Assn. of American Railroads	8,760,160
15	Ford Motor Co.	8,008,000
16	Boeing Co.	7,820,000
17	American Council of Life Insurance	7,712,090
18	Blue Cross/Blue Shield	7,655,822
19	AT&T	7,480,000
19	Pharmaceutical Research & Mfrs of America	7,480,000

Source: Reprinted by permission of the Center for Responsive Politics, *Influence, Inc.* 2000. There is considerable change from year to year in the list, depending on the nature of the legislation before Congress.

Some lobbying organizations rely heavily on their campaign contributions to achieve lobbying power; others rely on large memberships, and still others on politically active members who concentrate their attention on a narrow range of issues (see *Up Close:* "Washington's Most Powerful Lobbies").

Washington's army of lobbyists includes many former members of Congress. Lobbying is a favorite occupation of former members; they can command much higher salaries as lobbyists than they did as Congress members. Lobbying firms are pleased to have people who know the lawmaking process from the inside and who can easily "schmooze" with their former colleagues.

Regulation of Lobbies   The Constitution's First Amendment guarantee of the right "to petition the government for a redress of grievances" protects lobbying. But the government can and does regulate lobbying activities, primarily through disclosure laws. The Regulation of Lobbying Act requires lobbyists to register and to report how much they spend, but definitions of *lobbying* are unclear and enforcement is weak. Many large lobbying groups have never registered as lobbyists. These organizations claim that because lobbying is not their principal activity, they need not register under the law. In addition, financial reports of lobbyists grossly underestimate the extent of lobbying in Congress because the law requires reports of only money spent for *direct* lobbying before Congress, not money spent for public relations or grass-roots mobilization of members to pressure Congress. Another weakness in the law is that it applies only to attempts to influence Congress; it does not regulate lobbying activities in administrative agencies or litigation in the courts.

Tax laws require nonprofit organizations to refrain from direct lobbying in order to retain their tax-free status. Under current tax law, individual contributions to

UP CLOSE

Washington's Most Powerful Lobbies

Fortune magazine sponsored a survey of more than 2,000 Washington "insiders," including members of Congress, their staffs, and White House officials, asking them to rank the most powerful lobbyists in the capital. The results were as follows:

The "Power 25"

1. American Association of Retired Persons
2. American Israel Public Affairs Committee
3. National Federation of Independent Business
4. National Rifle Association of America
5. AFL-CIO
6. Association of Trial Lawyers of America
7. Christian Coalition
8. Credit Union National Association
9. National Right to Life Committee
10. American Medical Association
11. Chamber of Commerce of the U.S.A.
12. Independent Insurance Agencies of America
13. National Association of Manufacturers
14. American Farm Bureau Federation
15. National Restaurant Association
16. National Association of Home Builders of the U.S.
17. National Association of Realtors
18. National Association of Broadcasters
19. Motion Picture Association of America
20. American Bankers Association
21. National Education Association
22. Health Insurance Association of America
23. American Council of Life Insurance
24. National Beer Wholesalers Association
25. Veterans of Foreign Wars of the United States

Source: "Fat & Happy in DC: Washington's Most Powerful Lobbies," from *Fortune*, May 28, 2001. Copyright © 2001 by Time, Inc. Reprinted by permission of *Fortune*.

nonprofit charitable and educational organizations are tax deductible, and the income of these organizations is tax free. But these organizations risk losing these tax preferences if a "substantial part" of their activities is "attempting to influence legislation." Thus, for example, Washington think tanks such as the Brookings Institution, the American Enterprise Institute, and the Heritage Foundation refrain from direct lobbying even though they make policy recommendations. But the line between public affairs "education" and "lobbying" is very fuzzy.

Tightening Lobby Regulations Recent scandals involving lobbyists (see "Lobbying Ethics" later in this chapter) have led to proposals to curtail gifts by lobbyists to Congress members, including paid vacations, dinners, flights, and so forth. Another reform proposal has been to eliminate "earmarking" of appropriations for specific projects that have been heavily lobbied. Yet, so far, Congress has failed to adopt these reform proposals.

The Fine Art of Lobbying

Any activity directed at a government decision maker with the hope of influencing decisions is a form of **lobbying**. (The term arose from the practice of waiting in the lobbies of legislative chambers to meet and persuade legislators.) For organized interests, lobbying is continuous—in congressional committees, in congressional staff offices, at the White House, at executive agencies, at Washington cocktail parties. If a group loses a round in Congress, it continues the fight in the agency in charge of executing the policy, or it challenges the policy in the courts. The following year it resumes the struggle in Congress: It fights to repeal the offending legislation, to weaken amendments, or to reduce the agency's budget enough to cripple enforcement efforts.

Lobbying techniques are as varied as the imagination of interest-group leaders, but such activities generally fall into seven categories: (1) public relations;

American League of Lobbyists
Lobbyists have their own Web site, one devoted to "ethical conduct" in the lobbying process and the "advancement of the lobbying profession."
www.alldc.org

lobbying Activities directed at government officials with the hope of influencing their decisions.

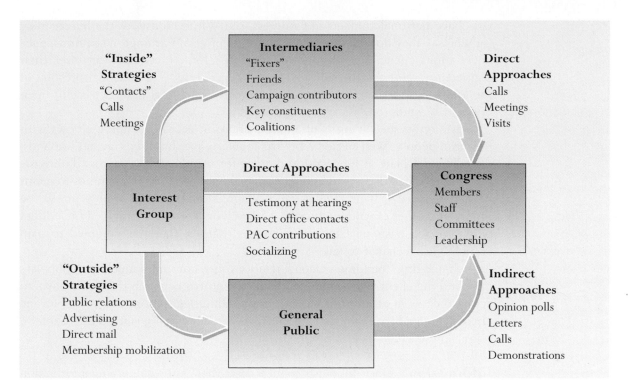

"Inside" Strategies
"Contacts"
Calls
Meetings

Intermediaries
"Fixers"
Friends
Campaign contributors
Key constituents
Coalitions

Direct Approaches
Calls
Meetings
Visits

Interest Group

Direct Approaches
Testimony at hearings
Direct office contacts
PAC contributions
Socializing

Congress
Members
Staff
Committees
Leadership

"Outside" Strategies
Public relations
Advertising
Direct mail
Membership mobilization

General Public

Indirect Approaches
Opinion polls
Letters
Calls
Demonstrations

Figure 9.2   A Guide to the Fine Art of Lobbying
Interest groups seek to influence public policy both directly through lobbying and campaign contributions (inside strategy) and indirectly through public relations efforts to mold public opinion (outside strategy).

(2) access; (3) information; (4) grass-roots mobilization; (5) protests and demonstrations; (6) coalition building; and (7) campaign support. In the real world of Washington power struggles, all these techniques may be applied simultaneously or innovative techniques may be discovered and applied at any time (see Figure 9.2).

Public Relations   Many interest groups actually spend more of their time, energy, and resources on **public relations**—developing and maintaining a favorable climate of opinion in the nation—than on direct lobbying of Congress. The mass media—television, magazines, newspapers—are saturated with expensive ads by oil companies, auto companies, chemical manufacturers, trade associations, teachers' unions, and many other groups, all seeking to create a favorable image for themselves with the general public. These ads are designed to go well beyond promoting the sale of particular products; they portray these organizations as patriotic citizens, protectors of the environment, providers of jobs, defenders of family values, and supporters of the American way of life. Generally, business interests have an advantage in the area of public relations because public relations and sales and marketing activities are synonymous. But paid advertising is less credible than news stories and media commentary. Hence interest groups generate a daily flood of press releases, media events, interviews, reports, and studies for the media. Media news stories appear to favor liberal public interest groups.[9]

public relations Building and maintaining goodwill with the general public.

Access   "Opening doors" is a major business in Washington. To influence decision makers, organized interests must first acquire **access** to them. Individuals

access Meeting and talking with decision makers, a prerequisite to direct persuasion.

who have personal contacts in Congress, the White House, or the bureaucracy (or who say they do) sell their services at high prices. Washington law firms, public relations agencies, and consultants—often former insiders—all offer their connections, along with their advice, to their clients. The personal prestige of the lobbyist, together with the group's perceived political influence, helps open doors in Washington.

Washington socializing is often an exercise in access—rubbing elbows with powerful people. Well-heeled lobbyists regularly pay hundreds, even thousands, of dollars per plate at fund-raising dinners for members of Congress. Lobbyists regularly provide dinners, drinks, travel, vacations, and other amenities to members of Congress, their families, and congressional staff, as well as to White House and other executive officials. These favors are rarely provided on a direct quid pro quo basis in exchange for votes. Rather, they are designed to gain access—"just a chance to talk."

"Schmoozing," building personal relationships, consumes much of a lobbyist's time and the client's money. It is difficult to know how much this contributes to actual success in passing, defeating, or amending legislation. But, to quote one client: "I figured that half of the money I spend on lobbying is wasted. Trouble is, I don't know which half."[10]

Information   Once lobbyists gain access, their knowledge and information become valuable resources to those they lobby. Members of Congress and their staff look to lobbyists for *technical expertise* on the issue under debate as well as *political information* about the group's position on the issue. Members of Congress must vote on hundreds of questions each year, and it is impossible for them to be fully informed about the wide variety of bills and issues they face. Consequently many of them (and administrators in the executive branch as well) come to depend on trusted lobbyists.

Lobbyists also spend considerable time and effort keeping informed about bills affecting their interests. They must be thoroughly familiar with the "ins and outs" of the legislative process—the relevant committees and subcommittees, their schedules of meetings and hearings, their key staff members, the best moments to act, the precise language for proposed bills and amendments, the witnesses for hearings, and the political strengths and weaknesses of the legislators themselves. In their campaign to win congressional and bureaucratic support for their programs, lobbyists engage in many different types of activities. Nearly all testify at congressional hearings and make direct contact with government officials on issues that affect them. In addition, lobbyists provide the technical reports and analyses used by congressional staffs in their legislative research. Engaging in protest demonstrations is a less common activity, in part because it involves a high risk of alienating some members of Congress.

Experienced lobbyists develop a reputation for accurate information. Most successful lobbyists do not supply faulty information; their success depends on maintaining the trust and confidence of decision makers. A reputation for honesty is as important as a reputation for influence.

Grass-Roots Mobilization   Many organized interests lobby Congress from both the *outside* and the *inside*. From the outside, organizations seek to mobilize **grass-roots lobbying** of members of Congress by their constituents. Lobbyists frequently encourage letters and calls from "the folks back home." Larger organized interests often have local chapters throughout the nation and can mobilize these local affiliates to apply pressure when necessary. Lobbyists encourage influential local people to visit the office of a member of Congress personally or to

AARP
The AARP site covers issues and provides information relevant to the concerns of citizens who are 50 years of age or older.
www.aarp.org

grass-roots lobbying
Attempts to influence government decision making by inspiring constituents to contact their representatives.

UP CLOSE

AARP: The Nation's Most Powerful Interest Group

The American Association of Retired Persons (AARP) is the nation's largest and most powerful interest group, with more than 36 million members. The AARP's principal interests are the Social Security and Medicare system programs, the nation's largest and most expensive entitlements.

Like many other interest groups, the AARP has grown in membership not only by appealing to the political interests of retired people but also by offering a wide array of material benefits. For a $12.50 annual fee, members are offered a variety of services, including discounted rates on home, auto, life and health insurance; discounted mail-order drugs, tax advisory services; discounted rates on hotels, rental cars, and so on; a newsletter, *The AARP Bulletin*; a semi-monthly magazine, *Modern Maturity*, and for babyboomers now reaching their 50s, a new magazine, *My Generation*.

The political power of senior citizens is so great that prospects for limiting current or even future increases in government benefits for the elderly are slim. President Bush's proposal to allow workers to invest part of their Social Security taxes in private accounts was defeated largely by the work of the AARP. Social Security is said to be the "third rail of American politics—touch it and you're dead."

Critics of the AARP argue that its lobbyists in Washington do not fairly represent the views of the nation's senior citizens, that few of its members know what its lobbying arm does at the nation's capital. Indeed, in the struggle over prescription drug coverage under Medicare in 2003, the AARP leadership was accused of favoring its own interest in selling private insurance over the interests of its members in receiving government-paid insurance. AARP keeps its dues low, and consequently its membership high, through its business ties with insurance companies, its magazine advertising revenue, and commercial royalties revenues for endorsing products and services.

Source: Reprinted, with permission, from the April 1997 issue of *Reason Magazine*, Copyright 2000 by the Reason Foundation, 3415 S. Sepulveda Blvd., Suite 400, Los Angeles, CA 90034, *www.reason.com*.

make a personal phone call on behalf of the group's position. And, naturally, members are urged to vote for or against certain candidates, based on their policy stances (see *Up Close:* "AARP: The Nation's Most Powerful Interest Group").

Experienced lawmakers recognize attempts by lobby groups to orchestrate "spontaneous" grass-roots outpourings of cards and letters. Pressure mail is often identical in wording and content. Nevertheless, members of Congress dare not

Senator John McCain (R-AZ) addresses the National Council of La Raza, a Latino interest group, in support of more aid to immigrants.

ignore a flood of letters and telegrams from home, for the mail shows that constituents are aware of the issue and care enough to sign their names.

Protests and Demonstrations Interest groups occasionally employ protests and demonstrations to attract media attention to their concerns and thereby apply pressure on officials to take action. For these actions to succeed in getting issues on the agenda of decision makers in Congress, in the White House, and in executive agencies, participation by the media, especially television, is essential. The media carry the message of the protest or demonstration both to the general public and directly to government officials (see "Protest as Political Participation" in Chapter 5).

Organized interest groups most often resort to protests and demonstrations when (1) they are frustrated in more traditional "inside" lobbying efforts; and/or (2) they wish to intensify pressure on officials at a specific point in time. Demonstrations typically attract media attention for a short time only. But media coverage of specific events can carry a clear message—for example, farmers driving tractors through Washington to protest farm conditions; motorcyclists conducting a giant "bike-in" to protest laws requiring helmets; cattle raisers driving steers down the Washington Mall to protest beef prices. The potential drawbacks to such activities are that the attention is short-lived and the group's reputation may be tarnished if the protest turns nasty or violent.

coalition A joining together of interest groups (or individuals) to achieve a common goal.

Coalition Building Interest groups frequently seek to build **coalitions** with other groups in order to increase their power. Coalitions tend to form among groups with parallel interests: for example, the National Organization for Women, the League of Women Voters, and NARAL Pro-Choice America on women's issues. Coalitions usually form temporarily around a single piece of legislation in a major effort to secure or prevent its passage.

Campaign Support Perhaps the real key to success in lobbying is the campaign contribution. Interest-group contributions not only help lobbyists gain access and a favorable hearing but also help elect people friendly to the group's goals. As the costs of campaigning increase, legislators must depend more heavily on the contributions of organized interests.

Most experienced lobbyists avoid making electoral threats. Amateur lobbyists sometimes threaten legislators by vowing to defeat them at the next election, but this tactic usually produces a hostile reaction among members of Congress. Legislators are likely to respond to crude pressures by demonstrating their independence and voting against the threatening lobbyist. Moreover, experienced members of Congress know that such threats are empty; lobbyists can seldom deliver enough votes to influence the outcome of an election.

Lobbying Ethics Experienced lobbyists also avoid offering a campaign contribution in exchange for a specific vote.[11] Crude "vote buying" (bribery) is illegal and risks repulsing politicians who refuse bribes. **Bribery**, when it occurs, is probably limited to very narrow and specific actions—payments to intervene in a particular case before an administrative agency; payments to insert a very specific break in a tax bill or a specific exemption in a trade bill; payments to obtain a specific contract with the government. Bribery on major issues is very unlikely; there is too much publicity and too many participants for bribery to be effective.

To the skeptical, "lobbying ethics" may seem to be an oxymoron. Lobbyists regularly send Congress members and even their staffs on expensive junkets around the world and entertain them back in Washington with golf outings, free meals at expensive restaurants, luxury skybox seats at sporting events, and a host of other perks. And, of course, they direct their clients' campaign contributions to Congress members who support their cause. Prudent lobbyists report these contributions and avoid any direct communications that would suggest that the contributions were made in exchange for a particular official action. But ethical problems remain. In 2005 lobbyist Jack Abramoff was indicted for defrauding Indian tribes of millions in fees and campaign contributions that had been given by the tribes to gain favorable treatment of their gambling enterprises. Abramoff kept millions for himself, but he also distributed millions to hundreds of Congress members both directly and indirectly through organizations he created. Following his indictment, many Congress members rushed to rid themselves of his contributions by giving them to charity.

PAC Power

Organized interest groups channel their campaign contributions through **political action committees (PACs)**. PACs are organized by corporations, labor unions, trade associations, ideological and issue-oriented groups, and cooperatives and nonprofit corporations to solicit campaign contributions and distribute them to political candidates.

Distributing PAC Money Because PAC contributions are in larger lumps than individual contributions, PAC contributions often attract more attention from members of Congress. The PACs listed in Table 9.4 gave millions of dollars to finance the campaigns of their potential allies in 2004.

Most PACs use their campaign contributions to acquire access and influence with decision makers. Corporate, trade, and professional PAC contributions go overwhelmingly to incumbents, regardless of party. Leaders of these PACs know that incumbents are rarely defeated, and they do not wish to antagonize even unsympathetic members of Congress by backing challengers. However, ideological and issue-oriented PACs are more likely to allocate funds according to the candidates' policy positions and voting records. Labor PACs give almost all of

---

Think Again

If a lobbyist makes a campaign contribution to a Congress member, hoping to gain support for a bill, is this a form of bribery?

bribery Giving or offering anything of value in an effort to influence government officials in the performance of their duties.

political action committees (PACs) Organizations that solicit and receive campaign contributions from corporations, unions, trade associations, and ideological and issue-oriented groups, and their members, and then distribute these funds to political candidates.

Table 9.4   The Big Money PACs in 2004

Rank	Organization	Total Amount	Dem Pct	Repub Pct
1	National Assn. of Realtors	$3,787,083	47%	52%
2	Laborers Union	$2,684,250	86	14
3	National Auto Dealers Assn.	$2,603,300	27	73
4	Intl. Brotherhood of Electrical Workers	$2,369,500	96	4
5	National Beer Wholesalers Assn.	$2,314,000	24	76
6	National Assn. of Home Builders	$2,201,500	33	67
7	Assn. of Trial Lawyers of America	$2,181,499	93	6
8	United Parcel Service	$2,142,679	28	72
9	American Medical Assn.	$2,092,425	21	79
10	United Auto Workers	$2,075,700	98	1
11	Carpenters & Joiners Union	$2,074,560	74	26
12	Credit Union National Assn.	$2,065,678	42	58
13	Service Employees International Union	$1,985,000	85	15
14	American Bankers Assn.	$1,978,013	36	64
15	SBC Communications	$1,955,116	35	65
16	Machinists/Aerospace Workers Union	$1,942,250	99	1
17	Teamsters Union	$1,917,413	88	11
18	American Hospital Assn.	$1,769,326	44	56
19	American Federation of Teachers	$1,717,372	97	3
20	Wal-Mart Stores	$1,677,000	22	78

Source: Reprinted by permission of Center for Responsive Politics.

EMILY's List
Political network for pro-choice Democratic women that raises early money for women candidates.
www.emilyslist.org

their contributions to Democrats. Ideological and issue-oriented PACs give money to challengers as well as incumbents; in recent years, these groups collectively favored Democrats as women's, environmental, abortion rights, and elderly groups proliferated. (See *Up Close:* "EMILY's List.") Business, trade and professional PACs usually split their contributions in order to ensure access to both Democrats and Republicans. But Republicans generally garner a larger share of the money from these PACs.

PAC money is less important in the Senate than in the House. PAC contributions account for about 35 percent of House campaign contributions; they account for only about 20 percent of Senate campaign contributions. Actually, PACs contribute more *dollars* to the average senator than to the average House member. But because Senate campaigns cost so much more than House campaigns, PAC contributions are *proportionally* less. Senators must rely more on individual contributions than House members do.

Payback   Representatives of organized interest groups say that their PAC contributions are designed to buy access—"a chance to talk"—with members of Congress, their staffs, and executives in the administration (see "What Do Contributors Buy?" in Chapter 8). Both interest groups and government officials usually deny that campaign contributions can "buy" support.

Nevertheless, the pattern of campaign contributions by major industries corresponds closely with the pattern of congressional voting on many key issues. Congress members who receive the largest PAC contributions from an industry group tend to vote in favor of that group's position. Congress members who oppose the industry's position generally receive far less (see *Up Close:* "Payback: Money and Medicare").

UP CLOSE

EMILY's List

Fund-raising is the greatest obstacle to mounting a successful campaign against an incumbent. And the most difficult problem facing challengers is raising money *early* in the campaign, when they have little name recognition and little or no standing in the polls.

EMILY's List is a politically adroit and effective effort to support liberal Democratic women candidates by infusing *early money* into their campaigns. EMILY stands for Early Money Is Like Yeast, because "it makes the dough rise." Early contributions provide the initial credibility that a candidate, especially a challenger, needs in order to solicit additional funds from individuals and organizations. EMILY is a fund-raising network of thousands of contributors, each of whom pays $100 to join and pledges to give at least $100 to two women from a list of candidates prepared by EMILY's leaders. Most of the contributors are professional women who appreciate EMILY's screening of pro-choice, liberal women candidates around the country.

EMILY's List was begun in 1985 by a wealthy heir to a founder of IBM, Ellen Malcolm. Women challengers for congressional races traditionally faced frustration in fund-raising. Incumbent male officeholders enjoyed a huge fund-raising advantage because contributors expected them to win and therefore opened their wallets to gain access and goodwill. EMILY's List has helped to overcome defeatism among both women candidates and contributors.

EMILY's List supports *only* Democratic women candidates who are strong supporters of abortion rights. When the list was founded, there were no women in the Senate and only a very few in the House. In 2006 there were thirteen women in the Senate (eleven supported by Emily's List) and forty-nine in the House (forty-three supported by Emily's list). EMILY's List currently boasts of more than 100,000 members; they have contributed more than $43 million dollars to pro-choice Democratic women.

Senator Barbara Milkulski, Democrat of Maryland and an early beneficiary of EMILY's List, at a news conference.

Lobbying the Bureaucracy

Lobbying does not cease after a law is passed. Rather, interest groups try to influence the implementation of the law. Interest groups know that bureaucrats exercise considerable discretion in policy implementation (see "Bureaucratic Power" in Chapter 12). Thus many interests spend as much as or more time and energy trying to influence executive agencies as they do Congress.

Lobbying the bureaucracy involves various types of activities, including monitoring regulatory agencies for notices of new rules and regulatory changes; providing reports, testimony, and evidence in administrative hearings; submitting contract and grant applications and lobbying for their acceptance; and monitoring the performance of executive agencies on behalf of group members.

Groups may try to influence the creation of a new agency to carry out the law or influence the assignment of implementation to an existing "friendly" agency. They may try to influence the selection of personnel to head the implementing agency. They may lobby the agency to devote more money and personnel to

UP CLOSE

Payback: Money and Medicare

After years of struggle, Congress finally passed a prescription drug benefit for Medicare recipients in 2003. The bill was one of the most heavily lobbied pieces of legislation in the Congress in many years. The House and Senate passed very different measures, and the conference committee required months of behind-the-scenes negotiations before sending the bill to both chambers for final passage.

The principal beneficiaries of the bill were supposed to be the nation's senior citizens. And indeed the AARP was heavily involved in every stage of the bill's progress. But the biggest campaign contributors, and arguably the biggest beneficiaries of the final bill, were the drug manufacturers, the health maintenance organizations (HMOs), and the insurance industry.

The House passed the final bill by a close vote of 220–215. An analysis of congressional voting on the bill shows that lawmakers who voted to approve the legislation received an average of roughly twice as much in campaign contributions from the drug companies, HMOs, and insurance companies, as those who voted against the bill.

Republicans controlled the House as well as the Senate, and Republicans were generally more favorable toward the positions taken by these industries. So it is no surprise that Republican Congress members on average received much larger contributions from these industries than Democrats, even Democrats who supported the industries' positions.

PAC Contributions and the Prescription Drug Vote in the House

| | Average Contributions 1990–2003 | |
	Supporters	Opponents
Drug manufacturers	$27,618	$11,308
HMOs	$11,582	$ 6,630
Health insurers	$19,510	$10,128

enforcement of the law (or less, depending on a group's preference). They may argue for strict rules and regulations—or loose interpretations of the law—by the implementing agencies. Lobbyists frequently appear at administrative hearings to offer information. They often undertake to sponsor test cases of administrative regulations on behalf of affected members. In short, lobbying extends throughout the government.[12]

Iron Triangles   In general, interest groups strive to maintain close working relationships with the departments and agencies that serve their members or regulate their industries. Conversely, bureaucracies seek to nourish relationships with powerful "client" groups that are capable of pressuring Congress to expand their authority and increase their budgets. Both bureaucracies and interest groups seek close working relationships with the congressional committees that exercise jurisdiction over their policy function. Finally, members of Congress seek the political and financial support of powerful interest groups, and members also seek to influence bureaucrats to favor supportive interest groups.

The mutual interests of congressional committee members, organized groups, and bureaucratic agencies come together to form what has been labeled the "iron triangles" of American government. **Iron triangles** refer to stable relationships among interest groups, congressional committees, and administrative agencies functioning in the same policy area. Each of the three sides of these triangles

iron triangles Mutually supportive relationships among interest groups, government agencies, and legislative committees with jurisdiction over a specific policy area.

Figure 9.3 Iron Triangles
The iron triangle approach provides a convenient way to look at the interrelationship among interest groups, executive agencies, and congressional committees. As this example shows, veterans' interest groups work closely with both the Department of Veterans Affairs (executive agency) and the House Veterans Affairs Committee.

depends on the support of the other two; their cooperation serves their own interests (see Figure 9.3).

In an iron triangle, bureaucracies, interest groups, and congressional committees "scratch each other's backs." Bureaucrats get political support from interest groups in their requests for expanded power and authority and increased budgetary allocations. Interest groups get favorable treatment of their members by the bureaucracy. Congressional committee members get political and financial support from interest groups, as well as favorable treatment for their constituents and contributors who are served or regulated by the bureaucracy.

Iron triangles are more likely to develop in specialized policy areas over which there is relatively little internal conflict. However, conflict, rather than cooperation, is more likely to characterize bureaucratic–congressional–interest-group relationships when powerful, diverse interests are at stake. For example, the Occupational Safety and Health Administration is caught between the demands of labor unions and industry groups. The U.S. Forest Service is caught between the demands of environmental groups and the lumber industry. The Environmental Protection Agency is pressured by environmental groups as well as by industry and agriculture. These kinds of conflicts break open the iron triangles or prevent them from forming in the first place.

Revolving Doors   It is not uncommon in Washington for people in a particular policy field to switch jobs, moving from a post in the government to a job in the private sector, or vice versa, or moving to different posts within the government. In one example, an individual might move from a job in a corporation (Pillsbury or General Mills) to the staff of an interest group (American Farm Bureau Federation), and then to the executive agency charged with implementing policy in the field (U.S. Department of Agriculture) or to the staff of a House or Senate committee with jurisdiction over the field (House Agricultural Committee or Senate Agriculture, Nutrition, and Forestry Committee). The common currency of moves within a network is both policy expertise and contacts within the field.

The term **revolving doors** is often used to criticize people who move from a government post (where they acquired experience, knowledge, and personal contacts) to a job in the private sector as a consultant, lobbyist, or salesperson. Defense contractors may recruit high-ranking military officers or Defense Department officials to help sell weapons to their former employers. Trade associations may recruit congressional staffers, White House staffers, or high-ranking

revolving doors The movement of individuals from government positions to jobs in the private sector, using the experience, knowledge, and contacts they acquired in government employment.

agency heads as lobbyists, or these people may leave government service to start their own lobbying firms. Attorneys from the Justice Department, the Internal Revenue Service, and federal regulatory agencies may be recruited by Washington law firms to represent clients in dealings with their former employers.

Former members of Congress are considered the most viable commodity a lobby firm can offer their clients. The Center for Responsive Politics reports that 125 to 150 former Congress members are lobbyists, many of them among the highest paid in the profession. When asked, lobbyists themselves, especially former members of Congress, acknowledge that their success depends mostly on "schmoozing" with their former colleagues.[13]

Concern about revolving doors centers not only on individuals cashing in on their knowledge, experience, and contacts obtained through government employment, but also on the possibility that some government officials will be tempted to tilt their decisions in favor of corporations, law firms, or interest groups that promise these officials well-paid jobs after they leave government employment.

The Ethics in Government Act limits postgovernment employment in an effort to reduce the potential for corruption. Former members of Congress are not permitted to lobby Congress for one year after leaving that body. Former employees of executive agencies are not permitted to lobby their agency for one year after leaving government service, and they are not permitted to lobby their agency for two years on any matter over which they had any responsibility while employed by the government.

Lobbying the Courts

litigation Legal dispute brought before a court.

Interest groups play an important role in influencing federal courts. Many of the key cases brought to the federal courts are initiated by interest groups. Indeed, **litigation** is becoming a favored instrument of interest-group politics. Groups that oppose a new law or an agency's action often challenge it in court as unconstitutional or as violating the law. Interest groups bring issues to the courts by (1) supplying the attorneys for individuals who are parties to a case; (2) bringing suits to the courts on behalf of classes of citizens; or (3) filing companion **amicus curiae** (literally "friend of the court") arguments in cases in which they are interested.

amicus curiae Person or group other than the defendant or the plaintiff or the prosecution that submits an argument in a case for the court's consideration.

The nation's most powerful interest groups all have legal divisions specializing in these techniques. The American Civil Liberties Union is one of the most active federal court litigants on behalf of criminal defendants (see *Up Close:* "Politics and the ACLU" in Chapter 14). The early civil rights strategy of the National Association for the Advancement of Colored People (NAACP) was directed by its Legal Defense and Education Fund under the leadership of Thurgood Marshall. The NAACP chose to sponsor a suit by Linda Brown against the Board of Education in her hometown—Topeka, Kansas—in order to win the historic 1954 desegregation decision.[14] NARAL Pro-Choice America is active in sponsoring legal challenges to abortion restrictions. The Environmental Defense Fund and the Natural Resources Defense Council specialize in environmental litigation.

The special rules of judicial decision making preclude direct lobbying of judges by interest groups (see "The Special Rules of Judicial Decision Making" in Chapter 13). Directly contacting federal judges about a case, letter writing, telephoning, and demonstrating outside of federal courtrooms are all considered inappropriate conduct. They inspire more resentment than support among federal judges. However, interest groups have been very active in direct lobbying of Congress over judicial appointments. Key interest groups supporting abortion rights—NARAL Pro-Choice America, People for the American Way, the National Organization for Women, and so on—have played a central role in confirmation battles (see *Up Close:* "The Confirmation of Clarence Thomas" in Chapter 13).

Politics as Interest-Group Conflict

Politics can be viewed as a struggle among interest groups over government policy. Interest groups, rather than individual citizens, can be viewed as the principal participants in American politics.

Pluralism as Democratic Politics   Pluralism (see Chapter 2) is the idea that democracy can be preserved in a large, complex society through individual membership in interest groups that compete, bargain, and compromise over government policy. Individuals are influential in politics only when they act as part of, or on behalf of, groups. (Only leaders of organizations participate directly in policy making.) The group becomes the essential bridge between the individual and the government. Pluralists argue that interest-group politics is a natural extension of the democratic ideals of popular participation in government, freedom of association, and competition over public policy.

Pluralism portrays public policy at any given time as the equilibrium reached in the struggle among interest groups to influence policy (see Figure 9.4). This equilibrium is determined by the relative influence of interest groups. Changes in the relative influence of any interest group can be expected to result in changes in public policy; policy will move in the direction desired by the groups gaining in influence and away from the desires of groups losing influence.

According to this view of political life, government plays a passive role, merely "refereeing" group struggles. Public policy at any given moment represents the "equilibrium" point of the group pressures—the balance of competing interests. The job of politicians is to function as brokers of group interests, arranging compromises and balancing interests.

Balancing Group Power   Pluralism assumes that compromises *can* be arranged and that interests *can* be balanced in relatively stable fashion. It assumes that no single interest will ever become so dominant that it can reject compromise and proceed to impose its will on the nation without regard for the interests of other people. This assumption is based on several beliefs. The first is that interest groups act as a check on each other and that a system of *countervailing*

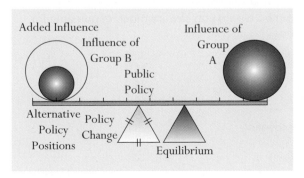

Figure 9.4 The Interest-Group Model

According to pluralist theorists, policy in a democracy is the result of various special-interest groups "reaching equilibrium"—arriving at a compromise position that requires all parties to give up something but gives all parties something they wanted.

power will protect the interests of all. For example, the power of big business will be checked by the countervailing power of big labor and big government.

A second belief is that *overlapping group membership* will tend to moderate the demands of particular groups and lead to compromise. Because no group can command the undivided loyalty of all its members, its demands will be less drastic and its leaders more amenable to compromise. If the leaders of any group go too far with their demands, those of its members who also belong to other groups endangered by these immoderate demands will balk.

A third belief is that radical programs and doctrinaire demands will be checked by the large, unorganized, but potentially significant *latent interest group* that is composed of all Americans who believe in toleration, compromise, and democratic processes.

Interest-Group Politics: How Democratic?   There are several problems with accepting pluralism as the legitimate heir to classic democratic theory. Democratic theory envisions public policy as the rational choice of *individuals* with equal influence who evaluate their needs and reach a majority decision with due regard for the rights of others. This traditional theory does not view public policy as a product of interest-group pressures. In fact, classic democratic theorists viewed interest groups and even political parties as intruders into an individualistic brand of citizenship and politics. Today critics of pluralism charge that interest groups dominate the political arena, monopolize access to governmental power, and thereby restrict individual participation rather than enhance it.

Another assumption of pluralism is that group membership enhances the individual's influence on policy. But only rarely are interest groups democratically governed. Individuals may provide the numerical strength for organizations, but interest groups are usually run by a small elite of officers and activists. Leaders of corporations, banks, labor unions, medical associations, and bar associations—whose views and agendas often differ from those of their memberships—remain in control year after year. Very few people attend meetings, vote in organizational elections, or make their influence felt within their organizations. Indeed, people believe that "special interest groups" are "what is wrong with government today" (see Table 9.5).

Finally, pluralists hope that the power of diverse institutions and organizations in society will roughly balance out and prevent the emergence of a power monopoly. Yet inequality of power among organizations is commonplace. Examples

---

Table 9.5   Public Views of Interest Groups

Among the following, which one or two would you say are most responsible for what is wrong with government today?

Special interest groups	38%
The media	29
Elected officials	24
Political parties	24
The public	14
Government employees	6
Other	8
Not sure	2

Source: As reported in *The Polling Report,* November 11, 2003.

A CONSTITUTIONAL NOTE

Controlling the Effects of Interest Groups

The Constitution's First Amendment includes a guarantee of "the right of the people to assemble and petition their government for redress of grievances." The Constitution, then, protects the formation of groups and their right to lobby in Washington on behalf of their own interests. Yet the Founders worried about "the mischiefs of faction," and James Madison defined a faction as "a number of citizens, whether amounting to a majority or minority of the whole, who are united and actuated by some common impulse of passion, or interests, adverse to the rights of other citizens, or the permanent and aggregate interests of the community." But Madison also understood that "the latent causes

of faction are thus sown in the nature of man." A faction could only be destroyed by destroying liberty itself, "by giving to every citizen the same opinions." According to Madison, a wiser and more practical approach would be to control the effects of faction by "first, the delegation of the government [in a republic] to a small number of citizens elected by the rest; secondly, the greater number of citizens and greater sphere of country over which [a republic] may be extended. The influence of factious leaders may kindle a flame within their particular States but will be unable to spread a general conflagration throughout the other States." Today, however, with national means of communication, interest groups are capable of doing exactly what Madison feared. They can mobilize mass opinion, intimidate elected representatives, and dominate the national political arena.

abound of narrow, organized interests achieving their goals at the expense of the broader, unorganized public. Furthermore, producer interests, bound together by economic ties, usually dominate less well-organized consumer groups and groups based on noneconomic interests. Special interests seeking governmental subsidies, payments, and "entitlements" regularly prevail over the broader yet unorganized interests of taxpayers.

> **Think Again**
>
> Is organized interest-group activity a cause of government gridlock?

Interest-Group Politics: Gridlock and Paralysis   Even if the pluralists are correct that the public interest is only the equilibrium of special-interest claims, some consensus among major interest groups is required if government is to function at all. Democracies require a sense of community and common purpose among the people. If the demands of special interests displace the public interest, government cannot function effectively. Uncompromising claims by conflicting special interests create policy *gridlock*. Yet if politicians try to placate every special interest, the result is confusing, contradictory, and muddled policy—or worse, no policy at all.

Interest-group paralysis and the resulting inability of government to act decisively to resolve national problems weaken popular confidence in government. "The function of government is to govern. A weak government, a government which lacks authority, fails to perform its function, is immoral in the same sense in which a corrupt judge, a cowardly soldier, or an ignorant teacher, is immoral."[15]

Over time, the continued buildup of special protections, privileges, and treatments in society results in "institutional sclerosis." Economist Mancur Olson argues that the accumulation of special interest subsidies, quotas, and protections leads to economic stagnation. Interest groups focus on gaining distributive advantages—a larger share of the pie for themselves—rather than on growth of the whole economy—a larger pie.[16] Major interest groups are more interested in winning income transfers to themselves through government action than in promoting the growth of national income. The more entrenched the interest-group system becomes, the slower the growth of the national economy.

Summary Notes

- Organizations concentrate power, and concentrated power prevails over diffused power. Interest groups are organizations that seek to influence government policy.

- The interest-group system supplements the electoral system as a form of representation. The electoral system is designed to respond to broad, majority preferences in geographically defined constituencies. The interest-group system represents narrower, minority interests in economic, professional, ideological, religious, racial, gender, and issue constituencies.

- Interest groups originated to protect economic interests, to advance social movements, to seek government benefits, and to respond to government activity. As government has expanded into more sectors of American life, more interest groups have formed to influence government policy.

- Washington lobbying groups represent a wide array of organized interests. But business, trade, and professional associations outnumber labor union, women's, public-interest, single-issue, and ideological groups.

- Interest-group formation has been aided in recent decades by entrepreneurs who create and build group memberships. They urge people to join organizations either by appealing to their sense of obligation or by providing an array of direct tangible benefits.

- Most organized groups are dominated by small groups of leaders and activists. Few groups are governed democratically; members who oppose the direction of the organization usually drop out rather than challenge the leadership. Group membership and especially group leadership overrepresent educated, upper-middle-class segments of the population.

- Lobbying activities include advertising and public relations, obtaining access to government officials, providing them with technical and political information, mobilizing constituents, building coalitions, organizing demonstrations, and providing campaign support. Bribery is illegal, and most lobbyists avoid exacting specific vote promises in exchange for campaign contributions.

- Organized political action committees (PACs) proliferated following the 1974 "reform" of campaign finance laws.

Most PAC money goes to incumbents; interest-group leaders know that incumbents are rarely defeated.

- The mutual interests of organized groups, congressional committees, and bureaucratic agencies sometimes come together to form "iron triangles" of mutual support and cooperation in specific policy areas. In many policy areas, loose "policy networks" emerge among people who share an interest and expertise—although not necessarily opinions—about a policy and are in regular contact with each other.

- The "revolving door" problem emerges when individuals use the knowledge, experience, and contacts obtained through government employment to secure high-paying jobs with corporations, law firms, lobbying and consulting firms, and interest groups doing business with their old agencies.

- Interest groups influence the nation's courts not only by providing financial and legal support for issues of concern to them but also by lobbying Congress over judicial appointments.

- Pluralism views interest-group activities as a form of democratic representation. According to the pluralists, public policy reflects the equilibrium of group influence and a reasonable approximation of society's preferences. Competition among groups, overlapping group memberships, and latent interest groups all combine to ensure that no single group dominates the system.

- Critics of pluralism warn that interest groups may monopolize power and restrict individual participation in politics rather than enhance it. They note that interest groups are not usually democratically governed, nor are their leaders or members representative of the general population. They warn that accommodation rather than competition may characterize group interaction and that narrow producer interests tend to achieve their goals at the expense of broader consumer (taxpayer) interests.

- The growing power of special interests, when combined with the declining power of parties and the fragmentation of government, may lead to gridlock and paralysis in policy making. The general public interest may be lost in the conflicting claims of special interests.

Key Terms

interest group   280
majoritarianism   280
organizational sclerosis   280
trade associations   285
public-interest groups   287
single-issue groups   287
ideological
   organizations   287
interest-group
   entrepreneurs   291
free-riders   291
lobbyist   292
lobbying   294
public relations   295
access   295
grass-roots lobbying   296
coalitions   298
bribery   299
political action committees
   (PACs)   299
iron triangles   302
revolving doors   303
litigation   304
amicus curiae   304

Suggested Readings

Berry, Jeffrey M. *The New Liberalism: The Rising Power of Citizen Groups*. Washington, D.C.: Brookings Institution Press, 1999. A description of the increasing number and activities of liberal interest groups in Washington and their success in defeating both business and conservative groups.

Cigler, Allan J., and Burdett A. Loomis, eds. *Interest Group Politics*. 6th ed. Washington, D.C.: CQ Press, 2002. A collection of essays examining interest-group politics.

Goldstein, Kenneth M. *Interest Groups, Lobbying and Participation in America*. New York: Cambridge University Press, 2003. When and why people join interest groups, how they are recruited, and how groups try to influence legislation.

Hernson, Paul S., Ronald G. Shaiko, and Clyde Wilcox. The *Interest Group Connection: Electioneering, Lobbying and Policy-making*. 2nd ed. Washington, D.C. CQ Press, 2004. Interest group activities in the electoral, legislative, judicial, and policy-making processes.

Lowi, Theodore J. *The End of Liberalism*. New York: Norton, 1969. The classic critique of "interest-group liberalism," describing how special interests contribute to the growth of government and the development of "clientism."

Olson, Mancur. *The Logic of Collective Action*. Cambridge, Mass.: Harvard University Press, 1965. A highly theoretical inquiry into the benefits and costs to individuals of joining groups and the obstacles (including the free-rider problem) to forming organized interest groups.

Olson, Mancur. *The Rise and Decline of Nations*. New Haven, Conn.: Yale University Press, 1982. Argues that, over time, the development of powerful special-interest lobbies has led to institutional sclerosis, inefficiency, and slowed economic growth.

Rozell, Mark J., Clyde Wilcox, and David Madland. *Interest Groups in American Campaigns*. Washington, D.C.: CQ Press, 2005. The role of interest groups in campaigns, including their adjustments to the Bipartisan Campaigns Reform Act of 2002 and the creation of "527s" to circumvent the act.

Wolpe, Bruce E., and Bertram J. Levine. *Lobbying Congress*. 2nd ed. Washington, D.C.: CQ Press, 1996. A practical guide to lobbying on Capitol Hill written by experienced lobbyists.

★ Make It Real

INTEREST GROUPS

This unit lets students represent an interest group and try to get their legislation passed.

Part Four

INSTITUTIONS

Price of Victory

ABCNEWS
Originally Aired: **March 15, 2005**
Program: **Nightline**
Running Time: **14:34**

It was meant to be a victory that could be savored all the way through the 2004 election. When the president signed the Medicare bill into law last December, it was a landmark event. This bill had managed to achieve what seniors had been demanding for years—prescription drug coverage. That's definitely something to celebrate. Well, a funny thing happened on the way to the bill's becoming law: accusations of bribery, lying, intimidation, political shenanigans—it has become quite a Washington drama. A bureaucrat who you probably wouldn't normally hear about testified on Capitol Hill. Richard Foster is the chief actuary of the Medicare program and he says that his boss threatened to fire him if he publicized his estimates of how much the Medicare bill would actually cost. His boss happens to be a political appointee. The bill that passed had a cost estimate of around $400 billion. Foster's estimate—$534 billion—became public a month after the signing of the bill. Needless to say, people are furious, including Republicans who now say if they knew then what they know now, they would not have voted for the bill.

Then there is the story of the endless vote in the House—a fifteen-minute roll call that stayed open for three hours. A lot of arm-twisting occurred that night, including allegations that retiring Congressman Nick Smith (R-Michigan) was told that if he voted for the bill his son would get $100,000 worth of help for his upcoming congressional race. Smith voted against the bill, but there is another investigation of this allegation.

There are some people who roll their eyes at the very thought of the congressional process. But this is a dramatic one. People are really emotional about it, as you will see in this program.

Critical Thinking Questions

1. In "Price of Victory," of what does Medicare actuary Richard Foster accuse the administration?

2. In the process of passing the 2003 Medicare bill, what was unusual in regard to the timing of the vote?

3. In "Price of Victory," of what does Representative Nick Smith accuse the House leadership?

4. Your text describes the process by which bills become laws. How does the process in the text differ from the process in the video?

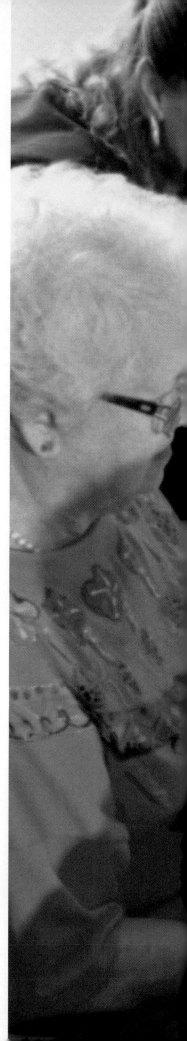

10 CONGRESS
Politics on Capitol Hill

Think About Politics

1 Should members of Congress be limited in the number of terms they can serve?
Yes ☐ No ☐

2 Should congressional districts be drawn to ensure that minorities win seats in Congress in rough proportion to their populations in the states?
Yes ☐ No ☐

3 Do Congress members spend too much time in their home districts seeking re-election?
Yes ☐ No ☐

4 Is the nation better served when the president and the majority in Congress are from the same party?
Yes ☐ No ☐

5 Is it ethical for Congress members to pay special attention to requests for assistance by people who make large campaign contributions?
Yes ☐ No ☐

6 Are there too many lawyers in Congress?
Yes ☐ No ☐

7 Are members of Congress obliged to vote the way their constituents wish, even if they personally disagree?
Yes ☐ No ☐

Who are the members of Congress? How did they get there, and how do they manage to stay there? How did Congress—the official institution for deciding who gets what in America—get its powers, and how does it use them?

The Powers of Congress

The Constitution gives very broad powers to Congress. "All legislative Powers herein granted shall be vested in a Congress of the United States, which shall consist of a Senate and House of Representatives." *The nation's Founders envisioned Congress as the first and most powerful branch of government.* They equated national powers with the powers of Congress and gave Congress the most clearly specified role in national government.

Article I empowers Congress to levy taxes, borrow and spend money, regulate interstate commerce, establish a national money supply, establish a post office, declare war, raise and support an army and navy, establish a court system, and pass all laws "necessary and proper" to implement these powers. Congress may also propose amendments to the Constitution or (with a two-thirds vote of both the House and the Senate) admit new states. In the event that no presidential candidate receives a majority of votes in the Electoral College, the House of Representatives selects the president. The Senate has two additional powers: It is called on for advice and consent to treaties, and it confirms presidential nominations to executive and judicial posts. The House has the power to impeach, and the Senate to try any officer of the U.S. government, including the president. Each **congressional session** convenes on January 3 following congressional elections in November of even-numbered years.

Institutional Conflict Over two centuries, the three separate branches of the national government—the Congress, the presidency and the executive branch, and the Supreme Court and federal judiciary—have struggled for power and preeminence in governing. This struggle for power among the separate institutions is precisely what the Founders envisioned. In writing the Constitution, they sought to create "opposite and rival interests" among the separate branches of the national government. "The constant aim," explained Madison, "is to divide and arrange the several offices in such a manner as that each may be a check on the other"[1] (see Appendix, *Federalist Papers*, No. 51). From time to time, first the Congress, then the presidency, and occasionally the Supreme Court have appeared to become the most powerful branch of government.

congressional session Each Congress elected in November of even-numbered years meets the following January 3 and remains in session for two years. Since the first Congress to meet under the Constitution in 1789, Congresses have been numbered by session (for example, 107th Congress 2001–2003, 108th Congress 2003–2005, 109th Congress 2005–2007).

U.S. House of Representatives
Official Web site of the House, with schedule of floor and committee actions, legislative information, and links to every Representative's Web site and every committee Web site.
www.house.gov

bicameral Any legislative body that consists of two separate chambers or houses; in the United States, the Senate represents 50 statewide voter constituencies, and the House of Representatives represents voters in 435 separate districts.

"The President Initiates, Congress Deliberates"   Throughout much of the twentieth century, Congress ceded leadership in national policy making to the president and the executive branch. Congress largely responded to the policy initiatives and spending requests originating from the president, executive agencies, and interest groups. Congress did not merely ratify or "rubber-stamp" these initiatives and requests; it played an independent role in the policymaking process. But this role was essentially a deliberative one, in which Congress accepted, modified, amended, or rejected the policies and budget requests initiated by others.

It is easier for the Congress to obstruct the policy initiatives of the president than it is to assume policy leadership itself. Congress can defeat presidential policy proposals, deny presidential budget requests, delay or reject presidential appointments, investigate executive agencies, hold committee hearings to spotlight improprieties, and generally immobilize the executive branch. It can investigate and question nominees for the Supreme Court and the federal judiciary; it can legislate changes in the jurisdiction of the federal courts; and it can try to reverse court decisions by amending laws or the Constitution itself. The Congress can even threaten to impeach the president or federal judges. But these are largely reactive, obstructionist actions, usually accompanied by a great deal of oratory.

Dividing Congressional Power: House and Senate   Congress must not only share national power with the executive and judicial branches of government; it must also share power within itself. The framers of the Constitution took the advice of the nation's eldest diplomat, Benjamin Franklin: "It is not enough that your legislature should be numerous; it should also be divided. . . . One division should watch over and control the other, supply its wants, correct its blunders, and cross its designs, should they be criminal or erroneous."[2] Accordingly, the U.S. Congress is **bicameral**—composed of two houses (see Figure 10.1).

No law can be passed and no money can be spent unless both the House of Representatives and the Senate pass identical laws. Yet the House and the Senate have very different constituencies and terms. The House consists of 435 voting members, elected from districts within each state apportioned on the basis of equal population. (The average congressional district since the 2000 census has a population of about 650,000; the House also includes nonvoting delegates from Puerto Rico, the District of Columbia, Guam, the Virgin Islands, and American Samoa.) All House members face election every two years. The Senate consists of 100 members serving six-year terms, elected by statewide constituencies. Senate terms are staggered so that one-third of senators are elected every two years (see Table 10.1).

The House of Representatives, with its two-year terms, was designed to be more responsive to the popular mood. Representatives are fond of referring to their chamber as "the people's House," and the Constitution requires that all revenue-raising bills originate in the House. The Senate was designed to be a smaller, more deliberative body, with its members serving six-year terms. Indeed, the Senate is the more prestigious body. House members frequently give up their seats to run for the Senate; the reverse has seldom occurred. Moreover, the Senate exercises certain powers not given to the House: the power to ratify treaties and the power to confirm federal judges, ambassadors, cabinet members, and other high executive officials.

Domestic versus Foreign and Defense Policy   Congress is more powerful in domestic than in foreign and military affairs. It is freer to reject presidential initiatives in domestic policy areas such as welfare, health, education, the envi-

HOUSE OF REPRESENTATIVES   SENATE

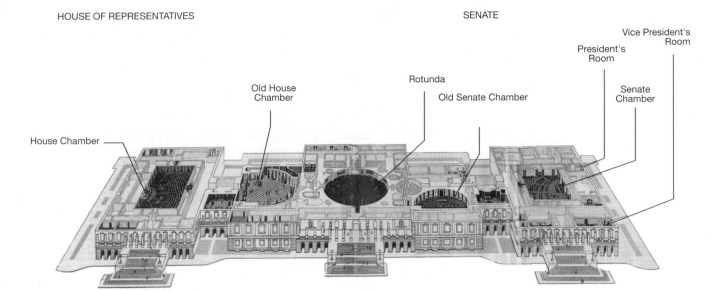

Figure 10.1   Corridors of Power in Congress
The architecture and floor plan of the Capitol Building in Washington reflect the
bicameral division of Congress, with one wing for the House of Representatives
and one for the Senate.

ronment, and taxation. But Congress usually follows presidential leadership in
foreign and defense policy even though constitutionally the president and
Congress share power in these arenas. The president is "Commander-in-Chief" of
the armed forces, but only Congress can "declare war." The president appoints
and receives ambassadors and "makes treaties," but the Senate must confirm
appointments and provide "advice and consent" to treaties. Historically presidents have led the nation in matters of war and peace.

U.S. Senate
Official Senate Web
site, with floor and
committee schedules, Senate
news, and links to each
Senator's Web site.
www.senate.gov

Table 10.1   Comparing the House and Senate

	House of Representatives	**Senate**
Terms	Two years	Six years
Members	435	100
Elections	All every two years	One-third every two years
Constituencies	Congressional districts	States
Unique powers	Originate tax bills Bring impeachment charges	Advise and consent to (ratify) treaties by two-thirds vote Confirm appointments Try impeachment charges
Debate on bills	Limited by Rules Committee	Unlimited, except by unanimous consent or vote of cloture (three-fifths)

Member prestige	Modest; smaller personal staffs, fewer
	  committee assignments
		High: larger personal staffs, more committee
		  assignments, always addressed as "Senator"

Leadership	Hierarchical, with speaker, majority and
	  minority leaders and whips and
	  committees, especially Rules, concen-
	  trating power
		Less hierarchical, with each senator exercising
		  more influence on leadership, committees,
		  and floor votes

Committees	Twenty standing and select committees Each member on about five committees Difficult to bypass	Twenty standing and select committees Each member on about seven committees Easier to bypass

The Vietnam experience inspired Congress to try to reassert its powers over war and peace. Military embarrassment, prolonged and indecisive fighting, and accumulating casualties—all vividly displayed on national television—encouraged Congress to challenge presidential war-making power. The War Powers Resolution of 1973, passed over the veto of President Richard Nixon, who was weakened by the Watergate scandal, sought to curtail the president's power to commit U.S. military forces to combat (see "Commander-in-Chief" in Chapter 11). But this legislation has not proven effective, and both Republican and Democratic presidents have continued to exercise war-making powers.

power of the purse
Congress's exclusive constitutional power to authorize expenditures by all agencies of the federal government.

The Power of the Purse Congress's real power in both domestic and foreign (defense) policy centers on its **power of the purse**—its power over federal taxing and spending. Only Congress can "lay and collect Taxes, Duties, Imposts and Excises" (Article I, Section 8), and only Congress can authorize spending: "No Money shall be drawn from the Treasury, but in Consequence of Appropriations made by Law" (Article I, Section 9).

Congress jealously guards these powers. Presidents initiate taxing and spending policies by sending their budgets to the Congress each year (see "The Budgetary Process" in Chapter 12 for details). But Congress has the last word on taxing and spending. The most important bills that Congress considers each year are usually the budget resolutions setting ceilings on various categories of expenditures and the later appropriations bills authorizing specific expenditures. It is often in these appropriations bills that Congress exercises its greatest influence over national policy. Thus, for example, the Congress's involvement in foreign affairs centers on its annual consideration of appropriations for foreign aid, its involvement in military affairs centers on its annual deliberations over the defense appropriations bill, and so on.

oversight Congressional monitoring of the activities of executive branch agencies to determine if the laws are being faithfully executed.

Oversight of the Bureaucracy Congressional **oversight** of the federal bureaucracy is a continuing process by which Congress reviews the activities of the executive branch. The *formal* rationale of oversight is to determine whether the purposes of laws passed by Congress are being achieved by executive agencies and whether appropriations established by Congress are being spent as intended. Often the *real* purpose is to influence executive branch decisions, secure favorable treatment for friends and constituents, embarrass presidential appointees, undercut political support for particular programs or agencies, lay the political groundwork for budgetary increases or decreases for an agency, or simply enhance the power of congressional committees and subcommittees and those who chair them.

Oversight is carried out primarily through congressional committees and subcommittees. Individual senators and representatives can engage in a form of oversight simply by writing or calling executive agencies, but committees and their staffs carry on the bulk of oversight activity. Because committees and subcommittees specialize in particular areas of policy making, each tends to focus its oversight activities on particular executive departments and agencies. Oversight is particularly intense during budget hearings. Subcommittees of both the House and the Senate Appropriations Committees are especially interested in how money is being spent by the agencies they oversee.

advice and consent The constitutional power of the U.S. Senate to reject or ratify (by a two-thirds vote) treaties made by the president.

Senate Advice and Consent and Confirmation of Presidential Appointments The Constitution provides that the president must obtain the **advice and consent** of the Senate for treaties "provided that two-thirds of the Senators present concur." In fact, the Senate has seldom provided "advice" to the

Senate committee confirmation hearings provide an opportunity for senators to lecture presidential nominees about how they should perform their jobs. The Senate must vote to confirm high executive branch nominees, including the Federal Reserve Board Chairman, Ben Bernanke, shown here testifying in 2005.

president regarding treaties prior to their submission to the Senate for "consent." The president enjoys a high degree of autonomy over U.S. foreign policy (see "Global Leader" in Chapter 11). The process of treaty ratification begins when a president submits an already negotiated treaty to the Senate. Once submitted, treaties are automatically referred to the Senate Foreign Relations Committee. That Committee cannot make changes in the treaty itself; it can either reject the treaty or forward it to the full Senate. The Senate itself cannot make changes in the formal treaty but must accept or reject it. Ratification requires a two-thirds vote. The Senate can, however, express its reservations to a treaty and/or instruct the president how the treaty is to be interpreted.[3]

The Senate also exercises a special power over the president and the executive branch of government through its constitutional responsibility for approving presidential appointments of key executive officers, including Cabinet members, ambassadors, and other high officials (see "Congressional Constraints on the Bureaucracy" in Chapter 12). And the Senate exercises a special power over the judicial branch through its constitutional responsibility for the **confirmation** of presidential appointments to the federal judiciary including the Supreme Court (see "The Politics of Selecting Judges" in Chapter 13).

confirmation The constitutionally required consent of the Senate to appointments of high-level executive officials by the president and appointments of federal judges.

Agenda Setting and Media Attention

Congressional hearings and investigations often involve agenda setting—bringing issues to the public's attention and placing them on the national agenda. For agenda-setting purposes, congressional committees or subcommittees need the assistance of the media. Televised hearings and investigations are perhaps the most effective means by which Congress can attract attention to issues as well as to itself and its members.

Hearings and investigations are similar in some ways, but hearings are usually held on a specific bill in order to build a record of both technical information (what is the problem and how legislation might be crafted to resolve it) and political information (who favors and who opposes various legislative options).

congressional hearings Congressional committee sessions in which members listen to witnesses who provide information and opinions on matters of interest to the committee, including pending legislation.

congressional investigation
Congressional committee hearings on alleged misdeeds or scandals.

In contrast, investigations are held on alleged misdeeds or scandals. Although the U.S. Supreme Court has held that there must be some "legislative purpose" behind a **congressional investigation**, that phrase has been interpreted very broadly indeed.[4]

The *formal* rationale for congressional investigations is that Congress is seeking information to assist in its lawmaking function. But from the earliest Congress to the present, the investigating powers of Congress have often been used for political purposes: to rally popular support for policies or programs favored by Congress; to attack the president, other high officials in the administration, or presidential policies or programs; to focus media attention and public debate on particular issues; or simply to win media coverage and popular recognition for members of Congress.

Congressional investigators have the legal power to subpoena witnesses (force them to appear), administer oaths, compel testimony, and initiate criminal charges for contempt (refusing to cooperate) and perjury (lying). These powers can be exercised by Congress's regular committees and subcommittees and by committees appointed especially to conduct a particular investigation.

Congress cannot impose criminal punishments as a result of its investigations. But the information uncovered in a congressional investigation can be turned over to the U.S. Department of Justice, which may proceed with its own criminal investigation and perhaps indictment and trial of alleged wrongdoers in federal courts.

Congressional investigations have long been used as an opportunity for Congress to expose wrongdoing on the part of executive branch officials. The first congressional investigation (1792) examined why General Arthur St. Clair had been defeated by the Indians in Ohio; the Crédit Mobilier investigations (1872–73) revealed scandals in the Grant administration; the Select Committee on Campaign Practices, known universally as the "Watergate Committee," exposed the activities of President Richard Nixon's inner circle that led to impeachment charges and Nixon's forced resignation; a House and Senate Joint Select Committee conducted the Iran-Contra investigation in the Reagan Administration; the Senate Special Whitewater Committee investigated matters related to Bill and Hillary Clinton's real estate investments in Arkansas.

Impeachment and Removal Potentially Congress's most formidable power is that of impeaching and removing from office the president, other officers of the United States, and federal judges, including Supreme Court justices. Congress can do so only for "Treason, Bribery or other High Crimes and Misdemeanors." The House of Representatives has the sole authority to bring charges of impeachment, by a simple majority vote. Impeachment is analogous to a criminal indictment; it does not remove an officer but merely subjects him or her to trial by the Senate. Only the Senate, following a trial, can remove the federal official from office, and then only by a two-thirds vote.

Bill Clinton is the second president in the nation's history to be impeached by the U.S. House of Representatives. (Andrew Johnson was the first in 1867; after a one-month trial in the Senate, the "guilty" vote fell one short of two-thirds needed for removal. President Richard Nixon resigned just prior to an impending impeachment vote in 1974.) The 1998 House impeachment vote split along partisan lines, with Republicans voting "yes" and Democrats voting "no." Two Articles of Impeachment were passed, one for perjury before a grand jury and one for obstruction of justice. In the subsequent Senate trial, only 45 senators (less than a majority and far less than the needed two-thirds) voted to convict

President Clinton on the first charge, and only 50 voted to convict on the second (see *Up Close:* "Sex, Lies, and Impeachment" in Chapter 11).

Congressional Apportionment and Redistricting

The Constitution states that "Representatives . . . shall be apportioned among the several states . . . according to their respective Numbers." It orders an "actual enumeration" (census) every ten years. And it provides that every state shall have at least one representative, in addition to two senators, regardless of population. But the Constitution is silent on the size of the House of Representatives. Congress itself determines its own size; for more than a century, it allowed itself to grow to accommodate new states and population growth. In 1910 it fixed the membership of the House at 435.

The effect of doing so has been to expand the population of House districts over the years. Following the 2000 census, House districts have populations of about 650,000. It is sometimes argued that such large House constituencies prevent meaningful communication between citizens and their representatives. (The Framers originally envisioned House districts of no more than 30,000 people.) But expanding the size of the House would complicate its work, reduce the influence of individual members, require more procedural controls, and probably strengthen the power of party leaders.

Apportionment   Apportionment refers to the allocation of House seats to the states after each ten-year census. The Constitution does not specify a mathematical method of apportionment; Congress adopted a complex "method of equal proportion" in 1929, which so far has withstood court challenges (see *Across the USA:* "Reapportionment, 2000," which shows the current apportionment, together with the states that gained and lost seats after the 2000 census).

Malapportionment   Historically, state legislatures were notorious for their **malapportionment**—congressional (and state legislative) districts with grossly unequal numbers of people. Some congressional districts had twice the average number of people per district, and others had only half as many. In a district twice the size of the average district, the value of an individual's vote was heavily diluted. In a district half the size of the average, the value of an individual's vote was greatly magnified.

Enter the Supreme Court   Prior to 1962, the Supreme Court refused to intervene in apportionment, holding that this question belonged to the state legislatures and that the federal courts should avoid this "political thicket." So the Supreme Court's decision in the landmark case *Baker v. Carr* (1962) came as a surprise. The Court ruled that inequalities in voters' influence resulting from different-size districts violated the Equal Protection Clause of the Fourteenth Amendment. The case dealt with a complaint about Tennessee's state legislative districts, but the Court soon extended its holding to congressional districts as well.[5] "The conception of political equality from the Declaration of Independence to Lincoln's Gettysburg Address, to the Fourteenth, Fifteenth, Seventeenth, and Nineteenth Amendments, can mean only one thing—one person, one vote."[6]

The shift in the Supreme Court's policy raised a new question: How equal must districts be in order to guarantee voters "equal protection of the law"? The

---

— Think Again —

Should congressional districts be drawn to ensure that minorities win seats in Congress in rough proportion to their populations in the states?

---

apportionment The allocation of legislative seats to jurisdictions based on population. Seats in the U.S. House of Representatives are apportioned to the states on the basis of their population after every ten-year census.

malapportionment Unequal numbers of people in legislative districts resulting in inequality of voter representation.

ACROSS THE USA

Reapportionment, 2000

Since 1910, the number of seats in the House of Representatives has remained constant at 435. Each ten-year census requires a reapportionment of seats among states based on their populations. States with rapid population growth such as Arizona, Texas, Georgia, and Florida gain seats (each of these states gained two seats following the 2000 census). States with slow population growth lose seats (New York and Pennsylvania both lost two seats). The newly apportioned House convened in January 2003.

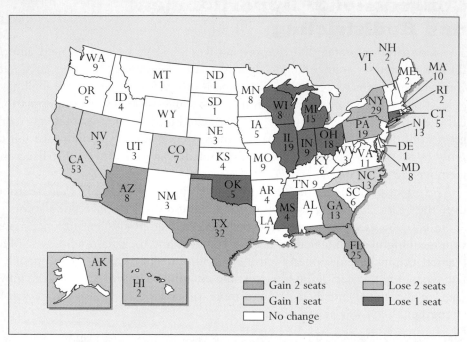

courts have ruled that only official U.S. Bureau of the Census figures may be used: estimated changes since the last census may *not* be used. In recent years, the courts have insisted on nearly exact mathematical equality in populations in congressional districts in a state.

"Enumeration"   The U.S. Constitution is very specific in its wording: It calls for an "actual Enumeration" (Article I, Section 2) of the population in each ten-year census. However, the U.S. Bureau of the Census has considered the use of samples and estimates to correct what it perceives to be "undercounts." Undercounting is said to occur when certain populations are difficult to identify and count on an individual basis, populations such as recent non-English-speaking immigrants or residents of neighborhoods likely to mistake government census takers for law enforcement officers or other unwelcome government officials. Political leaders (usually Democrats) of states and cities with large immigrant and minority populations have favored the substitution of samples and estimates for actual head counts. However, the U.S. Supreme Court held in 1999 that the Census Act of 1976 prohibits sampling for purposes of apportioning House members among the states.[7] Congress may use sampling for determining the allocation of grant-in-aid funds if it wishes.

redistricting Drawing of legislative district boundary lines following each ten-year census.

Redistricting   Redistricting refers to the drawing of boundary lines of congressional districts following the census. After each census, some states gain and others lose seats, depending on whether their populations have grown faster or slower than the nation's population. In addition, population shifts within a state

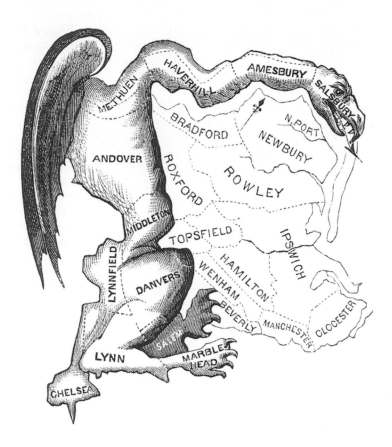

Figure 10.2 The Original Gerrymander

The term *gerrymander* immortalizes Governor Elbridge Gerry (1744–1814) of Massachusetts, who in 1811 redistricted the state legislature to favor Democrats over Federalists. A district north of Boston was designed to concentrate, and thus "waste," Federalist votes. This political cartoon from the *Boston Gazette,* March 26, 1812, depicted the new district lines as a salamander, dubbing the process the "gerrymander."

may force districting changes. Congressional district boundaries are drawn by state legislatures in each state; a state's redistricting act must pass both houses of the state legislature and win the governor's signature (or be passed over a gubernatorial veto). The U.S. Justice Department and the federal judiciary are also deeply involved in redistricting issues, particularly questions of whether or not redistricting disadvantages African Americans or other minorities.

Gerrymandering   Gerrymandering is the drawing of district lines for political advantage (see Figure 10.2). The population of districts may be equal, yet the district boundaries are drawn in such a fashion as to grant advantage or disadvantage to specific groups of voters. Gerrymandering has long been used by parties in control of the state legislatures to maximize their seats in Congress and state legislatures.

Gerrymandering, with the aid of sophisticated computer-mapping programs and data on past voting records of precincts, is a highly technical task. But consider a simple example where a city is entitled to three representatives and the eastern third of the city is Republican but the western two-thirds is Democratic (see Figure 10.3). If the Republicans could draw the district lines, they might draw them along a north-south direction to allow their party to win in one of the three districts. In contrast, if Democrats could draw the district lines, they might draw them along an east-west direction to allow their party to win all three districts by diluting the Republican vote. Such dividing up and diluting of a strong minority to deny it the power to elect a representative is called **splintering**. Often gerrymandering is not as neat as our example; district lines may twist and turn, creating grotesque patterns in order to achieve the desired effects. Another

gerrymandering Drawing district boundary lines for political advantage.

splintering Redistricting in which a strong minority is divided up and diluted to prevent it from electing a representative.

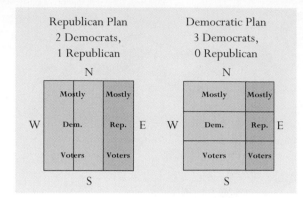

Republican Plan
2 Democrats,
1 Republican

Democratic Plan
3 Democrats,
0 Republican

Figure 10.3
Gerrymandering
in Action
Depending on how an area
is divided into districts, the
result may benefit one party
or the other. In this
example, dividing the area
so one district has virtually
all the Republicans gives
that party a victory in that
district while ceding the
other two districts to the
Democrats. In contrast,
Democrats benefit when
Republican voters are
divided among the three
districts so that their votes
are splintered.

packing Redistricting in
which partisan voters are
concentrated in a single
district, "wasting" their
majority vote and allowing
the opposition to win by
modest majorities in other
districts.

gerrymandering strategy—**packing**—is the heavy concentration of one party's
voters in a single district in order to "waste" their votes and allow modest majorities of the party doing the redistricting to win in other districts.

Partisan Gerrymandering   Partisan gerrymandering does not violate federal
court standards for "equal protection" under the Fourteenth Amendment. There is
no constitutional obligation to allocate seats "to the contending parties in proportion to what their anticipated statewide vote will be."[8] For several years the
Supreme Court threatened to intervene to correct partisan gerrymandering,[9] but
in 2004 it finally decided that the issue was "nonjusticiable"—there were no "judicially manageable standards for adjudicating [party] claims." The Court decided
that "'Fairness' is not a judicially manageable standard."[10] Parties are free to try to
advantage themselves in redistricting.

Reredistricting   The redrawing of congressional districts usually occurs after
each ten-year census. However, several states have been embroiled in a second
round of redistricting, notably Texas. (If one party dominated a state legislature
during the first redistricting after the census and drew district lines in a partisan
fashion, there is then a strong temptation for the opposition party to undertake a
second round of partisan redistricting if it subsequently wins control of the state
legislature.) It is theoretically possible that redistricting could be undertaken
every time a state legislature changes party control.

In a controversial case, the Supreme Court upheld the practice of reredistricting.
After a protracted partisan struggle in 2003, a new Republican majority in the
Texas Legislature redrew congressional boundaries that had been drawn by a
Democratic-controlled legislature after the 2000 Census. The result was a significant increase in Republican congressional seats and a corresponding decrease in
Democratic seats in that state. But the Supreme Court declined to intervene: "Neither the Constitution nor Congress has stated any explicit prohibition on mid-decade redistricting to change districts drawn earlier in conformance with a
decennial census.[11] And the Court approved of mid-decade redistricting when racial
or ethnic groups appeared to have been disadvantaged by earlier redistricting.

Incumbent Gerrymandering   Yet another problem confronting state legislatures in redistricting is the preservation of incumbent Congress members, that is, **incumbent gerrymandering**. Incumbents generally have sufficient political clout with their state parties to inspire efforts in the legislature to protect their districts.

Incumbent gerrymandering means drawing district lines in such a way as to ensure that districts of incumbents include enough supporters of their party to provide a high probability of their reelection. But often ensuring incumbents' security and maximizing the party's total number of seats are conflicting goals. It is not always possible to redraw district lines in such a way as to protect incumbents and at the same time ensure the largest number of party seats in a state. Incumbents themselves want the largest number of their party's voters packed in their district. But this tactic may result in losses for their party in other districts that have been robbed of party voters. Redistricting almost always confronts incumbents with new voters—voters who were previously in a different incumbent's district. As a result, incumbents usually have a somewhat more difficult reelection campaign following redistricting than in other elections.[12]

Racial Gerrymandering   Racial gerrymandering to disadvantage African Americans and other minorities violates both the Equal Protection Clause of the Fourteenth Amendment and the Voting Rights Act of 1965. The Voting Rights Act specifies that redistricting in states with a history of voter discrimination or low voter participation must be "cleared" in advance with the U.S. Justice Department. The act extends special protection not only to African American voters but also to Hispanic, Native American, Alaska Native, and Asian voters.

In 1982 Congress strengthened the Voting Rights Act by outlawing any electoral arrangement that has the effect of weakening minority voting power. This *effects test* replaced the earlier *intent test*, under which redistricting was outlawed only if boundaries were intentionally drawn to dilute minority political influence. In *Thornburg v. Gingles* (1986), the Supreme Court interpreted the effects test to require state legislatures to redistrict their states in a way that maximizes minority representation in Congress and the state legislatures.[13] The effect of this ruling was to require **affirmative racial gerrymandering**—the creation of predominantly African American and minority districts (labeled "majority-minority" districts) whenever possible. Following the 1990 census, redistricting in legislatures in states with large minority populations was closely scrutinized by the U.S. Justice Department and the federal courts. The result was a dramatic increase in African American and Hispanic representation in Congress (see Figure 10.7 later in this chapter).

However, the Supreme Court later expressed constitutional doubts about bizarre-shaped districts based *solely* on racial composition. In a controversial 5 to 4 decision in *Shaw v. Reno* (1993), Justice Sandra Day O'Connor wrote, "Racial gerrymandering, even for remedial purposes, may balkanize us into competing racial factions. . . . A reapportionment plan that includes in one district individuals who have little in common with one another but the color of their skin bears an uncomfortable resemblance to political apartheid"[14] (see Figure 10.4). Later the Court held that the use of race as the "predominant factor" in drawing district lines is unconstitutional: "When the state assigns voters on the basis of race, it engages in the offensive and demeaning assumption that voters of a particular race, because of their race, think alike, share the same political interests and will prefer the same candidates at the polls."[15] But the Court has stopped short of saying that *all* race-conscious districting is unconstitutional.

incumbent gerrymandering
Drawing legislative district boundaries to advantage incumbent legislators.

affirmative racial gerrymandering Drawing district boundary lines to maximize minority representation.

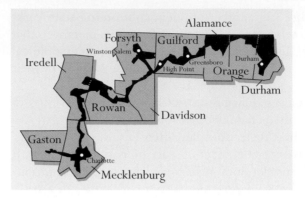

Figure 10.4 Affirmative Racial Gerrymandering
North Carolina's Twelfth Congressional District was drawn up to be a "majority-minority" district by combining African American communities over a wide region of the state. The U.S. Supreme Court in *Shaw v. Reno* (1993) ordered a court review of this district to determine whether it incorporated any common interest other than race. The North Carolina legislature redrew the district in 1997, lowering its black population from 57 to 46 percent, yet keeping its lengthy connection of black voters from Charlotte to Greensboro.

Partisanship Interacts with Race   Racial gerrymandering appears to help Republican congressional candidates. If African American voters are concentrated in heavily black districts, the effect is to "bleach" surrounding districts of Democratic-leaning black voters and thus improve the chances for Republican victories. Republican Party congressional gains in the South during the 1990s may be partly attributed to racial gerrymandering.[16] In what has been described as a "paradox of representation," the creation of majority-minority districts brought more minority members to Congress, but it also led to a more conservative House of Representatives, as Republicans gained seats previously held by white liberal Democrats.[17]

Republican-led efforts to "pack" black (Democratic) voters into relatively few districts suffered a setback in 2003 when the U.S. Supreme Court recognized that doing so might diminish the power of African American voters overall. The Court approved of a plan that "unpacked" some heavily concentrated majority-minority districts in Georgia. The Court reasoned that the result would be to create additional black "influence" districts where African American voters would not be in a majority but would be a large influential voting bloc.[18]

Getting to Capitol Hill

Members of Congress are independent political entrepreneurs—selling themselves, their services, and their personal policy views to the voters in 435 House districts and 50 states across the country. They initiate their own candidacies, raise most of their campaign funds from individual contributors, put together personal campaign organizations, and get themselves elected with relatively little help from their party. Their reelection campaigns depend on their ability to raise funds from individuals and interest groups and on the services and other benefits they provide to their constituents.

Every two years all House members and one-third of the Senate face reelection. Here Democratic House Minority Leader Nancy Pelosi (D-CA) and Representative Marty Meehan (D-MA) share a joke during a meeting at Pelosi's Capitol Hill office.

Who Runs for Congress?   Members of Congress come from a wide variety of backgrounds, ranging from acting and professional sports to medicine and the ministry. However, exceptionally high percentages of senators and representatives have prior experience in at least one of three fields—law, business, or public service (see Table 10.2). Members of Congress are increasingly career politicians, people who decided early in life to devote themselves to running for and occupying public office.[19] The many lawyers, by and large, are *not* practicing attorneys. Rather, the typical lawyer-legislator is a political activist with a law degree. These are people who graduated from law school and immediately sought public jobs— as federal or state prosecuting attorneys, as attorneys for federal or state agencies, or as staff assistants in congressional, state, or city offices. They used their early job experiences to make political contacts and learn how to organize a political campaign, find financial contributors, and deal with the media. Another group of Congress members are former businesspeople—not employees of large corporations, but people whose personal or family businesses brought them into close contact with government and their local community, in real estate, insurance, franchise dealerships, community banks, and so forth.

Competition for Seats   Careerism in Congress is aided by the electoral advantages enjoyed by incumbents over challengers. Greater name recognition, advantages in raising campaign funds, and the resources of congressional offices all combine to limit competition for seats in Congress and to reelect the vast majority of incumbents (see "The Advantages of Incumbency" in Chapter 8). The result is an incumbent reelection percentage for House members that usually exceeds 90 percent. The average reelection rate for U.S. senators is more than 80 percent (see Figure 10.5).

   Aspirants for congressional careers are well advised to wait for open seats. **Open seats** in the House of Representatives are created when incumbents retire or vacate the seat to run for higher office. These opportunities occur on average in about 10 percent of House seats in each election. But every ten years reapportionment creates many new opportunities to win election to Congress. Reappor-

—Think Again—
Are there too many lawyers in Congress?

Roll Call
www   This online magazine covers a variety of current topics about Congress but is especially strong on stories dealing with running for Congress and/or campaign financing. *www.rollcall.com*

open seat Seat in a legislature for which no incumbent is running for reelection.

Table 10.2 Backgrounds of Congress Members

Occupations

Many members cite more than one occupation. Members are especially likely to cite previous public service jobs as their principal occupation. (This is especially true for Democrats.) Traditionally, lawyers predominated, and they may still do so because many lawyers prefer to claim public service as their occupation. But as far as self-identification is concerned, public service prevails. Businessmen have a slight advantage over lawyers. An increasing number of congress members are coming from education.

	Total
Public service	254
Business	245
Law	242
Education	104
Real estate	42
Agriculture	34
Medicine	20
Journalism	18
Labor/blue collar	12
Law enforcement	9

Religion

Catholics have long been the single largest religious group in Congress. But all Protestants combined—Baptists, Methodists, Presbyterians, Episcopalians, Lutherans, and others—make up a solid majority. Jews comprise about 10 percent of the Congress.

Roman Catholics	153
Baptists	72
Methodists	62
Presbyterians	50
Episcopalians	42
Lutherans	21
Jews	37
Mormons	16
Other religions	81

Top 10 Universities in Congress

It might not always seem so, especially when Congress is in gridlock or unable to address itself to important national problems, but in fact Congress members on the whole are very well educated. Indeed, the largest number of university graduates obtained their degree at prestigious Harvard University, followed by Georgetown University and Yale University. The overall Top 10 are

Harvard University	39
Georgetown University	20
Yale University	16
University of Virginia	14
Stanford University	13
University of Michigan	12
George Washington University	11
University of Florida	10
University of Pittsburgh	10
University of Texas	9

Source: Congressional Quarterly Weekly Report, January 31, 2005.

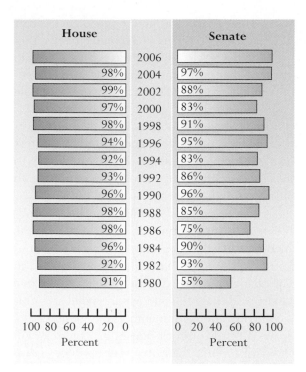

House		Senate
	2006	
98%	2004	97%
99%	2002	88%
97%	2000	83%
98%	1998	91%
94%	1996	95%
92%	1994	83%
93%	1992	86%
96%	1990	96%
98%	1988	85%
98%	1986	75%
96%	1984	90%
92%	1982	93%
91%	1980	55%

100 80 60 40 20 0   0 20 40 60 80 100
Percent   Percent

Figure 10.5 Incumbent Advantage
Despite periodic movements to "throw the bums out," voters in most districts and states routinely reelect their members of Congress. In recent years, more than 90 percent of representatives and 80 percent of senators who have sought reelection have been returned to Congress by votes in their districts or states.

tionment creates new seats in states gaining population, just as it forces out some incumbents in states losing population. Redistricting also threatens incumbents with new constituencies, where they have less name recognition, no history of casework, and perhaps no common racial or ethnic identification. Thus forced retirements and electoral defeats are more common in the first election following each ten-year reapportionment and redistricting of Congress.

Winning Big Not only do incumbent Congress members usually win, they usually also win big. Over 70 percent of House members win by margins of 60 percent or more or run unopposed. (In recent years, 10 to 18 percent of House members have had no opposition in the general election.) Senate races are somewhat more competitive. Senate challengers are usually people who have political experience and name recognition as members of the House, governors, or other high state officials. Even so, most Senate incumbents seeking reelection are victorious over their challengers. Most members of Congress, then, sit comfortably in **safe seats**—that is, they regularly win reelection by a large margin of the vote.

Turnover Despite a high rate of reelection of incumbents in Congress, about 15 percent of members arrive new to their jobs each session. **Turnover** occurs more frequently as a result of retirement, resignation (sometimes to run for higher office), or reapportionment (and the loss of an incumbent's seat) than it does as a result of an incumbent's defeat in a bid for reelection. Roughly 10 percent of Congress members voluntarily leave office when their term expires.[20]

Congressional Term Limits? Public distrust of government helped to fuel a movement in the states to limit congressional terms. Several states attempted to limit their state's House members to four two-year terms and their senators to

safe seat Legislative district in which the incumbent regularly wins by a large margin of the vote.

turnover Replacement of members of Congress by retirement or resignation, by reapportionment, or (more rarely) by electoral defeat, usually expressed as a percentage of members newly elected.

Think Again

Should members of
Congress be limited in the
number of terms they can
serve?

two six-year terms. Proponents of congressional term limits argued that career politicians become isolated from the lives and concerns of average citizens, that they acquire an "inside the Beltway" (the circle of highways that surround Washington) mentality. They also argued that term limits would increase competition, creating "open-seat" races on a regular basis and encouraging more people to seek public office.

Opponents of congressional term limits argued that they infringe on the voters' freedom of choice. If voters are upset with the performance of their Congress members, they can limit their terms by not reelecting them. But if voters wish to keep popular and experienced legislators in office, they should be permitted to do so. Opponents also argued that inexperienced Congress members would be forced to rely more on the policy information supplied them by bureaucrats, lobbyists, and staff people—thus weakening the institution of Congress.

But the U.S. Supreme Court ruled in 1995 that the states themselves cannot limit the terms of their members of Congress. "If the qualifications set forth in the text of the Constitution are to be changed, that text must be amended."[21] In a controversial 5 to 4 decision, the Court held that the Founders intended age, citizenship, and residency to be the *only* qualifications for members of Congress.

It is not likely that the necessary two-thirds of both houses of Congress will ever vote for a constitutional amendment to limit their own stay in office. Thus, the Supreme Court's decision effectively killed the movement for congressional term limits.

The Congressional Electorate Congressional elections generally fail to arouse much interest among voters. Indeed, only about 60 percent of the general public can name one U.S. senator from their state, and only about 40 percent can name both of their U.S. senators. Members of the House of Representatives fare no better: less than half of the general public can name their representative. But even constituents who know the names of their congressional delegation seldom know anything about the policy positions of these elected officials or about their votes on specific issues. Turnout in congressional *general elections* averages only about 35 percent in off-year (nonpresidential) elections. Turnout in congressional *primary elections* seldom exceeds 15 to 20 percent of persons eligible to vote. This lack of public attentiveness to congressional elections gives a great advantage to candidates with high name recognition, generally the incumbents (see *What Do You Think?* "Why Do Voters Reelect Members of an Unpopular Congress?").

Independence of Congressional Voting Congressional voting is largely independent of presidential voting. The same voters who elected Republican presidents in 1968, 1972, 1980, 1984, and 1988 simultaneously elected Democratic majorities to the House of Representatives. And while reelecting Democratic President Bill Clinton in 1996, voters simultaneously reelected Republican majorities in the House and Senate. In 2000, Republicans maintained a razor-thin margin in the House, despite Gore's popular vote victory. Only in 2004 did voters elect a Republican president and *add* to Republican majorities in the House and Senate. It is unlikely that voters deliberately seek to impose *divided party government* on the nation. Rather, they cast their presidential and congressional votes on the basis of differing expectations of presidents versus members of Congress. Divided party government reappeared in Washington in 2006, when Democrats captured control of both houses of Congress, confronting Republican George Bush with a legislature from the opposing party in his final two years in the White House.

WHAT DO YOU THINK?

Why Do Voters Reelect Members of an Unpopular Congress?

Congress is the least popular branch of government. Public approval of Congress is well below that of the presidency and the Supreme Court. What accounts for this lack of popularity? The belief that members of Congress "spend more time thinking about their own political futures than they do in passing legislation" may contribute to this sentiment.

But public disapproval of Congress may also arise from a misunderstanding of democratic government. "People do not wish to see uncertainty, conflicting options, long debate, competing interests, confusion and compromised imperfect solutions. . . . They often see a patently unrealistic form of democracy."[a]

But in an apparent paradox, most voters *approve of their own* representative (see figure below), even while Congress itself is the object of popular distrust and ridicule. A majority of voters believe that their own representatives "deserve reelection."

This apparent contradiction is explained in part by differing expectations: Americans expect Congress to deal with national issues, but they expect their own representatives to deal with local concerns and even personal problems. Members of Congress understand this concern and consequently devote a great deal of their time to constituent service. Indeed, many members of Congress try to dissociate themselves from Congress, attacking Congress in their own campaigns and contributing to negative images of the institution. Finally, the national news media are highly critical of Congress, but local news media frequently portray local members of Congress in a more favorable light.

Q. "Do you approve of the way the U.S. Congress is handling its job?"

Q. "Do you approve or disapprove of the way the representative from your own congressional district is handling his or her job?"

[a]John R. Hibbing and Elizabeth Theiss-Morse, *Congress as Public Enemy* (Cambridge: Cambridge University Press, 1995), p. 147. Also cited by Roger H. Davidson and Walter J. Oleszak, *Congress and Its Members* 9th ed. (Washington, D.C.: CQ Press, 2004), p. 487.

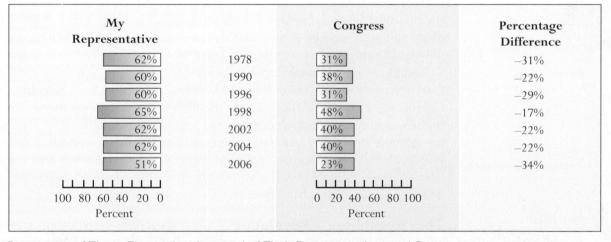

My Representative		Congress		Percentage Difference
62%	1978	31%		−31%
60%	1990	38%		−22%
60%	1996	31%		−29%
65%	1998	48%		−17%
62%	2002	40%		−22%
62%	2004	40%		−22%
51%	2006	23%		−34%

100 80 60 40 20 0   Percent   0 20 40 60 80 100   Percent

Percentage of Those Expressing Approval of Their Representatives and Congress.

Source: Data from various surveys, as reported in *www.thepollingreport.com*

Congressional Campaign Financing Raising the $900,000 it can take to win a House seat or the $5 to $10 million for a successful Senate campaign is a major job in and of itself (see "How Much Does It Cost to Get Elected?" in Chapter 8). Even incumbents who face little or no competition still work hard at fund-raising, "banking" contributions against some future challenger. Large campaign chests, assembled well in advance of an election, can also be used to frighten off would-be challengers. Campaign funds can be used to build a strong personal organization back home, finance picnics and other festivities for constituents, expand the margin of victory, and develop a reputation for invincibility that may someday protect against an unknown challenger.[23]

Does money buy elections? In about 90 percent of all congressional races, the candidate who spends the most money wins. However, because most winning candidates are incumbents, the money probably reflects the expected political outcome rather than shaping it. But even in open-seat races, the candidate who spends the most money usually wins.

Party Fortunes in Congress

For forty years (1954–94) Democrats enjoyed an advantage in congressional races; in fact, the Democratic Party was said to have a "permanent majority" in the House of Representatives (see Figure 10.6). The Republican victory in the congressional election of 1994 was widely described as a political "earthquake." It gave the GOP control of the House for the first time in four decades, as well as control of the Senate. Republicans remained in control of the House and the Senate (except for a brief period in 2001–2002) until the 2006 elections.

The Historic Democratic Party Dominance of Congress   The historic Democratic dominance of Congress was attributed to several factors. First, over those four decades more voters identified themselves with the Democratic Party than with the Republican Party (see Chapter 7). Party identification plays a significant role in congressional voting; it is estimated that 75 percent of those who identify themselves with a party cast their vote for the congressional candidate of their party.[24] Second, the Democratic advantage was buttressed by the fact that many voters considered local rather than national conditions when casting congressional votes. Voters may have wanted to curtail *overall* federal spending in Washington (a traditional Republican promise), but they wanted a member of Congress who would "bring home the bacon." Although both Republican and Democratic congressional candidates usually promised to bring money and jobs to their districts, Democratic candidates appeared more creditable on such promises because their party generally supported large domestic-spending programs. Finally, Democratic congressional candidates over those years enjoyed the many advantages of incumbency. It was thought that only death or retirement would dislodge many of them from their seats.

The Republican "Revolution"?   The sweeping Republican victory in 1994—especially the party's capturing control of the House of Representatives— surprised many analysts.[25] Just two years after a Democratic president won election and Democrats won substantial majorities in both houses of Congress, the GOP gained its most complete victory in many years. How did it happen?

First of all, the Republican congressional candidates, under the leadership of Newt Gingrich, largely succeeded in *nationalizing* the midterm congressional election. That is, Republican candidates sought to exploit the voters' general skepticism about government and disenchantment with its performance. Voters were often unfamiliar with specific Republican promises, but they correctly sensed that the Republicans favored "less government."

The GOP's capture of control of both houses of Congress in 1994 for the first time in forty years raised conservatives' hopes of a "revolution" in public policy.

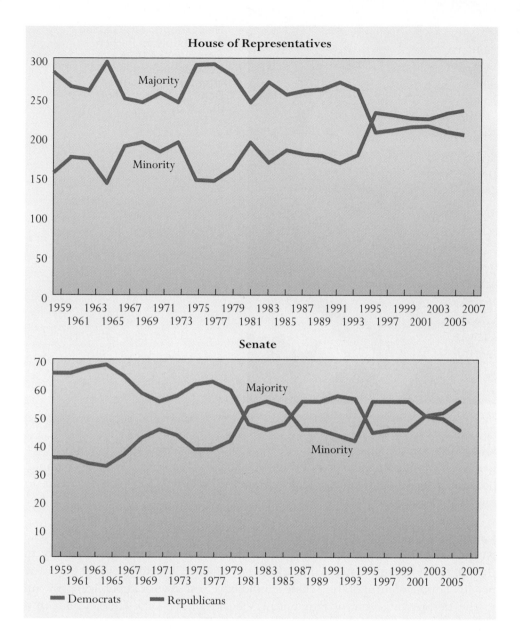

Figure 10.6 Party Control of the House and Senate

Except for two very brief periods, Democrats continuously controlled both the House of Representatives and the Senate for more than forty years. The Democratic Party's "permanent" control of Congress was ended in 1994, when Republicans won majorities in both houses. Republicans retained control of Congress despite President Clinton's victory in 1996, and retained control by a slim margin in the House in 1998, 2000, and 2002. President George W. Bush's reelection victory in 2004 increased Republican margins in both the House and Senate.

The new Republican House Speaker, Newt Gingrich, was the acknowledged leader of the revolution, with Republican Senate Majority Leader Bob Dole in tow. But soon the revolution began to fizzle out. Two key Republican campaign promises failed to pass the Congress: the House failed to muster the necessary two-thirds majority for a constitutional amendment to impose congressional term limits, and the Senate failed to do so on behalf of a balanced budget amendment.

The Democratic Revival Republicans succeeded in maintaining their control of Congress despite Clinton's reelection in 1996. But Democrats gained House seats in both the 1996 and 1998 congressional elections. Although the GOP retained a slim majority in the House of Representatives, the 1998 midterm election stunned Republicans. They had expected to benefit from

Newt Gingrich (R-Ga.) led the Republican Party to victory in the House of Representatives in 1994 after forty years of Democratic control of that body.

Clinton's acknowledged sexual misconduct and the House impeachment investigation. But voters generally sided with Clinton. Democrats were encouraged because historically the party controlling the White House had *lost* seats in midterm elections.

Congress Divided   The congressional elections of 2000 reflected the close partisan division of the nation. Republicans barely held on to their majority in the House of Representatives. The election produced a historic 50–50 tie in the Senate. Formal control of the Senate should have rested with Republicans, owing to the tie-breaking vote of Republican Vice President Dick Cheney. But in a precedent-shattering midsession shift of power, Democrats took control of the Senate in 2001, when Republican Senator Jim Jeffords from Vermont abandoned his party, declared himself an Independent, but gave his vote to the Democrats in the Senate. Other senators had defected from their party in the past, but no previous switch ever produced a change in party control. The new 51–49 Democratic majority took control of all Senate committees as well as the floor of that body.

Bush Leads GOP to Victories in 2002 and 2004   Traditionally, the party that had won the White House in the previous presidential election *lost* seats in the following midterm congressional election. (Indeed, since Abraham Lincoln was president, the party holding the presidency *lost* House seats in every midterm election except three—1902, 1934, and 1998.) It was theorized that presidential popularity tended to wane after two years in office, and that voters usually sought to check presidential power in the following midterm election. It was also believed that even popular presidents had little impact on midterm congressional elections; these elections were thought to be decided by the popularity of individual candidates and local district issues.

ACROSS THE USA

Urban, Suburban, and Rural Districts

Congressional House districts can be divided into urban, suburban, rural, and mixed, each with a distinctly Republican or Democratic tilt. Most residents of *urban districts* live in the central cities of metropolitan areas; most residents of *suburban districts* live in the metropolitan area but outside of the central city; most residents of *rural districts* live outside of metropolitan areas outside cities of more than 25,000; *mixed districts* are those in which there is no majority in any of the other categories.

Urban Districts		Suburban Districts	
Number 90		Number 220	
Party (2004)		Party (2004)	
Democrats	76%	Democrats	39%
Republicans	24%	Republicans	61%
Ethnicity		Ethnicity	
White	46%	White	73%
Black	20%	Black	10%
Hispanic	24%	Hispanic	11%
Other	10%	Other	4%

Rural Districts		Mixed Districts	
Number 61		Number 64	
Party (2004)		Party (2004)	
Democrats	44%	Democrats	44%
Republicans	56%	Republicans	66%
Ethnicity		Ethnicity	
White	83%	White	76%
Black	9%	Black	9%
Hispanic	4%	Hispanic	9%
Other	4%	Other	6%

Source: From *Congressional Quarterly Weekly Report*, Data for the 109th Congress, by Congressional Quarterly. Copyright © 2005 by Congressional Quarterly, Inc. Reproduced with permission of Congressional Quarterly Inc. in the format Textbook via Copyright Clearance Center.

But in 2002 President George W. Bush designated himself as "Campaigner-in-Chief," traveling about the country raising campaign money and lending his popularity to Republican House and Senate candidates. His continuing high approval rating throughout the year following the "9/11" terrorist attack on America made him a highly welcomed campaigner in districts and states across the nation. In his campaign stops, Bush talked about the war on terrorism and his need for "allies" in the Congress. President Bush appeared to influence just enough voters in key districts and states to reverse the historic pattern of presidential midterm congressional losses. The GOP won back control of the U.S. Senate and strengthened its majority in the House of Representatives.

Again in 2004 President Bush appeared to help GOP congressional candidates across the country. Republicans increased their control of the Senate from 51 to 55. They picked up several seats of retiring older-generation Southern Democrats. And they even succeeded in defeating the Democratic Senate Minority Leader, Tom Daschle of South Dakota. The 2004 election also made the Senate slightly more "diverse": African American Barack Obama was elected from Illinois, and Hispanic Mel Martinez was elected from Florida. In the House, Republicans also increased their margin of control. President Bush was quick to claim that winning the White House, the Senate, and the House of Representatives meant that the American People supported his "agenda."

After twelve years of Republican majorities in the House of Representatives, Democrats captured control of that body in 2006. Some 30 seats switched from Republican to Democratic. Although this was only about seven percent of the

UP CLOSE

Divided Government: The 110th Congress

Divided government does not *necessarily* mean policy gridlock, yet that is often the result. The bitter partisanship that has infected Washington in recent years may prevent the Republican president and the Democratic Congress from working together to pass much significant legislation.

The substantial Democratic majority in the House of Representatives is likely to be a major stumbling block to any policy initiatives by President Bush. And the president is likely to threaten vetoes to any major new social spending program initiated by the congressional leadership.

Democratic Speaker of the House Nancy Pelosi has a reputation for strong partisan attacks on Republicans. Leadership itself may tend to moderate her rhetoric, and many of the newly elected Democratic House members won office by projecting a "moderate" image. Yet the senior Democratic leadership in both the House and the Senate are committed to a liberal agenda, and the strong liberal base of the Democratic Party will push for that agenda to be enacted.

The president is the Commander-in-Chief, and there is little that Congress can do by itself to com-

pel changes in strategy in Iraq. In theory, Congress can cut off funds for the war, but it is politically unthinkable that Congress would vote to deny funds for American troops in the field.

The policy agenda for the congressional leadership includes strengthening congressional ethics rules, increasing the minimum wage, authorizing the government to negotiate with drug companies for lower prices, and reducing interest rates on student loans. And Bush's "comprehensive"immigration reform proposal—a guest worker program with earnable citizenship for immigrants who are here now, as well as increased border enforcement—may succeed with Democratic cooperation. (It was primarily congressional opposition from the president's own party that doomed efforts at comprehensive reform in the last Congress.)

Perhaps the most contentious issue between the Democratic-controlled Congress and the Republican president is taxation. Bush's first-term tax cuts are set to expire in 2010 unless Congress makes them permanent. Republicans characterize a failure to do so as a "tax increase." Democrats call Bush's cuts "tax cuts for the rich" and oppose making them permanent.

Bipartisanship is a popular term in political rhetoric, but it seldom describes what actually occurs in Washington, especially with divided party government.

Democratic senator Harry Reid of Nevada, center and House Minority Leader Nancy Pelosi, center, left, are surrounded by House and Senate Democrats during an event highlighting the Democrats' approach to homeland security.

Senator Barack Obama (D-IL) clasps hands with his grandmother, who lives in Kenya. Obama is a rapidly rising star in the Democratic Party.

435-member House, it was enough to change the balance of power in Washington. In the Senate only six seats switched from Republican to Democratic, but that too was enough to change party control of that chamber.

Life in Congress

"All politics is local," declared former House Speaker Thomas P. "Tip" O'Neill, himself once the master of both Boston ward politics and the U.S. House of Representatives. Attention to the local constituency is the key to survival and success in congressional politics. If Congress often fails to deal responsibly with national problems, the explanation lies in part with the design of the institution. House members must devote primary attention to their districts and Senate members to their states. Only *after* their constituencies are served can they turn their attention to national policy making.

The "Representativeness" of Congress   The Constitution requires only that members of the House of Representatives be (1) residents of the state they represent (they need not live in their congressional district, although virtually all do so); (2) U.S. citizens for at least seven years; and (3) at least twenty-five years old. Senators must also be residents of the state they represent, but they must be at least thirty years old and U.S. citizens for at least nine years.

■ *African Americans*   African Americans were first elected to Congress following the Civil War—seven black representatives and one black senator served in 1875. But with the end of Reconstruction, black membership in Congress fell to a single seat in the House from 1891 to 1955. Following the Civil Rights Act of 1964 and the Voting Rights Act of 1965, black membership in Congress rose steadily. Redistricting following the 1990 census resulted in many new "majority-minority" congressional districts. After the 1992 elections, black membership in the House rose dramatically (see Figure 10.7), with most elected from predominantly African American districts.[26] As a result, although African Americans today make up a little more than 12 percent of the U.S. population, they

Figure 10.7 Women, African Americans, and Hispanics in the House of Representatives

Although the House of Representatives is still far short of "looking like America," in recent years the number of African American, Hispanic, and female members has risen noticeably. Particularly impressive advances were made in the 1992 elections, following court-ordered creation of "majority–minority" districts.

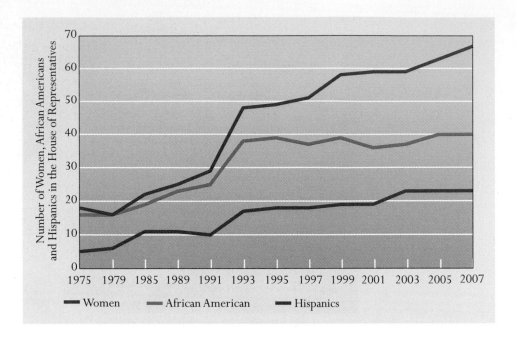

make up less than 9 percent of the House membership. African American Carol Moseley Braun of Illinois served in the Senate from 1993 to 1999, and Barack Obama won a Senate seat in the same state in 2004. He is currently the only African American in the U.S. Senate.

■ *Hispanics*   Hispanics now comprise the nation's largest minority, with slightly more than 12 percent of the U.S. population. But Hispanic representation in the Congress lags considerably behind their population growth. Currently only about 5 percent of House members are Hispanic, and just one Hispanic serves in the U.S. Senate. The Voting Rights Act of 1965 protects "language minorities" as well as racial and ethnic minorities. Prior to the 1990 census and the creation of many court-ordered "majority-minority" congressional districts, very few Hispanics served in the Congress. But with the creation of new Hispanic majority districts, Hispanic representation began to increase in the House of Representatives. Most Hispanic House members come from California, Florida, and Texas.

■ *Women*   Women have made impressive gains in both the House and the Senate in the last decade. The "year of the woman" election in 1992 brought a significant increase in the number of women in the House of Representatives. Since then, women's representation in the House continued upward; fifty-nine women serve in the House in the 108th Congress (2003–2005), divided between thirty-eight Democrats and twenty-one Republicans. In the Senate, fourteen women serve. California is represented by two Democratic women, Dianne Feinstein and Barbara Boxer. They are joined by seven other Democratic women Senators, including former First Lady Hillary Rodham Clinton. (See *People in Politics:* "Hillary Rodham Clinton in the Senate.") Five Republican women serve in the Senate: Elizabeth Dole from North Carolina, Kay Hutchinson from Texas, Olympia Snowe and Susan Collins from Maine, and Lisa Murkowski from Alaska. Although this is the largest delegation of women ever to serve together in the U.S. Senate, it is still only 14 percent of that body. The number of women in Congress has grown as a result of many factors, including strides that women

PEOPLE IN POLITICS

Hillary Rodham Clinton in the Senate

Hillary Rodham Clinton is the first First Lady ever elected to the Congress and the first woman senator from New York. Her celebrity attracts the media wherever she goes, sometimes causing resentment among her ninety-nine other Senate colleagues, all of whom think of themselves as stars in their own right. Her initial efforts in the Senate have been directed toward establishing herself as a serious, knowledgeable, and effective legislator. And she tries particularly hard to identify herself with the interests of her adopted state, New York.

Hillary Rodham grew up in suburban Chicago, the daughter of wealthy parents who sent her to the private, prestigious Wellesley College. A 1969 honors graduate with a counterculture image—horn-rimmed glasses, long, straggling hair, no makeup—she was chosen by her classmates to give a commencement speech—a rambling statement about "more immediate, ecstatic, and penetrating modes of living."

At Yale Law School Hillary met a long-haired, bearded Rhodes scholar from Arkansas, Bill Clinton, who was just as politically ambitious as she was. Both Hillary and Bill received their law degrees in 1973. Bill returned to Arkansas to build a career in state politics, and Hillary went to Washington as an attorney—first for a liberal lobbying group, the Children's Defense Fund, and later on the staff of the House Judiciary Committee seeking to impeach President Richard Nixon. But Rodham and other Yale grads traveled to Arkansas to help Clinton run, unsuccessfully, for Congress in 1974. Hillary decided to stay with Bill in Little Rock: they married before his next campaign, a successful run for state attorney general in 1976. Hillary remained Hillary Rodham, even as her husband went on to the governorship in 1978.

Her husband's 1980 defeat for reelection as governor was blamed on his liberal leanings; therefore, in his 1982 comeback Bill repackaged himself as a moderate and centrist. Hillary cooperated by becoming Mrs. Bill Clinton, shedding her horn-rims for contacts, blonding her hair, and echoing her husband's more moderate line. These tactics helped propel them back into the governor's mansion. Hillary soon became a full partner in Little Rock's Rose law firm, regularly earning more than $200,000 a year (while Bill earned only $35,000 as Arkansas governor). She won national recognition as one of the "100 most influential lawyers in the United States," according to the *American National Law Journal*. She chaired the American Bar Association's Commission on Women and the Profession.

Hillary's steadfast support of Bill during the White House sex scandals and subsequent impeachment by the House of Representatives in all likelihood saved his presidency. Her approval ratings in public opinion polls skyrocketed during the affair. Whatever she thought in private, she never chastised her husband in public and blamed much of the scandal on "a vast right-wing conspiracy."

Her Senate race attracted national media attention as well as campaign contributions from supporters throughout the nation. When New York City's Mayor Rudolph Giuliani announced that he would *not* run for the Senate, Hillary was relieved to confront a little-known opponent, Congressman Rick Lazio. New York voters were unimpressed with charges that Hillary was not a true New Yorker. She studied New York problems diligently, and overwhelmed Lazio in the campaign. Over $85 million were spent by the candidates, making the campaign the most expensive congressional campaign in history.

Senator Clinton has developed a reputation as an advocate for children and families. Her early work with the Children's Defense Fund and Marian Wright Edelman (see *People in Politics:* "Marian Wright Edelman, Lobbying for the Poor" in Chapter 9) was carried forward in her book *It Takes a Village* in 1997. She was prominently mentioned in all of the early 2004 presidential polls, but she declined to run. She crushed her Republican opponent in her 2006 reelection to the Senate, setting the stage for a possible presidential campaign in 2008.

have made in the workplace and other societal institutions. Yet stereotypes about women as politicians remain. Generally, voters view women as better able to handle "feminine" issues, such as health care, child care and education, but less able to handle "masculine" issues, including the economy and war. In the past, some women candidates tried to counter these stereotypes by emphasizing their toughness, especially on crime. But new evidence suggests that women candidates can use female stereotypes to their advantage by focusing the campaign on gender-owned issues—health, welfare, education, and other compassion issues.[27]

Congressional Staff   Congress is composed of a great deal more than 535 elected senators and representatives. Congressional staff and other support personnel now total some 25,000 people. Each representative has a staff of twenty or more people, usually headed by a chief of staff or administrative assistant and including legislative assistants, communications specialists, constituent-service personnel, office managers, secretaries, and aides of various sorts. Senators frequently have staffs of thirty to fifty or more people. All representatives and senators are provided with offices both in Washington and in their home districts and states. In addition, representatives receive more than $500,000 apiece for office expenses, travel, and staff; and senators receive $2 million or more, depending on the size of their state's population. Overall, Congress spends more than $2 *billion* on itself each year.

Congressional staff people exercise great influence over legislation. Many experienced "Hill rats" have worked for the same member of Congress for many years. They become very familiar with "their" member's political strengths and vulnerabilities and handle much of the member's contacts with interest groups and constituents. Staff people, more than members themselves, move the legislative process—scheduling committee hearings, writing bills and amendments, and tracking the progress of such proposals through committees and floor proceedings. By working with the staff of other members of Congress or the staff of committees and negotiating with interest-group representatives, congressional staff are often able to work out policy compromises, determine the wording of legislation, or even outline "deals" for their member's vote (all subject to later approval by their member). With multiple demands on their time, members of Congress come to depend on their staff not only for information about the content of legislation but also for political recommendations about what position to take regarding it.

Support Agencies   In addition to the thousands of personal and committee staff who are supposed to assist members of Congress in research and analysis, four congressional support agencies provide Congress with information:

- The Library of Congress and its Congressional Research Service (CRS) are the oldest congressional support agencies. Members of Congress can turn to the Library of Congress for references and information. The CRS responds to direct requests of members for factual information on virtually any topic. It tracks major bills in Congress and produces summaries of each bill introduced. This information is available on computer terminals in members' offices.

Government Accountability Office   The GAO Web site provides the latest reports evaluating government programs and spending. *www.gao.gov*

- The **Government Accountability Office** (GAO) has broad authority to oversee the operations and finances of executive agencies, to evaluate their programs, and to report its findings to Congress. Established as an arm of Congress in 1921, the GAO largely confined itself to financial auditing and management studies in its early years but expanded to more than five thousand employees in the 1970s and undertook a broad agenda of policy research and evaluation. Most GAO studies and reports are requested by members of Congress and congressional committees, but the GAO also undertakes some studies on its own initiative.

■ The Congressional Budget Office (CBO) was created by the Congressional Budget and Impoundment Act of 1974 to strengthen Congress's role in the budgeting process. It was designed as a congressional counterweight to the president's Office of Management and Budget (see Chapter 14). The CBO supplies the House and Senate budget committees with its own budgetary analyses and economic forecasts, sometimes challenging those found in the president's annual budget.

■ The Government Printing Office (GPO), created in 1860 as the publisher of the *Congressional Record*, now distributes over 20,000 different government publications in U.S. government bookstores throughout the nation.

Congressional Budget Office
The Web site of the CBO is an excellent source of data on federal finances, economic projections, and the budgetary process.
www.cbo.gov

Workload   Members of Congress claim to work twelve- to fifteen-hour days: two to three hours in committee and subcommittee meetings; two to three hours on the floor of the chamber; three to four hours meeting with constituents, interest groups, other members, and staff in their offices; and two to three hours attending conferences, events, and meetings in Washington.[28] Members of Congress may introduce anywhere from ten to fifty bills in a single session of Congress. Most bills are introduced merely to exhibit the member's commitment to a particular group or issue. Cosigning a popular bill is a common practice; particularly popular bills may have 100 or 200 cosigners in the House of Representatives. Although thousands of bills are introduced, only 400 to 800 are passed in a session.[29]

Pay and Perks   Taxpayers can relate directly to what members of Congress spend on themselves, even while millions—and even billions—of dollars spent on government programs remain relatively incomprehensible. Taxpayers thus were enraged when Congress, in a late-night session in 1991, raised its own pay from $89,500 to $129,000. Congress claimed the pay raise was a "reform," since it was coupled with a stipulation that members of Congress would no longer be allowed to accept honoraria from interest groups for their speeches and appearances, thus supposedly reducing members' dependence on outside income. Many angry taxpayers saw only a 44 percent pay raise, in the midst of a national recession, for a Congress that was doing little to remedy the nation's problems. By

Democratic House Member John Lewis is congratulated for success in passing a Voting Rights Act reauthorization bill. Lewis regularly wins his Atlanta congressional seat by large margins.

2006, automatic cost-of-living increases, also enacted by Congress, had raised members' pay to $165,200. House and Senate members receive the same pay; leaders in both houses receive $183,500 and the speaker of the House $212,000. Benefits, including retirement pay, are very generous.

As the pay-raise debate raged in Washington, several states resurrected a constitutional amendment originally proposed by James Madison. Although passed by the Congress in 1789, it had never been ratified by the necessary three-quarters of the states. The 203-year-old amendment, requiring a House election to intervene before a congressional pay raise can take effect, was added as the Twenty-seventh Amendment when ratified by four states (for a total of thirty-nine) in 1992.

Home Style

Members of Congress spend as much time politically cultivating their districts and states as they do legislating. **Home style** refers to the activities of senators and representatives in promoting their images among constituents and personally attending to constituents' problems and interests.[30] These activities include members' allocations of their personnel and staff resources to constituent services; members' personal appearances in the home district or state to demonstrate personal attention; and members' efforts to explain their Washington activities to the voters back home.

Casework   Casework is really a form of "retail" politics. Members of Congress can win votes one at a time by helping constituents on a personal level. Casework can involve everything from tracing lost Social Security checks and Medicare claims to providing information about federal programs, solving problems with the Internal Revenue Service, and assisting with federal job applications. Over time, grateful voters accumulate, giving incumbents an advantage at election time. Congressional staff do much of the actual casework, but letters go out over the signature of the member of Congress. Senators and representatives blame the growth of government for increasing casework, but it is also clear that members solicit casework, frequently reminding constituents to bring their problems to their member of Congress.[31]

Pork Barrel   Pork barreling describes the efforts of senators and representatives to "bring home the bacon"—to bring federally funded projects, grants, and contracts that primarily benefit a single district or state to their home constituencies. Opportunities for pork barreling have never been greater: roads, dams, parks, and post offices are now overshadowed by redevelopment grants to city governments, research grants to universities, weapons contracts to local plants, "demonstration" projects of all kinds, and myriad other "goodies" tucked inside each year's annual appropriations bills. Members of Congress understand the importance of supporting each other's pork barrel projects, cooperating in the "incumbent-protection society." Even though pork barreling adds to the public's negative image of Congress as an institution, individual members gain local popularity for the benefits they bring to home districts and states.

Pressing the Flesh   Senators and representatives spend a great deal of time in their home states and districts. Although congressional sessions last virtually all year, members of Congress find ways to spend more than a hundred days per year at home.[32] It is important to be seen at home—giving speeches and attending dinners, fund-raising events, civic occasions, and so on. To accommodate this

---

Think Again

Do Congress members spend too much time in their home districts seeking reelection?

home style Activities of Congress members specifically directed at their home constituencies.

casework Services performed by legislators or their staff on behalf of individual constituents.

pork barreling Legislation designed to make government benefits, including jobs and projects used as political patronage, flow to a particular district or state.

aspect of home style, Congress usually follows a Tuesday-to-Thursday schedule of legislative business, allowing members to spend longer weekends in their home districts. Congress also enjoys long recesses during the late summer and over holidays.

Puffing Images   To promote their images back home, members make generous use of their **franking privilege** (free mailing) to send their constituents newsletters, questionnaires, biographical material, and information about federal programs. Newsletters "puff" the accomplishments of the members; questionnaires are designed more to flatter voters than to assess opinions; and informational brochures tout federal services members claim credit for providing and defending. Congress's penchant for self-promotion has also kept pace with the media and electronic ages. Congress now provides its members with television studios and support for making videotapes to send to local stations in home districts, and all members maintain Web sites on the Internet designed to puff their images.

franking privilege   Free mail service afforded members of Congress.

Hill Styles and Home Styles   Members of Congress spend their lives "moving between two contexts, Washington and home, and between two activities, governing and campaigning."[33] They must regularly ask themselves how much time they should spend at home with their constituents versus how much time they should spend on lawmaking assignments in Washington. It is no surprise that freshman legislators spend more time in their districts; indeed, very few first-termers move their families to Washington. Long-term incumbents spend more time in Washington, but all Congress members spend more time at home in an election year.

Much of the time spent at home—with small groups of constituents, among contributors, in public speeches, and appearances on radio and television—is devoted to explaining issues and justifying the member's vote on them. "Often members defend their own voting record by belittling Congress—portraying themselves as knights errant battling sinister forces and feckless colleagues."[34]

 **Congressional Quarterly (CQ)**
The *Congressional Quarterly Weekly Report* provides the most comprehensive coverage of events in Congress, including key issues, House and Senate roll call votes, backgrounds of members, and political and election information. The CQ Press is a major publisher of books on politics and government. *www.cq.com*

Organizing Congress: Party and Leadership

Congress is composed of people who think of themselves as leaders, not followers. They got elected without much help from their party. Yet they realize that their chances of attaining their personal goals—getting reelected and influencing policy—are enhanced if they cooperate with each other.

Party Organizations in Congress   The Democratic and Republican party organizations within the House of Representatives and the Senate are the principal bases for organizing Congress (see Figure 10.8). The leadership of each house of Congress, although nominally elected by the entire chamber, is actually chosen by secret ballot of the members of each party at a "conference" or caucus (see Table 10.3).

The parties and their leaders do not choose congressional candidates, nor can they deny them renomination; all members of Congress are responsible for their own primary and general election success. But party leadership in each chamber can help incumbents achieve their reelection goals. Each party in the House and Senate sponsors a campaign committee that channels some campaign funding to party members seeking reelection, although these Republican and Democratic congressional and senatorial campaign committees contribute less money than either PACs or individuals to the candidates.[35] Rather, good relations between

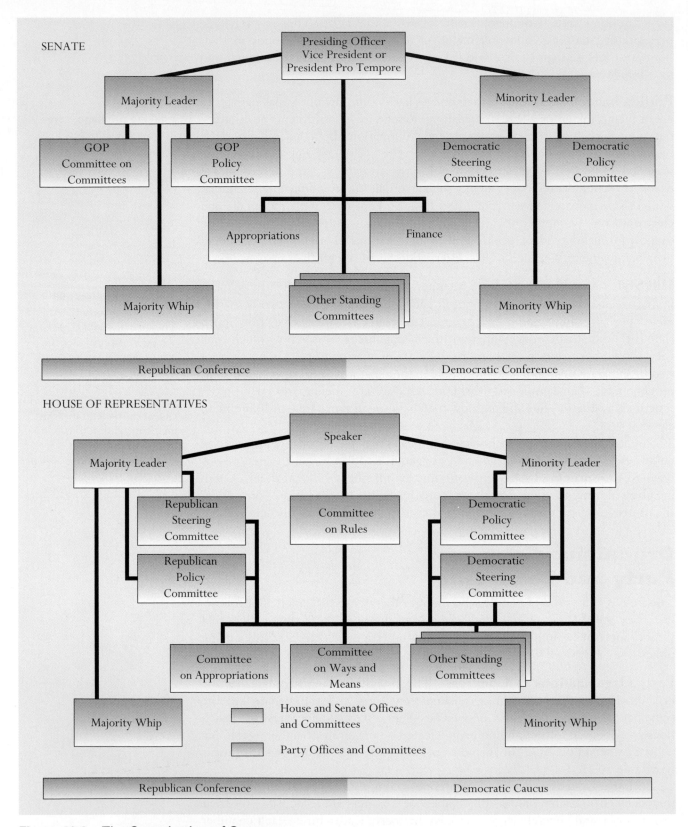

Figure 10.8   The Organization of Congress

Aside from naming the Speaker of the House as head of that body's operations and the vice president as overseer of Senate deliberations, the Constitution is silent on the organization of Congress. Political parties have filled this gap: both majority and minority parties have their own leadership, which governs the appointment of members to the various committees, where much of the work of Congress actually takes place.

Table 10.3   Leadership in Congress

	Senate
President Pro Tempore	An honorary post, usually the senior member of the majority party
Majority Leader	Top Senate post, elected by majority party members
Majority Whip	Second-ranking post in the majority party
Minority Leader	Leader of the minority opposition party
Minority Whip	Second-ranking post in the minority party
	House
Speaker	Powerful presiding officer, elected with the votes of the majority party
Majority Leader	Officially the leader of the majority party but second in power to the Speaker
Majority Whip	Third-ranking leader of the majority party
Minority Leader	Top post in the minority party
Minority Whip	Second-ranking post in the minority party

members and their party's leadership are more important in the quest for power and influence in Washington.

Majority status confers great power on the party that controls the House and the Senate. The majority party chooses the leadership in each body, selects the chairs of every committee, and ensures that every committee has a majority of members from the majority party. In other words, if Republicans are in the majority in either the House or the Senate or both, Republicans will occupy all leadership positions, chair every committee, and constitute a majority of the members of every committee, and, of course, the Democrats enjoy the same advantages when they capture a majority of either body. Majority-party members in each house even take in more campaign contributions than minority members.[36]

In the House: "Mr. Speaker"   In the House of Representatives, the key leadership figure is the **Speaker of the House,** who serves as both presiding officer of the chamber and leader of the majority party. In the House, the Speaker has many powers. The Speaker decides who shall be recognized to speak on the floor and rules on points of order (with advice from the parliamentarian), including whether a motion or amendment is germane (relevant) to the business at hand. The Speaker decides to which committees new bills will be assigned and can schedule or delay votes on a bill. The Speaker appoints members of select, special, and conference committees and names majority-party members to the Rules Committee. And the Speaker controls both patronage jobs and office space in the Capitol. Although the norm of fairness requires the Speaker to apply the rules of the House consistently, the Speaker is elected by the majority party and is expected to favor that party.

Over the years, different Speakers have displayed different leadership styles. Republican Speaker Newt Gingrich was an ideological leader with a dramatic and aggressive agenda—a "Contract with America"—who contributed to partisan rancor in the House. In contrast, Republican Speaker Dennis Hastert has been a pragmatic leader who deals with his colleagues in an accommodating fashion.[37] Republicans express fear that Democratic Speaker Nancy Pelosi will

Speaker of the House
Presiding officer of the House of Representatives.

Republican Dennis Hastert lost his post as Speaker of the House when Democrats took control of that body in 2006.

lead the House in a liberal direction (see *People in Politics:* "Nancy Pelosi, Leading House Democrats.")

majority leader In the House, the majority-party leader and second in command to the Speaker; in the Senate, the leader of the majority party.

House Leaders and Whips   The Speaker's principal assistant is the **majority leader.** The majority leader formulates the party's legislative program in consultation with other party leaders and steers the program through the House. The majority leader also must persuade committee leaders to support the aims of party leaders in acting on legislation before their committees. Finally, the majority leader arranges the legislative schedule with the cooperation of key party members.

minority leader In both the House and Senate, the leader of the opposition party.

The minority party in the House selects a **minority leader** whose duties correspond to those of the majority leader, except that the minority leader has no authority over the scheduling of legislation. The minority leader's principal duty has been to organize the forces of the minority party to counter the legislative program of the majority and to pass the minority party's bills. It is also the minority leader's duty to consult ranking minority members of House committees and to encourage them to adopt party positions and to follow the lead of the president if the minority party controls the White House.

whips In both the House and Senate, the principal assistants to the party leaders and next in command to those leaders.

In both parties, **whips** assist leaders in keeping track of the whereabouts of party members and in pressuring them to vote the party line. Whips are also responsible for ensuring the attendance of party members at important roll calls and for canvassing their colleagues on their likely support for or opposition to party-formulated legislation. Finally, whips are involved regularly in the formation of party policy and the scheduling of legislation.

In the Senate: "Mr. President"   The Constitution declares the vice president of the United States to be the presiding officer of the Senate. But vice presidents seldom exercise this senatorial responsibility, largely because the presiding officer of the Senate has very little power. Having only 100 members, the Senate usually does not restrict debate and has fewer scheduling constraints than the House. The only significant power of the vice president is the right to cast a deciding vote in the event of a tie on a Senate roll call. In the usual absence of the vice president, the Senate is presided over by a *president pro tempore.* This honorific position is traditionally granted by the majority party to one of its senior stalwarts. The job of presiding over the Senate is so boring that neither the vice president nor the president pro tempore is found very often in the chamber.

PEOPLE IN POLITICS

Nancy Pelosi, Leading House Democrats

Nancy Pelosi is the first woman in the history of the U.S. Congress to serve as Speaker of the House. In 2001 her Democratic colleagues elected her Minority Leader, the highest-ranking leadership position among Democratic members. Pelosi has represented her San Francisco district since her first election to the Congress in 1986.

Congresswoman Pelosi comes from a highly political family. Her father, Thomas D'Alesandro, served five terms in Congress and later 12 years as mayor of Baltimore. Pelosi's brother also served as mayor of Baltimore. Young Nancy grew up in Washington and graduated from that city's Trinity College in 1962. She served as a congressional intern to her Maryland senator. She married Paul Pelosi, moved to his hometown of San Francisco, and raised five children. Prior ·to her election to Congress, she served on the National Democratic Committee.

In her years in Congress, Pelosi built a solid liberal reputation, serving on the powerful Appropriations Committee. She won the post as Democratic whip in 2001 in a close election against a more moderate Democrat. But Pelosi's real strength within the Democratic Party has long been her fund-raising ability. Her San Francisco district is the home of some of the party's wealthiest individual donors, and Democrats across the nation rely heavily upon money from California. Pelosi created her own leadership PAC and handed out over $1 million to her Democratic colleagues in 2000. She spends relatively little (about $400,000) on her own reelection races in her heavily Democratic district.

In 2002, Pelosi was reelected with an astonishing 80 percent of the vote in her California district. She has continued to win by 80 percent or more of the vote through 2006.

Junior senators are often asked to assume the chore. Nevertheless, speeches on the Senate floor begin with the salutation "Mr. President," referring to the president of the Senate, *not* the president of the United States.

Senate Majority and Minority Leaders   Senate leadership is actually in the hands of the Senate majority leader, but the Senate majority leader is not as powerful in that body as the Speaker is in the House. With fewer members, all of whom perceive themselves as powerful leaders, the Senate is less hierarchically organized than the House. The Senate majority leader's principal power is scheduling the business of the Senate and recognizing the first speaker in floor debate. To be effective in policy making, the majority leader must be skilled in interpersonal persuasion and communication. Moreover, in the media age, the Senate majority leader must also be a national spokesperson for the party, along with the Speaker of the House. Republican Senate Leader Bill Frist and Republican Speaker of the House Dennis Hastert were their party's leading congressional spokesmen in the 109th Congress. The minority-party leader in the Senate represents the opposition in negotiations with the majority leader over Senate business. With the majority leader, the minority-party leader tends to dominate floor debate in the Senate.

Career Paths within Congress   Movement up the party hierarchy in each house is the most common way of achieving a leadership position. The traditional succession pattern in the House is from whip to majority leader to Speaker. In the Senate, Republicans and Democrats frequently resort to election contests in choosing their party leaders, yet both parties have increasingly adopted a two-step succession route from whip to leader.[38]

Leadership PACs   House and Senate leaders, and members who aspire to become leaders, often ingratiate themselves to their colleagues by distributing campaign funds to them. In recent years, *leadership PACs* have proliferated on Capitol Hill.

In Committee

Much of the real work of Congress is done in committee. The floor of Congress is often deserted; C-SPAN focuses on the podium, not the empty chamber. Members dash to the floor when the bell rings throughout the Capitol signaling a roll-call vote. Otherwise they are found in their offices or in the committee rooms, where the real work of Congress is done.

Standing Committees   The committee system provides for a division of labor in the Congress, assigning responsibility for work and allowing members to develop some expertise (see Table 10.4). The committee system is as old as the Congress itself: the very first Congress regularly assigned the task of wording bills to selected members who were believed to have a particular expertise. Soon a system of **standing committees**—permanent committees that specialize in a particular area of legislation—emerged. House committees have forty to sixty or more members and Senate committees fifteen to twenty-five members each. The proportions of Democrats and Republicans on each committee reflect the proportions of Democrats and Republicans in the House and Senate as a whole. Thus the majority party has a majority of members on every committee; and every committee is chaired by a member of the majority party. The minority membership on each committee is led by the **ranking minority member**, the minority-party committee member with the most seniority.

The principal function of standing committees is the screening and drafting of legislation. With 8,000 to 10,000 or more bills introduced each session, the screening function is essential. The standing committees are the gatekeepers of Congress; less than 10 percent of the legislation introduced will pass the Congress. With rare exceptions, bills are not submitted to a vote by the full membership of the House or Senate without prior approval by the majority of a standing committee. Moreover, committees do not merely sort through bills assigned to

Library of Congress
The Thomas system allows the tracing of bills from their introduction, through the committee system, floor schedule vote, and so on *http://thomas.loc.gov*

standing committee
Permanent committee of the House or Senate that deals with matters within a specified subject area.

ranking minority member
The minority-party committee member with the most seniority.

Congressional committee hearings provide an opportunity for members of Congress to gather information and at the same time promote their own images. Celebrity witnesses increase media coverage. Shown here testifying at a House committee hearing on steroid use in sports are baseball stars Curt Schilling, Rafael Palmeiro, Mark McGwire, and Sammy Sosa.

them to find what they like. Rather, committees—or more often their subcommittees—draft (write) legislation themselves. Committees may amend, rewrite, or write their own bills. Committees are "little legislatures" within their own policy jurisdictions. Each committee guards its own policy jurisdiction jealously; jurisdictional squabbles between committees are common.

The Pecking Order of Committees   The most powerful standing committees, and, therefore, the most sought-after committee assignments, are the Appropriations Committees in the House and the Senate. These committees hold the federal purse strings, arguably Congress's most important power. These committees are closely followed in influence and desirability by the Ways and Means Committee in the House and the Senate Finance Committee; these committees must pass on all tax matters, as well as Social Security and Medicare financing. In the House, the Rules Committee is especially powerful, owing to its control over floor consideration of every bill submitted to the full House. The Senate Judiciary Committee is especially influential because of its influence over all presidential nominees to the federal judiciary, including Supreme Court justices. The Senate Foreign Relations Committee is also a highly valued assignment. Perhaps the *least* desirable committee assignments are those on the Senate Ethics Committee and the House Standards of Official Conduct Committee; these ethics panels are obliged to sit in judgment of their own colleagues.

Decentralization and Subcommittees   Congressional **subcommittees** within each standing committee further decentralize the legislative process. At present, the House has about 90 subcommittees and the Senate about 70 subcommittees, each of which functions independently of its full committee (see Table 10.4). Subcommittees have fixed jurisdictions (for example, the House International Relations Committee has subcommittees on Africa, Asia and the Pacific, International Economic Policy, International Operations and Human Rights, and the Western Hemisphere); they meet and schedule their own hearings; and they have their own staffs and budgets. However, bills recommended by a subcommittee still require full standing-committee endorsement before being reported to the floor of the House or Senate. Full committees usually, but not always, ratify the decisions of their subcommittees.

> **subcommittees** Specialized committees within standing committees; subcommittee recommendations must be approved by the full standing committee before submission to the floor.

Chairing a committee or subcommittee gives members of Congress the opportunity to exercise power, attract media attention, and thus improve their chances of reelection. Often committees have become "fiefdoms" over which their chairs exercise complete control and jealously guard their power. This situation allows a very small number of House and Senate members to block legislation. Many decisions are not really made by the whole Congress. Rather, they are made by subcommittee members with a special interest in the policy under consideration. Although the committee system may satisfy the desire of members to gain power, prestige, and reelection opportunities, it weakens responsible government in the Congress as a whole.

Committee Membership   Given the power of the committee system, it is not surprising that members of Congress have a very keen interest in their committee assignments. Members strive for assignments that will give them influence in Congress, allow them to exercise power in Washington, and ultimately improve their chances for reelection. For example, a member from a big city may seek a seat on Banking, Housing, and Urban Affairs, a member from a farm district may seek a seat on Agriculture, and a member from a district with a large military base may seek a seat on National Security or Veterans Affairs. Everyone

---

Table 10.4 Committees in Congress

Senate

Agriculture, Nutrition, and Forestry	Health, Education, Labor and Pensions
Appropriations	Homeland Security and
Armed Services	Environmental Affairs
Banking, Housing, and Urban Affairs	Judiciary
Budget	Rules and Administration
Commerce, Science, and	Small Business and
Transportation	Entrepreneurship
Energy and Natural Resources	Select Aging
Environment and Public Works	Select Ethics
Finance	Select Indian
Foreign Relations	Select Intelligence
	Veterans Affairs

House

Agriculture	Judiciary
Appropriations	Resources
Armed Forces	Rules
Budget	Science
Energy and Commerce	Small Business
Education and the Workforce	Standards of Official Conduct
Financial Services	Transportation and Infrastructure
Government Reform	Veterans Affairs
Homeland Security	Ways and Means
House Administration	Select Intelligence
International Relations	

Joint Committees

Joint Economic Committee
Joint Taxation
Joint Committee on Printing
Joint Committee on the Library

---

seeks a seat on Appropriations, because both the House and the Senate Appropriations committees have subcommittees in each area of federal spending.[39]

    Party leadership in both the House and the Senate largely determines committee assignments. These assignments are given to new Democratic House members by the Democratic Steering and Policy Committee; new Democratic senators receive their assignments from the Senate Democratic Steering Committee. New Republican members receive their committee assignments from the Republican Committee on Committees in both houses. The leadership generally tries to honor new members' requests and improve their chances for reelection, but because incumbent members of committees are seldom removed, openings on powerful committees are infrequent.

Seniority Committee chairs are elected in the majority-party caucus. But the **seniority system** governs most movement into committee leadership positions. The seniority system ranks all committee members in each party according to the length

seniority system Custom whereby the member of Congress who has served the longest on the majority side of a committee becomes its chair and the member who has served the longest on the minority side becomes its ranking member.

of time they have served on the committee. If the majority-party chair exits the Congress or leaves the committee, that position is filled by the next *ranking majority-party member*. New members of a committee are initially added to the bottom of the ranking of their party; they climb the seniority ranking by remaining on the committee and accruing years of seniority. Members who stay in Congress but "hop" committees are usually placed at the bottom of their new committee's list.

The seniority system has a long tradition in the Congress. The advantage is that it tends to reduce conflict among members, who otherwise would be constantly engaged in running for committee posts. It also increases the stability of policy direction in committees over time. Critics of the system note, though, that the seniority system grants greater power to members from "safe" districts— districts that offer little electoral challenge to the incumbent. (Historically in the Democratic Party, these districts were in the conservative South, and opposition to the seniority system developed among liberal northern Democrats. But in recent years, many liberal Democrats gained seniority and the seniority system again became entrenched (see People in Politics: "Ted Kennedy, Keeping Liberalism Alive in the U.S. Senate"). The seniority rule for selecting committee chairs has been violated on only a few notable occasions.

Senator Joe Biden (left), of the Senate Foreign Relations Committee, speaks to reporters after meeting with President Bush about the arms treaty with Russia.

Committee Hearings   The decision of a congressional committee to hold public hearings on a bill or topic is an important one. It signals congressional interest in a particular policy matter and sets the agenda for congressional policy making. Ignoring an issue by refusing to hold hearings on it usually condemns it to oblivion. Public hearings allow interest groups and government bureaucrats to present formal arguments to Congress. Testimony comes mostly from government officials, lobbyists, and occasional experts recommended by interest groups or committee staff members. Hearings are usually organized by the staff under the direction of the chair. Staff members contact favored lobbyists and bureaucrats and schedule their appearances. Committee hearings are regularly listed in the *Washington Post* and are open to the public. Indeed, the purpose of many hearings is not really to inform members of Congress but instead to rally public support behind an issue or a bill. The media are the real target audience of many public hearings, with committee members jockeying in front of the cameras for a "sound bite" on the evening news.

Markup   Once hearings are completed the committee's staff is usually assigned the task of writing a report and **drafting a bill**. The staff's bill generally reflects the chair's policy views. But the staff draft is subject to committee **markup**, a line-by-line consideration of the wording of the bill. Markup sessions are frequently closed to the public in order to expedite work. Lobbyists are forced to stand in the hallways, buttonholing members as they go into and out of committee rooms.

It is in markup that the detailed work of lawmaking takes place. Markup sessions require patience and skill in negotiation. Committee or subcommittee chairs may try to develop consensus on various parts of the bill, either within the whole committee or within the committee's majority. In marking up a bill, members of a subcommittee must always remember that the bill must pass both in the full committee and on the floor of the chamber. Although they have considerable freedom in writing their own policy preferences into law, especially on the details of the legislation, they must give some consideration to the views of these larger bodies. Consultations with party leadership are not infrequent.

drafting a bill Actual writing of a bill in legal language.

markup Line-by-line revision of a bill in committee by editing each phrase and word.

PEOPLE IN POLITICS

Ted Kennedy: Keeping Liberalism Alive in the U.S. Senate

To the American public, Massachusetts Senator Edward M. "Ted" Kennedy is largely a symbol of his family's legendary triumphs and tragedies. But in the U.S. Senate, Kennedy has established himself over the years as the recognized leader of liberal Democrats and a highly effective legislator.

Ted Kennedy's father, Joseph P. Kennedy, was a wealthy banker and stock market manipulator who provided key financial backing for the 1932 presidential campaign of Franklin D. Roosevelt. FDR later appointed "Old Joe" as ambassador to England. The senior Kennedy fathered nine children, including Joseph P. Jr., who was killed in World War II; President John F. Kennedy, who was assassinated in 1963; Senator Robert F. Kennedy, who was assassinated in 1968; and the youngest, Edward M. "Ted" Kennedy.

Although born to great wealth (he received his first communion from the Pope), Ted Kennedy acquired the sense of competition fostered in the large Kennedy household. In 1951, suspended from Harvard for cheating on an examination, he joined the Army and served two years in Germany. He was later readmitted to Harvard from which he graduated in 1956. Rejected by Harvard Law School, he enrolled instead in the University of Virginia Law School and completed his law degree in 1959. When he was just 30 years old, the minimum age for a U.S. senator, he announced his candidacy for the Massa-

chusetts Senate seat formerly held by his brother, who was then president. His 1962 election to the U.S. Senate reflected the esteem that Massachusetts voters have always held for his family.

But Ted's personal life was marred by accident, tragedy, and scandal. He nearly died in a 1964 plane crash in which he suffered a broken back. He was frequently the object of romantic gossip in Washington. In 1969, a young woman died when the car Kennedy was driving plunged off a narrow bridge on Chappaquiddick Island after a late-night party. Missing for ten hours after the accident, Kennedy later made a dramatic national television appearance claiming that the tragedy had been an accident that he had been too confused to report until the next day. He pled guilty to the minor charge of leaving the scene of the accident. Senate Democrats removed Kennedy from his position as majority party whip.

Kennedy deliberately avoided Democratic presidential battles in both 1972 and 1976, believing that the public's memory of Chappaquiddick was still too fresh. However, in late 1979, with President Jimmy Carter standing at a near all-time low for presidents in opinion polls, Kennedy announced his presidential candidacy. But shortly thereafter, Soviet troops invaded neighboring Afghanistan. Support for the president was equated with support for America, and Carter benefited from this "rally round the flag" effect. Carter defeated Kennedy in the Democratic primaries.

As the ranking Democrat on the Senate Health, Education, and Labor Committee, Kennedy has undertaken the lead in a variety of important legislative issues. He helped pass the Family Leave Act of 1993, the Kennedy-Kassebaum Act of 1996 that mandated health insurance "portability" (see Chapter 17), and increases in the minimum wage. In 2006 he was elected to his eighth full term as U.S. senator from Massachusetts with fully 70 percent of the vote.

discharge petition Petition signed by at least 218 House members to force a vote on a bill within a committee that opposes it.

Most bills die in committee. Some are voted down, but most are simply ignored. Bills introduced simply to reassure constituents or interest groups that a representative is committed to "doing something" for them generally die quietly. But House members who really want action on a bill can be frustrated by committee inaction. The only way to force a floor vote on a bill opposed by a committee is to get a majority (218) of House members to sign a **discharge petition**. Out of hundreds of discharge petition efforts, only a few dozen have succeeded. The Senate also can forcibly "discharge" a bill from committee by simple majority vote; but because senators can attach any amendment to any bill they wish, there is generally no need to go this route.

Seniority is a valuable resource in the U.S. Senate. Senators Ted Kennedy (D-MA) and Robert Byrd (D-WV) together have served over eighty years in the Senate.

On the Floor

A favorable "report" by a standing committee of the House or Senate places a bill on the "calendar." The word *calendar* is misleading, because bills on the calendar are not considered in chronological order and many die on the calendar without ever reaching the floor.

House Rules Committee   Even after a bill has been approved by a standing committee, getting it to the floor of the House of Representatives for a vote by the full membership requires favorable action by the Rules Committee. The Rules Committee acts as a powerful "traffic cop" for the House. In order to reach the floor, a bill must receive a rule from the Rules Committee. The Rules Committee can kill a bill simply by refusing to give it a rule. A **rule** determines when the bill will be considered by the House and how long the debate on the bill will last. More important, a rule determines whether amendments from the floor will be permitted and, if so, how many. A **closed rule** forbids House members from offering any amendments and speeds up consideration of the bill in the form submitted by the standing committee. A **restricted rule** allows certain specified amendments to be considered. An **open rule** permits unlimited amendments. Most key bills are brought to the floor of the House with fairly restrictive rules. In recent sessions, about three-quarters of all bills reaching the floor were restricted, and an additional 10 to 15 percent were fully closed. Only a few bills were open.

Senate Floor Traditions   The Senate has no rules committee but relies instead on a **unanimous consent agreement** negotiated between the majority and minority leader to govern consideration of a bill. The unanimous consent agreement generally specifies when the bill will be debated, what amendments will be

rule Stipulation attached to a bill in the House of Representatives that governs its consideration on the floor, including when and for how long it can be debated and how many (if any) amendments may be appended to it.

closed rule Rule that forbids adding any amendments to a bill under consideration by the House.

restricted rule Rule that allows specified amendments to be added to a bill under consideration by the House.

open rule Rule that permits unlimited amendments to a bill under consideration by the House.

unanimous consent agreement Negotiated by the majority and minority leaders of the Senate, it specifies when a bill will be taken up on the floor, what amendments will be considered, and when a vote will be taken.

considered, and when the final vote will be taken. But as the name implies, a single senator can object to a unanimous consent agreement and thus hold up Senate consideration of a bill. Senators do not usually do so, because they know that a reputation for obstructionism will imperil their own favorite bills at a later date. Once accepted, a unanimous consent agreement is binding on the Senate and cannot be changed without another unanimous consent agreement. To get unanimous consent, Senate leaders must consult with all interested senators. Unanimous consent agreements have become more common in recent years as they have become more specific in their provisions.

The Senate cherishes its tradition of unrestricted floor debate. Senators may speak as long as they wish or even try to **filibuster** a bill to death by talking nonstop and tying up the Senate for so long that the leadership is forced to drop the bill in order to go on to other work. Senate rules also allow senators to place a "hold" on a bill, indicating their unwillingness to grant unanimous consent to its consideration. Debate may be ended only if *sixty* or more senators vote for **cloture**, a process of petition and voting that limits the debate. A cloture vote requires a petition signed by sixteen senators; two days must elapse between the petition's introduction and the cloture vote. If cloture passes, then each senator is limited to one hour of debate on the bill. But getting the necessary sixty votes for cloture is difficult. Recently Democrats, although a minority in the Senate, have defeated cloture motions in order to derail President Bush's nominees for federal judgeships (see *What Do You Think?* "Should Presidential Appointments of Judges, Including Supreme Court Justices, Be Thwarted by Senate Filibusters?").

Senate floor procedures also permit unlimited amendments to be offered, even those that are not germane to the bill. A **rider** is an amendment to a bill that is not germane to the bill's purposes.

These Senate traditions of unlimited debate and unrestricted floor amendments give individual senators considerably more power over legislation than individual representatives enjoy.

Floor Voting The key floor votes are usually on *amendments* to bills rather than on their final passage. Indeed, "killer amendments" are deliberately designed to defeat the original purpose of the bill. Other amendments may water down the bill so much that it will have little policy impact. Thus the true policy preferences of senators or representatives may be reflected more in their votes on amendments than their vote on final passage. Members may later claim to have supported legislation on the basis of their vote on final passage, even though they earlier voted for amendments designed to defeat the bill's purposes.

Members may also obscure their voting records by calling for a voice vote—simply shouting "aye" or "nay"—and avoiding recording of their individual votes. In contrast, a **roll-call vote** involves the casting of individual votes, which are reported in the *Congressional Record* and are available to the media and the general public. Electronic voting machines in the House allow members to insert their cards and record their votes automatically. The Senate, truer to tradition, uses no electronic counters.

Conference Committees The Constitution requires that both houses of Congress pass a bill with identical wording. However, many major bills pass each house in different forms, not only with different wording but sometimes with wholly different provisions. Occasionally the House or the Senate will resolve these differences by reconsidering the matter and passing the other chamber's

filibuster Delaying tactic by a senator or group of senators, using the Senate's unlimited debate rule to prevent a vote on a bill.

cloture Vote to end debate—that is, to end a filibuster—which requires a three-fifths vote of the entire membership of the Senate.

rider Amendment to a bill that is not germane to the bill's purposes.

roll-call vote Vote of the full House or Senate at which all members' individual votes are recorded and made public.

WHAT DO YOU THINK?

Should Presidential Appointments of Judges, Including Supreme Court Justices, Be Thwarted by Senate Filibusters?

The Constitution gives a president the power to make judicial appointments, including appointments to the Supreme Court, "by and with the Advice and Consent of the Senate." The Constitution requires only a majority vote of the Senate to consent to the president's appointment.

But from the earliest days of the Senate the idea of "unlimited debate" was enshrined in Senate rules and customs. For over a century, the "filibuster" was honored as "insurance against the will of a majority of states being imposed over the wishes of a minority of states." Over the years, liberals and progressives in the Senate came to loathe the filibuster rule. President Woodrow Wilson (formerly a political science professor at Princeton University and author of a book on Congress) persuaded the Senate to adopt a "cloture rule" (see p. 352 in this chapter) which called for cutting off debate with a two-thirds vote of Senators present and voting. For decades afterward, liberals sought to completely eliminate the filibuster, as it became an important tool of opponents of civil rights legislation. (The Civil Rights Act of 1964 was passed only after a successful cloture vote ended a Southern filibuster.) In 1975 the Senate lowered the vote requirement for cloture to sixty, that is, three-fifths rather than two-thirds.

By the 1990s filibusters became more common as partisanship in the Senate began to rise. Democrats and Republicans both regularly threatened filibusters to stop legislation they opposed. This meant that controversial bills could not get through the Senate without sixty votes, rather than a simple majority of fifty-one.

Senate Democrats began to use the filibuster to thwart judicial nominees submitted by Republican President George W. Bush. Republican Senate Majority Leader Bill Frist argued that such a use violated the Constitution, which requires only a majority vote for judicial confirmations. Several key appeals for court nominations were held up by Democrats threatening filibusters. Republicans had only fifty-five members in the Senate, not the sixty needed to end debate. So in 2005 Frist threatened "the nuclear option"—having the presiding officer of the Senate, Republican Vice President Richard Cheney, declare the filibuster rule for judicial nominations to be

Senate filibusters can be ended only by persuasion or by a three-fifths vote (60 members). Inasmuch as at least one filibustering member must remain continuously on the floor of the Senate, beds are often prepared in Senate offices for periodic alternating-member breaks.

unconstitutional. This ruling would then be upheld by a simple majority vote of the Senate.

But a temporary truce was fashioned in which several Bush judicial appointments were confirmed and the filibuster rule was undisturbed. Senators promised to use it only under "extraordinary circumstances," a phrase left undefined. Republicans promised not to use the nuclear option unless the Democrats fail to abide by the agreement.

Generally, Americans appear to support the filibuster, even against judicial nominees:

Q. *"As you know there are 100 senators. How many senators' votes should it take to move ahead to confirm a Supreme Court nominee? Should a majority of 51 votes be required, or is this something that should require a larger majority of 60 votes"?*

Favor	Oppose	Unsure
28%	37%	35%

Q. *"How do you feel about this issue? Do you favor or oppose changing the rules of the Senate to stop the use of filibusters against judicial nominees?"*

51 votes	60 votes	Unsure
31%	64%	5%

Source: From *Beyond Red and Blue,* Pew Research Center for the People and the Press, May 20, 2005. Copyright © 2005 by the Pew Research Center. Reprinted by permission.

conference committee
Meeting between representatives of the House and Senate to reconcile differences over provisions of a bill passed by both houses.

version of the bill. But about 15 percent of the time, serious differences arise and bills are assigned to **conference committees** to reach agreement on a single version for resubmission to both houses. Conference committees are temporary, with members appointed by the leadership in each house, usually from among the senior members of the committees that approved the bills.

Conference committees can be very powerful. Their final bill is usually (although not always) passed in both houses and sent to the president for approval. In resolving differences between the House and the Senate versions, the conference committee makes many final policy decisions. Although conference committees have considerable leeway in striking compromises, they focus on points of disagreement and usually do not change provisions already approved by both houses. Figure 10.9 summarizes the lawmaking process.

Decision Making in Congress

How do senators and representatives decide about how they will vote on legislation? From an almost limitless number of considerations that go into congressional decision making, a few factors recur across a range of voting decisions: party loyalty, presidential support or opposition, constituency concerns, interest-group pressures, and the personal values and ideologies of members themselves.

party vote Majority of Democrats voting in opposition to a majority of Republicans.

Party Voting   Party appears to be the most significant influence on congressional voting. **Party votes** are roll-call votes on which a majority of voting Democrats oppose a majority of voting Republicans. Traditionally, party votes occurred on roughly *half* of all roll-call votes in Congress. Partisanship in Congress, as reflected in the percentage of party votes, rose during the 1990s but may be moderating somewhat today (see Figure 10.10 on page 356).

party unity Percentage of Democrats and Republicans who stick with their party on party votes.

Party unity is measured by the percentage of Democrats and Republicans who stick by their party on party votes. Both Democratic and Republican Party unity have remained at fairly constant levels (85–95 percent) in both the House and the Senate over the past ten years. This is higher than in previous decades when party unity was regularly 50–60 percent in both the House and Senate. Greater party unity suggests increased partisan polarization in congress.

Sources of Partisanship   Why do Democrats and Republicans in Congress vote along party lines? First of all, the Democratic Party has become more liberal and the Republican Party has become more conservative over the years (see *Up Close:* "Polarization on Capitol Hill"). Conservative Democrats, once very common in southern politics, are rapidly disappearing. At the same time, the ranks of liberal Republicans, mostly from the Northeast, have thinned. Second, the decline in voter turnout, especially in primary elections, has added to the importance of well-organized and ideologically motivated groups. In primary elections Republicans must be more concerned with pleasing conservative activists (e.g., the Christian Coalition, National Right-to-Life Committee, National Rifle Association, etc.), and Democrats must be more concerned with pleasing liberal groups (National Education Association, American Federation of State, County, and Municipal Employees, Sierra Club, etc.). And third, the rising costs of campaigning make members ever more dependent upon the financial support of these interests.

Conflict between the parties occurs frequently on domestic social and economic issues—welfare, housing and urban affairs, health, business regulation, taxing, and

	HOUSE	SENATE
Bill Introduction	Bill is introduced and assigned to a committee, which refers it to the appropriate subcommittee.	Bill is introduced and assigned to a committee, which refers it to the appropriate subcommittee.
Subcommittee Hearings	**Subcommittee** Subcommittee holds hearings and "marks up" the bill. If the bill is approved in some form, it goes to the full committee.	**Subcommittee** Subcommittee holds hearings, debates provisions and "marks up" the bill. If a bill is approved, it goes to the full committee.
Committee Action	**Committee** Full committee considers the bill. If the bill is approved in some form, it is "reported" to the full House and placed on the House calendar.	**Committee** Full committee considers the bill. If the bill is approved in some form, it is "reported" to the full Senate and placed on the Senate calendar.
Floor Action	**Rules Committee** Rules Committee issues a rule to govern debate on the floor. Sends it to the full House. **Full House** Full House debates the bill and may amend it. If the bill passes and it is in a form different from the Senate version, it must go to a conference committee.	**Leadership** Majority and minority leaders negotiate "unanimous consent" agreements scheduling full Senate debate and vote on the bill. **Full Senate** Full Senate debates the bill. Senate may amend it. If the bill passes and is in a form different from the House version, it must go to a conference committee.
Conference Action	**Conference Committee** Conference committee of senators and representatives meets to reconcile differences between bills. When agreement is reached, a compromise bill is sent back to both the House and the Senate.	
Presidential Decision	**President** President signs or vetoes the bill. Congress can override a veto by a two-thirds majority vote in both the House and Senate.	

Figure 10.9 How a Bill Becomes a Law

This diagram depicts the major hurdles a successful bill must overcome in order to be enacted into law. Few bills introduced travel this full path; less than 10 percent of bills introduced are passed by Congress and sent to the president for approval or veto. Bills fail at every step along the path, but most die in committees and subcommittees, usually from inaction rather than from being voted down.

Figure 10.10 Party Voting in Congress

Partisanship varies over time in Congress. For many years, between 30 and 40 percent of votes in the House and Senate were party votes—votes on which a majority of Democrats were in opposition to a majority of Republicans—but during the 1990s the percentage rose, indicating an increasingly partisan environment in Congress.

Note: Data indicate the percentage of all recorded votes on which a majority of voting Democrats opposed a majority of voting Republicans.

Source: Based on data from *Congressional Quarterly Weekly Report,* January 12, 2002, p. 136; December 11, 2005, p. 29–53.

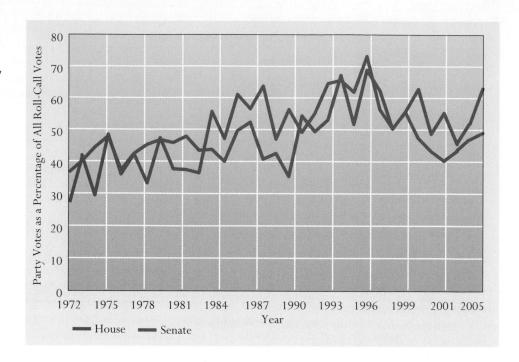

bipartisanship Agreement by members of both the Democratic and the Republican parties.

divided party government One party controls the presidency while the other party controls one or both houses of Congress.

spending. Traditionally, **bipartisanship** was the goal of both presidents and congressional leaders on foreign and defense policy issues. Since the Vietnam War, however, Democrats in the Congress have been more critical of U.S. military involvements (and defense spending in general) than have Republicans.

Presidential Support or Opposition   Presidential influence in congressional voting is closely tied to party. Presidents almost always receive their greatest support from members of their own party (see Figure 10.11). Indeed, policy gridlock is often associated with **divided party government**—in past decades, a Republican president and a Democratic-controlled Congress, but beginning in 1995 a Democratic president and a Republican-controlled Congress.

The decentralization of power in the congressional committee system also limits the president's ability to influence voting. The president cannot simply negotiate with the leadership of the House and Senate but instead must deal with scores of committee and subcommittee chairs and ranking members. To win the support of so many members of Congress, presidents often must agree to insert pork into presidential bills, promise patronage jobs, or offer presidential assistance in campaign fund raising.

If negotiations break down, presidents can "go over the heads" of Congress, using the media to appeal directly to the people to support presidential programs and force Congress to act. The president has better access to the media than Congress has. But such threats and appeals can only be effective when (1) the president himself is popular with the public; and (2) the issue is one about which constituents can be made to feel intensely.

Finally, presidents can threaten to veto legislation. This threat, expressed or implied, confronts congressional leaders, committee chairs, and sponsors of a bill with several options. They must decide whether to (1) modify the bill to overcome the president's objections; (2) try to get two-thirds of both houses to com-

UP CLOSE

Polarization on Capitol Hill

The Democratic and Republican parties in Congress are further apart ideologically than ever before. The Republicans are more uniformly conservative, and the Democrats more liberal, than in previous decades. "The proportion of political moderates—conservative Democrats or liberal Republicans—hovered at about 30 percent in the 1960s and 1970s. . . . Fewer than one in ten of today's lawmakers fall into this centrist category."[a] Conservative Southern Democrats once represented a third of their party's members, and a "conservative coalition" of Republicans and Southern Democrats was once a strong force in the Senate. Indeed, in the early 1980s President Ronald Reagan won the support of many moderate-to-conservative Democrats for his tax cutting measures. But today conservative Democrats account for less than 10 percent of their party's membership in Congress; with the retirement of several Southern Democratic senators in 2004, conservative Democrats have practically disappeared

from the Senate. An even rarer breed—the liberal Republican—is also nearing extinction.

Partisanship and ideology are closely connected in this polarization on Capitol Hill. The result is more conflict, less bipartisan cooperation, and more acrimony in the halls of Congress.

The most common explanation for this polarization is the realignment of Southern voters from the Democratic to the Republican party. Southern conservatives moved almost en bloc into the Republican Party in the 1980s. As conservatives in the Republican Party gained strength, liberal Republicans, mostly from the Northeast, lost ground. Geographically, the Republican Party became centered in the Mountain states and the South, while the Democratic Party held the Northeast and West Coast. Finally, more polarizing issues—abortion, term limits, budget balancing—and a more aggressive leadership style, beginning with Republican Speaker Newt Gingrich in the 1990s and carried on by Democratic leader Nancy Pelosi since 2004, also contributes to party polarization.[b]

[a]Roger H. Davidson and Walter Oleszek. *Congress and Its Members*. 9th ed. Washington, D.C.: CQ Press, 2004, p. 276.

[b]Jason M. Roberts and Steven S. Smith, "Procedure Contexts, Party Strategy, and Conditional Party Voting in the U.S. House of Representatives, 1971–2000." *American Journal of Political Science* 47 (April 2003): pp 305–317.

mit to overriding the threatened veto; or (3) pass the bill and dare the president to veto it, then make a political issue out of the president's opposition. Historically, less than 5 percent of vetoes have been overridden by the Congress. Unless the president is politically very weak (as Richard Nixon was during the Watergate scandal), Congress cannot count on overriding a veto. If members of Congress truly want to address an important problem and not just define a political issue, they must negotiate with the White House to write a bill the president will sign.

Constituency Influence   Constituency influence in congressional voting is most apparent on issues that attract media attention and discussion and generate intense feelings among the general public. If many voters in the home state or district know about an issue and have intense feelings about it, members of Congress are likely to defer to their constituents' feeling, regardless of the position of their party's leadership or even their own personal feelings. Members of Congress from *safe seats* seem to be just as attuned to the interests of their constituents as members from competitive seats (see *Up Close:* "Tips on Lobbying Congress").

Constituencies may also exercise a subtle influence by conditioning the personal views of members. Many members were born, were raised, and continue to live in the towns they represent; over a lifetime they have absorbed and internalized the views of their communities. Moreover, some members of Congress feel an obligation to represent their constituents' opinions even when they personally disagree.

constituency The votes in a legislator's home district.

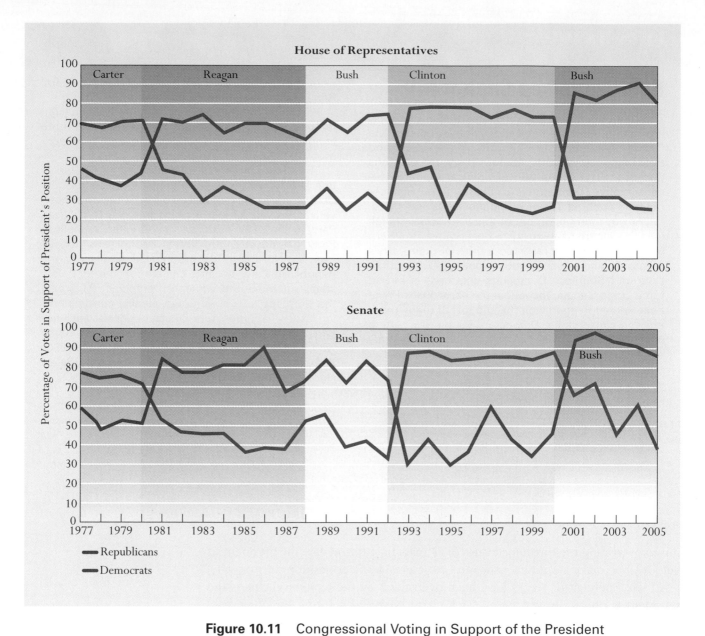

Figure 10.11   Congressional Voting in Support of the President

Presidents always receive more support in Congress from members of their own party. Democratic Presidents Jimmy Carter and Bill Clinton could count on winning large majorities of Democratic members' votes, Republican Presidents Ronald Reagan and George Bush won large majorities of GOP members' votes. Percentages indicate congressional votes supporting the president on votes on which the president took a position.

Source: Norman J. Ornstein, Thomas E. Mann, and Michael J. Malbin, Vital Statistics on Congress 1999–2000 (Washington, D.C.: CQ Press, 2000), pp. 254–55; and *Congressional Quarterly Weekly Report*, December 11, 1999, p. 2987, January 12, 2002, p. 136; December 14, 2003, p. 3275; January 3, 2004, p. 53; December 11, p. 2946;

However, members of Congress have considerable latitude in voting against their constituents' opinions if they choose to do so. Constituents, as noted earlier, lack information about most policy issues and the voting records of their senators and representatives. Even when constituents know about an issue and

UP CLOSE

Tips on Lobbying Congress

YourCongress.com has some good suggestions about how to lobby Congress.

1. Keep it short and to the point. (Good lobbyists tell exactly what they want and why, in the fewest amount of words.)
2. Say thank you. (So few people say anything positive to members of Congress or their staff. If you know that they've done something good, say thank you. They'll remember it.)
3. Get to know the staff. (Good lobbyists don't complain when they don't get to meet the member of Congress. The staff does most of the work anyway, and has a knack for making requests disappear if given a reason to do so.)
4. Tell the whole story. (Good lobbyists don't patronize. They acknowledge when something is difficult and are up front about the opposition.)
5. Timing is everything. (Good lobbyists know the process of Congress, mention the proper deadlines, and don't ask for requests at the last minute.)
6. Always one page, and always written up in advance. (Good lobbyists have already written a draft of what they want before they ask for it, and are always happy to leave it or send it over.)
7. Capitol Hill is the last place to burn bridges. (Good lobbyists don't go ballistic when they are told no. They regroup and wait for another chance. D.C. is a very small place, and being a jerk will only mean you quickly get a reputation for being a jerk.)

feel strongly about it, members can afford to cast a "wrong" vote from time to time. A long record of home style politics—casework, pork barreling, visits, public appearances, and so on—can isolate members of Congress from the wrath generated by their voting records. Only a long string of "wrong" votes on issues important to constituents is likely to jeopardize an incumbent.

Interest-Group Influence   Inside the Washington Beltway, the influence of interest groups, lobbyists, and fund raisers on members of Congress is well understood. This influence is seldom talked about back home or on the campaign trail, except perhaps by challengers. Lobbyists have their greatest effects on the *details* of public policy. Congressional decisions made in committee rooms, at markup sessions, and around conference tables can mean billions of dollars to industries and tens of millions to individual companies. Pressures from competing interest groups can be intense as lobbyists buttonhole lawmakers and try to win legislative amendments that can make or break business fortunes. One of the most potent tools in the lobbyist's arsenal is money. The prohibitive cost of modern campaigning has dictated that dollars are crucial to electoral victory, and virtually all members of Congress spend more time than they would like courting it, raising it, and stockpiling it for the next election. (See also Lobbying Ethics in Chapter 9.)

Voters may be wrong when they think that all members of Congress are crooks, but they are not far off the mark when they worry that their own representatives may be listening to two competing sets of constituents—the real constituents back home in the district and the "cash constituents" who come calling in Washington.[40]

Personal Values   It was the eighteenth-century English political philosopher Edmund Burke, himself a member of Parliament, who told his constituents; "You choose a member indeed; but when you have chosen him, he is not a member of Bristol, but he is a member of *Parliament.*" Burke defended the classic notion of representatives as **trustees** who feel obligated to use their own best judgment

Think Again

Are members of Congress obliged to vote the way their constituents wish, even if they personally disagree?

Think Again

Is it ethical for Congress members to pay special attention to requests for assistance by people who make large campaign contributions?

trustees Legislators who feel obligated to use their own best judgment in decision making.

delegates Legislators who feel obligated to present the views of their home constituents.

about what is good for the nation as a whole. In this theory, representatives are not obligated to vote the views of their constituents. This notion contrasts with the idea of representatives as **delegates** who feel obligated to vote according to the views of "the folks back home" regardless of their own personal viewpoint. Most legislators *claim* to be trustees, perhaps because of the halo effect generated by the independence implied in the term.

Democratic political philosophers have pondered the merits of trustee versus delegate representation over the centuries, but the question only rarely arises in actual congressional deliberations. In many cases, members' own personal views and those of their constituents are virtually identical. Even when legislators perceive conflicts between their own views and those of their constituents, most attempt to find a compromise between these competing demands rather than choose one role or another exclusively. The political independence of members of Congress—their independence from party, combined with the ignorance of their constituents about most policy issues—allows members to give great weight to their own personal ideologies in voting.

Customs and Norms

Over time, institutions develop customs and norms of behavior to assist in their functioning. These are not merely quaint and curious folkways; they promote the purposes of the institution. Congressional customs and norms are designed to help members work together, to reduce interpersonal conflict, to facilitate bargaining and promote compromise.

Civility   Traditionally, members of Congress understood that uncivil behavior—expressions of anger, personal attacks on character, ugly confrontations, flaming rhetoric—undermined the lawmaking function. Indeed, civility was encouraged by the longstanding custom of members of Congress referring to each other in elaborately courteous terms: "my distinguished colleague from Ohio," "the honorable representative from Pennsylvania," and the like. By custom, even bitter partisan enemies in Congress were expected to avoid harsh personal attacks on each other. The purpose of this custom was to try to maintain an atmosphere in which people who hold very different opinions can nevertheless function with some degree of decorum. Unfortunately, many of these customs and norms of behavior are breaking down. Individual ambition and the drive for power and celebrity have led to a decline in courtesy, cooperation, and respect for traditional norms. One result is that it has become increasingly difficult for Congress to reach agreement on policy issues. Another result is that life in Congress is increasingly tedious, conflict-filled, and unpleasant (see *A Conflicting View:* "Congress Can Act Responsibly on Occasion").

The Demise of the Apprenticeship Norm   Years ago, "the first rule"[41] of congressional behavior was that new members were expected to be seen but not heard on the floor, to be studious in their committee work, and to be cooperative with party leaders. But the institutional norm of apprenticeship has been swept aside as increasingly ambitious and independent senators and representatives arrive on Capitol Hill. Today new members of Congress feel free to grab the spotlight on the floor, in committee, and in front of television cameras. "The evidence is clear, unequivocal, and overwhelming: the [apprenticeship] norm is simply gone."[42] Nevertheless, experienced members are more active and influential in shaping legislation than are new members.[43]

A CONFLICTING VIEW

Congress Can Act Responsibly on Occasion

Congress is not always mired in partisanship, squabbling, and gridlock. On occasion it acts responsibly in the national interest. Indeed, consider the following congressional landmarks in U.S. history:

Louisiana Purchase (1803)

President Thomas Jefferson offered to purchase from France nearly 830,000 square miles between the Mississippi and the Rockies for $15 million—about three cents an acre. There is no constitutional provision authorizing the federal government to buy foreign territory, but the Senate, accepting Jefferson's broad interpretation of the Constitution, approved the purchase. The House appropriated the money to consummate the deal. On December 29, 1803, the United States took possession of North America's heartland, doubling the nation's size with territory that would comprise thirteen states.

Homestead Act (1862)

This Civil War–era legislation allowed any family head or adult male to claim 160 acres of prairie land for a $10 registration fee and a promise to live there continuously for five years. It opened up the midwestern United States for immediate settlement. The act drew thousands of English, Irish, Germans, Swedes, Danes, Norwegians, and Czechs to the United States, pushing settlement farther west.

Social Security Act (1935)

The act was designed to secure "the men, women, and children of the nation against certain hazards and vicissitudes of life," explained President Franklin Roosevelt. The act's best-known measure is the social insurance system that provides monthly checks to the elderly.

National Labor Relations Act (1935)

By declaring workers had a right to join unions and bargain collectively with employers for pay raises and improved working conditions, the act spurred the growth of the nation's major industrial unions. Labor's Magna Carta also provided workers with the legal weapons to improve plant conditions and protect themselves from employer harassment.

G.I. Bill of Rights (1944)

The G.I. Bill of Rights, known officially as the Serviceman's Readjustment Act of 1944, offered to pay tuition for college or trade education to ex–World War II servicemen. It also mandated that they receive up to $500 a year for tuition, books, and supplies. Nearly 8 million veterans took advantage of this first G.I. Bill and American higher education expanded rapidly as a result. Veterans also made use of the bill's guaranteed mortgages and low interest rates to buy new homes in the suburbs, inspiring a development boom.

Truman Doctrine (1947) and NATO (1949)

The Truman Doctrine initiated U.S. resistance to expansion of the Soviet Union into Western Europe following World War II, and the NATO treaty has provided the framework for European security for half a century. Truman declared to a joint session of Congress, "I believe that it must be the policy of the United States to support free people who are resisting attempted subjugation by armed minorities or by outside pressures."

Federal Highway Act (1956)

President Dwight D. Eisenhower was right when he said, "More than any single action by the government since the end of the war, this one would change the face of America." The most expensive public-works project in U.S. history, the highway act built the 41,000-mile nationwide interstate highway system.

Civil Rights Act of 1964

Only Congress could end racial segregation in privately owned businesses and facilities. It did so by an overwhelming vote of both houses in the Civil Rights Act of 1964. Injustices endure, but the end of segregated restaurants, theaters, and drinking fountains provided new opportunities for African Americans and helped change white attitudes. In addition, Title VII of the act prohibits gender discrimination and serves as the legal bulwark for women's rights.

Voting Rights Act of 1965

President Lyndon B. Johnson signed this act in the same room in the Capitol where Abraham Lincoln had penned the Emancipation Proclamation. This legislation guaranteed all Americans the most fundamental of all rights—the right to vote. Between the 1964 and 1968 presidential elections, black voter registration increased 50 percent across the nation, even in the reluctant Southern states, giving African Americans newfound political clout.

Medicare and Medicaid (1965)

Congress amended the Social Security Act of 1935 to provide for national health insurance for the aged (Medicare) and for the poor (Medicaid). In 2003 (28 years later) Congress added prescription drug coverage to Medicare.

Specialization and Deference   The committee system encourages members of Congress to specialize in particular policy areas. Even the most independent and ambitious members can perceive the advantage of developing power and expertise in an area especially relevant to their constituents. Traditionally, members who developed a special expertise and accumulated years of service on a standing committee were deferred to in floor proceedings. These specialists were "cue givers" for party members when bills or amendments were being voted on. Members are still likely to defer to specialized committee members when the issues are technical or complicated, or when the issue is outside of their own area of policy specialization, but deference is increasingly rare on major public issues.

Bargaining   Bargaining is central to the legislative process. Little could be achieved if individual members were unwilling to bargain with each other for votes both in committees and on the floor. A willingness to bargain is a long-standing functional norm of Congress.

Members of Congress are not expected to violate their consciences in the bargaining process. On the contrary, members respect one another's issues of conscience and receive respect in return. On most issues, however, members can and do bargain their support. "Horse trading" is very common in committee work. Members may bargain in their own personal interest, in the interests of constituents or groups, or even in the interests of their committee with members of other committees. Because most bargaining occurs in a committee setting, it is seldom a matter of public record. The success and reputation of committee chairs largely depend on their ability to work out bargains and compromises.

Bargaining can assume different forms. Explicit trade-offs such as "If you vote for my bill, I'll vote for yours" are the simplest form of bargaining, but implicit understandings may be more common. Members may help other members in anticipation of receiving reciprocal help at some future unspecified time. Moreover, representatives who refuse to cooperate on a regular basis may find little support for their own bills. Mutual "back scratching" allows members to develop a reservoir of IOUs for the future. Building credit is good business for most members; one can never tell when one will need help in the future.

Bargaining requires a certain kind of integrity. Members of Congress must stick to their agreements. They must not consistently ask too high a price for their cooperation. They must recognize and return favors. They must not renege on promises. They must be trustworthy.

Conference-committee bargaining is essential if legislation acceptable to both houses is to be written. Indeed, it is expected that conferees from each house will bargain and compromise their differences. "Every House-Senate conference is expected to proceed via the methods of 'give and take,' 'trading back and forth,' 'pulling and hauling,' 'horse-trading and compromise,' 'splitting the difference,' etc."[44]

Reciprocity   The norm of *reciprocity*—favors rendered should be repaid in kind—supports the bargaining process. Members willing to accept "half a loaf" traditionally accomplished more than those who insisted on a "whole loaf." But the norm of reciprocity may have weakened in recent years.

Logrolling   Perhaps the most celebrated and reviled form of reciprocity, **logrolling** is mutual agreement to support projects that primarily benefit individual members of Congress and their constituencies. Logrolling is closely associated with pork-barrel legislation. Yet it can occur in virtually any kind of

logrolling Bargaining for agreement among legislators to support each other's favorite bills, especially projects that primarily benefit individual members and their constituents.

legislation. Even interest-group lobbyists may logroll with each other, promising to support each other's legislative agendas.

Leader-Follower Relations   Because leaders have few means of disciplining members, they must rely heavily on their bargaining skills to solicit cooperation and get the work of Congress accomplished. Party leaders can appeal to members' concerns for their party image among the voters. Individual majority members want to keep their party in the majority—if for no other reason than to retain their committee and subcommittee chairs. Individual minority members would like their party to win control of their house in order to assume the power and privileges of committee and subcommittee chairs. Party leaders must appeal to more than partisanship to win cooperation, however.

To secure cooperation, leaders can grant—or withhold—some tangible benefits. A member of the House needs the Speaker's support to get recognition, to have a bill called up, to get a bill scheduled, to see to it that a bill gets assigned to a preferred committee, to get a good committee assignment, and to help a bill get out of the Rules Committee, for example.

Party leaders may also seek to gain support from their followers by doing favors that ease their lives in Washington, advance their legislative careers, and help them with their reelection. Favors from party leaders oblige members to respond to leaders' requests at a later time. Members themselves like to build up a reservoir of good feeling and friendship with the leadership, knowing that eventually they will need some favors from the leadership.

Gridlock   Congress is often criticized for legislative **gridlock**—the failure to enact laws, including appropriations acts, that are widely perceived to have merit. Indeed, much of the popular frustration with Congress relates to gridlock arising from policy and budgetary stalemates. Research has suggested that the following factors contribute to congressional gridlock:[15]

gridlock Political stalemate between the executive and legislative branches arising when one branch is controlled by one major political party and the other branch by the other party.

- Divided party control of the presidency and Congress

- Divided party control of the House and Senate

- Greater ideological polarization (liberal versus conservative) of the parties

- In the Senate, the willingness of members to filibuster against a bill, requiring 60 votes to overcome the opposition

In contrast, the factors that appear to lessen gridlock and encourage significant legislative accomplishment include

- Unified party control of the presidency, House, and Senate

- Larger numbers of moderates among Democrats and Republicans in Congress (as opposed to larger numbers of strong liberals and strong conservatives)

- Overwhelming public support for new legislation

Note that the constitutional structure of American government—separation of powers and checks and balances, as well as bicameralism—plays a major role in gridlock, as does the American two-party system. Overcoming gridlock requires a willingness of members of both parties in both houses of Congress, as well as the White House, to bargain and compromise over legislation. And it requires strong public opinion in support of congressional action.

Fourteen women served in the U.S. Senate in 2005–2006, nine Democrats and seven Republicans. But this number is only 14 percent of that 100-member body.

Congressional Ethics

Although critics might consider the phrase *congressional ethics* to be an oxymoron, the moral climate of Congress today is probably better than in earlier eras of American history. Nevertheless, Congress as an institution has suffered from well-publicized scandals that continue to prompt calls for reform.

Ethics Rules   Congress has an interest in maintaining the integrity of the institution itself and the trust of the people. Thus Congress has established its own rules of ethics. These rules include the following:

■ *Financial disclosure:* All members must file personal financial statements each year.

■ *Honoraria:* Members cannot accept fees for speeches or personal appearances.

■ *Campaign funds:* Surplus campaign funds cannot be put to personal use. (A loophole allowed members elected before 1980 to keep such funds if they left office before January 1, 1993. A record number of House members resigned in 1992; many of them kept substantial amounts of campaign money.)

■ *Gifts:* Members may not accept gifts worth more than $50 (with annual increases in these amounts for inflation).

■ *Free travel:* Members may not accept free travel from private corporations or individuals for more than four days of domestic travel and seven days of international travel per year. (Taxpayer-paid "junkets" to investigate problems at home or abroad or attend international meetings are not prohibited.)

■ *Lobbying:* Former members may not lobby Congress for at least one year after retirement.

But these limited rules have not gone very far in restoring popular trust in Congress.

Gray Areas: Services and Contributions Congress members are expected to perform services for their political contributors. However, a direct *quid pro quo*—receiving a financial contribution specifically for the performance of official duty—is illegal. Few Congress members would be so foolish as to openly state a price to a potential contributor for a specific service, and most contributors know not to state a dollar amount that would be forthcoming if the member performed a particular service for them. But what if the contribution and the service occur close together? A Senate Ethics Committee once found that a close relationship between a service and a contribution to be an "impermissible pattern of conduct [that] violated established norms of behavior in the Senate . . . [and] was improper and repugnant."[46] But the Ethics Committee offered little in the way of a future guidance in handling services for campaign contributors.

Expulsion The Constitution gives Congress the power to discipline its own members. "Each House may . . . punish its Members for disorderly Behaviour, and, with the Concurrence of two thirds, expel a Member." But the Constitution fails to define *disorderly behavior.*

It seems reasonable to believe that criminal conduct falls within the constitutional definition of disorderly behavior. Bribery is a criminal act: it is illegal to solicit or receive anything of value in return for the performance of a government duty. During its notorious Abscam investigation in 1980, the Federal Bureau of Investigation set up a sting operation in which agents posing as wealthy Arabs offered bribe money to members of Congress while secretly videotaping the transactions. Six representatives and one senator were convicted. But criminal conviction does not automatically result in expulsion from Congress. In the Abscam case, only one defendant, Representative Michael "Ozzie" Myers (D-Pa.), was expelled, becoming the first member to be expelled since the Civil War. (Two other House members and the senator resigned rather than face expulsion, and the other three representatives were defeated for reelection.) Perhaps the

Democrat Dan Rostenkowski was the powerful Chairman of the House Ways and Means (taxation) Committee before he was indicted and convicted of misuse of public funds in 1994. He refused to resign, but his Chicago constituents voted him out of office.

A CONSTITUTIONAL NOTE

Congress as the First Branch

The Founders believed that the Congress would be the first and most powerful branch of government. Thus, Article I establishes the Congress, describes its structure, and sets forth its powers. Note that its powers *are* the enumerated powers of the national government. Following the English precedent of two houses of the legislature, a House of Commons and a House of Lords, the Founders created two separate houses, a House of Representatives and a Senate. They did so in part as a result of the Connecticut Compromise, which balanced large population states in the House with the small population states' demands for equality in the Senate. But the Founders also wanted a Senate elected by state legislatures, not the people, "as a defense to the people against their own temporary errors and delusions."

The Founders believed that the Senate would balance the interests and numerical superiority of common citizens with the property interests of the less numerous landowners, bankers, and merchants, who they expected to be sent to the Senate by the state legislatures. This defense against "temporary errors and delusions" of the people was strengthened by different lengths of tenure for the House and Senate. All House members were elected every two years, but Senate members were elected for six-year terms, one-third of the Senate elected every two years. The longer terms of the Senate were designed to protect senators from temporary popular movements. Not until the Seventeenth Amendment was ratified in 1913, over a century later, were senators directly elected by the people. In short, the original Constitution of 1787 was careful to limit the role of the people in lawmaking.

most interesting result of the Abscam investigation: Only one member of Congress approached by the FBI, Democratic Senator Larry Presler of South Dakota, turned down the bribe. The powerful chair of the House Ways and Means Committee, Democrat Dan Rostenkowski (Ill.), was indicted by a federal grand jury in 1994 for misuse of congressional office funds; he refused to resign from Congress, but his Chicago constituents voted him out of office. Democratic Representative Mel Reynolds (Ill.) resigned in 1995, following his criminal conviction on charges of sexual misconduct. (A special election to fill his vacated seat was won by Jesse Jackson Jr., son of the popular preacher, commentator, and former Democratic presidential contender.) Republican Senator Robert Packwood (Oreg.) resigned in 1995 in order to avoid official expulsion following a Senate Ethics Committee report charging him with numerous counts of sexual harassment of female staff. Representative James A. Traficant (D-Ohio) was expelled in 2002 following his conviction on ten federal corruption charges. And Representative Randy Cunningham (D-Calif.) resigned in 2005 after pleading guilty to charges of accepting $2.4 million in bribes from lobbyists.

censure Public reprimand for wrongdoing, given to a member standing in the chamber before Congress.

Censure   A lesser punishment in the Congress than expulsion is official **censure**. Censured members are obliged to "stand in the well" and listen to the charges read against them. It is supposed to be a humiliating experience and fatal to one's political career. In 1983 two members of Congress, Barney Frank (D-Mass.) and Gerry Studds (D-Mass.), were censured for sexual misconduct with teenage congressional pages. Both were obliged to "stand in the well." In 2002 New Jersey Democratic Senator Robert Torricelli was "severely admonished" by the Senate Ethics Committee for "at least the appearance of impropriety" for improperly accepting gifts and campaign contributions. Torricelli abruptly dropped out of his reelection race.

Lesser forms of censure include a public reprimand or admonition by the

Ethics Committee expressing disapproval of the Congress member's behavior. And the Ethics Committee may also order a member to repay funds improperly received.

Summary Notes

- The Constitution places all of the delegated powers of the national government in the Congress. The Founders expected Congress to be the principal institution for resolving national conflicts, balancing interests, and deciding who gets what. Today, Congress is a central battleground in the struggle over national policy. Congress generally does not initiate but responds to policy initiatives and budget requests originating from the president, the bureaucracy, and interest groups. Over time, the president and the executive branch, together with the Supreme Court and federal judiciary, have come to dominate national policy making.

- The Congress represents local and state interests in policy making. The Senate's constituencies are the 50 states, and the House's constituencies are 435 separate districts. Both houses of Congress, but especially the House of Representatives, wield power in domestic and foreign affairs primarily through the "power of the purse."

- Congressional powers include oversight and investigation. These powers are exercised primarily through committees. Although Congress claims these powers are a necessary part of lawmaking, their real purpose is usually to influence agency decision making, to build political support for increases or decreases in agency funding, to lay the political foundation for new programs and policies, and to capture media attention and enhance the power of members of Congress.

- Congress is gradually becoming more "representative" of the general population in terms of race and gender. Redistricting, under federal court interpretations of the Voting Rights Act, has increased African American and Hispanic representation in Congress. And women have significantly increased their presence in Congress in recent years. Nevertheless, women and minorities do not occupy seats in Congress proportional to their share of the general population.

- Members of Congress are independent political entrepreneurs. They initiate their own candidacies, raise their own campaign funds, and get themselves elected with very little help from their party. Members of Congress are largely career politicians who skillfully use the advantages of incumbency to stay in office. Incumbents outspend challengers by large margins. Interest-group political action committees and individual contributors strongly favor incumbents. Congressional elections are seldom focused on

great national issues but rather on local issues and personalities and the ability of candidates to "bring home the bacon" from Washington and serve their constituents.

- Congress as an institution is not very popular with the American people. Scandals, pay raises, perks, and privileges reported in the media have hurt the image of the institution. Nevertheless, individual members of Congress remain popular with their districts' voters.

- Members of Congress spend as much time on "home style" activities—promoting their images back home and attending to constituents' problems—as they do legislating. Casework wins votes one at a time, gradually accumulating political support back home, and members often support each other's "pork-barrel" projects.

- Despite the independence of members, the Democratic and Republican party structures in the House and Senate remain the principal bases for organizing Congress. Party leaders in the House and Senate generally control the flow of business in each house, assigning bills to committees, scheduling or delaying votes, and appointing members to committees. But leaders must bargain for votes; they have few formal disciplinary powers. They cannot deny renomination to recalcitrant members.

- The real legislative work of Congress is done in committees. Standing committees screen and draft legislation; with rare exceptions, bills do not reach the floor without approval by a majority of a standing committee. The committee and subcommittee system decentralizes power in Congress. The system satisfies the desires of members to gain power, prestige, and electoral advantage, but it weakens responsible government in the Congress as a whole. All congressional committees are chaired by members of the majority party. Seniority is still the major determinant of power in Congress.

- In order to become law, a bill must win committee approval and withstand debate in both houses of Congress. The rules attached to a bill's passage in the House can significantly help or hurt its chances. Bills passed with differences in the two houses must be reworked in a conference committee composed of members of both houses and then passed in identical form in both.

- In deciding how to vote on legislation, Congress members are influenced by party loyalty, presidential support or opposition, constituency concerns, interest-group pressures, and their own personal values and ideology. Party majorities oppose each other on roughly half of all roll-call votes in Congress. Presidents receive the greatest support in Congress from members of their own party.

■ The customs and norms of Congress help reduce interpersonal conflict, facilitate bargaining and compromise, and make life more pleasant on Capitol Hill. They include the recognition of special competencies of members, a willingness to bargain and compromise, mutual "back scratching" and logrolling, reciprocity, and deference toward the

leadership. But traditional customs and norms have weakened over time as more members have pursued independent political agendas. And partisanship and incivility in Congress have risen in recent years.

■ Congress establishes its own rules of ethics. The Constitution empowers each house to expel its own members for "disorderly conduct" by a two-thirds vote, but expulsion has seldom occurred. Some members have resigned to avoid expulsion; others have been officially censured yet remained in Congress.

Key Terms

congressional
  session   314
bicameral   314
power of the purse   316
oversight   316
advice and consent   316
confirmation   317
congressional hearings   317
congressional
  investigation   318
apportionment   319
malapportionment   319
redistricting   320
gerrymandering   321
splintering   321
packing   322

incumbent
  gerrymandering   323
affirmative racial
  gerrymandering   323
open seat   325
safe seat   327
turnover   327
Government Accountability
  Office   338
home style   340
casework   340
pork barreling   340
franking privilege   341
Speaker of the
  House   343
majority leader   344

minority leader   344
whips   344
standing committee   346
ranking minority
  member   346
subcommittees   347
seniority system   348
drafting a bill   349
markup   349
discharge petition   350
rule   351
closed rule   351
restricted rule   351
open rule   351
unanimous consent
  agreement   351

filibuster   352
cloture   352
rider   352
roll-call vote   352
conference committees   354
party vote   354
party unity   354
bipartisanship   356
divided party
  government   356
constituency   357
trustees   359
delegates   360
logrolling   362
gridlock   363
censure   366

Suggested Readings

Bond, Jon R., and Richard Fleisher, eds. *Polarized Politics: Congress and the President in a Partisan Era.* Washington, D.C.: CQ Press, 2000. Essay on the rise of partisanship in Washington and its effect on congressional-presidential relations.

Davidson, Robert H., and Walter J. Oleszek. *Congress and Its Members.* 10th ed. Washington, D.C.: CQ Press, 2005. Authoritative text on Congress covering the recruitment of members, elections, House styles and Hill styles, leadership, decision making, and relations with interest groups, presidency, and courts. Emphasizes tension between lawmaking responsibilities and desire to be reelected.

Fenno, Richard F. *Home Style.* Boston: Little, Brown, 1978. The classic description of how attention to constituency by members of Congress enhances their reelection prospects. Home style activities, including casework, pork barreling, travel and appearances back home, newsletters, and surveys, are described in detail.

Herrnson, Paul S. *Playing Hardball: Campaigning for the U.S. Congress.* Upper Saddle River, N.J.: Prentice Hall, 2001.

Congressional candidates' strategies, targeting, fund raising, and getting out the vote.

Herrnson, Paul S. *Congressional Elections: Campaigning at Home and in Washington.* 4th ed. Washington, D.C.: CQ Press, 2003. Interviews with candidates, campaign aides, and political consultants to paint a comprehensive portrait of congressional campaigns.

Jones, Charles O. *Separate but Equal Branches: Congress and the Presidency.* 2nd ed. Washington, D.C.: CQ Press, 1999. Presidential–congressional relations under Johnson, Nixon, Ford, Carter, Reagan, Bush, and Clinton.

Oleszek, Walter J. *Congressional Procedures and Policy Processes.* 6th ed. Washington, D.C.: CQ Press, 2003. The definitive work on congressional rules, procedures and traditions and their effect on the course and content of legislation.

Ornstein, Norman J., Thomas E. Mann, and Michael J. Malbin. *Vital Statistics on Congress.* Washington, D.C.: CQ Press, 2006. Published biennially. Excellent source of data on members of Congress, congressional elections, campaign finance, committees and staff, workload, and voting alignments.

Sinclair, Barbara. *Unorthodox Lawmaking*. 2nd ed. Washington, D.C.: CQ Press, 2000. A description of the various detours and shortcuts a major bill is likely to take in Congress, including five case studies.

Stathis, Stephen W. *Landmark Legislation 1774–2002*. Washington, D.C.: CQ Press, 2003. A summary of major congressional legislation over 225 years, in a single volume.

Make It Real

CONGRESS
The simulation makes the student a member of Congress.

11 THE PRESIDENT
White House Politics

Think About Politics

1 Do you approve of the way the president is handling his job?
Yes ☐ No ☐

2 Should presidents have the power to take actions not specifically authorized by law or the Constitution that they believe necessary for the nation's well-being?
Yes ☐ No ☐

3 Should the American people consider private moral conduct in evaluating presidential performance?
Yes ☐ No ☐

4 Should Congress rally to support a president's decision to send U.S. troops into action even if it disagrees with the decision?
Yes ☐ No ☐

5 Should Congress have the authority to call home U.S. troops sent by the president to engage in military actions overseas?
Yes ☐ No ☐

6 Should Congress impeach and remove a president whose policy decisions damage the nation?
Yes ☐ No ☐

7 Is presidential performance more related to character and personality than to policy positions?
Yes ☐ No ☐

8 Do you think the situation in Iraq was worth going to war?
Yes ☐ No ☐

How much power does the president of the United States really have—over policies, over legislation, over the budget, over how this country is viewed by other nations, even over how it views itself?

★　　★　　★

Presidential Power

Americans look to their president for "Greatness." The presidency embodies the popular "great man" view of history and public affairs—attributing progress in the world to the actions of particular individuals. Great presidents are those associated with great events: George Washington with the founding of the nation, Abraham Lincoln with the preservation of the Union, Franklin D. Roosevelt with the nation's emergence from economic depression and victory in World War II (see *What Do You Think?* "How Would You Rate the Presidents?"). People tend to believe that the president is responsible for "peace and prosperity" as well as for "change." They expect their president to present a "vision" of America's future and to symbolize the nation.

The Symbolic President   The president personifies American government for most people. People expect the president to act decisively and effectively to deal with national problems. They expect the president to be "compassionate"—to show concern for problems confronting individual citizens.[1] The president, while playing these roles, is the focus of public attention and the nation's leading celebrity. Presidents receive more media coverage than any other person in the nation, for everything from their policy statements to their favorite foods to their dogs and cats.

Managing Crises   In times of crisis, the American people look to their president to take action, to provide reassurance, and to protect the nation and its people. It is the president, not the Congress or the courts, who is expected to speak on behalf of the American people in times of national triumph and tragedy.[2] The president gives expression to the nation's pride in victory. The nation's heroes are welcomed and its championship sports teams are feted in the White House Rose Garden.

The president also gives expression to the nation's sadness in tragedy and strives to help the nation go forward. How presidents respond to crises often defines their place in history. Franklin D. Roosevelt raised public morale during the Great Depression of the 1930s by reassuring Americans that "the only thing we have to fear is fear itself." Later he led the nation into war following the Japanese attack on Pearl Harbor, December 7, 1941, "a day which will live in infamy." When the *Challenger* spaceship disintegrated before the eyes of millions of television viewers in

How Would You Rate the Presidents?

From time to time, historians have been polled to rate U.S. presidents (see table). The survey ratings given the presidents have been remarkably consistent. Abraham Lincoln, George Washington, and Franklin Roosevelt are universally recognized as the greatest American presidents. It is more difficult for historians to rate recent presidents; the views of historians are influenced by their own (generally liberal and reformist) political views. Richard Nixon once commented, "History will treat me fairly. Historians probably won't."

Historians may tend to rank activist presidents who led the nation through war or economic crisis higher than passive presidents who guided the nation in peace and prosperity. Initially Dwight Eisenhower, who presided in the relatively calm 1950s, was ranked low by historians. But later, after comparing his performance with those who came after him, his steadiness and avoidance of war raised his ranking dramatically.

Arthur M. Schlesinger (1948)	Arthur M. Schlesinger, Jr. (1962)	Robert Murray (1982)	Arthur M. Schlesinger, Jr. (1996)	W. J. Ridings, S. B. McIver (1997)
Great	**Great**	**Presidential Rank**	**Great**	**Overall Ranking**
1. Lincoln	1. Lincoln	1. Lincoln	1. Lincoln	1. Lincoln
2. Washington	2. Washington	2. F. Roosevelt	2. Washington	2. F. Roosevelt
3. F. Roosevelt	3. F. Roosevelt	3. Washington	3. F. Roosevelt	3. Washington
4. Wilson	4. Wilson	4. Jefferson	**Near Great**	4. Jefferson
5. Jefferson	5. Jefferson	5. T. Roosevelt	4. Jefferson	5. T. Roosevelt
6. Jackson	**Near Great**	6. Wilson	5. Jackson	6. Wilson
Near Great	6. Jackson	7. Jackson	6. T. Roosevelt	7. Truman
7. T. Roosevelt	7. T. Roosevelt	8. Truman	7. Wilson	8. Jackson
8. Cleveland	8. Polk	9. J. Adams	8. Truman	9. Eisenhower
9. J. Adams	8. Truman (tie)	10. L. Johnson	9. Polk	10. Madison
10. Polk	10. J. Adams	11. Eisenhower	**High Average**	11. Polk
Average	11. Cleveland	12. Polk	10. Eisenhower	12. L. Johnson
11. J. Q. Adams	**Average**	13. Kennedy	11. J. Adams	13. Monroe
12. Monroe	12. Madison	14. Madison	12. Kennedy	14. J. Adams
13. Hayes	13. J. Q. Adams	15. Monroe	13. Cleveland	15. Kennedy
14. Madison	14. Hayes	16. J. Q. Adams	14. L. Johnson	16. Cleveland
15. Van Buren	15. McKinley	17. Cleveland	15. Monroe	17. McKinley
16. Taft	16. Taft	18. McKinley	16. McKinley	18. J. Q. Adams
17. Arthur	17. Van Buren	19. Taft	**Average**	19. Carter
18. McKinley	18. Monroe	20. Van Buren	17. Madison	20. Taft
19. A. Johnson	19. Hoover	21. Hoover	18. J. Q. Adams	21. Van Buren
20. Hoover	20. B. Harrison	22. Hayes	19. B. Harrison	22. Bush
21. B. Harrison	21. Arthur	23. Arthur	20. Clinton	23. Clinton
Below Average	21. Eisenhower (tie)	24. Ford	21. Van Buren	24. Hoover
22. Tyler	23. A. Johnson	25. Carter	22. Taft	25. Hayes
23. Coolidge	**Below Average**	26. B. Harrison	23. Hayes	26. Reagan
24. Fillmore	24. Taylor	27. Taylor	24. Bush	27. Ford
25. Taylor	25. Tyler	28. Tyler	25. Reagan	28. Arthur
26. Buchanan	26. Fillmore	29. Fillmore	26. Arthur	29. Taylor
27. Pierce	27. Coolidge	30. Coolidge	27. Carter	30. Garfield
Failure	28. Pierce	31. Pierce	28. Ford	31. B. Harrison
28. Grant	29. Buchanan	32. A. Johnson	**Below Average**	32. Nixon
29. Harding	**Failure**	33. Buchanan	29. Taylor	33. Coolidge
	30. Grant	34. Nixon	30. Coolidge	34. Tyler
	31. Harding	35. Grant	31. Fillmore	35. W. Harrison
		36. Harding	32. Tyler	36. Fillmore
			Failure	37. Pierce
			33. Pierce	38. Grant
			34. Grant	39. A. Johnson
			35. Hoover	40. Buchanan
			36. Nixon	41. Harding
			37. A. Johnson	
			38. Buchanan	
			39. Harding	

Note: These ratings result from surveys of scholars ranging in number from 55 to 950.

Sources: Arthur Murphy, "Evaluating the Presidents of the United States," *Presidential Studies Quarterly* 14 (1984): 117–26; Arthur M. Schlesinger, Jr., "Rating the Presidents: Washington to Clinton," *Political Science Quarterly* 112 (1997): 179–90; William J. Ridings and Stuart B. McIver, *Rating the Presidents* (Secaucus, N.J.: Citadel Press, 1997).

Crisis management is a key presidential responsibility. People look to the president for reassurance in times of national tragedy. President Bush is shown here during one of his many visits to the New Orleans area following Hurricane Katrina in 1995.

1986, Ronald Reagan gave voice to the nation's feelings about the disaster: "I want to say something to the schoolchildren of America who were watching the live coverage of the shuttle's takeoff. I know it is hard to understand, but sometimes painful things like this happen. The future doesn't belong to the faint-hearted. It belongs to the brave." And the terrorist attack on America, September 11, 2001, transformed President George W. Bush in the eyes of the nation:

> Tonight we are a country awakened to danger and called to defend freedom. Our grief has turned to anger, and anger to resolution. Whether we bring our enemies to justice, or bring justice to our enemies, justice will be done.[3]

The White House
This official White House site provides up-to-date information or news about the current president's policies, speeches, appointments, proclamations, and cabinet members.
www.whitehouse.gov

Providing Policy Leadership   The president is expected to set policy priorities for the nation. Most policy initiatives originate in the White House and various departments and agencies of the executive branch and then are forwarded to Congress with the president's approval. Presidential programs are submitted to Congress in the form of messages, including the president's annual State of the Union Address, and in the Budget of the United States Government, which the president presents each year to Congress.

As a political leader, the president is expected to mobilize political support for policy proposals. It is not enough for the president to send policy proposals to Congress. The president must rally public opinion, lobby members of Congress, and win legislative battles. To avoid being perceived as weak or ineffective, presidents must get as much of their legislative programs through Congress as possible. The president is responsible for "getting things done" in the policy arena.

Managing the Economy   The American people hold the president responsible for maintaining a healthy economy. Presidents are blamed for economic downturns, whether or not governmental policies had anything to do with market conditions. The president is expected to "Do Something!" in the face of high unemployment, declining personal income, high mortgage rates, rising inflation, high gasoline prices, or a stock market crash. Herbert Hoover in 1932, Gerald Ford in 1976, Jimmy Carter in 1980, and George Bush in 1992—all incumbent presidents defeated for reelection during recessions—learned the hard way that the general public holds the president responsible for hard economic times.

Presidents must have an economic "game plan" to stimulate the economy—tax incentives to spur investments, spending proposals to create jobs, plans to lower interest rates.

Managing the Government As the chief executive of a mammoth federal bureaucracy with 2.8 million civilian employees, the president is responsible for implementing policy, that is, for achieving policy goals. Policy making does not end when a law is passed. Policy implementation involves issuing orders, creating organizations, recruiting and assigning personnel, disbursing funds, overseeing work, and evaluating results. It is true that the president cannot perform all of these tasks personally. But the ultimate responsibility for implementation—in the words of the Constitution, "to take Care that the Laws be faithfully executed"—rests with the president.

The Global President Nations strive to speak with a single voice in international affairs; for the United States, the global voice is that of the president. As Commander-in-Chief of the armed forces of the United States, the president is a powerful voice in foreign affairs. Efforts by Congress to speak on behalf of the nation in foreign affairs and to limit the war-making power of the president have been generally unsuccessful. It is the president who orders American troops into combat (see *People in Politics*: "George Bush and the War on Terrorism").

Constitutional Powers of the President

Popular expectations of presidential leadership far exceed the formal constitutional powers granted to the president. Compared with the Congress, the president has only modest constitutional powers (see Table 11.1). Nevertheless, presidents have pointed to a variety of clauses in Article II to support their rights to do everything from doubling the land area of the nation (Thomas Jefferson) to routing out terrorists from Afghanistan and invading Iraq (George W. Bush).

Who May Be President? To become president, the Constitution specifies that a person must be a natural-born citizen at least thirty-five years of age and a resident of the United States for fourteen years.

Initially, the Constitution put no limit on how many terms a president could serve. George Washington set a precedent for a two-term maximum that endured until Franklin Roosevelt's decision to run for a third term in 1940 (and a fourth term in 1944). In reaction to Roosevelt's lengthy tenure, in 1947 Congress proposed the Twenty-second Amendment (ratified in 1951), which officially restricts the president to two terms (or one full term if a vice president must complete more than two years of the previous president's term).

Presidential Succession Until the adoption of the Twenty-fifth Amendment in 1967, the Constitution had said little about presidential succession, other than designating the vice president as successor to the president "in Case of the Removal, . . . Death, Resignation, or Inability" and giving Congress the power to decide "what Officer shall then act as President" if both the president and vice president are removed. The Constitution was silent on how to cope with serious presidential illnesses. It contained no provision for replacing a vice president. The incapacitation issue was more than theoretical: James A. Garfield lingered months after being shot in 1881; Woodrow Wilson was an invalid during his last years in office (1919–20); Dwight Eisenhower suffered major heart attacks in office; and Ronald Reagan was in serious condition following an assassination attempt in 1981.

American Presidents
Biographical facts and key events in the lives of all U.S. presidents.
www.americanpresidents.org

Table 11.1   The Constitutional Powers of the President

Chief Executive

Implement policy: "take Care that the Laws be faithfully executed" (Article II, Section 3)
Supervise executive branch of government
Appoint and remove executive officials (Article II, Section 2)
Prepare executive budget for submission to Congress (by law of Congress)

Chief Legislator

Initiate policy: "give to the Congress Information of the State of the Union, and recommend to their Consideration such Measures as he shall judge necessary and expedient" (Article II, Section 3)
Veto legislation passed by Congress, subject to override by a two-thirds vote in both houses
Convene special session of Congress "on extraordinary Occasions" (Article II, Section 3)

Chief Diplomat

Make treaties "with the Advice and Consent of the Senate" (Article II, Section 2)
Exercise the power of diplomatic recognition: "receive Ambassadors" (Article II, Section 3)
Make executive agreements (by custom and international law)

Commander-in-Chief

Command U.S. armed forces: "The president shall be Commander-in-Chief of the Army and Navy" (Article II, Section 2)
Appoint military officers

Chief of State

"The executive Power shall be vested in a President" (Article II, Section 1)
Grant reprieves and pardons (Article II, Section 2)
Represent the nation as chief of state
Appoint federal court and Supreme Court judges (Article II, Section 2)

The Twenty-fifth Amendment stipulates that when the vice president and a majority of the cabinet notify the Speaker of the House and the president pro tempore of the Senate in writing that the president "is unable to discharge the powers and duties of his office," then the vice president becomes *acting* president. To resume the powers of office, the president must then notify Congress in writing that "no inability exists." If the vice president and a majority of cabinet officers do not agree that the president is capable of resuming office, then the Congress "shall decide the issue" within twenty-one days. A two-thirds vote of both houses is required to replace the president with the vice president.

The disability provisions of the amendment have never been used, but the succession provisions have been. The Twenty-fifth Amendment provides for the selection of a new vice president by presidential nomination and confirmation by a majority vote of both houses of Congress. When Vice President Spiro Agnew resigned in the face of bribery charges in 1973, President Richard Nixon nominated the Republican leader of the House, Gerald Ford, as vice president; and when Nixon resigned in 1974, Ford assumed the presidency and made Nelson Rockefeller, governor of New York, his vice president. Thus Gerald Ford's two-year tenure in the White House marked the only time in history when the man serving as president had not been elected to either the presidency or the vice presidency. (If the offices of president and vice president are both vacated, then Congress by law has specified the next in line for the presidency as the Speaker of the House of Representatives, followed by the president pro tempore of the Senate, then the cabinet officers, beginning with the secretary of state.)

PEOPLE IN POLITICS

George Bush and the War on Terrorism

In times of crisis for the nation, presidents matter. What they say and what they do create indelible images that determine how their presidencies are viewed by history. George W. Bush's place in history will likely be measured by his ability to inspire and mobilize the American public for the war on terrorism.

An Unpromising Start

George W. Bush was born into his family's tradition of wealth, privilege, and public service. (Bush's grandfather, investment banker Prescott Bush, was a U.S. senator from Connecticut and chairman of the Yale Corporation, the university's governing board.)

He grew up in Midland, Texas, where his father had established himself in the oil business before going into politics—first as a Houston congressman, then Republican National Chairman, director of the CIA, ambassador to China, and finally vice president and president of the United States. George W. followed in his father's footsteps to Yale University, but he was not the scholar-athlete that his father had been. Rather, he was a friendly, likable, heavy-drinking president of his fraternity. Upon graduation in 1968, he joined the Texas Air National Guard, completed flight school, but never faced combat in Vietnam. He earned an [MBA] degree from Harvard Business School and returned to Midland to enter the oil business himself. Later in his career he would acknowledge his "youthful indiscretions," including a drunk driving arrest in 1976.

Texas Governor

George W. Bush had never held public office before running for governor of Texas in 1994. But he had gained valuable political experience serving as an unofficial adviser to his father during his presidential

campaigns. He went up against the sharp-tongued incumbent Democratic Governor Ann Richards, who ridiculed him as the "shrub" (little Bush). Bush heavily outspent Richards and won 54 percent of the vote, to become Texas's second Republican governor in modern times.

George W.'s political style fit comfortably with the Texas "good old boys" in both parties. Although the Texas legislature was controlled by Democrats, Bush won most of his early legislative battles. Bush's style was to meet frequently and privately with his Democratic opponents and to remain on friendly personal terms with them. He easily won reelection as governor in 1998.

Running for President

Bush denies that his father ever tried to influence his decision to run for president, but many of his father's friends and political associates did, believing that only he could reclaim the White House for the GOP. They compared "Dubya" to Ronald Reagan—amiable, charming, and good-humored, even if a little vague on the details of public policy. His mother's 10,000-name Christmas card list of closest family friends helped in building a bankroll of more than $100 million before the campaign even began. And the GOP establishment stuck with him when he was challenged in the early primary elections by maverick Arizona Republican Senator and Vietnam war hero John McCain.

His Father's Friends

While "Dubya's" father remained in the background, the president's White House and cabinet appointments indicated his reliance on experienced people to run the government. People who served in the Reagan and earlier Bush administrations surround George W. Bush. Bush chose Richard Cheney as his vice president, even though Cheney, as a former small state (Wyoming) congressman, brought no significant electoral votes to the ticket. But Cheney had won the confidence of the Bushes as secretary of defense during the Gulf War. Bush also brought the former chairman of the Joint Chiefs of Staff, Colin Powell, into his administration as secretary of state. Presi-

---

impeachment Equivalent of a criminal charge against an elected official; removal of the impeached official from office depends on the outcome of a trial.

Impeachment   The Constitution grants Congress the power of **impeachment** over the president, vice president, and "all civil Officers of the United States" (Article II, Section 4). Technically, impeachment is a charge similar to a criminal indictment brought against an official. The power to bring charges of impeachment is given to the House of Representatives. The power to try all impeachments is given to the Senate, and "no Person shall be convicted without the Concurrence

dent Gerald Ford's secretary of defense, Donald Rumsfeld, was reappointed to his old job. National Security Adviser Condoleezza Rice brought a reputation for brilliance and independence to her position. It was clear that "Dubya" was not afraid of being overshadowed by "heavyweights" in his administration.

"9/11"

The terrorist attack on America, September 11, 2001, dramatically changed the political landscape in Washington and the nation. The attack became the defining moment in the presidency of George W. Bush. He grew in presidential stature, respect, and decisiveness. His public appearances and statements reassured the American people. He promptly declared a "War on Terrorism" against both the terrorist organizations themselves and the nations that harbor and support them.

Military action in Afghanistan followed quickly. Bush showed no hesitation, no indecision, no willingness to negotiate with terrorists. His public approval ratings skyrocketed: 90 percent of Americans approved of the way he was handling his job, a figure that even exceeded his father's approval ratings during the Gulf War. The rapid collapse of the hated Taliban government in Afghanistan seemed to confirm the wisdom of Bush's actions.

Good Versus Evil

George Bush convinced the American people that the war on terrorism is "a monumental struggle of good versus evil." In his 2002 State of the Union message he specifically identified an "axis of evil"—Iraq, Iran, and North Korea. While many in the media scoffed at Bush's portrayal of the war on terrorism as a struggle between good and evil, most Americans heralded what they saw as Bush's "moral clarity" and the firmness of his convictions. Bush failed to win the support of the United Nations to oust Saddam Hussein from power in Iraq. (Only Britain, under the leadership of Tony Blair, gave Bush significant support.) But Bush succeeded in getting Congress to pass the joint resolution granting him authority to launch a preemptive military strike against Iraq. The early military phase of the war in Iraq went well; U.S. forces captured Baghdad in a mere 21 days, with precious few casualties. But remnants of Saddam's forces together with terrorists and other hard-line organizations began a guerrilla war against American and other coalition forces. Confronted with a prolonged struggle, costing lives and money, critics at home and abroad questioned American purposes in Iraq. Bush's high approval ratings began a slow decline. Throughout most of 2004, polls showed Bush running neck and neck with John Kerry in the presidential race. Kerry won the debates, but Bush remained "better at handling the war on terrorism." Election day brought the highest turnout in almost thirty years, and exit polls reported that "moral values" were the single most important concern of voters. These voters seemed to appreciate Bush's commitment to faith and family. He won 51 percent of the popular vote.

Second Term Troubles

But Bush's second term turned out to be troublesome. His approval ratings plummeted into the 30s, and a majority of people turned against his "stay the course" policy in Iraq. He failed to get any significant legislation passed by a Republican Congress, despite impassioned pleas for Social Security and immigration reform. The election of a Democratic-controlled Congress in 2006 promised even more difficulties in his final two years in office. Bush was obliged to signal changes in Iraq policy by accepting the resignation of Defense Secretary Donald Rumsfeld the day after the midterm election.

After the September 11 terrorist attacks, U.S. troops moved quickly into Afghanistan to eliminate the Taliban.

of two thirds of the Members present" (Article I, Section 3). Impeachment by the House and conviction by the Senate only remove an official from office; a subsequent criminal trial is required to inflict any other punishment.

The Constitution specifies that impeachment and conviction can only be for "Treason, Bribery, or other High Crimes and Misdemeanors." These words indicate that Congress is not to impeach presidents, federal judges, or any other officials simply because Congress disagrees with their decisions or policies. Indeed, the phrase implies that only serious criminal offenses, not political conflicts, can result in impeachment. Nevertheless, politics was at the root of the impeachment of President Andrew Johnson in 1867. Johnson was a southern Democrat who had remained loyal to the Union. Lincoln had chosen him as vice president in 1864 as a gesture of national unity. A Republican House impeached him on a party-line vote, but after a month-long trial in the Senate, the "guilty" vote fell one short of the two-thirds needed for removal.[4] And partisan politics played a key role in the House impeachment and later Senate trial of Bill Clinton (see *Up Close:* "Sex, Lies, and Impeachment").

Presidential Pardons   The Constitution grants the president the power to "grant Reprieves and Pardons." This power derives from the ancient right to appeal to the king to reverse errors of law or justice committed by the court system. It is absolute: The president may grant pardons to anyone for any reason. The most celebrated use of the presidential pardon was President Ford's blanket pardon of former President Nixon "for all offenses against the United States which he, Richard Nixon, has committed or may have committed or taken part in." Ford defended the pardon as necessary to end "the bitter controversy and divisive national debate," but his actions may have helped cause his defeat in the 1976 election.

Executive Power   The Constitution declares that the "executive Power" shall be vested in the president, but it is unclear whether this statement grants the president any powers that are not specified later in the Constitution or given to the president by acts of Congress. In other words, does the grant of "executive Power" give presidents constitutional authority to act as they deem necessary *beyond* the actions specified elsewhere in the Constitution or specified in laws passed by Congress?

Contrasting views on this question have been offered over two centuries. President William Howard Taft provided the classic narrow interpretation of executive power: "The president can exercise no power which cannot be fairly and reasonably traced to some specific grant of power or justly implied and included within such express grant as proper and necessary to its exercise.[5] Theodore Roosevelt, Taft's bitter opponent in a three-way race for the presidency in 1912, expressed the opposite view: "My belief was that it was not only his right but his duty to do anything that the needs of the nation demanded, unless such action was forbidden by the Constitution or by the laws."[6] Although the constitutional question has never been fully resolved, history has generally sided with those presidents who have taken an expansive view of their powers.

Some Historical Examples   U.S. history is filled with examples of presidents acting independently, beyond specific constitutional powers or laws of Congress. Among the most notable:

- George Washington issued a Proclamation of Neutrality during the war between France and Britain following the French Revolution, thereby establishing the president's power to make foreign policy.

- Thomas Jefferson, who prior to becoming president argued for a narrow interpretation of presidential powers, purchased the Louisiana Territory despite the fact that the Constitution contains no provision for the acquisition of territory, let alone authorizing presidential action to do so.

Think Again

Should presidents have the power to take actions not specifically authorized by law or the Constitution that they believe necessary for the nation's well-being?

Center for the Study of the Presidency

Studies of the presidency and publication of the scholarly journal *Presidential Studies Quarterly*.

www.thepresidency.org

UP CLOSE

Sex, Lies, and Impeachment

Bill Clinton is the second president in the nation's history (following Andrew Johnson in 1867) to be impeached by the U.S. House of Representatives. (President Richard Nixon resigned just prior to an impeachment vote in 1974.)

Clinton's impeachment followed a report to the House by Independent Counsel Kenneth Starr in 1998 that accused the president of perjury, obstruction of justice, witness tampering, and "abuse of power." The Starr Report describes in graphic and lurid detail Clinton's sexual relationship with young White House intern Monica Lewinsky.

Does engaging in extramartial sex and lying about it meet the Constitution's standard for impeachment—"Treason, Bribery, or other High Crimes and Misdemeanors"? Perjury—knowingly giving false testimony in a sworn legal proceeding—is a criminal offense. But does the Constitution envision more serious misconduct? According to Alexander Hamilton in the *Federalist*, No. 65, impeachment should deal with "the abuse or violation of some public trust." Is Clinton's acknowledged "inappropriate behavior" a private affair or a violation of the public trust?

How are such questions decided? Despite pious rhetoric in Congress about the "search for truth," "impartial investigation," and "unbiased constitutional judgment," the impeachment process, whatever the merits of the charges against a president, is *political,* not judicial.

The House vote to impeach Clinton on December 19, 1998 (228 to 205), was largely along partisan lines, with all but five Republicans voting "yes" and all but five Democrats voting "no." And the vote in Clinton's Senate "trial" on February 12, 1999, was equally partisan. Even on the strongest charge—that Clinton had tried to obstruct justice—the Senate failed to find the president guilty. Removing Clinton failed to win even a majority of Senate votes, far less than the required two-thirds. All forty-five Democrats were joined by five Republicans to create a 50–50 tie vote that left Clinton tarnished but still in office.

Most Americans believed the president had a sexual affair in the White House and subsequently lied about it; however, they also *approved* of the way Clinton was performing his job as president. Indeed, the public appeared to rally around the president following the allegations of sexual misconduct.

Various explanations have been offered for this apparent paradox—a public that believed the president had an affair in the White House and lied about it, yet gave the president the highest approval ratings of his career. Many Americans believe that private sexual conduct is irrelevant to the performance

President Clinton greets well-wishers, including Monica Lewinsky, at a Democratic Party event in January 1996. Clinton's acknowledged "inappropriate behavior" and his efforts to conceal his relationship with Lewinsky were the subjects of the impeachment investigation opened against him by the House in 1998.

of public duties. Private morality is viewed as a personal affair about which Americans should be nonjudgmental. Some people said, "If it's okay with Hillary, why should we worry?" Haven't we had adulterous presidents before, from Thomas Jefferson to John F. Kennedy, presidents who were ranked highly in history? And many Americans believe that "they all do it."

Others argue, nonetheless, that private character counts in presidential performance, indeed, that it is a prerequisite for public trust. The president, in this view, performs a symbolic role that requires dignity, honesty, and respect. A president publicly embarrassed by sexual scandal, diminished by jokes, and laughed at by late-night television audiences cannot perform this role. The acceptance of a president's adulterous behavior, according to one commentator, lowers society's standards of behavior. "The president's legacy . . . will be a further vulgarization and demoralization of society."[a]

[a]Gertrude Himmelfarb, "Private Lives, Public Morality," *New York Times*, February 9, 1998.

- Andrew Jackson ordered the removal of federal funds from the national bank and removed his secretary of the treasury from office, establishing the president's power to *remove* executive officials, a power not specifically mentioned in the Constitution.

- Abraham Lincoln, asking, "Was it possible to lose the nation yet preserve the Constitution?" established the precedent of vigorous presidential action in national emergencies: He blockaded southern ports, declared martial law in parts of the country, and issued the Emancipation Proclamation—all without constitutional or congressional authority.

- Franklin D. Roosevelt, battling the Great Depression during the 1930s, ordered the nation's banks to close temporarily. Following the Japanese attack on Pearl Harbor in 1941, he ordered the incarceration without trial of many thousands of Americans of Japanese ancestry living on the West Coast.

Checking Presidential Power   President Harry Truman believed that "the president has the right to keep the country from going to hell," and he was willing to use means beyond those specified in the Constitution or authorized by Congress. In 1952, while U.S. troops were fighting in Korea, steelworkers at home were threatening to strike. Rather than cross organized labor by forbidding the strike under the terms of the Taft-Hartley Act of 1947 (which he had opposed), Truman chose to seize the steel mills by executive order and continue their operations under U.S. government control. The U.S. Supreme Court ordered the steel mills returned to their owners, however, acknowledging that the president may have inherent powers to act in a national emergency but arguing that Congress had provided a legal remedy, however distasteful to the president. Thus the president can indeed act to keep the country from "going to hell," but if Congress has already acted to do so, the president must abide by the law.[7]

The most dramatic illustration of the checking of presidential power was the forced resignation of Richard M. Nixon in 1974 (for details, see *Up Close:* "Watergate and the Limits of Presidential Power"). Nixon's conduct inspired the intense hostility of the nation's media, particularly the prestigious *Washington Post.* His high public approval ratings following the Vietnam peace agreement plummeted. A Democratic-controlled Senate created a special committee to investigate **Watergate** that produced damaging revelations almost daily. Congressional Republicans began to desert the embattled president. The Supreme Court ordered him to turn over White House audiotapes to a special investigator, tapes that implicated Nixon in cash payments to the men who had burglarized the Democratic National Committee offices during his 1972 reelection campaign. Facing the enmity of the media, the loss of public approval, opposition from his own party in the Congress, and the failure of his constitutional claim of "executive privilege" in the Supreme Court, Nixon became the only president of the United States ever to resign that office.

Executive Privilege   Over the years, presidents and scholars have argued that the Constitution's establishment of a separate executive branch of government entitles the president to **executive privilege**—the right to keep confidential communications from other branches of government. Public exposure of internal executive communications would inhibit the president's ability to obtain candid advice from subordinates and would obstruct the president's ability to conduct negotiations with foreign governments or to command military operations.

— Think Again —
Should Congress have the authority to call home U.S. troops sent by the president to engage in military actions overseas?

Watergate The scandal that led to the forced resignation of President Richard M. Nixon. Adding "gate" as a suffix to any alleged corruption in government suggests an analogy to the Watergate scandal.

executive privilege Right of a president to withhold from other branches of government confidential communications within the executive branch; although posited by presidents, it has been upheld by the Supreme Court only in limited situations.

UP CLOSE

Watergate and the Limits of Presidential Power

Richard Nixon was the only president ever to resign the office. He did so to escape certain impeachment by the House of Representatives and a certain guilty verdict in trial by the Senate. Yet Nixon's first term as president included a number of historic successes. He negotiated the first ever strategic nuclear arms limitation treaty, SALT I, with the Soviet Union. He changed the global balance of power in favor of the Western democracies by opening relations with the People's Republic of China and dividing the communist world. In his second term, he withdrew U.S. troops from Vietnam, negotiated a peace agreement, and ended one of America's longest and bloodiest wars. But his remarkable record is forever tarnished by his failure to understand the limits of presidential power.

On the night of June 17, 1972, five men with burglary tools and wiretapping devices were arrested in the offices of the Democratic National Committee in the Watergate Building in Washington. Also arrested were E. Howard Hunt Jr., G. Gordon Liddy, and James W. McCord Jr., all employed by the Committee to Reelect the President (CREEP). All pleaded guilty and were convicted, but U.S. District Court Judge John J. Sirica believed that the defendants were shielding whoever had ordered and paid for the operation.

Although there is no evidence that Nixon himself ordered or had prior knowledge of the break-in, he discussed with his chief of staff, H. R. Haldeman, and White House advisers John Ehrlichman and John Dean the advisability of payoffs to buy the defendants' silence. Nixon hoped his landslide electoral victory in November 1972 would put the matter to rest.

But a series of sensational revelations in the *Washington Post* kept the story alive. Using an inside source known only as Deep Throat, Bob Woodward and Carl Bernstein, investigative reporters for the *Post,* alleged that key members of Nixon's reelection committee, including its chairman, former Attorney General John Mitchell, and White House staff were actively involved in the break-in and, more important, in the subsequent attempts at a cover-up.

In February 1973 the U.S. Senate formed a Special Select Committee on Campaign Activities—the "Watergate Committee"—to delve into Watergate and related activities. The committee's nationally televised hearings enthralled millions of viewers with lurid stories of "the White House horrors." John Dean broke with the White House and testified

Richard Nixon was the only president ever to resign the office. He did so in 1974 to avoid impeachment following the Watergate scandal. He is shown here leaving the White House for the last time.

before the committee that he had earlier warned Nixon the cover-up was "a cancer growing on the presidency." Then, in a dramatic revelation, the committee—and the nation—learned that President Nixon maintained a secret tape-recording system in the Oval Office. Hoping that the tapes would prove or disprove charges of Nixon's involvement in the cover-up, the committee issued a subpoena to the White House. Nixon refused to comply, arguing that the constitutional separation of powers gave the president an "executive privilege" to withhold his private conversations from Congress. However, the U.S. Supreme Court, voting 8 to 0 in *United States v. Richard M. Nixon,* ordered Nixon to turn over the tapes.

Despite the rambling nature of the tapes, committee members interpreted them as confirming Nixon's involvement in the payoffs and cover-up. Informed by congressional leaders of his own party that impeachment by a majority of the House and removal from office by two-thirds of the Senate were assured, on August 9, 1974, Richard Nixon resigned his office.

On September 8, 1974, new President Gerald R. Ford pardoned former President Nixon "for all offenses against the United States which he, Richard Nixon, has committed or may have committed or taken part in" during his presidency. Upon his death in 1994, Nixon was eulogized for his foreign policy successes.

But Congress has never recognized executive privilege. It has frequently tried to compel the testimony of executive officials at congressional hearings. Presidents have regularly refused to appear themselves at congressional hearings and have frequently refused to allow other executive officials to appear or divulge specific information, citing executive privilege. The federal courts have generally refrained from intervening in this dispute between the executive and legislative branches. However, the Supreme Court has ruled that the president is not immune from court orders when illegal acts are under investigation. In *United States v. Nixon* (1974), the U.S. Supreme Court acknowledged that although the president might legitimately claim executive privilege where military or diplomatic matters are involved, such a privilege cannot be invoked in a criminal investigation. The Court ordered President Nixon to surrender tape recordings of White House conversations between the president and his advisors during the Watergate scandal.[8] (See *Up Close:* "Watergate and the Limits of Presidential Power.")

Presidential Impoundment   The Constitution states that "no Money shall be drawn from the Treasury, but in Consequence of appropriations made by Law" (Article I, Section 9). Clearly the president cannot spend money *not* appropriated by Congress. But the Constitution is silent on whether the president *must* spend all of the money appropriated by Congress for various purposes. Presidents from Thomas Jefferson onward frequently refused to spend money appropriated by Congress, an action referred to as **impoundment**. But taking advantage of a presidency weakened by the Watergate scandal, the Congress in 1974 passed the Budget and Impoundment Control Act, which requires the president to spend all appropriated funds. The act does provide, however, that presidents may send Congress a list of specific **deferrals**—items on which they wish to postpone spending—and **rescissions**—items they wish to cancel altogether. Congress by *resolution* (which cannot be vetoed by the president) may restore the deferrals and force the president to spend the money. Both houses of Congress must approve a rescission; otherwise the government must spend the money.

impoundment Refusal by a president to spend monies appropriated by Congress; outlawed except with congressional consent by the Budget and Impoundment Control Act of 1974.

deferrals Items on which a president wishes to postpone spending.

rescissions Items on which a president wishes to cancel spending.

Responsibility to the Courts   The president is not "above the law"; that is, his conduct is not immune from judicial scrutiny. The president's official conduct must be lawful; federal courts may reverse presidential actions found to be unconstitutional or violative of laws of Congress. And presidents are not immune from criminal prosecution; they cannot ignore demands to provide information in criminal cases. However, the Supreme Court has held that the president has "absolute immunity" from civil suits "arising out of the execution of official duties."[9] In other words, the president cannot be sued for damages caused by actions or decisions that are within his constitutional or legal authority.

But can the president be sued for *private* conduct beyond the scope of his official duties? In 1997 the U.S. Supreme Court rejected the notion of presidential immunity from civil claims arising from actions outside of the president's official duties.[10] (See *Up Close:* "William Jefferson Clinton v. Paula Corbin Jones," in Chapter 13.)

Political Resources of the President

The real sources of presidential power are not found in the Constitution. The president's power is the *power to persuade.* As Harry Truman put it, "I sit here all day trying to persuade people to do things they ought to have sense enough to do without my persuading them. . . . That's all the powers of the president amount to."[11]

The president's political resources are potentially very great. The nation looks to the president for leadership, for direction, for reassurance. The president is the focus of public and media attention. The president has the capacity to mobilize public opinion, to communicate directly with the American people, and to employ the symbols of office to advance policy initiatives in both foreign and domestic affairs.

The Reputation for Power   A reputation for power is itself a source of power. Presidents must strive to maintain the image of power in order to be effective. A president perceived as powerful can exercise great influence abroad with foreign governments and at home with the Congress, interest groups, and the executive bureaucracy. A president perceived as weak, unsteady, bumbling, or error prone will soon become unpopular and ineffective.

Presidential Popularity   Presidential popularity with the American people is a political resource. Popular presidents cannot always transfer their popularity into foreign policy successes or legislative victories, but popular presidents usually have more success than unpopular presidents.

Presidential popularity is regularly tracked in national opinion polls. For more than forty years, national surveys have asked the American public: "Do you approve or disapprove of the way _____ is handling his job as president?" (see Figures 11.1 and 11.2). Analyses of variations over time in these poll results suggest some generalizations about presidential popularity (see Figure 11.1).

Presidential popularity is usually high at the beginning of a president's term of office, but this period can be very brief. The American public's high expectations

— Think Again —
Is presidential performance more related to character and personality than to policy positions?

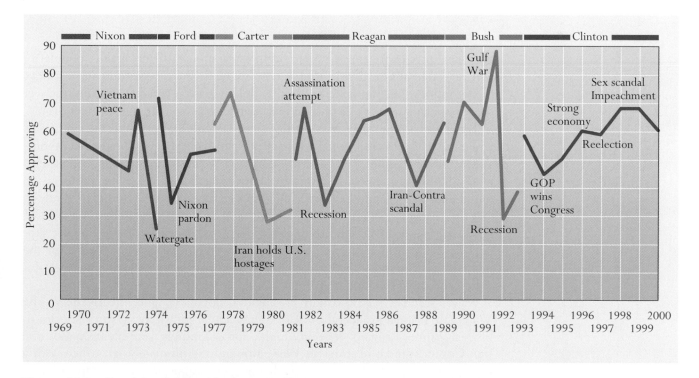

Figure 11.1   Presidential Popularity over Time

Americans expect a great deal from their presidents and are quick to give these leaders the credit—and the blame—for major events in the nation's life. In general; public approval (as measured by response to the question "Do you approve or disapprove of the way _____ is handling the job of president?") is highest at the beginning of a new president's term in office and declines from that point. Major military confrontations generally raise presidential ratings initially but can (as in the case of Lyndon Johnson) cause dramatic decline if the conflict drags on. In addition, public approval of the president is closely linked to the nation's economic health. When the economy is in recession, Americans tend to take a negative view of the president.

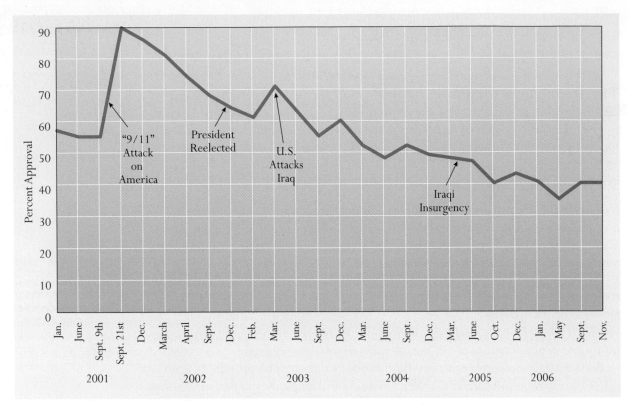

Figure 11.2   George W. Bush's Approval Ratings
Source: Various polls reported in *The Polling Report.*

for a new president can turn sour within a few months. A president's popularity will vary a great deal during a term in office, with sharp peaks and steep valleys in the ratings. But the general trend is downward.[12] Presidents usually recover some popularity at the end of their first term as they campaign for reelection.

Presidential popularity rises during crises. People "rally 'round the president" when the nation is confronted with an international threat or the president initiates a military action.[13] President George H.W. Bush, for example, registered nearly 90 percent approval during the Persian Gulf War. Likewise, the invasion of Grenada in 1983 and Panama in 1989 rallied support to the president. And the "9/11" terrorist attack on America rallied the American people behind George W. Bush (see Figure 11.2). But prolonged warfare and stalemate erode popular support. In both the Korean and the Vietnam wars, initial public approval of the president and support for the war eroded over time as military operations stalemated and casualties mounted.[14]

Major scandals *may* also hurt presidential popularity and effectiveness. The Watergate scandal produced a low of 22 percent approval for Nixon just prior to his resignation. Reagan's generally high approval ratings were blemished by the Iran-Contra scandal hearings in 1987, although he ultimately left office with a high approval rate. But highly publicized allegations of sexual improprieties against President Clinton in early 1998 appeared to have the opposite effect; Clinton's approval ratings went *up*. Perhaps the public differentiates between private sexual conduct and performance in office.

Finally, economic recessions erode presidential popularity. Every president in office during a recession has suffered loss of popular approval, including President Reagan during the 1982 recession. But no president suffered a more precipitous decline in approval ratings than George H.W. Bush, whose popularity plummeted from its Gulf War high of 89 percent in 1991 to a low of 37 percent in only a year, largely as a result of recession.

Access to the Media   The president dominates the news more than any other single person. All major television networks, newspapers, and newsmagazines have reporters (usually their most experienced and skilled people) covering the "White House beat." The presidential press secretary briefs these reporters daily, but the president also may appear in person in the White House press room at any time. Presidents regularly use this media access to advance their programs and priorities.[15]

The **White House press corps** is an elite group of reporters assigned to cover the president. It includes the prestige press—the *New York Times, Washington Post, Wall Street Journal, Time, Newsweek, U.S. News and World Report*, as well as the television networks—ABC, CBS, NBC, CNN, FOX, and even the foreign press. Indeed, more than 1,800 journalists have White House press credentials. Fortunately, however, not all show up at once (there are only 48 seats in the White House briefing room, and attendance at press conferences is usually about 300). The great majority of daily newspapers have no Washington correspondents, but instead rely on national news services such as the Associated Press.

Formal press conferences are a double-edged sword for the president. They *can* help mobilize popular support for presidential programs. Presidents often try to focus attention on particular issues, and they generally open press conferences with a policy statement on these issues. But reporters' questions and subsequent reporting often refocus the press conference in other directions. Often the lead media story emerging from a press conference has nothing to do with the president's purpose in holding the conference. The president cannot control questions or limit the subject matter of press conferences.

Presidents may also use direct television addresses from the White House. (President Reagan made heavy use of national prime time television appeals to mobilize support for his programs; he was exceptionally successful in generating telephone calls, wires, and letters to Congress in support of his programs.) President George W. Bush has also used direct addresses to try to mobilize support for the war on terrorism, including military actions in Afghanistan and Iraq.

However, there is some evidence that with the multiplication of channels available to the public, presidential addresses may have less impact today on public opinion than in previous years. Television ratings for presidential addresses have been declining, and in reaction some broadcast networks have declined to cover presidential addresses.[16] Even the State of the Union Address attracts fewer viewers than in the past. Nonetheless, presidents continue to receive more television and press coverage than any other political figure. And a combination of national speeches, press conferences, speeches to various groups around the country, and media interviews, together with public appearances by members of their administrations, can move public opinion in the president's direction.[17]

White House press corps
Reporters from both print and broadcast media assigned to regularly cover the president.

Personality versus Policy

A president with an engaging personality—warmth, charm, and good humor—can add to his political power. And, of course, a president who seems distant, uncaring, or humorless can erode his political resources. (Richard Nixon's seeming mean-spiritedness contributed to the collapse of his approval ratings during the Watergate scandal; Jimmy Carter's often cold and distant appearance failed

President George W. Bush answers questions during a press conference. These meetings with the press can be a double-edged sword. They give the president an opportunity to present his point of view to the public, but they also allow the press to raise issues a president might rather avoid.

to inspire much popular support for his programs; and George H. W. Bush appeared to be uncaring about the economic circumstances of ordinary Americans.) The public evaluates presidents as much on style as on policy substance.[18] (Perhaps no other president in recent times enjoyed such personal popularity while pursuing relatively unpopular policies as Ronald Reagan.) If the public thinks the president understands and cares about their problems, they may be willing to continue to approve of the job he is doing despite policy setbacks. In other words, the public evaluates the president by how much they like him as a person. (President Bill Clinton's likability kept his public approval ratings high during the sex scandal and impeachment effort.) Yet, as we have seen, public approval ratings of presidents can rise or fall based on wars and crises, scandals, and economic prosperity or recession, even while their personal style remains unaltered.

Bush's presidential campaigns, both against Al Gore in 2000 and John Kerry in 2004, rested largely on his personal appeal to voters—his perceived trustworthiness, warmth, good humor, and general "likability." With a strong economy, budget surpluses, relative peace, and a popular president to follow, Al Gore should have won the 2000 presidential election. But compared to Bush, Gore seemed stiff, wooden, artificial, and out of touch with common people. Bush mangled his sentences (and even joked about it) and offered fewer details about public policy issues.

Bush never hid his religious faith. He admitted to giving up drinking and carousing and finding religion earlier in his life. In 2004 Democratic Presidential candidate John Kerry appeared presidential, strong-voiced, articulate, and well-informed on the issues. He won the presidential debates but failed to shed his image as aloof, austere, and lacking in strong commitment to issues that mattered. Bush was able to characterize him as a "waffler" and a "flip-flopper." Bush, despite all his flaws, was seen as strong, uncomplicated, and "willing to take a stand."

Party Leadership Presidents are leaders of their party, but this role is hardly a source of great strength. It is true that presidents select the national party chair, control the national committee and its Washington staff, and largely direct the national party convention. Incumbent presidents can use this power to help defeat challengers *within* their own parties. President Ford used this power to help defeat challenger Ronald Reagan in 1976; President Carter used it to help defeat challenger Ted Kennedy in 1980; and President Bush used it against challenger Pat Buchanan in 1992. But the role of party leader is of limited value to a president because the parties have few direct controls over their members (see Chapter 7).

Nevertheless, presidents enjoy much stronger support in Congress from members of their own party than from members of the opposition party (see "Decision Making in Congress" in Chapter 10). Some of the president's party support in Congress is a product of shared ideological values and policy positions. But Republican Congress members do have some stake in the success of a Republican president, as do Democratic members in the success of a Democratic president. Popular presidents may produce those few extra votes that make the difference for party candidates in close congressional districts.

Policy Leadership   Presidents feel an obligation to exercise policy leadership—develop a policy agenda, to present it to the Congress, sell it to the American people, and lobby it through to success. Presidents are less likely than most politicians to pander to public opinion. Rather, they expect to be able to manipulate public opinion themselves.[19]

Nevertheless, there are times when presidents prudently decide to follow public opinion, rather than try to change it. First of all, presidents who are approaching a reelection contest become more responsive to public opinion. They are less likely to go off into new policy directions or to support unpopular policies. Generally, presidents present their policy initiatives at the beginning of their terms. This period usually corresponds to a president's high public approval rating. Indeed, throughout a presidential term, the higher their approval rating, the more likely they are to present new policy directions and even to take unpopular policy positions. In contrast, presidents experiencing low approval ratings are much less likely to present new policy initiatives or to pursue unpopular policies.[20]

Chief Executive

The president is the chief executive of the nation's largest bureaucracy: 2.8 million civilian employees, 60 independent agencies, 15 departments, and the large Executive Office of the President. The formal organizational chart of the federal government places the president at the head of this giant structure (see Figure 12.1, "The Federal Bureaucracy," in Chapter 12). But the president cannot command this bureaucracy in the fashion of a military officer or a corporation president. When Harry Truman was preparing to turn over the White House to Dwight Eisenhower, he predicted that the general of the army would not understand the presidency: "He'll sit here and say 'Do this! Do that!' and nothing will happen. Poor Ike—it won't be a bit like the army. He'll find it very frustrating." Truman vastly underestimated the political skills of the former general, but the crusty Missourian clearly understood the frustrations confronting the nation's chief executive. The president does not command the executive branch of government but rather stands at its center—persuading, bargaining, negotiating, and compromising to achieve goals (see *Up Close:* "Contrasting Presidential Styles").

The Constitutional Executive   The Constitution is vague about the president's authority over the executive branch. It vests executive power in the presidency and grants the president authority to appoint principal officers of the government "by and with the Advice and Consent of the Senate." Under the Constitution, the president may also "require the Opinion, in writing, of the principal

Officer in each of the executive Departments, upon any Subject relating to the Duties of their respective Offices." This awkward phrase presumably gives the president the power to oversee operations of the executive departments. Finally, and perhaps most important, the president is instructed to "take Care that the Laws be faithfully executed."

At the same time, Congress has substantial authority over the executive branch. Through its lawmaking abilities, Congress can establish or abolish executive departments and regulate their operations. Congress's "power of the purse" allows it to determine the budget of each department each year and thus to limit or broaden or even "micromanage" the activities of these departments. Moreover, Congress can pressure executive agencies by conducting investigations, calling administrators to task in public hearings, and directly contacting agencies with members' own complaints or those of their constituents.

executive order Formal regulation governing executive branch operations issued by the president.

Executive Orders   Presidents frequently use **executive orders** to implement their policies. Executive orders may direct specific federal agencies to carry out the president's wishes, or they may direct all federal agencies to pursue the president's preferred course of action. In any case, they must be based on either a president's constitutional powers or on powers delegated to the president by laws of Congress. Presidents regularly issue 50 to 100 executive orders each year, but some stand out. In 1942 President Franklin D. Roosevelt issued Executive Order 9066 for the internment of Japanese Americans during World War II. In 1948 President Harry Truman issued Executive Order 9981 to desegregate the U.S. armed forces. In 1965 President Lyndon Johnson issued Executive Order 11246 to require that private firms with federal contracts institute affirmative action programs. A president can even declare a national emergency by executive order, a step that authorizes a broad range of unilateral actions.

Executive orders have legal force when they are based on the president's constitutional or statutory authority. And presidents typically take an expansive view of their own authority. (President George Washington issued an executive order declaring American neutrality in the war between France and England in 1793. While the Constitution gave the power to "declare war" to Congress, Washington assumed the authority to declare neutrality.) Federal courts have generally upheld presidential executive orders. However, the Supreme Court overturned an order by President Harry Truman in 1951 during the Korean War seizing the nation's steel mills.[21] Research on the frequency of executive orders suggests that: Democratic presidents issue more orders than Republican presidents; presidents may issue executive orders to circumvent Congress but only when they believe that Congress will not overturn their orders; and presidents issue more executive orders when they are running for reelection.[22]

Appointments   Presidential power over the executive branch derives in part from the president's authority to appoint and remove top officials. Presidents can shape policy by careful attention to top appointments—cabinet secretaries, assistant secretaries, agency heads, and White House staff. The key is to select people who share the president's policy views and who have the personal qualifications to do an effective job. However, in cabinet appointments political considerations weigh heavily: unifying various elements of the party; appealing for interest-group support; rewarding political loyalty; providing a temporary haven for unsuccessful party candidates; achieving a balance of racial, ethnic, and gender representation.[23] The appointment power gives the president only limited control over the executive branch of government. Of the executive branch's 2.8 million civilian employees, the president actually appoints only about 3,000. The

UP CLOSE

Contrasting Presidential Styles

Every president brings to the White House his own personal administrative style. Some presidents work almost constantly, putting in twelve to fourteen hour days (Carter, Clinton). Others pursue a more leisurely schedule, leaving the Oval Office at 5 or 6 P.M. and spending weekends at the presidential retreat at Camp David or their home (Eisenhower, Reagan, Bush). Some presidents delegate a great deal of responsibility to Cabinet members and White House aides (Eisenhower, Reagan, Bush). Others closely monitor what is happening in executive depart-

ments and agencies (Johnson, Carter, Clinton). Some pursue a great many policy initiatives (Clinton), while others focus on a few key priorities (Reagan, Bush). Some are well informed about the specifics of public policy (Carter, Clinton), while others care more about overall goals and directions of their administration (Reagan, Bush). Some operate informally, communicating frequently with staff, Cabinet members, and others (Clinton). Other presidents function in a more business-like fashion, communicating mostly through their chief-of-staff (Eisenhower, Reagan). Below are the differences between the Bush and Clinton administrative styles as seen by two prominent political scientists.

Differences Between the Bush and Clinton Presidencies

George W. Bush	Bill Clinton
Disciplined White House	Less disciplined White House
Scripted presidency	Unscripted presidency
Strict focus on few key priorities	Wide-ranging policy focus
More reliance on vice president	Less reliance on vice president
Punctuality required for meetings with clear starting and ending times	Meetings start late and seldom end on time
Little use of the bully pulpit	More use of the bully pulpit
Direct public communicator	Skillful public communicator
Frequent reliance on experts to provide policy overviews	Well informed on policy issues
Somewhat more attentive to Congress and its members	Less attentive to Congress and its members
Large responsibilities delegated to aides	Close supervisory role maintained over all top aides
Preference for executive summaries	Enamored of thick briefing books
Regular working days observed insofar as practicable	A "24/7" president

Source: Roger H. Davidson and Walter J. Oleszak, *Congress and Its Members*. 9th ed. (Washington, D.C.: CQ Press, 2004), p. 302.

vast majority of federal executive branch employees are civil servants—recruited, paid, and protected under civil service laws—and are not easily removed or punished by the president. Cabinet secretaries and heads of independent regulatory agencies require congressional confirmation, but presidents can choose their own White House staff without the approval of Congress.

Presidents have only limited power to remove the heads of independent regulatory agencies. By law, Congress sets the terms of these officials. Federal Communications Commission members are appointed for five years; Securities and Exchange Commission members for five years; and Federal Reserve Board members, responsible for the nation's money supply, enjoy the longest term of any executive officials—fourteen years. Congress's responsibility for term length for regulatory agencies is supposed to insulate those agencies, in particular their quasi-judicial responsibilities, from "political" influence.

Budget Presidential authority also derives from the president's role in the budgetary process. The Constitution makes no mention of the president with regard to expenditures; rather, it grants the power of the purse to Congress. Indeed, for nearly 150 years, executive departments submitted their budget requests directly to the Congress without first submitting them to the president. But with the passage of the Budget and Accounting Act in 1921, Congress established the Office of Management and Budget (OMB) (originally named the Bureau of the Budget) to assist the president in preparing an annual Budget of the United States Government for presentation to the Congress. The president's budget is simply a set of recommendations to the Congress. Congress must pass appropriations acts before the president or any executive department or agency may spend money. Congress can and frequently does alter the president's budget recommendations (see "The Politics of Budgeting" in Chapter 12).

cabinet The heads (secretaries) of the executive departments together with other top officials accorded cabinet rank by the president; only occasionally does it meet as a body to advise and support the president.

Cabinet
The White House site provides the names of the current president's cabinet as well as those individuals with "cabinet-rank" status.
www.whitehouse.gov/ government/cabinet.html

The Cabinet The **cabinet** is not mentioned in the U.S. Constitution; it has no formal powers. It consists of the secretaries of the fifteen executive departments and others the president may designate, including the vice president, the Administrator of the Environmental Protection Agency, the Director of the Office of Management and Budget, the Director of National Drug Control Policy, and the Special Trade Representative. According to custom, cabinet officials are ranked by the date their departments were created (see Table 11.2). Thus the secretary of state is the senior cabinet officer, followed by the secretary of the treasury. They sit next to the president at cabinet meetings; heads of the newest departments sit at the far ends of the table.

The cabinet rarely functions as a decision-making body. Cabinet officers in the United States are powerful because they head giant administrative organizations. The secretary of state, the secretary of defense, the secretary of the treasury, the attorney general, and, to a lesser extent, the other departmental secretaries are all people of power and prestige. But seldom does a strong president hold a cabinet meeting to decide important policy questions. More

Table 11.2   The Cabinet Departments

Department	Created
State	1789
Treasury	1789
Defense*	1947
Justice	1789
Interior	1849
Agriculture†	1889
Commerce	1913
Labor	1913
Health and Human Services‡	1953
Housing and Urban Development	1965
Transportation	1966
Energy	1977
Education	1979
Veterans' Affairs	1989
Homeland Security	2002

*Formerly the War and Navy Departments, created in 1789 and 1798, respectively.

†Agriculture Department created in 1862, made part of cabinet in 1889.

‡Originally Health, Education, and Welfare; reorganized in 1979, with the creation of a separate Department of Education.

The Constitution designates the president as the nation's chief executive officer. The president names his cabinet secretaries (with the confirmation of the Senate). But the cabinet rarely meets as a body, and when it does, it is usually to allow the president to promote his views. President Bush is shown here with his cabinet in 2005.

frequently, presidents know what they want and hold cabinet meetings only to help promote their views.

The Constitution requires that "Officers of the United States" be confirmed by the Senate. In the past, the Senate rarely rejected a presidential cabinet nomination; the traditional view was that presidents were entitled to pick their own people and even make their own mistakes. In recent years, however, the confirmation process has become more partisan and divisive, with the Senate conducting lengthy investigations and holding public hearings on presidential cabinet nominees. The intense public scrutiny and potential for partisan attacks, together with financial disclosure and conflict-of-interest laws, may be discouraging some well-qualified people from accepting cabinet posts.

The National Security Council   The National Security Council (NSC) is really an "inner cabinet" created by law in 1947 to advise the president and coordinate foreign, defense, and intelligence activities. The president is chair, and the vice president, Secretary of State, Secretary of Defense and Secretary of the Treasury are participating members. The chair of the Joint Chiefs of Staff and the Director of Central Intelligence serve as advisers to the NSC. The President's National Security Advisor also sits on the NSC and heads its staff. The purposes of the council are to advise and coordinate policy; but in the Iran-Contra scandal in 1987, a staff member of the NSC, Lt. Col. Oliver North, undertook to *implement* security policy by directly channeling funds and arms to Nicaraguan "contras" fighting a communist-dominated government. Various investigative committees strongly recommended that the NSC staff confine itself to an advisory role.

National Security Council (NSC) "Inner cabinet" that advises the president and coordinates foreign, defense, and intelligence activities.

 **National Security Council**
Site provides brief history of NSC plus new releases dealing with national security.
www.whitehouse.gov/nsc

White House Staff   Today, presidents exercise their powers chiefly through the White House staff. This staff includes the president's closest aides and advisers. Over the years, the White House staff has grown from Roosevelt's small "brain trust" of a dozen advisers to several hundred people.

Senior White House staff members are trusted political advisers, often personal friends and long-time associates of the president. Some enjoy office space in the White House itself and daily contact with the president (see Figure 11.3). Appointed without Senate confirmation, they are loyal to the president alone, not to departments, agencies, or interest groups. Their many tasks include the following:

- Providing the president with sound advice on everything from national security to congressional affairs, policy development, and electoral politics.

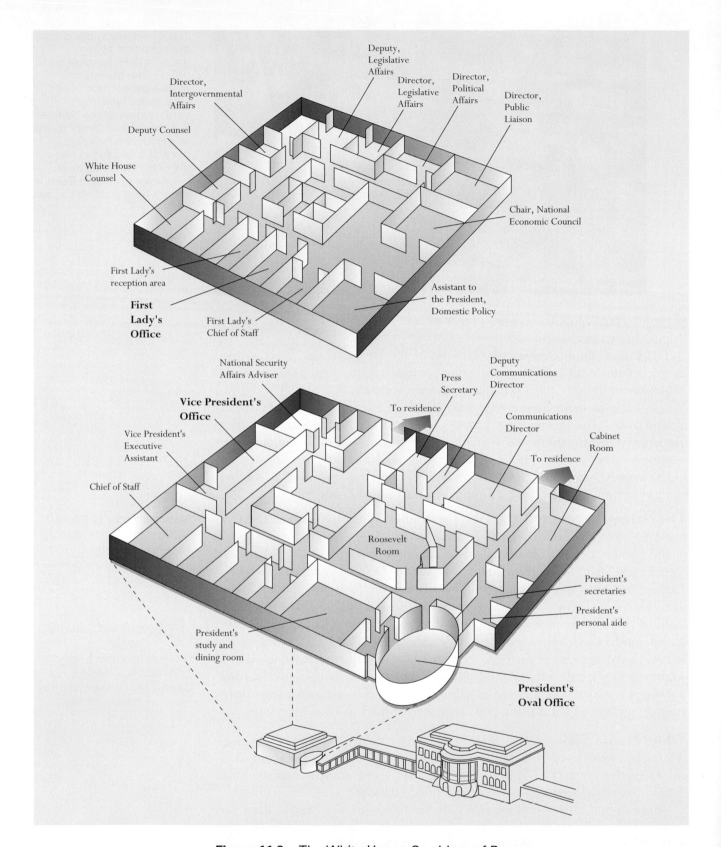

Figure 11.3 The White House Corridors of Power

Presidents allocate office space in the White House according to their own desires. An office located close to the president's is considered an indication of the power of the occupant. This diagram shows the office assignments during the Clinton Administration.

- Monitoring the operations of executive departments and agencies and evaluating the performance of key executive officials.

- Setting the president's schedule, determining whom the president will see and call, where and when the president will travel, and where and to whom the president will make personal appearances and speeches.

- Above all, the staff must protect their boss, steering the president away from scandal, political blunders, and errors of judgment.

The senior White House staff normally includes a chief of staff, the national security adviser, a press secretary, the counsel to the president (an attorney), a director of personnel (patronage appointments), and assistants for political affairs, legislative liaison, management, and domestic policy. Staff organization depends on each president's personal taste. Some presidents have organized their staffs hierarchically, concentrating power in the chief of staff. Others have maintained direct contact with several staff members.

Presidential Perks   Presidential perks are many, from the use of Air Force One to the living quarters of the White House. The president receives a salary of $400,000 per year, including a $50,000 expense allowance. Many presidential expenses are shifted to the budgets of other departments, especially the Department of Defense. Even after leaving the White House, benefits are generous; former President Bill Clinton receives an annual pension of $151,800 plus $150,000 for expenses. Presidents, First Ladies, and their children under 16, receive round-the-clock protection from the Secret Service.

Chief Legislator and Lobbyist

The president has the principal responsibility for the initiation of national policy. Indeed, about 80 percent of the bills considered by Congress originate in the executive branch. Presidents have a strong incentive to fulfill this responsibility: the American people hold them responsible for anything that happens in the nation during their term of office, whether or not they have the authority or capacity to do anything about it.

Policy Initiation   The Founders understood that the president would be involved in policy initiation. The Constitution requires the president to "give to the Congress Information of the State of the Union," to "recommend to their Consideration such Measures as he shall judge necessary and expedient" (Article II, Section 3). "On extraordinary Occasions" the president may call a recessed Congress into special session. Each year the principal policy statement of the president comes in the State of the Union message to Congress. It is followed by the president's Budget of the United States Government, which sets forth the president's programs with price tags attached. Many other policy proposals are developed by executive departments and agencies, transmitted to the White House for the president's approval or "clearance," and then sent to Congress.

Congress may not accept all or even most of the president's proposals. Indeed, from time to time it may even try to develop its own legislative agenda in competition with the president's. But the president's legislative initiatives usually set the agenda of congressional decision making. As one experienced Washington lobbyist put it, "Obviously when the president sends up a bill, it takes first place in the queue. All other bills take second place."[24]

Presidents are expected to provide policy leadership and to work for congressional passage of their policy proposals. President Bush is shown here with the leadership of both the Democratic and Republican parties in the House and Senate.

White House Lobbying   Presidents do not simply send their bills to Congress and then await the outcome. The president is also expected to be the chief lobbyist on behalf of the administration's bills as they make their way through the legislative labyrinth. The White House staff includes "legislative liaison" people—lobbyists for the president's programs. They organize the president's legislative proposals, track them through committee and floor proceedings, arrange committee appearances by executive department and agency representatives, count votes, and advise the president on when and how to "cut deals" and "twist arms."

Presidents are not without resources in lobbying Congress. They may exchange many favors, large and small, for the support of individual members. They can help direct "pork" to a member's district, promise White House support for a member's pet project, and assist in resolving a member's problems with the bureaucracy. Presidents also may issue or withhold invitations to the White House for prestigious ceremonies, dinners with visiting heads of state, and other glittering social occasions—an effective resource because most members of Congress value the prestige associated with close White House "connections."

The president may choose to "twist arms" individually—by telephoning and meeting with wavering members of Congress. Arm twisting is generally reserved for the president's most important legislative battles. There is seldom time for a president to contact individual members of Congress personally about many bills in various stages of the legislative process—in subcommittee, full committee, floor consideration, conference committee, and final passage—in both the House and the Senate. Instead, the president must rely on White House staff for most legislative contacts and use personal appeals sparingly.

honeymoon period Early months of a president's term in which his popularity with the public and influence with the Congress are generally high.

The Honeymoon   The **honeymoon period** at the very start of a president's term offers the best opportunity to get the new administration's legislative proposals enacted into law. Presidential influence in Congress is generally highest at this time both because the president's personal popularity is typically at its height and because the president can claim the recent election results as a popular mandate for key programs. Sophisticated members of Congress know that votes cast for a presidential candidate are not necessarily votes cast for that candidate's policy position (see "The Voter Decides" in Chapter 8). But election results signal members of Congress, in a language they understand well, that the president is politically popular and that they must give the administration's programs careful consideration. President Lyndon Johnson succeeded in getting the bulk of his Great Society program enacted in the year following his landslide victory in 1964. Ronald Reagan pushed through the largest tax cut in American history in

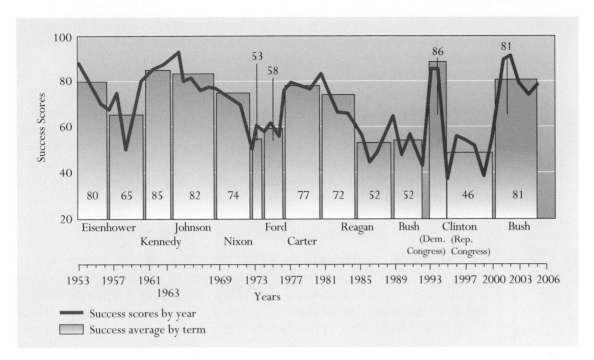

Figure 11.4   Presidential Success Scores in Congress

Presidential "box scores"—the percentage of times that a bill endorsed by the president is enacted by Congress—are closely linked to the strength of the president's party in Congress. For example, both Dwight D. Eisenhower and Ronald Reagan benefited from having a Republican majority in the Senate in their first terms and suffered when Democrats gained control of the Senate in their second terms. Democratic control of both houses of Congress resulted in significantly higher box scores for Democratic presidents John Kennedy, Lyndon Johnson, and Jimmy Carter than for Republicans Richard Nixon, Gerald Ford, and George Bush. Clinton was very successful in his first two years, when the Democrats controlled Congress, but when the Republicans won control following the 1994 midterm election, Clinton's box score plummeted. Bush enjoyed a Republican Congress and therefore succeeded in passing over 80 percent of his bills.

the year following his convincing electoral victory over incumbent president Jimmy Carter in 1980. Bill Clinton was most successful with the Congress during his first year in office, in 1993, even winning approval for a major tax increase as part of a deficit-reduction package. And George W. Bush succeeded in getting a tax cut through Congress in his first six months in office. Both Democrat Clinton and Republican Bush benefited from having their party control the Congress during their first months in office.

Presidential "Box Scores"   How successful are presidents in getting their legislation through Congress? *Congressional Quarterly* regularly compiles "box scores" of presidential success in Congress—percentages of presidential victories on congressional votes on which the president took a clear-cut position. The measure does not distinguish between bills that were important to the president and bills that may have been less significant. But viewed over time (see Figure 11.4), the presidential box scores provide interesting insights into the factors affecting the president's legislative success.

The most important determinant of presidential success in Congress is party control. Presidents are far more successful when they face a Congress controlled by their own party. Democratic presidents John F. Kennedy and Lyndon Johnson enjoyed the support of Democratic-controlled Congresses and posted average success scores over 80 percent. Jimmy Carter was hardly a popular president, but he enjoyed the support of a Democratic Congress and an average of 76.8 percent presidential support. Republican presidents Richard Nixon and Gerald Ford fared poorly with Democratic-controlled Congresses. Republican president Ronald Reagan was very successful in his first term when he faced a Democratic House and a Republican Senate, but after Democrats took over both houses of Congress, Reagan's success rate plummeted. During the Reagan and Bush presidencies, divided party control of government (Republicans in the White House and Democrats controlling one or both houses of Congress) was said to produce **gridlock**, the political inability of the government to act decisively on the nation's problems. President Bill Clinton's achievements when Democrats controlled the Congress (1993–94), contrasted with his dismal record in dealing with Republican-controlled Congresses (1995–99), provide a vivid illustration of the importance of party in determining a president's legislative success.

The Veto Power   The **veto** is the president's most powerful weapon in dealing with Congress. The veto is especially important to a president facing a Congress controlled by the opposition party. Even the *threat* of a veto enhances the president's bargaining power with Congress.[25] Confronted with such a threat, congressional leaders must calculate whether they can muster a two-thirds vote of both houses to override the veto.

To veto a bill passed by the Congress, the president sends to Congress a veto message specifying reasons for not signing it. If the president takes no action for ten days (excluding Sundays) after a bill has been passed by Congress, the bill becomes law without the president's signature. However, if Congress has adjourned within ten days of passing a bill and the president has not signed it, then the bill does not become law; this outcome is called a **pocket veto**.

A bill returned to Congress with a presidential veto message can be passed into law over the president's opposition by a two-thirds vote of both houses. (A bill that has received a pocket veto cannot be overridden because the Congress is no longer in session.) In other words, the president needs only to hold the loyalty of more than one-third of *either* the House or the Senate to sustain a veto. If congressional leaders cannot count on the votes to **override**, they are forced to bargain with the president. "What will the president accept?" becomes a key legislative question.

The president's bargaining power with Congress has been enhanced over the years by a history of success in sustaining presidential vetoes.[26] From George Washington to Bill Clinton, more than 96 percent of all presidential vetoes have been sustained (see Table 11.3). For example, although George H.W. Bush was unable to achieve much success in getting his own legislative proposals enacted by a Democratic Congress, he was extraordinarily successful in saying no. Of Bush's many vetoes, only one (regulation of cable TV) was overridden by Congress. Clinton did not veto any bills when Democrats controlled Congress, but he began a series of vetoes in his struggle with the Republican Congress elected in 1994. He was able to sustain almost all of his vetoes because Republicans did not have two-thirds of the seats in both houses and most Democratic Congress members stuck with their president.

Line-Item Veto Power Denied   For many years, presidents, both Democratic and Republican, petitioned Congress to give them the **line-item veto**, the ability to veto some provisions of a bill while accepting other provisions. The lack of presidential line-item veto power was especially frustrating when dealing with appropriations bills because the president could not veto specific pork-barrel provisions from major spending bills for defense, education, housing, welfare, and so on. Finally, in 1996 Congress granted the president authority to

---

gridlock Political stalemate between the executive and legislative branches arising when one branch is controlled by one major political party and the other branch by the other party.

veto Rejection of a legislative act by the executive branch; in the U.S. federal government, overriding of a veto requires a two-thirds majority in both houses of Congress.

pocket veto Effective veto of a bill when Congress adjourns within ten days of passing it and the president fails to sign it.

override Voting in Congress to enact legislation vetoed by the president; requires a two-thirds vote in both the House and Senate.

line-item veto Power of the chief executive to reject some portions of a bill without rejecting all of it.

Table 11.3   Presidential Vetoes

President	Total Vetoes[*]	Vetoes Overridden	Percentage of Vetoes Sustained
F. Roosevelt	633	9	99%
Truman	250	12	95
Eisenhower	181	2	99
Kennedy	21	0	100
L. Johnson	30	0	100
Nixon	43	5	90
Ford	66	12	85
Carter	31	2	94
Reagan	78	8	91
Bush	46	1	98
Clinton	37	2	95
Bush	1	0	—

[*]Regular vetoes plus pocket vetoes.

Source: Harold W. Stanley and Richard G. Niemi, *Vital Statistics on American Politics, 1999–2000* (Washington, D.C.: CQ Press, 2000), p. 256. Updated by author.

"cancel" spending items in any appropriation act and any limited tax benefit. Such cancellation would take effect immediately unless blocked by a special "disapproval bill" passed by Congress.

However, opponents of the line-item veto successfully challenged its constitutionality, arguing that it transfers legislative power—granted by the Constitution only to Congress—to the president. The U.S. Supreme Court agreed: "There is no provision in the Constitution that authorizes the president to enact or amend or repeal statutes." The line-item veto, the Court said, "authorizes the president himself to elect to repeal laws, for his own policy reasons" and therefore violates the law-making procedures set forth in Article I of the Constitution.[27]

Global Leader

The president of the United States is the leader of the world's largest and most powerful democracy. During the Cold War, the president of the United States was seen as the leader of the "free world." The threat of Soviet expansionism, the huge military forces of the Warsaw Pact, and Soviet-backed guerrilla wars around the world all added to the global role of the American president as the defender of democratic values. In today's post–Cold War world, Western Europe and Japan are formidable economic competitors and no longer routinely defer to American political leadership. But if a new stable world order based on democracy and self-determination is to emerge, the president of the United States must provide the necessary leadership.

Global leadership is based on a president's powers of persuasion. Presidents are more persuasive when the American economy is strong, when American military forces are perceived as ready and capable, and when the president is seen as having the support of the American people and Congress. America's allies as well as its enemies perceive the president as the controlling force over U.S. foreign and military policy. Only occasionally do they seek to bypass the president and appeal to the Congress or to American public opinion.

The president is recognized throughout the world as the American "head of state"; this power aids him in dominating American foreign and defense policy making. British Prime Minister Tony Blair was one of the very few foreign leaders to support Bush's policies in Iraq, support that eventually led to Blair's replacement.

Presidents sometimes prefer their global role to the much more contentious infighting of domestic politics. Abroad, presidents are treated with great dignity as head of the world's most powerful state. In contrast, at home presidents must confront hostile and insulting reporters, backbiting bureaucrats, demanding interest groups, and contentious members of Congress.

State Department Official site includes news, travel warnings, international issues, and background notes on countries of the world. *www.state.gov*

diplomatic recognition Power of the president to grant "legitimacy" to or withhold it from a government of another nation (to declare or refuse to declare it "rightful").

Foreign Policy   As the nation's chief diplomat, the president has the principal responsibility for formulating U.S. foreign policy. The president's constitutional powers in foreign affairs are relatively modest. Presidents have the power to make treaties with foreign nations "with the Advice and Consent of the Senate." Presidents may negotiate with nations separately or through international organizations such as the North Atlantic Treaty Organization (NATO) or the United Nations, where the president determines the U.S. position in that body's deliberations. The Constitution also empowers the president to "appoint Ambassadors, other public Ministers, and Consuls" and to "receive Ambassadors." This power of **diplomatic recognition** permits a president to grant legitimacy to or withhold it from ruling groups around the world (to declare or refuse to declare them "rightful"). Despite controversy, President Franklin Roosevelt officially recognized the communist regime in Russia in 1933, Richard Nixon recognized the communist government of the People's Republic of China in 1972, and Carter recognized the communist Sandinistas' regime in Nicaragua in 1979. To date, all presidents have withheld diplomatic recognition of Fidel Castro's government in Cuba.

Presidents have expanded on these modest constitutional powers to dominate American foreign policy making. In part, they have done so as a product of their role as Commander-in-Chief. Military force is the ultimate diplomatic language. During wartime, or when war is threatened, military and foreign policy become inseparable. The president must decide on the use of force and, equally important, when and under what conditions to order a cease-fire or an end to hostilities.

Presidents have also come to dominate foreign policy as a product of the customary international recognition of the head of state as the legitimate voice of a government. Although nations may also watch the words and actions of the American Congress, the president's statements are generally taken to represent the official position of the U.S. government.

Treaties   Treaties the president makes "by and with the Advice and Consent of the Senate" are legally binding upon the United States. The Constitution specifies that "all Treaties made . . . under the Authority of the United States, shall be the supreme Law of the Land, and the Judges in every State shall be bound thereby" (Article VI). Thus treaty provisions are directly enforceable in federal courts.

Although presidents may or may not listen to "advice" from the Senate on foreign policy, no formal treaty is valid unless "two-thirds of the Senators present concur" to its ratification. Although the Senate has ratified the vast majority of treaties, presidents must be sensitive to Senate concerns. The Senate defeat of the Versailles Treaty in 1920, which formally ended World War I and established the League of Nations, prompted Presidents Roosevelt and Truman to include prominent Democratic and Republican members of the Senate Foreign Relations Committee in the delegation that drafted the United Nations Charter in 1945 and the NATO Treaty in 1949.

President Clinton was sharply reminded of the need to develop bipartisan support for treaties in the Senate in 1999 when that body rejected the Comprehensive Test Ban Treaty. This treaty would have prohibited all signatory nations from conducting any tests of nuclear weapons. Most Western European nations had already signed and ratified the nuclear test ban, but North Korea, Iraq, Iran, India, and Pakistan, among other nations, had rejected it. China and Russia appeared to be waiting for the United States to act first. The president argued that the United States should take moral leadership in worldwide nonproliferation of nuclear weapons. His opponents in the Senate argued that too many rogue nations would ignore the treaty and continue their own nuclear testing. Despite the Senate's rejection of the treaty, Clinton continued by executive order his own moratorium on nuclear testing by the United States (see Chapter 18).

Treaties in Force
Complete list of all treaties of the U.S. in force as of January 1, 2000.
www.state.gov/www/global/legalaffairs

Executive Agreements   Over the years, presidents have come to rely heavily on **executive agreements** with other governments rather than formal treaties. An executive agreement signed by the president of the United States has much the same effect in international relations as a treaty. However, an executive agreement does not require Senate ratification. Presidents have asserted that their constitutional power to execute the laws, command the armed services, and determine foreign policy gives them the authority to make agreements with other nations and heads of state without obtaining approval of the U.S. Senate. However, unlike treaties, executive agreements do not supersede laws of the United States or of the states with which they conflict, but they are otherwise binding on the United States.

executive agreement
Agreement with another nation signed by the president of the United States but less formal (and hence potentially less binding) than a treaty because it does not require Senate confirmation.

The use of executive agreements in important foreign policy matters was developed by President Franklin Roosevelt. Prior to his administration, executive agreements had been limited to minor matters. But in 1940, Roosevelt agreed to trade fifty American destroyers to England in exchange for naval bases in Newfoundland and the Caribbean. Roosevelt was intent on helping the British in their struggle against Nazi Germany, but before the Japanese attack on Pearl Harbor in 1941, isolationist sentiment in the Senate was too strong to win a two-thirds ratifying vote for such an agreement. Toward the end of World War II, Roosevelt at the Yalta Conference and Truman at the Potsdam Conference negotiated secret executive agreements dividing the occupation of Germany between the Western Allies and the Soviet Union.

Congress has sometimes objected to executive agreements as usurping its own powers. In the Case Act of 1972, Congress required the president to inform Congress of all executive agreements within sixty days, but the act does not limit the president's power to make agreements. It is easier for Congress to renege on executive agreements than on treaties that the Senate has ratified. In 1973

President Nixon signed an executive agreement with South Vietnamese President Nguyen Van Thieu pledging that the United States would "respond with full force" if North Vietnam violated the Paris Peace Agreement that ended American participation in the Vietnam War. But when North Vietnam reinvaded the south in 1975, Congress rejected President Gerald Ford's pleas for renewed military aid to the South Vietnamese government, and Ford knew that it had become politically impossible for the United States to respond with force.

Intelligence   The president is responsible for the intelligence activities of the United States. Presidents have undertaken intelligence activities since the founding of the nation. During the Revolutionary War, General George Washington nurtured small groups of patriots living behind British lines who supplied him with information on Redcoat troop movements.[28] Today, the National Intelligence Director (NID) is appointed by the president (subject to Senate confirmation) and reports directly to the president.

The NID coordinates the activities of the "intelligence community" (see *Up Close:* "Reorganizing Intelligence After 9/11" in Chapter 12). Some elements of the intelligence community—the Central Intelligence Agency, the Defense Intelligence Agency, the National Security Agency, the National Reconnaissance Office, and the National Geo-Spacial Agency—deal exclusively with intelligence collection, analysis and distribution. Other elements of the intelligence community are located in the Department of Defense, Department of Homeland Security, Federal Bureau of Investigation, Department of State, Department of Energy, and Department of the Treasury. Indeed, the fragmentation of the intelligence community may be its principal weakness.[29]

The Central Intelligence Agency   The CIA provides intelligence on national security to the president, the NID, the National Security Council, and other top Washington decision makers. The CIA is responsible for (1) assembly, analysis, and dissemination of intelligence information from all agencies in the intelligence community; (2) collection of human intelligence from abroad; (3) with specific "presidential findings," the conduct of **covert actions**, including paramilitary special operations.

Covert actions refer to activities in support of the national interest of the United States that would be ineffective if their sponsorship were made public. For example, one of the largest covert actions ever undertaken by the United States was the support, for nearly ten years, of the Afghan rebels fighting Soviet occupation of their country during the Afghanistan war (1978–88). Public acknowledgment of such aid would have assisted the Soviet-backed regime in Afghanistan to claim that the rebels were not true patriots but rather "puppets" of the United States. The rebels themselves did not wish to acknowledge U.S. aid publicly, even though they knew it was essential to the success of their cause. Hence Presidents Carter and Reagan aided the Afghan rebels through covert action.

Covert action is, by definition, secret. And secrecy spawns elaborate conspiracy theories and flamboyant tales of intrigue and deception. In fact, most covert actions consist of routine transfers of economic aid and military equipment to pro-U.S. forces that do not wish to acknowledge such aid publicly. Although most covert actions would have widespread support among the American public if they were done openly, secrecy opens the possibility that a president will undertake to do by covert action what would be opposed by Congress and the American people if they knew about it.

In the atmosphere of suspicion and distrust engendered by the Watergate scandal, Congress passed intelligence oversight legislation in 1974 requiring a

covert action Secret intelligence activity outside U.S. borders undertaken with specific authorization by the president; acknowledgment of U.S. sponsorship would defeat or compromise its purpose.

 **Central Intelligence Agency**
The CIA site provides information about the agency's mission, organization, values, press releases, and congressional testimony along with employment possibilities.
www.CIA.gov

Although still part of the "Big Three," along with Prime Minister Winston Churchill of Great Britain (right) and Marshal Josef Stalin of the Soviet Union (left), it was a gravely ill President Franklin Roosevelt (middle) who traveled to Yalta, a port on Russia's Crimean peninsula, and negotiated secret executive agreements dividing Germany among the Allies in 1945. Germany remained divided until 1989, when protesters tore down the Berlin Wall and the Soviet Union under Mikhail Gorbachev acquiesced in the unification of Germany under a democratic government.

written "presidential finding" for any covert action and requiring that members of the House and Senate Intelligence Committees be informed of all covert actions. The president does not have to obtain congressional approval for covert actions; but Congress can halt such actions if it chooses to do so.

Commander-in-Chief

Global power derives primarily from the president's role as Commander-in-Chief of the armed forces of the United States. Presidential command over the armed forces is not merely symbolic; presidents may issue direct military orders to troops in the field. As president, Washington personally led troops to end the Whiskey Rebellion in 1794; Abraham Lincoln issued direct orders to his generals in the Civil War; Lyndon Johnson personally chose bombing targets in Vietnam; and George H. W. Bush personally ordered the Gulf War cease-fire after 100 hours of ground fighting. All presidents, whether they are experienced in world affairs or not, soon learn after taking office that their influence throughout the world is heavily dependent upon the command of capable military forces.

War-making Power   Constitutionally, war-making power is divided between the Congress and the president. Congress has the power "to declare war," but the president is the "Commander-in-Chief of the Army and Navy of the United States."

In reality, however, presidents have exercised their powers as Commander-in-Chief to order U.S. forces into military action overseas on many occasions—from John Adams's ordering of U.S. naval forces to attack French ships (1798–99) to Harry Truman's decision to intervene in the Korean War (1951–53) to Lyndon Johnson's and Richard Nixon's conduct of the Vietnam War (1965–73), to George H. W. Bush's Operation Desert Storm (1991), to Bill Clinton's interventions in Bosnia and Kosovo (1998–99), to George W. Bush's military actions in Afghanistan

www DefenseLink
Official site of U.S. Department of Defense, with news and links to Army, Navy, Air Force, and Marine Corps Web sites and other defense agencies and commands.
www.defenselink.gov

(2001) and Iraq (2003). The Supreme Court has consistently refused to hear cases involving the war powers of the president and Congress.[30]

Thus, although Congress retains the formal power to "declare war," in modern times wars are seldom "declared." Instead, they begin with direct military actions, and the president, as Commander-in-Chief of the armed forces, determines what those actions will be. Historically, Congress accepted the fact that only the president has the information-gathering facilities and the ability to act with the speed and secrecy required for military decisions during periods of crisis. Not until the Vietnam War was there serious congressional debate over whether the president has the power to commit the nation to war.

War Powers Resolution   In the early days of the Vietnam War, the liberal leadership of the nation strongly supported Democratic President Lyndon Johnson's power to commit the nation to war. By 1969, however, many congressional leaders had withdrawn their support of the war. With a new Republican president, Richard Nixon, and a Democratic Congress, congressional attacks on presidential policy became much more partisan.

Antiwar members of Congress made several attempts to end the war by cutting off money for U.S. military activity in Southeast Asia. Such legislation only passed after President Nixon announced a peace agreement in 1973, however. It is important to note that Congress has *never* voted to cut off funds to support American armies while they were in the field.

Congress also passed the **War Powers Resolution**, designed to restrict presidential war-making powers, in 1973. (President Nixon vetoed the bill, but the Watergate affair undermined his support in Congress, which overrode his veto.) The act has four major provisions:

1. In the absence of a congressional declaration of war, the president can commit armed forces to hostilities or to "situations where imminent involvement in hostilities is clearly indicated by the circumstances" only:

   - To repel an armed attack on the United States or to forestall the "direct and imminent threat of such an attack."

   - To repel an armed attack against U.S. armed forces outside the United States or to forestall the threat of such attack.

   - To protect and evacuate U.S. citizens and nationals in another country if their lives are threatened.

2. The president must report promptly to Congress the commitment of forces for such purposes.

3. Involvement of U.S. forces must be no longer than sixty days unless Congress authorizes their continued use by specific legislation.

4. Congress can end a presidential commitment by resolution, an action that does not require the president's signature.

Presidential Noncompliance   The War Powers Resolution raises constitutional questions. A Commander-in-Chief clearly can order U.S. forces to go anywhere. Presumably, Congress cannot constitutionally command troops, yet that is what the act attempts to do by specifying that troops must come home if Congress orders them to do so or if Congress simply fails to endorse the president's decision to commit them. No president—Democrat or Republican—can allow Congress to usurp this presidential authority. Thus, since the passage of the War

War Powers Resolution Bill passed in 1973 to limit presidential war-making powers; it restricts when, why, and for how long a president can commit U.S. forces and requires notification of and, in many cases, approval by Congress.

— Think Again —

Should Congress have the authority to call home U.S. troops sent by the president to engage in military actions overseas?

Powers Resolution, presidents have continued to undertake military actions on their own initiative (see Table 18.1 in Chapter 18).

Politically, it is often important for the president to show the world, and especially enemies of the United States, that he has congressional support for going to war. For this reason, presidents have asked Congress for resolutions in support of using military means to achieve specific goals. President George H. W. Bush asked for and received (by a close vote) a resolution of support to use military force to oust Iraqi forces from Kuwait in 1991. President George W. Bush won strong support for a congressional resolution in 2002 to allow him to use military force to make Saddam Hussein comply with U.N. resolutions. Both presidents claimed that they had the constitutional authority as Commander-in-Chief to use military force even *without* such resolutions. But politically such resolutions strengthen the president when he chooses to use military force. (See "Political Support for War in Iraq" in Chapter 18.)

Presidential Use of Military Force in Domestic Affairs   Democracies are generally reluctant to use military force in domestic affairs. Yet the president has the constitutional authority to "take Care that the Laws be faithfully executed" and, as Commander-in-Chief of the armed forces, can send them across the nation as well as across the globe. The Constitution appears to limit presidential use of military forces in domestic affairs to protecting states "against domestic Violence" and only "on Application of the [state] Legislature or the [state] Executive (when the Legislature cannot be convened)" (Article IV, Section 4). Although this provision would seem to require states themselves to request federal troops before they can be sent to quell domestic violence, historically presidents have not waited for state requests to send troops when federal laws, federal court orders, or federal constitutional guarantees are being violated.

Despite a Supreme Court ruling that segregation in education was illegal, many southern states continued to try to keep their schoolhouse doors closed to black students. Here Elizabeth Eckford, a fifteen-year-old resident of Little Rock, Arkansas, is denied entry to Central High School by a member of the National Guard under the orders of Governor Orval Faubus. Not until President Dwight Eisenhower sent the 101st Airborne Division to Little Rock were the high court's desegregation orders enforced.

Relying on their constitutional duty to "faithfully execute" federal laws and their command over the nation's armed forces, presidents have used military force in domestic disputes since the earliest days of the Republic. Perhaps the most significant example of a president's use of military force in domestic affairs was Dwight Eisenhower's 1957 dispatch of U.S. troops to Little Rock, Arkansas, to enforce a federal court's desegregation order. In this case, the president acted directly *against* the expressed wishes of the state's governor, Orval Faubus, who had posted state units of the National Guard at the entrance of Central High School to prevent the admission of black students, which had been ordered by the federal court. Eisenhower officially called Arkansas's National Guard units into federal service, took personal command of them, and then ordered them to leave the high school. Ike then replaced the Guard units with U.S. federal troops under orders to enforce desegregation. Eisenhower's action marked a turning point in the struggle over school desegregation. The Supreme Court's historic desegregation decision in *Brown v. Board of Education of Topeka* might have been rendered meaningless had not the president chosen to use military force to secure compliance.

The Vice Presidential Waiting Game

Historically, the principal responsibility of the vice president is to be prepared to assume the responsibilities of the president. Eight vice presidents have become president following the death of their predecessor. But vice presidents have not always been well prepared: Harry Truman, who succeeded Franklin Roosevelt while World War II still raged, had never even been informed about the secret atomic bomb project.

Political Selection Process The political process surrounding the initial choice of vice presidential candidates does not necessarily produce the persons best qualified to occupy the White House. It is, indeed, a "crap shoot"[31]; if it produces a person well qualified to be president, it is only by luck. Candidates may *claim* that they select running mates who are highly qualified to take over as president, but this claim is seldom true.

Traditionally, vice presidential candidates have been chosen to give political "balance" to the ticket, to attract voters who might otherwise desert the party or stay home. Democratic presidential candidates sought to give ideological and geographical balance to the ticket. Northern liberal presidential candidates (Adlai Stevenson, John Kennedy) selected southern conservatives (John Sparkman, Estes Kefauver, Lyndon Johnson) as their running mates. Walter Mondale selected New York Congresswoman Geraldine Ferraro in a bold move to exploit the gender gap. Liberal Massachusetts Governor Michael Dukakis returned to the earlier Democratic tradition, choosing to run with conservative Texas Senator Lloyd Bentsen. Bill Clinton sought a different kind of balance: Al Gore's military service in Vietnam and his unimpeachable family life helped offset reservations about Clinton's avoidance of the draft and his past marital troubles. Massachusetts Senator John Kerry was viewed as serious, sober, and reserved, so the choice of the cheerful, enthusiastic, and outgoing North Carolinian John Edwards seemed to balance the ticket in both image and geography.

Republican presidential candidates sought to accommodate either the conservative or moderate wing of their party in their vice presidential selections. Moderate Eisenhower chose conservative Nixon. Conservative Barry Goldwater's selection of William Miller, an unknown conservative member of the

House, ensured his loss of moderate support in 1964. In 1980 conservative Reagan first asked his moderate predecessor Gerald Ford to join him on the ticket before turning to his moderate primary opponent George Bush, who in 1988 tapped conservative Senator Dan Quayle. In 1996 Bob Dole gambled big in choosing the popular and charismatic—but opinionated and unpredictable— Jack Kemp as his running mate. Far behind in the polls, Dole could not afford a "safe" choice. He needed the former star quarterback of the Buffalo Bills to add excitement to the ticket, even at the risk of seeing Kemp call plays not approved by the coach.

Running behind in the polls prior to the 2000 Democratic convention, Al Gore believed he needed a dramatic choice of a running mate to stir interest in his campaign. Connecticut Senator Joe Lieberman would make history as the first Jew to run on a major party national ticket. Moreover, his moderate voting record balanced Gore's appeal to liberals.

Bush's dream running mate, General Colin Powell, turned down the offer. So Bush turned to Dick Cheney, secretary of defense in his father's administration during the Gulf War. It was hoped that Cheney would add *gravitas* (experience and wisdom) to the ticket. And Cheney's conservative voting record, as a former Congressman from Wyoming, helped reassure conservatives in the Republican Party that Bush was not overlooking them. Cheney's public approval ratings dropped as the Iraq war lengthened. Bush was urged to replace him with the popular former New York City Mayor Rudolph Giuliani. But Bush remained loyal to his family's old adviser.

Vice Presidential Roles   Presidents determine what role their vice presidents will play in their administration. Constitutionally, the only role given the vice president is to preside over the Senate and to vote in case of a tie in that body. Presiding over the Senate is so tiresome that vice presidents perform it only on rare ceremonial occasions, but they have occasionally cast important tie-breaking votes. If the president chooses not to give the vice president much responsibility, the vice presidency becomes what its first occupant, John Adams, described as "the most insignificant office that ever the invention of man contrived or his imagination conceived." One of Franklin Roosevelt's three vice presidents, the salty Texan John Nance Garner, put it more pithily, saying that the job "ain't worth a bucket of warm spit" (reporters of that era may have substituted "spit" for Garner's actual wording).

The political functions of vice presidents are more significant than their governmental functions. Vice presidents are obliged to support their president and the administration's policies. But sometimes a president will use the vice president to launch strongly partisan political attacks on opponents while the president remains "above" the political squabbles and hence more "presidential." Richard Nixon served as a partisan "attack dog" for Eisenhower, and then gave Spiro Agnew this task in his own administration. George Bush was a much more reserved vice president, but Dan Quayle renewed the tradition of the vice president as political "hit man." The attack role allows the vice president also to help cement political support for the president among highly partisan ideologues. Vice presidents are also useful in campaign fund-raising. Large contributors expect a personal touch; the president cannot be everywhere at once, so the vice president is frequently a guest at political fund-raising events. Presidents also have traditionally sent their vice presidents to attend funerals of world leaders and placed them at the head of governmental commissions.

PEOPLE IN POLITICS

Dick Cheney, Presidential Confidant

For many weeks after the "9/11" attack on America, Vice President Dick Cheney remained out of sight "in a secure undisclosed location." A direct attack on the White House was viewed as a distinct possibility, and Cheney's absence from Washington was designed to ensure "continuity of government."

Yet during the crisis—indeed, throughout George W. Bush's presidency—Dick Cheney has been his chief's closest adviser—a prime minister, a *consigliere,* pal, tutor, and big brother to the president. Reportedly, Cheney and Bush confer several times a day, and Cheney's recommendations are seldom ignored. Cheney exercises more influence in the White House than perhaps any previous vice president.

Why does Bush place so much trust in his vice president? Cheney served as secretary of defense for Bush's father and served in the Nixon and Ford administrations. He also served as a Republican Congress member from Wyoming and a leader of the conservatives in the House of Representatives. But perhaps his most valued characteristic as vice president is his absence of political ambition. Unlike any other recent vice president, Cheney has no plans to run for president, no personal agenda other than to give his best advice to his president. This elevates the level of trust between the two men.

Dick Cheney has experienced four heart attacks and quadruple bypass heart surgery and wears a surgically implanted heart pacemaker. Yet he follows a very demanding schedule, including lengthy trips to the Middle East and elsewhere in the world.

Cheney was reported to be a strong supporter of the Iraq invasion, and his public approval ratings tumbled as the war lengthened. When he accidentally wounded a friend on a hunting trip, the media ridiculed him and his approval ratings fell even further. But he remained Bush's closest adviser.

Vice presidents themselves strive to play a more significant policy-making role, often as senior presidential adviser and confidant. Recent presidents have encouraged the development of the vice presidency along these lines. Walter Mondale, the first modern vice president to perform this function, had an office in the White House next to the president's, had access to all important meetings and policy decisions, and was invited to lunch privately each week with President Carter. Vice President Al Gore was routinely stationed behind President Clinton during major policy pronouncements. Clinton reportedly gave great weight to Gore's views on the environment, on cost savings in government, and on information technology. Gore also spoke out aggressively in defense of Clinton's policies. Thus the senior advisory role is becoming institutionalized over time (see *People in Politics:* "Dick Cheney, Presidential Confidant").

The Waiting Game   Politically ambitious vice presidents are obliged to play a torturous waiting game. They can use their time in office to build a network of contacts that can later be tapped for campaign contributions, workers, and support in their own race for the presidency, should they decide to run. But winning the presidency following retirement of their former boss requires a delicate balance. They must show loyalty to the president in order to win the president's endorsement and also to help ensure that the administration in which they participated is judged a success by voters. At the same time, vice presidents must demonstrate that they have independent leadership qualities and a policy agenda of their own to offer voters. This dilemma becomes more acute as their boss's term nears its end.

A CONSTITUTIONAL NOTE

How Broad Is the "Executive Power"?

The Constitution states that "The executive Power shall be vested in a President of the United States of America" (Article II). The Constitution also gives the president specific powers; for example "to take care that the laws be faithfully executed"; to appoint and remove executive officials; "to give to the Congress information on the State of the Union and recommend to their Consideration such Measures as he shall judge necessary and expedient"; to veto legislation passed by Congress, subject to override by a two-thirds vote of both houses; to convene special sessions of Congress; to make treaties "with the Advice and Consent of the Senate"; to receive ambassadors; to grant pardons; to appoint federal court and Supreme Court judges, subject to Senate confirmation; and to serve as Commander-in-Chief of the Armed Forces. And the Congress may by law add to the president's powers. But does the Constitution's general grant of "executive power" give the president any powers that are not specified later in the Constitution or given to the president by acts of Congress? Most presidents have asserted a general "executive power," or, as Theodore Roosevelt said, "My belief was that it was not only his right but his duty to do anything that the needs of the nation demanded, unless such action was forbidden by the Constitution or by the laws." But when the Congress has addressed a problem by law, the president is obliged to follow the law, whether he likes it or not.[a] Closely related to the question of executive power is the question of "executive privilege." Can a president withhold information from the Congress or the courts to preserve confidentiality within the executive branch? The Supreme Court has acknowledged a constitutional protection for the "president's need for complete candor and objectivity from advisers" and for "military, diplomatic, or sensitive national security secrets,"[b] But the president cannot withhold information from the courts in a criminal investigation not related to defense or diplomacy, as Richard Nixon found to his dismay in the Watergate affair.

[a]*Youngstown Sheet & Tube Co. v. Sawyer*, 343 U.S. 579 (1952).

[b]*United States v. Nixon*, 418 U.S. 683 (1974).

Historically, only a few sitting vice presidents have won election to the White House: John Adams (1797), Thomas Jefferson (1801), Martin Van Buren (1837), and George H. W. Bush (1988). In addition, four vice presidents won election in their own right after entering the Oval Office as a result of their predecessors' death: Theodore Roosevelt (1901), Calvin Coolidge (1923), Harry Truman (1945), and Lyndon Johnson (1963). Only one nonsitting former vice president has been elected president: Richard Nixon (1968, after losing to Kennedy in 1960). Thus, out of the forty-seven men who served the nation as vice president through 2000, only nine were ever elected to higher office.

Summary Notes

- The American presidency is potentially the most powerful office in the world. As head of state, the president symbolizes national unity and speaks on behalf of the American people to the world. And as Commander-in-Chief of the armed forces, the president has a powerful voice in national and international affairs. The president also symbolizes government for the American people, reassuring them in times of hardship and crises.

- As head of the government, the president is expected to set forth policy priorities for the nation, to manage the economy, to mobilize political support for the administration's programs in Congress, to manage the giant federal bureaucracy, and to recruit people for policy-making positions in both the executive and judicial branches of government.

- Popular expectations of presidential leadership far exceed the formal constitutional powers of the president: chief administrator, chief legislator, chief diplomat, Commander-in-Chief, and chief of state. The vague reference in the Constitution to "executive Power" has been used by presidents to justify actions beyond those specified elsewhere in the Constitution or in laws of Congress.

- It is the president's vast political resources that provide the true power base of the presidency. These include the president's reputation for power, personal popularity with the public, access to the media, and party leadership position.

- Presidential popularity and power are usually highest at the beginning of the term of office. Presidents are more likely to be successful in Congress during this honeymoon period. Presidents' popularity also rises during crises, especially during international threats and military actions. But prolonged indecision and stalemate erode popular support, as do scandals and economic recessions.

- As chief executive, the president oversees the huge federal bureaucracy. Presidential control of the executive branch is exercised through executive orders, appointments and removals, and budgetary recommendations to Congress. But the president's control of the executive branch is heavily circumscribed by Congress, which establishes executive departments and agencies, regulates their activities by law, and determines their budgets each year.

- Presidents are expected not only to initiate programs and policies but also to shepherd them through Congress. Presidential success scores in Congress indicate that presidents are more successful early in their term of office. Presidents who face a Congress controlled by the opposition party are far less successful in winning approval for their programs than presidents whose party holds a majority.

- The veto is the president's most powerful weapon in dealing with Congress. The president needs to hold the loyalty of only one more than one-third of either the House or the Senate to sustain a veto. Few vetoes are overridden. The threat of a veto enables the president to bargain in Congress for more acceptable legislation.

- During the long years of the Cold War, the president of the United States was the leader of the "free world." In the post–Cold War world, the president is still the leader of the world's most powerful democracy and is expected to exercise global leadership on behalf of a stable world order.

- Presidents have come to dominate foreign policy through treaty making, executive agreements, control of intelligence activities, and international recognition of their role as head of state. Above all, presidents have used their power as Commander-in-Chief of the armed forces to decide when to make war and when to seek peace.

- The global power of presidents derives primarily from this presidential role as Commander-in-Chief. Constitutionally, war-making power is divided between Congress and the president, but historically it has been the president who has ordered U.S. military forces into action. In the War Powers Resolution, Congress tried to reassert its war-making power after the Vietnam War, but the act has failed to restrain presidents. Presidents have also used the armed forces in domestic affairs to "take Care that the Laws be faithfully executed."

- The principal responsibility of the vice president is to be prepared to assume the responsibilities of the president. However, the selection of the vice president is dominated more by political concerns than by consideration of presidential qualifications. Aside from officially presiding over the U.S. Senate, vice presidents perform whatever roles are assigned them by the president.

Key Terms

impeachment 376
Watergate 380
executive privilege 380
impoundment 382
deferrals 382
rescissions 382

White House press
  corps 385
executive order 388
cabinet 390
National Security
  Council (NSC) 391

honeymoon period 394
gridlock 396
veto 396
pocket veto 396
override 396
line-item veto 396

diplomatic recognition 398
executive agreement 399
covert action 400
War Powers Resolution 402

Suggested Readings

Barber, James David. *The Presidential Character: Predicting Performance in the White House*. 4th ed. Upper Saddle River, N.J.: Prentice Hall, 1992. Barber's original thesis that a president's performance in office is largely a function of active/passive and positive/negative character; includes classifications of twentieth-century presidents through Reagan.

Brody, Richard A. *Assessing Presidents: The Media, Elite Opinion, and Public Support*. Stanford, Calif.: Stanford University Press, 1991. Develops the thesis that media and elite interpretations of presidential actions shape public evaluations of the president; includes analysis of the president's "honeymoon," "rally round the president" events, and the rise and fall of public approval ratings.

DiClerico, Robert E. *The American President*. 5th ed. Upper Saddle River, N.J.: Prentice Hall, 2000. Comprehensive text on the presidency, focusing on selection, power, accountability, decision making, personality, and leadership.

Edwards, George C. and Stephen J. Wayne. *Presidential Leadership*. 6th ed. Belmont, Calif.: Wadsworth, 2003. Comprehensive text covering nomination and election of the president, relations with the public, the media, the bureaucracy, Congress and the courts.

Lowi, Theodore. *The Personal President*. Ithaca, N.Y.: Cornell University Press, 1987. An examination of the presidency from the perspective of the public and its reliance on the president for reassurance in crises.

Milkus, Stanley, and Michael Nelson. *The American Presidency: Origins and Development, 1776–2002*. 4th ed. Washington, D.C.: CQ Press, 2003. A comprehensive history of the presidency that argues that the institution is best understood by examining its development over time, describes the significant presidential actions in the early days of the Republic that shaped the office, as well as the modern era in which the president has replaced Congress and the political parties as the leading instrument of popular rule.

Nelson, Michael, ed. *The Presidency and the Political System*. 8th ed. Washington, D.C.: CQ Press, 2005. A series of influential essays on the presidency.

Neustadt, Richard E. *Presidential Power*. New York: Wiley, 1960. The classic argument that the president's power is the power to persuade, that the formal constitutional powers of the presidency provide only a framework for the president's use of persuasion, public prestige, reputation for power, and other personal attributes to exercise real power.

Pika, Joseph A., John Maltese, and Norman C. Thomas. *The Politics of the Presidency*. Rev. 6th ed. Washington, D.C.: CQ Press, 2005. An overview of the institution of the presidency, including George W. Bush as a wartime president.

Schultz, Jeffrey D. *Presidential Scandals*. Washington, D.C.: CQ Press, 1999. An historical survey of scandals in presidential administrations, from George Washington to Bill Clinton.

Van Tassel, Emily Field, and Paul Finkelman. *Impeachable Offenses*. Washington, D.C.: CQ Press, 1999. A documentary history of impeachment from 1787 to the present.

Make It Real

THE PRESIDENT
This module allows students to pick the next Supreme Court Justice.

12 THE BUREAUCRACY
Bureaucratic Politics

Think About Politics

1 Do bureaucrats in Washington have too much power?
Yes ☐ No ☐

2 Should the federal bureaucracy be managed by nonpartisan professionals rather than people politically loyal to the president?
Yes ☐ No ☐

3 Should the federal bureaucracy at all levels reflect the gender and minority ratios of the total civilian work force?
Yes ☐ No ☐

4 Do you believe the bureaucrats in Washington waste a lot of the money we pay in taxes?
Yes ☐ No ☐

5 Do you believe the federal government is spending more money but delivering less service?
Yes ☐ No ☐

6 Do you believe that the overall costs of federal regulatory activity are justified by the benefits?
Yes ☐ No ☐

7 Do you believe bureaucratic regulations of all kinds are hurting America's competitiveness in the global economy?
Yes ☐ No ☐

Power in Washington is not only exercised by the president, Congress, and courts, but also by 2.8 million federal bureaucrats—neither elected nor accountable to ordinary citizens—who determine in large measure who gets what in America.

★   ★   ★

Bureaucratic Power

Political conflict does not end after a law has been passed by Congress and signed by the president. The arena for conflict merely shifts from Capitol Hill and the White House to the **bureaucracy**—to the myriad departments, agencies, and bureaus of the federal executive branch that implement the law. Despite the popular impression that policy is decided by the president and Congress and merely implemented by the federal bureaucracy, in fact policy is also made by the bureaucracy. Indeed, it is often remarked that "implementation is the continuation of policy making by other means." The Washington bureaucracy is a major base of power in the American system of government—independent of Congress, the president, the courts, and the people. Indeed, controlling the bureaucracy has become a major challenge of democratic government.

The Nature of Bureaucracy   "Bureaucracy" has become a negative term equated with red tape,[1] paper shuffling, duplication of effort, waste and inefficiency, impersonality, senseless regulations, and unresponsiveness to the needs of "real" people. But bureaucracy is really a form of social organization found not only in governments but also in corporations, armies, schools, and many other societal institutions. The German sociologist Max Weber described bureaucracy as a "rational" way for society to organize itself that has the following characteristics: a **chain of command** (hierarchical structure of authority in which command flows downward); a **division of labor** (work divided among many specialized workers in an effort to improve productivity); and **impersonality** (all persons within the bureaucracy treated on "merit" principles, and all "clients" served by the bureaucracy treated equally according to rules; all activities undertaken according to rules; records maintained to assure rules are followed).[2] Thus, according to Weber's definition, General Motors and IBM, the U.S. Marine Corps, the U.S. Department of Education, and all other institutions organized according to these principles are "bureaucracies."

The Growth of Bureaucratic Power   Bureaucratic power has grown with advances in technology and increases in the size and complexity of society. There are a variety of explanations for this growth of power.

First Gov
Official Web portal to all federal departments and agencies, information on government benefits, agency links, and so forth.
www.firstgov.gov

bureaucracy Departments, agencies, bureaus, and offices that perform the functions of government.

chain of command Hierarchical structure of authority in which command flows downward; typical of a bureaucracy.

division of labor Division of work among many specialized workers in a bureaucracy.

impersonality Treatment of all persons within a bureaucracy on the basis of "merit" and of all "clients" served by the bureaucracy equally according to rules.

— Think Again —
Do bureaucrats in Washington have too much power?

implementation
Development by the federal bureaucracy of procedures and activities to carry out policies legislated by Congress; it includes regulation as well as adjudication.

1. *Needed Expertise and Technological Advances*   Congress and the president do not have the time, energy, or expertise to handle the details of policy making. A related explanation is that the increasing complexity and sophistication of technology require technical experts ("technocrats") to actually carry out the intent of Congress and the president. Neither the president nor the 535 members of Congress can look after the myriad details involved in environmental protection, occupational safety, air traffic control, or thousands of other responsibilities of government. So the president and Congress create bureaucracies, appropriate money for them, and authorize them to draw up detailed rules, regulations, and "guidelines" that actually govern the nation. Bureaucratic agencies receive only vague and general directions from the president and Congress. Actual governance is in the hands of the Environmental Protection Agency, the Occupational Safety and Health Administration, the Federal Aviation Administration, and hundreds of similar agencies (see Figure 12.1).

2. *Symbolic Politics*   But there are also political explanations for the growth of bureaucratic power. Congress and the president often deliberately pass vague and ambiguous laws. These laws allow elected officials to show symbolically their concerns for environmental protection, occupational safety, and so on, yet avoid the controversies surrounding actual application of those lofty principles. Bureaucracies must then give practical meaning to these symbolic measures by developing specific rules and regulations. If the rules and regulations prove unpopular, Congress and the president can blame the bureaucrats and pretend that these unpopular decisions are a product of an "ungovernable" Washington bureaucracy (see *What Do You Think?* "How Would You Rate These Federal Agencies?")

3. *Bureaucratic Explanation*   There is also a bureaucratic explanation of the growth in the size and influence of government agencies. Bureaucracy has become its own source of power. Bureaucrats have a personal stake in expanding the size of their own agencies and budgets and adding to their own regulatory authority. They can mobilize their "client" groups (interest groups that directly benefit from the agency's programs, such as environmental groups on behalf of the Environmental Protection Agency, farm groups for the Department of Agriculture, the National Education Association for the Department of Education) in support of larger budgets and expanded authority.

4. *Popular Demands*   Finally, it has been argued that "big government" is really an expression of democratic sentiments. People want to use the power of government to improve their lives—to regulate and develop the economy, to guarantee civil rights, to develop their communities, and so on. Conservative opponents of the government are really expressing their disdain for popular demands.[3]

Bureaucratic Power: Implementation   Bureaucracies are not *constitutionally* empowered to decide policy questions. But they do so, nevertheless, as they perform their tasks of implementation, regulation, and adjudication.

Implementation is the development of procedures and activities to carry out policies legislated by Congress. It may involve creating new agencies or bureaus or assigning new responsibilities to old agencies. It often requires bureaucracies to translate laws into operational rules and regulations and usually to allocate resources—money, personnel, offices, supplies—to the new function. All of these tasks involve decisions by bureaucrats, decisions that drive how the law

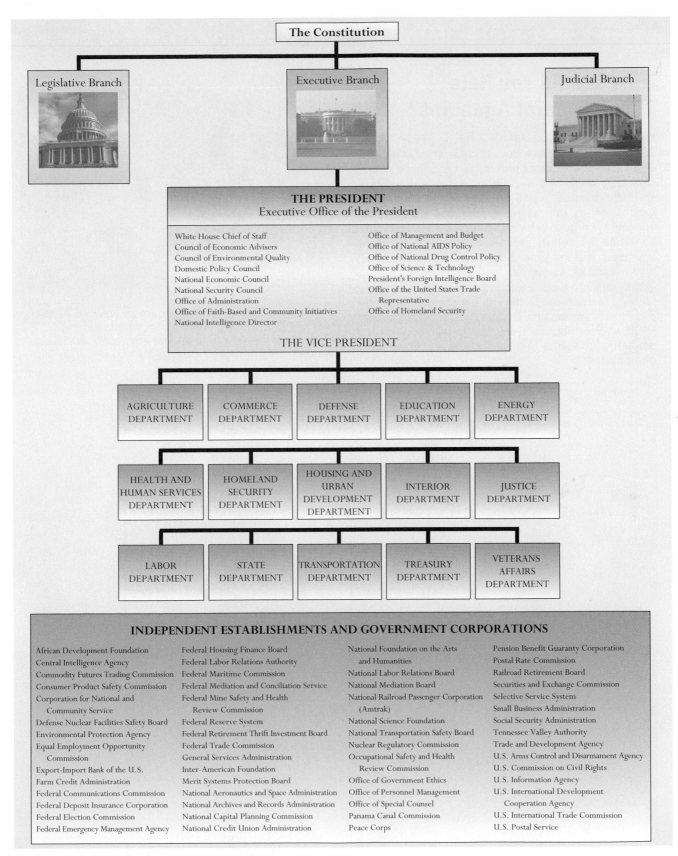

Figure 12.1 The Federal Bureaucracy

Although the president has constitutional authority over the operation of the executive branch, Congress creates departments and agencies and appropriates their funds, and Senate approval is needed for presidential appointees to head departments.

WHAT DO YOU THINK?

How Would You Rate These Federal Agencies?

Many federal agencies have come under close scrutiny following the devastating terrorist attacks of 9/11, deadly anthrax letters, and economic recession, the threat of a bird flu epidemic, and a space shuttle explosion. A poll near the end of 2003 asked Americans to rate some of the key government agencies charged with protecting the American public. While the poll did not ask about all government agencies, it does give a sense of how the public views some of the more prominent of them.

Overall, Americans rate individual agencies fairly highly. Even though the opinion polls regularly report that Americans believe "the federal government in Washington" has "too much power" (60 percent), individual agencies are given reasonably good marks.

The Federal Emergency Management Agency, FEMA, was charged with bureaucratic mismanagement during Hurricane Katrina and its aftermath. Survivors endured long lines and inadequate service.

Q. How would you rate the job being done by _____? Would you say it is doing an excellent, good, only fair, or poor job?

Percent saying "excellent" or "good"

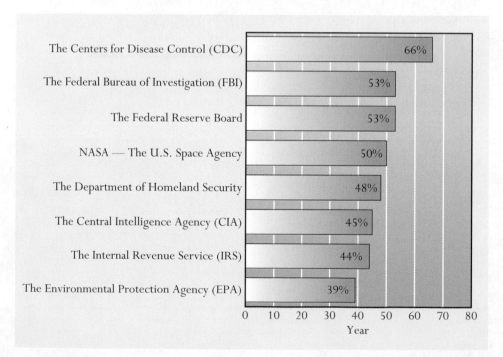

Agency	Percent
The Centers for Disease Control (CDC)	66%
The Federal Bureau of Investigation (FBI)	53%
The Federal Reserve Board	53%
NASA — The U.S. Space Agency	50%
The Department of Homeland Security	48%
The Central Intelligence Agency (CIA)	45%
The Internal Revenue Service (IRS)	44%
The Environmental Protection Agency (EPA)	39%

Year

Source: Gallup poll, September 30, 2003. Copyright © 1996–2004 by The Gallup Organization.

will actually affect society. In some cases, bureaucrats delay the development of regulations based on a new law, assign enforcement responsibility to existing offices with other higher priority tasks, and allocate few people with limited resources to the task. In other cases, bureaucrats act forcefully in making new regulations, insist on strict enforcement, assign responsibilities to newly created aggressive offices with no other assignments, and allocate a great deal of staff time and agency resources to the task. Interested groups have a strong stake in these decisions, and they actively seek to influence the bureaucracy.

Bureaucratic Power: Regulation   Regulation involves the development of formal rules for implementing legislation. The federal bureaucracy publishes about 80,000 pages of rules in the *Federal Register* each year. The Environmental Protection Agency (EPA) is especially active in developing regulations governing the handling of virtually every substance in the air, water, or ground. The rule-making process for federal agencies is prescribed by an Administrative Procedures Act, first passed in 1946 and amended many times. Generally, agencies must:

1. Announce in the *Federal Register* that a new regulation is being considered.
2. Hold hearings to allow interested groups to present evidence and arguments regarding the proposed regulation.
3. Conduct research on the proposed regulation's economic and environmental impacts.
4. Solicit "public comments" (usually the arguments of interest groups).
5. Consult with higher officials, including the Office of Management and Budget.
6. Publish the new regulation in the *Federal Register.*

regulation Development by the federal bureaucracy of formal rules for implementing legislation.

American Society for Public Administration
Organization of scholars and practitioners in public administration. Site includes information on careers, job listings, etc. *www.apsanet.org*

Regulatory battles are important because formal regulations that appear in the *Federal Register* have the effect of law. Congress can amend or repeal a regulation only by passing new legislation and obtaining the president's signature. Controversial bureaucratic regulations often remain in place because Congress is slow to act, because key committee members block corrective legislation, or because the president refuses to sign bills overturning the regulation.

Bureaucratic Power: Adjudication   Adjudication involves bureaucratic decisions about individual cases. Rule making resembles the legislative process, and adjudication resembles the judicial process. In adjudication, bureaucrats decide whether a person or firm is failing to comply with laws or regulations and, if so, what penalties or corrective actions are to be applied. Regulatory agencies and commissions—for example, the National Labor Relations Board, the Federal Communications Commission, the Equal Employment Opportunity Commission, the Federal Trade Commission, the Securities and Exchange Commission—are heavily engaged in adjudication. Their elaborate procedures and body of previous decisions closely resemble the court system. Losers may appeal to the federal courts, but the record of agency success in the federal courts discourages many appeals.

adjudication Decision making by the federal bureaucracy as to whether or not an individual or organization has complied with or violated government laws and/or regulations.

Bureaucratic Power: Administrative Discretion   Much of the work of bureaucrats is administrative routine—issuing Social Security checks, printing forms, delivering the mail. Routines are repetitive tasks performed according to established rules and procedures. Yet bureaucrats almost always have some discretion in performing even the most routine tasks. Discretion is greatest when cases do not exactly fit established rules, or when more than one rule might be applied to the same case, resulting in different outcomes. The Internal Revenue

An Internal Revenue Service processing center. The IRS administers the nation's complex tax code, leaving wide discretion to its agents to determine how to apply the rules to individual taxpayers.

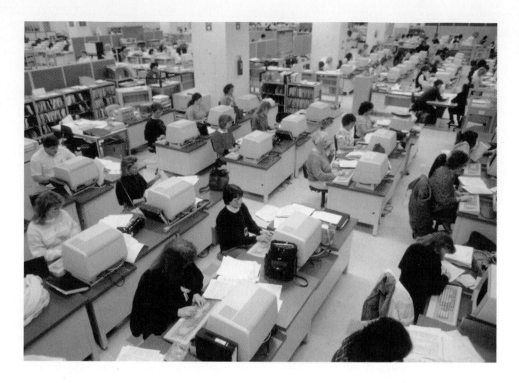

Service administers the hundreds of thousands of rules developed to implement the U.S. Tax Code, but each IRS auditing agent has wide discretion in deciding which rules to apply to a taxpayer's income, deductions, business expenses, and so on. Indeed, identical tax information submitted to different IRS offices almost always results in different estimates of tax liability. But even in more routine tasks, from processing Medicare applications to forwarding mail, individual bureaucrats can be friendly and helpful or hostile and obstructive.[4]

Bureaucratic Power and Budget Maximization   Bureaucrats generally believe strongly in the value of their programs and the importance of their tasks. Senior military officers and civilian officials of the Department of Defense believe in the importance of a strong national defense, and top officials in the Social Security Administration are committed to maintaining the integrity of the retirement system and serving the nation's senior citizens. Beyond these public-spirited motives, bureaucrats, like everyone else, seek higher pay, greater job security, and added power and prestige for themselves.

These public and private motives converge to inspire bureaucrats to seek to expand the powers, functions, and budgets of their departments and agencies. Rarely do bureaucrats request a reduction in authority, the elimination of a program, or a decrease in their agency's budget. Rather, over time, **budget maximization**—expanding the agency's budget, staff, and authority as much as possible—becomes a driving force in government bureaucracies. This is especially true of discretionary funds. **Discretionary funds** are those that bureaucrats have flexibility in deciding how to spend, rather than money committed by law to specific purposes.[5] Thus, bureaucracies continually strive to add new functions, acquire more authority and responsibility, and increase their budgets and personnel. Bureaucratic expansion is just one of the reasons that government grows over time.

budget maximization
Bureaucrats' tendencies to expand their agencies' budgets, staff, and authority.

discretionary funds
Budgeted funds not earmarked for specific purposes but available to be spent in accordance with the best judgment of a bureaucrat.

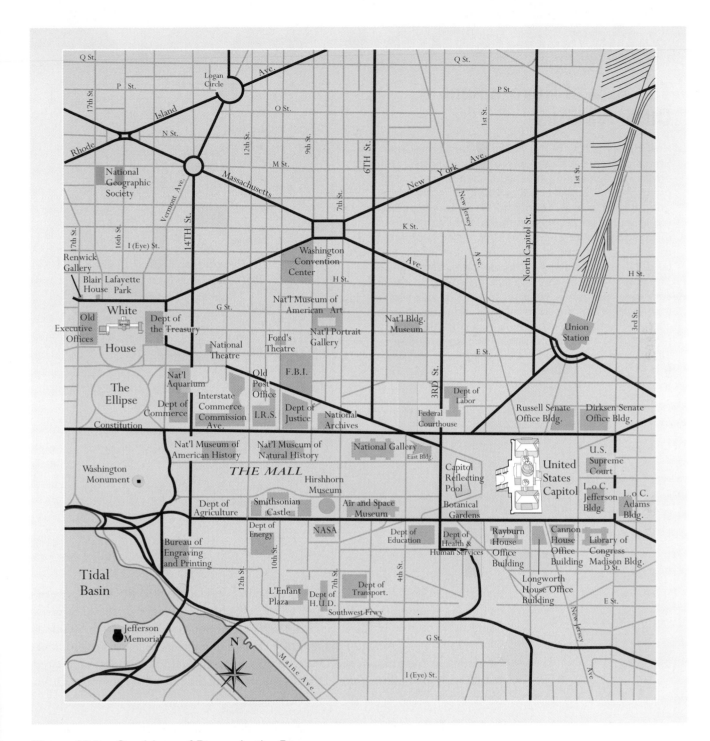

Figure 12.2 Corridors of Power in the Bureaucracy

This map shows the Capitol, the White House, and the major departments of the federal bureaucracy in Washington, D.C.

The Federal Bureaucracy

The federal bureaucracy—officially part of the executive branch of the U.S. government—consists of about 2.8 million civilian employees (plus 1.4 million persons in the armed forces) organized into 15 cabinet departments, more than 60 independent agencies, and a large Executive Office of the President (see Figure 12.2). The expenditures of *all* governments in the United States—the fed-

COMPARED TO WHAT?

The Size of Government in Other Nations

How does the size of the public sector in the United States compare with the size of the public sector in other economically advanced, democratic countries? There is a great deal of variation in the size of government across countries. Government spending accounts for nearly two-thirds of the total output in Sweden. Government spending exceeds one-half of the total output of Denmark, Netherlands, Finland, Germany, Italy, Austria, Belgium, and France. The high level of government spending in these countries primarily reflects greater public-sector involvement in the provision of housing, health care, retirement insurance, and aid to the unemployed. The sizes of the public sectors in Australia, Japan, and Switzerland are only slightly higher than that of the United States.

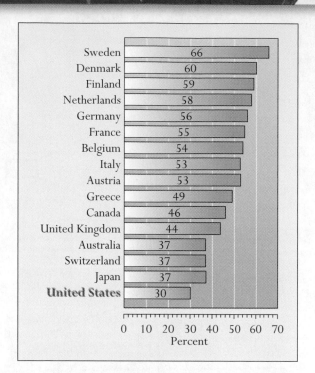

Governmental Percentage of Gross Domestic Product

Source: Joint Economic Committee of Congress, "The Size and Function of Government" (Washington, D.C.: 1998). United States updated to 2002.

eral government, the 50 state governments, and some 86,000 local governments—now amount to about *$4.0 trillion* (roughly 30 percent of the U.S. gross domestic product, or GDP, of *$13.4 trillion*). About two-thirds of this—about *$2.8 trillion* a year (about 20 percent of GDP)—is spent by the *federal* government. Government spending in the United States remains relatively modest compared to that of many nations (see *Compared to What?* "The Size of Government in Other Nations").

Cabinet Departments Cabinet departments employ about 60 percent of all federal workers (see Table 12.1). Each department is headed by a secretary (with the exception of the Justice Department, which is headed by the attorney general) who is appointed by the president and must be confirmed by the Senate. Each department is hierarchically organized; each has its own organization chart.

Cabinet status confers great legitimacy on a governmental function and prestige on the secretary, thus strengthening that individual's voice in the government. Therefore the elevation of an executive agency to cabinet level often reflects political considerations as much as or more than national needs. Strong pressures from "client" interest groups (groups principally served by the department), as well as presidential and congressional desires to pose as defenders and promoters of particular interests, account for the establishment of all of the

Fed World
Run by the U.S. Commerce Department, this site contains information about federal/state–local agency links, government jobs, IRS forms, Supreme Court decisions, and the vast array of governmental services. *www.fedworld.gov*

Table 12.1   Cabinet Departments and Functions

Department and Date Created	Function
State (1789)	Advises the president on the formation and execution of foreign policy; negotiates treaties and agreements with foreign nations; represents the United States in the United Nations and in more than fifty major international organizations and maintains U.S. embassies abroad; issues U.S. passports and, in foreign countries, visas to the United States.
Treasury (1789)	Serves as financial agent for the U.S. government; issues all payments of the U.S. government according to law; manages the debt of the U.S. government by issuing and recovering bonds and paying their interest; collects taxes owed to the U.S. government; collects taxes and enforces laws on alcohol, tobacco, and firearms and on customs duties; manufactures coins and currency.
Defense (1947: formerly the War Department, created in 1789, and the Navy Department, created in 1798)	Provides the military forces needed to deter war and protect the national security interest; includes the Departments of the Army, Navy, and Air Force.
Justice (1789)	Enforces all federal laws, including consumer protection, antitrust, civil rights, drug, and immigration and naturalization; maintains federal prisons.
Interior (1849)	Has responsibility for public lands and natural resources, for American Indian reservations, and for people who live in island territories under U.S. administration; preserves national parks and historical sites.
Agriculture (1889)	Works to improve and maintain farm income and to develop and expand markets abroad for agricultural products; safeguards standards of quality in the food supply through inspection and grading services; administers rural development, credit, and conservation programs; administers food stamp program.
Commerce (1913)	Encourages the nation's international trade, economic growth, and technological advancement; conducts the census; provides social and economic statistics and analyses for business and government; maintains the merchant marine; grants patents and registers trademarks.
Labor (1913)	Oversees working conditions; administers federal labor laws; protects workers' pension rights; sponsors job training programs; keeps track of changes in employment, price, and other national economic indicators.
Health and Human Services (1953 as Health, Education, and Welfare; reorganized with Education as a separate department in 1979)	Administers social welfare programs for the elderly, children, and youths; protects the health of the nation against impure and unsafe foods, drugs, and cosmetics; operates the Centers for Disease Control; funds the Medicare and Medicaid programs.
Housing and Urban Development (1965)	Is responsible for programs concerned with housing needs, fair housing opportunities, and the improvement and development of the nation's communities; administers mortgage insurance programs, rental subsidy programs, and neighborhood rehabilitation and preservation programs.
Transportation (1966)	Is responsible for the nation's highway planning, development, and construction; also urban mass transit, railroads, aviation, and the safety of waterways, ports, highways, and oil and gas pipelines.
Energy (1977)	Is responsible for the research, development, and demonstration of energy technology; marketing of federal electric power; energy conservation; the nuclear weapons program; regulation of energy production and use; and collection and analysis of energy data.
Education (1979)	Administers and coordinates most federal assistance to education.
Veterans Affairs (1989)	Operates programs to benefit veterans and members of their families.
Homeland Security (2002)	Prevents terrorist attacks within the United States, reduces the vulnerability of the nation to terrorism, and minimizes the damage and assists in recovery from terrorist attacks.

Source: The United States Government Manual (Washington, D.C.: Government Printing Office, annual).

UP CLOSE

The Department of Homeland Security

Presidents often create new bureaucratic organizations to symbolize their commitment to a policy direction. On October 8, 2001, less than one month after the "9/11" terrorist attack on America, President George W. Bush issued an executive order establishing the Office of Homeland Security and naming Pennsylvania's popular governor Tom Ridge as its director with "cabinet-level" status. Ridge was expected to coordinate the counterterrorism activities of 46 separate bureaucracies, but he was not given direct control over any government department or agency.

In 2002, in response to growing concerns that he had not done enough to reassure the American public of the federal government's commitment to protect them from terrorism, President Bush proposed a new Department of Homeland Security. Its mission is to prevent terrorist attacks within the United States, to reduce vulnerability of the United States to terrorism, and to minimize damage and assist recovery when and if terrorist attacks occur within the country.

The new department does more than just "coordinate" other federal agencies. In a major reorganization, the Department of Homeland Security has been given responsibility over agencies concerned with border protection, transportation security, and emergency preparedness, including the U.S. Border Patrol, the U.S. Customs Service, the Immigration and Naturalization Service, the U.S. Coast Guard, the Secret Service, the Federal Emergency Management Agency, and the newly created Transportation Security Administration.

But the Department of Homeland Security does *not* have authority over the Federal Bureau of Investigation in the Justice Department or the independent Central Intelligence Agency. So questions

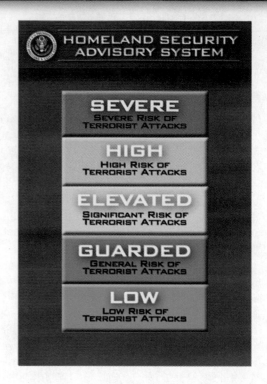

remain as to whether these two law enforcement and intelligence organizations can coordinate information among themselves and with the new Department of Homeland Security.

A new secretary was named in early 2005—former U.S. Court of Appeals Judge Michael Chertoff. But Chertoff had little time to prepare the department, especially the Federal Emergency Management Agency (FEMA), for the devastating Hurricane Katrina that laid waste to vast areas of New Orleans and the Mississippi Coast. The failures of FEMA in that disaster tarnished the image of the new Department (see *Up Close*: "Katrina: Federalism Fails in a Crisis" in Chapter 4).

newer departments. President Woodrow Wilson appealed to the labor movement in 1913 when he separated out a Department of Labor from the earlier business-dominated Department of Commerce and Labor. In 1965 President Lyndon Johnson created the Department of Housing and Urban Development to demonstrate his concern for urban problems. Seeking support from teachers and educational administrators, President Jimmy Carter created a separate Department of Education in 1979 and changed the name of the former Department of Health, Education, and Welfare to the Department of Health and Human Services (perhaps finding the phrase "human services" more politically acceptable than "welfare"). President Ronald Reagan tried, and failed, to "streamline" government by abolishing the Department of Education. But Reagan himself added a cabinet post, elevating the Veterans Administration to the Department of Veterans Affairs in an attempt to ingratiate himself with veterans. President George W. Bush created a new Department of Homeland Security in 2002 in response to the "9/11" terrorist attack on America and the threat of future attacks directly on the soil of the United States (see *Up Close:* "The Department of Homeland Security").

Cabinet Department Functions   The relative power and prestige of each cabinet-level department is a product not only of its size and budget but also of the importance of its function. By custom, the "pecking order" of departments—and therefore the prestige ranking of their secretaries—is determined by their years of origin. Thus the Departments of State, Treasury, Defense (War), and Justice, created by the First Congress in 1789, head the protocol list of departments. Overall, the duties of the fifteen cabinet-level departments of the executive branch cover an enormous range—everything from providing mortgage insurance, to overseeing the armed forces of the United States (see Table 12.1).

Cabinet Appointments   The Constitution requires that "Officers of the United States" be confirmed by the Senate. In the past, the Senate rarely rejected a presidential cabinet nomination; the traditional view was that presidents were entitled to pick their own people and even make their own mistakes. In recent years, however, the confirmation process has become more partisan and divisive, with the Senate conducting lengthy investigations and holding public hearings on presidential cabinet nominees. In 1989 the Senate rejected President Bush's nomination of John Tower as secretary of defense in a partisan battle featuring charges that the former Texas senator was a heavy drinker. The intense public scrutiny and potential for partisan attacks, together with financial disclosure and conflict-of-interest laws, may be discouraging some well-qualified people from accepting cabinet posts.

Independent Regulatory Commissions   Independent regulatory commissions differ from cabinet departments in their function, organization, and accountability to the president. Their function is to *regulate* a sector of society—transportation, communications, banking, labor relations, and so on (see Table 12.2). These commissions are empowered by Congress both to make and to enforce rules, and they thus function in a legislative and judicial fashion. To symbolize their impartiality, many of these organizations are headed by *commissions,* usually with five to ten members, rather than by a single secretary. Major policy decisions are made by majority vote of the commission. Finally, these agencies are more independent of the president than are cabinet departments. Their governing commissions are appointed by the president and confirmed by the Senate in the same fashion as cabinet secretaries, but their terms are fixed; they cannot be removed by the president.[6] These provisions are designed to insulate regulators from direct partisan or presidential pressures in their decision making.

A few powerful regulatory agencies remain inside cabinet departments. The most notable are the Food and Drug Administration (FDA), which remains in the Department of Health and Human Services and has broad authority to prevent the sale of drugs not deemed by the agency to be both "safe" and "effective"; the Occupational Health and Safety Administration (OSHA) in the Department of Labor, with authority to make rules governing any workplace in America; and

 Internal Revenue Service
The tax-collecting IRS is potentially the most powerful of all government agencies, with financial records on every tax-paying American. *www.irs.gov*

Food and Drug Administration
The Food and Drug Administration site is a reflection of the agency's mission "to promote and protect the public health by helping safe and effective products reach the market in a timely way." *www.fda.gov*

Table 12.2 Major Regulatory Bureaucracies

Commission	Date Created	Primary Functions
Federal Communications Commission (FCC)	1934	Regulates interstate and foreign communications by radio, television, wire, and cable.
Food and Drug Administration (FDA)	1930	Sets standards of safety and efficacy for foods, drugs, and medical devices.
Federal Home Loan Bank	1932	Regulates savings and loan associations that specialize in making home mortgage loans.
Federal Maritime Commission	1961	Regulates the waterborne foreign and domestic offshore commerce of the United States.
Federal Reserve Board (FRB)	1913	Regulates the nation's money supply by making monetary policy, which influences the lending and investing activities of commercial banks and the cost and availability of money and credit.
Federal Trade Commission (FTC)	1914	Regulates business to prohibit unfair methods of competition and unfair or deceptive acts or practices.
National Labor Relations Board (NLRB)	1935	Protects employees' rights to organize; prevents unfair labor practices.
Securities and Exchange Commission (SEC)	1934	Regulates the securities and financial markets (such as the stock market).
Occupational Safety and Health Administration (OSHA)	1970	Issues workplace regulations; investigates, cites, and penalizes for noncompliance.
Consumer Product Safety Commission (CPSC)	1972	Protects the public against product-related deaths, illnesses, and injuries.
Commodity Futures Trading Commission	1974	Regulates trading on the futures exchanges as well as the activities of commodity exchange members, public brokerage houses, commodity salespersons, trading advisers, and pool operators.
Nuclear Regulatory Commission (NRC)	1974	Regulates and licenses the users of nuclear energy.
Federal Energy Regulatory Commission (formerly Federal Power Commission)	1977	Regulates the transportation and sale of natural gas, the transmission and sale of electricity, the licensing of hydroelectric power projects, and the transportation of oil by pipeline.
Equal Employment Opportunity Commission (EEOC)	1964	Investigates and rules on charges of racial, gender, and age discrimination by employers and unions, in all aspects of employment.
Environmental Protection Agency (EPA)	1970	Issues and enforces pollution control standards regarding air, water, solid waste, pesticides, radiation, and toxic substances.
Federal Elections Commission (FEC)	1975	Administers and enforces federal campaign finance laws.

Source: FirstGov, www.firstgov.gov/agencies

the most powerful government agency of all, the Internal Revenue Service in the Treasury Department, with its broad authority to interpret the tax code, maintain records on every American, and investigate and punish alleged violations of the tax code.

Independent Agencies Congress has created a number of independent agencies outside of any cabinet department. Like cabinet departments, these agencies are hierarchically organized with a single head—usually called an "administrator"—who is appointed by the president and confirmed by the Senate. Administrators have no fixed terms of office and can be dismissed by the president; thus they are independent only insofar as they report directly to the

CHAPTER 12 • THE BUREAUCRACY: BUREAUCRATIC POLITICS

Cleaning up an oil spill on a California beach. The Environmental Protection Agency is perhaps the most powerful independent agency in the bureaucracy.

president rather than through a cabinet secretary. Politically, this independence ensures that their interests and budgets will not be compromised by other concerns, as may occur in agencies located within departments. (For more on their operations, see ""Regulatory Battles"" later in this chapter.)

One of the most powerful independent agencies is the Environmental Protection Agency (EPA), which is responsible for implementing federal legislation dealing with clean air, safe drinking water, solid waste disposal, pesticides, radiation, and toxic substances. EPA establishes and enforces comprehensive and complex standards for thousands of substances in the environment. It enjoys the political support of influential environmental interest groups, including the Environmental Defense Fund, Friends of the Earth, National Audubon Society, National Wildlife Federation, Natural Resources Defense Council, Sierra Club, and the Wilderness Society.

The Federal Reserve System is the most independent of all federal government agencies. The function of the "Fed" is to regulate the supply of money and thereby avoid both inflation and recession (see Chapter 16). The Federal Reserve System is independent of either the president or Congress. Its seven-member Board of Governors is appointed for *14-year terms*. Members are appointed by the president, with the consent of the Senate, but they may not be removed from the board except for "cause." No member has ever been removed since the creation of the board in 1913. The chairman of the board serves only a four-year term, but the chairman's term overlaps that of the president, so that new presidents

UP CLOSE

Managing the Nation's Money

Economist Alan Greenspan served as Chairman of the Board of Governors of the Federal Reserve System for eighteen years. He was initially appointed by President Ronald Reagan and served under four presidents—Reagan, Bush, Clinton, and Bush. His management of the Fed was widely praised by both Democrats and Republicans. He successfully fought inflationary trends during the nation's economic expansion in the 1990s by raising interest rates. When recession threatened in 2001, he led the Fed in bringing down interest rates to an all-time low, preventing a deep recession. During Greenspan's years inflation averaged only a modest 3 percent per year and unemployment averaged only 5.5 percent. (This compares with an inflation rate of 6.5 percent and an unemployment rate of 6.8 percent in the eighteen years prior to his assuming the job.) Greenspan received his Ph.D. in economics from New York University; prior to serving as Fed Chairman, he had served as a member of the Council of Economic Advisors.

Ben Bernanke received his Ph.D. from MIT and also served on the Council of Economic Advisors before being appointed Fed chairman to replace the retiring Greenspan in 2005. Bernanke promptly announced his intention to "maintain continuity" with Greenspan's policies. But trying to keep a balance between inflation and recession requires "reading the tea leaves"—carefully evaluating economic reports to estimate the direction of the economy and initiate stabilizing policies as early as possible. Economists agree that Greenspan was a master at the art. It remains to be seen whether Bernanke will be as successful as his predecessor.

Occupational Safety and Health Administration
This site covers news and information directly related to OSHA's mission "to ensure safe and healthful workplaces in America." *www.osha.gov*

Federal Reserve System
This Federal Reserve System site covers general information about "Fed" operations, including monetary policy, reserve bank services, international banking, and supervisory and regulatory functions. *www.federalreserve.gov*

Amtrak
The Amtrak Web site provides valuable information about trip planning, reservations, train schedules, and train fares. *www.amtrak.com*

cannot immediately name their own chair (see *Up Close:* "Managing the Nation's Money").

Government Corporations   Government corporations are created by Congress to undertake independent commercial enterprises. They resemble private corporations in that they typically charge for their services. Like private corporations, too, they are usually governed by a chief executive officer and a board of directors, and they can buy and sell property and incur debts.

Presumably, government corporations perform a service that the private enterprise system has been unable to carry out adequately. The first government corporation was the Tennessee Valley Authority, created by President Franklin Roosevelt during the Depression to build dams and sell electricity at inexpensive rates to impoverished citizens in the mid-South. In 1970 Congress created Amtrak to restore railroad passenger service to the United States. The U.S. Post Office had originally been created as a cabinet-level department, but in 1971 it became the U.S. Postal Service, a government corporation with a mandate from Congress to break even.

Contractors and Consultants   How has the federal government grown enormously in power and size, yet kept its number of employees at roughly the same level in recent years? The answer is found in the spectacular growth of private firms that live off federal contracting and consulting fees. Nearly one-fifth of all federal government spending flows through private contractors: for supplies, equipment, services, leases, and research and development. An army of scientists, economists, education specialists, management consultants, transportation experts, social scientists, and others are scattered across the country in universities, think tanks, consulting firms, and laboratories. Many are concentrated in the "beltway bandit" firms surrounding Washington, D.C.

The federal grant and contracting system is enormously complex; an estimated 150,000 federal contracting offices in nearly 500 agencies oversee thousands of outside contractors and consultants.[7] Although advertised bidding is sometimes required by law, most contracts and grants are awarded without competition through negotiation with favored firms or "sole source contracts" with organizations believed by bureaucrats to be uniquely qualified. Even when federal agencies issue public requests for proposals (RFPs), often a favored contractor has been alerted and advised by bureaucrats within the agency about how to win the award.

Bureaucracy and Democracy

Traditionally, conflict over government employment centered on the question of partisanship versus competence. Should the federal bureaucracy be staffed by people politically loyal to the president, the president's party, or key members of Congress? Or should it be staffed by nonpartisan people selected on the basis of merit and protected from "political" influence?

The Spoils System   Historically, government employment was allocated by the **spoils system**—selecting employees on the basis of party loyalty, electoral support, and political influence. Or, as Senator William Marcy said in 1832, "They see nothing wrong in the rule that to the victors belong the spoils of the enemy."[8] The spoils system is most closely associated with President Andrew Jackson, who viewed it as a popular reform of the earlier tendency to appoint officials on the basis of kinship and class standing. Jackson sought to bring into government many of the common people who had supported him. Later in the nineteenth century, the bartering and sale of government jobs became so scandalous and time-consuming that presidents complained bitterly about the task. When President James Garfield was shot and killed in 1881 by a disgruntled job seeker, the stage was set for reform.

The Merit System   The **merit system**—government employment based on competence, neutrality, and protection from partisanship—was introduced in the Pendleton Act of 1883. The act created the Civil Service Commission to establish a system for selecting government personnel based on merit, as determined by competitive examinations. In the beginning, "civil service" coverage included only about 10 percent of total federal employees. Over the years, however, more and more positions were placed under civil service, primarily at the behest of presidents who sought to "freeze in" their political appointees. By 1978 more than 90 percent of federal employees were covered by civil service or other merit systems.

The civil service system established a uniform General Schedule (GS) of job grades from GS 1 (lowest) to GS 15 (highest), with an Executive Schedule added later for top managers and pay ranges based on an individual's time in the grade. Each grade has specific educational requirements and examinations. College graduates generally begin at GS 5 or above; GS 9 through GS 12 are technical and supervisory positions; and GS 13, 14, and 15 are midlevel management and highly specialized positions. The Executive Schedule (the "supergrades") are reserved for positions of greatest responsibility. (In 2006 annual pay ranged from roughly $32,000 to $44,000 for Grades 5–8, up to $85,000 to $120,000 for Grades 13–15, and $183,500 for some Executive Schedule positions.)

About two-thirds of all federal civilian jobs come under the General Schedule system, with its written examinations and/or training, experience, and educational requirements. Most of the other one-third of federal civilian employees are

spoils system Selection of employees for government agencies on the basis of party loyalty, electoral support, and political influence.

—Think Again—

Should the federal bureaucracy be managed by nonpartisan professionals rather than people politically loyal to the president?

merit system Selection of employees for government agencies on the basis of competence, with no consideration of an individual's political stance and/or power.

USA Jobs
This site is the official source for federal employment information.
www.usajobs.opm.gov

During the administration of Andrew Jackson, the spoils system was perhaps more overt than at any other time in the history of the U.S. federal government. Jackson claimed he was trying to involve more of the "common folk" in the government, but his selection of advisers on the basis of personal friendship rather than qualifications sometimes caused him difficulties.

part of the "excepted services"; they are employed by various agencies that have their own separate merit systems, such as the Federal Bureau of Investigation, the Central Intelligence Agency, the U.S. Postal Service, and the State Department Foreign Service. The military also has its own system of recruitment, promotion, and pay.

Political Involvement   Congress passed the Hatch Act in 1939, a law that prohibited federal employees from engaging in partisan political activity, including running for public office, soliciting campaign funds, or campaigning for or against a party or candidate. It also protected federal merit system employees from dismissal for partisan reasons. But over the years many federal employees came to believe that the Hatch Act infringed on their rights as citizens. In 1993, a Democratic-controlled Congress repealed major portions of the Hatch Act, allowing civil servants to hold party positions and involve themselves in political fund-raising and campaigning. They still may not be candidates for public office in partisan elections, or solicit contributions from subordinate employees or people who do business with—or have cases before—their agencies.

The Problem of Responsiveness   The civil service system, like most other "reforms," eventually created problems at least as troubling as those in the system it replaced. First of all, there is the problem of a *lack of responsiveness* to presidential direction. Civil servants, secure in their protected jobs, can be less than cooperative toward their presidentially appointed department or agency heads. They can slow or obstruct policy changes with which they personally disagree. Each bureau and agency develops its own "culture," usually in strong support of the governmental function or client group served by the organization. Changing the culture of an agency is extremely difficult, especially when a presidential administration is committed to reducing its resources, functions, or services. Bureaucrats' powers of policy obstruction are formidable: They can help mobilize interest-group support against the president's policy; they can "leak" damaging information to sympathizers in Congress or the media to undermine the president's policy; they can delay and/or "sabotage" policies with which they disagree.

The Problem of Productivity   Perhaps the most troublesome problem in the federal bureaucracy has involved *productivity*—notably the inability to improve job performance because of the difficulties in rewarding or punishing civil servants. "Merit" salary rewards have generally proven ineffective in rewarding the performance of federal employees. More than 99 percent of federal workers regularly receive annual "merit" pay increases. Moreover, over time, federal employees have secured higher grade classifications and hence higher pay for most of the job positions in the General Schedule. This "inflation" in GS grades, combined with regular increases in salary and benefits, has resulted in many federal employees enjoying higher pay and benefits than employees in the private sector performing similar jobs.

At the same time, very poor performance often goes largely unpunished. Once hired and retained through a brief probationary period, a federal civil servant cannot be dismissed except for "cause." Severe obstacles to firing a civil servant result in a rate of dismissal of about one-tenth of 1 percent of all federal employees (see Table 12.3). It is doubtful that only such a tiny fraction are performing unsatisfactorily. A federal executive confronting a poorly performing or nonperforming employee must be prepared to spend more than a year in extended proceedings to secure a dismissal. Often costly substitute strategies are devised to work around or inspire the resignation of unsatisfactory federal employees—assigning them meaningless or boring tasks, denying them promotions, transferring them to distant or undesirable locations, removing secretaries or other supporting resources, and the like.

Civil Service Reform   Presidents routinely try to remedy some of the problems in the system. The Civil Service Reform Act of 1978, initiated by President Jimmy Carter, replaced the Civil Service Commission with the Office of Personnel Management (OPM) and made OPM responsible for recruiting, examining, training, and promoting federal employees. Unlike the Civil Service Commission, OPM is headed by a single director responsible to the president. The act

---

Table 12.3   Firing a Bureaucrat: What Is Required to Dismiss a Federal Employee

- Written notice at least thirty days in advance of a hearing to determine incompetence or misconduct.
- A statement of cause, indicating specific dates, places, and actions cited as incompetent or improper.
- The right to a hearing and decision by an impartial official, with the burden of proof falling on the agency that wishes to fire the employee.
- The right to have an attorney and to present witnesses in the employee's favor at the hearing.
- The right to appeal any adverse action to the Merit Systems Protection Board.
- The right to appeal any adverse action by the board to the U.S. Court of Appeals.
- The right to remain on the job and be paid until all appeals are exhausted.

Table 12.4   Women and Minorities in the Federal Bureaucracy

	Percentage Female	Percentage White, Non-Hispanic	Percentage African American	Percentage Hispanic
Overall	44.4%	68.6%	16.9%	7.3%
By pay grade				
GS 1–4	64.8	56.7	24.2	9.3
GS 5–8	65.9	59.5	24.6	8.8
GS 9–11	46.2	68.7	16.1	8.7
GS 12–13	—	74.9	13.3	5.5
GS 14–15	32.3	80.7	8.9	3.9
Executive	9.1	86.0	6.5	3.5
U.S. population (2000)	50.9	75.2	12.3	12.5

Table excludes Native Americans, Alaska Natives, and Asian and Pacific Islanders.

Source: Office of Personnel Management. Demographic Profile of the Federal Workforce. *www.opm.gov*

also sought to (1) streamline procedures through which individuals could be disciplined for poor performance; (2) establish merit pay for middle-level managers; and (3) create a Senior Executive Service (SES) composed of about 8,000 top people designated for higher Executive Schedule grades and salaries who also might be given salary bonuses, transferred among agencies, or demoted, based on performance.

But like many other reforms, this act failed to resolve the major problems—the responsiveness and productivity of the bureaucracy. No senior executives were fired, demoted, or involuntarily transferred. The bonus program proved difficult to implement: There are few recognized standards for judging meritorious work in public service, and bonuses often reflect favoritism as much as merit. Because the act created a separate Merit Systems Protection Board to hear appeals by federal employees from dismissals, suspensions, and demotions, rates of dismissal for all grades have not changed substantially from earlier days.

Bureaucracy and Representation   In addition to the questions of responsiveness and productivity, there is also the question of the representativeness of the federal bureaucracy. About 45 percent of the total civilian workforce is female, 16.9 percent is black, and 7.3 percent is Hispanic. However, a close look at *top* bureaucratic positions reveals far less diversity. As Table 12.4 shows, only 9.1 percent of federal "executive" positions (levels GS 16–18) are filled by women, only 6.5 percent by blacks, and only 3.5 percent by Hispanics. Thus the federal bureaucracy, like other institutions in American society, is *un*representative of the general population in its top executive positions.

Bureaucratic Politics

To whom is the federal bureaucracy really accountable? The president, Congress, or itself? Article II, Section 2, of the Constitution places the president at the head of the executive branch of government, with the power to "appoint Ambassadors, other public Ministers and Consuls, Judges of the Supreme Court, and all other Officers of the United States . . . which shall be established by Law." Appointment of these officials requires "the Advice and Consent of the Senate"—that is, a

— Think Again —

Should the federal bureaucracy at all levels reflect the gender and minority ratios of the total civilian work force?

majority vote in the Senate. The Constitution also states that "the Congress may by Law vest the Appointment of such inferior Officers, as they think proper, in the President alone." If the bureaucracy is to be made accountable to the president, we would expect the president to directly appoint *policy-making* executive officers. But it is difficult to determine exactly how many positions are truly "policy making."

Presidential "Plums"   The president retains direct control over about 3,000 federal jobs. Some 700 of these jobs are considered policy-making positions. They include presidential appointments authorized by law—cabinet and subcabinet officers, judges, U.S. marshals, U.S. attorneys, ambassadors, and members of various boards and commissions. The president also appoints a large number of "Schedule C" jobs throughout the bureaucracy, described as "confidential or policy-determining" in character. Each new administration goes through many months of high-powered lobbying and scrambling to fill these posts. Applicants with congressional sponsors, friends in the White House, or a record of loyal campaign work for the president compete for these "plums." Political loyalty must be weighed against administrative competence.[9]

Rooms at the Top   The federal bureaucracy has "thickened" at the top, even as total federal employment has declined. Over time, departments and agencies have added layers of administrators, variously titled "deputy secretary," "under-secretary," "assistant secretary," "deputy assistant secretary," and so on. Cabinet departments have become top-heavy with administrators, and the same multiplication of layers of executive management has occurred in independent agencies as well.[10]

Whistle-Blowers   The question of bureaucratic responsiveness is complicated by the struggle between the president and Congress to control the bureaucracy. Congress expects federal agencies and employees to respond fully and promptly to its inquiries and to report candidly on policies, procedures, and expenditures. Whistle-blowers are federal employees (or employees of a firm supplying the government) who report government waste, mismanagement, or fraud to the media or to congressional committees or who "go public" with their policy disputes with their superiors. Congress generally encourages whistle-blowing as a means of getting information and controlling the bureaucracy, but the president and agency heads whose policies are under attack are often less kindly disposed toward whistle-blowers. In 1989 Congress passed the Whistleblower Protection Act, which established an independent agency to guarantee whistle-blowers protection against unjust dismissal, transfer, or demotion.

Agency Cultures   Over time, every bureaucracy tends to develop its own "culture"—beliefs about the values of the organization's programs and goals and close associations with the agency's client groups and political supporters. Many government agencies are dominated by people who have been in government service most of their lives, and most of these people have worked in the same functional field most of their lives. They believe their work is important, and they resist efforts by either the president or Congress to reduce the activities, size, or budget of their agency. Career bureaucrats tend to support enlargement of the public sector—to enhance education, welfare, housing, environmental and consumer protection, and so on. Bureaucrats not only share a belief in the need for government expansion but also stand to benefit directly from increased authority, staffing, and funding as government takes on new and enlarged responsibilities.

 Center for Public Integrity
Reform organization committed to "exposing" corruption, mismanagement, and waste in government.
www.publicintegrity.org

whistle-blower Employee of the federal government or of a firm supplying the government who reports waste, mismanagement, and/or fraud by a government agency or contractor.

Friends and Neighbors   Bureaucracies maintain their own cultures in part by staffing themselves. Informal practices in recruitment often circumvent civil service procedures. Very few people ever get hired by taking a federal civil service examination administered by OPM and then sitting and waiting to be called for an interview by an agency. Most bureaucratic hiring actually comes about through "networks" of personal friends and professional associates. People inside an agency contact their friends and associates when a position first becomes vacant; they then send their friends to OPM to formally qualify for the job. Thus inside candidates learn about an opening well before it appears on any list of vacant positions and can tailor their applications to the job description. Agencies may even send a "name request" to OPM, ensuring that the preselected person will appear on the list of qualified people. In this way, individuals sometimes move through many jobs within a specific policy network—for example, within environmental protection, within transportation, or within social welfare— shifting between the federal bureaucracy, state or local government, and private firms or interest groups in the same field. Network recruiting generally ensures that the people entering a bureaucracy will share the same values and attitudes of the people already there.

"Reinventing" Government   Reformers lament "the bankruptcy of bureaucracy"—the waste, inefficiency, impersonality, and unresponsiveness of large government organizations. They decry "the routine tendency to protect turf, to resist change, to build empires, to enlarge one's sphere of control, to protect projects and programs regardless of whether or not they are any longer needed."[11] Many bureaucratic reform efforts have foundered, from Hoover Commission studies in the Truman and Eisenhower years to the Grace Commission work in the Reagan Administration. Clinton assigned a "reinventing government" task to Vice President Al Gore. Gore produced a report designed to put the "customer" (U.S. citizen) first, to "empower" government employees to get results, to cut red tape, to introduce competition and a market orientation wherever possible, and to decentralize government decision making.[12] The most impressive result was the overall decline in federal employment during the Clinton Administration, from 3.1 million to 2.8 million civilian employees.

Presidential Initiative   Presidents can create some new agencies by executive order. Often Congress gives presidents the authority to reorganize agencies by legislation (see *Up Close:* "Reorganizing Intelligence After 9/11"). But presidents have also acted on their own to create new agencies. Indeed, one study concludes that presidents have created about 40 percent of all new agencies[13]— perhaps the most famous was President Kennedy's Peace Corps. Of course, Congress has the last word, inasmuch as the continuation of a presidentially created agency requires funding and Congress controls the purse strings. It can end an agency's existence by cutting off its funds.

The Budgetary Process

── Think Again ──
Do you believe the
bureaucrats in Washington
waste a lot of the money
we pay in taxes?

The federal government's annual budget battles are the heart of the political process. Budget battles decide who gets what and who pays the cost of government. The budget is the single most important policy statement of any government.

The president is responsible for submitting the annual *Budget of the United States Government*—with estimates of revenues and recommendations for expenditures— for consideration, amendment, and approval by the Congress. But the president's budget reflects the outcome of earlier bureaucratic battles over who gets what. Despite highly publicized wrangling between the president and Congress each year—and occasional declarations that the president's budget is "DOA" (dead on arrival)—final congressional appropriations rarely deviate by more than 2 or 3 percent from the original presidential budget. Thus the president and the Office of Management and Budget in the Executive Office of the President have real budgetary power.

UP CLOSE

Reorganizing Intelligence After 9/11

"Imagination is not a gift usually associated with bureaucracies." There were reports at lower levels of the intelligence community prior to 9/11 that Al Qaeda was planning a major attack on the United States, that the World Trade Center might be a target because it had been a target of a car bomb in 1992, that Muslim fanatics were in the country and some had been taking flying lessons, and that various intelligence agencies had considered the possibilities of terrorists using aircraft as weapons. But no specifics were reported—time, location, or individuals involved—and the *9/11 Commission: The National Commission on Terrorist Attacks upon the United States* concluded that no agency or individual was to blame for the failure to anticipate the tragedy. Simply, "No one connected the dots."

9/11 Commission

President Bush authorized the 9/11 Commission in 2002, after pressure mounted in Washington for a thorough investigation of the 9/11 attack. The Commission's Final Report makes for exciting reading; it carefully reconstructs what happened in the days and months prior to the tragedy, as well as the events on that day itself; and it describes what each relevant federal agency knew and did not know about the possibility of such an attack. Finally, the commission issued a series of recommendations regarding reorganization of the intelligence community: to unify the intelligence community and operational planning against terrorists; to unify the many agencies participating in counterterrorism; and to strengthen homeland defense.

The Intelligence Community

The intelligence community consists of a series of agencies, each with a specialized responsibility, together with elements of the Department of Defense, the Department of Homeland Security, the

Federal Bureau of Investigation, the Department of State, the Department of Energy, and the Department of the Treasury. The Central Intelligence Agency (CIA) was the lead agency in assembly, analysis, and dissemination of intelligence from all other agencies in the intelligence community. It prepared the President's Daily Briefing (PDB), which summarizes all intelligence reports from all agencies for the president each day. The CIA also prepared National Intelligence Estimates (NIE's)—more thorough studies of specific topics, for example, North Korea's nuclear capabilities. In addition the CIA is charged with responsibility for human intelligence collection (recruiting agents around the world and supervising their work), and it also has responsibility for covert operations under the direction of the president (see "The Central Intelligence Agency" in Chapter 11). The National Security Agency (NSA) collects and processes foreign signals intelligence—all electronic emissions from radio to satellite communication. The National Reconnaissance Office (NRO) collects information from satellite reconnaissance. The National Imagery and Mapping Agency (NIMA) is responsible for geographic and geospatial intelligence. The Defense Intelligence Agency (DIA) is responsible for delivering tactical military intelligence directly to war fighters as well as policy makers.

National Intelligence Director

The key recommendation of the 9/11 Commission was the creation of a new office—the National Intelligence Director (NID)—to oversee the entire intelligence community. The new NID would replace the CIA director's role as the principal intelligence advisor to the president. The CIA director would concentrate on the responsibilities of the CIA itself. The NID would unify the budget for national intelligence as well as approve and submit nominations for individuals to head various agencies of the intelligence community. The NID would also manage the nation's counterterrorism effort, with the assistance of a new National Counterterrorism Center, which would assemble and analyze information on terrorists gathered both at home and abroad.

Military Intelligence

The Defense Department objected to giving the NID budget and personnel responsibility for intelligence agencies located within the department. Army, Navy, Air Force, and Marine intelligence are closely integrated with their respective military commands. The issue was compromised in Congress, with the military retaining direct control over intelligence activities within the Defense Department and the NID only consulting on these issues. The same compromise was reached regarding intelligence activities in the Department of Homeland Security, Department of State, Department of Energy, and Department of the Treasury.

Integrating Foreign and Domestic Intelligence

Perhaps the most troublesome problem in intelligence and counterterrorism in the past had been the lack of coordination between the CIA and the FBI. Fighting global terrorism requires close surveillance of individuals and terrorist organizations both within and outside of the United States. But in the original National Security Act of 1947, establishing the CIA, this agency was specifically prohibited from engaging in any activities, including surveillance of individual organizations, *inside the borders of the United States*. Only the FBI has the authority to act against terrorists inside the United States. Intelligence reorganization encouraged greater cooperation between these agencies. And the USA PATRIOT Act now permits both agencies to undertake surveillance of communications relevant to terrorism both within the United States and abroad. In a separate reorganization within the FBI, a new National Security Center was established with responsibility for counterterrorism. The NID was given budgetary and personnel authority over the new center. However, the FBI and the intelligence community each continue to operate largely separately from the other, and it is not clear whether the problems of communication and coordination between these agencies have been resolved.

FISA and Domestic Surveillance

In the Foreign Intelligence Surveillance Act of 1978 (FISA) Congress created a special FISA court to oversee the collection of electronic intelligence within the United States. It required all intelligence agencies, including the National Security Agency, which is responsible for the collection of electronic intelligence, to obtain warrants upon a showing that the surveillance is required for investigation of possible attacks upon the nation. The FISA court is secret and the persons under surveillance are not notified.

Nevertheless, President Bush authorized the National Security Agency to intercept international calls to and from Americans—calls involving known or suspected terrorists—without a FISA warrant. The president claimed that he has inherent constitutional powers as Commander-in-Chief to gather intelligence during war or armed conflict, and that the United States is currently at war with international terrorists. The president also claims that a joint resolution of Congress passed following the 9/11 terrorist attack on American included "authorization for the use of military force" and that such authorization includes warrantless survelliance of suspected terrorists both inside and outside of the United States.

Opponents of warrantless surveillance argue that the president is bound by the FISA Act, which specifically requires court warrants for surveillance within United States, including international calls. Congress did not authorize warrantless surveillance in its 9/11 joint resolution. Moreover, Congress did authorize surveillance of American citizens in terrorist investigations *but only* with a warrant issued by the FISA court. Congress was direct and specific on the subject of domestic surveillance in the FISA Act even during wartime. And as far back as 1952, the Supreme Court held that when Congress has addressed a specific issue by law, the president is obliged to follow that law in dealing with the issue.[a] The president, opponents claim, is acting unconstitutionally and unlawfully in authorizing warrantless surveillance of American citizens.

[a]*Youngstown Sheet & Tube Co. v. Sawyer*, 343 U.S. 579 (1952).

Office of Management and Budget (OMB) The OMB site includes all budget documents and information on regulatory oversight. *www.omb.gov*

The Office of Management and Budget The Office of Management and Budget (OMB) has the key responsibility for budget preparation. In addition to this major task, OMB has related responsibilities for improving the organization and management of the executive agencies, for coordinating the extensive statistical services of the federal government, and for analyzing and reviewing proposed legislation.

Preparation of the budget begins when OMB, after preliminary consultations with the executive agencies and in accord with presidential policy, develops targets or ceilings within which the agencies are encouraged to build their requests

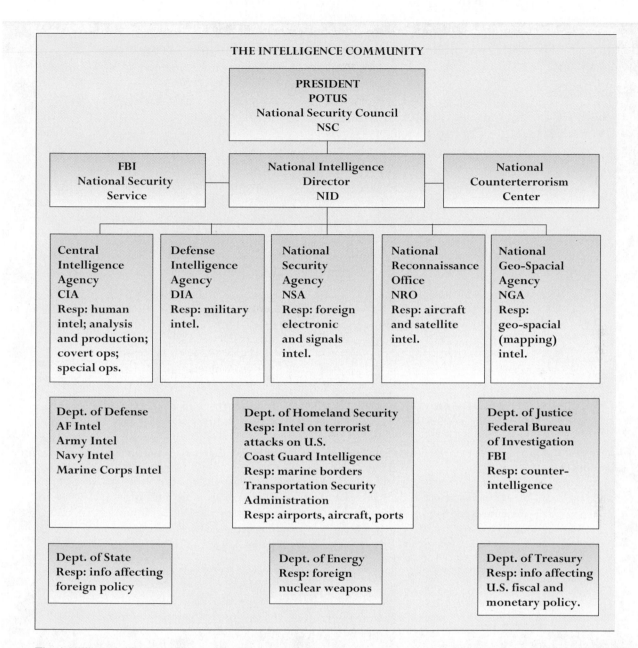

The Intelligence Community

Note: The CIA, DIA, NSA, NRO, and NGA are concerned exclusively with intelligence. The Departments of Defense, Homeland Security, Justice, State, Energy, and Treasury are concerned primarily with other missions but do have some intelligence responsibilities.

(see Figure 12.3). Budget materials and instructions then go to the agencies, with the request that the forms be completed and returned to OMB. This request is followed by about three months of arduous work by agency budget officers, department heads, and the "grass-roots" bureaucracy in Washington, D.C., and out in the field. Budget officials at the bureau and departmental levels check requests from the smaller units, compare them with previous years' estimates, hold conferences, and make adjustments. The heads of agencies are expected to submit their completed requests to OMB by July or August. Although these requests usually remain within target levels, occasionally they include some

	WHO	WHAT	WHEN
Presidential budget making	President and OMB	OMB presents long-range forecasts for revenues and expenditures to the president. President and OMB develop general guidelines for all federal agencies. Agencies are sent guidelines and forms for their budget requests.	January February March
	Executive agencies	Agencies prepare and submit budget requests to OMB.	April May June July
	OMB and agencies	OMB reviews agency requests and holds hearings with agency officials.	August September October
	OMB and president	OMB presents revised budget to president. President and OMB write budget message for Congress.	November December January
	President	President presents budget for the next fiscal year to Congress.	February
Congressional budget process	CBO and congressional committees	CBO reviews taxing and spending proposals and reports to House and Senate budget committees.	February–April
	Congress; House and Senate budget committees	Committees present first concurrent resolution, which sets overall total for budget outlays in major categories. Full House and Senate vote on resolution. Committees are instructed to stay within Budget Committee's resolution.	May June
	Congress; House and Senate appropriations committees and budget committees	Appropriations committees and subcommittees draw up detailed appropriations bills and submit them to budget committees for second concurrent resolution. The full House and Senate vote on "reconciliations" and second (firm) concurrent resolution.	July August September
	Congress and president	House and Senate pass various appropriations bills (nine to sixteen bills, by major functional category, such as "defense"). Each is sent to president for signature. (If successfully vetoed, a bill is revised and resubmitted to the president.)	September October
Executive budget implementation	Congress and president	Fiscal year for all federal agencies begins October 1. If no appropriations bill for an agency has been passed by Congress and signed by the president, Congress must pass and the president sign a continuing resolution to allow the agency to spend at last year's level until a new appropriations bill is passed. If no continuing resolution is passed, the agency must officially cease spending government funds and must officially shut down.	After October 1

Figure 12.3   The Budget Process
Development, presentation, and approval of the federal budget for any fiscal year takes almost two full years. The executive branch spends more than a year on the process before Congress even begins its review and revision of the president's proposals. The problems of implementing the budgeted programs then fall to the federal bureaucracy.

"overceiling" items (requests above the suggested ceilings). With the requests of the spending agencies at hand, OMB begins its own budget review, including hearings at which top agency officials support their requests as convincingly as possible. Frequently OMB must say "no," that is, reduce agency requests. On rare occasions, dissatisfied agencies may ask the budget director to take their cases to the president.

The President's Budget   In December, the president and the OMB director devote much time to the key document, *The Budget of the United States Government*, which by now is approaching its final stages of assembly. Each budget is named for the **fiscal year** in which it *ends*. The federal fiscal year begins on October 1 and ends the following September 30. (Thus *The Budget of the United States Government Fiscal Year* 2009 begins October 1, 2008, and ends September 30, 2009.) Although the completed document includes a revenue plan with general estimates for taxes and other income, it is primarily an expenditure budget. (Revenue and tax policy staff work centers in the Treasury Department, not in the Office of Management and Budget.) In late January, the president presents Congress with

fiscal year Yearly government accounting period, not necessarily the same as the calendar year. The federal government's fiscal year begins October 1 and ends September 30.

The 2005 Budget of the United States government shows total outlays of $2.4 trillion, with a deficit of nearly $365 billion. The deficit is in part a product of increased spending for defense and homeland security.

The Budget of the United States Government for the fiscal year beginning October 1. After the budget is in legislative hands, the president may recommend further alterations as needs dictate.

House and Senate Budget Committees   The Constitution gives Congress the authority to decide how the government should spend its money: "No money shall be drawn from the Treasury, but in Consequence of Appropriations made by Law" (Article 1, Section 9). The president's budget is sent initially to the House and Senate Budget Committees, which rely on their own bureaucracy, the Congressional Budget Office (CBO), to review the president's budget. Based on the CBO's assessment, these committees draft a first **budget resolution** (due May 15) setting forth target goals to guide congressional committees regarding specific appropriations and revenue measures. If proposed spending exceeds the targets in the budget resolution, the resolution comes back to the floor in a reconciliation measure. A second budget resolution (due September 15) sets binding budget figures for committees and subcommittees considering appropriations. In practice, however, these two budget resolutions are often folded into a single measure because Congress does not want to argue the same issues twice.

Congressional Appropriations Committees   Congressional approval of each year's spending is usually divided into thirteen separate appropriations bills (acts), each covering separate broad categories of spending (for example, defense, labor, human services and education, commerce, justice). These appropriations bills are drawn up by the House and Senate Appropriations Committees and their specialized subcommittees, which function as overseers of agencies included in their appropriations bills. Committee work in the House of Representatives is usually more thorough than it is in the Senate; the committee in the Senate tends to be a "court of appeal" for agencies opposed to House action. Each committee, moreover, has about ten largely independent subcommittees, each reviewing the requests of a particular agency or a group of related functions. Specific appropriations bills are taken up by the subcommittees in hearings. Departmental officers answer questions on the conduct of their programs and defend their requests for the next fiscal year; lobbyists and other witnesses testify. Although committees and subcommittees have broad discretion in allocating funds to the agencies they monitor, they must stay within overall totals set forth in the second budget resolution adopted by Congress.

Appropriations Acts   In examining the interactions between Congress and the federal bureaucracy over spending, it is important to distinguish between appropriations and authorization. An **authorization** is an act of Congress that establishes a government program and defines the amount of money it may spend. Authorizations may be for one or several years. However, an authorization does not actually provide the money that has been authorized; only an **appropriations act** can do that. In fact, appropriations acts, which are usually for a single fiscal year, are almost always *less* than authorizations; deciding how much less is the real function of the Appropriations Committees and subcommittees. (By its own rules, Congress cannot appropriate money for programs it has not already authorized.) Appropriations acts include both obligational authority and outlays.

Obligational authority permits a government agency to enter into contracts that will require the government to make payments beyond the fiscal years in question. **Outlays** must be spent in the fiscal year for which they are appropriated.

Continuing Resolutions and "Shutdowns"   All appropriations acts *should* be passed by both houses and signed by the president into law before October 1,

---

budget resolution
Congressional bill setting forth target budget figures for appropriations to various government departments and agencies.

authorization   Act of Congress that establishes a government program and defines the amount of money it may spend.

appropriations act
Congressional bill that provides money for programs authorized by Congress.

obligational authority
Feature of some appropriations acts by which an agency is empowered to enter into contracts that will require the government to make payments beyond the fiscal year in question.

outlays   Actual dollar amounts to be spent by the federal government in a fiscal year.

Much of the work of the federal bureaucracy is routine, including the printing of money.

the date of the start of the fiscal year. However, it is rare for Congress to meet this deadline, so the government usually finds itself beginning a new fiscal year without a budget. Constitutionally, any U.S. government agency for which Congress does not pass an appropriations act may not draw money from the Treasury and thus is obliged to shut down. To get around this problem, Congress usually adopts a **continuing resolution** that authorizes government agencies to keep spending money for a specified period at the same level as in the previous fiscal year.

A continuing resolution is supposed to grant additional time for Congress to pass, and the president to sign, appropriations acts. But occasionally this process has broken down in the heat of political combat over the budget: the time period specified in a continuing resolution has expired without agreement on appropriations acts or even on a new continuing resolution. Shutdowns occurred during the bitter battle between President Bill Clinton and the Republican-controlled Congress over the Fiscal Year 1996 budget. In theory, the absence of either appropriations acts or a continuing resolution should cause the entire federal government to "shut down," that is, to cease all operations and expenditures for lack of funds. But in practice, such shutdowns have been only partial, affecting only "nonessential" government employees and causing relatively little disruption.

continuing resolution
Congressional bill that authorizes government agencies to keep spending money for a specified period at the same level as in the previous fiscal year; passed when Congress is unable to enact final appropriations measures by October 1.

The Politics of Budgeting

Budgeting is very political. Being a good "bureaucratic politician" involves (1) cultivating a good base of support for requests among the public at large and among people served by the agency; (2) developing interest, enthusiasm, and support for one's program among top political figures and congressional leaders; (3) winning favorable coverage of agency activities in the media; and (4) following strategies that exploit opportunities (see *Up Close:* "Bureaucratic Budget Strategies").

UP CLOSE

Bureaucratic Budget Strategies

How do bureaucrats go about "maximizing" their resources? Some of the most common budgetary strategies of bureaucrats are listed here. Remember that most bureaucrats believe strongly in the importance of their tasks; they pursue these strategies not only to increase their own power and prestige but also to better serve their client groups and the entire nation.

■ **Spend it all:** Spend all of your current appropriation. Failure to use up an appropriation indicates the full amount was unnecessary in the first place, which in turn implies that your budget should be cut next year.

■ **Ask for more:** Never request a sum less than your current appropriation. It is easier to find ways to spend up to current appropriation levels than it is to explain why you want a reduction. Besides, a reduction indicates your program is not growing, an embarrassing admission to most government administrators. Requesting an increase, at least enough to cover "inflation," demonstrates the continued importance of your program.

■ **Put vital programs in the "base":** Put top priority programs into the basic budget—that is, that part of the budget within current appropriation

levels. The Office of Management and Budget (OMB) and legislative committees seldom challenge programs that appear to be part of existing operations.

■ **Make new programs appear "incremental":** Requested increases should appear to be small and should appear to grow out of existing operations. Any appearance of a fundamental change in a budget should be avoided.

■ **Give them something to cut:** Give the OMB and legislative committees something to cut. Normally it is desirable to submit requests for substantial increases in existing programs and many requests for new programs, in order to give higher political authorities something to cut. This approach enables authorities to "save" the public untold millions of dollars and justify their claim of promoting "economy" in government. Giving them something to cut also diverts attention from the basic budget with its vital programs.

■ **Make cuts hurt:** If your agency is faced with a real budget cut—that is, a reduction from last year's appropriation—announce pending cuts in vital and popular programs in order to stir up opposition to the cut. For example, the National Park Service might announce the impending closing of the Washington Monument. Never acknowledge that cuts might be accommodated by your agency without reducing basic services.

Budgeting Is "Incremental" The most important factor determining the size and content of the budget each year is last year's budget. Decision makers generally use last year's expenditures as a *base*; active consideration of budget proposals generally focuses on new items and requested increases over last year's base. The budget of an agency is almost never reviewed as a whole. Agencies are seldom required to defend or explain budget requests that do *not* exceed current appropriations; but requested increases *do* require explanation and are most subject to reduction by OMB or Congress.

The result of **incremental budgeting** is that many programs, services, and expenditures continue long after there is any real justification for them. When new needs, services, and functions arise, they do not displace older ones but rather are *added* to the budget. Budget decisions are made incrementally because policy makers do not have the time, energy, or information to review every dollar of every budget request every year. Nor do policy makers wish to refight every political battle over existing programs every year. So they generally accept last year's base spending level as legitimate and focus attention on proposed increases for each program.

incremental budgeting
Method of budgeting that focuses on requested increases in funding for existing programs, accepting as legitimate their previous year's expenditures.

WHAT DO YOU THINK?

How Much Money Does the Government Waste?

Bureaucracy is often associated in the public's mind with waste and inefficiency. But it is very difficult to determine objectively how much money government really wastes. People disagree on the value of various government programs. What is "waste" to one person may be a vital governmental function to another. But even those who believe a government program is necessary may still believe some of the money going to that program is wasted by the bureaucracy.

Indeed, over the last twenty years, nearly two-thirds of Americans have described the government as wasting "a lot" of money rather than "some" or "not very much" (see graph). Americans believe that there is more waste in domestic spending than in military spending.

Is public opinion correct in estimating that "a lot" of money is wasted? The Government Accountability Office (GAO) is an arm of Congress with broad authority to audit the operations and finances of federal agencies. GAO audits have frequently found fraud and mismanagement amounting to 10 percent or more of the spending of many agencies it has reviewed, which suggests that *$200 billion* of the overall federal budget of $2.1 trillion may be wasted.[a] Citizens' commissions studying the federal bureaucracy place an even higher figure on waste. The

Grace Commission estimated waste at more than 20 percent of federal spending.[b]

[a]General Accounting Office, *Federal Evaluation Issues* (Washington, D.C., 1989).

[b]*President's Private Sector Survey on Cost Control* (Grace Commission Report) (Washington, D.C.: Government Printing Office, 1984).

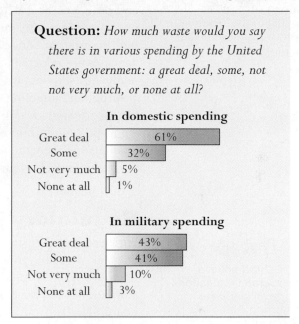

Question: *How much waste would you say there is in various spending by the United States government: a great deal, some, not not very much, or none at all?*

In domestic spending

Great deal	61%
Some	32%
Not very much	5%
None at all	1%

In military spending

Great deal	43%
Some	41%
Not very much	10%
None at all	3%

Source: Copyright © 2001, *The Washington Post.* Reprinted by permission.

Reformers have proposed "sunset" laws requiring bureaucrats to justify their programs every five to seven years or else the programs go out of existence, as well as **zero-based budgeting** that would force agencies to justify every penny requested—not just requested increases. In theory, sunset laws and zero-based budgeting would regularly prune unnecessary government programs, agencies, and expenditures and thus limit the growth of government and waste in government (see *What Do You Think?* "How Much Money Does the Government Waste?"). But in reality, sunset laws and zero-based budgeting require so much effort in justifying already accepted programs that executive agencies and legislative committees grow tired of the effort and return to incrementalism.

The "incremental" nature of budgetary politics helps reduce political conflicts and maintain stability in governmental programs. As bruising as budgetary battles are today, they would be much worse if the president or Congress undertook to review the value of *all* existing expenditures and programs each year. Comprehensive budgetary review would "overload the system" with political conflict by refighting every policy battle every year.

Budgeting Is Nonprogrammatic   Budgeting is *nonprogrammatic* in that an agency budget typically lists expenditures under ambiguous phrases: "personnel

zero-based budgeting
Method of budgeting that demands justification for the entire budget request of an agency, not just its requested increase in funding.

services," "contractual services," "travel," "supplies," "equipment." It is difficult to tell from such a listing exactly what programs the agency is spending its money on. Such a budget obscures policy decisions by hiding programs behind meaningless phrases. Even if these categories are broken down into line items (for example, under "personnel services," the line-item budget might say, "John Doaks, Assistant Administrator, $85,000"), it is still next to impossible to identify the costs of various programs.

For many years, reformers have called for budgeting by programs. **Program budgeting** would require agencies to present budgetary requests in terms of the end products they will produce or at least to allocate each expense to a specific program. However, bureaucrats are often unenthusiastic about program budgeting; it certainly adds to the time and energy devoted to budgeting, and many agencies are reluctant to describe precisely what it is they do and how much it really costs to do it. Moreover, some political functions are best served by *non*program budgeting. Agreement comes more easily when the items in dispute can be treated in dollars instead of programmatic differences. Congressional Appropriations Committees can focus on increases or decreases in overall dollar amounts for agencies rather than battle over even more contentious questions of which individual programs are worthy of support.

program budgeting
Identifying items in a budget according to the functions and programs they are to be spent on.

Regulatory Battles

Bureaucracies regulate virtually every aspect of American life. Interest rates on loans are heavily influenced by the Federal Reserve Board. The National Labor Relations Board protects unions and prohibits "unfair labor practices." Safety in automobiles and buses is the responsibility of the National Transportation Safety Board. The Federal Deposit Insurance Corporation insures bank accounts. The Federal Trade Commission orders cigarette manufacturers to place a health warning on each pack. The Equal Employment Opportunity Commission investigates complaints about racial and sexual discrimination in jobs. The Consumer Product Safety Commission requires that toys be large enough that they cannot be swallowed by children. The Federal Communications Commission bans tobacco advertisements on television. The Environmental Protection Agency requires automobile companies to limit exhaust emissions. The Occupational Safety and Health Administration requires construction firms to place portable toilets at work sites. The Food and Drug Administration decides what drugs your doctor can prescribe. The list goes on and on. Indeed, it is difficult to find an activity in public or private life that is not regulated by the federal government (see *A Conflicting View:* "Bureaucratic Regulations Are Suffocating America").

Federal regulatory bureaucracies are legislators, investigators, prosecutors, judges, and juries—all wrapped into one. They issue thousands of pages of rules and regulations each year; they investigate thousands of complaints and conduct thousands of inspections; they require businesses to submit hundreds of thousands of forms each year; they hold hearings, determine "compliance" and "noncompliance," issue corrective orders, and levy fines and penalties. Most economists agree that regulation adds to the cost of living, is an obstacle to innovation and productivity, and hinders economic competition. Most regulatory commissions are independent; they are not under an executive department, and their members are appointed for long terms by a president who has little control over their activities.

Traditional Agencies: Capture Theory   The **capture theory of regulation** describes how some regulated industries come to benefit from government

---Think Again---
Do you believe bureaucratic regulations of all kinds are hurting America's competitiveness in the global economy?

---Think Again---
Do you believe that the overall costs of federal regulatory activity are justified by the benefits?

capture theory of regulation   Theory describing how some regulated industries come to benefit from government regulation and how some regulatory commissions come to represent the industries they are supposed to regulate rather than representing "the people."

A CONFLICTING VIEW

Bureaucratic Regulations Are Suffocating America

Today, bureaucratic regulations of all kinds—environmental controls, workplace safety rules, municipal building codes, government contracting guidelines—have become so numerous, detailed, and complex that they are stifling initiative, curtailing economic growth, wasting billions of dollars, and breeding popular contempt for law and government.

Consider, for example, the Environmental Protection Agency's rules and regulations, now *seventeen volumes* of fine print. Under one set of rules, before any land on which "toxic" waste was once used can be reused by anyone for any purpose, it must be cleaned to near perfect purity. The dirt must be made cleaner than soil that has never been used for anything. The result is that most new businesses choose to locate on virgin land rather than incur the enormous expense of cleaning dirt, and a great deal of land previously used by industry sits vacant while new land is developed.

These and similar examples of "the death of common sense" in bureaucratic regulations are set forth by critic Philip K. Howard, who argues, "We have constructed a system of regulatory law that basically outlaws common sense."[a]

The explosive growth in federal regulations in the last two decades has added heavy costs to the American economy. The costs of regulations do not appear in the federal budget: rather, they are paid for by businesses, employees, and consumers.

[a]Philip K. Howard. *The Death of Common Sense: How Law Is Suffocating America* (New York: Random House, 1995), pp. 10–11.

Indeed, politicians prefer a regulatory approach to the environment, health, and safety precisely because it forces costs on the private sector—costs that are largely invisible to voters and taxpayers. Yet as the costs of regulation multiply for American businesses, the prices of their products rise in world markets.

How large is the regulatory bill? Proponents of a regulatory activity usually object to estimating its cost. Politicians who wish to develop an image as protectors of the environment, of consumers, of the disabled, and so on, do not want to call attention to the costs of their legislation. Only recently has the Office of Management and Budget (OMB) even attempted to estimate the costs of federal regulatory activity. Overall, regulatory activity costs Americans between $300 billion (OMB estimate) and $700 billion a year (estimate by Center for the Study of American Business), an amount equal to over one-third of the total federal budget.

Regulation also places a heavy burden on innovations and productivity. The costs and delays in winning permission for a new product tend to discourage invention and to drive up prices. For example, new drugs are difficult to introduce in the United States because the Food and Drug Administration (FDA) typically requires up to ten years of testing. Western European nations are many years ahead in their number of life-saving drugs available; they speak of the "drug lag" in the United States. Critics charge that if aspirin were proposed for marketing today, it would not be approved by the FDA. Recently activists have succeeded in speeding up FDA approval of drugs to treat AIDS, but the agency has continued to delay the introduction of drugs to treat other diseases.

regulation and how some regulatory commissions come to represent the industries they are supposed to regulate rather than representing "the people." Historically, regulatory commissions have acted against only the most wayward members of an industry. By attacking those businesses that gave the industry bad publicity, the commissions actually helped improve the public's opinion of the industry as a whole. Regulatory commissions provided symbolic reassurance to the public that the behavior of the industry was proper. Among the traditional regulatory agencies that have been accused of becoming too close to their regulated industry are the Federal Communications Commission (FCC, regulator of the communications industry, including the television networks), the Securities and Exchange Commission (SEC, the securities industry and stock exchanges), the Federal Reserve Board (FRB, the banking industry), and National Labor Relations Board (NLRB, unions).

Agencies need not be actually "captured" by the industries they regulate but rather simply provide "protection" to these industries, especially to the largest corporations within them. Larger corporations are better able to meet agency requirements and to respond to changes in these requirements than smaller corporations or individual firms. In product approval, licensing, permitting, and grant making, for example, larger corporations are better able to jump through bureaucratic hoops.[14]

Commission members often come from the industry they are supposed to regulate, and after a few years in government, the "regulators" return to high-paying jobs in the industry, creating the *revolving door problem* described in Chapter 9. Over the years, then, some industries have come to support their regulatory bureaucracies. Industries have often strongly opposed proposals to reduce government controls. Proposals to deregulate railroads, interstate trucking, and airlines have met with substantial opposition from both the regulatory bureaucracies and the regulated industries, working together.

The Newer Regulators: The Activists   In recent decades, Congress created several new "activist" regulatory agencies in response to the civil rights movement, the environmental movement, and the consumer protection movement. Unlike traditional regulatory agencies, the activist agencies do not regulate only a single industry; rather, they extend their jurisdiction to all industries. The Equal Employment Opportunity Commission (EEOC), the Environmental Protection Agency (EPA), and the Occupational Safety and Health Administration (OSHA) pose serious challenges to the business community. Many businesspeople argue that EEOC rules designed to prevent racial and sexual discrimination in employment and promotion (affirmative action guidelines) ignore the problems of their industry or their labor market and overlook the costs of training or the availability of qualified minorities. Likewise, many of OSHA's thousands of safety regulations appear costly and ridiculous to people in industry. The complaint about EPA is that it seldom considers the cost of its rulings to business or the consumer. Industry representatives contend that EPA should weigh the costs of its regulations against the benefits to the environment.

Deregulation   The demand to deregulate American life was politically very popular during President Ronald Reagan's administration in the 1980s. But **deregulation** made only limited progress in curtailing the power of the regulatory bureaucracies. Arguments for deregulation centered on the heavy costs of compliance with regulations, the burdens these costs imposed on innovation and productivity, and the adverse impact of regulatory activity on the global competitiveness of American industry. In 1978 Jimmy Carter succeeded in getting Congress to deregulate the airline industry. Against objections by the industry itself, which *wanted* continued regulation, the Civil Aeronautics Board was stripped of its powers to allocate airline routes to various carriers and to set rates. At the end of 1984, the board went out of existence, the first major regulatory agency ever to be abolished. With the airlines free to choose where to fly and what to charge, competition on heavily traveled routes (such as from New York to Los Angeles) reduced fares dramatically while prices rose on less traveled routes served by a single airline. Overall the cost of airline travel declined by 25 to 30 percent.[15] Competition caused airline profits to decline and financially weak airlines to declare bankruptcy. Also, during the 1980s the Interstate Commerce Commission (ICC), the first regulatory commission ever established by the federal government, dating from 1887, was stripped of most of its power to set railroad and trucking rates. The ICC itself was finally abolished in 1995. Prices to consumers of railroad and trucking services declined dramatically.

deregulation Lifting of government rules and bureaucratic supervision from business and professional activity.

The deregulation of the airline industry contributed to the development of the hub-and-spoke system currently used by most airlines to reduce their costs. Here American Airlines aircraft congregate at the airline's hub in Dallas/Fort Worth. Although deregulation has caused fares to decrease on heavily competitive routes, critics charge that it has contributed to higher rates on noncompetitive routes.

Reregulation   Deregulation threatens to diminish politicians' power and to eliminate bureaucrats' jobs. It forces industries to become competitive and diminishes the role of interest group lobbyists. So in the absence of strong popular support for deregulation, pressures to continue and expand regulatory activity will always be strong in Washington.

Airline deregulation brought about a huge increase in airline travel. The airlines doubled their seating capacity and made more efficient use of their aircraft through the development of "hub-and-spoke" networks. Air safety continued to improve; fatalities per millions of miles flown declined; and by taking travelers away from far more dangerous highway travel, overall transportation safety was enhanced. But these favorable outcomes were overshadowed by complaints about congestion at major airports and increased flight delays, especially at peak hours. The major airports are publicly owned, and governments have been very slow in responding to increased air traffic. Congestion and delays are widely publicized, and politicians respond to complaints by calling for reregulation of airline travel.

The political incentives to create new regulatory agencies, grant additional powers to existing agencies, and add to the accumulation of federal regulations are great. Politicians want to be seen "doing something" about any well-publicized problem in America. When the media reports accidents, health scares, environmental dangers, etc., politicians are interviewed for their response, and most feel obliged to call for new laws and regulations, with little regard to their likely costs or effectiveness.

Regulating America

Federal regulatory agencies continually add more rules to American life. Roughly 4,000 new rules, all with the force of law, are issued by regulatory agencies each year. The Environmental Protection Agency (EPA) leads in making new rules,

www **Code of Federal Regulations**
All fifty titles of federal regulations can be found at the Cornell Law School site.
www.cfr.law.cornell.edu

closely followed by the Internal Revenue Service (IRS) and the Federal Communications Commission (FCC).

Over 50 federal agencies have rule-making power. These agencies must publish proposed rules in the *Federal Register* and allow time for interested groups to "comment" on them. "Major rules," those estimated to cost Americans at least $100 or more per year in compliance, are sent to the Office of Management and Budget before being finalized.

Multiplying Regulations   Inasmuch as proposed new regulations must be published in the *Federal Register,* the size of this publication is often used as an indicator of overall federal regulatory activity. In 1970, the *Federal Register* included roughly 20,000 pages; by 1980 it had expanded to over 73,000 pages. Only during the presidency of Ronald Reagan, who promised to reduce federal regulatory activity, did the size of the *Federal Register* decline somewhat. But by 2000 it was again over 80,000 pages.

The accumulated regulations of federal government are published in the Code of Federal Regulations. The Code includes all regulations currently in effect. The Code has now expanded to over 150,000 pages, 50 titles, and 205 volumes.

The Costs of Regulation   Regulatory activity incurs costs for American businesses, employers, and consumers—costs which do not appear in the federal budget. (The official budgets of all federal regulatory agencies combined add up to "only" about $15 billion.) Indeed, it is precisely because these costs do not appear in the federal budget that politicians prefer a regulatory approach to many of the nation's problems. Regulation shifts costs from the government itself onto the private sector, costs that are largely invisible to voters and taxpayers. Even when agencies themselves are supposed to calculate the costs of their regulations, their calculations vary in quality and almost always underestimate the true costs.[16] One independent estimate of the total costs of federal regulation sets the figure at $700 *billion,* or about 7 percent of the nation's Gross Domestic Product.[17]

Regulations impose costs on Americans in a variety of ways. First of all, there are the direct costs of compliance. Direct costs include everything from adding pollution control devices and making businesses accessible to the disabled, to the overhead costs of paperwork, attorney and accounting fees, and staff time needed to negotiate the federal regulatory maze. Secondly, there are indirect economic costs—costs incurred by devoting resources to compliance that otherwise would be used to increase productivity. This lost economic output may amount to $1 *trillion* per year.[18] All of these costs, which typically are imposed on businesses, are ultimately passed on to American consumers in the form of higher prices.

Congressional Constraints on the Bureaucracy

Bureaucracies are unelected hierarchical organizations, yet they must function within democratic government. To wed bureaucracy to democracy, ways must be found to ensure that bureaucracy is responsible to the people. Controlling the bureaucracy is a central concern of democratic government. The federal bureaucracy is responsible to all three branches of government—the president, the Congress, and the courts. Although the president is the nominal head of the executive agencies, Congress—through its power to create or eliminate and fund or fail to fund these agencies—exerts its full share of control. Most of the structure of the executive branch of government (see Figure 12.1) is determined by

The Director of the Office of Management and Budget is one of the most influential bureaucrats in Washington. Yet he is seldom seen on national television. Here, President Bush's OMB Director Joshua B. Bolten (now White House Chief of Staff) testifies before a congressional committee.

laws of Congress. Congress has the constitutional power to create or abolish executive departments and independent agencies, or to transfer their functions, as it wishes. Congress can by law expand or contract the discretionary authority of bureaucrats. It can grant broad authority to agencies in vaguely written language, thereby adding to the power of bureaucracies, which can then determine themselves how to define and implement their own authority. In contrast, narrow and detailed laws place constraints on the bureaucracy.

In addition to specific constraints on particular agencies, Congress has placed a number of general constraints on the entire federal bureaucracy. Among the more important laws governing bureaucratic behavior are the following:

- *Administrative Procedures Act (1946):* Requires that agencies considering a new rule or policy give public notice in the *Federal Register,* solicit comments, and hold public hearings before adopting the new measures.

- *Freedom of Information Act (1966):* Requires agencies to allow citizens (and the media) to inspect all public records, with some exceptions for intelligence, current criminal investigations, and personnel actions (see *Up Close:* "How to Use the Freedom of Information Act").

- *Privacy Act (1974):* Requires agencies to keep confidential the personal records of individuals, notably their Social Security files and income tax records.

Senate Confirmation of Appointments   The U.S. Senate's power to confirm presidential appointments gives it some added influence over the bureaucracy.[19] It is true that once nominated and confirmed, cabinet secretaries and

UP CLOSE

How to Use the Freedom of Information Act

The Freedom of Information Act (FOIA) of 1966 requires agencies of the federal government to provide any member of the public records of the agencies. As amended by the Privacy Act of 1974, individuals can obtain their personal records held by government agencies and are given the right to correct information that is inaccurate. The FOIA does not apply to Congress, the federal courts, state and local government agencies (unless a state has a similar law), military plans and weapons, law enforcement investigations, records of financial institutions, or records which would invade the privacy of others. An agency must respond within ten days to an FOIA request, but it may charge fees for the costs of searching for the documents and duplicating them.

A good request must "reasonably describe" the records that are being sought; it must be specific enough that an agency employee will be able to locate the records within a reasonable amount of time. A good FOIA request letter includes:

Attention: Freedom of Information/Privacy Request Name and Address of Agency

This is a request under the Freedom of Information Act, 5 U.S.C. Sec.552

I request a copy of the following documents be provided for me.

_____

_____

I am aware that if my request is denied I am entitled to know the grounds for this denial and make an administrative appeal.

I am willing to pay fees for this request up to a maximum of $___. If you estimate that fees will exceed this limit, please inform me first.

Thank you for your prompt attention.

Signature

Address

regulatory commission members can defy the Congress; only the president can remove them from office. Senators usually try to impress their own views on presidential appointees seeking confirmation, however. Senate committees holding confirmation hearings often subject appointees to lengthy lectures on how the members believe their departments or agencies should be run. In extreme cases, when presidential appointees do not sufficiently reflect the views of Senate leaders, their confirmation can be held up indefinitely or, in very rare cases, defeated in a floor vote on confirmation.

Congressional Oversight Congressional oversight of the federal bureaucracy is a continuing activity.[20] Congress justifies its oversight activities on the grounds that its lawmaking powers require it to determine whether the purposes of the laws it passed are being carried out. Congress has a legitimate interest in communicating legislative *intent* to bureaucrats charged with the responsibility for implementing laws of Congress. But often oversight activities are undertaken to influence bureaucratic decision making. Members of Congress may seek to secure favorable treatment for friends and constituents, try to lay the political groundwork for increases or decreases in agency appropriations, or simply strive to enhance their own power or the power of their committees or subcommittees over the bureaucracy.

Oversight is lodged primarily in congressional committees and subcommittees (see "In Committee" in Chapter 10) whose jurisdictions generally parallel those of executive departments and agencies. However, all too frequently, agencies are

Protests are frequent in Washington, especially near the White House in Lafayette Park. Topics of protests vary widely. The war in Iraq has spawned more protests in recent years than any other issue.

required to respond to multiple committee inquiries in both the House and the Senate.

Congressional Appropriations   The congressional power to grant or to withhold the budget requests of bureaucracies and the president is perhaps Congress's most potent weapon in controlling the bureaucracy. Spending authorizations for executive agencies are determined by standing committees with jurisdiction in various policy areas, such as armed services, judiciary, education, and labor (see Table 10.4 in Chapter 10), and appropriations are determined by the House and Senate Appropriations Committees and, more specifically, their subcommittees with particular jurisdictions. These committees and subcommittees exercise great power over executive agencies. The Defense Department, for example, must seek *authorizations* for new weapons systems from the House and Senate Armed Services Committees and *appropriations* to actually purchase these weapons from the House and Senate Appropriations Committees, especially their Defense Appropriations subcommittees.

Congressional Investigation   Congressional investigations offer yet another tool for congressional oversight of the bureaucracy. Historically, congressional investigations have focused on scandal and wrongdoing in the executive branch (see "Oversight of the Bureaucracy" in Chapter 10). Occasionally, investigations even produce corrective legislation, although they more frequently produce changes in agency personnel, procedures, or policies. Investigations are more likely to follow media reports of waste, fraud, or scandal than to uncover previously unknown problems. In other words, investigations perform a political function for Congress—assuring voters that the Congress is taking action against bureaucratic abuses. Studies of routine bureaucratic performance are likely to be undertaken by the Government Accountability Office (GAO), an arm of Congress and frequent critic of executive agencies. GAO may undertake studies of the operations of executive agencies on its own initiative but more often responds to requests for studies by specific members of Congress.

casework Services performed by legislators and their staffs on behalf of individual constituents.

Casework   Perhaps the most frequent congressional oversight activities are calls, letters, and visits to the agencies by individual members of Congress seeking to influence particular actions on behalf of themselves or their constituents. A great deal of congressional **casework** involves intervening with executive agencies on behalf of constituents[21] (see Chapter 10). Executive departments and agencies generally try to deal with congressional requests and inquiries as favorably and rapidly as the law allows. Pressure from a congressional office will lead bureaucrats to speed up an application, correct an error, send information, review a case, or reinterpret a regulation to favor a client with congressional contacts. But bureaucrats become very uncomfortable when asked to violate established regulations on behalf of a favored person or firm. The line between serving constituents and unethical or illegal attempts to influence government agencies is sometimes very difficult to discern.

Interest Groups and Bureaucratic Decision Making

Interest groups understand that great power is lodged in the bureaucracy. Indeed, interest groups exercise an even closer oversight of bureaucracy than do the president, Congress, and courts, largely because their interests are directly affected by day-to-day bureaucratic decisions. Interest groups focus their attention on the particular departments and agencies that serve or regulate their own members or that function in their chosen policy field. For example, the American Farm Bureau Federation monitors the actions of the Department of Agriculture; environmental lobbies—such as the National Wildlife Federation, the Sierra Club, and the Environmental Defense Fund—watch over the Environmental Protection Agency as well as the National Park Service; the American Legion, Veterans of Foreign Wars, and Vietnam Veterans "oversee" the Department of Veterans Affairs. Thus, specific groups come to have a proprietary interest in "their" specific departments and agencies. Departments and agencies understand that their "client" groups have a continuing interest in their activities.

Many bureaucracies owe their very existence to strong interest groups that successfully lobbied Congress to create them. The Environmental Protection Agency owes its existence to the environmental groups, just as the Equal Employment Opportunity Commission owes its existence to civil rights groups. Thus, many bureaucracies nourish interest groups' support to aid in expanding their authority and increasing their budgets (see "Iron Triangles and Policy Networks" in Chapter 9).

Interest groups can lobby bureaucracies directly by responding to notices of proposed regulations, testifying at public hearings, and providing information and commentary. Or interest groups can lobby Congress either in support of bureaucratic activity or to reverse a bureaucratic decision. Interest groups may also seek to "build fires" under bureaucrats by holding press conferences, undertaking advertising campaigns, and soliciting media support for agency actions. Or interest groups may even seek to influence bureaucracies through appeals to the federal courts.

Judicial Constraints on the Bureaucracy

Judicial oversight is another source of restraint on the bureaucracy. Bureaucratic decisions are subject to review by the federal courts. Federal courts can even issue *injunctions* (orders) to an executive agency *before* it issues or enforces a regulation or undertakes a particular action. Thus, the judiciary poses a check on bureaucratic power.

A CONSTITUTIONAL NOTE

Congress and the Budget

The Constitution places "the power of the purse" firmly in the hands of Congress: "No money shall be drawn from the Treasury, but in Consequence of Appropriations made by Law" (Article I, Section 9). The Congress has multiple means of controlling the bureaucracy. It can create, eliminate, or reorganize agencies, and it can alter their functions and rules of operation as it sees fit. And the Senate can confirm or withhold confirmation of presidential appointments. In the exercise of these powers Congress can hold hearings, conduct investigations, and interrogate executive officials. But the power over appropriations for departments and agencies remains the most important instrument of congressional control over the bureaucracy. The president, of course, is head of the executive branch and the Constitution charges him to "take care that the laws be faithfully executed" (Article II, Section 3). Prior to 1921, executive departments and agencies submitted their budgets directly to the Congress with very little presidential input or control. But the Budget and Accounting Act of that year established a Bureau of the Budget which later was placed in the White House directly under the president. The act required all executive agencies to submit their budgets to the Bureau of the Budget, now called the Office of Management and Budget (OMB), and to the president. The president and OMB draw up the *Budget of the United States Government* each year for submission to Congress. The Budget Committees of the House and Senate by resolution set overall totals for budget outlays in major categories. These committees are under no obligation to follow the president's budget recommendations. Later, the Appropriations Committees and subcommittees of each house write up specific appropriations bills. If it wishes, Congress can ignore items in the president's budget and appropriate whatever funds to whatever agencies it chooses. The Appropriations Committees of the House and Senate jealously guard Congress's "power of the purse."

Judicial Standards for Bureaucratic Behavior Historically, the courts have stepped in when agency actions have violated laws passed by Congress, when agencies have exceeded the authority granted them under the laws, when the agency actions have been adjudged "arbitrary and unreasonable," and when agencies have failed in their legal duties under the law. The courts have also restrained the bureaucracy on procedural grounds—ensuring proper notice, fair hearings, rights of appeal, and so on. In short, appeals to the courts must cite failures of agencies to abide by substantive or procedural laws.

Judicial oversight tends to focus on (1) whether or not agencies are acting beyond the authority granted them by Congress; and (2) whether or not they are abiding by rules of procedural fairness. It is important to realize that the courts do not usually involve themselves in the *policy* decisions of bureaucracies. If policy decisions are made in accordance with the legal authority granted agencies by Congress, and if they are made with procedural fairness, the courts generally do not intervene.

Bureaucrats' Success in Court Bureaucracies have been very successful in defending their actions in federal courts.[22] Individual citizens and interest groups seeking to restrain or reverse the actions or decisions of executive agencies have been largely *unsuccessful*. What accounts for this success? Bureaucracies have established elaborate administrative processes to protect their decisions from challenge on procedural grounds. Regulatory agencies have armies of attorneys, paid for out of tax monies, who specialize in these narrow fields of law. It is very expensive for individual citizens to challenge agency actions. Corporations and interest groups must weigh the costs of litigation against the costs of compliance before undertaking a legal challenge of the bureaucracy. Excessive delays in court proceedings, sometimes extending to several years, add to the time and expense of challenging bureaucratic decisions.

Summary Notes

- The Washington bureaucracy—the departments, agencies, and bureaus of the executive branch of the federal government—is a major base of power in American government. Political conflict does not end when a law is passed by Congress and signed by the president. The arena merely shifts to the bureaucracy.

- Bureaucratic power has grown with increases in the size of government, advances in technology, and the greater complexity of modern society. Congress and the president do not have the time, resources, or expertise to decide the details of policy across the wide range of social and economic activity in the nation. Bureaucracies must draw up the detailed rules and regulations that actually govern the nation. Often laws are passed for their symbolic value; bureaucrats must give practical meaning to these laws. And the bureaucracy itself is now sufficiently powerful to get laws passed adding to its authority, size, and budget.

- Policy implementation is the development of procedures and activities and the allocation of money, personnel, and other resources to carry out the tasks mandated by law. Implementation includes regulation—the making of detailed rules based on the law—as well as adjudication—the application of laws and regulations to specific cases. Bureaucratic power increases with increases in administrative discretion.

- Bureaucracies usually seek to expand their own powers, functions, and budgets. Most bureaucrats believe strongly in the value of their own programs and the importance of their tasks. And bureaucrats, like everyone else, seek added power, pay, and prestige. Bureaucratic expansion contributes to the growth of government.

- The federal bureaucracy consists of 2.8 million civilian employees in fourteen cabinet departments and more than sixty independent agencies, as well as a large Executive Office of the President. Federal employment is not growing, but federal spending, especially for Social Security, Medicare, and Medicaid, is growing rapidly.

- Today federal spending amounts to about 20 percent of GDP, and federal, state, and local government spending combined amounts to about 30 percent of GDP.

- Historically, political conflict over government employment centered on the question of partisanship versus competence. Over time, the "merit system" replaced the "spoils system" in federal employment, but the civil service system raised problems of responsiveness and productivity in the bureaucracy. Civil service reform efforts have not really resolved these problems.

- The president's control of the bureaucracy rests principally on the powers to appoint and remove policy-making officials, to recommend increases and decreases in agency budgets, and to recommend changes in agency structure and function.

- But the bureaucracy has developed various means to insulate itself from presidential influence. Bureaucrats have many ways to delay and obstruct policy decisions with which they disagree. Whistle-blowers may inform Congress or the media of waste, mismanagement, or fraud. A network of friends and professional associates among bureaucrats, congressional staffs, and client groups helps create a "culture" within each agency and department. The bureaucratic culture is highly resistant to change.

- Women and minorities are represented in overall federal employment in proportion to their percentages of the U.S. population. However, women and minorities are not proportionately represented in the higher levels of the bureaucracy.

- Budget battles over who gets what begin in the bureaucracy as departments and agencies send their budget requests forward to the president's Office of Management and Budget. OMB usually reduces agency requests in line with the president's priorities. The president submits spending recommendations to Congress early each year in *The Budget of the United States Government*. Congress is supposed to pass its appropriations acts prior to the beginning of the fiscal year, October 1, but frequently falls behind schedule.

- Budgeting is incremental, in that last year's agency expenditures are usually accepted as a base and attention is focused on proposed increases. Incrementalism saves time and effort and reduces political conflict by not requiring agencies to justify every dollar spent, only proposed increases each year. Nonprogrammatic budgeting also helps reduce conflict over the value of particular programs. The result, however, is that many established programs continue long after the need for them has disappeared.

- Bureaucracies regulate virtually every aspect of our lives. The costs of regulation are borne primarily by business and consumers; they do not appear in the federal budget. In part for this reason, a regulatory approach to national problems appeals to elected officials who seek to obscure the costs of government activity. It is difficult to calculate the true costs and benefits of much regulatory activity. After a brief period of deregulation in the 1980s, regulation has regained popular favor.

- Congress can exercise control over the bureaucracy in a variety of ways: by creating, abolishing, or reorganizing departments and agencies; by altering their authority and functions; by requiring bureaucrats to testify before congressional committees; by undertaking investigations and studies through the Government Accountability Office; by intervening directly on behalf of constituents; by instructing presidential nominees in Senate confirmation hearings and occasionally delaying or defeating nominations; and especially by withholding or threatening to withhold agency appropriations or by writing very specific provisions into appropriations acts.

■ Interest groups also influence bureaucratic decision making directly by testifying at public hearings and providing information and commentary, and indirectly by contacting the media, lobbying Congress, and initiating lawsuits.

■ Judicial control of the bureaucracy is usually limited to determining whether agencies have exceeded the authority granted them by law or have abided by the rules of procedural fairness. Federal bureaucracies have a strong record of success in defending themselves in court.

Key Terms

bureaucracy 412	budget maximization 416	authorization 436	zero-based
chain of command 412	discretionary funds 416	appropriations act 436	budgeting 439
division of labor 412	spoils system 425	obligational	program budgeting 440
impersonality 412	merit system 425	authority 436	capture theory of
implementation 412	whistle-blowers 429	outlays 436	regulation 440
regulation 415	fiscal year 435	continuing resolution 437	deregulation 442
adjudication 415	budget resolution 436	incremental budgeting 438	casework 448

Suggested Readings

Henry, Nicholas. *Public Administration and Public Affairs.* 9th ed. Upper Saddle River, N.J.: Prentice Hall, 2004. Authoritative introductory textbook on public organizations (bureaucracies), public management, and policy implementation.

Howard, Philip K. *The Death of Common Sense: How Law Is Suffocating America.* New York: Random House, 1995. Outrageous stories of bureaucratic senselessness coupled with a plea to allow bureaucrats flexibility in achieving the purposes of laws and holding them accountable for outcomes.

Kettl, Donald F., and James W. Fesler. *The Politics of the Administrative Process.* 3rd ed. Washington, D.C.: CQ Press, 2005. Introduction to bureaucracy and public administration, including a case appendix with illustrations complementing each chapter.

Kerwin, Cornelius M. *Rulemaking: How Government Agencies Write Law and Make Policy.* 3rd ed. Washington, D.C.: CQ Press, 2003. Argues that rulemaking actually defines the laws of Congress and describes the political activity surrounding rulemaking.

Maxwell, Bruce. *CQ's Insider's Guide to Finding a Job in Washington.* Washington, D.C.: CQ Press, 2000. How to locate job vacancies, make contacts, "market" oneself, and build a career in the Washington bureaucracy.

Neiman, Max. *Defending Government: Why Big Government Works.* Upper Saddle River, N. J.: Prentice Hall, 2000. A spirited defense of big government as a product of people's desire to improve their lives.

Osborne, David, and Ted Gaebler. *Reinventing Government.* New York: Addison-Wesley, 1992. The respected manual of the "reinventing government" movement, with recommendations to overcome the routine tendencies of bureaucracies and inject "the entrepreneurial spirit" into them.

Schick, Allen. *The Federal Budget: Politics, Policy, Process.* Rev. ed. Washington, D.C.: Brookings Institution, 2000. A comprehensive explanation of the federal budgetary process.

Smith, Robert W., and Thomas D. Lynch. *Public Budgeting in America.* 5th ed. Upper Saddle River, N.J.: Prentice Hall, 2004. Standard text describing public budget processes, behaviors, and administration.

Wilson, James Q. *Bureaucracy: What Government Agencies Do and Why They Do It.* New York: Basic Books, 1989. In the author's words, "an effort to depict the essential features of bureaucratic life in the government agencies of the United States." Examining what really motivates middle-level public servants, Wilson argues that congressional attempts to "micromanage" government activities hamper the ability of bureaucrats to do their jobs.

Make It Real

BUREAUCRACY

In this unit, the student plays the role of a bureaucrat.

13 COURTS
Judicial Politics

Think About Politics

1 Have the federal courts grown too powerful?
Yes ☐ No ☐

2 Is it really democratic to allow federal court judges, who are appointed, not elected, and who serve for life, to overturn laws of an elected Congress and president?
Yes ☐ No ☐

3 Should the Constitution be interpreted in terms of the original intentions of the Founders rather than the morality of society today?
Yes ☐ No ☐

4 Are the costs of lawsuits in America becoming too burdensome on the economy?
Yes ☐ No ☐

5 Should presidents appoint only judges who agree with their judicial philosophy?
Yes ☐ No ☐

6 Should the Senate confirm Supreme Court appointees who oppose abortion?
Yes ☐ No ☐

7 Should the Supreme Court overturn the law of Congress that prohibits federal funding of abortions for poor women?
Yes ☐ No ☐

8 Is there a need to appoint special prosecutors to investigate presidents and other high officials?
Yes ☐ No ☐

Do the Supreme Court and the federal judiciary in fact have the real power to shape public policies in the United States?

★   ★   ★

Judicial Power

"There is hardly a political question in the United States which does not sooner or later turn into a judicial one."[1] This observation by French diplomat and traveler Alexis de Tocqueville, although made in 1835, is even more accurate today. It is the Supreme Court and the federal judiciary, rather than the president or Congress, that has taken the lead in deciding many of the most heated issues of American politics. It has undertaken to:

- Eliminate racial segregation and decide about affirmative action.

- Ensure separation of church and state and decide about prayer in public schools.

- Determine the personal liberties of women and decide about abortion.

- Define the limits of free speech and free press and decide about obscenity, censorship, and pornography.

- Ensure equality of representation and require legislative districts to be equal in population.

- Define the rights of criminal defendants, prevent unlawful searches, limit the questioning of suspects, and prevent physical or mental intimidation of suspects.

- Protect private homosexual acts between consenting adults from criminal prosecution.

- Decide the life-or-death issue of capital punishment.

Courts are "political" institutions. Like Congress, the president, and the bureaucracy, courts decide who gets what in American society. Judges do not merely "apply" the law to specific cases. Years ago, former Supreme Court Justice Felix Frankfurter explained why this mechanistic theory of judicial objectivity fails to describe court decision making.

> The meaning of "due process" and the content of terms like "liberty" are not re-
> vealed by the Constitution. It is the Justices who make the meaning. They read

into the neutral language of the Constitution their own economic and social views. . . . Let us face the fact that five Justices of the Supreme Court are the molders of policy rather than the impersonal vehicles of revealed truth.[2]

─Think Again─

Have the federal courts grown too powerful?

Constitutional Power of the Courts The Constitution grants "the judicial Power of the United States" to the Supreme Court and other "inferior Courts" that Congress may establish. The Constitution guarantees that the Supreme Court and federal judiciary will be politically independent: judges are appointed, not elected, and hold their appointments for life (barring commission of any impeachable offenses). It also guarantees that their salaries will not be reduced during their time in office. The Constitution goes on to list the kinds of cases and controversies that the federal courts may decide. Federal judicial power extends to any case arising under the Constitution and federal laws and treaties, to cases in which officials of the federal government or of foreign governments are a party, and to cases between states or between citizens of different states.

Interpreting the Constitution: Judicial Review The Constitution is the "supreme Law of the Land" (Article VI). Judicial power is the power to decide cases and controversies and, in doing so, to decide what the Constitution and laws of Congress really mean. This authority—together with the guaranteed independence of judges—places great power in the Supreme Court and the federal judiciary. Indeed, because the Constitution takes precedence over laws of Congress as well as state constitutions and laws, it is the Supreme Court that ultimately decides whether Congress, the president, the states, and their local governments have acted constitutionally.

judicial review Power of the courts, especially the Supreme Court, to declare laws of Congress, laws of the states, and actions of the president unconstitutional and invalid.

The power of **judicial review** is the power to invalidate laws of Congress or of the states that conflict with the U.S. Constitution. Judicial review is not specifically mentioned in the Constitution but has long been inferred from it. Even before the states had approved the Constitution, Alexander Hamilton wrote in 1787 that "limited government . . . can be preserved in practice no other way than through the medium of courts of justice, whose duty it is to declare all acts contrary to the manifest tenor of the Constitution void."[3] But it was the historic decision of *Marbury v. Madison* (1803)[4] that officially established judicial review as the most important judicial check on congressional power (see *People in Politics:* "John Marshall and Early Supreme Court Politics"). Writing for the majority, Chief Justice Marshall constructed a classic statement in judicial reasoning as he proceeded step by step to infer judicial review from the Constitution's Supremacy (Article VI) and Judicial Power (Article III, Section 1) clauses:

- The Constitution is the supreme law of the land, binding on all branches of government: legislative, executive, and judicial.

- The Constitution deliberately establishes a government with limited powers.

- Consequently, "an act of the legislature repugnant to the Constitution is void." If this were not true, the government would be unchecked and the Constitution would be an absurdity.

- Under the judicial power, "It is emphatically the province and duty of each of the judicial departments to say what the law is."

- "So if a law be in opposition to the Constitution . . . the court must determine which of these conflicting rules governs the case. This is the very essence of judicial duty."

PEOPLE IN POLITICS

John Marshall and Early Supreme Court Politics

John Marshall was a dedicated Federalist. A prominent Virginia lawyer, he was elected a delegate to Virginia's Constitution-ratifying convention, where he was instrumental in winning his state's approval of the document in 1788. Later Marshall served as secretary of state in the administration of John Adams, where he came into conflict with Adams's vice president, Thomas Jefferson.

In the election of 1800, Jefferson's Democratic-Republicans crushed Adams's Federalist Party. But Adams, taking advantage of the fact that his term of office would not expire until the following March,[a] sought to pack the federal judiciary with Federalists. The lame duck Federalist majority in the Senate confirmed the appointments, and John Marshall was sworn in as Chief Justice of the Supreme Court on February 4, 1801. Many of these "midnight appointments" came at the very last hours of Adams's term of office.

At that time, a specified task of the secretary of state was to deliver judicial commissions to new judges. When Marshall left his position as secretary of state to become Chief Justice, several of these commissions were still undelivered. Jefferson and the Democratic-Republicans were enraged over this last-minute Federalist chicanery, so when Jefferson assumed office in March, he ordered his new secretary of state, James Madison, not to deliver the remaining commissions. William Marbury, one of the disappointed Federalist appointees, brought a lawsuit to the Supreme Court, asking it to issue a writ of mandamus ("we command") to James Madison, ordering him to do his duty and deliver the valid commission.

The Judiciary Act of 1789, which established the federal court system, had included a provision granting original jurisdiction to the Supreme Court to issue writs of mandamus. The case, therefore, came directly to new Chief Justice John Marshall, who had failed to deliver the commission in the first place. (Today, we expect justices who are personally involved in a case to "recuse" themselves—that is, not to participate in that case, allowing the other justices to make the decision—but Marshall's actions were typical of his time.)

John Marshall realized that if he issued a direct order to Madison to deliver the commission, Madison would probably ignore it. The Court had no way to enforce such an order, and Madison had the support of President Jefferson. Issuing the writ would create a constitutional crisis in which the Supreme Court would most likely lose power. But if the Court failed to pronounce Madison's actions unlawful, it would lose legitimacy.

Marshall resolved his political dilemma with a brilliant judicial ploy. Writing for the majority in *Marbury v. Madison,* he announced that Madison was wrong to withhold the commission but that the Supreme Court could not issue a writ of mandamus because Section 13 of the Judiciary Act of 1789, which gave the Court *original* jurisdiction in the case, was unconstitutional. Giving the Supreme Court *original* jurisdiction conflicted with Article III, Section 2, of the Constitution, which gives the Supreme Court original jurisdiction only in cases affecting "Ambassadors, other public Ministers and Consuls, and those in which a State shall be a Party." "In all other Cases," the Constitution states that the Court shall have appellate jurisdiction. Thus Section 13 of the Judiciary Act was unconstitutional.

By declaring part of an act of Congress unconstitutional, Marshall accomplished multiple political objectives. He avoided a showdown with the executive branch that would undoubtedly have weakened the Court. He left Jefferson and Madison with no Court order to disobey. At the same time, Marshall forced Jefferson and the Democratic-Republicans to acknowledge the Supreme Court's power of judicial review—the power to declare an act of Congress unconstitutional. (To do otherwise would have meant acknowledging Marbury's claim.) Thus Marshall sacrificed Marbury's commission to a greater political goal, enhancing the Supreme Court's power.

[a]Not until the adoption of the Twentieth Amendment in 1933 was the president's inauguration moved up to January.

■ "If, then, the courts are to regard the Constitution, and the Constitution is superior to any ordinary act of the legislature, the Constitution, and not such ordinary act, must govern the case to which they both apply."

■ Hence, if a law is repugnant to the Constitution, the judges are duty bound to declare that law void in order to uphold the supremacy of the Constitution.

Judicial Review of State Laws   The power of the federal courts to invalidate *state* laws and constitutions that conflict with federal laws or the federal Constitution is easily defended. Article VI states that the Constitution and federal laws and treaties are the supreme law of the land, "any Thing in the Constitution or Laws of any State to the Contrary notwithstanding." Indeed, the Constitution specifically obligates state judges to be "bound" by the Constitution and federal laws and to give these documents precedence over state constitutions and laws in rendering decisions. Federal court power over state decisions is probably essential to maintaining national unity: fifty different state interpretations of the meaning of the Constitution or of the laws and treaties of Congress would create unimaginable confusion. Thus the power of federal judicial review over state constitutions, laws, and court decisions is seldom questioned.

The Supreme Court has used its power of judicial review more frequently to invalidate state laws than laws of Congress. Some of these decisions had impact far beyond the individual states on trial. For example, the historic 1954 decision in *Brown v. Board of Education of Topeka*, declaring segregation of the races in public schools to be unconstitutional, struck down the laws of twenty-one states[5] (see Chapter 12). The 1973 *Roe v. Wade* decision, establishing the constitutional right to abortion, struck down antiabortion laws in more than forty states.[6] In 2003 the Court again struck down the laws of more than forty states by holding that private homosexual acts by consenting adults were protected by the constitution.[7]

Judicial Review of Laws of Congress   Judicial review is potentially the most powerful weapon in the hands of the Supreme Court. It enables the Court to assert its power over the Congress, the president, and the states and to substitute its own judgment for that of other branches of the federal government and the states. However, the Supreme Court has been fairly restrained in its use of judicial review to void acts of Congress. Prior to the Civil War, the Supreme Court invalidated very few laws of any kind. Since that time, however, the general trend has been for the U.S. Supreme Court to strike down more *state* laws as unconstitutional. In contrast, the Court has been relatively restrained in its rejection of *federal* laws; over two centuries the Court has struck down fewer than 150 of the more than 60,000 laws passed by Congress.

Nevertheless, some of the laws overturned by the Supreme Court have been very important. In *Buckley v. Valeo* (1976)[8] the Court struck down provisions of the Federal Election Campaign Act that had limited the amount individuals could spend to finance their own campaigns or express their own independent political views. In *United States v. Morrison* (2000), the Supreme Court struck down Congress's Violence Against Women Act[9] as an unconstitutional expansion of the interstate commerce power and an invasion of powers reserved to the states (see *What Do You Think?* "Should Violence Against Women Be a Federal Crime?" in Chapter 4). Overall, however, the Supreme Court's use of judicial review against the Congress has been restrained.

Judicial Review of Presidential Actions   The Supreme Court has only rarely challenged presidential power. The Court has overturned presidential

UP CLOSE

William Jefferson Clinton v. Paula Corbin Jones

The president is not "above the law"; that is, his conduct is not immune from judicial scrutiny. The president's official conduct must be lawful; federal courts may reverse presidential actions found to be unconstitutional or violative of laws of Congress. And presidents are not immune from criminal prosecution; they cannot ignore demands to provide information in criminal cases.[a] However, the Supreme Court has held that the president has "absolute immunity" from civil suits "arising out of the execution of official duties."[b] In other words, the president cannot be sued for damages caused by actions or decisions that are within his constitutional or legal authority.

But can the president be sued for *private* conduct beyond the scope of his official duties? In 1994 Paula Corbin Jones sued William Jefferson Clinton in federal district court in Arkansas, alleging that he made "abhorrent" sexual advances toward her in Little Rock in 1991 while he was governor and she was a state employee.

The president's lead attorney, Robert Bennett (brother of conservative commentator and former Reagan cabinet official William Bennett), stated that Clinton "has no recollection of ever meeting this woman" and "did not engage in any inappropriate or sexual conduct with this woman." But the president's defense team also argued that the president should be immune from civil actions, especially those arising from events alleged to occur *before* he assumed office. They argued that the president's constitutional responsibilities are so important and demanding that he must devote his undivided time and attention to them. He cannot be distracted by civil suits; otherwise a large volume of politically motivated frivolous litigation might undermine his ability to function effectively in office. At the very least, the president's attorney argued, the president should be given "temporary immunity" by postponing the case until after he leaves office.

However, in 1997 the U.S. Supreme Court rejected the notion of presidential immunity (as well as temporary immunity) from civil claims arising from actions outside of the president's official duties. Although advising lower courts to give "utmost deference to Presidential responsibilities" in handling the case, the Court held that "the doctrine of separation of powers does not require federal courts to stay all private actions against the president until he leaves office."[c]

Subsequently, after reviewing the case, federal district judge Susan Wright dismissed Jones's charges as insufficient to prove sexual assault or harassment.[d] Clinton later settled the case with a financial payment to Jones, but with no admission or apology. The settlement ended Jones's appeals and avoided possible reopening of the case.

[a]*United States v. Nixon* (1974).
[b]*Nixon v. Fitzgerald* (1982).
[c]*Clinton v. Jones,* May 27, 1997.
[d]*Jones v. Clinton,* April 1, 1998.

---

policies both on the grounds that they conflicted with laws of Congress and on the grounds that they conflicted with the Constitution. In *Ex parte Milligan* (1866)[10] for example, the Court held (somewhat belatedly) that President Abraham Lincoln could not suspend the writ of habeas corpus in rebellious states during the Civil War. In *Youngstown Sheet & Tube Co. v. Sawyer,* in 1952,[11] it declared President Harry Truman's seizure of the nation's steel mills during the Korean War to be illegal. In 1974 it ordered President Richard Nixon to turn over taped White House conversations to the special Watergate prosecutor, leading to Nixon's forced resignation.[12] And in 1997 the Court held that President Bill Clinton was obliged to respond to a civil suit even while serving in the White House.[13] (See *Up Close:* "William Jefferson Clinton versus Paula Corbin Jones.")

Interpreting Federal Laws The power of the Supreme Court and the federal judiciary does not rest on judicial review alone. The courts also make policy in their interpretation of **statutory laws**—the laws of Congress. Frequently, Congress decides that an issue is too contentious to resolve. Members of Congress cannot themselves agree on specific language, so they write, sometimes deliberately,

statutory laws Laws made by act of Congress or the state legislatures, as opposed to constitutional law.

vague, symbolic language into the law—words and phrases like "fairness," "equitableness," "good faith," "good cause," and "reasonableness"—effectively shifting policy making to the courts by giving courts the power to read meaning into these terms.

Activism versus Self-Restraint

Supreme Court Justice Felix Frankfurter once wrote: "The only check upon our own exercise of power is our own sense of self-restraint. For the removal of unwise laws from the statute books, appeal lies not to the courts but to the ballot and to the processes of democratic government."[14]

Judicial Self-Restraint   The idea behind **judicial self-restraint** is that judges should not read their own philosophies into the Constitution and should avoid direct confrontations with Congress, the president, and the states whenever possible. The argument for judicial self-restraint is that federal judges are not elected by the people and therefore should not substitute their own views for the views of elected representatives. The courts should defer to the judgments of the other branches of government unless there is a clear violation of constitutional principle. The benefit of the doubt should be given to actions taken by elected officials. Courts should only impose remedies that are narrowly tailored to correct specific legal wrongs. As Justice Sandra Day O'Connor argued in her Senate confirmation hearings, "The courts should interpret the laws, not make them. . . . I do not believe it is a function of the Court to step in because times have changed or social mores have changed."[15]

Wisdom versus Constitutionality   A law may be unwise, unjust, or even stupid and yet still be constitutional. One should not equate the wisdom of a law with its constitutionality, and the Court should decide only the constitutionality and not the wisdom of a law. Justice Oliver Wendell Holmes once lectured a younger colleague, sixty-one-year-old Justice Harlan Stone, on this point:

> Young man, about 75 years ago I learned that I was not God. And so, when the people . . . want to do something I can't find anything in the Constitution expressly forbidding them to do, I say, whether I like it or not, "Goddamn it, let 'em do it."[16]

However, the actual role of the Supreme Court in the nation's power struggles suggests that the Court indeed often equates wisdom with constitutionality. People frequently cite broad phrases in the Fifth and Fourteenth Amendments establishing constitutional standards of "due process of law" and "equal protection of the laws" when attacking laws they believe are unfair or unjust. Most Americans have come to believe that unwise laws must be unconstitutional. If so, then the courts must be the final arbiters of fairness and justice.

Original Intent   Should the Constitution be interpreted in terms of the intentions of the Founders or according to the morality of society today? Most jurists agree the Constitution is a living document, that it must be interpreted by each generation in the light of current conditions, and to do otherwise would soon render the document obsolete. But in interpreting the document, whose values should prevail—the values of the judges or the values of the Founders? The doctrine of **original intent** takes the values of the Founders as expressed in the text of the Constitution and attempts to apply these values to current conditions. Defenders of original intent argue that the words in the document must be given

---

judicial self-restraint Self-imposed limitation on judicial power by judges deferring to the policy judgments of elected branches of government.

original intent Judicial philosophy under which judges attempt to apply the values of the Founders to current issues.

their historical meaning and that meaning must restrain the courts as well as the legislative and executive branches of government. That is, the Supreme Court should not set aside laws made by elected representatives unless they conflict with the original intent of the Founders. Judges who set aside laws that do not accord with their personal views of today's moral standards are simply substituting their own morality for that of elected bodies. Such decisions lack democratic legitimacy because there is no reason why judges' moral views should prevail over those of elected representatives.

Judicial Activism   However, the doctrine of original intent carries little weight with proponents of judicial activism. The idea behind **judicial activism** is that the Constitution is a living document whose strength lies in its flexibility, and judges should shape constitutional meaning to fit the needs of contemporary society. The argument for judicial activism is that viewing the Constitution as a broad and flexible document saves the nation from having to pass dozens of new constitutional amendments to accommodate changes in society. Instead, the courts need to give contemporary interpretations to constitutional phrases, particularly general phrases such as "due process of law" (Fifth Amendment), "equal protection of the laws" (Fourteenth Amendment), "establishment of religion" (First Amendment), and "cruel and unusual punishment" (Eighth Amendment). Courts have the responsibility to review the actions of other branches of government vigorously, to strike down unconstitutional acts, and to impose far-reaching remedies for legal wrongs whenever necessary.[17]

judicial activism Making of new law through judicial interpretations of the Constitution.

Stare Decisis   Conflicts between judicial activism and judicial self-restraint are underscored by questions of whether to let past decisions stand or to find constitutional support for overturning them. The principle of **stare decisis**, which means the issue has already been decided in earlier cases, is a fundamental notion in law. Reliance on **precedent** gives stability to the law; if every decision were new law, then no one would know what the law is from day to day. Yet the Supreme Court has discarded precedent in many of its most important decisions: *Brown v. Board of Education* (1954), which struck down laws segregating the races; *Baker v. Carr* (1962), which guaranteed equal representation in legislatures; *Roe v. Wade* (1973), which made abortion a constitutional right; and many other classic cases. Former Justice William O. Douglas, a defender of judicial activism, justified disregard of precedent as follows:

stare decisis Judicial precept that the issue has already been decided in earlier cases and the earlier decision need only be applied in the specific case before the bench; the rule in most cases, it comes from the Latin for "the decision stands."

precedent Legal principle that previous decisions should determine the outcome of current cases; the basis for stability in law.

> The decisions of yesterday or of the last century are only the starting points. . . . A judge looking at a constitutional decision may have compulsions to revere the past history and accept what was once written. But he remembers above all else that it is the Constitution which he swore to support and defend, not the gloss which his predecessors may have put on it. So he comes to formulate his own laws, rejecting some earlier ones as false and embracing others. He cannot do otherwise unless he lets men long dead and unaware of the problems of the age in which he lives do his thinking for him.[18]

Rules of Restraint   Even an activist Supreme Court adheres to some general rules of judicial self-restraint, however, including the following:

- The Court will pass on the constitutionality of legislation only in an actual case; it will not advise the president or Congress on constitutional questions.

- The Court will not anticipate a question on constitutional law; it does not decide hypothetical cases.

- The Court will not formulate a rule of constitutional law broader than that required by the precise facts to which it must be applied.

- The Court will not decide on a constitutional question if some other ground exists on which it may dispose of the case.

- The Court will not decide on the validity of a law if the complainants fail to show that they have been injured by the law.

- When doubt exists about the constitutionality of a law, the Court will try to interpret the law so as to give it a constitutional meaning and avoid the necessity of declaring it unconstitutional.

- Complainants must have exhausted all remedies available in lower federal courts or state courts before the Supreme Court will accept review.

- The Court will invalidate a law only when a constitutional issue is crucial to the case and is substantial, not trivial.

- Occasionally the Court defers to Congress and the president, classifies an issue as a political question, and refuses to decide it. The Court has generally stayed out of foreign and military policy areas.

- If the Court holds a law unconstitutional, it will confine its decision to the particular section of the law that is unconstitutional; the rest of the statute stays intact.

jurisdiction Power of a court to hear a case in question.

original jurisdiction Refers to a particular court's power to serve as the place where a given case is initially argued and decided.

appellate jurisdiction Particular court's power to review a decision or action of a lower court.

appeal In general, requests that a higher court review cases decided at a lower level. In the Supreme Court, certain cases are designated as appeals under federal law; formally, these must be heard by the Court.

www U.S. Courts
The goal of this site is "to function as a clearinghouse for information from and about the Judicial Branch of the U.S. government." The site covers the U.S. Supreme Court, U.S. Courts of Appeals, U.S. District Courts, and U.S. Bankruptcy Courts.
www.uscourts.gov

district courts Original jurisdiction trial courts of the federal system.

Structure and Jurisdiction of Federal Courts

The federal court system consists of three levels of courts—the Supreme Court, the Courts of Appeals, and the district courts—together with various special courts (see Figure 13.1). Only the Supreme Court is established by the Constitution, although the number of justices is determined by Congress. Article III authorizes Congress to establish such "inferior Courts" as it deems appropriate. Congress has designed a hierarchical system with a U.S. Court of Appeals divided into twelve regional circuit courts, a federal circuit, and ninety-four district courts in the fifty states and one each in Puerto Rico and the District of Columbia. Table 13.1 describes their **jurisdiction** and distinguishes between **original jurisdiction**—where cases are begun, argued, and initially decided—and **appellate jurisdiction**—where cases begun in lower courts are argued and decided on **appeal**.

The Supreme Court is the "court of last resort" in the United States, but it hears only a very small number of cases each year. In a handful of cases, the Supreme Court has original jurisdiction; these concern primarily disputes between states (or states and residents of other states), disputes between a state and the federal government, and disputes involving foreign dignitaries. However, most Supreme Court cases are appellate decisions involving cases from state supreme courts or cases tried first in a U.S. district court.

District Courts District courts are the original jurisdiction trial courts of the federal system. Each state has at least one district court, and larger states have more (New York, for example, has four). There are about eight hundred federal district judges, each appointed for life by the president and confirmed by the Senate. The president also appoints a U.S. marshal for each district to carry out orders of the court and maintain order in the courtroom. District courts hear criminal cases prosecuted by the Department of Justice as well as civil cases. As

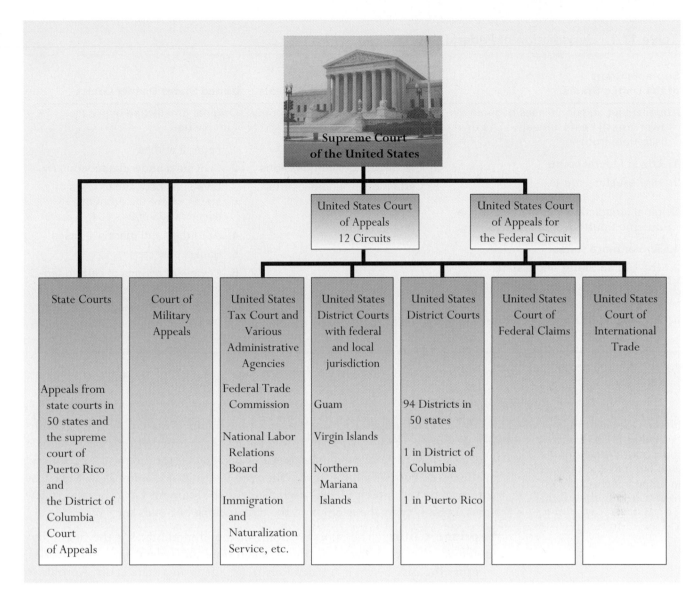

Figure 13.1   Structure of Federal Courts

The federal court system of the United States is divided into three levels: the courts of original jurisdiction (state courts, military courts, tax courts, district courts, claims courts, and international trade courts), U.S. Courts of Appeals (which hear appeals from all lower courts except state and military panels), and the U.S. Supreme Court, which can hear appeals from all sources.

trial courts, the district courts make use of both **grand juries** (called to hear evidence and, if warranted, to indict a defendant by bringing formal criminal charges) and **petit (regular) juries** (which determine guilt or innocence). District courts may hear 270,000 civil cases in a year and 70,000 criminal cases.

Courts of Appeals   Federal **circuit courts** (see *Across the USA:* "Geographic Boundaries of Federal Courts") are appellate courts. They do not hold trials or accept new evidence but consider only the records of the trial courts and oral or written arguments (**briefs**) submitted by attorneys. Federal law guarantees everyone the right to appeal, so the Court of Appeals has little discretion in this regard. Appellate judges themselves estimate that more than 80 percent of all appeals are frivolous—that is, without any real basis. There are more than a

grand juries Juries called to hear evidence and decide whether defendants should be indicted and tried.

petit (regular) juries Juries called to determine guilt or innocence.

circuit courts The twelve appellate courts that make up the middle level of the federal court system.

Table 13.1   Jurisdiction of Federal Courts

Supreme Court of the United States	United States Courts of Appeals	United States District Courts
Appellate jurisdiction (cases begin in a lower court); hears appeals, at its own discretion, from: 1. Lower federal courts 2. Highest state courts Original jurisdiction (cases begin in the Supreme Court) over cases involving: 1. Two or more states 2. The United States and a state 3. Foreign ambassadors and other diplomats 4. A state and a citizen of a different state (if begun by the state)	No original jurisdiction; hear only appeals from: 1. Federal district courts 2. U.S. regulatory commissions 3. Certain other federal courts	Original jurisdiction over cases involving: 1. Federal crimes 2. Civil suits under the federal law 3. Civil suits between citizens of states where the amount exceeds $75,000 4. Admiralty and maritime cases 5. Bankruptcy cases 6. Review of actions of certain federal administrative agencies 7. Other matters assigned to them by Congress

briefs Documents submitted by an attorney to a court, setting out the facts of the case and the legal arguments in support of the party represented by the attorney.

www Supreme Court Cases

This Cornell Law School's Legal Information Institute site contains up-to-date information about important legal decisions rendered by federal and state courts along with an exhaustive online law library available to researchers. *www.law.cornell.edu*

hundred circuit judges, each appointed for life by the president subject to confirmation by the Senate. Normally, these judges serve together on a panel to hear appeals. More than 90 percent of the cases decided by the Court of Appeals end at this level. Further appeal to the Supreme Court is not automatic; it must be approved by the Supreme Court itself. Because the Supreme Court hears very few cases, in most cases the decision of the circuit court becomes law.

Supreme Court   The Supreme Court of the United States is the final interpreter of all matters involving the Constitution and federal laws and treaties, whether the case began in a federal district court or in a state court. Appeals to the U.S. Supreme Court may come from a state court of last resort (usually a state's supreme court) or from lower federal courts. The Supreme Court determines whether to accept an appeal and consider a case. It may do so when there is a "substantial federal question" presented in a case or when there are "special and important reasons," or it may reject a case—with or without explaining why.

In the early days of the Republic, the size of the Supreme Court fluctuated, but since 1869 the membership has remained at nine: the Chief Justice and eight associate justices. The Supreme Court is in session each year from October through June, hearing oral arguments, accepting written briefs, conferring, and rendering opinions.

Appeals from State Courts   Each of the fifty states maintains its own courts. The federal courts are not necessarily superior to those courts; state and federal courts operate independently. State courts have original jurisdiction in most criminal and civil cases. Because the U.S. Supreme Court has appellate jurisdiction over state supreme courts as well as over lower federal courts, the Supreme Court oversees the nation's entire judicial system, but the great bulk of cases begin and end in the state court systems. The federal courts do not interfere once a case has been started in a state court except in very rare circumstances. And Congress has stipulated that legal disputes between citizens of different

ACROSS THE USA

Geographic Boundaries of Federal Courts

For administrative convenience, the U.S. District Courts are organized into twelve circuits (regions), plus the Federal Circuit (Washington, D.C.). Within each region, circuit court judges form panels to hear appeals from district courts. U.S. Circuit Courts of Appeals are numbered. U.S. District Courts are named for geographic regions of the states (East, West, North, South, Middle), for example, U.S. District Court for Northern California.

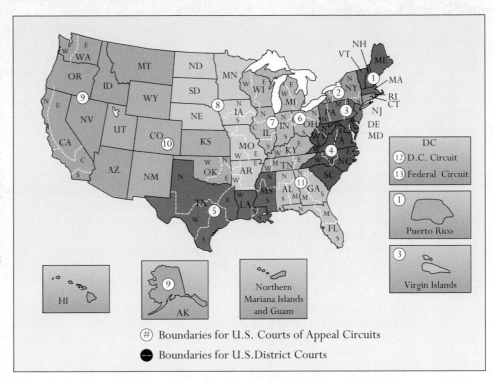

(#) Boundaries for U.S. Courts of Appeal Circuits

⊖ Boundaries for U.S. District Courts

states must involve $75,000 or more to be heard in federal courts. Moreover, parties to cases in state courts must "exhaust their remedies"—that is, appeal their case all the way through the state court system—before the federal courts will hear an appeal. Appeals from state supreme courts go directly to the U.S. Supreme Court and not to a federal district or circuit court. Such appeals are usually made on the grounds that a federal question is involved in the case—that is, a question has arisen regarding the application of the Constitution or a federal law.

Federal Cases   Some 10 million civil and criminal cases are begun in the nation's courts each year (see *A Conflicting View:* "America Is Drowning Itself in a Sea of Lawsuits" on page 464). About 270,000 (3 percent) of the cases are begun in the federal courts. About 8,000 are appealed to the Supreme Court each year, but only about 125 of them are openly argued and decided by signed opinions. The Constitution "reserves" general police powers to the states. That is, civil disputes and most crimes—murder, robbery, assault, and rape—are normally state offenses rather than federal crimes and thus are tried in state and local courts.

Federal court caseloads have risen in recent years (see Figure 13.2), in part because more civil disputes are being brought to federal courts. In addition, the U.S. Justice Department is prosecuting more criminal cases as federal law enforcement agencies—such as the Federal Bureau of Investigation (FBI), Drug Enforcement Administration (DEA), Internal Revenue Service (IRS), and Bureau of Alcohol,

 **The U.S. Supreme Court**
Official site provides recent decisions, case dockets, oral arguments, public information, etc.
www.supremecourtus.gov

Law Info
Web site offering legal documents, legal help guides, attorney references, and so forth. *www.lawinfo.com*

A CONFLICTING VIEW

America Is Drowning Itself in a Sea of Lawsuits

America is threatening to drown itself in a sea of lawsuits. Civil suits in the nation's courts exceed *10 million* per year. There are more than 805,000 lawyers in the United States (compared to about 650,000 physicians). These lawyers are in business, and their business is litigation. Generating business means generating lawsuits. And just as businesses search for new products, lawyers search for new legal principles on which to bring lawsuits. They seek to expand legal liability for civil actions—that is, to expand the definition of civil wrongdoings, or torts.

Unquestionably, the threat of lawsuits is an important safeguard for society, compelling individuals, corporations, and government agencies to behave responsibly toward others. Because victims require compensation for *actual* damages incurred by the wrongdoing of others, liability laws protect all of us.

But we need to consider the social costs of frivolous lawsuits, especially those brought without any merit but initiated in the hope that individuals or firms will offer a settlement just to avoid the expenses of defending themselves. Legal expenses

and excessive jury awards leveled against corporations increase insurance premiums for businesses and service providers. The Insurance Information Institute estimates that the overall costs of civil litigation in America is many times more than that of other industrial nations, perhaps amounting to over 2 percent of our nation's GDP. For example, the risk of lawsuits forces physicians to practice "defensive medicine," ordering expensive tests, multiple consultations with specialists, and expensive procedures, not because they are adjudged medically necessary, but rather to protect themselves from the possibility of a lawsuit.

Insurance premiums have risen sharply for physicians seeking malpractice insurance, as have premiums for recreation facilities, nurseries and day-care centers, motels, and restaurants.

Reforming the nation's liability laws presents major challenges to the political system. The reform movement can count on support from some normally powerful interest groups—insurance companies, manufacturers, drug companies, hospitals, and physicians. But legal reform is an anathema to the legal profession itself, notably the powerful Association of Trial Lawyers. And lawyers compose the single largest occupational background of Congress members—indeed, of politicians generally.

Figure 13.2 Caseloads in Federal Courts

Increasing caseloads in the federal courts have placed a heavy burden on prosecutors and judges. Although the increase in civil suits in the federal courts is the result of more plaintiffs insisting on taking their cases to the federal level both originally and on appeal, the increase in criminal cases is the result of Congress's decision to make more crimes— especially drug-related crimes—federal offenses and to pursue such criminals more vigorously.

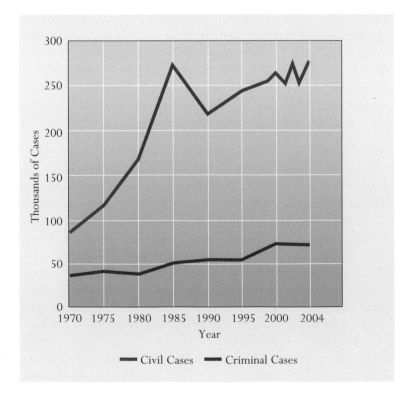

Tobacco, Firearms, and Explosives (ATF)—have stepped up their investigations. Most of this recent increase is attributable to enforcement of federal drug laws.

Traditionally, federal crimes were offenses directed against the U.S. government, its property, or its employees or were offenses involving the crossing of state lines. Over the years, however, Congress has greatly expanded the list of federal crimes so that federal and state criminal court jurisdictions often overlap, as they do, for example, in most drug violations.

The Special Rules of Judicial Decision Making

Courts are political institutions that resolve conflict and decide about public policy. But unlike Congress, the presidency, and the bureaucracy, the courts employ highly specialized rules in going about their work.

Cases and Controversies   Courts do not initiate policy but rather wait until a case or controversy is brought to them for resolution. A case must involve two disputing parties, one of which must have incurred some real damage as a result of the action or inaction of the other. They do *not* issue policy declarations or decide hypothetical cases. Rather, the courts wait until disputing parties bring a case to them that requires them to interpret the meaning of a law or determine its constitutionality in order to resolve the case. Only then do courts render opinions.

The vast majority of cases do *not* involve important policy issues. Courts determine the guilt or innocence of criminal defendants. Courts enforce contracts and award damages to victims of negligence in **civil cases**. And courts render these decisions on the basis of established law. Only occasionally do courts make significant policy decisions.

civil cases Noncriminal court proceedings in which a plaintiff sues a defendant for damages in payment for harm inflicted.

Adversarial Proceedings   Underlying judicial decision making is the assumption that the best way to decide an issue is to allow two disputing parties to present arguments on each side. Judges in the United States do not investigate cases, question witnesses, or develop arguments themselves (as they do in some European countries). This **adversarial system** depends on quality of argument on each side, which means it often depends on the capabilities of attorneys. There is no guarantee that the adversarial process will produce the best policy outcomes.

adversarial system Method of decision making in which an impartial judge or jury or decision maker hears arguments and reviews evidence presented by opposite sides.

Standing   To bring an issue into court as a case, individuals or firms or interest groups must have **standing**; that is, they must be directly harmed by a law or action. People cannot "go to court" simply because they do not like what the government is doing. Merely being taxpayers does not entitle people to claim that they are damaged by government actions.[19] Individuals or firms automatically have standing when they are prosecuted by the government for violation of laws or regulations. Thus, one way to gain standing in order to challenge the legality of a regulation or the constitutionality of a law is to violate the regulation or law and invite the government to prosecute.

To sue the government, plaintiffs must show they have suffered financial damages, loss of property, or physical or emotional harm as a direct result of the government's action. (The party initiating a suit and claiming damages is the **plaintiff**; the party against whom a suit is brought is the **defendant**.) The ancient legal doctrine of **sovereign immunity** means that one cannot sue the government without the government's consent. But by law, the U.S. government allows itself to be sued in a wide variety of contract and negligence cases. A citizen can also personally sue to force government officials to carry out acts that they are

standing Requirement that the party who files a lawsuit have a legal stake in the outcome.

plaintiff Individual or party who initiates a lawsuit.

defendants Parties against whom a criminal or civil suit is brought.

sovereign immunity Legal doctrine that individuals can sue the government only with the government's consent.

required by law to perform or for acting contrary to law. The government does not allow suits for damages as a result of military actions.

class action suits Cases initiated by parties acting on behalf of themselves and all others similarly situated.

—Think Again—

Are the costs of lawsuits in America becoming too burdensome on the economy?

Class Action Suits   Class action suits are cases brought into court by individuals on behalf not only of themselves but also of all other persons "similarly situated." That is, the party bringing the case is acting on behalf of a "class" of people who have suffered the same damages from the same actions of the defendant. One of the most famous and far-reaching class action suits was *Brown v. Board of Education of Topeka* (1954). The plaintiff, Linda Brown of Topeka, Kansas, sued her local board of education on behalf of herself and all other black pupils who were forced to attend segregated schools, charging that such schools violated the Equal Protection Clause of the Fourteenth Amendment. When she won the case, the Court's ruling affected not only Linda Brown and the segregated public schools in Topeka but also all other black pupils similarly situated across the nation (see Chapter 12).

Class action suits have grown in popularity. These suits have enabled attorneys and interest groups to bring multimillion-dollar suits against corporations and governments for damages to large numbers of people, even when none of them has individually suffered sufficient harm to merit bringing a case to court. For example, an individual overcharged by an electric utility would not want to incur the expense of suing for the return of a few dollars. But if attorneys sue the utility on behalf of a large number of customers similarly overcharged, the result may be a multimillion-dollar settlement from which the attorneys can deduct their hefty fees.

Legal Fees   Going to court requires financial resources. Criminal defendants are guaranteed an attorney, without charge if they are poor, by the Sixth Amendment's guarantee of "Assistance of Counsel" (see Chapter 12).[20] However, persons who wish to bring a *civil* suit against governments or corporations must still arrange for the payment of legal fees. The most common arrangement is the

The Supreme Court of the United States is the final interpreter of the Constitution and federal laws and treaties. Two new members were added to the Court in 2005 and 2006: Chief Justice John Roberts (center, bottom) and Associate Justice Samuel Alito Jr. (top, right).

contingency fee, in which plaintiffs agree to pay expenses and share one-third or more of the money damages with their lawyers if the case is won. If the case is lost, neither plaintiffs nor their lawyers receive anything for their labors. Lawyers do not usually participate in such arrangements unless the prospects for winning the case are good and the promised monetary reward is substantial. Civil suits against the government have increased since Congress enacted a law requiring governments to pay the attorneys' fees of citizens who successfully bring suit against public officials for violation of their constitutional rights.

Remedies and Relief   Judicial power has vastly expanded through court determination of **remedies and relief**. These are the orders of a court following a decision that are designed to correct a wrong. In most cases, judges simply fine or sentence criminal defendants to jail or order losing defendants in civil suits to pay monetary damages to the winning plaintiffs. In recent years, however, federal district court judges have issued sweeping orders to governments to correct constitutional violations. For example, a federal district judge took over operation of the Boston public schools for more than ten years to remedy *de facto* (an existing, although not necessarily deliberate, pattern of) racial segregation. A federal district judge ordered the city of Yonkers, New York, to build public housing in white neighborhoods. A federal district judge took over the operation of the Alabama prison system to ensure proper prisoner treatment. A federal district judge ordered the Kansas City, Missouri, school board to increase taxes to pay for his desegregation plan.[21]

Independent Counsels?   The Ethics in Government Act of 1978 (passed in the wake of the Watergate scandal) granted federal courts the power, upon request of the attorney general, to appoint an **independent counsel**, or "special prosecutor," to investigate and prosecute violations of federal law by the president and other high officials. This act was challenged in the U.S. Supreme Court as a transferral of executive power ("to take care that the laws be faithfully executed"—Article II) to the judicial branch of government in violation of the separation of powers in the U.S. Constitution. But the Court upheld the law, noting that the attorney general, an executive branch official appointed by the president, had to request the judiciary to appoint the independent counsel.[22]

Whatever the original intent of the act, special prosecutors were often accused of *bringing politics into* the criminal justice system. Indeed, special prosecutor Kenneth Starr's dogged pursuit of Bill and Hillary Clinton (in "Whitewater" real estate deals and later the Monica Lewinsky sex scandal) was deemed a "witch hunt" by friends of the president. The First Lady linked Starr to "a vast right-wing conspiracy" trying to reverse the outcome of two presidential elections.

Congress allowed the independent counsel law to lapse in 1999. Democrats, infuriated by Starr's investigations, joined Republicans, who had earlier complained when Reagan and Bush administration officials were the targets of prosecution, in killing the act. Getting rid of the law, said its opponents, will help to "decriminalize" politics in Washington.

The Politics of Selecting Judges

The Constitution specifies that all federal judges, including justices of the Supreme Court, shall be appointed by the president and confirmed by a majority vote of the Senate. Judicial recruitment is a political process: presidents almost always appoint members of their own party to the federal courts. More than 80 percent of federal judges have held some political office prior to their appointment to the court. More important, political philosophy now plays a major role in

contingency fees Fees paid to attorneys to represent the plaintiff in a civil suit and receive in compensation an agreed-upon percentage of damages awarded (if any).

remedies and relief Orders of a court to correct a wrong, including a violation of the Constitution.

independent counsel ("special prosecutor") A prosecutor appointed by a federal court to pursue charges against a president or other high official. This position was allowed to lapse by Congress in 1999 after many controversial investigations by these prosecutors.

Class action suits initiated by attorneys or interest groups on behalf of large numbers of people are increasingly popular. Here an attorney announces a suit against the nation's tobacco companies on behalf of flight attendants previously subjected to smoke.

the selection of judges. Thus the appointment of federal judges has increasingly become an arena for conflict between presidents and their political opponents in the Senate.

The Politics of Presidential Selection   Presidents have a strong motivation to select judges who share their political philosophy. Judicial appointments are made for life. The Constitution stipulates that federal judges "shall hold their Offices during good Behaviour." A president cannot remove a judge for any reason, and Congress cannot impeach judges just because it dislikes their decisions.

This independence of the judiciary has often frustrated presidents and Congresses. Presidents who have appointed people they thought were liberals or conservatives to the Supreme Court have sometimes been surprised by the decisions of their appointees. An estimated one-quarter of the justices of the Supreme Court have deviated from the political expectations of the presidents who appointed them.[23]

It is important to recognize that presidents' use of political criteria in selecting judges has a democratic influence on the courts. Presidents can campaign on the pledge to make the courts more liberal or conservative through their appointive powers, and voters are free to cast their ballots on the basis of this pledge.

Political Litmus Test   Traditionally, presidents and senators have tried to discern where a Supreme Court candidate fits on the continuum of liberal activism versus conservative self-restraint. Democratic presidents and senators usually prefer liberal judges who express an activist philosophy. Republican presidents usually prefer conservative judges who express a philosophy of judicial self-restraint. Until very recently, both the president and the Senate denied using any political "litmus test" in judicial recruitment. A **litmus test** generally refers to recruitment based on a nominee's stand on a single issue. Since the Supreme Court ruling on *Roe v. Wade* (1973), however, the single issue of abortion has come to dominate the politics of judicial recruitment. President Clinton was forthright in his pledge to nominate only justices who specifically support the *Roe v. Wade* decision. Republican presidents have denied using a litmus test, but they have insisted that nominees generally support a philosophy of judicial self-restraint.

—Think Again—

Should presidents appoint only judges who agree with their judicial philosophy?

litmus test In political terms, a person's stand on a key issue that determines whether he or she will be appointed to public office or supported in electoral campaigns.

The Politics of Senate Confirmation   All presidential nominations for the federal judiciary, including the Supreme Court, are sent to the Senate for confirmation. The Senate refers them to its powerful Judiciary Committee, which holds hearings, votes on the nomination, and then reports to the full Senate, where floor debate may precede the final confirmation vote.

The Senate's involvement in federal district judgeships traditionally centered on the practice of **senatorial courtesy**. If senators from the president's party from the same state for which an appointment was being considered disapproved of a nominee, their Senate colleagues would defeat the nomination. But if the president and senators from that party agreed on the nomination, the full Senate, even if controlled by the opposition, customarily confirmed the nomination. During the Reagan-Bush years, however, partisan divisions between these Republican presidents and Senate Democrats eroded the tradition of senatorial courtesy.

senatorial courtesy Custom of the U.S. Senate with regard to presidential nominations to the judiciary to defer to the judgment of senators from the president's party from the same state as the nominee.

Supreme Court nominations have always received close political scrutiny in the Senate. Over the last two centuries, the Senate has rejected or refused to confirm about 20 percent of presidential nominees to the high court, but only five nominees in this century (see Table 13.2). In the past, most senators believed that presidents deserved to appoint their own judges; the opposition party would get its own opportunity to appoint judges when it won the presidency. Only if the Senate found some personal disqualification in a nominee's background (for example, financial scandal, evidence of racial or religious bias, judicial incompetence) would a nominee likely be rejected. But publicity and partisanship over confirmation of Supreme Court nominees have increased markedly in recent years.[24]

The Bork Battle   The U.S. Senate's rejection of President Ronald Reagan's nomination of Judge Robert H. Bork in 1987 set a new precedent in Senate confirmation of Supreme Court nominees. The Senate rejected Bork because of his views, not because he lacked judicial qualifications. Bork had a reputation for "conservative activism"—a desire better to reflect the "original intent" of the Constitution's Framers by rolling back some of the Supreme Court's broad interpretations of privacy rights, including *Roe v. Wade*, free speech, and equal protection of the law. Unlike previous nominees, Bork was subjected by the Senate Judiciary Committee to extensive case-by-case questioning in nationally televised confirmation hearings. The Democrat-controlled U.S. Senate rejected his nomination. Victory in the Bork battle encouraged liberal interest groups to closely scrutinize the personal lives and political views of subsequent nominees. Indeed, the Bork battle set the stage for an even more controversial political struggle—the confirmation of Justice Clarence Thomas (see *Up Close:* "The Confirmation of Clarence Thomas").

Filibustering Court Nominees   The Constitution requires only a majority vote of the Senate to "advise and consent" to a presidential nominee for a federal court judgeship, including a seat on the Supreme Court. However, recent partisan battles over nominees have centered on the Senate's filibuster rule and the sixty votes required for cloture to end a filibuster. The Democrats in the Senate control more than forty votes, so they can deny the majority the ability to end debate. This means they can deny the vote on a federal court nominee indefinitely and thereby effectively kill the nomination. The president cannot force an up-or-down vote on a court nominee.[25]

President George W. Bush suffered several key defeats of judicial nominees for seats on the U.S. Court of Appeals by failing to get sixty votes to end filibusters

Table 13.2   Senate Confirmation Votes on Supreme Court Nominations since 1950

Nominee	President	Year	Vote
Earl Warren	Eisenhower	1954	NRV[a]
John Marshall Harlan	Eisenhower	1955	71–11
William J. Brennan	Eisenhower	1957	NRV
Charles Whittaker	Eisenhower	1957	NRV
Potter Stewart	Eisenhower	1959	70–17
Byron White	Kennedy	1962	NRV
Arthur Goldberg	Kennedy	1962	NRV
Abe Fortas	Johnson	1965	NRV
Thurgood Marshall	Johnson	1967	69–11
Abe Fortas[b]	Johnson	1968	Withdrawn[c]
Homer Thornberry	Johnson	1968	No action
Warren Burger	Nixon	1969	74–3
Clement Haynsworth	Nixon	1969	Defeated 45–55
G. Harrold Carswell	Nixon	1970	Defeated 45–51
Harry Blackmun	Nixon	1970	94–0
Lewis Powell	Nixon	1971	89–1
William Rehnquist	Nixon	1971	68–26
John Paul Stevens	Nixon	1975	98–0
Sandra Day O'Connor	Reagan	1981	99–0
William Rehnquist[b]	Reagan	1986	65–33
Antonin Scalia	Reagan	1986	98–0
Robert Bork	Reagan	1987	Defeated 42–58
Douglas Ginsburg	Reagan	1987	Withdrawn
Anthony Kennedy	Reagan	1988	97–0
David Souter	Bush	1990	90–9
Clarence Thomas	Bush	1991	52–48
Ruth Bader Ginsburg	Clinton	1993	96–3
Stephen G. Breyer	Clinton	1994	87–9
John G. Roberts Jr.	Bush	2005	78–22
Harriet Miers	Bush	2005	Withdrawn
Samuel Alito Jr.	Bush	2005	58–42

[a]No recorded vote.

[b]Elevation to Chief Justice.

[c]Nomination withdrawn after Senate vote failed to end filibuster against nomination; vote was 45 to 43 to end filibuster, and two-thirds majority was required.

Source: Congressional Quarterly, *The Supreme Court: Justice and the Law* (Washington, D.C.: Congressional Quarterly, 1983), p. 179; updated by the author.

over these nominations. All of his nominations were qualified from a judicial point of view, but all were considered conservatives by leading Democrats in the Senate. Republican Majority Leader Bill Frist threatened to try to end the filibuster rule for judicial nominations. He argued that the constitution itself specifies a "majority vote of the Senate," not a three-fifths vote for confirmation. But ending the filibuster rule, even for only judicial nominations, would challenge a sacred tradition of the Senate. (Some senators referred to it as the "nuclear option.") A shaky compromise was reached in 2005 when some previously rejected appellate court nominees were confirmed, and Democrats in the Senate promised to use the filibuster only in extraordinary cases. The Democrats chose *not* to filibuster the Supreme Court nomination of John Roberts or Samuel Alito.

WHAT DO YOU THINK? ★ ★ ★

Should Supreme Court Nominees Reveal Their Views on Key Cases before the Senate Votes to Confirm Them?

U.S. Senators on the Judiciary Committee, questioning presidents' Supreme Court nominees, have traditionally been frustrated by the refusal of nominees to comment on issues that are likely to come before the court in future cases. The nominees have argued that giving specific opinions may impinge upon their judicial impartiality when faced with specific cases. A true judicial approach requires that they examine specific facts in a case, listen to the arguments on both sides, and confer with their colleagues on the Court before rendering an opinion. They should not approach cases with preconceived opinions. Thus, when asked if he supported *Roe v. Wade*, John Roberts simply stated that the case was now precedent in constitutional law and entitled to "due respect." "I should stay away from issues that may come before the court again."

But Democratic Sen. Joseph R. Biden Jr. insisted that Roberts could at least discuss his views about abortion and the right of privacy, as well as other general legal views. "Without any knowledge of your understanding of the law, because you will not share it with us, we are rolling the dice with you, judge."

Polls reveal that the general public wants to know the Supreme Court nominee's views on important issues.

Q. "When the Senate votes on a nominee for the U.S. Supreme Court should it consider only that person's legal qualifications and background, or, along with legal background, should the Senate also consider how that nominee might vote on major issues the Supreme Court decides?"

Legal background only	Issues too	Unsure
36%	51%	10%

Q. "Before senators vote on whether John Roberts should be confirmed as the Chief Justice of the Supreme Court, how important do you think it is for the Senate to know his position on issues such as abortion and affirmative action?"

Very Important	Somewhat Important	Not Very Important	Not At All Important	Unsure
46%	31%	9%	13%	1%

Sources: Congressional Quarterly Weekly Report, September 19, 2005, p. 2497; *New York Times*, September 14, 2005.

Who Is Selected?

What background and experiences are brought to the Supreme Court? Despite often holding very different views on the laws, the Constitution, and their interpretation, the justices of the U.S. Supreme Court tend to share a common background of education at the nation's most prestigious law schools and prior judicial experience.

Law Degrees   There is no constitutional requirement that Supreme Court justices be attorneys, but every person who has ever served on the High Court has been trained in law. Moreover, a majority of the justices have attended one or another of the nation's most prestigious law schools (see Table 13.3).

Judicial Experience   Historically, about half of all Supreme Court justices have been federal or state court judges. Many justices have served some time as U.S. attorneys in the Department of Justice early in their legal careers. Relatively few have held elected political office, but one chief justice—William Howard Taft—previously held the nation's highest elected post, the presidency.

Age   Most justices have been in their fifties when appointed to the Court. Presumably this is the age at which people acquire the necessary prominence and experience to bring themselves to the attention of the White House and Justice

Find Law for Students
Law school information for schools A–Z, state bar information, job listings, law school rankings, and so forth.
http://stu.findlaw.com

UP CLOSE

Bush Scores, Then Fumbles, Then Scores Again

President George W. Bush was successful in his first Supreme Court nomination, John G. Roberts Jr. as Chief Justice. Roberts was eminently qualified: B.A., Harvard; J.D., Harvard Law School; editor of the *Harvard Law Review*; clerk for Supreme Court Justice William Rehnquist; assistant to the Attorney General; partner in the prestigious Washington law firm of Hogan and Harrison; Deputy Solicitor General; and since 2003 Judge on the D.C. Circuit Court of Appeals. As a lawyer he argued thirty-one cases before the Supreme Court. At the Senate Judiciary Committee hearings he was pleasant, courteous, and extraordinarily knowledgeable about the law. He testified for days without any notes. He promised judicial restraint—to interpret the law, not make it—but appeared more moderate than conservative in judicial philosophy. He declined, with grace and deference to the committee, to answer questions that might come before the Court in the future. His nomination was confirmed by 78–22, with all Republicans and half of the Democrats supporting him.

But President Bush followed Roberts's nomination with the nomination of Harriet Miers, a long-time personal friend serving as counselor to the president. Miers received her B.A. and law degrees from Southern Methodist University, worked at a Dallas law firm, served two years on the Dallas City Commission, and was appointed Texas Lottery Commissioner. She had never served in a judicial capacity; she had no record of past decisions. Lacking any public record, the Senate Judiciary Committee summoned all her communications with the president while she had served in the White House. Many conservative Republicans expressed their disappointment; they wanted a strong voice for conservatism on the Court. Democrats complained that "her lack of judicial experience, coupled with close personal ties to President Bush, cast a shadow over her nomination." Finally after weeks of personal visits with Senators, Miers withdrew her nomination, citing the Senate's demand for White House internal documents, a demand "that would undermine the president's ability to receive candid counsel."

President Bush promptly nominated Samuel A. Alito Jr., a judge with fifteen years of experience on the Third Circuit Court of Appeals. Alito received his B.A. from Princeton and his law degree from Yale. Yale was a hothouse of liberal activism while Alito was a student (Bill and Hillary Clinton were two years ahead of him). But Alito remained above the fray, concentrating on the complexities of the law, precedent, and reason. Following graduation, he became a Reagan Justice Department official and wrote many

Presidential appointments to the Supreme Court require Senate confirmation. Here Senator Robert Byrd (D-WV) meets with Supreme Court nominee John Roberts prior to Roberts's confirmation in 2005.

This television image shows the final confirmation vote on the nomination of Samuel Alito Jr. to the Supreme Court in 2006. Alito replaced retiring Justice Sandra Day O'Connor.

memos in support of Reagan policies. Liberals would later accuse him of personally endorsing these policies, but Alito responded that he was only serving his client as any lawyer would do. Later, on the Third Circuit Court of Appeals, his decisions were consistently narrow and respectful of precedent. He did not inject his personal views into his decisions. Liberal opponents of his nomination were unable to focus on any controversial decisions or statements. At the Senate Judiciary Committee hearings he was respectful of questioning Senators but stopped short of providing any views on pending cases that might later come before the Court (as had all preceding nominees). Regarding *Roe v. Wade* (the 1973 case declaring abortion a constitutional right), he declined to say whether he "supported" it, but he acknowledged that it was established precedent, that it had been relied upon by the Court many times, and that it was entitled to due respect. Overall he gave the impression that he would be a moderate on the Court, rather than a regular member of the conservative block. His nomination was confirmed by the Senate by a 58 to 42 vote.

The Confirmation of Clarence Thomas

Television coverage of Senate confirmation hearings on Clarence Thomas's appointment to the Supreme Court in 1991 captivated a national audience. The conflict raised just about every "hot-button" issue in American politics, from abortion rights and affirmative action to sexual harassment.

Born to a teenage mother who earned $10 a week as a maid, Clarence Thomas and his brother lived in a dirt-floor shack in Pin Point, Georgia, where they were raised by strict, hardworking grandparents who taught young Clarence the value of education and sacrificed to send him to a Catholic school. He excelled academically and went on to mostly white Immaculate Conception Seminary College in Missouri to study for the Catholic priesthood. But when he overheard a fellow seminarian express satisfaction at the assassination of Dr. Martin Luther King Jr., Thomas left the seminary in anger and enrolled at College of the Holy Cross, where he helped found the college's Black Student Union, and went on to graduate with honors and to win admission to Yale Law School.

Upon graduating from Yale, Thomas took a job as assistant attorney general in Missouri and later became a congressional aide to Republican Missouri Senator John Danforth. In 1981 he accepted the post as head of the Office of Civil Rights in the Department of Education. In 1982 he was named chair of the Equal Employment Opportunity Commission (EEOC), where he successfully eliminated much of that agency's financial mismanagement and aggressively pursued individual cases of discrimination. But at the same time, he spoke out against racial "quotas." In 1989 President Bush nominated him to the U.S. Court of Appeals, and he was easily confirmed by the Senate.

In tapping Thomas for the Supreme Court, the White House reasoned that the liberal groups who had blocked the earlier nomination of conservative Robert Bork would be reluctant to launch personal attacks on an African American. With the opposition fractured, the White House saw an opportunity to push a strong conservative nominee through the Democrat-dominated Senate Judiciary Committee and win confirmation by the full Senate.

But behind the scenes, liberal interest groups, including the National Abortion Rights Action League, People for the American Way, and the National Organization for Women, were searching for evidence to discredit Thomas. A University of Oklahoma law professor, Anita Hill, a former legal assistant to Thomas both at the Department of Education and later at the Equal Employment Opportunity Commission, charged, in a nationally televised press conference, that Thomas had sexually harassed her in both jobs. Thomas himself flatly denied the charges.

Democrats on the committee treated Hill with great deference, asking her to talk about her feelings and provide even more explicit details of Thomas's alleged misconduct. Given an opportunity to rebut Hill's charges, Thomas did so very emphatically: "This is a circus. It's a national disgrace. And from my standpoint as a black American, as far as I'm concerned, it is a high-tech lynching for uppity blacks who in any way deign to think for themselves."

In the end, there was no way to determine who was telling the truth, and "truth" in Washington is, at any rate, often determined by opinion polls. A majority of blacks as well as whites, and a majority of women as well as men, sided with the nominee.[a] In a fitting finale to the bitter and sleazy conflict, the final Senate confirmation vote was 52 to 48, the closest vote in the history of such confirmations. The best that can be said about the affair was that it placed the issue of sexual harassment on the national agenda.

[a]*Gallup Opinion Reports*, October 15, 1991, p. 209.

Table 13.3 **The Supreme Court**

Justice	Age at Appointment	President Who Appointed	Law School	Position at Time of Appointment	Years as a Judge before Appointment
John Paul Stevens	50	Ford (1976)	Northwestern	U.S. Court of Appeals	5
Antonin Scalia	50	Reagan (1988)	Harvard	U.S. Court of Appeals	4
Anthony M. Kennedy	51	Reagan (1988)	Harvard	U.S. Court of Appeals	12
David H. Souter	50	Bush (1990)	Harvard	State Supreme Court	13
Clarence Thomas	43	Bush (1991)	Yale	U.S. Court of Appeals	2
Ruth Bader Ginsburg	60	Clinton (1993)	Columbia	U.S. Court of Appeals	13
Stephen G. Breyer	56	Clinton (1994)	Harvard	U.S. Court of Appeals	14
John G. Roberts Jr. Chief Justice	50	Bush (2005)	Harvard	U.S. Court of Appeals	2
Samuel A. Alito Jr.	55	Bush (2005)	Yale	U.S. Court of Appeals	15

Department as potential candidates. At the same time, presidents seek to make a lasting imprint on the Court, and candidates in their fifties can be expected to serve on the Court for many more years than older candidates with the same credentials.

Race and Gender No African American had ever served on the Supreme Court until President Lyndon Johnson's appointment of Thurgood Marshall in 1967. A Howard University Law School graduate, Marshall had served as counsel for the National Association for the Advancement of Colored People Legal Defense Fund and had personally argued the historic *Brown v. Board of Education* case before the Supreme Court in 1954. He served as solicitor general of the United States under President Lyndon Johnson before his elevation to the high court. Upon Marshall's retirement in 1991, President George Bush sought to retain minority representation on the Supreme Court, yet at the same time to reinforce conservative judicial views, with his selection of Clarence Thomas.

No woman had served on the Supreme Court prior to the appointment of Sandra Day O'Connor by President Ronald Reagan in 1981. O'Connor was Reagan's first Supreme Court appointment. Although a relatively unknown Arizona state court judge, she had the powerful support of Arizona Republican Senator Barry Goldwater and Stanford classmate Justice William Rehnquist. The second woman to serve on the High Court, Ruth Bader Ginsburg, had served as an attorney for the American Civil Liberties Union while teaching at Columbia Law School and had argued and won several important gender discrimination cases. President Jimmy Carter appointed her in 1980 to the U.S. Court of Appeals; President Bill Clinton elevated her to the Supreme Court in 1993.

Supreme Court Decision Making

The Supreme Court sets its own agenda: it decides what it wants to decide. Of the more than 8,000 requests for hearing that come to its docket each year, the

Court issues opinions on only about 150 cases. Another 150 or so cases are decided *summarily* (without opinion) by a Court order either affirming or reversing the lower court decision. The Supreme Court refuses to rule at all on the vast majority of cases that are submitted to it. Thus the rhetorical threat to "take this all the way to the Supreme Court" is usually an empty one. It is important, however, to realize that a refusal to rule also creates law by allowing the decision of the lower court to stand. That is why the U.S. Circuit Courts of Appeals are powerful bodies.

Setting the Agenda: Granting Certiorari   Most cases reach the Supreme Court when a party in a case appeals to the Court to issue a **writ of certiorari** (literally to "make more certain"), a decision by the Court to require a lower federal or state court to turn over its records on a case.[26] To "grant certiorari"—that is, to decide to hear arguments in a case and render a decision—the Supreme Court relies on its **rule of four**: four justices must agree to do so. Deciding which cases to hear takes up a great deal of the Court's time.

What criteria does the Supreme Court use in choosing its policy agenda—that is, in choosing the cases it wishes to decide? The Court rarely explains why it accepts or rejects cases, but there are some general patterns. First, the Court accepts cases involving issues that the justices are interested in. The justices are clearly interested in the area of First Amendment freedoms—speech, press, and religion. Members of the Court are also interested in civil rights issues under the Equal Protection Clause of the Fourteenth Amendment and the civil rights laws and in overseeing the criminal justice system and defining the Due Process Clauses of the Fifth and Fourteenth Amendments.

In addition, the Court seems to feel an obligation to accept cases involving questions that have been decided differently by different circuit courts of appeals. The Supreme Court generally tries to see to it that "the law" does not differ from one circuit to another. Likewise, the Supreme Court usually acts when lower courts have made decisions clearly at odds with Supreme Court interpretations in order to maintain control of the federal judiciary. Finally, the Supreme Court is more likely to accept a case in which the U.S. government is a party and requests a review, especially when an issue appears to be one of overriding importance to the government. In fact, the U.S. government is a party in almost half of the cases decided by the Supreme Court.

Hearing Arguments   Once the Supreme Court places a case on its decision calendar, attorneys for both sides submit written briefs on the issues. The Supreme Court may also allow interest groups to submit **amicus curiae** (literally, "friend of the court") briefs. This process allows interest groups direct access to the Supreme Court. In the affirmative action case of *University of California Regents v. Bakke* (1978)[27] the Court accepted 59 *amicus curiae* briefs representing more than 100 interest groups. The U.S. government frequently submits *amicus curiae* arguments in cases in which it is not a party. The **solicitor general** of the United States is responsible for presenting the government's arguments both in cases in which the government is a party and in cases in which the government is merely an *amicus curiae*.

Oral arguments before the Supreme Court are a time-honored ritual of American government. They take place in the marble "temple"—the Supreme Court building across the street from the U.S. Capitol in Washington, D.C. (see Figure 13.3). The justices, clad in their black robes, sit behind a high "bench" and peer down at the attorneys presenting their arguments. Arguing a case before the

writ of certiorari Writ issued by the Supreme Court, at its discretion, to order a lower court to prepare the record of a case and send it to the Supreme Court for review. Most cases come to the Court as petitions for writs of certiorari.

rule of four At least four justices must agree to hear an appeal (writ of certiorari) from a lower court in order to get a case before the Supreme Court.

amicus curiae Literally, "friend of the court"; a person, private group or institution, or government agency that is not a party to a case but participates in the case (usually through submission of a brief) at the invitation of the court or on its own initiative.

solicitor general Attorney in the Department of Justice who represents the U.S. government before the Supreme Court and any other courts.

Figure 13.3 Corridors of Power in the Supreme Court
This cutaway shows the location of the principal offices and chambers of the Supreme Court building.

THE SUPREME COURT

1. Courtyards
2. Solicitor General's Office
3. Lawyers' Lounge
4. Marshal's Office
5. Main Hall
6. Courtroom
7. Conference and Reception Rooms

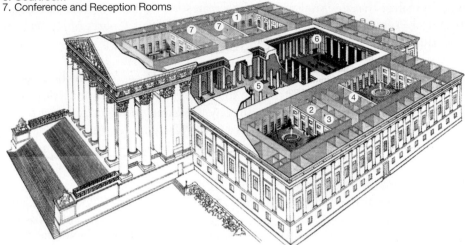

majority opinion Opinion in a case that is subscribed to by a majority of the judges who participated in the decision.

Supreme Court is said to be an intimidating experience. Each side is usually limited to either a half-hour or an hour of argument, but justices frequently interrupt with their own pointed questioning. Court watchers sometimes try to predict the Court's decision from the tenor of the questioning. Oral argument is the most public phase of Supreme Court decision making, but no one really knows whether these arguments ever change the justices' minds.

In Conference The actual decisions are made in private conferences among the justices. These conferences usually take place on Wednesdays and Fridays and cover the cases argued orally during the same week. The Chief Justice presides, and only justices (no law clerks) are present. It is customary for the Chief Justice to speak first on the issues, followed by each associate justice in order of seniority. A majority must decide which party wins or loses and whether a lower court's decision is to be affirmed or reversed.

Writing Opinions The *written* opinion determines the actual outcome of the case (votes in conference are not binding). When the decision is unanimous, the Chief Justice traditionally writes the opinion. In the case of a split decision, the Chief Justice may take on the task of writing the **majority opinion** or assign it to another justice in the majority. If the Chief Justice is in the minority, the senior justice in the majority makes the assignment. Writing the opinion of the Court is the central task in Supreme Court policy making. Broadly written opinions may effect sweeping policy changes; narrowly written opinions may decide a particular case but have very little policy impact. The reasons cited for the decision become binding law, to be applied by lower courts in future cases. Yet despite the crucial role of opinion writing in Court policy making, most opinions are actually written by law clerks who are only recent graduates of the nation's prestigious law schools. The justices themselves read, edit, correct, and sometimes rewrite drafts prepared by clerks, but clerks may have a strong influence over the position taken by justices on the issues.

A draft of the opinion is circulated among members of the majority. Any majority member who disagrees with the reasoning in the opinion, and thus disagrees with the policy that is proposed, may either negotiate changes in the opinion with others in the majority or write a concurring opinion. A **concurring opinion** agrees with the decision about which party wins the case but sets forth a different reason for the decision, proposing, in effect, a different policy position.

Justices in the minority often agree to present a **dissenting opinion**. The dissenting opinion sets forth the views of justices who disagree with both the decision and the majority reasoning. Dissenting opinions do not have the force of law. They are written both to express opposition to the majority view and to appeal to a future Court to someday modify or reverse the position of the majority. Occasionally, the Court is unable to agree on a clear policy position on particularly vexing questions. If the majority is strongly divided over the reasoning behind their decision and as many as four justices dissent altogether from the decision, lower courts will lack clear guidance and future cases will be decided on a case-by-case basis, depending on multiple factors occurring in each case (see, for example, "Affirmative Action in the Courts" in Chapter 15). The absence of a clear opinion of the Court, supported by a unified majority of the justices, invites additional cases, keeping the issue on the Court's agenda until such time (if any) as the Court establishes a clear policy on the issue.

concurring opinion
Opinion by a member of a court that agrees with the result reached by the court in the case but disagrees with or departs from the court's rationale for the decision.

dissenting opinion Opinion by a member of a court that disagrees with the result reached by the court in the case.

American Bar Association (ABA)
ABA news and views; information for law students.
www.abanet.org

Politics and the Supreme Court

The political views of Supreme Court justices have an important influence on Court decisions. Justices are swayed primarily by their own ideological views; but public opinion, the president's position, and the arguments of interest groups all contribute to the outcome of cases.

Liberal and Conservative Voting Blocs   Although liberal and conservative voting blocs on the Court are visible over time, on any given case particular justices may deviate from their perceived ideological position. Many cases do not present a liberal-conservative dimension. Each case presents a separate set of facts, and even justices who share a general philosophy may perceive the central facts of a case differently. Moreover, the liberal-versus-conservative dimension sometimes clashes with the activist-versus-self-restraint dimension. Although we generally think of liberals as favoring activism and conservatives self-restraint, occasionally those who favor self-restraint are obliged to approve of legislation that violates their personal conservative beliefs because opposing it would substitute their judgment for that of elected officials. So ideological blocs are not always good predictors of voting outcomes on the Court.

Over time, the composition of the Supreme Court has changed, as has the power of its various liberal and conservative voting blocs (see Table 13.4). The liberal bloc, headed by Chief Justice Earl Warren, dominated Court decision making from the mid-1950s through the end of the 1960s. The liberal bloc gradually weakened following President Richard Nixon's appointment of Warren Burger as Chief Justice in 1969, but not all of Nixon's appointees joined the conservative bloc; Justice Harry Blackmun and Justice Lewis Powell frequently joined in voting with the liberal bloc. Among Nixon's appointees, only William Rehnquist consistently adopted conservative positions. President Gerald Ford's only appointee to the Court, John Paul Stevens, began as a moderate and drifted to the liberal bloc. As a result, the Burger Court, although generally not as activist as the Warren Court, still did not reverse any earlier liberal holdings.

Table 13.4   Liberal and Conservative Voting Blocs on the Supreme Court

	The Warren Court	The Burger Court	The Rehnquist Court	The Roberts Court*
Liberal	1968 Earl Warren Hugo Black William O. Douglas Thurgood Marshall William J. Brennan Abe Fortas	1975 William O. Douglas Thurgood Marshall William J. Brennan	2004 John Paul Stevens Ruth Bader Ginsburg Stephen G. Breyer	2006 John Paul Stevens Ruth Bader Ginsburg Stephen G. Breyer David Souter
Moderate	Potter Stewart Byron White	Potter Stewart Byron White Lewis Powell Harry Blackmun	Anthony Kennedy Sandra Day O'Connor David Souter	Anthony Kennedy John Roberts
Conservative	John Marshall Harlan	Warren Burger William Rehnquist	William Rehnquist Antonin Scalia Clarence Thomas	Samuel Alito Antonin Scalia Clarence Thomas

*All blocs have been designated by the author; blocs on the Roberts Court are more speculative, inasmuch as this court has yet to decide many cases.

President Ronald Reagan, who had campaigned on a pledge to restrain the liberal activism of the Court, tried to appoint conservatives. His first appointee, Sandra Day O'Connor, turned out to be less conservative than expected, especially on women's issues and abortion rights. When Chief Justice Burger retired in 1986, Reagan seized on the opportunity to strengthen the conservative bloc by elevating Rehnquist to Chief Justice. Reagan also appointed Antonin Scalia, another strong conservative, to the Court. Reagan added Anthony Kennedy to the Court in 1988, hoping to give Rehnquist and the conservative bloc the opportunity to form a majority. Had President Reagan succeeded in getting the powerful conservative voice of Robert Bork on the Court, it is possible that many earlier liberal decisions, including *Roe v. Wade*, would have been reversed. But the Senate rejected Bork; David Souter, the man ultimately confirmed, eventually drifted toward the liberal bloc.

Liberals worried that the appointment of conservative Clarence Thomas as a replacement for the liberal Thurgood Marshall would give the conservative bloc a commanding voice in Supreme Court policy making. But no solid conservative majority emerged. Justices Rehnquist, Scalia, and Thomas were considered the core of the conservative bloc, but they had to win over at least two of the more moderate justices in order to form a majority in a case. President Bill Clinton's appointees, Ruth Bader Ginsburg and Stephen G. Breyer, have consistently supported liberal views on the Supreme Court. On key questions, the moderate bloc has the deciding vote.

While the moderate bloc currently holds the balance of power on the Court, the Court as a whole has moved in a conservative direction since the high-watermark of judicial liberalism during the era of Chief Justice Earl Warren (1953–68). Liberalism on the Court—as measured by pro-individual rights decisions against the government in civil liberties cases, pro-defendant decisions in criminal cases, and pro-women and minorities decisions in civil rights cases—has declined significantly since the 1960s.[28] It has yet to be determined whether the Roberts Court will continue in a conservative direction.

Public Opinion   "By all arguable evidence of the modern Supreme Court, the Court appears to reflect public opinion about as accurately as other policy makers."[29] And indeed, on the liberal-conservative dimension, it can be argued that Supreme Court decisions have generally followed shifts in American public opinion. However, the Court appears to lag behind public opinion. It is doubtful that the justices read opinion polls; their jobs do not depend on public approval ratings. Rather, it is more likely that the justices, whose nomination and confirmation depended on an elected president and Senate, generally share the views of those who put them on the bench. Thus, public opinion affects the Court only indirectly, through the nomination and confirmation process.

Presidential Influence   Even after a president's initial appointment of a Justice to the High Court, a president may exercise some influence over judicial decision making. The Office of the **U.S. Solicitor General** is charged with the responsibility of presenting the government's (the president's) views in cases not only to which the U.S. government is a party, but also in cases in which the president and the Attorney General have a strong interest and present their arguments in amicus curiae briefs. The Solicitor General's Office, in both Democratic and Republican presidential administrations, has compiled an enviable record in Supreme Court cases. When representing federal agencies that are parties to cases, the Solicitors General have won two-thirds of their cases before the Supreme Court over the years. And in cases where the Solicitor General has offered an amicus curiae brief, he has won about three-quarters of the cases. In contrast, the states have won fewer than half of the cases before the Supreme Court in which a state has been a party.

U.S. Solicitor General The U.S. government's chief legal counsel, presenting the government's arguments in cases in which it is a party or in which it has an interest.

Interest-Group Influence   Interest groups have become a major presence in Supreme Court cases. First of all, interest groups (for example, Planned Parenthood, National Association for the Advancement of Colored People, American Civil Liberties Union) sponsor many cases themselves. They find persons they believe to be directly damaged by a public policy, initiate litigation on their behalf, and provide the attorneys and money to pursue these cases all the way to the Supreme Court. Secondly, it is now a rare case that comes to the Court without multiple amicus curiae briefs filed by interest groups.

How influential are interest groups in Supreme Court decisions? Certainly interest groups have a significant influence in bringing issues before the Supreme Court through their sponsorship of cases. It is unlikely that the Court would have acted when it did on many key issues from racial segregation in 1954 (*Brown v. Board of Education* sponsored by the NAACP) to abortion in 1992 (*Planned Parenthood v. Casey* sponsored by Planned Parenthood) in the absence of interest-group activity. And interest-group *amicus curiae* briefs are now mentioned (cited) in about two-thirds of the written decisions of the Court. However, these briefs may not have much *independent* effect on decisions, that is, they may not have convinced the justices to decide a case one way or another. Several studies have found that interest-group briefs have had very little effect on Supreme Court decisions.[30]

Checking Court Power

Many people are concerned about the extent to which we now rely on a nonelected judiciary to decide key policy issues rather than depending on a democratically elected president or Congress.

Legitimacy as a Restraint on the Judiciary   Court authority derives from legitimacy rather than force. By that we mean that the courts depend on their authority being seen as rightful, on people perceiving an obligation to abide by court decisions whether they agree with them or not. The courts have no significant force at their direct command. Federal marshals, who carry out the orders of federal courts, number only a few thousand. Courts must rely primarily on the executive branch for enforcement of their decisions.

Today most Americans believe that Supreme Court decisions are authoritative statements about the Constitution and that people have an obligation to obey these decisions whether they agree with them or not.[31] Thus public opinion constrains other public officials—from the president, to governors, to school superintendents, to law enforcement officials—to obey Supreme Court decisions. Their constituents do not hold them personally responsible for unpopular actions ordered by the Supreme Court or federal judges. On the contrary, their constituents generally expect them to comply with court decisions.

Compliance with Court Policy   Federal and state court judges must apply Supreme Court policies when ruling on cases in their own courts. Occasionally lower courts express their disagreement with the Supreme Court in an opinion, even when they feel obliged to carry out the High Court's policy. At times, lower federal and state courts try to give a narrow interpretation to a Supreme Court decision with which they disagree. But judges who seek to defy the Supreme Court face the ultimate sanction of reversal on appeal by the losing party. Professional pride usually inspires judges to avoid reversals of their judgments by higher courts even though a long record of reversals is not grounds for impeachment or removal of a federal judge.

Public officials who defy Supreme Court rulings risk lawsuits and court orders mandating compliance. Persons injured by noncompliance are likely to file suit against noncomplying officials, as are interest groups that monitor official compliance with the policies they support. These suits are expensive, time consuming, and potentially embarrassing to government officials and agencies. Once a court order is issued, continued defiance can result in fines and penalties for contempt of court.

The president of the United States is subject to federal court orders. Historically, this notion has been challenged: early presidents believed they were separate and at least co-equal to the courts and that their own determination about the legality or constitutionality of their own acts could not be overturned by the courts. President Andrew Jackson could—and did—say: "John Marshall has made his decision. Now let him enforce it," expressing the view that the president was not obliged to enforce court decisions he disagreed with.[32] But in the course of 200 years, the courts—not the president—have gained in legitimacy as the final authority on the law and the Constitution. Today a president who openly defied the Supreme Court would lose any claims to legitimacy and would risk impeachment by Congress.

The case of Richard Nixon illustrates the weakness of a modern president who would even consider defying the Supreme Court. When Nixon sought to invoke executive privilege to withhold damaging tapes of White House conversations in the Watergate investigation (see *Up Close:* "Watergate and the Limits of Presidential Power" in Chapter 11), federal district judge John Sirica rejected his claim and ordered that the tapes be turned over to the special prosecutor in the case. In arguments before the Supreme Court, Nixon's lawyers contended that the president would not have to comply with a Supreme Court decision to turn over the tapes.

UP CLOSE

Bush v. Gore in the U.S. Supreme Court

The presidential election of 2000 was unique in American history in that the outcome was decided by the Supreme Court of the United States. The Supreme Court's decision on December 12, 2000, in *Bush v. Gore,* rested on constitutional issues, but the 5–4 decision of the justices raised the question of the High Court's political partisanship.[a]

"Too Close to Call"

On the morning after Election Day, it became clear that the outcome of the presidential election depended on Florida's twenty-five electoral votes. Florida's Secretary of State (separately elected Republican Katherine Harris) initially reported a margin of 1,784 for Bush out of over 6 million votes cast in the state. But because Florida law provides for a recount when the margin of victory is less than one-half of 1 percent, the recount of machine votes was conducted as well as a count of absentee ballots. Bush's lead was reduced to a slim 930 votes. The Florida Secretary of State declined to accept any recount returns from the counties after November 14, the date set by Florida law as the final date for submission of returns to the Secretary.

Judicial Maneuvering

But immediately after Election Day armies of lawyers descended on Florida's capital city, Tallahassee. The stakes were high—the presidency of the United States. Gore's legal team was headed by former Secretary of State Warren Christopher, and the Bush team by former Secretary of State James Baker (although neither argued directly before the courts). The Gore team demanded *manual* recounts of the ballots in the state's three largest (and most Democratic) counties—Miami-Dade, Broward (Fort Lauderdale), and Palm Beach. The case was first argued before a Leon County (Tallahassee) trial judge, who dismissed Gore's petition. But the case was quickly appealed to the Florida Supreme Court (with its seven justices, all appointed by Democratic governors). That Court set aside the state's legal deadline for recounts, and county canvassing boards began a tedious hand count of punch card ballots.

The Bush legal team appealed directly to the U.S. Supreme Court, arguing first of all that the U.S. Constitution gives the power to appoint presidential electors "in such Manner as the *Legislature* thereof may direct" (Article II, Section 1), and that the Florida Supreme Court overreached its authority

when it set aside legislative-enacted provisions of the election laws of the state, including the deadline for recounts. They also argued that hand counts in counties were late, unreliable, subjective, and open to partisan bias. The U.S. Supreme Court responded initially by ordering a halt to the recounts and remanding (sending back) the case to the Florida Supreme Court for clarification as to the grounds on which it had been decided.

The Florida Supreme Court was apparently not intimidated by the U.S. Supreme Court's implied judgment that it had erred in its decision. It ordered a manual recount of all legal votes in the state, especially undercounts (where ballots failed to register a vote for president). It specified that "the intent of the voter" should be the criterion for deciding how to count a ballot. The Florida Supreme Court decision, Gore v. Harris,[b] was immediately appealed to the U.S. Supreme Court.

By now more than a month had passed with the nation not knowing who would be its next president. It became clear that Al Gore had won the nationwide popular vote. But most Americans acknowledged that the popular vote was of secondary importance to the Constitution of the United States in its provisions for choosing the president by state electoral votes. Only the U.S. Supreme Court seemed to possess sufficient legitimacy to resolve the first contested presidential election in over a century.

A Divided Supreme Court

The Supreme Court held that "the use of standardless manual recounts violates the Equal Protection and Due Process Clauses [of the U.S. Constitution] . . . . Moreover, the [Florida] court's interpretation of "legal vote," and hence its decision to order a contest-period recount, plainly departed from the legislative scheme. Florida statutory law cannot reasonably be thought to require the counting of improperly marked ballots. The judgment of the Supreme Court of Florida is reversed."

The narrow 5–4 decision appeared to follow partisan lines, with Justices O'Connor, Kennedy, Rehnquist, Scalia, and Thomas voting in the majority to allow Florida's Secretary of State to certify that state's electoral votes for Bush. Justices Souter, Stevens, Ginsburg, and Breyer dissented, arguing that the U.S. Supreme Court should not interfere with the Florida Supreme Court's order for a manual recount. Indeed, Justice Stevens implied that the Supreme Court's decision would undermine "the nation's confidence in the judge as an impartial guardian of the rule of law."

---

[a]*Bush v. Gore*, 531 U.S. 98, 2000.

[b]*Gore v. Harris*, Florida Supreme Court, December 8, 2000.

Yet when the Court ruled unanimously against him, Nixon felt bound to comply and released tapes that were very damaging to his cause. But Nixon understood that refusal to abide by a Supreme Court decision would most assuredly have resulted in impeachment. Under the circumstances, compliance was the better of two unattractive choices.

Presidential Influence on Court Policy   The president and Congress can exercise some restraint over court power through the checks and balances built into the Constitution. Using the office's powers of appointment, presidents have effectively modified the direction of Supreme Court policy and influenced lower federal courts as well. Certainly presidents must await the death or retirement of Supreme Court justices and federal judges, and presidents are constrained by the need to secure Senate confirmation of their appointees. However, over time presidential influence on the courts can be significant. During their combined twelve years in the White House, Ronald Reagan and his successor George H. W. Bush were able to fill 70 percent of federal district and appellate court judgeships and six of nine Supreme Court positions with their own appointees. As noted earlier, however, their appointees did not always reflect these presidents' philosophy of judicial self-restraint in rendering decisions. Nevertheless, the federal courts tilted in a somewhat more conservative direction. President Bill Clinton's appointments generally strengthened liberal, activist impulses throughout the federal judiciary, and George W. Bush's appointees generally supported a conservative, restrained judiciary.

Congressional Checks on the Judiciary   The Constitution gives Congress control over the structure and jurisdiction of federal district and appellate courts, but congressional use of this control has been restrained. Only the Supreme Court is established by the Constitution; Article III gives Congress the power to "ordain and establish" "inferior" courts. In theory, Congress could try to limit court jurisdiction to hear cases that Congress did not wish it to decide. Congress has used this power to lighten the federal courts' workload; for example, Congress has limited the jurisdiction of federal courts in cases between citizens of different states by requiring that the dispute involve more than $50,000. But Congress has never used this power to change court policy—for example, by removing federal court jurisdiction over school prayer cases or desegregation cases. Indeed federal courts would probably declare unconstitutional any congressional attempt to limit their power to interpret the Constitution by limiting jurisdiction.

Likewise, although Congress could, in theory, expand membership on the Supreme Court, the custom of a nine-member Supreme Court is now so deeply ingrained in American government that "court packing" is politically unthinkable. Franklin Roosevelt's unsuccessful 1937 attempt to expand the Supreme Court was the last serious assault on its membership.

A more common congressional constraint on the Supreme Court is amending statutory laws to reverse federal court interpretations of these laws that Congress believes are in error. Thus when the Supreme Court decided that civil rights laws did not mandate a cutoff of *all* federal funds to a college upon evidence of discrimination in a single program but only the funds for that program,[33] Congress amended its own laws to require the more sweeping remedy. Although members of Congress frequently berate the Court for what they see as misreading of the laws, all Congress needs to do to reverse a Court interpretation of those laws is to pass amendments to them.

Constitutional amendment is the only means by which the Congress and the states can reverse a Supreme Court interpretation of the Constitution itself. After

A CONSTITUTIONAL NOTE

The Power of Judicial Review

Nowhere in the Constitution do we find any mention of the power of "judicial review." It is true that the Constitution's Supremacy Clause (Article VI, Section 2) makes the Constitution and national laws and treaties "the supreme law of the land, anything in the Constitution or laws of any *state* to the contrary notwithstanding." The Founders clearly believed that federal court power over state decisions was essential to maintaining national unity. But at the *national* level, why should an appointed court's interpretation of the Constitution prevail over the views of an elected Congress and an elected president? All are pledged to uphold the Constitution. The answer is that the Founders distrusted popular majorities and elected officials subject to their influence. So the Founders deliberately insulated the courts from popular majorities; by appointing judges for life terms, they sought to ensure their independence. Alexander Hamilton viewed the federal courts as a final bulwark against threats to prin-

ciple and property. Writing in *The Federalist* in late 1787 he said: "Limited government. . . can be preserved in practice no other way than through the medium of courts of justice, whose duty it is to declare all acts contrary to the manifest tenor of the Constitution void." But it was not until the case of *Marbury v. Madison* in 1803 that John Marshall first assumed the power of Judicial review. He argued persuasively that (1) the Constitution is declared "the supreme law of the land," and national as well as state laws must be congruent with it; (2) Article III gives the Supreme Court the "judicial power," which includes the power to interpret the meaning of laws and, in case of conflict between laws, to decide which law shall prevail; and (3) the courts are sworn to uphold the Constitution, so they must declare void any law that conflicts with the Constitution. Despite the logic of the argument, judicial review—the ability of an *un*elected judiciary, serving for life, to invalidate laws of Congress and actions of the president—would appear to be an undemocratic feature of the Constitution.

the Civil War, the Thirteenth Amendment abolishing slavery reversed the Supreme Court's *Dred Scott* decision (1857) that slavery was constitutionally protected. The Sixteenth Amendment (1913) gave Congress the power to impose an income tax, thus reversing the Supreme Court's earlier decision in *Pollock v. Farmer's Loan*[34] holding income taxes unconstitutional (1895). But recent attempts to reverse Supreme Court interpretations of the Constitution by passing constitutional amendments on the issues of prayer in public schools, busing, and abortion have all failed to win congressional approval. The barriers to a constitutional amendment are formidable: a two-thirds vote of both houses of Congress and ratification by three-quarters of the states. Thus, for all practical purposes, the Constitution is what the Supreme Court says it is.

Congress can impeach federal court judges, but only for "cause" (committing crimes), not for their decisions. Although impeachment is frequently cited as a constitutional check on the judiciary, it has no real influence over judicial policy making. Only five federal court judges have ever been impeached by the House, convicted by the Senate, and removed from office, although two others were impeached and another nine resigned to avoid impeachment. In 1989 Federal District Court Judge Alcee Hastings became the first sitting judge in more than fifty years to be impeached, tried, and found guilty by the Congress. He was convicted by the Senate of perjury and conspiracy to obtain a $150,000 bribe; but a federal district court judge later ruled that he should have been tried by the full Senate, not a special committee of the Senate. Hastings declared the ruling a vindication; in 1992 he won a congressional seat in Florida, becoming the first person ever to become a member of the House after being impeached by that same body. Even criminal convictions do not ensure removal from office, although judges have resigned under fire.

Summary Notes

- Great power is lodged in the Supreme Court of the United States and the federal judiciary. These courts have undertaken to resolve many of the most divisive conflicts in American society. The judicial power is the power to decide cases and controversies, and in so doing to decide the meaning of the Constitution and laws of Congress.

- The power of judicial review is the power to invalidate laws of Congress or of the states that the federal courts believe conflict with the U.S. Constitution. This power is not specifically mentioned in the Constitution but was derived by Chief Justice John Marshall from the Supremacy Clause and the meaning of judicial power in Article III.

- The Supreme Court has been fairly restrained in its use of judicial review with regard to laws of Congress and actions of presidents; it has more frequently overturned state laws. The federal courts also exercise great power in the interpretation of the laws of Congress, especially when statutory language is vague.

- Arguments over judicial power are reflected in the conflicting philosophies of judicial activism and judicial self-restraint. Advocates of judicial restraint argue that judges must not substitute their own views for those of elected representatives and the remedy for unwise laws lies in the legislature, not the courts. Advocates of judicial activism argue that the courts must view the Constitution as a living document and its meaning must fit the needs of a changing society.

- The federal judiciary consists of three levels of courts—the Supreme Court, the U.S. Courts of Appeals, and the U.S. District Courts. The district courts are trial courts that hear both civil and criminal cases. The courts of appeals are appellate courts and do not hold trials but consider only the record of trial courts and the arguments (briefs) of attorneys. More than 90 percent of federal cases end in appeals courts. The Supreme Court can hear appeals from state high courts as well as lower federal courts. The Supreme Court hears only about 200 cases a year.

- Courts function under general rules of restraint that do not bind the president or Congress. The Supreme Court does not decide hypothetical cases or render advisory opinions. The principle of stare decisis, or reliance on precedent, is not set aside lightly.

- The selection of Supreme Court justices and federal judges is based more on political considerations than legal qualifications. Presidents almost always appoint judges from their own party, and presidents increasingly have sought judges who share their ideological views. However, because of the independence of judges once they are appointed, presidents have sometimes been disappointed in the decisions of their appointees. In addition, Senate approval of

- nominees has become increasingly politicized, with problems most evident when different parties control the White House and the Senate.

- The Supreme Court sets its own agenda for policy making, usually by granting or withholding certiorari. Generally four justices must agree to grant certiorari for a case to be decided by the Supreme Court. The Supreme Court has been especially active in policy making in interpreting the meaning of the Fourteenth Amendment's guarantee of "equal protection of the laws," as well as of the civil rights and voting rights acts of Congress. It has also been active in defining the meaning of freedom of press, speech, and religion in the First Amendment and "due process of law" in the Fifth Amendment. The federal courts are active in overseeing government regulatory activity. But federal courts have generally left the areas of national security and international relations to the president and Congress. In addition, the Court tends to accept cases involving questions decided differently by different courts of appeal, cases in which lower courts have challenged Supreme Court interpretations, and cases in which the U.S. government is a party and it requests review.

- Liberal and conservative blocs on the Supreme Court can be discerned over time. Generally, liberals have been judicial activists and conservatives have been restraintists. Today a moderate bloc appears to hold the balance of power.

- The Supreme Court risked its reputation for political impartiality when it intervened in the 2000 presidential election and issued a decision that in effect gave Florida's 25 electoral votes to George W. Bush and by so doing won him a majority in the Electoral College.

- Court power derives primarily from legitimacy rather than force. Most Americans believe that Supreme Court decisions are authoritative statements about the Constitution and people have an obligation to obey these decisions whether they agree with them or not. Although early presidents thought of themselves as constitutional co-equals with the Supreme Court and not necessarily bound by Court decisions, today it would be politically unthinkable for a president to ignore a court order.

- There are very few checks on Supreme Court power. Presidents may try to influence Court policy through judicial nominations, but once judges are confirmed by the Senate they can pursue their own impulses. Congress has never used its power to limit the jurisdiction of federal courts in order to influence judicial decisions.

- Only by amending the Constitution can Congress and the states reverse a Supreme Court interpretation of its meaning. Congress can impeach federal judges only for committing crimes, not for their decisions.

Key Terms

Suggested Readings

Baum, Lawrence. *The Supreme Court.* 8th ed. Washington, D.C.: CQ Press, 2003. Readable introduction to the Supreme Court as a political institution, covering the selection and confirmation of judges, the nature of the issues decided by courts, the process of judicial decision making, and the impact of Supreme Court decisions.

Bork, Robert H. *Coercing Virtue.* Washington, D.C.: AEI Press, 2003. An argument that judges, rather than legislators, are making and repealing law and deciding cases with partisan and ideological subjectivity.

Carp, Robert A., and Ronald Stidham. *The Federal Courts.* 4th ed. Washington, D.C.: CQ Press, 2001. Overview of the federal judicial system, arguing that federal judges and Supreme Court justices function as part of the political system and engage in policy making that influences all our lives.

Epstein, Lee, and Thomas G. Walker. *Constitutional Law for a Changing America: Institutional Power and Constraints.* 5th ed. Washington, D.C.: CQ Press, 2004. Commentary and selected excerpts from cases dealing with the structure and powers of government.

Johnson, Charles, and Danette Buickman. *Independent Counsel: The Law and the Investigations.* Washington, D.C.: CQ Press, 2001. A comprehensive history of the independent counsel law and the investigations conducted under it since 1978, from Watergate to Whitewater.

Neubauer, David W. and Stephen S. Weinhold. *Judicial Politics: Law, Courts, and Politics in the United States.* Belmont, Calif.: Wadsworth, 2004. Introduction to the judicial process with controversial cases in each chapter.

U.S. Supreme Court decisions are available at most public and university libraries as well as at law libraries in volumes of *United States Reports.* Court opinions are cited by the names of the parties, for example, *Brown v. Board of Education of Topeka,* followed by a reference number such as 347 U.S. 483 (1954). The first number in the citation (347) is the volume number; "U.S." refers to *United States Reports;* the subsequent number is the page on which the decision begins; the year the case was decided is in parentheses.

Make It Real

THE JUDICIARY

This module allows students to become Supreme Court Justices.

Part Five

OUTCOMES

Illegal Immigrant Workers

ABCNEWS

Originally Aired: **December 14, 2004**
Program: **Nightline**
Running Time: **15:22**

When Bernard Kerik, President Bush's first choice to run the Department of Homeland Security, withdrew his nomination because of a nanny who was an undocumented worker that he hired and failed to pay taxes on, it was a story that probably sounded familiar. Cabinet nominees have been tripped on this issue before in both the Clinton and Bush administrations. So the question is, why does this keep happening?

One of the reasons it keeps happening is that it is pretty easy to get by hiring undocumented workers. It seems that the only way to get tripped up is if you undergo a background check for an important government post. You would be hard pressed to find any aspect of the nation's economy where undocumented workers are not making a contribution. It could be in the service industry or the construction business. You will eat something today that has been brought to you as a result of the labor of illegal immigrants working here. A conservative estimate is that at least 50 percent of agricultural laborers are undocumented workers. So is this a result of American employers being cheap, or is it a result of the efficiency of market forces? Many employers say it is not easy to find Americans willing to do a lot of the low-paying, menial, and tedious tasks that immigrants are willing to do. Labor advocates say that illegal immigrants depress the wage market so Americans are shut out of these jobs. Everyone can find statistics to back their argument.

So what is the solution? When the president announced a proposal in 2006 to grant legal status to millions of undocumented workers in the United States, it wasn't greeted with unanimous enthusiasm. "Out of common sense and fairness, our laws should allow willing workers to enter our country and fill jobs that Americans are not filling," the president said. He wasn't calling for amnesty but a temporary guest worker program. But will that satisfy both sides? Michel Martin examines the arguments advanced on something that has always been a hot-button issue. We also speak with Senator John McCain of Arizona. His state has addressed the illegal immigration issue by voting for a sweeping proposition that bans all government services to illegal immigrants. He says that this is an issue that the nation has to wake up to and start dealing with as a high priority.

Critical Thinking Questions

1. Why aren't immigration laws more strictly enforced?

2. Explain the "geographic" component to immigration law enforcement.

3. The inability to bar illegal aliens from entering the country is not a question of power. Rather, the problems are political and practical. Briefly explain what this means.

14 POLITICS AND PERSONAL LIBERTY

Power and Individual Liberty

To the authors of the Declaration of Independence, individual liberty was inherent in the human condition. It was not derived from governments or even from constitutions. Rather, governments and constitutions existed to make individual liberty more secure.

> We hold these truths to be self-evident, that all men are created equal, that they are endowed by their Creator with certain unalienable Rights, that among these are Life, Liberty and the pursuit of Happiness. That to secure these rights, Governments are instituted among Men, deriving their just powers from the consent of the governed.

The authors of the Bill of Rights (the first ten amendments to the Constitution) did *not* believe that they were creating individual rights, but rather that they were recognizing and guaranteeing rights that belonged to individuals by virtue of their humanity.

Authority and Liberty To avoid the brutal life of a lawless society, where the weak are at the mercy of the strong, people form governments and endow them with powers to secure peace and self-preservation. People voluntarily relinquish some of their individual freedom to establish a government that is capable of protecting them from their neighbors as well as from foreign aggressors. This government must be strong enough to maintain its own existence or it cannot defend the rights of its citizens.

But what happens when a government becomes too strong and infringes on the liberties of its citizens? How much liberty must individuals surrender to secure an orderly society? This is the classic dilemma of free government: People must create laws and governments to protect their freedom, but the laws and governments themselves restrict freedom.

Democracy and Personal Liberty When democracy is defined only as a *decision-making process*—widespread popular participation and rule by majority—it offers little protection for individual liberty. Democracy must also be defined to include *substantive values*—a recognition of the dignity of all individuals and their equality under law. Otherwise, some

Think About Politics

1 Do you think the government has become so large and powerful that it poses a threat to the rights and freedoms of ordinary citizens?
Yes ☐ No ☐

2 Do you believe that using tax funds to pay tuition at church-affiliated schools violates the separation of church and state?
Yes ☐ No ☐

3 Do we have a constitutional right to physician-assisted suicide?
Yes ☐ No ☐

4 Do law-abiding citizens have a constitutional right to carry a handgun for self-protection?
Yes ☐ No ☐

5 Should persons captured on a foreign battlefield in the war on terrorism be entitled to constitutional protections?
Yes ☐ No ☐

6 Do you believe that the seizure of property believed by police to be used in drug trafficking, without a judicial hearing or trial, violates civil liberty?
Yes ☐ No ☐

7 Is the death penalty a "cruel and unusual" punishment?
Yes ☐ No ☐

Government power defends your most basic rights to life, liberty, and the pursuit of happiness while at the same time ensuring that all other Americans have the same rights. The Founders guaranteed individual liberty in the earliest days of our nation through the first ten amendments to the Constitution— our Bill of Rights.

First Amendment Center
Vanderbilt University center provides sources of information on First Amendment issues.
www.firstamendmentcenter.org

incorporation In constitutional law, the application of almost all of the Bill of Rights to the states and all of their subdivisions through the Fourteenth Amendment.

people, particularly "the weaker party, or an obnoxious individual," would be vulnerable to deprivations of life, liberty, or property simply by decisions of majorities (see "The Paradox of Democracy" in Chapter 1). Indeed, the "great object" of the Constitution, according to James Madison, was to preserve popular government yet at the same time to protect individuals from "unjust" majorities.[1]

The purpose of the Constitution—and especially its Bill of Rights, passed by the First Congress in September 1789—is to limit governmental power over the individual, that is, to place personal liberty beyond the reach of government (see Table 14.1). Each individual's rights to life, liberty, and property, due process of law, and equal protection of the law are not subject to majority vote. Or, as Supreme Court Justice Robert Jackson once declared, "One's right to life, liberty, and property, to free speech, a free press, freedom of worship and assembly, and other fundamental rights may not be submitted to vote: they depend on the outcome of no elections."[2]

Nationalizing the Bill of Rights   The Bill of Rights begins with the words *"Congress* shall make no law . . .," indicating that it was originally intended to limit only the powers of the federal government. The Bill of Rights was added to the Constitution because of fear that the *federal* government might become too powerful and encroach on inIndividual liberty. But what about encroachments by state and local governments and their officials?

The Fourteenth Amendment includes the words "No *State* shall . . ."; its provisions are directed specifically at states. Initially, the U.S. Supreme Court rejected the argument that the Fourteenth Amendment's Privileges or Immunities Clause[3] and the Due Process Clause[4] incorporated the Bill of Rights. But beginning in the 1920s, the Court handed down a long series of decisions that gradually brought about the **incorporation** of almost all of the protections of the Bill of Rights into the "liberty" guaranteed against state actions by the due process clause of the Fourteenth Amendment. In *Gitlow v. New York* (1925), the Court ruled that "freedom of speech and of the press—which are protected by the First Amendment from abridgment by Congress—are among the fundamental personal rights and liberties protected by the due process clause of the Fourteenth Amendment from impairment by the states."[5] Over time, the Court applied the same reasoning in incorporating almost all provisions of the Bill of Rights into the Fourteenth Amendment's Due Process Clause. States and all of their subdivisions—cities, counties, townships, school districts, and so forth—are bound by the Bill of Rights.

Freedom of Religion

Americans are a very religious people. Belief in God and church attendance are more widespread in the United States than in any other advanced industrialized nation. Although many early American colonists came to the new land to escape religious persecution, they frequently established their own government-supported churches and imposed their own religious beliefs on others. Puritanism was the official faith of colonial Massachusetts, and Virginia officially established the Church of England. Only two colonies (Maryland and Rhode Island) provided for full religious freedom. In part to lessen the potential for conflict among the states, the Framers of the Bill of Rights sought to prevent the new national government from establishing an official religion or interfering with religious exercises.[6] The very first words of the First Amendment set forth *two*

Table 14.1   Constitutionally Protected Rights

The Bill of Rights

The first ten amendments to the Constitution of the United States, passed by the First Congress of the United States in September 1789 and ratified by the states in December 1791.

Amendments	Protections
First Amendment: Religion, Speech, Press, Assembly, Petition Congress shall make no law respecting an establishment of religion, or prohibiting the free exercise thereof, or abridging the freedom of speech, or of the press; or the right of the people peaceably to assemble, and to petition the Government for a redress of grievances.	Prohibits government establishment of religion. Protects the free exercise of religion. Protects freedom of speech. Protects freedom of the press. Protects freedom of assembly. Protects the right to petition government "for a redress of grievances."
Second Amendment: Right to Bear Arms A well regulated Militia, being necessary to the security of a free State, the right of the people to keep and bear Arms, shall not be infringed.	Protects the right of people to bear arms and states to maintain militia (National Guard) units.
Third Amendment: Quartering of Soldiers No Soldier shall, in time of peace, be quartered in any house, without the consent of the Owner, nor in time of war, but in a manner to be prescribed by law.	Prohibits forcible quartering of soldiers in private homes in peacetime, or in war without congressional authorization.
Fourth Amendment: Searches and Seizures The right of the people to be secure in their persons, houses, papers, and effects, against unreasonable searches and seizures, shall not be violated, and no Warrants shall issue, but upon probable cause, supported by Oath or affirmation, and particularly describing the place to be searched, and the persons or things to be seized.	Protects against "unreasonable searches and seizures." Requires warrants for searches of homes and other places where there is a reasonable expectation of privacy. Judges may issue search warrants only with "probable cause," and such warrants must be specific regarding the place to be searched and the things to be seized.
Fifth Amendment: Grand Juries, Double Jeopardy, Self-Incrimination, Due Process, Protection against Government Takings of Property No person shall be held to answer for a capital, or otherwise infamous crime, unless on a presentment or indictment of a grand jury, except in cases arising in the land or naval forces, or in the Militia, when in actual service in time of war or public danger; nor shall any person be subject for the same offence to be twice put in jeopardy of life or limb, nor shall he be compelled in any criminal case to be a witness against himself, nor be deprived of life, liberty, or property, without due process of law; nor shall private property be taken for public use, without just compensation.	Requires that, before trial for a serious crime, a person (except military personnel) must be indicted by a grand jury. Prohibits double jeopardy (trial for the same offense a second time after being found innocent). Prohibits the government from forcing any person in a criminal case to be a witness against himself or herself. Prohibits the government from taking life, liberty, or property "without due process of law." Prohibits government from taking private property without paying "just compensation."

(continued)

Table 14.1   Constitutionally Protected Rights (continued)

Amendments	Protections
Sixth Amendment: Fair Trial	
In all criminal prosecutions, the accused shall enjoy the right to a speedy and public trial, by an impartial jury of the State and district wherein the crime shall have been committed, which district shall have been previously ascertained by law, and to be informed of the nature and cause of the accusation; to be confronted with the witnesses against him; to have compulsory process for obtaining witnesses in his favor, and to have the Assistance of Counsel for his defense.	Requires that the accused in a criminal case be given a speedy and public trial, and thus prohibits prolonged incarceration without trial or secret trials. Requires that trials be by jury and take place in the district where the crime was committed. Requires that the accused be informed of the charges, have the right to confront witnesses, have the right to force supporting witnesses to testify, and have the assistance of counsel.
Seventh Amendment: Trial by Jury in Civil Cases	
In Suits at common law, where the value in controversy shall exceed twenty dollars, the right of trial by jury shall be preserved, and no fact tried by a jury, shall be otherwise reexamined in any Court of the United States, than according to the rules of the common law.	Requires a jury trial in civil cases involving more than $20. Limits the degree to which factual questions decided by a jury may be reviewed by another court.
Eighth Amendment: Bail, Fines and Punishment	
Excessive bail shall not be required, nor excessive fines imposed, nor cruel and unusual punishments inflicted.	Prohibits excessive bail. Prohibits excessive fines. Prohibits cruel and unusual punishment.
Ninth Amendment: Unspecified Rights Retained by People	
The enumeration in the Constitution, of certain rights, shall not be construed to deny or disparage others retained by the people.	Protection of unspecified rights (including privacy) that are not listed in the Constitution. The Constitution shall not be interpreted to be a complete list of rights retained by the people.
Tenth Amendment: Rights Reserved to the States	
The powers not delegated to the United States by the Constitution, nor prohibited by it to the States, are reserved to the States respectively, or to the people.	States retain powers that are not granted by the Constitution to the national government or prohibited by it to the states.

Rights in the Text of the Constitution

Several rights were written into the text of the Constitution in 1787 and thus precede in time the adoption of the Bill of Rights.

Article 1 Section 9: Habeas Corpus, Bills of Attainder, and Ex Post Facto Laws	
The privilege of the Writ of Habeas Corpus shall not be suspended, unless when in Cases of Rebellion or Invasion the public Safety may require it. No Bill of Attainder or ex post facto Law shall be passed.	Habeas corpus prevents imprisonment without a judge's determination that a person is being lawfully detained. Prohibition of bills of attainder prevents Congress (and states) from deciding people guilty of a crime and imposing punishment without trial. Prohibition of ex post facto laws prevents Congress (and states) from declaring acts to be criminal that were committed before the passage of a law making them so.

Table 14.1   Constitutionally Protected Rights (continued)

Thirteenth and Fourteenth Amendments

The Bill of Rights begins with the words "Congress shall make no law . . ." indicating that it initially applied only to the *federal* government. Although states had their own constitutions that guarantee many of the same rights, for more than a century the Bill of Rights did not apply to state and local governments. Following the Civil War, the Thirteenth, Fourteenth, and Fifteenth (voting rights) Amendments were passed, restricting *state* governments and their local subdivisions. But not until many years later did the U.S. Supreme Court, in a long series of decisions, apply the Bill of Rights against the states.

Thirteenth Amendment

Neither slavery nor involuntary servitude, except as a punishment for crime whereof the party shall have been duly convicted, shall exist within the United States, or any place subject to their jurisdiction.	Prohibits slavery or involuntary servitude except for punishment by law; applies to both governments and private citizens.

Fourteenth Amendment

All persons born or naturalized in the United States, and subject to the jurisdiction thereof, are citizens of the United States and of the State wherein they reside. No State shall make or enforce any law which shall abridge the privileges or immunities of citizens of the United States; nor shall any State deprive any person of life, liberty, or property, without due process of law; nor deny to any person within its jurisdiction the equal protection of the laws.	Protects "privileges and immunities of citizenship." Prevents deprivation of life, liberty, or property "without due process of law"; this phrase incorporates virtually all of the rights specified in the Bill of Rights. Prevents denial of "equal protection of the laws" for all persons.

separate prohibitions on government: "Congress shall make no law respecting an *establishment of religion*, or prohibiting the *free exercise* thereof." These two restrictions on government power—the Free Exercise Clause and the No Establishment Clause—guarantee separate religious freedoms.

Free Exercise of Religion   The **Free Exercise Clause** prohibits government from restricting religious beliefs or practices. Although the wording of the First Amendment appears absolute ("Congress shall make *no* law . . ."), the U.S. Supreme Court has never interpreted the phrase to protect any conduct carried on in the name of religion. In the first major decision involving this clause, the Court ruled in 1879 that polygamy could be outlawed by Congress in Utah Territory even though some Mormons argued that it was part of their religious faith. The Court distinguished between belief and behavior, saying that "Congress was deprived of all legislative power over mere opinion [by the First Amendment], but was left free to reach actions which were in violation of social duties."[7] The Court also employed the Free Exercise Clause to strike down as unconstitutional an attempt by a state to prohibit private religious schools and force all children to attend public schools.[8] This decision protects the entire structure of private religious schools in the nation.

Later, the Supreme Court elaborated on its distinction between religious belief and religious practice. *Beliefs* are protected absolutely, but with regard to religious *practices*, the Court has generally upheld governmental restrictions when enacted for valid secular purposes.[9] Thus the government can outlaw religious practices

Free Exercise Clause Clause in the First Amendment to the Constitution that prohibits government from restricting religious beliefs and practices that do not harm society.

that threaten health, safety, or welfare. The Free Exercise Clause does *not* confer the *right* to practice human sacrifice or even the ceremonial use of illegal drugs.[10] Individuals must comply with valid and neutral laws even if these laws restrict religious practices.

But the Supreme Court has continued to face many difficulties in applying its "valid secular test" to specific infringements of religious freedom. When some Amish parents refused to allow their children to attend any school beyond the eighth grade, the state of Wisconsin argued that its universal compulsory school attendance law had a valid purpose: the education of children. The Amish parents argued that high school exposed their children to worldly influences and values contrary to their religious beliefs. The Supreme Court sided with the Amish, deciding that their religious claims outweighed the legitimate interests of the state in education.[11] When a Florida city attempted to outlaw the Santeria (a mix of Catholicism and voodoo) practice of slaughtering animals in religious ceremonies, the Supreme Court held that the city's ordinance was "not neutral" and "targeted" a particular religious ceremony and was therefore unconstitutional.[12]

Yet the Supreme Court has upheld government actions that were challenged as infringements of religious freedom in several key cases. The Court approved an Internal Revenue Service action revoking the tax-exempt status of Bob Jones University because of its rules against interracial dating or marriage among its students. The school argued that its rule was based on religious belief, but the Court held that the government had "an overriding interest in eradicating racial discrimination in education."[13] And the Court upheld an Oregon law that prohibited the possession of peyote (a hallucinogenic drug made from cactus plants) against the claims of a Native American church that its use was a religious sacrament.[14] The Court also upheld an Air Force dress code regulation that prevented orthodox Jews from wearing a yarmulke while in uniform. The Court rejected the argument that the regulation violated the Free Exercise Clause, holding instead that "the mission of the military . . . [including fostering] obedience, unity, commitment and esprit de corps" overrides the individual freedom that would protect civilians from such a government regulation.[15]

No Establishment of Religion
Various meanings have been ascribed to the First Amendment's **No Establishment Clause**.

1. The first meaning—what the writers of the Bill of Rights had in mind—is that it merely prohibits the government from officially recognizing and supporting a national church, like the Church of England in that nation.

2. A second meaning is somewhat broader: the government may not prefer one religion over another or demonstrate favoritism toward or discrimination against any particular religion, but it might recognize and encourage religious activities in general.

3. The most expansive meaning is that the clause creates "a wall of separation between church and state" that prevents government from endorsing, aiding, sponsoring, or encouraging any or all religious activities.

The phrase "separation of church and state" does *not* appear in the Constitution. It was first used by Thomas Jefferson in a letter to a Baptist Church in 1802 assuring them that the federal government would not establish a national church. The current meaning derives from a 1947 decision by Justice Hugo Black, who, writing for the Supreme Court majority, gave the following definition of the **wall-of-separation doctrine**:

Think Again

Do you believe that using tax funds to pay tuition at church-affiliated schools violates the separation of church and state?

No Establishment Clause
Clause in the First Amendment to the Constitution that is interpreted to require the separation of church and state.

wall-of-separation doctrine
The Supreme Court's interpretation of the No Establishment Clause that laws may not have as their purpose aid to one religion or aid to all religions.

Neither a state nor the Federal Government can set up a church. Neither can pass laws which aid one religion, aid all religions, or prefer one religion over another. Neither can force nor influence a person to go to or to remain away from church . . . or force him to profess a belief or disbelief in any religion. . . . No tax in any amount, large or small, can be levied to support any religious activities or institutions, whatever they may be called, or whatever form they may adopt to teach or practice religion.[16]

Although the Supreme Court has generally voiced its support for the wall-of-separation doctrine, on several occasions it has permitted cracks to develop in the wall. In allowing public schools to give pupils regular releases from school to attend religious instructions given outside of the school, Justice William O. Douglas wrote that the state and religion need not be "hostile, suspicious or even unfriendly."[17]

What Constitutes "Establishment"? It has proven difficult for the Supreme Court to reconcile this wall-of-separation interpretation of the First Amendment with the fact that religion plays an important role in the life of most Americans. Public meetings, including sessions of the Congress, often begin with prayers;[18] coins are inscribed with the words "In God We Trust"; and the armed forces provide chaplains for U.S. soldiers.

The Supreme Court has set forth a three-part **Lemon test** for determining whether a particular state law constitutes "establishment" of religion and thus violates the First Amendment. To be constitutional, a law affecting religious activity:

1. Must have a secular purpose.
2. As its primary effect, must neither advance nor inhibit religion.
3. Must not foster "an excessive government entanglement with religion."[19]

Using this three-part test, the Supreme Court held that it was unconstitutional for a state to pay the costs of teachers' salaries or instructional materials in parochial schools. The justices argued that this practice would require excessive government

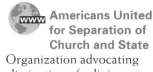

Americans United for Separation of Church and State
Organization advocating elimination of religious activity from public life.
www.au.org

Lemon test To be constitutional, a law must have a secular purpose; its primary effect must neither advance nor inhibit religion; and it must not foster excessive government entanglement with religion.

A Menorah lighting ceremony celebrating Chanukah on public property near the White House. The Supreme Court is divided over whether such public displays violate the No Establishment Clause of the First Amendment.

controls and surveillance to ensure that funds were used only for secular instruction and thus involved "excessive entanglement between government and religion."

However, the Court has upheld the use of tax funds to provide students attending church-related schools with nonreligious textbooks, lunches, transportation, sign-language interpreting, and special education teachers. And the Court has upheld a state's granting of tax credits to parents whose children attend private schools, including religious schools.[20] The Court has also upheld government grants of money to church-related colleges and universities for secular purposes.[21] The Court has ruled that if public buildings are open to use for secular organizations, they must also be opened to use by religious organizations.[22] And the Court has held that a state institution (the University of Virginia) not only can but must grant student activity fees to religious organizations on the same basis as it grants these fees to secular organizations.[23]

The Supreme Court has upheld tax exemptions for churches on the grounds that "the role of religious organizations as charitable associations, in furthering the secular objectives of the state, has become a fundamental concept in our society."[24] It held that schools must allow after-school meetings on school property by religious groups if such a privilege is extended to nonreligious groups.[25] Deductions on federal income tax returns for church contributions are also constitutional. The Supreme Court allows states to close stores on Sundays and otherwise set aside that day, as long as there is a secular purpose—such as "rest, repose, recreation and tranquility"—in doing so.[26]

But the Court has not always acted to "accommodate" religion. In a controversial case, the Court held that a Christmas nativity scene sitting alone on public property was an official "endorsement" of Christian belief and therefore violated the No Establishment Clause. However, if the Christian display was accompanied by a Menorah, a traditional Christmas tree, Santa Claus and reindeer, it would simply be "taking note of the season" and not an unconstitutional endorsement of religion.[27] And in another case, the Supreme Court held that a Louisiana law requiring the teaching of "creationism" along with evolution in the public schools was an unconstitutional establishment of a religious belief.[28]

Prayer in the School   The Supreme Court's most controversial interpretation of the No Establishment Clause involved the question of prayer and Bible-reading ceremonies conducted by public schools. The practice of opening the school day with prayer and Bible-reading ceremonies was once widespread in American

Although the Supreme Court ruled in 1962 (*Engel v. Vitale*) that even voluntary prayer in public schools was an unconstitutional violation of the separation of church and state under the First Amendment, the question of prayer in the schools remains a heated one. Indeed, recent court rulings regarding nondenominational prayers at graduation ceremonies and sporting events have, if anything, further confused the issue.

public schools. To avoid the denominational aspects of these ceremonies, New York State's Board of Regents substituted the following nondenominational prayer, which it required to be said aloud in each class in the presence of a teacher at the beginning of each school day: "Almighty God, we acknowledge our dependence upon Thee, and we beg Thy blessings upon us, our parents, our teachers, and our country." New York argued that this brief prayer did not violate the No Establishment Clause, because the prayer was denominationally neutral and because student participation in the prayer was voluntary. However, in *Engel v. Vitale* (1962), the Supreme Court stated that "the constitutional prohibition against laws respecting an establishment of a religion must at least mean in this country it is no part of the business of government to compose official prayers for any group of the American people to recite as part of a religious program carried on by government." The Court pointed out that making prayer voluntary did not free it from the prohibitions of the No Establishment Clause, and that clause prevented the *establishment* of a religious ceremony by a government agency regardless of whether the ceremony was voluntary.[29]

One year later, in the case of *Abington Township v. Schempp*, the Court considered the constitutionality of Bible-reading ceremonies in the public schools. Here again, even though the children were not required to participate, the Court found that Bible reading as an opening exercise in the schools was a religious ceremony. The justices went to some trouble in the majority opinion to point out that they were not "throwing the Bible out of the schools." They specifically stated that the *study* of the Bible or of religion, when presented objectively and as part of a secular program of education, did not violate the First Amendment; but religious *ceremonies* involving Bible reading or prayer established by a state or school did.[30]

"Voluntary" Prayer   State efforts to encourage "voluntary prayer" in public schools have also been struck down by the Supreme Court as unconstitutional. When the state of Alabama authorized a period of silence for "meditation or voluntary prayer" in public schools, the Court ruled that this action was an "establishment of religion." The Court said the law had no secular purpose, that it conveyed "a message of state endorsement and promotion of prayer," and that its real intent was to encourage prayer in public schools.[31] In a stinging dissenting opinion, Justice William Rehnquist noted that the Supreme Court itself opened its session with a prayer and that both houses of Congress opened every session with prayers led by official chaplains paid by the government. In 1992 the Court held that invocations and benedictions at public high school graduation ceremonies were an unconstitutional establishment of religion.[32] And in 2000 the Court ruled that student-led "invocations" at football games were unconstitutional. A Texas school district that allowed students to use its public address system at football games "to solemnize the event" was violating the No Establishment Clause. "The Constitution demands that schools not force on students the difficult choice between whether to attend these games or to risk facing a personally offensive religious ritual."[33] (See *Up Close:* "Are We One Nation Under God"?)

State Vouchers to Attend Religious Schools   Another important issue arising under the No Establishment Clause is the granting of educational vouchers to parents to spend at any school they choose, including religious schools. State governments redeem the vouchers submitted by schools by paying specific amounts for each student enrolled. When Ohio initiated a "Scholarship Program"

Christian Coalition
Organization dedicated to "take America back" from the "judicial tyranny" that would remove religion from public life.
www.cc.org

UP CLOSE

Are We One Nation "Under God"?

For over one hundred years the years the Pledge of Allegiance has been recited in public school rooms at the beginning of each day. In 1954, at the height of the Cold War, Congress added the words "under God" after "one nation," to emphasize that the United States acknowledged spiritual values in contrast to "godless communism." President Dwight D. Eisenhower, upon signing the bill, said it would strengthen "those spiritual weapons which forever will be our country's most powerful resource in peace and war."

As early as 1943, the Supreme Court declared that public school pupils could not be *required* to recite the pledge. The opinion was widely praised as an expression of our constitutional freedoms: "If there is any fixed star in our constitutional constellation, it is that no official, high or petty, can prescribe what shall be orthodox in politics, nationalism, religion, or other matters of opinion, or force citizens to confess by word or act their faith therein."[a] Pupils who did not wish to take the pledge were free to stand silent in the classroom while the pledge was being recited.

The Supreme Court was called upon to review the phrase "under God" in 2002 when the father of a public school pupil argued that these words constituted an establishment of religion by an instrument of the government, namely the schools, whether or not his daughter was required to participate in the ceremony. He argued that the pledge with "under God" constituted "a ritual proclaiming that there is a God" and therefore violated the No Establishment Clause of the First Amendment. The Words "under God" asserted monotheism and possibly offended atheists, the nonreligious, and others who did not wish to swear an oath of allegiance to a monotheistic deity.

The U.S. Court of Appeals for the Ninth Circuit (with jurisdiction for California and other West Coast states and arguably the most liberal Circuit Court in the nation) agreed that the words "under God" were not neutral and represented a swearing of allegiance to monotheism. The effect of this appeals court's opinion was to remove the words "under God" from the Pledge. However, subsequently it

was revealed that the father (who was divorced) did not have custody over his daughter, and that the custodial mother did not wish her daughter to bring suit over this issue. The Supreme Court, therefore, dismissed the case on this technicality and avoided the substantive issue of whether or not the words "under God" in the Pledge of Allegiance violated the No Establishment Clause.[b] The effect of the Supreme Court's decision was to retain the words.

It can be argued that these words do not refer to any specific religion or deity but simply acknowledge the nation's religious heritage. References to God have long been part of our national identity. Our coins invoke the blessing "In God We Trust," chaplains are provided for the Armed Forces, prayers open the sessions of both chambers of Congress as well as the Supreme Court itself. A strong majority (84 percent) of Americans support the inclusion of the words "under God" in the Pledge of Allegiance.

[a]*West Virginia Board of Education v. Barnette*, 319 U.S. 624 (1943).

[b]*El Grove United School District v. Newdow*, 542 U.S. 277 (2004).

that provided tuition aid to certain students in the Cleveland City School District who could choose to use this aid to attend either public or private or religious schools of their parents' choosing, opponents challenged the program in federal court, arguing that it "advanced a religious mission" in violation of the No Establishment Clause. Although parents could use the vouchers to send their children to other public schools or nonreligious private schools, over 90 percent of the students participating in the scholarship program were enrolled in religiously affiliated schools. In 2002 the U.S. Supreme Court held (in a narrow 5–4 decision) that the program did *not* violate the Constitution.[34] The Court reasoned that the program was neutral with respect to religion and provided assistance directly to citizens who, in turn, directed this aid to religious schools wholly as a result of their own independent private choices. The incidental advancement of a religious mission is reasonably attributed to the individual recipients, not the government, "whose role ends with the distribution of benefits."

Freedom of Speech

Although the First Amendment is absolute in its wording ("Congress shall pass no law . . . abridging the freedom of speech"), the Supreme Court has never been willing to interpret this statement as a protection of *all* speech. What kinds of speech does the First Amendment protect from government control, and what kinds of speech may be constitutionally prohibited?

Think Again

Do you believe that using tax funds to pay tuition at church-affiliated schools violates the separation of church and state?

Clear and Present Danger Doctrine   The classic example of speech that can be prohibited was given by Justice Oliver Wendell Holmes in 1919: "The most stringent protection of free speech would not protect a man in falsely shouting 'fire' in a theater and causing a panic."[35] Although Holmes recognized that the government may prevent speech that creates a serious and immediate danger to society, he objected to government attempts to stifle critics of its policies, such as the Espionage Act of 1917 and the Sedition Act of 1918. The Sedition Act prohibited, among other things, speech that was meant to discourage the sale of war bonds and "disloyal" speech about the government, the Constitution, the military forces, or the flag of the United States. In the case of *Gitlow v. New York*, the majority supported the right of the government to curtail any speech that "tended to subvert or imperil the government," but Holmes dissented, arguing that "every idea is an incitement. It offers itself for belief and if believed it is acted on unless some other belief outweighs it."[36] Unless the expression of an idea created a *serious and immediate danger*, Holmes argued that it should be tolerated and combated or defeated only by the expression of better ideas. This standard for determining the limits of free expression became known as the **clear and present danger doctrine**. Government should not curtail speech merely because it *might tend* to cause a future danger: "The question in every case is whether the words used are used in such circumstances and are of such a nature as to create a clear and present danger that they will bring about the substantive evils that Congress has a right to prevent."[37] Holmes's dissent inspired a long struggle in the courts to strengthen constitutional protections for speech and press (see *Up Close:* "The American Civil Liberties Union").

Although Holmes was the first to use the phrase "clear and present danger," it was Justice Louis D. Brandeis who later developed the doctrine into a valuable constitutional principle that the Supreme Court gradually came to adopt. Brandeis explained that the doctrine involved two elements: (1) the clearness or

clear and present danger doctrine Standard used by the courts to determine whether speech may be restricted; only speech that creates a serious and immediate danger to society may be restricted.

UP CLOSE

The American Civil Liberties Union

The American Civil Liberties Union (ACLU) is one of the largest and most active interest groups devoted to litigation. Its Washington offices employ a staff of several hundred people; it counts on some five thousand volunteer lawyers across the country; and it has affiliates in every state and most large cities. The ACLU claims that its sole purpose is defense of civil liberty, that it has no other political agenda, that it defends the Communist Party and the Ku Klux Klan alike—not because it endorses their beliefs but because "the Bill of Rights is the ACLU's only client."[a] And indeed on occasion it has defended the liberties of Nazis, Klansmen, and other right-wing extremists to express their unpopular views. But most ACLU work has involved litigation on behalf of liberal causes, such as abortion rights, resistance to military service, support for affirmative action, and opposition to the death penalty.

The ACLU was founded in 1920 by Roger Baldwin, a wealthy radical activist who opposed both capitalism and war. Baldwin graduated from Harvard University and briefly taught sociology at Washington University in St. Louis. He refused to be drafted during World War I and served a year's imprisonment for draft violation. In prison, Baldwin joined the Industrial Workers of the World (IWW, or the "Wobblies"), a radical labor union that advocated violence to achieve its goals. In the early 1920s, the ACLU defended socialists, "Bolsheviks," labor organizers, and pacifists against government coercion, including those arrested in the "Red Scare" raids of Attorney General Alexander Mitchell Palmer.

Later the ACLU concentrated its efforts on the defense of First Amendment freedoms of speech, press, religion, and assembly. ACLU member Felix Frankfurter, later a Supreme Court justice, set the tone: "Civil liberty means liberty for those whom we do not like or even detest." In the famous "Monkey Trial" of 1925, the ACLU helped defend schoolteacher John Scopes for having taught the theory of evolution in violation of Tennessee state law. Later, it played a supporting role in the litigation efforts of the National Association for the Advancement of Colored People in the elimination of segregation; it defended Vietnam War protesters; it brought cases to court to ban prayer and religious exercise in pub-

Leigh Johnson, 24, left, a student at the University of California at Berkeley, and Kot Hordynski, 20, right, a student at the University of California at Santa Cruz, answer questions about alleged government spying on student-led protests during a news conference at the offices of the ACLU in San Francisco, Feb. 1, 2006.

lic schools; it has opposed the death penalty and fought for abortion rights; and it defended the rights of people to burn the American flag as a form of symbolic speech.

The ACLU's decision to defend the right of the American Nazi Party to march through Skokie, Illinois, a Chicago suburb with a large Jewish population, including some Holocaust survivors, created a crisis in the organization. The ACLU had defended Nazis and Klansmen before, but the Skokie case engendered more publicity than any earlier cases involving right-wing extremists. Many members quit the organization and financial contributions temporarily declined.

Today, the ACLU is racked by internal arguments over politically correct speech codes and over whether "hate crimes" (crimes committed with racist, sexist, antihomosexual, or similar motives) should invoke harsher sentences than the same crimes committed for other motives. "Pure" First Amendment defenders in the organization oppose speech codes and hate crime legislation, while many liberal members rationalize these penalties on speech and thought.

Former Supreme Court Chief Justice Earl Warren once said of the ACLU, "It is difficult to appreciate how far our freedoms might have eroded had it not been for the Union's valiant representation in the courts of the constitutional rights of people of all persuasions."[b]

[a]William A. Donohue. *The Politics of the American Civil Liberties Union* (New Brunswick, N.J.: Transaction Books, 1985), p. 3.

[b]Quoted in *ACLU Annual Report*, 1977, cited in ibid., p. 2.

seriousness of the expression; and (2) the immediacy of the danger flowing from the speech. With regard to immediacy he wrote,

> No danger flowing from speech can be deemed clear and present, unless the incidence of the evil apprehended is so imminent that it may befall before there is opportunity for full discussion. If there be time to expose through discussion the falsehood and fallacies, to avert the evil by the processes of education, the remedy to be applied is more speech, not enforced silence.

And with regard to seriousness he wrote,

> Moreover, even imminent danger cannot justify resort to prohibition [of speech] . . . unless the evil apprehended is relatively serious. Prohibition of free speech and assembly is a measure so stringent that it would be inappropriate as the means for averting a relatively trivial harm to society. . . . There must be the probability of serious injury to the State.[38]

Preferred Position Doctrine   Over the years, the Supreme Court has given the First Amendment freedoms of speech, press, and assembly a special **preferred position** in constitutional law. These freedoms are especially important to the preservation of democracy. If speech, press, or assembly are prohibited by government, the people have no way to correct the government through democratic processes. Thus the burden of proof rests on the *government* to justify any restrictions on speech, writing, or assembly.[39] In other words, any speech or writing is presumed constitutional unless the government proves that a serious and immediate danger would ensue if the speech were allowed.

preferred position Refers to the tendency of the courts to give preference to the First Amendment rights to speech, press, and assembly when faced with conflicts.

The Cold War Challenge   Despite the Supreme Court's endorsement of the clear and present danger and preferred position doctrines, in times of perceived national crisis the courts have been willing to permit some government restrictions of speech, press, and assembly. At the outbreak of World War II, just prior to U.S. entry into that world conflict, Congress passed the Smith Act, which stated,

> It shall be unlawful for any person to knowingly or willfully advocate, abet, advise, or teach the duty, necessity, desirability, or propriety of overthrowing or destroying any government in the United States by force or violence, or by the assassination of any officer of any such government.

Congress justified its action in terms of national security, initially as a protection against fascism during World War II, then later as a protection against communism in the early days of the Cold War.

In 1949 the Department of Justice prosecuted Eugene V. Dennis and ten other top leaders of the Communist Party of the United States for violation of the Smith Act. A jury found them guilty of violating the act, and the party leaders were sentenced to jail terms ranging from one to five years. In 1951 the case of *Dennis v. United States* came to the Supreme Court on appeal. In upholding the conviction of the Communist Party leaders, the Court seemed to abandon Brandeis's idea that "present" meant "before there is opportunity for full discussion."[40] It seemed to substitute clear and *probable* for clear and *present*.

Since that time, however, the Supreme Court has returned to a policy closer to the original clear and present danger doctrine. As the Cold War progressed, Americans grew to view communism as a serious threat to democracy, but not a *present* danger. The overthrow of the American government advocated by

The Supreme Court ruled in 2003 that cross burning was meant to intimidate and was therefore *not* protected as symbolic speech by the First Amendment.

freedom of expression
Collectively, the First Amendment rights to free speech, press, and assembly.

symbolic speech Actions other than speech itself but protected by the First Amendment because they constitute political expression.

 **American Civil Liberties Union (ACLU)**
This American Civil Liberties Union Web site provides ample information about the ACLU as an organization and the issues it deals with.
www.aclu.org

communists was not an incitement to *immediate* action. A democracy must not itself become authoritarian to protect itself from authoritarianism. In later cases, the Supreme Court held that the mere advocacy of revolution, apart from unlawful action, is protected by the First Amendment.[41] It struck down federal laws requiring communist organizations to register with the government,[42] laws requiring individuals to sign "loyalty oaths,"[43] laws prohibiting communists from working in defense plants,[44] and laws stripping passports from Communist Party leaders.[45] In short, once the perceived Cold War crisis began to fade, the Supreme Court reasserted the First Amendment rights of individuals and groups.

Symbolic Speech   The First Amendment's guarantees of speech, press, and assembly are broadly interpreted to mean **freedom of expression**. Political expression encompasses more than just words. For example, when Mary Beth Tinker and her brothers were suspended for wearing black armbands to high school to protest the Vietnam War, they argued that the wearing of armbands constituted **symbolic speech** protected by the First Amendment. The Supreme Court agreed, noting that the school did not prohibit all wearing of symbols but instead singled out this particular expression for disciplinary action.[46]

The Supreme Court continues to wrestle with the question of what kinds of conduct are symbolic speech protected by the First Amendment and what kinds of conduct are outside of this protection (see *Up Close:* "We Can Burn the Flag But Not the Cross"). Symbolic speech, like speech itself, cannot be banned just because it offends people. "If there is only one bedrock principle underlying the First Amendment, it is that the Government may not prohibit the expression of an idea simply because society finds the idea itself offensive or disagreeable."[47]

Speech and Public Order   The Supreme Court has wrestled with the question of whether speech can be prohibited when it stirs audiences to public disorder, not because the speaker urges lawless action but because the audience reacts to the speech with hostility. In short, can a speaker be arrested because of the *audience's* disorderly behavior? In an early case, the Supreme Court fashioned a *fighting words doctrine*, to the effect that words that "ordinary men know are likely to cause a fight" may be prohibited.[48] But later the Court seemed to realize that this doctrine, if broadly applied, could create a huge constitutional hole in the First Amendment guarantee of free speech. Authorities could curtail speech simply because it met with audience hostility. The Court recognized that "speech is often provocative and challenging. It may . . . have profound unsettling effects. . . . That is why freedom of speech, while not absolute, is nevertheless protected against censorship."[49] The Court has also held that the First Amendment protects the use of four-letter words when used to express an idea: "One man's vulgarity may be another's lyric."[50] And the Court has consistently refused to allow government authorities to ban speech *before* it has occurred simply because they believe it *may* create a disturbance.

Campus Speech   Many colleges and universities have undertaken to ban speech that is considered racist, sexist, homophobic, or otherwise "insensitive" to the feelings of women and minorities. Varieties of "speech codes," "hate codes," and sexual harassment regulations that prohibit verbal expressions raise serious constitutional questions, especially at state-supported colleges and universities. The First Amendment includes insulting or offensive racist or sexist words or comments in its protection (see *Up Close:* "Political Correctness versus Free Speech on Campus"). Many of these college and university regulations would not withstand a judicial challenge if students or faculty undertook to oppose them in federal court.

UP CLOSE

We Can Burn the Flag but Not the Cross

Symbolic speech continues to create difficulties for the Supreme Court. Two separate cases illustrate the problems in protecting symbolic speech.

Burning the Flag

Flag desecration is a physical act, but it also has symbolic meaning—for example, hatred of the United States or opposition to government policies. At the 1984 Republican national convention in Dallas, Gregory Lee Johnson joined a protest march against Reagan Administration policies and then doused an American flag with kerosene and set fire to it. As it burned, he and others chanted, "America, the red, white, and blue, we spit on you." Police arrested Johnson and charged him with violating a Texas law against flag desecration. The American Civil Liberties Union came to Johnson's defense, arguing that flag burning is "symbolic speech" protected by the First Amendment.

In the case of Texas v. Johnson (1989), a majority of Supreme Court justices argued that "Johnson's burning of the flag was conduct sufficiently imbued with elements of communication to implicate the First Amendment." They declared that when speech and conduct are combined in the same expressive act, the government must show that it has "a sufficiently important interest in regulating the non-speech element to justify incident limitations on First Amendment freedoms." In this case, "preserving the flag as a symbol of nationhood and national unity" was not deemed sufficiently important to justify limiting Johnson's freedom of expression.[a] A later effort in Congress to pass a constitutional amendment banning flag desecration failed to garner enough votes.

Burning the Cross

The Supreme Court has long recognized that threats to commit unlawful violence on a particular individual or group of individuals is unlawful speech. In an early case the Court had held that wearing Ku Klux Klan hoods and gathering to burn a cross were protected symbolic speech. However, in 2003 the Court upheld a Virginia statute that prohibited the burning of a cross "with the intent of intimidating any person or group" and asserting that "any such burning . . . shall be prima facie evidence of an intent to intimidate." The Supreme Court cited the long history of cross burnings as a form of intimidation and a threat of impending violence. "As the history of cross burning in this country shows, that act is often intimidating, intended to create a pervasive fear in victims that they are a target of violence." Therefore, "The First Amendment permits Virginia to outlaw cross burnings done with the intent to intimidate because burning a cross is a particularly virulent form of intimidation."[b]

[a]*Texas v. Johnson*, 491 U.S. 397 (1989).
[b]*Virginia v. Black*, 538 U.S. 343 (2003).

Hate Speech and Hate Crimes   "Hate" speech is usually defined as hostile or prejudicial attitudes expressed toward another person's or group's characteristics, notably sex, race, ethnicity, religion, or sexual orientation. Banning hate speech is now common at colleges and universities, in business employment and sports enterprises, on radio and television, and in the press. But do *government* prohibitions on hate speech violate the First Amendment?

Historically the Supreme Court viewed prohibitions on offensive speech as unconstitutional infringements of First Amendment freedoms. "The remedy to be applied is more speech, not enforced silence."[51]

The Supreme Court was called upon to review prohibitions on hate speech in 1992 when the city of St. Paul, Minnesota, enacted an ordinance prohibiting any communication that "arouses anger, alarm, or resentment among others on the basis of race, color, creed, religion, or gender." The ordinance defined such expressions as "disorderly conduct" and made them misdemeanors punishable by law. But the Supreme Court, in a unanimous decision, struck down the city's effort to prohibit expressions only because they cause "hurt feelings, offense, or resentment." Speech expressing racial, gender, or religious intolerance is still speech, and it is protected by the First Amendment.[52]

National Association of Scholars
Advocacy organization opposing speech codes and other PC violations of individual freedom on campuses. *www.nas.org*

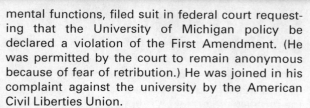

UP CLOSE

Political Correctness Versus Free Speech on Campus

Universities have a very special responsibility to protect freedom of expression. The free and unfettered exchange of views is essential to the advancement of knowledge—the very purpose of universities. For centuries universities have fought to protect academic freedom from pressures arising from the world *outside* of the campus—governments, interest groups, financial contributors—arguing that the university must be a protected enclave for free expression of ideas. But today's threat to academic freedom arises from *within* universities— from efforts by administrations, faculty, and campus groups to suppress ideas, opinions, and language that are not "politically correct" (PC). PC activists seek to suppress opinions and expressions they consider to be racist, sexist, "homophobic," or otherwise "insensitive" to specified groups.[a]

Speech Codes

The experience at the University of Michigan with its "Policy on Discrimination and Discriminatory Harassment" illustrates the battles occurring on many campuses over First Amendment rights. In 1988 a series of racial incidents on campus prompted the university to officially ban "any behavior verbal or physical" that "stigmatized" an individual "on the basis of race, ethnicity, religion, sex, sexual orientation, creed, national origin, ancestry, age, marital status, handicap, or Vietnam-era veteran status" or that created "an intimidating, hostile, or demeaning environment for educational pursuits." A published guide provided examples of banned activity, which included the following:

- A male student makes remarks in class like "women just aren't as good in this field as men."
- Jokes about gay men and lesbians.
- Commenting in a derogatory way about a particular person or group's physical appearance or sexual orientation, or their cultural origins, or religious beliefs.

Free Speech

In 1989 "John Doe," a psychology graduate student studying gender differences in personality traits and mental functions, filed suit in federal court requesting that the University of Michigan policy be declared a violation of the First Amendment. (He was permitted by the court to remain anonymous because of fear of retribution.) He was joined in his complaint against the university by the American Civil Liberties Union.

In its decision, the court acknowledged that the university had a legal responsibility to prevent racial or sexual discrimination or harassment. However, it did not have a right to

> establish an anti-discrimination policy which had the effect of prohibiting certain speech because it disagreed with ideas or messages sought to be conveyed. . . . Nor could the University proscribe speech simply because it was found to be offensive, even gravely so, by large numbers of people. . . . These principles acquire a special significance in the University setting, where the free and unfettered interplay of competing views is essential to the institution's educational mission. . . . While the Court is sympathetic to the University's obligation to ensure educational opportunities for all of its students, such efforts must not be at the expense of free speech.[b]

It seems ironic that students and faculty now must seek the protection of the federal courts from attempts by universities to limit speech. Traditionally, universities themselves fought to protect academic freedom. Academic freedom included the freedom of faculty and students to express themselves in the classroom, on the campus, and in writing, on controversial and sensitive topics, including race and gender. It was recognized that students often express ideas that are biased or ill informed, immature, or crudely expressed. But students were taught that the remedy for offensive language or off-color remarks or ill-chosen examples was more enlightened speech, not the suppression of speech.

[a]Dinesh D'Souza, *Illiberal Education: The Politics of Race and Sex on Campus* (New York: Vintage Books, 1992).
[b]*John Doe v. University of Michigan*, 721 F. Supp. 852 (1989).

However, the Supreme Court is willing to recognize that bias-motivated crimes—crimes intentionally directed at a victim because of his or her race, religion, disability, national origin, or sexual orientation—may be more heavily punished than the same crimes inspired by other motives. The Court held that a criminal defendant's "abstract beliefs, however obnoxious to most people, may not be taken into consideration by a sentencing judge."[53] But a defendant's *motive* for committing a particular criminal act has traditionally been a factor in sentencing, and a defendant's verbal statements can be used to determine motive.

Commercial Speech   Do First Amendment freedoms of expression apply to commercial advertising? The Supreme Court has frequently asserted that **commercial speech** is protected by the First Amendment. The Court held that states cannot outlaw price advertising by pharmacists[54] or advertising for services by attorneys[55] and that cities cannot outlaw posting "For Sale" signs on property, even in the interests of halting white flight and promoting racially integrated neighborhoods. Advertising is the "dissemination of information" and is constitutionally protected.[56]

> **commercial speech**
> Advertising communications given only partial protection under the First Amendment to the Constitution.

However, the Court has also been willing to weigh the First Amendment rights of commercial advertisers against the public interest served by regulation. In other words, the Court seems to suspend its preferred position doctrine with regard to commercial advertising and to call for a "balancing of interests." Thus, the Supreme Court has allowed the Federal Communications Commission to regulate the contents of advertising on radio and television and even to ban advertising for cigarettes. The Federal Trade Commission enforces "truth" in advertising by requiring commercial packages and advertisers to prove all claims for their products.

Libel and Slander   Libel and slander have never been protected by the First Amendment against subsequent punishment (see "Libel and Slander" in Chapter 6). Once a communication is determined to be libelous or slanderous, it is outside of the protection of the First Amendment. The courts have traditionally defined "libel" as a "damaging falsehood." However, if plaintiffs are public officials they must prove that the statements made about them are not only false and damaging but also "made with actual malice"—that is, with knowledge that they are false or with "reckless disregard" of the truth—in order to prove libel.[57]

Privacy, Abortion, and the Constitution

A right of "privacy" is not expressly provided for anywhere in the Constitution. But does the word *liberty* in the First and Fourteenth Amendments include a constitutional right to privacy?

Finding a Right to Privacy   The U.S. Supreme Court found a right of privacy in the Constitution when it struck down a Connecticut law prohibiting the use of contraceptives in 1965. Estelle Griswold had opened a birth control clinic on behalf of the Planned Parenthood League of that state and was distributing contraceptives in violation of the state statute prohibiting their use. She challenged the constitutionality of the statute, even though there is no direct reference to birth control in the Bill of Rights. The Supreme Court upheld Griswold's challenge, finding a right of privacy, according to Justice William O. Douglas, in the "penumbras formed by the emanations from" the First, Third, Fourth, Fifth, Ninth, and Fourteenth Amendments. "Various guarantees create a zone of

Pro-life and pro-choice activists confront each other outside the Supreme Court in 1992 after the justices issued their ruling in *Planned Parenthood of Pennsylvania v. Casey.*

privacy. . . . Would we allow the police to search the sacred precincts of marital bedrooms for telltale signs of the use of contraceptives? The very idea is repulsive to the notion of privacy surrounding the marriage relationship." In concurrent opinions, other justices found the right of privacy in the Ninth Amendment: "The enumeration in the Constitution of certain rights, shall not be construed to deny or disparage others retained by the people."[58]

Roe v. Wade   The fact that the *Griswold Case* dealt with reproduction gave encouragement to groups advocating abortion rights. In 1969 Norma McCorvey sought an abortion in Texas but was refused by doctors who cited a state law prohibiting abortion except to save a woman's life. McCorvey challenged the Texas law in federal courts on a variety of constitutional grounds, including the right to privacy. McCorvey became "Jane Roe," and the case became one of the most controversial in the Supreme Court's history.[59]

The Supreme Court ruled that the constitutional right of privacy as well as the Fourteenth Amendment's guarantee of "liberty" included a woman's decision to bear or not to bear a child. The Court held that the word "person" in the Constitution did *not* include the unborn child; therefore, the Fifth and Fourteenth Amendments' guarantee of "life, liberty, or property" did not protect the "life" of the fetus. The Court also ruled that a state's power to protect the health and safety of the mother could not justify any restriction on abortion in the first three months of pregnancy. Between the third and sixth months of pregnancy, a state could set standards for abortion procedures in order to protect the health of women, but a state could not prohibit abortions. Only in the final three months could a state prohibit or regulate abortion to protect the unborn.

Rather than end the political controversy over abortion, *Roe v. Wade* set off a conflagration. Congress defeated efforts to pass a constitutional amendment restricting abortion or declaring that life begins at conception. However, when Congress banned the use of federal funds under Medicaid (medical care for the poor) for abortions except to protect the life of a woman, the Supreme Court upheld the ban, holding that there was no constitutional obligation for governments to *pay* for abortions.[60]

Pro-Choice America
Formerly the National Abortion Rights Action League (NARAL), with information on current legislation and court cases.
www.prochoiceamerica.org

National Right to Life Committee
Leading anti-abortion organization with information on current legislation and court cases.
www.nrlc.org

Reaffirming *Roe v. Wade* Abortion has become such a polarizing issue that "pro-choice" and "pro-life" groups are generally unwilling to search out a middle ground. Yet the current Supreme Court appears to have chosen a policy of affirming a woman's right to abortion while upholding modest restrictions, as evidenced by the Court's ruling in *Planned Parenthood of Pennsylvania v. Casey* (1992).[61]

In this case, the Supreme Court considered a series of restrictions on abortion enacted by Pennsylvania: Physicians must inform women of risks and alternatives; women must wait twenty-four hours after requesting an abortion before having one; and the parents of minors must be notified. It struck down a requirement that spouses be notified. Later, the court struck drawn a parental notification law that did not provide an exception for a judge to withhold notification when it would not be in the best interest of the minor.

Justice Sandra Day O'Connor took the lead in forming a moderate, swing bloc on the Court. Her majority opinion strongly reaffirmed the fundamental right of abortion, both on the basis of the Fourteenth Amendment and on the principle of stare decisis. But the majority also upheld states' rights to protect any fetus that reached the point of "viability." The Court went on to establish a new standard for constitutionally evaluating restrictions: they must not impose an "undue burden" on women seeking abortion or place "substantial obstacles" in her path. All of Pennsylvania's restrictions met this standard and were upheld except spousal notification.

"Partial Birth Abortion" A number of states have attempted to outlaw an abortion procedure known as "intact dilation and evacuation" or "partial birth" abortion. This procedure, which is used in very few abortions, involves partial delivery of the fetus feet-first, then vacuuming out the brain and crushing the skull to ease complete removal. In a surprise 5 to 4 decision, with Justice O'Connor supporting the majority, the Supreme Court declared a Nebraska law prohibiting the procedure to be an unconstitutional "undue burden" on a woman's right to an abortion. The Nebraska law failed to make an exception in its prohibition of the procedure "for the preservation of the health of the mother."[62]

Congress passed a ban on partial birth abortions in 2003 and President George Bush signed it into law. (Earlier bans passed by Congress had been vetoed by President Bill Clinton.) The new law provides an exception—allowing the method if it is necessary to save a mother's life. Proponents of the law hope that this exception will make it acceptable to a majority of the Supreme Court.

Sexual Conduct "Liberty gives substantial protection to adult persons in deciding how to conduct their lives in matters pertaining to sex." This Supreme Court ruling in *Lawrence v. Texas* (2003) struck down a state law against homosexual sodomy. The ruling overturned an earlier case in which the Court held that the Constitution granted no "fundamental right to homosexuals to engage in acts of consensual sodomy."[63] Rather, the Supreme Court decided that "The liberty protected by the Constitution allows homosexual persons the right to choose to enter upon relationships in the confines of their homes and their own private lives and still retain their dignity as free persons."[64]

Other Private Activities How far does the right of privacy extend? The Supreme Court appears to have left this question open to argument. In 1969 the Court held that privacy may be constitutionally protected where there is a "reasonable expectation of privacy," notably in one's own home. The Court overturned a criminal conviction for the "mere private possession of obscene material," that is, the possession and viewing of pornography at home.[65]

Gay Marriage   The Supreme Court has not yet spoken out on gay marriages—marriages between persons of the same sex. Several state courts, including the Supreme Court of Massachusetts, have held that the Equal Protection Clause of the Fourteenth Amendment entitles gay couples to marry, that to deny them marriage rights while recognizing heterosexual marriages amounts to discrimination. The issue is complicated by the constitutional provision that requires all states to give "Full Faith and Credit" to judicial proceedings of other states (see *What Do You Think:* "Federalism and Same-Sex Marriages" in Chapter 4). This provision implies that gay marriages in any state must be recognized in all states. Congress passed a Defense of Marriage Act in 1996 declaring that no state need recognize a gay marriage. But Congress failed to pass a constitutional amendment banning same-sex marriage (see *What Do You Think?:* "Should We Amend the Constitution to Ban Gay Marriages?").

A Right to Die?   In most states, for most of the nation's history, it has been a crime to help another person to commit suicide. Michigan's prosecution of Dr. Jack Kevorkian for publicly participating in physician-assisted suicides launched a nationwide debate on the topic. More important, a group of physicians in Washington, along with their gravely ill patients, filed suit in federal court seeking a declaration that their state's law banning physician-assisted suicide violated the "liberty" guaranteed by the Fourteenth Amendment. They argued that mentally competent, terminally ill patients had the "right to die"; that is, they had a privacy right to request and receive aid in ending their life. They relied on the Supreme Court's previous rulings on abortion, contending that Washington's law placed an undue burden on the exercise of a privacy right. But the U.S. Supreme Court held that there is no *constitutional right* to physician-assisted suicide.[66] The Court implied that if the laws governing the practice are to be changed, they must be changed by legislatures, not by reinterpreting the Constitution.

Patients have a right to refuse treatment, even if by so doing they ensure their own deaths. Life-sustaining procedures can be ended at the request of a family member only if there is "clear and convincing evidence" that the patient would not want these procedures.[67] Most states now recognize "living wills" in which people express their wishes while still of sound mind. The absence of a living will, and disputes within the family over what a comatose patient would wish, can cause prolonged and bitter court fights.

Obscenity and the Law

Obscene materials of all kinds—words, publications, photos, videotapes, films— are *not* protected by the First Amendment. Most states ban the publication, sale, or possession of obscene material, and Congress bans its shipment in the mails. Because obscene material is not protected by the First Amendment, it can be banned without even an attempt to prove that it results in antisocial conduct. In other words, it is not necessary to show that obscene material would result in a clear and present danger to society, the test used to decide the legitimacy of *speech*. In order to ban obscene materials, the government need only prove that they are *obscene*.

Defining "obscenity" has confounded legislatures and the courts for years, however. State and federal laws often define pornography and obscenity in such terms as "lewd," "lascivious," "filthy," "indecent," "disgusting"—all equally as vague as "obscene." "Pornography" is simply a synonym for "obscenity." *Soft-core pornography* usually denotes nakedness and sexually suggestive poses; it is less

WHAT DO YOU THINK?

Should We Amend the Constitution to Ban Gay Marriages?

President George W. Bush asked Congress to pass a constitutional amendment to be sent to the states for ratification, an amendment that would ban gay marriages: "After more than two centuries of American jurisprudence and a millennium of human experience, a few judges and local authorities are presuming to change the most fundamental institution of civilization." Congress has before it an amendment which says: "Marriage in the United States shall consist only of the union of a man and a woman. Neither this Constitution or the Constitution of any state, nor state or federal law, shall be construed to require that marital status or the legal incidents thereof be conferred upon unmarried couples or groups."

In general, Americans oppose same-sex marriages. Various polls over time indicate that almost two-thirds of the public oppose gay marriages.

Q. Should same-sex marriages be recognized by law as valid with the same rights as traditional marriages?

Yes 32%   No 64%

However, many Americans are reluctant to amend the Constitution to define marriage as strictly between a man and a woman.

Q. Do you favor a constitutional amendment that would define marriage as being between a man and a woman, thus barring same-sex marriages?

Yes 53%   No 44%

And Americans are divided over whether federal or state laws should govern same-sex marriage.

Q. Do you think laws regarding same-sex marriage should be determined by the federal government or individual state governments?

Federal 48%   State 46%

Source: As reported in *USA Today*, February 25, 2004.

Despite protests in support of gay marriage, most states and the Congress in its Protection of Marriage Act declare that a legal marriage can be only "between a man and a woman."

likely to confront legal barriers. *Hard-core pornography* usually denotes explicit sexual activity. After many fruitless efforts by the Supreme Court to come up with a workable definition of "pornography" or "obscenity," a frustrated Justice Potter Stewart wrote in 1974, "I shall not today attempt further to define [hard-core pornography]. . . . But *I know it when I see it.*"[68]

Slackening Standards: *Roth v. United States*   The Court's first comprehensive effort to define "obscenity" came in *Roth v. United States* (1957). Although the Court upheld Roth's conviction for distributing pornographic magazines through the mails, it defined "obscenity" somewhat narrowly: "Whether to the average person applying contemporary community standards, the dominant theme of the material, taken as a whole, appeals to prurient interests."[69]

Note that the material must be obscene to the *average* person, not to children or particular groups of adults who might be especially offended by pornography. The standard is "contemporary," suggesting that what was once regarded as obscene might be acceptable today. Later, the *community standard* was clarified to mean the "society at large," not a particular state or local community.[70] The material must be "considered as a whole," meaning that even if a work includes some obscene material, it is still acceptable if its "dominant theme" is something other than "prurient." The Court added that a work must be "utterly without redeeming social or literary merit" in order to be judged obscene.[71] The Court never really said what a "prurient" interest was but reassured everyone that "sex and obscenity are not synonymous."

Tightening Standards: *Miller v. California*   The effect of the Roth decision, and the many and varied attempts by lower courts to apply its slippery standards, tended to limit law enforcement efforts to combat pornography during the 1960s and 1970s. The Supreme Court itself came under ridicule when it was learned that the justices had set up a movie room in the basement of the Supreme Court building to view films that had been brought before them in obscenity cases.[72]

So the Supreme Court tried again, in *Miller v. California* (1973), to give law-enforcement officials some clearer standards in determining obscenity. Although the Court retained the "average person" and "contemporary" standards, it redefined "community" to mean the *local* community rather than the society at large. It also defined "prurient" as "patently offensive" representations or descriptions of "ultimate sex acts, normal or perverted, actual or simulated," as well as "masturbation, excretory functions, and lewd exhibition of the genitals." It rejected the earlier requirement that the work had to be "utterly without redeeming social value" in order to be judged obscene, and it substituted instead "lacks serious literary, artistic, political, or scientific value."[73]

The effect of the Supreme Court's *Miller* standards has been to increase the likelihood of conviction in obscenity-pornography cases. It is easier to prove that a work lacks serious value than to prove that it is utterly without redeeming merit. Moreover, the *local community standard* allows prosecution of adult bookstores and X-rated video stores in some communities, while allowing the same stores to operate in other communities. The Supreme Court has also upheld local ordinances that ban nudity in public places, including bars and lounges. The Court rejected the argument that nude dancing was "expressive" conduct.[74]

Porn on the Internet   New technologies continue to challenge courts in the application of First Amendment principles. Currently the Internet, the global computer communication network, allows users to gain access to information

Internet Freedom Organization opposed to all forms of censorship and content regulation on the Internet. *www.netfreedom.org*

UP CLOSE

Child Pornography

In 1982 the U.S. Supreme Court struck a hard blow against child pornography—the "dissemination of material depicting children engaged in sexual conduct regardless of whether the material is obscene."[a] Such material includes any visual depiction of children performing sexual acts or lewdly exhibiting their genitals. The Court reasoned that films or photographs of sexual exploitation and abuse of children were "intrinsically related" to criminal activity; such material was evidence that crime has been committed. Thus the test for *child* pornography was much stricter than the standards set for obscene material. It is not necessary to show that the sexual depiction of children is "obscene" (under the *Miller* standards) in order to ban such material; it is only necessary to show that children were used in the production of the material.

But what if the images of children involved in sexual activity are produced by means other than using real children, such as the use of youthful-looking adults or computer-imaging technology? In the Child Pornography Prevention Act of 1996, Congress tried to prohibit "any visual depiction, including any photograph, film, video, picture, or computer or computer-generated image . . . [that] is, or appears to be, of a minor engaging in sexually explicit conduct." Congress did not construct this act to meet the *Miller* standards; it prohibited *any* depictions of sexually explicit activity by children, whether or not they contravened community standards or had serious redeeming value.

But the Supreme Court, in a highly controversial (6–3) decision, held that there was an important distinction between actual and virtual child pornography. Virtual child pornography and adults posing as minors do not directly involve the exploitation or abuse of children. The Court held that the congressional definition of child pornography was overly broad; the mere assertion that such material might encourage pedophiles to seduce children was not sufficient to prohibit it. "The First Amendment requires a more precise restriction."[b]

[a]*New York v. Ferber,* 458 U.S. 747 (1982).

[b]*Ashcroft v. Free Speech Coalition,* 535 U.S. 234 (2002).

---

worldwide. Thousands of electronic bulletin boards give computer users access to everything from bomb-making instructions and sex conversations to obscene photos and even child pornography. Many commercial access services ban obscene messages and exclude bulletin boards with sexually offensive commentary. Software programs that screen out pornography Web sites are readily available to consumers. But can *government* try to ban such material from the Internet without violating First Amendment freedoms?

Congress tried unsuccessfully to ban "indecent" and "patently-offensive" communications from the Internet in its Communications Decency Act of 1996. Proponents of the law cited the need to protect children from pornography. But in 1997 the Supreme Court held the act unconstitutional: "Notwithstanding the legitimacy and importance of the Congressional goal of protecting children from harmful materials, we agree that the statute abridges freedom of speech protected by the First Amendment." Government cannot limit Internet messages "to only what is fit for children." The Supreme Court agreed with the assertion that "as the most participatory form of mass speech yet developed [the Internet] deserves the highest protection from government intrusion."[75] (See also *Up Close: "Child Pornography"*).

Freedom of the Press

Democracy depends on the free expression of ideas. Authoritarian regimes either monopolize the media or subject them to strict licensing and censorship of their content. The idea of a free and independent press is deeply rooted in the evolution of democratic government.

prior restraint Government actions to restrict publication of a magazine, newspaper, or books on grounds of libel, obscenity, or other legal violations prior to actual publication of the work.

No-Prior-Restraint Doctrine   Long before the Bill of Rights was written, English law protected newspapers from government restrictions or licensing prior to publication—a practice called **prior restraint**. This protection, however, does not mean that publishers are exempt from *subsequent punishment* for libelous, obscene, or other illegal publications. Prior restraint is more dangerous to free expression because it allows the government to censor the work prior to publication and forces the defendants to *prove* that their material should *not* be censored. In contrast, subsequent punishment requires a trial in which the government must prove that the defendant's published materials are unlawful.

In *Near v. Minnesota* (1931), a muckraking publication that accused local officials of trafficking with gangsters was barred from publishing under a Minnesota law that prohibited the publication of a "malicious, scandalous or defamatory newspaper." The Supreme Court struck down the law as unconstitutional, affirming the *no-prior-restraint doctrine*. However, a close reading of the majority opinion reveals that the doctrine is not absolute. Chief Justice Charles Evans Hughes noted that prior government censorship might be constitutional "if publication . . . threatened the country's safety in times of war."[76]

Yet the question of whether or not the government can restrain publication of stories that present a serious threat to national security remains unanswered. For example, can the government restrain the press from reporting in advance on the time and place of an impending U.S. military action, thereby warning an enemy and perhaps adding to American casualties? In the most important case on this question, *New York Times v. United States* (1971), the Supreme Court upheld the right of the newspaper to publish secret documents that had been stolen from State Department and Defense Department files. The material covered U.S. policy decisions in Vietnam, and it was published while the war was still being waged. But five separate (concurring) opinions were written by justices in the majority as well as two dissenting opinions. Only two justices argued that government can *never* restrain any publication regardless of the seriousness or immediacy of the harm. Others in the majority cited the government's failure to show proof in this case that publication "would surely result in direct, immediate, and irreparable damage to our nation or its people."[77] Presumably, if the government had produced such proof, the case might have been decided differently. The media interpret the decision as a blanket protection to publish anything they wish regardless of harm to government or society.

Film Censorship   The no-prior-restraint doctrine was developed to protect the print media—books, magazines, newspapers. When the motion picture industry was in its infancy, the Supreme Court held that films were "business, pure and simple" and were not entitled to the protection of the First Amendment.[78] But as films grew in importance, the Court gradually extended First Amendment freedoms to cover motion pictures.[79] However, the Supreme Court has not given the film industry the same strong no-prior-restraint protection it has given the press. The Court has approved government requirements for prior submission of films to official censors, so long as (1) the burden of proof that the film is obscene rests with the censor; (2) a procedure exists for judicial determination of the issue; and (3) censors are required to act speedily.[80] To avoid government-imposed censorship the motion picture industry adopted its own system of rating films:

> *G:* suitable for all audiences
>
> *PG:* parental guidance suggested

PG-13: parental guidance strongly suggested for children under thirteen

R: restricted to those seventeen or older unless accompanied by a parent or guardian

NC-17: no one under seventeen admitted

Some city governments have sought to restrict showing of NC-17 films, and their restrictions have been upheld by the Courts.[81]

Radio and Television Censorship The Federal Communications Commission was created in 1934 to allocate broadcast frequencies and to license stations. The exclusive right to use a particular frequency is a "public trust." Thus, broadcasters, unlike newspapers and magazines, are licensed by the government and subject to government rules. Although the First Amendment protects broadcasters, the Supreme Court has recognized the special obligations that may be imposed on them in exchange for the exclusive right to use a broadcast frequency. "No one has a First Amendment right to a license or to monopolize a radio frequency; to deny a station license because 'the public interest' requires it, is not a denial of free speech."[82] Thus the Court has upheld FCC-imposed "equal time" and "fairness" rules against broadcasters, even while striking down government attempts to impose the same rules on newspapers.[83]

Media Claims for Special Rights The news media make various claims to special rights arising out of the First Amendment's guarantee of a free press. Reporters argue, for example, that they should be able to protect their news sources and are not obliged to give testimony in criminal cases when they have obtained evidence in confidence. However, the only witnesses the Constitution exempts from compulsory testimony are defendants themselves, who enjoy the Fifth Amendment's protection against "self-incrimination." The Supreme Court has flatly rejected reporters' claims to a privilege against compulsory testimony. "We cannot seriously entertain the notion that the First Amendment protects a newsman's agreement to conceal the criminal conduct of his source, or evidence thereof, on the theory that it is better to write about a crime than to do something about it."[84]

Despite these rulings, reporters regularly boast of their willingness to go to jail to protect sources, and many have done so. But the media have also pressured the nation's legislatures for protection. Congress has passed the Privacy Protection Act, which sharply limits the ability of law-enforcement officials to search press offices, and many states have passed **shield laws** specifically protecting reporters from giving testimony in criminal cases.

shield laws Laws in some states that give reporters the right to refuse to name their sources or to release their notes in court cases; may be overturned by the courts when such refusals jeopardize a fair trial for a defendant.

Television networks hope to avoid government-imposed censorship by offering warnings such as "viewer discretion advised."

Freedom of Assembly and Petition

The First Amendment guarantees "the right of the people peaceably to assemble, and to petition the government for redress of grievances." The right to organize political parties and interest groups derives from the right of assembly. And freedom of petition protects most lobbying activities.

The Right of Association   Freedom of assembly includes the right to form and join organizations and associations. In an important case during the early civil rights movement, the state of Alabama attempted to harass the National Association for the Advancement of Colored People by requiring it to turn over its membership lists to authorities. The Supreme Court held the state's action to be an unconstitutional infringement of the freedom of association.[85]

The Supreme Court has also protected the right of students to form organizations. "First Amendment rights . . . are available to teachers and students. It can hardly be argued that either teachers or students shed their constitutional rights at the school house gate."[86] Attempts by a college or university to deny official recognition to a student organization based on its views violates the right of association.

Protests, Parades, and Demonstrations   Freedom of assembly includes the right to peacefully protest, parade, and demonstrate. Authorities may, within reasonable limits, enact restrictions regarding the "time, place, and manner" of an assembly so as to preserve public order, smooth traffic flow, freedom of movement, and even peace and quiet. But these regulations cannot be unevenly applied to groups with different views. Thus authorities may require a permit to parade, but they cannot deny a permit to a group because of the nature of their views or content of their message. For example, the Supreme Court held that city authorities in Skokie, Illinois, acted unconstitutionally in prohibiting the American Nazi Party from holding a march in that city even though it was populated with large numbers of Jewish survivors of the Holocaust.[87]

Picketing   Assemblies of people have a high potential for creating a public disturbance. Parades block traffic and litter the streets; loudspeakers assault the ears of local residents and bystanders; picket lines may block the free passage of others. Although the right of assembly is protected by the First Amendment, its exercise involves conduct as well as expression, and therefore it is usually subject to greater government regulation than expression alone. The Court has generally upheld reasonable use of public property for assembly, but it has not forced *private* property owners to accommodate speeches or assemblies. Airport terminals, shopping malls, and other open forums, which may or may not be publicly owned, have posed problems for the courts.

Freedom of assembly is currently being tested by opponents of abortion who picket abortion clinics, hoping to embarrass and dissuade women from entering them. Generally the courts have allowed limits on these demonstrations to ensure that people can move freely in and out of the clinics. Freedom of assembly does not include the right to block access to public or private buildings. And when abortion opponents demonstrated at the residence of a physician who performed abortions, the Supreme Court upheld a local ordinance barring assemblies in residential neighborhoods.[88] Physically obstructing access to buildings almost always violates state or local laws, as does the threat or use of force by picketers. The Supreme Court made a distinction between a "fixed buffer zone," prohibiting assembly around a building entrance, and a "floating buffer zone" (of 15 feet), prohibiting demonstrators from approaching individuals in public places. The "fixed"

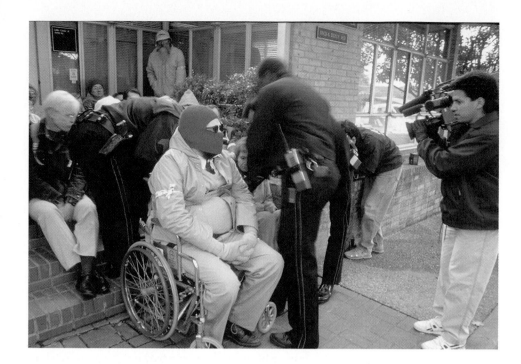

No rights are absolute. The freedom to assemble does not include the right to block public access to buildings. Congress reaffirmed this limitation in 1994 in a law guaranteeing access to abortion clinics.

zone was held to be a constitutional limit on assembly but the "floating" zone was held to be an unconstitutional limit on free speech.[89] In 1994 Congress passed a federal law guaranteeing access to abortion clinics, arguing that the federal government should act to guarantee a recognized constitutional right.

Protecting Property Rights

The Fifth Amendment provides specific protection for private property against government confiscation: "nor shall private property be taken for public use without just compensation." This **takings clause** recognizes that occasionally governments—federal, state, or local—may be obliged to take property from private owners for public uses, for example, streets, roads, public buildings, parks and the like. But the Founders wanted to be certain that even these "takings" from private owners would have some constitutional protection. Taking land from private owners who do not wish to sell it to the government is known as eminent domain. The Fifth Amendment's takings clause guarantees that the taking of private property by the government for public use can only be done with just compensation being paid to the owner. Usually a city or state tries to purchase land from the owners in a mutually agreed transaction. But if the owners do not wish to sell or do not agree with the government's offered price, the issue is determined by a court in what is known as **eminent domain** proceedings. In these proceedings a city or state must go to court and show that the land is needed for a legitimate public purpose; the court will then establish a fair price (just compensation) based on testimony from the owner, the city or state, and impartial appraisers.

takings clause The Fifth Amendment's prohibition against government taking of private property without just compensation.

eminent domain The action of a government to take property for public use with just compensation even if the owner does not wish to sell.

Public Use   Takings under eminent domain are valid only when the property is to be put to "public use." But what constitutes a "public use"? Traditionally, public use referred to goods that served the general public, including schools, highways, public buildings, public memorials, and other facilities open to the public generally. Over time, however, the public use clause was given expanded meaning. Eminent domain was used in urban renewal projects to eliminate slums and blighted areas of a city.

But what if the property taken under eminent domain is not a slum or blighted area but rather a residential area not unlike residential areas elsewhere in the city, and the government proposes to give the taken property to private developers to build new residences and offices and facilities for new businesses—"city revitalization"? The city of New London, Connecticut, exercised its eminent domain power by taking a number of residential properties from owners who did not wish to sell for the purposes of economic development. The city proposed to give these properties to private developers for projects that would create new jobs and garner new revenues for the city. The Supreme Court, in reviewing the city's action, acknowledged that "the sovereign may not take the property of A for the sole purpose of transferring it to another private party B, even if A is paid just compensation." The Court seemed to say that if the only beneficiary of the government taking of private property was another private party, it would violate the Fifth Amendment's takings clause. But the Court reasoned that economic development was a public purpose, arguing that the definition of "public use" can be "broad and inclusive" and that the legislative body rather than the courts should make the determination of whether a project would generally serve the public interest.[90] The fact that a taking benefited some private parties more than others did not make it unconstitutional.

This Supreme Court decision allowing an eminent domain taking for sale to private developers seemed to undermine the Fifth Amendment's takings clause. It caused a stir among politicians, the media, and the general public. Some states have considered more restrictive definitions of "public use" than the Supreme Court's, a legislative action that the Court said it would allow.

Takings   What if the government does not "take" ownership of a property but instead restricts the owner's use of it through regulation? Zoning ordinances, environmental regulations, or building and housing codes may reduce the value of a property to the owner. Should the owner be compensated for the loss of full use?

Courts have recognized that governments can make laws to protect the health, safety, and general welfare of its citizens. Owners of property have never been entitled to any compensation for obeying laws or ordinances with a clear public purpose. Yet it was still argued that some city regulations, especially those designed for beauty and aesthetics, had no relation to public health or safety, but rather they simply enacted somebody's preferences over those of their neighbor. But in 1954 the Supreme Court upheld a very broad interpretation of the police power: "It is within the power of the Legislature to determine that the community should be beautiful as well as healthy, spacious as well as clean, well-balanced as well as carefully patrolled."[91] The Court made it difficult to challenge the constitutionality of local planning and zoning ordinances as a "taking" of private property without compensation even though it reduced the value of property to the owner.

Yet in 1992 the Supreme Court stepped in to hold that a regulation that denies a property owner of *all* economically beneficial use of his land (for example, a state coastal zone management regulation preventing any construction on a beach lot) was a "taking" that requires just compensation to the owner in order to be constitutional.[92] But the court did not address the question of how far governments can go in regulating land use without compensating property owners.

Depriving land owners of *all* beneficial uses of their land without compensation is clearly unconstitutional. But what if their use of land is devalued by 50 percent or 25 percent? In recent years both Congress and the federal courts, as well as some states, have undertaken to reconsider "how far" governments can go in depriving property owners of value uses of their land.

The Right to Bear Arms

The Second Amendment to the U.S. Constitution states: "A well regulated Militia, being necessary to the security of a free State, the right of the people to keep and bear Arms, shall not be infringed."

Bearing Arms   What is meant by the right of the people "to keep and bear arms"? One view is that the Second Amendment confers on Americans an *individual* constitutional right, like the First Amendment freedom of speech or press. The history surrounding the adoption of the Second Amendment reveals the concern of colonists with attempts by despotic governments to confiscate the arms of citizens and render them helpless to resist tyranny. James Madison wrote in the *Federalist Papers*, No. 46 that "the advantage of being armed which the Americans possess over the people of almost every other nation, forms a barrier against the enterprise of [tyrannical] ambition.[93] The Second Amendment was adopted with little controversy; most state constitutions at the time, like Pennsylvania's, declared that "the people have a right to bear arms for the defense of themselves and the state." Early American political rhetoric was filled with praise for an armed citizenry able to protect its freedoms by force if necessary.

State Militias   But many constitutional scholars argue that the Second Amendment protects only the *collective* right of the states to form militias—that is, their right to maintain National Guard units. They focus on the qualifying phrase

— Think Again —

Do law-abiding citizens have a constitutional right to carry a handgun for self-protection?

 **Right to Keep and Bear Arms**
Organizations advocating self-defense rights with information on legislation, court cases, and so forth.
www.rkba.org

www **Brady Campaign**
The nation's leading gun control organization, with facts, legislation, and a "report card" on each state.
www.bradycampaign.org

The Second Amendment's "right to bear arms" can be interpreted to guarantee an individual's right to own guns (as asserted by these protestors), or only as a grant of power to the states to maintain National Guard units.

WHAT DO YOU THINK?

Gun Control?

New controls on guns are a common policy demand following highly publicized murders or assassination attempts. The Federal Gun Control Act of 1968 was a response to the assassinations of Sen. Robert F. Kennedy and Martin Luther King Jr. in that year, and efforts to legislate additional restrictions occurred after attempts to assassinate presidents Gerald Ford and Ronald Reagan. Today various federal gun control laws include the following:

- A ban on interstate and mail-order sales of handguns
- Prohibition of the sale of firearms to convicted felons
- A requirement that all firearms *dealers* be licensed by the federal Bureau of Alcohol, Tobacco, Firearms, and Explosives
- Requirements that manufacturers record the serial number of all firearms and that dealers record all sales
- Restrictions of private ownership of automatic weapons and military weapons.

Finally there is the *Brady Law* requirement for a five-day waiting period for the purchase of a handgun. (The law was named for James S. Brady, former press secretary to President Ronald Reagan, who was severely wounded in the 1981 attempted assassination of the president.) Handgun dealers must send police agencies a form completed by the buyer; police agencies have five days to make certain the purchaser is not a convicted felon.

Gun Laws and Crime

There is no systematic evidence that gun control laws reduce violent crime. If we compare violent crime rates in jurisdictions with very restrictive gun laws (for example, New York, Massachusetts, New Jersey, Illinois, and the District of Columbia, all of which prohibit the possession of handguns by citizens) to crime rates in jurisdictions with very loose controls, we find no difference in rates of violent crime that cannot be attributed to social conditions.[a]

The Second Amendment

Proponents of gun control cite the 1939 Supreme Court decision in *United States v. Miller*, a case in which a defendant challenged a federal law prohibiting the transportation of sawed-off shotguns in interstate commerce.[b] The defendant claimed that the law infringed upon his right to keep and bear arms. But the Supreme Court held that a sawed-off shotgun had no "relationship to the preservation or efficiency of a well regulated militia" and rejected the defendant's challenge to the law. The clear implication of this decision is that the right to bear arms refers only to a state's right to maintain a militia. However, a U.S. Court of Appeals in 2001 ruled that: "All of the evidence indicates that the Second Amendment like other parts of the Bill of Rights, applies to and protects individual Americans ... in their right to keep and bear arms whether or not they are a member of a select militia or performing active military service."[c]

Public Opinion

Public opinion clearly opposes a nationwide prohibition on the sale of handguns to citizens. Various polls report that 65 to 75 percent of the public does *not* wish to deprive citizens of the right to own guns. However, there is considerable support for various laws respecting gun owners.[d]

[a]Douglas R. Murray, "Handguns, Gun Control Laws and Firearms Violence," *Social Problems*, 23 (June 1975, 26–35); James D. Wright and Peter H. Rossi, *Weapons, Crime and Violence in America* (Washington, D.C.: National Institute of Justice, 1981); Gary Kleck, *Targeting Guns* (New York: Aldine de Gruyter, 1997).
[b]*United States v. Miller*, 307 U.S. 174 (1939).
[c]*United States v. Emerson*, 5th Cir., Oct. 2001.
[d]Various polls from Public Agenda, *www.publicagenda.org*.

	Favor	Oppose
Background checks on people buying guns	92%	6%
Trigger locks on stored guns	81	15
A ban on the sale of assault weapons	71	27
Requiring gun owners to attend a course on gun safety	84	12
A ban on people carrying concealed weapons	49	48

Perhaps most controversial is the proposal to require all gun owners to register with the government. The National Rifle Association (NRA) believes that this is the first step in the government effort to seize all citizen-owned guns. However, the general public seems to favor gun registration.

Requiring gun owners to register with the government	75	24

"a well-regulated Militia, being necessary to the security of a free State." The Second Amendment merely prevents Congress from denying the states the right to organize their own military units. If the Founders had wished to create an individual right to bear arms, they would not have inserted the phrase about a "well-regulated militia." (Opponents of this view argue that the original definition of a militia included all free males over eighteen.) Interpreted in this fashion, the Second Amendment does *not* protect private groups who form themselves into militias, nor does it guarantee citizens the right to own guns.

Rights of Criminal Defendants

While society needs the protection of the police, it is equally important to protect society from the police. Arbitrary searches and arrests, imprisonment without trial, forced confessions, beatings and torture, secret trials, tainted witnesses, excessive punishments, and other human rights violations are all too common throughout the world. The U.S. Constitution limits the powers of the police and protects the rights of the accused (see Table 14.2). (See also *What Do You Think?:* "Should Victims' Rights Be Added to the Constitution?")

The Guarantee of the Writ of Habeas Corpus   One of the oldest and most revered rights in English common law is the right to obtain a **writ of habeas corpus**, which is a court order directing public officials who are holding a person in custody to bring the prisoner into court and explain the reasons for confinement. If a judge finds that the prisoner is being unlawfully detained, or finds insufficient evidence that a crime has been committed or that the prisoner could have committed it, the judge must order the prisoner's release. Thus the writ of habeas corpus is a means to test the legality of any imprisonment (see *What Do You Think?:* "Are Persons Captured on the Battlefields of Afghanistan and Iraq Entitled to Protections of the U.S. Constitution?").

The writ of habeas corpus was considered so fundamental to the Framers of the Constitution that they included it in the original text of Article I: "The privilege of the Writ of Habeas Corpus shall not be suspended, unless when in Cases of Rebellion or Invasion the public Safety may require it." Despite the qualifying phrase, the Supreme Court has never sanctioned suspension of the writ of habeas corpus even during wartime. President Abraham Lincoln suspended the writ of habeas corpus in several areas during the Civil War, but in the case of *Ex parte Milligan* (1866), the Supreme Court ruled that the president had acted unconstitutionally.[94] (With the war over, however, the Court's decision had no practical effect.) Again, in 1946, the Supreme Court declared that the military had had no right to substitute military courts for ordinary courts in Hawaii during World War II, even though Hawaii was in an active theater of war.[95] State courts cannot issue writs of habeas corpus to federal officials, but federal judges may issue such writs to state officials whenever there is reason to believe that a person is being held in violation of the Constitution or laws of the United States.

The Prohibition of Bills of Attainder and Ex Post Facto Laws   Like the guarantee of habeas corpus, protection against bills of attainder and ex post facto laws was considered so fundamental to individual liberty that it was included in the original text of the Constitution. A **bill of attainder** is a legislative act inflicting punishment without judicial trial. An **ex post facto law** is a retroactive criminal law that works against the accused—for example, a law that makes an act criminal after the act is committed or a law that increases the punishment

www **Bureau of Alcohol, Tobacco, Firearms, and Explosives**
Federal agency responsible for regulation of alcohol, tobacco, firearms, and explosives; site includes publications on gun crimes.
www.atf.gov

— Think Again —

Do you believe that the seizure of property believed by police to be used in drug trafficking, without a judicial hearing or trial, violates civil liberty?

writ of habeas corpus
Court order directing public officials who are holding a person in custody to bring the prisoner into court and explain the reasons for confinement; the right to habeas corpus is protected by Article I of the Constitution.

bill of attainder   Legislative act inflicting punishment without judicial trial; forbidden under Article I of the Constitution.

ex post facto law
Retroactive criminal law that works against the accused; forbidden under Article I of the Constitution.

Table 14.2 Individual Rights in the Criminal Justice Process

Rights	Process
Fourth Amendment: Protection against unreasonable searches and seizures Warranted searches for sworn "probable cause." Exceptions: consent searches, safety searches, car searches, and searches incident to a valid arrest.	**Investigation by law-enforcement officers** Expectation that police act lawfully.
Fifth Amendment: Protection against self-incrimination Miranda rules (see Figure 14.1, p. 527). **Habeas corpus** Police holding a person in custody must bring that person before a judge with cause to believe that a crime was committed and the prisoner committed it.	**Arrest** Arrests based on warrants issued by judges and magistrates. Arrests based on crimes committed in the presence of law enforcement officials. Arrests for "probable cause."
Eighth Amendment: No excessive bail Defendant considered innocent until proven guilty; release on bail and amount of bail depends on seriousness of crime, trustworthiness of defendant, and safety of community.	**Hearing and bail** Preliminary hearing in which prosecutor presents testimony that a crime was committed and probable cause for charging the accused.
Fifth Amendment: Grand jury (federal) Federal prosecutors (but not necessarily state prosecutors) must convince a grand jury that a reasonable basis exists to believe the defendant committed a crime and he or she should be brought to trial.	**Indictment** Prosecutor, or a grand jury in federal cases, issues formal document naming the accused and specifying the charges.
Sixth Amendment: Right to counsel Begins in investigation stage, when officials become "accusatory"; extends throughout criminal justice process. Free counsel for indigent defendants.	**Arraignment** Judge reads indictment to the accused and ensures that the accused understands charges and rights and has counsel. Judge asks defendant to choose a plea: Guilty, *nolo contendere* (no contest), or not guilty. If defendant pleads guilty or no contest, a trial is not necessary and defendant proceeds to sentencing.
Sixth Amendment: Right to a speedy and public trial Impartial jury. Right to confront witnesses. Right to compel favorable witnesses to testify. **Fourth Amendment: Exclusionary rule** Illegally obtained evidence cannot be used against defendant.	**Trial** Impartial judge presides as prosecuting and defense attorneys present witnesses and evidence relevant to guilt or innocence of defendant and make arguments to the jury. Jury deliberates in secret and issues a verdict.
Eighth Amendment: Protection against cruel and unusual punishments	**Sentencing** If the defendant is found not guilty, the process ends. Defendants who plead guilty or no contest and defendants found guilty by jury are sentenced by fine, imprisonment, or both by the judge. Sentences imposed must be commensurate to the crimes committed.
Fifth Amendment: Protection against double jeopardy Government cannot try a defendant again for the same offense.	**Appeal** Defendants found guilty may appeal to higher courts for reversal of verdict or a new trial based on errors made anywhere in the process.

WHAT DO YOU THINK

Should Victims' Rights Be Added to the Constitution?

The U.S. Constitution includes fifteen specific guarantees of the rights of the accused. It makes no mention of victims' rights.

Liberal California Democratic U.S. Senator Dianne Feinstein and conservative Arizona Republican U.S. Senator Jon Kyl have co-sponsored an amendment to the Constitution that would guarantee to victims of violent crime:

- To be informed of and not be excluded from critical proceedings including:
  arraignment
  preliminary hearing
  trial
  sentencing
  appeals hearing
  parole hearings
- To be heard at proceedings involving a release from custody, sentencing, or acceptance of a negotiated plea
- To notice of any release or escape of the offender
- To a disposition free from unreasonable delay
- To an order of restitution from the convicted offender
- To have the safety of the victims considered in determining a release from custody
- To notice of the victim's rights.

Supporters of a constitutional amendment, a "Crime Victims' Bill of Rights," argue that each year there are millions of victims of violent crime, many of whom are victimized a second time by the criminal justice system itself. They are not notified of the arrest, arraignment, or trial of the person accused of harming them, nor are they guaranteed a hearing at crucial stages of the judicial process— plea-bargaining, sentencing, or parole. Polls show that victims' rights are overwhelmingly supported by the American people. The Senate Judiciary Committee has approved of the victims' rights amendment to the Constitution, and it has the support of President George W. Bush.

But to date the sponsors of the amendment have failed to gather the necessary two-thirds vote of both houses of Congress to send the amendment to the states for ratification. Opponents argue that more than half the states already have added victims' rights amendments to their state constitutions. They argue that it is unnecessary to further clutter the U.S. Constitution with a lengthy amendment that is likely to cause additional litigation and delay in criminal cases.

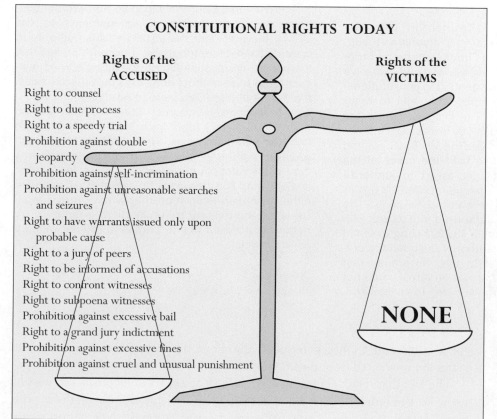

CONSTITUTIONAL RIGHTS TODAY

Rights of the
ACCUSED

Right to counsel
Right to due process
Right to a speedy trial
Prohibition against double
jeopardy
Prohibition against self-incrimination
Prohibition against unreasonable searches
and seizures
Right to have warrants issued only upon
probable cause
Right to a jury of peers
Right to be informed of accusations
Right to confront witnesses
Right to subpoena witnesses
Prohibition against excessive bail
Right to a grand jury indictment
Prohibition against excessive fines
Prohibition against cruel and unusual punishment

Rights of the
VICTIMS

NONE

*The Need for a Victims'
Rights Amendment*

Source: From the Office of U.S.
Senator Dianne Feinstein.

WHAT DO YOU THINK?

Are Persons Captured on the Battlefields of Afghanistan and Iraq Entitled to the Protections of the U.S. Constitution?

The United States has held 6,000 or more "enemy combatants" captured on the battlefields of Afghanistan and Iraq for several years. Some are held at the U.S. base in Guantanamo Bay, Cuba.

Prisoners of war have never been entitled to constitutional protection. Prisoners of war are uniformed members of the military forces of a nation. (The U.S. held tens of thousands of German and Japanese prisoners of war during World War II.) They are entitled only to "humane treatment" under the Geneva Accords. They are not released until the war is ended.

"Detainees" from the war on terrorism are not officially prisoners of war, inasmuch as they are not uniformed soldiers of any nation. The United States has pledged humane treatment even though the government argues that these detainees are not protected by the Geneva Accords. They are not held on U.S. soil. As military detainees, they were not given lawyers or access to courts or, in most cases, even identified by name.

But in a controversial decision in 2004 the Supreme Court held that enemy combatants captured on the battlefield and "imprisoned in territory over which the United States exercises an exclusive jurisdiction and control" are entitled to constitutional rights including habeas corpus—the right to bring their case to U.S. courts. "The fact that petitioners are being held in military custody is immaterial."[a]

In response, President George W. Bush created special military tribunals to hear the cases of the detainees. Congress was not asked to authorize these tribunals. Rather, the president cited his power as Commander-in-Chief in wartime to do so. He noted that Congress had authorized him to use military force to fight terrorism in its 2001 congressional resolution and that such authority included the creation of special military tribunals. He argued that "enemy combatants" in the war on terror could not be brought to trial in criminal cases in civilian U.S.

Detainees in the war on terrorism do not have the same procedural rights as American citizens. Prisoners at the U.S. base in Guantanamo Bay are to be tried in special military tribunals established by Congress in 2006, following a Supreme Court decision that the president alone cannot decide how to try them.

courts. The procedures used in these tribunals did not incorporate the Uniform Code of Military Justice (UCMJ), which was established by congressional statute. (For example, the accused was not entitled to see and hear all of the evidence against him, on the grounds that to do so might jeopardize intelligence sources and methods.)

The Supreme Court held in 2006 that without congressional authorization or amendments to the UCMJ, the president had exceeded his authority in creating the military tribunals.[b] The court implied that there were no reasons why the military should conduct these trials without applying court-martial rules. If the rules of the UCMJ were to be changed, it would have to be done by Congress. Congress had made no mention of military tribunals in its 2001 resolution to fight terrorism. Moreover, the Court held that certain provisions of the Geneva Accords did protect persons "in a conflict not of an international character."

Following the decision, President Bush pledged either to obtain legislation that would form a legal basis for the military tribunals or to arrange to try detainees accused of war crimes in regular military courts-martial.

[a]*Rasul v. Bush*, 542 U.S. 466 (2004).
[b]*Hamdan v. Rumsfeld*, June 29, 2006.

for a crime and applies it retroactively. Both the federal government and the states are prevented from passing such laws.

The fact that relatively few cases of bills of attainder or ex post facto laws have come to the federal courts does not diminish the importance of these protections. Rather, it testifies to the widespread appreciation of their importance in a free society.

Unreasonable Searches and Seizures   Individuals are protected by the Fourth Amendment from "unreasonable searches and seizures" of their private "persons, houses, papers, and effects." The Fourth Amendment lays out specific rules for searches and seizures of evidence: "No warrants shall issue, but upon probable cause, supported by Oath or affirmation, and particularly describing the place to be searched, and the persons or things to be seized." Judges cannot issue a **search warrant** just to let police see *if* an individual has committed a crime; there must be "probable cause" for such issuance. The indiscriminate searching of whole neighborhoods or groups of people is unconstitutional and is prevented by the Fourth Amendment's requirement that the place to be searched must be specifically described in the warrant. The requirement that the things to be seized must be described in the warrant is meant to prevent "fishing expeditions" into an individual's home and personal effects on the possibility that some evidence of unknown illegal activity might crop up. The only exception is if police, in the course of a valid search for a specified item, find other items whose very possession is a crime—for example, illicit drugs.

But the courts also permit police to undertake various other "reasonable" searches *without* a warrant: searches in connection with a valid arrest; searches to protect the safety of police officers; searches to obtain evidence in the immediate vicinity and in the suspect's control; searches to preserve evidence in danger of being immediately destroyed; and searches with the consent of a suspect. Indeed, most police searches today take place without warrant under one or another of these conditions. The Supreme Court has also allowed automobile searches and searches of open fields without warrants in many cases. The requirement of "probable cause" has been very loosely defined; even a "partially corroborated anonymous informant's tip" qualifies as "probable cause" to make a search, seizure, or arrest.[96] And if the police, while making a warranted search, or otherwise lawfully on the premises, see evidence of a crime "in plain view," they may seize such evidence without further authorization.[97] And the Court recently approved "no-knock searches," reversing a long tradition of requiring police to knock and identify themselves before breaking into a home. However, the Court has held that merely stopping a car for a traffic violation does not give police excuse for a search of the car for drugs.[98]

Wiretapping and Electronic Surveillance   For many years the Supreme Court refused to view wiretapping as a search and seizure within the meaning of the Fourth Amendment.[99] However, over time as electronic surveillance techniques became more common and more sophisticated, the Court changed its position. The Court began to view wiretapping and electronic surveillance as a challenge to privacy rights implied by the Fourth Amendment; the Court held that such law enforcement techniques required "probable cause" and a warrant. The government may not undertake to eavesdrop where a person has "a reasonable expectation of privacy" without first showing probable cause and obtaining a warrant.[100] Congress has also enacted a law prohibiting federal agents from intercepting a wire, oral, or electronic communication without first obtaining a warrant.

FISA and Domestic Surveillance   In the Foreign Intelligence Surveillance Act of 1978 (FISA), Congress created a special FISA court to oversee the collection of electronic intelligence within the United States. It required all intelligence agencies, including the National Security Agency, which is responsible for the collection of electronic intelligence, to obtain warrants upon a showing that

search warrant   Court order permitting law-enforcement officials to search a location in order to seize evidence of a crime; issued only for a specified location, in connection with a specific investigation, and on submission of proof that "probable cause" exists to warrant such a search.

New technologies continuously challenge the right of privacy implied by the Fourth Amendment. Here, a video camera monitors a Connecticut preschool.

the surveillance is required for investigation of possible attacks upon the nation. The FISA court is secret, and the persons under surveillance are not notified.

Nevertheless, President Bush authorized the National Security Agency to intercept international calls to and from Americans—calls involving known or suspected terrorists—without a FISA warrant. The president claimed that he has inherent constitutional powers as Commander-in-Chief to gather intelligence during war or armed conflict and that the United States is currently at war with international terrorists. The president also claims that a joint resolution of Congress passed following the 9/11 terrorist attack on America included "authorization for the use of military force" and that such authorization includes warrantless surveillance of suspected terrorists both inside and outside of the United States.

Opponents of warrantless surveillance argue that the president is bound by the FISA Act, which specifically requires court warrants for surveillance within United States, including international calls. Congress did not authorize warrantless surveillance in its 9/11 joint resolution. Moreover, Congress did authorize surveillance of American citizens in terrorist investigations *but only* with a warrant issued by the FISA court. Congress was direct and specific on the subject of domestic surveillance in the FISA Act even during wartime. And as far back as 1952, the Supreme Court held that when Congress has addressed a specific issue by law, the president is obliged to follow that law in dealing with the issue.[101] The president, opponents claim, is acting unconstitutionally and unlawfully in authorizing warrantless surveillance of American citizens.

Drug Testing   "Unreasonable" drug testing violates the Fourth Amendment. But the Supreme Court has held that it is reasonable to impose mandatory drug testing on railroad workers, federal law-enforcement agents, and even students participating in athletics.[102] However, when the state of Georgia enacted a law requiring drug testing for candidates for public office, the Court found it to be an "unreasonable" search in violation of the Fourth Amendment.[103] Apparently mandatory drug testing in occupations affecting public safety and drug testing in schools to protect children are reasonable, while suspicionless drug testing of the general public is not.

A CONFLICTING VIEW

Terrorism Requires Restrictions on Civil Liberties

The terrorist attack on America of September 11, 2001, was the most horrific violence committed against innocent American citizens in recent times. It created a new examination of Americans' commitment to personal freedoms and their willingness to trade these freedoms for the safety and security of society. All of the polls taken shortly after the attack indicated that Americans were prepared to accept many new restrictions on their freedom—more surveillance of their papers and communications, more searches of their belongings, roundups of suspected immigrants, and even prolonged detention without recourse to the courts. As time passed, however, fewer Americans expressed a willingness to sacrifice basic civil liberties to prevent additional acts of terrorism.[a]

Following the attack, Congress moved swiftly to enact the "PATRIOT" Act, officially the Uniting and Strengthening America Act by Providing Appropriate Tools Required to Intercept and Obstruct Terrorism of 2001. President Bush and Attorney General John Ashcroft successfully lobbied Congress to increase the federal government's powers of search, seizure, surveillance, and detention of suspects. The concerns of civil libertarians were largely swept aside. The act was passed nearly unanimously in the Senate (98–1) and overwhelmingly in the House (357–66), with the support of both Democrats and Republicans. The Act was extended in 2005, with only minor changes.

Among the key provisions of the USA PATRIOT Act:

- *Roving wiretaps:* Allows wiretaps of any telephones that suspects might use instead of requiring separate warrants for each line.
- *Internet tracking:* Allows law enforcement authorities to track Internet communications, that is, to "surf the Web" without obtaining warrants.
- *Business records:* Allows investigators to obtain information from credit cards, bank records, con-

sumer purchases, hospitals, libraries, schools and colleges, and so forth with secret warrants.

- *Foreign Intelligence Surveillance Court:* A special Foreign Intelligence Surveillance Court, originally established in 1978 to separate intelligence investigations from criminal investigation, may issue search warrants on an investigator's assertion that the information sought is relevant to a terrorist investigation. No showing of "probable cause" is required. The warrant is not made public, in order to avoid "tipping off" the subject.
- *Property seizure:* Authorizes the seizure of the property of suspected terrorists. Persons whose property is seized bear the burden of proof that the property was not used for terrorist purposes in order to secure the return of their property.
- *Detention:* Allows the detention of suspected terrorists for lengthy periods without judicial recourse.
- *Aliens reporting and detention:* Authorizes the Immigration and Customs Enforcement, or ICE (formerly the Immigration and Naturalization Service, or INS) to indefinitely detain illegal aliens suspected of terrorist connections.
- *Prohibits harboring of terrorists:* Creates a new federal crime—knowingly harboring persons who have committed, or are about to commit, a terrorist act.

What factors affect Americans' willingness to trade off restrictions on civil liberties in order to provide for safety and security from terrorism? Political science research suggests that the greater people's sense of threat, the greater their support for restrictions on civil liberties. The lower people's trust in government, the less willing they are to trade off civil liberties for security. Liberals are less willing to trade off civil liberties than moderates or conservatives. Overall it seems clear that Americans' commitment to civil liberties is highly contingent on their concerns about threats to national or personal security.

[a]Darren W. Davis and Brian D. Silver, "Civil Liberties vs. Security: Public Opinion in the Context of the Terrorist Attacks on America," *American Journal of Political Science* 48 (January 2004): 28–46.

Arrests The Supreme Court permits *arrests without warrants* (1) when a crime is committed in the presence of an officer; and (2) when an arrest is supported by "probable cause" to believe that a crime has been committed by the person apprehended.[104] However, the Court has held that police may not enter a home to arrest its occupant without either a warrant for the arrest or the consent of the owner.[105]

indictment Determination by a grand jury that sufficient evidence exists to warrant trial of an individual on a felony charge; necessary before an individual can be brought to trial.

grand jury Jury charged only with determining whether sufficient evidence exists to support indictment of an individual on a felony charge; the grand jury's decision to indict does not represent a conviction.

grant of immunity from prosecution Grant by the government to an individual of freedom from prosecution on a particular charge in return for testimony by that individual that might otherwise be self-incriminating.

Indictment The Fifth Amendment requires that an **indictment** be issued by a **grand jury** before a person may be brought to trial on a felony offense. This provision was designed as a protection against unreasonable and harassing prosecutions by the government. In principle, the grand jury is supposed to determine whether the evidence submitted to it by government prosecutors is sufficient to place a person on trial. In practice, however, grand juries spend very little time deliberating on the vast majority of cases. Neither defendants nor their attorneys are permitted to testify before grand juries without the prosecution's permission, which is rarely given. Thus the prosecutor controls the information submitted to grand juries and instructs them in their duties. In almost all cases, grand juries accept the prosecution's recommendations with little or no discussion. Thus grand juries, whose hearings are secret, do not provide much of a check on federal prosecutors, and their refusal to indict is very rare.

Self-Incrimination and the Right to Counsel Freedom from self-incrimination had its origin in English common law; it was originally designed to prevent persons from being tortured into confessions of guilt. It is also a logical extension of the notion that individuals should not be forced to contribute to their own prosecution, that the burden of proof rests on the state. The Fifth Amendment protects people from both physical and psychological coercion.[106] It protects not only accused persons at their own trial but also witnesses testifying in trials of other persons, civil suits, congressional hearings, and so on. Thus "taking the Fifth" has become a standard phrase in our culture: "I refuse to answer that question on the grounds that it might tend to incriminate me." The protection also means that judges, prosecutors, and juries cannot use the refusal of people to take the stand at their own trial as evidence of guilt. Indeed, a judge or attorney is not even permitted to imply this to a jury, and a judge is obligated to instruct a jury not to infer guilt from a defendant's refusal to testify.

It is important to note that individuals may be forced to testify when they are not themselves the object of a criminal prosecution. Government officials may also extend a **grant of immunity from prosecution** to a witness in order to compel testimony. Under a grant of immunity, the government agrees not to use any of the testimony against the witness; in return, the witness provides information that the government uses to prosecute others who are considered more dangerous or more important than the immune witness. Because such grants ensure that nothing the witnesses say can be used against them, immunized witnesses cannot refuse to answer under the Fifth Amendment.

The Supreme Court under Chief Justice Earl Warren greatly strengthened the Fifth Amendment protection against self-incrimination and the right to counsel in a series of rulings in the 1960s:

- *Gideon v. Wainwright* (1963): Equal protection under the Fourteenth Amendment requires that free legal counsel be appointed for all indigent defendants in all criminal cases.[107]

- *Escobedo v. Illinois* (1964): Suspects are entitled to confer with counsel as soon as police investigation focuses on them or once "the process shifts from investigatory to accusatory."[108]

- *Miranda v. Arizona* (1966): Before questioning suspects, a police officer must inform them of all their constitutional rights, including the right to counsel (appointed at no cost to the suspect if necessary) and the right to remain silent. Although suspects may knowingly waive these rights, the police cannot question anyone who at any point asks for a lawyer or declines "in any manner" to be

METROPOLITAN POLICE DEPARTMENT
Warning As To Your Rights

You are under arrest. Before we ask you any questions you must understand what your rights are.

You have the right to remain silent. You are not required to say anything to us at any time or to answer any questions. Anything you say can be used against you in court.

You have the right to talk to a lawyer for advice before we question you and to have him with you during questioning.

If you cannot afford a lawyer and want one, a lawyer will be provided for you.

If you want to answer questions now without a lawyer present, you will still have the right to stop answering at any time. You also have the right to stop answering at any time until you talk to a lawyer.

WAIVER

1. Have you read or had read to you the warning as to your rights?_____

2. Do you understand these rights? _____

3. Do you wish to answer any questions? _____

4. Are you willing to answer questions without having an attorney present? _____

5. Signature of defendant on line below.

_____

6. Time _____   Date _____

7. Signature of officer _____

8. Signature of witness _____

Figure 14.1   The Miranda Warning
Since the U.S. Supreme Court's ruling in the case of *Miranda v. Arizona* in 1966, law-enforcement officials at all levels have routinely carried "Miranda rights" cards, which they read to accused individuals immediately after their arrest. This procedure has largely eliminated defendants' abilities to obtain dismissals and/or acquittals on the basis of ignorance of their rights or lack of proper counsel. The Supreme Court reaffirmed the *Miranda* rule in 2000.

questioned. If the police commit an error in these procedures, the accused goes free, regardless of the evidence of guilt.[109] Figure 14.1 shows a typical **Miranda warning** card carried by police to ensure that they issue the proper warnings to those under arrest.

The Exclusionary Rule   Illegally obtained evidence and confessions may not be used in criminal trials. If police find evidence of a crime in an illegal search or if they elicit statements from suspects without informing them of their rights to remain silent or to have counsel, the evidence or statements produced are not admissible in a trial. This **exclusionary rule** is one of the more controversial procedural rights that the Supreme Court has extended to criminal defendants. The rule is also unique to the United States: in Great Britain evidence obtained illegally may be used against the accused, although the accused may bring charges against the police for damages.

The rule provides *enforcement* for the Fourth Amendment guarantee against unreasonable searches and seizures, as well as the Fifth Amendment guarantee against compulsory self-incrimination and the guarantee of counsel. Initially applied only in federal cases, in *Mapp v. Ohio* (1961) the Supreme Court extended the exclusionary rule to all criminal cases in the United States.[110] A *good faith*

Miranda warning
Requirement that persons arrested be informed of their rights immediately after arrest.

exclusionary rule   Rule of law that evidence found in an illegal search or resulting from an illegally obtained confession may not be admitted at trial.

exception is made "when law enforcement officers have acted in objective good faith or their transgressions have been minor."[111] And police are *not* prohibited from tricking a suspect into giving them incriminating evidence.[112] But the exclusionary rule is frequently attacked for the high price it extracts from society—the release of guilty criminals. Why punish society because of the misconduct of police? Why not punish police directly, perhaps with disciplinary measures imposed by courts that discover errors, instead of letting guilty persons go free?

Bail Requirements   The Eighth Amendment says only that *"excessive* bail shall not be required." This clause does not say that pretrial release on **bail** will be available to all. The Supreme Court has held that "in our society liberty is the norm, and detention prior to trial or without trial is the carefully limited exception." Pretrial release on bail can be denied on the basis of the seriousness of the crime (bail is often denied in murder cases), the trustworthiness of the defendant (bail is often denied when the prosecution shows that the defendant is likely to flee before trial), or, in a more controversial exception, when release would threaten "the safety of any other person or the community."[113] If the court does not find any of these exceptions, it must set bail no higher than an amount reasonably calculated to ensure the defendant's later presence at trial.

Most criminal defendants cannot afford the bail money required for pretrial release. They must seek the services of a bail bondsman, who charges a heavy fee for filing the bail money with the court. The bail bondsman receives all of the bail money back when the defendant shows up for trial. But even if the defendant is found innocent, the bail bondsman retains the charge fee. (Thus the system is said to discriminate against poor defendants who cannot afford the bondsman's fee.) The failure of a criminal defendant to appear at his or her trial is itself a crime and subjects the defendant to immediate arrest as well as forfeiture of bail. Most states authorize bail bondsmen to find and arrest persons who have "jumped bail," return them to court, and thereby recover the bail money.

Fair Trial   The original text of the Constitution guaranteed jury trials in criminal cases, and the Sixth Amendment went on to correct weaknesses the Framers saw in the English justice system at that time—closed proceedings, trials in absentia (where the defendant is not present), secret witnesses, long delays

bail Release of an accused person from custody in exchange for promise to appear at trial, guaranteed by money or property that is forfeited to court if defendant does not appear.

Dollree Mapp was arrested in 1957, but police seized vital evidence against her during an unwarranted, unconstitutional search. In *Mapp v. Ohio* (1961), the U.S. Supreme Court held that evidence obtained illegally could not be used in a criminal trial.

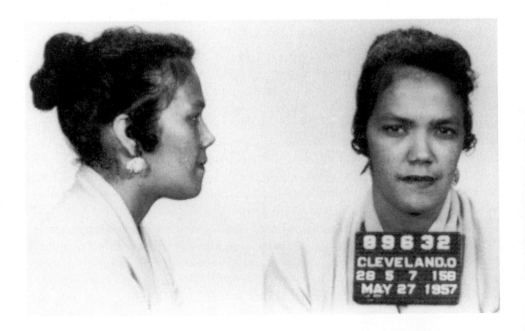

between arrest and trial, biased juries, and the absence of defense counsel. Specifically, the Sixth Amendment guarantees the following:

- The right to a speedy and public trial. ("Speedy" refers to the time between arrest and trial, not the time between the crime itself and trial,[114] but the Supreme Court has declined to set a specific time limit that defines "speedy."[115])

- An impartial jury chosen from the state or district where the crime was committed.

- The right to confront (cross-examine) witnesses against the accused.

- The right of the accused to compel (subpoena) favorable witnesses to appear.

- The right of the accused to be represented by counsel.

Over the years the courts have elaborated on these elements of a fair trial so that today trial proceedings follow a rigidly structured format. First, attorneys make opening statements. The prosecution describes the crime and how it will prove beyond a reasonable doubt that the defendant committed it. The defense attorney argues either that the crime did not occur or that the defendant did not do it. Next, each side, again beginning with the prosecution, calls witnesses who first testify on "direct examination" for their side, then are cross-examined by the opposing attorney. Witnesses may be asked to verify evidence that is introduced as "exhibits." Defendants have a right to be present during their own trials (although an abusive and disruptive defendant may be considered to have waived his or her right to be present and be removed from the courtroom).[116] Prosecution witnesses must appear in the courtroom and submit to cross-examination (although special protection procedures, including videotaped testimony, may be used for children).[117] Prosecutors are obliged to disclose any information that might create a reasonable doubt about the defendant's guilt,[118] but the defendant may not be compelled to disclose incriminating information.

After all of the witnesses offered by both sides have been heard and cross-examined, prosecution and defense give their closing arguments. The burden of proof "beyond a reasonable doubt" rests with the prosecution; the defense does not need to prove that the accused is innocent, only that reasonable doubt exists regarding guilt. (However, see *A Conflicting View:* "The War on Drugs Threatens Individual Liberty.")

Juries must be "impartial": they must not have prejudged the case or exhibit bias or prejudice or have a personal interest in the outcome. Judges can dismiss jurors for "cause." During jury selection, attorneys for the prosecution and defense are allowed a fixed number of "peremptory" challenges of jurors (although they cannot do so on the basis of race or gender).[119] Jury selection is often regarded by attorneys as the key to the outcome of a case; both sides try to get presumed sympathetic people on the jury. In well-publicized cases, judges may "sequester" a jury (keep them in a hotel away from access to the mass media) in order to maintain impartiality. Judges may exclude press or television to prevent trials from becoming spectacles if they wish.[120] By tradition, English juries have had twelve members; however, the Supreme Court has allowed six-member juries in non-death-penalty cases.[121] Also by tradition, juries should arrive at a unanimous decision. If a jury cannot do so, judges declare a "hung" jury and the prosecutor may schedule a retrial. Only a "not guilty" prevents retrial of a defendant. Traditionally, it was believed that a lack of unanimity raised "reasonable doubt" about the defendant's guilt. But the Supreme Court has permitted nonunanimous verdicts in some cases.[122]

A CONFLICTING VIEW

The War on Drugs Threatens Individual Liberty

Drug offenses currently account for over half of all prison sentences meted out by federal courts. The average federal sentence for drug crimes—possession, trafficking, or manufacturing of illegal substances—is seven years; the federal minimum sentence for possession of illegal drugs is five years. More than 1 million persons are arrested each year for drug violations.[a] The United States imprisons a larger proportion of its population than any other advanced nation.

The greatest threat arising from the "war on drugs," however, is the loss of personal liberty that has accompanied efforts to "take the profit out of crime." Congress passed a Racketeer Influenced and Corrupt Organizations Act (RICO) in 1970, following a 1968 presidential campaign in which President Richard Nixon made "getting tough on crime" a key issue. RICO authorizes federal agents to seize cash, bank accounts, homes, cars, boats, businesses, and other assets on "probable cause" to believe that they were used in criminal activity or were obtained with profits from criminal activity. People may be stopped in an airport terminal, a bus station, or on the street on suspicion of drug trafficking, and have their cash and cars seized by law enforcement agencies. Boats and airplanes are also favored targets of seizure, but RICO also allows the seizure of bank accounts, homes, and businesses. Assets seized by federal law-enforcement agencies—FBI, DEA, Customs Service, Treasury and Justice Departments—are usually retained by these agencies (or the profits of selling these assets at auction), and proceeds are often shared with state and local law-enforcement agencies that cooperated in the investigation. Thus, there is a strong bureaucratic incentive for agencies to concentrate on cases likely to result in forfeiture of these assets—primarily drug cases—and to overlook other law-enforcement activities.

RICO permits the government to seize property *before* any adjudication of guilt. Indeed a subsequent guilty verdict in a criminal trial is not necessary for the government to retain possession of the property seized. The only requirement is that government agents have "probable cause" to believe that the property was used in a crime or was purchased with the profits of crime. People whose property is seized under RICO must initiate a suit against the government. They have the burden of proving that they are innocent of any crime and, more importantly, that officers had no probable cause to seize their property. The proceedings are considered a civil suit by an individual against the government, not a criminal case by the government against the individual. The government, therefore, need not prove "beyond a reasonable doubt" that the person was involved in criminal activity or the property was used in commission of a crime. Rather, the person must prove his or her own innocence and the government's lack of probable cause to seize the property.

In a decision that seriously endangers personal liberty in America, the Supreme Court upheld RICO.[b] The Court ruled that the government's seizure of property is a civil and not a criminal punishment. This means that individuals whose property is seized are not afforded the constitutional rights of criminal defendants. They have no right to "due process of law" (Fifth Amendment), protection against double jeopardy (Fifth Amendment), or protection against "excessive fines" (Eighth Amendment).

Efforts in Congress to reform RICO have consistently failed. Members of Congress wish to avoid being labeled "soft on crime." And law-enforcement agencies—federal, state, and local—lobby heavily against reform.

[a]*Statistical Abstract of the United States, 2004–2005*, p. 196.

[b]*U.S. v. Ursery* 518 U.S. 267 (1996).

plea bargaining Practice of allowing defendants to plead guilty to lesser crimes than those with which they were originally charged in return for reduced sentences.

Plea Bargaining Few criminal cases actually go to trial. More than 90 percent of criminal cases are plea bargained.[123] In **plea bargaining**, the defendant agrees to plead guilty and waives the right to a jury trial in exchange for concessions made by the prosecutor, perhaps the dropping of more serious charges against the defendant or a pledge to seek a reduced sentence or fine. Some critics of plea bargaining view it as another form of leniency in the criminal justice system that reduces its deterrent effects. Other critics view plea bargaining as a violation of the

Constitution's protection against self-incrimination and guarantee of a fair jury trial. Prosecutors, they say, threaten defendants with serious charges and stiff penalties in order to force a guilty plea. Still other critics see plea bargaining as an "under-the-table" process that undermines respect for the criminal justice system.

Yet it is vital to the nation's court system that most defendants plead guilty. The court system would quickly break down from overload if any substantial proportion of defendants insisted on jury trials.

Double Jeopardy   The Constitution appears to bar multiple prosecutions for the same offense: "Nor shall any person be subject for the same offense to be twice put in jeopardy of life or limb" (Fifth Amendment). But very early the Supreme Court held that this clause does not protect an individual from being tried a second time if jurors are deadlocked and cannot reach a verdict in the first trial (a "hung" jury).[124] Moreover, the Supreme Court has held that federal and state governments may separately try a person for the same offense if it violates both federal and state laws.[125] Thus, in the well-publicized Rodney King case in 1992, in which police officers were videotaped beating King, a California court found the officers not guilty of assault, but later the U.S. Justice Department won convictions against the officers in a federal court for violating King's civil rights. Finally, a verdict of guilt or innocence in a criminal trial does not preclude a civil trial in which plaintiffs (private citizens) sue for damages inflicted by the accused. Thus, O.J. Simpson was found not guilty of murder in a criminal trial but was later found to be responsible for the deaths of two people in a civil trial. Civil courts, of course, can only impose monetary awards; they cannot impose criminal penalties.

The Death Penalty

Perhaps the most heated debate in criminal justice policy today concerns capital punishment. Opponents of the death penalty argue that it violates the prohibition against "cruel and unusual punishments" in the Eighth Amendment to the Constitution. They also argue that the death penalty is applied unequally. A large proportion of those executed have been poor, uneducated, and nonwhite. In contrast, many Americans feel that justice demands strong retribution for heinous crimes—a life for a life. A mere jail sentence for a multiple murderer or rapist-murderer seems unjust compared with the damage inflicted on society and the victims. In many cases, a life sentence means less than ten years in prison under the current early-release and parole policies in many states. Convicted murderers have been set free, and some have killed again.

Prohibition against Unfair Application   Prior to 1971, the death penalty was officially sanctioned by about half of the states. Federal law also retained the death penalty. However, no one had actually suffered the death penalty since 1967 because of numerous legal tangles and direct challenges to the constitutionality of capital punishment.

In *Furman v. Georgia* (1972), the Supreme Court ruled that capital punishment, as then imposed, violated the Eighth and Fourteenth Amendment prohibitions against cruel and unusual punishment and due process of law. The justices' reasoning in the case was very complex. Only Justices William J. Brennan and Thurgood Marshall declared that capital punishment itself is cruel and unusual. The other justices in the majority felt that death sentences had been applied unfairly; some individuals received the death penalty for crimes for which many others received much lighter sentences. These justices left open the possibility that capital punishment would be constitutional if it was specified for certain kinds of crime and applied uniformly.[126]

---Think Again---

Is the death penalty a "cruel and unusual" punishment?

 The National Coalition to Abolish the Death Penalty This site provides information about public policies, institutions, and individuals that collectively work toward the "unconditional rejection of capital punishment." *www.ncadp.org*

After this decision, a majority of states rewrote their death penalty laws to try to ensure fairness and uniformity of application. Generally, these laws mandate the death penalty for murders committed during rape, robbery, hijacking, or kidnapping; murder of prison guards; murder with torture; and multiple murders. They call for two trials to be held—one to determine guilt or innocence and another to determine the penalty. At the second trial, evidence of "aggravating" and "mitigating" factors must be presented; if there are aggravating factors but no mitigating factors, the death penalty is mandatory.

Death Penalty Reinstated   The revised death penalty laws were upheld in a series of cases that came before the Supreme Court in 1976. The Court concluded that "the punishment of death does *not* invariably violate the Constitution." The majority decision noted that the Framers of the Bill of Rights had accepted death as a common penalty for crime. Although acknowledging that the Constitution and its amendments must be interpreted in a dynamic fashion, reflecting changing moral values, the Court's majority noted that most state legislatures have been willing to reenact the death penalty and hundreds of juries have been willing to impose that penalty. Thus "a large proportion of American society continues to regard it as an appropriate and necessary criminal sanction." Moreover, the Court held that the social purposes of retribution and deterrence justify the use of the death penalty; this ultimate sanction is "an expression of society's moral outrage at particularly offensive conduct."[127]

The Court reaffirmed that *Furman v. Georgia* struck down the death penalty only where it was invoked in "an arbitrary and capricious manner." A majority of the justices upheld the death penalty in states where the trial is a two-part proceeding, provided that during the second part the jury is given relevant information and standards for deciding whether to impose the death penalty. The Court approved the consideration of "aggravating and mitigating circumstances." Later the Court held that the jury, not a judge acting alone, must find aggravating circumstances in order to impose the death sentence.[128] The Court also called for automatic review of all death sentences by state supreme courts to ensure that none is imposed under the influence of passion or prejudice, that aggravating factors are supported by the

 **Bureau of Justice Statistics**
Federal statistics on jails, prisons, probation, and capital punishment. Click to capital punishment for numbers of executions and persons under sentence of death. *www.ojp.usdoj.gov/bjs*

Do retribution and deterrence justify the use of the death penalty? Perhaps the most heated debate in criminal justice policy today concerns capital punishment.

ACROSS THE USA

The Death Penalty

Today the death penalty is rarely imposed. Twelve states have no death penalty in their laws. An additional seven states have the death penalty in their laws but have not carried out any executions since 1977 (following the Supreme Court's 1976 decision in *Gregs v. Georgia*). The federal government itself has a death penalty, but the executions of Timothy McVeigh and Juan Garza in 2001 marked the first death sentences carried out by the federal government in several decades. There are more than 3,500 prisoners across the country convicted and sentenced to death. Over half of these "death row" inmates have been held for more than five years. Executions have slowed as judges and governors have reviewed cases with new DNA evidence.

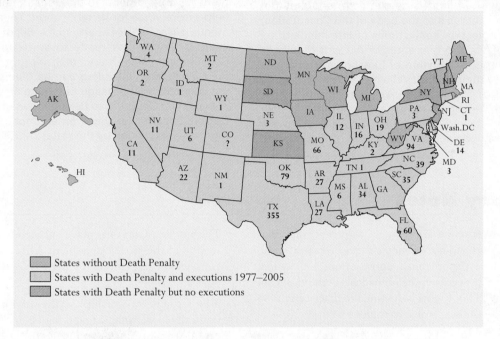

States without Death Penalty
States with Death Penalty and executions 1977–2005
States with Death Penalty but no executions

Note: In 2005 the New York Supreme Court ruled that the death penalty violated that state's constitution. Connecticut held its first execution in 2005. The year 2005 saw the one hundredth execution since the death penalty was resumed in 1976.

evidence, and that the sentence is not disproportionate to the crime. However, the court disapproved of state laws making the death penalty mandatory in all first-degree murder cases, holding that such laws were "unduly harsh and unworkably rigid." The Court has held that executions of the mentally retarded are "cruel and unusual punishments" prohibited by the Eighth Amendment. And in 2005 the Court held that the Eighth Amendment prohibited executions of offenders who were under age 18 when their crimes were committed.[129]

Racial Bias   The death penalty has been challenged as a violation of the Equal Protection Clause of the Fourteenth Amendment because of racial bias in the application of the punishment. White murderers are just as likely to receive the death penalty as black murderers. However, some statistics show that if the *victim* is white there is a greater chance that the killer will be sentenced to death than if the victim is black. Nevertheless, the U.S. Supreme Court has ruled that statistical disparity in the race of victims by itself does not bar the use of the death penalty in all cases. There must be evidence of racial bias against a particular defendant in order for the Court to reverse a death sentence.[130]

A CONSTITUTIONAL NOTE

The Origins of the Bill of Rights

The Constitution that emerged from the Philadelphia Convention of 1787 did not include a Bill of Rights. This was a particularly glaring omission because the idea of a bill of rights was popular at the time, and most constitutions contain one. The Founders certainly believed in limited government, and they did write a few liberties into the body of the Constitution, including protection against bills of attainder and ex post facto laws, the guarantee of the writ of habeas corpus, a limited definition of treason, and the guarantee of jury trials. But they dismissed the notion of a written Bill of Rights as unnecessary, claiming that the national government, as a government of only enumerated powers, could not exercise any powers not expressly delegated to it. And the power to infringe on free speech or press or otherwise restrain liberty was not among the enumerated powers. It was therefore not necessary to specifically deny the new government the power to interfere with individual liberty. But this logic was unconvincing to Anti-Federalist opponents of the new Constitution; they wanted much firmer written guarantees of liberty in the Constitution. So Federalist supporters of the Constitution made a solemn promise to add a Bill of Rights as amendments to the Constitution in order to help secure votes for its ratification. Thus, the fundamental guarantees of liberty in the Bill of Rights were political concessions made to win support for the Constitution itself. True to their word, supporters of the Constitution, including James Madison, secured the congressional passage of twelve amendments in the very first Congress to be convened under the new Constitution. Ten of these amendments—the Bill of Rights—were ratified by the states by 1791.

Summary Notes

- Laws and government are required to protect individual liberty. Yet laws and governments themselves restrict liberty. To resolve this dilemma, constitutions seek to limit governmental power over the individual. In the U.S. Constitution, the Bill of Rights is designed to place certain liberties beyond the reach of government.

- Initially the Bill of Rights applied against only the federal government, not state or local governments. But over time, the Bill of Rights was nationalized, as the Supreme Court applied the Due Process Clause of the Fourteenth Amendment to all governments in the United States.

- Freedom of religion encompasses two separate restrictions on government: government must not establish religion or prohibit its free exercise. Although the wording of the First Amendment is absolute ("Congress shall make no law . . ."), the Supreme Court has allowed some restrictions on religious practices that threaten health, safety, or welfare.

- The Supreme Court's efforts to maintain "a wall of separation" between church and state have proven difficult and controversial. The Court's banning of prayer and religious ceremony in public schools more than thirty years ago remains politically unpopular today.

- The Supreme Court has never adopted the absolutist position that all speech is protected by the First Amendment. The Court's clear and present danger doctrine and its preferred position doctrine recognize the importance of free expression in a democracy, yet the Court has permitted some restrictions on expression, especially in times of perceived national crisis.

- The Supreme Court has placed obscenity outside the protection of the First Amendment, but it has encountered considerable difficulty in defining "obscenity."

- Freedom of the press prevents government from imposing prior restraint (censorship) on the news media except periodically in wartime, when it has been argued that publication would result in serious harm or loss of life. The Supreme Court has allowed greater government authority over radio and television than over newspapers, on the grounds that radio and television are given exclusive rights to use specific broadcast frequencies.

- The First Amendment guarantee of the right of assembly and petition protects the organization of political parties and interest groups. It also protects the right of people to peacefully protest, parade, and demonstrate. Governments may, within reasonable limits, restrict these activities for valid reasons but may not apply different restrictions to different groups based on the nature of their views.

- The Second Amendment guarantees "the right of the people to keep and bear arms." However, it is frequently argued that this is not an individual right to possess a gun, but rather a collective right of the states to maintain National Guard units.

- Crime rates in the United States are currently declining. Yet a free society must balance any remedies to the crime problem against potential infringements of the rights of its citizens.

- The Constitution includes a number of important procedural guarantees in the criminal justice system: the writ of habeas corpus; prohibitions against bills of attainder and ex post facto laws; protection against unreasonable searches and seizures; protection against self-incrimination; guarantee of legal counsel; protection against excessive bail; guarantee of a fair public and speedy trial by an impartial jury; the right to confront witnesses and to compel favorable witnesses to testify; and protection against cruel or unusual punishment.

- The Supreme Court's exclusionary rule helps to enforce some of these procedural rights by excluding illegally obtained evidence and self-incriminating statements from criminal trials. In the 1960s, Court interpretations of the Fourth and Fifth Amendments strengthened the rights of

criminal defendants. Police procedures adjusted quickly, and today there is little evidence that procedural rights greatly hamper law enforcement.

- Few criminal cases go to trial. Most are plea bargained, with the defendant pleading guilty in exchange for reduced charges and/or a lighter sentence. Although this practice is frequently criticized, without plea bargaining the nation's criminal court system would break down from case overload.

- The Supreme Court has ruled that the death penalty is not a "cruel and unusual punishment," but the Court has insisted on fairness and uniformity of application.

Key Terms

incorporation 490
Free Exercise Clause 493
No Establishment Clause 494
wall-of-separation doctrine 494
Lemon test 495

clear and present danger doctrine 499
preferred position 501
freedom of expression 502
symbolic speech 502
commercial speech 505
prior restraint 512

shield laws 513
takings clause 515
eminent domain 515
writ of habeas corpus 519
bill of attainder 519
ex post facto law 519
search warrant 523

indictment 526
grand jury 526
grant of immunity from prosecution 526
Miranda warning 527
exclusionary rule 527
bail 528
plea bargaining 530

Suggested Readings

Bruce, Tammy. *The New Thought Police.* New York: Prima Lyfestyles, 2003. A liberal feminist confronts the Left's assault on free speech.

Epstein, Lee, and Thomas G. Walker. *Constitutional Law for a Changing America: Rights, Liberties and Justice.* 5th ed. Washington, D.C.: CQ Press, 2003. An authoritative text on civil liberties and the rights of the criminally accused. It describes the political context of Supreme Court decisions and provides key excerpts from the most important decisions.

Garrow, David. *Liberty and Sexuality: The Right to Privacy and the Making of Roe v. Wade.* New York: Macmillan, 1994. Historical account of the background and development of the right to sexual privacy.

Hentoff, Nat. *Free Speech for Me—But Not for Thee.* New York: HarperCollins, 1992. Account of how both the right and the left in America try to suppress the opinions of those who disagree with them.

Kobylka, Joseph F. *The Politics of Obscenity.* Westport, Conn.: Greenwood Press, 1991. Comprehensive review of Supreme Court obscenity decisions, arguing that the *Miller* case in 1973 was a turning point away from a more permissive to a

more restrictive approach toward sexually oriented material. It examines the litigation strategies of the American Civil Liberties Union and other groups in obscenity cases.

Lewis, Anthony. *Gideon's Trumpet.* New York: Random House, 1964. The classic story of Clarence Gideon and how his handwritten habeas corpus plea made its way to the U.S. Supreme Court, resulting in the guarantee of free legal counsel for poor defendants in felony cases.

Savage, David. *The Supreme Court and Individual Rights.* Washington, D.C.: CQ Press, 2004. An overview of individual rights—freedom of ideas, political participation, due process and criminal rights, equal rights, and personal liberties.

Shiell, Timothy C. *Campus Hate Speech on Trial.* Lawrence: University of Kansas Press, 1998. Traditional academic values emphasizing the free exchange of ideas are being sacrificed on campus by anti-hate speech codes.

Sullivan, Harold J. *Civil Rights and Liberties: Provocative Questions and Evolving Answers.* 2nd ed. Upper Saddle River, N.J.: Prentice Hall, 2005. Contemporary issues in civil liberties discussed in a question-and-answer format.

Make It Real

CIVIL LIBERTIES
The simulation puts the student in the role of NSA policy-maker.

15 POLITICS AND CIVIL RIGHTS

Think About Politics

1 Does the U.S. Constitution require the government to be color blind with respect to different races in all its laws and actions?
Yes ☐ No ☐

2 If a city's schools are mostly black and the surrounding suburban schools are mostly white, should busing be used to achieve a better racial balance?
Yes ☐ No ☐

3 Are differences between blacks and whites in average income mainly a product of discrimination?
Yes ☐ No ☐

4 Do you generally favor affirmative action programs for women and minorities?
Yes ☐ No ☐

5 Do you believe racial and sexual preferences in employment and education discriminate against white males?
Yes ☐ No ☐

6 Should gender equality receive the same level of legal protection as racial equality?
Yes ☐ No ☐

7 Do dirty jokes and foul language at work constitute sexual harassment?
Yes ☐ No ☐

Equality has long been the central issue of American politics. What do we mean by equality? And what, if anything, should government do to achieve it?

The Politics of Equality

Equality has been the central issue of American politics throughout the history of the nation. It is the issue that sparked the nation's only civil war, and it continues today to be the nation's most vexing political concern.

Conflict begins over the very definition of "equality" (see "Dilemmas of Equality" in Chapter 2). Although Americans agree in the abstract that everyone is equal, they disagree over what they mean by "equality." Traditionally, equality meant "equality of *opportunity*": an equal opportunity to develop individual talents and abilities and to be rewarded for work, initiative, merit, and achievement. Over time, the issue of equality has shifted to "equality of *results*": an equal sharing of income and material rewards. With this shift in definition has come political conflict over the question of what, if anything, government should do to narrow the gaps between rich and poor, men and women, blacks and whites, and all other groups in society.

The nation's long struggle over equality has produced a number of constitutional and legal milestones in civil rights. These are summarized in Table 15.1. Much of the politics of civil rights centers on the development and interpretation of these guarantees of equality.

Slavery, Segregation, and the Constitution

In penning the Declaration of Independence in 1776, Thomas Jefferson affirmed that "All men are created equal." Yet from 1619, when the first slaves were brought to Jamestown, Virginia, until 1865, when the Thirteenth Amendment to the Constitution outlawed the practice, slavery was a way of life in the United States. Africans were captured, enslaved, transported to America, bought and sold, and used as personal property.

Table 15.1   Guarantees of Civil Rights

Thirteenth Amendment (1865)

Neither slavery nor involuntary servitude, except as a punishment for crime whereof the party shall have been duly convicted, shall exist within the United States, or any place subject to their jurisdiction.

Fourteenth Amendment (1868)

No State shall make or enforce any law which shall abridge the privileges or immunities of citizens of the United States; nor shall any State deprive any person of life, liberty, or property, without due process of law; nor deny to any person within its jurisdiction the equal protection of the laws.

Fifteenth Amendment (1870)

The rights of the citizens of the United States to vote shall not be denied or abridged by the United States or by any State on account of race, color, or previous condition of servitude.

Nineteenth Amendment (1920)

The right of the citizens of the United States to vote shall not be denied or abridged by the United States or by any State on account of sex.

Civil Rights Acts of 1866, 1871, and 1875

Acts passed by the Reconstruction Congress following the Civil War. The Civil Rights Act of 1866 guaranteed newly freed persons the right to purchase, lease, and use real property. The Civil Rights Act of 1875 outlawed segregation in privately owned businesses and facilities, but in the Civil Rights Cases (1883), the Supreme Court declared the act an unconstitutional expansion of federal power, ruling that the Fourteenth Amendment limits only "State" actions. Other provisions of these acts were generally ignored for many decades. But the Civil Rights Act of 1871 has been revived in recent decades; the act makes it a federal crime for any person acting under the authority of state law to deprive another of rights protected by the Constitution.

Civil Rights Act of 1957

The first civil rights law passed by Congress since Reconstruction. It empowers the U.S. Justice Department to enforce voting rights, established the Civil Rights Division in the Justice Department, and created the Civil Rights Commission to study and report on civil rights in the United States.

Civil Rights Act of 1964

A comprehensive enactment designed to erase racial discrimination in both public and private sectors of American life. Major titles of the act: I. outlaws arbitrary discrimination in voter registration and expedites voting rights suits; II. bars discrimination in public accommodations, such as hotels and restaurants, that have a substantial relation to interstate commerce; III. and IV. authorizes the national government to bring suits to desegregate public facilities and schools; V. extends the life and expands the power of the Civil Rights Commission; VI. provides for withholding federal funds from programs administered in a discriminatory manner; VII. establishes the right to equality in employment opportunities.

Civil Rights Act of 1968

Prohibits discrimination in the advertising, financing sale, or rental of housing, based on race, religion, or national origin and, as of 1974, sex. A major amendment to the act in 1988 extended coverage to the handicapped and to families with children.

Voting Rights Act

Enacted by Congress in 1965 and renewed and expanded in 1970, 1975, and 1982, this law has sought to eliminate restrictions on voting that have been used to discriminate against blacks and other minority groups. Amendments in 1975 (1) required bilingual ballots in all states; (2) required approval by the Justice Department or a federal court of any election law changes in states covered by the act; (3) extended legal protection of voting rights to Hispanic Americans, Asian Americans, and Native Americans. The 1982 act provides that *intent* to discriminate need not be proven if the *results* demonstrate otherwise. Although the 1982 extension does not require racial quotas for city councils, school boards, or state legislatures, a judge may under the law redraw voting districts to give minorities maximum representation.

— Think Again —

Does the U.S. Constitution require the government to be color blind with respect to different races in all its laws and actions?

Slavery and the Constitution   The Constitution of 1787 recognized and protected slavery in the United States. Article I stipulated that slaves were to be counted as three-fifths of a person for purposes of representation and taxation; it also prohibited any federal restriction on the importation of slaves until 1808. Article IV even guaranteed the return of escaped slaves to their owners. The Founders were aware that the practice of slavery contradicted their professed belief in "equality," and this contradiction caused them some embarrassment. Thus they avoided the word "slave" in favor of the euphemism "person held to Service or Labour" in writing the Constitution.

Supreme Court Chief Justice Roger Taney, ruling in the notorious case of *Dred Scott v. Sandford* in 1857, reflected the racism that prevailed in early America:

> They had for more than a century before been regarded as beings of an inferior order, and altogether unfit to associate with the white race, either in social or political relations; and so far inferior, that they had no rights which the white man was bound to respect; and that the negro might justly and lawfully be reduced to slavery for his benefit.[1]

Taney's decision in this case interpreted the Constitution in terms of the *original intent* of the Founders. The ruling upheld slavery and the constitutional guarantee given slave owners for the return of slaves escaping to nonslave states.

The Supreme Court's 1896 decision in *Plessy v. Ferguson* allowed "separate but equal" public facilities. But segregated facilities were seldom equal, and segregation itself was often a humiliating experience.

Emancipation and Reconstruction   A growing number of Americans, especially members of the **abolition movement**, disagreed with Taney. In 1860 internal party divisions over the slavery issue led to a four-way race for the presidency and the election of Abraham Lincoln. Although personally opposed to slavery, Lincoln had promised during the campaign not to push for abolition of slavery where it existed. Many southerners were unconvinced, however, and on December 20, 1860 (three months before Lincoln's inauguration), South Carolina became the first state to secede from the Union, touching off the Civil War.

The Civil War was the nation's bloodiest war. (Combined deaths of Union and Confederate forces matched the nation's losses in World War II, even though the nation's population in 1860 was only 31 million compared to 140 million during World War II.) Very few families during the Civil War did not experience a direct loss from that conflict. As casualties mounted, northern Republicans joined abolitionists in calling for emancipating, or freeing, the slaves simply to punish the Rebels. They knew that much of the South's power depended on slave labor. Lincoln also knew that if he proclaimed the war was being fought to free the slaves, military intervention by the British on behalf of the South was less likely. Accordingly, on September 22, 1862, Lincoln issued his **Emancipation Proclamation**. Claiming his right as Commander-in-Chief of the army and navy, he declared that, as of January 1, 1863, "all persons held as slaves within any State, or designated part of a State, the people whereof shall then be in rebellion against the United States, shall be then, thenceforward, and forever free." The Emancipation Proclamation did not come about as a result of demands by the people. It was a political and military action by the president intended to help preserve the Union.

The Emancipation Proclamation freed slaves in the seceding states, and the Thirteenth Amendment in 1865 abolished slavery everywhere in the nation. But freedom did not mean civil rights. The post–Civil War Republican Congress attempted to "reconstruct" southern society. The Fourteenth Amendment, ratified in 1868, made "equal protection of the laws" a command for every state to obey. The Fifteenth Amendment, passed in 1869 and ratified in 1870, prohibited federal and state governments from abridging the right to vote "on account of race, color, or previous condition of servitude." In addition, Congress passed a series of civil rights laws in the 1860s and 1870s guaranteeing the newly freed slaves protection in the exercise of their constitutional rights. Between 1865 and the early 1880s, the success of **Reconstruction** was evident in widespread black voting throughout the South, the presence of many blacks in federal and state offices, and the admission of blacks to theaters, restaurants, hotels, and public transportation.[2]

abolition movement Social movement before the Civil War whose goal was to abolish slavery throughout the United States.

Emancipation Proclamation Lincoln's 1862 Civil War declaration that all slaves residing in rebel states were free. It did not abolish all slavery; that would be done by the Thirteenth Amendment in 1865.

Reconstruction The Post–Civil War period when the Southern states were occupied by federal troops and newly freed African Americans occupied many political offices and exercised civil rights.

The Imposition of Segregation   But political support for Reconstruction policies soon began to erode. In the Compromise of 1877, the national government agreed to end military occupation of the South, give up its efforts to rearrange Southern society, and lend tacit approval to white supremacy in that region. In

The Thirteenth, Fourteenth, and Fifteenth Amendments to the Constitution, as well as other legislation passed during Reconstruction, opened the ballot box and access to political office to the freedmen of the South. However, these gains were soon largely reversed by Jim Crow laws and segregation.

Jim Crow Second-class-citizen status conferred on blacks by southern segregation laws; derived from a nineteenth-century song-and-dance act (usually performed by a white man in blackface) that stereotyped blacks.

separate but equal Ruling of the Supreme Court in the case of *Plessy v. Ferguson* (1896) to the effect that segregated facilities were legal as long as the facilities were equal.

return, the Southern states pledged their support to the Union, accepted national supremacy, and agreed to permit the Republican presidential candidate, Rutherford B. Hayes, to assume the presidency, although the Democratic candidate, Samuel Tilden, had received more popular votes in the disputed election of 1876.

As white Southerners regained political power and blacks lost the protection of federal forces, the Supreme Court moved to strike down Reconstruction laws. In the Civil Rights Cases of 1883, the Supreme Court declared federal civil rights laws preventing discrimination by private individuals to be unconstitutional.[3] By denying Congress the power to protect blacks from discrimination by businesses and individuals, the Court paved the way for the imposition of segregation as the prevailing social system of the South. In the 1880s and 1890s, white southerners imposed segregation in public accommodations, housing, education, employment and almost every other sector of private and public life. By 1895 most southern states had passed laws *requiring* racial segregation in education and in public accommodations. At the time, more than 90 percent of the African American population of the United States lived in these states.

Segregation became the social instrument by which African Americans were "kept in their place"—that is, denied social, economic, educational, and political equality. In many states, **Jim Crow** followed them throughout life: birth in segregated hospital wards, education in segregated schools, residence in segregated housing, employment in segregated jobs, eating in segregated restaurants, and burial in segregated graveyards. Segregation was enforced by a variety of public and private sanctions, from lynch mobs to country club admission committees. But government was the principal instrument of segregation in both the Southern and the border states of the nation. (For a look at the political reactions of African Americans to segregation, see *Up Close:* "African American Politics in Historical Perspective" on page 542.)

Early Court Approval of Segregation   Segregation was imposed despite the Fourteenth Amendment's guarantee of "equal protection of the laws." In the 1896 case of *Plessy v. Ferguson*, the Supreme Court upheld state laws requiring segregation. Although segregation laws involved state action, the Court held that segregation of the races did not violate the Equal Protection Clause of the Fourteenth Amendment as long as people in each race received equal treatment. Schools and other public facilities that were **separate but equal** were constitutional, the Court ruled.

> The object of the amendment was undoubtedly to enforce the absolute equality of the two races before the law, but in the nature of things it could not have been intended to abolish distinctions based upon color, or to enforce social, as distinguished from political, equality, or a commingling of the two races upon terms unsatisfactory to either. Laws permitting, and even requiring, their separation in places where they are liable to be brought into contact do not necessarily imply the inferiority of either race to the other, and have been generally, if not universally, recognized as within the competency of the state legislatures in the exercise of their police power.[4]

The effect of this decision was to give constitutional approval to segregation; the decision was not reversed until 1954.

Equal Protection of the Laws

The initial goal of the civil rights movement was to eliminate segregation laws, especially segregation in public education. Only after this battle was well under way could the civil rights movement turn to the fight against segregation and discrimination in all sectors of American life, *private* as well as *governmental*.

The NAACP and the Legal Battle   The National Association for the Advancement of Colored People (NAACP) and its Legal Defense and Education Fund led the fight to abolish lawful segregation. As chief legal counsel to the fund, Thurgood Marshall, later to become the first African American to sit on the U.S. Supreme Court, began a long legal campaign to ensure equal protection of the law for African Americans. Initially, the NAACP's strategy focused on achieving the "equal" portion of the separate-but-equal doctrine. Segregated facilities, including public schools, were seldom "equal," even with respect to physical conditions, teachers' salaries and qualifications, curricula, and other tangible factors. In other words, southern states failed to live up even to the segregationist doctrine of separate but equal. In a series of cases, Marshall and other NAACP lawyers convinced the Supreme Court to act when segregated facilities were clearly unequal. For example, the Court ordered the admission of individual blacks to white public universities where evidence indicated that separate black institutions were inferior or nonexistent.[5]

But Marshall's goal was to prove that segregation *itself* was inherently unequal whether or not facilities were equal in all tangible respects. In other words, Marshall sought a reversal of *Plessy v. Ferguson* and a ruling that separation of the races was unconstitutional. In 1952 Marshall led a team of NAACP lawyers in a suit to admit Linda Brown to the white public schools of Topeka, Kansas, one of the few segregated school systems where white and black schools were equal with respect to buildings, curricula, teachers' salaries, and other tangible factors. In choosing the *Brown* suit, the NAACP sought to prevent the Court from simply ordering the admission of black pupils because tangible facilities were not equal and to force the Court to review the doctrine of segregation itself.

Brown v. Board of Education of Topeka   On May 17, 1954, the Court rendered its historic decision in the case of *Brown v. Board of Education of Topeka*:

> Segregation of white and colored children in public schools has a detrimental effect upon the colored children. The impact is greater when it has the sanction of law, for the policy of separating the races is usually interpreted as denoting the inferiority of the Negro group. A sense of inferiority affects the motivation of a child to learn. Segregation with the sanction of law, therefore, has a tendency to retard the educational and mental development of Negro children and to deprive them of some of the benefits they would receive in a racially integrated school system. Whatever may have been the extent of psychological knowledge of the time of *Plessy v. Ferguson*, this finding is amply supported by modern authority. Any language in *Plessy v. Ferguson* contrary to this source is rejected. . . . We conclude that in the field of public education the doctrine of "separate but equal" has no place. Separate educational facilities are inherently unequal.[6]

The Supreme Court decision in *Brown* was symbolically very important. Although it would be many years before any significant number of black children would attend previously all-white schools in the South, the decision by the nation's highest court stimulated black hopes and expectations. Indeed, *Brown* started the modern civil rights movement. As the African American psychologist Kenneth Clark wrote, "This [civil rights] movement would probably not have existed at all were it not for the 1954 Supreme Court school desegregation decision, which provided a tremendous boost to the morale of blacks by its clear affirmation that color is irrelevant to the rights of American citizens."[7]

Enforcing Desegregation   The *Brown* ruling struck down the laws of twenty-one states as well as congressional laws segregating the schools of the District of

NAACP Legal Defense Fund
Founded in 1940 by Thurgood Marshall to provide legal assistance to poor African Americans. Originally affiliated with the NAACP; now a separate organization.
www.naacpldf.org

Think Again
If a city's schools are mostly black and the surrounding suburban schools are mostly white, should busing be used to achieve a better racial balance?

Brown Matters   Chronology of *Brown vs. Board of Education*, 1957.
www.brownmatters.org

UP CLOSE

African American Politics in Historical Perspective

Many early histories of Reconstruction paid little attention to the political responses of African Americans to the imposition of segregation. But there were at least three distinct types of response: accommodation to segregation; the formation of a black protest movement and resort to legal action; and migration out of the South (to avoid some of the worst consequences of white supremacy) coupled with political mobilization of black voters in large Northern cities.

Accommodation

The foremost African American advocate of accommodation to segregation was well-known educator Booker T. Washington (1856–1915). Washington enjoyed wide popularity among both white and black Americans. An adviser to two presidents (Theodore Roosevelt and William Howard Taft), he was highly respected by white philanthropists and government officials. In his famous Cotton States' Exposition speech in Atlanta in 1895, Washington assured whites that blacks were prepared to accept a separate position in society: "In all things that are purely social we can be as separate as the fingers, yet one as the hand in all things essential to mutual progress."[a]

Washington's hopes for black America lay in a program of self-help through education. He himself had attended Hampton Institute in Virginia, where the curriculum centered around practical trades for African Americans. Washington obtained some white philanthropic support in establishing his own Tuskegee Institute in Tuskegee, Alabama, in 1881. His first students helped build the school. Early curricula at Tuskegee emphasized immediately useful vocations, such as farming, teaching, and blacksmithing. One of Tuskegee's outstanding faculty members, George Washington Carver, researched and developed uses for southern crops. Washington

urged his students to stay in the South, to acquire land, and to build homes, thereby helping to eliminate ignorance and poverty.

Protest

While Booker T. Washington was urging African Americans to make the best of segregation, a small group was organizing in support of a declaration of black resistance and protest that would later rewrite American public policy. The leader of this group was W.E.B. Du Bois (1868–1963), a historian and sociologist at Atlanta University. In 1905 Du Bois and a few other black intellectuals met in Niagara Falls, Canada, to draw up a platform intended to "assail the ears" and sear the consciences of white Americans. The Niagara Statement listed the major injustices perpetrated against African Americans since Reconstruction: the loss of voting rights, the imposition of Jim Crow laws and segregated public schools, the denial

Booker T. Washington

Columbia (see Figure 15.1).[8] Such a far-reaching exercise of judicial power was bound to meet with difficulties in enforcement, and the Supreme Court was careful not to risk its own authority. It did not order immediate national desegregation but rather required state and local authorities, under the supervision of federal district courts, to proceed with "all deliberate speed" in desegregation.[9] For more than fifteen years, state and school districts in the South waged a campaign of resistance to desegregation. Delays in implementing school desegregation continued until 1969, when the Supreme Court rejected a request by Mississippi officials

W.E.B. Du Bois

of equal job opportunities, the existence of inhumane conditions in southern prisons, the exclusion of blacks from West Point and Annapolis, and the federal government's failure to enforce the Fourteenth and Fifteenth Amendments. Out of the Niagara meeting came the idea of a nationwide organization dedicated to fighting for African Americans, and on February 12, 1909, the one hundredth anniversary of Abraham Lincoln's birth, the National Association for the Advancement of Colored People (NAACP) was founded.

Du Bois himself was on the original board of directors of the NAACP, although a majority of the early board members and financial contributors were white. Du Bois was also the NAACP's first director of research and the editor of its magazine, *Crisis*. The NAACP began a long and eventually successful campaign to establish black rights through legal action. Over the years, this organization brought hundreds of court cases at the local, state, and federal court levels on behalf of African Americans denied their constitutional rights.

Migration and Political Mobilization

World War I provided an opportunity for restive blacks in the South to escape the worst abuses of white supremacy by migrating en masse to northern cities. Between 1916 and 1918, an estimated half-million African Americans moved north to fill the labor shortage caused by the war effort. Most arrived in big northern cities only to find more poverty and segregation, but at least they could vote, and they did not encounter laws requiring segregation in public places.

The progressive "ghettoization" of African Americans—their migration from the rural South to the urban North and their increasing concentration in central cities—had profound political, as well as social, implications. The ghetto provided an environment conducive to political mobilization. As early as 1928, African Americans in Chicago were able to elect one of their own to the U.S. House of Representatives. The election of Oscar de Priest, the first black member of Congress from the North, signaled a new turn in American urban politics by announcing to white politicians that they would have to reckon with the black vote in northern cities. The black ghettos would soon provide an important element in a new political coalition that was about to take form: the Democratic Party of Franklin Delano Roosevelt.

The increasing concentration of African Americans in large, politically competitive, "swing" states provided black voters with new political power—not only to support the Democratic Party coalition in national politics but also to elect African Americans to local public office. Today African American mayors serve, or have served, in cities as diverse as New York, Chicago, Los Angeles, Detroit, Philadelphia, Atlanta, and New Orleans.

---

[a]Quoted in Henry Steele Commager, ed., *The Struggle for Racial Equality* (New York: Harper & Row, 1967), p. 19.

---

for further delay, declaring that all school districts were obligated to end their dual school systems "at once" and "now and hereafter" to operate only integrated schools.[10]

Busing and Racial Balancing   Federal district judges enjoy wide freedom in fashioning remedies for past or present discriminatory practices by governments. If a federal district court anywhere in the United States finds that any actions by governments or school officials have contributed to racial imbalances (for example,

Figure 15.1
Segregation Laws in the
United States in 1954

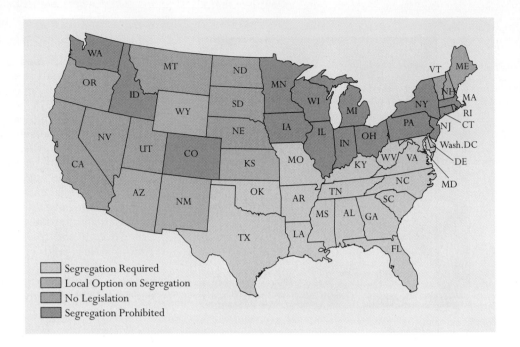

☐ Segregation Required
☐ Local Option on Segregation
☐ No Legislation
☐ Segregation Prohibited

drawing school district attendance lines that separate black and white pupils), the
judge may order the adoption of a desegregation plan to overcome racial imbalances produced by official action. A large number of cities have come under federal
district court orders to improve racial balances in their schools through busing.

In the important case of *Swann v. Charlotte-Mecklenburg County Board of Education*
(1971), the Supreme Court approved of the following:

- The use of racial balance requirements in schools and the assignment of pupils
  to schools based on race.

- "Close scrutiny" by judges of schools that are predominantly of one race.

- Gerrymandering of school attendance zones as well as "clustering" or "grouping" of schools to achieve racial balance.

- Court-ordered busing of pupils to achieve racial balance.[11]

The Court was careful to note, however, that racial imbalance in schools is not itself grounds for ordering these remedies unless it is also shown that some present
or past governmental action contributed to the imbalance.

De Facto Segregation   However, in the absence of any past or present governmental actions contributing to racial imbalance, states and school districts are not
required by the Fourteenth Amendment to integrate their schools. For example,
where central-city schools are predominantly black and suburban schools are predominantly white owing to residential patterns, cross-district busing is not required
unless some official action brought about these racial imbalances. Thus in 1974 the
Supreme Court threw out a lower federal court order for massive busing of students
between Detroit and fifty-two suburban school districts.[12] Although Detroit city
schools were 70 percent black and the suburban schools almost all white, none of
the area school districts segregated students within their own boundaries. This
important decision means that largely black central cities surrounded by largely

Although the first conflicts over integration in the public schools erupted in the segregated Southern states, Northern cities later became the focus of unrest over school integration. When federal judges ordered the busing of schoolchildren outside their neighborhoods in order to achieve racial balances citywide, parents and politicians in some Northern cities responded with a ferocity equal to earlier Southern protests. In Boston, many parents initially boycotted a busing order in 1974, refusing to send their children to school at all or establishing private schools and even attacking busloads of minority children arriving at formerly white schools.

white suburbs will remain segregated in practice because there are not enough white students living within the city boundaries to achieve integration.

De facto segregation is more common in the northern metropolitan areas than in the South. The states with the largest percentages of African American students attending schools that have 90 to 100 percent minority enrollments are Illinois, Michigan, New York, and New Jersey. The persistence of de facto segregation, together with a renewed interest in the quality of education, has caused many civil rights organizations to focus their attention on improving the quality of schools in urban areas rather than trying to desegregate these schools.

Many school districts in the South and elsewhere have operated under federal court supervision for many years. How long should court supervision continue, and what standards are to be used in determining when desegregation has been achieved once and for all? The Supreme Court in recent years has undertaken to free some school districts from direct federal court supervision. Where the last vestiges of state-sanctioned discrimination have been removed "as far as practicable," the Supreme Court has allowed lower federal courts to dissolve racial balancing plans even though imbalances due to residential patterns may continue to exist.[13]

de facto segregation Racial imbalances not directly caused by official actions but rather by residential patterns.

The Civil Rights Acts

The early goal of the civil rights movement was to eliminate discrimination and segregation practiced by *governments*, particularly states and school districts. When the civil rights movement turned to *private* discrimination—discrimination practiced by private owners of restaurants, hotels, motels, and stores; private employers, landlords, and real estate agents; and others who were not government officials—it had to take its fight to the Congress. The Constitution does not govern the activities of private individuals. Only Congress at the national level could outlaw discrimination in the private sector. Yet prior to 1964, Congress had been content to let the courts struggle with the question of civil rights. New political tactics and organizations were required to put the issue of equality on the agenda of Congress.

www **The King Center**
Biography of M. L. K. Jr., together with news and information from Atlanta King Center.
http://thekingcenter.com

Martin Luther King Jr., and Nonviolent Direct Action   Leadership in the struggle to eliminate discrimination and segregation from private life was provided by a young African American minister, Martin Luther King Jr. (see *People in Politics:* "Martin Luther King Jr., 'I Have a Dream' "). Under King, the civil rights movement developed and refined political techniques for use by American minorities, including **nonviolent direct action**. Nonviolent direct action is a form of protest that involves breaking "unjust" laws in an open, "loving," nonviolent fashion. The purpose of nonviolent direct action is to call attention—to "bear witness"—to the existence of injustice. In the words of Martin Luther King Jr., such civil disobedience "seeks to dramatize the issue so that it can no longer be ignored"[14] (see also *A Conflicting View:* "Sometimes It's Right to Disobey the Law" in Chapter 1).

King formed the Southern Christian Leadership Conference (SCLC) in 1957 to develop and direct the growing nonviolent direct action movement. During the next few years, the SCLC overshadowed the older NAACP in leading the fight against segregation. Where the NAACP had developed its strategy of court litigation to combat discrimination by *governments*, now the SCLC developed nonviolent direct action tactics to build widespread popular support and to pressure Congress to outlaw discrimination by *private businesses*.

The year 1963 was perhaps the most important for nonviolent direct action. The SCLC focused its efforts in Birmingham, Alabama, where King led thousands of marchers in a series of orderly and peaceful demonstrations. When police attacked the marchers with fire hoses, dogs, and cattle prods—in full view of national television cameras—millions of viewers around the country came to understand the injustices of segregation. The Birmingham action set off demonstrations in many parts of the country. The theme remained one of nonviolence, and it was usually whites rather than blacks who resorted to violence in these demonstrations. Responsible black leaders remained in control of the movement and won widespread support from the white community.

The culmination of King's nonviolent philosophy was a huge yet orderly march on Washington, D.C., held on August 28, 1963. More than 200,000 blacks and whites participated in the march, which was endorsed by many civic leaders, religious groups, and political figures. The march ended at the Lincoln Memorial, where Martin Luther King Jr. delivered his most eloquent appeal, entitled "I Have a Dream." Congress passed the Civil Rights Act of 1964 by better than a two-thirds favorable vote in both houses; it won the overwhelming support of both Republican and Democratic members of Congress.

The Civil Rights Act of 1964   Signed into law on July 4, 1964, the Civil Rights Act of 1964 ranks with the Emancipation Proclamation, the Fourteenth Amendment, and the *Brown* case as one of the most important steps toward full equality for all minorities, including African Americans. Among its most important provisions are the following:

> *Title II:* It is unlawful to discriminate against or segregate persons on the grounds of race, color, religion, or national origin in any public accommodation, including hotels, motels, restaurants, movies, theaters, sports arenas, entertainment houses, and other places that offer to serve the public. This prohibition extends to all business establishments whose operations affect interstate commerce or whose discriminatory practices are supported by state action.

> *Title VI:* Each federal department and agency is to take action to end discrimination in all programs or activities receiving federal financial assistance in any form. This action may include termination of financial assistance to persistently discriminatory agencies.

nonviolent direct action
Strategy used by civil rights leaders such as Martin Luther King Jr., in which protesters break "unjust" laws openly but in a "loving" fashion in order to bring the injustices of such laws to public attention.

U.S. Department of Justice, Civil Rights Division
Responsible for enforcement of U.S. civil rights laws. Site includes information on cases. *www.usdoj.gov/crt*

PEOPLE IN POLITICS

Martin Luther King Jr., "I Have a Dream"

If a man hasn't discovered something he will die for, he isn't fit to live.[a]

For Martin Luther King Jr. (1929–1968), civil rights was something to die for, and before he died for the cause, he would shatter a century of Southern segregation and set a new domestic agenda for the nation's leaders. King's contributions to the development of nonviolent direct action won him international acclaim and the Nobel Peace Prize.

King's father was the pastor of one of the South's largest and most influential African American congregations, the Ebenezer Baptist Church in Atlanta, Georgia. Young Martin was educated at Morehouse College in Atlanta and received a Ph.D. in religious studies at Boston University. Shortly after beginning his career as a Baptist minister in Montgomery, Alabama, in 1955, a black woman, Rosa Parks, refused to give up her seat to whites on a Montgomery bus, setting in motion a year-long bus boycott in that city. Only twenty-six years old, King was thrust into national prominence as the leader of that boycott, which ended in the elimination of segregation on the city's buses. In 1957 King founded the Southern Christian Leadership Conference (SCLC) to provide encouragement and leadership to the growing nonviolent protest movement against segregation.

Perhaps the most dramatic application of nonviolent direct action occurred in Birmingham, Alabama, in the spring of 1963. Thousands of African Americans, ranging from schoolchildren to senior citizens, marched in protest. Although the demonstrators conducted themselves in a nonviolent fashion, police and firefighters attacked the demonstrators with fire hoses, cattle prods, and police dogs, all in clear view of national television cameras. Thousands of demonstrators were dragged off to jail, including King. (It was at this time that King wrote his "Letter from Birmingham Jail," explaining and defending nonviolent direct action.) Pictures of police brutality flashed throughout the nation and

the world, touching the consciences of many white Americans.

King was also the driving force behind the most massive application of nonviolent direct action in U.S. history: the great "March on Washington" in August 1963, during which more than 200,000 black and white marchers converged on the nation's capital. The march ended at the Lincoln Memorial, where King delivered his most eloquent appeal, entitled "I Have a Dream."

> I still have a dream. It is a dream deeply rooted in the American dream. I have a dream that one day this nation will rise up and live out the true meaning of its creed: "We hold these truths to be self-evident, that all men are created equal."[b]

It was in the wake of the March on Washington that President John F. Kennedy sent to the Congress a strong civil rights bill that would be passed after his death—the Civil Rights Act of 1964. That same year, King received the Nobel Peace Prize.

White racial violence in the early 1960s, including murders and bombings of black and white civil rights workers, shocked and disgusted many whites in both the North and the South. In 1963 Medgar Evers, the NAACP's state chair for Mississippi, was shot to death by a sniper as he entered his Jackson home. That same year, a bomb killed four young black girls attending Sunday school in Birmingham. On the evening of April 3, 1968, King spoke to a crowd in Memphis, Tennessee, in eerily prophetic terms. "I just want to do God's will. And He's allowed me to go to the mountain. And I've looked over, and I've seen the promised land. I may not get there with you. But I want you to know tonight, that we, as a people will get to the promised land. So I'm happy tonight. I'm not worried about anything. I'm not fearing any man." On the night of April 4, 1968, the world's leading exponent of nonviolence was killed by an assassin's bullet.[c]

[a]Martin Luther King Jr., speech, June 23, 1963, Detroit, Michigan.

[b]Martin Luther King Jr., "I Have a Dream" speech, August 28, 1963, at the Lincoln Memorial, Washington, D.C., printed in David J. Garrow, *Bearing the Cross: Martin Luther King, Jr., and the Southern Christian Leadership Conference* (New York: Vintage Books, 1988), pp. 283–84.

[c]Martin Luther King Jr., speech, April 3, 1968, Memphis, Tennessee, ibid., p. 621.

In the civil rights march of 1963 more than 200,000 people marched peacefully on Washington, D.C., to end segregation. It was here that Martin Luther King Jr. delivered his famous "I Have a Dream" speech.

Title VII: It is unlawful for any employer or labor union to discriminate against any individual in any fashion in employment because of the individual's race, color, religion, sex, or national origin. The Equal Employment Opportunity Commission is established to enforce this provision by investigation, conference, conciliation, persuasion, and, if need be, civil action in federal court.

The Civil Rights Act of 1968 For many years "fair housing" had been considered the most sensitive area of civil rights legislation. Prospects for a fair housing law were poor at the beginning of 1968. However, when Martin Luther King Jr. was assassinated on April 4, the mood of Congress and the nation changed dramatically. Congress passed a fair housing law as tribute to the slain civil rights leader. The Civil Rights Act of 1968 prohibited discrimination in the sale or rental of a dwelling to any person on the basis of race, color, religion, or national origin.

Equality: Opportunity versus Results

Although the gains of the civil rights movement were immensely important, these gains were primarily in *opportunity* rather than in *results*. The civil rights movement of the 1960s did not bring about major changes in the conditions under which most African Americans lived in the United States. Racial politics today center around the *actual* inequalities between blacks and whites in incomes, jobs, housing, health, education, and other conditions of life.

Continuing Inequalities The issue of inequality today is often posed as differences in the "life chances" of blacks and whites. Figures can reveal only the bare outline of an African American's "life chances" in this society (see Table 15.2). The average income of a black family is 63 percent of the average white family's income. Over 20 percent of all black families live below the recognized poverty line, whereas less than 10 percent of white families do so. The black unemployment rate is more than twice as high as the white unemployment rate. Blacks are less likely to hold prestigious executive jobs in professional, managerial, clerical, or sales work. They do not hold many skilled craft jobs in industry but

www **U.S. Commission on Civil Rights**
National clearinghouse on information regarding discrimination because of race, color, religion, sex, age, disability, or national origin. Publishes reports, findings and recommendations.
www.usccr.gov

Table 15.2   Minority Life Chances

	Median Income of Families				
	1970	**1975**	**1980**	**1985**	**2004**
White	$10,236	$14,268	$21,904	$29,152	$49,000
Black	6,279	8,779	12,674	16,786	30,100
Hispanic	(NA)	9,551	14,716	19,027	34,200

	Percentage of Persons below Poverty Level			
	1975	**1980**	**1985**	**2004**
White	9.7%	10.2%	11.4%	8.6%
Black	31.3	32.5	31.3	24.7
Hispanic	26.9	25.7	29.0	21.3

	Unemployment Rate		
	1980	**1985**	**2005**
White	6.3%	6.2%	4.0%
Black	14.3	15.1	10.5
Hispanic	10.1	10.5	6.0

	Education: Percentage of Persons over Twenty-Five Who Have Completed High School				
	1960	**1970**	**1980**	**1990**	**2004**
White	43%	55%	69%	79%	85%
Black	20	31	51	66	80
Hispanic	(NA)	32	44	51	57

	Education: Percentage of Persons over Twenty-Five Who Have Completed College				
	1960	**1970**	**1980**	**1990**	**2004**
White	8%	11%	17%	22%	28%
Black	3	4	8	11	17
Hispanic	(NA)	4	8	9	11

Source: Statistical Abstract of the United States, various issues; U.S. Census Bureau, *www.census/population;* Bureau of Labor Statistics, *www.bls.gov.*

are concentrated in operative, service, and laboring positions. The civil rights movement opened up new opportunities for African Americans. But equality of *opportunity* is not the same as equality of *results*.

Explaining Inequalities   African American and Hispanic minorities have improved their economic condition in recent years. However, the income *disparity* between whites and minorities has remained about the same. Note that in 1970 black median family income was approximately 61 percent of white median family income, almost the same percentage as in 2004. This income gap remains despite a significant narrowing of differences in educational levels between whites and minorities.

Much, but certainly not all, of the disparity in income between whites and minorities disappears when educational levels are taken into account. Comparing the income of whites and minorities *at same educational levels* suggests that some

---Think Again---

Are differences between blacks and whites in average income mainly a product of discrimination?

Table 15.3   White and Minority Income by Educational Attainment

	Annual Mean Income				
	White	**Black**	**Hispanic**	**Black/White Ratio**	**Hispanic/White Ratio**
Professional Degree	$115,523	$96,368	$81,186	83%	75%
Bachelor's Degree	52,479	42,285	40,949	81	78
High School Degree	28,145	22,823	24,163	81	86
No High School Degree	19,264	16,516	18,981	86	98

Source: U.S. Bureau of the Census, 2005. Data for 2002.

discrimination may remain. Black college graduates on average earn about 77 percent of the income of white college graduates; black high school graduates earn about 80 percent of the income of white high school graduates. The average income of Hispanics is even closer to that of whites at the same educational levels. But neither African Americans nor Hispanics earn the same income as whites with the same educational background (see Table 15.3).

Policy Choices   What public policies should be pursued to achieve equality in America? Is it sufficient that government eliminate discrimination, guarantee equality of opportunity, and apply color-blind standards to both blacks and whites? Or should government take **affirmative action** to overcome the results of past unequal treatment of blacks—preferential or compensatory treatment to assist black applications for university admissions and scholarships, job hiring and promotion, and other opportunities for advancement in life?

affirmative action Any program, whether enacted by a government or by a private organization, whose goal is to overcome the results of past unequal treatment of minorities and/or women by giving members of these groups preferential treatment in admissions, hiring, promotions, or other aspects of life.

Shifting Goals in Civil Rights Policy   For decades, the emphasis of government policy was on equal *opportunity*. This early nondiscrimination approach began with President Harry Truman's decision to desegregate the armed forces in 1948 and carried through to Title VI and Title VII of the Civil Rights Act of 1964, which eliminated discrimination in federally aided projects and private employment. Gradually, however, the goal of the civil rights movement shifted from the traditional aim of equality of opportunity through nondiscrimination alone to affirmative action involving the establishment of "goals and timetables" to achieve greater equality of results between blacks and whites. While avoiding the term **quota**, the notion of affirmative action tests the success of equal opportunity by observing whether blacks achieve admissions, jobs, and promotions in proportion to their numbers in the population.

quota Provision of some affirmative action programs in which specific numbers or percentages of positions are open only to minorities and/or women.

Affirmative Action   Affirmative action programs were initially developed in the federal bureaucracy. Federal executive agencies were authorized by the Civil Rights Act of 1964 to develop "rules and regulations" for desegregating any organization or business receiving federal funds. In 1965 President Lyndon B. Johnson signed Executive Order 11246, requiring all federal agencies and businesses contracting with the federal government to practice affirmative action. In 1972 the U.S. Office of Education issued guidelines that mandated "goals" for university admissions and faculty hiring of minorities and women. The Equal Employment Opportunity Commission (EEOC), established by the Civil Rights Act of 1964, is responsible for monitoring affirmative action programs in private employment.

Equal Employment Opportunity Commission (EEOC) Federal EEOC site with information on what constitutes discrimination by age, disability, race, ethnicity, religion, gender; how to file a charge; and guidance for employers. *www.eeoc.gov*

Federal officials generally measure "progress" in affirmative action in terms of the number of disadvantaged group members admitted, employed, or promoted. The pressure to show "progress" can result in relaxation of traditional measures of qualifications, such as test scores and educational achievement. Advocates of affirmative action argue that these measures are not good predictors of performance on the job or in school and are biased in favor of white culture. State and local governments, schools, colleges and universities, and private employers are under pressure to revise these standards.

Affirmative Action in the Courts

The constitutional question posed by affirmative action programs is whether or not they discriminate against whites in violation of the Equal Protection Clause of the Fourteenth Amendment. A related question is whether or not affirmative action programs discriminate against whites in violation of the Civil Rights Act of 1964, which prohibits discrimination "on account of race," not just discrimination against blacks. Clearly, these are questions for the Supreme Court to resolve.

The Bakke Case   In the absence of a history of racial discrimination, the Supreme Court has been willing to scrutinize affirmative action programs to ensure that they do not directly discriminate against whites. In *University of California Regents v. Bakke* (1978), the Supreme Court struck down a special admissions program for minorities at a state medical school on the grounds that it excluded a white applicant because of his race and violated his rights under the Equal Protection Clause.[15] Allan Bakke applied to the University of California Davis Medical School two consecutive years and was rejected; in both years, black applicants with significantly lower grade point averages and medical aptitude test scores were accepted through a special admissions program that reserved sixteen minority places in a class of one hundred.[16] The University of California did not deny that its admissions decisions were based on race. Instead, it argued that its racial classification was "benign," that is, designed to assist minorities. The special admissions program was designed to (1) "reduce the historical deficit of traditionally disfavored minorities in medical schools and the medical profession"; (2) "counter the effects of societal discrimination"; (3) "increase the number of physicians who will practice in communities currently underserved"; and (4) "obtain the educational benefits that flow from an ethnically diverse student body."

The Supreme Court held that these objectives were legitimate and that race and ethnic origin *may* be considered in reviewing applications to a state school without violating the Fourteenth Amendment's Equal Protection Clause. However, the Court also held that a separate admissions program for minorities with a specific quota of openings that were unavailable to white applicants *did* violate the Equal Protection Clause. The Court ordered the university to admit Bakke to its medical school and to eliminate the special admissions program. It recommended that California consider an admissions program developed at Harvard, which considered disadvantaged racial or ethnic background as a "plus" in an overall evaluation of an application but did not set numerical quotas or exclude any person from competing for all positions.

Reaction to the decision was predictable: supporters of affirmative action emphasized the Supreme Court's willingness to allow minority status to be considered a positive factor; opponents emphasized the Supreme Court's unwillingness to allow quotas that exclude whites from competing for some positions. Because **Bakke** had "won" the **case**, many observers felt that the Supreme Court was not going to permit racial quota systems.

---Think Again---

Do you generally favor affirmative action programs for women and minorities?

***Bakke* case** U.S. Supreme Court case challenging affirmative action.

WHAT DO YOU THINK?

Do You Favor Affirmative Action?

Americans are divided on the issue of affirmative action. Polls reveal that whites are almost equally divided when the question is posed as general support for "affirmative action." In contrast, blacks and Hispanics are strongly supportive of affirmative action programs for racial minorities.

Q. "Do you generally favor or oppose affirmative action programs for racial minorities?"

	Favor	Oppose	Unsure
All	49	43	8
Whites	44	49	7
Blacks	70	21	9
Hispanics	83	28	9

But when the question is phrased in a way that implies minority preference over merit for admission to colleges and universities, then a strong majority of whites favor admission "solely on the basis of merit." Hispanics also favor merit over racial preference, but blacks appeared to be split on the issue.

Q. "Which comes closer to your view about evaluating students for admission into a college or university? Applicants should be admitted solely on the basis of merit, even if that results in few minority students being admitted. Or, an applicant's race and ethnic background should be considered to help promote diversity on college campuses, even if that means admitting some minority students who otherwise would not be admitted."

	Solely Merit	Race/ Ethnicity	Unsure
All	69	27	4
Whites	75	22	3
Blacks	44	49	7
Hispanics	59	36	5

Whites believe that black applicants to colleges and universities have the same as or a better chance of admission than white applicants, but blacks believe that white applicants have the advantage.

Q. "If two equally qualified students, one white and one black, applied to a major U.S. college or university, who do you think would have the better chance of being accepted to the college: the white student, the black student, or would they have the same chance?"

	White Student	Black Student	Same Chance	Unsure
All	31	29	36	4
Whites	24	34	38	4
Blacks	67	5	24	4
Hispanics	44	14	38	4

Source: As reported in The Polling Report, *www.pollingreport.com*, July 15, 2005.

Barbara Grutter and Jennifer Gratz challenged the affirmative action policies of the University of Michigan. The Supreme Court rejected Grutter's challenge, holding that the law school's admission policy was "narrowly tailored" to achieve a "compelling interest"— diversity. But the high court upheld Gratz's claim that making race the "decisive factor" in undergraduate admissions was unconstitutional.

Affirmative Action as a Remedy for Past Discrimination The Supreme Court has continued to approve of affirmative action programs where there is evidence of past discriminatory practices. In *United Steelworkers of America v. Weber* (1979), the Supreme Court approved a plan developed by a private employer and a union to reserve 50 percent of higher paying, skilled jobs for minorities. The Court held that "employers and unions in the private sector [are] free to take such race-conscious steps to eliminate manifest racial imbalances in traditionally segregated job categories. We hold that Title VII does not prohibit such . . . affirmative action plans." According to the Court, it would be "ironic indeed" if the Civil Rights Act were used to prohibit voluntary private race-conscious efforts to overcome the past effects of discrimination.[17] In *United States v. Paradise* (1987), the Court upheld a rigid 50 percent black quota system for promotions in the Alabama Department of Safety, which had excluded blacks from the ranks of state troopers prior to 1972 and had not promoted any blacks higher than corporal prior to 1984. In a 5-to-4 decision, the majority stressed the long history of discrimination in the agency as a reason for upholding the quota system. Whatever burdens imposed on innocent parties were outweighed by the need to correct the effects of past discrimination.[18]

Cases Questioning Affirmative Action However, the Supreme Court has continued to express concern about whites who are directly and adversely affected by government action solely because of their race. In *Firefighters Local Union 1784 v. Stotts* (1984), the Court ruled that a city could not lay off white firefighters in favor of black firefighters with less seniority.[19] In *City of Richmond v. Crosen Co.* (1989), the Supreme Court held that a minority **set-aside program** in Richmond, Virginia, which mandated that 30 percent of all city construction contracts must go to "blacks, Spanish-speaking, Orientals, Indians, Eskimos, or Aleuts," violated the Equal Protection Clause of the Fourteenth Amendment.[20]

Moreover, the Court has held that racial classifications in law must be subject to "**strict scrutiny.**" This means that race-based actions by government—any disparate treatment of the races by federal, state, or local public agencies—must be found necessary to remedy past proven discrimination, or to further clearly identified, legitimate and "compelling" government interests. Moreover, race-based actions must be "narrowly tailored" and "least restrictive" so as to minimize adverse effects on rights of other individuals. In striking down a federal construction contract set-aside program for small businesses owned by racial minorities, the Court expressed skepticism about governmental racial classifications: "There is simply no way of determining what classifications are 'benign' and 'remedial' and what classifications are in fact motivated by illegitimate notions of racial inferiority or simple racial politics."[21]

The Reverend Jesse Jackson leads a group of marchers protesting California's anti-affirmative action policies. Pictured alongside Jackson are radio personality Kasey Kasem and Delores Huerta, co-founder of the United Farm Workers' Union.

set-aside program Program in which a specified number or percentage of contracts must go to designated minorities.

strict scrutiny Supreme Court holding that race-based actions by governments can be done only to remedy past discrimination or to further a "compelling" interest and must be "narrowly tailored" to minimize effects on the rights of others.

Affirmative Action and "Diversity" in Higher Education

Most colleges and universities in United States—public as well as private—identify "**diversity,**" a term that refers to racial and ethnic representation in the student body and faculty, as an institutional goal.

University administrators argue that students benefit when they interact with others from different cultural heritages. "Students must be engaged with diverse peers if we expect learning and development to occur," and the existence of a racially and ethnically diverse student body is "a necessary condition" for such engagement. There is some evidence that students admitted under policies

diversity Term in higher education that refers to racial and ethnic representation among students and faculty.

designed to increase diversity do well in their post-college careers. And there are claims that racial and ethnic diversity on the campus improve students' "self-evaluation," "social-historical thinking," and "intellectual engagement."

But despite numerous efforts to develop scientific evidence that racial or ethnic diversity on the campus improves learning, no definitive conclusions have emerged. Educational research on this topic is clouded by political and ideological conflict. There is no evidence that racial diversity does in fact promote the expression of ideas on the campus or change perspectives or viewpoints of students.

Diversity and Affirmative Action   Even if diversity provides educational benefits, the question arises as to how to achieve it. Diversity is closely linked to affirmative action programs on campuses throughout the nation. When affirmative action programs are designed as special efforts to recruit and encourage qualified minority students to attend college, they enjoy widespread public support. But when affirmative action programs include preferences for minority applicants over equally or better qualified nonminorities, public support falters and constitutional questions arise.

Diversity as a Constitutional Question   The U.S. Supreme Court has held that the Equal Protection Clause of the Fourteenth Amendment requires that racial classifications be subject to "strict scrutiny." This means that race-based actions by governments—any disparate treatment of the racial or ethnic group by federal, state, or local public agencies, including colleges and universities—must be found necessary to advance a "compelling government interest" and must be "narrowly tailored" to further that interest.[22]

The U.S. Supreme Court held in 2003 that diversity may be a compelling government interest because it "promotes cross-racial understanding, helps to break down racial stereotypes, and enables [students] to better understand persons of different races." This opinion was written by Justice Sandra Day O'Connor in a case involving the University of Michigan Law School's affirmative action program. In a 5–4 decision, O'Connor, writing for the majority, said the Constitution "does not prohibit the law school's narrowly tailored use of race in admissions decisions to further a compelling interests in obtaining the educational benefits that flow from a diverse student body."[23]

However, in a case involving the University of Michigan's affirmative action program for *undergraduate admissions*, the Supreme Court held that the admissions policy was "not narrowly tailored to achieve respondents' asserted interest in diversity" and therefore violated the Equal Protection Clause of the Fourteenth Amendment. The Court again recognized that diversity may be a compelling interest, but *rejected an affirmative action plan that made race the decisive factor* for even minimally qualified minority applicants. Yet the Supreme Court restated its support for limited affirmative action programs that use race as a "plus" factor, the position the court has held since the *Bakke* case in 1978.[24]

Race-Neutral Approaches to Diversity   There is a variety of ways in which diversity can be achieved without using racial preferences in the admission of students. The U.S. Department of Education recommends (1) preferences based on socioeconomic status; (2) recruitment outreach efforts targeted at students from traditionally low-performing schools; and (3) admission plans for students who finish at the top of their high school classes without regard to SAT or ACT scores.[25] California, Texas, and Florida currently give preference to students who stand at or near the top of their class in each of the states' high schools. All three

FIRE: Foundation for Equal Rights in Education
Advocacy organization defending individual rights on campus and opposing racial preferences.
www.thefire.org

states officially abandoned racial preferences. Yet currently all three states enroll roughly the same numbers of minorities in their colleges and universities that they did before abandoning racial preferences.

The Absence of a Clear Constitutional Principle   The Supreme Court's decisions on affirmative action have not yet established a clear and coherent interpretation of the Constitution. No clear rule of law or constitutional principle tells us exactly what is permissible and what is prohibited in the way of racially conscious laws and practices. Nevertheless, over time some general tendencies in Supreme Court policy can be identified. Affirmative action programs are *more likely to be found constitutional* when

- They are adopted in response to a past proven history of discrimination.

- They do not absolutely bar whites or ban them from competing or participating.

- They serve a clearly identified, legitimate, and "compelling governmental interest."

- They are "narrowly tailored" to achieve the government's compelling interest and represent the "least restrictive" means of doing so.

It is important to note that the Supreme Court has never adopted the color-blind doctrine, first espoused by Justice Harlan in his *dissent* from *Plessy v. Ferguson*, that "Our Constitution is color-blind, and neither knows nor tolerates classes among the citizens." If the Equal Protection Clause required the laws of the United States and the states to be truly color-blind, then no racial guidelines, goals, or quotas would be tolerated. Occasionally this view has been expressed in recent minority dissents (see *A Conflicting View:* "The Constitution Should Be Color-Blind").

The California Civil Rights Initiative   National rethinking of affirmative action was inspired by a citizens' initiative placed on the ballot in California by popular petition and approved by 54 percent of the state's voters in 1996. The California Civil Rights Initiative added the following phrase to that state's constitution:

> Neither the state of California nor any of its political subdivisions or agents shall use race, sex, color, ethnicity or national origin as a criterion for either discriminating against, or granting preferential treatment to, any individual or group in the operation of the State's system of public employment, public education or public contracting.[26]

The key words are "or granting preferential treatment to . . ." Opponents argued that a constitutional ban on preferential treatment of minorities and women eliminates affirmative action programs in government, prevents governments from acting to correct historic racial or gender imbalances, and denies minorities and women the opportunity to seek legal protections in education and employment. Opponents challenged the California Civil Rights Initiative in federal courts, arguing that by preventing minorities and women from seeking preferential treatment under law, the initiative violated the Equal Protection Clause of the Fourteenth Amendment. But a Circuit Court of Appeals held, and the U.S. Supreme Court affirmed, that "[A] ban on race or gender preferences, as a matter of law or logic does not violate the Equal Protection Clause in any conventional sense. . . Impediments to preferential treatment do not deny equal protection."[27] The Court reasoned that the Constitution allows some race-based preferences to correct past discrimination, but it does not prevent states from banning racial preferences altogether.

Demonstrators at the Florida state capitol in Tallahassee chant "Shame on Bush" over Governor Jeb Bush's effort to ban racial preferences in university admissions and state contracting.

www **Center for Individual Rights**
Advocacy organization opposing racial preferences.
www.cir-usa.org

556 CHAPTER 15 • POLITICS AND CIVIL RIGHTS

A CONFLICTING VIEW

The Constitution Should Be Color-Blind

In 1896 a single voice spoke out against *all* racial classifications—Supreme Court Justice John Harlan opposing segregation: "Our Constitution is color-blind and neither knows nor tolerates classes among the citizens." He was *dissenting* from the Supreme Court's majority opinion in the infamous case of *Plessy v. Ferguson,* which approved the segregationist doctrine of "separate but equal." Unfortunately, the ideal of a color-blind society remains almost as elusive today as it was more than a hundred years ago.

Martin Luther King Jr. had a dream that "our children will one day live in a nation where they will not be judged by the color of their skin but by the content of their character." Can that dream be made a reality?

Over time, the civil rights movement shifted its focus from *individual rights* to *group benefits.* Affirmative action programs classify people by group membership, thereby challenging a belief widely held in the United States—that people be judged on individual attributes such as character and achievement, rather than on race or gender. Racial and gender preferences are currently encountered in hiring and promotion practices in private and public employment and in college and university admissions, scholarships, and faculty recruitment.

Affirmative action programs divide Americans into two classes—those who enjoy legally mandated preferential treatment and those who do not. Majority support for civil rights laws is weakening under growing resentment among those who are denied preferential treatment.

Some early supporters of affirmative action have come to view race-conscious programs as no longer necessary. They argue that disadvantages in society today are based more on class than on race. If preferences are to be granted at all, in their view, they should be based on economic disadvantage, not race.

Misgivings also have been expressed by a few African American scholars about the unfair stigmatizing of the supposed beneficiaries of affirmative action—a resulting negative stereotyping of blacks as unable to advance on merit alone. Race-conscious government policies, they argue, have done more harm than good. African American economist Glenn Loury claims that proponents of affirmative action have an inferiority complex: "When blacks say we have to have affirmative action, please don't take it away from us, it's almost like saying, you're right, we can't compete on merit. But I know that we can compete." Conservative columnist William Bennett says that "toxic" race relations, aggravated by affirmative action, have led to damaging forms of new segregation: "Affirmative action has not brought us what we want—a color-blind society. It has brought us an extremely color-conscious society. In our universities we have separate dorms, separate social centers. What's next—water fountains? That's not good and everybody knows it."

Many argue that affirmative action has caused the civil rights movement to lose widespread public support and instead become contentious and divisive. In fact, civil rights has become such a hot topic that most elected officials now prefer to avoid it. As one anonymous member of Congress put it, "The problem is political correctness—you can't talk openly."

Source: Quotations reported in *Newsweek,* February 13, 1996.

Hispanics in America

Hispanics—a term the U.S. Census Bureau uses to refer to Mexican Americans, Puerto Ricans, Cubans, and others of Spanish-speaking ancestry and culture—are now the nation's largest minority (see Table 15.4). The largest Hispanic subgroup is Mexican Americans. Some are descendants of citizens who lived in the Mexican territory annexed to the United States in 1848, but most have come to the United States in accelerating numbers in recent years. The largest Mexican American populations are found in Texas, Arizona, New Mexico, and California. Puerto Ricans constitute the second largest Hispanic subgroup. Many still retain ties to the commonwealth and move back and forth from Puerto Rico to New York. Cubans make up the third largest subgroup; most have fled from Fidel Castro's Cuba and live mainly in the Miami metropolitan area. Each of these Hispanic groups has encountered a different experience in American life. Indeed, some evidence indicates that these groups identify themselves separately, rather than as Hispanics.[28]

Table 15.4   Minorities in America in 2010

	Number (000)	Percent of Population (%)
Hispanics	47,756	15.5
African Americans	40,454	13.1
Asians	14,241	4.6
All other races[a]	9,246	3.0
Total Population	308,936	100[b]

[a]Includes American Indian and Alaska Native, Pacific Islanders, and persons identified as being of two or more races.

[b]White alone, not Hispanic = 65.1%.

Source: U.S. Bureau of the Census, estimates as of March 18, 2004.

If all Hispanics are grouped together for statistical comparisons, their median family income level is well below that of whites (see Table 15.2). Hispanic poverty and unemployment rates are also higher than those of whites. The percentage of Hispanics completing high school and college education is well below that of both whites and blacks, suggesting language or other cultural obstacles in education. Yet within these overall racial comparisons, there are wide disparities among subgroups as well as among individuals.

Mexican Americans   The Mexican American population in the southwestern United States is growing very rapidly; it doubled in size between 1980 and 2000. For many years, agricultural business encouraged immigration of Mexican farm laborers willing to endure harsh conditions for low pay. Many others came to the United States as *indocumentados*—undocumented, or illegal, aliens. In the Immigration Reform Act of 1986 Congress offered amnesty to all undocumented workers who had entered the United States prior to 1982.

Economic conditions in Mexico and elsewhere in Central America continue to fuel immigration, legal and illegal, to the United States. But with lower educational levels, average incomes of Mexican American families in the United States are lower and the poverty rate is higher than the general population. Although Mexican Americans have served as governors of Arizona and New Mexico and have won election to the U.S. Congress, their political power does not yet match their population percentages. Mexican American voter turnout is lower than other ethnic groups, perhaps because many are resident aliens or illegal immigrants not eligible to vote, or perhaps because of cultural factors that discourage political participation.[29]

Puerto Ricans   Residents of Puerto Rico are American citizens because Puerto Rico is a commonwealth of the United States. Puerto Rico's commonwealth government resembles that of a state, with a constitution and elected governor and legislature, but the island has no voting members of the U.S. Congress and no electoral votes for president. As citizens, Puerto Ricans can move anywhere in the United States; many have immigrated to New York City.

Median family income in Puerto Rico is higher than anywhere else in the Caribbean, but only half that of the poorest state in the United States. Puerto Ricans have not fared as well economically as other Hispanic groups within the United States: Puerto Ricans have lower median family incomes and higher poverty percentages, in part perhaps because of lower work force participation.

Despite efforts to improve Hispanic voter turnout, it still remains significantly lower than that of Anglos or of African Americans.

ACROSS THE USA

Hispanic Populations

The Hispanic population of the United States is concentrated in relatively few states, notably California, Arizona, New Mexico, Texas, and Florida. These are states in which Hispanics exceed 10 percent of the population. In addition Hispanics are 5 to 10 percent of the populations of New York, Massachusetts, Rhode Island, Connecticut, New Jersey, Illinois, Hawaii, Kansas, Colorado, Utah, Wyoming, Nevada, and Washington. Among the states, only Florida, where Cubans predominate in the Hispanic population, regularly votes Republican. In all other states, Hispanics tend to vote Democratic. Texas Hispanics split their vote almost evenly in the 2004 presidential election between Texan George Bush and Massachusetts Senator John Kerry.

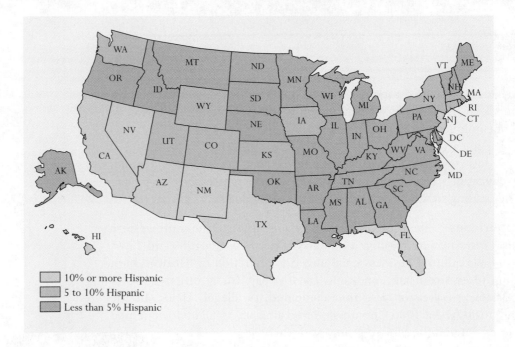

- 10% or more Hispanic
- 5 to 10% Hispanic
- Less than 5% Hispanic

Mexican American Legal Defense League

Advocacy and litigation on behalf of Latinos, with information on cases dealing with immigration rights.
www.maldef.org

One explanation centers on the history of access to federal welfare programs on the island and the resulting social dependency it fostered among some Puerto Rican families.[30]

Puerto Ricans have long debated whether to remain a commonwealth of the United States, apply for statehood, or seek complete independence from the United States. As citizens of a commonwealth, Puerto Ricans pay no U.S. income tax (although their local taxes are substantial) while receiving all the benefits that U.S. citizens are entitled to—Social Security, welfare assistance, food stamps, Medicaid, Medicare, and so forth. If Puerto Rico chose to become a state, its voters could participate in presidential and congressional elections, but its taxpayers would not enjoy the same favorable cost-benefit ratio they enjoy under commonwealth status. Some Puerto Ricans also fear that statehood would dilute the island's cultural identity and force English on them as the national language.

As a state, Puerto Rico would have two U.S. senators and perhaps six U.S. representatives. The island's majority party, the Popular Democratic Party, is closely identified with the Democratic Party, so most of these new members would likely be Democrats. But the island's New Progressive Party, identified with the Republican Party, supports statehood, and many GOP leaders believe their party should appeal to Hispanic voters. If Puerto Ricans were to choose independence,

Feelings run high over immigration reform at a 2006 meeting of the National Council of La Raza. The NCLA is the nation's largest Hispanic civil rights organization.

a new constitution for the Republic of Puerto Rico would be drawn up by the islanders themselves.

Only Congress can admit a new state, but Congress is unlikely to act without the full support of Puerto Ricans themselves. Several nonbinding referenda votes have been held in Puerto Rico over the years, the most recent in 1998. Opinion today appears to be closely divided, with commonwealth status edging out statehood by a small margin; independence has never received more than one percent of the vote.

Cuban Americans   Many Cuban Americans, especially those in the early waves of refugees from Castro's revolution in 1959, were skilled professionals and businesspeople, and they rapidly set about building Miami into a thriving economy. Although Cuban Americans are the smallest of the Hispanic subgroups, today they are better educated and enjoy higher incomes than the others. They are well organized politically, and they have succeeded in electing Cuban Americans to local office in Florida and to the U.S. Congress.

Hispanic Politics

Mexican Americans constitute the largest portion, nearly three-quarters, of the nation's Hispanic population. Most reside in the southwestern United States—California, Texas, Arizona, New Mexico, and Colorado. Puerto Ricans in New York, and Cubans and other Central and South Americans in Florida, constitute only about one-quarter of the Hispanic population. Thus, generalizations about Hispanic politics are heavily influenced by Mexican Americans.

Organizing for Political Activity   For many decades American agriculture encouraged Mexican American immigration, both legal and illegal, to labor in fields as *braceros*. Most of these migrant farm workers lived and worked under very difficult conditions; they were paid less than minimum wages for backbreaking labor. Farm workers were not covered by the federal National Labor Relations Act and therefore not protected in the right to organize labor unions. But civil rights activity among Hispanics, especially among farm workers, grew during the 1960s under the leadership of Cesar Chavez and his United Farm Workers union. Chavez organized a national boycott of grapes from California vineyards that refused to recognize the union or improve conditions. *La Raza*, as the movement was called, finally ended in a union contract with the growers and later a California law protecting the right of farm workers to organize unions and bargain

La Raza
National Council of La Raza. Issue positions, programs, news, dedicated to improving life experiences of Hispanic Americans.
www.nclr.org

collectively with their employers. More importantly, the movement galvanized Mexican Americans throughout the Southwest to engage in political activity.[31]

However, inasmuch as many Mexican American immigrants were noncitizens, and many were *indocumentados* (undocumented residents of the United States), the voting strength of Mexican Americans never matched their numbers in the population. The Immigration Reform and Control Act of 1986 granted amnesty to illegal aliens living in the United States in 1982. But the same act also imposed penalties on employers who hired illegal aliens. The effect of these threatened penalties on many employers was to make them wary of hiring Hispanics, especially as permanent employees. At the same time, industries in need of cheap labor—agriculture, health and hospitals, restaurants, clothing manufacturers, and so on—continued to encourage legal and illegal immigration to fill minimum and even subminimum wage level jobs with few if any benefits.

Hispanic Political Power Most Hispanics today believe that they confront less prejudice and discrimination than their parents. Nonetheless, in 1994 California voters approved a referendum, Proposition 187, that would have barred welfare and other benefits to persons living in the state illegally. Most Hispanics opposed the measure, believing that it was motivated by prejudice. A federal court later declared major portions of Proposition 187 unconstitutional. And the U.S. Supreme Court has held that a state may not bar the children of illegal immigrants from attending public schools.[32]

Mexican American voter turnout remains weak. Various explanations have been advanced for the lower voter participation of Mexican Americans. Language barriers may still discourage some voters, even though ballots in many states are now available in Spanish. Illegal immigrants, of course, cannot vote.

Table 15.5   Hispanic Politics

	Total	Mexican	Puerto Rican	Cuban	Other
"In politics today do you consider yourself a Republican, a Democrat, an Independent, or something else?"					
Democrat	37%	33%	52%	29%	39%
Republican	16	15	17	34	12
Independent	33	37	17	27	35
"Do you think abortion should be legal in all cases, illegal in most cases, or illegal in all cases?"					
Legal	40	36	60	49	32
Illegal	58	61	39	49	66
"Do you think the government should provide health insurance for Americans without insurance, or is this something the government should not do?"					
Should	83	83	84	87	86
Should not	14	14	15	11	11
"Should colleges sometimes take a student's racial and ethnic background into consideration when they decide which students to admit, or should they select students without considering their racial or ethnic backgrounds?					
Consider	22	21	17	17	21
Don't consider	75	76	78	82	76
"Do you favor or oppose offering government financial aid or 'vouchers' to pay parents some of the cost of sending their children to private and parochial schools?					
Favor	40	40	46	49	37
Oppose	18	16	12	22	23

Source: Copyright © *Public Perspective*, a publication of the Roper Center for Public Opinion Research, University of Connecticut, Storrs. Reprinted by permission of Roper Center for Public Opinion Research.

UP CLOSE

Republicans and the Latino Vote

Winning the Hispanic vote is increasingly important for the Republican Party. With African American voters regularly giving Democratic candidates 90 percent or more of their vote, the Republican Party cannot afford to lose the vote of what is now the nation's largest minority. It is true that so far Hispanics voters make up only 6 to 8 percent of all voters in presidential elections, even though Hispanics constitute over 12 percent of the nation's population. (African Americans constitute about 12 percent of the population and comprise about 11 percent of the voters on Election Day.) But over time, the growth of the Hispanic population, together with an increase in voter education and participation, will become crucial to Republican victories.

Bush's Efforts

President George W. Bush has been particularly committed to winning the hearts of Latinos for the GOP. The bilingual president won substantial numbers of Hispanic voters while serving as governor of Texas. In 2000, against democrat Al Gore, Bush won about 36 percent of Hispanic voters nationwide, and in 2004, against Democrat John Kerry, Bush increased that margin to about 42 percent.

Immigration

President Bush has long supported a new immigration initiative that would allow temporary "guest" workers to cross the border and work in the United States for up to six years. He has also proposed that illegal immigrants be allowed to apply for work visas good for six years, after which they could apply for permanent residency if their taxes are paid and they have no criminal records. The Bush proposal has met with substantial opposition within his own party's Congress members, many of whom oppose giving legal status to people who broke the law to enter the United States. And after 9/11 any effort to relax immigration standards appeared doomed.

Issues Cited By Latino Voters in 2004

But interestingly, immigration reform appears to be only a modest concern to Hispanic voters. A national survey of Hispanic voters in 2004 reported the following issues of greatest concern to them:

Education	54%
Economy/Jobs	51
Health Care	51
War on Terror	45
Crime	40
Social Security	39
Moral Values	31
Taxes	33
Immigration	27

The issues of concern to Hispanic voters do not appear to be much different from those of non-Hispanic voters.

Source: Pew Hispanic Center, Kaiser Family Foundation Survey of Latinos 2004. *www.cis.org/articles*

Lower education and income levels are also associated with lower voter turnout. Nonetheless, Hispanic voting is on the increase throughout the nation, and both Democratic and Republican candidates are increasingly aware of the importance of the Hispanic vote.

Overall, most Hispanics identify with the Democratic Party (see Table 15.5). Mexican Americans in the Southwestern states and Puerto Ricans in New York have traditionally supported Democratic candidates, while the strong anticommunist heritage among Cuban Americans has fostered a Republican voting tradition in Florida. Hispanics are generally conservative on social issues (opposing abortion, opposing racial preferences, favoring government vouchers to pay parochial school tuitions) but liberal on economic issues (favoring government provision of health insurance for all, favoring a larger federal government with many services). (See *Up Close:* "Republicans and the Latino Vote.")

The Voting Rights Act of 1965, as later amended and as interpreted by the U.S. Supreme Court, extends voting rights protections to "language minorities," including Hispanics (see "Congressional Apportionment and Redistricting" in

The American Indian Movement, AIM, has emerged as the leading activist organization supporting Native Americans.

Chapter 10). Following redistricting after the 1990 census, Hispanic representation in Congress rose substantially; today there are nineteen Hispanic members of the House of Representatives—about 4 percent, still well below the 11 percent of the U.S. population which is Hispanic. Hispanics have been elected governors of Arizona, New Mexico, and Florida.

Native Americans: Trail of Tears

Christopher Columbus, having erred in his estimate of the circumference of the globe, believed he had arrived in the Indian Ocean when he first came to the Caribbean. He mistook the Arawaks there for people of the East Indies, calling them *Indios,* and this Spanish word passed into English as "Indians"—a word that came to refer to all Native American peoples. But at the time of the first European contacts, these peoples had no common ethnic identity; hundreds of separate cultures and languages were thriving in the Americas. Although estimates vary, most historians believe 7 million to 12 million people lived in the land that is now the United States and Canada; 25 million more lived in Mexico; and as many as 60 million to 70 million in all lived in the Western Hemisphere, a number comparable to Europe's population at the time.

In the centuries that followed, the Native American population of the Western Hemisphere was devastated by warfare, by famine, and, most of all, by epidemic diseases brought from Europe. Overall, the Native population fell by 90 percent, the greatest known human disaster in world history. By 1910 only 210,000 Native Americans lived in the United States. Their population has slowly recovered to the current 2.2 million (less than 1 percent of the U.S. population). Many live on reservations and trust lands, the largest of which is the Navajo and Hopi enclave in the southwestern United States (see *Across the USA:* "Native American Peoples").

The Trail of Broken Treaties   In the Northwest Ordinance of 1787, Congress, in organizing the western territories of the new nation, declared, "The utmost good faith shall always be observed toward the Indians. Their lands and property shall never be taken from them without their consent." And later, in the Intercourse Act of 1790, Congress declared that public treaties between the United States government and the independent Native nations would be the only legal means of obtaining Indian land.

As president, George Washington forged a treaty with the Creeks: in exchange for land concessions, the United States pledged to protect the boundaries of the Creek nation and to allow the Creeks themselves to punish all violators of their laws within these boundaries. This semblance of legality was reflected in hundreds of treaties that followed. (Indeed, in recent years some Native American nations have successfully sued in federal court for reparations and return of lands obtained in violation of the Intercourse Act of 1790 and subsequent treaties.) Yet Native lands were constantly invaded by whites. The resulting Native resistance typically led to wars that ultimately resulted in great loss of life among warriors and their families and the further loss of Native land. The cycle of invasion, resistance, military defeat, and further land concessions continued for a hundred years.

"Indian Territories"   Following the purchase of the vast Louisiana Territory in 1803, President Thomas Jefferson sought to "civilize" the Natives by promoting farming in "reservations" that were located west of the Mississippi River. But soon, peoples who had been forced to move from Ohio to Missouri were forced to move again to survive the relentless white expansion. President James Monroe designated as "Indian territory" most of the Great Plains west of the Missouri

ACROSS THE USA

Native American Peoples

This map shows the locations of the principal Native American reservations in the United States. Tribal governments officially govern these reservations. (Alaska Natives, including Aleuts and Eskimos, live mostly in 200 villages widely scattered across rural Alaska; twelve regional Native American corporations administer property and mineral rights on behalf of Native peoples in that state.)

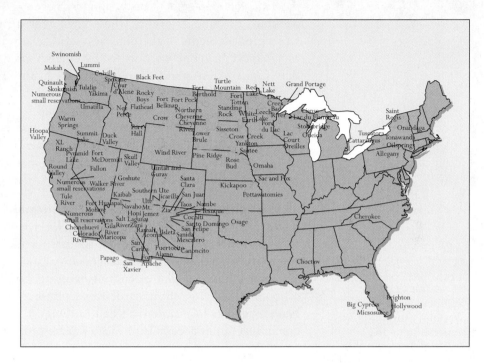

River. Native peoples increasingly faced three unattractive choices: assimilation, removal, or extinction.

In 1814 the Creeks, encouraged by the British during the War of 1812 to attack American settlements, faced an army of Tennessee volunteer militia led by Andrew Jackson. At the Battle of Horseshoe Bend, Jackson's cannon fire decimated the Creek warriors. In the uneven Treaty of Fort Jackson, the Creeks, Choctaws, and Cherokees were forced to concede millions of acres of land.

By 1830 the "Five Civilized Tribes" of the southeastern United States (Cherokees, Chickasaws, Choctaws, Creeks, and Seminoles) had ceded most but not all of their lands. When gold was discovered on Cherokee land in northern Georgia in 1829, whites invaded their territory. Congress, at the heeding of the old "Indian fighter" President Andrew Jackson, passed the Removal Act, ordering the forcible relocation of the Natives to Oklahoma Indian Territory. The Cherokees tried to use the whites' law to defend their land, bringing their case to the U.S. Supreme Court. When Chief Justice John Marshall held the Cherokees were a "domestic dependent nation" that could not be forced to give up its land, President Jackson replied scornfully, "John Marshall has made his decision. Now let him enforce it." He sent a 7,000-strong army to pursue Seminoles into the huge Florida Everglades swamp and forced 16,000 Cherokees and other peoples on the infamous "Trail of Tears" march to Oklahoma in 1838.

"Indian Wars" The "Indian Wars" were fought between the Plains nations and the U.S. Army between 1864 and 1890. Following the Civil War, the federal government began to assign boundaries to each nation and authorized the Bureau of Indian Affairs (BIA) to "assist and protect" Native peoples on their "reservations." But the reservations were repeatedly reduced in size until subsistence by hunting became impossible. Malnutrition and demoralization of the Native peoples were accelerated by the mass slaughter of the buffalo; vast herds, numbering perhaps as many as 70 million, were exterminated over the years. The most storied engagement of the long war occurred at the Little Bighorn River in Montana on June 25, 1876, where Civil War hero General George Armstrong Custer led elements of the U.S. Seventh Cavalry to destruction at the hands of Sioux and Cheyenne warriors led by chiefs Crazy Horse, Sitting Bull, and Gall. But "Custer's last stand" inspired renewed army campaigns against the Plains peoples; the following year, Crazy Horse was forced to surrender. In 1881 destitute Sioux under Chief Sitting Bull returned from exile in Canada to surrender themselves to reservation life. Among the last peoples to hold out were the Apaches, whose famous warrior Geronimo finally surrendered in 1886. Sporadic fighting continued until 1890, when a small malnourished band of Lakota Sioux were wiped out at Wounded Knee Creek.

The Attempted Destruction of Traditional Life The Dawes Act of 1887 governed federal Native American policy for decades. The thrust of the policy was to break up Native lands, allotting acreage for individual homesteads in order to assimilate Natives into the white agricultural society. Farming was to replace hunting, and traditional Native customs were to be shed for English language and schooling. But this effort to destroy culture never really succeeded. Although Native peoples lost more than half of their 1877 reservation land, few lost their communal ties or accumulated much private property. Life on the reservations was often desperate. Natives suffered the worst poverty of any group in the United States, with high rates of infant mortality, alcoholism, and other diseases. The Federal Bureau of Indian Affairs (BIA), notoriously corrupt and mismanaged, encouraged dependency and regularly interfered with religious affairs and customs.

The New Deal The New Deal under President Franklin D. Roosevelt came to Native Americans in the form of the Indian Reorganization Act of 1934. This act sought to restore Native tribal structures by recognizing these nations as instruments of the federal government. Landownership was restored, and elected Native tribal councils were recognized as legal governments. Efforts to force assimilation were largely abandoned. The BIA became more sensitive to Native culture and began employing Native Americans in larger numbers. Yet the BIA remained "paternalistic," frequently interfering in tribal "sovereignty."

The American Indian Movement The civil rights movement of the 1960s inspired a new activism among Native American groups. The American Indian Movement (AIM) was founded in 1968 and attracted national headlines by occupying Alcatraz Island in San Francisco Bay. Violence flared in 1972 when AIM activists took over the site of the Wounded Knee battle and fought with FBI agents. Several Native nations succeeded in federal courts and Congress at winning back lands and/or compensation for lands taken from them in treaty violations.

Native Americans Today The U.S. Constitution (Article I, Section 8) grants Congress the full power "to regulate Commerce . . . with the Indian Tribes." States are prevented from regulating or taxing Native peoples or extending their courts' jurisdiction over them unless authorized by Congress. The Supreme Court recognizes Native Americans "as members of quasi-sovereign tribal entities"[33] with powers to regulate their own internal affairs, establish their

Bureau of Indian Affairs
Government agency with responsibility for administration of 562 federally recognized tribal governments in the United States. *www.doi.gov/bureau-Indian-affairs*

American Indian Movement
Advocacy organization for Native Americans, with news and views on treaties and treaty violations.
www.aimovement.org

own courts, and enforce their own laws, all subject to congressional supervision. Thus, for example, many Native peoples chose to legalize gambling, including casino gambling, on reservations in states that otherwise prohibited the activity. As citizens, Native Americans have the right to vote in state as well as national elections. Those living off reservations have the same rights and responsibilities as other citizens. Ben Nighthorse Campbell, former U.S. senator from Colorado, was the only tribal member (Northern Cheyenne) to serve in Congress.

The Bureau of Indian Affairs in the Department of the Interior continues to supervise reservation life, and Native Americans enrolled as members of nations and living on reservations are entitled to certain benefits established by law and treaty. Nevertheless, these peoples remain the poorest and least healthy in the United States, with high incidences of infant mortality, suicide, and alcoholism. Approximately half of all Native Americans live below the poverty line.

The Rights of Disabled Americans

Disabled Americans were *not* among the classes of people protected by the landmark Civil Rights Act of 1964. Throughout most of the nation's history, little thought was given to making public or private buildings or facilities accessible to blind, deaf, or mobility-impaired people.[34] Not until the Education of Handicapped Children Act of 1975 did the federal government mandate that the nation's public schools provide free education to handicapped children.

Americans with Disabilities Act The Americans with Disabilities Act (ADA) of 1990 is a sweeping law that prohibits discrimination against disabled people in private employment, government programs, public accommodations, and telecommunications. The act is vaguely worded in many of its provisions, requiring "reasonable accommodations" for disabled people that do not involve "undue hardship." This means disabled Americans do not have exactly the same standard of protection as minorities or women, who are protected from discrimination *regardless* of hardship or costs. (It also means that attorneys, consultants, and

The most recent Americans to pressure Congress and the courts for protection of rights long denied them are the nation's disabled citizens. In 1990 disability rights activists succeeded in getting Congress to pass the Americans with Disabilities Act, which mandates the removal of many barriers that have kept handicapped people from working, traveling, and enjoying leisure activities. Nevertheless, many obstacles remain. Here, activists demonstrate in favor of the act.

bureaucrats will make handsome incomes over the years interpreting the meaning of these phrases.) Specifically the ADA includes the following protections:

- *Employment:* Disabled people cannot be denied employment or promotion if, with "reasonable accommodation," they can perform the duties of the job. Reasonable accommodation need not be made if doing so would cause "undue hardship" on the employer.

- *Government programs:* Disabled people cannot be denied access to government programs or benefits. New buses, taxis, and trains must be accessible to disabled persons, including those in wheelchairs.

- *Public accommodations:* Disabled people must enjoy "full and equal" access to hotels, restaurants, stores, schools, parks, museums, auditoriums, and the like. To achieve equal access, owners of existing facilities must alter them "to the maximum extent feasible"; builders of new facilities must ensure that they are readily accessible to disabled persons unless doing so is structurally impossible.

- *Communications:* The Federal Communications Commission is directed to issue regulations that will ensure telecommunications devices for hearing- and speech-impaired people are available "to the extent possible and in the most efficient manner."

Mental and Learning Disabilities   The ADA protects the rights of people with learning and psychiatric disabilities, as well as physical disabilities. The U.S. Equal Employment Opportunity Commission has received almost as many complaints about workplace discrimination against the mentally disabled as it has received from people claiming back injuries.[35] But it is far more difficult for employers to determine how to handle a depressed or anxiety-ridden employee than an employee with a visible physical disability. How can employers distinguish uncooperative employees from those with psychiatric disorders?

The American Council on Education reports that the percentage of students in colleges and universities claiming a "learning disability" has jumped from 3 to 10 percent.[36] A recent decision by the U.S. Department of Education that "attention deficit disorder" is covered by the ADA is expected to result in another significant rise in students claiming disabilities. Colleges and universities are required to provide special accommodations for students with disabilities, including tutors, extra time on examinations, oral rather than written exams, and the like.

Gender Equality and the Fourteenth Amendment

The historical context of the Fourteenth Amendment implies its intent to guarantee equality for newly freed slaves, but the wording of its Equal Protection Clause applies to "any person." Thus the text of the Fourteenth Amendment could be interpreted to bar any gender differences in the law, in the fashion of the once proposed yet never ratified Equal Rights Amendment. But the Supreme Court has not interpreted the Equal Protection Clause to give the same level of protection to gender equality as to racial equality. Indeed, in 1873 the Supreme Court specifically rejected arguments that this clause applied to women. The Court once upheld a state law banning women from practicing law, arguing that "the natural and proper timidity and delicacy which belongs to the female sex evidently unfits it for many of the occupations of civil life. . . . The paramount

ADA Home Page
Federal agency site with guide to disability rights laws. *www.usdoj.gov/crt/ada*

American Council on Education
Information on a wide range of educational issues, including diversity, testing, admissions, and so forth. *www.acenet.edu*

— Think Again —
Should gender equality receive the same level of legal protection as racial equality?

destiny and mission of women are to fulfill the noble and benign offices of wife and mother. This is the law of the Creator."[37]

Early Feminist Politics   The earliest active feminist organizations grew out of the pre–Civil War antislavery movement. There the first generation of feminists— including Lucretia Mott, Elizabeth Cady Stanton, Lucy Stone, and Susan B. Anthony—learned to organize, hold public meetings, and conduct petition campaigns. After the Civil War, women were successful in changing many state laws that abridged the property rights of married women and otherwise treated them as "chattel" (property) of their husbands. By the early 1900s activists were also successful in winning some protections for women in the workplace, including state laws limiting women's hours of work, working conditions, and physical demands. At the time, these laws were regarded as "progressive."

The most successful feminist efforts of the 1800s centered on protection of women in families. The perceived threats to women's well-being were their husbands' drinking, gambling, and consorting with prostitutes. Women led the Anti-Saloon League, succeeded in outlawing gambling and prostitution in every state except Nevada, and provided the major source of moral support for the Eighteenth Amendment (Prohibition).

In the early twentieth century, the feminist movement concentrated on women's suffrage—the drive to guarantee women the right to vote. The early suffragists employed mass demonstrations, parades, picketing, and occasional disruption and civil disobedience—tactics similar to those of the civil rights movement of the 1960s. The culmination of their efforts was the 1920 passage of the Nineteenth Amendment to the Constitution: "The right of citizens of the United States to vote shall not be denied or abridged by the United States or by any State on account of sex." The suffrage movement spawned the League of Women Voters; in addition to women's right to vote, the League has sought protection of women in industry, child welfare laws, and honest election practices.

Judicial Scrutiny of Gender Classifications   In the 1970s, the Supreme Court became responsive to arguments that sex discrimination might violate the

Elizabeth Cady Stanton addresses a meeting. Stanton, with Lucretia Mott and others, organized one of the defining moments in feminist politics in the United States—the Seneca Falls convention of 1848. Participants at the convention approved a Declaration of Sentiments, modeled on the Declaration of Independence, that demanded legal and political rights for women, including the right to vote.

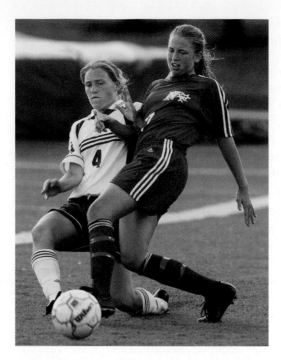

The high school girls' national soccer finals in 2004. These girls can now compete for college athletic scholarships, made more accessible by Title IX.

Equal Protection Clause of the Fourteenth Amendment. In *Reed v. Reed* (1971), it ruled that sexual classifications in the law "must be reasonable and not arbitrary, and must rest on some ground of difference having fair and substantial relation to . . . important governmental objectives."[38] This is a much more relaxed level of scrutiny than the Supreme Court gives to racial classification in the law.

The Supreme Court continues to wrestle with the question of whether some gender differences can be recognized in law. The question is most evident in laws dealing with sexual activity and reproduction. The Court has upheld statutory rape laws that make it a crime for an adult male to have sexual intercourse with a female under the age of eighteen, regardless of her consent. "We need not to be medical doctors to discern that young men and young women are not similarly situated with respect to the problems and the risks of sexual intercourse. Only women may become pregnant, and they suffer disproportionately the profound physical, emotional and psychological consequences of sexual activity."[39]

Women's participation in military service, particularly combat, raises even more controversial questions regarding permissible gender classifications. The Supreme Court appears to have bowed out of this particular controversy. In upholding Congress's draft registration law for men only, the Court ruled that "the constitutional power of Congress to raise and support armies and to make all laws necessary and proper to that end is broad and sweeping."[40] Congress and the Defense Department are responsible for determining assignments for women in the military. Women have won assignments to air and naval combat units but remain excluded from combat infantry, armor, artillery, special forces, and submarine duty.

Title IX and Women's Athletics   Perhaps no other gender-related law has had more impact on the nation's colleges and universities than **Title IX**, part of the Education Act Amendments of 1972. Title IX prohibits discrimination against women in college and university athletic programs. But what exactly does this mean? It was not until 1978 that the federal government attempted to set forth regulations concerning intercollegiate athletics. Among the stated goals of these regulations were (1) financial support substantially proportionate to the number of male and female athletes; (2) the provision of opportunities to participate

---

www **National Organization for Women (NOW)** Advocacy organization for feminist activists working to protect abortion rights, end discrimination against women, and "eradicate racism, sexism, and homophobia." *www.now.org*

Title IX A provision in the Federal Education Act forbidding discrimination against women in college athletic programs.

in athletics for men and women substantially proportionate to their enrollments; (3) or, where these conditions were not met, a continuing practice of program expansion for female athletes. Football was recognized as unique, because it produces the revenues needed to maintain the entire athletic program of most colleges and universities, so football programs could continue to outspend women's athletics.

The results of Title IX have been impressive. In 2005 there were more than 150,000 female student athletes, a dramatic increase over the 30,000 when the law was passed. Women's teams in the National Collegiate Athletic Association nearly doubled from about 4,800 to 8,400.

But to maintain the proportionality required by the law, the number of men's sports at many universities have failed to expand and indeed many have been cut, especially nonrevenue producing sports such as wrestling. Critics of the law have urged that it be amended to account for perceived differences in interest in athletics between male and female college students.

The Equal Rights Amendment   The proposed **Equal Rights Amendment** to the U.S. Constitution, passed by Congress in 1972 but never ratified by the states, was worded very broadly: "Equality of rights under the law shall not be denied or abridged by the United States or any State on account of sex." Had it been ratified by the necessary thirty-eight states, it would have eliminated most, if not all, gender differences in the law. Without the ERA, many important guarantees of equality for women rest on laws of Congress rather than on the Constitution.

Gender Equality in the Economy

As cultural views of women's roles in society have changed and economic pressures on family budgets have increased, women's participation in the labor force has risen. The gap between women's and men's participation in the nation's workforce is closing over time.[41] With the movement of women into the workforce, feminist political activity has shifted toward economic concerns—gender equality in education, employment, pay, promotion, and credit.

Gender Equality in Civil Rights Laws   Title VII of the Civil Rights Act of 1964 prevents sexual (as well as racial) discrimination in hiring, pay, and promotions. The Equal Employment Opportunity Commission, the federal agency charged with eliminating discrimination in employment, has established guidelines barring stereotyped classifications of "men's jobs" and "women's jobs." The courts have repeatedly struck down state laws and employer practices that differentiate between men and women in hours, pay, retirement age, and so forth.

The Federal Equal Credit Opportunity Act of 1974 prohibits sex discrimination in credit transactions. Federal law prevents banks, credit unions, savings and loan associations, retail stores, and credit card companies from denying credit because of sex or marital status. However, these businesses may still deny credit for a poor or nonexistent credit rating, and some women who have always maintained accounts in their husband's name may still face credit problems if they apply in their own name.

The Earnings Gap   Despite protections under federal laws, women continue to earn substantially less than men do. Today women, on average, earn about 76 percent of what men do (see Figure 15.2). This earnings gap has been closing very slowly: In 1985 women earned an average 68 percent of men's earnings. The earnings gap is not primarily a product of **direct discrimination**; women in the same job with the same skills, qualifications, experience, and work record are not

Employees of the Mitsubishi automobile plant in Normal, Illinois, demonstrated outside the offices of the Equal Employment Opportunity Commission in Chicago in April 1996 in support of the company after it became the target of a sexual harassment investigation. The company provided transportation to the demonstration and paid the workers for the day.

Equal Rights Amendment (ERA)
A proposed constitutional amendment, passed by Congress but never ratified by three-quarters of the states, that would have explicitly guaranteed equal rights for women.

direct discrimination Now illegal practice of differential pay for men versus women even when those individuals have equal qualifications and perform the same job.

Figure 15.2 The Earnings Gap: Median Weekly Earnings of Men and Women

The continuing "earnings gap" between men and women reflects a division in the labor market between traditionally male higher paying occupations and traditionally female lower paying positions.

Note: Figures in parentheses indicate the ratio of women's to men's median weekly earnings.

Source: Bureau of Labor Statistics, *www.bls.gov.*

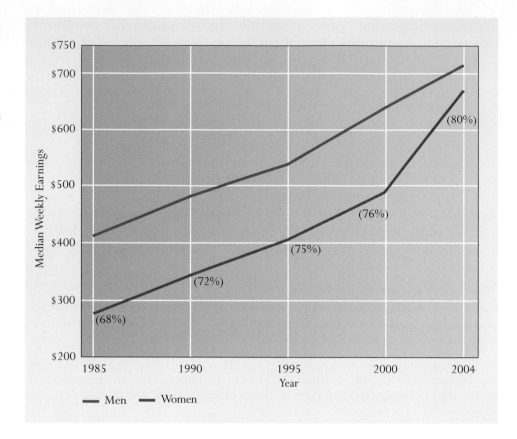

generally paid less than men. Such direct discrimination has been illegal since the Civil Rights Act of 1964. Rather, the earnings gap is primarily a product of a division in the labor market between traditionally male and female jobs, with lower salaries paid in traditionally female occupations.

The Dual Labor Market and "Comparable Worth" The existence of a "dual" labor market, with male-dominated "blue-collar" jobs distinguishable from female-dominated "pink-collar" jobs, continues to be a major obstacle to economic equality between men and women. These occupational differences result from cultural stereotyping, social conditioning, and training and education—all of which narrow the choices available to women. Although significant progress has been made in reducing occupational sex segregation (see Figure 15.3), many observers nevertheless doubt that sexually differentiated occupations will be eliminated in the foreseeable future.

As a result of a growing recognition that the wage gap is more a result of occupational differentiation than direct discrimination, some feminist organizations have turned to a new approach—the demand that pay levels in various occupations be determined by **comparable worth** rather than by the labor market. Comparable worth goes beyond paying men and women equally for the same work and calls for paying the same wages for jobs of comparable value to the employer. Advocates of comparable worth argue that governmental agencies or the courts should evaluate traditionally male and female jobs to determine their "worth" to the employer, perhaps by considering responsibilities, effort, knowledge, and skill requirements. Jobs adjudged to be "comparable" would be paid equal wages. Government agencies or the courts would replace the labor market in determining wage rates.

Feminist.Com
Web site promoting women's business development, with information and advice.
www.feminist.com

comparable worth
Argument that pay levels for traditionally male and traditionally female jobs should be equalized by paying equally all jobs that are "worth about the same" to an employer.

WHAT DO YOU THINK?

What Constitutes Sexual Harassment?

Various surveys report that up to one-third of female workers say they have experienced sexual harassment on the job.[a] But it is not always clear exactly what kind of behavior constitutes "sexual harassment."

The U.S. Supreme Court has provided some guidance in the development of sexual harassment definitions and prohibitions. Title VII of the Civil Rights Act of 1964 makes it "an unlawful employment practice to discriminate against any individual with respect to his [sic] compensation, terms, conditions or privileges of employment because of such individual's race, color, religion, sex, or national origin." In the employment context, the U.S. Supreme Court has approved the following definition of sexual harassment:

> Unwelcome sexual advances, requests for sexual favors, and other verbal or physical conduct of a sexual nature constitute sexual harassment when (1) submission to such conduct is made either explicitly or implicitly a term or condition of an individual's employment; (2) submission to or rejection of such conduct by an individual is used as the basis for employment decisions affecting such individual; or (3) such conduct has the purpose or effect of unreasonably interfering with an individual's work performance or creating an intimidating, hostile, or offensive working environment.[b]

There are no great difficulties in defining sexual harassment when jobs or promotions are conditional on the granting of sexual favors. But several problems arise in defining a "hostile working environment." This phrase may include offensive utterances, sexual innuendoes, dirty jokes, the display of pornographic material, and unwanted proposals for dates. First, it would appear to include speech and hence raise First Amendment questions regarding how far speech may be curtailed by law in the workplace. Second, the definition depends more on the subjective feelings of the individual employee about what is "offensive" and "unwanted" than on an objective standard of behavior easily understood by all. Justice Sandra Day O'Connor wrestled with the definition of a "hostile work environment" in *Harris v. Forklift* in 1993. She held that a plaintiff need not show that the utterances caused psychological injury but that a "reasonable person," not just the plaintiff, must perceive the work environment to be hostile or abusive. Presumably a single incident would not constitute harassment; rather, courts should consider "the frequency of the discriminatory conduct," "its severity," and whether it "unreasonably interferes with an employee's work performance."[c]

What behaviors does a "reasonable person" believe to be sexual harassment? Some polls indicate that women are somewhat more likely to perceive sexual harassment in various behaviors than men (see figure). But neither women nor men are likely to perceive it to include repeated requests for a date, the telling of dirty jokes, or comments on attractiveness—even though these behaviors often inspire formal complaints.

Many university policies go well beyond both Supreme Court rulings and opinion polls in defining what constitutes sexual harassment, including the following: "remarks about a person's clothing" "suggestive or insulting sounds," and "leering at or ogling of a person's body."

[a]*Washington Post National Weekly Edition:* March 7, 1993.
[b]*Mentor Savings Bank v. Vinson,* 477 U.S. 57 (1986).
[c]*Harris v. Forklift Systems,* 126 L. Ed. 2d 295 (1993).

Question: *Here is a list of some different situations. We're interested in knowing whether you think they are forms of sexual harassment— not just inappropriate or in bad taste, but sexual harassment.*

Definitely is sexual harassment:

Situation	Men	Women
If a male boss makes it clear to a female employee that she must go to bed with him for a promotion	91%	92%
If a male boss asks very direct questions of a female employee about her personal sexual practices and preferences	59%	68%
If a female boss asks very direct questions of a male employee about his personal sexual practices and preferences	47%	57%
If a man once in a while asks a female employee of his to go out on dates, even though she has said no in the past	15%	21%
If a man once in a while tells dirty jokes in the presence of female employees	15%	16%
If a male boss tells a female employee that she looks very attractive today	3%	5%

■ Men   ■ Women

Source: Roper Organization as reported in *American Enterprise.* September/October 1993, p. 93.

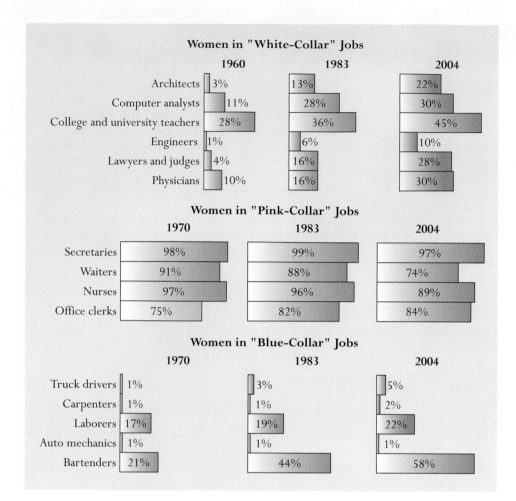

Figure 15.3 Gender Differentiation in the Labor Market

Most of the earnings gap between men and women in the U.S. labor force today is the result of the different job positions held by the two sexes. Although women are increasingly entering "white-collar" occupations long dominated by men, they continue to be disproportionately concentrated in "pink-collar" service positions. "Blue-collar" jobs have been the most resistant to change, remaining a male bastion, although women bartenders now outnumber men.

Sources:Statistical Abstract of the United States, 2001, pp. 380–82; 2004-2005, pp. 388–390.

A CONSTITUTIONAL NOTE

The Fourteenth Amendment

The Constitution of 1787 not only recognized slavery by counting slaves as three-fifths of a person for apportionment of representatives and direct taxes (Article I, Section 2) but also protected slavery by requiring states to return escaped slaves to their owners (Article IV, Section 2). (The Founders appear to have been embarrassed by the word "slave" and employed the euphemism "person held to service or labor.") Following the Civil War the Thirteenth Amendment prohibited slavery and the Fifteenth Amendment prohibited states from denying the right to vote on account of race, color, or previous condition of servitude. But it was the Fourteenth Amendment that eventually became the basis of the

civil rights movement in America and the source of the most important guarantees of equality:

> No State shall make or enforce any law which shall abridge the privileges or immunities of citizens of the United States; nor shall any state deprive any person of life, liberty, or property, without due process of law; nor deny to any person within its jurisdiction the equal protection of the laws.

What are the meanings of words such as "liberty," "due process of law," and "equal protection of the laws"? Constitutionally, the history of the civil rights movement centers around definitions of these terms, as does the history of the women's movement.

The "Glass Ceiling" The barriers to women's advancement to top positions in the corporate and financial worlds are often very subtle, giving rise to the phrase **glass ceiling.** In explaining "why women aren't getting to the top," one observer argues that "at senior management levels competence is assumed. What you're looking for is someone who fits, someone who gets along, someone you trust. Now that's subtle stuff. How does a group of men feel that a woman is going to fit? I think it's very hard." Or, as a woman bank executive says, "The men just don't feel comfortable."[42] And at all levels, increasing attention has been paid to sexual harassment (see *What Do You Think?* "What Constitutes Sexual Harassment?"). Finally, it is important to note that affirmative action efforts by governments—notably the EEOC—are directed primarily at entry-level positions rather than senior management posts.

glass ceiling "Invisible" barriers to women rising to the highest positions in corporations and the professions.

Summary Notes

- Equality has long been the central issue of American politics. Today, most Americans agree that all individuals should have an equal opportunity to make of their lives whatever they can without artificial barriers of race, class, gender, or ethnicity. Political conflict arises over what, if anything, government should do to achieve greater equality of results—the reduction of gaps between rich and poor, men and women, blacks and whites, and other groups in society.

- The original Constitution of 1787 recognized and protected slavery. Not until after the Civil War did the Thirteenth Amendment (1865) abolish slavery. But the Fourteenth Amendment's guarantee of "equal protection of the laws" and the Fifteenth Amendment's guarantee of voting rights were largely ignored in Southern states after the federal government's Reconstruction efforts ended. Segregation was held constitutional by the U.S. Supreme Court in its "separate but equal" decision in *Plessy v. Ferguson* in 1896.

- The NAACP led the long legal battle in the federal courts to have segregation declared unconstitutional as a violation of the Equal Protection Clause of the Fourteenth Amendment. Under the leadership of Thurgood Marshall, a major victory was achieved in the case of *Brown v. Board of Education of Topeka* in 1954.

- The struggle over school desegregation continues even today. Federal courts are more likely to issue desegregation orders (including orders to bus pupils to achieve racial balance in schools) in school districts where present or past actions by government officials contributed to racial imbalances. Courts are less likely to order desegregation where racial imbalances are a product of residential patterns.

- The courts could eliminate *governmental* discrimination by enforcing the Fourteenth Amendment of the Constitution; but only Congress could end private discrimination

through legislation. Martin Luther King Jr.'s campaign of nonviolent direct action helped bring remaining racial injustices to the attention of Congress. Key legislation includes the Civil Rights Act of 1964, which bans discrimination in public accommodations, government-funded programs, and private employment; the Voting Rights Act of 1965, which authorizes strong federal action to protect voting rights; and the Civil Rights Act of 1968, which outlaws discrimination in housing.

- Today, racial politics center around continuing inequalities between blacks and whites in the areas of income, jobs, housing, health, education, and other conditions of life. Should the government concentrate on "equality of opportunity" and apply "color-blind" standards to both blacks and whites? Or should government take "affirmative action" to assist blacks and other minorities to overcome the results of past unequal treatment?

- Generally the Supreme Court is likely to approve of affirmative action programs when these programs have been adopted in response to a past proven history of discrimination, when they are narrowly tailored so as not to adversely affect the rights of individuals, when they do not absolutely bar whites from participating, and when they serve clearly identified, compelling, and legitimate government objectives.

- Economic conditions in Mexico and other Spanish-speaking nations of the Western Hemisphere continue to fuel large-scale immigration, both legal and illegal, into the United States. But the political power of Mexican Americans, the nation's largest Hispanic group, does not yet match their population percentage. Their voter turnout remains lower than that of other ethnic groups in the United States.

- Since the arrival of the first Europeans on this continent, Native American peoples have experienced cycles of invasion, resistance, military defeat, and land concessions. Today Native American peoples collectively remain the poorest and least healthy of the nation's ethnic groups.

■ The most recent major civil rights legislation is the Americans with Disabilities Act of 1990, which prohibits discrimination against disabled persons in private employment, government programs, public accommodations, and communications.

■ The Equal Protection Clause of the Fourteenth Amendment applies to "any person," but traditionally the Supreme Court has recognized gender differences in laws. Nevertheless, in recent years the Court has struck down gender differences where they are unreasonable or arbitrary and unrelated to legitimate government objectives.

■ Gender discrimination in employment has been illegal since the passage of the Civil Rights Act of 1964. Nevertheless, differences in average earnings of men and women persist, although these differences have narrowed somewhat over time. The earnings gap appears to be mainly a product of lower pay in occupations traditionally dominated by women and higher pay in traditionally male occupations. Although neither Congress nor the courts have mandated wages based on comparable worth of traditional men's and women's jobs in private employment, many governmental agencies and some private employers have undertaken to review wage rates to eliminate gender differences.

■ The Equal Protection Clause does not bar government from treating persons in various income classes differently. However, governments must treat every individual in a class equally, and the classifications must not be "arbitrary" or "unreasonable." The poor cannot demand benefits or services as a matter of constitutional rights; but once government establishes a social welfare program by law, it must provide equal access to all persons "similarly situated."

Key Terms

abolition movement 539	de facto	*Bakke* case 551	Equal Rights Amendment
Emancipation	segregation 545	set-aside	(ERA) 569
Proclamation 539	nonviolent direct	program 553	direct discrimination 569
Reconstruction 539	action 546	strict scrutiny 553	comparable worth 570
Jim Crow 540	affirmative action 550	diversity 553	glass ceiling 573
separate but equal 540	quota 550	Title IX 568	

Suggested Readings

Barker, Lucius J., and Mack H. Jones. *African Americans and the American Political System*. 4th ed. Upper Saddle River, N.J.: Prentice Hall, 1999. Comprehensive analysis of African American politics, examining access to the judicial arena, the interest-group process, political parties, Congress, and the White House.

Bowen, William G., and Derek Curtis Bok. *The Shape of the River*. Princeton, N.J.: Princeton University Press, 1999. An argument by two university presidents that preferential treatment of minorities in admissions to prestigious universities has led to the subsequent success in life by the beneficiaries of the preferences.

Conway, M. Margaret, Gertrude A. Steurnagel, and David W. Ahern. *Women and Political Participation*. 2d ed. Washington, D.C.: CQ Press, 2004. A wide-ranging review of changes in American political culture brought about by women's increasing political clout. Continuing gender differences in representation are explored.

Fox-Genovese, Elizabeth. *Feminism Is Not the Story of My Life*. New York: Doubleday, 1995. Critique of radical feminism for failing to understand the central importance of marriage and motherhood in women's lives, and a discussion of how public policy could ease the clashing demands of work and family on women.

Harrison, Brigid C. *Women in American Politics*. Belmont, Calif.: Wadsworth, 2003. Comprehensive text on role of women in interest groups, parties, elections, Congress, the executive branch, and the judiciary.

Hero, Rodney E. *Latinos and the U.S. Political System*. Philadelphia: Temple University Press, 1992. General history of political participation of major Latino groups, arguing that different cultural behaviors limit their ability to participate in the interest-group system and policy-making process as currently structured.

LeMay, Michael, *Perennial Struggle: Race, Ethnicity and Minority Group Relations in the United States*, 2nd ed. Upper Saddle River, N.J.: Prentice Hall, 2005. A description and assessment of minority group strategies—accommodation, separatism, radicalism—in coping with their political and economic status.

Sigelman, Lee, and Susan Welch. *Black Americans' Views of Racial Inequality*. Cambridge, Mass.: Cambridge University Press,

1991. Analysis of survey research showing that black perceptions of racial inequality in America are considerably different from white perceptions. Although remaining optimistic about the future, blacks see discrimination as commonplace and are much more likely than whites to attribute black-white differences in education, occupation, and income to racism.

Thernstrom, Stephen, and Abigail Thernstrom. *America in Black and White*. New York: Simon & Schuster, 1997. Information-rich analysis tracing social and economic progress of African Americans and arguing that gains in education and employment were greater *before* the introduction of affirmative action programs.

Walton, Hanes, and Robert C. Smith. *American Politics and the African-American Quest for Freedom*. 3rd ed. New York: Longman, 2005. Comprehensive text arguing the profound influence that African-Americans have on American politics.

Make It Real

CIVIL RIGHTS

This module contains an excellent interactive timeline on civil rights movements.

16 POLITICS AND THE ECONOMY

Politics and Economics

Earlier, we observed that one of America's foremost political scientists, Harold Lasswell, defined "politics" as "who gets what, when, and how." One of America's foremost economists, Paul Samuelson, defined "economics" as "deciding what shall be produced, how, and for whom."[1] The similarity between these definitions is based on the fact that both the political system and the economic system provide society with means for deciding about the production and distribution of goods and services. The political system involves *collective* decisions—choices made by communities, states, or nations—and relies on government coercion through laws, regulations, taxes, and so on to implement them. A free-market economic system involves *individual* decisions—choices made by millions of consumers and thousands of firms—and relies on *voluntary exchange* through buying, selling, borrowing, contracting, and trading to implement them (see *People in Politics:* "Milton Friedman, In Defense of Free Markets"). Both politics and markets function to transform popular demands into goods and services, to allocate costs, and to distribute goods and services.

One of the key questions in any society is how much to rely on government versus the marketplace to provide goods and services. This question of the proper relationship between governments and markets—that is, between politics and economics—is the subject of political economy. The United States is primarily a free-market economy, but the federal government strongly influences economic activity.

Economic Decision Making

Economic decision making involves both fiscal and monetary policy. **Fiscal policy** refers to the taxing, spending, and borrowing activities of the national government. Fiscal policy making takes place within the same system of separated powers and checks and balances that governs other areas of federal policy making (see "Separation of Powers and Checks and Balances" in Chapter 3), with both the Congress and the president sharing responsibility.

Monetary policy refers to decisions regarding the supply of money in the economy, including private borrowing, interest rates, and banking activity. Monetary policy is a principal responsibility of the powerful and independent Federal Reserve Board. Congress established the Federal Reserve Board in 1913 and its power rests on congressional legislation.

PEOPLE IN POLITICS

Milton Friedman, In Defense of Free Markets

Economist Milton Friedman is perhaps the world's most influential spokesperson on behalf of free-market economics. He has spent a lifetime arguing that free markets are indispensable for human freedom and dignity. In 1976 Friedman was awarded a Nobel Prize in economics for his work in monetary policy.

Friedman was born in Brooklyn, New York, the son of working-class immigrants who stressed the importance of education. Young Friedman was an excellent high school student who went on to major in economics at Rutgers University, where he worked his way through college with a number of odd jobs. Upon graduation in 1932, Friedman was awarded a scholarship to attend graduate school at the University of Chicago. After earning his M.A. in economics, he worked in Washington, D.C., at various posts before returning to Columbia University for his Ph.D. in 1943. In 1946 he joined the faculty at the University of Chicago.

In his book *Studies in the Quantity Theory of Money* (1956) and in testimony before the Joint Congressional Economic Committee, Friedman argued against the prevailing economic philosophy of John Maynard Keynes and its prescription of increased government borrowing and spending to stimulate the economy. Friedman contended that a gradual, steady, continuous rate of increase in the money supply would be the best policy for achieving stable economic growth. Friedman and other economists who support this theory are known as *monetarists*.

In Friedman's view, the chief cause of recession and inflation is fluctuation in the nation's money supply. In an influential book, *A Monetary History of the United States* (1963), Friedman presented extensive historical evidence of the effect of money supply on the economic health of the nation. But Friedman's most widely read works are his cogent defenses of individual freedom and dignity. In *Capitalism and Freedom* (1962), he argued convincingly that free markets are essential to individual freedom and that government intervention in the marketplace inevitably curtails individual liberty and substitutes the judgment of a privileged few for the decisions of the people. In his television series *Free to Choose,* he brought his free-market ideas to a wide audience. According to Friedman, "The preservation of freedom requires limiting narrowly the role of government and placing primary reliance on private property, free markets and voluntary arrangements."

fiscal policy Economic policies involving taxing, spending, and deficit levels of the national government.

monetary policy Economic policies involving the money supply, interest rates, and banking activity.

Congress could, if it wished, reduce its power or even abolish the Fed. But no serious effort has ever been undertaken to do so.

Congress, the President, and Fiscal Policy   The Constitution of the United States places all taxing, borrowing, and spending powers in the hands of Congress. Article I grants Congress the "Power to lay and collect Taxes, Duties, Imposts and Excises, to pay the Debts and provide for the common Defence and general Welfare of the United States," and "to borrow Money on the Credit of the United States." It also declares that "No Money shall be drawn from the Treasury, but in Consequence of Appropriations made by Law." For nearly 150 years the power to spend was interpreted in a limited fashion: Congress could only spend money to perform powers specifically enumerated in Article I, Section 8, of the Constitution. But the Supreme Court has since ruled that the phrase "to pay the Debts and provide for the common Defence and general Welfare" may be broadly interpreted to authorize congressional spending for any purpose that serves the general welfare. Thus today there are no constitutional limits on Congress's spending power. Congress's borrowing power has always been unlimited constitutionally; *there is no constitutional requirement for a balanced budget.*

The Constitution gives the president no formal powers over taxing and spending or borrowing, stating only that the president shall . . . recommend to [Congress's] Consideration such Measures as he shall judge necessary and expedient"

(Article II, Section 3). From this meager constitutional grant of power, however, presidents have gradually acquired leadership over national economic policy. The principal instrument of executive economic policy making is the Budget of the United States Government, which the president submits annually to Congress. The budget sets forth the president's recommendations for spending for the forthcoming fiscal year; revenue estimates, based on existing taxes or recommendations for new or increased tax levels; and estimates of projected deficits and the need for borrowing when, as has usually been the case of late, spending recommendations exceed revenue estimates (see Figure 12.4, "The Budgetary Process," for more detail).

The President's Economic Team   The *president's* recommendations to Congress regarding taxing, spending, and borrowing are influenced by advice received from three sources:

1. The Office of Management and Budget (OMB), responsible for preparing the Budget of the United States Government, exerts a powerful influence on the expenditure side of the budget. OMB supervises the year-long process of checking, reviewing, and modifying the budget requests of every federal department and agency.

2. The Department of the Treasury and the secretary of the Treasury have the principal responsibility for estimating revenues and, if requested by the president, for drawing up new tax proposals and forecasting how much revenue they might produce. The Treasury Department also manages the nation's huge national debt—the result of past annual deficits. The Treasury must continually sell **government bonds** to banks and other investors, both foreign and domestic, in order to cover payments on previous deficits as well as to fund current deficits. In doing so, the Treasury Department determines interest rates on federal bonds, and it pays out interest charges on the national debt—charges that now amount to 9 percent of all federal spending.

3. The Council of Economic Advisers (CEA), which forecasts economic conditions and recommends economic policies, is composed of three professional economists and a small staff. In theory, the CEA gives the president unbiased forecasts of economic trends and impartial analyses of economic issues. It does so principally in the annual Economic Report of the President, which the CEA prepares. But because the president chooses the members of the CEA, it often produces economic reports that reflect the president's thinking.

The Fed and Monetary Policy   Most economically advanced democracies have central banks whose principal responsibility is to regulate the supply of money, both currency in circulation and bank deposits. And most of these democracies have found it best to remove this responsibility from the direct control of elected politicians. Politicians everywhere are sorely tempted to inflate the supply of money in order to fund projects and programs with newly created money instead of new taxes. Nations pay for this approach with a general rise in prices and a reduction in goods and services available to private firms and individuals—inflation. Indeed, nations whose control of the money supply has fallen victim to irresponsible governments have experienced inflation rates of 500 to 1,000 percent per year, which is to say that their money became worthless.

The Federal Reserve System of the United States is largely independent of either the president or Congress. Its independent status is a result not only of law but also of its structure. It is run by a seven-member board of governors who are appointed by the president, with the consent of the Senate, for *fourteen-year*

 Council of Economic Advisors (CEA)
Official CEA site, with latest *Economic Report of the President* and mostly economic indicators.
www.whitehouse.gov/cea

government bonds
Certificates of indebtedness that pay interest and promise repayment on a future date.

 Federal Reserve System
Official site of the Fed, with data on money supply, interest rates, and banking regulation.
www.federalreserve.gov

Senator Chuck Schumer (D-NY) holding a news conference at a gas station to bash Republicans over high gas prices.

Federal Reserve Board (the Fed) Independent agency of the executive branch of the federal government charged with overseeing the nation's monetary policy.

terms. Members may not be removed from the board except for "cause"; no member has ever been removed since the creation of the board in 1913. The board's chair serves only a four-year term, but the chair's term overlaps that of the president, so that new presidents cannot immediately name their own chair.

The task of the **Federal Reserve Board (the Fed)** is to regulate the money supply and by so doing to help avoid both inflation and recession. The Fed oversees the operation of the nation's twelve Federal Reserve Banks, which actually issue the nation's currency, called "Federal Reserve Notes." The Federal Reserve Banks are bankers' banks; they do not directly serve private citizens or firms. They hold the deposits, or "reserves," of banks; lend money to banks at "discount rates" that the Fed determines; buy and sell U.S. Government Treasury bonds; and assure regulatory compliance by private banks and protection of depositors against fraud. The Fed determines the reserve requirements of banks and otherwise monitors the health of the banking industry. The Fed also plays an important role in clearing checks throughout the banking system.

inflation Rise in the general level of prices; not just the prices of some products.

The Fed's influence over the economy is mainly through monetary policy—increasing or decreasing the supply of money and hence largely determining interest rates. When **inflation** threatens, the Fed typically acts to limit ("tighten") the supply of money and raise interest rates by (1) raising the reserve requirement of banks and thereby reducing the amount of money they have to loan out; or (2) raising the discount rate and thereby the cost of borrowing by banks; or (3) selling off government bonds to banks and others in "open market operations," thereby reducing the funds banks can lend to individuals and businesses. When **recession** threatens, the Fed typically acts to expand ("ease") the money supply and lower interest rates by taking the opposite of each action just described.

recession Decline in the general level of economic activity.

Although it is the Fed that makes monetary policy, voters typically hold the president responsible for recessions. Hence presidents frequently try to persuade ("jawbone") the independent Fed into lowering interest rates, especially in an election year, believing a temporary stimulus to help win the election is worth whatever inflationary effects it might create after the election.[2]

The Performance of the American Economy

Underlying the power of nations and the well-being of their citizens is the strength of their economy—their total productive capacity. The United States produces about $12 *trillion* worth of goods and services in a single year for its 300 million people—more than $40,000 worth of output for every person.

gross domestic product (GDP) Measure of economic performance in terms of the nation's total production of goods and services for a single year, valued in terms of market prices.

Economic Growth   Gross domestic product (GDP) is a widely used measure of the performance of the economy.[3] GDP is a nation's total production of goods and services for a single year valued in terms of market prices. It is the sum of all the goods and services that people have been willing to pay for, from wheat production to bake sales, from machine tools to maid service, from aircraft manufacturing to bus rides, from automobiles to chewing gum. GDP counts only final purchases of goods and services (that is, it ignores the purchase of steel by car makers until it is sold as a car) to avoid double counting in the production process. GDP also excludes financial transactions (such as the sale of bonds and stocks) and income transfers (such as Social Security, welfare, and pension payments) that do not add to the production of goods and services. Although GDP is expressed in current dollar prices, it is often recalculated in constant dollar terms to reflect real values over time, adjusting for the effect of inflation. GDP estimates are prepared each quarter by the U.S. Department of Commerce; these figures are widely reported and closely watched by the business and financial community.

Growth in real (constant dollar) GDP measures the performance of the overall economy. Economic recessions and recoveries are measured as fluctuations or swings in the growth of GDP. For example, a recession is usually defined as negative GDP growth in two or more consecutive quarters. Historical data reveal that periods of economic growth have traditionally been followed by periods of contraction, giving rise to the notion of **economic cycles**. Prior to 1950, economic cycles in the United States produced extreme ups and downs, with double-digit swings in real GDP. In recent decades, however, economic fluctuations have been more moderate. The United States still experiences economic cycles, but many economists believe that countercyclical government fiscal and monetary policy has succeeded in achieving greater stability (see Figure 16.1).

Unemployment   From a political standpoint, the **unemployment rate** may be the most important measure of the economy's performance. The unemployment rate is the percentage of the civilian labor force who are looking for work or waiting to return to or begin a job. Unemployment is different from not working; people who have retired or who attend school and people who do not work because of sickness, disability, or unwillingness are not considered part of the labor force and so are not counted as unemployed. People who are so discouraged about finding a job that they have quit looking for work are also not counted in the official unemployment rate. The unemployed do include people who have been terminated from their last job or temporarily laid off from work, as well as people who voluntarily quit and those who have recently entered or reentered the labor force and are now seeking employment.

The unemployment rate is measured each month by the U.S. Department of Labor. It does so by contacting a random sample of more than 50,000 households in many locations throughout the country. Trained interviewers ask a variety of questions to determine how many (if any) members of the household are

economic cycles
Fluctuations in real GDP growth followed by contraction.

**Bureau of Economic Analysis**
Source of official economic statistics, listed A–Z.
www.bea.gov

unemployment rate
Percentage of the civilian labor force who are not working but who are looking for work or waiting to return to or to begin a job.

**Bureau of Labor Statistics**
The U.S. Department of Labor's Bureau of Labor Statistics site contains monthly information about the nation's employment rate plus a wealth of supporting data. *www.bls.gov*

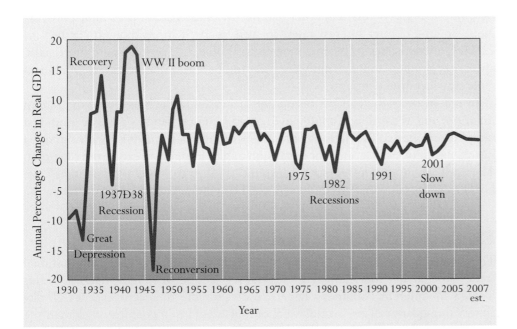

Figure 16.1
Economic Growth
The tendency for periods of economic growth to alternate with periods of contraction has led to the concept of the business cycle—the idea that at least some fluctuation is normal, even healthy, helping to keep the economy growing in the long run by keeping prices from getting too high. In recent decades, government intervention in the economy appears to have succeeded in reducing, although not in altogether eliminating, the depths of recessions to which the nation was formerly prone.

Source: Data from Bureau of Economic Analysis, 2005.

Figure 16.2
Unemployment
and Inflation

Economic growth during the 1980s lowered both the inflation and unemployment rates, freeing the nation from the stagflation (combined inflation and high unemploy-ment) that had characterized much of the 1970s. Un-employment rose during the recession of 1990–91 and again in 2002–2003. Inflation has remained relatively low in recent years.

Source: Data from Bureau of Labor Statistics, 2005.

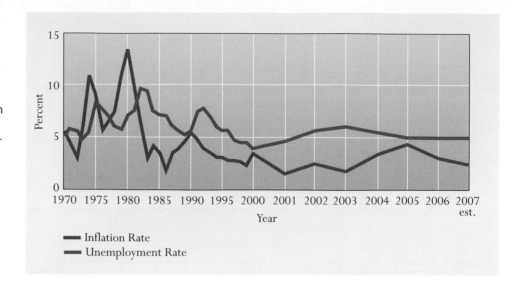

Just how bad can inflation get? Between the two world wars, inflation in Germany reached such levels that the nation's currency was often weighed, rather than counted, in order to speed transactions.

international trade The buying and selling of goods and services between individuals or firms located in different countries.

either working or have a job but did not work at it because of sickness, vacation, strike, or personal reasons (employed); or whether they have no job but are available for work and actively seeking a job (unemployed). The unemployment rate fluctuates with the business cycle, reflecting recessions and recoveries (see Figure 16.2). Generally, unemployment lags behind GDP growth, going down only after the recovery has begun. Following years of economic growth in the 1990s, the nation's unemployment rate fell to near record lows, below 5 percent. The economic slowdown of 2001–2002 temporarily pushed unemployment above 5 percent again (see Figure 16.2).

Inflation   Inflation erodes the value of the dollar because higher prices mean that the same dollars can now purchase fewer goods and services. Thus inflation erodes the value of savings, reduces the incentive to save, and hurts people who are living on fixed incomes. When banks and investors anticipate inflation, they raise interest rates on loans in order to cover the anticipated lower value of repay-ment dollars. Higher interest rates, in turn, make it more difficult for new or expanding businesses to borrow money, for home buyers to acquire mortgages, and for consumers to make purchases on credit. Thus inflation and high interest rates slow economic growth.

In recent years the Fed has been very successful in keeping down the rate of inflation, and as a result, keeping down overall interest rates as well. Low interest rates contributed to the nation's booming economy in the 1990s by encouraging businesses to borrow money for expansion and consumers to buy more on credit. The "soft" economy in 2001–2002 inspired the Fed to lower interest rates even further. As the economy strengthened, the Fed gradually raised interest rates.

Economic Globalization

The American economy is a major force in the global economy. **International trade**—the buying and selling of goods and services between individuals and firms located in different countries—has expanded rapidly in recent decades. Today almost one-quarter of the world's total output is sold in a country other than the one in which it was produced. The United States exports about 11 percent of the value of its gross domestic product (GDP) and imports about 12 percent. As late as 1970, exports and imports were only about 3 percent of GDP (see Figure 16.3).

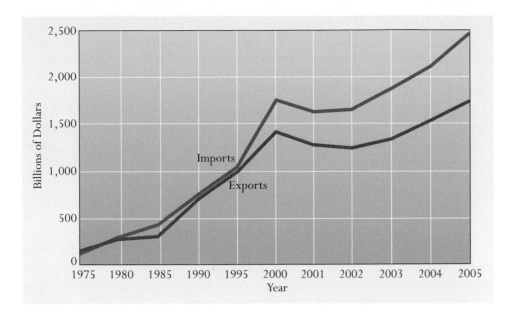

Figure 16.3
U.S. World Trade

Source: U.S. Bureau of Economic Analysis, December, 2005.

Historic Protectionism   Historically, American business supported high tariffs—taxes on foreign imports. Prior to World War II, U.S. tariffs on imported goods averaged 30 to 50 percent in various decades. This eliminated most foreign competition from U.S. markets. American firms could raise prices to levels just below the price of imported goods with their high tariffs attached. Not only did this improve the profit margins of American manufacturers, it also allowed them to be less efficient than foreign producers and yet survive and prosper under the protection of tariffs. The pressure to cut wages and downsize work forces was less than it would be if U.S. firms had to face foreign competition directly. American consumers, of course, paid higher prices than they otherwise would if foreign goods could come into the country without tariffs. The policy of high tariffs and quotas—limits on the number of units of specific goods imported into the country—was referred to as **protectionism**.

Free Trade   But after World War II, the American economy became the most powerful in the world, and American businesses sought to expand their markets overseas. In order to lower trade barriers in other countries, the United States reduced or eliminated almost all of its own tariffs and import quotas. In effect, the United States became an open market. "Free trade" became a byword of American business, and "protectionism" became a derogatory term.

The argument for **free trade** is that it lowers the price of goods and improves the standard of living in nations that choose to trade with each other. Trade shifts resources (investment capital, jobs, technology, raw materials, etc.) in each nation toward what each does best. If one nation is much better at producing aircraft and another better at producing clothing, then each nation will benefit more from trading than from trying to produce both airplanes and clothing. The efficiencies achieved by trading are said to directly benefit consumers by making available cheaper imported goods. Export industries also benefit when world markets are opened to their products. It is also argued that the pressure from competition from foreign-made goods in the American marketplace forces our own industries to become more efficient—cutting their costs and improving the quality of their goods. Finally, trade expands the menu of goods and services available to trading countries. American consumers gain access to everything from exotic foods and foreign-language movies to Porsches, BMWs, and Toyotas.

Think Again

Do you think the trend toward a global economy is a good thing or a bad thing for the United States?

protectionism A policy of high tariffs and quotas on imports to protect domestic industries.

free trade A policy of reducing or eliminating tariffs and quotas on imports to stimulate international trade.

Uneven Benefits of Globalization While the U.S. economy has performed very well in recent years, the benefits of that performance have been unevenly distributed. A global economy inspires worldwide competition not only among corporations and businesses but also among workers. America's best educated and most highly skilled workers compete well in the global economy. U.S. export industries have thrived on international trade expansion, adding jobs to the American economy and raising the incomes of their executives, professionals, and skilled high-tech workers. But the global economy offers a huge supply of unskilled and semiskilled workers at very low wages. Increased trade, especially with less developed economies such as Mexico, China, and India, with their huge numbers of low-wage workers, creates competition with America's unskilled and semiskilled workers. It is difficult to maintain the wage levels of American jobs, especially in labor-intensive industries, in the face of competition from low-wage countries. And U.S. corporations can move their manufacturing plants to low-wage countries, for example to northern Mexico, where the transportation costs of moving these products back into the United States are minimal. Harvard economist Richard B. Freeman summarizes the problem:

> An economic disaster has befallen low-skilled Americans, especially young men. Researchers using several data sources—including household survey data from the Current Population Survey, other household surveys, and establishment surveys—have documented that wage inequality and skill differentials in earnings and employment increased sharply in the United States from the mid-1970s through the 1980s and into the 1990s. The drop in the relative position of the less skilled shows up in a number of ways: greater earnings differentials between those with more and less education; greater earnings differentials between older and younger workers; greater differentials between high-skilled and low-skilled occupations; in a wider earnings distribution overall and within demographic and skill groups; and in less time worked by low-skill and low-paid workers.[4]

Income inequality has worsened in America along with the growth of international trade (see "Inequality of Wealth and Income" in Chapter 2). Figure 16.4 shows the percentage of losses and gains between 1980 and 2000 for American

Figure 16.4
Worsening Inequality
Change in percent distribution of family income by quintile, 1980–2000.

Source: Statistical Abstract of the United States, 2002 p. 437.

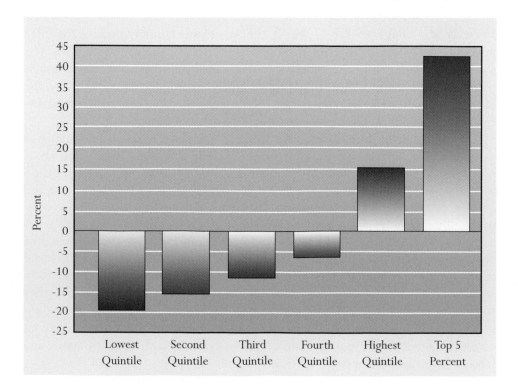

families in each income class. The nation's lowest income families lost 22 percent of their real income over these years, while the highest income families gained 33 percent in real income. Not all of this increase in inequality can be attributed to the growth of international trade. But, clearly, America's less educated and less skilled workers are at a disadvantage in global competition.[5]

The Politics of Free Trade   Over the years both Democratic and Republican presidential administrations have advanced free trade. And Congress has approved the major treaties and organizations designed to institutionalize the global economy (see Table 16.1). The task of the cabinet-level position, International Trade

> **World Trade Organization (WTO)**
> Official WTO site, with trade agreements, including General Agreement on Tariffs and Trade (GATT).
> *www.wto.org*

Table 16.1   Major International Trade Agreements

The World Trade Organization and GATT

The World Trade Organization (WTC) was created in 1993. Today the WTO includes 149 nations that agree to a governing set of global trade rules. (China joined in 2001.) The WTO is given power to adjudicate trade disputes among countries and monitor and enforce trade agreements, including GATT. GATT, the multinational General Agreement on Tariffs and Trade, was created following World War II for the purpose of encouraging international trade. Over the years GATT has been dominated by banking, business, and commercial interests in Western nations seeking multilateral tariff reductions and the relaxation of quotas. In 1993 the GATT "Uruguay Round" eliminated quotas on textile products; established more uniform standards for proof of dumping; set rules for the protection of intellectual property rights (patents and copyrights on books, movies, videos, and so on); reduced tariffs on wood, paper, and some other raw materials; and scheduled a gradual reduction of government subsidies for agricultural products.

The International Monetary Fund (IMF) and the World Bank

The IMF's purpose is to facilitate international trade, allowing nations to borrow to stabilize their balance of trade payments. When economically weak nations, however, incur chronic balance of trade deficits and perhaps face deferral or default on international debts, the IMF may condition its loans on changes in a nation's economic policies. It may require a reduction in a nation's government deficits by reduced public spending and/or higher taxes; or it may require a devaluation of its currency, making its exports cheaper and imports more expensive. It may also require the adoption of noninflationary monetary policies. Currently, the IMF as well as the World Bank are actively involved in assisting Russia and other states of the former Soviet Union to convert to free-market economies.

The World Bank makes long-term loans, mostly to developing nations, to assist in economic development. It works closely with the IMF in investigating the economic conditions of nations applying for loans and generally imposes IMF requirements on these nations as conditions for loans.

North American Free Trade Agreement (NAFTA)

In 1993 the United States, Canada, and Mexico signed the North American Free Trade Agreement (NAFTA). Objections by labor unions in the United States were drowned out in a torrent of support by the American corporate community, Democrats and Republicans in Congress, President Bill Clinton, and former President George Bush. NAFTA envisions the removal of tariffs on virtually all products by all three nations over a period of ten to fifteen years. It also allows banking, insurance, and other financial services to cross these borders.

FTAA AND CAFTA

Currently the United States and the nations of North, Central, and South America are engaged in negotiations designed to create a free trade area throughout most of the Western Hemisphere. The Free Trade Area of the Americas (FTAA) is to resemble NAFTA. Barriers to trade and investment are to be progressively eliminated. The rules of the World Trade Organization will constitute a base for the FTAA agreements.

Recent U.S. presidents, both Democrats and Republicans, have pressed Congress for "fast-track authority" for trade agreements, essentially requesting that Congress pass presidentially negotiated trade agreements without amendments. In 2002, Congress granted President Bush's request for something quite similar— "trade promotion authority."

While negotiations on FTAA continue, President Bush signed a trade agreement—the Central American Free Trade Agreement (CAFTA)—with five Central American nations (Guatemala, El Salvador, Honduras, Costa Rica, and Nicaragua). CAFTA is based on the NAFTA model and is looked upon in Washington as a stepping stone to the broader FTAA.

WHAT DO YOU THINK?

Does Globalization Help or Hurt America?

While Democratic and Republican presidents and Congresses have supported free trade and given their approval to two major trade agreements, the American public appears to be divided over the benefits of economic globalization.

Q. Based on what you know or may have heard, do you think the globalization of the world economy is mostly good for the United States, mostly bad for the United States, or doesn't make much difference?

Bad	22%
Good	38
No difference	25
Haven't heard/don't know	14

More Americans believe that free trade agreements cost U.S. jobs rather than create U.S. jobs.

Q. Do you think the trade agreements between the United States and other countries have helped create more jobs in the United States, or have they cost the U.S. jobs, or haven't they made much of a difference?

Cost U.S. jobs	49%
Haven't made much difference	23
Helped create more U.S. jobs	21
Don't know	7

It comes as no surprise that higher-income Americans voice greater support for globalization than lower-income Americans. Nor is it much of a surprise that public policy more closely reflects the views of higher-income Americans.

Question: *Do you think the trend toward a global economy is a good thing or a bad thing for the country?*

	Good thing	Bad thing
$75,000 and up	69%	31%
$50-75,000	65%	35%
$30-49,000	61%	39%
$20-29,000	60%	40%
Under $20,000	56%	44%
Total	61%	39%

Sources: Washington Post/Newsweek survey, October 2000 (for first and second questions); Princeton Survey Research, September 1998 (for third question). See Public Agenda Online at www.publicagenda.org

---

Think Again

Which is more important: holding down the size of government or providing needed services?

Representative, has been to open up foreign markets to American products. Occasionally the United States has threatened to limit the importation of foreign products in order to force other nations to open up their own markets. And occasionally Congress members from districts adversely affected by foreign competition have opposed specific trade arrangements or, alternatively, called upon the federal government to assist workers displaced by foreign competition. But the thrust of U.S. policy has been to expand free trade.

Democrats in Congress have expressed more reservations about free trade than Republicans. (Democrats often call for "fair trade" in lieu of "free trade.") Democratic Congress members often reflect the views of their party's core constituencies, including labor unions, that fear the adverse effect on wages created by globalization. Environmentalists also complain that foreign corporations are not governed by strong or well-enforced environmental laws in their own countries. An array of other groups frequently demonstrates against globalization at meetings of the World Trade Organization and other international bodies (see *What Do You Think?:* "Does Globalization Help or Hurt America?").

Government Spending, Budget Priorities, and Debt

The expenditures of all governments in the United States—federal, state, and local governments combined—today amount to about 30 percent of GDP. The federal government itself spends more than $2.4 trillion each year—about 20 percent of GDP.

"Mandatory" Spending   Much of the growth of federal government spending over the years is attributed to **mandatory spending** items in the federal budget. These "uncontrollables" are budget items committed to by past policies of Congress that are not easily changed in annual budget making. Sources of mandatory spending include the following:

- *Entitlement programs:* Federal programs that provide classes of people with a legally enforceable right to benefits are called **entitlement programs**. Entitlement programs account for more than half of all federal spending, including Social Security, Medicare and Medicaid, food stamps, federal employees' retirement pensions, and veterans' benefits (see *Up Close:* "Transfers and Entitlements Drive Government Spending"). These entitlements are benefits that past Congresses have pledged the federal government to pay. Entitlements are not really uncontrollable. Congress can always amend the basic laws that established them, but doing so is politically difficult and might be regarded as abandonment of a public trust. As more people become "entitled" to government benefits—for example, as more people reach retirement ages and claim Social Security benefits, federal spending increases.

- *Indexing of benefits:* Another reason that spending increases each year is that Congress has authorized automatic increases in benefits to match inflation. Benefits under such programs as Social Security are tied to the Consumer Price Index. This **indexing** pushes up the cost of entitlement programs each year, even when the number of recipients stays the same, thus running counter to federal efforts to restrain inflation. Moreover, because the Consumer Price Index includes interest payments for new housing and the cost of new cars and appliances, it generally overestimates the needs of older recipients for cost-of-living increases.

- *Increasing costs of in-kind benefits:* Rises in the cost of major **in-kind (noncash) benefits**, particularly the medical costs of Medicaid and Medicare, also guarantee growth in federal spending. These in-kind benefit programs have risen faster in cost than cash benefit programs.

- *Interest on the national debt:* The federal government has a long history of deficits. In 1998 the president sent the first **balanced budget** to the Congress in thirty years. Deficit spending resumed in 2002. The accumulated deficits leave the government with a national debt of over $8 trillion. Interest payments on this debt now make up about 8 percent of total federal spending.

- *Backdoor spending and loan guarantees:* Some federal spending does not appear on the budget. For example, spending by the Postal Service is not included in the federal budget. No clear rule explains why some agencies are in the budget and others are not, but "off-budget" agencies have the same economic effects as other government agencies. Another form of **backdoor spending** is found in government-guaranteed loans. Initially government guarantees for loans—Federal Housing Administration (FHA) housing loans, Guaranteed Student Loans, veterans' loans, and so forth—do not require federal money. The government merely promises to repay the loan if the borrower fails to do so. Yet these loans create an obligation against the government.

Federal Budget Priorities   Federal budget shares (the percentage of outlays devoted to various functions) reflect the spending priorities of the national government. Entitlements and other mandatory spending (principally interest on the

mandatory spending
Spending for program commitments made by past congresses.

entitlement programs
Social welfare programs that provide classes of people with legally enforceable rights to benefits.

indexing Tieing of benefit levels in social welfare programs to the general price level.

in-kind (noncash) benefits
Benefits of a social welfare program that are not cash payments, including free medical care, subsidized housing, and food stamps.

balanced budget
Government budget in which expenditures and revenues are equal, so that no deficit or surplus exists.

backdoor spending
Spending by agencies of the federal government whose operations are not included in the federal budget.

UP CLOSE

Transfers and Entitlements Drive Government Spending

Traditionally, governments in the United States have provided for national defense, police and fire protection, roads, education, and other public goods and services. These "public goods" cannot readily be provided by private markets because if one individual or firm purchased them, everyone else would get a "free ride"—that is, would use them without paying. Government involvement in these areas is not surprising. But these traditional public functions are not responsible for the growth of government in recent years.

Income Transfers

Expansion in the relative size of government over the years has been the result of increased governmental involvement in "income transfer" activities. The government has become a redistributor of income from one group to another—from the working population to retirees, from the employed to the unemployed, from the taxpayers to the disadvantaged (such as low-income households with dependent children).

Entitlements

Entitlement spending—payments to people entitled by law to receive them—account for more than 60 percent of all federal spending. Note that most entitlement payments do not go to the poor. The largest share of entitlements—Social Security, Medicare, veterans' and federal retirement—goes to retirees. These programs alone account for two-thirds of all entitlement payments. Payments to the poor and unemployed—welfare, Medicaid, and unemployment insurance—account for less than one-third of federal entitlement spending.

Entitlements in the Federal Budget

	Billions of Dollars	Percentage
Entitlements, Total	1,699	61.3
Social Security	586	21.1
Medicare	392	14.1
Medicaid	280	10.1
Federal retirement	104	3.7
Welfare entitlement (housing, food, cash assistance)	223	8.1
Veterans' benefits	74	2.6
Unemployment insurance	40	1.4
Defense	527	19.0
Domestic	264	9.6
Interest	247	8.9
International	33	1.2
Total Federal Spending	2,770	100.0

Source: Budget of the United States Government, 2007.

---

discretionary spending Spending for programs not previously mandated by law.

Center on Budget and Policy Priorities Data on budget items, projected costs of federal programs, etc. *www.cbpp.org*

deficit Imbalance in the annual federal budget in which spending exceeds revenues.

national debt Total debt accumulated by the national government over the years.

national debt) heavily outweighs defense and **discretionary spending** combined (see Figure 16.5). Spending on programs designed to assist senior citizens (Social Security and Medicare) heavily outweighs defense spending, welfare spending, and all discretionary spending. Today Social Security payments are the largest single item in the federal budget. Over time defense spending declined from over 50 percent of the federal budget at the height of the Cold War in the early 1960s to 14 percent in the 1990s. The war on terror, including military operations in Iraq and Afghanistan, has increased defense spending to about 19 percent of the budget. Medical costs—Medicare for the elderly and Medicaid for the poor—are currently the fastest growing items in the federal budget.

The Debt Burden The U.S. federal government incurred a **deficit** every year from 1969 to 1998—that is, its expenditure exceeded its revenues (see Figure 16.6). The accumulated **national debt** is over $8 trillion, or $20,000 for every man, woman, and child in the nation. This government debt is owed mostly to U.S. banks and financial institutions and private citizens who buy Treasury bonds. Only about 15 percent of the debt is owed to foreign banks and individuals. As old debt comes due, the U.S. Treasury Department sells new bonds to pay off the old; that is, it continues to "roll over" or "float" the debt. Despite its size in dollars, the debt today is smaller as a percentage of GDP than at some periods in U.S. history. For

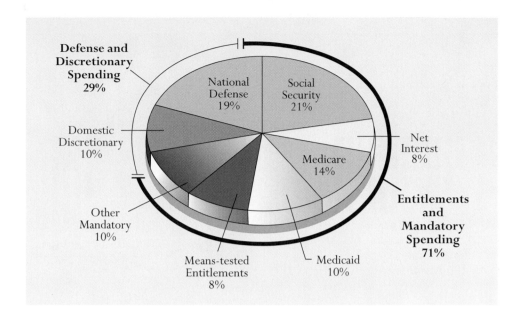

Figure 16.5   Federal Budget Shares
Mandatory spending—spending commitments in existing laws, notably Social Security, Medicare, Medicaid, and other entitlements, plus interest on the national debt—accounts for about two-thirds of the federal budget. Discretionary spending, including defense, accounts for only a little over one-third of the budget.

Source: Budget of the United States Government, 2007.

example, to pay the costs of fighting World War II, the U.S. government ran up a debt equivalent to over 100 percent of GDP. The current $8 trillion debt, although the highest in history in dollar terms, is equal to about 65 percent of GDP.

The ability to float such a huge debt depends on public confidence in the U.S. government—confidence that it will continue to pay interest on its debt, that it will pay off the principal of bonds when they come due, and that the value of the bonds will not decline over time because of inflation.

Interest Burden for Future Generations   Interest payments on the national debt come from current taxes and so divert money away from *all* other government programs. Even if the federal government manages to balance future budgets, these payments will remain obligations of the children and grandchildren of the current generation of policy makers and taxpayers. Interest payments on the national debt, currently about 8 percent of the federal budget, do not purchase any government goods or services. This means that for every dollar paid in federal taxes, taxpayers currently receive only 92 cents in government goods and services.

The Long-Sought Balanced Budget   Economic growth began to shrink annual deficits after the 1991–92 recession. The nation's booming economy increased tax revenues. And in 1993, President Clinton succeeded in getting a Democratic-controlled Congress to pass a major increase in tax rates (see "Tax Politics," later in this chapter). After 1994, a Republican-controlled Congress slowed the growth of federal spending. Budget "caps" were enacted by Congress and worked surprisingly well during the 1990s in holding down overall spending. President Clinton did not introduce any major new spending programs after his comprehensive health care program failed to pass Congress in 1993 (see Chapter 17). So both Democrats and Republicans claimed credit for reducing annual deficits.

Concord Coalition Nonpartisan advocacy organization promoting fiscal responsibility and balanced federal budget.
www.concordcoalition.org

Politics, Deficits, and Spending   Federal budget surpluses lasted for only four years, 1998–2001. During those years, Democrats and Republicans in Washington fought over what to do with the surplus revenues. Both parties pledged to use part of the surplus to strengthen Social Security and Medicare for the coming retirement of the "baby-boom" generation. But Republicans and conservatives argued that surpluses should also be used to reduce taxes or to pay off part of the national debt, or some combination of both. In contrast, Democrats argued that

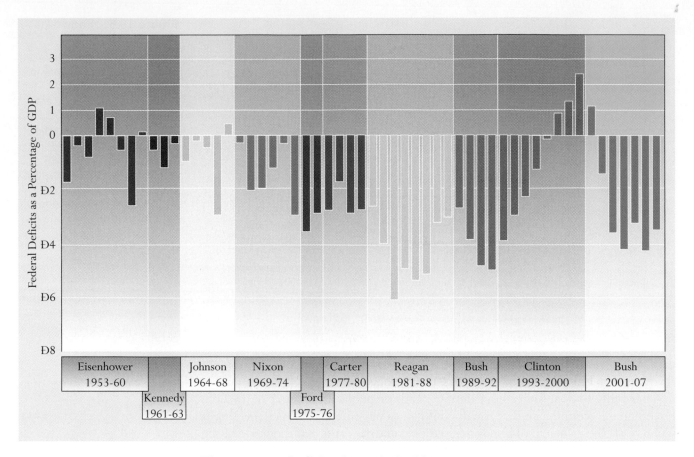

Figure 16.6   Deficits through the Years

This figure shows annual federal deficits as percentages of the GDP. Note that the federal government incurred deficits for thirty years, under both Republican and Democratic presidential administrations. A strong economy, and resulting increases in revenues flowing to the federal government, created budget surpluses from 1998 to 2001. An economic slowdown and added security costs after the 9/11 attack on America put the federal budget back in the red.

Note: Figures for 2006 and 2007 are estimates. Estimated figures tend to gyrate, but not much.
Source: Budget of the United States Government, 2007.

the surpluses should be used for investment in education, job skills, federal health insurance, and environmental protection. The result of the stalemate was a modest automatic reduction in the national debt.

But an economic slowdown, combined with the added security spending after the 9/11 attack on America, brought a return of red ink to federal budgets. Outlays for national defense increased dramatically, as did spending for homeland security— border and airport security, terrorism preparedness, aid to police, fire, and rescue teams, and the like. Democrats also blamed the return of deficits on Bush's tax cuts of 2001 and 2003 (see "Bush Tax Cuts" later in this chapter). But Republicans argued that these tax cuts helped avoid an even deeper economic recession.

Both parties now support increased spending for the military and for homeland security. Both seem willing to set aside the goal of a balanced budget in order to do so. But it is likely that conflict between Democrats, who seek to spend more on social programs, and Republicans, who seek further tax reductions, is likely to continue. The general public remains ambivalent over conflicting budget goals; they want both increased government services *and* reduced taxes.

The Tax Burden

The tax burden in the United States is modest compared to burdens in other advanced democracies (see *Compared to What?*: "Tax Burdens in Advanced Democracies" on page 592). Federal revenues are derived mainly from (1) individual income taxes, (2) corporate income taxes, (3) Social Security payroll taxes, (4) estate and gift taxes, and (5) excise taxes and custom duties.

Individual Income Taxes   The **individual income tax** is the federal government's largest source of revenue (see Figure 16.7). Following tax cuts enacted by Congress in 2001 and 2003, individual income is now taxed at six rates: 10, 15, 25, 28, 33, and 35 percent. These are *marginal rates*, a term that economists use to mean additional. That is, income up to the top of the lowest bracket is taxed at 10 percent; additional income in the next bracket is taxed at 15 percent, up to a top marginal rate of 35 percent on income over $311,950 (in 2006). A personal exemption for each taxpayer and dependent, together with a standard deduction for married couples and a refundable earned income tax credit, ensure that low income earners pay no income tax. (However, they still must pay Social Security taxes on wages.) Tax brackets, as well as the personal exemption and standard deduction, are indexed annually to protect against inflation.

The income tax is automatically deducted from the paychecks of employees. This "withholding" system is the backbone of the individual income tax. There is no withholding of nonwage income such as dividends on investments, but taxpayers with such income must file a "Declaration of Estimated Taxes" and pay this estimate in quarterly installments. Before April 15 of each year, all income-earning Americans must report their taxable income for the previous year to the Internal Revenue Service on its 1040 Form.

Americans are usually surprised to learn that half of all personal income is not taxed. To understand why, we must know how the tax laws distinguish between *adjusted gross income* (an individual's total money income minus expenses incurred in earning that income) and *taxable income* (that part of adjusted gross income subject to taxation). Federal tax rates apply only to *taxable* income.

Tax expenditures are tax revenues lost to the federal government because of exemptions, exclusions, deductions, and special treatments in tax laws. Federal government revenues from individual and business income taxes would be substantially higher were it not for special provisions in tax laws that enable taxpayers to avoid paying taxes on often substantial sums of income. Although each of these "loopholes" supposedly has a larger social goal behind it (for example, the deductibility of mortgage interest is supposed to stimulate the purchase and construction of homes, keeping up the value of those assets for current homeowners and keeping the construction industry employed), critics charge that many cost far more than they are worth to society. These are the major tax expenditures in federal tax law:

- Personal exemptions for taxpayer, spouse, and children
- Deductibility of mortgage interest on homes
- Deductibility of property taxes on first and second homes
- Deferral of capital gains on home sales
- Deductibility of charitable contributions
- Credit for child-care expenses
- Tax-free deposits for educational savings accounts

individual income tax Taxes on individuals' wages and other earned income, the primary source of revenue for the U.S. federal government.

tax expenditures Revenues lost to the federal government because of exemptions, exclusions, deductions, and special-treatment provisions in tax laws.

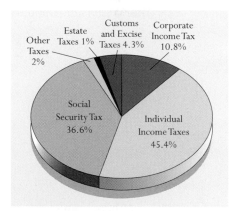

Figure 16.7 Sources of Federal Income

Individual income taxes make up the largest portion of the federal government's revenues (43 percent). The government also relies heavily on the second largest source of its revenues, Social Security taxes.

Source: Budget of the United States Government, 2007.

COMPARED TO WHAT?

Tax Burdens in Advanced Democracies

Americans complain a lot about taxes. But from a global perspective, overall tax burdens in the United States are relatively low (see figure). Federal, state, and local taxes in the United States amount to about 30 percent of the gross domestic product (GDP), slightly below the burden carried by the nation's leading competitors, Japan and Germany. U.S. taxes are well below the burdens imposed in Sweden, Denmark, and other nations with highly developed welfare systems.

Top marginal tax rates in many nations were reduced during the 1980s and 1990s. For example, the top rate in Great Britain was lowered from 60 to 40 percent, in Japan from 70 to 30 percent, and in Sweden from 80 to 55 percent. Both in the United States and abroad, the notion that excessively high tax rates discourage work, savings, and investment, as well as slow economic growth, won acceptance (although how high is "excessive" is obviously open to different interpretations). Moreover, in a global economy, with increased mobility of individuals and firms, pressures push nations to keep their top tax rates within reasonable limits. Corporations can shift their assets to low-tax jurisdictions, and high personal income tax rates can even threaten a "brain drain" of talented individuals.

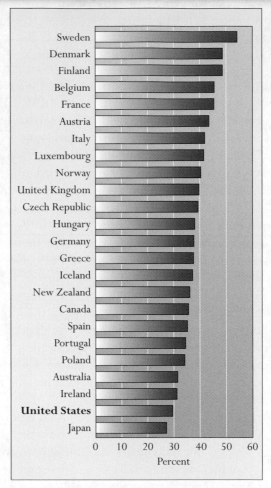

Tax Revenues as a Percentage of GDP

Source: OECD, *Figures for 2000. www.oecd.org.*

- Exclusion of employer contributions to pension plans and medical insurance

- Partial exclusion of Social Security benefits

- Exclusion of interest on public-purpose state and local bonds

- Deductibility of state and local income taxes

- Exclusion of income earned abroad

- Accelerated depreciation of machinery, equipment, and structures

- Deductible contributions to IRAs and 401(K) retirement plans, and accrued interest and profits in these plans. (But taxes must be paid when cash is taken from these plans.)

There is a continual struggle between proponents of special tax exemptions to achieve social goals and those who believe the tax laws should be simplified and social goals met by direct government expenditures. Much of the political infighting in Washington involves the efforts of interest groups to obtain exemptions, exclusions, deductions, and special treatments in tax laws.[6]

In addition to these multiple means of **tax avoidance** (legal means), an "underground economy" that facilitates **tax evasion** (illegal means of dodging taxes) costs the federal government many billions of dollars. The federal Internal Revenue Service itself estimates that it is losing about $200 billion per year in revenue due to the failure of people to report income and pay taxes on it. Independent estimates of the size of the underground economy are much higher, perhaps $350 billion, or 15 percent of all taxes due.[7] Many citizens receive cash for goods and services they provide, and it simply does not occur to them to report these amounts as income in addition to the wage statements they receive from their employer. Many others receive all or most of their income from cash transactions; they have a strong incentive to underreport their income. And, of course, illegal criminal transactions such as drug dealing are seldom reported on personal income tax forms. As tax rates rise, hiding income becomes more profitable.

Corporate Income Taxes   The corporate income tax provides only about 10 percent of the federal government's total revenue. The Tax Reform Act of 1986 reduced the top corporate income tax from 46 to 34 percent (raised to 35 percent in 1993). However, corporations find many ways of reducing their taxable income often to zero. The result is that many very large and profitable corporations pay little in taxes. Religious, charitable, and educational organizations, as well as labor unions, are exempt from corporate income taxes except for income they may derive from "unrelated business activity."

Who really bears the burden of the corporate income tax? Economists differ over whether the corporate income tax is "shifted" to consumers or whether corporations and their stockholders bear its burden. The evidence on the **incidence**—that is, who actually bears the burden—of this tax is inconclusive.[8]

Social Security Taxes   The second largest source of federal revenue is the Social Security tax. It is withheld from paychecks as the "FICA" deduction, an acronym that helps hide the true costs of Social Security and Medicare from wage earners. To keep up with the rising number of beneficiaries and the higher levels of benefits voted for by Congress, including generous automatic cost-of-living increases each year, the Social Security taxes rose to 15.3 percent. (The Social Security tax is 12.4 percent and the Medicare tax is 2.9 percent; all wage income is subject to the Medicare tax, but wage income above a certain level $94,200 in 2006—is not subject to the Social Security tax.)

Taxes collected under FICA are earmarked (by Social Security number) for the account of each taxpayer. Workers thus feel they are receiving benefits as a right rather than as a gift of the government. However, less than 15 percent of the benefits being paid to current recipients of Social Security can be attributed to their prior contributions. Current taxpayers are paying more than 85 percent of the benefits received by current retirees.

Today a majority of taxpayers pay more in Social Security taxes than income taxes. Indeed, combined employer and employee Social Security taxes now amount to over $14,400 for each worker at the top of the wage base. If we assume that the employer's share of the tax actually comes out of wages that would otherwise be paid to the employee, then more than 75 percent of all taxpayers pay more in Social Security taxes than in income taxes.

Estate and Gift Taxes   Taxation of property left to heirs is one of the oldest forms of taxation in the world. Federal estate taxes begin on estates of $1 million and levy a tax rate that starts at 18 percent and rises to 45 percent for estates

tax avoidance Taking advantage of exemptions, exclusions, deductions, and special treatments in tax laws (legal).

tax evasion Hiding income and/or falsely claiming exemptions, deductions, and special treatments (illegal).

incidence Actual bearer of a tax burden.

 **National Taxpayers Union**
Advocacy organization for taxpayers "to keep what they have earned," with policy papers and data on tax burdens. *www.ntu.org*

worth more than $3 million. Because taxes at death otherwise could be avoided by simply giving estates to heirs while the giver is still alive, a federal gift tax is also levied on anyone who gives gifts in excess of $11,500 annually.

Excise Taxes and Custom Duties   Federal excise taxes on the consumption of liquor, tobacco, gasoline, telephones, air travel, and other so-called luxury items, together with customs taxes on imports, provide about 3 percent of total federal revenues.

Tax Politics

The politics of taxation centers around the question of who actually bears the heaviest burden of a tax—especially which income groups must devote the largest proportion of their income to taxes. **Progressive taxation** requires high-income groups to pay a larger percentage of their incomes in taxes than low-income groups. **Regressive taxation** takes a larger share of the income of low-income groups. **Proportional (flat) taxation** requires all income groups to pay the same percentage of their income in taxes. Note that the *percentage of income* paid in taxes is the determining factor. Most taxes take more money from the rich than the poor, but a progressive or regressive tax is distinguished by the percentages of income taken from various income groups.

The Argument for Progressivity   Progressive taxation is generally defended on the principle of ability to pay; the assumption is that high-income groups can afford to pay a larger *percentage* of their incomes in taxes at no more of a sacrifice than that required of lower income groups to devote a smaller proportion of their income to taxation. This assumption is based on what economists call *marginal utility theory* as it applies to money; each additional dollar of income is slightly less valuable to an individual than preceding dollars. For example, a $5,000 increase in the income of an individual already earning $100,000 is much less valuable than a $5,000 increase to an individual earning only $10,000 or to an individual with no income at all. Hence, it is argued that added dollars of income can be taxed at higher rates without violating equitable principles.

The Argument for Proportionality   Opponents of progressive taxation generally assert that equity can only be achieved by taxing everyone at the same percentage of their income, regardless of the size of their income. Progressivity penalizes initiative, enterprise, and the risk taking necessary to create new products and businesses. It also reduces incentives to expand and develop the nation's economy. Highly progressive taxes curtail growth and make everyone poorer (see *A Conflicting View:* "We Should Enact a Flat Tax").

Reagan's Reductions in Progressivity   Certainly the most dramatic change in federal tax laws during the Reagan years was the reduction in the progressivity of individual income tax rates (see Figure 16.8). The top marginal tax rate fell from 70 percent when President Reagan took office to 28 percent following enactment of tax reform in 1986. The Tax Reform Act of 1986 reduced fourteen rate brackets to only two rate brackets, 15 and 28 percent.

"Read My Lips"   At the Republican national convention in 1988, presidential nominee George H. W. Bush made a firm pledge to American voters that he would veto any tax increases passed by the Democratic-controlled Congress: "Read my lips! No new taxes." Yet in a 1990 budget summit with Democratic congressional leaders, President Bush agreed to add a top marginal rate of 31 percent

progressive taxation
System of taxation in which higher income groups pay a larger percentage of their incomes in taxes than do lower income groups.

regressive taxation System of taxation in which lower income groups pay a larger percentage of their incomes in taxes than do higher income groups.

proportional (flat) taxation
System of taxation in which all income groups pay the same percentage of their income in taxes.

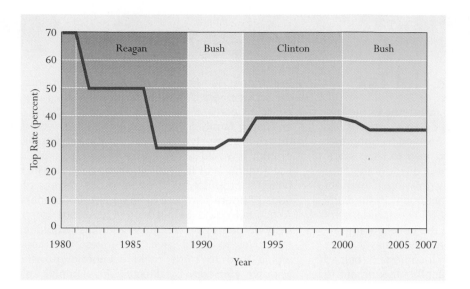

Figure 16.8 Top Personal Income Tax Rates
The top marginal personal income tax rate fell dramatically during the Reagan Administration, then began to creep upward again under Presidents Bush and Clinton. George W. Bush lowered the top rate in 2001 and again in 2003.

to the personal income tax. Breaking his solemn pledge on taxes contributed heavily to Bush's defeat in the 1992 presidential election.

"Soak the Rich"   Proposals to "soak the rich" are always politically very popular. President Clinton pushed Congress to raise the top marginal tax rates to 39.6 percent for families earning $250,000. But these new top rates do not raise much revenue, partly because very few people have annual incomes in these categories. Moreover, high rates encourage people to seek tax-sheltered investments—to use their capital less efficiently to create tax breaks for themselves rather than to promote new business and new jobs.

Bush Tax Cuts   George W. Bush came into office vowing *not* to make the same mistake as his father, raising tax rates in an effort to compromise with the Democrats. On the contrary, Bush was strongly committed to lowering taxes, arguing first in 2001 that the American people should receive some part of the government's surpluses. Congress responded with a small tax cut, bringing the top marginal rate from 39.6 percent to 38.6 percent.

By 2003 the economy appeared to be in a slide. Bush argued that an "economic stimulus" package of additional tax cuts would revive the economy. He believed that federal deficits were the result of slow economic growth; tax reductions might temporarily add to deficits, but eventually the economic growth inspired by lower taxes would increase government revenues and eliminate deficits.

Bush moved the Republican-controlled Congress to lower the top marginal rate to 35 percent, and restructure rates through six brackets—10, 15, 25, 28, 33, and 35 percent (see Table 16.2). And the Bush 2003 tax package also contained a variety of new credits and special treatments:

George Bush's pledge "Read my lips, no new taxes" helped him to victory in 1988. But breaking the pledge in 1990 contributed heavily to his defeat in 1992.

> *Dividends:* Corporate stock dividends are to be taxed at a low 15 percent rather than at the same rate as earned income. Bush and the Republicans in Congress initially proposed eliminating all taxes on dividends. They argued that corporations already paid taxes on corporate profits, and inasmuch as dividends come out of profits, taxing them as personal income amounted to "double taxation." They also recognized that nearly one-half of all American families now own stock or mutual funds, and they hoped that this new tax break would be politically popular. The 15 percent tax rate on dividends is less than half of the top marginal rate of 35 percent on earned income.

A CONFLICTING VIEW

We Should Enact a Flat Tax

More than a hundred years ago, Supreme Court Justice Stephen J. Field, in striking down as unconstitutional a progressive income tax enacted by Congress, predicted that such a tax would lead to class wars: "Our political contests will become a war of the poor against the rich, a war constantly growing in intensity and bitterness."[a] But populist sentiment in the early twentieth century—the anger of Midwestern farmers toward Eastern rail tycoons and the beliefs of impoverished Southerners that they would never have incomes high enough to pay an income tax—helped secure the passage of the Sixteenth Amendment to the U.S. Constitution. The federal income tax passed by Congress in 1914 had a top rate of 7 percent; less than 1 percent of the population had incomes high enough to be taxed. Today the top rate is 35 percent (actually over 42 percent when mandated phaseouts of deductions are calculated); about half of the population pays income taxes.

The current income tax progressively penalizes all the behaviors that produce higher incomes—work, savings, investment, and initiative. And whenever incomes are taxed at different rates, people will figure out ways to take advantage of the differential. They will hire lawyers, accountants, and lobbyists to find or create exemptions, exclusions, deductions, and preferential treatments for their own sources of income. The tax laws will become increasingly lengthy and complex. Today about half of all personal income is excluded from federal income taxation.

The Internal Revenue Service (IRS) is the most intrusive of all government agencies, overseeing the finances of every tax-paying citizen and corporation in America. It maintains personal records on more than 100 million Americans and requires them to submit more than a billion forms each year. It may levy fines and penalties and collect taxes on its own initiative; in disputes with the IRS, the burden of proof falls on the taxpayer, not the agency. Its 110,000 employees spend $8 billion per year reviewing tax returns, investigating taxpayers, and collecting revenue. Americans pay an additional $30 billion for the services of tax accountants and preparers, and they waste some $200 billion in hours of record keeping and computing their taxes.

We should replace the current federal income tax system with a simple flat tax that could be calculated on a postcard. The elimination of all exemptions, exclusions, deductions, and special treatments, and the replacement of current progressive tax rates with a flat 19 percent tax on all forms of income, even excluding family incomes under $25,000, would produce just as much revenue as the current complicated system. It would sweep away the nation's army of tax accountants and lawyers and lobbyists and increase national productivity by relieving taxpayers of millions of hours of record keeping and tax preparation. A flat tax could be filed on a postcard form (see below). Removing progressive rates would create incentives to work, save, and invest in America. It would lead to more rapid economic growth and improve efficiency by directing investments to their most productive uses rather than to tax avoidance. It would eliminate current incentives to underreport income, overstate exemptions, and avoid and evade taxation. Finally, by exempting a generous personal and family allowance, the flat tax would be made fair.

Form 1	Individual Wage Tax		2000
Your first name and initial (if joint return, also give spouse's name and initial)		Last name	Your social security number
Home address (number and street including apartment number or rural route)			Spouse's social security number
City, town, or post office, state, and ZIP code			Your occupation
			Spouse's occupation
1 Wages and salary		1	
2 Pension and retirement benefits		2	
3 Total compensation (*line 1 plus line 2*)		3	
4 Personal allowance			
(a) 0 $16,500 for married filing jointly		4a	
(b) 0 $9,500 for single		4b	
(c) 0 $14,000 for single head of household		4c	
5 Number of dependents, not including spouse		5	
6 Personal allowances for dependents (*line 5 multiplied by $4,500*)		6	
7 Total personal allowances (*line 4 plus line 6*)		7	
8 Taxable compensation (*line 3 less line 7, if positive; otherwise zero*)		8	
9 Tax (*19% of line 8*)		9	
10 Tax withheld by employer		10	
11 Tax due (*line 9 less line 10, if positive*)		11	
12 Refund due (*line 10 less line 9, if positive*)		12	

[a]*Pollock v. Farmer's Loan,* 158 U.S. 601 (1895).

Marriage penalty: For married couples the new law made the standard personal deduction twice that of a single person. This change corrected a flaw in the tax law that had long plagued married persons filing joint returns.

Child tax credit: The per child tax credit was raised to $1,000 (from $600). This was a politically popular change supported by many Democrats as well as Republicans.

Table 16.2   Marginal Individual Income Tax Rates

	Before 2001	2001	2007
Lowest	15%	10%	10%
to	28	15	15
Highest	31	27	25
Income	36	30	28
Brackets	39.6	35	33
		38.6	35

Capital gains: Finally, the Bush tax package chipped away again at the tax on capital gains—profits from the sale of investments held at least one year. The capital gains tax was reduced from 20 to 15 percent, a rate less than half of the top marginal rate on earned income of 35 percent.

The Bush tax package was approved in the Republican-controlled House and Senate on largely party line votes. Most Democrats were opposed to the package, arguing that it primarily benefited the rich, that it would do little to help the economy, and that it would add to the already huge annual federal deficits. Republicans argued that the package benefited all taxpayers, and inasmuch as the rich pay most of the taxes it is only fair that they should benefit from tax reductions. And they argued that the child credit and marriage penalty breaks would continue to ensure that families with incomes under $40,000 would pay little or no federal income taxes.

Who Pays the Federal Income Tax?   The federal income tax continues to be highly progressive. Progressive rates, together with the personal and standard deductions for families and the earned income tax credit for low-income earners, combined to remove most of the income tax burden on middle- and low-income Americans. Indeed, the lower half of the nation's taxpayers pay less than 4 percent of total income taxes paid to the federal government (see Figure 16.9).

Even though marginal tax rates have been reduced substantially since 1980, upper-income Americans pay a much larger share of the federal income tax today than was previously the case. Although top marginal tax rates were reduced from 70 percent to 35 percent, the richest Americans are now paying more of the personal income tax even though their rates are lower than those in effect in 1980. How can one explain the fact that the rich are paying more now even though their tax rates are lower? The answer is that the incentive to earn additional income increases when tax rates decrease. Moreover, the incentive to find loopholes in the tax laws, to avoid receiving taxable income, and even to hide income (that is, to cheat), is reduced when top marginal rates are lowered.

Note that today the top 50 percent of income earners pay virtually all of the nation's personal income tax. Indeed, the top 10 percent of income earners pay about 66 percent of all of the income taxes collected by the federal government, and the top 1 percent pay about a third of all income taxes. This was not the case in 1980 when marginal tax rates were high. At that time the top 10 percent of income earners paid only 49 percent of all income taxes, and the top 1 percent paid only 19 percent of all income taxes.

Capital Gains Taxation   All income is *not* taxed equally under federal income tax laws. (Indeed, interest income from municipal bonds is totally tax free, encouraging many wealthy investors to put their money into these "munies.") The Tax

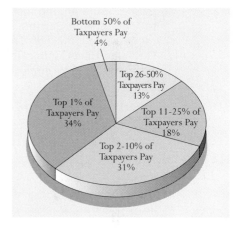

Figure 16.9   Who Pays the Federal Personal Income Tax?
Percentage of Total Federal Income Taxes Paid by Income Levels

Source: Based on data from The Tax Foundation at *http://www.taxfoundation.org.html.*

 **Tax Foundation Advocacy**
Organization devoted to making the public "tax conscious," with information, "fiscal facts," and "tax freedom day." *www.taxfoundation.org*

A CONSTITUTIONAL NOTE

The Constitution and Private Property

The protection of private property was one of the principal motives in convening the Constitutional Convention of 1787. Among the powers set forth in Article I, Section 8, are the "power to lay and collect taxes, duties, imposts, and excises"; "to borrow money"; "to regulate commerce with foreign nations and among the several states and with the Indian Tribes"; "to establish . . . uniform rules of bankruptcy"; "to coin money, regulate the value thereof"; "to provide for the punishment of counterfeiting." And among the powers specifically denied to the states in Section 10 are the powers to "coin money; emit Bills of Credit; make any Thing but Gold and Silver Coin a Tender in Payment of Debts; pass any . . . Law impairing the Obligation of Con-

tracts. . . ." In addition, the Constitution of 1787 created what we call today a *common market* or *free trade area* among the states: "No state shall . . . lay any Imports or Duties on Imports or Exports. . . ." This prevents states taxing goods or services moving across state lines or from taxing foreign commerce. In short, the Constitution places power over the economy in the hands of the national government and prevents the states from interfering with commerce. However, for well over a century the Supreme Court interpreted the Interstate Commerce Clause narrowly to include only the regulation of goods and services that actually moved across state lines. It was not until 1937 that the Court, in the important case of *National Labor Relations Board v. Jones and Locklin Steel Co.*, extended the commerce power to include production and manufacturing which occurred *within* a state but nonetheless affected interstate commerce.

---

capital gains Profits from buying and selling property including stocks, bonds, and real estate.

Code distinguishes between earned income and **capital gains**—profits from the buying and selling of property, including stocks, bonds, and real estate. Currently capital gains are taxed at a top marginal rate of 15 percent, compared to the top marginal rate of 35 percent for earned income in 2006.

Why should income earned from *working* be taxed at a higher rate than income earned from *investing*? The real estate industry, together with investment firms and stockbrokers, argue that high tax rates on capital gains discourage investment and economic growth. (But if it is true that high taxes discourage investment, high taxes must also discourage work, and both capital and labor are required for economic growth.) But the political power of investors, especially in the Republican Party, places heavy downward pressure on capital gains tax rates.

Capital gains are concentrated among the rich. More than half of all capital gains go to persons with incomes in excess of $1 million. That means that any reduction in capital gains taxes go disproportionately to the rich. Of course, the rich pay virtually all capital gains taxes.

Summary Notes

- A central policy issue is deciding how much to rely on government versus the marketplace to produce and distribute goods and services. The United States is primarily a free-market economy, but federal fiscal and monetary policies exercise a strong influence over economic activity.

- Fiscal policy—decisions about government taxing, spending, and deficits or surpluses—is decided in the president's budget recommendations and in the appropriations acts passed by Congress. Monetary policy is largely decided by the independent Federal Reserve Board.

- The performance of the economy can be measured by GDP growth and the unemployment and inflation

rates. Politically the unemployment rate may be the most important of these measures of economic performance.

- Imports and exports grow each year as a percentage of the gross domestic product of the United States. This trend toward globalization has been fostered by U.S. participation in the World Trade Organization, the International Monetary Fund, the World Bank, the North American Free Trade Agreement, and other agreements and treaties in support of free trade. Free trade may benefit the economy as a whole, but it appears to disadvantage poorly educated, low-skilled American workers.

- Annual federal budget deficits over thirty years led to a national debt of more than $5 trillion, an amount equal to almost half the nation's GDP. A strong economy produced budget surpluses from 1998 through 2001, but an economic slowdown combined with the effects of the 9/11 terrorist attack, and perhaps also the effects of tax cuts enacted by the Republican-controlled Congress and President George W. Bush, led to a return of annual budget deficits.

- Tax politics centers on the question of who actually bears the burden of a tax. The individual income tax, the largest source of federal government revenue, is progressive, with higher rates levied at higher income levels. Progressive taxation is defended on the ability-to-pay principle. But half of all personal income, and a great deal of corporate income, is untaxed, owing to a wide variety of exemptions, exclusions, deductions, and special treatments on tax laws. These provisions are defended in Washington by a powerful array of interest groups.

- The Reagan Administration reduced top income tax rates from 70 to 28 percent, believing high rates discouraged work, savings, and investment, and thereby curtailed economic growth. But George Bush agreed to an increase in the top rate to 31 percent. Bill Clinton pushed Congress to raise the top rates to 39.6 percent, arguing that rich people had benefited from Reagan's "trickle down" policies and must now be forced to bear their "fair share." George W. Bush succeeded in getting two tax cut bills through Congress in 2001 and 2003. The bills lowered the top marginal income tax rate to 35 percent, eliminated the marriage penalty, increased child exemptions, and lowered the capital gain rate to 15 percent.

Key Terms

fiscal policy   578
monetary policy   578
government bonds   579
Federal Reserve Board
   (the Fed)   580
inflation   580
recession   580
gross domestic product
   (GDP)   580

economic cycles   581
unemployment rate   581
international trade   582
protectionism   583
free trade   583
mandatory spending   587
entitlement
   programs   587
indexing   587

in-kind (noncash)
   benefits   587
balanced budget   587
backdoor spending   587
discretionary
   spending   588
deficit   588
national debt   588
individual income tax   591

tax expenditures   591
tax avoidance   593
tax evasion   593
incidence   593
progressive taxation   594
regressive taxation   594
proportional (flat)
   taxation   594
capital gains   598

Suggested Readings

Issak, Robert A., *Globalization Gap*. Upper Saddle River, N.J.: Prentice Hall, 2005. Antiglobalization argument that rich nations get richer and poor nations get poorer as a result of international trade.

Jacobs, Laurence R., and Theda S. Kocpol, eds. *Inequality and American Democracy*. New York: Russell Sage Foundation, 2005. A series of essays describing increasing inequality in America and its political and social consequences.

Langren, Robert and Martin Snitzer. *Government, Business and the American Economy*. Upper Saddle River, N.J.: Prentice Hall, 2001. Comprehensive text on the government's role in the economy.

Rothgeb, John M. Jr. *U.S. Trade Policy*. Washington, D.C.: CQ Press, 2001. Concise text on international trade, including history of GATT, WTO, and NAFTA.

Sowell, Thomas. *Basic Economics: A Citizen's Guide to the Economy*. New York: Basic Books, 2003. Introduction to economics with an emphasis on public policy. No jargon or equations.

Steger, Manfred B. *Globalism*. Boston: Rowman & Littlefield, 2002. The politics of pro- and antiglobalist groups, with a sharp critique of the ideology of globalism.

Wolff, Edward N. *Top Heavy* (updated edition). New York: Century Foundation, 2002. The study of the increasing inequality of wealth in United States and an argument for taxing financial wealth (bank accounts, stocks, bonds, property, houses, cars, etc.) as well as income.

Make It Real

ECONOMIC POLICY
The simulation allows student to try to balance the federal budget.

17 POLITICS AND SOCIAL WELFARE

Chapter Outline

- Power and Social Welfare
- Poverty in the United States
- Social Welfare Policy
- Senior Power
- Politics and Welfare Reform
- Health Care in America
- Politics and Health Care Reform

Think About Politics

1 Do you think government welfare programs perpetuate poverty?
Yes ☐ No ☐

2 Should all retirees receive Social Security benefits regardless of their personal wealth or income?
Yes ☐ No ☐

3 Do you believe the Social Security system will still be solvent when you retire?
Yes ☐ No ☐

4 Should Medicare benefits be expanded to include prescription drugs?
Yes ☐ No ☐

5 Should the government pay for nursing home care without forcing beneficiaries to use up all their savings and income?
Yes ☐ No ☐

6 Should the states rather than the federal government decide about welfare policy?
Yes ☐ No ☐

7 Should there be a time limit on how long a person can receive welfare payments?
Yes ☐ No ☐

8 Should government provide health care insurance for all Americans?
Yes ☐ No ☐

Through its social welfare policies, the federal government has the power to redistribute income among people. But most government payments to individuals do not go to poor people but rather to senior citizens whose voting power heavily influences elected officials.

Power and Social Welfare

Social welfare policy largely determines who gets what from government—who benefits from government spending on its citizens and how much they get. This vast power has made the federal government a major *redistributor* of income from one group to another—from the working population to retirees, from the employed to the unemployed, from taxpayers to poor people. Direct payments to individuals—Social Security, welfare, pension, and other **transfer payments**—now account for about 60 percent of all federal government outlays.

When most Americans think of social welfare programs, they think of poor people. An estimated 35 million to 40 million people in the United States (11 to 15 percent of the population) have incomes below the official **poverty line**—that is, their annual cash income falls below what is required to maintain a decent standard of living (see Figure 17.1). If the approximately $1 trillion spent per year for social welfare were directly distributed to the nation's poor people, each poor person—man, woman, and child—would receive $25,000 per year.

Why does poverty persist in a nation where total social welfare spending is more than four times the amount needed to eliminate poverty? Because poor people are not the principal beneficiaries of social welfare spending. Most social welfare spending, including the largest programs—Social Security and Medicare—goes to the *non*poor (see Figure 17.2). Less than one-third of federal social welfare spending is **means-tested spending**—that is, distributed on the basis of the recipient's income. The middle classes, not the poor, are the major beneficiaries of the nation's social welfare system.

Poverty in the United States

How much poverty really exists in the United States? It depends on how you define the term "poverty." The official definition used by the federal government focuses on the cash income needed to maintain a "decent standard of living." The official poverty line is only a little more than one-third of the median income of all American families. It takes into account the effects of inflation, rising each year with the rate of inflation. (For example, in 1990, the official poverty line for an urban family of four was $13,359 per year; by 2005 the poverty line had risen to about $20,000.)

Temporary Poverty   Poor people are often envisioned as a permanent "underclass" living most of their lives in poverty. But most poverty is not

Figure 17.1   Number of Poor and Poverty Rate

Source: http://www.census.gov/hhes/poverty00/pov00.html

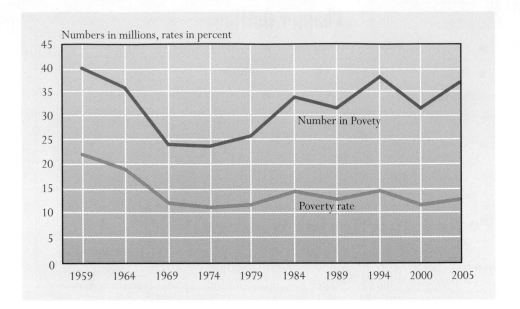

long term. Tracing poor families over time presents a different picture of the nature of poverty from the "snapshot" view taken in any one year. For example, over the last decade 11 to 15 percent of the nation's population has been officially classified as poor in any one year. However, only *some* poverty is persistent: about 6 to 8 percent of the population remains in poverty for more than five years. Thus about half of the people who are counted as poor are experiencing poverty for only a short period of time. For these temporary poor, welfare is a "safety net" that helps them through hard times.

Persistent Poverty   About half of the people on welfare rolls at any one time are *persistently poor,* that is, likely to remain on welfare for five or more years. For these people, welfare is a more permanent part of their lives.

Because they place a disproportionate burden on welfare resources, persistently poor people pose serious questions for social scientists and policy makers. Prolonged poverty and welfare dependency create an **underclass** that suffers from many social ills—teen pregnancy, family instability, drugs, crime, alienation, apathy, and irresponsibility.[1] Government educational, training, and jobs programs, as well as many other social service efforts, fail to benefit many of these people.

Family Structure   Poverty and welfare dependency are much more frequent among female-headed households with no husband present than among husband-wife households (see *Up Close:* "Who Are the Poor?"). Traditionally, "illegitimacy" was held in check by powerful religious and social structures. But these structures weakened over time (see Figure 17.3), and the availability of welfare cash benefits, food stamps, medical care, and government housing removed much of the economic hardship once associated with unwed motherhood. Indeed, it was sometimes argued that government welfare programs, however well meaning, ended up perpetuating poverty and social dependency. This argument inspired welfare reform in 1996 (see "Politics and Welfare Reform" later in this chapter).

Teen Pregnancy   Teenage motherhood is usually a path to poverty. "Babies having babies" is closely associated with social welfare dependency. But births to

---

transfer payments Direct payments (either in cash or in goods and/or services) by governments to individuals as part of a social welfare program, not as a result of any service or contribution rendered by the individual.

poverty line Official standard regarding what level of annual cash income is sufficient to maintain a "decent standard of living"; those with incomes below this level are eligible for most public assistance programs.

means-tested spending Spending for benefits that is distributed on the basis of the recipient's income.

underclass People who have remained poor and dependent on welfare over a prolonged period of time.

National Center for Children in Poverty Columbia University Center with studies and data on children in poverty.
www.nccp.org

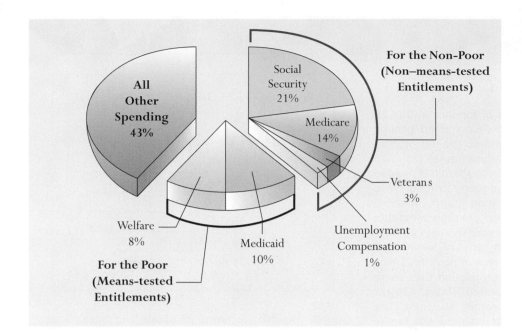

Figure 17.2   Social Welfare Entitlement Programs in the Federal Budget

Source: Budget of the United States Government, 2007.

teenage mothers—the number of births per 1,000 women fifteen to nineteen years of age—has actually *declined* in recent years. Liberals claim that this modest victory is a product of better sex education and condom distribution in schools. Conservatives claim that it is a result of teaching abstinence, as well as welfare reforms requiring teenagers to reside with their parents and continue schooling as conditions for cash payments. According to federal survey data, teenage girls are having less sex *and* making more use of birth control.

The "Truly Disadvantaged"   The nation's largest cities have become the principal location of virtually all of the social problems confronting our society— poverty, homelessness (see *Up Close:* "Homelessness in America"), racial tension, drug abuse, delinquency, and crime. These problems are all made worse by their concentration in large cities. Yet the concentration of social ills in cities is a relatively recent occurrence; as late as 1970, there were higher rates of poverty in rural America than in the cities.

Institute for Research on Poverty
University of Wisconsin
Institute leads in research on extent and causes of poverty.
www.ssc.wsc.edv/irp

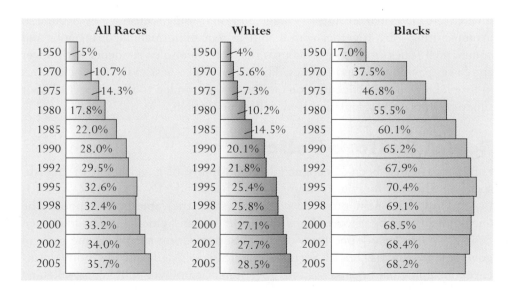

	All Races		Whites		Blacks
1950	5%	1950	4%	1950	17.0%
1970	10.7%	1970	5.6%	1970	37.5%
1975	14.3%	1975	7.3%	1975	46.8%
1980	17.8%	1980	10.2%	1980	55.5%
1985	22.0%	1985	14.5%	1985	60.1%
1990	28.0%	1990	20.1%	1990	65.2%
1992	29.5%	1992	21.8%	1992	67.9%
1995	32.6%	1995	25.4%	1995	70.4%
1998	32.4%	1998	25.8%	1998	69.1%
2000	33.2%	2000	27.1%	2000	68.5%
2002	34.0%	2002	27.7%	2002	68.4%
2005	35.7%	2005	28.5%	2005	68.2%

Figure 17.3   Births to Unmarried Women

The rate of children born to unmarried women rose through 1995. Recent reports indicate a leveling off of births to unmarried women, at approximately one-third of all births.

Source: Centers for Disease Control, www.cdc.gov; Statistical Abstract of the United States, 2004–2005, p. 64.

UP CLOSE

Who Are the Poor?

Poverty occurs in many kinds of families and in all races and ethnic groups. However, some groups experience poverty (low income) in greater proportions than the national average (see figure).

Poverty is most common among families headed by women. The incidence of poverty among these families is four times greater than that for married couples. These women and their children constitute over two-thirds of all of the persons living in poverty in the United States. About one of every five children in the United States lives in poverty. These figures describe what has been labeled the "feminization of poverty" in the United States. Clearly, poverty is closely related to family structure. The disintegration of the traditional husband-wife family is the single most influential factor contributing to poverty today.

Blacks also experience poverty in much greater proportions than whites. Over the years, the poverty rate among blacks in the United States has been almost three times higher than the poverty rate among whites. Poverty among Hispanics is also significantly greater than among whites.

In contrast, elderly people in America experience less poverty than the nonaged. The aged are not poor, despite the popularity of the phrase "the poor and the aged." The percentage of persons over sixty-five years of age with low incomes is below the national average. Moreover, elderly people are

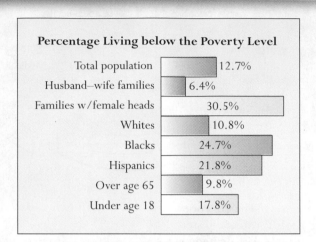

Percentage Living below the Poverty Level

Total population	12.7%
Husband–wife families	6.4%
Families w/female heads	30.5%
Whites	10.8%
Blacks	24.7%
Hispanics	21.8%
Over age 65	9.8%
Under age 18	17.8%

much wealthier in terms of assets and have fewer expenses than the nonaged. They are more likely than younger people to own homes with paid-up mortgages. Medicare pays a large portion of their medical expenses. With fewer expenses, elderly people, even with relatively smaller cash incomes, experience poverty differently from the way a young mother with children experiences it. The declining poverty rate among elderly people is a relatively recent occurrence, however. Continuing increases in Social Security benefits over the years are largely responsible for this singular "victory" in the war against poverty.

Source: U.S. Bureau of the Census, 2005.

Why has the inner city become the locus of social problems? Some observers argue that changes in the labor market from industrial goods–producing jobs to professional, financial, and technical service–producing jobs have increasingly divided the labor market into low-wage and high-wage sectors.[2] The decline in manufacturing jobs, together with a shift in remaining manufacturing jobs and commercial (sales) jobs to the suburbs, has left inner-city residents with fewer and lower paying job opportunities. The rise in joblessness in the inner cities has in turn increased the concentration of poor people, added to the number of poor single-parent families, and increased welfare dependency.

Social Welfare Policy

Public welfare has been a recognized responsibility of government in English-speaking countries for many centuries. As far back as the Poor Relief Act of 1601, the English Parliament provided workhouses for the "able-bodied poor" (the unemployed) and poorhouses for widows and orphans, elderly and handicapped people.[3] Today, nearly one-third of the U.S. population receives some form of government benefits: Social Security, Medicare or Medicaid, disability insurance, unemployment compensation, government employee retirement, veterans'

UP CLOSE

Homelessness in America

The most visible social welfare problem in the United States is the nation's homeless people, who wander about in the larger cities suffering exposure, alcoholism, drug abuse, and chronic mental illness.

The issue of homelessness has become so politicized that an accurate assessment of the problem and a rational strategy for dealing with it have become virtually impossible. The term "homeless" is used to describe many different situations.[a] Many are street people who sleep in subways, bus stations, parks, or the streets. Some of them are temporarily traveling in search of work; some have left home for a few days or are youthful runaways; others have roamed the streets for months or years. In contrast sheltered homeless people have obtained housing in shelters operated by local governments or private charities. As the number of shelters has grown over the years, the number of sheltered homeless people has also grown. But most of the sheltered homeless people come from other housing, not the streets. These are people who have recently been evicted from rental units or have previously lived with family or friends. They often include families with children; the street people are virtually all single persons.

About half of all street people are chronic alcohol and drug abusers; an additional one-fourth to one-third are mentally ill.[b] Moreover, homeless people who are alcohol and drug abusers and/or mentally ill are by far the most likely to remain on the streets for long periods of time.

The current plight of homeless people is primarily a result of various "reforms" in public policy, notably the "deinstitutionalization" of care for the mentally ill and the newly recognized rights of individuals to refuse treatment; the "decriminalization" of vagrancy and public intoxication; and urban renewal, which has eliminated many low-rent apartments and cheap hotels.

Deinstitutionalization, a policy advanced by mental health care professionals and social welfare activists in the 1960s and 1970s after the introduction of new psychotropic drug therapies, has resulted in the release of all but the most dangerous mental patients from state-run mental hospitals.

Decriminalization of public intoxication has also added to the numbers of street people. Involuntary confinement of substance abusers is now banned

A family eating a Christmas Eve lunch for the needy and homeless, prepared by a Washington, D.C., mission.

unless a person is arrested while possessing an illegal substance or is found in court to be "a danger to himself or others," which means a person must commit a serious act of violence before the courts will intervene.

Community-based care has failed for many substance abusers and chronically mentally ill street people. Many are "uncooperative"; they are isolated from society; they have no family members or doctors or counselors to turn to for help. The nation's vast social welfare system provides them little help. They cannot handle forms, appointments, or interviews; the welfare bureaucracy is intimidating. Lacking a permanent address, many receive no Social Security, welfare, or disability checks. Shelters provided by private charities, such as the Salvation Army, or by city governments are more helpful to the temporarily homeless than to chronic alcohol or drug abusers or mentally ill people. Few shelters offer treatment for alcohol or drug abusers, and some refuse disruptive people.

[a]Peter H. Rossi, *Down and Out in America* (Chicago: University of Chicago Press, 1989).

[b]As reported in a twenty-seven-city survey by the U.S. Conference of Mayors. See *U.S. News & World Report*, January 15, 1990, pp. 27–29.

social insurance programs
Social welfare programs to which beneficiaries have made contributions so that they are entitled to benefits regardless of their personal wealth.

public assistance programs
Those social welfare programs for which no contributions are required and only those living in poverty (by official standards) are eligible; includes food stamps, Medicaid, and Family Assistance.

entitlements Any social welfare program for which there are eligibility requirements, whether financial or contributory.

Social Security Social insurance program composed of the Old Age and Survivors Insurance program, which pays benefits to retired workers who have paid into the program and their dependents and survivors, and the Disability Insurance program, which pays benefits to disabled workers and their families.

unemployment compensation Social insurance program that temporarily replaces part of the wages of workers who have lost their jobs.

Supplemental Security Income (SSI) Public assistance program that provides monthly cash payments to the needy elderly (sixty-five or older), blind, and disabled.

benefits, food stamps, school lunches, job training, public housing, or cash public assistance payments (see Table 17.1). More than half of all families in the United States include at least one person who receives a government check. Thus the "welfare state" now encompasses a very large part of our society.

The major social welfare programs can be classified as either **social insurance** or **public assistance**. This distinction is an important one that has on occasion become a major political issue. If the beneficiaries of a government program are required to have made contributions to it before claiming any of its benefits, and if they are entitled to the benefits regardless of their personal wealth—as in Social Security and Medicare—then the program is said to be financed on the social insurance principle. If the program is financed out of general tax revenues and if recipients are required to show that they are poor before claiming its benefits—as in Temporary Assistance to Needy Families, Supplemental Security Income, and Medicaid—then the program is said to be financed on the public assistance principle. Public assistance programs are generally labeled as "welfare."

Entitlements   Entitlements are government benefits for which Congress has set eligibility criteria—age, income, retirement, disability, unemployment, and so on. Everyone who meets the criteria is "entitled" to the benefit.

Most of the nation's major entitlement programs were launched either in the New Deal years of the 1930s under President Franklin D. Roosevelt (Social Security, Unemployment Compensation, Aid to Families with Dependent Children, now called Temporary Assistance to Needy Families, and Aid to Aged, Blind, and Disabled, now called Supplemental Security Income) or in the Great Society years of the 1960s under President Lyndon B. Johnson (food stamps, Medicare, Medicaid).

Social Security   Begun during the Depression (1935), **Social Security** is now the largest of all entitlements; it comprises two distinct programs. The Old Age and Survivors Insurance program provides monthly cash benefits to retired workers and their dependents and to survivors of insured workers. The Disability Insurance program provides monthly cash benefits for disabled workers and their dependents. An automatic, annual cost-of-living adjustment (COLA) for both programs matches any increase in the annual inflation rate.

With more than 46 million beneficiaries, Social Security is the single largest spending program in the federal budget. About 96 percent of the nation's paid workforce is covered by the program, which is funded by a payroll tax on employers and employees. Retirees can begin receiving benefits at age sixty-two (full benefits at age sixty-five), regardless of their personal wealth or income (see "Senior Power" in this chapter).

Unemployment Compensation   Unemployment compensation temporarily replaces part of the wages of workers who lose their jobs involuntarily and helps stabilize the economy during recessions. The U.S. Department of Labor oversees the system, but states administer their own programs, with latitude within federal guidelines to define weekly benefits and other program features. Benefits are funded by a combination of federal and state unemployment taxes on employers.

Supplemental Security Income   Supplemental Security Income (SSI) is a means-tested, federally administered income assistance program that provides monthly cash payments to needy elderly (sixty-five or older), blind, and disabled people. A loose definition of "disability"—including alcoholism, drug abuse, and attention deficiency among children—has led to a rapid growth in the number of SSI beneficiaries.

Table 17.1 Beneficiaries of Major Federal Social Welfare Programs

Social Insurance Programs	Beneficiaries (millions)	Public Assistance Programs	Beneficiaries (millions)
Social Security		**Cash Aid**	
Retirement	33.0	Assistance to Families	5.1
Survivors	6.9	Supplemental Security Income (SSI)	6.9
Disabled	8.0	**Medical Care**	
Total	47.7	Medicaid	50.9
Unemployment Compensation		Veterans	1.6
Total	9.9	Indians	1.6
		Maternal and child health	9.0
Government and Military Retirement		**Food Benefits**	
Military	3.5	Food stamps	20.1
Federal employees	3.5	School lunches	16.0
State and local	14.1	Women, Infants, Children (WIC)	7.5
		Child and adult care food	2.0
Medicare		**Housing Benefit**	
Total	39.5	Total	3.3
		Education Aid	
		Pell Grants	4.8
		Stafford Loans	5.6
		Head Start	0.9
		Work Study	2.0
		Job Training	
		Total	0.8
		Energy Assistance	
		Total	4.6
		Earned Income Tax Credit	
		Total	16.8

Source: U.S. Bureau of the Census, *Statistical Abstract of the United States,* 2006, pp. 109, 362, 365.

Family Assistance Family Assistance, officially Temporary Assistance to Needy Families (formerly AFDC, or Aid to Families with Dependent Children), is a grant program to enable the states to assist needy families. States now operate the program and define "need"; they set their own benefit levels and establish (within federal guidelines) income and resource limits. Prior to welfare reform in 1996, AFDC was a *federal* entitlement program. The federal government now mandates a two-year limit on benefits, a five-year lifetime limit, and other requirements (see "Politics and Welfare Reform" later in this chapter).

Food Stamps The Food Stamp program provides low-income household members with coupons that they can redeem for enough food to provide a minimal nutritious diet. The program is overseen by the federal government but administered by the states.

Earned Income Tax Credit The Earned Income Tax Credit (EITC) is designed to assist the working poor. It not only refunds their payroll taxes but also provides larger refunds than they actually paid during the previous tax year. Thus, the EITC is in effect a "negative" income tax. It was originally passed by a

Family Assistance Public assistance program that provides monies to the states for their use in helping needy families with children.

 **Food Stamp Program**
This U.S. Department of Agriculture's Food Stamp program site contains information about application procedures, recipient eligibility guidelines, and other relevant subjects.
www.fns.usda.gov/fsp

Most of America's social welfare programs began in either the Great Depression of the 1930s or the War on Poverty in the 1960s. At the outset of the Depression, millions of unemployed Americans, like the New Yorkers in a bread line in the photo at left, had only private charities to turn to for survival. The War on Poverty of the 1960s was a reaction to the persistence of extreme poverty, like that of the rural family in the photograph at right in the midst of the prosperity that followed World War II.

Food Stamp program
Public assistance program that provides low-income households with coupons redeemable for enough food to provide a minimal nutritious diet.

Earned Income Tax Credit
Tax refunds in excess of tax payments for low-income workers.

Medicaid Public assistance program that provides health care to the poor.

Democratic-controlled Congress and signed by Republican President Gerald Ford in 1975. Over the years EITC payments have increased substantially. However, the program applies only to those poor who actually work and who apply for the credit when filing their income tax.

Medicaid   Medicaid is a joint federal-state program providing health services to low-income Americans. Most Medicaid spending goes to elderly and nonelderly disabled people. However, women and children receiving benefits under TANF automatically qualify for Medicaid, as does anyone who gets cash assistance under SSI. States can also offer Medicaid to the "medically needy"—those who face crushing medical costs but whose income or assets are too high to qualify for SSI or Family Assistance, including pregnant women and young children not receiving Family Assistance. Medicaid also pays for long-term nursing home care, but only after beneficiaries have used up virtually all of their savings and income.

Senior Power

Senior citizens are the most politically powerful age group in the population. They constitute 28 percent of the voting-age population, but, more important, because of their high voter turnout rates, they constitute more than one-third of the voters on election day. Persons over age sixty-five average a 68 percent turnout rate in presidential elections and a 61 percent rate in congressional elections. By comparison, those aged eighteen to twenty-one have a turnout rate of 36 percent in presidential elections and 19 percent in congressional elections, so the voting power of senior citizens is twice that of young people. Moreover, seniors are well represented in Washington; the American Association of Retired Persons (AARP) is the nation's largest organized interest group (see *Up Close:* "AARP: The Nation's Most Powerful Interest Group" in Chapter 9). No elected officials can afford to offend seniors, and seniors strongly support generous Social Security benefits.

— Think Again —

Should all retirees receive Social Security benefits regardless of their personal wealth or income?

— Think Again —

Do you believe the Social Security system will still be solvent when you retire?

Senior citizens enjoy enormous influence over the nation's politicians. Social Security is sacrosanct to the elderly. Any proposed changes in it bring about powerful reactions. Even a proposal to allow workers to allocate part of their Social Security taxes to stock market investments generates controversy.

The Aged in the Future   The baby boom from 1945 to 1960 produced a large generation of people who crowded schools and colleges in the 1960s and 1970s and encountered stiff competition for jobs in the 1980s. During the baby boom, women averaged 3.5 births during their lifetime. Today, the birthrate is only 1.8 births per woman, less than the 2.1 figure required to keep the population from declining. (Current U.S. population growth is a product of immigration.) The baby-boom generation will be retiring beginning in 2010, and by 2030 they will constitute more than 80 million people, 20 percent of the population (see Figure 17.4). Changes in lifestyle—less smoking, more exercise, better weight control—may increase the aged population even more. Medical advances may also extend life expectancy.

The Generational Compact   The framers of the Social Security Act of 1935 created a "trust fund" with the expectation that a reserve would be built up from social insurance taxes paid by working persons. The reserve would earn interest, and the interest and principal would be used in later years to pay benefits. In theory, Social Security is an insurance program. (Payments are recorded by name and Social Security number.) Many people believe that they get back what they paid during their working years. Reality, however, has proven much different.

Social Security is now financed on a pay-as-you-go system, rather than a reserve system. Today, the income from all social insurance premiums (taxes) pays for current Social Security benefits. This generation of workers is paying for the benefits of the last generation, and this generation must hope that its future benefits will be financed by the next generation of workers. Taxing current workers to pay benefits to current retirees may be viewed as a compact between generations. Each generation of workers in effect agrees to pay benefits to an earlier generation of retirees and expects the next generation will pay for its retirement.

The Rising Dependency Ratio   Because current workers must pay for the benefits of current retirees and other beneficiaries, the **dependency ratio** becomes an important component of evaluating the future of Social Security. The dependency ratio for Social Security is the number of recipients as a percentage of the number of contributing workers. Americans are living longer and increasing the

---Think Again---

Should the government pay for nursing home care without forcing beneficiaries to use up all their savings and income?

AARP Social Security
AARP's Social Security Center site provides information about the Social Security system including such items as the system's future solvency and a tutorial on how the system works.
www.aarp.org/socialsecurity

dependency ratio In the Social Security system, the number of recipients as a percentage of the number of contributing workers.

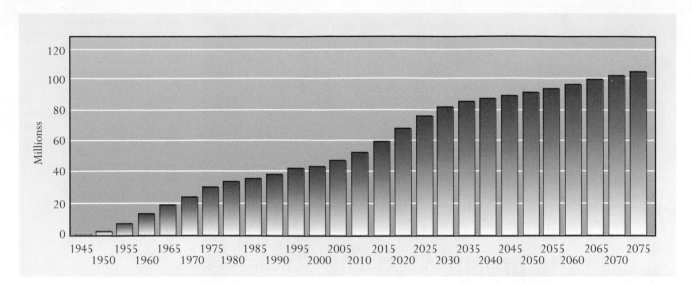

Figure 17.4   Growing Number of Social Security Beneficiaries

Millions of Old-Age, Survivors, and Disability Insurance (OASDI) recipients, 1945–2075.

Note: Numbers for 2000 onwards are estimates based on intermediate assumptions.

Source: "2000 Annual Report." March 2000, Board of Trustees, Federal Old-Age and Survivors Insurance and Disability Insurance Trust Funds.

 **Social Security Reform**
CATO Institute think tank urges private investment of Social Security premiums.
www.socialsecurity.org

COLAs Annual cost-of-living adjustments mandated by law in Social Security and other welfare benefits.

dependency ratio. A child born in 1935, when the Social Security system was created, could expect to live only to age sixty-one, four years *less* than the retirement age of sixty-five. The life expectancy of a child born in 1990 is seventy-four years, nine years beyond the retirement age. In the early years of Social Security, there were ten workers supporting each retiree—a dependency ratio of 10 to 1. But today, as the U.S. population grows older—due to lower birthrates and longer life spans—there are only three workers for each retiree, and by 2010 the dependency ratio will be two workers for each retiree.

Social Security Taxes   Social Security taxes are levied on workers' earnings. Combined Social Security and Medicare taxes amount to 15.3 percent of wage earnings. (The Social Security tax is 12.4 percent and the Medicare tax is 2.9 percent.) Half is paid directly by the employer, and half is deducted from the employees' check as the FICA deduction. All wage income is subject to the Medicare tax, but wage income above a certain level—$94,200 in 2006—is not subject to Social Security taxes. This wage limit increases every year.

Cost-of-Living Increases   Currently, the annual Social Security cost-of-living adjustments (**COLAs**) are based on the Consumer Price Index, which estimates the cost of all consumer items each year. These costs include home buying, mortgage interest, child rearing, and other costs that many retirees do not confront. Moreover, most workers do not have the same protection against inflation as retirees; average wage rates do not always match increases in the cost of living. Hence, over the years, COLAs have improved the economic well-being of Social Security recipients relative to all American workers.

Wealthy Retirees   Social Security benefits are paid to *all* eligible retirees, regardless of whatever other income they may receive. There is no means test for

Social Security benefits. As a result, large numbers of affluent Americans receive government checks each month. They paid into Social Security during their working years, and they can claim these checks as an entitlement under the social insurance principle. But currently their benefits far exceed their previous payments.

Because elderly people experience less poverty than today's workers (see *Up Close:* "Who Are the Poor?" on page 604) and possess considerably more wealth, Social Security benefits constitute a "negative" redistribution of income—that is, a transfer of income from poorer to richer people. The elderly are generally better off than the people supporting them.

"Saving" Social Security   The income from Social Security taxes *currently* exceeds payments to beneficiaries—that is, it produces a "surplus." But Social Security taxes are lumped together with general tax revenues in federal budgets; the Social Security surplus is used to hide a portion of overall federal deficits. Democrats and Republicans alike have promised to create a "lock box" and not "dip into Social Security" in order to fund current programs. But the Social Security "trust fund" is merely an accounting gimmick: current Social Security taxes are used to fund current government spending, and future retirement benefits will be paid from future revenues.

The Social Security system appears to be adequately financed for the next several decades. (In 1983 a National Commission on Social Security Reform, appointed by President Reagan, recommended an increase in Social Security taxes and a gradual increase in the retirement age from sixty-five to sixty-seven beginning in 2000. Congress adopted these recommendations.) But with the aging of the population and the resulting increases in the dependency ratio expected in the twenty-first century, Social Security will become a heavy burden on working Americans.

"Saving" Social Security is a popular political slogan in Washington. But agreement on exactly how to reform the system continues to evade lawmakers. In theory, Congress could reform Social Security by limiting COLAs to the true increases in the cost of living for retirees, or it could introduce means tests to deny benefits to high-income retirees. But politically these reforms are very unlikely. Yet another approach to reform is to allow the Social Security trust fund to invest in the private stock market with the expectation that stock values will increase over time. But if stock market investment decisions were made by the government itself, presumably the Social Security Administration, controversies would be bound to arise over these decisions. And critics object to the idea of the government making private investment decisions for Americans. Another reform frequently recommended is to allow American workers to deposit all or part of their Social Security payroll tax into an individual retirement account to buy securities of their own choosing. But such a plan would expose those individuals to the risk of bad investment decisions. (See *What Do You Think?:* "How Should We Reform Social Security?")

Politics and Welfare Reform

Americans confront a clash of values in welfare policy. Americans are a generous people; they believe government should aid those who are unable to take care of themselves, especially children, disabled people, and elderly people. But Americans are worried that welfare programs encourage dependency, undermine the work ethic, and contribute to illegitimate births and the breakup of families.

Think Again
Do you think government welfare programs perpetuate poverty?

Think Again
Should the states rather than the federal government decide about welfare policy?

Think Again
Should there be a time limit on how long a person can receive welfare payments?

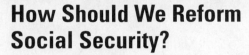

WHAT DO YOU THINK?

How Should We Reform Social Security?

Politicians want to make Social Security reform as painless as possible. The topic of Social Security reform in Washington is so sensitive that Congress has been unable to adopt any long-term reform proposals since 1983, when a presidential commission recommended a gradual increase in the retirement age. But most Americans do recognize the seriousness of the problem. Polls show that fewer than half of the American public believes the Social Security system will have money to provide benefits when

they retire. Yet despite their skepticism about the future of Social Security, relatively few Americans save enough for retirement.

Specific proposals for reforming Social Security receive mostly negative support among the general public (see below). Americans do not want to cut Social Security benefits, or increase taxes, or raise the eligibility age. Support for allowing individuals to invest part of their Social Security taxes in private investments (stocks or bonds) has actually declined in recent years despite President George Bush's active support at the proposal. The rate proposals that get majority support are those that "tax the rich."

	Favor	Oppose
Changing Social Security from a system where the government collects the taxes to a system where individuals invest some of their payroll tax contributions themselves	40%	54%
Raise the retirement age	31%	68%
Reduce the rate of growth in benefits for future retirees	30%	68%
Increase the amount employers and workers pay in taxes	40%	59%
Increase the eligibility age to receive full benefits	35%	63%
Reduce benefits for people currently under age 55	29%	67%
Increase Social Security taxes for all workers	37%	60%
Limit benefits for wealthy retirees	68%	29%
Require higher income workers to pay taxes on all of their wages	67%	30%

Source: Various polls reported at Public Agenda, www.publicagenda.org (2005).

Although social insurance programs (Social Security, Medicare, and Unemployment Compensation) are politically popular and enjoy the support of large numbers of active beneficiaries, public assistance programs (Family Assistance, SSI, Medicaid) are far less popular. A variety of controversies surround welfare policy in the United States.

Conflict Over What Causes Poverty Americans have different ideas about what causes poverty (see Table 17.2). Some attribute poverty to characteristics of individuals—drug use, declining moral values, lack of motivation. Others blame the economy—too many part-time and low-wage jobs and a shortage of good jobs. Still others place blame on the welfare system itself. Indeed, prior to welfare reform in 1996, some scholars argued that government itself was a major cause of poverty—that social welfare programs destroyed incentives to work, encouraged teenage pregnancies, and made people dependent on government handouts.[4] They argued that the combination of cash payments, food stamps, Medicaid, and housing assistance unintentionally discouraged people from forming families, taking low-paying jobs, and, perhaps, with hard work and perseverance, gradually pulling themselves and their children into the mainstream of American life.

Table 17.2   Public Opinion about the Causes of Poverty

Question: For each of the following, please tell me if this is a major cause of poverty, a minor cause of poverty, or not a cause at all.

	Major	Minor	Not a Cause	Don't Know
Drug abuse	70%	24%	5%	2%
Medical bills	58%	32%	7%	2%
Decline in moral values	57%	29%	12%	3%
Too many part-time or low-wage jobs	54%	32%	10%	4%
Too many single parents	54%	32%	12%	2%
Poor people lacking motivation	52%	35%	9%	4%
Poor public schools	47%	38%	13%	4%
The welfare system	46%	37%	11%	7%
A shortage of jobs	34%	41%	23%	2%

Source: Data copyrighted by International Communications Research for the Kaiser Family Foundation. Graphic copyright © 2002 by Public Agenda. *www.publicagenda.org*. Reprinted by permission of Public Agenda.

There is little doubt that poverty and welfare dependency are closely related to family structure. As noted earlier, poverty is much more frequent among female-headed households with no husband present than among husband-wife households. As births to unmarried women rose, poverty and social dependency increased. (In 1970 only 11 percent of births were to unmarried women; by 2000 this figure had risen to 33 percent of all births and 69 percent of minority births.) The troubling question was whether the welfare system ameliorated some of the hardships confronting unmarried mothers and their children, or whether it actually contributed to social dependency by mitigating the consequences of unmarried motherhood. For example, were teenage pregnancies more common because teenagers knew that government benefits were available to young mothers and their children?

The Politics of Welfare Reform   A political consensus grew over the years that long-term social dependency had to be addressed in welfare policy. The fact that most nonpoor mothers work convinced many *liberals* that welfare mothers had no special claim to stay at home with their children. And many *conservatives* acknowledged that some transitional assistance—education, job training, continued health care, and day care for children—might be necessary to move welfare mothers into the work force.

Although President Clinton had once promised "to end welfare as we know it," it was the Republican-controlled Congress elected in 1994 that proceeded to do so. The Republican-sponsored welfare reform bill ended the sixty-year-old federal "entitlement" for low-income families with children—the venerable AFDC program. In its place the Republicans devised a "devolution" of responsibility to the states through federal block grants—**Temporary Assistance to Needy Families**—lump sum allocations to the states for cash welfare payments, with benefits and eligibility requirements decided by the states. Conservatives in Congress imposed tough-minded "strings" to state aid, including a two-year limit

Temporary Assistance to Needy Families Welfare reform program replacing federal cash entitlement with grants to the states for welfare recipients.

on continuing cash benefits and a five-year lifetime limit; a "family cap" that would deny additional cash benefits to women already on welfare who bear more children; the denial of cash welfare to unwed parents under 18 years of age unless they live with an adult and attend school. President Clinton vetoed the first welfare reform bill passed by Congress in early 1996, but as the presidential election neared, he reversed himself and signed the Welfare Reform Act, establishing the Temporary Assistance to Needy Families program. Food stamps, SSI, and Medicaid were continued as federal "entitlements" (see *Up Close:* "Is Welfare Reform Working?").

More Reform?   Public sentiment is strongly behind the concept of working in exchange for receiving public assistance. It is unlikely that public policy will ever return to welfare as we used to know it. But Democrats and liberals and Republicans and conservatives continue to argue over additional reforms. Democrats and liberals argue for expanded subsidized day care, increases in the minimum wage, spending more on medical care for the poor, and making food stamps more available. Republicans and conservatives propose toughening the work requirements for cash welfare assistance and closing many of the loopholes that allow states to continue paying benefits to persons whose time limit has expired.

President George W. Bush established an Office of Faith-Based and Community Initiatives in the White House to eliminate "federal barriers to churches, synagogues, mosques and charities" from receiving federal grants to assist them in providing food, job training and counseling, substance abuse programs, and other aid. The Office is supposed to "identify and act to remedy statutes, regulations, and bureaucratic barriers that stand in the way of effective faith-based and community programs." But it is not supposed to direct government funds toward "inherently religious activities like sectarian worship or proselytizing." But critics worry that government-funded faith-based organizations promote religious messages and violate the No Establishment Clause of the First Amendment.

"As far as I'm concerned, they can do what they want with the minimum wage, just as long as they keep their hands off the maximum wage."

UP CLOSE

Is Welfare Reform Working?

Welfare reform, officially Temporary Assistance to Needy Families, was passed by Congress in 1996; its provisions took effect in 1997. By early 1998 the Clinton Administration, as well as Republican congressional sponsors of welfare reform, was declaring it a success.

The number of cash welfare recipients in the nation has dropped below 5 million—the lowest number in more than twenty-five years. Only about 2 percent of Americans are now on cash welfare—the smallest proportion since 1970. No doubt some of this decline is attributable to strong growth of the economy: declines in welfare rolls began *before* Congress passed its welfare reform law, and some decline may have occurred without reform. Many states had initiated their own reforms under "waivers" from the federal government even before Congress acted.

All states have now developed work programs for welfare recipients. Applicants for welfare benefits are now generally required to enter job-search programs, to undertake job training, and to accept jobs or community service positions.

Yet, although nearly everyone agrees that getting people off welfare rolls and onto payrolls is the main goal of reform, there are major obstacles to the achievement of this goal. First of all, a substantial portion (perhaps 25 to 40 percent) of long-term welfare recipients have handicaps—physical disabilities, chronic illnesses, learning disabilities, alcohol or drug abuse problems—that prevent them from holding a full-time job. Many long-term recipients have no work experience (perhaps 40 per-

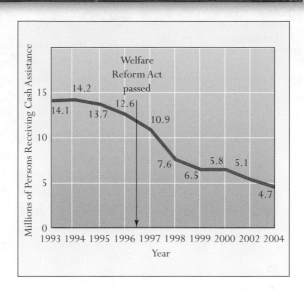

Source: Department of Health and Human Services, 2006.

cent), and two-thirds of them did not graduate from high school. Almost half have three or more children, making day-care arrangements a major obstacle. It is unlikely that any counseling, education, job training, or job placement programs could ever succeed in getting these people into productive employment.

Early studies of people who left the welfare rolls following welfare reform suggest that over half and perhaps as many as three-quarters have found work, although most at minimum or near-minimum wages.[a]

[a]*Governing* (April 1999), pp. 21–26.

Programs such as this Riverside, California, "Jobs Club" try to help welfare recipients find jobs in the wake of reforms intended to reduce welfare dependency.

—Think Again—

Should government
provide health care
insurance for all
Americans?

Health Care in America

The United States spends more of its resources on health care than any other nation (see *Compared to What?* "Health and Health Care Costs in Advanced Democracies"). Nevertheless, the United States ranks well below other advanced democracies in key measures of the health of its people such as life expectancy and infant death rate. Moreover, unlike most other advanced democracies, which make provision for health care for all citizens, Americans have no guarantee of access to medical care. In short, the American health care system is the most expensive and least universal in its coverage in the world.

The Health of Americans Historically, most reductions in death rates have resulted from public health and sanitation improvements, including immunizations, clean public water supplies, sanitary sewage disposal, improved diets, and increased standards of living. Many of the leading causes of death today (see Table 17.3), including heart disease, cancer, stroke, and AIDS, are closely linked to heredity, personal habits and lifestyles (smoking, eating, drinking, exercise, stress, sexual practices), and the physical environment—factors over which doctors and hospitals have no direct control. Thus some argue that the greatest contribution to better health is likely to be found in altered personal habits and lifestyles rather than in more medical care. Thanks to improved health care habits as well as breakthroughs in medical technology, Americans are living longer than ever before.

Access to Care A major challenge in health care is to extend coverage to all Americans. Today, about 85 percent of the nation's population is covered by either government or private health insurance. Government pays about 43 percent of all health care costs—through Medicare for the aged, Medicaid for the poor, and other government programs, including military and veterans' care. Private insurance pays for about 40 percent of the nation's health costs; the remaining 17 percent is paid directly by patients (see Figure 17.5).

But about 15 percent of the U.S. population—an estimated 45 million Americans—have *no* medical insurance. These include workers and their dependents

Table 17.3 Leading Causes of Death

	Deaths per 100,000 Population per Year				
	1960	**1970**	**1980**	**1990**	**2004**
All causes	954.7	945.3	883.4	863.8	847.3
Heart disease	369.0	362.0	336.0	368.3	241.9
Stroke (cerebrovascular)	108.0	101.9	75.5	57.9	56.4
Cancer	149.2	162.8	183.9	203.2	197.2
Accidents	52.3	56.4	46.7	37.0	37.0
Pneumonia/Influenza	37.3	30.9	24.1	32.0	22.3
Diabetes	16.7	18.9	15.5	19.2	25.4
Alzheimers	N.A.	N.A.	N.A.	N.A.	20.4
AIDS	N.A.	N.A.	N.A.	17.6	4.9
Suicide	10.6	11.6	11.9	12.4	11.0
Homicide	4.7	8.3	10.7	10.0	6.1

Source: Centers for Disease Control, www.cdc.gov/nchs/data.

COMPARED TO WHAT?

Health and Health Care Costs in Advanced Democracies

Americans spend more than any other nation in the world for health care (see figure). They spend over 50 percent more than Canadians and nearly 100 percent more than Japanese. Few people object to heavy spending for health care if they get their money's worth. But cross-national comparisons of health statistics indicate that Americans on the average are less healthy than citizens in other advanced democracies. The United States ranks *below* many other advanced

nations in life expectancy and infant death rates—two commonly used measures of national health.

The United States offers some of the most advanced and sophisticated medical care in the world, attracting patients from the countries that rank well ahead of it in various health measures. The United States is the locus of some of the most advanced medical research, attracting medical researchers from throughout the world. But the high quality of medical care available in the United States, combined with the poor health statistics of the general public, suggests that the nation's health care problems center more on access to care and education and prevention of health problems than on the quality of care available.

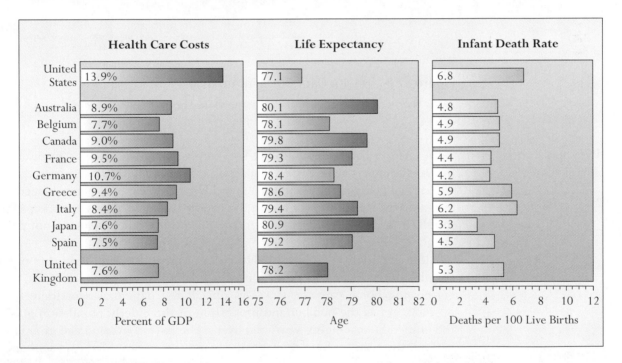

Source: Statistical Abstract of the United States, 2004–2005, pp. 846, 849.

whose employers do not offer a health insurance plan, as well as unemployed people who are not eligible for Medicare or Medicaid. People who lack health insurance may postpone or go without needed medical care or may be denied medical care by hospitals and physicians in all but emergency situations. Confronted with serious illness, they may be obliged to impoverish themselves in order to become eligible for Medicaid. Any unpaid medical bills must be absorbed by hospitals or shifted to paying patients and their insurance companies.

Coverage Gaps   Even people who *do* have health insurance often confront serious financial problems in obtaining medical care owing to inadequate coverage. Medicare, like most private insurance plans, requires patients to pay some

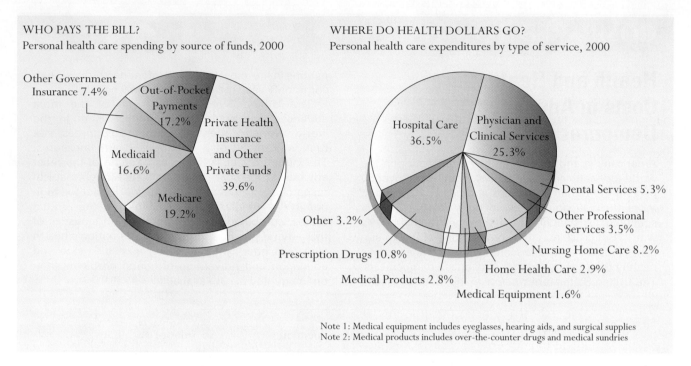

WHO PAYS THE BILL?
Personal health care spending by source of funds, 2000

WHERE DO HEALTH DOLLARS GO?
Personal health care expenditures by type of service, 2000

Other Government Insurance 7.4%
Out-of-Pocket Payments 17.2%
Private Health Insurance and Other Private Funds 39.6%
Medicaid 16.6%
Medicare 19.2%

Hospital Care 36.5%
Physician and Clinical Services 25.3%
Dental Services 5.3%
Other Professional Services 3.5%
Nursing Home Care 8.2%
Home Health Care 2.9%
Medical Equipment 1.6%
Medical Products 2.8%
Prescription Drugs 10.8%
Other 3.2%

Note 1: Medical equipment includes eyeglasses, hearing aids, and surgical supplies
Note 2: Medical products includes over-the-counter drugs and medical sundries

Figure 17.5   Health Care Costs in America

Source: "National Health Expenditures Tables." Health Care Financing Administration.

deductibles Initial charges in insurance plans, paid by beneficiaries.

initial charges called **deductibles**. The purpose of deductibles is to discourage unnecessary treatment. Patients must also make up any difference between doctors' actual charges and the rates allowed by their insurance plans. Indeed, only an estimated half of the doctors in the nation accept Medicare rates as payment in full. In addition, Medicare and many private insurance plans do not pay for eyeglasses, hearing aids, or routine physical examinations.

More important, perhaps, Medicare does *not* pay for long-term care or catastrophic illness. Medicare covers only the first 60 days of hospitalization; it covers nursing home care for 100 days only if the patient is sent there from a hospital. Yet as the number and proportion of the elderly population grows in the United States (eighty years and over is the fastest growing age group in the nation), the need for long-term nursing home care grows. Medicaid assistance to needy people is paid for nursing home patients, but middle-class people cannot qualify for Medicaid without first "spending down" their savings. Long-term nursing home care threatens their assets and their children's inheritance. Private insurance policies covering long-term care are said to be too expensive. So senior citizen groups have lobbied heavily for long-term nursing home care to be paid for by taxpayers under Medicare.

Health Care Costs   No system of health care can provide as much as people will use. Anyone whose health and life may be at stake will want the most thorough diagnostic testing, the most constant care, the most advanced treatment. Sworn to preserve life, doctors, too, want the most advanced diagnostic and treatment facilities available for their patients. Under conditions of uncertainty in a medical situation—and there is always some uncertainty—physicians are trained to seek more consultations, run more tests, and try new therapeutic approaches. Any tendency for doctors to limit testing and treatment is countered by the threat of malpractice suits; it is always easier to order one more test or procedure than to risk even the tiniest chance that failing to do so will some day be cause for a court suit. So in the absence of restraints, both patients and doctors will push up the costs of health care. Currently, health care costs appear to have stabilized at about 13 percent of the nation's GDP.

Managed Care Controversies   Both private and government insurers have made efforts to counter rising costs through **managed care**. Private insurers have negotiated discounts with groups of physicians and with hospitals—**preferred provider organizations (PPOs)**—and have implemented rules to guide physicians about when patients should and should not receive costly diagnostic and therapeutic procedures. Medicare no longer pays hospitals based on costs incurred; instead it pays fixed fees based on primary and secondary diagnoses at the time of admission. Both government and private insurers have encouraged the expansion of **health maintenance organizations (HMOs)**, groups that promise to provide a stipulated list of services to patients for a fixed fee and that are able to provide care at lower total costs than can other providers. Today over 30 percent of Americans are enrolled in HMOs.

But many of the efforts by both private insurers and governments to control costs have created new problems. These include cost-control regulations and restrictions that add to administrative costs and create a mountain of paperwork for physicians and hospitals, and frustration and anger among both health care workers and patients. Doctors and hospitals argue that the *administrative* costs imposed by these cost-control measures far exceed whatever savings are achieved. Patients and doctors complain that preapproval of treatment by insurance companies often removes medical decisions from the physician and patient and places them in the hands of insurance company employees.

Medicare   Medicare is a two-part program that helps elderly and disabled people pay acute-care (as opposed to long-term-care) health costs. Hospital insurance (Part A) helps pay the cost of hospital inpatient and skilled nursing care. Anyone sixty-five or older who is eligible for Social Security is automatically eligible for Part A benefits. Also eligible are people under sixty-five who receive Social Security disability or railroad retirement disability and people who have end-stage kidney disease. Part A is financed primarily by the 1.45 percent payroll tax collected with Social Security (FICA) withholding. Supplemental Medical Insurance (Part B) is an optional add-on taken by virtually all those covered by Part A. It pays 80 percent of covered doctor and outpatient charges. Small monthly premiums are deducted from Social Security benefit checks to finance it.

Medicare has tried to control rising costs in a variety of ways. Currently Medicare offers beneficiaries:

- *Original Medicare plan (fee-for-services).*   Patients choose any physician or specialist, but pay a higher patient co-payment.

- *Managed care plans.*   Patients join an HMO that receives the patient's monthly Medicare premiums from the government in exchange for an insurance plan that covers many items not covered by original Medicare, for example, eye exams, hearing aids, routine physicals, and (until newly enacted for 2006) prescription drugs. However, patients must see only HMO doctors and obtain their recommendation before seeing specialists.

- *Medicare plus Medigap plans.*   Patients remain in original Medicare plan, choosing their own physicians and specialists but purchase a separate "medigap" plan from a private insurer to cover most of the gaps in Medicare.

managed care   Programs designed to keep health care costs down by the establishment of strict guidelines regarding when and what diagnostic and therapeutic procedures should be administered to patients under various circumstances.

preferred provider organizations (PPOs)   Groups of hospitals and physicians who have joined together to offer their services to private insurers at a discount.

health maintenance organizations (HMOs)   Health care provider groups that provide a stipulated list of services to patients for a fixed fee that is usually substantially lower than such care would otherwise cost.

Medicare   Social insurance program that provides health care insurance to elderly and disabled people.

🌐 Medicare
Official government site explaining eligibility, plan options, appeals, and so forth. *www.medicare.gov*

Figure 17.6 Projected Medicare Costs

Source: Congressional Budget Office.

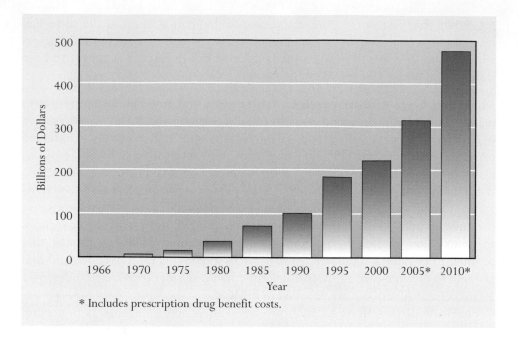

* Includes prescription drug benefit costs.

But Medicare costs are expected to rise dramatically in future years as the baby boom generation expands the population age sixty-five and over and people live longer (see Figure 17.6). The addition of prescription drug coverage will add even more to Medicare costs.

Politics and Health Care Reform

Health care reform centers on two central problems: controlling costs and expanding access. These problems are related: expanding access to Americans who are currently uninsured and closing gaps in coverage requires increased costs, even while a central thrust of reform is to control overall health care costs.

National Health Insurance Plans   Liberals have long sought the creation of a Canadian-style health care system in which the federal government would provide health insurance for all Americans in a single national plan paid for by general tax increases. Under **national health insurance** all Americans would be entitled to a stipulated list of services from physicians, hospitals, and nursing homes, regardless of their employment, age, medical status, or income level. The federal government would be the "single payer" of health care costs through increased taxes. Hospitals would operate on budgets periodically negotiated with the government. Government fee schedules would dictate payments to physicians. Patients also might have to pay some share of the costs at the time of illness. This approach to health care would shift most costs from the private to the public sector. Although these plans are generally popular in Canada and Western Europe, proposals for federal nationwide insurance systems have consistently failed to win political support in Washington (see *What Do You Think?:* "Should We Enact a National Health Care System Covering All Americans?").

national health insurance
Government-provided insurance to all citizens paid from tax revenues.

Employer-Based Plans   Others have advanced the notion of universal coverage through mandated employer-based insurance for most workers combined with government subsidies to pay the insurance costs for people living below the poverty line and to assist others in purchasing insurance.

WHAT DO YOU THINK?

Should We Enact a National Health Care System Covering All Americans?

Most Americans say that they would support a government-run universal health care system covering all Americans, not just the aged and the poor. Presumably such a program would resemble the Canadian health care system. However, when confronted with some of the common difficulties encountered in such programs—for example, long lines for non-emergency treatment and little choice of doctors—support for a Canadian-style system plummets among Americans.

Question: *Which would you prefer — the current health insurance system in the U.S., in which most people get their health insurance from private employers but some people have no insurance, or a universal health insurance program, in which everyone is covered under a program like Medicare that's run by the government and financed by taxpayers?*

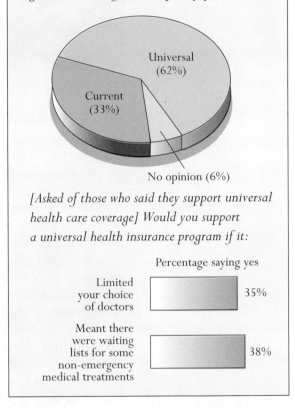

[Asked of those who said they support universal health care coverage] Would you support a universal health insurance program if it:

Percentage saying yes

Limited your choice of doctors	35%
Meant there were waiting lists for some non-emergency medical treatments	38%

Source: Derived from *ABC News/Washington Post* poll, October, 2003.

A majority of American employees are currently enrolled in employer-based plans, but these plans vary a great deal in coverage and cost to employees. And, of course, they do not cover the self-employed or unemployed. The federal government has never *mandated* employers to provide health insurance to their workers.

Modest Reforms Some modest reforms were enacted in 1996 in the Kennedy–Kassebaum Act, named for its bipartisan sponsorship by liberal Democratic Senator Edward M. Kennedy and moderate Republican Senator Nancy Kassebaum. This act guarantees the "portability" of health insurance—allowing workers to maintain their insurance coverage if they lose or change jobs. Their new employer's health insurance company cannot deny them insurance for "preexisting conditions."

Lack of health insurance forces many Americans to postpone regular visits to a doctor and to rely on crowded hospital emergency rooms when they become sick.

A Patients' Bill of Rights The growth of managed care health plans, and their efforts to control costs, have fueled a drive for a "patients' bill of rights." Various proposals have been put forward for inclusion in a patients' bill of rights. The most common proposals are those allowing patients to see specialists without first obtaining permission from a representative of their health plan; providing emergency care without securing prior approval from a health plan representative; allowing immediate appeals when a patient is denied coverage for a particular treatment; and giving patients the right to sue their health plans for medical mistakes. The health insurance industry, including HMOs, argues that these proposals would significantly increase costs of health insurance. They oppose giving the federal government such a large role in overseeing health care plans. And they are particularly concerned about opening themselves to patients' lawsuits—"just a lawyers' bill of rights."

Prescription Drug Coverage under Medicare The long battle over adding prescription drug coverage to Medicare reached a turning point in 2004 when Congress finally passed by wide margins and President Bush signed such a bill. Americans have long supported the addition of prescription drug benefits to Medicare. And in every election over the previous twenty years both Democrats and Republicans had pledged their support for such a benefit. But it was not until after a prolonged battle over the details of the legislation that Congress finally added the long-awaited prescription drug benefit to Medicare. (The Medicaid program for the poor has paid for prescription drugs since its inception.)

The bill was passed by a Republican-controlled Congress and signed by a Republican president; most Democrats in Congress opposed the bill, claiming that it failed to go far enough in protecting seniors. The AARP provided crucial support for the bill, arguing that later amendments could cure any defects.

To receive prescription drug benefits under Medicare, seniors must enroll in a private plan offered by insurance companies. Participants must pay a modest monthly premium of about $35, as well as an annual deductible of $250. After the deductible is paid, the insurance plan must pay 75 percent of yearly drug costs up to $2,850. The patient must pay all drug costs between $2,850 and $3,600 out-of-pocket—the so-called "coverage gap." After $3,600 in drug costs the plan pays all added costs. All private insurers must at least offer this plan to participate; they may compete by offering additional incentives. In addition to

A CONSTITUTIONAL NOTE

Rights versus Entitlements

The Constitution *limits* government. It does not oblige the government to provide any benefits or services to people, such as education, welfare, Social Security, medical care, and so on. Constitutionally speaking, there is no *right* to these benefits. The states, for example, are not obliged by the Constitution to provide public education; the national government is not obliged by the Constitution to provide Social Security or Medicare. These governments do so as a matter of legislation, not as a mandate of the U.S. Constitution. (Of course, if the national or state governments decide to provide such services, they must provide them equally to all persons "similarly situated," that is, they cannot discriminate but must provide "equal protection of laws" under the Fourteenth Amendment.) Political rhetoric often claims a *right* to an education, or to Social Security, or to medical care, or to other important programs. But there are no such rights set forth in the Constitution. Although politically unthinkable, states could abolish public education altogether; Congress could abolish Social Security or Medicare.

However, governments over time have provided benefits and services that people have come to depend upon. The laws granting these benefits set eligibility requirements—age, income, disability, unemployment, and so forth. Everyone who meets these requirements is said to be *entitled* to these benefits by law. Indeed, we have come to refer to these benefits as *entitlements*. But it is important to distinguish between *rights*—limits on government power to protect individuals—and *entitlements*—benefits that governments have enacted for persons who meet specific requirements.

the "coverage gap," critics of the plan note that the federal government does not negotiate with drug companies for lower costs.

Prescription Drug Costs   Prescription drugs are more costly in the United States than anywhere else in the developed world. The American pharmaceutical industry argues that the higher prices that Americans pay help to fund research on new drugs, and that forcing down drug prices would curtail the development of new and potentially life-saving drugs. In effect, Americans are asked to subsidize drug research that benefits the entire world.

Many Americans have resorted to importing drugs from Canada or other nations that have much lower prices than those being charged in the United States. The Food and Drug Administration contends that this practice is illegal, and both the FDA and drug companies claim that imported drugs may not be safe (a highly dubious claim, inasmuch as they are the same drugs shipped by American drug companies to Canada and other nations).

Interest-Group Battles   Interest-group battles over the details of health care policy have been intense. Virtually everyone has a financial stake in any proposal to reorganize the nation's health care system.

- Employers, especially small businesses, are fearful of added costs.

- Physicians strongly oppose price controls and treatment guidelines, as well as programs that take away patient choice of physician or force all physicians into health maintenance organizations (HMOs). Support is stronger among those physicians most likely to benefit from low-cost plans—general family practitioners—and weakest among those most likely to lose—medical specialists.

- Psychiatrists, psychologists, mental health and drug abuse counselors, physical therapists, chiropractors, optometrists, and dentists all want their own services covered. Providing such "comprehensive" services greatly increases costs.

- Drug companies want to see prescription drugs paid for, but they vigorously oppose price controls on drugs.

■ Hospitals want all patients to be insured but oppose government payment schedules.

■ Medical specialists fear that proposals for managed care will result in fewer consultations, and medical manufacturers fear it will limit use of high-priced equipment.

■ The powerful senior citizens' lobby wants added benefits—including coverage for drugs, eyeglasses, dental care, and nursing homes—but fears folding Medicare into a larger health care system.

■ Veterans' groups want to retain separate VA hospitals and medical services.

■ Opponents of abortion rights are prepared to do battle to keep national coverage from including such procedures, whereas many supporters of abortion rights will not back any plan that excludes abortion services.

Although polls show that a majority of Americans are willing to pay higher taxes for comprehensive health care, many are willing to see increases only in "sin taxes"—taxes on alcohol, tobacco, and guns.

Summary Notes

■ Social welfare policy largely determines who gets what from government; over half of the federal budget is devoted to "human resources." The government is a major redistributor of income from group to group.

■ The poor are *not* the principal beneficiaries of social welfare spending. Only about one-third of all federal social welfare spending is means tested. Most social welfare spending, including the largest programs—Social Security and Medicare—goes to the middle class.

■ About 11 to 15 percent of the U.S. population falls below the annual cash income level that the federal government sets as its official definition of poverty.

■ Poverty is temporary for many families, but some poverty is persistent—lasting five years to a lifetime. Prolonged poverty and welfare dependency create an "underclass" beset by many social and economic problems. Poverty is most frequent among families headed by single mothers.

■ Nearly one-third of the U.S. population receives some form of government payments or benefits. Entitlements are government benefits for which Congress has set eligibility criteria by law. Social Security and Medicare are the largest entitlement programs. The elderly are entitled to these benefits regardless of their income or wealth.

■ Senior citizens are politically powerful; they vote more often than younger people and they have powerful lobbying organizations in Washington. Social Security is the largest single item in the federal budget. Yet proposals to modify Social Security or Medicare benefits are politically dangerous.

■ Public assistance programs, including Family Assistance, Supplemental Security Income, and food stamps, require

recipients to show that they are poor in order to claim benefits.

■ Social welfare policies seek to alleviate hardship; at the same time they seek to avoid creating disincentives to work. Cash welfare payments may, for example, encourage teenage pregnancies, undermine family foundations, and contribute to long-term social dependency. Welfare reform centers on moving former welfare recipients into the work force. But doing so may require increased spending on education, job training, health care, and child care, and some recipients may never be able to work.

■ Welfare reform in 1996 replaced federal entitlements to cash payments with block grants to the states. It also set time limits on welfare enrollment.

■ Americans spend more on health care than citizens of any other nation, yet we fail to insure about 15 percent of the population. And the United States ranks below many other advanced nations in common health measures.

■ Health care reform centers on two related problems—extending health insurance coverage to all Americans and containing the costs of health care. Proposals for extending coverage have included national health insurance and mandatory employer-sponsored health insurance. But only more modest proposals, for example, extending government programs to children and making insurance "portable," have been enacted.

■ A modest prescription drug insurance plan was added to Medicare for seniors. It is administered through private insurance companies, but fails to cover all drug costs.

Key Terms

transfer payments 602
poverty line 602
means-tested spending 602
underclass 602
social insurance
    programs 606
public assistance programs
    606
entitlements 606

Social Security 606
unemployment
    compensation 606
Supplemental Security
    Income (SSI) 606
Family Assistance 607
Food Stamp
    program 608
Earned Income Tax

Credit (EITC) 608
Medicaid 608
dependency
    ratio 609
COLAs 610
Temporary Assistance to
    Needy Families 613
deductibles 618
managed care 619

preferred provider
    organizations
    (PPOs) 619
health maintenance
    organizations
    (HMOs) 619
Medicare 619
national health
    insurance 620

Suggested Readings

DiNitto, Diana M. *Social Welfare Politics and Policy*. 8th ed. New York: Allyn & Bacon, 2003. A comprehensive overview of social welfare programs—Social Security, Medicare, SSI, cash assistance, Medicaid, food stamps, and so on—and the political controversies surrounding them.

Gilens, Martin. *Why Americans Hate Welfare*. Chicago: University of Chicago Press, 2000. An argument that racial stereotypes, aided by the media, encourage opposition to welfare.

Hays, Sharon. *Flat Broke With Children: Women in the Age of Welfare Reform*. New York: Oxford Press, 2003. Stories of single mothers and welfare workers trying to cope with the harsher rules of welfare reform.

MacManus, Susan A. *Young v. Old*. Boulder, CO: Westview Press, 1996. An argument based on polling data that "generational combat" is likely in the twenty-first century over taxing and spending for Social Security, Medicare, education, health care, and so on.

Murray, Charles. *Losing Ground*, 10th American ed. New York: Basic Books, 1994. Controversial, classic thesis, first put forth in 1984, that government social welfare programs, by encouraging social dependence, had the unintended and perverse effect of slowing and even reversing earlier progress in reducing poverty, crime, ignorance, and discrimination. Often cited as the inspiration for welfare reform.

Rector, Robert E., and Sarah E. Youssef. *The Impact of Welfare Reform*. Washington, D.C.: Heritage Foundation, 1999. Statistical analysis of the effects of welfare reform, including state-by-state data.

Schiller, Bradley R. *The Economics of Poverty and Discrimination*. 9th ed. Upper Saddle River, NJ: Prentice Hall, 2004. Leading text on poverty and welfare in America.

Weissert, Carol S., and William G. Weissert. *Governing Health: The Politics of Health Policy*. 2d ed. Baltimore, MD: Johns Hopkins University Press, 2002. Health care policymaking, including the roles of Congress, the president, interest groups, and the bureaucracy.

Wilson, William Julius. *The Truly Disadvantaged*. Chicago: University of Chicago Press, 1987. Classic thesis that the growth of the underclass is primarily a result of the decline of manufacturing jobs and their shift to the suburbs, and the resulting concentration of poor, jobless, isolated people in the inner city.

Make It Real

SOCIAL POLICY
In this unit, students consider immigration policy options.

18 POLITICS AND NATIONAL SECURITY

Chapter Outline

- Power among Nations
- The Legacy of the Cold War
- Nuclear Threats
- When to Use Military Force?
- The War on Terrorism
- Political Support for War in Iraq

Think About Politics

1 Has the United Nations been effective in maintaining world peace?
Yes ☐ No ☐

2 Should the United States and NATO intervene in regional conflicts in Eastern Europe?
Yes ☐ No ☐

3 Should the United States build a ballistic missile defense system even if it is very costly?
Yes ☐ No ☐

4 Is the president justified in placing U.S. troops in danger where U.S. vital interests are not at stake?
Yes ☐ No ☐

5 Do you approve of the military attacks led by the United States against targets in Afghanistan?
Yes ☐ No ☐

6 Do you favor the U.S. invading Iraq?
Yes ☐ No ☐

7 Are U.S. military force levels today sufficient to deal with potential regional aggressors such as Iran, Iraq, and North Korea?
Yes ☐ No ☐

8 Should the United States destroy all of its nuclear weapons now that the Cold War is over?
Yes ☐ No ☐

America must decide how to use its national power in world affairs. Should we intervene with military forces in pursuit of humanitarian goals and to keep the peace in war-torn lands? Or should we only use military force when vital national interests are at stake?

Power among Nations

International politics, like all politics, is a struggle for power. The struggle for power is global; it involves all the nations and peoples of the world, whatever their goals or ideals. As the distinguished political scientist Hans Morgenthau once observed,

> Whatever the ultimate aims of international politics, power is always the immediate aim. Statesmen and peoples may ultimately seek freedom, security, prosperity or power itself. They may define their goals in terms of a religious, philosophic, economic, or social ideal. . . . But whenever they strive to realize their goal by means of international politics, they are striving for power.[1]

The struggle for power among nations has led to many attempts to bring order to the international system.

Collective Security Originally, **collective security** meant that *all* nations would join together to guarantee each other's "territorial integrity and existing political independence" against "external aggression" by any nation. This was the idea behind the League of Nations, established in 1919. However, opposition to international involvement was so great in the United States after World War I that, after a lengthy debate, the Senate refused to enroll the United States in the League of Nations. More important, the League of Nations failed to deal with acts of aggression by the Axis Powers—Germany, Japan, and Italy—in the 1930s. During that decade, Japan invaded Manchuria, Italy invaded Ethiopia, and Germany dismembered Czechoslovakia. Finally, when Germany invaded Poland in 1939, World War II began. It cost more than 40 million lives, both civilian and military.

Formation of the United Nations Even after World War II, the notion of collective security remained an ideal of the victorious Allied Powers. The Charter of the United Nations, signed in 1945, provided for the following organization:

- The Security Council, with eleven member nations, five of them being permanent members—the United States, the **Soviet Union** (whose membership is now held by Russia), Britain, France, and China—and each having the power to veto any action by the Security Council.

- The General Assembly, composed of all the member nations, each with a single vote.

collective security Attempt to bring order to international relations by all nations joining together to guarantee each other's "territorial integrity" and "independence" against "external aggression."

Soviet Union The Union of Soviet Socialist Republics (USSR) consisting of Russia and its bordering lands and ruled by the communist regime in Moscow, officially dissolved in 1991.

State Department This U.S. Department of State Web site contains background notes on the countries and regions of the world. *www.state.gov*

superpowers Refers to the United States and the Soviet Union after World War II, when these two nations dominated international politics.

United Nations This United Nations site contains basic information about the world body's mission, member states, issues of concern, institutions, and accomplishments. *www.un.org*

regional security Attempt to bring order to international relations during the Cold War by creating regional alliances between a superpower and nations of a particular region.

North Atlantic Treaty Organization (NATO) Mutual-security agreement and joint military command uniting the nations of Western Europe, initially formed to resist Soviet expansionism.

- The Secretariat, headed by a Secretary General with a staff at United Nations headquarters in New York.

- Organizations to handle specialized affairs—for example, the Economic and Social Council, the Trusteeship Council, and the International Court of Justice at The Hague in the Netherlands.

The Security Council has the "primary responsibility" for maintaining "international peace and security." The General Assembly has authority over "any matter affecting the peace of the world," although it is supposed to defer to the Security Council when the council has already taken up a particular security matter. No nation has a veto in the General Assembly; every nation has one vote regardless of its size or power. Most resolutions can be passed by a majority vote.

The United Nations in the Cold War   The United Nations (UN) proved largely ineffective during the long Cold War confrontation between the communist nations, led by the Soviet Union, and the Western democracies, led by the United States. The UN grew from its original 51 member nations to more than 150 (191 in 2005), but most of those nations were headed by authoritarian regimes of one kind or another. The Western democracies were outnumbered in the General Assembly, and the Soviet Union frequently used its veto to prevent action by the Security Council. Anti-Western and antidemocratic speeches became common in the General Assembly.

During the Cold War, the UN was overshadowed by the confrontation of the world's two **superpowers**: the United States and the Soviet Union. Indeed, international conflicts throughout the world—in the Middle East, Africa, Latin America, Southeast Asia, and elsewhere—were usually influenced by some aspect of the superpower struggle.

Regional Security   The general disappointment with the United Nations as a form of collective security gave rise as early as 1949 to a different approach, **regional security**. In response to aggressive Soviet moves in Europe, the United States and the democracies of Western Europe created the **North Atlantic Treaty Organization (NATO)**. In the NATO treaty, fifteen Western nations agreed to collective regional security: they agreed that "an armed attack against one or more [NATO nations] . . . shall be considered an attack against them all." The United States made a specific commitment to defend Western Europe in the event of a Soviet attack. A joint NATO military command was established (with Dwight D. Eisenhower as its first commander) to coordinate the defense of Western Europe.

After the formation of NATO, the Soviets made no further advances into Western Europe. The Soviets themselves, in response to NATO, drew up the Warsaw Pact, a comparable treaty with their own Eastern European satellite nations. But for many years the real deterrent to Warsaw Pact expansion was not the weak NATO armies, but rather the pledge of the United States to use its strategic nuclear bomber force to inflict "massive retaliation" on the Soviet Union itself in the event of an attack on Western Europe.

The Warsaw Pact disintegrated following the dramatic collapse of the communist governments of Eastern Europe in 1989. Former Warsaw Pact nations—Poland, Hungary, Romania, Bulgaria, and East Germany—threw out their ruling communist regimes and demanded the withdrawal of Soviet troops from their territory. The Berlin Wall was dismantled in 1989, and Germany was formally reunified in 1990, bringing together the 61 million prosperous people of West Germany and the 17 million less affluent people of East Germany. (Unified

Germany continues as a member of NATO.) The Communist Party was ousted from power in Moscow, and the Soviet Union collapsed in 1991.

NATO Today   The United States and its Western European allies agree that NATO continues to play an important role in the security of Europe. Indeed, the continued deployment of some level of U.S. troops to NATO is widely considered to be reassurance that the United States remains committed to this security.

In recent years NATO has made the key decision to expand its security protections to the newly democratic nations of Eastern Europe. Three nations—Poland, Hungary, and the Czech Republic—were admitted to NATO in 1998. At that time Russia strongly objected to NATO expansion, viewing it as an incursion of Western powers in the East and a threat to Russia's security. A NATO-Russia Council was created in 2002 to calm Russian fears about NATO's intentions. In 2004 seven additional countries—Bulgaria, Estonia, Latvia, Lithuania, Romania, Slovakia, and Slovenia—were admitted to membership. All of these nations were formerly under the domination of the Soviet Union. NATO now has 26 members.

Yet another question confronting NATO is what role it should play in trying to resolve religious and ethnic conflicts in Eastern Europe. A combination of security and humanitarian concerns drew NATO, with heavy U.S. participation, into the former Yugoslavian province of Bosnia in 1995 to assist in resolving the war among the Serbs, Croats, and Muslims. This was the first deployment of NATO forces *outside* the national boundaries of NATO nations. NATO began acting militarily to halt ethnic conflicts in Kosovo in 1999. NATO forced Serbian President Slobodan Milosovic to withdraw his forces from the largely Muslim province. U.S. air power played the principal role in this engagement.

The UN Today   Russia inherited the UN Security Council seat of the former Soviet Union, and its government has generally cooperated in UN efforts to bring stability to various regional conflicts. No longer are these conflicts "proxy" wars between the superpowers. The UN has sent blue-helmeted "peacekeeping" forces to monitor cease-fires in many troubled areas of the world. Yet the United Nations and its Security Council must rely on "the last remaining superpower," the United States, to take the lead in enforcing its resolutions. However, a top-heavy bureaucracy at UN headquarters in New York, together with scandal and inefficiency in UN spending, has eroded support for the UN in the United States.

The Legacy of the Cold War

For more than forty years following the end of World War II, the United States and the Soviet Union confronted each other in the protracted political, military, and ideological struggle known as the **Cold War**.

Origins   During World War II, the United States and the Soviet Union joined forces to eliminate the Nazi threat to the world. The United States dismantled its military forces at the end of the war in 1945, but the Soviet Union, under the brutal dictatorship of Josef Stalin, used the powerful Red Army to install communist governments in the nations of Eastern Europe in violation of wartime agreements to allow free elections. Stalin also ignored pledges to cooperate in a unified allied occupation of Germany; Germany was divided, and in 1948 Stalin unsuccessfully tried to oust the United States, Britain, and France from Berlin in a year-long "Berlin Blockade." Former British Prime Minister Winston Churchill warned the United States as early as 1946 that the Soviets were dividing Europe with an "Iron Curtain." When Soviet-backed communist forces threatened Greece and Turkey

The U.N. Building in New York City symbolizes the hope that nations can resolve problems through collective action. But the United Nations has achieved only limited success in the worldwide war on terror.

NATO
The official "North Atlantic Treaty Organization" site contains basic facts about the alliance, current NATO news and issues, and important NATO policies.
www.nato.int

Cold War   Political, military, and ideological struggle between the United States and the Soviet Union following the end of World War II and ending with the collapse of the Soviet Union's communist government in 1991.

Think Again

Should the United States and NATO intervene in regional conflicts in Eastern Europe?

Truman Doctrine U.S. foreign policy, first articulated by President Harry S Truman, that pledged the United States to "support free peoples who are resisting attempted subjugation by armed minorities or by outside pressures."

containment Policy of preventing an enemy from expanding its boundaries and/or influence, specifically the U.S. foreign policy vis-à-vis the Soviet Union during the Cold War.

Marshall Plan U.S. program to rebuild the nations of Western Europe in the aftermath of World War II in order to render them less susceptible to communist influence and takeover.

Korean War Project Organization
Dedicated to the memory of sacrifices of Americans in Korea, with links to battles, units, and memorials.
www.koreanwar.org

Korean War Communist North Korea invaded non-Communist South Korea in June 1950, causing President Harry S Truman to intervene militarily, with U.N. support. General Douglas MacArthur defeated the North Koreans, but with China's entry into the war, a stalemate resulted. An armistice was signed in 1953, with Korea divided along nearly original lines.

Cuban Missile Crisis The 1962 confrontation between the Soviet Union and the U.S. over Soviet placement of nuclear missiles in Cuba.

in 1947, President Harry S Truman responded with a pledge to "support free people who are resisting attempted subjugation by armed minorities or by outside pressures," a policy that became known as the **Truman Doctrine**.

Containment The United States had fought two world wars to maintain democracy in Western Europe. The new threat of Soviet expansionism and communist world revolution caused America to assume world leadership on behalf of the preservation of democracy. In an influential article in the Council on Foreign Relations' journal *Foreign Affairs*, the State Department's Russia expert George F. Kennan called for a policy of **containment**:

> It is clear that the main element of any United States policy toward the Soviet Union must be that of a long-term, vigilant containment of Russian expansive tendencies. . . .[2]

To implement the containment policy, the United States first initiated the **Marshall Plan**, named for Secretary of State George C. Marshall, to rebuild the economies of the Western European nations. Marshall reasoned that *economically* weak nations were more susceptible to communist subversion and Soviet intimidation. The subsequent formation of NATO provided the necessary *military* support to contain the Soviet Union.

The Korean War The first military test of the containment policy came in June 1950, when communist North Korean armies invaded South Korea. President Truman assumed that the North Koreans were acting on behalf of their sponsor, the Soviet Union. The Soviets had already aided Chinese communists under the leadership of Mao Zedong in capturing control of mainland China in 1949. The United States quickly brought the Korean invasion issue to the Security Council. With the Soviets boycotting this meeting because the council had refused to seat the new communist delegation from China, the council passed a resolution calling on member nations to send troops to repel the invasion.

America's conventional (nonnuclear) military forces had been largely dismantled after World War II. Moreover, President Truman insisted on keeping most of the nation's forces in Europe, fearing that the Korean invasion was a diversion to be followed by a Soviet invasion of Western Europe. But General Douglas MacArthur, in a brilliant amphibious landing at Inchon behind North Korean lines, destroyed a much larger enemy army, captured the North Korean capital, and moved northward toward the Chinese border. Then in December 1950, disaster struck American forces as a million-strong Chinese army entered the conflict. Chinese troops surprised the Americans, inflicting heavy casualties, trapping entire units, and forcing U.S. troops to beat a hasty retreat. General MacArthur urged retaliation against China, but Truman sought to keep the war "limited." When MacArthur publicly protested political limits to military operations, Truman dismissed the popular general. The **Korean War** became a bloody stalemate.

Dwight Eisenhower was elected president in 1952 in large measure because he promised to "go to Korea" to end the increasingly unpopular war. He also threatened to use nuclear weapons in the conflict but eventually agreed to a truce along the original border between North and South Korea. Communist expansion in Korea was "contained," but at a high price: the United States lost more than 38,000 men in the war.

The Cuban Missile Crisis The most serious threat of nuclear holocaust during the entire Cold War was the **Cuban Missile Crisis**. In 1962 Soviet Premier Nikita Khrushchev sought to secretly install medium-range nuclear missiles in Cuba in an effort to give the Soviet Union nuclear capability against U.S. cities. In October 1962 intelligence photos showing Soviet missiles at Cuban bases touched off a thirteen-day crisis. President Kennedy rejected advice to launch an air strike to destroy the missiles before they could be activated. Instead, he publicly announced a naval blockade of Cuba, threatening to halt Soviet missile-carrying vessels at sea by force if necessary. The prospect of war appeared imminent; U.S. nuclear forces went on alert. Secretly, Kennedy proposed to withdraw U.S. nuclear missiles from Turkey in exchange for Soviet withdrawal of nuclear missiles from Cuba. Khrushchev's agreement to the deal appeared to the world as a backing down; Kennedy would be hailed for his statesmanship in the crisis, while Khrushchev would soon lose his job.

The Vietnam War   When communist forces led by Ho Chi Minh defeated French forces at the battle of Dien Bien Phu, the resulting Geneva Accords divided that country into North Vietnam, with a communist government, and South Vietnam, with a U.S.-backed government. When South Vietnamese communist (Vietcong) guerrilla forces threatened the South Vietnamese government in the early 1960s, President Kennedy sent a force of more than 12,000 advisers and counterinsurgency forces to assist in every aspect of training and support for the Army of the Republic of Vietnam (ARVN) in South Vietnam and authorized a gradual increase in air strikes against North Vietnam. Washington committed more than 500,000 troops to a war of attrition, a war in which U.S. firepower was expected to inflict sufficient casualties on the enemy to force a peace settlement. But over time, the failure to achieve any decisive military victories eroded popular support for the **Vietnam War**.

On January 31, 1968, the Vietnamese holiday of Tet, Vietcong forces blasted their way into the U.S. embassy compound in Saigon and held the courtyard for six hours. The attack was part of a massive, coordinated Tet offensive against all major cities of South Vietnam. U.S. forces responded and inflicted very heavy casualties on the Vietcong. By any military measure, the Tet offensive was a "defeat" for the enemy and a "victory" for U.S. forces. Yet the Tet offensive was Hanoi's greatest *political* victory. Television pictures of bloody fighting in Saigon and Hue seemed to mock President Johnson's promises of an early end to the war.

On March 31, 1968, President Johnson went on national television to make a dramatic announcement: He halted the bombing of North Vietnam and asked Hanoi for peace talks, concluding, "I shall not seek, and I will not accept, the nomination of my party for another term as your president." Formal peace talks opened in Paris on May 13.

The new president, Richard Nixon, and his national security adviser, Henry Kissinger, knew the war must be ended, but they sought to end it "honorably." Even in the absence of a settlement with the communists in Vietnam, Nixon began the withdrawal of U.S. troops under the guise of "Vietnamization" of the war effort. Unable to persuade Hanoi to make even the slightest concession at Paris, President Nixon sought to demonstrate American strength and resolve. In December 1972 the United States unleashed a devastating air attack directly on Hanoi for the first time. Critics at home labeled Nixon's action "the Christmas bombing," but when negotiations resumed in Paris in January, the North Vietnamese quickly agreed to peace on the terms that Kissinger and Le Duc Tho had worked out earlier.

The South Vietnamese government lasted two years after the agreement. In early 1975 Hanoi decided that the Americans would not "jump back in" and therefore "the opportune moment" was at hand for a new invasion. President Gerald Ford's requests to Congress for emergency military aid to the South Vietnamese fell on deaf ears. Saigon (now Ho Chi Minh City) fell to the North Vietnamese in April 1975, and the United States abandoned hundreds of thousands of loyal Vietnamese who had fought alongside the Americans for years.[3] The

www **Cuban Crisis**   The October 1962 nuclear missile crisis described day to day, with photos. *www.cubacrisis.net*

Vietnam War War between non-Communist South Vietnam and Communist North Vietnam from 1956 to 1975, with increasing U.S. involvement, ending with U.S. withdrawal in 1973 and Communist victory in 1975. The war became unpopular in the United States after 1968 and caused President Johnson not to run for a second term. More than 58,000 Americans died in the war.

The Vietnam War inflicted more than 47,000 battle deaths on U.S. forces. Units of Army Infantry and Marines slogged through the jungles of Southeast Asia for more than eight years. The Paris Peace Accord, signed in 1973, was ignored by the communist regime in Hanoi; its renewed invasion in 1975 succeeded in capturing all of Vietnam.

spectacle of U.S. Marines using their rifle butts to keep desperate Vietnamese from boarding helicopters on the roof of the U.S. embassy "provided a tragic epitaph for twenty-five years of American involvement in Vietnam."[4]

The Vietnam Syndrome   America's humiliation in Vietnam had lasting national consequences. The United States suffered 47,378 battle deaths and missing-in-action among the 2.8 million U.S. personnel who served in Vietnam. A new isolationism permeated American foreign policy following defeat in Vietnam. The slogan "No more Vietnams" was used to oppose any U.S. military intervention, whether or not U.S. vital interests were at stake. Disillusionment replaced idealism. American leaders had exaggerated the importance of Vietnam; now Americans were unwilling to believe their leaders when they warned of other dangers.

Rebuilding America's Defenses   The decision to rebuild Western military forces and reassert international leadership on behalf of democratic values gained widespread support in the Western world in the early 1980s. President Ronald Reagan, British Prime Minister Margaret Thatcher, French President François Mitterrand, and German Chancellor Helmut Kohl all pledged to increase their defense efforts and all held fast against a "nuclear freeze" movement that would have locked in Soviet superiority in European-based nuclear weapons.

The Reagan defense buildup extended through 1985—with increases in defense spending, improvements in strategic nuclear weapons, and, perhaps more important, the rebuilding and reequipping of U.S. conventional forces. The American and NATO defense buildup, together with the promise of a new, expensive, and technologically sophisticated race for ballistic missile defenses, forecast heavy additional strains on the weak economy of the Soviet Union. Thus, in 1985, when new Soviet President Mikhail Gorbachev came to power, the stage was set for an end to the Cold War.

Gorbachev announced reductions in the size of the Soviet military and reached agreements with the United States on the reduction of nuclear forces More important, in 1988 he announced that the Soviet Union would no longer use its military forces to keep communist governments in power in Eastern European nations. This stunning announcement, for which he received the Nobel Peace Prize in 1990, encouraged opposition democratic forces in Poland (the Solidarity movement), Czechoslovakia, Hungary, Bulgaria, Romania, and East Germany. Gorbachev refused to intervene to halt the destruction of the Berlin Wall, despite pleas by the East German hard-line communist leader Erich Honecker.

The Collapse of Communism   When hardliners in the Communist Party, the military, and the KGB attempted the forcible removal of Gorbachev in August 1991, democratic forces rallied to his support. Led by Boris Yeltsin, the first elected president of the Russian Republic, thousands of demonstrators took to the streets; Soviet military forces stood aside. Yeltsin emerged as the most influential leader in the nation. The failed coup hastened the demise of the Communist Party. The party lost legitimacy with the peoples of Russia and the other republics.

The Disintegration of the Soviet Union   Strong independence movements in the republics of the Soviet Union emerged as the authority of the centralized Communist Party in Moscow waned. Lithuania, Estonia, and Latvia—nations that had been forcibly incorporated into the Soviet Union in 1939—led the way to independence in 1991. Soon all of the fifteen republics of the Soviet Union declared their independence, and the Union of Soviet Socialist Republics officially ceased to exist after December 31, 1991. The red flag with its hammer and sickle atop the Kremlin was replaced with the flag of the Russian Republic.

The Vietnam War Memorial in Washington, D.C., is inscribed with the names of the nearly 50,000 Americans who died in Vietnam. America's defeat fostered a lasting skepticism about the wisdom of foreign military intervention, leading to a new isolationism in foreign policy.

Presidents Vladimir Putin of Russia and George W. Bush of the United States reached agreement in 2002 to reduce their nations' nuclear stockpiles by over 80 percent from Cold War levels.

Russia after Communism   The transition from a centralized state-run economy to free markets turned out to be more painful for Russians than expected. Living standards for most people declined, alcoholism and death rates increased, and even average life spans shortened. Ethnic conflict and political separatism, especially in the largely Muslim province of Chechnya, added to Russia's problems. Yeltsin was able to overcome these political challenges and win reelection as president in 1996. But corruption, embezzlement, graft, and organized crime continue to undermine democratic reforms. Poor health eventually forced Yeltsin to turn over power to Vladimir Putin, who himself won election as president of Russia in 2000.

> **Russia EIN News**
> Business, cultural, political, and scientific news from Russia.
> *www.einnews.com/russia*

Nuclear Threats

Nuclear weaponry has made the world infinitely more dangerous. During the Cold War, the nuclear arsenals of the United States and the Soviet Union threatened a human holocaust. Yet, paradoxically, the very destructiveness of nuclear weapons caused leaders on both sides to exercise extreme caution in their relations with each other. Scores of wars, large and small, were fought by different nations during the Cold War years, yet American and Soviet troops never engaged in direct combat against each other.

> —**Think Again**—
> Should the United States destroy all of its nuclear weapons now that the Cold War is over?

Deterrence   To maintain nuclear peace during the Cold War, the United States relied primarily on the policy of **deterrence**. Deterrence is based on the notion that a nation can dissuade a *rational* enemy from attacking by maintaining the capacity to destroy the enemy's homeland even *after* the nation has suffered a well-executed surprise attack by the enemy. Deterrence assumes that the worst may happen—a surprise first strike against a nation's nuclear forces. It emphasizes **second-strike capability**—the ability of a nation's forces to survive a surprise attack by the enemy and then to inflict an unacceptable level of destruction on the enemy's homeland. Deterrence is really a *psychological* defense against attack; no effective physical defense against a ballistic missile attack exists even today.

deterrence U.S. approach to deterring any nuclear attack from the Soviet Union by maintaining a second-strike capability.

second-strike capability Ability of a nation's forces to survive a surprise nuclear attack by the enemy and then to retaliate effectively.

Limiting Nuclear Arms: SALT   The United States and the Soviet Union engaged in negotiations over nuclear arms control for many years. The development of reconnaissance satellites in the 1960s made it possible for each nation to

Intercontinental Ballistic Missiles (ICBMs) with multiple nuclear warheads, like this MX Peacekeeper being test-fired, threatened a nuclear holocaust during the long Cold War. The START II Treaty in 1993 called for the dismantling of all multiple-warhead missiles, and the Treaty of Moscow in 2002 called for the reduction of total nuclear warheads by 80 percent from Cold War levels.

SALT I First arms limitation treaty between the United States and the Soviet Union, signed in 1972, limiting the total number of offensive nuclear missiles; it included the ABM Treaty that reflected the theory that the population centers of both nations should be left undefended.

ABM Treaty A formal treaty in 1972 between the United States and the Soviet Union in which each side agreed not to build or deploy antiballistic missiles.

monitor the strategic weapons possessed by the other. Space photography made cheating on agreements more difficult and thus opened the way for both nations to seek stability through arms control.

Following the election of Richard Nixon as president in 1968, the United States, largely guided by former Harvard professor Henry Kissinger (national security adviser to the president and later secretary of state), began negotiations with the Soviet Union over strategic nuclear arms. In 1972 the two nations concluded two and a half years of Strategic Arms Limitation Talks (SALT) about limiting the nuclear arms race. The agreement, **SALT I**, consisted of a treaty limiting antiballistic missiles (ABMs) and an agreement placing a numerical ceiling on offensive missiles. In the **ABM Treaty** both nations pledged *not* to build ballistic missile defenses. This meant that the populations of both nations in effect would be held hostage against a first strike by either nation.

SALT I was the first step forward on the control of nuclear arms; both sides agreed to continue negotiations. After seven years of difficult negotiations, the United States and the Soviet Union produced the lengthy and complicated **SALT II** treaty in 1979. It set an overall limit on "strategic nuclear launch vehicles"—ICBMs, SLBMs, bombers, and long-range cruise missiles—at 2,250 for each side. It also limited the number of missiles that could have multiple warheads (MIRVs). But when the Soviet Union invaded Afghanistan in 1979, President Carter withdrew the SALT II treaty from Senate consideration. However, President Carter, and later President Reagan, announced that the United States would abide by the provisions of the unratified SALT II treaty as long as the Soviet Union did so.

Reducing Nuclear Arms: START In negotiations with the Soviets, the Reagan administration established three central principles of arms control—reductions, equality, and verification. The new goal was to be *reductions* in missiles and warheads, not merely limitations on future numbers and types of weapons, as in previous SALT talks. To symbolize this new direction, President Reagan renamed the negotiations the Strategic Arms *Reduction* Talks, or START.

The **START I** Treaty signed in Moscow in 1991 by Presidents George H.W. Bush and Mikhail Gorbachev was the first agreement between the nuclear powers that actually resulted in the reduction of strategic nuclear weapons. The START I Treaty reduced the total number of deployed strategic nuclear delivery systems to no more than 1,600, a 30 percent reduction from the SALT II level.

A far-reaching **START II** agreement, signed in 1993 by U.S. President George H.W. Bush and Russian President Yeltsin, promised to eliminate the threat of a first-strike nuclear attack by either side. Its most important provision was the agreement to eliminate all multiwarhead (MIRVed) land-based missiles. START II also called for the reduction of overall strategic warheads to 3,500.

The Treaty of Moscow The capstone of strategic nuclear arms reductions is the Treaty of Moscow, signed by Russian President Vladimir Putin and U.S. President George W. Bush in 2002. This new treaty calls for an overall limit of nuclear warheads at 1,700–2,200 by 2012. Each side may determine for itself the composition and structure of its strategic forces consistent with this limit. The provisions of the START treaties remain unchanged. The effect of the Moscow Treaty, together with earlier reductions in nuclear weapons under the START treaties, will be to reduce the nuclear arsenals of the former adversaries by over 80 percent from Cold War levels (see Figure 18.1).

Nuclear Terrorism Even as the threat of a large-scale nuclear attack recedes, the threats arising from "nondeterrable" sources are increasing. Today, the principal

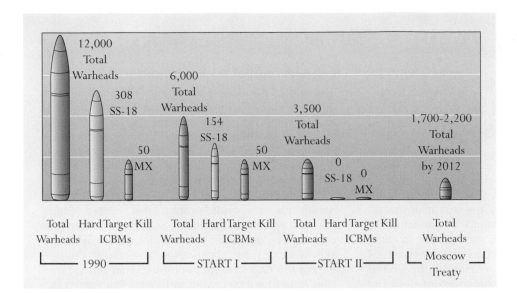

Figure 18.1 Strategic Nuclear Arms under START Treaties

Implementation of the START II Treaty will reduce the total number of warheads in both the United States and Russia by over two-thirds and will completely eliminate hard target kill ICBMs.

nondeterrable threats are estimated to be (1) missiles launched by a terrorist nation; (2) unauthorized missile launches by terrorist organizations, and (3) accidental missile launches. Over time global nuclear and ballistic missile proliferation steadily increases the likelihood of these types of threats. Terrorist launches are considered "nondeterrable" because the threat of nuclear retaliation is largely meaningless.

The threat of mass terror weapons—nuclear, chemical, or biological weapons, especially those carried by medium- or long-range missiles—is likely to increase dramatically in the years ahead. North Korea is reported to possess nuclear weapons and to be developing long-range missiles to carry them. Iran has announced its intention to acquire materials for the development of nuclear weapons. Defending against terrorist missile attacks requires the development and deployment of **ballistic missile defense (BMD)** systems, weapons capable of detecting, intercepting, and destroying ballistic missiles while they are in flight. At present there is no defense against a ballistic missile attack on American cities (see *A Conflicting View:* "We Should Defend Ourselves against a Ballistic Missile Attack").

When to Use Military Force?

All modern presidents have acknowledged that the most agonizing decisions they have made were to send U.S. military forces into combat. These decisions cost lives. The American people are willing to send their sons and daughters into danger—and even to see some of them wounded and killed—but *only* if a president convinces them that the outcome "is worth dying for." A president must be able to explain why they lost their lives and to justify their sacrifice.

To Protect Vital Interests   The U.S. military learned many bitter lessons in its long bloody experience in Vietnam. Among those lessons are what became known as the Powell Doctrine, advanced by then Chair of the Joint Chiefs of Staff, General Colin Powell:

- The United States should commit its military forces only in support of vital national interests.

- If military forces are committed, they must have clearly defined military objectives—the destruction of enemy forces and/or the capture of enemy-held territory.

- Any commitment of U.S. forces must be of sufficient strength to ensure overwhelming and decisive victory with the fewest possible casualties.

SALT II Lengthy and complicated treaty between the United States and the Soviet Union, agreed to in 1979 but never ratified by the U.S. Senate, that set limits on all types of strategic nuclear launch vehicles.

START I First treaty between the United States and the Soviet Union that actually reduced the strategic nuclear arms of the superpowers, signed in 1991.

START II A treaty between the United States and Russia eliminating all multiwarhead land missiles and reducing nuclear weapons stockpiles; signed in 2003.

ballistic missile defense (BMD) Weapons systems capable of detecting, intercepting, and destroying missiles in flight.

— Think Again —

Is the president justified in placing U.S. troops in danger where U.S. vital interests are not at stake?

A CONFLICTING VIEW

We Should Defend Ourselves against a Ballistic Missile Attack

For over a half-century, since the terrible nuclear blasts at Hiroshima and Nagasaki in Japan in 1945, the world has avoided nuclear war. Peace has been maintained by deterrence—by the threat of devastating nuclear attacks that would be launched in retaliation to an enemy's first strike. But in 1983 President Ronald Reagan urged that instead of deterring war through fear of retaliation, the United States should seek a technological defense against nuclear missiles.

> Our nuclear retaliating forces have deterred war for forty years. The fact is, however, that we have no defense against ballistic missile attack. . . . In the event that deterrence failed, a president's only recourse would be to surrender or to retaliate. Nuclear retaliation, whether massive or limited, would result in the loss of millions of lives. . . .[a]

"Star Wars"

Reagan's Strategic Defense Initiative (SDI) was a research program designed to explore means of destroying enemy nuclear missiles in space before they could reach their targets. Following President Reagan's initial announcement of SDI in March 1983, the press quickly labeled the effort "Star Wars." In theory, a ballistic missile defense (BMD) system could be based in space, orbiting over enemy missile-launching sites. Should an enemy missile get through the space-based defense, a ground-based BMD system would attempt to intercept warheads as they reentered the atmosphere and approached their targets. SDI included research on laser beams, satellite surveillance, computerized battle-management systems, and "smart" and "brilliant" weapons systems. SDI under President Reagan was a very ambitious program with the goal of creating an "impenetrable shield" that would protect not only the population of the United States but the population of our allies as well.

Protection against Nuclear Terrorism

The end of the Cold War refocused SDI away from defense against a massive Russian missile attack to more limited yet more likely threats. Today the principal nuclear threats are missiles launched by terrorists or a "rogue state." President Bush redirected SDI toward defending against these more limited yet potentially devastating attacks.

The Gulf War experience demonstrated that deterrence may not protect the United States against a ballistic missile attack by a terrorist regime. The success of the Patriot antiballistic missile in destroying short-range Iraqi Scud missiles during the Gulf War demonstrated that enemy missiles could be intercepted in flight. (The Patriot is a ground-based "tactical" weapon designed to protect specific military targets.) However, developing an effective antiballistic missile that can intercept and destroy another missile in space has proven to be more difficult, although not impossible.

The Future of BMDs

As a Reagan-era initiative, partisanship has tended to cloud the debate over BMDs. In 1993 President Clinton announced the termination of the separate SDI organization, but he reassured the nation that research would continue on the ground-based ballistic missile defenses. President George W. Bush notified the Russians in 2002 that the United States was withdrawing from provisions of the ABM Treaty of 1972 that prohibited the development, testing, or deployment of new ballistic missile defense systems.

Advanced testing has met with both successes and failures. Intercepting an incoming missile has been compared to "hitting a bullet with a bullet." Even this daunting challenge is further complicated by the likelihood of enemy decoys masking the real warhead; a reliable ballistic missile defense must be able to discriminate between decoys and actual warheads.

President George W. Bush announced a limited deployment of sea-based and ground-based missile interceptors and advanced Patriot missiles in 2004. The president spoke of an incremental growth of U.S. anti-ballistic missile capability directed at potential terrorist attacks.

[a]President Ronald Reagan, *The President's Strategic Defense Initiative*, The White House, January 3, 1985.

■ Before committing U.S. military forces, there must be some reasonable assurances that the effort has the support of the American people and their representatives in Congress.

■ The commitment of U.S. military forces should be a last resort, after political, economic, and diplomatic efforts have proven ineffective.

President George H.W. Bush argued that his decision to use military force in the Gulf War in 1990–91 met these guidelines: that preventing Iraq's Saddam Hussein from gaining control of the world's oil supply and developing nuclear and chemical weapons were vital national interests; that political and economic sanctions were not effective; and that he had defined clear military objectives— the removal of Iraqi troops from Kuwait and the destruction of Iraq's nuclear and chemical weapon capabilities (see *Up Close:* "The Use of Force: Operation Desert Storm"). And he authorized a large military commitment that led to a speedy and decisive victory.

These guidelines for the use of military force are widely supported within the U.S. military itself.[5] Contrary to Hollywood stereotypes, military leaders are extremely reluctant to go to war when no vital interest of the United States is at stake, where there are no clear-cut military objectives, without the support of Congress or the American people, or without sufficient force to achieve speedy and decisive victory with minimal casualties. They are wary of seeing their troops placed in danger merely to advance diplomatic goals, or to engage in "peacekeeping," or to "stabilize governments," or to "show the flag." They are reluctant to undertake humanitarian missions while being shot at. They do not like to risk their soldiers' lives under "rules of engagement" that limit their ability to defend themselves.

In Support of Important Political Objectives In contrast to military leaders, political leaders and diplomats often reflect the view that "war is a continuation of politics by other means"—a view commonly attributed to nineteenth-century German theorist of war Karl von Clausewitz. Military force may be used to protect interests that are important but not necessarily vital. Otherwise, the United States would be rendered largely impotent in world affairs. A diplomat's ability to achieve a satisfactory result often depends on the expressed or implied threat of military force. The distinguished international political theorist Hans Morgenthau wrote, "Since military strength is the obvious measure of a nation's power, its demonstration serves to impress others with that nation's power."[6]

Currently American military forces must be prepared to carry out a variety of missions in addition to the conduct of conventional war:

- Demonstrating U.S. resolve in crisis situations.

- Demonstrating U.S. support for democratic governments.

- Protecting U.S. citizens living abroad.

- Peacemaking among warring factions or nations.

- Peacekeeping where hostile factions or nations have accepted a peace agreement.

- Providing humanitarian aid often under warlike conditions.

- Assisting in an international war against drug trafficking.

In pursuit of such objectives, recent U.S. presidents have sent troops to Lebanon in 1982 to stabilize the government (Reagan), to Grenada in 1983 to rescue American medical students and restore democratic government (Reagan), to Panama in 1989 to oust drug-trafficking General Manuel Antonio Noriega from power and to protect U.S. citizens (Bush); to Somalia in 1992–93 to provide emergency humanitarian aid (Bush and Clinton); to Haiti in 1994 to restore constitutional government (Clinton) and again to Haiti in 2004 (Bush); and to Bosnia and Kosovo for peacekeeping among warring ethnic factions (see Table 18.1).

CIA World Factbook
Nations listed A–Z with geography, people, economy, government, military, and so on, information.
www.cia.gov/publications/ factbook

UP CLOSE

The Use of Force: Operation Desert Storm

Saddam Hussein's invasion of Kuwait on August 2, 1990, was apparently designed to restore his military prestige after an indecisive war against Iran, to secure additional oil revenues to finance the continued buildup of Iraqi military power, and to intimidate (and perhaps invade) Saudi Arabia and the Gulf states, thereby securing control over a major share of the world's oil reserves.

The Iraqi invasion met with a surprisingly swift response by the United Nations, with Security Council resolutions condemning the invasion, demanding an immediate withdrawal, and imposing a trade embargo and economic sanctions. President George H.W. Bush immediately set to work to stitch together a coalition military force that would eventually include thirty nations. Early on, the president described the U.S. military deployment as "defensive," but he soon became convinced that neither diplomacy nor an economic blockade would dislodge Saddam from Kuwait and so ordered the military to prepare an "offensive" option.

The top U.S. military commanders—including the chair of the Joint Chiefs of Staff, General Colin Powell, and the commander in the field, General Norman Schwartzkopf—had been field officers in Vietnam, and they were resolved not to repeat the mistakes of that war. They were reluctant to go into battle without the full support of the American people. If ordered to fight, they wanted to employ overwhelming and decisive military force; they wanted to avoid the gradual escalation, protracted conflict, target limitations, and political interference in the conduct of the war that had characterized the U.S. military's efforts in Vietnam. Accordingly, they presented the president with a plan that called for a very large military buildup involving nearly 500,000 troops. Coalition forces also included British and French heavy armored units, and Egyptian, Syrian, Saudi, and other Arab forces.

From Baghdad, CNN reporters Bernard Shaw and Peter Arnett were startled on the night of January 16 when Operation Desert Storm began with an air attack on key installations in the city. Iraqi forces were also surprised, despite the prompt timing of the attack; Saddam had assured them that the United States lacked the resolve to fight.

The success of the coalition air force was spectacular. American TV audiences saw videotapes of laser-guided bombs entering the doors and air shafts of enemy bunkers. Civilian damage was lower than in any previous air war. After five weeks of air war, intelligence estimated that nearly half the Iraqi tanks and artillery in the field had been

The Gulf War, labeled "Operation Desert Storm" by the U.S. military, destroyed Iraqi troops in Kuwait and eastern Iraq. President George H. W. Bush ordered a ceasefire after only 100 hours of ground operations. It was hoped that the Iraqi defeat would lead to the ouster of Saddam Hussein, but he survived and strengthened his hold on the Iraqi people.

destroyed, demoralized troops were hiding in deep shelters, and the battlefield had been isolated and "prepared" for ground operations.

General Schwartzkopf's plan for the ground war emphasized deception and maneuver. While Iraqi forces prepared for attacks from the south and the east coast, he sent heavily armed columns in a "Hail Mary" play—a wide sweep to the west, outflanking and cutting off Iraqi forces in the battle area. On the night of February 24, the ground attack began. Marines breached ditches and minefields and raced directly to the Kuwait airport; army helicopter air assaults lunged deep into Iraq; armored columns raced northward across the desert to outflank Iraqi forces and then attack them from the west, while a surge in air attacks kept Iraqi forces holed up in their bunkers. Iraqi troops surrendered in droves, highways from Kuwait city became a massive junkyard of Iraqi vehicles, and Iraqi forces that tried to fight were quickly destroyed. After 100 hours of ground fighting, President Bush ordered a cease-fire.

The United States had achieved a decisive military victory quickly and with remarkably few casualties. The president resisted calls to expand the original objectives of the war and go on to capture Baghdad, to destroy the Iraqi economy, to encourage Iraq's disintegration as a nation, or to kill Saddam, although it was expected that his defeat would lead to his ouster. Although the war left many political issues unresolved, it was the most decisive military outcome the United States had achieved since the end of World War II.[a] President Bush chose to declare victory and celebrate the return of American troops.

[a]See Harry G. Summers Jr., *On Strategy II: A Critical Analysis of the Gulf War* (New York: Dell, 1992).

Table 18.1   Major Deployments of U.S. Military
                 Forces Since World War II

Year	Area	President
1950–53	Korea	Truman
1958	Lebanon	Eisenhower
1961–64	Vietnam	Kennedy
1962	Cuban waters	Kennedy
1965–73	Vietnam	Johnson, Nixon
1965	Dominican Republic	Johnson
1970	Laos	Nixon
1970	Cambodia	Nixon
1975	Cambodia	Ford
1980	Iran	Carter
1982–83	Lebanon	Reagan
1983	Grenada	Reagan
1989	Panama	Bush
1990–91	Persian Gulf	Bush
1992–93	Somalia	Bush, Clinton
1994–95	Haiti	Clinton
1995–2000	Bosnia	Clinton
1999–2000	Kosovo	Clinton
2001–	Afghanistan	Bush
2002–	Philippines	Bush
2003–	Iraq	Bush
2004	Haiti	Bush

In Support of the War on Terrorism   The War on Terrorism creates new
conditions for the use of military force.[7] Currently U.S. forces are prepared for:

- Direct attacks against terrorist forces to capture or kill them. These operations
  are usually carried out by highly trained Special Forces.

- Attacks on nations that harbor terrorists, allow terrorists to maintain bases, or
  supply and equip terrorist organizations. In 1986, the United States struck at
  Libya in a limited air attack in response to various Libyan-supported acts of terrorism around the world. In 1993, the United States struck Iraq's intelligence
  center in Baghdad in response to a foiled plot to assassinate former President
  George Bush. In 2001, the United States relied principally on Special Forces
  working in conjunction with tribal forces in Afghanistan to attack Al Qaeda
  terrorists and to topple the Taliban government that had harbored and supported Al Qaeda.

- **Preemptive attacks** on regimes that threaten to use weapons of mass instruction—chemical, biological, or nuclear weapons—against the United States or
  its allies, or to supply terrorist organizations with these weapons. Preemptive military action represents a reversal of traditional U.S. policy. Historically the
  United States acted militarily only in response to a direct attack on its own
  forces or those of its allies. But it is argued that the Terrorist Attack of 9/11 initiated the current War on Terrorism and that American military actions in the
  Middle East, including those in Afghanistan and Iraq, are related to the 9/11 attack on America. The argument for preemptive military action was summarized
  by Secretary of State Condoleezza Rice: "We cannot wait until the smoking gun
  becomes a mushroom cloud."

— Think Again —
Do you approve of the
military attacks led by the
United States against
targets in Afghanistan?

— Think Again —
Do you favor the United
States invading Iraq?

preemptive attack The
initiation of military action
by the United States to
prevent terrorists or rogue
nations from inflicting heavy
damage on the United States.

The War on Terrorism

Terrorism is a political act. The deliberate targeting of civilians, the infliction of widespread destruction, and the resulting media portrayals of the pain and suffering of victims are designed to call attention to political grievances and to instill fear in people. (The Latin root of the term, *terrere*, means "to frighten.") The horror of terrorist acts and their unpredictability add to public fear—people can neither anticipate nor prepare for tragedies inflicted upon them. Terrorists hope to undermine the confidence of people in their government to protect them, and so they will conclude that submission to the terrorists' demands is preferable to living in a continuing climate of anxiety and uncertainty.

Global Terrorism   Global terrorism has evolved over the years into highly sophisticated networks operating in many countries. The most notable terrorist attacks extend back over thirty years, but the death and destruction wrought by terrorists have dramatically increased (see Table 18.2). Prior to the attacks on New York's World Trade Center and the Pentagon on September 11, 2001, most Americans thought of terrorism as foreign. Terrorist acts on American soil had been rare; the most destructive attack—the Oklahoma City bombing of a federal building in 1995—had been carried out by domestic terrorists. But the 9/11 attacks were on an unprecedented scale and they revealed a sophisticated global plot against America.

A loose-knit network of terrorist cells (Al Qaeda) organized by a wealthy Saudi Arabian, Osama bin Laden, was engaged in global terrorism. Their political grievances included America's support of Israel in Middle East conflicts and an American presence in Islamic holy lands, notably Saudi Arabia. Several nations share these grievances and, more importantly, provided support and haven to Al Qaeda and similar terrorist organizations. The principal base of support and sanctuary for Al Qaeda was the repressive and violent Taliban regime of Afghanistan.

Declaring War on Terrorism   On the evening of September 11, President George W. Bush spoke to the American people from the Oval Office in a nationally televised address:

> The pictures of airplanes flying into buildings, fires burning, huge structures collapsing, have filled us with disbelief, terrible sadness, and a quiet, unyielding anger. These mass murders were intended to frighten our nation into chaos and retreat. But they failed; our country is strong. . . . These deliberate and deadly attacks were more than acts of terror. They were acts of war.

The president outlined a broad "response to terrorism" to be fought both at home and abroad through diplomatic, military, financial, investigative, homeland security, and humanitarian means. He warned that the new war on terrorism would require a long-term sustained effort. It would require Americans to accept new restrictions on their lives (see "Terrorism's Threat to Democracy" in Chapter 1). It would require new legislation—an Airport Security Act federalizing security at U.S. airports and instituting new strict security measures, and a Patriot (antiterrorism) Act expanding the authority of the attorney general and federal law-enforcement agencies to fight domestic terrorism (see *A Conflicting View:* "Terrorism Requires Restrictions on Civil Liberties" in Chapter 14). It would require the creation of a new Department of Homeland Security designed to coordinate many federal, state, and local law-enforcement agencies charged with responsibility for dealing with acts of terror (see "The Department of Homeland Security" in Chapter 12).

Operation "Enduring Freedom"   The military phase of the war on terrorism began October 7, 2001, when U.S. Air Force and Navy aircraft began attacks

terrorism Title 22 of the U.S. Code, Section 2656 (d): "The term 'terrorism' means premeditated, politically motivated violence perpetrated against noncombatant targets by subnational groups or clandestine agents, usually intended to influence an audience."

 **Terrorism Research Center**

The "Terrorism Research Center" Web site is dedicated to "informing the public of the phenomena of terrorism and information warfare." It contains news, analytical essays on terrorist issues, and many links to other terrorism materials and research sources. *www.terrorism.com*

 **Defenselink Terrorism**

Official Defense Department site link to information on terrorism. *www.defenselink.mil/terrorism*

CIA-Terrorism   Reports, news, facts, regarding terrorism. *www.cia.gov/terrorism*

PEOPLE IN POLITICS

Condoleezza Rice

Condoleezza Rice was a trusted Bush insider well before her appointment as secretary of state in 2005. She had served as national security adviser under President Bush in his first term, and along with Vice President Dick Cheney, Secretary of Defense Donald Rumsfeld, and others, she was a staunch supporter of the invasion of Iraq. She lectures in broad terms about "implanting democracy in the Middle East," but, like the president, she defines only a vague strategy to achieve that elusive goal.

Condoleezza Rice was born in Birmingham, Alabama, in 1954, and she observed the violence of early desegregation, including the Birmingham Church bombing that killed four children. Her father was a pastor and her mother a music teacher. Young Condoleezza was a child prodigy who entered college at age fifteen intending to become a concert pianist. But her interests soon turned to international politics, and she graduated Phi Beta Kappa from the University of Denver with a major in political science. She received her master's degree from Notre Dame and then returned to the University of Denver for her Ph.D. in 1981. She accepted a professorship at Stanford University and later became that university's provost. She also joined the staff of the Hoover Institution, a think tank on the Stanford campus occasionally labeled conservative because of its commitment to individualism and free markets around the world. She became a member of the Council on Foreign Relations and joined the boards of Chevron, J.P. Morgan, Transamerica, Hewlett-

Packard, the Hewlett Foundation, the RAND Corporation, and the Carnegie Corporation. (Chevron initially named an oil tanker for her but later changed its name when she went to Washington.)

Rice has been exceptionally well received in world capitals. She speaks several foreign languages, impresses world leaders with her keen intellect, and puts people at ease with her congeniality. She has been instrumental in negotiations, getting the Chinese to side with the United States in pressuring North Korea to give up its nuclear weapons program. But inevitably her legacy as secretary of state will be judged by the outcome in Iraq. Her expressed optimism in democracy is not likely in itself to bring peace to that country. But if significant progress can be achieved in Iraq by 2008, she may be a leading prospect for a place on the Republican presidential ticket.

on known Al Qaeda bases in Afghanistan and U.S. Special Forces organized and led anti-Taliban fighters, including several tribal groups in a campaign against the Taliban regime. A coalition of nations participated in Operation "Enduring Freedom"; some, including Britain and Canada, contributed troops, while others, including Pakistan, Saudi Arabia, and Uzbekistan, informally allowed U.S. forces to base operations on their territory. Kabul, the capital of Afghanistan, was occupied by anti-Taliban forces on November 13, 2001.

President Bush made it clear that the United States was prepared to act militarily against governments that harbored or gave sanctuary to terrorists. The Taliban regime was ousted from power. By April 2002—six months into Operation Enduring Freedom—Al Qaeda and Taliban forces had been either destroyed or scattered into small groups in the mountainous areas of Afghanistan and neighboring Pakistan. Osama bin Laden himself, however, escaped capture.

A meeting in Bonn, Germany, of various Afghan political and military groups produced general agreement on the installation of a new government in Kabul, headed by Hamid Karzai. But today the Karzai government has less than full control over Afghanistan; various tribal military chiefs, or "warlords," exercise independent power throughout the country.

Table 18.2   Notable Global Terrorist Attacks

Date	Number of People Killed	Description	Prime suspect[s]
September 5, 1972	17	Israeli athletes are killed during the Olympics in Munich, Germany	Black September, a Palestinian guerrilla group
April 18, 1983	63	The American Embassy in Beirut, Lebanon, is bombed	Hezbollah [Party of God]
September 23, 1983	112	A plane crashes in United Arab Emirates after a bomb explodes in the baggage compartment	Unknown
October 23, 1983	299	Two truck bombs kill U.S. Marines and French paratroopers in Beirut, Lebanon	U.S. blames groups aligned with Iran and Syria
June 23, 1985	329	An Air India jet explodes over the Atlantic Ocean, off the coast of Ireland	The Royal Canadian Mounted Police charge Ajaib Singh Bagri and Ripudaman, two Sikh dissidents, in 2000
November 29, 1987	115	A Korean Air Lines jet explodes over the Burma coast	South Korea suspects North Korean involvement
December 21, 1988	270	Pan Am 103 explodes over Lockerbie, Scotland	One Libyan intelligence officer is convicted in a trial in The Hague in 2001, another is acquitted
September 19, 1989	171	A French U.T.A. jet explodes over Niger	The Lebanese Islamic Holy War claims responsibility, France holds Libya responsible
October 2, 1990	128	A hijacked Xiamen Airlines plane crashes into other parked planes in an airport in China	Unknown
March 17, 1992	29	A bomb demolishes the Israeli Embassy in Buenos Aires, Argentina	Unknown
February 26, 1993	6	A van filled with explosives explodes in the garage of the World Trade Center, leaving more than 1,000 people wounded	Ramzi Yousef receives a life sentence plus 240 years in 1998; the FBI suspects Osama bin Laden is behind the plot
April 19, 1995	168	Oklahoma City truck bomb destroys the Alfred P. Murrah federal building	Timothy McVeigh, executed June 11, 2001
August 7, 1998	224	Car bombs destroy U.S. embassies in Nairobi, Kenya, and Dar Es Salaam, Tanzania	Al Qaeda (Osama bin Laden)
October 12, 2000	17	Rubber boat filled with explosives detonates next to USS *Cole* in Yemen	Al Qaeda (Osama bin Laden)
September 11, 2001	3,000+	Four U.S. commercial airlines hijacked. Two destroy World Trade Center, one hits the Pentagon, one crashes in Pennsylvania	Al Qaeda (Osama bin Laden)
March 11, 2004	191	Bombing of train in Madrid, Spain	Al Qaeda
September 3, 2004	355 (176 children)	Chechen terrorists attack school in Beslan, Russia	Chechen
July 7, 2005	58	Terrorists set off four bombs in London's transit system	Unknown
Nov 9, 2005	57	Three hotels bombed in Amman, Jordan	Al Zarqawi, right arm of Osama bin Laden
July 11, 2006	147+	Train stations bombed in Mumbai (Bombay), India	Kashmir Muslim separatists

Source: U.S. Department of State, Office of Counterterrorism.

COMPARED TO WHAT?

World Opinion about America's War against Terrorism

Europeans were generally sympathetic with the United States following the terrorist attack of 9/11, and generally supported the U.S. military campaign

against terrorists in Afghanistan. But opinion in Europe, as well as in the Muslim world, opposed U.S. military action in Iraq. Indeed, over time ratings of the United States have grown markedly less favorable among Europeans, and the United States is now strongly disliked in the Muslim world. An important factor in world opinion about America is the perception that the United States acts internationally without taking into account the interests of other nations.

Ratings of the United States

	2002		2004	
	Favorable	Unfavorable	Favorable	Unfavorable
Great Britain	75%	16%	58%	34%
France	63	34	37	62
Germany	61	35	38	59
Russia	61	33	47	44
Turkey	30	42	30	45
Pakistan	10	58	21	50
Jordan	25	57	5	67
Morocco	27	46	27	46

Source: Pew Research Center for the People and the Press. *http://www.people-press.org*. Reprinted by permission of Pew Research Center for the People and the Press.

Operation Iraqi Freedom At the end of the Gulf War in 1991, the Iraqi regime of Saddam Hussein agreed to destroy all of its chemical and biological weapons and to end its efforts to acquire nuclear weapons. United Nations inspectors were to verify Iraqi compliance with these conditions. But Saddam's regime refused to cooperate; in 1998 he ordered the inspectors out of the country. Over a twelve-year period Iraq violated at least a dozen U.N. resolutions. Following a U.S. military buildup in the region in late 2002, Saddam allowed U.N. inspectors to return but continued to obstruct their work. On March 19, 2003, after giving Saddam a forty-eight hour warning to leave Iraq, the United States and Great Britain launched air strikes designed to eliminate Saddam and his top command.

At different times President Bush stated the purposes of "Operation Iraqi Freedom" as (1) the elimination of Iraq's weapons of mass destruction, (2) a "regime change" for Iraq to end the threat that Saddam posed for his neighbors and to free the Iraqi people from his oppressive rule, and (3) to ensure that Saddam would not harbor or assist terrorist organizations. But President Bush and Secretary of State Colin Powell failed to secure U.N. Security Council approval for military action. Among the permanent members of the Security Council, only the British, with the strong support of Prime Minister Tony Blair, were prepared to offer significant military support for the war against Saddam. Public opinion in America supported military action, but public opinion in Europe opposed it (see *Compared to What:* "World Opinion about America's War against Terrorism"). France and Germany led the diplomatic opposition; Turkey refused to let U.S. troops use its territory to

American and British soldiers and Marines swept into Baghdad in just twenty-one days in 2003 with relatively few casualties. But the subsequent occupation of that country was poorly prepared for, incompetently executed, and terribly costly in soldiers' lives lost.

attack Iraq; and the United States was obliged to rely primarily on Kuwait, Qatar, and the other smaller Gulf states for regional support.

The U.S. military wanted to wage war in the fashion of the successful Gulf War—a period of heavy air bombardment to "prepare the battlefield," followed by a massive ground attack using overwhelming military force. But Secretary of Defense Donald Rumsfeld wanted a "leaner" fighting force in Iraq. He deployed fewer than half of the air, ground, and naval forces that had been used in the Gulf War. And he began the air and ground attacks simultaneously.

American and British soldiers and Marines took just twenty-one days to sweep the 350 miles from the Kuwait border to downtown Baghdad. The British 3rd Armored Division, with Australian support, captured the port city of Basra; the U.S. 3rd Infantry Division moved up the west side of the Euphrates River; and the U.S. 1st Marine Division moved up the east side. Special Operations Forces, together with elements of the 101st Airborne Division, joined Kurdish forces in northern Iraq. Special Operations Forces also acted quickly to secure Iraq's oil fields and prevent their destruction. At first progress was hindered by the requirement that soldiers wear heavy chemical protection gear and carry decontamination equipment. But neither chemical nor biological weapons were used against U.S. forces. The advance on Baghdad was speeded up and the city was captured with precious few casualties.

But the subsequent occupation of Iraq by American troops and attempts to construct a more democratic government in that nation turned out badly. U.S. troops suffered more casualties in the aftermath of the war than during the war itself. Insurgent activity against American and British and other coalition nations' forces, and against Iraqis who appeared to cooperate in the reconstruction of their country, inflicted heavy damage and loss of life. The United States officially turned over sovereignty to an interim Iraqi government before June 30, 2004. The Iraqis voted to ratify a constitution in 2005 and later in the year elected a parliament under that constitution. But no firm plans were announced for the withdrawal of American troops from Iraq.

 **American Security Council**

Organization providing summary information on national security threats.
www.ascusa.org

— Think Again —

Are U.S. military force levels today sufficient to deal with potential regional aggressors such as Iran, Iraq, and North Korea?

Political Support for War in Iraq

Americans demand quick victory in war. With the exception of World War II, American public support for wars, notably Korea (1950–53) and Vietnam (1965–73), declined steadily as casualties rose and no end appeared in sight. The initial "rally 'round the flag" support for military action begins to wane after the first year of combat. Quick victories with few casualties, as in the Gulf War (1991), inspire support for the president and his decision to go to war. Prolonged stalemates with mounting casualties gradually erode public support for war.

The insurgency in Iraq following the capture of Baghdad in 2003 seemed to surprise Secretary of Defense Donald Rumsfeld. Planning for post-war Iraq appeared nonexistent. Rumsfeld steadfastly refused to send additional U.S. troops to Iraq to handle the insurgency and insisted that a new Iraqi government could eventually recruit and train enough troops to contain the insurgency. President Bush held steady throughout years of rising casualties. By late 2004, polls indicated that Americans, who had strongly supported going to war, had concluded that the war was "not worth it" (see Figure 18.2).

Bush's critics at home and abroad complained bitterly of the president's "unilateralism"—his willingness to go to war without the support of the United Nations. They charged that he misled Congress, the UN and the American

A CONSTITUTIONAL NOTE

Congress versus the Commander-in-Chief

The Constitution of 1787 divided war-making powers between the Congress and the president. Article I, Section 8 states that "Congress shall have Power... to provide for the common Defense... to declare War.... to raise and support Armies... to provide and maintain a Navy... to make Rules for the Government and Regulation of the land and naval forces." However, Article II, Section 2, states that "the President shall be the Commander-in-Chief of the Army and Navy of the United States." But today wars are not "declared"; instead they begin with military action, and the president is responsible for the actions of the Armed Forces of the United States. Presidents have sent U.S. troops beyond the borders of the United States in military actions on more than 200 occasions. In contrast, Congress has formerly declared war only five times: the War of 1812, the Mexican War in 1846, the Spanish-American War in 1898, World War I in 1917, and World War II in 1941. Congress did *not* declare war in the Korean War (1950–53), the Vietnam War (1965–73), the Persian Gulf War (1991), or the wars in Afghanistan (2002–) or Iraq (2003–). While presidents asked for the support of Congress in these wars, no formal declarations of war were ever made. The Supreme Court has consistently refused to hear cases involving the war powers of the president and Congress.

people about the existence of weapons of mass destruction. Bush's actions alienated our traditional allies—France and Germany—and were opposed by Russia and China and most of the Muslim world. Finally, critics charged that Bush had "no plan" for the reconstruction of Iraq after the fall of Saddam.

Secretary of Defense Rumsfeld continued to refuse to send additional troops to Iraq. He argued that eventually American-trained Iraqi troops would be able to take over the task of providing security for a new, more democratic Iraqi government. He pointed to the successful efforts to write a new Iraqi constitution, the heavy turnout of voters to ratify that constitution, and the even heavier turnout to elect a parliament in 2005. Yet American casualties continued from insurgent attacks, and insurgents attacked newly formed Iraqi troops as well as

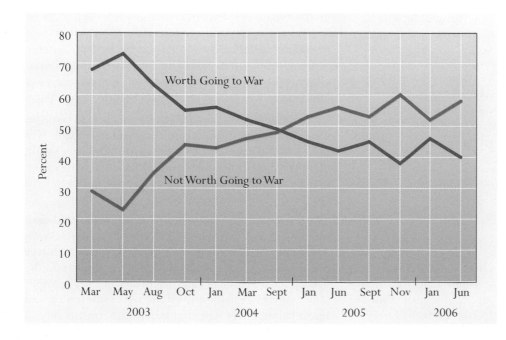

Figure 18.2 Changing Public Opinion about the War in Iraq

Q. All in all, do you think it was worth going to war in Iraq, or not?

Dates of Polls: 2003–March, May, August, October; 2004–January, March, June, September; 2005–January, June, September, November; 2005–June.

Source: www.pollingreport.com.

vital infrastructure, including oil supplies, damaging U.S. efforts to create a stable democracy in that country.

Nevertheless, President Bush argued that the war in Iraq was central to the worldwide war against terrorism. The "regime change" in Baghdad (Saddam was captured and placed on trial) removed a base of operations for terrorists. More importantly, President Bush argued forcefully that an abrupt withdrawal ("cut and run") would encourage radical Islamic terrorists around the world.

> Failure is not an option. Iraq would become a safe haven from which terrorists could plan attacks against American interests abroad, and our allies. Middle East reformers would never again fully trust American assurances of support for democracy in human rights in the region. Iraq is the central front in the global war on terror.[8]

Even the Western powers that had initially opposed going to war in Iraq came to see that any defeat of the United States in that country would prove calamitous to the Western world.

Summary Notes

- The struggle for power is global. Leaders and peoples of the world protect and advance their goals and ideals through the exercise of power.

- There is no world government capable of legislating and enforcing rules of international politics. But various efforts to stabilize relations among nations have been attempted, including the balance-of-power system of alliances in the eighteenth and nineteenth centuries, the collective security arrangements of the League of Nations and the United Nations in the twentieth century, and the regional security approach of the North Atlantic Treaty Organization.

- The United Nations was largely ineffective during the Cold War, the confrontation between the Western democracies led by the United States and communist bloc nations led by the Soviet Union. During these years, the Western nations relied principally on the strength of the North Atlantic Treaty Organization (NATO) to deter war in Europe.

- For nearly fifty years, the Cold War largely directed U.S. foreign and defense policy. The United States sought to contain Soviet military expansionism and world communist revolutionary forces in all parts of the globe. U.S. involvement in the Korean and Vietnam wars grew out of this containment policy.

- During the Cold War years, U.S. and Soviet military forces never engaged in direct combat against each other, although many "proxy" conflicts took place throughout the world. The most serious threat of nuclear war occurred during the Cuban missile crisis in 1962.

- To maintain nuclear peace, the United States relied primarily on the policy of deterrence—dissuading the Soviets from launching a nuclear attack by maintaining survivable second-strike forces capable of inflicting unacceptable levels of destruction in a retaliatory attack.

- In 1970 President Richard Nixon and National Security Adviser Henry Kissinger began negotiations with the Soviet Union with a view to limiting the nuclear arms race. These Strategic Arms Limitation Talks produced the SALT I agreement in 1972, and later, under President Jimmy Carter, the SALT II agreement in 1979. Both agreements set limits on future strategic weapons development but failed to reduce existing weapons stockpiles.

- President Ronald Reagan renamed the negotiations START, emphasizing the goal of reductions in weapons rather than limitations, and stressing equality and verification. The START I (1991) and START II (1993) treaties called for reducing nuclear arsenals by two-thirds from Cold War levels.

- The end of the Cold War followed the ouster of communist governments in Eastern Europe in 1989, the unification of Germany in 1990, the collapse of the Warsaw Pact communist military alliance in 1991, and the dissolution of the Soviet Union in 1991. Russia has inherited most of the nuclear weapons and military forces of the former Soviet Union as well as its seat on the UN Security Council.

- Current threats to peace and security are likely to be posed by regional aggressors. U.S. involvement in the Gulf War in 1990–91 is representative of the type of military action most likely to be undertaken in the future. Current defense policy calls for the United States to be prepared to fight two "Iraqi equivalent wars" "nearly simultaneously."

- The military phase of America's War on Terrorism began October 7, 2001, when U.S. aircraft began attacks on Al Qaeda bases in Afghanistan and U.S. special forces organized and led anti-Taliban Afghan fighters to oust the Taliban regime that had harbored the terrorists. These military actions largely destroyed the terrorist infrastructure in Afghanistan; yet scattered groups of terrorists remain in that country and neighboring Pakistan.

- President George W. Bush warned that the War on Terrorism would be a continuing one, but the variety of ways and means and places of potential terrorist attack make it impossible for the United States to guarantee an end to international terrorism.

- Following the Vietnam War, many military leaders argued that U.S. forces should be used only to protect vital American interests, only in support of clearly defined military objectives, only with sufficient strength to ensure decisive victory with the fewest possible casualties, only with the support of the American people and Congress, and only as a last resort.

- Recent presidents, however, have used military forces to carry out a variety of missions in addition to conventional war, including peacekeeping, antiterrorist, and humanitarian activities. They have argued that the risks were worth taking in light of the importance of the goals.

Key Terms

collective security   628
Soviet Union   628
superpowers   628
regional security   628
North Atlantic Treaty
   Organization
   (NATO)   628

Cold War   629
Truman Doctrine   630
containment   630
Marshall Plan   630
Korean War   630
Cuban Missile
   Crisis   631

Vietnam War   631
deterrence   633
second-strike
   capability   633
SALT I   634
ABM Treaty   634
SALT II   635

START I   635
START II   635
ballistic missile defense
   (BMD)   635
preemptive attack   639
terrorism   640

Suggested Readings

Clausewitz, Karl von. *On War*. Edited and translated by Michael Howard and Peter Paret. Princeton, N.J.: Princeton University Press, 1984. The classic theory of war and military operations, emphasizing their political character; first published in 1832.

Combs, Cynthia C. *Terrorism in the 21st Century*. 4th ed. Upper Saddle River, N.J.: Prentice Hall, 2006. History of terrorism, terrorist operations and responses to terrorism, written for those not familiar with the topic.

Hastedt, Glenn P. *American Foreign Policy: Past, Present, Future*. 6th ed. Upper Saddle River, N.J.: Prentice Hall, 2006. A foreign policy text that deals with national security issues within the broader context of foreign policy.

International Institute for Strategic Studies. *The Military Balance*. London: International Institute for Strategic Studies, published annually. Careful description of the military forces of more than 160 countries; this book is considered the most authoritative public information available.

Kegley, Charles W. *The New Global Terrorism*. Upper Saddle River, N.J.: Prentice Hall, 2003. Describing post-9/11 terrorism, its multiple roots, and leading ideas for winning the "war on global terrorism."

Magstadt, Thomas M. *An Empire If You Can Keep It: Power and Principle in American Foreign Policy*. Washington, D.C.: CQ Press, 2004. Comprehensive text on American foreign policy, describing its history, the Cold War, the Gulf War, September 11, and the War on Terrorism.

Snow, Donald M. *When America Fights: The Uses of U.S. Military Force*. Washington, D.C.: CQ Press, 2000. Questions U.S. military involvement in "peacekeeping" operations. Discusses the use of force in relation to U.S. national interests.

Summers, Harry G., Jr. *On Strategy II: A Critical Analysis of the Gulf War*. New York: Dell, 1992. Analysis of the Gulf War based on Clausewitz's classic principles of war. The strategic decisions leading to victory in the Gulf contrast markedly with the decisions in Vietnam that led to defeat, a topic covered in Summers's groundbreaking first book, *On Strategy: A Critical Analysis of the Vietnam War* (New York: Dell, 1984).

APPENDIX

The Declaration of Independence

Drafted mainly by Thomas Jefferson, this document, adopted by the Second Continental Congress and signed by John Hancock and fifty-five others, outlined the rights of man and the rights to rebellion and self-government. It declared the independence of the colonies from Great Britain, justified rebellion, and listed the grievances against George III and his government. What is memorable about this famous document is not only that it declared the birth of a new nation, but that it set forth with eloquence our basic philosophy of liberty and representative democracy.

IN CONGRESS, JULY 4, 1776 (The unanimous Declaration of the Thirteen United States of America)

Preamble

When, in the course of human events, it becomes necessary for one people to dissolve the political bands which have connected them with another, and to assume, among the powers of the earth, the separate and equal station to which the laws of nature and of nature's God entitle them, a decent respect to the opinions of mankind requires that they should declare the causes which impel them to the separation.

New Principles of Government

We hold these truths to be self-evident; that all men are created equal, that they are endowed by their Creator with certain unalienable rights, that among these are life, liberty, and the pursuit of happiness.

That, to secure these rights, governments are instituted among men, deriving their just powers from the consent of the governed.

That whenever any form of government becomes destructive of these ends, it is the right of the people to alter or to abolish it, and to institute new government, laying its foundation on such principles, and organizing its powers in such form, as to them shall seem most likely to effect their safety and happiness. Prudence, indeed will dictate that governments long established should not be changed for light and transient causes; and accordingly all experience hath shown that mankind are more disposed to suffer while evils are sufferable, than to right themselves by abolishing the forms to which they are accustomed. But when a long train of abuses and usurpations, pursuing invariably the same object, evinces a design to reduce them under absolute despotism, it is their right, it is their duty, to throw off such government, and to provide new guards for their future security.

Reasons for Separation

Such has been the patient sufferance of these colonies; and such is now the necessity which constrains them to alter their former systems of government. The history of the present king of Great Britain is a history of repeated injuries and usurpations, all having in direct object the establishment of an absolute tyranny over these states. To prove this, let facts be submitted to a candid world.

He has refused his assent to laws, the most wholesome and necessary for the public good.

He has forbidden his governors to pass laws of immediate and pressing importance unless suspended in their operation till his assent should be obtained; and when so suspended, he has utterly neglected to attend to them.

He has refused to pass other laws for the accommodation of large districts of people, unless those people would relinquish the right of representation in the legislature, a right inestimable to them, and formidable to tyrants only.

He has called together legislative bodies at places unusual, uncomfortable, and distant for the depository of their public records, for the sole purpose of fatiguing them into compliance with his measures.

He has dissolved representative houses repeatedly, for opposing, with manly firmness, his invasions on the rights of people.

He has refused, for a long time after such dissolutions, to cause others to be elected; whereby the legislative powers incapable of annihilation, have returned to the people at large for their exercise; the state remaining, in the mean-time, exposed to all the dangers of invasion from without and convulsions within.

He has endeavored to prevent the population of these states; for that purpose obstructing the laws of naturalization of foreigners, refusing to pass others to encourage their migration hither, and raising the conditions of new appropriations of lands.

He has obstructed the administration of justice, by refusing his assent to laws for establishing judiciary powers.

He has made judges dependent on his will alone for the tenure of their offices, and the amount and payment of their salaries.

He has erected a multitude of new offices, and sent hither swarms of officers to harass our people and eat out their substance.

He has kept among us, in times of peace, standing armies, without the consent of our legislature.

He has affected to render the military independent of, and superior to, the civil power.

He has combined with others to subject us to jurisdiction foreign to our constitution and unacknowledged by our laws, giving his assent to their acts of pretended legislation:

For quartering large bodies of armed troops among us;

For protecting them, by a mock trial, from punishment for any murders which they should commit on the inhabitants of these states;

For cutting off our trade with all parts of the world;

For imposing taxes on us without our consent;

For depriving us, in many cases, of the benefits of trial by jury;

For transporting us beyond seas, to be tried for pretended offenses;

For abolishing the free system of English laws in a neighboring province, establishing therein an arbitrary government, and enlarging its boundaries, so as to render it at once an example and fit instrument for introducing the same absolute rule into these colonies;

For taking away our charters, abolishing our most valuable laws, and altering, fundamentally, the forms of our governments;

For suspending our own legislatures, and declaring themselves invented with power to legislate for us in all cases whatsoever.

He has abdicated government here, by declaring us out of his protection and waging war against us.

He has plundered our seas, ravaged our coasts, burned our towns, and destroyed the lives of our people.

He is at this time transporting large armies of foreign mercenaries to complete the works of death, desolation, and tyranny already begun with circumstances of cruelty and perfidy scarcely paralleled in the most barbarous ages and totally unworthy of the head of a civilized nation.

He has constrained our fellow-citizens, taken captive on the high seas, to bear arms against their country, to become the executioners of their friends and brethren, or to fall themselves by their hands.

He has excited domestic insurrections among us, and has endeavored to bring on the inhabitants of our frontiers the merciless Indian savages, whose known rule of warfare is an undistinguished destruction of all ages, sexes, and conditions.

In every stage of these oppressions we have petitioned for redress in the most humble terms; our repeated petitions have been answered only by repeated injury. A prince whose character is thus marked by every act which may define a tyrant is unfit to be the ruler of a free people.

Nor have we been wanting in attention to our British brethren. We have warned them, from time to time, of attempts by their legislature to extend an unwarrantable jurisdiction over us. We have reminded them of the circumstances of our emigration and settlement here. We have appealed to their native justice and magnanimity; and we have conjured them, by the ties of our common kindred, to disavow these usurpations, which would inevitably interrupt our connections and correspondence. They, too, have been deaf to the voice of justice and of consanguinity. We must, therefore, acquiesce in the necessity which denounces our separation, and hold them, as we hold the rest of mankind, enemies in war, in peace, friends.

We, therefore, the representatives of the United States of America, in General Congress assembled, appealing to the Supreme Judge of the world for the rectitude of our intentions, do, in the name and by authority of the good people of these colonies, solemnly publish and declare, that these united colonies are, and of right ought to be, free and independent states; that they are absolved from all allegiance to the British crown, and that all political connection between them and the state of Great Britain is, and ought to be, totally dissolved; and that, as free and independent states, they have full power to levy war, conclude peace, contract alliances, establish commerce, and do all other acts and things which independent states may of a right do. And, for the support of this declaration, with a firm reliance on the protection of Divine Providence, we mutually pledge to each other our lives, our fortunes, and our sacred honor.

The Federalist, No. 10, James Madison

To the People of the State of New York: Among the numerous advantages promised by a well-constructed union, none deserves to be more accurately developed than its tendency to break and control the violence of faction. The friend of popular governments, never finds himself so much alarmed for their character and fate, as when he contemplates their propensity to this dangerous vice. He will not fail, therefore, to set a due value on any plan which, without violating the principles to which he is attached, provides a proper cure for it. The instability, injustice, and confusion introduced into the public councils, have, in truth, been the mortal diseases under which popular governments have everywhere perished; as they continue to be the favourite and fruitful topics from which the adversaries to liberty derive their most specious declamations. The valuable improvements made by the American constitutions on the popular models, both ancient and modern, cannot certainly be too much admired; but it would be an unwarrantable partiality, to contend that they have as effectually obviated the danger on this side, as was wished and expected. Complaints are everywhere heard from our most considerate and virtuous citizens, equally the friends of public and private faith, and of public and personal liberty, that our governments are too unstable; that the public good is disregarded in the conflicts of rival parties; and that measures are too often decided, not according to the rules of justice, and the rights of the minor party, but by the superior force of an interested and over-bearing majority. However anxiously we may wish that these complaints had no foundation, the evidence of known facts will not permit us to deny that they are in some degree true. It will be found, indeed, on a candid review of our situation, that some of the distresses under which we labour have been erroneously charged on the operation of our governments; but it will be found, at the same time, that other causes will not alone account for many of our heaviest misfortunes; and, particularly, for that prevailing and increasing distrust of public engagements, and alarm for private rights, which are echoed from one end of the continent to the other. These must be chiefly, if not wholly, effects of the unsteadiness and injustice, with which a factious spirit has tainted our public administrations.

By a faction, I understand a number of citizens, whether amounting to a majority or minority of the whole, who are united and actuated by some common impulse of passion, or of interest, adverse to the rights of other citizens, or to the permanent and aggregate interests of the community.

There are two methods of curing the mischiefs of faction: the one, by removing its causes; the other, by controlling its effects.

There are again two methods of removing the causes of faction: the one, by destroying the liberty which is essential to its existence; the other, by giving to every citizen the same opinions, the same passions, and the same interests.

It could never be more truly said, than of the first remedy, that it was worse than the disease. Liberty is to faction what air is to fire, an aliment without which it instantly expires. But it could not be a less folly to abolish liberty, which is essential to political life, because it nourishes faction, than it would be to wish the annihilation of air, which is essential to animal life, because it imparts to fire its destructive agency.

The second expedient is as impracticable, as the first would be unwise. As long as the reason of man continues fallible, and he is at liberty to exercise it, different opinions will be formed. As long as the connection subsists between his reason and his self-love, his opinions and his passions will have a reciprocal influence on each other; and the former will be objects to which the latter will attach themselves. The diversity in the faculties of men, from which the rights of property originate, is not less an insuperable obstacle to an uniformity of interests. The protection of these faculties is the first object of government. From the protection of different and unequal faculties of acquiring property, the possession of different degrees and kinds of property immediately results; and from the influence of these on the sentiments and views of the respective proprietors, ensues a division of the society into different interests and parties.

The latent causes of faction are thus sown in the nature of man; and we see them everywhere brought into different degrees of activity, according to the different circumstances of civil society. A zeal for different opinions concerning religion, concerning government, and many other points, as well of speculation as of practice; an attachment to different leaders ambitiously contending for preeminence and power; or to persons of other descriptions whose fortunes have been interesting to the human passions, have, in turn, divided mankind into parties, inflamed them with mutual animosity, and rendered them much more disposed to vex and oppress each other, than to cooperate for their common good. So strong is this propensity of mankind, to fall into mutual animosities, that where no substantial occasion presents itself, the most frivolous and fanciful distinctions have been sufficient to kindle their unfriendly passions and excite their most violent conflicts. But the most common and durable source of factions, has been the various and unequal distribution of property. Those who hold, and those who are without property, have ever formed distinct interests in society. Those who are creditors, and those who are debtors, fall under a like discrimination. A landed interest, a manufacturing interest, a mercantile interest, a moneyed interest, with many lesser interests, grow up of necessity in civilized nations, and divide them into different classes, actuated by different sentiments and views. The regulation of these various and interfering interests forms the principal task of modern legislation, and involves the spirit of the party and faction in the necessary and ordinary operations of the government.

No man is allowed to be a judge in his own cause; because his interest will certainly bias his judgment, and, not improbably, corrupt his integrity. With equal, nay, with greater reason, a body of men are unfit to be both judges and parties at the same time; yet what are many of the most important acts of legislation, but so many judicial determinations, not indeed concerning the right of single persons, but concerning the rights of large bodies of citizens? And what are the different classes of legislators, but advocates and parties to the causes which they determine? Is a law proposed concerning private debts? It is a question to which the creditors are parties on one side, and the debtors on the other. Justice ought to hold the balance between them. Yet the parties are, and must be, themselves the judges; and the most numerous party, or, in other words, the most powerful faction, must be expected to prevail. Shall domestic manufacturers be encouraged, and in what degree, by restrictions on foreign manufacturers are questions which would be differently decided by the landed and the manufacturing classes; and probably by neither with a sole regard to justice and the public good. The apportionment of taxes, on the various descriptions of property, is an act which seems to require the most exact impartiality; yet there is, perhaps, no legislative act, in which greater opportunity and temptation are given to a predominant party to trample on the rules of justice. Every shilling, with which they overburden the inferior number, is a shilling saved to their own pockets.

It is in vain to say, that enlightened statesmen will be able to adjust these clashing interests, and render them all subservient to the public good. Enlightened statesmen will not always be at the helm; nor, in many cases, can such an adjustment be made at all, without taking into view indirect and remote considerations, which will rarely prevail over the immediate interest which one party may find in disregarding the rights of another, or the good of the whole.

The inference to which we are brought is, that the *causes* of faction cannot be removed; and that relief is only to be sought in the means of controlling its *effects*.

If a faction consists of less than a majority, relief is supplied by the republican principle, which enables the majority to defeat its sinister views, by regular vote. It may clog the administration, it may convulse the society; but it will be unable to execute and mask its violence under the forms of the Constitution. When a majority is included in a faction, the form of popular government, on the other hand, enables it to sacrifice to its ruling passion or interest, both the public good and the rights of other citizens. To secure the public good, and private rights, against the danger of such a faction, and at the same time to preserve the spirit and the form of popular government, is then the great object to which our inquiries are directed. Let me add, that it is the great desideratum, by which alone this form of government can be rescued from the opprobrium under which it has so long laboured, and be recommended to the esteem and adoption of mankind.

By what means is this object attainable? Evidently by one of two only. Either the existence of the same passion or interest in a majority, at the same time, must be prevented; or the majority, having such coexistent passion or interest, must be rendered, by their number and local situation, unable to concert and carry into effect schemes of oppression. If the impulse and the opportunity be suffered to coincide, we well know that neither moral nor religious motives can be relied on as an adequate control. They are not found to be such on the injustice and violence of individuals, and lose their efficacy in proportion to the number combined together; that is, in proportion as their efficacy becomes needful.

From this view of the subject, it may be concluded, that a pure democracy, by which I mean a society consisting of a small number of citizens, who assemble and administer the government in person, can admit of no cure for the mischiefs of faction. A common passion or interest will, in almost every case, be felt by a majority of the whole; a communication and concert, results from the form of government itself; and there is nothing to check the inducements to sacrifice the weaker party, or an obnoxious individual. Hence, it is, that such democracies have ever been spectacles of turbulence and contention; have ever been found incompatible with personal security, or the rights of property; and have in general been as short in their lives, as they have been violent in their deaths. Theoretic politicians, who have patronized this species of government, have erroneously supposed, that by reducing mankind to a perfect equality in their political rights, they would, at the same time, be perfectly equalized and assimilated in their possessions, their opinions, and their passions.

A republic, by which I mean a government in which the scheme of representation takes place, opens a different prospect, and promises the cure for which we are seeking. Let us examine the points in which it varies from pure democracy, and we shall comprehend both the nature of the cure and the efficacy which it must derive from the union.

The two great points of difference, between a democracy and a republic, are, first, the delegation of the government, in the latter, to a small number of citizens, elected by the rest; secondly, the greater number of citizens, and greater sphere of country, over which the latter may be extended.

The effect of the first difference is, on the one hand, to refine and enlarge the public views, by passing them through the medium of a chosen body of citizens, whose wisdom may best discern the true interest of their country, and whose patriotism and love of justice, will be least likely to sacrifice it to temporary or partial considerations. Under such a regulation, it may well happen, that the public voice, pronounced by the representatives of the people, will be more consonant to the public good, than if pronounced by the people themselves, convened for the purpose. On the other hand the effect may be inverted. Men of factious tempers, of local prejudices, or of sinister designs, may by intrigue, by corruption, or by other means, first obtain the suffrages, and then betray the interest of the people. The question resulting is, whether small or extensive republics are most favourable to the election of proper guardians of the public weal; and it is clearly decided in favour of the latter by two obvious considerations.

In the first place, it is to be remarked that, however small the republic may be, the representatives must be raised to a certain number, in order to guard against the cabals of a few; and that however large it may be, they must be limited to a certain number, in order to guard against the confusion of a multitude. Hence, the number of representatives in the two cases not being in proportion to that of the constituents, and being proportionally greatest in the small republic, it follows, that if the proportion of fit characters be not less in the large than in the small republic, the former will present a greater option, and consequently a greater probability of a fit choice.

In the next place, as each representative will be chosen by a greater number of citizens in the large than in the small republic, it will be more difficult for unworthy candidates to practice with success the vicious arts, by which elections are too often carried; and the suffrages of the people being more free, will be more likely to centre in men who possess the most attractive merit, and the most diffusive and established characters.

It must be confessed, that in this, as in most other cases, there is a mean, on both sides of which inconveniences will be found to lie. By enlarging too much the number of electors, you render the representatives too little acquainted with all their local circumstances and lesser interests; as by reducing it too much, you render him unduly attached to these, and too little fit to comprehend and pursue great and national objects. The federal constitution forms a happy combination in this respect; the great and aggregate interests being referred to the national, the local and particular to the state legislatures.

The other point of difference is, the greater number of citizens, and extent of territory, which may be brought within the compass of republican, than of democratic government; and it is this circumstance principally which renders factious combinations less to be dreaded in the former, than in the latter. The smaller the society, the fewer probably will be the distinct parties and interests composing it; the fewer the distinct parties and interests, the more frequently will a majority be found of the same party; and the smaller the number of individuals composing a majority, and the smaller the compass within which they are placed, the more easily will they concert and execute their plans of oppression. Extend the sphere, and you take in a greater variety of parties and interests; you make it less probable that a majority of the whole will have a common motive to invade the rights of other citizens; or if such a common motive exists, it will be more difficult for all who feel it to discover their own strength, and to act in unison with each other. Besides other impediments, it may be remarked, that where there is a consciousness of unjust or dishonourable purposes, communication is always checked by distrust, in proportion to the number whose concurrence is necessary.

Hence, it clearly appears, that the same advantage, which a republic has over a democracy, in controlling the effects of faction, is enjoyed by a large over a small republic—is enjoyed by the union over the states composing it. Does this advantage consist in the substitution of representatives, whose enlightened views and virtuous sentiments render them superior to local prejudices, and to schemes of injustice? It will not be denied that the representation of the union will be most likely to possess these requisite endowments. Does it consist in the greater security afforded by a greater variety of parties, against the event of any one party being able to outnumber and oppress the rest? In an equal degree does the increased variety of parties, comprised within the union, increase the security? Does it, in fine, consist in the greater obstacles opposed to the concert and

accomplishment of the secret wishes of an unjust and interested majority? Here, again, the extent of the union gives it the most palpable advantage.

The influence of factious leaders may kindle a flame within their particular states, but will be unable to spread a general conflagration through the other states; a religious sect may degenerate into a political faction in a part of the confederacy; but the variety of sects dispersed over the entire face of it, must secure the national councils against any danger from that source; a rage for paper money, for an abolition of debts, for an equal division of property, or for any other improper or wicked project, will be less apt to pervade the whole body of the union than a particular member of it; in the same proportion as such a malady is more likely to taint a particular county or district, than an entire state.

In the extent and proper structure of the union, therefore, we behold a republican remedy for the diseases most incident to republican government. And according to the degree of pleasure and pride we feel in being republicans, ought to be our zeal in cherishing the spirit, and supporting the character of federalists.

The Federalist, No. 51, James Madison

To what expedient, then, shall we finally resort, for maintaining in practice the necessary partition of power among the several departments as laid down in the Constitution? The only answer that can be given is that as all these exterior provisions are found to be inadequate the defect must be supplied, by so contriving the interior structure of the government as that its several constituent parts may, by their mutual relations, be the means of keeping each other in their proper places. Without presuming to undertake a full development of this important idea I will hazard a few general observations which may perhaps place it in a clearer light, and enable us to form a more correct judgment of the principles and structure of the government planned by the convention.

In order to lay a due foundation for that separate and distinct exercise of the different powers of government, which to a certain extent is admitted on all hands to be essential to the preservation of liberty, it is evident that each department should have a will of its own; and consequently should be so constituted that the members of each should have as little agency as possible in the appointment of the members of the others. Were this principle rigorously adhered to, it would require that all the appointments for the supreme executive, legislative, and judiciary magistracies should be drawn from the same fountain of authority, the people, through channels having no communication whatever with one another. Perhaps such a plan of constructing the several departments would be less difficult in practice than it may in contemplation appear. Some difficulties, however, and some additional expense would attend the execution of it. Some deviations, therefore, from the principle must be admitted. In the constitution of the judiciary department in particular, it might be inexpedient to insist rigorously on the principle: first, because peculiar qualifications being essential in the members, the primary consideration ought to be to select that mode of choice which best secures these qualifications; second, because the permanent tenure by which the appointments are held in that department must soon destroy all sense of dependence on the authority conferring them.

It is equally evident that the members of each department should be as little dependent as possible on those of the others for the emoluments annexed to their offices. Were the executive magistrate, or the judges, not independent of the legislature in this particular, their independence in every other would be merely nominal.

But the great security against a gradual concentration of the several powers in the same department consists in giving to those who administer each department the necessary constitutional means and personal motives to resist encroachments of the others. The provision for defense must in this, as in all other cases, be made commensurate to the danger of attack. Ambition must be made to counteract ambition. The interest of the man must be connected with the constitutional rights of the place. It may be a reflection on human nature that such devices should be necessary to control the abuses of government. But what is government itself but the greatest of all reflections on human nature? If men were angels, no government would be necessary. If angels were to govern men, neither external nor internal controls on government would be necessary. In framing a government which is to be administered by men over men, the great difficulty lies in this: you must first enable the government to control the governed; and in the next place oblige it to control itself. A dependence on the people is, no doubt, the primary control on the government; but experience has taught mankind the necessity of auxiliary precautions.

This policy of supplying, by opposite and rival interests, the defect of better motives, might be traced through the whole system of human affairs, private as well as public. We see it particularly displayed in all the subordinate distributions of power, where the constant aim is to divide and arrange the several offices in such a manner as that each may be a check on the other—that the private interest of every individual may be a sentinel over the public rights. These inventions of prudence cannot be less requisite in the distribution of the supreme powers of the State.

But it is not possible to give to each department an equal power of self-defense. In republican government, the legislative authority necessarily predominates. The remedy for this inconveniency is to divide the legislature into different branches; and to render them, by modes of election and different principles of action, as little connected with each other as the nature of their common functions and their common dependence on the society will admit. It may even be necessary to guard against dangerous encroachments by still further precautions. As the weight of the legislative authority requires that it should be thus divided, the weakness of the executive may require, on the other hand, that it should be fortified. An absolute negative on the legislature appears, at first view, to be the natural defense with which the executive magistrate should be armed. But perhaps it would be neither altogether safe nor alone sufficient. On ordinary occasions it might not be exerted with the requisite firmness, and on extraordinary occasions it might be perfidiously abused. May not this defect of an absolute negative be supplied by some qualified connection between this weaker department and the weaker branch of the stronger department, by which the latter may be led to support the constitutional rights of the former, without being too much detached from the rights of its own department?

If the principles on which these observations are founded be just, as I persuade myself they are, and they be applied as a criterion to the several State constitutions, and to the federal Constitution, it will be found that if the latter does not perfectly correspond with them, the former are infinitely less able to bear such a test.

There are, moreover, two considerations particularly applicable to the federal system of America, which place that system in a very interesting point of view.

First. In a single republic, all the power surrendered by the people is submitted to the administration of a single government; and the usurpations are guarded against by a division of the government into distinct and separate departments. In the compound republic of America, the power surrendered by the people is first divided between two distinct governments, and then the portion allotted to each subdivided among distinct and separate departments. Hence a double security arises to the rights of the people. The different governments will control each other, at the same time that each will be controlled by itself.

Second. It is of great importance in a republic not only to guard the society against the oppression of its rulers, but to guard one part of the society against the injustice of the other part. Different interests necessarily exist in different classes of citizens. If a majority be united by a common interest, the rights of the minority will be insecure. There are but two methods of providing against this evil: the one by creating a will in the community independent of the majority—that is, of the society itself; the other, by comprehending in the society so many separate descriptions of citizens as will render an unjust combination of a majority of the whole very improbable, if not impracticable. The first method prevails in all governments possessing an hereditary or self-appointed authority. This, at best, is but a precarious security; because a power independent of the society may as well espouse the unjust views of the major as the rightful interests of the minor party, and may possibly be turned against both parties. The second method will be exemplified in the federal republic of the United States. Whilst all authority in it will be derived from and dependent on the society, the society itself will be broken into so many parts, interests and classes of citizens, that the rights of individuals, or of the minority, will be in little danger from interested combinations of the majority. In a free government the security for civil rights must be the same as that for religious rights. It consists in the one case in the multiplicity of interests, and in the other in the multiplicity of sects. The degree of security in both cases will depend on the number of interests and sects; and this may be presumed to depend on the extent of country and number of people comprehended under the same government. This view of the subject must particularly recommend a proper federal system to all the sincere and considerate friends of republican government, since it shows that in exact proportion as the territory of the Union may be formed into more circumscribed Confederacies, or States, oppressive combinations of a majority will be facilitated; the best security, under the republican forms, for the rights of every class of citizen, will be diminished; and consequently the stability and independence of some member of the government, the only other security, must be proportionally increased. Justice is the end of government. It is the end of civil society. It ever has been and ever will be pursued until it be obtained, or until liberty be lost in the pursuit. In a society under the forms of which the stronger faction can readily unite and oppress the weaker, anarchy may as truly be said to reign as in a state of nature, where the weaker individual is not secured against the violence of the stronger; and as, in the latter state, even the stronger individuals are prompted, by the uncertainty of their condition, to submit to a government which may protect the weak as well as themselves; so, in the former state, will the more powerful factions or parties be gradually induced, by a like motive, to wish for a government which will protect all parties, the weaker as well as the more powerful. It can be little doubted that if the State of Rhode Island was separated from the Confederacy and left to itself, the insecurity of rights under the popular form of government within such narrow limits would be displayed by such reiterated oppressions of factious majorities that some power altogether independent of the people would soon be called for by the voice of the very factions whose misrule had proved the necessity of it. In the extended republic of the United States, and among the great variety of interests, parties, and sects which it embraces, a coalition of a majority of the whole society could seldom take place on any other principles than those of justice and the general good; whilst there being thus less danger to a minor from the will of a major party, there must be less pretext, also, to provide for the security of the former, by introducing into the government a will not dependent on the latter, or, in other words, a will independent of the society itself. It is no less certain that it is important, notwithstanding the contrary opinions which have been entertained that the larger the society, provided it lie within a practicable sphere, the more duly capable it will be of self-government. And happily for the *republican cause*, the practicable sphere may be carried to avery great extent by a judicious modification and mixture of the *federal principle*.

PRESIDENTS AND VICE PRESIDENTS

1. George Washington (1789)
   John Adams (1789)

2. John Adams (1797)
   Thomas Jefferson (1797)

3. Thomas Jefferson (1801)
   Aaron Burr (1801)
   George Clinton (1805)

4. James Madison (1809)
   George Clinton (1809)
   Elbridge Gerry (1813)

5. James Monroe (1817)
   Daniel D. Tompkins (1817)

6. John Quincy Adams (1825)
   John C. Calhoun (1825)

7. Andrew Jackson (1829)
   John C. Calhoun (1829)
   Martin Van Buren (1833)

8. Martin Van Buren (1837)
   Richard M. Johnson (1837)

9. William H. Harrison (1841)
   John Tyler (1841)

10. John Tyler (1841)

11. James K. Polk (1845)
    George M. Dallas (1845)

12. Zachary Taylor (1849)
    Millard Fillmore (1849)

13. Millard Fillmore (1850)

14. Franklin Pierce (1853)
    William R. King (1853)

15. James Buchanan (1857)
    John C. Breckinridge (1857)

16. Abraham Lincoln (1861)
    Hannibal Hamlin (1861)
    Andrew Johnson (1865)

17. Andrew Johnson (1865)

18. Ulysses S. Grant (1869)
    Schuyler Colfax (1869)
    Henry Wilson (1873)

19. Rutherford B. Hayes (1877)
    William A. Wheeler (1877)

20. James A. Garfield (1881)
    Chester A. Arthur (1881)

21. Chester A. Arthur (1881)

22. Grover Cleveland (1885)
    T.A. Hendricks (1885)

23. Benjamin Harrison (1889)
    Levi P. Morton (1889)

24. Grover Cleveland (1893)
    Adlai E. Stevenson (1893)

25. William McKinley (1897)
    Garret A. Hobart (1897)
    Theodore Roosevelt (1901)

26. Theodore Roosevelt (1901)
    Charles Fairbanks (1905)

27. William H. Taft (1909)
    James S. Sherman (1909)

28. Woodrow Wilson (1913)
    Thomas R. Marshall (1913)

29. Warren G. Harding (1921)
    Calvin Coolidge (1921)

30. Calvin Coolidge (1923)
    Charles G. Dawes (1925)

31. Herbert C. Hoover (1929)
    Charles Curtis (1929)

32. Franklin D. Roosevelt (1933)
    John Nance Garner (1933)
    Henry A. Wallace (1941)
    Harry S Truman (1945)

33. Harry S Truman (1945)
    Alben W. Barkley (1949)

34. Dwight D. Eisenhower (1953)
    Richard M. Nixon (1953)

35. John F. Kennedy (1961)
    Lyndon B. Johnson (1961)

36. Lyndon B. Johnson (1963)
    Hubert H. Humphrey (1965)

37. Richard M. Nixon (1969)
    Spiro T. Agnew (1969)
    Gerald R. Ford (1973)

38. Gerald R. Ford (1974)
    Nelson A. Rockefeller (1974)

39. James E. Carter Jr. (1977)
    Walter F. Mondale (1977)

40. Ronald W. Reagan (1981)
    George H.W. Bush (1981)

41. George H.W. Bush (1989)
    James D. Quayle III (1989)

42. William J.B. Clinton (1993)
    Albert Gore (1993)

43. George W. Bush (2001)
    Richard Cheney (2001)

SUPREME COURT JUSTICES

Current Supreme Court Justices

1. John G. Roberts (Chief Justice)
2. Antonin Scalia (Associate Justice)
3. John Paul Stevens (Associate Justice)
4. Samuel A. Alito Jr. (Associate Justice)
5. Anthony M. Kennedy (Associate Justice)
6. Ruth Bader Ginsburg (Associate Justice)
7. David H. Souter (Associate Justice)
8. Clarence Thomas (Associate Justice)
9. Stephen G. Breyer (Associate Justice)

Former Supreme Court Chief Justices

1. John Jay (1779–1795)
2. John Rutledge (1795)
3. Oliver Ellsworth (1996–1800)
4. John Marshall (1801–1835)
5. Roger Brooke Tancy (1836–1864)
6. Salmon Portland Chase (1864–1873)
7. Morrison R. Waite (1874–1888)
8. Melville Weston Fuller (1888–1910)
9. Edward Douglas White (1910–1921)
10. William Howard Taft (1921–1930)
11. Charles Evans Hughes (1930–1941)
12. Harlan Fiske Stone (1941–1946)
13. Fred M. Vison (1946–1953)
14. Earl Warren (1953–1969)
15. Warren E. Burger (1969–1986)
16. William H. Rehnquist (1986–2005)

Former Supreme Court Associate Judges

1. James Wilson (1789–1798)
2. William Cushing (1790–1810)
3. John Blair Jr. (1790–1796)
4. James Iredell (1790–1799)
5. Thomas Johnson (1792–1793)
6. William Paterson (1793–1806)
7. Samuel Chase (1796–1811)
8. Bushrod Washington (1799–1829)
9. Alfred Moore (1800–1804)
10. William Johnson (1804–1834)
11. H. Brockholst Livingston (1807–1328)
12. Thomas Todd (1807–1826)
13. Gabriel Duvall (1811–1835)
14. Joseph Story (1812–1845)
15. Smith Thompson (1823–1843)
16. Robert Trimble (1826–1828)
17. John McLean (1830–1861)
18. Henry Baldwin (1830–1844)
19. James M. Wayne (1835–1867)
20. Philip P. Barbour (1836–1841)
21. John Catron (1837–1865)
22. John McKinley (1838–1852)
23. Peter V. Daniel (1842–1860)
24. Samuel Nelson (1845–1872)
25. Levi Woodbury (1845–1851)
26. Robert C. Grier (1846–1870)
27. Benjamin R. Curtis (1851–1857)
28. John A. Campbell (1853–1861)
29. Nathan Clifford (1858–1881)
30. Noah H. Swayne (1862–1881)
31. Samuel F. Miller (1862–1890)
32. David Davis (1862–1877)
33. Stephen J. Field (1863–1897)
34. William Strong (1870–1880)
35. Joseph P. Bradley (1870–1892)
36. Ward Hunt (1873–1882)
37. John Marshall Harlan (1877–1911)
38. William B. Woods (1881–1887)
39. Stanley Matthews (1881–1889)
40. Horace Gray (1882–1902)
41. Samuel Blatchford (1882–1893)
42. Lucius Q. C. Lamar (1888–1893)
43. David J. Brewer (1890–1910)
44. Henry B. Brown (1891–1906)
45. George Shiras Jr. (1892–1903)
46. Howell E. Jackson (1893–1895)
47. Rufus W. Peckham (1896–1909)
48. Joseph McKenna (1898–1925)
49. Oliver Wendell Holmes Jr. (1902–1932)
50. William R. Day (1903–1922)
51. William H. Moody (1906–1910)
52. Horace H. Lurton (1910–1914)
53. Willis Van Devanter (1911–1937)
54. Joseph Rucker Lamar (1911–1916)
55. Mahlon Pitney (1912–1922)
56. James Clark McReynolds (1914–1941)
57. Louis D. Brandeis (1916–1939)
58. John H. Clark (1916–1922)
59. George Sutherland (1922–1938)
60. Pierce Butler (1923–1939)
61. Edward T. Sanford (1923–1930)
62. Owen J. Roberts (1930–1945)
63. Benjamin Nathan Cardozo (1932–1938)
64. Hugo Black (1937–1971)
65. Stanley F. Reed (1938–1957)

66. Felix Frankfurter (1939–1962)
67. William O. Douglas (1939–1975)
68. Frank W. Murphy (1940–1949)
69. James F. Byrnes (1941–1942)
70. Robert H. Jackson (1941–1954)
71. Wiley B. Rutledge (1943–1949)
72. Harold H. Burton (1945–1958)
73. Tom C. Clark (1949–1967)
74. Sherman Minton (1949–1956)
75. William J. Brennan Jr. (1956–1990)
76. John Marshall Harlan II (1955–1971)
77. Charles E. Whittaker (1957–1962)
78. Potter Stewart (1958–1981)
79. Byron R. White (1962–1993)
80. Arthur J. Goldberg (1962–1965)
81. Abe Fortas (1965–1969)
82. Thurgood Marshall (1967–1991)
83. Harry A. Blackmun (1970–1994)
84. Lewis F. Powell Jr. (1972–1987)
85. Sandra Day O'Connor (1981–2005)

PRESIDENTIAL ELECTIONS AND VOTING

Year	Number of States	Candidates	Party	Popular Vote*	Electoral Vote†	Percentage of Popular Vote
1789	11	**George Washington**	No party designations		69	
		John Adams			34	
		Other Candidates			35	
1792	15	**George Washington**	No party designations		132	
		John Adams			77	
		George Clinton			50	
		Other Candidates			5	
1796	16	**John Adams**	Federalist		71	
		Thomas Jefferson	Democratic Republican		68	
		Thomas Pinckney	Federalist		59	
		Aaron Burr	Democratic Republican		30	
		Other Candidates			48	
1800	16	**Thomas Jefferson**	Democratic Republican		73	
		Aaron Burr	Democratic Republican		73	
		John Adams	Federalist		65	
		Charles C. Pinckney	Federalist		64	
		John Jay	Federalist		1	
1804	17	**Thomas Jefferson**	Democratic Republican		162	
		Charles C. Pinckney	Federalist		14	
1808	17	**James Madison**	Democratic Republican		122	
		Charles C. Pinckney	Federalist		47	
		George Clinton	Democratic Republican		6	
1812	18	**James Madison**	Democratic Republican		128	
		DeWitt Clinton	Federalist		89	
1816	19	**James Monroe**	Democratic Republican		183	
		Rufus King	Federalist		34	
1820	24	**James Monroe**	Democratic Republican		231	
		John Quincy Adams	Independent Republican		1	
1824	24	**John Quincy Adams**		108,740	84	30.5
		Andrew Jackson		153,544	99	43.1
		William H. Crawford		46,618	41	13.1
		Henry Clay		47,136	37	13.2
1828	24	**Andrew Jackson**	Democrat	647,286	178	56.0
		John Quincy Adams	National Republican	508,064	83	44.0
1832	24	**Andrew Jackson**	Democrat	687,502	219	55.0
		Henry Clay	National Republican	530,189	49	42.4
		William Wirt	Anti-Masonic		7	
		John Floyd	National Republican	33,108	11	2.6
1836	26	**Martin Van Buren**	Democrat	765,483	170	50.9
		William H. Harrison	Whig		73	
		Hugh L. White	Whig		26	
		Daniel Webster	Whig	739,795	14	49.1
		W. P. Mangum	Whig		11	
1840	26	**William H. Harrison**	Whig	1,274,624	234	53.1
		Martin Van Buren	Democrat	1,127,781	60	46.9

(continued on page A-12)

PRESIDENTIAL ELECTIONS AND VOTING

Year	Number of States	Candidates	Party	Popular Vote*	Electoral Vote†	Percentage of Popular Vote
1844	26	**James K. Polk**	Democrat	1,338,464	170	49.6
		Henry Clay	Whig	1,300,097	105	48.1
		James G. Birney	Liberty	62,300		2.3
1848	30	**Zachary Taylor**	Whig	1,360,967	163	47.4
		Lewis Cass	Democrat	1,222,342	127	42.5
		Martin Van Buren	Free Soil	291,263		10.1
1852	31	**Franklin Pierce**	Democrat	1,601,117	254	50.9
		Winfield Scott	Whig	1,385,453	42	44.1
		John P. Hale	Free Soil	155,825		5.0
1856	31	**James Buchanan**	Democrat	1,832,955	174	45.3
		John C. Frémont	Republican	1,339,932	114	33.1
		Millard Fillmore	American ("Know Nothing")	871,731	8	21.6
1860	33	**Abraham Lincoln**	Republican	1,865,593	180	39.8
		Stephen A. Douglas	Democrat	1,382,713	12	29.5
		John C. Breckinridge	Democrat	848,356	72	18.1
		John Bell	Constitutional Union	592,906	39	12.6
1864	36	**Abraham Lincoln**	Republican	2,206,938	212	55.0
		George B. McClellan	Democrat	1,803,787	21	45.0
1868	37	**Ulysses S. Grant**	Republican	3,013,421	214	52.7
		Horatio Seymour	Democrat	2,706,829	80	47.3
1872	37	**Ulysses S. Grant**	Republican	3,596,745	286	55.6
		Horace Greeley	Democrat	2,843,446	*	43.9
1876	38	**Rutherford B. Hayes**	Republican	4,036,572	185	48.0
		Samuel J. Tilden	Democrat	4,284,020	184	51.0
1880	38	**James A. Garfield**	Republican	4,453,295	214	48.5
		Winfield S. Hancock	Democrat	4,414,082	155	48.1
		James B. Weaver	Greenback-Labor	308,578		3.4
1884	38	**Grover Cleveland**	Democrat	4,879,507	219	48.5
		James G. Blaine	Republican	4,850,293	182	48.2
		Benjamin F. Butler	Greenback-Labor	175,370		1.8
		John P. St. John	Prohibition	150,369		1.5
1888	38	**Benjamin Harrison**	Republican	5,447,129	233	47.9
		Grover Cleveland	Democrat	5,537,857	168	48.6
		Clinton B. Fisk	Prohibition	249,506		2.2
		Alson J. Streeter	Union Labor	146,935		1.3
1892	44	**Grover Cleveland**	Democrat	5,555,426	277	46.1
		Benjamin Harrison	Republican	5,182,690	145	43.0
		James B. Weaver	People's	1,029,846	22	8.5
		John Bidwell	Prohibition	264,133		2.2
1896	45	**William McKinley**	Republican	7,102,246	271	51.1
		William J. Bryan	Democrat	6,492,559	176	47.7
1900	45	**William McKinley**	Republican	7,218,491	292	51.7
		William J. Bryan	Democrat; Populist	6,356,734	155	45.5
		John C. Woolley	Prohibition	208,914		1.5

PRESIDENTIAL ELECTIONS AND VOTING

Year	Number of States	Candidates	Party	Popular Vote*	Electoral Vote†	Percentage of Popular Vote
1904	45	**Theodore Roosevelt**	Republican	7,628,461	336	57.4
		Alton B. Parker	Democrat	5,084,223	140	37.6
		Eugene V. Debs	Socialist	402,283		3.0
		Silas C. Swallow	Prohibition	258,536		1.9
1908	46	**William H. Taft**	Republican	7,675,320	321	51.6
		William J. Bryan	Democrat	6,412,294	162	43.1
		Eugene V. Debs	Socialist	420,793		2.8
		Eugene W. Chafin	Prohibition	253,840		1.7
1912	48	**Woodrow Wilson**	Democrat	6,296,547	435	41.9
		Theodore Roosevelt	Progressive	4,118,571	88	27.4
		William H. Taft	Republican	3,486,720	8	23.2
		Eugene V. Debs	Socialist	900,672		6.0
		Eugene W. Chafin	Prohibition	206,275		1.4
1916	48	**Woodrow Wilson**	Democrat	9,127,695	277	49.4
		Charles E. Hughes	Republican	8,533,507	254	46.2
		A. L. Benson	Socialist	585,113		3.2
		J. Frank Hanly	Prohibition	220,506		1.2
1920	48	**Warren G. Harding**	Republican	16,143,407	404	60.4
		James M. Cox	Democrat	9,130,328	127	34.2
		Eugene V. Debs	Socialist	919,799		3.4
		P. P. Christensen	Farmer-Labor	265,411		1.0
1924	48	**Calvin Coolidge**	Republican	15,718,211	382	54.0
		John W. Davis	Democrat	8,385,283	136	28.8
		Robert M. La Follette	Progressive	4,831,289	13	16.6
1928	48	**Herbert C. Hoover**	Republican	21,391,993	444	58.2
		Alfred E. Smith	Democrat	15,016,169	87	40.9
1932	48	**Franklin D. Roosevelt**	Democrat	22,809,638	472	57.4
		Herbert C. Hoover	Republican	15,758,901	59	39.7
		Norman Thomas	Socialist	881,951		2.2
1936	48	**Franklin D. Roosevelt**	Democrat	27,752,869	523	60.8
		Alfred M. Landon	Republican	16,674,665	8	36.5
		William Lemke	Union	882,479		1.9
1940	48	**Franklin D. Roosevelt**	Democrat	27,307,819	449	54.8
		Wendell L. Willkie	Republican	22,321,018	82	44.8
1944	48	**Franklin D. Roosevelt**	Democrat	25,606,585	432	53.5
		Thomas E. Dewey	Republican	22,014,745	99	46.0
1948	48	**Harry S Truman**	Democrat	24,105,812	303	49.5
		Thomas E. Dewey	Republican	21,970,065	189	45.1
		J. Strom Thurmond	States' Rights	1,169,063	39	2.4
		Henry A. Wallace	Progressive	1,157,172		2.4
1952	48	**Dwight D. Eisenhower**	Republican	33,936,234	442	55.1
		Adlai E. Stevenson	Democrat	27,314,992	89	44.4
1956	48	**Dwight D. Eisenhower**	Republican	35,590,472	457*	57.6
		Adlai E. Stevenson	Democrat	26,022,752	73	42.1

(continued on page A-14)

PRESIDENTIAL ELECTIONS AND VOTING

Year	Number of States	Candidates	Party	Popular Vote*	Electoral Vote†	Percentage of Popular Vote
1960	50	John F. Kennedy	Democrat	34,227,096	303†	49.9
		Richard M. Nixon	Republican	34,108,546	219	49.6
1964	50	Lyndon B. Johnson	Democrat	42,676,220	486	61.3
		Barry M. Goldwater	Republican	26,860,314	52	38.5
1968	50	Richard M. Nixon	Republican	31,785,480	301	43.4
		Hubert H. Humphrey	Democrat	31,275,165	191	42.7
		George C. Wallace	American Independent	9,906,473	46	13.5
1972	50	Richard M. Nixon‡	Republican	47,165,234	520	60.6
		George S. McGovern	Democrat	29,168,110	17	37.5
1976	50	Jimmy Carter	Democrat	40,828,929	297	50.1
		Gerald R. Ford	Republican	39,148,940	240	47.9
		Eugene McCarthy	Independent	739,256		0.9
1980	50	Ronald Reagan	Republican	43,201,220	489	50.9
		Jimmy Carter	Democrat	34,913,332	49	41.2
		John B. Anderson	Independent	5,581,379		6.6
1984	50	Ronald Reagan	Republican	53,428,357	525	59.0
		Walter F. Mondale	Democrat	36,930,923	13	41.0
1988	50	George H. W. Bush	Republican	48,901,046	426	53.4
		Michael Dukakis	Democrat	41,809,030	111	45.6
1992	50	Bill Clinton	Democrat	43,728,275	370	43.2
		George Bush	Republican	38,167,416	168	37.7
		H. Ross Perot	United We Stand, America	19,237,247		19.0
1996	50	Bill Clinton	Democrat	45,590,703	379	49.0
		Bob Dole	Republican	37,816,307	159	41.0
		H. Ross Perot	Reform	7,866,284		8.0
2000	50	George W. Bush	Republican	50,456,169	271	48.0
		Al Gore	Democrat	50,996,116	266	48.0
		Ralph Nader	Green	2,767,176	0	3.0
2004	50	George W. Bush	Republican	62,040,606	286	50.7
		John Kerry	Democrat	59,028,109	251	48.3
		Ralph Nader	Independent	411,304	0	1.0

*Percentage of popular vote given for any election year may not total 100 percent because candidates receiving less than 1 percent of the popular vote have been omitted.

†Prior to the passage of the Twelfth Amendment in 1904, the electoral college voted for two presidential candidates; the runner-up became Vice President. Data from Historical Statistics of the United States, Colonial Times to 1957 (1961), pp. 682–683, and The World Almanac.

*Because of the death of Greeley, Democratic electors scattered their votes.

*Walter B. Jones received 1 electoral vote.

†Harry F. Byrd received 15 electoral votes.

‡Resigned August 9, 1974: Vice President Gerald R. Ford became President.

PARTY CONTROL OF CONGRESS

Congress	Years	Party and President	Senate DEM.	REP.	OTHER	House DEM.	REP.	OTHER
57th	1901–03	R T. Roosevelt	29	56	3	153	198	5
58th	1903–05	R T. Roosevelt	32	58	—	178	207	—
59th	1905–07	R T. Roosevelt	32	58	—	136	250	—
60th	1907–09	R T. Roosevelt	29	61	—	164	222	—
61st	1909–11	R Taft	32	59	—	172	219	—
62d	1911–13	R Taft	42	49	—	228	162	1
63d	1913–15	D Wilson	51	44	1	290	127	18
64th	1915–17	D Wilson	56	39	1	230	193	8
65th	1917–19	D Wilson	53	42	1	200	216	9
66th	1919–21	D Wilson	48	48	1	191	237	7
67th	1921–23	R Harding	37	59	—	132	300	1
68th	1923–25	R Coolidge	43	51	2	207	225	3
69th	1925–27	R Coolidge	40	54	1	183	247	5
70th	1927–29	R Coolidge	47	48	1	195	237	3
71st	1929–31	R Hoover	39	56	1	163	267	1
72d	1931–33	R Hoover	47	48	1	216	218	1
73d	1933–35	D F. Roosevelt	59	36	1	313	117	5
74th	1935–37	D F. Roosevelt	69	25	2	322	103	10
75th	1937–39	D F. Roosevelt	75	17	4	333	89	13
76th	1939–41	D F. Roosevelt	69	23	4	262	169	4
77th	1941–43	D F. Roosevelt	66	28	2	267	162	6
78th	1943–45	D F. Roosevelt	57	38	1	222	209	4
79th	1945–47	D Truman	57	38	1	243	190	2
80th	1947–49	D Truman	45	51	—	188	246	1
81st	1949–51	D Truman	54	42	—	263	171	1
82d	1951–53	D Truman	48	47	1	234	199	2
83d	1953–55	R Eisenhower	47	48	1	213	221	1
84th	1955–57	R Eisenhower	48	47	1	232	203	—
85th	1957–59	R Eisenhower	49	47	—	234	201	—
86th	1959–61	R Eisenhower	64	34	—	283	154	—
87th	1961–63	D Kennedy	64	36	—	263	174	—
88th	1963–65	D { Kennedy / Johnson	67	33	—	258	176	—
89th	1965–67	D Johnson	68	32	—	295	140	—
90th	1967–69	D Johnson	64	36	—	248	187	—
91st	1969–71	R Nixon	58	42	—	243	192	—
92d	1971–73	R Nixon	55	45	—	255	180	—
93d	1973–75	R { Nixon / Ford	57	43	—	243	192	—
94th	1975–77	R Ford	61	38	—	291	144	—
95th	1977–79	D Carter	62	38	—	292	143	—
96th	1979–81	D Carter	59	41	—	277	158	—
97th	1981–83	R Reagan	47	53	—	243	192	—
98th	1983–85	R Reagan	46	54	—	269	166	—
99th	1985–87	R Reagan	47	53	—	253	182	—
100th	1987–89	R Reagan	55	45	—	258	177	—
101st	1989–91	R Bush	55	45	—	260	175	—
102d	1991–93	R Bush	57	43	—	267	167	1
103d	1993–95	D Clinton	59	43	—	258	176	1
104th	1995–97	D Clinton	46	54	—	204	230	1
105th	1997–99	D Clinton	45	55	—	207	227	1
106th	1999–01	D Clinton	45	55	—	211	223	1
107th	2001–03	R Bush	50	50	—	212	221	2
108th	2003–05	R Bush	49[a]	51	—	206	228	1
109th	2005–07	R Bush	45[a]	55	—	202	230	1
110th	2007–09	R Bush	51[b]	49	—	230	205	—

[a]Including Vermont independent Jim Jeffords.
[b]Including Vermont independent Bernie Sanders and Connecticut independent Joe Lieberman.

GLOSSARY

ABM Treaty Treaty in 1972 between the U.S. and the Soviet Union in which each side agreed not to build or deploy antiballistic missiles.

abolition movement Social movement before the Civil War whose goal was to abolish slavery throughout the United States.

access Meeting and talking with decision makers, a prerequisite to direct persuasion.

adjudication Decision making by the federal bureaucracy as to whether or not an individual or organization has complied with or violated government laws and/or regulation.

adversarial system Method of decision making in which an impartial judge or jury or decision maker hears arguments and reviews evidence presented by opposite sides.

advice and consent The constitutional power of the U.S. Senate to reject or ratify (by a two-thirds vote) treaties made by the president.

affirmative action Any program, whether enacted by a government or by a private organization, whose goal is to overcome the results of past unequal treatment of minorities and/or women by giving members of these groups preferential treatment in admissions, hiring, promotions, or other aspects of life.

affirmative racial gerrymandering Drawing district boundary lines to maximize minority representation.

agenda setting Deciding what will be decided, defining the problems and issues to be addressed by decision makers.

amendment Formal change in a bill, law, or constitution.

amicus curiae Literally, "friend of the court"; a person, private group or institution, or government agency that is not a party to a case but participates in the case (usually through submission of a brief) at the invitation of the court or on its own initiative.

Anti-Federalists Those who opposed the ratification of the U.S. Constitution and the creation of a strong national government.

appeal In general, requests that a higher court review cases decided at a lower level. In the Supreme Court, certain cases are designated as appeals under federal law; formally, these must be heard by the Court.

appellate jurisdiction Particular court's power to review a decision or action of a lower court.

apportionment The allocation of legislative seats to jurisdictions based on population. Seats in the U.S. House of Representatives are apportioned to the states on the basis of their population after every ten-year census.

appropriations act Congressional bill that provides money for programs authorized by Congress.

authoritarianism Monopoly of political power by an individual or small group that otherwise allows people o go about their private lives as they wish.

authorization Act of Congress that establishes a government program and defines the amount of money it may spend.

backdoor spending Spending by agencies of the federal government whose operations are not included in the federal budget.

bail Release of an accused person from custody in exchange for promise to appear at trial, guaranteed by money or property that is forfeited to court if defendant does not appear.

***Bakke* case** U.S. Supreme Court case challenging affirmative action.

balanced budget Government budget in which expenditures and revenues are equal, so that no deficit or surplus exists.

ballistic missile defense (BMD) Weapons systems capable of detecting, intercepting, and destroying missiles in flight.

beliefs Shared ideas about what is true.

bicameral Any legislative body that consists of two separate chambers or houses; in the United States, the Senate represents 50 statewide voter constituencies, and the House of Representatives represents voters in 435 separate districts.

big-state strategy Presidential political campaign strategy in which a candidate focuses on winning primaries in large states because of their high delegate counts.

bill of attainder Legislative act inflicting punishment without judicial trial; forbidden under Article I of the Constitution.

Bill of Rights Written guarantees of basic individual liberties; the first ten amendments to the U.S. Constitution.

bipartisanship Agreement by members of both the Democratic and the Republican parties.

bloc Group of legislators who act together for a common goal regardless of party affiliation.

bribery Giving or offering anything of value in an effort to influence government officials in the performance of their duties.

briefs Documents submitted by an attorney to a court, setting out the facts of the case and the legal arguments in support of the party represented by the attorney.

budget maximization Bureaucrats' tendencies to expand their agencies' budgets, staff, and authority.

budget resolution Congressional bill setting forth target budget figures for appropriations to various government departments and agencies.

bureaucracy Departments, agencies, bureaus, and offices that perform the functions of government.

cabinet The heads (secretaries) of the executive departments together with other top officials accorded cabinet rank by the president; only occasionally does it meet as a body to advise and support the president.

campaign strategy Plan for a political campaign, usually including a theme, an attempt to define the opponent or the issues, and an effort to coordinate images and messages in news broadcasts and paid advertising.

capital gains Profits from buying and selling property including stocks, bonds, and real estate.

capitalism Economic system asserting the individual's right to own private property and to buy, sell, rent, and trade that property in a free market.

capture theory of regulation Theory describing how some regulated industries come to benefit from government regulation and how some regulatory commissions come to represent the industries they are supposed to regulate rather than representing "the people."

careerism In politics, a reference to people who started young working in politics, running for and holding public office, and made politics their career.

casework Services performed by legislators or their staff on behalf of individual constituents.

caucus Nominating process in which party leaders select the party's nominee.

censure Public reprimand for wrongdoing, given to a member standing in the chamber before Congress.

centralized federalism Model of federalism in which the national government assumes primary responsibility for determining national goals in all major policy areas and directs state and local government activity through conditions attached to money grants.

chain of command Hierarchical structure of authority in which command flows downward; typical of a bureaucracy.

challengers In politics, a reference to people running against incumbent officeholders.

checks and balances Constitutional provisions giving each branch of the national government certain checks over the actions of other branches.

circuit courts The twelve appellate courts that make up the middle level of the federal court system.

civil cases Noncriminal court proceedings in which a plaintiff sues a defendant for damages in payment for harm inflicted.

civil disobedience Form of public protest involving the breaking of laws believed to be unjust.

class action suits Cases initiated by parties acting on behalf of themselves and all others similarly situated.

class conflict Conflict between upper and lower social classes over wealth and power.

class consciousness Awareness of one's class position and a feeling of political solidarity with others within the same class in opposition to other classes.

classical liberalism Political philosophy asserting the worth and dignity of the individual and emphasizing the rational ability of human beings to determine their own destinies.

clear and present danger doctrine Standard used by the courts to determine whether speech may be restricted; only speech that creates a serious and immediate danger to society may be restricted.

closed primaries Primary elections in which voters must declare (or have previously declared) their party affiliation and can cast a ballot only in their own party's primary election.

closed rule Rule that forbids adding any amendments to a bill under consideration by the House.

cloture Vote to end debate—that is, to end a filibuster—which requires a three-fifths vote of the entire membership of the Senate.

coalition A joining together of interest groups (or individuals) to achieve a common goal.

COLAs Annual cost-of-living adjustments mandated by law in Social Security and other welfare benefits.

Cold War Political, military, and ideological struggle between the United States and the Soviet Union following the end of World War II and ending with the collapse of the Soviet Union's communist government in 1991.

collective security Attempt to bring order to international relations by all nations joining together to guarantee each other's "territorial integrity" and "independence" against "external aggression."

commercial speech Advertising communications given only partial protection under the First Amendment to the Constitution.

common market Unified trade area in which all goods and services can be sold or exchanged free from customs or tariffs.

communism System of government in which a single totalitarian party controls all means of production and distribution of goods and services.

comparable worth Argument that pay levels for traditionally male and traditionally female jobs should be equalized by paying equally all jobs that are "worth about the same" to an employer.

concurrent powers Powers exercised by both the national government and state governments in the American federal system.

concurring opinion Opinion by a member of a court that agrees with the result reached by the court in the case but disagrees with or departs from the court's rationale for the decision.

confederation Constitutional arrangement whereby the national government is created by and relies on subnational governments for its authority.

conference committee Meeting between representatives of the House and Senate to reconcile differences over provisions of a bill passed by both houses.

confirmation The constitutionally required consent of the Senate to appointments of high-level executive officials by the president and appointments of federal judges.

congressional hearings Congressional committee sessions in which members listen to witnesses who provide information and opinions on matters of interest to the committee, including pending legislation.

congressional investigation Congressional committee hearings on alleged misdeeds or scandals.

congressional session Each Congress elected in November of even-numbered years meets the following January 3 and remains in session for two years. Since the first Congress to meet under the Constitution in 1789, Congresses have been numbered by session (for example,

107th Congress 2001–2003, 108th Congress 2003–2005, 109th Congress 2005–2007).

conservatism Belief in the value of free markets, limited government, and individual self-reliance in economic affairs, combined with a belief in the value of tradition, law, and morality in social affairs.

constituency The votes in a legislator's home district.

constitution The legal structure of a political system, establishing governmental bodies, granting their powers, determining how their members are selected, and prescribing the rules by which they make their decisions. Considered basic or fundamental, a constitution cannot be changed by ordinary acts of governmental bodies.

constitutionalism A government of laws, not people, operating on the principle that governmental power must be limited and government officials should be restrained in their exercise of power over individuals.

containment Policy of preventing an enemy from expanding its boundaries and/or influence, specifically the U.S. foreign policy vis-à-vis the Soviet Union during the Cold War.

contingency fees Fees paid to attorneys to represent the plaintiff in a civil suit and receive in compensation an agreed-upon percentage of damages awarded (if any).

continuing resolution Congressional bill that authorizes government agencies to keep spending money for a specified period at the same level as in the previous fiscal year; passed when Congress is unable to enact final appropriations measures by October 1.

convention Nominating process in which delegates from local party organizations select the party's nominees.

cooperative federalism Model of federalism in which national, state, and local governments work together exercising common policy responsibilities.

council-manager Form of city government in which policy is set by an elected city council, which hires a professional city manager to head the daily administration of city government.

council of government (COG) Council comprised of representatives of other governments in a defined region of the state.

covert action Secret intelligence activity outside U.S. borders undertaken with specific authorization by the president; acknowledgment of U.S. sponsorship would defeat or compromise its purpose.

Cuban Missile Crisis The 1962 confrontation between the Soviet Union and the U.S. over Soviet placement of nuclear missiles in Cuba.

de facto segregation Racial imbalances not directly caused by official actions but rather by residential patterns.

dealignment Declining attractiveness of the parties to the voters, a reluctance to identify strongly with a party, and a decrease in reliance on party affiliation in voter choice.

deductibles Initial charges in insurance plans, paid by beneficiaries.

defendants Parties against whom a criminal or civil suit is brought.

deferrals Items on which a president wishes to postpone spending.

deficit Imbalance in the annual federal budget in which spending exceeds revenues.

delegated, or enumerated, powers Powers specifically mentioned in the Constitution as belonging to the national government.

delegates Accredited voting members of a party's national presidential nominating convention.

democracy Governing system in which the people govern themselves, from the Greek term meaning "rule by the many."

democratic ideals Individual dignity, equality before the law, widespread participation in public decisions, and public decisions by majority rule, with one person having one vote.

Democratic Leadership Council Organization of party leaders who sought to create a "new" Democratic Party to appeal to middle-class, moderate voters.

Democratic Party One of the main parties in American politics; it traces its origins to Thomas Jefferson's Democratic-Republican Party, acquiring its current name under Andrew Jackson in 1828.

dependency ratio In the Social Security system, the number of recipients as a percentage of the number of contributing workers.

deregulation Lifting of government rules and bureaucratic supervision from business and professional activity.

deterrence U.S. approach to deterring any nuclear attack from the Soviet Union by maintaining a second-strike capability.

devolution Passing down of responsibilities from the national government to the states.

diplomatic recognition Power of the president to grant "legitimacy" to or withhold it from a government of another nation (to declare or refuse to declare it "rightful").

direct democracy Governing system in which every person participates actively in every public decision, rather than delegating decision making to representatives.

direct discrimination Now illegal practice of differential pay for men versus women even when those individuals have equal qualifications and perform the same job.

discharge petition Petition signed by at least 218 House members to force a vote on a bill within a committee that opposes it.

discretionary funds Budgeted funds not earmarked for specific purposes but available to be spent in accordance with the best judgment of a bureaucrat.

discretionary spending Spending for programs not previously mandated by law.

dissenting opinion Opinion by a member of a court that disagrees with the result reached by the court in the case.

district court Primary trial court in Texas. It has jurisdiction over criminal felony cases and civil disputes.

diversity Term in higher education that refers to racial and ethnic representation among students and faculty.

divided party government One party controls the presidency while the other party controls one or both houses of Congress.

division of labor Division of work among many specialized workers in a bureaucracy.

division votes Votes taken on the computerized voting boards in the Texas house but erased without being permanently recorded.

drafting a bill Actual writing of a bill in legal language.

dual federalism Early concept of federalism in which national and state powers were clearly distinguished and functionally separate.

Earned Income Tax Credit (EITC) Tax refunds in excess of tax payments for low-income workers.

economic cycles Fluctuations in real GDP growth followed by contraction.

Electoral College The 538 presidential electors apportioned among the states according to their congressional representation (plus 3 for the District of Columbia) whose votes officially elect the president and vice president of the United States.

elitism Political system in which power is concentrated in the hands of a relatively small group of individuals or institutions.

Emancipation Proclamation Lincoln's 1862 Civil War declaration that all slaves residing in rebel states were free. It did not abolish all slavery; that would be done by the Thirteenth Amendment.

end of history The collapse of communism and the worldwide movement toward free markets and political democracy.

entitlement programs Social welfare programs that provide classes of people with legally enforceable rights to benefits.

entitlements Any social welfare program for which there are eligibility requirements, whether financial or contributory.

enumerated powers Powers specifically mentioned in the Constitution as belonging to the national government.

Equal Rights Amendment (ERA) Proposed amendment to the Constitution guaranteeing that equal rights under the law shall not be denied or abridged on account of sex. Passed by Congress in 1972, the amendment failed to win ratification by three of the necessary three-fourths of the states.

equality of opportunity Elimination of artificial barriers to success in life and the opportunity for everyone to strive for success.

equality of results Equal sharing of income and material goods regardless of one's efforts in life.

equal-time rule Federal Communications Commission (FCC) requirement that broadcasters who sell time to any political candidate must make equal time available to opposing candidates at the same price.

ex post facto law Retroactive criminal law that works against the accused; forbidden under Article I of the Constitution.

exclusionary rule Rule of law that evidence found in an illegal search or resulting from an illegally obtained confession may not be admitted at trial.

executive agreement Agreement with another nation signed by the president of the United States but less formal (and hence potentially less binding) than a treaty because it does not require Senate confirmation.

executive order Formal regulation governing executive branch operations issued by the president.

executive privilege Right of a president to withhold from other branches of government confidential communications within the executive branch; although posited by presidents, it has been upheld by the Supreme Court only in limited situations.

externalities Costs imposed on people who are not direct participants in an activity.

extremism Rejection of democratic politics and the assertion of the supremacy of the "people" over laws, institutions, and individual rights.

Fair Deal Policies of President Harry Truman extending Roosevelt's New Deal and maintaining the Democratic Party's voter coalition.

Family Assistance Public assistance program that provides monies to the states for their use in helping needy families with children.

fascism Political ideology in which the state and/or race is assumed to be supreme over individuals.

Federal Election Commission (FEC) Agency charged with enforcing federal election laws and disbursing public presidential campaign funds.

Federal Reserve Board (the Fed) Independent agency of the executive branch of the federal government charged with overseeing the nation's monetary policy.

federalism A constitutional arrangement whereby power is divided between national and subnational governments, each of which enforces its own laws directly on its citizens and neither of which can alter the arrangement without the consent of the other.

Federalists Those who supported the U.S. Constitution during the ratification process and who later formed a political party in support of John Adams's presidential candidacy.

"feeding frenzy" Intense media coverage of a scandal or event that blocks out most other news.

filibuster Delaying tactic by a senator or group of senators, using the Senate's unlimited debate rule to prevent a vote on a bill.

first reading Introduction of a bill in the house or the senate and its referral to a committee by the presiding officer.

fiscal policy Economic policies involving taxing, spending, and deficit levels of the national government.

fiscal year Yearly government accounting period, not necessarily the same as the calendar year. The federal government's fiscal year begins October 1 and ends September 30.

focus group In a political context, a small number of people brought together in a comfortable setting to discuss and respond to themes and issues, allowing campaign managers to develop and analyze strategies.

Food Stamp Program Public assistance program that provides low-income households with coupons redeemable for enough food to provide a minimal nutritious diet.

franking privilege Free use of the U.S. mails granted to members of Congress to promote communication with constituents.

Free Exercise Clause Clause in the First Amendment to the Constitution that prohibits government from restricting religious beliefs and practices.

free market Free competition for voluntary exchange among individuals, firms, and corporations.

free-riders People who do not belong to an organization or pay dues, yet nevertheless benefit from its activities.

free trade A policy of reducing or eliminating tariffs and quotas on imports to stimulate international trade.

freedom of expression Collectively, the First Amendment rights to free speech, press, and assembly.

front-end strategy Presidential political campaign strategy in which a candidate focuses on winning early primaries to build momentum.

front loading The scheduling of presidential primary elections early in the year.

gender gap Aggregate differences in political opinions of men and women.

general election Election to choose among candidates nominated by parties and/or independent candidates who gained access to the ballot by petition.

generation gap Differences in politics and public opinion among age groups.

gerrymandering Drawing district boundary lines for political advantage.

glass ceiling "Invisible" barriers to women rising to the highest positions in corporations and the professions.

GOP "Grand Old Party"—popular label for the Republican Party.

government Organization extending to the whole society that can legitimately use force to carry out its decisions.

government bonds Certificates of indebtedness that pay interest and promise repayment on a future date.

grand jury Jury charged only with determining whether sufficient evidence exists to support indictment of an individual on a felony charge; the grand jury's decision to indict does not represent a conviction.

grant of immunity from prosecution Grant by the government to an individual of freedom from prosecution on a particular charge in return for testimony by that individual that might otherwise be self-incriminating.

grants-in-aid Payments of funds from the national government to state or local governments or from a state government to local governments for specific purposes.

grass-roots lobbying Attempts to influence government decision making by inspiring constituents to contact their representatives.

Great Society Policies of President Lyndon Johnson that promised to solve the nation's social and economic problems through government intervention.

gridlock Political stalemate between the executive and legislative branches arising when one branch is controlled by one major political party and the other branch by the other party.

gross domestic product (GDP) Measure of economic performance in terms of the nation's total production of goods and services for a single year, valued in terms of market prices.

halo effect Tendency of survey respondents to provide socially acceptable answers to questions.

health maintenance organizations (HMOs) Health care provider groups that provide a stipulated list of services to patients for a fixed fee that is usually substantially lower than such care would otherwise cost.

home rule Power of local government to pass laws affecting local affairs, so long as those laws do not conflict with state or federal laws.

home style Activities of Congress members specifically directed at their home constituencies.

honeymoon period Early months of a president's term in which his popularity with the public and influence with the Congress are generally high.

horse-race coverage Media coverage of electoral campaigns that concentrates on who is ahead and who is behind, and neglects the issues at stake.

ideological organizations Interest groups that pursue ideologically based (liberal or conservative) agendas.

ideological party Third party that exists to promote an ideology rather than to win elections.

ideology Consistent and integrated system of ideas, values, and beliefs.

impeachment Equivalent of a criminal charge against an elected official; removal of the impeached official from office depends on the outcome of a trial.

impersonality Treatment of all persons within a bureaucracy on the basis of "merit" and of all "clients" served by the bureaucracy equally according to rules.

implementation Development by the federal bureaucracy of procedures and activities to carry out policies legislated by Congress; it includes regulation as well as adjudication.

implied powers Powers not mentioned specifically in the Constitution as belonging to Congress but inferred as necessary and proper for carrying out the enumerated powers.

impoundment Refusal by a president to spend monies appropriated by Congress; outlawed except with congressional consent by the Budget and Impoundment Control Act of 1974.

incidence Actual bearer of a tax burden.

income transfers Government transfers of income from taxpayers to persons regarded as deserving.

incorporation In constitutional law, the application of almost all of the Bill of Rights to the states and all of their subdivision through the Fourteenth Amendment.

incremental budgeting Method of budgeting that focuses on requested increases in funding for existing programs, accepting as legitimate their previous year's expenditures.

incumbent Candidate currently in office seeking reelection.

incumbent gerrymandering Drawing legislative district boundaries to advantage incumbent legislators.

independent counsel ("special prosecutor") A prosecutor appointed by a federal court to pursue charges against a president or other high official. This position was allowed to lapse by Congress in 1999 after many controversial investigations by these prosecutors.

indexing Tying of benefit levels in social welfare programs to the general price level.

indictment Determination by a grand jury that sufficient evidence exists to warrant trial of an individual on a felony charge; necessary before an individual can be brought to trial.

individual income tax Taxes on individuals' wages and other earned income, the primary source of revenue for the U.S. federal government.

inflation Rise in the general level of prices; not just the prices of some products.

information Document formally charging a person with a misdemeanor.

information overload Situation in which individuals are subjected to so many communications that they cannot make sense of them.

in-kind (noncash) benefits Benefits of a social welfare program that are not cash payments, including free medical care, subsidized housing, and food stamps.

interest group Organization seeking to influence government policy.

interest-group entrepreneurs Leaders who create organizations and market memberships.

intergovernmental relations Network of political, financial, and administrative relationships between units of the federal government and those of state and local governments.

international trade The buying and selling of goods and services between individuals or firms located in different countries.

iron triangles Mutually supportive relationships among interest groups, government agencies, and legislative committees with jurisdiction over a specific policy area.

issue ads Ads that advocate policy positions rather than explicitly supporting or opposing particular candidates.

Jim Crow Second-class-citizen status conferred on blacks by Southern segregation laws; derived from a nineteenth-century song-and-dance act (usually performed by a white man in blackface) that stereotyped blacks.

judicial activism Making of new law through judicial interpretations of the Constitution.

judicial review Power of the courts, especially the Supreme Court, to declare laws of Congress, laws of the states, and actions of the president unconstitutional and invalid.

judicial self-restraint Self-imposed limitation on judicial power by judges deferring to the policy judgments of elected branches of government.

jurisdiction Power of a court to hear a case in question.

Korean War Communist North Korea invaded non-Communist South Korea in June, 1950, causing President Harry S Truman to intervene militarily, with U.N. support. General Douglas MacArthur defeated the North Koreans, but with China's entry into the war, a stalemate resulted. An armistice was signed in 1953, with Korea divided along nearly original lines.

laboratories of democracy A reference to the ability of states to experiment and innovate in public policy.

left A reference to the liberal, progressive, and/or socialist side of the political spectrum.

legitimacy Widespread acceptance of something as necessary, rightful, and legally binding.

Lemon test To be constitutional, a law must have a secular purpose; its primary effect must neither advance nor inhibit religion; and it must not foster excessive government entanglement with religion.

Leninism The theories of Vladimir Lenin, among them that advanced capitalist countries turned toward war and colonialism to make their own workers relatively prosperous.

libel Writings that are false and malicious and are intended to damage an individual.

liberalism Belief in the value of strong government to provide economic security and protection for civil rights, combined with a belief in personal freedom from government intervention in social conduct.

libertarian Opposing government intervention in both economic and social affairs, and favoring minimal government in all sectors of society.

limited government Principle that government power over the individual is limited, that there are some personal liberties that even a majority cannot regulate, and that government itself is restrained by law.

line-item veto Power of the chief executive to reject some portions of a bill without rejecting all of it.

literacy test Examination of a person's ability to read and write as a prerequisite to voter registration, outlawed by Voting Rights Act (1965) as discriminatory.

litigation Legal dispute brought before a court.

litmus test In political terms, a person's stand on a key issue that determines whether he or she will be appointed to public office or supported in electoral campaigns.

lobbying Activities directed at government officials with the hope of influencing their decisions.

lobbyist Person working to influence government policies and actions.

logrolling Bargaining for agreement among legislators to support each other's favorite bills, especially projects that primarily benefit individual members and their constituents.

machine Tightly disciplined party organization, headed by a boss, that relies on material rewards—including patronage jobs—to control politics.

majoritarianism Tendency of democratic governments to allow the faint preferences of the majority to prevail over the intense feelings of minorities.

majority Election by more than 50 percent of all votes cast in the contest.

majority leader In the House, the majority-party leader and second in command to the Speaker; in the Senate, the leader of the majority party.

majority opinion Opinion in a case that is subscribed to by a majority of the judges who participated in the decision.

malapportionment Unequal numbers of people in legislative districts resulting in inequality of voter representation.

managed care Programs designed to keep health care costs down by the establishment of strict guidelines regarding when and what diagnostic and therapeutic procedures should be administered to patients under various circumstances.

mandate Perception of popular support for a program or policy based on the margin of electoral victory won by a candidate who proposed it during a campaign; direct federal orders to state and local governments requiring them to perform a service or to obey federal laws in the performance of their functions.

mandatory spending Spending for program committments made by past congresses.

markup Line-by-line revision of a bill in committee by editing each phrase and word.

Marshall Plan U.S. program to rebuild the nations of Western Europe in the aftermath of World War II in order to render them less susceptible to communist influence and takeover.

Marxism The theories of Karl Marx, among them that capitalists oppress workers and that worldwide revolution and the emergence of a classless society are inevitable.

mass media All means of communication with the general public, including television, newspapers, magazines, radio, books, recordings, motion pictures, and the Internet.

means-tested spending Spending for benefits that is distributed on the basis of the recipient's income.

Medicaid Public assistance program that provides health care to the poor.

Medicare Social insurance program that provides health care insurance to elderly and disabled people.

merit system Selection of employees for government agencies on the basis of competence, with no consideration of an individual's political stance and/or power.

metro government Local government in which city and county governments consolidate to avoid duplication of public services.

minority leader In both the House and Senate, the leader of the opposition party.

Miranda warning Requirement that persons arrested be informed of their rights immediately after arrest.

mobilize In politics, to activate supporters to work for candidates and turn out on Election Day.

monetary policy Economic policies involving the money supply, interest rates, and banking activity.

"Motor Voter Act" Federal mandate that states offer voter registration at driver's licensing and welfare offices.

muckraking Journalistic exposés of corruption, wrongdoing, or mismanagement in government, business, and other institutions of society.

name recognition Public awareness of a candidate—whether they even know his or her name.

national debt Total debt accumulated by the national government over the years.

national health insurance Government-provided insurance to all citizens paid from tax revenues.

National Security Council (NSC) "Inner cabinet" that advises the president and coordinates foreign, defense, and intelligence activities.

National Supremacy Clause Clause in Article VI of the U.S. Constitution declaring the constitution and laws of the national government "the supreme law of the land" superior to the constitutions and laws of the states.

nationalism Belief that shared cultural, historical, linguistic, and social characteristics of a people justify the creation of a government encompassing all of them; the resulting nation-state should be independent and legally equal to all other nation-states.

Necessary and Proper Clause Clause in Article I, Section 8, of the U.S. Constitution granting Congress the power to enact all laws that are "necessary and proper" for carrying out those responsibilities specifically delegated to it. Also referred to as the Implied Powers Clause.

negative campaigning Speeches, commercials, or advertising attacking a political opponent during a campaign.

New Deal Policies of President Franklin D. Roosevelt during the depression of the 1930s that helped form a Democratic Party coalition of urban working-class, ethnic, Catholic, Jewish, poor, and Southern voters.

new federalism Attempts to return power and responsibility to the states and reduce the role of the national government in domestic affairs.

newsmaking Deciding what events, topics, presentations, and issues will be given coverage in the news.

No Establishment Clause Clause in the First Amendment to the Constitution that is interpreted to require the separation of church and state.

nomination Political party's selection of its candidate for a public office.

nominee Political party's entry in a general election race.

nonpartisan elections Elections in which candidates do not officially indicate their party affiliation; often used for city, country, school board, and judicial elections.

nonviolent direct action Strategy used by civil rights leaders such as Martin Luther King Jr., in which protesters break "unjust" laws openly but in a "loving" fashion in order to bring the injustices of such laws to public attention.

North Atlantic Treaty Organization (NATO) Mutual-security agreement and joint military command uniting the nations of Western Europe, initially formed to resist Soviet expansionism.

obligational authority Feature of some appropriations acts by which an agency is empowered to enter into contracts that will require the government to make payments beyond the fiscal year in question.

open primaries Primary elections in which a voter may cast a ballot in either party's primary election.

open rule Rule that permits unlimited amendments to a bill under consideration by the House.

open seat Seat in a legislature for which no incumbent is running for reelection.

organizational sclerosis Society encrusted with so many special benefits to interest groups that everyone's standard of living is lowered.

original intent Judicial philosophy under which judges attempt to apply the values of the Founders to current issues.

original jurisdiction Refers to a particular court's power to serve as the place where a given case is initially argued and decided.

outlays Actual dollar amounts to be spent by the federal government in a fiscal year.

override Voting in Congress to enact legislation vetoed by the president; requires a two-thirds vote in both the House and Senate.

oversight Congressional monitoring of the activities of executive branch agencies to determine if the laws are being faithfully executed.

packing Redistricting in which partisan voters are concentrated in a single district, "wasting" their majority vote and allowing the opposition to win by modest majorities in other districts.

paradox of democracy Potential for conflict between individual freedom and majority rule.

parole Early release of an inmate from prison, subject to certain conditions.

partial preemption Federal government's assumption of some regulatory powers in a particular field, with the stipulation that a state law on the same subject as a federal law is valid if it does not conflict with the federal law in the same area.

party identification Self-described identification with a political party, usually in response to the question, "Generally speaking, how would you identify yourself: as a Republican, Democrat, independent, or something else?"

party organization National and state party officials and workers, committee members, convention delegates, and others active in the party.

party-in-the-electorate Voters who identify themselves with a party.

party-in-the-government Public officials who were nominated by their party and who identify themselves in office with their party.

party polarization The tendency of the Democratic Party to take more liberal positions and the Republican Party to take more conservative positions on key issues.

party unity Percentage of Democrats and Republicans who stick with their party on party votes.

party vote Majority of Democrats voting in opposition to a majority of Republicans.

passport Evidence of U.S. citizenship, allowing people to travel abroad and reenter the United States.

patronage Appointment to public office based on party loyalty.

petit (regular) jury Panel of citizens that hears evidence in a civil lawsuit or a criminal prosecution and decides the outcome by issuing a verdict.

photo ops Staged opportunities for the media to photograph the candidate in a favorable setting.

plaintiffs Parties initiating suits and claiming damages. In criminal cases, the state acts as plaintiff on behalf of an injured society and requests fines and/or imprisonment as damages. In civil suits, the plaintiff is the injured party and seeks monetary damages.

platform Statement of principles adopted by a political party at its national convention (specific portions of the platform are known as planks); a platform is not binding on the party's candidates.

plea bargaining Practice of allowing defendants to plead guilty to lesser crimes than those with which they were originally charged in return for reduced sentences.

pluralism Theory that democracy can be achieved through competition among multiple organized groups and that individuals can participate in politics through group memberships and elections.

plurality Election by at least one vote more than any other candidate in the race.

pocket veto Effective veto of a bill when Congress adjourns within ten days of passing it and the president fails to sign it.

policy networks Interaction in a common policy area among lobbyists, elected officials, staff personnel, bureaucrats, journalists, and private-sector experts.

political action committees (PACs) Organizations that solicit and receive campaign contributions from corporations, unions, trade associations, and ideological and issue-oriented groups, and their members, then distribute these funds to political candidates.

political alienation Belief that politics is irrelevant to one's life and that one cannot personally affect public affairs.

political culture Widely shared views about who should govern, for what ends, and by what means.

political equality Belief that the law should apply equally to all and that every person's vote counts equally.

political organizations Parties and interest groups that function as intermediaries between individuals and government.

political parties Organizations that seek to achieve power by winning public office.

political science The study of politics: who governs, for what ends, and by what means.

politically correct (PC) Repression of attitudes, speech, and writings that are deemed racist, sexist, homophobic (anti-homosexual), or otherwise "insensitive."

politics Deciding who gets what, when, and how.

poll taxes Taxes imposed as a prerequisite to voting; prohibited by the Twenty-fourth Amendment.

pork barreling Legislation designed to make government benefits, including jobs and projects used as political patronage, flow to a particular district or state.

poverty line Official standard regarding what level of annual cash income is sufficient to maintain a "decent standard of living"; those with incomes below this level are eligible for most public assistance programs.

power of the purse Congress's exclusive, constitutional power to authorize expenditures by all agencies of the federal government.

precedent Legal principle that previous decisions should determine the outcome of current cases; the basis for stability in law.

precinct Subdivision of a city, county, or ward for election purposes.

preemption Total or partial federal assumption of power in a particular field, restricting the authority of the states.

preferred position Refers to the tendency of the courts to give preference to the First Amendment rights to speech, press, and assembly when faced with conflicts.

preferred provider organizations (PPOs) Groups of hospitals and physicians who have joined together to offer their services to private insurers at a discount.

presidential primaries Primary elections in the states in which voters in each party can choose a presidential candidate for its party's nomination. Outcomes help determine the distribution of pledged delegates to each party's national nominating convention.

primary elections Elections to choose party nominees for public office; may be open or closed.

prior restraint Government actions to restrict publication of a magazine, newspaper, or books on grounds of libel, obscenity, or other legal violations prior to actual publication of the work.

professionalism In politics, a reference to the increasing number of officeholders for whom politics is a full-time occupation.

program budgeting Identifying items in a budget according to the functions and programs they are to be spent on.

progressive taxation System of taxation in which higher income groups pay a larger percentage of their incomes in taxes than do lower income groups.

proportional (flat) taxation System of taxation in which all income groups pay the same percentage of their income in taxes.

proportional representation Electoral system that allocates seats in a legislature based on the proportion of votes each party receives in a national election.

prosecution Conduct of legal proceedings against an individual charged with a crime.

protectionism A policy of high tariffs and quotas on imports to protect domestic industries.

protest party Third party that arises in response to issues of popular concern which have not been addressed by the major parties.

protests Public marches or demonstrations designed to call attention to an issue and motivate others to apply pressure on public officials.

public assistance programs Those social welfare programs for which no contributions are required and only those living in poverty (by official standards) are eligible; includes food stamps, Medicaid, and Family Assistance.

public goods Goods and services that cannot readily be provided by markets, either because they are too expensive for a single individual to buy or because if one person bought them, everyone else would use them without paying.

public-interest groups Interest groups that claim to represent broad classes of people or the public as a whole.

public opinion Aggregate of preferences and opinions of individuals on significant issues.

public relations Building and maintaining goodwill with the general public.

quota Provision of some affirmative action programs in which specific numbers or percentages of positions are open only to minorities and/or women.

radicalism Advocacy of immediate and drastic changes in society, including the complete restructuring of institutions, values, and beliefs. Radicals may exist on either the extreme left or extreme right.

raiding Organized efforts by one party to get its members to cross over in a primary and defeat an attractive candidate in the opposition party's primary.

ratification Power of a legislature to approve or reject decisions made by other bodies. State legislators or state conventions must ratify constitutional amendments submitted by Congress. The U.S. Senate must ratify treaties made by the president.

Reagan Coalition Combination of economic and social conservatives, religious fundamentalists, and defense-minded anticommunists who rallied behind Republican President Ronald Reagan.

realignment Major shift in political party support or identification that usually occurs around a critical election. In Texas, realignment took place as a gradual transformation from a one-party system dominated by Democrats to a two-party system in which Republicans became competitive in elections.

recession Decline in the general level of economic activity.

Reconstruction The Post–Civil war period when the Southern states were occupied by federal troops and newly freed African Americans occupied many political offices and exercised civil rights.

redistricting Drawing of legislative district boundary lines following each ten-year census.

referenda Proposed laws or constitutional amendments submitted to the voters for their direct approval or rejection, found in state constitutions but not in the U.S. Constitution.

regional security Attempt to bring order to international relations during the Cold War by creating regional alliances between a superpower and nations of a particular region.

registration Requirement that prospective voters establish their identity and place of residence prior to an election in order to be eligible to vote.

regressive taxation System of taxation in which lower income groups pay a larger percentage of their incomes in taxes than do higher income groups.

regulation Development by the federal bureaucracy of formal rules for implementing legislation.

remedies and reliefs Orders of a court to correct a wrong, including a violation of the Constitution.

representational federalism Assertion that no constitutional division of powers exists between the nation and the states but the states retain their constitutional role merely by selecting the president and members of Congress.

representative democracy Governing system in which public decision making is delegated to representatives of the people chosen by popular vote in free, open, and periodic elections.

Republican Party One of the two main parties in American politics, it traces its origins to the antislavery and nationalist forces that united in the 1850s and nominated Abraham Lincoln for president in 1860.

republicanism Government by representatives of the people rather than directly by the people themselves.

rescissions Items on which a president wishes to cancel spending.

reserved powers Powers not granted to the national government or specifically denied to the states in the Constitution that are recognized by the Tenth Amendment as belonging to the state governments. This guarantee, known as the Reserved Powers Clause, embodies the principle of American federalism.

responsible party model System in which competitive parties adopt a platform of principles, recruiting candidates and directing campaigns based on the platform, and holding their elected officials responsible for enacting it.

restricted rule Rule that allows specified amendments to be added to a bill under consideration by the House.

retail politics Direct candidate contact with individual voters.

retrospective voting Voting for or against a candidate or party on the basis of past performance in office.

revolving doors The movement of individuals from government positions to jobs in the private sector, using the experience, knowledge, and contacts they acquired in government employment.

rider Amendment to a bill that is not germane to the bill's purposes.

right A reference to the conservative, traditional, anticommunist side of the political spectrum.

roll-call vote Vote of the full House or Senate on which all members' individual votes are recorded and made public.

rule Stipulation attached to a bill in the House of Representatives that governs its consideration on the floor, including when and for how long it can be debated and how many (if any) amendments may be appended to it.

rule of four At least four justices must agree to hear an appeal (writ of certiorari) from a lower court in order to get a case before the Supreme Court.

runoff primary Additional primary held between the top two vote-getters in a primary where no candidate has received a majority of the vote.

safe seat Legislative district in which the incumbent regularly wins by a large margin of the vote.

salient issues Issues about which most people have an opinion.

SALT I First arms limitation treaty between the United States and the Soviet Union, signed in 1972, limiting the total number of offensive nuclear missiles; it included the ABM Treaty that reflected the theory that the population centers of both nations should be left undefended.

SALT II Lengthy and complicated treaty between the United States and the Soviet Union, agreed to in 1979 but never ratified by the U.S. Senate, that set limits on all types of strategic nuclear launch vehicles.

search warrant Court order permitting law-enforcement officials to search a location in order to seize evidence of a crime; issued only for a specified location, in connection with a specific investigation, and on submission of proof that "probable cause" exists to warrant such a search.

second-strike capability Ability of a nation's forces to survive a surprise nuclear attack by the enemy and then to retaliate effectively.

secular In politics, a reference to opposition to religious practices and symbols in public life.

selective perception Mentally screening out information or opinions with which one disagrees.

senatorial courtesy Custom of the U.S. Senate with regard to presidential nomina-

tions to the judiciary to defer to the judgment of senators from the president's party from the same state as the nominee.

seniority system Custom whereby the member of Congress who has served the longest on the majority side of a committee becomes its chair and the member who has served the longest on the minority side becomes its ranking member.

separate but equal Ruling of the Supreme Court in the case of *Plessy v. Ferguson* (1896) to the effect that segregated facilities were legal as long as the facilities were equal.

separation of powers Constitutional division of powers among the three branches of the national government—legislative, executive, and judicial.

set-aside program Program in which a specified number or percentage of contracts must go to designated minorities.

shield laws Laws in some states that give reporters the right to refuse to name their sources or to release their notes in court cases; may be overturned by the courts when such refusals jeopardize a fair trial for a defendant.

single-issue groups Organizations formed to support or oppose government action on a specific issue.

single-issue party Third party formed around one particular cause.

slander Oral statements that are false and malicious and are intended to damage an individual.

social contract Idea that government originates as an implied contract among individuals who agree to obey laws in exchange for protection of their rights.

social insurance programs Social welfare programs to which beneficiaries have made contributions so that they are entitled to benefits regardless of their personal wealth.

social mobility Extent to which people move upward or downward in income and status over a lifetime or generations.

Social Security Social insurance program composed of the Old Age and Survivors Insurance program, which pays benefits to retired workers who have paid into the program and their dependents and survivors, and the Disability Insurance program, which pays benefits to disabled workers and their families.

socialism System of government involving collective or government ownership of economic enterprise, with the goal being equality of results, not merely equality of opportunity.

socialization The learning of a culture and its values.

solicitor general Attorney in the Department of Justice who represents the U.S. government before the Supreme Court and any other courts.

sound bites Concise and catchy phrases that attract media coverage.

sovereign immunity Legal doctrine that individuals can sue the government only with the government's consent.

Soviet Union The Union of Soviet Socialist Republics (USSR) consisting of Russia and its bordering lands and ruled by the communist regime in Moscow, officially dissolved in 1991.

Speaker of the House Presiding officer of the House of Representatives.

spin doctor Practitioner of the art of spin control, or manipulation of media reporting to favor one's own candidate.

splinter party Third party formed by a dissatisfied faction of a major party.

splintering Redistricting in which a strong minority is divided up and diluted to prevent it from electing a representative.

spoils system Selection of employees for government agencies on the basis of party loyalty, electoral support, and political influence.

standard partial preemption Form of partial preemption in which the states are permitted to regulate activities already regulated by the federal government if the state regulatory standards are at least as stringent as the federal government's.

standing Requirement that the party who files a lawsuit have a legal stake in the outcome.

standing committee Permanent committee of the House or Senate that deals with matters within a specified subject area.

stare decisis Judicial precept that the issue has already been decided in earlier cases and the earlier decision need only be applied in the specific case before the bench; the rule in most cases, it comes from the Latin for "the decision stands."

START I First treaty between the United States and the Soviet Union that actually reduced the strategic nuclear arms of the superpowers, signed in 1991.

START II A treaty between the United States and Russia eliminating all multiwarhead land missiles and reducing nuclear weapons stockpiles; signed in 2003.

statutory laws Laws made by act of Congress or the state legislatures, as opposed to constitutional law.

strict scrutiny Supreme Court holding that race-based actions by government can be done only to remedy past discrimination or to further a "compelling" interest and must be "narrowly tailored" to minimize effects on the rights of others.

subcommittees Specialized committees within standing committees; subcommittee recommendations must be approved by the full standing committee before submission to the floor.

subcultures Variations on the prevailing values and beliefs in a society.

subpoenas Court orders requiring people to testify in court or before grand juries or to produce certain documents.

suffrage Legal right to vote.

Sullivan rule Court guideline that false and malicious statements regarding public officials are protected by the First Amendment unless it can be proven they were known to be false at the time they were made or were made with "reckless disregard" for their truth or falsehood.

superdelegates Delegates to the Democratic Party national convention selected because of their position in the government or the party and not pledged to any candidate.

superpowers Refers to the United States and the Soviet Union after World War II, when these two nations dominated international politics.

Supplemental Security Income (SSI) Public assistance program that provides monthly cash payments to the needy elderly (sixty-five or older), blind, and disabled.

survey research Gathering of information about public opinion by questioning a representative sample of the population.

swing states States that are not considered to be firmly in the Democratic or Republican column.

symbolic speech Actions other than speech itself but protected by the First Amendment because they constitute political expression.

tag Rule that allows an individual senator to postpone a committee hearing on any bill for at least forty-eight hours, a delay that can be fatal to a bill during the closing days of a legislative session.

takings clause The Fifth Amendment's prohibition against government taking of private property without just compensation.

tariff Tax imposed on imported products (also called a customs duty).

tax avoidance Taking advantage of exemptions, exclusions, deductions, and special treatments in tax laws (legal).

tax evasion Hiding income and/or falsely claiming exemptions, deductions, and special treatments (illegal).

tax expenditures Revenues lost to the federal government because of exemptions, exclusions, deductions, and special-treatment provisions in tax laws.

taxes Compulsory payments to the government.

television malaise Generalized feelings of distrust, cynicism, and powerlessness stemming from television's emphasis on the negative aspects of American life.

Temporary Assistance to Needy Families Welfare reform program replacing federal cash entitlement with grants to the states for welfare recipients.

terrorism Title 22 of the U.S. Code, Section 2656 (d): "The term 'terrorism' means premeditated, politically motivated violence perpetrated against noncombatant targets by subnational groups or clandestine agents, usually intended to influence an audience."

Texas court of criminal appeals Nine-member court with final appellate jurisdiction over criminal cases.

Texas supreme court Nine-member court with final appellate jurisdiction over civil lawsuits.

third party Political party that challenges the two major parties in an election.

third reading Final presentation of a bill before the full house or senate.

ticket splitter Person who votes for candidates of different parties for different offices in a general election.

Title IX A provision in the Federal Education Act forbidding discrimination against women in college athletic programs.

total preemption Federal government's assumption of all regulatory powers in a particular field.

totalitarianism Rule by an elite that exercises unlimited power over individuals in all aspects of life.

trade associations Interest groups composed of businesses in specific industries.

transfer payments Direct payments (either in cash or in goods and/or services) by governments to individuals as part of a social welfare program, not as a result of any service or contribution rendered by the individual.

Truman Doctrine U.S. foreign policy, first articulated by President Harry S Truman, that pledged the United States to "support free peoples who are resisting attempted subjugation by armed minorities or by outside pressures."

trustees Legislators who feel obligated to use their own best judgment in decision making.

turnout Number of voters who actually cast ballots in an election, as a percentage of people eligible to register and vote.

turnover Replacement of members of Congress by retirement or resignation, by reapportionment, or (more rarely) by electoral defeat, usually expressed as a percentage of members newly elected.

unanimous consent agreement Negotiated by the majority and minority leaders of the Senate, it specifies when a bill will be taken up on the floor, what amendments will be considered, and when a vote will be taken.

underclass People who have remained poor and dependent on welfare over a prolonged period of time.

unemployment compensation Social insurance program that temporarily replaces part of the wages of workers who have lost their jobs.

unemployment rate Percentage of the civilian labor force who are not working but who are looking for work or waiting to return to or to begin a job.

unfunded mandates Mandates that impose costs on state and local governments (and private industry) without reimbursement from the federal government.

unitary system Constitutional arrangement whereby authority rests with the national government, subnational governments have only those powers given to them by the national government.

U.S. Solicitor General The U.S. government's chief legal council, presenting the government's arguments in cases in which it is a party or in which it has an interest.

urbanization Process by which a predominantly rural society or area becomes urban.

values Shared ideas about what is good and desirable.

veto Rejection of a legislative act by the executive branch; in the U.S. federal government, overriding of a veto requires a two-thirds majority in both houses of Congress.

Vietnam War War between non-Communist South Vietnam and Communist North Vietnam from 1956 to 1975, with increasing U.S. involvement, ending with U.S. withdrawal in 1973 and Communist victory in 1975. The war became unpopular in the U.S. after 1968 and caused President Johnson not to run for a second term. More than 58,000 Americans died in the war.

visa A document or stamp on a passport allowing a person to visit a foreign country.

wall-of-separation doctrine The Supreme Court's interpretation of the No Establishment Clause that laws may not have as their purpose aid to one religion or aid to all religions.

War Powers Resolution Bill passed in 1973 to limit presidential war-making powers; it restricts when, why, and for how long a president can commit U.S. forces and requires notification of and, in many cases, approval by Congress.

ward Division of a city for electoral or administrative purposes or as a unit for organizing political parties.

Watergate The scandal that led to the forced resignation of President Richard M. Nixon. Adding "gate" as a suffix to any alleged corruption in government suggests an analogy to the Watergate scandal.

whips In both the House and Senate, the principal assistants to the party leaders and next in command to those leaders.

whistle-blower Employee of the federal government or of a firm supplying the government who reports waste, mismanagement, and/or fraud by a government agency or contractor.

White House press corps Reporters from both print and broadcast media assigned to regularly cover the president.

white primary Democratic Party primary elections in many Southern counties in the early part of the twentieth century that excluded black people from voting.

writ of certiorari Writ issued by the Supreme Court, at its discretion, to order a lower court to prepare the record of a case and send it to the Supreme Court for review. Most cases come to the Court as petitions for writs of certiorari.

writ of habeas corpus Court order directing public officials who are holding a person in custody to bring the prisoner into court and explain the reasons for confinement; the right to habeas corpus is protected by Article I of the Constitution.

zero-based budgeting Method of budgeting that demands justification for the entire budget request of an agency, not just its requested increase in funding.

NOTES

Chapter 1

1. Harold Lasswell, *Politics: Who Gets What, When, How* (New York: McGraw-Hill, 1936).
2. For a discussion of various aspects of legitimacy and its measurement in public opinion polls, see M. Stephen Weatherford, "Measuring Political Legitimacy," *American Political Science Review* 86 (March 1992): 140–55.
3. Thomas Hobbes, *Leviathan* (1651).
4. John Locke, *Treatise on Government* (1688).
5. See Barbara S. Gamble, "Putting Civil Rights to a Popular Vote," *American Journal of Political Science* 41 (January 1997): 245–69.
6. James Madison, Alexander Hamilton, and John Jay, *The Federalist Papers* (New York: Mentor Books, 1961), No. 10, p. 81. Madison's *Federalist Papers*, No. 10 and No. 51, are reprinted in the Appendix.
7. E. E. Schattschneider, *Two Hundred Million Americans in Search of a Government* (New York: Holt, Rinehart & Winston, 1969), p. 63.
8. Harold Lasswell and Daniel Lerner, *The Comparative Study of Elites* (Stanford, Calif.: Stanford University Press, 1952), p. 7.
9. C. Wright Mills's classic study, *The Power Elite* (New York: Oxford University Press, 1956), is widely cited by Marxist critics of American democracy, but it can be read profitably by anyone concerned with the effects of large bureaucracies—corporate, governmental, or military—on democratic government.
10. In *Who Rules America?* (New York: Prentice Hall, 1967) and its sequel, *Who Rules America Now?* (New York: Prentice Hall, 1983), sociologist G. William Domhoff argues that America is ruled by an "upper class" who attend the same prestigious private schools, intermarry among themselves, and join the same exclusive clubs. In *Who's Running America?* (New York: Prentice Hall, 1976) and *Who's Running America? The Clinton Years* (New York: Prentice Hall, 1995), political scientist Thomas R. Dye documents the concentration of power and the control of assets in the hands of officers and directors of the nation's largest corporations, banks, law firms, networks, foundations, and so forth. Dye argues, however, that most of these "institutional elites" were not born into the upper class but instead climbed the ladder to success.
11. Yale political scientist Robert A. Dahl is an important contributor to the development of pluralist theory, beginning with his *Preface to Democratic Theory* (Chicago: University of Chicago Press, 1956). He often refers to a pluralist system as a *polyarchy*—literally, a system with many centers of power. See his *Polyarchy* (New Haven, Conn.: Yale University Press, 1971), and for a revised defense of pluralism, see his *Democracy and Its Critics* (New Haven, Conn.: Yale University Press, 1989).

Chapter 2

1. Gunnar Myrdal, *An American Dilemma* (New York: Harper, 1944).
2. See Martin Luther King, Jr., "Letter from Birmingham City Jail," April 16, 1963.
3. For a discussion of the sources and consequences of intolerance in the general public, see James L. Gibson, "The Political Consequences of Intolerance: Cultural Conformity and Political Freedom," *American Political Science Review* 86 (June 1992): 338–52.
4. Alexis deTocqueville, *Democracy in America*, orig. 1835 (New York: Penguin Classic Books, 2003). See also Aurelian Craiutu and Jeremy Jennings, "The Third Democracy: Tocqueville's Views of America After 1840," *American Journal of Political Science* 98 (August 2004): 391–404.
5. Quoted in *The Ideas of Equality*, ed. George Abernathy (Richmond, Va.: John Knox Press, 1959), p. 185; also in Herbert McClosky and John Zaller, *The American Ethos: Public Attitudes toward Capitalism and Democracy* (Cambridge, Mass.: Harvard University Press, 1984), p. 72.
6. Quoted in Richard Hofstadter, *The American Political Tradition* (New York: Knopf, 1948), p. 45. Historian Hofstadter describes the thinking of American political leaders from Jefferson and the Founders to Franklin D. Roosevelt.
7. For a discussion of how people balance the values of individualism and opposition to big government with humanitarianism and the desire to help others, see Stanley Feldman and John Zaller, "The Political Culture of Ambivalence: Ideological Responses to the Welfare State," *American Journal of Political Science* 36 (February 1992): 268–307.
8. Lawrence R. Jacobs and Theda Skocpol, eds., *Inequality and American Democracy* (New York: Russell Sage Foundation, 2005).
9. Greg J. Duncan, *Years of Poverty, Years of Plenty* (Ann Arbor: University of Michigan Press, 1984); Isabel Sawhill, *Income Mobility in the United States* (Washington, D.C.: Urban Institute, 1996).
10. American Security Council, *The Illegal Immigration Crisis* (Washington, D.C.: ASC, 1994).
11. *Sale v. Haitian Centers Council*, 125 L. Ed. 2d 128 (1993).
12. Poll figures in this section are derived from the Pew Research Center for the People and the Press, "Religion and American Life," August 24, 2004. *www.people-press.org*
13. *Congressional Quarterly*, March 7, 2005.
14. See Stephen Earl Bennett, "Americans' Knowledge of Ideology, 1980–92," *American Politics Quarterly* 23 (July 1995): 259–78.
15. For evidence that ideological consistency increases with educational level, see William G. Jacoby, "Ideological Identification and Issue Attitude," *American Journal of Political Science* 35 (February 1991): 178–205.
16. Richard Hofstadter, *The Paranoid Style in American Politics* (New York: Knopf, 1965).
17. Francis Fukuyama, *The End of History and the Last Man* (New York: Free Press, 1992).
18. See Robert Kimball, *Tenured Radicals* (New York: Harper & Row, 1990).
19. Herbert Marcuse, *One-Dimensional Man* (Boston: Beacon Press, 1964).
20. Allan Bloom, *The Closing of the American Mind* (New York: Simon & Schuster, 1987), p. 15.

Chapter 3

1. In *Federalist Papers*, No. 53, James Madison distinguishes a "constitution" from a law: a constitution is "established by the people and unalterable by the government, and a law established by the government and alterable by the government."
2. Another important decision on opening day of the Constitutional Convention was to keep the proceedings secret. James Madison made his own notes on the convention proceedings, and they were published many years later. See Max Ferrand, ed., *The Records of the Federal Convention of 1787* (New Haven, Conn.: Yale University Press, 1911).
3. See Edward Millican, *One United People: The Federalist Papers and the National Idea* (Lexington: University Press of Kentucky, 1990).
4. See David Brian Robertson, "Madison's Opponents and Constitutional Design," *American Political Science Review* 99 (May 2005): 225–43.
5. Charles A. Beard, *An Economic Interpretation of the Constitution* (New York: Macmillan, 1913).
6. Robert E. Brown, *Charles Beard and the Constitution* (Princeton, N.J.: Princeton University Press, 1956).
7. James Madison, *Federalist Papers*, No. 10, reprinted in the Appendix.
8. Alexander Hamilton, *Federalist Papers*, No. 78.

Chapter 4

1. The states are listed in the order in which their legislatures voted to secede. While occupied by Confederate troops, secessionist legislators in Missouri and Kentucky also voted to secede, but Unionist representatives from these states remained in Congress.
2. *Texas v. White*, 7 Wallace 700 (1869).
3. James Madison, *Federalist Papers*, No. 51, reprinted in the Appendix.
4. Ibid.
5. The arguments for "competitive federalism" are developed at length in Thomas R. Dye, *American Federalism: Competition among Governments* (Lexington, Mass.: Lexington Books, 1990).
6. David Osborne, *Laboratories of Democracy* (Cambridge, Mass.: Harvard Business School, 1988).
7. Morton Grodzins, *The American System* (Chicago: Rand McNally, 1966), pp. 8–9.
8. Ibid., p. 265.
9. Charles Press, *State and Community Governments in the Federal System* (New York: Wiley, 1979), p. 78.
10. *Garcia v. San Antonio Metropolitan Transit Authority*, 469 U.S. 528 (1985).
11. See Michael S. Greve, *Real Federalism: Why It Matters, How It Could Happen* (Washington, D.C.: AEI Press, 1999).
12. *U.S. v. Lopez*, 514 U.S. 549 (1995).
13. *Seminole Tribe of Florida v. Florida*, 517 U.S. 44 (1996).
14. *Alden v. Maine*, 67 U.S.L.W. 1401 (1999).
15. *Printz v. U.S.* 521 U.S. 890 (1997).
16. *Brzonkala v. Morrison* (2000).
17. *Federal-State-Local Relations: Federal Grants in Aid*, House Committee on Government Operations, 85th Cong., 2d sess., p. 7.
18. Craig Volden, "Intergovernmental Political Competition in American Federalism," *American Journal of Political Science* 49 (April 2005): 327–42.

Chapter 5

1. See James A. Stimson, Michael B. MacKuen, and Robert S. Erikson, "Dynamic Representation," *American Political Science Review* 89 (September 1995): 543–61.
2. Robert S. Erikson and Kent L. Tedin, *American Public Opinion*, 7th ed. (New York: Longman, 2005).
3. Ibid. p. 35.
4. For a summary of literature on public opinion, see James Stimson, "Opinion and Representation," *American Political Science Review* 89 (March 1995): 179–83.
5. Sandra K. Schwartz, "Preschoolers and Politics," in *New Directions in Political Socialization*, eds. David C. Schwartz and Sandra K. Schwartz (New York: Free Press, 1975), p. 242.
6. David O. Sears and Carolyn Funk, "Evidence of the Long-Term Persistence of Adults' Political Predispositions," *Journal of Politics* 61 (February 1999): 1–28.
7. Robert D. Hess and Judith V. Torney, *The Development of Political Attitudes in Children* (Chicago: Aldine, 1977), p. 42.
8. See also Ted G. Jelen, "The Political Consequences of Religious Group Attitudes," *Journal of Politics* 55 (February 1993): 178–90.
9. Geoffrey C. Longman, "Religion and Political Behavior in the United States," *Public Opinion Quarterly* 61 (Summer 1997): 288–316.
10. See John C. Green, "The Christian Right in the 1994 Elections," *P.S.: Political Science and Politics* 28 (March 1995): 5–23.
11. See also James A. Stimson, *Public Opinion in America: Moods, Cycles, and Swings* (Boulder, Colo.: Westview Press, 1991).
12. Janet M. Box-Steffensmeier, Suzanna De Boef, and Tse-Min Lin, "The Dynamics of the Partisan Gender Gap," *American Political Science Review* 98 (August 2004): 515–28.
13. Jon Horwitz and Mark Peffley, "Explaining the Great Racial Divide: Perceptions of Fairness in the U.S. Criminal Justice System," *Journal of Politics*, 67 (August 2005): 768–83.
14. V.O. Key Jr., *Public Opinion and American Democracy* (New York: Knopf, 1967), p. 536.
15. *Smith V. Allwright*, 321 U.S. 649 (1944).
16. *Harper v. Virginia State Board of Elections*, 383 U.S. 663 (1966).
17. Congress had earlier passed the Voting Rights Act of 1970, which (1) extended the vote to eighteen-year-olds regardless of state law; (2) abolished residency requirements in excess of thirty days; and (3) prohibited literacy tests. However, there was some constitutional debate about the power of Congress to change state laws on voting age. Although Congress could end racial discrimination, extending the vote to eighteen-year-olds was a different matter. All previous extensions of the vote had come by constitutional amendment. Hence Congress quickly passed the Twenty-sixth Amendment.
18. Staci L. Rhine, "Registration Reform and Turnout," *American Politics Quarterly* 23 (October 1995): 409–26; Stephen Knack, "Does 'Motor Voter' Work?" *Journal of Politics* 57 (August 1995): 796–811; Michael D. Martinez and David B. Hill, "Did Motor Voter Work?" *American Politics Quarterly* 27 (February 1997): 296–315.
19. Richard G. Niemi and Paul S. Herrnson, "Beyond the Butterfly: The Complexity of U.S. Ballots," *Perspectives on Politics* 1 (June, 2003): 317–26.
20. See Dennis F. Thompson, "Election Time: Normative Implications of Temporal Properties of the Election Process in the United States," *American Political Science Review* 98 (February 2004): 51–64.
21. *General Social Survey, 1998* (Chicago: National Opinion Research Center, 1999).

22. John E. Filer, Lawrence W. Kenny, and Rebecca B. Morton, "Redistribution, Income, and Voting," *American Journal of Political Science* 37 (February 1993): 63–87.

23. Sidney Verba, Kay Scholzman, Henry Brady, and Norman Nie, "Citizen Activity: Who Participates? What Do They Say?" *American Political Science Review* 87 (June 1993): 303–18.

24. See Katherine Tate, "Black Political Participation in the 1984 and 1988 Presidential Elections," *American Political Science Review* 85 (December 1991): 1159–76.

25. John Stuart Mill, *Considerations on Representative Government* (Chicago: Regnery, Gateway, 1962; original publication 1859), p. 144.

26. Ibid., p. 130.

27. Quotation from Austin Ranney in "Non-Voting Is Not a Social Disease," *Public Opinion* 6 (November/December 1983): 18.

28. Martin Luther King Jr., "Letter from Birmingham City Jail," April 16, 1963.

Chapter 6

1. For an overview of the mass media in American politics, see Doris A. Graber, *Mass Media and American Politics*, 6th ed. (Washington, D.C.: CQ Press, 2002).

2. Pew Research Center for People and the Press. http://people-press.org June, 2000.

3. See Lance Bennett, *News: The Politics of Illusion*, 4th ed. (White Plains, N.Y.: Longman, 2001).

4. E. E. Schattschneider, *The Semisovereign People* (New York: Holt, Rinehart & Winston, 1961), p. 68.

5. William A. Henry, "News as Entertainment," in *What's News*, ed. Elie Abel (San Francisco: Institute for Contemporary Studies, 1981), p. 133.

6. Shanto Iyengar, *Is Anyone Responsible? How Television Frames Political Issues* (Chicago: University of Chicago Press, 1991).

7. Graber, *Mass Media*, p. 35.

8. Matthew A. Baum, "Sex, Lies, and War: How Soft News Brings Foreign Policy to the Inattentive Public," *American Political Science Review* 96 (March, 2002): 91–109.

9. Larry Sabato, Mark Stencel, and S. Robert Lichter, *Peep Show? Media Politics in an Age of Scandal* (Lanham, Md.: Rowman & Little-field, 2001).

10. Ben J. Wattenberg, *The Good News Is the Bad News Is Wrong* (New York: Simon & Schuster, 1984).

11. Ted Smith, "The Watchdog's Bite," *American Enterprise* 2 (January/February 1990): 66.

12. Larry Sabato, *Feeding Frenzy: How Attack Journalism Has Transformed American Politics* (New York: Free Press, 1991).

13. Graber, *Mass Media*, p. 946.

14. S. Robert Lichter, Stanley Rothman, and Linda S. Lichter, *The Media Elite* (Bethesda, Md.: Adler and Adler, 1986).

15. David Prindle, "Hollywood Liberalism" *Social Science Quarterly* 71 (March 1993): 121.

16. David C. Barker, "Rushed Decisions: Political Talk Radio and Vote Choice," *Journal of Politics* 61 (May 1999): 527–39.

17. Diana C. Mutz and Byron Reeves, "The New Videomalaise: Effects of Televised Incivility on Political Trust," *American Political Science Review* 99 (February 2005): 1–15.

18. Marcus Prior, "News Versus Entertainment; How Increasing Media Choice Widens Gaps in Political Knowledge and Turnout," *American Journal of Political Science* 49 (July 2005): 577–592.

19. Julianne F. Flowers, Audrey A. Haynes, and Michael H. Crespin, "The Media, the Campaign, and the Message," *American Journal of Political Science* 47 (April 2003): 259–73.

20. See David S. Castle, "Media Coverage of Presidential Primaries," *American Politics Quarterly* 19 (January 1991): 13–42; Christine F. Ridout, "The Role of Media Coverage of Iowa and New Hampshire," *American Politics Quarterly* 19 (January 1991): 43–58.

21. *Media Monitor* Vol. 14 (November/December, 2000).

22. *New York Times v. U.S.*, 376 U.S. 713 (1971).

23. *New York Times v. Sullivan*, 376 U.S. 254 (1964).

24. See Arthur Lupia and Tasha S. Philpot "Views from Inside the Net," *Journal of Politics* 67 (November, 2005): 1122–42.

25. *Reno v. American Civil Liberties Union* 117 S.Ct. 2329 (1997).

26. Bernard Cohen, *The Press and Foreign Policy* (Princeton, N.J.: Princeton University Press, 1963), p. 16.

27. Austin Ranney, *Channels of Power* (New York: Basic Books, 1983), p. 81.

28. Benjamin J. Page, Robert Y. Shapiro, and Glen R. Dempsey, "What Moves Public Opinion," *American Political Science Review* 81 (March 1987): 23–43.

29. National Institute of Mental Health, *Television and Behavior* (Washington, D.C.: Government Printing Office, 1982).

30. Brandon Centerwall, "Exposure to Television as a Risk Factor for Violence," *American Journal of Epidemiology* 129 (April 1989): 643–52.

Chapter 7

1. Gaetano Mosca, *The Ruling Class* (New York: McGraw-Hill, 1939), p. 51.

2. James Madison, *Federalist Papers*, No. 10, reprinted in the Appendix.

3. George Washington, Farewell Address, September 17, 1796, in *Documents on American History*, 10th ed., eds. Henry Steele Commager and Milton Cantor (Upper Saddle River, N.J.: Prentice Hall, 1988), 1: 172.

4. Colleen A. Sheehan and *Madison v. Hamilton*, "The Battle over Republicanism and the Role of Public Opinion," *American Political Science Review* 98 (August 2004), 405–24.

5. E. E. Schattschneider, *Party Government* (New York: Holt, Rinehart & Winston, 1942), p. 1.

6. Geofrey C. Layman and Thomas M. Carsey, "Party Polarization and Conflict Extension in the American Electorate," *American Journal of Political Science* 46 (October 2002): 786–802.

7. Since 1954, only Presidents Kennedy, Johnson, and Carter (all Democrats) worked with their party's majorities in both houses of Congress; President Clinton enjoyed Democratic Party control of the Congress only in his first two years in office. George W. Bush is the only Republican president in a half century to serve with a Republican majority in both the House and Senate. See Harold W. Stanley and Richard C. Niemi, *Vital Statistics on American Politics* (Washington, D.C.: CQ Press, 2003).

8. See Thomas R. Dye and Susan MacManus, *Politics in States and Communities*, 11th ed. (Upper Saddle River, N.J.: Prentice Hall, 2003).

9. *National Election Study*, 2000.

10. Conventions continue to play a modest role in nominations in some states:
   • Colorado: Parties may hold a preprimary convention to designate a candidate to be listed first on the primary ballot. All candidates receiving at least 30 percent of the delegate vote will be listed on the primary ballot.
   • Connecticut: Party conventions are held to endorse candidates. If no one challenges the endorsed candidate, no primary election is held. If a challenger receives 20 percent of the delegate

vote, a primary election will be held to determine the party's nominee in the general election.

- New York: Party conventions choose the party's "designated" candidate in primary elections. Anyone receiving 25 percent of the delegates also appears on the ballot.
- Utah: Party conventions select party's nominees.
- Illinois, Indiana, Michigan, and South Carolina: Party conventions nominate candidates for some minor state offices.

11. For an argument that primary elections force parties to be more responsive to voters, see John G. Geer and Mark E. Shere, "Party Competition and the Prisoner's Dilemma: An Argument for the Direct Primary," *Journal of Politics* 54 (August 1992): 365–74.

12. For an up-to-date listing of state primaries and relevant information about them, see *The Book of the States*, published biannually by the Council of State Governments, Lexington, Kentucky.

13. The U.S. Supreme Court declared that the "blanket primary" violated the First Amendment freedom of association right of political parties to choose their own candidates. California had adopted a primary system that gave all voters, regardless of party affiliation, ballots that included the names of *all* candidates in *both* parties. Candidates of each party who received the most votes were to become the nominees of those parties and move on to face each other in the general election. But the Supreme Court held that the blanket primary violated the First Amendment right of association (*California Democratic Party v. Jones*, 530 U.S. 567 (2000).

14. Congressional Quarterly, *National Party Conventions 1811–1996* (Washington, D.C.: CQ Press, 1997).

15. For evidence that the national party conventions raise the poll standings of their presidential nominees, see James E. Campbell, Lynna L. Cherry, and Kenneth A. Wink, "The Convention Bump," *American Politics Quarterly* 20 (July 1992): 287–307.

16. See John A. Clark, John M. Bruce, John H. Kessel, and William G. Jacoby, "I'd Rather Switch Than Fight: Lifelong Democrats and Converts to Republicanism among Campaign Activists," *American Journal of Political Science* 35 (August 1991): 577–97.

17. For a scholarly debate over realignment, see Byron E. Schafer, ed., *The End of Realignment: Interpreting American Election Eras* (Madison: University of Wisconsin Press, 1991).

18. Gary Miller and Norman Schofield, "Activists and Partisan Realignment in the United States," *American Political Science Review* 97 (May 2003): 245–60.

Chapter 8

1. Gerald Pomper, *Elections in America* (New York: Dodd, Mead, 1968).

2. Morris P. Fiorina, *Retrospective Voting in American National Elections* (New Haven, Conn.: Yale University Press, 1988).

3. Quoted in *Congressional Quarterly Almanac, 1965* (Washington, D.C.: Congressional Quarterly, Inc., 1966), p. 267.

4. Alan Ehrenhalt, *The United States of Ambition: Politicians, Power and the Pursuit of Office* (New York: Random House, 1991), p. 22.

5. See Jamie L. Carson, "Strategy, Selection and Candidate Competition in U.S. House and Senate Elections", *Journal of Politics* 67 (February 2005): 1–26.

6. Alan I. Abramowitz, "Incumbency, Campaign Spending, and the Decline of Competition in U.S. House Elections," *Journal of Politics* 53 (February 1991): 55–70.

7. Herbert Alexander, as quoted in Richard R. Lau et al., "The Effects of Negative Political Advertisements," *American Political Science Review* 93 (December 1999): 851–75.

8. Lee Sigelman and Emmett H. Buell Jr., "You Take the High Road and I'll Take the Low Road? The Interplay of Attack Strategies and Tactics in Presidential Campaigns," *The Journal of Politics* 46 (May 2003): 518–31; Richard R. Lau and Gerald M. Pomper, "Effectiveness of Negative Campaigning in U.S. Senate Elections," *American Journal of Political Science* 46 (January 2002): 47–66.

9. Ted Brader, "Striking a Responsive Chord: How Political Ads Motivate and Persuade Voters by Appealing to Emotions," *American Journal of Political Science* 49 (April 2005): 388–405.

10. Paul Friedman, Michael Franz, and Kenneth Goldstein, "Campaign Advertising and Democratic Citizenship," *American Journal of Political Science* 48 (October 2004): 723–41.

11. Thomas M. Holbrook and Scott D. McClung, "The Mobilization of Core Supporters," *American Journal of Political Science*, 49 (October 2005): 689–703.

12. Center for Responsive Politics, *The Big Picture: The Money Behind the 2000 Elections* (Washington, D.C., 2001).

13. In the important U.S. Supreme Court decision in *Buckley v. Valeo* in 1976, James L. Buckley, former U.S. senator from New York, and his brother, William F. Buckley, the well-known conservative commentator, argued successfully that the laws limiting an individual's right to participate in political campaigns—financially or otherwise—violated First Amendment freedoms. Specifically, the U.S. Supreme Court held that no government could limit individuals' rights to spend money or publish or broadcast their own views on issues or elections. Candidates can spend as much of their own money as they wish on their own campaigns. Private individuals can spend as much as they wish to circulate their own views on an election, although their contributions to candidates and parties can still be limited. The Court, however, permitted governmental limitations on parties and campaign organizations and allowed the use of federal funds for financing campaigns. *Buckley v. Valeo*, 424 U.S. 1 (1976).

14. Sanford C. Gordon and Catherine Hafer, "Flexing Muscles: Corporate Political Expenditures As Signals to the Bureaucracy," *American Political Science Review* 99 (May 2005): 245–61.

15. *McConnell v. Federal Elections Commission* 540 U.S. 93 (2003).

16. *Randall v. Sorrell*, June 26, 2006.

17. See Paul-Henri Guvian and Audrey A. Haynes, "Presidential Nominating Campaigns," *P.S. Political Science and Politics* 36 (April 2003): 175–80.

18. Lynn Vavreck, Constantine J. Spiliotes and Linda L. Fowler, "The Effects of Retail Politics in the New Hampshire Primary," *American Journal of Political Science* 46 (July 2002): 595–610.

19. William G. Mayer, "Forecasting Presidential Nominations," *P.S. Political Science and Politics* 36 (April 2003): 153–58.

20. Matthew A. Baum, "Talking the Vote: Why Presidential Candidates Hit the Talk Show Circuit," *American Journal of Political Science* 49 (April 2005): 213–34.

21. University-based political scientists rely heavily on a series of National Election Studies, originated at the Survey Research Center at the University of Michigan, which have surveyed the voting-age population in every presidential election and most congressional elections since 1952.

22. See Martin P. Wattenberg, *The Rise of Candidate-Centered Politics* (Cambridge, Mass.: Harvard University Press, 1991).

23. Responsibility for the economy, however, is also affected by the voters' partisanship, ideology and views about whether the president or Congress is chiefly responsible. See Joseph J. Rudolph, "Who's Responsible for the Economy?," *American Journal of Political Science* 47 (October, 2003): 698–713.

24. For an argument that voters look ahead to the economic future and reward or punish the president based on rational expectations, see Michael B. MacKuen, Robert S. Erickson, and James A. Stimson, "Peasants or Bankers? The American Electorate and the U.S. Economy," *American Political Science Review* 86 (September 1992): 680–95.

25. See Herbert F. Weisberg, "The Structure and Effects of Moral Predispositions in Contemporary American Politics", *Journal of Politics* 67 (August 2005): 646–68.

Chapter 9

1. Political scientist David Truman's classic definition of an interest group: "any group that is based on one or more shared attitudes and makes certain demands upon other groups or organizations in society." See *The Governmental Process* (New York: Knopf, 1971), p. 33.

2. James Madison, *Federalist Papers*, No. 10, reprinted in the Appendix.

3. Gale Research Company, *Encyclopedia of Associations* (Detroit: Gale Research, 2004).

4. Frank R. Baumgartner and Beth L. Leech, "Interest Niches and Policy Bandwagons: Patterns of Interest Group Involvement in National Politics," *The Journal of Politics* 63 (November 2001): 1191–1213.

5. Jeffrey M. Berry, *The New Liberalism: The Rising Power of Citizen Groups* (Washington, D.C.: Brookings Institution Press, 1999).

6. For both theory and survey data on the sources of interest-group mobilization, see Jack L. Walker, *Mobilizing Interest Groups in America: Patrons, Professions, and Social Movements* (Ann Arbor: University of Michigan Press, 1991).

7. Kay Lehmann Scholzman, "What Accent the Heavenly Chorus? Political Equality and the American Pressure System," *Journal of Politics* 46 (November 1984): 1006–32; see also Jeffrey M. Berry, Kent E. Portney, and Ken Thomson, *The Case for Participatory Democracy* (Washington, D.C.: Brookings Institution Press, 1994).

8. Center for Responsive Politics, *Influence, Inc.* 2000 (Washington, D.C., 2001).

9. Jeffrey M. Berry, *The New Liberalism* (Washington D.C.: Brookings Institution Press, 1999).

10. Quotation from Roger Kersh, "Corporate Lobbyists as Political Actors," in *Interest Group Politics*, 6th ed., ed. Allan J. Cigler and Burdett A. Loomis (Washington, D.C.: CQ Press, 2002).

11. For evidence that vote buying on congressional roll calls is rare, see Janet M. Grenzke, "Shopping in the Congressional Supermarket: The Currency Is Complex," *American Journal of Political Science* 33 (February 1989): 1–24. But for evidence that committee participation by members of Congress is influenced by political action committee money, see Richard L. Hall and Frank W. Wayman, "Buying Time: Moneyed Interests and the Mobilization of Bias in Congressional Committees," *American Political Science Review* 84 (September 1990): 797–819.

12. See, for example, Mark E. Patterson, "The Presidency and Organized Interests: White House Patterns of Interest Group Liaison," *American Political Science Review* 86 (September 1992): 612–22.

13. Robert H. Salisbury, "Who You Know versus What You Know: The Use of Government Experience by Washington Lobbyists," *American Journal of Political Science* 33 (February 1989): 175–95.

14. *Brown v. Board of Education of Topeka,* 349 U.S. 294 (1955).

15. Samuel Huntington, *Political Order in Changing Societies* (New Haven, Conn.: Yale University Press, 1965), p. 28.

16. Mancur Olson, *The Rise and Decline of Nations.* (New Haven, Conn.: Yale University Press, 1982).

Chapter 10

1. James Madison, *Federalist Papers*, No. 10, reprinted in the Appendix.

2. Quoted in Jay M. Schafritz, *The Harper Collins Dictionary of American Government and Politics* (New York: HarperCollins, 1992), p. 56.

3. See David Auerswald and Forrest Maltzman, "Policymaking through Advice and Consent: Treaty Consideration by the United States Senate," *Journal of Politics* 65 (November 2003): 1097–1110.

4. *McGrain v. Doughtery,* 273 U.S. 13J (1927).

5. *Baker v. Carr,* 369 U.S. 186 (1962), *Wesberry v. Sanders,* 370 U.S. 1 (1964).

6. *Gray v. Sanders,* 322 U.S. 368 (1963).

7. *Department of Commerce v. U.S. House of Representatives,* 525 U.S. 316 (1999).

8. *Gaffney v. Cummings,* 412 U.S. 763 (1973).

9. *Davis v. Bandemer* 478 U.S. 109 (1986).

10. *Vieth v. Jubelirer* 241 F. Supp. 2d 478 (2004).

11. *League of United Latin American Citizens v. Perry,* June 28, 2006.

12. Scott W. Desposato and John R. Petrocik, "The Variable Incumbency Advantage: New Voters, Redistricting, and Personal Vote," *American Journal of Political Science* 47 (January 2003): 18–32

13. *Thornburg v. Gingles,* 478 U.S. 30 (1986).

14. *Shaw v. Reno,* 125 l. Ed. 2d 511 (1993).

15. *Miller v. Johnson,* 115 S. Ct. 2475 (1995).

16. See Roger H. Davidson and Walter J. Oleszek, *Congress and Its Members,* 9th ed. (Washington, D.C.: CQ Press, 2004).

17. David Lublin, *The Paradox of Representation: Racial Gerrymandering and Minority Interests in Congress* (Princeton, NJ.: Princeton University Press, 1997). See also David Lublin and D. Stephen Voss, "The Missing Middle," *Journal of Politics* 65 (February 2003). 227–37.

18. *Georgia v. Ashcroft,* 539 U.S. 461 (2003).

19. For an in-depth analysis of who decides to run for Congress and who does not, see Linda L. Fowler and Robert D. McClure, *Political Ambition: Who Decides to Run for Congress* (New Haven, Conn.: Yale University Press, 1990).

20. See Michael K. Moore and John R. Hibbing, "Situational Dissatisfaction in Congress: Explaining Voluntary Departures," *Journal of Politics* 60 (November 1998): 1088–1107.

21. *U.S. Term Limits v. Thornton,* 115 S.C. 1842, (1995).

22. See Gary Jacobson, *The Politics of Congressional Elections,* 5th ed. (New York: HarperCollins, 2000).

23. See David Epstein and Peter Zemsky, "Money Talks: Deterring Quality Challengers in Congressional Elections," *American Political Science Review* 89 (June 1995): 295–322.

24. See Thomas E. Mann and Raymond Wolfinger, "Candidates and Parties in Congressional Elections," *American Political Science Review* 84 (September 1990): 545–64.

25. See Mary T. Hanna, "Political Science Caught Flat-Footed by Midterm Elections," *Chronicle of Higher Education,* November 30, 1994, pp. B1–2.

26. See Richard Fenno, *Going Home: Black Representatives and Their Constituents* (Chicago: University of Chicago Press, 2003).

27. Paul S. Herrnson, J. Celeste Lay, and Atiya Kai Stokes, "Women Running 'As Women'," *Journal of Politics* 65 (February 2003): 244–55.

28. See Glen S. Krutz, "Issues and Institutions: 'Winnowing' in the U.S. Congress," *American Journal of Political Science* 49 (April 2005) 313–26.

29. U.S. House of Representatives, Commission on Administrative Review, *Administrative Reorganization and Legislative Management,* 95th Cong., 1st sess, H. Doc. 95–232, pp. 17–19.

30. Richard F. Fenno, *Home Style* (Boston: Little, Brown, 1978).

31. Roger H. Davidson and Walter J. Oleszek, *Congress and Its Members* 814 (Washington, D.C.: CQ Press, 2000).

32. Glenn R. Parker, *Characteristics of Congress* (Upper Saddle River, N.J.: Prentice Hall, 1989), p. 30.

33. Richard F. Fenno, *The Making of a Senator: Dan Quayle* (Washington, D.C.: CQ Press, 1989), p. 119. Also cited in Davidson and Oleszek, *Congress and Its Members,* 9th ed., p. 120.

34. Davidson and Oleszek, *Congress and Its Members*, 9th ed., p. 129.
35. Barbara Sinclair, "The Emergence of Strong Leadership in the House of Representatives," *Journal of Politics* 54 (August 1992): 657–84.
36. Gary W. Cox and Eric Magar, "How Much Is Majority Status in the U.S. Congress Worth?" *American Political Science Review* 93 (June 1999): 299–310.
37. Davidson and Oleszek, *Congress and Its Members*, 9th ed. p. 161.
38. John R. Hibbing, *Congressional Careers* (Chapel Hill: University of North Carolina Press, 1991).

39. See Charles Stewart and Tim Groseclose, "The Value of Committee Seats in the United States Senate," *American Journal of Political Science* 43 (July 1999): 963–73.
40. Larry Markinson, *The Cash Constituents of Congress* (Washington, D.C.: CQ Press, 1992).
41. Donald Matthews, *U.S. Senators and Their World* (New York: Vintage Books, 1960).
42. David Rohde, Norman J. Ornstein, and Robert L. Peabody, "Political Change and Legislative Norms," in *Studies of Congress*, ed. Glenn R. Parker (Washington, D.C.: CQ Press, 1985), p. 175.

43. See John R. Hibbing, "Contours of the Modern Congressional Career," *American Political Science Review* 85 (June 1991): 405–28.
44. Richard Fenno, *Power of the Purse* (Boston: Little, Brown, 1965), p. 620.
45. See David R. Mayhew, *Divided We Govern* (New Haven, Conn.: Yale University Press, 1991); Sarah A. Binder, "The Dynamics of Legislative Gridlock," *American Political Science Review* 93 (September 1999): 519–33.
46. *Congressional Quarterly Weekly Report*, November 23, 1991, p. 3437.

Chapter 11

1. For an argument that presidents encourage people to think of them as "the single head of government and moral leader of the nation who speaks for all of the people," see Barbara Hinckley, *The Symbolic Presidency: How Presidents Portray Themselves* (New York: Routledge, 1991).
2. See Theodore Lowi, *The Personal President* (Ithaca, N.Y.: Cornell University Press, 1987).
3. Presidential address to Congress, September 20, 2001.
4. See Michael Less Benedict, *The Impeachment and Trial of Andrew Johnson* (New York: Norton, 1973).
5. William Howard Taft, *Our Chief Magistrate and His Powers* (New York: Columbia University Press, 1938), p. 138, reprinted in *The Presidency*, ed. John P. Roche (New York: Harcourt Brace Jovanovich, 1964), p. 23.
6. Quoted in Arthur B. Tourtellot, *Presidents on the Presidency* (New York: Doubleday, 1964), pp. 55–56.
7. *Youngstown Sheet & Tube Co. v. Sawyer*, 343 U.S. 579 (1952).
8. *United States v. Nixon*, 418 U.S. 683 (1974).
9. *Nixon v. Fitzgerald*, 457 U.S. 731 (1982).
10. *Clinton v. Jones*, 520 U.S. 681 (1997).
11. Quoted in Richard Neustadt, *Presidential Power* (New York: Wiley, 1960), p. 9.
12. See Paul Brace and Barbara Hinckley, "The Structure of Presidential Approval," *Journal of Politics* 53 (November 1991): 993–1017.
13. See Suzanne L. Pancer, "Toward an Understanding of 'Rally' Effect," *Public Opinion Quarterly* 59 (September, 1995):

526–46; Wave J. Aetherington and Michael Nelson: "Anatomy of a Rally Effect," *P.S. Political Science and Politics* 36 (January, 2003): 37–42.
14. John Mueller, *War, Presidents, and Public Opinion* (New York: Wiley, 1973).
15. See George C. Edwards and B. Dan Wood, "Who Influences Whom," *American Political Science Review* 93 (June 1999): 327–44.
16. Garry Young and William B. Perkins, "Presidential Rhetoric, the Public Agenda, and the End of Presidential Television's 'Golden Age,'" *Journal of Politics* 67 (November 2005): 1190–1205.
17. Michael Bailey, Lee Sigelman, and Clyde Wilcox, "Presidential Persuasion on Social issues," *Political Research Quarterly* 56 (March 2003): 49–58.
18. George C. Edwards and Stephen J. Wayne, *Presidential Leadership*. 6th ed. (Belmont, Calif.: Wadsworth, 2003), p. 118.
19. Lawrence R. Jacobs and Robert Y. Schapiro, *Politicians Don't Pander* (Chicago: University of Chicago Press, 2000).
20. Brandice Canes-Wrone and Kenneth W. Shotts, "The Conditional Nature of Presidential Responsiveness to Public Opinion," *American Journal of Political Science* 48 (October 2004): 690–706.
21. *Youngstown Sheet & Tube Co. v. Sawyer*, 343 U.S. 579 (1952).
22. Kenneth R. Mayer, "Executive Orders and Presidential Power," *Journal of Politics* 61 (May 1999): 445–66; Christopher J. Deering and Forrest Maltzman, "The Politics of Executive Orders," *Political*

Research Quarterly 52 (December 1999): 767–83.
23. See also Jeffrey E. Cohen, *The Politics of the U.S. Cabinet* (Pittsburgh: University of Pittsburgh Press, 1988).
24. John Kingdon, *Agenda, Alternatives, and Public Policies* (Boston: Little, Brown, 1984), p. 25.
25. See Daniel E. Ingberman and Dennis A. Yao, "Presidential Commitment and the Veto," *American Journal of Political Science* 35 (May 1991): 357–89; and Samuel B. Hoff, "Saying No," *American Politics Quarterly* 19 (July 1991): 310–23.
26. For a discussion of the factors affecting the use of the presidential veto, see John T. Woolley, "Institutions, the Election Cycle, and the Presidential Veto," *American Journal of Political Science* 35 (May 1991): 279–304.
27. *Clinton v. City of New York*, 524 U.S. 417 (1998).
28. G.J.A. O'Toole, *Honorable Treachery: A History of U.S. Intelligence from the American Revolution to the CIA* (New York: Atlantic Monthly Press, 1991).
29. National Commission on Terrorist Attacks upon the United States, *The 9/11 Commission Report*, New York: W.W. Norton, 2004.
30. *Mora v. McNamara*, 389 U.S. 934 (1964); *Massachusetts v. Laird*, 400 U.S. 886 (1970). The Court specifically refused to intervene in the conduct of the Vietnam War by presidents Johnson and Nixon.
31. Jules Witcover, *Crap Shoot: Rolling the Dice on the Vice Presidency* (New York: Crow Publishing, 1992).

Chapter 12

1. "Red tape" derives its meaning from the use of reddish tape by seventeenth-century English courts to bind legal documents. Unwrapping court orders entangled one in "red tape." See Herbert Kaufman, *Red Tape: Its Uses and Abuses* (Washington, D.C.: Brookings Institution, 1977).

2. H. H. Gerth and C. Wright Mills, *From Max Weber* (New York: Oxford Press, 1958).

3. Max Neiman, *Defending Government: Why Big Government Works* (Upper Saddle River, N.J.: Prentice Hall, 2000).

4. James Q. Wilson, *Bureaucracy: What Government Agencies Do and Why They Do It* (New York: Basic Books, 1989).

5. William Niskanen, *Bureaucracy and Representative Government* (Chicago: Aldine, 1971).

6. The constitutional question of whether Congress can establish an executive branch commission and protect its members from dismissal by the president was settled in *Humphrey's Executor v. United States* (1935). Franklin Roosevelt fired Humphrey from the Federal Trade Commission despite a fixed term set by Congress. Humphrey died shortly afterward, and when the executors of his estate sued for his back pay, the Supreme Court ruled that his firing was illegal.

7. See Nicholas Henry, *Public Administration and Public Affairs*, 7th ed. (Upper Saddle River, N.J.: Prentice Hall, 1999), Chapter 11.

8. Quoted in U.S. Civil Service Commission, *Biography of an Ideal: A History of the Civil Service System* (Washington, D.C.: Government Printing Office, 1973), p. 16.

9. See John D. Huber and Nalan McCarty, "Bureaucratic Capacity, Delegation, and Political Reform," *American Political Science Review* 98 (August 2004) 481–494.

10. Paul C. Light, *Thickening Government: Federal Hierarchy and the Diffusion of Accountability* (Washington, D.C.: Brookings Institution, 1995).

11. David Osborne and Ted Gaebler, *Reinventing Government* (New York: Addison-Wesley, 1992).

12. Al Gore, *Creating a Government That Works Better and Costs Less* (Washington, D.C.: Government Printing Office, 1993).

13. William G. Howell and David E. Lewis, "Agencies by Presidential Design," *Journal of Politics* 64 (November 2002): 1098–1114.

14. Daniel P. Carpenter, "Protection Without Capture," *American Political Science Review* 98 (November 2004): 613–31.

15. Robert Crandell and Jerry Ellig, *Economic Deregulation and Consumer Choice* (Fairfax, Va.: Center for Market Processes, 1997).

16. General Accounting Office, *Regulatory Enforcement Fairness Act Report*, 1999.

17. Thomas D. Hopkins, *Regulatory Costs in Profile* (Washington, D.C.: Center for the Study of American Business, 1996).

18. Richard K. Vedder, "Federal Regulation's Impact on the Productivity Slowdown: A Trillion Dollar Drag," *Policy Study*, Center for the Study of American Business, July 1996.

19. For research suggesting that the appointive power is a more important instrument of political control of the bureaucracy than budgets or legislation, see B. Dan Wood and Richard W. Waterman, "The Dynamics of Political Control of the Bureaucracy," *American Political Science Review* 83 (September 1991): 801–28.

20. See Joel D. Aberbach, *Keeping a Watchful Eye: The Politics of Congressional Oversight* (Washington, D.C.: Brookings Institution, 1990).

21. Evidence of the effectiveness of interventions by members of Congress in local offices of federal agencies is provided by John T. Scholz, Jim Twombly, and Barbara Headrick, "Street-Level Political Controls over Federal Bureaucracy," *American Political Science Review* 85 (September 1991): 829–50.

22. Bradley Cannon and Michael Giles, "Recurring Litigants: Federal Agencies before the Supreme Court," *Western Political Quarterly* 15 (September 1972): 183–91; Reginald S. Sheehan, "Federal Agencies and the Supreme Court," *American Politics Quarterly* 20 (October 1992): 478–500.

Chapter 13

1. Alexis de Tocqueville, *Democracy in America* (1835; New York: Mentor Books, 1956), p. 75.

2. Felix Frankfurter, "The Supreme Court and the Public," *Forum* 83 (June 1930): 332.

3. Alexander Hamilton, *Federalist Papers*, No. 78 (New York: Modern Library, 1937), p. 505.

4. *Marbury v. Madison*, 1 Cranch 137 (1803).

5. *Brown v. Board of Education of Topeka*, 347 U.S. 483 (1954).

6. *Roe v. Wade*, 410 U.S. 113 (1973).

7. *Lawrence v. Texas* (June 26, 2003).

8. *Buckley v. Valeo*, 424 U.S. 1 (1976).

9. *U.S. v. Morrison* (May 15, 2000).

10. *Ex parte Milligan*, 4 Wallace 2 (1866).

11. *Youngstown Sheet & Tube Co. v. Sawyer*, 343 U.S. 579 (1952).

12. *United States v. Nixon*, 418 U.S. 683 (1974).

13. *Clinton v. Jones*, 520 U.S. 681 (1997).

14. *West Virginia Board of Education v. Barnette*, 319 U.S. 624 (1943).

15. Quoted in Henry J. Abraham, *Justices and Presidents*, 3rd ed. (New York: Oxford University Press, 1992), p. 7.

16. Quoted in Charles P. Curtis, *Lions under the Throne* (Boston: Houghton Mifflin, 1947), p. 281.

17. Lee Epstein and Thomas G. Walker, *Constitutional Law for a Changing America*, 3rd ed. (Washington, D.C.: CQ Press, 1998), pp. 33–34.

18. William O. Douglas, "Stare Decisis," *Record*, April 1947, cited in Henry J. Abraham, *The Judicial Process* (New York: Oxford University Press, 1968), p. 58.

19. *Flast v. Cohen*, 392 U.S. 83 (1968).

20. *Gideon v. Wainwright*, 372 U.S. 335 (1963).

21. *Missouri v. Jenkins*, 110 S.C. 1651 (1990).

22. *Morrison v. Olson*, 487 U.S. 654 (1988).

23. Robert Scigliano, *The Supreme Court and the Presidency* (New York: Free Press, 1971), pp. 147–48.

24. See Bryon J. Moraski and Charles R. Shipan, "The Politics of Supreme Court Nominations," *American Journal of Political Science* 43 (October 1999): 1069–95.

25. See Charles R. Shipan and Megan L. Shannon, "Delaying Justices, *American Journal of Political Science* 47 (October, 2003): 654–68; Sarah A. Binder and Forrest Maltzman, "Senatorial Delay in Confirming Federal Judges," *American Journal of Political Science* 46 (January 2002): 190–99.

26. At one time the U.S. Supreme Court was legally required to accept certain "writs of appeal," but today very few cases come to the Court in this fashion.

27. *University of California Regents v. Bakke*, 438 U.S. 265 (1978).

28. See Lee Epstein et al., *The Supreme Court Compendium*, 3rd ed. (Washington, D.C.: CQ Press, 2002).

29. Thomas Marshall, *Public Opinion and the Supreme Court* (New York: Unwin Hyman, 1989), p. 97.

30. Lee Epstein and C. K. Rowland, "Debunking the Myth of Interest Group

Invincibility," *American Political Science Review* 85 (1991): 205–17.

31. James L. Gibson et al., "Measuring Attitudes toward the United States Supreme Court," *American Journal of Political Science* 47 (April 2003): 354–67; Stephen P. Nicholson and Robert H. Howard, "Framing Support for the Supreme Court in the Aftermath of *Bush v.*

Gore," *Journal of Politics* 65 (August 2003): 676–95.

32. President Andrew Jackson's comments came in response to the Court's ruling in the case of *Cherokee Nation v. Georgia* (1831) and *Worcester v. Georgia* (1832), which forbade the federal or state governments from seizing Native American lands and forcing the people to move. Refusal by

Jackson, an old "Indian fighter," to enforce the Court's decisions resulted in the infamous "Trail of Tears," the forced march of the Georgia Cherokees that left one-quarter of them dead along the path west.

33. *Grove City College v. Bell*, 465 U.S. 555 (1984).

34. *Pollock v. Farmer's Loan*, 158 U.S. 601 (1895).

Chapter 14

1. James Madison, *Federalist Papers*, No. 10, reprinted in the Appendix.
2. *West Virginia Board of Education v. Barnette*, 319 U.S. 624 (1943).
3. *Slaughter-House Cases*, 16 Wallace 36 (1873).
4. *Hurtado v. California*, 110 U.S. 516 (1884).
5. *Gitlow v. New York*, 268 U.S. 652 (1925).
6. For an argument that Madison and some other framers not only were concerned with lessening religious conflict but also were hostile to religion generally, see Thomas Lindsay, "James Madison on Religion and Politics," *American Political Science Review* 85 (December 1991): 1051–65.
7. *Reynolds v. United States*, 98 U.S. 145 (1879).
8. *Pierce v. Society of Sisters*, 268 U.S. 510 (1925).
9. *Cantwell v. Connecticut*, 310 U.S. 296 (1940).
10. *Employment Division v. Smith*, 494 U.S. 872 (1990).
11. *Wisconsin v. Yoder*, 406 U.S. 295 (1972).
12. *Church of Lukumi Babalu Aye v. City of Hialeah* 508 U.S. 520 (1993).
13. *Bob Jones University v. United States*, 461 U.S. 574 (1983).
14. *Employment Division of Oregon v. Smith*, 494 U.S. 872 (1990).
15. *Goldman v. Weinberger*, 475 U.S. 503 (1986).
16. *Everson v. Board of Education*, 330 U.S. 1, 15, 16 (1947).
17. *Zorach v. Clausen*, 343 U.S. 306 (1952).
18. Opening public meetings with prayer was ruled constitutional as "a tolerable acknowledgment of beliefs widely held among the people of this country." *Marsh v. Chambers*, 463 U.S. 783 (1983).
19. *Lemon v. Kurtzman*, 403 U.S. 602 (1971).
20. *Mueller v. Adams*, 463 U.S. 388 (1983).
21. *Tilton v. Richardson*, 403 U.S. 672 (1971).
22. *Lambs Chapel v. Center Moriches Union Free School District*, 508 U.S. 384 (1993).
23. *Rosenberger v. University of Virginia*, 515 U.S. 819 (1995).
24. *Walz v. Tax Commission*, 397 U.S. 664 (1970).
25. *Board of Education v. Mergens*, 497 U.S. 111 (1990).
26. *McGowan v. Maryland*, 366 U.S. 429 (1961), and *Braunfeld v. Brown*, 366 U.S. 599 (1961).

27. *County of Allegheny v. ACLU*, 492 U.S. 573 (1989).
28. *Edwards v. Aguillard*, 482 U.S. 578 (1987).
29. *Engel v. Vitale*, 370 U.S. 421 (1962).
30. *Abington School District v. Schempp*, 374 U.S. 203 (1963).
31. *Wallace v. Jaffree*, 472 U.S. 38 (1985).
32. *Lee v. Weisman*, 505 U.S. 577 (1992).
33. *Santa Fe Independent School District v. Doe*, 120 S.Ct. 2266 (2000).
34. *Zelman v. Simmons-Harris*, June 27, 2002.
35. *Schenck v. United States*, 249 U.S. 47 (1919).
36. *Gitlow v. New York*, 268 U.S. 652 (1925).
37. *Schenck v. United States*, 249 U.S. 47, 52 (1919).
38. *Whitney v. California*, 274 U.S. 357, 377 (1927), concurring opinion.
39. *Thomas v. Collins*, 323 U.S. 516 (1945).
40. *Dennis v. United States*, 341 U.S. 494 (1951).
41. *Yates v. United States*, 354 U.S. 298 (1957).
42. *Albertson v. Subversive Activities Control Board*, 382 U.S. 70 (1965).
43. *Whitehill v. Elkins*, 389 U.S. 54 (1967).
44. *United States v. Robel*, 389 U.S. 258 (1967).
45. *Aptheker v. Secretary of State*, 378 U.S. 500 (1964).
46. *Tinker v. Des Moines Independent Community School District*, 393 U.S. 503 (1969).
47. *Texas v. Johnson*, 491 U.S. 397 (1989).
48. *Chaplinsky v. New Hampshire*, 315 U.S. 568 (1942).
49. *Terminiello v. Chicago*, 337 U.S. 1 (1949).
50. *Cohen v. California*, 403 U.S. 15 (1971).
51. Justice Louis D. Brandeis opinion in *Whitney v. California*, 274 U.S. 357 (1927).
52. *R. A. V. v. City of St. Paul, Minnesota*, 505 U.S. 377 (1992).
53. *Wisconsin v. Mitchell*, 508 U.S. 476 (1993).
54. *Virginia State Board of Pharmacy v. Virginia Consumer Council, Inc.*, 425 U.S. 748 (1976).
55. *Bates v. Arizona State Bar*, 433 U.S. 350 (1977).
56. *Linmark Associates, Inc. v. Township of Willingboro*, 431 U.S. 85 (1977).
57. *New York Times v. Sullivan*, 376 U.S. 254 (1964).
58. *Griswold v. Connecticut*, 381 U.S. 479 (1965).
59. *Roe v. Wade*, 410 U.S. 113 (1973).
60. *Harris v. McRae*, 448 U.S. 297 (1980).
61. *Planned Parenthood v. Casey*, 510 U.S. 110 (1992).
62. *Stenberg v. Carhart*, June 28, 2000.
63. *Bowers v. Hardwick*, 478 U.S. 186 (1986).

64. *Lawrence v. Texas* (June 26, 2003).
65. *Stanley v. Georgia* (1969).
66. *Washington v. Glucksberg*, 117 S.Ct. 2258 (1997).
67. *Cruzan v. Missouri Department of Health*, 497 U.S. 261 (1990).
68. *Gertz v. Robert Welch, Inc.*, 418 U.S. 323 (1974).
69. *Roth v. United States*, 354 U.S. 476 (1957).
70. *Jacobellis v. Ohio*, 378 U.S. 184 (1964).
71. *Jacobellis v. Ohio*, 378 U.S. 184 (1964).
72. Bob Woodward and Scott Armstrong, *The Brethren* (New York: Avon, 1979), p. 233.
73. *Miller v. California*, 5413 U.S. 15 (1973).
74. *Barnes v. Glenn Theatre*, 501 U.S. 560 (1991).
75. *Reno v. American Civil Liberties Union*, 117 S.Ct. 2329 (1997).
76. *Near v. Minnesota*, 283 U.S. 697 (1931).
77. *New York Times v. United States*, 403 U.S. 713 (1971).
78. *Mutual Film Corp. v. Industrial Commission*, 236 U.S. 230 (1915).
79. *Times Film Corporation v. Chicago*, 365 U.S. 43 (1961).
80. *Freedman v. Maryland*, 380 U.S. 51 (1965).
81. *Young v. American Mini Theaters, Inc.*, 427 U.S. 50 (1976).
82. *Red Lion Broadcasting Co. v. Federal Communications Commission*, 395 U.S. 367 (1969).
83. *Miami Herald Publishing Co. v. Tornillo*, 418 U.S. 241 (1974).
84. *Branzburg v. Hayes*, 408 U.S. 665 (1972).
85. *NAACP v. Alabama ex rel. Patterson*, 357 U.S. 449 (1958).
86. *Healy v. James*, 408 U.S. 169 (1972).
87. *National Socialist Party of America v. Skokie*, 432 U.S. 43 (1977).
88. *Frisby v. Schultz*, 487 U.S. 474 (1988).
89. *Schenck v. Pro Choice Network of Western New York*, 519 U.S. 357 (1997).
90. *Kelo v. New London*, June 23, 2005.
91. *Village of Euclid v. Amber Realty*, 272 U.S. 365 (1954).
92. *Lucas v. South Carolina Coastal Council*, 112 Sup. Ct. 2886 (1992).
93. James Madison, *Federalist Papers*, No. 46.
94. *Ex parte Milligan*, 4 Wallace 2 (1866).
95. *Duncan v. Kahanamosby*, 327 U.S. 304 (1946).
96. *Illinois v. Gates*, 462 U.S. 213 (1983).
97. *Arizona v. Hicks*, 480 U.S. 321 (1987).
98. *Knowles v. Iowa*, 525 U.S. 113 (1998).

99. *Olmstead v. U.S.*, 277 U.S. 438 (1928).
100. *Katz v. U.S.*, 309 U.S. 347 (1967).
101. *Youngstown Sheet & Tube Co. v. Sawyer*, 343 U.S. 579 (1952).
102. *Veronia School District v. Acton*, 515 U.S. 646 (1995).
103. *Chandler v. Miller*, 520 U.S. 305 (1997).
104. *United States v. Watson*, 423 U.S. 411 (1976).
105. *Payton v. New York*, 445 U.S. 573 (1980).
106. *Spano v. New York*, 360 U.S. 315 (1959).
107. *Gideon v. Wainwright*, 372 U.S. 335 (1963).
108. *Escobedo v. Illinois*, 378 U.S. 478 (1964).
109. *Miranda v. Arizona*, 384 U.S. 436 (1966).
110. *Mapp v. Ohio*, 367 U.S. 643 (1961).
111. *United States v. Leon*, 468 U.S. 897 (1984).
112. *Illinois v. Perkins*, 497 U.S. 177 (1990).
113. *United States v. Salerno*, 481 U.S. 739 (1987).
114. *U.S. v. Marion*, 404 U.S. 307 (1971).
115. *Barker v. Wingo*, 407 U.S. 514 (1972).
116. *Illinois v. Allen*, 397 U.S. 337 (1970).
117. *Maryland v. Craig*, 497 U.S. 1 (1990).
118. *Brady v. Maryland*, 373 U.S. 83 (1963).
119. *Batson v. Kentucky*, 476 U.S. 79 (1986).
120. *Sheppard v. Maxwell*, 384 U.S. 333 (1966).
121. *Williams v. Florida*, 399 U.S. 78 (1970).
122. *Johnson v. Louisiana*, 406 U.S. 356 (1970); *Apodaca v. Oregon*, 406 U.S. 404 (1972).
123. U.S. Department of Justice, *The Prevalence of Guilty Pleas* (Washington, D.C.: Government Printing Office, 1984).
124. *U.S. v. Perez*, 9 Wheat 579 (1824).
125. *Heath v. Alabama*, 474 U.S. 82 (1985).
126. *Furman v. Georgia*, 408 U.S. 238 (1972).
127. *Gregg v. Georgia*, 428 U.S. 153 (1976); *Proffitt v. Florida*, 428 U.S. 242 (1976); *Jurek v. Texas*, 428 U.S. 262 (1976).
128. *Ring v. Arizona*, June 24, 2002.
129. *Atkins v. Virginia*, June 20, 2002.
130. *Roper v. Simmons*, March 1, 2005.

Chapter 15

1. *Dred Scott v. Sandford*, 60 U.S. 393 (1857).
2. See C. Vann Woodward, *Reunion and Reaction* (Boston: Little, Brown, 1951), and Woodward, *The Strange Career of Jim Crow* (New York: Oxford University Press, 1957).
3. *Civil Rights Cases*, 100 U.S. 3 (1883).
4. *Plessy v. Ferguson*, 163 U.S. 537 (1896).
5. *Sweatt v. Painter*, 339 U.S. 629 (1950).
6. *Brown v. Board of Education of Topeka*, 347 U.S. 483 (1954).
7. Kenneth Clark, *Dark Ghetto* (New York: Harper & Row, 1965), p. 75.
8. The Supreme Court ruled that Congress was bound to respect the Equal Protection Clause of the Fourteenth Amendment even though the amendment is directed at states, because equal protection is a liberty guaranteed by the Fifth Amendment. *Bolling v. Sharpe*, 347 U.S. 497 (1954).
9. *Brown v. Board of Education of Topeka* (II), 349 U.S. 294 (1955).
10. *Alexander v. Holmes Board of Education*, 396 U.S. 19 (1969).
11. *Swann v. Charlotte-Mecklenburg County Board of Education*, 402 U.S. (1971).
12. *Milliken v. Bradley*, 418 U.S. 717 (1974).
13. *Board of Education v. Dowell*, 498 U.S. 550 (1991).
14. Martin Luther King Jr., "Letter from Birmingham City Jail," April 16, 1963.
15. *University of California Regents v. Bakke*, 438 U.S. 265 (1978).
16. Bakke's overall grade point average was 3.46, and the average for special admissions students was 2.62. Bakke's MCAT scores were verbal, 96; quantitative, 94; science, 97; general information, 72. The average MCAT scores for special admissions students were verbal, 34; quantitative, 30; science, 37; general information, 18.
17. *United Steelworkers of America v. Weber*, 443 U.S. 193 (1979).
18. *United States v. Paradise*, 480 U.S. 149 (1987).
19. *Firefighters Local Union 1784 v. Stotts*, 467 U.S. 561 (1984).
20. *City of Richmond v. Crosen Co.*, 488 U.S. 469 (1989).
21. *Adarand Construction v. Pena*, 132 L. Ed., 2d 158 (1995).
22. *Hopwood v. Texas*, 116 S.Ct. 2581 (1996).
23. *Grutter v. Bollinger* (June 23, 2003).
24. *Gratz v. Bollinger* (June 23, 2003).
25. U.S. Department of Education, Office of Civil Rights, "Race-neutral Alternatives in Postsecondary Education," March 2003.
26. State of California, Proposition 209 "Prohibition Against Discrimination or Preferential Treatment by State and Other Public Entities," http://vote96.ss.ca.gov.
27. *Coalition for Economic Equity v. Pete Wilson*, Ninth Circuit Court of Appeals, April 1997.
28. Rudolpho O. de la Garza et al., *Latino Voices: Mexican, Puerto Rican, and Cuban Perspectives on American Politics* (Boulder, Colo.: Westview Press, 1992).
29. See F. Luis Garcia, *Latinos in the Political System* (Notre Dame, Ind.: Notre Dame University Press, 1988).
30. Linda Chavez, "Tequila Sunrise: The Slow but Steady Progress of Hispanic Immigrants," *Policy Review* (Spring 1989): 64–67.
31. Peter Mathiessen, *Sal Si Puedes: Cesar Chavez and the New American Revolution* (New York: Random House, 1969).
32. *Plyer v. Doe*, 457 U.S. 202 (1982).
33. *Morton v. Mancari*, 417 U.S. 535 (1974).
34. See Joseph P. Shapiro, *No Pity: People with Disabilities Forging a New Civil Rights Movement* (New York: Times Books/Random House, 1993).
35. *U.S. News & World Report*, February 9, 1998.
36. *The Chronicle of Higher Education*, December 8, 2000.
37. *Bradwell v. Illinois*, 16 Wall 130 (1873).
38. *Reed v. Reed*, 404 U.S. 71 (1971).
39. *Michael M. v. Superior Court of Sonoma County*, 450 U.S. 464 (1981).
40. *Rostker v. Goldberg*, 453 U.S. 57 (1981).
41. *Statistical Abstract of the United States*, 2002, p. 440.
42. Susan Fraker, "Why Women Aren't Getting to the Top," *Fortune*, April 16, 1984, pp. 40–45.

Chapter 16

1. Paul Samuelson, *Economics*, 12th ed. (New York: McGraw-Hill, 1985), p. 5.
2. For an argument that the money supply expands in election years in most democracies, see Edward R. Tufte, *Political Control of the Economy* (Princeton, N.J.: Princeton University Press, 1978).
3. GDP differs very little from gross national product, GNP, which is often used to compare the performance of national economies.
4. Richard B. Freeman, "Are Your Wages Set in Beijing?" *Journal of Economic Perspectives* 9 (Summer 1995): 15.
5. Laurence R. Jacobs and Theda Skocpol, eds., *Inequality and American Democracy* (New York: Russell Sage Foundation, 2005).
6. For a revealing case study of interest-group efforts to maintain tax breaks during the struggle over the Tax Reform Act of 1986, see Jeffrey H. Birnbaum and Alan S. Murray, *Showdown at Gucci Gulch* (New York: Random House, 1986).
7. "The Underground Economy," National Center for Policy Analysis, 1998.
8. Joseph A. Pechman, *Federal Tax Policy*, 5th ed. (Washington, D.C.: Brookings Institution, 1987).

Chapter 17

1. Christopher Jenks and Paul E. Peterson, eds., *The Urban Underclass* (Washington, D.C.: Brookings Institution, 1991). See also William A. Kelso, *Poverty and the Underclass* (New York: New York University Press, 1994).

2. See William Julius Wilson, *The Truly Disadvantaged* (Chicago: University of Chicago Press, 1987).

3. See Michael B. Katz, *In the Shadow of the Poorhouse* (New York: Basic Books, 1996).

4. See Charles Murray, *Losing Ground* (New York: Basic Books, 1984).

Chapter 18

1. Hans Morgenthau, *Politics among Nations*, 5th ed. (New York: Knopf, 1973), p. 27.

2. George F. Kennan, writing under the pseudonym "X," "Sources of Soviet Conduct," *Foreign Affairs* 25 (July 1947): 25.

3. Frank Snepp, *Decent Interval* (New York: Random House, 1977).

4. George C. Herring, *America's Longest War* (New York: Random House, 1979), p. 262.

5. See Caspar W. Weinberger, "The Uses of Military Force," *Defense* (Arlington, Va.: American Forces Information Services Survey, 1985), pp. 2–11.

6. Morgenthau, *Politics among Nations*, p. 80.

7. President George W. Bush, *National Security Strategy 2006*, March 16, 2006, www.whitehouse.gov.

8. President George W. Bush, *National Strategy for Victory in Iraq*, November 1, 2005, www.whitehouse.gov.

PHOTO CREDITS

INDEX

ELECTORAL COLLEGE VOTES IN THE 2004 ELECTION

THE UNITED STATES
A Political Map
States drawn in proportion
to number of electoral votes

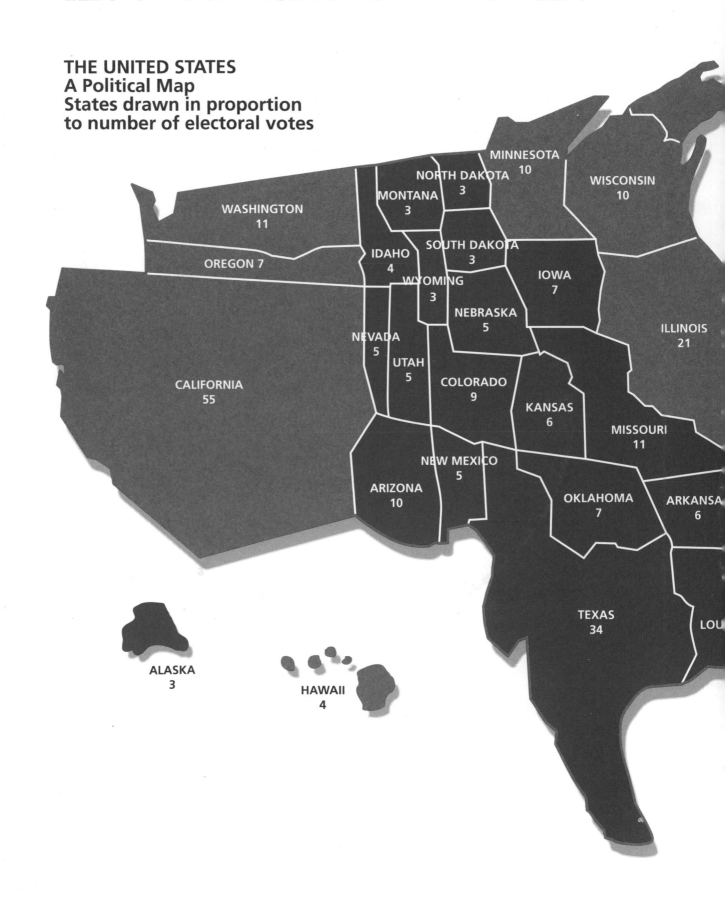